About Wolters Kluwer Legal & Regulatory U.S.

Wolters Kluwer Legal & Regulatory U.S. delivers expert content and solutions in the areas of law, corporate compliance, health compliance, reimbursement, and legal education. Its practical solutions help customers successfully navigate the demands of a changing environment to drive their daily activities, enhance decision quality and inspire confident outcomes.

Serving customers worldwide, its legal and regulatory portfolio includes products under the Aspen Publishers, CCH Incorporated, Kluwer Law International, ftwilliam.com and MediRegs names. They are regarded as exceptional and trusted resources for general legal and practice-specific knowledge, compliance and risk management, dynamic workflow solutions, and expert commentary.

For
Suzie
and
Joan
and
Debra

SUMMARY OF CONTENTS

PART THREE

INDIRECT CONTROLS   885

APPENDIX   943

CONTENTS

CHAPTER II

JUDICIAL REVIEW OF ADMINISTRATIVE DECISIONS 117

CHAPTER III

AVAILABILITY OF JUDICIAL REVIEW   277

PART TWO
ADMINISTRATIVE FUNCTIONS   **415**

CHOICE OF POLICYMAKING INSTRUMENTS   **417**

CHAPTER V

RULEMAKING   479

CHAPTER VI

ADJUDICATION   619

CHAPTER VII

ENFORCEMENT AND LIABILITY   739

CHAPTER VIII

LICENSING   841

PART THREE
INDIRECT CONTROLS   885

CHAPTER IX

PUBLIC ACCESS   887

APPENDIX   943

PREFACE

These are truly momentous times in the field of administrative law. Powerful forces of globalization, technological change, economic dislocation, social unrest, and political conflict all seem to be converging on the administrative state. Mechanisms designed primarily to fill statutory interstices and administer stable policies are now called upon to address problems like climate change, illegal immigration, financial instability, economic inequality, and the breakdown of the health care system. With the political branches often immobilized by partisan gridlock and the judiciary constrained by institutional limitations, the burden of addressing these issues falls increasingly on our nation's vast array of administrative agencies.

The efforts of administrators to respond to these contemporary challenges place increasing strains on the system of legal principles that have evolved over the past century to legitimize and control our "fourth branch of government." The challenge of administrative law has always been to balance the need for efficiency, flexibility, and discretion in the exercise of administrative authority against the need for due process, rationality, and accountability. The task of an introductory course in administrative law is not only to acquaint law students with those historic principles, but to equip future lawyers to apply those principles to the rapidly changing environment of administrative practice that they will soon confront. This casebook seeks to provide the platform for achieving both of those goals. Further, with the movement in many law schools to include a regulatory component in the first year, such as a course on Legislation and Regulation, this casebook is also designed to contain sufficient advanced materials to be used in an intermediate or advanced course on administrative law.

As a field of academic study, administrative law is forever in search of itself, hovering uneasily between vacuous platitudes about the place of administrative government in a constitutional democracy and the numbing detail of daily bureaucratic life in the regulatory state. Those who teach and write about administrative law are constantly challenged to strike the appropriate balance between abstraction and concreteness. In the formative era of administrative law, when administrative agencies were fewer in number and less complex in operation, textbook and casebook authors tended to favor concreteness. Materials were often grouped by particular agency or substantive topic. Since the watershed period of the New Deal, when the number of agencies multiplied, many of which were given broad powers to address a host of social problems, however, the emphasis has shifted toward the abstract. Administrative lawyers have attempted to capture the growing profusion and complexity of administrative life in a handful of universal legal principles, such as a uniform (*State Farm*) formulation of the "arbitrary and capricious" review standard, *Chevron* deference to agencies' interpretations of laws they administer, resistance to "formalizing" informal rulemaking, and the presumption of reviewability. While these efforts at constructing overarching principles have given coherence to discussion of some administrative law problems, they also are often a source of confusion and dissatisfaction when they seemingly fail to produce determinate results or to fit particular situations.

The attempt to filter the rich and changing variety of administrative life through a handful of doctrinal categories can have three unfortunate consequences. One is the sense of redundancy, or worse, superfluity that so often characterizes students' perceptions of administrative law. A second ill effect is the distorted view of administrative agencies when seen exclusively through the prism of appellate review. And, finally, formal doctrines frequently offer an incomplete or erroneous picture, causing many students to view administrative law "doctrines" as pedagogical abstractions, not genuinely explanatory constructs.

As a result, all too often students end a course in administrative law without understanding how administrative agencies behave, without appreciating the working of nonjudicial controls over agency behavior, and without even understanding the judicial controls themselves. In preparing teaching materials for the course in administrative law, then, we have been guided by a determination to overcome these deficiencies.

At the same time, we recognize the essential importance of teaching traditional doctrine: courts and agencies approach issues in doctrinal terms and couch decisions in that language; students will need to be familiar with these doctrines, and skilled at deploying them, once they enter practice. We have tried here to retain the benefits of doctrinal discussion while avoiding the difficulties of relying exclusively on it. To that end, we have used case studies to put many important cases in a larger political and policy context, enabling students to see the gritty reality in which sometimes abstract doctrinal questions arise. And we have organized administrative action into certain useful categories, or grouped it according to certain functions agencies are seen to perform, as a way of enriching otherwise abstract doctrinal points.

Part One of the book introduces the institutional framework of the course. The first chapter acquaints students with the basic issues of social policymaking and governmental organization that underlie all of administrative law. After discussing the origin and nature of administrative agencies, the chapter focuses on their continuing relationships to the legislative and executive branches, and the means by which these branches try to exert supervisory control. The next two chapters explore in greater depth the role of the courts in supervising administrative behavior. Although these chapters introduce students to the conventional rules and principles governing the scope and availability of judicial review, they serve more as vehicles to explore basic themes of comparative institutional competence that run throughout the succeeding chapters.

Part Two is the heart of the book's emphasis on the *functions* agencies perform, where we examine legal problems and doctrinal responses by grouping them into four generic administrative activities: policy formation (covered in two chapters, one on choice of policymaking instruments, the second on rulemaking), adjudication, enforcement (including private alternatives to agency enforcement), and licensing. Although government activities are of almost infinite variety, most can be classified to fit within these four functional headings. Despite obvious differences from one agency to another, these functions tend, wherever they are used, to elicit similar patterns of behavior and to create similar relationships between governmental and nongovernmental parties. It is these commonalities that the chapters in Part Two seek to illuminate.

In Part Three, we shift the spotlight from direct judicial supervision to indirect legal control of administrative behavior. While modes of indirect controls are legion, this part focuses on one mechanism that has generated extensive litigation and controversy: public access rules. Chapter IX focuses on the use of information and open meeting laws to increase public access to the decisionmaking process.

The other approach we use to compensate for the deficiencies of traditional administrative law materials is the case study method. Much of the book is divided into self-contained units centering around a particular episode, situation, or conflict. Most case studies focus on litigated disputes, including the controversies that have produced the leading modern judicial precedents in the field of administrative law. As in traditional treatments, we present sufficient excerpts from the appellate court decision to illuminate the issues presented and the doctrinal development for which the case stands. But we typically provide a much fuller presentation of background information on the political, legal, institutional, and technical context than is found in other texts.

In sum, our effort is not to abandon legal doctrine, but to infuse it with flesh and blood — to orient the course around what is peculiar to the formation and operation of administrative agencies, to place administrative law issues in the political and social contexts that are so critical to their resolution, to suggest alternative theoretical frameworks that can inform both positive and normative discussion of administrative behavior, and to facilitate the learning process by providing a fuller, less judicially biased group of materials drawn from a smaller number of disputes.

While adhering to the basic architecture of previous editions, this eighth edition makes significant changes to most chapters. Many of these changes are designed, by highlighting contemporary developments, to convey a sense of the dynamism discussed in the opening paragraph of this Preface. Other changes are designed simply to improve the flow, organization, and teachability of the book. In particular, we have tried in the current edition to highlight especially important secondary cases by presenting them in squib format and to streamline the notes and questions following leading cases. Highlights of changes made in this edition include the following:

Chapter I. The basic structure of this chapter has been retained, and the material updated and tightened. In the nondelegation doctrine unit, we have added an extended excerpt from Justice Gorsuch's dissent in Gundy v. United States, which may signal an impending revival of the doctrine. The appropriations materials include a note on Patchak v. Zinke. In the unit on executive control of agencies, we have relocated the "executive command" materials (featuring *Youngstown* and the Tobacco Marketing Rule case study) to the beginning of that unit and added an excerpt from San Francisco v. Trump (the "sanctuary cities" case). In the appointments unit we have added notes on such recent decisions as Lucia v. SEC, Ortiz v. United States, and NLRB v. Southwest General, as well as a lengthy note on PHH Corp. v. CFPB, on the constitutionality of the appointment of the director of the Consumer Financial Protection Bureau.

Chapter II. We have inserted as new major cases two important decisions from the Supreme Court's October 2018 Term: Department of Commerce v. New York (the *Census* case), the Court's most important pronouncement on the meaning and application of "arbitrary, capricious" review since *State Farm*, including its novel theory of "pretextual" reasoning; and Kisor v. Wilkie, replacing the *Decker* decision as the vehicle for revisiting the justifications for and limitations on the *Auer* doctrine of deference to agencies' interpretations of their own rules. We have also inserted an extended excerpt from Biestek v. Berryhill, an important contemporary examination of the "substantial evidence" standard of review. Other additions include notes on several other recent decisions, including extended excerpts from Encino Motor Cars v. Navarro and Cuozzo Speed Technologies v. Lee, further elaborating (or complicating) the *Chevron* doctrine. Also in the *Chevron* unit we inserted a new subsection on the question of whether a reviewing court should defer to a changed agency interpretation or one that conflicts with a prior judicial interpretation, using an excerpt from the Thomas-Scalia debate in *Brand X* (shifted from Chapter VIII) as the vehicle.

Chapter III. In the unit on statutory preclusion of review, we have inserted *Cuozzo Speed Technologies* as a leading case that provides an excellent vehicle for wrestling with the interpretation of preclusionary statutes. The unit on review of actions "committed to agency discretion" includes several recent pronouncements on that topic, including generous excerpts from the *Census* case and Texas v. United States (the Fifth Circuit opinion on the DAPA program). In the rest of the chapter, we have added brief descriptions of significant recent decisions including the *Mach Mining, Gill, Hawkes, Clean Air Council, PDR Network*, and *Smith* cases. And we trimmed some of the lengthy notes from the standing and ripeness material.

Chapter IV. This chapter remains essentially as it was in the seventh edition, with minor changes and updates.

Chapter V. The materials on rulemaking procedures have been updated with notes on recent cases, including excerpts from the *Census, Kisor,* and *Texas* cases. We have inserted a new subsection on "Agency Authority to Stay Promulgated Rules," using the NRDC v. NHTSA case as the principal vehicle for exploring a technique deployed on several occasions by agencies seeking to implement the deregulatory policies of the Trump Administration. We updated the units on negotiated rulemaking, alternatives to negotiated rulemaking, and presidential oversight of rulemaking to account for recent developments, including President Trump's issuance of Executive Order 13,771, requiring agencies to identify two rules to rescind for each new one adopted. Finally, the NEPA unit has been tightened, by reducing *Strycker's Bay* to a note, and updated.

Chapter VI. Aside from our decision to "demote" the *O'Bannon* case to a note (reflecting our view that the "indirect benefits" issue is relatively marginal to Due Process analysis), changes to the adjudication chapter consist primarily of notes on significant recent rulings. These include Wellness International Network v. Sharif, Oil States Energy Services v. Greene's Energy Group, Regents of the University of California v. Department of Homeland Security, Kerry v. Din, and Williams v. Pennsylvania. We have amended the note on administrative law judges, just before the *AALJ* case, to take account of the *Lucia* decision and the executive order issued in response to it.

Chapter VII. Aside from condensing the introductory materials on enforcement theory, the changes to Chapter VII all fall into the "updating" category. We have inserted notes on Los Angeles v. Patel (dealing with administrative searches), McClane Co. v. EEOC (administrative subpoenas), Virginia Uranium v. Warren ("field" preemption), Thacker v. TVA ("sue and be sued" clauses), and Ziglar v. Abbasi (officer immunity).

Chapter VIII. We have restructured the unit on business licensing to make it more coherent and more teachable. The final subsection of the business licensing unit, on regulatory expansion, had previously focused on Internet regulation (using *Brand X* as the major case). We feel that a better vehicle for discussing regulatory expansion (or the "regulatory ratchet," as we call it) is the *Southwestern Cable* case, both because it established the "ancillary jurisdiction" doctrine and because it arose in the more familiar context of broadcast regulation. Thus, we have reduced to an extended note the topic of regulatory expansion (and contraction) in the world of Internet regulation. The unit on rate regulation in the telephone context remains essentially the same with editorial changes in the explanatory note preceding *MCI*.

Chapter IX is unchanged except for reducing the *Forsham* case to a note and inserting notes on two recent decisions dealing with the definition of "record" for FOIA purposes (*American Immigration Lawyers Ass'n*) and the meaning of "confidential" in FOIA exemption 4 (*Food Marketing Inst.*).

No undertaking of this magnitude could possibly be completed, much less succeed, without the dedicated effort of many people. At the unavoidable risk of slighting some by inadvertent omission, we would like to acknowledge with gratitude the assistance of the following: Susan Banks, Charles Bennett, Larry Boisvert, Briana Cardwell, Melissa Connell, Eric Dannenmaier, Rob Evans, Shirin Everett, Deborah Fawcett, Marcia Fleschel, Kristen Fontaine, Lydia French, Mike Fricklas, Maria Gonzalez, Alan Gordee, Howard Haas, Caroline Hayday, Ben Jones, Robert Kanapka, Erica Larence, Marie Martineau, Michelle Melton, Bruce Meyer, Carla Munroe, Ben Narodick, David Nirenberg, Scott Owens, David Palamé, Ken Parsigian, Christopher Parsons, Nina Pickering, Tom Pfeifle, Beth Pollack, James Pollack, Dee Price, John Re, Tal Ron, Adam Rowland, Susan Silberberg, Joshua Simon, Risa Sorkin, Daniel Suraci, Patricia Washienko, Courtney Worcester, and William Zolla II for their diligent research assistance; Holly Escott, Shantelle Evans, Charlotte Gliksman, William Kaleva, Susan Michals, and Lisa Vogel for their superb clerical and administrative assistance; Renée Barnow, Jeffrey Lubbers, and David Pritzker for help and guidance; Professors Robert Anthony, Betsy Foote, Gary Lawson, Ron Levin, Marc Poirier, Robert Rabin, and Adam White for advice, criticisms, and good counsel; and Professors Clark Byse and Glen Robinson for their general inspiration.

Ronald A. Cass
Colin S. Diver
Jack M. Beermann
Jody Freeman

December 2019

ACKNOWLEDGMENTS

The authors gratefully acknowledge the permissions granted to reproduce the following materials.

Calame, B., Everybody Favors Job Safety, but . . . , Wall St. J., Nov. 17, 1970, at 27, col. 4. Reprinted by permission of The Wall Street Journal, © Dow Jones & Company, Inc. 1970. All rights reserved worldwide.

Congressional Quarterly, 1968 Cong. Q. Almanac 677. Copyright © 1968 by Congressional Quarterly Inc. Reprinted by permission.

Friedman, M., Capitalism and Freedom 139, 144-145 (1962). Copyright © 1962 by The University of Chicago Press. Reprinted by permission of the publisher and the author.

Morrall, Cotton Dust: An Economist's View, in The Scientific Basis of Health and Safety Regulation 93, 100-101 (R. Crandall & L. Lave, eds. 1981). Copyright © 1981 by the Brookings Institution Press. Reprinted by permission.

ADMINISTRATIVE LAW

PART ONE

INSTITUTIONAL FRAMEWORK

We live in an administrative state. At a minimum, that statement connotes the enormous size and pervasiveness of modern government. Together, the federal, state, and local governments employ roughly one of every six American workers, consume about 40 percent of the gross domestic product, regulate every significant industry, and provide services, assistance, and benefits to every American. But, more than that, invocation of the "administrative state" connotes the peculiar *form* in which governmental growth has occurred. For the hallmark of the administrative state is the immense number, variety, and power of administrative agencies. As Justice Robert H. Jackson said many years ago:

> The rise of administrative bodies probably has been the most significant legal trend of the last century. . . . They have become a veritable fourth branch of the Government, which has deranged our three-branch legal theories.

Federal Trade Commission v. Ruberoid Co., 343 U.S. 470, 487 (1952) (Jackson, J., dissenting).

Part One of this book is about our legal system's response to that "derangement"—the century-long effort to create a satisfactory theory of the place of administrative agencies in our tripartite constitutional order. As we shall observe, such a theory requires us to define the legal relationships between Justice Jackson's "fourth branch" and the three constitutional branches or to find a way to fit legal rules respecting the administrative bodies into the constitutional three-branch system. Chapter I focuses on the first two of these three institutional linkages: the relationships between administrative agencies and both the Congress and the President. The third linkage—that between court and agency—is the subject of the succeeding two chapters. In Chapter II we explore the substantive standards applied by courts when they review the actions of administrators, while in Chapter III we examine the circumstances in which courts will exercise their power of review.

CHAPTER I

THE NATURE AND FUNCTIONS OF ADMINISTRATIVE AGENCIES

The administrative state did not spring from the soil or descend from the heavens. It was created piece by piece over the past two centuries, mostly by legislatures, sometimes by elected executive officials, judges, or the electorate acting by referendum. At the federal level—which for reasons of prominence and convenience will be our primary focus—the process began when the very first Congress authorized the President to appoint an administrative officer to "estimate the duties payable on imports." Act of July 31, 1789, 1 Stat. 36. During Washington's administration, three executive departments were created—State, War, and Treasury—as well as the Post Office Department and the Attorney General's office. Prior to the Civil War, the administrative branch grew quite slowly, with most of the growth attributable to expansion of the Post Office Department. The pace of growth accelerated after 1860 as new departments were added (e.g., Agriculture in 1862, Labor in 1888) and federal civilian employment ballooned from 37,000 in 1861 to 95,000 in 1881. Still, as late as 1889, Lord Bryce could write: "It is a great merit of American government that it relies very little on officials and arms them with little power of arbitrary interference." James Bryce, The American Commonwealth, vol. II, p. 465 (1889).

Ironically, just two years earlier an event occurred that would eventually be seen as the birth of the administrative era. With the enactment of the Interstate Commerce Act of 1887, Congress created the first "modern" regulatory agency—the Interstate Commerce Commission (ICC). Although small, the ICC had clout. In the hands of a few political appointees it concentrated broad and expansive authority to affect the fortunes of an industry—railroads—crucial to the nation's development. Building on that model, Congress gradually expanded its regulatory surveillance of the American economy during the next four decades—regulating food and drugs in 1906, unfair methods of competition in 1914, shipping in 1916, hydroelectric projects in 1920, commodity trading in 1922, and radio in 1927.

The New Deal era brought with it unprecedented growth in the number and influence of federal agencies. Not only did federal regulatory tentacles continue to reach into new industries—securities markets (1934), wholesale electric power (1935), labor relations (1935), trucking (1935), airlines (1938), natural gas (1938)—but the welfare state began in earnest with major federal initiatives in social insurance, public assistance, health care, farm price supports, and housing subsidies. Another quantum leap in administrative power occurred in the 1960s and 1970s as Congress embarked on a massive campaign of "social regulation" to combat discrimination, consumer fraud, and health, safety, and environmental risks of every stripe.

The growing enchantment with economy-wide social regulation was accompanied, however, by a growing disenchantment with earlier forms of industry-specific regulation. As a result, in the 1980s and 1990s, Congress deregulated several industries, such as airlines, trucking, and railroads. Ironically, the ICC, whose creation launched the administrative state, was abolished in 1996. After decades of steady growth, federal civilian employment peaked at about 3.1 million in 1990 and thereafter declined slightly. It stood at about 2.6 million in 2014. State and local government employment, however, continued to grow throughout that period, rising from about 13 million in the early 1990s, to 19.3 million in 2014.

As is usually the case, legal theory lagged well behind onrushing reality. Well into the last century, observers tended to view these agencies and their statutory mandates as isolated phenomena, each a tailor-made response to a unique social problem. It was not until the turn of that century that various writers began to see unifying threads in this legal tangle. The emergence of the "public administration" movement hastened that awareness. In a pioneering essay, Woodrow Wilson set the agenda for a generation by proclaiming the separation of "politics" and "administration." Woodrow Wilson, The Study of Administration, 2 Pol. Sci. Q. 197 (1887). Not surprisingly, the search for a distinctive "science" of administration led to a search for a distinctive "law" of administration as well. Indeed, Frank Goodnow, the author of the first public administration text (Politics and Administration (1900)), also authored two of the earliest treatises on administrative law: Comparative Administrative Law (1893), and The Principles of the Administrative Law of the United States (1905).

Early books on administrative law focused on two subjects: the legal sources of administrative and executive power and the Byzantine system of judicial remedies for abuses of that power. As late as 1932, Felix Frankfurter and J. Forrester Davison devoted two-thirds of their influential casebook to questions relating to the uncertain place of agencies in our constitutional system. Felix Frankfurter & J. Forrester Davison, Cases and Other Materials on Administrative Law (1932). The other third was devoted to judicial review of agency action, organized by type of agency.

The proliferation of agencies during the New Deal prompted the first official studies of the administrative process with the object of establishing uniform rules for the exercise of administrative power. The Brownlow Committee, appointed by President Franklin D. Roosevelt, recommended in 1937 that the numerous multimember commissions (the "headless fourth branch" of government) be abolished and their functions transferred to executive agencies. It also recommended separating the adjudicatory and prosecutorial functions of agencies by transferring the former to an independent administrative tribunal comparable to the French Conseil d'État or the Italian Consiglio di Stato. President's Committee on Administrative Management, Report with Special Studies (1937). Although President Roosevelt repudiated its recommendations, Congress, increasingly concerned with the concentration of power in administrative hands, passed a bill in 1940 (the Walter-Logan bill) that would have implemented many of the Brownlow Committee's proposals. Roosevelt vetoed the bill, however, arguing that it would overjudicialize the administrative process.

In 1941 a distinguished committee appointed by the President in 1939 to study the administrative process issued its recommendations. Attorney General's Committee on Administrative Procedure, Final Report: Administrative Procedure in Government Agencies, S. Doc. No. 8, 77th Cong., 1st Sess. (1941). After protracted deliberations delayed by the Second World War, Congress finally adopted a compromise version of the committee's proposal, known as the Administrative Procedure Act of 1946 (APA), *now codified at* 5 U.S.C. §§551-559, 701-706, and excerpted in the Appendix. That same year (1946), the National Conference of Commissioners on Uniform State Laws adopted a "Model State Administrative Procedure Act" based largely on a draft submitted by the American Bar Association, but also drawing on the work of the Attorney General's Committee. Though the Model Act was slow to catch on in the states, virtually every state has adopted some form of centralized statute on administrative procedure, a majority of them based on the Model Act. The Model Act was revised in 1961, 1981, and 2010, with each revision departing slightly more from the APA approach. For discussion of the Model Act's evolution, impact, and relation to federal law, *see* Arthur E. Bonfield, The Federal APA and State Administrative Law, 72 Va. L. Rev. 297 (1986). Our focus principally is on federal law. Thus, the APA but not the Model Act will be a subject of continued attention.

Since enacting the APA in 1946, Congress has enacted many other statutes that specify procedures to be followed by federal administrative agencies, some of them codified as amendments to the APA. The most significant of these, most of them discussed in the pages that follow (see Index), are:

- Freedom of Information Act of 1967, providing for public disclosure of agency records and publication of many agency rulings;
- National Environmental Policy Act of 1969, requiring agencies to consider the impacts of their actions on the environment;
- Federal Advisory Committee Act of 1972, requiring that committees created to give advice to federal agencies conduct their meetings in public;
- Government in the Sunshine Act of 1976, requiring meetings of multimember federal agencies to be open to the public;
- Regulatory Flexibility Act of 1980, requiring agencies to examine and seek to reduce the impact of their rules on small businesses;
- Administrative Dispute Resolution Act of 1990, establishing alternative procedures for the resolution of administrative disputes;
- Regulatory Negotiation Act of 1990, establishing a rulemaking procedure that includes negotiation among private parties likely to be affected by the rule;

- Unfunded Mandate Reform Act of 1995, requiring agencies to consider the costs that their rules will impose on state and local governments; and
- Contract with America Advancement Act of 1996, establishing an expedited procedure for Congress to nullify an agency regulation by enacting a joint resolution of disapproval.

In addition, Congress has continued to enact special procedural provisions applicable only to individual agencies or programs. Yet, in the midst of this proliferating variety, the APA has maintained a central position as the "constitution" of federal administrative law, the bedrock on which its doctrinal superstructure still stands. It has maintained this role, as we shall see, precisely because of its flexibility to respond to the ever-changing complexion of the administrative state. For a description of the origins of the APA, its evolution, and its effects on administrative law, *see* Symposium, The Administrative Procedure Act: A Fortieth Anniversary Symposium, 72 Va. L. Rev. 215 (1986); Special Issue: The APA at Fifty, 63 U. Chi. L. Rev. 1463 (1995).

A.   THE ORIGIN AND MANDATE OF ADMINISTRATIVE AGENCIES

The administrative state is so firmly established today that it may seem purely academic to inquire into the causes of its emergence and growth. Yet, administrative agencies are continuously being created or abolished, their mandates enlarged or curtailed. Each of those events calls forth a demand for explanation. Furthermore, any effort to develop a normative theory of administrative power must rest in some antecedent descriptive account.

1.   *Theories of the Origin of Administrative Agencies*

Administrative agencies perform a bewildering variety of functions in our society. They regulate the personal behavior of individuals and the conduct of businesses, distribute subsidies and benefits, provide services, collect revenues, and manage and develop resources. They issue licenses, promulgate rules, conduct inspections, seize goods and people, prosecute offenders, and adjudicate claims. They deal with transportation, energy, employment, housing, mental and physical health, education, natural resources, and foreign and military affairs. Any attempt to explain their origins, it would seem, will quickly bog down in endless detail. Indeed, the explanations one encounters are as varied as the forms of administration they describe. Yet, one can perceive two distinct kinds of argument running through these accounts. The first focuses on an underlying social problem or need to which the administrative apparatus is viewed as the response. According to this view, administrative agencies are created to serve some kind of "public interest" or promote some "public value." The second type of explanation views the creation of an administrative agency as the outcome of a struggle among self-serving legislators and the factions, interest groups, and powerful individuals that compete for legislative prizes. This is the "public choice" story of agency origin.

Professor Frank Michelman attempts to capture the distinction between public interest and public choice explanations in the following passage:

> In the economic or public choice model, all substantive values or ends are regarded as strictly private and subjective. The legislature is conceived as a market-like arena in which votes instead of money are the medium of exchange. The rule of majority rule arises strictly in the guise of a technical device for prudently controlling the transaction costs of individualistic exchanges. Legislative intercourse is not public-spirited but self-interested. Legislators do not deliberate towards goals, they dicker towards terms. There is no right answer, there are only struck bargains. There is no public or general or social interest, there are only concatenations of particular interests or private preferences. . . .
>
> The opposed, public-interest model depends at bottom on a belief in the reality—or at least the possibility—of public or objective values and ends for human action. In this public-interest model the legislature is regarded as a forum for identifying or defining, and acting towards those ends. The process is one of mutual search through joint deliberation, relying on the use of reason supposed to have persuasive force. Majority rule is experienced as the natural way of taking action as and for a group—or as a device for filtering the reasonable from the unreasonable, the persuasive from the unpersuasive, the right from the wrong and the good from the bad.

Frank I. Michelman, Political Markets and Community Self-Determination: Competing Judicial Models of Local Government Legitimacy, 53 Ind. L.J. 145, 148-149 (1977).

These two perspectives produce strikingly different accounts of legislative decisions both to intervene in a particular area and to utilize the administrative form as its chosen instrument. Consider the enactment of the Interstate Commerce Act of 1887, widely acclaimed as the prototype for the modern regulatory statute. Why did Congress choose to intervene in a field—transportation by railroad—previously consigned to a combination of the unregulated market and selective state regulation? The public interest account stresses the widespread "abuses" by railroads resulting from "market failures" such as monopoly power in the railroad industry. By this account, regulation promoted the public value of "efficiency" or perhaps "individual autonomy." *See, e.g.,* I.L. Sharfman, The Interstate Commerce Commission: An Appraisal, 46 Yale L.J. 915 (1937). Public choice theorists, by contrast, explain the Act's passage as an attempt by the nation's leading railroads to impose a legally binding cartel on their newer or more aggressive rivals, or as an attempt by a coalition of disfavored shippers to gain pricing and service advantages at the expense of their competitors. *See, e.g.,* Gabriel Kolko, Railroads and Regulation: 1877-1916 (1965).

The divergent explanations of railroad regulation illustrate the different focus of each theory. Public interest theory endeavors to identify benefits to the general welfare of society that flow from a government action. The two principal strands of public interest theory derive from welfare economics and moral theory.

Welfare economists have identified four public interest rationales to justify most government regulation of the marketplace: natural monopoly, public goods, external effects, and asymmetric information. The first explanation ostensibly justifies regulation of "public utilities," such as cable communications or natural gas pipelines, that might otherwise exploit their monopoly power to charge excessive prices. The public goods rationale observes that, without government subsidies or other inducements, the market will underproduce certain goods or services—such as police protection or parks—whose enjoyment cannot easily be restricted to those who pay for them. The external effects explanation is the reverse side of the public goods rationale: without government regulation, public "bads"—such as air or water pollution—will be overproduced. The theory of asymmetric information arguably justifies government regulation of goods and services—such as health care or pharmaceuticals—whose quality, safety, or cost is difficult for consumers to evaluate.

In contrast to theories derived from welfare economics, moral theorists have invoked the principles of human dignity, autonomy, and equality to justify government programs such as provision of food and housing to the poor, protection of procreative freedom, or prohibition of invidious discrimination based on race, gender, or sexual identity.

Public choice theory, by contrast, focuses on the way in which individual preferences will be aggregated and expressed through public decisionmaking processes, rather than the way in which overall social welfare will be advanced. From assumptions about the distribution and intensity of voter preferences, opportunities for and costs of political participation, and the mechanics of legislative decisionmaking, public choice theorists seek to explain how a process such as our majoritarian-representative system of government systematically favors certain interests over others.

The explanations for legislative behavior generated by public choice theorists are often quite divergent from public interest explanations. Thus, public utility franchises are often viewed as a form of "unnatural" monopoly granted by the state to a dominant firm in a formative industry seeking to perpetuate its position. Public choice theory also predicts that, while genuine public goods will be underprovided by the political process, legislatures will often provide private goods masquerading as public goods. Much of public television programming is sold as propagation of "culture," when in fact it is highbrow entertainment for the affluent few. One can likewise explain much regulation of adverse external effects as self-serving. Eastern coal producers, for example, supported stringent air pollution controls as a way of protecting their markets against competition from "cleaner" Western coal. Asymmetric information interests public choice theorists, too: not as a justification for regulation, however, but as a source of political advantage enjoyed by particular groups with specialized training or knowledge.

In addition to these disparate explanations for legislative decisions to regulate, the public interest and public choice accounts produce different answers to the question of why a legislature elects to place enforcement authority in the hands of an administrative body, rather than, say, to rely solely on private actions brought in the courts. The typical public interest answer stresses such values as efficiency and effectiveness. A specialized agency like the (now-defunct) ICC, the argument runs, can better provide "continuous expert supervision, capable of ad hoc development to parallel the development of the subject matter involved." Walter Gellhorn, Federal Administrative Proceedings 9 (1941). The distinguishing feature of the ICC, public choice theorists would reply, is not its expertise or its expeditiousness, but its amenability to influence. A political body like the ICC would be much more responsive than the courts to the coalition of carriers and shippers who won the legislative prize, or to the legislators whose constituents stood to benefit most from its rulings.

Both approaches, clearly, have their limitations. The public interest theory has been justly criticized for failing to articulate any coherent conception of "public interest" and for failing to contain any explicit assumptions about the motivations of legislators and lobbyists. *See* Richard A. Posner, Theories of Economic Regulation, 5 Bell J. Econ. & Mgmt. Sci. 335 (1974). It has done a poor job of explaining the highly protectionist, anticompetitive behavior of many "economic" regulatory agencies, like the ICC, the Federal Communications Commission, or the (now-defunct) Civil Aeronautics Board, at least during their early years. In contrast, the public choice model has struggled to explain the dramatic reversal of form by these same agencies at times, as well as the spate of health, safety, and environmental regulatory programs enacted during the 1960s and 1970s. While general theories about government processes may provide a useful starting place, those who seek to explain administrative origins must remain sensitive to the irreducible complexity of a messy reality.

2.   A Case Study: The Occupational Safety and Health Act

On December 29, 1970, President Richard M. Nixon signed into law the Occupational Safety and Health Act of 1970, Pub. L. No. 91-596, 84 Stat. 1590, *codified at* 29 U.S.C. §§651-678 (1980). The Act's passage culminated a three-year struggle to enact comprehensive federal legislation "to assure so far as possible every working man and woman in the Nation safe and healthful working conditions" (§1). The story of the Act's passage and subsequent implementation serves as an excellent vehicle for exploring the process by which administrative agencies are created and empowered.

The Occupational Safety and Health Act (the OSH Act) applies to every private employer "engaged in a business affecting commerce" in the United States or its territories (§3(5)), estimated in 2009 as 8.9 million workplaces, employing 135 million workers. The Act authorizes the Secretary of Labor to promulgate mandatory "occupational safety and health standards" that require employers to maintain certain conditions or to adopt certain practices "reasonably necessary or appropriate to provide safe or healthful employment" (§§3(8), 6(b)). In addition to requiring compliance with these standards, the Act imposes on every employer a general duty to "furnish to each of his employees employment and a place of employment which are free from recognized hazards that are causing or are likely to cause death or serious physical harm" (§5(a)).

The Secretary may contract with state occupational safety agencies to enforce the Act, provided that the state's enforcement plan meets federal standards (§§18(b), 23). In all other states, the Labor Department is responsible for enforcing the Act directly. The Secretary is authorized to conduct regular unannounced inspections of workplaces (§8(a)). In addition, the Act seeks to encourage workers to file complaints by protecting complainants against employer retaliation and by requiring an inspection in response to a reasonable complaint (§§8(f), 11(c)). Upon detecting a violation of the standards, the Secretary may seek either civil or criminal penalties (§§13, 17). The chief sanction contemplated by the Act is the assessment of "civil money penalties" up to $7,000 per violation ($70,000 for "willful" or "repeated" violations). To adjudicate claims for penalties initiated by the Labor Department, the Act (§12) created an independent agency, the Occupational Safety and Health Review Commission (OSHRC) headed by three commissioners appointed by the President for staggered six-year terms.

While the Act also encourages promotion of safety by other means, such as employee education (§21) and research (§§22, 23, 24), its dominant thrust is regulatory. It stands as a modern classic in the genre of "command and control" regulatory legislation. Thomas Schelling, Command and Control, in Social Responsibility and the Business Predicament 79 (James McKie ed., 1974).

Passage of the OSH Act in 1970 was by no means the first or even the most significant government action to protect worker safety and health. For the first two centuries of the Republic, protection of workers was primarily entrusted to the states, where the initial government response to worker injury came from the courts. Applying general principles of tort law, state courts recognized the right of workers to recover damages for injuries suffered because of the negligence of their employers. In the latter decades of the nineteenth century, state legislatures began to supplement common law tort rules with specific measures aimed at promoting safer workplaces. Massachusetts enacted the first factory inspection law in 1877, requiring machine guards, fire escapes, and elevator doors. By the early 1900s most industrialized states had enacted some form of safety legislation, and by 1970 virtually all states had regulatory programs, although the coverage, stringency, and aggressiveness of enforcement varied widely.

Around the turn of the twentieth century, states began to adopt workers' compensation laws, which replaced the fault-based tort system with a form of compulsory no-fault insurance administered by special administrative tribunals. Workers injured in the course of their employment received compensation based on fixed schedules of injury payments. By 1970, roughly 85 percent of workers were covered by such programs, at a cost to employers of $4.9 billion.

Federal regulation of workplace safety developed much more slowly and selectively. Beginning with the creation of the Bureau of Mines in 1910, Congress gradually established a special federal concern for mine safety, authorizing federal inspections in 1941, promulgation of advisory safety codes in 1947, and issuance of mine closure orders in 1952. Following the infamous Farmington Disaster of 1968 that claimed the lives of 78 miners, Congress enacted the extremely stringent Federal Coal Mine Health and Safety Act of 1969, which authorized the Secretary of the Interior to set and enforce mandatory mine safety standards. In 1927 Congress enacted the Longshoremen's and Harbor Workers' Compensation Act to fill the gap left by the inapplicability of state workers' compensation laws to workers on navigable waterways. Workplace safety received an indirect federal boost with the passage of the Wagner Act in 1935, guaranteeing workers the right to organize and bargain collectively. The federal presence in the workplace was further strengthened by the Walsh-Healey Act of 1936, which directed the Secretary of Labor to establish safety regulations for workers on federal contracts. By 1969 these regulations covered some 27 million employees working in 75,000 establishments.

The initial impetus for a comprehensive regulatory program in the mid-1960s came, not from organized labor, but from officials in the Labor Department dissatisfied with the limited scope of their authority to regulate workplace safety. They succeeded in persuading President Lyndon B. Johnson's advisors to include a workplace safety bill in the Administration's 1968 legislative program. In a January 23, 1968, message to Congress, Johnson offered a rather cautious legislative proposal that would empower the Labor Department to conduct inspections comparable to those being performed by the states and would direct the Department of Health, Education, and Welfare to conduct research on occupational hazards. In support of his proposal, Johnson cited alarming statistics on the annual toll taken by workplace injury: 14,500 workers killed, 2.2 million injured, $1.5 billion in lost wages, and $8 billion in lost national product.

Although House and Senate committees held hearings on the Administration's bill, in neither house did it reach the floor. This account of the lobbying effort appeared in Congressional Quarterly:

> The President's occupational safety proposal came under sharp assault by powerful business interests. A broad front of business groups including the Chamber of Commerce of the United States, the National Assn. of Manufacturers (NAM), American Iron and Steel Institute, American Medical Assn., Manufacturing Chemists' Assn., and others, lobbied hard against the bill and succeeded in watering the measure down considerably in the House Education and Labor Committee and keeping it bottled up altogether in the Senate Committee on Labor and Public Welfare.

> Despite the House Committee's changes, business groups still opposed the bill. The Chamber of Commerce, regarded as the leading opponent of the measure, issued a position paper asserting that ". . . the changes have not turned a poor bill into a good bill." The only satisfactory solution, the Chamber indicated, would be to knock out the Secretary [of Labor's] authority altogether. The Chamber and other groups based their attack primarily on a contention that the federal standards invade an area that traditionally had been the domain of the states.

> Throughout the spring and summer, business lobbyists paid frequent visits to key members of the House and Senate committees, and a flood of constituent mail, reflecting material printed in Chamber and other business publications, was reported. . . .

> Rep. Elmer J. Holland (D. Pa.) . . . said he had received a large number of letters "ranging from the merely outraged to the downright abusive" opposing [the Administration's bill]. But he said "support has begun to appear for the measure."

> Holland inserted into the Congressional Record letters of support from the National Consumers League, the National Education Assn., the International Union of Operating Engineers and state nursing associations in Maryland, Florida, Vermont and West Virginia. . . .

> In a related development, 50 representatives of the National Council of Senior Citizens . . . picketed the U.S. Chamber of Commerce in Washington to protest the Chamber's opposition to the pending bill.

> The Administration's big ally in the battle was the AFL-CIO.

1968 Cong. Q. Almanac 677.

Concern about health and safety hazards was much more prevalent in the
91st Congress, which began in January 1969. More than 1,000 safety-related
bills were introduced in that session, including several relating to occupational
safety. In May 1969, the Democrats submitted "majority" bills in both houses,
to concentrate standard-setting and remedial powers in the Secretary of Labor.
President Nixon countered in August with a proposal to create an independent
five-member commission to regulate workplace safety, while preserving considerable room for continued state regulation. While organized labor staunchly
defended the Democrats' version, business leaders urged a more "flexible"
program that relied on "guidelines" rather than mandatory standards and displaced state regulation only where states failed to act.

By mid-1970, committees in both houses reported out occupational safety
legislation, the House version based on the Administration bill, the Senate version based on the majority bill. Most business lobbies had come around to offering at least conditional support for the Administration bill. But the differences
were still sharp, as this news account illustrates:

> WASHINGTON—Job safety, like motherhood and apple pie, is hardly the
> sort of thing anyone opposes.
>
> Organized labor and the Democrats are for improved safety on the job. So
> are the Nixon Administration, the GOP and the U.S. Chamber of Commerce. . . .
>
> This unanimity can quickly evaporate, however, in the heat of fashioning leg-
> islation and deciding precisely who will set and enforce Federal safety standards.
> And since the Nixon Administration proposed a job safety bill last year, the differ-
> ing views of organized labor and the Administration have so hardened that Con-
> gress may not be able to pass any job safety bill in this session.
>
> The showdown in what Sen. Javits (R., N.Y.) calls "the most bitter labor-
> management fight in years" is expected this week, as the Senate heads for a final
> vote on the matter today or tomorrow.
>
> [M]ost of the controversy centers on who would set and enforce the stan-
> dards. Labor leaders contend that this responsibility must be "centralized" in one
> agency. That agency should be the Labor Department, argues AFL-CIO President
> George Meany, because it "exists to protect the interests of workers." And, union
> officials concede privately, it's obviously the spot where organized labor normally
> has the most political clout.
>
> As for the Administration's idea of separate panels, federation Secretary-
> Treasurer Lane Kirkland charges that "the point of this many-headed administra-
> tive monstrosity is to make sure that as little as possible gets done." The United
> Auto Workers union contends that the Administration bill "is an anti-labor legal
> trap written by the U.S. Chamber of Commerce."
>
> The Administration and Chamber of Commerce say independent standard-
> setting and enforcement panels are needed to provide a "separation of powers"
> that will assure "fairness and due process" for employers and employees. Laurence
> H. Silberman, Undersecretary of Labor, claims the independent board of experts
> proposed by the Administration would provide more "high-level" attention for
> standard-setting.
>
> Labor Secretary Hodgson contends there's "the possibility of serious abuse
> inherent" in calling on his office "to perform all roles from lawmaker to police-
> man, to prosecutor, to jury, to judge in setting, administering and enforcing stan-
> dards." The Chamber of Commerce protests that the bill "would open the door to
> extreme harassment of business."

Organized labor is convinced that time is working in its favor, that it can afford to refuse to compromise. "Even if a bill isn't passed in this session, the one that will eventually be passed is certain to be stronger," argues one labor lobbyist. Though the union strategists don't say so publicly, many of them figure the increased publicity being given factory accidents and health by consumer advocate Ralph Nader and others will continue to generate greater citizen concern. And this, they reason, will arouse growing sympathy for their contention that "you can't compromise where people's lives are at stake."

Byron E. Calame, Everybody Favors Job Safety, But . . . , Wall St. J., Nov. 17, 1970, at 22, col. 4.

That very day (November 17), the Senate adopted, on an 83-3 roll call vote, a compromise engineered by Senator Javits to keep standard-setting and inspection in the Labor Department, but shift adjudication to an independent body. The next week, the House, by a vote of 220-172, adopted an Administration-backed compromise splitting standard-setting and enforcement between two independent boards. The conference committee adopted the Senate version, however, and its version was finally approved in the House on December 17. Having already antagonized labor by vetoing a public jobs bill earlier that month, a reluctant President Nixon signed the bill on December 29.

To administer the Act, the Secretary of Labor created a new division within the Labor Department called the Occupational Safety and Health Administration (OSHA). OSHA is headed by an "Assistant Secretary for Occupational Safety and Health," who, like the Secretary of Labor, is appointed by the President subject to Senate confirmation and serves at the President's pleasure.

QUESTIONS

1. Why did Congress pass the OSH Act of 1970? In trying to answer that question, it is useful to split it into its component parts. First, why did Congress feel that *any* form of government intervention was warranted? Many economists argue that society can rely on the marketplace to achieve an appropriate level of industrial safety, without the necessity for active government involvement. If job A (say, driving truckloads of explosives) is more dangerous than job B (driving truckloads of fruits and vegetables), so the argument runs, workers will demand a higher wage (or other benefits) for job A, in compensation for the greater risk they assume. The amount of "risk premium" that they demand will just equal the expected cost to them of assuming that risk (that is, the extra cost of the injuries or diseases that they are exposed to, multiplied by their probability of occurrence). Workers will not demand anything less than this amount because, at any lower wage, job B becomes preferable to job A. Nor will they demand more than this amount because, if they do, the employer will find someone else willing to take the job for a little less. Employers, in turn, will be willing to pay this risk premium only if two conditions exist. First, there must be no cheaper way to reduce the risk (such as installing safety equipment or giving safety-related training). If such a method exists, the employer will adopt it, thereby making the job safer. Second, the value of the output produced by the workers in job A must equal or exceed the (higher) wage that they demand. If

not, capital and labor will shift to other activities (like job *B*) that are safer or more valuable. The end result will be that workers will incur only those risks for which they are compensated and for which the social benefit exceeds the cost.

What assumptions does this theory rest on? How realistic are they? In what occupations or sectors of the economy are they likely to be most suspect? Would there be any justification for government regulation *even if* the assumptions on which the market theory rests were all realistic?

Second, why did Congress feel that intervention by the *federal government* was warranted? Most states already had programs in place to compensate injured workers (workers' compensation or tort law) and to set regulatory standards for local workplaces. Economists have argued that the federal government should intervene only when there are significant "externalities" or "spillovers" between states. The classic example is regulating pollution of interstate waterways. Because the upstream state will bear all of the costs of pollution control, but realize only part of the benefits, it will adopt too lax a program of regulation. Thus, national regulation is needed. Does this logic apply to occupational safety and health regulation?

Some public interest advocates have occasionally defended federal regulation by suggesting that state governments are less competent or honest than the federal government. Is that a plausible justification for federal intervention in this context?

Third, why did Congress rely primarily on a strategy of "command and control" regulation? It could have chosen one of several alternative approaches. One strategy would have been simply to give employers and workers better information about workplace hazards. During hearings on the OSH Act, several union officials had testified that unions lacked sufficient expertise to bargain for improvements in workplace safety. Another approach might have been to correct perceived defects in the compensation system. Workers' compensation systems had been criticized for providing excessively low awards relative to actual injury costs, presenting difficult burdens of proof on the work-relatedness of certain injuries and diseases, and failing to structure insurance premiums so as to give employers incentives to reduce injuries. A third alternative was to impose some form of "injury tax." Economists long have argued that the efficient way to correct unwanted externalities is to tax them in an amount equal to the social harm they cause. Thus, producers are forced to internalize—pay in full for—the costs they impose on others. Does command-and-control regulation have any inherent advantages over these techniques of social control?

Fourth, having selected the regulatory approach, why did Congress delegate such broad policymaking authority to an administrative agency? The hearings were full of testimony on specific occupational hazards like asbestos and specific dangerous industries like foundries. Why didn't Congress write concrete standards for those hazards into the law itself?

Finally, why did Congress choose that particular institutional structure for administering the statute? Why did Congress split off standard-setting and monitoring from adjudication? Why did it assign the former to the Labor Department rather than, say, a new agency or some other existing agency (like the Department of Health, Education, and Welfare)? Why did it assign the latter function to an administrative tribunal rather than the courts?

2. As you answer those questions, do you find yourself making "public interest" arguments or "public choice" arguments? In what sense is there a "public" interest in the answers to those questions? What "public"? How do we know its interest?

What are the "private" interests involved in the legislative struggle? Who won? Who lost? Why did the winners prevail over the losers?

Last, do you think that your answers, based on the information from this case study, would be the same if Congress were addressing the same issues today?

B. LEGISLATIVE CONTROL OF ADMINISTRATIVE AGENCIES

Congress exercises control over federal administrative agencies through a variety of mechanisms. For organizational convenience we have grouped these powers under four headings in this section: "Authorization," "Revision," "Appropriations," and "Legislative Oversight." First and most important, Congress creates and empowers administrative agencies through legislative authorization. A statute that provides for the creation of a particular agency or confers upon it a particular set of powers and responsibilities is usually called an "authorizing act" or "enabling act." In the first section of this subchapter we discuss authorization, with particular attention to the constitutional dilemma posed by "delegation" of policymaking authority to an administrative agency.

A second form of legislative control is through revision of the powers conferred by enabling acts or of the actions taken pursuant to those powers. The primary means of revision is, of course, through enactment of legislation amending the agency's enabling act or otherwise redefining the scope of the agency's powers. But, as we shall see, Congress has experimented with another method — the "legislative veto" — for correcting what it perceives to be misuses of administrative authority.

A third form of control is through the power of the purse. Legal authority means little without the funds to implement that authority. By determining — almost always on an annual basis — the amounts of money that an agency will have to spend, and by specifying the purposes for which those funds can be expended, Congress can exercise considerable ongoing supervision of an agency. Finally, we consider a catchall category of "oversight" that embraces a variety of additional, often quite informal, indirect, or even invisible techniques by which Congress or members of Congress influence the behavior of administrators.

1. *Authorization: The Problem of Delegation*

The notion of what we now call administrative agencies was hardly foreign to the framers of the Constitution. Article I, §8, explicitly authorizes Congress to create "Post Offices," "Armies," and a "Navy." Article II, §2, cl. 2, provides for presidential appointment of "Ambassadors," "public Ministers," and "Officers of the United States," and refers generically to "Departments." Yet, aside from those and a few other sparse references, the Constitution is relatively silent about the origin and powers of administrative agencies. The Founding generation clearly assumed that an act of Congress was required to create a federal administrative agency and that Congress could unproblematically confer on agencies such traditional "executive" functions as collecting taxes and duties, coining money, building post roads, and prosecuting violators of the law. As the number and functions of administrative agencies proliferated, however, questions began to arise about the limitations on the range of powers that Congress could confer upon administrative bodies. The most troublesome of these questions concerned the extent to which Congress could utilize administrative agencies to perform functions more typically associated with legislatures and courts. That is, could Congress empower agencies to issue general commands having the force of law, comparable to the legislative enactments of Congress itself? Could Congress authorize agencies to adjudicate specific controversies of the sort that courts ordinarily handle? In this section of Chapter I, we address the answers that the Supreme Court has given to the first of those questions, reserving to Chapter VI a discussion of the second question.

As the materials on the OSH Act suggest, legislatures often create an administrative agency to implement public policy in a particular arena when they lack the expertise, foresight, or political will to determine precisely what that policy should be. Situations like that typically breed vague statutory delegations that confer broad policymaking power on the agency. In some sense, the entire field known as "administrative law" represents the efforts of courts and legislatures to come to terms with that fact.

The Supreme Court flatly declared the following in 1892: "That Congress cannot delegate legislative power . . . is a principle universally recognized as vital to the integrity and maintenance of the system of government ordained by the Constitution." Field v. Clark, 143 U.S. 649, 692 (1892). This "universally recognized principle" has come to be known as the "nondelegation doctrine." Its constitutional basis is found in the Article I, §1, directive that "[a]ll legislative power herein granted shall be vested in a Congress. . . ," combined with considerable constitutional detail specifying the way that Congress is to be composed and the methods by which it can enact laws.

Although courts consistently have asserted that Congress cannot delegate its "legislative" power, they have struggled to define the contours of legislative power. In The Brig Aurora, 11 U.S. (7 Cranch) 382 (1813), the Supreme Court upheld a delegation of power to the President to lift an embargo of European trade when he found that the Europeans had "ceased to violate the neutral commerce of the United States." Embargo Act of 1809, ch. 5, 2 Stat. 605. The Court accepted the delegation of power as contingent solely on a finding of facts, since the statute specified both the act to be performed and the condition for its performance. Wayman v. Southard, 23 U.S. (10 Wheat.) 1 (1825), dealt with a delegation of power to the federal courts to make their own rules of process. The Court supported the delegation on the theory that the delegate was assigned merely to "fill up the details" on a matter of slight importance.

The next significant case, Field v. Clark, 143 U.S. 649 (1892), concerned the Tariff Act of 1890 (known as the McKinley Tariff), which eliminated tariffs on a set of agricultural products, but directed the President to reimpose certain specified duties on each product whenever he was "satisfied" that another country placed duties on U.S. agricultural exports that were "reciprocally unequal and unreasonable" in light of the tariffs eliminated in the law. Once again, the Court reasoned that the power delegated was not "legislative" because it was rooted in finding facts to effectuate the congressional will.

J.W. Hampton, Jr. & Co. v. United States, 276 U.S. 394 (1928), for the first time acknowledged that Congress could delegate policymaking authority, so long as the statute furnished "an intelligible principle" to guide the delegate's discretion. *Id.* at 409. That case upheld a statute authorizing the President to revise certain tariff duties whenever he determined revision to be necessary to "equalize the costs of production in the United States and the principal competing country." *Hampton* upheld this delegation of broad power largely because the determinations delegated seemed so complex as to defy legislators' competence (at least in Chief Justice Taft's view).

The limits of the "intelligible principle" doctrine were tested by two 1935 cases involving the National Industrial Recovery Act (NIRA), a centerpiece of President Roosevelt's New Deal legislation enacted in the depths of the Great Depression. The two cases represent the climax in an epic struggle between a conservative judiciary and the political branches. Section 9(c) of the NIRA gave the President authority to exclude from interstate commerce petroleum products "produced or withdrawn from storage in excess of the amount permitted . . . by any state law or valid regulation. . . ." In Panama Refining Co. v. Ryan, 293 U.S. 388 (1935), the Supreme Court sustained a challenge to the constitutionality of the statute for its failure to guide the President's decision whether, and when, to use this power: "the Congress has declared no policy, has established no standard, has laid down no rule. There is no requirement, no definition of circumstances and conditions in which the transportation is to be allowed or prohibited." *Id.* at 430. As for the government necessity theory, the Court observed: "The constant recognition of the necessity [of delegations] and the wide range of administrative authority which has been developed by means of them, cannot be allowed to obscure the limitations of the authority to delegate, if our constitutional system is to be maintained." *Id.* at 421. Justice Benjamin Cardozo's lone dissent found sufficient guidelines in the goal of industrial recovery itself, whose attainment the President could promote by imposing a temporary restriction based on an objective study of the facts in the "typical and classic form" of *Field* and *Hampton. Id.* at 438.

Later in the same term, the Supreme Court revisited the NIRA in the *Schechter Poultry* decision, this time delivering an even more emphatic rejection of broad congressional delegations of power.

A.L.A. SCHECHTER POULTRY CORP. v. UNITED STATES, 295 U.S. 495 (1935):   Section 3 of the NIRA authorized the President to approve "codes of fair competition" for trades and industries. Such codes could be approved, upon application by industry trade associations, if the President found (1) that such associations "impose no inequitable restrictions on admission to membership therein and are truly representative," and (2) that such codes are not designed "to promote monopolies or to eliminate or oppress small enterprises and will not operate to discriminate against them, and will tend to effectuate the policy" of Title I of the Act. Section 1 of Title I enumerated a long list of statutory purposes, including: removing "obstructions" to commerce, promoting "the

organization" of industry and labor, eliminating "unfair competitive practices," increasing consumption and production, decreasing unemployment, improving "standards of labor," "rehabilita[ting]" industry, and conserving natural resources. Violation of an approved code was a misdemeanor punishable by a fine of not more than $500 for each offense.

Petitioners, slaughterhouse operators in New York City, were charged with violating the so-called "Live Poultry Code," drafted by trade associations representing about 90 percent of New York's live poultry industry, and approved by President Roosevelt on April 13, 1934. Petitioners were convicted on 18 counts, including violating the Code's minimum wage and maximum hour provisions, selling unfit or uninspected chickens, selling to unlicensed dealers, and permitting customers to select particular chickens in violation of a requirement that chickens be sold by the "coop." The convictions on most of the counts were upheld by the Court of Appeals. The Supreme Court, in an opinion by Chief Justice Hughes, reversed petitioners' convictions, finding that §3 of the Act constituted an unconstitutional delegation of legislative power to the President:

> What is meant by "fair competition" as the term is used in the Act? . . . We think the conclusion is inescapable that the authority sought to be conferred by Section 3 was not merely to deal with "unfair competitive practices" which offend against existing law, and could be the subject of judicial condemnation without further legislation, or to create administrative machinery for the application of established principles of law to particular instances of violation. Rather, the purpose is clearly disclosed to authorize new and controlling prohibitions through codes of laws which would embrace what the formulators would propose, and what the President would approve, or prescribe, as wise and beneficent measures for the government of trades and industries in order to bring about their rehabilitation, correction and development, according to the general declaration of policy in section one. . . .
>
> The Government urges that the codes will "consist of rules of competition deemed fair for each industry by representative members of that industry—by the persons most vitally concerned and most familiar with its problems." . . . But would it be seriously contended that Congress could delegate its legislative authority to trade or industrial associations or groups so as to empower them to enact the laws they deem to be wise and beneficent for the rehabilitation and expansion of their trade or industries? Could trade or industrial associations or groups be constituted legislative bodies for that purpose because such associations or groups are familiar with the problems of their enterprises? . . . The answer is obvious. Such a delegation of legislative power is unknown to our law and is utterly inconsistent with the constitutional prerogatives and duties of Congress.
>
> The question, then, turns upon the authority which Section 3 of the Recovery Act vests in the President to approve or prescribe. If the codes have standing as penal statutes, this must be due to the effect of the executive action. But Congress cannot delegate legislative power to the President to exercise an unfettered discretion to make whatever laws he thinks may be needed or advisable for the rehabilitation and expansion of trade or industry. . . .

Examining the provisions of §3, Chief Justice Hughes concluded that its "representativeness" and "antimonopoly" provisions provided only minor restraints on the content or scope of codes, leaving the proponents of a code to "roam at will" and the President to "approve or disapprove their proposals as he may see fit." Furthermore, the Chief Justice asserted:

[T]he President in approving a code may impose his own conditions, adding to or taking from what is proposed, as "in his discretion" he thinks necessary "to effectuate the policy" declared by the Act. . . . And this authority relates to a host of different trades and industries, thus extending the President's discretion to all the varieties of laws which he may deem to be beneficial in dealing with the vast array of commercial and industrial activities throughout the country.

Such a sweeping delegation of legislative power finds no support in the decisions upon which the Government especially relies. . . . Section 3 of the Recovery Act is without precedent. It supplies no standards for any trade, industry or activity. It does not undertake to prescribe rules of conduct to be applied to particular states of fact determined by appropriate administrative procedure. Instead of prescribing rules of conduct, it authorizes the making of codes to prescribe them. For that legislative undertaking, Section 3 sets up no standards, aside from the statement of the general aims of rehabilitation, correction and expansion described in section one. In view of the scope of that broad declaration, and of the nature of the few restrictions that are imposed, the discretion of the President in approving or prescribing codes, and thus enacting laws for the government of trade and industry throughout the country, is virtually unfettered. We think that the code-making authority thus conferred is an unconstitutional delegation of legislative power. . . .

Even Justice Cardozo agreed. In a concurring opinion he said:

The delegated power of legislation which has found expression in this code is not canalized within banks that keep it from overflowing. . . . Here, in the case before us, is an attempted delegation not confined to any single act nor to any class or group of acts identified or described by reference to a standard. Here in effect is a roving commission to inquire into evils and upon discovery correct them. . . .

The code does not confine itself to the suppression of methods of competition that would be classified as unfair according to accepted business standards or accepted norms of ethics. It sets up a comprehensive body of rules to promote the welfare of the industry, if not the welfare of the nation, without reference to standards, ethical or commercial, that could be known or predicted in advance of its adoption. . . .

NOTES AND QUESTIONS

1. *The constitutional basis for the nondelegation doctrine.* What is the constitutional basis for the nondelegation principle? Is the principle, as articulated by Chief Justice Hughes, logically implied by the "vesting" of "all legislative powers" in the Congress by Article I, §1? Is it implicit in the separation of the government into three branches, as established by the first three Articles? Why cannot President Roosevelt reply to Chief Justice Hughes that he is merely "taking care that the laws be faithfully executed," as the President is commanded by Article II, §3? Is the nondelegation doctrine implied by more general principles inherent in the constitutional framework? If so, what are those principles, and how do they operate in the context of the NIRA?

2. *"Intelligible" principles.* In his opinion in *Schechter,* Chief Justice Hughes distinguished other facially broad delegations that had previously been upheld by the Court. One example was the Federal Radio Act of 1927, which created a

Federal Radio Commission to regulate the nascent radio broadcasting industry. The Commission was empowered to allocate frequencies and grant licenses "as public convenience, interest or necessity requires"—a verbal formulation that Congress used in several regulatory enactments of the early twentieth century. Is the NIRA's standard for approving codes of fair competition really any less "intelligible" than that? Or is "intelligibility" not the real criterion being applied? Chief Justice Hughes noted that, unlike the NIRA, the Radio Act established an expert administrative agency to exercise the broad policymaking powers delegated by Congress. Why should that make a difference? Are the purposes of the delegation principle better served by delegating powers to an unelected independent regulatory commission than to an elected President?

3. *Delegation to private parties.* Although not expressly resting his decision on this basis, Chief Justice Hughes seemed troubled by the influential role played by industry in sponsoring codes of fair competition. Was he assuming that the President did not really exercise independent policymaking discretion in approving the live poultry code? Is that assumption fair? The issue of delegating lawmaking power to private groups came to a head a year later, in the case of Carter v. Carter Coal Co., 298 U.S. 238 (1936). The case involved a provision of the Bituminous Coal Conservation Act of 1935, specifying a peculiar procedure for setting maximum working hours for coal miners. Under the Act, once a particular maximum-hour provision had been adopted in collective bargaining agreements among unions representing over one-half of all miners in America and companies producing over two-thirds of all coal tonnage mined in America, that provision would automatically become effective for all other miners and all other coal producers in the nation. The Court found this provision unconstitutional:

> The power conferred upon the majority is, in effect, the power to regulate the affairs of an unwilling minority. This is legislative delegation in its most obnoxious form; for it is not even delegation to an official or an official body, presumptively disinterested, but to private persons whose interests may be and often are adverse to the interests of others in the same business. . . . The difference between producing coal and regulating its production is, of course, fundamental. The former is a private activity; the latter is necessarily a governmental function, since, in the very nature of things, one person may not be entrusted with the power to regulate the business of another, and especially of a competitor. And a statute which attempts to confer such power undertakes an intolerable and unconstitutional interference with personal liberty and private property. The delegation is so clearly arbitrary, and so clearly a denial of rights safeguarded by the due process clause of the Fifth Amendment . . . .

Id. at 311.

After a long period of dormancy, the *Carter Coal* principle was recently invoked in a case involving a statute empowering Amtrak to exercise regulatory authority over its private railroad competitors. Amtrak (formally, the "National Railroad Passenger Corporation") is a creature of Congress sharing both public and private attributes. Section 207 of the Passenger Rail Investment and Improvement Act of 2008 confers upon Amtrak and the Federal Railroad Administration (FRA, a division of the Department of Transportation) joint authority to establish binding rules for allocating use of the nation's rail network by Amtrak and private railroads. An association of private railroads challenged rail-use standards jointly issued by Amtrak and the FRA, alleging that Amtrak is essentially a private corporation, and that the delegation of regulatory power to it thus violated the *Carter Coal* principle. The railroads relied heavily on provisions in Amtrak's enabling act stating that Amtrak "shall be operated and managed as a for-profit corporation," and that it "is not a department, agency, or instrumentality of the United States Government." 49 U.S.C. §§24301(a)(2) & (3). The Supreme Court disagreed, however, finding that, notwithstanding congressional labels, Amtrak is in reality a government entity for purposes of constitutional separation-of-powers analysis. Department of Transportation v. Association of American Railroads, 135 S. Ct. 1225 (2015). In so finding, the Court noted that eight of the nine members of Amtrak's governing board are appointed by the President with advice and consent of the Senate; Amtrak is required by statute to provide various unremunerative services to the public; and it receives large annual subsidies from Congress. Though the Court's decision dodged the *Carter Coal* issue, the factual setting of the case illustrates the occasional difficulty of locating the boundary line between "public" and "private" regulation. Throughout the materials in this book we will see regulatory systems that rely, sometimes quite heavily, on private input into regulatory decisionmaking. A common example is provided by state occupational licensing regimes, such as those described in the *Gibson* and *North Carolina Dental* cases, excerpted in Chapters VI and VII, *infra*, in which members of the licensed profession serve on the governing board of the agency that regulates them and their competitors. Would a federal regulatory regime structured in this way constitute an unconstitutional delegation to private parties? Would it matter if the members of the licensing board were elected by its licensees?

4. *The decline (and revival?) of the nondelegation doctrine.* The Supreme Court's brief dalliance with a forceful application of nondelegation principles came to an abrupt halt after *Panama Refining* and *Schechter*. For example, in Yakus v. United States, 321 U.S. 414 (1944), the Court upheld a statute empowering the wartime Office of Price Administration to fix "generally fair and equitable" rent and price ceilings. The Court found that Congress had "specified the basic conditions of fact upon whose existence or occurrence, ascertained from relevant data by a designated administrative agency, it directs that its statutory command shall be effective." *Id.* at 425. After *Yakus*, the Supreme Court routinely upheld delegations of policymaking power to administrative agencies—so routinely, in fact, as to lead many commentators to conclude that the nondelegation doctrine had become a dead letter. Yet, as the following two cases illustrate, members of the Court would occasionally send signals hinting that news of the doctrine's demise might be premature.

INDUSTRIAL UNION DEPT., AFL-CIO v. AMERICAN PETROLEUM INSTITUTE, 448 U.S. 607 (1980) (THE *BENZENE* CASE): *Benzene* involved the interplay of two sections of the Occupational Safety and Health Act. Section 3(8) requires that all workplace safety and health standards promulgated by the Secretary of Labor be "reasonably necessary and appropriate" to protect worker health and safety. Section 6(b)(5), dealing specifically with harmful toxic substances in the workplace, directs the Secretary to select the standard that "most adequately assures, to the extent feasible, that no employee will suffer material impairment of health or functional capacity." The Secretary had issued a standard relating to airborne concentrations of benzene, a chemical believed to cause leukemia and other disorders, and for which no safe exposure level was known to exist. The standard set a maximum exposure limit of one part benzene per million parts of air (1 ppm). Relying on §3(8), representatives of the petrochemical industry argued that in setting the standard, the Secretary should quantify the benefits (in terms of diseases or deaths prevented) and compare them to the costs of compliance. The Secretary refused to quantify the benefits or compare them to costs. Instead, he had set the standard at the lowest level he considered "technologically achievable at a cost that will not impair the viability of the industries subject to the regulation." The Supreme Court struck down the standard. A plurality of four Justices, in an opinion by Justice Stevens, said that the Secretary, before setting the benzene standard, should have made a threshold finding that, at concentrations in excess of 1 ppm, benzene poses a "significant risk of harm." In explaining why it imposed this interpretive gloss on the statutory language, the plurality said:

> If the Government were correct in arguing that [the Act does not require] that the risk from a toxic substance be quantified sufficiently to enable the Secretary to characterize it as significant in an understandable way, the statute would make such a "sweeping delegation of legislative power" that it might be unconstitutional under the Court's reasoning in [*Schechter*].

448 U.S. at 646.

Justice Rehnquist, concurring, urged the Court to declare that §6(b)(5) was unconstitutional as an excessive delegation of legislative power. In Rehnquist's view, the insertion of the "feasibility" constraint, as an amendment to the original, absolutist version of the provision, rendered "what had been a clear, if somewhat unrealistic, standard largely, if not entirely, precatory." As such, in his view, the statute violated the three purposes served by the nondelegation doctrine: namely, (1) to ensure that "important choices of social policy are made by Congress, the branch of our Government most responsive to the popular will," (2) to provide the recipient of a delegation an "'intelligible principle' to guide the exercise of the delegated discretion," and (3) to enable reviewing courts to "test that exercise against ascertainable standards." *Id.* at 685-686. Four members of the Court, in a dissenting opinion by Justice Marshall, concluded that the meaning of the Act was sufficiently clear to present no delegation problem and, therefore, to provide no justification for adding the "substantial risk of harm" gloss inserted by the plurality.

A year later, in American Textile Manufacturers Institute v. Donovan, 452 U.S. 490 (1981) (the *Cotton Dust* Case) (excerpted in Chapter II, *infra*), the Court squarely addressed the issue sidestepped in *Benzene,* by ruling that, so long as the Secretary has found a "significant risk of harm," he is not further required to compare the costs and benefits of a standard issued under §6(b)(5). Justice Rehnquist, this time joined by Chief Justice Burger, strenuously dissented, once again attacking the Act as an improper delegation of legislative power:

> Congress simply abdicated its responsibility for the making of a fundamental and most difficult policy choice—whether and to what extent "the statistical probability of future deaths should . . . be disregarded in light of the economic costs of

preventing those deaths." . . . That is a "quintessential legislative" choice and must be made by the elected representatives of the people, not by nonelected officials in the Executive branch.

452 U.S. at 549. Those who read *Benzene* to signal a resurrection of the nondelegation doctrine were disappointed. But at least the Rehnquist view had picked up another vote.

MISTRETTA v. UNITED STATES, 488 U.S. 361 (1989):   In an attempt to impose greater uniformity in the sentences dispensed by federal judges in criminal cases, Congress enacted the Sentencing Reform Act of 1984 (Act), *as amended,* 18 U.S.C. §§3551 *et seq.,* and 28 U.S.C. §§991-998. The Act established the United States Sentencing Commission, and directed it to promulgate sentencing "guidelines" (permissible ranges) for determining the length of sentences. Once promulgated, the guidelines were binding on sentencing judges, allowing them only very limited discretion to consider aggravating or mitigating factors not adequately reflected in the guidelines. The Commission was established by the Act "as an independent commission in the judicial branch of the United States," §991(a), and consisted of seven voting members appointed by the President, with the advice and consent of the Senate, at least three of whom had to be sitting federal judges. Commission members were subject to removal by the President "only for neglect of duty or malfeasance in office or for other good cause shown." *Id.*

Mistretta, indicted for certain drug offenses, claimed that the sentencing guidelines could not be applied to him because the Act was unconstitutional. Among other claims, he argued that the Act constituted an invalid delegation of legislative powers to the Commission. Justice Blackmun, writing for an eight-Justice majority, easily dismissed the argument, noting that the Act contained sufficient standards—including enumeration of seven "offense" factors for establishing the severity of the offense, and eleven personal factors for establishing the risk posed by the defendant—to provide an "intelligible principle" for the exercise of the Commission's standard-setting power. Justice Scalia dissented:

> I can find no place within our constitutional system for an agency created by Congress to exercise no governmental power other than the making of laws. . . . The whole theory of *lawful* congressional "delegation" is not that Congress is sometimes too busy or too divided, and can therefore assign its responsibility of making law to someone else, but rather that a certain degree of discretion, and thus of lawmaking, *inheres* in most executive or judicial action, and it is up to Congress, by the relative specificity or generality of its statutory commands, to determine—up to a point—how small or how large that degree shall be. . . .
>
> In the present case, however, [it] is irrelevant whether the standards are adequate, because they are not standards related to the exercise of executive or judicial powers; they are, plainly and simply, standards for further legislation.
>
> The lawmaking function of the Sentencing Commission is completely divorced from any responsibility for execution of the law or adjudication of private rights under the law. It is divorced from responsibility for execution of the law not only because the Commission is not said to be "located in the Executive Branch" . . . but, more importantly, because the Commission neither exercises any executive power on its own, nor is subject to the control of the President, who does.

[T]he Commission's lawmaking is completely divorced from the exercise of judicial powers since, not being a court, it has no judicial powers itself, nor is it subject to the control of any other body with judicial powers. The power to make law at issue here, in other words, is not ancillary, but quite naked. The situation is no different in principle from what would exist if Congress gave the same power of writing sentencing laws to a congressional agency such as the General Accounting Office, or to members of its staff.

The delegation of lawmaking authority to the Commission is, in short, unsupported by any legitimating theory to explain why it is not a delegation of legislative power. To disregard structural legitimacy is wrong in itself—but since structure has purpose, the disregard also has adverse practical consequences. In this case, as suggested earlier, the consequence is to facilitate and encourage judicially uncontrollable delegation. . . . By reason of today's decision, I anticipate that Congress will find delegation of its lawmaking powers much more attractive in the future. If rulemaking can be entirely unrelated to the exercise of judicial or executive powers, I foresee all manner of "expert" bodies, insulated from the political process, to which Congress will delegate various portions of its lawmaking responsibility. How tempting to create an expert Medical Commission (mostly M.D.'s, with perhaps a few Ph.D.'s in moral philosophy) to dispose of such thorny, "now-in" political issues as the withholding of life-support systems in federally funded hospitals, or the use of fetal tissue for research. This is an undemocratic precedent that we set—not because of the scope of the delegated power, but because its recipient is not one of the three Branches of Government. The only governmental power the Commission possesses is the power to make law; and it is not the Congress. . . . [Rather, it is] a sort of junior varsity Congress. . . .

NOTES AND QUESTIONS

1. *The functions served by the nondelegation doctrine.* Do you agree with Justice Rehnquist's list of the three functions served by the doctrine in his *Benzene* dissent? If so, why couldn't he obtain the support of more of his colleagues on the Court? Did the plurality's tactic of narrowly interpreting the OSH Act satisfy the three purposes enunciated by Rehnquist? Is Justice Scalia, in his *Mistretta* dissent, adding a fourth function: namely, to distinguish between the policymaking "inherent" in "executive" action and the "naked" policymaking characteristic of a legislature? Is his theory compelling? Useful? Does it merely shift the burden of doctrinal uncertainty to the definition of "executive"?

2. *Can the nondelegation doctrine be applied selectively?* In addition to *Benzene* and *Mistretta*, the Supreme Court has on occasion hinted that the nondelegation principle may have special force in certain contexts, such as taxation and criminal law. In National Cable Television Assn. v. United States, 415 U.S. 336 (1974), the Court narrowly construed a statute authorizing agencies to set fees for their services, implying that delegation of revenue-raising powers to agencies might pose special delegation issues. But in Skinner v. Mid-American Pipeline Co., 490 U.S. 212 (1989), another user-fee case, the Court seemed to put that notion to rest. In the words of Justice O'Connor, writing for the Court (490 U.S. at 223):

Even if the user fees are a form of taxation, we hold that the delegation of discretionary authority under Congress' taxing power is subject to no Constitutional scrutiny greater than what we have applied to other nondelegation challenges.

In Touby v. United States, 500 U.S. 160 (1991), the Court reviewed a statute delegating to the Attorney General the power to designate certain drugs as "controlled substances," with the result that their manufacture or sale would be subject to criminal penalties. In upholding the delegation, the Court assumed *arguendo* that greater congressional specificity might be required in delegating power to agencies to issue rules that are subject to criminal enforcement, but nonetheless found the delegation sufficiently specific. Shortly thereafter, however, in Loving v. United States, 517 U.S. 748 (1996), a case involving a delegation to the President to determine factors that can elevate murder to capital murder in military cases, the Court specifically rejected the contention that delegations of authority to fix criminal punishments must be judged by a higher standard.

There matters stood, when the D.C. Circuit issued a surprising decision in a case involving the Clean Air Act that gave the Supreme Court yet another opportunity to consider the meaning and scope of the nondelegation doctrine.

The Clean Air Act of 1970 (CAA) stands as perhaps the paradigmatic example of the "new regulation" of the 1960s and 1970s. A huge, sweeping, dense statute, the CAA sought nothing less than to clean the air breathed by every American within a decade. The Act required the newly established Environmental Protection Agency to set "national ambient air quality standards" (NAAQS) for certain pollutants harmful to public health (the agency named carbon monoxide, ozone, nitrogen oxide, sulfur dioxide, and two sizes of "particulate matter" as fitting the statutory criteria). By establishing an NAAQS, EPA specifies the maximum allowable concentration of the pollutant in the ambient air throughout the United States. Under §109 of the Act, the EPA was to set a "primary standard" (a concentration level "requisite to protect the public health" with an "adequate margin of safety") and a "secondary standard" (a concentration level "requisite to protect the public welfare"). For most NAAQS, the primary and secondary standards are the same. To take account of changes in circumstances and scientific knowledge, the Act required the EPA to review the standards at least every five years and revise them as frequently as warranted.

In order to achieve the NAAQS, the Act set forth a complex implementation scheme that divides enforcement responsibilities between the EPA and the state governments. The states must promulgate detailed "state implementation plans" (subject to EPA approval) for regulating pollution sources within their boundaries so as to achieve the NAAQS for each regulated pollutant, while the EPA sets standards for new mobile sources of pollution (primarily motor vehicles) and new stationary sources (such as factories and power plants). Initially, Congress intended to achieve the NAAQS within a mere seven years. No more old-fashioned, open-ended, permissive delegations: this was delegation with teeth—and a hammer!

As the 1977 deadline approached, it was apparent that many states—including almost all populous, industrial states—would not meet the deadline. Congress amended the CAA in 1977, postponing the deadlines for attaining air quality standards for some pollutants until 1982 and for other pollutants until 1987, but authorizing the EPA to impose severe penalties on states that failed to submit acceptable implementation plans. The 1977 amendments also attempted to reconcile the conflict between pollution reduction and economic development by allowing limited growth of pollution sources, subject to a rigorous permit-application process. After even the new deadlines were missed in many states, Congress again amended the Act in 1990, further extending compliance deadlines and specifying particular actions that noncomplying states and the EPA must take in an effort to attain the Act's goals.

The regulation of ozone illustrates the complexities of establishing air quality standards. Ozone (O3) is an airborne molecule that occurs naturally in the upper atmosphere, where it performs the highly salutary function of screening the sun's harmful ultraviolet radiation. Ground-level ozone or smog is harmful, however, reducing visibility and causing respiratory problems (including aggravating asthma and reducing lung function among other things). Smog is produced when sunlight reacts with nitrogen oxides and at least one volatile organic compound in the atmosphere. Nitrogen oxides come from car exhaust, coal power plants, and factory emissions. As a result, reducing smog requires regulating emissions from a variety of industrial and mobile sources.

In 1971, the EPA established, as the air quality standard for ozone, a maximum concentration of 0.08 ppm, sustained for a one-hour period. 36 Fed. Reg. 8136 (1971). Eight years later, the EPA revised the standard to set a maximum concentration of 0.12 ppm. 42 Fed. Reg. 20,493 (1979). In 1994, it undertook a new review of the ozone standard, specifically inviting comments from the public on the wisdom of shifting from a one-hour standard to an eight-hour standard, and setting the eight-hour concentration level at either 0.09 ppm (roughly, the status quo), 0.08 ppm, or 0.07 ppm. Three years later, after extensive research and analysis, the EPA set the ozone NAAQS at a maximum 0.08 ppm over an eight-hour period. 62 Fed. Reg. 38,856 (1997). In setting the standard, the EPA adhered to its consistent policy of setting NAAQS solely on the basis of benefits to the public health and public welfare and ignored the cost of compliance (which are considered later in the implementation process). Nonetheless, the EPA did estimate the costs and benefits of its new standard in a "regulatory impact analysis" in order to comply with a presidential executive order requiring the identification of the costs and benefits of major regulatory actions (discussed in Chapter V, *infra*). The EPA estimated the annual benefits of its new ozone standard as ranging from $400 million to $2.1 billion, and the annual costs at $1.1 billion. Thus, it projected that the standard's economic impact could range from a net *cost* of $700 million to a net *benefit* of $1 billion.

A diverse group of parties adversely affected by the revision to the ozone standard promptly challenged the EPA's action in federal court. In addition to making several statutory claims, the petitioners argued that §109 of the Clean Air Act constituted an unconstitutional delegation of legislative power to the EPA. The D.C. Circuit ruled in favor of the EPA on the statutory claims, but agreed with the petitioners on the delegation claim. American Trucking Assns., Inc. v. EPA, 175 F.3d 1027 (D.C. Cir. 1999). In finding a violation of the nondelegation doctrine, the court focused less on the language of the Clean Air Act than on the EPA's construction of its obligation to establish NAAQS that are "requisite to protect the public health" with an "adequate margin of safety." The court criticized the EPA for failing to apply a "determinate criterion" for deciding how much ozone was too much:

Here it is as though Congress commanded EPA to select "big guys," and EPA announced that it would evaluate candidates based on height and weight, but revealed no cut-off point. The announcement, though sensible in what it does say, is fatally incomplete. The reasonable person responds, "How tall? How heavy?" . . . EPA's explanations for its decisions amount to assertions that a less stringent standard would allow the relevant pollutant to inflict a greater quantum of harm on public health, and that a more stringent standard would result in less harm. Such arguments only support the intuitive proposition that more pollution will not benefit public health, not that keeping pollution at or below any particular level is "requisite" or not requisite to "protect the public health" with an "adequate margin of safety," the formula set out by §109(b)(1).

175 F.3d at 1034-1035. Rather than declaring the statute unconstitutional, however, the court took the unusual step of ordering the EPA to articulate an "intelligible principle" to fill the statutory gap, and even suggested several criteria that the EPA might consider in doing so. Christine Whitman, the EPA Administrator, petitioned for review by the Supreme Court.

WHITMAN v. AMERICAN TRUCKING ASSNS., INC.
531 U.S. 457 (2001)

Justice Scalia delivered the opinion of the Court.

These cases present the following questions: (1) Whether §109(b)(1) of the Clean Air Act (CAA) delegates legislative power to the Administrator of the Environmental Protection Agency (EPA). (2) Whether the Administrator may consider the costs of implementation in setting national ambient air quality standards (NAAQS) under §109(b)(1). (3) Whether the Court of Appeals had jurisdiction to review the EPA's interpretation of Part D of Title I of the CAA, 42 U.S.C. §§7501-7515, with respect to implementing the revised ozone NAAQS. (4) If so, whether the EPA's interpretation of that part was permissible.

I

[Justice Scalia here summarized the facts and litigation history of the case. In Part II of his opinion, excerpted in Chapter V, *infra*, the Court held that the D.C. Circuit was correct in ruling that the EPA is not permitted to consider costs of implementation in setting ambient air standards.]

III

Section 109(b)(1) of the CAA instructs the EPA to set "ambient air quality standards the attainment and maintenance of which in the judgment of the Administrator, based on [the] criteria [documents of §108] and allowing an adequate margin of safety, are requisite to protect the public health." 42 U.S.C. §7409(b)(1). The Court of Appeals held that this section as interpreted by the

Administrator did not provide an "intelligible principle" to guide the EPA's exercise of authority in setting NAAQS. . . . We disagree.

In a delegation challenge, the constitutional question is whether the statute has delegated legislative power to the agency. Article I, §1, of the Constitution vests "all legislative Power herein granted . . . in a Congress of the United States." This text permits no delegation of those powers, Loving v. United States, 517 U.S. 748, 771 (1996); *see id.* at 776-777 (Scalia, J., concurring in part and concurring in judgment), and so we repeatedly have said that when Congress confers decisionmaking authority upon agencies Congress must "lay down by legislative act an intelligible principle to which the person or body authorized to [act] is directed to conform." J. W. Hampton, Jr., & Co. v. United States, 276 U.S. 394, 409 (1928). We have never suggested that an agency can cure an unlawful delegation of legislative power by adopting in its discretion a limiting construction of the statute. . . . The idea that an agency can cure an unconstitutionally standardless delegation of power by declining to exercise some of that power seems to us internally contradictory. The very choice of which portion of the power to exercise—that is to say, the prescription of the standard that Congress had omitted—would itself be an exercise of the forbidden legislative authority. Whether the statute delegates legislative power is a question for the courts, and an agency's voluntary self-denial has no bearing upon the answer.

We agree with the Solicitor General that the text of §109(b)(1) of the CAA at a minimum requires that "for a discrete set of pollutants and based on published air quality criteria that reflect the latest scientific knowledge, [the] EPA must establish uniform national standards at a level that is requisite to protect public health from the adverse effects of the pollutant in the ambient air." Tr. of Oral Arg. in No. 99-1257, p. 5. Requisite, in turn, "means sufficient, but not more than necessary." *Id.* at 7. These limits on the EPA's discretion are strikingly similar to the ones we approved in Touby v. United States, 500 U.S. 160 (1991), which permitted the Attorney General to designate a drug as a controlled substance for purposes of criminal drug enforcement if doing so was "necessary to avoid an imminent hazard to the public safety." *Id.* at 163. They also resemble the Occupational Safety and Health Act provision requiring the agency to "set the standard which most adequately assures, to the extent feasible, on the basis of the best available evidence, that no employee will suffer any impairment of health"—which the Court upheld in Industrial Union Dept., AFL-CIO v. American Petroleum Institute, 448 U.S. 607, 646 (1980), and which even then-Justice Rehnquist, who alone in that case thought the statute violated the nondelegation doctrine, *see id.* at 671 (opinion concurring in judgment), would have upheld if, like the statute here, it did not permit economic costs to be considered. *See* American Textile Mfrs. Institute, Inc. v. Donovan, 452 U.S. 490, 545 (1981) (Rehnquist, J., dissenting).

The scope of discretion §109(b)(1) allows is in fact well within the outer limits of our nondelegation precedents. In the history of the Court we have found the requisite "intelligible principle" lacking in only two statutes, one of which provided literally no guidance for the exercise of discretion, and the other of which conferred authority to regulate the entire economy on the basis of no more precise a standard than stimulating the economy by assuring "fair competition." *See* Panama Refining Co. v. Ryan, 293 U.S. 388 (1935); A.L.A. Schechter Poultry Corp. v. United States, 295 U.S. 495 (1935). We have, on the other hand, upheld the validity of §11(b)(2) of the Public Utility Holding Company Act of 1935, 49 Stat. 821, which gave the Securities and Exchange Commission authority to modify the structure of holding company systems so as to ensure that they are not "unduly or unnecessarily complicated" and do not "unfairly or inequitably distribute voting power among security holders." American Power & Light Co. v. SEC, 329 U.S. 90, 104 (1946). We have approved the wartime conferral of agency power to fix the prices of commodities at a level that "'will be generally fair and equitable and will effectuate the [in some respects conflicting] purposes of the Act.'" Yakus v. United States, 321 U.S. 414, 420 (1944). And we have found an "intelligible principle" in various statutes authorizing regulation in the "public interest." *See, e.g.,* National Broadcasting Co. v. United States, 319 U.S. 190, 225-226 (1943) (FCC's power to regulate airwaves); New York Central Securities Corp. v. United States, 287 U.S. 12, 24-25 (1932) (ICC's power to approve railroad consolidations). In short, we have "almost never felt qualified to second-guess Congress regarding the permissible degree of policy judgment that can be left to those executing or applying the law." Mistretta v. United States, 488 U.S. 361, 416 (1989) (Scalia, J., dissenting); *see id.* at 373 (majority opinion).

It is true enough that the degree of agency discretion that is acceptable varies according to the scope of the power congressionally conferred. . . . While Congress need not provide any direction to the EPA regarding the manner in which it is to define "country elevators," which are to be exempt from new-stationary-source regulations governing grain elevators, see §7411(i), it must provide substantial guidance on setting air standards that affect the entire national economy. But even in sweeping regulatory schemes we have never demanded, as the Court of Appeals did here, that statutes provide a "determinate criterion" for saying "how much [of the regulated harm] is too much." 175 F.3d at 1034. In *Touby,* for example, we did not require the statute to decree how "imminent" was too imminent, or how "necessary" was necessary enough, or even—most relevant here—how "hazardous" was too hazardous. 500 U.S. at 165-167. Similarly, the statute at issue in Lichter [v. United States, 334 U.S. 742 (1948)] authorized agencies to recoup "excess profits" paid under wartime Government contracts, yet we did not insist that Congress specify how much profit was too much. 334 U.S. at 783-786. It is therefore not conclusive for delegation purposes that, as respondents argue, ozone and particulate matter are "nonthreshold" pollutants that inflict a continuum of adverse health effects at any airborne concentration greater than zero, and hence require the EPA to make judgments of degree. . . . Section 109(b)(1) of the CAA, which to repeat we interpret as requiring the EPA to set air quality standards at the level that is "requisite"—that is, not lower or higher than is necessary—to protect the public health with an adequate margin of safety, fits comfortably within the scope of discretion permitted by our precedent.

We therefore reverse the judgment of the Court of Appeals remanding for reinterpretation that would avoid a supposed delegation of legislative power. It will remain for the Court of Appeals—on the remand that we direct for other reasons—to dispose of any other preserved challenge to the NAAQS under the judicial-review provisions contained in 42 U.S.C. §7607(d)(9).

IV

[The Court then examined the EPA's decision to implement its revised ozone standards in so-called "nonattainment" areas of the country—namely, areas whose ozone levels currently exceed the maximum level permitted by its previous ozone standard. The Court ruled that: (1) the Court of Appeals had jurisdiction to review this decision by the EPA, and (2) on the merits, the EPA had misinterpreted the portions of the Clean Air Act dealing with setting ozone standards in nonattainment areas. Accordingly, the Court ordered that, on remand, the agency "develop a reasonable interpretation" of those provisions.]

The judgment of the Court of Appeals is affirmed in part and reversed in part, and the cases are remanded for proceedings consistent with this opinion.

It is so ordered.

JUSTICE THOMAS, concurring.

I agree with the majority that §109's directive to the agency is no less an "intelligible principle" than a host of other directives that we have approved. I also agree that the Court of Appeals' remand to the agency to make its own corrective interpretation does not accord with our understanding of the delegation issue. I write separately, however, to express my concern that there may nevertheless be a genuine constitutional problem with §109, a problem which the parties did not address.

The parties to this case who briefed the constitutional issue wrangled over constitutional doctrine with barely a nod to the text of the Constitution. Although this Court since 1928 has treated the "intelligible principle" requirement as the only constitutional limit on congressional grants of power to administrative agencies, *see* J. W. Hampton, Jr., & Co. v. United States, 276 U.S. 394, 409 (1928), the Constitution does not speak of "intelligible principles." Rather, it speaks in much simpler terms: "*All* legislative Powers herein granted shall be vested in a Congress." U.S. Const., Art. 1, §1 (emphasis added). I am not convinced that the intelligible principle doctrine serves to prevent all cessions of legislative power. I believe that there are cases in which the principle is intelligible and yet the significance of the delegated decision is simply too great for the decision to be called anything other than "legislative."

As it is, none of the parties to this case has examined the text of the Constitution or asked us to reconsider our precedents on cessions of legislative power. On a future day, however, I would be willing to address the question whether our delegation jurisprudence has strayed too far from our Founders' understanding of separation of powers.

JUSTICE STEVENS, with whom JUSTICE SOUTER joins, concurring in part and concurring in the judgment. . . .

[T]he Court convincingly explains why the Court of Appeals erred when it concluded that §109 effected "an unconstitutional delegation of legislative power." I wholeheartedly endorse the Court's result and endorse its explanation of its reasons, albeit with the following caveat.

The Court has two choices. We could choose to articulate our ultimate disposition of this issue by frankly acknowledging that the power delegated to the EPA is "legislative" but nevertheless conclude that the delegation is constitutional because adequately limited by the terms of the authorizing statute. Alternatively, we could pretend, as the Court does, that the authority delegated to the EPA is somehow not "legislative power." Despite the fact that there is language in our opinions that supports the Court's articulation of our holding, I am persuaded that it would be both wiser and more faithful to what we have actually done in delegation cases to admit that agency rulemaking authority is "legislative power."

The proper characterization of governmental power should generally depend on the nature of the power, not on the identity of the person exercising it. If the NAAQS that the EPA promulgated had been prescribed by Congress, everyone would agree that those rules would be the product of an exercise of "legislative power." The same characterization is appropriate when an agency exercises rulemaking authority pursuant to a permissible delegation from Congress.

My view is not only more faithful to normal English usage, but is also fully consistent with the text of the Constitution. In Article I, the Framers vested "All legislative Powers" in the Congress, Art. I, §1, just as in Article II they vested the "executive Power" in the President, Art. II, §1. Those provisions do not purport to limit the authority of either recipient of power to delegate authority to others. . . . Surely the authority granted to members of the Cabinet and federal law enforcement agents is properly characterized as "Executive" even though not exercised by the President. . . .

It seems clear that an executive agency's exercise of rulemaking authority pursuant to a valid delegation from Congress is "legislative." As long as the delegation provides a sufficiently intelligible principle, there is nothing inherently unconstitutional about it. Accordingly, . . . I would hold that when Congress enacted §109, it effected a constitutional delegation of legislative power to the EPA.

Justice Breyer, concurring in part and concurring in the judgment. [Omitted.]

NOTES AND QUESTIONS

1. *How much is too much?* Was the D.C. Circuit panel correct in saying that a principle is not "intelligible" unless it says how much is too much? Is its "big guys" example instructive or distracting? Assuming (as the EPA did) that ozone is harmful at all levels of concentration, even negligible levels, does the statutory standard—"requisite to protect the public health"—permit the EPA to set the ozone standard at any level above zero? If so, what criteria exist to tell the EPA (and the courts) where to set the standard? Note that the EPA, the D.C. Circuit, and the Supreme Court all agreed that the Act forbids the EPA to consider the cost of implementing an NAAQS. That being the case, how else could the EPA decide how much ozone is "too much"?

2. *The nondelegation doctrine and the constitutional text.* One striking feature of the *Whitman* decision is the disagreement between Justices Scalia and Stevens over the textual basis for the nondelegation doctrine in Article I, §1, of the Constitution. How do the two Justices read the words "vest" and "legislative power"? Whose reading is most plausible? Does it matter? Would the choice of textual

readings actually affect the outcome of any of the cases we have encountered? Does one reading better serve the purposes of the doctrine?

3. *"Curing" unconstitutional delegations by agency standard-setting.* Justice Scalia deals rather dismissively with the D.C. Circuit's novel idea that the EPA could "cure" an unconstitutional delegation by promulgating standards that fill in the missing "intelligible principle." Is there more to be said for that idea? In fact, the idea was suggested three decades earlier in a famous article by Kenneth C. Davis, A New Approach to Delegation, 36 U. Chi. L. Rev. 715 (1969). Rather than focus exclusively on the substantive standards written into statutes, he said, the courts should look at the full range of "safeguards"—procedural as well as substantive, administrative and judicial as well as legislative—that prevent agencies from exercising "uncontrolled discretionary power." In particular, Davis urged that, where Congress has failed to articulate substantive standards for the exercise of delegated powers, courts should require the agency to write its own standards.

4. *Delegation and statutory interpretation.* Even though the Court has refused since 1935 to strike down any statutes on delegation grounds, it has invoked the doctrine from time to time as a basis for narrowly interpreting broad statutes. Some commentators have referred to this practice as having created a nondelegation "canon," which results in narrow constructions of statutory authority. The *Benzene* and *National Cable* decisions are good illustrations of this approach. Another celebrated example is Kent v. Dulles, 357 U.S. 116 (1958). Secretary of State Dulles had refused to issue a passport to a member of the Communist Party, invoking a provision of the Passport Act authorizing the Secretary to issue passports "under such rules as the President shall designate and prescribe." The Court interpreted this language, despite its apparent breadth, not to encompass the power asserted. Noting that the right to travel is a "liberty" interest protected by the Fifth Amendment, the Court concluded that "we will not readily infer that Congress gave the Secretary of State unbridled discretion to grant or withhold it." *Id.* at 129.

The Court retreated from this strong stance in Zemel v. Rusk, 381 U.S. 1 (1965), where it upheld Secretary of State Rusk's refusal to validate U.S. citizens' passports for travel to Cuba. There was no delegation problem, the Court found, because Rusk was not indiscriminately abridging a citizen's constitutional right, but rather was protecting valid "foreign policy considerations affecting all citizens." *Id.* at 13. *See also* Regan v. Wald, 468 U.S. 222 (1984) (upholding the President's power to prevent the flow of U.S. currency to Cuba). The Court further limited *Kent* with its ruling in Haig v. Agee, 453 U.S. 280 (1983), that the Secretary of State may deny a passport to anyone "whose *conduct* is damaging the national security and foreign policy of the United States." *Id.* at 304.

5. *The nondelegation principle refuses to die?* In Gundy v. United States, 139 S. Ct. 2116 (2019), four Justices signaled that a revival of the nondelegation principle may be in the offing. At issue was a provision of the Sex Offender Registration and Notification Act that authorized the Attorney General, by rule, to determine whether the Act's registration requirements applied to persons convicted of sex crimes prior to the Act's adoption. Writing for a four-Justice plurality, Justice Kagan applied the familiar "intelligible principle" test and found that the delegation "easily passes constitutional muster." Justice Gorsuch, however, writing for himself, the Chief Justice, and Justice Thomas, argued that

the Act effected an unconstitutional delegation of legislative power. He first explained why the nondelegation doctrine is important as a corollary to constitutionally mandated separation of powers, exemplified by the Constitution's vesting clauses, but also inherent in various constitutional structures. The most important of these are the specific impediments to legislation:

> [To the framers,] Article I's detailed and arduous processes for new legislation . . . were bulwarks of liberty. . . . Because men are not angels and majorities can threaten minority rights, the framers insisted on a legislature composed of different bodies subject to different electorates as a means of ensuring that any new law would have to secure the approval of a supermajority of the people's representatives. This, in turn, assured minorities that their votes would often decide the fate of proposed legislation. . . .
>
> If Congress could pass off its legislative power to the executive branch, the "[v]esting [c]lauses, and indeed the entire structure of the Constitution," would "make no sense."[29] Without the involvement of representatives from across the country or the demands of bicameralism and presentment, legislation would risk becoming nothing more than the will of the current President. And if laws could be simply declared by a single person, they would not be few in number, the product of widespread social consensus, likely to protect minority interests, or apt to provide stability and fair notice. Accountability would suffer too. Legislators might seek to take credit for addressing a pressing social problem by sending it to the executive for resolution, while at the same time blaming the executive for the problems that attend whatever measures he chooses to pursue. . . .

139 S. Ct. at 2134 (Gorsuch, J., dissenting). Justice Gorsuch then urged the Court to return to the nondelegation tests formulated by the Court prior to 1928. He summarized those tests in these terms:

> First, we know that as long as Congress makes the policy decisions when regulating private conduct, it may authorize another branch to "fill up the details." . . . Second, once Congress prescribes the rule governing private conduct, it may make the application of that rule depend on executive fact-finding. . . . Third, Congress may assign the executive and judicial branches certain non-legislative responsibilities. While the Constitution vests all federal legislative power in Congress alone, Congress's legislative authority sometimes overlaps with authority the Constitution separately vests in another branch. . . .

139 S. Ct. at 2136. Justice Gorsuch then lamented the emergence of what he viewed as the much more expansive "intelligible principle" test after 1928:

> This Court first used that phrase in 1928 in *J. W. Hampton, Jr. & Co. v. United States,* where it remarked that a statute "lay[ing] down by legislative act an intelligible principle to which the [executive official] is directed to conform" satisfies the separation of powers. No one at the time thought the phrase meant to effect some revolution in this Court's understanding of the Constitution. . . . [T]he Court's reference to an "intelligible principle" was just another way to describe the traditional rule that Congress may leave the executive the responsibility to find facts and fill up details.

---

29. Lawson, Delegation and Original Meaning, 88 Va. L. Rev. 327, 340 (2002).

Still, it's undeniable that the "intelligible principle" remark eventually began to take on a life of its own. We sometimes chide people for treating judicial opinions as if they were statutes, divorcing a passing comment from its context, ignoring all that came before and after, and treating an isolated phrase as if it were controlling. But that seems to be exactly what happened here. For two decades, no one thought to invoke the "intelligible principle" comment as a basis to uphold a statute that would have failed more traditional separation-of-powers tests. In fact, the phrase sat more or less silently entombed until the late 1940s. Only then did lawyers begin digging it up in earnest and arguing to this Court that it had somehow displaced (*sub silentio* of course) all prior teachings in this area.

This mutated version of the "intelligible principle" remark has no basis in the original meaning of the Constitution, in history, or even in the decision from which it was plucked. Judges and scholars representing a wide and diverse range of views have condemned it as resting on "misunderst[ood] historical foundations."[61] They have explained, too, that it has been abused to permit delegations of legislative power that on any other conceivable account should be held unconstitutional. Indeed, where some have claimed to see "intelligible principles" many "less discerning readers [have been able only to] find gibberish."[62]

139 S. Ct. at 2139-2140.

Justice Alito wrote separately, stating that while he concurred that the delegation upheld in *Gundy* fell easily within the scope of those previously approved by the Court as fitting the intelligible principle test, he was open to reconsidering that test in a suitable future case. Justice Kavanaugh did not participate in the decision.

Look back at the questions above in Note 2. Do your answers to them change after reading *Gundy*? Whose approach to nondelegation is more likely to provide a justiciable standard?

Where does the nondelegation doctrine stand after *Gundy*? Is it awaiting rebirth? Or has it had a last chance at redemption? While academic writing does not always predict the direction of judicial decisions, the two decades preceding Gundy did see a revival of interest in nondelegation. *See, e.g.*, Larry Alexander & Saikrishna Prakash, Delegation Really Running Riot, 93 Va. L. Rev. 1035 (2007); Ronald A. Cass, Delegation Reconsidered: A Delegation Doctrine for the Modern Administrative State, 40 Harv. J.L. & Pub. Pol'y 147 (2016); Cynthia R. Farina, Deconstructing Nondelegation, 33 Harv. J.L. & Pub. Pol'y 87 (2010); Gary Lawson, Delegation and Original Meaning, 88 Va. L. Rev. 327 (2002); Eric A. Posner & Adrian Vermeule, Interring the Nondelegation Doctrine, 69 U. Chi. L. Rev. 1721 (2002); Neomi Rao, Administrative Collusion: How Delegation Diminishes the Collective Congress, 90 N.Y.U. L. Rev. 1463 (2015).

---

61. *Association of American Railroads*, 575 U.S. at (Thomas, J., concurring in judgment) (slip op., at 17)....

62. Lawson, 88 Va. L. Rev. at 329 ....

2. *Revision: The Legislative Veto*

Broad delegations, however constitutionally defensible or politically expedient, have nonetheless troubled many members of Congress who have seen control over lawmaking gradually shift to an unaccountable "fourth branch" of government. Theoretically, this problem is answered by the continuing opportunity of Congress to narrow and revise broad delegations by legislative amendment. But many members of Congress view the cumbersome process of legislating as an inadequate tool for overseeing the proliferating administrative branch.

A remedy to which Congress increasingly turned prior to 1983 was the "legislative veto." The term "legislative veto" describes a variety of mechanisms for requiring the approval of Congress, or some entity within Congress, before a proposed administrative action can become effective. A one-house veto provision gave either house of Congress the power to block an agency's proposed action, while other provisions required concurrent resolutions of both houses. (The latter differed from regular legislation by the absence of an opportunity for presidential veto and by a few procedural rules.) Other variations delegated veto power to a congressional committee or a committee chairperson.

As early as 1895, Congress authorized one of its committees to take "such measures as may be deemed necessary to remedy any neglect or delay" in government printing, thus overseeing the Public Printer's activities. Ch. 23, 28 Stat. 601. The modern legislative veto dates from the first executive reorganization statute of 1932. In that act, and many of its ensuing revisions, Congress granted the President authority to reorganize executive departments and agencies subject to some form of congressional veto. Thereafter, inclusion of legislative veto provisions in statutes accelerated. Congress enacted 5 statutes containing legislative veto provisions in the 1930s, 19 in the 1940s, 34 in the 1950s, 49 in the 1960s, and 248 in the 1970s. Between 1932 and 1982, Congress exercised the veto power a total of 230 times. Most of these involved deportation of aliens (111), budget alterations (65), or executive reorganizations (24). The remainder involved foreign relations, international trade, and administrative rulemaking.

Fully appreciating the potential intrusion into their prerogatives, Presidents consistently have objected to the legislative veto from the time of its inception. Many of their objections have been couched in constitutional terms. Even so, the prevalence of legislative veto provisions testifies to a parallel history of presidential acquiescence. Although some Presidents have vetoed bills containing legislative veto provisions, most have accepted such provisions as a political concession necessary to gain support for desired legislation.

Despite a history of disputes over the constitutionality of legislative veto provisions, judicial commentary was slow to develop. In a 1980 case brought by an alien whose right to remain in this country had been terminated by a one-house veto, the Ninth Circuit became the first federal court to strike down a legislative veto. Chadha v. Immigration & Naturalization Service, 634 F.2d 408 (9th Cir. 1980). The *Chadha* case arose under a statute, §244 of the Immigration and Nationality Act, that authorized the Attorney General, upon making certain findings, to "suspend" the deportation of an alien and adjust the alien's status to "lawfully admitted for permanent residence." Once he had issued an order suspending an alien's deportation, the Attorney General had to transmit it to

Congress. If, within the current or succeeding legislative session, either house passed a resolution disapproving the order, the alien would be deported.

As it stood in 1980, §244 was the latest in a long history of legislative attempts to infuse some humane flexibility into the nation's rather severe immigration laws. The Immigration Act of 1924, the first major legislative attempt to close our borders, provided no flexibility whatsoever: an alien who entered or remained in the United States illegally had to be deported. Responding to pleas of hardship, members of Congress began filing "private bills" seeking to adjust the status of particular named immigrants living within their districts. Like general legislation, these private bills had to be adopted by both houses and presented to the President. Tiring of having to deal with a growing flood of such private bills, Congress, in the Alien Registration Act of 1940, conferred upon the Attorney General the power to suspend deportation in a narrow category of cases. The Act provided, however, that a suspension order could be overturned if both houses of Congress disapproved the order by concurrent resolution. Eight years later, Congress amended the Act, broadening the category of aliens who would be eligible for suspension, but providing that a suspension order would not be effective unless affirmatively approved by concurrent resolution of both houses. The requirement of affirmative legislative concurrence proved to be almost as onerous on Congress as the old private bills regime. As a result, Congress almost immediately reversed itself once again, establishing, in the Immigration and Nationality Act of 1952, the one-house veto system in effect at the time of the *Chadha* case.

IMMIGRATION AND NATURALIZATION SERVICE v. CHADHA
462 U.S. 919 (1983)

Chief Justice Burger delivered the opinion of the Court. . . .

Chadha is an East Indian who was born in Kenya and holds a British passport. He was lawfully admitted to the United States in 1966 on a nonimmigrant student visa. His visa expired on June 30, 1972. On October 11, 1973, the District Director of the Immigration and Naturalization Service ordered Chadha to show cause why he should not be deported for having "remained in the United States for a longer time than permitted." App. 6. Pursuant to §242(b) of the Immigration and Nationality Act (Act), 8 U.S.C. §1252(b), a deportation hearing was held before an Immigration Judge on January 11, 1974. Chadha conceded that he was deportable for overstaying his visa and the hearing was adjourned to enable him to file an application for suspension of deportation under §244(a)(1) of the Act, 8 U.S.C. §1254(a)(1). Section 244(a)(1), at the time in question, provided:

> As hereinafter prescribed in this section, the Attorney General may, in his discretion, suspend deportation and adjust the status to that of an alien lawfully admitted for permanent residence, in the case of an alien who applies to the Attorney General for suspension of deportation and —
> (1) is deportable under any law of the United States except the provisions specified in paragraph (2) of this subsection; has been physically present in the United States for a continuous period of not less than seven years immediately preceding the date of such application, and proves that during all of such

period he was and is a person of good moral character; and is a person whose deportation would, in the opinion of the Attorney General, result in extreme hardship to the alien or to his spouse, parent, or child, who is a citizen of the United States or an alien lawfully admitted for permanent residence.[1]

After Chadha submitted his application for suspension of deportation, the deportation hearing was resumed on February 7, 1974. On the basis of evidence adduced at the hearing, affidavits submitted with the application, and the results of a character investigation conducted by the INS, the Immigration Judge, on June 25, 1974, ordered that Chadha's deportation be suspended. The Immigration Judge found that Chadha met the requirements of §244(a)(1): he had resided continuously in the United States for over seven years, was of good moral character, and would suffer "extreme hardship" if deported.

Pursuant to §244(c)(1) of the Act, 8 U.S.C. §1254(c)(1), the Immigration Judge suspended Chadha's deportation and a report of the suspension was transmitted to Congress. Section 244(c)(1) provides:

> Upon application by any alien who is found by the Attorney General to meet the requirements of subsection (a) of this section the Attorney General may in his discretion suspend deportation of such alien. If the deportation of any alien is suspended under the provisions of this subsection, a complete and detailed statement of the facts and pertinent provisions of law in the case shall be reported to the Congress with the reasons for such suspension. Such reports shall be submitted on the first day of each calendar month in which Congress is in session.

Once the Attorney General's recommendation for suspension of Chadha's deportation was conveyed to Congress, Congress had the power under §244(c)(2) of the Act, 8 U.S.C. §1254(c)(2), to veto the Attorney General's determination that Chadha should not be deported. Section 244(c)(2) provides:

> (2) In the case of an alien specified in paragraph (1) of subsection (a) of this subsection —
>
> if during the session of the Congress at which a case is reported, or prior to the close of the session of the Congress next following the session at which a case is reported, either the Senate or the House of Representatives passes a resolution stating in substance that it does not favor the suspension of such deportation, the Attorney General shall thereupon deport such alien or authorize the alien's voluntary departure at his own expense under the order of deportation in the manner provided by law. If, within the time above specified, neither the Senate nor the House of Representatives shall pass such a resolution, the Attorney General shall cancel deportation proceedings.

The June 25, 1974, order of the Immigration Judge suspending Chadha's deportation remained outstanding as a valid order for a year and a half. For reasons not disclosed by the record, Congress did not exercise the veto authority reserved to it under §244(c)(2) until the first session of the 94th Congress.

---

1. Congress delegated the major responsibilities for enforcement of the Immigration and Nationality Act to the Attorney General, 8 U.S.C. §1103(a). The Attorney General discharges his responsibilities through the Immigration and Naturalization Service, a division of the Department of Justice. *Ibid.*

This was the final session in which Congress, pursuant to §244(c)(2), could act to veto the Attorney General's determination that Chadha should not be deported. The session ended on December 19, 1975. 121 Cong. Rec. 42014, 42277 (1975). Absent congressional action, Chadha's deportation proceedings would have been canceled after this date and his status adjusted to that of a permanent resident alien. *See* 8 U.S.C. §1254(d).

On December 12, 1975, Representative Eilberg, Chairman of the Judiciary Subcommittee on Immigration, Citizenship, and International Law, introduced a resolution opposing "the granting of permanent residence in the United States to [six] aliens," including Chadha. H. Res. 926, 94th Cong., 1st Sess.; 121 Cong. Rec. 40247 (1975). The resolution was referred to the House Committee on the Judiciary. On December 16, 1975, the resolution was discharged from further consideration by the House Committee on the Judiciary and submitted to the House of Representatives for a vote. 121 Cong. Rec. 40800. The resolution had not been printed and was not made available to other Members of the House prior to or at the time it was voted on. *Ibid.* So far as the record before us shows, the House consideration of the resolution was based on Representative Eilberg's statement from the floor that

> [i]t was the feeling of the committee, after reviewing 340 cases, that the aliens contained in the resolution [Chadha and five others] did not meet these statutory requirements, particularly as it relates to hardship; and it is the opinion of the committee that their deportation should not be suspended.

Ibid. The resolution was passed without debate or recorded vote.[3] Since the House action was pursuant to §244(c)(2), the resolution was not treated as an

---

3. It is not at all clear whether the House generally, or Subcommittee Chairman Eilberg in particular, correctly understood the relationship between H. Res. 926 and the Attorney General's decision to suspend Chadha's deportation. Exactly one year previous to the House veto of the Attorney General's decision in this case, Representative Eilberg introduced a similar resolution disapproving the Attorney General's suspension of deportation in the case of six other aliens. H. Res. 1518, 93d Cong., 2d Sess. (1974). The following colloquy occurred on the floor of the House:

Mr. Wylie.   Mr. Speaker, further reserving the right to object, is this procedure to expedite the ongoing operations of the Department of Justice, as far as these people are concerned? Is it in any way contrary to whatever action the Attorney General has taken on the question of deportation; does the gentleman know?

Mr. Eilberg.   Mr. Speaker, the answer is no to the gentleman's final question. These aliens have been found to be deportable and the Special Inquiry Officer's decision denying suspension of deportation has been reversed by the Board of Immigration Appeals. We are complying with the law since all of these decisions have been referred to us for approval or disapproval, and there are hundreds of cases in this category. In these six cases however, we believe it would be grossly improper to allow these people to acquire the status of permanent resident aliens.

Mr. Wylie.   In other words, the gentleman has been working with the Attorney General's office?

Mr. Eilberg.   Yes.

Mr. Wylie.   This bill then is in fact a confirmation of what the Attorney General intends to do?

Mr. Eilberg.   The gentleman is correct insofar as it relates to the determination of deportability which has been made by the Department of Justice in each of these cases.

Mr. Wylie.   Mr. Speaker, I withdraw my reservation of objection.

120 Cong. Rec. 41412 (1974). Clearly, this was an obfuscation of the effect of a veto under §244(c)(2). Such a veto in no way constitutes "a confirmation of what the Attorney General intends to do." To the contrary, such a resolution was meant to overrule and set aside, or "veto," the Attorney General's determination that, in a particular case, cancellation of deportation would be appropriate under the standards set forth in § 244(a)(1).

Art. I legislative act; it was not submitted to the Senate or presented to the President for his action.

After the House veto of the Attorney General's decision to allow Chadha to remain in the United States, the Immigration Judge reopened the deportation proceedings to implement the House order deporting Chadha. Chadha moved to terminate the proceedings on the ground that §244(c)(2) is unconstitutional. The Immigration Judge held that he had no authority to rule on the constitutional validity of §244(c)(2). On November 8, 1976, Chadha was ordered deported pursuant to the House action.

Chadha appealed the deportation order to the Board of Immigration Appeals, again contending that §244(c)(2) is unconstitutional. The Board held that it had "no power to declare unconstitutional an act of Congress" and Chadha's appeal was dismissed. App. 55-56.

Pursuant to §106(a) of the Act, 8 U.S.C. §1105a(a), Chadha filed a petition for review of the deportation order in the United States Court of Appeals for the Ninth Circuit. The Immigration and Naturalization Service agreed with Chadha's position before the Court of Appeals and joined him in arguing that §244(c)(2) is unconstitutional. In light of the importance of the question, the Court of Appeals invited both the Senate and the House of Representatives to file briefs amici curiae.

After full briefing and oral argument, the Court of Appeals held that the House was without constitutional authority to order Chadha's deportation; accordingly it directed the Attorney General "to cease and desist from taking any steps to deport this alien based upon the resolution enacted by the House of Representatives." 634 F.2d 408, 436 (1980). The essence of its holding was that §244(c)(2) violates the constitutional doctrine of separation of powers.

We granted certiorari in Nos. 80-2170 and 80-2171, and postponed consideration of our jurisdiction over the appeal in No. 80-1832, 454 U.S. 812 (1981), and we now affirm. . . .

We turn now to the question whether action of one House of Congress under §244(c)(2) violates strictures of the Constitution. . . .

Justice White undertakes to make a case for the proposition that the one-House veto is a useful "political invention," and we need not challenge that assertion. We can even concede this utilitarian argument although the long-range political wisdom of this "invention" is arguable. . . . But policy arguments supporting even useful "political inventions" are subject to the demands of the Constitution which defines powers and, with respect to this subject, sets out just how those powers are to be exercised.

Explicit and unambiguous provisions of the Constitution prescribe and define the respective functions of the Congress and of the Executive in the legislative process.

These provisions of Art. I are integral parts of the constitutional design for the separation of powers.

[W]e see that the purposes underlying the Presentment Clauses, Art. I, §7, cls. 2, 3, and the bicameral requirement of Art. I, §1, and §7, cl. 2, guide our resolution of the important question presented in these cases. The very structure of the Articles delegating and separating powers under Arts. I, II, and III exemplifies the concept of separation of powers, and we now turn to Art. I.

THE PRESENTMENT CLAUSES

The records of the Constitutional Convention reveal that the requirement that all legislation be presented to the President before becoming law was uniformly accepted by the Framers. Presentment to the President and the Presidential veto were considered so imperative that the draftsmen took special pains to assure that these requirements could not be circumvented. During the final debate on Art. I, §7, cl. 2, James Madison expressed concern that it might easily be evaded by the simple expedient of calling a proposed law a "resolution" or "vote" rather than a "bill." 2 Farrand 301-302. As a consequence, Art. I, §7, cl. 3, . . . was added.

The decision to provide the President with a limited and qualified power to nullify proposed legislation by veto was based on the profound conviction of the Framers that the powers conferred on Congress were the powers to be most carefully circumscribed. . . .

The President's role in the lawmaking process also reflects the Framers' careful efforts to check whatever propensity a particular Congress might have to enact oppressive, improvident, or ill-considered measures. The President's veto role in the legislative process was described later during public debate on ratification:

> It establishes a salutary check upon the legislative body, calculated to guard the community against the effects of faction, precipitancy, or of any impulse unfriendly to the public good, which may happen to influence a majority of that body.
>   . . . The primary inducement to conferring the power in question upon the Executive is to enable him to defend himself; the secondary one is to increase the chances in favor of the community against the passing of bad laws, through haste, inadvertence, or design.

The Federalist No. 73, at 458 (A. Hamilton). *See also* The Pocket Veto Case, 279 U.S. 655, 678 (1929); Myers v. United States, 272 U.S. 52, 123 (1926). The Court also has observed that the Presentment Clauses serve the important purpose of assuring that a "national" perspective is grafted on the legislative process:

> The President is a representative of the people just as the members of the Senate and of the House are, and it may be, at some times, on some subjects, that the President elected by all the people is rather more representative of them all than are the members of either body of the Legislature whose constituencies are local and not countrywide. . . .

Myers v. United States, *supra*, at 123.

BICAMERALISM

The bicameral requirement of Art. I, §§1, 7, was of scarcely less concern to the Framers than was the Presidential veto and indeed the two concepts are interdependent. By providing that no law could take effect without the concurrence of the prescribed majority of the Members of both Houses, the Framers reemphasized their belief, already remarked upon in connection with the

Presentment Clauses, that legislation should not be enacted unless it has been carefully and fully considered by the Nation's elected officials. In the Constitutional Convention debates on the need for a bicameral legislature, James Wilson, later to become a Justice of this Court, commented:

> Despotism comes on mankind in different shapes, sometimes in an Executive, sometimes in a military, one. Is there danger of a Legislative despotism? Theory & practice both proclaim it. If the Legislative authority be not restrained, there can be neither liberty nor stability; and it can only be restrained by dividing it within itself, into distinct and independent branches. In a single house there is no check, but the inadequate one, of the virtue & good sense of those who compose it.

1 Farrand 254. . . .

However familiar, it is useful to recall that apart from their fear that special interests could be favored at the expense of public needs, the Framers were also concerned, although not of one mind, over the apprehensions of the smaller states. Those states feared a commonality of interest among the larger states would work to their disadvantage; representatives of the larger states, on the other hand, were skeptical of a legislature that could pass laws favoring a minority of the people. See 1 Farrand 176-177, 484-491. It need hardly be repeated here that the Great Compromise, under which one House was viewed as representing the people and the other the states, allayed the fears of both the large and small states.

The Constitution sought to divide the delegated powers of the new Federal Government into three defined categories, Legislative, Executive, and Judicial, to assure, as nearly as possible, that each branch of government would confine itself to its assigned responsibility. The hydraulic pressure inherent within each of the separate Branches to exceed the outer limits of its power, even to accomplish desirable objectives, must be resisted.

Although not "hermetically" sealed from one another, Buckley v. Valeo, 424 U.S., at 121, the powers delegated to the three Branches are functionally identifiable. . . . Whether actions taken by either House are, in law and fact, an exercise of legislative power depends not on their form but upon "whether they contain matter which is properly to be regarded as legislative in its character and effect." S. Rep. No. 1335, 54th Cong., 2d Sess., 8 (1897).

Examination of the action taken here by one House pursuant to §244(c)(2) reveals that it was essentially legislative in purpose and effect. In purporting to exercise power defined in Art. I, §8, cl. 4, to "establish an uniform Rule of Naturalization," the House took action that had the purpose and effect of altering the legal rights, duties, and relations of persons, including the Attorney General, Executive Branch officials and Chadha, all outside the Legislative Branch. Section 244(c)(2) purports to authorize one House of Congress to require the Attorney General to deport an individual alien whose deportation otherwise would be canceled under §244. The one-House veto operated in these cases to overrule the Attorney General and mandate Chadha's deportation; absent the House action, Chadha would remain in the United States. Congress has *acted* and its action has altered Chadha's status.

The legislative character of the one-House veto in these cases is confirmed by the character of the congressional action it supplants. Neither the House of Representatives nor the Senate contends that, absent the veto provision in §244(c)(2), either of them, or both of them acting together, could effectively require the Attorney General to deport an alien once the Attorney General, in the exercise of legislatively delegated authority,[16] had determined the alien should remain in the United States. Without the challenged provision in §244(c)(2), this could have been achieved, if at all, only by legislation requiring deportation. Similarly, a veto by one House of Congress under §244(c)(2) cannot be justified as an attempt at amending the standards set out in §244(a)(1), or as a repeal of §244 as applied to Chadha. Amendment and repeal of statutes, no less than enactment, must conform with Art. I.

The nature of the decision implemented by the one-House veto in these cases further manifests its legislative character. After long experience with the clumsy, time-consuming private bill procedure, Congress made a deliberate choice to delegate to the Executive Branch, and specifically to the Attorney General, the authority to allow deportable aliens to remain in this country in certain specified circumstances. It is not disputed that this choice to delegate authority is precisely the kind of decision that can be implemented only in accordance with the procedures set out in Art. I. Disagreement with the Attorney General's decision on Chadha's deportation—that is, Congress' decision to deport Chadha—no less than Congress' original choice to delegate to the Attorney General the authority to make that decision, involves determinations of policy that Congress can implement in only one way: bicameral passage followed by presentment to the President. Congress must abide by its delegation of authority until that delegation is legislatively altered or revoked.

Finally, we see that when the Framers intended to authorize either House of Congress to act alone and outside of its prescribed bicameral legislative role, they narrowly and precisely defined the procedure for such action. There are four provisions in the Constitution, explicit and unambiguous, by which one House may act alone with the unreviewable force of law, not subject to the President's veto:

(a) The House of Representatives alone was given the power to initiate impeachments. Art. I, §2, cl. 5;
(b) The Senate alone was given the power to conduct trials following impeachment on charges initiated by the House and to convict following trial. Art. I, §3, cl. 6;

---

16. Congress protests that affirming the Court of Appeals in these cases will sanction "lawmaking by the Attorney General. . . . Why is the Attorney General exempt from submitting his proposed changes in the law to the full bicameral process?" Brief for Petitioner in No. 80-2170, p.40. . . . The bicameral process is not necessary as a check on the Executive's administration of the laws because his administrative activity cannot reach beyond the limits of the statute that created it—a statute duly enacted pursuant to Art. I, §§1, 7. The constitutionality of the Attorney General's execution of the authority delegated to him by §244 involves only a question of delegation doctrine. . . . It is clear, therefore, that the Attorney General acts in his presumptively Art. II capacity when he administers the Immigration and Nationality Act. Executive action under legislatively delegated authority that might resemble "legislative" action in some respects is not subject to the approval of both Houses of Congress and the President for the reason that the Constitution does not so require. That kind of Executive action is always subject to check by the terms of the legislation that authorized it; and if that authority is exceeded it is open to judicial review as well as the power of Congress to modify or revoke the authority entirely. A one-House veto is clearly legislative in both character and effect and is not so checked; the need for the check provided by Art. I, §§1, 7, is therefore clear. Congress' authority to delegate portions of its power to administrative agencies provides no support for the argument that Congress can constitutionally control administration of the laws by way of a congressional veto.

(c) The Senate alone was given final unreviewable power to approve or to disapprove Presidential appointments. Art. II, §2, cl. 2;

(d) The Senate alone was given unreviewable power to ratify treaties negotiated by the President. Art. II, §2, cl. 2.

Clearly, when the Draftsmen sought to confer special powers on one House, independent of the other House, or of the President, they did so in explicit, unambiguous terms. . . . These exceptions are narrow, explicit, and separately justified; none of them authorize the action challenged here. On the contrary, they provide further support for the conclusion that congressional authority is not to be implied and for the conclusion that the veto provided for in §244(c)(2) is not authorized by the constitutional design of the powers of the Legislative Branch.

Since it is clear that the action by the House under §244(c)(2) was not within any of the express constitutional exceptions authorizing one House to act alone, and equally clear that it was an exercise of legislative power, that action was subject to the standards prescribed in Art. I.[22] . . .

The veto authorized by §244(c)(2) doubtless has been in many respects a convenient shortcut; the "sharing" with the Executive by Congress of its authority over aliens in this manner is, on its face, an appealing compromise. In purely practical terms, it is obviously easier for action to be taken by one House without submission to the President; but it is crystal clear from the records of the Convention, contemporaneous writings and debates, that the Framers ranked other values higher than efficiency. . . .

The choices we discern as having been made in the Constitutional Convention impose burdens on governmental processes that often seem clumsy, inefficient, even unworkable, but those hard choices were consciously made by men who had lived under a form of government that permitted arbitrary governmental acts to go unchecked. . . .

With all the obvious flaws of delay, untidiness, and potential for abuse, we have not yet found a better way to preserve freedom than by making the exercise of power subject to the carefully crafted restraints spelled out in the Constitution.

We hold that the congressional veto provision in §244(c)(2) is severable from the Act and that it is unconstitutional. Accordingly, the judgment of the Court of Appeals is affirmed.

---

22. Justice Powell's position is that the one-House veto in this case is a *judicial* act and therefore unconstitutional as beyond the authority vested in Congress by the Constitution. We agree that there is a sense in which one-House action pursuant to §244(c)(2) has a judicial cast, since it purports to "review" Executive action. In this case, for example, the sponsor of the resolution vetoing the suspension of Chadha's deportation argued that Chadha "did not meet [the] statutory requirements" for suspension of deportation. To be sure, it is normally up to the courts to decide whether an agency has complied with its statutory mandate. But the attempted analogy between judicial action and the one-House veto is less than perfect. Federal courts do not enjoy a roving mandate to correct alleged excesses of administrative agencies; we are limited by Art. III to hearing cases and controversies and no justiciable case or controversy was presented by the Attorney General's decision to allow Chadha to remain in this country. We are aware of no decision, and Justice Powell has cited none, where a federal court has reviewed a decision of the Attorney General suspending deportation of an alien pursuant to the standards set out in §244(a)(1). This is not surprising, given that no party to such action has either the motivation or the right to appeal from it.

JUSTICE POWELL, concurring in the judgment.

The Court's decision, based on the Presentment Clauses, Art. I, §7, cls. 2 and 3, apparently will invalidate every use of the legislative veto. The breadth of this holding gives one pause. Congress has included the veto in literally hundreds of statutes, dating back to the 1930s. Congress clearly views this procedure as essential to controlling the delegation of power to administrative agencies. One reasonably may disagree with Congress' assessment of the veto's utility, but the respect due its judgment as a coordinate branch of Government cautions that our holding should be no more extensive than necessary to decide these cases. In my view, the cases may be decided on a narrower ground. When Congress finds that a particular person does not satisfy the statutory criteria for permanent residence in this country it has assumed a judicial function in violation of the principle of separation of powers. Accordingly, I concur only in the judgment. . . .

On its face, the House's action appears clearly adjudicatory. The House did not enact a general rule; rather it made its own determination that six specific persons did not comply with certain statutory criteria. It thus undertook the type of decision that traditionally has been left to other branches. Even if the House did not make a *de novo* determination, but simply reviewed the Immigration and Naturalization Service's findings, it still assumed a function ordinarily entrusted to the federal courts.[8] . . .

The impropriety of the House's assumption of this function is confirmed by the fact that its action raises the very danger the Framers sought to avoid — the exercise of unchecked power. In deciding whether Chadha deserves to be deported, Congress is not subject to any internal constraints that prevent it from arbitrarily depriving him of the right to remain in this country.[9] Unlike the judiciary or an administrative agency, Congress is not bound by established substantive rules. Nor is it subject to the procedural safeguards, such as the right to counsel and a hearing before an impartial tribunal, that are present when a court or an agency adjudicates individual rights. The only effective constraint on Congress' power is political, but Congress is most accountable politically when it prescribes rules of general applicability. When it decides rights of specific persons, those rights are subject to "the tyranny of a shifting majority."

JUSTICE WHITE, dissenting.

Today the Court not only invalidates §244(c)(2) of the Immigration and Nationality Act, but also sounds the death knell for nearly 200 other statutory

---

8. The Court reasons in response to this argument that the one-House veto exercised in this case was not judicial in nature because the decision of the Immigration and Naturalization Service did not present a justiciable issue that could have been reviewed by a court on appeal. The Court notes that since the administrative agency decided the case in favor of Chadha, there was no aggrieved party who could appeal. Reliance by the Court on this fact misses the point. Even if review of the particular decision to suspend deportation is not committed to the courts, the House of Representatives assumed a function that generally is entrusted to an impartial tribunal. In my view, the Legislative Branch in effect acted as an appellate court by overruling the Service's application of established law to Chadha. And unlike a court or an administrative agency, it did not provide Chadha with the right to counsel or a hearing before acting. Although the parallel is not entirely complete, the effect on Chadha's personal rights would not have been different in principle had he been acquitted of a federal crime and thereafter found by one House of Congress to have been guilty.

9. When Congress grants particular individuals relief or benefits under its spending power, the danger of oppressive action that the separation of powers was designed to avoid is not implicated. Similarly, Congress may authorize the admission of individual aliens by special Acts, but it does not follow that Congress unilaterally may make a judgment that a particular alien has no legal right to remain in this country.

provisions in which Congress has reserved a "legislative veto." For this reason, the Court's decision is of surpassing importance. And it is for this reason that the Court would have been well advised to decide the cases, if possible, on the narrower grounds of separation of powers, leaving for full consideration the constitutionality of other congressional review statutes operating on such varied matters as war powers and agency rulemaking, some of which concern the independent regulatory agencies.

The prominence of the legislative veto mechanism in our contemporary political system and its importance to Congress can hardly be overstated. It has become a central means by which Congress secures the accountability of executive and independent agencies. Without the legislative veto, Congress is faced with a Hobson's choice: either to refrain from delegating the necessary authority, leaving itself with a hopeless task of writing laws with the requisite specificity to cover endless special circumstances across the entire policy landscape, or in the alternative, to abdicate its lawmaking function to the Executive Branch and independent agencies. To choose the former leaves major national problems unresolved; to opt for the latter risks unaccountable policymaking by those not elected to fill that role. Accordingly, over the past five decades, the legislative veto has been placed in nearly 200 statutes. The device is known in every field of governmental concern: reorganization, budgets, foreign affairs, war powers, and regulation of trade, safety, energy, the environment, and the economy. . . .

The history of the legislative veto also makes clear that it has not been a sword with which Congress has struck out to aggrandize itself at the expense of the other branches—the concerns of Madison and Hamilton. Rather, the veto has been a means of defense, a reservation of ultimate authority necessary if Congress is to fulfill its designated role under Art. I as the Nation's lawmaker. . . . The Court's holding today that all legislative-type action must be enacted through the lawmaking process ignores that legislative authority is routinely delegated to the Executive Branch, to the independent regulatory agencies, and to private individuals and groups. . . .

If Congress may delegate lawmaking power to independent and Executive agencies, it is most difficult to understand Art. I as prohibiting Congress from also reserving a check on legislative power for itself. Absent the veto, the agencies receiving delegations of legislative or quasi-legislative power may issue regulations having the force of law without bicameral approval and without the President's signature. It is thus not apparent why the reservation of a veto over the exercise of that legislative power must be subject to a more exacting test. In both cases, it is enough that the initial statutory authorizations comply with the Art. I requirements. . . . If the effective functioning of a complex modern government requires the delegation of vast authority which, by virtue of its breadth, is legislative or "quasi-legislative" in character, I cannot accept that Art. I—which is, after all, the source of the nondelegation doctrine—should forbid Congress to qualify that grant with a legislative veto.[21]

---

21. The Court's other reasons for holding the legislative veto subject to the presentment and bicameral passage requirements require but brief discussion. First, the Court posits that the resolution of disapproval should be considered equivalent to new legislation because absent the veto authority of §244(c)(2) neither House could, short of legislation, effectively require the Attorney General to deport an alien once the Attorney General has determined that the alien should remain in the United States. . . . The statement is neither accurate nor meaningful. The Attorney General's power under the Act is only

The Court also takes no account of perhaps the most relevant consideration: However resolutions of disapproval under §244(c)(2) are formally characterized, in reality, a departure from the status quo occurs only upon the concurrence of opinion among the House, Senate, and President. Reservations of legislative authority to be exercised by Congress should be upheld if the exercise of such reserved authority is consistent with the distribution of and limits upon legislative power that Art. I provides. . . .

The history of the Immigration and Nationality Act makes clear that §244(c)(2) did not alter the division of actual authority between Congress and the Executive. At all times, whether through private bills, or through affirmative concurrent resolutions, or through the present one-House veto, a permanent change in a deportable alien's status could be accomplished only with the agreement of the Attorney General, the House, and the Senate.

The central concern of the presentation and bicameralism requirements of Art. I is that when a departure from the legal status quo is undertaken, it is done with the approval of the President and both Houses of Congress—or, in the event of a Presidential veto, a two-thirds majority in both Houses. This interest is fully satisfied by the operation of §244(c)(2). The President's approval is found in the Attorney General's action in recommending to Congress that the deportation order for a given alien be suspended. The House and the Senate indicate their approval of the Executive's action by not passing a resolution of disapproval within the statutory period. Thus, a change in the legal status quo—the deportability of the alien—is consummated only with the approval of each of the three relevant actors. The disagreement of any one of the three maintains the alien's pre-existing status: the Executive may choose not to recommend suspension; the House and Senate may each veto the recommendation. The effect on the rights and obligations of the affected individuals and upon the legislative system is precisely the same as if a private bill were introduced but failed to receive the necessary approval.

[I]t may be asserted that Chadha's status before legislative disapproval is one of nondeportation and that the exercise of the veto, unlike the failure of a private bill, works a change in the status quo. This position plainly ignores the statutory language. At no place in §244 has Congress delegated to the Attorney General any final power to determine which aliens shall be allowed to remain in the United States. Congress has retained the ultimate power to pass on such changes in deportable status. . . .

---

to "suspend" the order of deportation; the "suspension" does not cancel the deportation or adjust the alien's status to that of a permanent resident alien. Cancellation of deportation and adjustment of status must await favorable action by Congress. More important, the question is whether §244(c)(2) as written is constitutional, and no law is amended or repealed by the resolution of disapproval which is, of course, expressly authorized by that section.

The Court also argues that the legislative character of challenged action of one House is confirmed by the fact that "when the Framers intended to authorize either House of Congress to act alone and outside of its prescribed bicameral legislative role, they narrowly and precisely defined the procedure for such action." Leaving aside again the above-refuted premise that all action with a legislative character requires passage in a law, the short answer is that all of these carefully defined exceptions to the presentment and bicameralism strictures do not involve action of the Congress pursuant to a duly enacted statute. Indeed, for the most part these powers—those of impeachment, review of appointments, and treaty ratification—are not legislative powers at all. The fact that it was essential for the Constitution to stipulate that Congress has the power to impeach and try the President hardly demonstrates a limit upon Congress' authority to reserve itself a legislative veto, through statutes, over subjects within its lawmaking authority.

The Court of Appeals struck §244(c)(2) as violative of the constitutional principle of separation of powers. It is true that the purpose of separating the authority of Government is to prevent unnecessary and dangerous concentration of power in one branch. . . .

Section 244(c)(2) survives this test. The legislative veto provision does not "preven[t] the Executive Branch from accomplishing its constitutionally assigned functions." [Nixon v. Administrator of General Services, 433 U.S. 425, 433 (1977).] First, it is clear that the Executive Branch has no "constitutionally assigned" function of suspending the deportation of aliens. "'[O]ver no conceivable subject is the legislative power of Congress more complete than it is over' the admission of aliens." Kleindienst v. Mandel, 408 U.S. 753, 766 (1972), *quoting* Oceanic Steam Navigation Co. v. Stranahan, 214 U.S. 320, 339 (1909). Nor can it be said that the inherent function of the Executive Branch in executing the law is involved. The Steel Seizure Case resolved that the Art. II mandate for the President to execute the law is a directive to enforce the law which Congress has written. Youngstown Sheet & Tube Co. v. Sawyer, 343 U.S. 579 (1952). . . . Here, §244 grants the Executive only a qualified suspension authority, and it is only that authority which the President is constitutionally authorized to execute. . . .

Nor does §244 infringe on the judicial power, as Justice Powell would hold. Section 244 makes clear that Congress has reserved its own judgment as part of the statutory process. Congressional action does not substitute for judicial review of the Attorney General's decisions. The Act provides for judicial review of the refusal of the Attorney General to suspend a deportation and to transmit a recommendation to Congress. INS v. Jong Ha Wang, 450 U.S. 139 (1981) (per curiam). But the courts have not been given the authority to review whether an alien should be given permanent status; review is limited to whether the Attorney General has properly applied the statutory standards for essentially denying the alien a recommendation that his deportable status be changed by the Congress. Moreover, there is no constitutional obligation to provide any judicial review whatever for a failure to suspend deportation. . . .

I do not suggest that all legislative vetoes are necessarily consistent with separation-of-powers principles. A legislative check on an inherently executive function, for example, that of initiating prosecutions, poses an entirely different question. But the legislative veto device here—and in many other settings—is far from an instance of legislative tyranny over the Executive. It is a necessary check on the unavoidably expanding power of the agencies, both Executive and independent, as they engage in exercising authority delegated by Congress.

I regret that I am in disagreement with my colleagues on the fundamental questions that these cases present. But even more I regret the destructive scope of the Court's holding. It reflects a profoundly different conception of the Constitution than that held by the courts which sanctioned the modern administrative state. Today's decision strikes down in one fell swoop provisions in more laws enacted by Congress than the Court has cumulatively invalidated in its history.

JUSTICE REHNQUIST, with whom JUSTICE WHITE joins, dissenting.

A severability clause creates a presumption that Congress intended the valid portion of the statute to remain in force when one part is found to be invalid. Carter v. Carter Coal Co., 298 U.S. 238, 312 (1936). . . .

The Court finds that the legislative history of §244 shows that Congress intended §244(c)(2) to be severable because Congress wanted to relieve itself of the burden of private bills. But the history elucidated by the Court shows that Congress was unwilling to give the Executive Branch permission to suspend deportation on its own. Over the years, Congress consistently rejected requests from the Executive for complete discretion in this area. Congress always insisted on retaining ultimate control, whether by concurrent resolution, as in the 1948 Act, or by one-House veto, as in the present Act. Congress has never indicated that it would be willing to permit suspensions of deportation unless it could retain some sort of veto.

It is doubtless true that Congress has the power to provide for suspensions of deportation without a one-House veto. But the Court has failed to identify any evidence that Congress intended to exercise that power. On the contrary, Congress' continued insistence on retaining control of the suspension process indicates that it has never been disposed to give the Executive Branch a free hand. . . .

Because I do not believe that §244(c)(2) is severable, I would reverse the judgment of the Court of Appeals.

NOTES AND QUESTIONS

1. *Presentment and bicameralism.* The Immigration and Nationality Act of 1952, containing the legislative-veto provision, was approved by both houses of Congress and presented to the President. Why isn't that fact a sufficient answer to the challenges based on the Presentment and Bicameralism Clauses? Chief Justice Burger and Justice White strenuously disagree over the question of whether the House veto resolution is an "action" (changing Chadha's legal status) or an "inaction" (failing to change Chadha's legal status). Who is right? Why isn't Justice Powell correct in characterizing the action of the House in disapproving the suspension of Chadha's deportation as "judicial"? Could Congress delegate to the House of Representatives the authority to determine, in the first instance, whether a deportable alien qualified for suspension of deportation? If not, how is this any different?

2. *Formalism and functionalism.* The reasoning employed in Chief Justice Burger's majority opinion has been criticized as excessively "formalistic." *See, e.g.,* E. Donald Elliott, *INS v. Chadha*: The Administrative Constitution, the Constitution, and the Legislative Veto, 1983 Sup. Ct. Rev. 125, 131-147; Peter L. Strauss, Was There a Baby in the Bathwater? A Comment on the Supreme Court's Legislative Veto Decision, 1983 Duke L.J. 789, 794-801. Do you agree? How does Chief Justice Burger define "legislative"? Would that definition also apply to the Attorney General's decision to suspend or not to suspend deportation? Would it apply to the Supreme Court's action in rendering its decision in *Chadha*? Can you frame a more acceptable definition of "legislative"?

3. *The judicial and legislative aftermath of Chadha.* The Supreme Court quickly made it clear that its ruling had the sweeping effect predicted by Justices Powell and White, when, two weeks after issuing its *Chadha* decision, it summarily affirmed two D.C. Circuit decisions that had struck down the use of legislative vetoes in the context of administrative rulemaking. Process Gas Consumers

Group v. Consumer Energy Council of America, 463 U.S. 1216 (1983), *af'g* Consumer Energy Council of America v. FERC, 673 F.2d 425 (D.C. Cir. 1982); and United States Senate v. FTC, 463 U.S. 1216 (1983), *af'g* Consumers Union v. FTC, 691 (D.C. Cir. 1982).

The legislative reaction to Chadha, according to then-Senator Joseph Biden, "was near panic." Joseph R. Biden, Jr., Who Needs a Legislative Veto? 35 Syracuse L. Rev. 685 (1984). Congressional reactions ranged from denunciations of the Supreme Court, to proposals for constitutional amendments, to a scramble to find alternative mechanisms for congressional review of agency rules. Although a number of bills were filed and considered, Congress took no action until 1996. The so-called Contract with America Advancement Act of 1996, Pub. L. No. 104-121, 110 Stat. 847, established a mechanism for Congress to oversee and potentially disapprove federal agency regulations. Enacted as part of the Small Business Regulatory Enforcement Fairness Act and codified at 5 U.S.C. §§801-808, the Congressional Review Act (CRA), creates expedited procedures allowing Congress to nullify agency rules before they become legally effective. Under the Act, agencies must submit to both houses of Congress and the Government Accountability Office a report containing a copy of the rule and information on the rule, including a summary, a designation of whether the rule is "major," and the proposed effective date of the rule. For "major" rules (defined as having a significant impact on the economy or otherwise determined to be major by the Office of Management and Budget) the agency must allow additional time for congressional review to be completed before the rule can be legally effective. Congress may nullify any rule by passing a joint resolution of disapproval. Joint resolutions are considered under special "fast-track" procedures that provide for expedited consideration and passage. If a resolution is adopted by both houses, it must be submitted to the President for approval or veto, like any other legislation.

Prior to 2017, the only use of the CRA to disapprove an agency rule occurred in March 2001, when President George W. Bush signed into law Senate Joint Resolution 6, Pub L. No. 107-5, 107th Cong. 1st Sess., rescinding an OSHA "ergonomics" rule designed to combat the widespread problem of workplace injuries causing musculoskeletal disorders. The Secretary of Labor had issued the rule during the final months of the Clinton Administration when, in response to a veto threat, Congress omitted the rider to OSHA's annual appropriations bills that had prohibited OSHA from issuing an ergonomics rule for several years. The Joint Resolution of Disapproval was passed by the Senate and House on largely party lines, with a handful of Democrats joining the Republican majorities in support. Had the rule been issued earlier, President Clinton would have been able to veto the Joint Resolution.

It was not until 2017 that the CRA was employed again, after the election of Donald J. Trump gave Republicans control of the Presidency and both Houses of Congress. Following through on campaign promises to break sharply with the regulatory policies of the Obama Administration, by May 2017 President Trump had signed sixteen Joint Resolutions disapproving rules promulgated in the final months of the Obama era, including rules concerning the taking of wildlife on wildlife refuges, protecting streams from pollution, reporting by the Social Security Administration on the mental health of gun purchasers and drug testing of unemployment compensation applicants. Is it surprising that every successful use of the CRA has occurred in the immediate aftermath of a presidential transition?

4. *The legislative veto and presidential signing statements.* Despite the Court's clear ruling in *Chadha* that legislative veto provisions are unconstitutional, and despite the procedure created by the Contract with America Act, Congress has continued to insert provisions in many statutes purporting to authorize a committee or single house of Congress to veto various executive actions. In most instances, Presidents have signed such statutes, while attaching a "presidential signing statement" expressing disapproval of the offending provision. For example, when President Barack Obama signed the Omnibus Appropriations Act of 2009, he released a statement that said:

> Numerous provisions of the legislation purport to condition the authority of officers to spend or reallocate funds on the approval of congressional committees. These are impermissible forms of legislative aggrandizement in the execution of the laws other than by enactment of statutes. Therefore, although my Administration will notify the relevant committees before taking the specified actions, and will accord the recommendations of such committees all appropriate and serious consideration, spending decisions shall not be treated as dependent on the approval of congressional committees.

Statement by the President on Signing the Omnibus Appropriations Act, 2009, Mar. 11, 2009, available at *http://www.whitehouse.gov/the-press-office/statement-president-signing-hr-1105.*

Presidential "signing statements" are not new. Since early in the Republic, Presidents have issued statements expressing opinions about the significance or meaning of a piece of legislation that they were signing. But recent Presidents, beginning with Ronald Reagan, developed a practice of using such signing statements to express either a narrowing interpretation or an outright unwillingness to enforce certain provisions that they claimed violated the Constitution. This practice reached a zenith with the administration of George W. Bush, who issued hundreds of signing statements, many of them grounded on his strong view of the inherent constitutional powers of the Executive. Scholars have differed in their view of the legitimacy and wisdom of presidential signing statements. *Compare* Curtis A. Bradley & Eric A. Posner, Presidential Signing Statements and Executive Power, 23 Const. Comment. 307 (2006) (endorsing the practice), *and* Ronald A. Cass & Peter Strauss, The Presidential Signing Statements Controversy, 17 Wm. & Mary Bill of Rts. J. 11 (2007) (generally supportive of the practice), *with* Philip J. Cooper, George W. Bush, Edgar Allan Poe, and the Use and Abuse of Presidential Signing Statements, 35 Presidential Stud. Q. 515 (2005) (generally critical of the practice).

5. *"Sunset" provisions and the abolition of agencies.* Another method of exercising ongoing legislative oversight is the mechanism of so-called "sunset" review. Following the lead of Colorado, a number of states have enacted legislation requiring all or most administrative agencies to justify their existence at stated periodic intervals. Congress has never enacted generic sunset legislation of this sort, but it sometimes puts specific limits on the authorized lifetime of a particular agency. When first established in 1927, the Federal Radio Commission was given a one-year life. Transformed (in 1934) into the Federal Communications Commission, it is still going strong today (and regulating an array of technologies unimaginable to those who passed the initial law nearly a century ago).

Sometimes agencies authorized for a limited span of time are, however, allowed to die. The Office of Independent Counsel, discussed in section C.2.c. of this chapter, *infra*, is a conspicuous example. Even without systematic sunset provisions, Congress has occasionally abolished federal agencies, most notably the Civil Aeronautics Board in 1985 (via the Airline Deregulation Act of 1978, Pub. L. No. 95-504, 92 Stat. 1705) and the ICC in 1996 (via the ICC Termination Act, Pub. L. No. 104-88, 109 Stat. 83). Though the ICC and some of its historic functions died, most of its functions survived, reassigned to other agencies or to the ICC's successor, the Surface Transportation Board, a statutorily separate agency within the Department of Transportation. Do you think broader use of sunset provisions would be helpful? Do you think that shorter authorization periods for agencies (or for particular administrative programs) would promote more or less serious attention from legislators to an agency's functioning?

3. Appropriations: Riders and the Line-Item Veto

Congress can, in principle, exercise a good deal of control over administrative action through the annual appropriation process. There are three dimensions to the influence wielded via the appropriations process. First, of course, is the sheer size of the appropriation. If the sum appropriated is extremely stingy, relative to the range of programmatic duties imposed by law or political expectation on an agency, the agency may be effectively prevented from undertaking new initiatives or expanding the scope of its activities. The second dimension is the specificity or generality of the budgetary categories used in the appropriations act. The more general the appropriation category—the limiting case being a single lump-sum appropriation for an entire agency, or a large division of an agency—the greater the effective discretion bestowed on the agency.

Finally, appropriations acts often contain "riders," or specific statutory language placing additional constraints or conditions on agency powers beyond those contained in its enabling acts. Most riders take the form of an explicit prohibition on the use of appropriated funds for a particular project or activity that is disfavored by a majority of Congress (or at least those most influential in the appropriations process of Congress). OSHA's controversial ergonomics regulation, discussed above, provides an illustration. Occasionally, by contrast, Congress uses appropriations riders to confirm an agency action of which it approves, and thereby insulate it from judicial review. In either case, the interaction between the specific language of an appropriations rider and the general language of the agency's underlying enabling act can raise tricky issues of statutory interpretation, as the following case illustrates.

ROBERTSON v. SEATTLE AUDUBON SOCIETY, 503 U.S. 429 (1992): The case arose from a widely publicized fight over logging in forests, managed by the U.S. Forest Service and Bureau of Land Management (BLM), that are habitat to the northern spotted owl, an endangered species. The Forest Service and BLM devised compromise plans to allow logging in some portions of the forests, while preserving some of the owl's habitat. Environmental groups challenged the plans in federal court, claiming that the plans violated several environmental statutes, including §2 of the Migratory Bird Treaty Act, 40 Stat. 755 (MBTA), which prohibits any agency action that will "kill" or "take" any member of a protected species. Logging interests also challenged the plans, claiming they were unnecessarily restrictive. After lower courts issued preliminary injunctions against the logging, and while the cases were pending on appeal to the Ninth Circuit, Congress essentially approved the agencies' compromise plans in a rider attached to the agencies' appropriations bill, §318 of the Department of the Interior and Related Agencies Appropriations Act, 1990, 103 Stat. 745. Sections 318(a)(1) and (a)(2) required the Forest Service and the BLM to offer for sale specified quantities of timber from certain designated sections of the national forests before the end of fiscal year 1990, while §§318(b)(3) and (b)(5) prohibited harvesting altogether from various other designated areas. Subsection (b)(3) provided:

> No timber sales offered pursuant to this section from the thirteen national forests in Oregon and Washington known to contain northern spotted owls may occur within SOHAs [spotted owl habitat areas] identified pursuant to the [Forest Service's timber management plan] as adjusted by this subsection:
>
> (A) For the Olympic Peninsula Province, which includes the Olympic National Forest, SOHA size is to be 3,200 acres; . . .
>
> [Subsequent subsections specified SOHA sizes for other named federal forests; and subsection (b)(5) contained similar language applicable to BLM lands in western Oregon.]

Subsection (b)(6)(A) provided:

> the Congress hereby determines and directs that management of areas according to [agency plans] on the thirteen national forests in Oregon and Washington and Bureau of Land Management lands in western Oregon is adequate consideration for the purpose of meeting the statutory requirements that are the basis for the consolidated cases captioned Seattle Audubon Society et al. v. F. Dale Robertson, Civil No. 89-160 and Washington Contract Loggers Assoc. et al. v. F. Dale Robertson, Civil No. 89-99 . . . and the case Portland Audubon Society et al. v. Manuel Lujan Jr., Civil No. 87-1160-FR.

Congress also stated in this subsection that it was not passing upon the "legal and factual adequacy" of the agency documents involved in the litigation.

The court of appeals struck down this rider on the grounds that it unconstitutionally interfered with judicial review by dictating the outcome in pending cases without actually amending the underlying statutes (including the MBTA) that were the basis for the litigation. The Supreme Court, in an opinion by Justice Thomas, unanimously reversed:

> We describe the operation of subsection (b)(6)(A) by example. The plaintiffs in both cases alleged violations of MBTA §2. . . . Before the Compromise was enacted, the courts adjudicating these MBTA claims were obliged to determine whether the challenged harvesting would "kill" or "take" any northern spotted owl, within the meaning of §2. Subsection (b)(6)(A), however, raised the question whether the harvesting would violate different prohibitions—those described in subsections (b)(3) and (b)(5). If not, then the harvesting would constitute "management . . . according to" subsections (b)(3) and (b)(5), and would therefore be deemed to "mee[t]" MBTA §2 regardless of whether or not it would cause

an otherwise prohibited killing or taking. Thus, under subsection (b)(6)(A), the agencies could satisfy their MBTA obligations in either of two ways: by managing their lands so as neither to "kill" nor "take" any northern spotted owl within the meaning of §2, or by managing their lands so as not to violate the prohibitions of subsections (b)(3) and (b)(5)....

We conclude that subsection (b)(6)(A) compelled changes in law, not findings or results under old law. Before subsection (b)(6)(A) was enacted, the original claims would fail only if the challenged harvesting [did not violate MBTA §2]. Under subsection (b)(6)(A), by contrast, those same claims would fail if the harvesting violated neither of two new provisions [*i.e.*, subsections (b)(3) and (b)(5) of §318]. Its operation, we think, modified [MBTA §2]. Moreover, we find nothing in subsection (b)(6)(A) that purported to direct any particular findings of fact or applications of law, old or new, to fact. For challenges to sales offered before or after fiscal year 1990, subsection (b)(6)(A) expressly reserved judgment upon "the legal and factual adequacy" of the administrative documents authorizing the sales. For challenges to sales offered during fiscal year 1990, subsection (g)(1) expressly provided for judicial determination of the lawfulness of those sales. Section 318 did not instruct the courts whether any particular timber sales would violate subsections (b)(3) and (b)(5), just as the MBTA, for example, does not instruct the courts whether particular sales would "kill" or "take" any northern spotted owl....

Respondents ... argue that subsection (b)(6)(A) did not modify old requirements, because it deemed compliance with new requirements to "mee[t]" the old requirements. We fail to appreciate the significance of this observation. Congress might have modified MBTA directly, for example, in order to impose a new obligation of complying either with the current §2 or with subsections (b)(3) and (b)(5). Instead, Congress enacted an entirely separate statute deeming compliance with subsections (b)(3) and (b)(5) to constitute compliance with §2—a "modification" of the MBTA, we conclude, through operation of the canon that specific provisions qualify general ones, *see, e.g.*, Simpson v. United States, 435 U.S. 6, 15 (1978).... [Respondents also] emphasize that subsection (b)(6)(A) explicitly made reference to pending cases identified by name and caption number. The reference to *Seattle Audubon* and *Portland Audubon*, however, served only to identify the [provisions of the five environmental statutes] that are the basis for those cases.... To the extent that subsection (b)(6)(A) affected the adjudication of the cases, it did so by effectively modifying the provisions at issue in those cases.

In the alternative, the Ninth Circuit held that subsection (b)(6)(A) "could not" effect an implied modification of substantive law, because it was embedded in an appropriations measure. *See* 914 F.2d at 1317. This reasoning [is erroneous. Although] repeals by implication are especially disfavored in the appropriations context, *see, e.g.*, TVA v. Hill, 437 U.S. 153, 190 (1978), Congress nonetheless may amend substantive law in an appropriations statute, as long as it does so clearly. [B]ecause subsection (b)(6)(A) provided by its terms that compliance with certain new law constituted compliance with certain old law, the intent to modify was not only clear, but express....

NOTES AND QUESTIONS

1. *The Gun Lake Trust Land Reaffirmation Act.* For a more recent case that is very similar to *Robertson, see* Patchak v. Zinke, 138 S. Ct. 897 (2018), upholding the Gun Lake Trust Land Reaffirmation Act, which "reaffirmed" the Secretary of Interior's decision to take certain property in trust for the

Match-E-Be-Nash-She-Wish Band of Pottawatomi Indians. One striking feature of the Act is that, in addition to reaffirming the land as trust land, it provides that "an action . . . relating to [that] land shall not be filed or maintained in a Federal court and shall be promptly dismissed," § 2(b). Although this seems to direct the outcome of an already pending challenge to the Secretary's decision, a plurality, in an opinion by Justice Thomas, found that the Act changed the law rather than compelled "results under old law" and thus satisfied the test in *Robertson*. Justices Ginsburg and Sotomayor rested their concurrence in the result on the federal government's sovereign immunity. Chief Justice Roberts, joined by Justices Kennedy and Gorsuch dissented, arguing that the statute violates separation of powers by "dictat[ing] the outcome of a single pending case." 138 S. Ct. at 914 (Roberts, C.J. dissenting).

2. *Repeals by implication in appropriations acts.* The issue in TVA v. Hill, cited by the Court in *Robertson*, was whether the Endangered Species Act (ESA) required the Tennessee Valley Authority to cease construction of a dam because of a determination that the dam would imperil an endangered species of fish. The TVA argued, *inter alia,* that continued congressional appropriations for the dam, even after the endangerment finding was issued, indicated Congress's judgment that there should be an implied exception from the ESA for the dam. The Supreme Court disagreed, saying:

> The doctrine disfavoring repeals [of statutes] by implication . . . applies with even greater force when the claimed repeal rests solely on an Appropriations Act. We recognize that both substantive enactments and appropriations measures are "Acts of Congress," but the latter have the limited and specific purpose of providing funds for authorized programs. When voting on appropriations measures, legislators are entitled to operate under the assumption that the funds will be devoted to purposes which are lawful and not for any purpose forbidden. Without such an assurance, every appropriations measure would be pregnant with prospects of altering substantive legislation, repealing by implication any prior statute which might prohibit the expenditure. Not only would this lead to the absurd result of requiring Members to review exhaustively the background of every authorization before voting on an appropriation, but it would flout the very rules the Congress carefully adopted to avoid this need.

437 U.S. at 190-191. Does the logic of *TVA* apply equally to the effect of §318 on the MBTA?

3. *Disciplining legislative budget-making by the "line-item veto."* In a formal sense, appropriations legislation is just like any other legislation: it must be passed by both houses of Congress and submitted to the President for approval or veto. But the sheer size of most appropriations acts, coupled with the time pressures under which they are usually adopted, sometimes produce sloppy or ill-advised statutory language. The difficulty of resolving disputes among members, each championing his or her pet projects, often leads to egregious "log-rolling" and "pork barrel" behavior.

Congress has from time to time experimented with various mechanisms to improve the budget-making process, including the Congressional Budget and Impoundment Control Act of 1974, discussed following Clinton v. New York, *infra,* and the Balanced Budget and Emergency Deficit Control Act of 1985, discussed in *Bowsher v. Synar, infra.*

In theory, the presidential veto stands as a means of combating the worst excesses of the appropriations process. But the same factors of enormity of scope and time pressure that cause Congress to enact ill-considered budget measures render the veto power almost useless. Vetoing an entire appropriations act so as to correct a handful of misguided appropriations is like using a hand grenade to kill a cockroach (tempting at times, but . . .). To render the veto more effective, many commentators have recommended that the President should have "line-item veto" authority: that is, the authority to veto specific sections of an omnibus appropriations act, without affecting the rest of the act.

Not surprisingly, the line-item veto has been championed most enthusiastically by fiscal conservatives, who view it as a valuable restraint on the congenital inability of legislatures to discipline themselves. Throughout his tenure in office, for example, President Reagan repeatedly called on Congress to give him line-item veto power, but to no avail. With the ascendancy of a conservative majority in Congress in 1994, however, the idea at last found favor on Capitol Hill. The result was the enactment of the Line Item Veto Act, Pub. L. No. 104-130, 110 Stat. 1200, *codified at* 2 U.S.C. §691 *et seq.* (1997 Supp.). The Act gave the President authority to "cancel" certain spending and tax benefit provisions of a duly enacted appropriations bill within five days after signing the bill into law, provided that he determined, with respect to each cancellation, that it would "(i) reduce the Federal budget deficit; (ii) not impair any essential Government functions; and (iii) not harm the national interest." Congress declared, in §691e of the Act, that a cancellation prevents the canceled item "from having legal force or effect." The cancellation could be overridden by enactment of a "disapproval bill" (which would have to be adopted in the usual manner for enacting legislation, subject only to the condition that it be considered on an expedited schedule). In the two years following the Act's passage, President Clinton exercised his new authority by canceling some 82 items in enacted budget bills. Legal challenges to two of those cancellations quickly landed in the Supreme Court's lap.

CLINTON v. CITY OF NEW YORK, 524 U.S. 417 (1998):   Acting under authority of the Line Item Veto Act, President Clinton canceled a provision of the Balanced Budget Act of 1997 that effectively terminated a $2.6 billion Medicaid repayment claim by the U.S. Department of Health and Human Services against New York State and New York City. He also canceled a provision of the Taxpayer Relief Act of 1997 that conferred a "limited tax benefit" on farmers' cooperatives. The would-be beneficiaries of these two canceled provisions brought suits against the President, challenging his cancellation orders. The Supreme Court, in an opinion by Justice Stevens, ruled that the cancellations violated the Presentment Clause of the Constitution, Article I, §7:

> In both legal and practical effect, the President has amended two Acts of Congress by repealing a portion of each. "[R]epeal of statutes, no less than enactment, must conform with Art. I." INS v. Chadha, 462 U.S. 919, 954 (1983). There is no provision in the Constitution that authorizes the President to enact, to amend, or to repeal statutes. . . .
>
> There are important differences between the President's "return" of a bill pursuant to Article I, §7, and the exercise of the President's cancellation authority pursuant to the Line Item Veto Act. The constitutional return takes place before the bill becomes law; the statutory cancellation occurs after the bill becomes law.

The constitutional return is of the entire bill; the statutory cancellation is of only a part. Although the Constitution expressly authorizes the President to play a role in the process of enacting statutes, it is silent on the subject of unilateral Presidential action that either repeals or amends parts of duly enacted statutes.

[R]elying primarily on Field v. Clark, 143 U.S. 649 (1892), the Government contends that the cancellations were merely exercises of discretionary authority granted to the President by the Balanced Budget Act and the Taxpayer Relief Act read in light of the previously enacted Line Item Veto Act. . . .

In Field v. Clark, the Court upheld the constitutionality of the Tariff Act of 1890. That statute contained a "free list" of almost 300 specific articles that were exempted from import duties "unless otherwise specially provided for in this act." 26 Stat. 602. Section 3 was a special provision that directed the President to suspend that exemption for sugar, molasses, coffee, tea, and hides "whenever, and so often" as he should be satisfied that any country producing and exporting those products imposed duties on the agricultural products of the United States that he deemed to be "reciprocally unequal and unreasonable. . . ." 26 Stat. 612.

[There are] three critical differences between the power to suspend the exemption from import duties and the power to cancel portions of a duly enacted statute. First, the exercise of the suspension power was contingent upon a condition that did not exist when the Tariff Act was passed: the imposition of "reciprocally unequal and unreasonable" import duties by other countries. In contrast, the exercise of the cancellation power within five days after the enactment of the Balanced Budget and Tax Reform Acts necessarily was based on the same conditions that Congress evaluated when it passed those statutes. Second, under the Tariff Act, when the President determined that the contingency had arisen, he had a duty to suspend; in contrast, while it is true that the President was required by the Act to make three determinations before he canceled a provision, those determinations did not qualify his discretion to cancel or not to cancel. Finally, whenever the President suspended an exemption under the Tariff Act, he was executing the policy that Congress had embodied in the statute. In contrast, whenever the President cancels an item of new direct spending or a limited tax benefit he is rejecting the policy judgment made by Congress and relying on his own policy judgment. Thus, the conclusion in Field v. Clark that the suspensions mandated by the Tariff Act were not exercises of legislative power does not undermine our opinion that cancellations pursuant to the Line Item Veto Act are the functional equivalent of partial repeals of Acts of Congress that fail to satisfy Article I, §7. . . .

Neither are we persuaded by the Government's contention that the President's authority to cancel new direct spending and tax benefit items is no greater than his traditional authority to decline to spend appropriated funds. The Government has reviewed in some detail the series of statutes in which Congress has given the Executive broad discretion over the expenditure of appropriated funds. . . . In those statutes, . . . the President was given wide discretion with respect to both the amounts to be spent and how the money would be allocated among different functions. It is argued that the Line Item Veto Act merely confers comparable discretionary authority over the expenditure of appropriated funds. The critical difference between this statute and all of its predecessors, however, is that unlike any of them, this Act gives the President the unilateral power to change the text of duly enacted statutes. None of the Act's predecessors could even arguably have been construed to authorize such a change. . . .

Justice Scalia, joined by Justice O'Connor and joined in part by Justice Breyer, dissented, arguing that the Line Item Veto Act did not violate the Presentment Clause:

There is no question that enactment of the Balanced Budget Act complied with [the Clause's] requirements: the House and Senate passed the bill, and the President signed it into law. It was only after the requirements of the Presentment Clause had been satisfied that the President exercised his authority under the Line Item Veto Act to cancel the spending item. Thus, the Court's problem with the Act is not that it authorizes the President to veto parts of a bill and sign others into law, but rather that it authorizes him to "cancel"—prevent from "having legal force or effect"—certain parts of duly enacted statutes.

Article I, §7 of the Constitution obviously prevents the President from canceling a law that Congress has not authorized him to cancel. . . . But that is not this case. . . . [The Presentment Clause] no more categorically prohibits the Executive reduction of congressional dispositions in the course of implementing statutes that authorize such reduction, than it categorically prohibits the Executive augmentation of congressional dispositions in the course of implementing statutes that authorize such augmentation—generally known as substantive rulemaking. There are, to be sure, limits upon the former just as there are limits upon the latter—and I am prepared to acknowledge that the limits upon the former may be much more severe. Those limits are established, however, not by some categorical prohibition of Art. I, §7, which our cases conclusively disprove, but by what has come to be known as the doctrine of unconstitutional delegation of legislative authority: When authorized Executive reduction or augmentation is allowed to go too far, it usurps the nondelegable function of Congress and violates the separation of powers.

It is this doctrine, and not the Presentment Clause, that was discussed in the *Field* opinion, and it is this doctrine, and not the Presentment Clause, that is the issue presented by the statute before us here. . . .

Insofar as the degree of political, "law-making" power conferred upon the Executive is concerned, there is not a dime's worth of difference between Congress's authorizing the President to cancel a spending item, and Congress's authorizing money to be spent on a particular item at the President's discretion. And the latter has been done since the Founding of the Nation. . . . The constitutionality of such appropriations has never seriously been questioned. . . .

The short of the matter is this: Had the Line Item Veto Act authorized the President to "decline to spend" any item of spending contained in the Balanced Budget Act of 1997, there is not the slightest doubt that authorization would have been constitutional. What the Line Item Veto Act does instead—authorizing the President to "cancel" an item of spending—is technically different. But the technical difference does not relate to the technicalities of the Presentment Clause, which have been fully complied with; and the doctrine of unconstitutional delegation, which is at issue here, is preeminently not a doctrine of technicalities. The title of the Line Item Veto Act, which was perhaps designed to simplify for public comprehension, or perhaps merely to comply with the terms of a campaign pledge, has succeeded in faking out the Supreme Court. The President's action it authorizes in fact is not a line-item veto and thus does not offend Art. I, §7; and insofar as the substance of that action is concerned, it is no different from what Congress has permitted the President to do since the formation of the Union. . . .

In a separate dissent, Justice Breyer argued that the delegation of cancellation authority to the President did not violate the nondelegation doctrine:

[T]he broadly phrased limitations in the Act, together with its evident deficit reduction purpose, and a procedure that guarantees Presidential awareness of the reasons for including a particular provision in a budget bill, taken together, guide the President's exercise of his discretionary powers. . . .

The President, unlike most agency decisionmakers, is an elected official. He is responsible to the voters, who, in principle, will judge the manner in which he exercises his delegated authority. Whether the President's expenditure decisions, for example, are arbitrary is a matter that in the past has been left primarily to those voters to consider. [J]udicial review is less appropriate when the President's own discretion, rather than that of an agency, is at stake. . . . These matters reflect in part the Constitution's own delegation of "executive Power" to "a President," U.S. Const., Art. II, §1 . . . , and we must take this into account when applying the Constitution's nondelegation doctrine to questions of Presidential authority. . . .

NOTES AND QUESTIONS

1. *Formalism versus functionalism II.* Once again, the differences among the Justices can be characterized as a debate between formal and functional approaches to interpreting the Constitution. Is it fair to say that, in *Clinton* as in *Chadha*, formalism carries the day? From a formalist perspective, is it necessarily true, as Justice Stevens argues, that the cancellation procedure authorized by the Act does not fit the form for presidential "return" of legislation prescribed by Article I, §7, and is therefore an "amendment" or "repeal" of legislation? Is Justice Scalia's argument, that enactment of the Line Item Veto Act satisfied the Presentment Clause, a convincing rejoinder? Look back at the material on nondelegation earlier in this chapter. Is the nature of the argument here different from questions about how much authority Congress can assign to administrative agencies without violating Article I's vesting clause?

From a functionalist perspective, is the cancellation procedure identical to a decision of the President not to exercise a discretionary spending authority, as suggested by Justice Scalia? Even if it is a good idea (or constitutionally permissible) for the President to have discretion not to expend particular appropriations, does it necessarily follow that it is a good thing (or constitutionally permissible) to give him blanket authority to cancel line items in future appropriation acts?

2. *Presidential spending authority.* It is true, as Justice Scalia argues, that there is a long history of conferring broad discretion on the President to decide whether to expend appropriated funds. But the more recent history also evidences at least an episodic desire by Congress to curtail such discretion. Richard Nixon's presidency gave rise to one notable episode. Frustrated at the "spendthrift" ways of a Democratic Congress, President Nixon adopted a practice of "impounding" portions of appropriations in order to achieve overall fiscal discipline. In response, Congress enacted the Congressional Budget and Impoundment Control Act of 1974, Pub. L. No. 93-344, 88 Stat. 302, *codified at* 2 U.S.C. §§601 *et seq.* (1994). The Act severely restricted the power of the President to impound appropriated funds. *See* 2 U.S.C. §621. In addition, the Act sought to centralize control over spending decisions in Congress, by establishing a new Congressional Budget Committee, advised by a Congressional Budget Office. The Congressional Budget Committee was intended to serve as a counterweight to the separate appropriations committees in the House and Senate, whose control over the drafting of budget bills gave them immense influence.

The Congressional Budget Office, likewise, was intended to serve as a kind of congressional counterweight to the Executive Branch's Office of Management and Budget, whose centralized control over agency budget requests gives the President enormous de facto power over the administrative branch. A more recent conflict over spending authority arose when President Donald J. Trump issued an executive order directing portions of federal funding to "sanctuary jurisdictions" to be withheld. This conflict is discussed later in this chapter in the section on Executive Control.

4. *Legislative Oversight*

Not surprisingly, students of government tend to focus most of their attention on the most visible methods of legislative control of agencies, such as enabling acts, legislative vetoes, and appropriations riders. In fact, however, there is considerable evidence that the most effective methods of congressional influence are the least visible. This thesis was advanced in a pair of influential articles by Barry Weingast and Mark Moran: The Myth of the Runaway Bureaucracy, Regulation, May/June 1982, at 33; and Bureaucratic Discretion or Congressional Control? Regulatory Policymaking by the Federal Trade Commission, 91 J. Pol. Econ. 775 (1983). In the former (at p. 34), they wrote:

> Congress need not direct agencies solely by "textbook" means—public hearings, investigations, policy pronouncements, and the like. It may also do so through a subtle bureaucratic incentive system—an "invisible (congressional) hand." In this view appropriations subcommittees channel budgetary rewards to agencies that successfully pursue congressional constituency interests. Oversight committees affect agency appointments by manipulating the selection process, not by making a last-minute effort at the confirmation hearings. Congressional staff members monitor agency activities regularly but informally. Finally, and perhaps most important, Congress reserves its powerful club of hearings and investigations for agencies that get out of hand. . . . [T]hey are tools for imposing sanctions on errant agencies.

Weingast and Moran base this conclusion on empirical evidence about the Federal Trade Commission (FTC) during the 1970s. By 1979, the FTC was "widely viewed as the prototypical runaway agency." *Id.* at 34. Weingast and Moran conclude that the agency did not run away; it was ridden. They assert that the FTC had followed quite closely the activist views of the members of the Senate Subcommittee on Consumer Affairs from 1966 to 1976. In 1977, though, there was a nearly total turnover of membership on this subcommittee. Only 2 out of 14 members from 1976 returned in 1977, and as a result the committee switched from being activist to being conservative. Rather than being out of control, the FTC was simply caught in the wake of this change.

In another much-cited article, political scientists Mathew McCubbins and Thomas Schwartz distinguished between two modes of congressional oversight that they fetchingly dubbed "police-patrol" and "fire alarm":

> [P]olice-patrol oversight is comparatively centralized, active, and direct: at its own initiative, Congress examines a sample of executive-agency activities, with the aim

of detecting and remedying any violation of legislative goals and, by its surveillance, discouraging such violations. An agency's activities might be surveyed by any of a number of means, such as reading documents, commissioning scientific studies, conducting field observations, and holding hearings to question officials and affected citizens.

. . . [F]ire-alarm oversight is less centralized. . . . [I]nstead of examining a sample of administrative decisions, looking for violations of legislative goals, Congress establishes a system of rules, procedures, and informal practices that enable individual citizens and organized interest groups to examine administrative decisions (sometimes in prospect), to charge executive agencies with violating congressional goals, and to seek remedies from agencies, courts, and Congress itself. . . . Congress' role consists in creating and perfecting this decentralized system and, occasionally, intervening in response to complaints. Instead of sniffing for fires, Congress places fire-alarm boxes on street corners, builds neighborhood fire houses, and sometimes dispatches its own hook-and-ladder in response to an alarm.

Mathew D. McCubbins & Thomas Schwartz, Congressional Oversight Overlooked: Police Patrols Versus Fire Alarms, 2 Am. J. Pol. Sci. 165, 166 (1984). The authors suggest that members of Congress exhibit a strong preference for fire alarm oversight, which efficiently alerts them to the agency actions that they will care most intensely about. Does that seem likely? Professor Beermann suggests that Congress engages in more "police patrol" oversight than the model suggests: "The high volume of reports that agencies are required to file with Congress and the constant monitoring of agencies that Congress performs indicates that some more generalized, police patrol type oversight is worthwhile." Jack M. Beermann, Congressional Administration, 43 San Diego L. Rev. 61, 66 (2006).

The Weingast-Moran and McCubbins-Schwartz articles helped spawn a huge literature on the "positive political theory" of legislative delegation and oversight. In this body of literature, McCubbins and Weingast have teamed up with fellow political scientist Roger Noll so often that they have formed a pseudonym, "McNollgast," to identify their authorship. Of particular relevance for our purposes is their attempt to explain how the choice of administrative procedures enables Congress to maximize the effectiveness, while minimizing the cost, of its oversight. *See, e.g.,* McNollgast, Administrative Procedures as Instruments of Political Control, 3 J.L. Econ. & Org. 243 (1987); Structure and Process: Politics and Policy: Administrative Arrangements and the Political Control of Agencies, 75 Va. L. Rev. 431 (1989); The Political Origins of the Administrative Procedure Act, 15 J.L. Econ. & Org. 180 (1999).

C.   EXECUTIVE CONTROL OF ADMINISTRATIVE AGENCIES

Article II, §1, of the Constitution provides that "The Executive Power shall be vested in a President of the United States of America." That sweeping mandate is followed by a delineation of specific powers granted to the President. The Executive is given broad authority in foreign affairs, but his domestic powers grow out of Article II, §3, which requires the President to "take Care that the Laws be faithfully executed." The Framers obviously did not expect that the President himself or herself would execute the laws without assistance from others performing functions necessary to that end. Article II also refers to the President's authority to "require the Opinion, in writing, of the principal Officer in each of the executive Departments, upon any Subject relating to the Duties of their respective Offices," Article II, §2, and permits Congress to assign appointment of inferior officers to "the Heads of Departments," "the President alone, or the Courts of Law." *Id.* Looking just at the constitutional language, does Article II make all of the executive powers subject to presidential control, or does it suggest that the Heads of Departments may have executive authority separate from the President? This question is at the heart of arguments over executive control that start early in the nation's history and continue today.

Alexander Hamilton seized upon the unconditional language in §1 to conclude that the subsequent enumerated powers "ought therefore to be considered, as intended merely to specify the principal articles implied in the definition of executive power; leaving the rest to flow from the general grant of that power, interpreted in conformity with other parts of the Constitution." 7 Works of Alexander Hamilton 76, 80-81 (C. Hamilton ed., 1851). Others, focusing on the Framers' apprehensions of a supreme ruler, have insisted that the enumerated powers are the President's only constitutional source of power. *See, e.g.,* 2 Farrand, Records of the Federal Convention 171, 185 (rev. ed. 1937) (contending that the purpose of §1 was merely to determine whether there should be a single or multiple executive, and to give that executive a title).

The tension between these two views underlies an ongoing controversy over the extent to which Congress may insulate administrative agencies from presidential control. For the first century of the Republic, Congress delegated most administrative functions to "departments," like the War Department, headed by officials who served at the President's pleasure. While Congress often created nondepartmental agencies (like the Customs Bureau or the Patent Office), it typically assigned them to a department and made their heads directly responsible to the Secretary of that department.

With the creation of the Interstate Commerce Commission (ICC) in 1887, this pattern began to change. Although governed by a multimember board appointed by the President for fixed terms, the ICC was initially assigned to the Interior Department and made accountable to the Secretary in matters concerning budget, staff, and internal management. Two years later, however, with little fanfare or explanation, Congress amended the Commerce Act, severing all ties between the ICC and the Interior Department. Act of March 2, 1889, 25 Stat. 8961. Thus, the first "independent" federal agency was born.

The intellectual justification for "independence" came later. In debates on Commerce Act amendments in 1910, several members of Congress argued that the ICC must remain free of presidential control because it performs a "legislative function" (namely, setting railroad rates). For this reason, it was regarded as an "arm of Congress," not the Executive. *See* Robert E. Cushman, The Independent Regulatory Commissions 101-114 (1941).

The next major independent agency created by Congress was the Federal Trade Commission. While echoing the sentiments expressed in 1910, sponsors of the Federal Trade Commission Act advanced an additional argument for independent status: the need for "expertise" and the corresponding necessity for "insulation" from "political influence." As one advocate remarked:

> Whatever we do in regulating business should be removed as far as possible from political influence. It will be far safer to place this power in the hands of a great independent commission that will go on while administrations may change . . . [thereby] taking these business matters out of politics.

Cushman, *supra*, at 190.

Although that argument seems quaintly naive today, it was invoked frequently in the succeeding decades as Congress increasingly turned to the independent commission as its chosen instrument for carrying out important regulatory policies. Many of the best-known independent regulatory commissions were born in the New Deal Era, when Congress established such commissions as the Federal Communications Commission (1934), Securities and Exchange Commission (1934), and National Labor Relations Board (1935).

Shortly thereafter, the intellectual tide began to turn, as more and more observers began to criticize the independent commissions for their lack of political accountability, fragmentary policies, inflexibility, and administrative inefficiency. *See, e.g.,* Marver H. Bernstein, Regulating Business by Independent Commission (1955); James M. Landis, The Administrative Process (1938). In recent decades, Congress generally has preferred to assign major new regulatory functions to existing executive departments (OSHA is an example) or to new agencies directly accountable to the President (such as the Environmental Protection Agency, headed by a single presidential appointee). But the creation of independent agencies like the Consumer Product Safety Commission indicates that the congressional dalliance with the independent form is not over. An intriguing contemporary example is the Bureau of Consumer Financial Protection (CFPB), created by the Dodd-Frank Wall Street Reform and Consumer Protection Act of 2010, Pub. L. No. 111-203, 124 Stat. 1376. The Act gives the CFPB sweeping authority to regulate practices of financial institutions providing credit to individuals through such instruments as credit cards, home mortgages, and consumer loans. Section 1011 of the Act establishes the CFPB as an "independent bureau" within the Federal Reserve System, funded by revenues of the Fed, but not subject to supervision by the Fed's Board of Governors. The CFPB is headed by a Director, appointed by the President with the advice and consent of the Senate. The Director serves for a five-year term, and is removable by the President during that term of office only for "inefficiency, neglect of duty, or malfeasance in office."

Below, we consider the scope of the executive powers constitutionally committed to the President, which also informs much of the debate over the president's power over to appoint and remove officials.

1.   *Executive Command*

In a very early case, Kendall v. United States, 37 U.S. (12 Pet.) 524 (1838), the Supreme Court ruled that the President did not have authority to order the Postmaster-General to withhold payment on a disputed claim against the

United States because the statute creating the Post Office Department did not make the Postmaster a subordinate of the President. Despite that parsimonious reading of executive authority, however, over the succeeding century Presidents steadily pushed the envelope of executive power, repeatedly asserting independent authority not only to undertake military actions and manage the foreign affairs of the United States, but even to shape its domestic policy. It was inevitable that a constitutional confrontation would eventually result.

YOUNGSTOWN SHEET & TUBE CO. v. SAWYER, 343 U.S. 579 (1952): In 1952, while this country was fighting a war in Korea, steelworkers were threatening a nationwide strike. President Harry S. Truman, fearful that a strike would jeopardize national security, issued an executive order directing Secretary of Commerce Charles Sawyer to take charge of operating most of the nation's steel mills. Presidents had legally seized industrial property before, but always under the auspices of a statute. Here, Truman invoked only the powers inherently vested in the President under Article II of the Constitution. The President immediately notified Congress of his edict and acknowledged that body's power to overrule his order. Congress, however, did nothing, despite having specifically denied the President this very authority just five years earlier when it passed the Taft-Hartley Act. The steel companies sued Sawyer in federal district court seeking injunctive relief. The case reached the Supreme Court after the district court issued an injunction, but the appeals court stayed the judgment.

The Supreme Court ruled, 6-3, that Truman exceeded his constitutional authority. Writing for the majority, Justice Hugo Black saw the problem in direct and simple terms. The President was not acting with statutory license, he argued, and the power to effect such a seizure was not deducible from his constitutional power to "see that the laws are faithfully executed" or as commander-in-chief of the armed forces. Because Truman was exercising a "lawmaking" power, not an "executive" power, Black wrote, the order was an infringement on Congress's realm and thus a violation of the separation-of-powers doctrine.

In a famous concurring opinion, Justice Robert H. Jackson articulated a more complex framework for determining the reach of presidential power. Jackson argued that "Presidential powers are not fixed but fluctuate, depending upon their disjunction or conjunction with those of Congress." 343 U.S. at 635. Jackson distinguished three types of presidential actions:

> 1. When the President acts pursuant to an express or implied authorization of Congress, his authority is at its maximum, for it includes all that he possesses in his own right plus all that Congress can delegate. In these circumstances, and in these only, may he be said (for what it may be worth) to personify the federal sovereignty. If his act is held unconstitutional under these circumstances, it usually means that the Federal Government as an undivided whole lacks power. A seizure executed by the President pursuant to an Act of Congress would be supported by the strongest of presumptions and the widest latitude of judicial interpretation, and the burden of persuasion would rest heavily upon any who might attack it.
>
> 2. When the President acts in absence of either a congressional grant or denial of authority, he can only rely upon his own independent powers, but there is a zone of twilight in which he and Congress may have concurrent authority, or in which its distribution is uncertain. Therefore, congressional inertia, indifference or quiescence may sometimes, at least as a practical matter, enable, if not invite,

measures on independent presidential responsibility. In this area, any actual test of power is likely to depend on the imperatives of events and contemporary imponderables rather than on abstract theories of law.

3. When the President takes measures incompatible with the expressed or implied will of Congress, his power is at its lowest ebb, for then he can rely only upon his own constitutional powers minus any constitutional powers of Congress over the matter. Courts can sustain exclusive presidential control in such a case only by disabling the Congress from acting upon the subject. Presidential claim to a power at once so conclusive and preclusive must be scrutinized with caution, for what is at stake is the equilibrium established by our constitutional system.

Id. at 635-638. Finding that Congress "has not left seizure of private property an open field but has covered it by three statutory policies inconsistent with this seizure," *id.* at 639, Jackson concluded that the seizure fell within the third category. Applying the "severe tests" of this category, Jackson rejected the Government's arguments that the seizure could be justified as an exercise of either the President's inherent "executive" power, his authority as commander-in-chief, or his duty of faithful execution of the laws.

Chief Justice Vinson, joined by Justices Minton and Reed, dissented, finding inherent executive power in the exigent circumstances surrounding prosecution of a war and also finding implicit congressional authorization (or at least acquiescence) in broad presidential power through Congress' support of the war.

NOTES AND QUESTIONS

1. *Jackson's taxonomy and presidential prerogatives. Youngstown* is most famous for Justice Jackson's three-part taxonomy for determining the lawful limits of presidential action. His second and third categories theoretically leave room for the President to define the powers and duties of administrative agencies in ways that go beyond (or even contradict) what Congress has authorized. But, after over two centuries of congressional enactments on all manner of subjects, one wonders how much practical leeway those categories afford to Presidents eager to place their stamp on the administrative state. Inherent presidential power is most often claimed, and conceded, in foreign and military affairs. For example, in Dames & Moore v. Regan, 453 U.S. 654 (1981), the Court upheld a series of executive orders issued by President Carter implementing a presidential agreement with the Iranian government to settle the Iranian hostage crisis, including an order suspending all claims against the Iranian government pending in American courts and referring them to an international forum. Although unable to find explicit statutory authorization for the suspension order, the Court found in a long history of congressional acquiescence "that Congress has implicitly approved the practice of claim settlement by executive agreement." 453 U.S. at 680. While some believe that the "twilight zone" encompasses only the President's foreign affairs functions, others have interpreted it to extend to any context in which there is a consistent and visible tradition of presidential action and congressional acquiescence. *See* Harold H. Bruff, Judicial Review and the President's Statutory Powers, 68 Va. L. Rev. 1, 36 (1982).

2. *Presidential executive orders.* The elusive boundary between Jackson's second and third categories has also been tested in a series of lower court decisions concerning the authority of the President, by executive order, to dictate the employment practices of government contractors. For example, Chamber of Commerce v. Reich, 74 F.3d 1322 (D.C. Cir. 1996), dealt with a Clinton executive order prohibiting federal agencies from contracting with employers that hired permanent strike-replacement workers. The D.C. Circuit struck the order down as incompatible with the National Labor Relations Act. But in Building & Construction Trades Dept., AFL-CIO v. Allbaugh, 295 F.3d 28 (D.C. Cir. 2002), the D.C. Circuit upheld, as not incompatible with the NLRA, a Bush executive order that made it easier for federal agencies to contract with non-unionized government contractors. Interestingly, in upholding the order, the court relied solely on the President's inherent executive power under the vesting clause of Article II, §1, invoking the *Myers* opinion's strong language about the President's constitutional "supervisory" authority.

Another conflict over the scope of presidential authority came from President Trump's executive order directing the Attorney General and the Secretary of the Department of Homeland Security to withhold portions of federal funding to "sanctuary jurisdictions" (more commonly "sanctuary cities") that "willfully violate Federal law in an attempt to shield aliens from removal from the United States." Exec. Order 13,768, 82 Fed. Reg. 8799 (Jan. 25, 2017). In particular, the order expressed concern with actions by state and local governments that violate 8 U.S.C. §1373(a), which prohibits government entities from prohibiting the sharing of "information regarding the citizenship or immigration status, lawful or unlawful, of any individual." The order instructed the departments of Justice and Homeland Security to implement its terms in a manner "consistent with applicable law and subject to the availability of appropriations." Numerous potentially affected jurisdictions and interested groups challenged the executive order and actions taken to implement it.

Among the more notable decisions resulting from these challenges was San Francisco v. Trump, 897 F.3d 1225 (9th Cir. 2018), affirming in part a district court injunction prohibiting withholding funds pursuant to E.O. 13,768. The majority opinion rejected both the administration's claim that the President had authority to restrict spending without clear delegation from Congress and its claim that the "consistent with applicable law" language in the E.O. insulated the order from conflict with any plain legislative direction to spend the particular funds at issue. Chief Judge Sidney Thomas stated the critical considerations in this way:

> The President's authority to act "must stem either from an act of Congress or from the Constitution itself." Youngstown Sheet & Tube Co. v. Sawyer, 343 U.S. 579, 585 (1952). Justice Jackson's Youngstown concurrence provides the operative test in this context:
>
> > When the President takes measures incompatible with the expressed or implied will of Congress, his power is at its lowest ebb, for then he can rely only upon his own constitutional powers minus any constitutional powers of Congress over the matter. Courts can sustain exclusive presidential control in such a case only by disabling the Congress from acting upon the subject. Presidential claim to a power at once so conclusive and preclusive must be

scrutinized with caution, for what is at stake is the equilibrium established by our constitutional system.

Youngstown, 343 U.S. at 637-638 (Jackson, J., concurring).

In this instance, because Congress has the exclusive power to spend and has not delegated authority to the Executive to condition new grants on compliance with §1373, the President's "power is at its lowest ebb." . . . Rather, the President has a corresponding obligation—to "take Care that the Laws be faithfully executed." U.S. Const. art. II, §3. Because Congress's legislative power is inextricable from its spending power, the President's duty to enforce the laws necessarily extends to appropriations. . . .

The *San Francisco* panel majority rejected the administration's claim that the "savings clause" in the E.O., coupled with an interpretation of the E.O. in a Department of Justice memorandum that limited the effective portions of the E.O. to restrictions on grants from the Departments of Justice and of Homeland Security, prevented any conflict with statutes, taking the administration's actions out of Justice Jackson's "lowest ebb" category. In Chief Judge Thomas' words, that interpretation must be rejected because it "renders the Executive Order a toothless threat."

Judge Ferdinand Fernandez, dissenting, quoted at length from §1373, part of the Illegal Immigration Reform and Immigrant Responsibility Act of 1996, Pub. L. No. 104-208 (Division C), 110 Stat. 3009, which prohibits various sorts of interference with the communication to or from the federal government of information respecting immigration or citizenship status. Each quoted provision began with the words "[n]otwithstanding any other provision of Federal, State, or local law." In Judge Fernandez's view, the E.O. was a direction to the President's subordinates to act in ways consistent with the law. Far from being in derogation of statutory directives, this served the President's "duty to see that duly adopted laws were faithfully executed."

Note that the majority viewed the conflict as one over who has primary authority to direct spending, while the dissent saw the issue as a matter of the President acting to prevent interference with implementation of substantive law. Who has the better argument? Does Youngstown control this argument? Should it make a difference whether the President takes actions to implement the law through spending limitations, through conditions on eligibility for non-monetary federal benefits or through imposition of penalties for violating §1373? Look back to the discussion of TVA v. Hill following the *Roberston* decision in the section on appropriations. Does *TVA* provide help in answering whether the majority or dissent has the better position?

3. *Prosecutorial discretion and executive power.* As we have seen in cases like *Buckley* and *Morrison*, the power to enforce the law has long been viewed as a central "executive" function. A corollary is the principle of "prosecutorial discretion," discussed in detail in Chapters III and VII, *infra*. A particularly controversial invocation of this principle was an "executive action" on immigration reform announced by President Obama on November 20, 2014, known as "Deferred Action for Parents of Americans" (DAPA). *See http://www.whitehouse.gov/the-press-office/2014/11/20/fact-sheet-immigration-accountability-executive-action*, accessed on

February 12, 2015. In his order, the President directed the Department of Homeland Security (DHS, the agency now primarily responsible for policing the borders and enforcing the immigration laws) to take a series of actions that would provide temporary relief from the threat of deportation for about 5 million of the estimated 11 million undocumented aliens present in the United States. The President decided to act unilaterally following an extended standoff with Congress over proposed legislation that would have provided a pathway to legal status for many undocumented resident aliens. The DAPA order dramatically expanded a pre-existing program (Deferred Action for Childhood Arrivals (DACA), also created by executive action). Both orders declared that certain categories of undocumented aliens could apply for "deferred action," a renewable three-year status that protects them against deportation and that, in many cases, qualifies them to obtain permits to obtain lawful employment.

The President claimed as the legal authority for his action the inherent prosecutorial discretion of executive agencies to establish priorities for their enforcement efforts. In justifying the action as an exercise of prosecutorial discretion, DHS noted that it had budgetary resources sufficient to pursue deportation of only about 400,000 of the nation's 11 million illegal aliens, that all applications for deferred status would be determined on a case-by-case basis, and that deferred status did not purport to change the legal status of any alien. The State of Texas, later joined by a majority of states and several municipalities, filed suit in federal court to challenge the legality of the President's action, claiming that the "executive action" was so sweeping in its effect as to constitute a change in the immigration law. As such, the plaintiffs asserted, the action exceeded the President's inherent executive power. The district court agreed, enjoining the continued operation of DAPA, a decision upheld by the U.S. Court of Appeals for the Fifth Circuit and, by an equally divided Court, by the Supreme Court as well. Texas v. United States, Civ. No. B-14-254 (S.D. Tex. 2015), *aff'd*, United States v. Texas, 787 F.3d 733 (5th Cir. 2015), *aff'd by an equally divided Court*, 136 S. Ct. 2271 (2016) (mem.). Litigation over the DACA program continues as of this writing.

While President Obama's administration was not wholly successful in persuading courts that these initiatives fell within the President's authority over enforcement decisions, they are not by any means the only controversial presidential actions seeking to direct results in agency proceedings. Another example comes from an earlier initiative respecting tobacco marketing. As with immigration reform, many observers lauded the substantive inclination behind the initiative, but questions arose about the President's legal authority, particularly the relation between the President's directives and congressional enactments. That is the episode described below.

THE TOBACCO MARKETING RULE: A CASE STUDY IN "PRESIDENTIAL ADMINISTRATION"

In an influential article, then-Professor (now Justice) Elena Kagan discussed what she refers to as "presidential administration"—that is, the tendency of some modern Presidents directly and personally to exercise (or at least, appear to exercise) the authority delegated by statute to the head of a department or agency. Elena Kagan, Presidential Administration, 114 Harv. L. Rev. 2245 (2001). A leading example is described in the case study that follows.

At a press conference on August 10, 1995, President Bill Clinton made the following announcement:

> Today I am announcing broad executive action to protect the young people of the United States from the awful dangers of tobacco. . . . [B]y executive authority, I will restrict sharply the advertising, promotion, distribution, and marketing of cigarettes to teenagers. I do this on the basis of the best available scientific evidence, the findings of the American Medical Association, the American Cancer Society, the American Heart Association, the American Lung Association, the Centers for Disease Control. Fourteen months of study by the Food and Drug Administration confirms what we all know: Cigarettes and smokeless tobacco are harmful, highly addictive, and aggressively marketed to our young people. The evidence is overwhelming, and the threat is immediate. . . . So today I am authorizing the Food and Drug Administration to initiate a broad series of steps all designed to stop sales and marketing of cigarettes and smokeless tobacco to children. As a result, the following steps will be taken. First, young people will have to prove their age with an I.D. card to buy cigarettes. Second, cigarette vending machines which circumvent any ban on sales to kids will be prohibited. Third, schools and playgrounds will be free of tobacco advertising on billboards in their neighborhoods. Fourth, images such as Joe Camel will not appear on billboards or in ads in publications that reach substantial numbers of children and teens. Fifth, teens won't be targeted by any marketing gimmicks, ranging from single cigarette sales to T-shirts, gym bags, and sponsorship of sporting events. And finally, the tobacco industry must fund and implement an annual $150 million campaign aimed at stopping teens from smoking through educational efforts.

The President's News Conference (Aug. 10, 1995), available at *http://www. presidency.ucsb.edu/ws/index.php?pid=51727.*

The following day, the Food and Drug Administration (FDA, a division of the Department of Health and Human Services) published a proposed regulation seeking to accomplish the various steps outlined by President Clinton, and requesting public comment pursuant to the "notice-and-comment" procedure for rulemaking specified by the APA (and discussed in Chapter V, *infra*). Regulations Restricting the Sale and Distribution of Cigarettes and Smokeless Tobacco Products to Children and Adolescents, Proposed Rule, 60 Fed. Reg. 41, 313 (Aug. 11, 1995).

A year later, after receiving and digesting over 700,000 public comments, the FDA issued a final rule regulating tobacco marketing to young people. *See* 61 Fed. Reg. 44, 395 (Aug. 28, 1996). As if to emphasize his personal role in the tobacco rulemaking, President Clinton announced the issuance of the rule in a Rose Garden ceremony five days before it was published in the Federal Register. Remarks Announcing the Final Rule to Protect Youth from Tobacco, 2 Pub. Papers 1332 (Aug. 23, 1996).

The legal authority invoked by the FDA in issuing the rule was the Federal Food, Drug, and Cosmetic Act of 1938 (FDCA). The FDCA creates an elaborate framework for the regulation of "drugs" and "drug delivery devices." By its terms, the FDCA delegates authority to regulate drugs and devices to "the Secretary" (of Health and Human Services). For example, the rulemaking provision reads: "The authority to promulgate regulations for the efficient enforcement of this Act . . . is hereby vested in the Secretary." FDCA §701, 21 U.S.C. §371. The Secretary had, in turn, delegated to the Commissioner of the FDA authority to execute the powers conferred on the Secretary by the FDCA. 21 C.F.R. §§5.10-5.11 (1996). Like the Secretary, the FDA commissioner is a direct appointee of the President, subject to confirmation by the Senate.

The tobacco companies immediately challenged the rule in court, and the rule was eventually thrown out by the Supreme Court in FDA v. Brown & Williamson Corp., 529 U.S. 120 (2000), excerpted in Chapter II, *infra*. In concluding that the FDCA did not give the FDA authority to regulate tobacco products in this manner, Justice O'Connor, speaking for a five-Justice majority, cited the long history of congressional regulation of cigarette marketing by other means, as well as the "enormous social consequences" of a ruling that nicotine is a "drug," making it potentially subject to outright prohibition under the FDCA. O'Connor never addressed the issue of potentially undue presidential interference. The only—rather oblique—mention of presidential involvement occurred in Justice Breyer's dissent:

> [O]ne might claim that courts, when interpreting statutes, should assume in close cases that a decision with "enormous social consequences" should be made by democratically elected Members of Congress rather than by unelected agency administrators. If there is such a background canon of interpretation, however, I do not believe it controls the outcome here.
>
> Insofar as the decision to regulate tobacco reflects the policy of an administration, it is a decision for which that administration, and those politically elected officials who support it, must (and will) take responsibility. And the very importance of the decision taken here, as well as its attendant publicity, means that the public is likely to be aware of it and to hold those officials politically accountable. Presidents, just like Members of Congress, are elected by the public. Indeed, the President and Vice President are the only public officials whom the entire Nation elects. I do not believe that an administrative agency decision of this magnitude—one that is important, conspicuous, and controversial—can escape the kind of public scrutiny that is essential in any democracy. And such a review will take place whether it is the Congress or the Executive Branch that makes the relevant decision.

529 U.S. at 189-190.

NOTES AND QUESTIONS

1. *Overseer or decider?* Did President Clinton overstep the bounds of his legal authority, given the fact that Congress delegated the authority to regulate drugs and devices under the FDCA, not to the President, but to the Secretary of HHS? In the words of Peter Strauss, is the President merely an "overseer" of the Executive Branch, or may he be the "decider"? Peter Strauss, Overseer, or "The Decider"? The President in Administrative Law, 75 Geo. Wash. L. Rev. 696 (2007).

Is Justice Breyer, in the excerpt quoted above, implicitly endorsing "the decider" model of executive power, as democratically superior to "the overseer" model? Is the Court's majority, by implication, rejecting the "decider" model?

2. *The political denouement.* David Kessler, Clinton's FDA Commissioner, argues in his memoir that the FDA was hardly a passive vehicle for Clinton's personal crusade. Indeed it was Kessler who eventually convinced a skeptical Clinton to make tobacco marketing a major presidential priority. *See* David A. Kessler, A Question of Intent: A Great American Battle with a Deadly Industry (2001). The Clinton-Kessler position was eventually vindicated when President Obama convinced Congress to adopt legislation giving the FDA the authority the Court said it lacked in 2000. *See* Family Smoking Prevention and Tobacco Control Act of 2009, Pub. L. No. 111-31, 123 Stat. 1776 (2009).

3. *Procedural limitations on presidential administration.* Even advocates of the strongest version of executive power acknowledge limitations on the President's authority to intervene directly in certain kinds of administrative decisions. The clearest example — acknowledged by Chief Justice Taft in *Myers* — is an action of a "quasi-judicial character." When, as a matter of either constitutional or statutory command, a decision must be made on the record of an adjudicative hearing, neither the President nor any member of his staff may seek to persuade the decisionmaker, except by appearing as a witness or submitting documentary evidence in the hearing itself. *See, e.g.,* Portland Audubon Soc'y v. Endangered Species Comm., 984 F.2d 1534 (9th Cir. 1993), excerpted in Chapter VI, *infra.* As a general matter the courts have reached a different conclusion with regard to presidential interventions in informal rulemaking proceedings, such as the FDA tobacco rulemaking. The leading authority on this issue is Sierra Club v. Costle, 657 F.2d 298 (D.C. Cir. 1981), excerpted in Chapter V, *infra.*

4. *The President as "agency."* The discussion in this section of the casebook assumes a separation between "the President" (in both the personal and institutional form) and "agencies." This assumption is usually justified. When Congress creates a government program that requires government "administration," it almost always assigns responsibility for its administration to an entity other than the "President" or even the "Executive Office of the President."

But not always. Sometimes, Congress confers upon the President direct responsibility for administering a government program. When the President exercises a power directly delegated to him by Congress, should he be considered an "agency" for purposes of the application of the APA? Would a presidential decision be subject, for example, to judicial review under 5 U.S.C. §§701-706? Curiously, that question remained unanswered for 46 years, until the Supreme Court decided, in Franklin v. Massachusetts, 505 U.S. 788 (1992), that the President was not an agency within the meaning of APA §551(1). Noting that the APA definition of "agency" neither expressly included nor excluded the President, the Court ruled: "Out of respect for the separation of powers and unique constitutional position of the President, we find that textual silence is not enough to subject the President to the provisions of the APA." The Court did note the well-established proposition that the President's actions are reviewable for constitutionality.

Looking at the text of APA §551(1), in the Appendix, *infra,* do you see any real ambiguity on the question of whether Congress intended the President to be covered? If Congress can freely choose to delegate a power to either the President or an administrative agency, why is there any separation-of-powers sensitivity about judicial review of the President's exercise of delegated power?

2. *Appointment and Removal Powers*

As we saw above, the growth of the independent agency form raised serious questions about the constitutional authority of Congress to insulate administrative agencies from presidential control. The Court has explored the extent of congressional control primarily in a small group of cases involving the President's appointment and removal powers, the subject of Section 2 below. Curiously, the Supreme Court did not address those questions until rather recently, and, as the following materials indicate, many of them remain unresolved even today.

a. Appointment Power

The President's power to supervise administrative actions begins with his constitutional power of appointment. Article II, §2, cl. 2, of the Constitution provides that the President "shall appoint . . . Officers of the United States." The President's appointment power is heavily dependent upon actions of Congress. In the first place, with the exception of so-called "recess appointments," discussed in connection with the *Noel Canning* case, *infra*, presidential appointments must be made "by and with the Advice and Consent of the Senate." There is no constitutional mechanism whereby the President can override a vote of the Senate defeating a proposed appointment. Second, Clause 2 expressly empowers Congress to "vest the Appointment of such inferior Officers, as they think proper, in the President alone, in the Courts of Law, or in the Heads of Departments." By implication, the President's exclusive constitutional power of appointment extends only to some undefined class of superior (or "principal") officers. Third, Congress must first establish the "office" to which the President may make an appointment. The power to create and define an office implies at least some degree of control over the qualifications and term of the office.

Throughout most of our history, the courts had surprisingly few occasions to explore the limits of the President's appointment power. Whenever Congress created a new administrative agency, it routinely provided for presidential appointment of its top-level personnel, subject, of course, to senatorial confirmation. In 1974, however, Congress created a rather exotic inter-branch entity to police federal elections that provided the Supreme Court an occasion to explore the meaning and scope of the appointment power.

BUCKLEY v. VALEO, 424 U.S. 1 (1975): In 1974 President Richard Nixon resigned his office on the eve of being impeached by the House of Representatives for allegedly impeding a criminal investigation. The investigation had started with a burglary of the Democratic National Committee's headquarters in Washington's Watergate apartment building, and eventually led to a number of high-ranking members of Nixon's administration and, perhaps, to the President himself.

In the wake of the Watergate scandal, Congress in 1974 passed sweeping amendments to the Federal Election Campaign Act. The 1974 Amendments imposed new limits on campaign contributions and candidates' expenditures, strengthened the reporting provisions, and expanded public financing of presidential election campaigns. To enforce the 1974 Amendments, Congress created the Federal Election Commission (FEC), consisting of six voting members—two members each appointed by the President *pro tempore* of the Senate, the Speaker of the House, and the President. Each pair of appointments had to include one Democrat and one Republican. The appointments by the President *pro tempore* of the Senate and by the Speaker of the House were required to be made upon the recommendation of the majority and minority leaders of each house. All six voting members were subject to confirmation by both houses of Congress. The commission also had two nonvoting members—the Secretary of the Senate and Clerk of the House, *ex officiis.*

Individual candidates for federal office and conservative political organizations brought suit in federal district court challenging the constitutionality of the 1974 Amendments on a number of grounds, including a claim that composition of the FEC violated the Appointments Clause of Article II. In a *per curiam* opinion, the Supreme Court agreed. The Court began by describing in some detail the functions delegated to the Commission by the Act:

> Chapter 14 of Title 2 [of the 1974 Amendments] makes the Commission the principal repository of the numerous reports and statements which are required by that chapter to be filed by those engaging in the regulated political activities. Its duties under §438(a) with respect to these reports and statements include filing and indexing, making them available for public inspection, preservation, and auditing and field investigations. It is directed to "serve as a national clearinghouse for information in respect to the administration of elections." §438(b).
>
> Beyond these recordkeeping, disclosure, and investigative functions, however, the Commission is given extensive rulemaking and adjudicative powers. Its duty under §438(a)(10) is "to prescribe suitable rules and regulations to carry out the provisions of . . . chapter [14]." Under §437d(a)(8) the Commission is empowered to make such rules "as are necessary to carry out the provisions of this Act." Section 437d(a)(9) authorizes it to "formulate general policy with respect to the administration of this Act" and enumerated sections of Title 18's Criminal Code, as to all of which provisions the Commission "has primary jurisdiction with respect to [their] civil enforcement." §437c(b). The Commission is authorized under §437f(a) to render advisory opinions with respect to activities possibly violating the Act, the Title 18 sections, or the campaign funding provisions of Title 26. . . .
>
> The Commission's enforcement power is both direct and wide ranging. It may institute a civil action for (i) injunctive or other relief against "any acts or practices which constitute or will constitute a violation of this Act," §437g(a)(5); (ii) declaratory or injunctive relief "as may be appropriate to implement or con[s]true any provisions" of Chapter 95 of Title 26, governing administration of funds for Presidential election campaigns and national party conventions, 26 U.S.C. §9011(b)(1) (1970 ed., Supp. IV); and (iii) "such injunctive relief as is appropriate to implement any provision" of Chapter 96 of Title 26, governing the payment of matching funds for Presidential primary campaigns, 26 U.S.C. §9040(c) (1970 ed., Supp. IV). . . . In no respect do the foregoing civil actions require the concurrence of or participation by the Attorney General; conversely, the decision not to seek judicial relief in the above respects would appear to rest solely with the Commission. . . .

The Court then examined the question whether the manner by which members of the Commission were appointed violated the Appointments Clause, concluding that it did:

> The Appointments Clause could, of course, be read as merely dealing with etiquette or protocol in describing "Officers of the United States," but the drafters had a less frivolous purpose in mind. This conclusion is supported by language from United States v. Germaine, 99 U.S. 508, 509-510 (1879):
>
>> The Constitution for purposes of appointment very clearly divides all its officers into two classes. The primary class requires a nomination by the President and confirmation by the Senate. But foreseeing that when offices became numerous, and sudden removals necessary, this mode might be inconvenient, it was provided that, in regard to officers inferior to those specially mentioned, Congress might by law vest their appointment in the President alone, in the courts of law, or in the heads of departments. That all persons who can be said to hold an office under the government about to be established under the Constitution were intended to be included within one or the other of these modes of appointment there can be but little doubt.
>
> We think that the term "Officers of the United States" as used in Art. II, defined to include "all persons who can be said to hold an office under the government" in United States v. Germaine, *supra*, is a term intended to have substantive meaning. We think its fair import is that any appointee exercising significant authority pursuant to the laws of the United States is an "Officer of the United States," and must, therefore, be appointed in the manner prescribed by §2, cl. 2, of that Article.
>
> If "all persons who can be said to hold an office under the government about to be established under the Constitution were intended to be included within one or the other of these modes of appointment," United States v. Germaine, *supra*, it is difficult to see how the members of the Commission may escape inclusion. If a postmaster first class, Myers v. United States, 272 U.S. 52 (1926), and the clerk of a district court, *Ex parte* Hennen, 13 Pet. 230 (1839), are inferior officers of the United States within the meaning of the Appointments Clause, as they are, surely the Commissioners before us are at the very least such "inferior Officers" within the meaning of that Clause.[162]
>
> Although two members of the Commission are initially selected by the President, his nominations are subject to confirmation not merely by the Senate, but by the House of Representatives as well. The remaining four voting members of the Commission are appointed by the President *pro tempore* of the Senate and by the Speaker of the House. While the second part of the Clause authorizes Congress to vest the appointment of the officers described in that part in "the Courts of Law, or in the Heads of Departments," neither the Speaker of the House nor the President *pro tempore* of the Senate comes within this language.
>
> The phrase "Heads of Departments," used as it is in conjunction with the phrase "Courts of Law," suggests that the Departments referred to are themselves

---

162. "Officers of the United States" does not include all employees of the United States, but there is no claim made that the Commissioners are employees of the United States rather than officers. Employees are lesser functionaries subordinate to officers of the United States, *see* Auffmordt v. Hedden, 137 U.S. 310, 327 (1890); United States v. Germaine, 99 U.S. 508 (1879), whereas the Commissioners, appointed for a statutory term, are not subject to the control or direction of any other executive, judicial, or legislative authority.

in the Executive Branch or at least have some connection with that branch. While the Clause expressly authorizes Congress to vest the appointment of certain officers in the "Courts of Law," the absence of similar language to include Congress must mean that neither Congress nor its officers were included within the language "Heads of Departments" in this part of cl. 2.

Thus with respect to four of the six voting members of the Commission, neither the President, the head of any department, nor the Judiciary has any voice in their selection. . . .

Insofar as the powers confided in the Commission are essentially of an investigative and informative nature, falling in the same general category as those powers which Congress might delegate to one of its own committees, there can be no question that the Commission as presently constituted may exercise them. . . .

But when we go beyond this type of authority to the more substantial powers exercised by the Commission, we reach a different result. The Commission's enforcement power, exemplified by its discretionary power to seek judicial relief, is authority that cannot possibly be regarded as merely in aid of the legislative function of Congress. A lawsuit is the ultimate remedy for a breach of the law, and it is to the President, and not to the Congress, that the Constitution entrusts the responsibility to "take Care that the Laws be faithfully executed." Art. II, §3. . . .

We hold that these provisions of the Act, vesting in the Commission primary responsibility for conducting civil litigation in the courts of the United States for vindicating public rights, violate Art. II, §2, cl. 2, of the Constitution. Such functions may be discharged only by persons who are "Officers of the United States" within the language of that section. . . .

NOTES AND QUESTIONS

1. *Congressional restrictions on the qualification of officers.* Congress has unquestioned authority to create and define the scope of authority of the federal "offices" to which the President may make appointments, pursuant to Article II, §2, cl. 2. Does it follow that Congress has unrestricted authority to impose statutory qualifications for appointment to those offices? Although Congress has done so repeatedly throughout our history, the courts have had very few occasions to address the issue and, on those occasions, have been reluctant to interfere with Congress's specification of statutory qualifications. An example is FEC v. NRA Political Victory Fund, 6 F.3d 821 (D.C. Cir. 1993). In response to the Supreme Court's decision in *Buckley,* Congress reconstituted the FEC as an independent agency, its six members appointed by the President, with the advice and consent of the Senate. No more than three commissioners could be affiliated with the same political party, and members were prohibited from engaging in substantial outside business activities. The D.C. Circuit declined to rule on the question of whether these restrictions on the qualifications of commissioners violated the Appointments Clause, finding it unclear from the evidence that the restrictions in fact had prevented the President from making appointments he would have preferred. The court, did, however, hold the new FEC unconstitutional because it contained two nonvoting, ex officio members, the Secretary of the Senate and Clerk of the House of Representatives. The court found that Congress, in legislating its agents into the commission, even as nonvoting members, must have expected them to influence the commission's

actions. The court concluded that "the mere presence of agents of Congress on an entity with executive powers offends the Constitution." *Id.* at 827.

2. *Principal officers versus inferior officers.* As the *Germaine* case (quoted in *Buckley*) noted, the Appointments Clause distinguishes between (principal) "officers" and "inferior officers." In *Buckley*, the Court observed that FEC commissioners were "at the very least" inferior officers. In Morrison v. Olson, 487 U.S. 76 (1988), excerpted at section c. of this part, *infra*, the Court ruled that a special prosecutor was an inferior officer based on "several factors," including that she was subject to removal by a higher Executive Branch official (the Attorney General) and that the enabling statute conferred on her only "limited" duties, jurisdiction, and tenure. Later, in Edmond v. United States, 520 U.S. 651 (1997), discussed *infra*, the Court, in an opinion by Justice Scalia, announced a more definitive test: "'inferior officers' are officers whose work is directed and supervised at some level by others who were appointed by presidential nomination with the advice and consent of the Senate." 520 U.S. at 662-663. Applying this standard, it appears clear that FEC commissioners were in fact principal officers.

3. *Officers versus employees.* In note 162, the *Buckley* Court recognized a further distinction between "officers" and "employees." The Constitution is silent about the appointment of employees. Why? Does that mean that Congress could strip the President of power to appoint, or oversee the appointment, of "employees" of executive agencies? The Supreme Court explored the line between inferior officers and employees in Freytag v. Commissioner of Internal Revenue, 501 U.S. 868 (1991). A statute authorized the Chief Judge of the U.S. Tax Court to appoint "special trial judges" (STJs) to preside at hearings and prepare proposed findings and opinions, which are then submitted to Tax Court Judges (who render the actual decision). The Tax Court is an Article I court. In a challenge to a decision of the Tax Court, the Supreme Court *sua sponte* raised the issue of whether the STJs had been appointed in a constitutionally permissible manner. The Court ruled that STJs are "inferior officers," not "employees," because their positions are "established by law" and they "exercise significant discretion." The Court was also unanimous in concluding that the power to appoint STJs could, constitutionally, be conferred on the head of the Tax Court. But the Justices split on the reason. Five Justices concluded that the Tax Court was a "Court of Law" as that term is used in the Appointments Clause (even though not an Article III "court"); four Justices concluded that the Tax Court is a "Department." Is it plausible that the Framers would mean something different by the word "Court" as used in Article II, §2, cl. 2, and in Article III, §1?

The Supreme Court reaffirmed part of *Freytag* in Lucia v. Securities and Exchange Commission, 138 S. Ct. 2044 (2018), finding that the SEC's administrative law judges (ALJs) were "officers," not "employees," and that, therefore, their appointment by SEC staff members violated the Appointments Clause. The Court held that under *Buckley*, *Freytag*, and *Germaine*, the SEC's ALJs are officers because they occupy continuing positions established by law and exercise significant discretion when presiding over adjudicatory hearings, even though their "initial decisions" are subject to SEC review. Does review of ALJ initial decisions by the Commission go to the distinction between officers and employees or the distinction between principal officers and inferior officers? What is the test now for each of these categories?

In anticipation of the *Lucia* decision, the SEC ratified the appointments of its ALJs, attempting to satisfy the Appointments Clause's requirement that, with Congress's permission, inferior officers may be appointed by a department head. Going even further, on July 10, 2018, President Trump issued an Executive Order removing ALJ appointments across the government from the competitive civil service process and placing their appointment in the hands of their respective department heads. See Executive Order Excepting Administrative Law Judges from the Competitive Service (July 10, 2018), discussed further in Chapter VI, *infra.*

4. *Appointment of members of Congress to executive agencies.* Could the President, if he so desired, appoint a member of Congress to sit on a body such as the Federal Election Commission? The answer is pretty clearly no. Article I, §6, cl. 2, of the Constitution provides:

> No Senator or Representative shall, during the Time for which he was elected, be appointed to any civil Office under the Authority of the United States, which shall have been created, or the Emoluments whereof shall have been increased during such time; and no Person holding any Office under the United States, shall be a member of either House during his Continuance in Office.

The first part of this provision—known as the "Ineligibility Clause"—appears to be an anticorruption provision, preventing members of Congress from creating executive positions for themselves or voting to raise the pay of an executive position they expect to occupy. The second part—the so-called "Incompatibility Clause"—is an important element of separation of powers, disallowing the common practice in parliamentary regimes of filling important Executive Branch positions from the ranks of the legislature.

The Incompatibility Clause has received virtually no authoritative judicial construction. In Reservists Committee to Stop the War v. Laird, 323 F. Supp. 833 (D.D.C. 1971), District Judge Gerhard Gesell held that the Clause prohibited members of Congress from simultaneously holding commissions in the Armed Forces Reserve, but the Supreme Court reversed on the ground that the complainants lacked standing to challenge the alleged violation. Schlesinger v. Reservists Comm. to Stop the War, 418 U.S. 208 (1974). In Metropolitan Washington Airports Auth. v. Citizens for Abatement of Aircraft Noise, Inc., 501 U.S. 252 (1991), the Supreme Court held that Congress could not subject decisions of the Washington Airports Authority to veto by a Board of Review, consisting of nine members of Congress. The Court reasoned that Congress was either attempting to participate in the execution of law, in violation of the assignment of executive powers to the President and his subordinates, or it was legislating in violation of *Chadha*'s insistence on bicameralism and presentment. Why did the Court not rest its decision on the Incompatibility Clause?

Is there any constitutional problem with the same person serving simultaneously as a principal and inferior officer, assuming Appointments Clause and statutory formalities are observed? Apparently not. In Ortiz v. United States, 138 S. Ct. 2165, 2183 (2018), the Supreme Court rejected a challenge to such simultaneous service, stating that "[t]his Court has never read the Appointments Clause to impose rules about dual service, separate and distinct from methods of appointment. Nor has it ever recognized principles of 'incongruity' or 'incompatibility' to test the permissibility of holding two offices."

5. *Appointment of judges to executive agencies.* Could the President, if he so desired, appoint a sitting federal judge to an administrative agency? There is no comparably explicit prohibition against judges' holding nonjudicial offices or performing nonjudicial functions. The Supreme Court has, however, applied general separation-of-powers principles to police limits on the nonjudicial activities of Article III judges. For example, in the *Mistretta* case, excerpted in part B.1., *supra,* the Supreme Court decided that appointment of three sitting federal judges to the United States Sentencing Commission did not violate the separation-of-powers doctrine. While conceding that the appointment of the sitting judges to such an agency is "somewhat troublesome," the Court took solace in the facts that service by any particular judge is voluntary and that sentencing policy is a traditional matter of judicial concern. Thus, the Act in effect pursues a policy of "reciprocity" among the branches, by "enlisting" judicial participation in policy concerning a "uniquely judicial subject." The Court also concluded that the President's power under the Act to remove commissioners for good cause did not impair the independence of the judiciary. Even though the President could threaten to remove or actually remove a judicial member *from the Commission,* he could not affect that member's tenure or compensation *as a judge.*

6. *Recess appointments.* As noted above, the only exception to the requirement of senatorial advice and consent for appointment of principal officers is the so-called "Recess Appointments Clause" of the Constitution, Art. II, §2, cl. 3, which provides:

> The President shall have Power to fill up all Vacancies that may happen during the Recess of the Senate, by granting Commissions which shall expire at the End of their next Session.

During the nineteenth century, when the Senate met for relatively brief annual "sessions," Presidents utilized this authority to make appointments during the lengthy breaks between sessions ("inter-session appointments"). But it was not until the twentieth century that Presidents began to make recess appointments during breaks within sessions ("intra-session appointments"). The practice accelerated in the decades after World War II, as Presidents of both parties made thousands of such appointments. While many observers questioned whether the practice of intra-session appointments complied with the constitutional language, the courts did not have occasion to explore the issue until a controversy erupted over a group of recess appointments to the National Labor Relations Board (NLRB) by President Obama.

The NLRB is responsible for establishing and policing the conditions necessary for workers and employers to engage peacefully in collective bargaining. The Board consists of five members, appointed to staggered five-year terms by the President, with advice and consent of the Senate. The Board can act only if it has at least a three-member quorum. Largely because of partisan political disagreements, President Obama had difficulty in obtaining senatorial confirmation of his nominees to the Board, with the result that there were only three sitting Board members in late 2011. Faced with the prospect that the Board would lack a quorum to conduct business when one of the remaining members' terms expired, President Obama made three appointments to the Board on

January 4, 2012, during a three-day break between two "*pro forma*" sessions of the Senate. The President did not seek or obtain the Senate's advice and consent, claiming that the Senate was in "recess." A challenge to the legality of that action soon reached the Supreme Court.

NATIONAL LABOR RELATIONS BOARD v. NOEL CANNING, 134 S. Ct. 2550 (2014):   The NLRB found that Noel Canning, a Pepsi-Cola distributor, had committed an unfair labor practice and ordered it to take certain remedial actions. On petition for review, the D.C. Circuit vacated the Board's order on the grounds that the Board lacked a lawful quorum to issue the order, because three of its five members had been invalidly appointed. As presented to the Supreme Court, the case turned on the answer to three questions: 1. Does the phrase "the Recess of the Senate," as used in the Recess Appointments Clause, mean only the period between annual sessions of the Senate or also include intra-session breaks of sufficient duration (and, if the latter, how long must a break last, in order to constitute a "recess")? 2. Does the Clause apply only to vacancies that *first occur* during a recess (however defined) or does it also apply more broadly to vacancies that *exist* during a recess (even if they first occurred while the Senate was in session)? 3. In determining whether an intra-session break in the Senate's activities is long enough to constitute a "recess," should *pro forma* sessions (in which no business is typically conducted) be included or ignored? In an opinion by Justice Breyer, the Court ruled in favor of the government on the first two questions but against the government on the third. Thus, because the Senate was not in recess during the period of *pro forma* sessions, the appointments were invalid:

> Presidents have made recess appointments since the beginning of the Republic. Their frequency suggests that the Senate and President have recognized that recess appointments can be both necessary and appropriate in certain circumstances. We have not previously interpreted the Clause, and, when doing so for the first time in more than 200 years, we must hesitate to upset the compromises and working arrangements that the elected branches of Government themselves have reached. . . .

III

> In our view, the phrase "the recess" includes an intra-session recess of substantial length. Its words taken literally can refer to both types of recess. Founding-era dictionaries define the word "recess," much as we do today, simply as "a period of cessation from usual work." The Founders themselves used the word to refer to intra-session, as well as to inter-session, breaks.
>
> We recognize that the word "the" in "the recess" might suggest that the phrase refers to the single break separating formal sessions of Congress. That is because the word "the" frequently (but not always) indicates "a particular thing." But the word can also refer "to a term used generically or universally." . . . And we believe the Clause's purpose demands the broader interpretation. The Clause gives the President authority to make appointments during "the recess of the Senate" so that the President can ensure the continued functioning of the Federal Government when the Senate is away. The Senate is equally away during both an inter-session and an intra-session recess, and its capacity to participate in the appointments process has nothing to do with the words it uses to signal its departure. . . .

The greater interpretive problem is determining how long a recess must be in order to fall within the Clause. Is a break of a week, or a day, or an hour too short to count as a "recess"? The Clause itself does not say. And Justice Scalia claims that this silence itself shows that the Framers intended the Clause to apply only to an intersession recess. [But] the lack of a textual floor raises a problem that plagues *both* interpretations—Justice Scalia's and ours. Today a brief inter-session recess is just as possible as a brief intra-session recess. . . .

Even the Solicitor General, arguing for a broader interpretation, acknowledges that there is a lower limit applicable to both kinds of recess. He argues that the lower limit should be three days by analogy to the Adjournments Clause of the Constitution. That Clause says: "Neither House, during the Session of Congress, shall, without the Consent of the other, adjourn for more than three days." Art. I, §5, cl. 4. We agree with the Solicitor General that a 3-day recess would be too short. The Adjournments Clause reflects the fact that a 3-day break is not a significant interruption of legislative business. . . . A Senate recess that is so short that it does not require the consent of the House is not long enough to trigger the President's recess-appointment power.

That is not to say that the President may make recess appointments during any recess that is "more than three days." [T]hough Congress has taken short breaks for almost 200 years, and there have been many thousands of recess appointments in that time, we have not found a single example of a recess appointment made during an intra-session recess that was shorter than 10 days. . . . We therefore conclude, in light of historical practice, that a recess of more than 3 days but less than 10 days is presumptively too short to fall within the Clause. We add the word "presumptively" to leave open the possibility that some very unusual circumstance—a national catastrophe, for instance, that renders the Senate unavailable but calls for an urgent response—could demand the exercise of the recess-appointment power during a shorter break. . . .

IV

The second question concerns the scope of the phrase "vacancies *that may happen* during the recess of the Senate." All agree that the phrase applies to vacancies that initially occur during a recess. But does it also apply to vacancies that initially occur before a recess and continue to exist during the recess? In our view the phrase applies to both kinds of vacancy. . . . We concede that the most natural meaning of "happens" as applied to a "vacancy" (at least to a modern ear) is that the vacancy "happens" when it initially occurs. But that is not the only possible way to use the word. . . .

The Clause's purpose strongly supports the broader interpretation. That purpose is to permit the President to obtain the assistance of subordinate officers when the Senate, due to its recess, cannot confirm them. . . . Examples are not difficult to imagine: An ambassadorial post falls vacant too soon before the recess begins for the President to appoint a replacement; the Senate rejects a President's nominee just before a recess, too late to select another. . . .

Historical practice over the past 200 years strongly favors the broader interpretation. The tradition of applying the Clause to pre-recess vacancies dates at least to President James Madison. [T]he President has consistently and frequently interpreted the Recess Appointments Clause to apply to vacancies that initially occur before, but continue to exist during, a recess of the Senate. The Senate as a body has not countered this practice for nearly three-quarters of a century, perhaps longer. . . .

V

The third question concerns the calculation of the length of the Senate's "recess." On December 17, 2011, the Senate by unanimous consent adopted a resolution to convene "*pro forma* session[s]" only, with "no business . . . transacted," on every Tuesday and Friday from December 20, 2011, through January 20, 2012. . . . During that period, the Senate . . . held pro forma sessions on December 20, 23, 27, and 30, and on January 3, 6, 10, 13, 17, and 20; and at the end of each pro forma session, it adjourned until the time and date of the next.

The President made the recess appointments before us on January 4, 2012, in between the January 3 and the January 6 *pro forma* sessions. We must determine the significance of these sessions—that is, whether, for purposes of the Clause, we should treat them as periods when the Senate was in session or as periods when it was in recess. . . .

In our view, . . . the *pro forma* sessions count as sessions, not as periods of recess. We hold that, for purposes of the Recess Appointments Clause, the Senate is in session when it says it is, provided that, under its own rules, it retains the capacity to transact Senate business. The Senate met that standard here.

The standard we apply is consistent with the Constitution's broad delegation of authority to the Senate to determine how and when to conduct its business. The Constitution explicitly empowers the Senate to "determine the Rules of its Proceedings." Art. I, §5, cl. 2. . . .

In addition, the Constitution provides the Senate with extensive control over its schedule. There are only limited exceptions. *See* Amdt. 20, §2 (Congress must meet once a year on January 3, unless it specifies another day by law); Art. II, §3 (Senate must meet if the President calls it into special session); Art. I, §5, cl. 4 (neither House may adjourn for more than three days without consent of the other). *See also* Art. II, §3 ("[I]n Case of Disagreement between [the Houses], with Respect to the Time of Adjournment, [the President] may adjourn them to such Time as he shall think proper"). The Constitution thus gives the Senate wide latitude to determine whether and when to have a session, as well as how to conduct the session. This suggests that the Senate's determination about what constitutes a session should merit great respect. . . .

For these reasons, we conclude that we must give great weight to the Senate's own determination of when it is and when it is not in session. But our deference to the Senate cannot be absolute. When the Senate is without the capacity to act, under its own rules, it is not in session even if it so declares. In that circumstance, the Senate is not simply unlikely or unwilling to act upon nominations of the President. It is *unable* to do so. . . .

Applying this standard, we find that the *pro forma* sessions were sessions for purposes of the Clause. First, the Senate said it was in session. . . . Second, the Senate's rules make clear that during its *pro forma* sessions, despite its resolution that it would conduct no business, the Senate retained the power to conduct business. During any *pro forma* session, the Senate could have conducted business simply by passing a unanimous consent agreement. . . . It is consequently unsurprising that the Senate has enacted legislation during *pro forma* sessions even when it has said that no business will be transacted.

[T]he Solicitor General warns that our holding may "'disrup[t] the proper balance between the coordinate branches by preventing the Executive Branch from accomplishing its constitutionally assigned functions.'" Brief for Petitioner 64 (quoting Morrison v. Olson, 487 U.S. 654, 695 (1988); alteration in original). We do not see, however, how our holding could significantly alter the constitutional balance. Most appointments are not controversial and do not produce friction between the branches. Where political controversy is serious, the Senate unquestionably has other methods of preventing recess appointments. As the Solicitor General concedes, the Senate could preclude the President from making recess appointments by holding a series of twice-a-week ordinary (not *pro forma*) sessions. . . . Regardless, the Recess Appointments Clause is not designed to overcome serious institutional friction. It simply provides a subsidiary method for appointing officials when the Senate is away during a recess. Here, as in other contexts, friction between the branches is an inevitable consequence of our constitutional structure. . . .

Given our answer to the last question before us, we conclude that the Recess Appointments Clause does not give the President the constitutional authority to make the appointments here at issue. . . .

In an opinion concurring in the judgment, Justice Scalia, joined by Chief Justice Roberts and Justices Thomas and Alito, agreed that the appointments were invalid, but disagreed with the Court's determinations that recess appointments may be made during an intra-session adjournment and that vacancies that occurred before the recess may be filled by recess appointments:

Today's Court agrees that the appointments were invalid, but for the far narrower reason that they were made during a 3-day break in the Senate's session. On its way to that result, the majority sweeps away the key textual limitations on the recess-appointment power. . . . The Court's decision transforms the recess-appointment power from a tool carefully designed to fill a narrow and specific need into a weapon to be wielded by future Presidents against future Senates. . . .

I. Our Responsibility

Today's majority disregards two overarching principles that ought to guide our consideration of the questions presented here.

First, the Constitution's core, government-structuring provisions are no less critical to preserving liberty than are the later adopted provisions of the Bill of Rights. . . . Second and relatedly, when questions involving the Constitution's government-structuring provisions are presented in a justiciable case, [t]his Court does not defer to the other branches' resolution of such controversies. . . . Since the separation of powers exists for the protection of individual liberty, its vitality "does not depend" on "whether 'the encroached-upon branch approves the encroachment.'" [Free Enterprise Fund v. Public Company Accounting Oversight Board, 561 U.S. 471, 497 (2010)] (quoting New York v. United States, 505 U.S. 144, 182 (1992)). . . .

Of course, where a governmental practice has been open, widespread, and unchallenged since the early days of the Republic, the practice should guide our interpretation of an ambiguous constitutional provision. . . . But "'[p]ast practice does not, by itself, create power.'" Medellín v. Texas, 552 U.S. 491, 532 (2008) (quoting Dames & Moore v. Regan, 453 U.S. 654, 686 (1981)). That is a necessary corollary of the principle that the political branches cannot by agreement alter the constitutional structure. Plainly, then, a self-aggrandizing practice adopted by one branch well after the founding, often challenged, and never before blessed by this Court—in other words, the sort of practice on which the majority relies in this case—does not relieve us of our duty to interpret the Constitution in light of its text, structure, and original understanding. . . .

II.   INTRA-SESSION BREAKS

. . . A sensible interpretation of the Recess Appointments Clause should start by recognizing that the Clause uses the term "Recess" in contradistinction to the term "Session." . . . In the founding era, the terms "recess" and "session" had well-understood meanings in the marking-out of legislative time. The life of each elected Congress typically consisted (as it still does) of two or more formal sessions separated by adjournments "*sine die*," that is, without a specified return date. The period between two sessions was known as "the recess." . . . By contrast, other provisions of the Constitution use the verb "adjourn" rather than "recess" to refer to the commencement of breaks during a formal legislative session. *See, e.g.*, Art. I, §5, cl. 1; *id.*, §5, cl. 4. . . .

The dictionary definitions of "recess" on which the majority relies . . . make clear that in colloquial usage, a recess could include any suspension of legislative business, no matter how short. The notion that the Constitution empowers the President to make unilateral appointments every time the Senate takes a half-hour lunch break is so absurd as to be self-refuting.

[T]he majority contends that the Clause's supposed purpose of keeping the wheels of government turning demands that we interpret the Clause to maintain its relevance in light of the "new circumstance" of the Senate's taking an increasing number of intra-session breaks that exceed three days. Even if I accepted the canard that courts can alter the Constitution's meaning to accommodate changed circumstances, I would be hard pressed to see the relevance of that notion here. The rise of intra-session adjournments has occurred in tandem with the development of modern forms of communication and transportation that mean the Senate "is always available" to consider nominations, even when its Members are temporarily dispersed for an intra-session break. The Recess Appointments Clause therefore is, or rather, should be, an anachronism . . . . The need it was designed to fill no longer exists, and its only remaining use is the ignoble one of enabling the President to circumvent the Senate's role in the appointment process. . . .

To avoid the absurd results that follow from its colloquial reading of "the Recess," the majority is forced to declare that some intra-session breaks—though undisputedly within the phrase's colloquial meaning—are simply "too short to trigger the Recess Appointments Clause." But it identifies no textual basis whatsoever for limiting the length of "the Recess," nor does it point to any clear standard for determining how short is too short. . . .

An interpretation that calls for this kind of judicial adventurism cannot be correct. Indeed, if the Clause really did use "Recess" in its colloquial sense, then there would be no "judicially discoverable and manageable standard for resolving" whether a particular break was long enough to trigger the recess-appointment power, making that a nonjusticiable political question. Zivotofsky [v. Clinton, 132 S. Ct. 1431, 1435 (2012)] (internal quotation marks omitted). . . .

The majority . . . insists that history "offers strong support" for its interpretation. The historical practice of the political branches is, of course, irrelevant when the Constitution is clear. But even if the Constitution were thought ambiguous on this point, history does not support the majority's interpretation. [After surveying the historical record, Justice Scalia concludes:] Intra-session recess appointments were virtually unheard of for the first 130 years of the Republic, were deemed unconstitutional by the first Attorney General to address them, were not openly defended by the Executive until 1921, were not made in significant numbers until after World War II, and have been repeatedly criticized as unconstitutional by Senators of both parties. . . .

III.   PRE-RECESS VACANCIES

[N]o reasonable reader would have understood the Recess Appointments Clause to use the word "happen" in the majority's "happen to be" sense, and thus to empower the President to fill all vacancies that might exist during a recess, regardless of when they arose. For one thing, the Clause's language would have been a surpassingly odd way of giving the President that power. The Clause easily could have been written to convey that meaning clearly: It could have referred to "all Vacancies that may exist during the Recess," or it could have omitted the qualifying phrase entirely and simply authorized the President to "fill up all Vacancies during the Recess." . . .

For another thing, the majority's reading not only strains the Clause's language but distorts its constitutional role, which was meant to be subordinate. As Hamilton explained, appointment with the advice and consent of the Senate was to be "the general mode of appointing officers of the United States." The Federalist No. 67, at 455. . . .

The Constitution is not a road map for maximally efficient government, but a system of "carefully crafted restraints" designed to "protect the people from the improvident exercise of power." *Chadha*, 462 U.S. at 957, 959. . . .

IV.   CONCLUSION

. . . The real tragedy of today's decision is not simply the abolition of the Constitution's limits on the recess-appointment power and the substitution of a novel framework invented by this Court. It is the damage done to our separation-of-powers jurisprudence more generally. It is not every day that we encounter a proper case or controversy requiring interpretation of the Constitution's structural provisions. Most of the time, the interpretation of those provisions is left to the political branches—which, in deciding how much respect to afford the constitutional text, often take their cues from this Court. We should therefore take every opportunity to affirm the primacy of the Constitution's enduring principles over the politics of the moment. Our failure to do so today will resonate well beyond the particular dispute at hand. Sad, but true: The Court's embrace of the adverse-possession theory of executive power (a characterization the majority resists but does not refute) will be cited in diverse contexts, including those presently unimagined, and will have the effect of aggrandizing the Presidency beyond its constitutional bounds and undermining respect for the separation of powers.

I concur in the judgment only.

NOTES AND QUESTIONS

1. *Minimum duration of a "recess."* The majority's reading of the Recess Appointments Clause forces the courts to articulate standards for determining when a "break" becomes a "recess." Shouldn't the Court have waited for lower courts to grapple with this issue in the context of subsequent cases before articulating its presumptive ten-day rule? Is there any plausible constitutional source for the selection of ten days? In subsequent cases challenging actions taken by NLRB panels that included recess appointees, the lower courts have rather mechanically applied the ten-day cut-off. *See, e.g.,* Mathew Enterprise, Inc. v.

NLRB, 771 F.3d 812 (D.C. Cir. 2014) (upholding a decision involving a board member appointed during a 17-day break in the Senate during March 2010). Given the Court's conclusion that the Senate was in fact in session, was it necessary for the Court to reach the question of whether the Clause applies to intra-session appointments? If not, should the lower courts treat as dicta everything but the conclusion that the Senate was not in recess while holding *pro forma* sessions?

2. *The functions served by senatorial confirmation.* Justice Scalia notes that the Constitution's structural provisions on governance are both designed for and important to the preservation of liberty and serve functions just as important as the Bill of Rights. Do you think that senatorial confirmation helps "preserve liberty"? In what way? Is it an equal concern for liberty that the Senate can effectively nullify a statute enacted by Congress by refusing to confirm appointees to run the agency charged with administering it? Does the Constitution provide the President with a means to make recess appointments by forcing the Senate to take a recess? Consider Article II, §3, cl. 2: "he may, on extraordinary Occasions, convene both Houses, or either of them and in Case of Disagreement between them, with Respect to the Time of Adjournment, he may adjourn them to such Time as he shall think proper." What role do you think this provision was designed to play? How would you interpret that provision in light of the reasoning in *Noel Canning*?

Separate from the Recess Appointments Clause, since the Founding, Congress has statutorily granted the President limited power to make temporary appointments to fill vacancies to "offices of the United States," pending nomination and appointment with Senatorial advice and consent. The latest version of this authority is in the Federal Vacancies Reform Act of 1998, 5 U.S.C. §§3345 et seq. (FVRA). Section 3345(a)(1) creates a presumptive rule that the "first assistant" to the vacant office shall perform that office's functions, but subsections (a)(2) and (a)(3) give the President discretion to appoint two other categories of senior officers in such a capacity. Section (b)(1) provides, however, that "notwithstanding section (a)(1)," a person may not serve in an acting capacity if the President has nominated him or her for permanent appointment (subject to senatorial advice and consent). In NLRB v. SW General, Inc., 137 S. Ct. 929 (2017), the Supreme Court, by a vote of 6-2, ruled that this disqualification also applied to a person temporarily appointed under authority of §3345(a)(3). Although the case turned on a complex and rather narrow issue of statutory interpretation, the Court evinced a reluctance to interpret the Act broadly with its opening description of senatorial confirmation as "'an excellent check upon a spirit of favoritism in the President' and a guard against 'the appointment of unfit characters . . . from family connection, from personal attachment, or from a view to popularity,'" quoting from The Federalist No. 76, p. 457 (C. Rossiter ed. 1961) (A. Hamilton). Justice Thomas, in a concurring opinion, declared that the FVRA violates the Appointments Clause insofar as it purports to authorize the President to appoint "acting" Principal Officers without the advice and consent of the Senate.

What do you think the constitutional basis would be for "acting" appointments? Is there a tension between permitting such appointments without clear limits while restricting the opportunity for recess appointments which are clearly based in constitutional text? What is the principal objection to recess appointments? To "acting" appointments? Which is more likely to be a source of the sorts of appointments the Constitution's framers worried about?

3. *The historical record and interpretive styles.* Justice Breyer acknowledges that there were very few recess appointments until the 1950s, but gives positive weight to the fact that there have been many recess appointments (by Presidents of both parties) in subsequent decades. You will recall that in *Chadha* the Court gave no apparent weight to the fact that Congress (with presidential acquiescence in most cases) had made frequent use of so-called "legislative veto" provisions in the decades prior to that decision. Is the Court being inconsistent in its use of history, or is there a sensible distinction between the two contexts? How would you characterize the reasoning styles used by Justices Breyer and Scalia to interpret the Recess Appointments Clause? Does it track the distinction between "formalist" and "functional" reasoning discussed in connection with cases like *Chadha* and Clinton v. New York?

4. *Filibusters and recess appointments.* One contributor to the recent spate of recess appointments was the Senate's filibuster policy, which permitted a minority of Senators to block presidential nominations with which they disagreed. For over a century from the date of the Founding, the United States Senate had permitted even a single Senator to block action on a bill or presidential nomination by filibustering. In 1917, the Senate provided that a filibuster could be overridden by a vote of two-thirds of Senators, and in 1975 the Senate lowered the cut-off ratio to three-fifths. Despite the reduction, the filibuster rule in force at the time of the *Noel Canning* appointments still made it possible for a minority coalition with 40 or more votes to block presidential appointments.

Although no filibuster was used to block a judicial appointment until the administration of President George W. Bush, filibusters — and the threat of filibusters — of presidential appointments had become frequent weapons in the increased partisan bickering of recent decades. In November 2013, frustrated at the difficulty of overcoming Republican opposition to President Obama's executive and judicial nominations, a slim Democratic majority in the Senate invoked what had been referred to as the "nuclear option" by eliminating the 60 percent rule, and substituting a simple majority rule, for all presidential nominations to executive offices and judicial positions other than the Supreme Court. (Enactment of legislation is still subject to the 60 percent rule.) While doing nothing to reduce partisan bickering — and indeed, arguably exacerbating it — this rule change made it much easier for the President to obtain confirmation of appointments, thus significantly reducing the pressure to make recess appointments. For example, applying its new rules, the Senate confirmed three appointments to the NLRB in August of 2014.

b.   Removal Power

Arguably the power to appoint is incomplete — perhaps even empty — without the power to remove. Yet the Constitution is strangely silent about the power to remove officials. In the very first Congress, James Madison relied on the sweeping mandate of Article II, §1, to find inherent authority for the President to remove, unilaterally, officers whom he had appointed with the advice and consent of the Senate. *See* Edward S. Corwin, The President: Office and

Powers 102-114, 428 (3d ed. 1948). In Marbury v. Madison, 5 U.S. (1 Cranch) 137 (1803), the Supreme Court adopted a narrower interpretation. Chief Justice John Marshall wrote that although the President generally had the power to remove such officers, that power did not extend to officers whose commissions granted them the right to serve a specified time without subjecting them to presidential removal. That portion of *Marbury* implicitly decides that Congress could restrict the President's authority of removal, but it does not expressly analyze that question. The next major Supreme Court decision on the subject came more than a century later.

MYERS v. UNITED STATES, 272 U.S. 52 (1926): In 1917, Frank Myers was appointed as a postmaster first class for Portland, Oregon, for a term of four years. In 1920, the Postmaster General, acting on orders of the President, fired Myers. Myers sued in the Court of Claims to recover back pay, claiming that his removal was unlawful because the Postmaster General had not obtained the consent of the Senate for the discharge, as required by the governing statute. The Supreme Court dismissed the claim, declaring the statute unconstitutional. Writing expansively about the executive power, Chief Justice William Howard Taft declared:

> The ordinary duties of officers prescribed by statute come under the general administrative control of the President by virtue of the general grant to him of the executive power, and he may properly supervise and guide their construction of the statutes under which they act in order to secure that unitary and uniform execution of the laws which Article II of the Constitution evidently contemplated in vesting general executive power in the President alone. Laws are often passed with specific provisions for the adoption of regulations by a department or bureau head to make the law workable and effective. The ability and judgment manifested by the official thus empowered, as well as his energy and stimulation of his subordinates, are subjects which the President must consider and supervise in his administrative control. Finding such officers to be negligent and inefficient, the President should have the power to remove them. Of course there may be duties so peculiarly and specifically committed to the discretion of a particular officer as to raise a question whether the President may overrule or revise the officer's interpretation of his statutory duty in a particular instance. Then there may be duties of a quasi-judicial character imposed on executive tribunals whose decisions . . . affect interests of individuals, the discharge of which the President cannot in a particular case properly influence or control. But even in such a case he may consider the decision after its rendition as a reason for removing the officer, on the ground that the discretion regularly entrusted to that officer by statute has not been on the whole intelligently or wisely exercised. Otherwise he does not discharge his own constitutional duty of seeing that the laws be faithfully executed.

Id. at 135. Nor was Taft impressed by the argument that a local postmaster held an "inferior" office:

> The power to remove inferior executive officers, like that to remove superior executive officers, is an incident of the power to appoint them, and is in its nature an executive power. The authority of Congress . . . to vest the appointment of such inferior officers in the heads of departments carries with it authority incidentally to invest the heads of departments with power to remove. . . . Congress, in

committing the appointment of such inferior officers to the heads of departments, may prescribe incidental regulations controlling and restricting the latter in the exercise of the power of removal. But the Court never has held, nor reasonably could hold, . . . that the . . . Congress [may] draw to itself, or to either branch of it, the power to remove or the right to participate in the exercise of that power. To do this would be to . . . infringe the constitutional principle of the separation of governmental powers.

Id. at 161.

HUMPHREY'S EXECUTOR v. UNITED STATES, 295 U.S. 602 (1935):   The broad sweep of Taft's language was tested nine years later, when President Franklin D. Roosevelt attempted to dismiss a member of the Federal Trade Commission named William E. Humphrey, a man characterized by one observer as "one of the most colorful (if least effective) commissioners in the history of federal regulation." Thomas K. McCraw, Prophets of Regulation 151 (1984). McCraw describes the events leading up to the confrontation in these terms:

> Appointed by President Coolidge in 1925, Humphrey had been a congressman and lumber lobbyist. After joining the commission, the garrulous and acerbic new chairman missed no opportunity to broadcast his view that the FTC's job was not so much to police business practices as to assist executives in doing what they already wanted to do. An unrestrained partisan of Old Guard Republicanism, Humphrey often publicly berated his fellow commissioners. He also attacked progressive Democrats and Republicans in Congress and generally disrupted whatever atmosphere of calm deliberation might otherwise have settled over the FTC. . . .
>
> Despite Humphrey's clowning, incompetence, and violent partisanship, President Hoover appointed him to a second [seven]-year term, beginning in 1931. This act, perhaps more than any other single episode during the commission's first generation of existence, hammered home a message that already had been indicated by repeated actions on the part of Congress and the courts: the Federal Trade Commission was not to be taken seriously.

Id. at 151-152. Shortly after taking office in 1933, Roosevelt wrote to Humphrey requesting his resignation. Roosevelt's letter stated: "I do not feel that your mind and my mind go along together on either policies or the administering of the Federal Trade Commission, and, frankly, I think it is best for the people of this country that I should have full confidence." *Humphrey's Executor*, 295 U.S. at 619. When Humphrey refused to step down, Roosevelt summarily fired him. Humphrey challenged the dismissal on the ground that the Federal Trade Commission Act permitted the President to remove a sitting commissioner only for "inefficiency, neglect of duty, or malfeasance in office." After Humphrey's death, his executor brought suit in the Court of Claims to recover Humphrey's salary as a commissioner for the period following his allegedly unauthorized dismissal. In reply, the United States asserted the President's inherent constitutional right to remove an officer. In rejecting the President's claim of inherent authority under Article II to remove FTC members, the Court carefully distinguished *Myers*:

> [T]he narrow point actually decided was only that the President had power to remove a postmaster of the first class, without the advice and consent of the Senate as required by act of Congress. In the course of the opinion of the court,

expressions occur which tend to sustain the government's contention, but these are beyond the point involved and, therefore, do not come within the rule of stare decisis. In so far as they are out of harmony with the views here set forth, these expressions are disapproved. . . .

The office of a postmaster is so essentially unlike the office now involved that the decision in the *Myers* case cannot be accepted as controlling our decision here. A postmaster is an executive officer restricted to the performance of executive functions. He is charged with no duty at all related to either the legislative or judicial power. . . .

The Federal Trade Commission is an administrative body created by Congress to carry into effect legislative policies embodied in the statute in accordance with the legislative standard therein prescribed, and to perform other specified duties as a legislative or as a judicial aid. Such a body cannot in any proper sense be characterized as an arm or an eye of the executive. Its duties are performed without executive leave and, in the contemplation of the statute, must be free from executive control. In administering the provisions of the statute in respect of "unfair methods of competition"— that is to say in filling in and administering the details embodied by that general standard— the commission acts in part quasi-legislatively and in part quasi-judicially. . . .

The fundamental necessity of maintaining each of the three general departments of government entirely free from the control or coercive influence, direct or indirect, of either of the others, has often been stressed and is hardly open to serious question. . . .

The power of removal here claimed for the President falls within this principle, since its coercive influence threatens the independence of a commission, which is not only wholly disconnected from the executive department, but which, as already fully appears, was created by Congress as a means of carrying into operation legislative and judicial powers, and as an agency of the legislative and judicial departments. . . .

Id. at 626-630.

The Court did not have occasion to examine the question of the President's removal power again until 1958. In Wiener v. United States, 357 U.S. 349 (1958), the Court reaffirmed *Humphrey's Executor* in ruling invalid the President's attempt to remove a member of the War Claims Commission, on the ground that the commission was an "adjudicating body." Interestingly, the Court implied a "for cause" limitation on the President's removal power, even though there was none in the statute. Nearly three more decades would pass before the Court again considered the allocation of removal power between Congress and the President.

BOWSHER v. SYNAR, 478 U.S. 714 (1986):   In response to growing federal deficits, Congress enacted the Balanced Budget and Emergency Deficit Control Act of 1985, Pub. L. No. 99-177, 99 Stat. 1038 (better known as the Gramm-Rudman Act). The Act created a rather elaborate procedure designed to achieve statutory deficit-reduction goals and placed central responsibility to achieve these goals in the hands of the Comptroller General. The Comptroller General headed the General Accounting Office (now, renamed the "Government Accountability Office"), an agency generally considered to be located within the legislative branch. Its primary responsibility is to report to Congress on the way in which recipients of federal appropriations are using the funds. The

Gramm-Rudman Act set annual targets for deficit reduction and directed the Comptroller General to report periodically to Congress on whether it appeared likely that those targets would be met. If not, he was directed to calculate amounts by which administrative agencies should reduce spending below those levels appropriated by Congress in the most recent appropriation act. Under certain statutory conditions, those reductions could then be binding on the agencies. Congressman Mike Synar, an opponent of the Act, later joined by 11 other members of Congress and a federal labor union, challenged the Act's constitutionality in court. At issue was whether the Act's deficit-reduction functions could constitutionally be delegated to an officer like the Comptroller General who was subject to the control of Congress. In an opinion by Chief Justice Burger, the Court ruled that it could not:

> The Constitution does not contemplate an active role for Congress in the supervision of officers charged with the execution of the laws it enacts. The President appoints "Officers of the United States" with the "Advice and Consent of the Senate. . . ." Article II, §2. Once the appointment has been made and confirmed, however, the Constitution explicitly provides for removal of Officers of the United States by Congress only upon impeachment by the House of Representatives and conviction by the Senate. An impeachment by the House and trial by the Senate can rest only on "Treason, Bribery or other high Crimes and Misdemeanors." Article II, §4. A direct congressional role in the removal of officers charged with the execution of the laws beyond this limited one is inconsistent with separation of powers. . . .
>
> To permit the execution of the laws to be vested in an officer answerable only to Congress would, in practical terms, reserve in Congress control over the execution of the laws. As the District Court observed, "Once an officer is appointed, it is only the authority that can remove him, and not the authority that appointed him, that he must fear and, in the performance of his functions, obey." 626 F. Supp. at 1401. The structure of the Constitution does not permit Congress to execute the laws; it follows that Congress cannot grant to an officer under its control what it does not possess.

The Court read the law governing removal of the Comptroller General to give Congress exactly the sort of control that it cannot have:

> Although the Comptroller General is nominated by the President from a list of three individuals recommended by the Speaker of the House of Representatives and the President pro tempore of the Senate, see 31 U.S.C. §703(a)(2),[6] and confirmed by the Senate, he is removable only at the initiative of Congress. He may be removed not only by impeachment but also by Joint Resolution of Congress "at any time" . . . for "inefficiency," "neglect of duty," or "malfeasance." These terms are very broad and, as interpreted by Congress, could sustain removal of a Comptroller General for any number of actual or perceived transgressions of the legislative will. The Constitutional Convention chose to permit impeachment of executive officers only for "Treason, Bribery, or other high Crimes and Misdemeanors." It rejected language that would have permitted impeachment for

---

6. Congress adopted this provision in 1980 because of "the special interest of both Houses in the choice of an individual whose primary function is to provide assistance to Congress." S. Rep. 96-570, 96th Cong., 2d Sess., 10 (1980).

"maladministration," with Madison arguing that "[s]o vague a term will be equivalent to a tenure during pleasure of the Senate." 2 Farrand 550. . . .

Justice Byron White, dissenting, urged that, as a practical matter, the Comptroller General was no more subservient to Congress than to the President:

> Congress' substantively limited removal power will undoubtedly be less of a spur to subservience than Congress' unquestionable and unqualified power to enact legislation reducing the Comptroller's salary, cutting the funds available to his department, reducing his personnel, limiting or expanding his duties, or even abolishing his position altogether.
>
> More importantly, the substantial role played by the President in the process of removal through joint resolution reduces to utter insignificance the possibility that the threat of removal will induce subservience to the Congress. . . .
>
> The practical result of the removal provision is not to render the Comptroller unduly dependent upon or subservient to Congress, but to render him one of the most independent officers in the entire federal establishment. . . .

NOTES AND QUESTIONS

1. *"Executive" functions.* Is the distinction between *Myers* and *Humphrey's Executor* that the postmaster was performing "executive" functions, while the FTC was performing "legislative" and "judicial" functions? In *Bowsher,* the Court says that the Comptroller General was engaged in "execution of the laws." Couldn't exactly the same thing be said of FTC Commissioner Humphrey? How would this analysis fit the framework offered by Justice Scalia's dissenting opinion in *Mistretta,* excerpted, *supra,* in part B.1. of this chapter?

It has always been assumed that there are some officers who must, as a constitutional matter, serve at the President's pleasure. A clear example would be the President's Chief of Staff. But what about, say, the Secretary of Labor or the Administrator of the EPA? In numerous enabling acts (such as the OSH Act and the Clean Air Act), Congress has bestowed on Executive Branch officers rulemaking and adjudicative powers, that is, the power to act "in part quasi-legislatively and in part quasi-judicially," to quote from *Humphrey's Executor.* Can Congress, by bestowing such powers, convert any department of the Executive Branch into an "independent agency"?

2. *How "independent"?* Are there *any* constitutional restrictions on the kinds of constraints Congress can impose on the removal of an officer? *Humphrey's Executor* upheld a statute permitting removal only for "inefficiency, neglect of duty, or malfeasance in office." Could Congress provide that an FTC commissioner may not be removed from office, period (except by impeachment and conviction)? *Bowsher* makes it clear that Congress may not directly participate in the removal of an Executive Branch officer, except through the constitutional process of impeachment and conviction. Is that, in retrospect, the correct rationale for the decision in *Myers*? If Congress can remove an officer by impeachment, why cannot it also participate in the decision to remove him by dismissal?

3. *The Consumer Financial Protection Bureau.* Prior to his appointment to the Supreme Court, then-Judge Brett Kavanaugh played a key role in a recent challenge to the structure of the Consumer Financial Protection Bureau (CFPB),

the independent agency created by Congress in the wake of the 2007-08 financial crisis, described in part C of this chapter, *supra*. The CFPB is headed by a single director with statutory protection from removal without cause and as noted earlier has broad authority over consumer protection in financial transactions including mortgages and other loans. In 2016, a panel of the D.C. Circuit, in an opinion by Judge Kavanaugh, held that this structure—a single director with for-cause removal protection—was unconstitutional:

> The CFPB's concentration of enormous executive power in a single, unaccountable, unchecked Director not only departs from settled historical practice, but also poses a far greater risk of arbitrary decisionmaking and abuse of power, and a far greater threat to individual liberty, than does a multi-member independent agency.

PHH Corp. v. Consumer Fin. Prot. Bureau, 839 F.3d 1, 8 (D.C. Cir. 2016). The panel's remedy for this defect was not to add members to the CFPB but to strike down the Director's removal protection, thus making the Director removable at will by the President.

The full D.C. Circuit, sitting *en banc*, disagreed with the panel and replaced its decision with an opinion upholding both the CFPB's structure and the Director's protection from removal without cause. PHH Corp. v. Consumer Fin. Prot. Bureau, 881 F.3d 75 (D.C. Cir. 2018) (*en banc*). The court's opinion noted that:

> The Supreme Court eighty years ago sustained the constitutionality of the independent Federal Trade Commission, a consumer-protection financial regulator with powers analogous to those of the CFPB. Humphrey's Executor v. United States, 295 U.S. 602 (1935). In doing so, the Court approved the very means of independence Congress used here: protection of agency leadership from at-will removal by the President.

881 F.3d at 77. The *en banc* court determined that the fact that the CFPB is headed by a single Director has no constitutional significance:

> [T]he constitutional distinction PHH proposes between the CFPB's leadership structure and that of multi-member independent agencies is untenable. That distinction finds no footing in precedent, historical practice, constitutional principle, or the logic of presidential removal power. The relevance of "internal checks" as a substitute for at-will removal by the President is no part of the removal-power doctrine, which focuses on executive control and accountability to the public, not the competing virtues of various internal agency design choices. Congress and the President have historically countenanced sole-headed financial regulatory bodies. And the Supreme Court has upheld Congress's assignment of even unmistakably executive responsibilities—criminal investigation and prosecution—to a sole officer protected from removal at the President's will. [*See* Morrison v. Olson, 487 U.S. 654, (686-696 1988).]

Judge Kavanaugh, among others, dissented from the *en banc* decision. In a lengthy and wide-ranging opinion reaching back to first principles of separation of powers, Judge Kavanaugh reiterated his contention that the CFPB's single member structure is unconstitutional because it lacks the check against arbitrary action provided by the deliberation and agreement inherent in the multimember structure of every other independent agency. As Judge Kavanaugh put it:

> Because the CFPB is an independent agency headed by a single Director and not by a multi-member commission, the Director of the CFPB possesses more unilateral authority—that is, authority to take action on one's own, subject to no check—than any single commissioner or board member in any other independent agency in the U.S. Government. Indeed, other than the President, the Director enjoys more unilateral authority than any other official in any of the three branches of the U.S. Government.

881 F.3d at 165-166 (Kavanaugh, J., dissenting). In a parallel case, the Ninth Circuit adopted the reasoning of the D.C. Circuit majority in *PHH*, upholding the Bureau's governing structure. CFPB v. Seila Law, LLC, 923 F.3d 680 (9th Cir. 2019). The Supreme Court granted certiorari in the *Seila Law* case. Its decision, pending at the time of publication, is widely anticipated.

c.   Appointment and Removal Reconsidered: The Independent Counsel and the Accounting Board

The Watergate scandal spawned a spate of "good government" legislation designed to combat perceived abuses of public power. One example that we have already encountered was the 1974 act amending the Federal Election Campaign Act, which was struck down in *Buckley*. Another was the Ethics in Government Act of 1978, Pub. L. No. 95-521, 92 Stat. 1873, *codified at* 28 U.S.C. §§49, 591 *et seq.* The Act addressed a dilemma that featured prominently in the Watergate scandal: How can one trust the Attorney General, an appointee of the President, to investigate and prosecute allegations of wrongdoing by officials in positions of authority in the Executive Branch, including perhaps the President himself? That problem was "solved" in the early stages of the Watergate episode when the Attorney General appointed Professor Archibald Cox as a "special prosecutor" to conduct the investigation, then focused primarily at high-level staffers in the White House. When Cox got too independent for President Nixon's taste, however, he was summarily fired. Bowing to public pressure, Nixon approved the appointment of another special prosecutor, whose investigation was instrumental in establishing the criminal misconduct of several high-level officials and eventually bringing down the President himself. Thus, the idea of an independent prosecutor was born and took flower in the Ethics in Government Act.

The Act created an elaborate mechanism for the appointment of an "independent counsel" (IC) to investigate and prosecute allegations of official wrongdoing. The process began with the receipt by the Attorney General of an allegation of official wrongdoing, a complaint, or a request for appointment of an IC from a member of Congress. If, in the Attorney General's opinion, the allegation was "sufficient to constitute grounds to investigate," he was required to conduct a preliminary investigation. If (and only if) the Attorney General found that there were "reasonable grounds to believe that further investigation or prosecution is warranted," he was required by the Act to apply to a special court, known as the "Special Division," for the appointment of an IC. The

Special Division was designated by the Act as a division of the D.C. Circuit, and consisted of three Circuit Court judges or Supreme Court Justices appointed by the Chief Justice of the United States for two-year terms.

The Special Division would thereupon appoint a suitably qualified individual to serve as IC to conduct the investigation. In making the appointment, the Special Division would also define the scope of her jurisdiction. In conducting the investigation, the IC would have all of the powers (for example, the power to compel testimony, subpoena records, offer immunity, and the like) possessed by the Attorney General or a U.S. Attorney. The Attorney General could, from time to time, refer to the IC additional matters related to the original allegations; and the IC could, from time to time, apply to the Special Division to expand the scope of her investigation to include additional, unrelated allegations.

An IC could be removed from office in one of two primary ways. First, upon "completion" of her work, the Special Division could terminate the position if the counsel did not voluntarily cease her work. Second, the Attorney General could remove an IC at any time under §596(a)(1) of the Act:

> An independent counsel appointed under this chapter may be removed from office, other than by impeachment and conviction, only by the personal action of the Attorney General and only for good cause, physical disability, mental incapacity, or any other condition that substantially impairs the performance of such independent counsel's duties.

The constitutionality of the Act was much debated at the time of its passage and for several years thereafter. But it was not until 1988 that the Supreme Court finally had occasion to address the issue. The case involved allegations that Theodore Olson, then Assistant Attorney General for the Office of Legal Counsel, had violated federal law by giving false testimony to Congress. The accusation grew out of a political standoff between the administration of President Ronald Reagan and the Democratic-controlled House over the manner in which the EPA and the Justice Department were enforcing the "superfund" law, which governs the cleanup of toxic waste—a dispute exacerbated by disagreements over the president's power to exert executive privilege to deny Congress access to "enforcement-sensitive" information from executive branch discussions. Responding to a complaint from the Chairman of the House Judiciary Committee, the Attorney General applied for appointment of an IC to investigate the matter. The Special Division appointed lawyer Alexia Morrison as the IC. When Morrison obtained subpoenas compelling the production of evidence by Olson, he refused to comply on the ground that the Act was unconstitutional. The District Court found him in contempt, but the Court of Appeals reversed on the grounds that the Act violated the Appointments Clause and the principle of separation of powers.

MORRISON v. OLSON
487 U.S. 654 (1988)

CHIEF JUSTICE REHNQUIST delivered the opinion of the Court.

This case presents us with a challenge to the independent counsel provisions of the Ethics in Government Act of 1978, 28 U.S.C.A. §§49, 591 *et seq.*

(Supp. 1988). We hold today that these provisions of the Act do not violate the Appointments Clause of the Constitution, Art. II, §2, cl. 2, or the limitations of Article III, nor do they impermissibly interfere with the President's authority under Article II in violation of the constitutional principle of separation of powers. . . .

III

. . . The initial question [under the Appointments Clause] is . . . whether appellant is an "inferior" or a "principal" officer. If she is the latter, as the Court of Appeals concluded, then the Act is in violation of the Appointments Clause.

The line between "inferior" and "principal" officers is one that is far from clear, and the Framers provided little guidance into where it should be drawn. . . . We need not attempt here to decide exactly where the line falls between the two types of officers, because in our view appellant clearly falls on the "inferior officer" side of that line. Several factors lead to this conclusion.

First, appellant is subject to removal by a higher Executive Branch official. Although appellant may not be "subordinate" to the Attorney General (and the President) insofar as she possesses a degree of independent discretion to exercise the powers delegated to her under the Act, the fact that she can be removed by the Attorney General indicates that she is to some degree "inferior" in rank and authority. Second, appellant is empowered by the Act to perform only certain, limited duties. An independent counsel's role is restricted primarily to investigation and, if appropriate, prosecution for certain federal crimes. Admittedly, the Act delegates to appellant "full power and independent authority to exercise all investigative and prosecutorial functions and powers of the Department of Justice." §594(a). But this grant of authority does not include any authority to formulate policy for the Government or the Executive Branch, nor does it give appellant any administrative duties outside of those necessary to operate her office. The Act specifically provides that in policy matters appellant is to comply to the extent possible with the policies of the Department. §594(f).

Third, appellant's office is limited in jurisdiction. Not only is the Act itself restricted in applicability to certain federal officials suspected of certain serious federal crimes, but an independent counsel can only act within the scope of the jurisdiction that has been granted by the Special Division pursuant to a request by the Attorney General. Finally, appellant's office is limited in tenure. There is concededly no time limit on the appointment of a particular counsel. Nonetheless, the office of independent counsel is "temporary" in the sense that an independent counsel is appointed essentially to accomplish a single task, and when that task is over the office is terminated, either by the counsel herself or by action of the Special Division. . . .

Appellees argue that even if appellant is an "inferior" officer, the Clause does not empower Congress to place the power to appoint such an officer outside the Executive Branch. They contend that the Clause does not contemplate congressional authorization of "interbranch appointments," in which an officer of one branch is appointed by officers of another branch. The relevant language of the Appointments Clause is worth repeating. It reads: ". . . but the

Congress may by Law vest the Appointment of such inferior Officers, as they think proper, in the President alone, in the Courts of Law, or in the Heads of Departments." On its face, the language of this "excepting clause" admits of no limitation on interbranch appointments. Indeed, the inclusion of "as they think proper" seems clearly to give Congress significant discretion to determine whether it is "proper" to vest the appointment of, for example, executive officials in the "Courts of Law." . . .

We do not mean to say that Congress' power to provide for interbranch appointments of "inferior officers" is unlimited. In addition to separation of powers concerns, Congress' decision to vest the appointment power in the courts would be improper if there was some "incongruity" between the functions normally performed by the courts and the performance of their duty to appoint. . . . In this case, however, we do not think it impermissible for Congress to vest the power to appoint independent counsels in a specially created federal court. . . . Congress of course was concerned when it created the office of independent counsel with the conflicts of interest that could arise in situations when the Executive Branch is called upon to investigate its own high-ranking officers. If it were to remove the appointing authority from the Executive Branch, the most logical place to put it was in the Judicial Branch. In the light of the Act's provision making the judges of the Special Division ineligible to participate in any matters relating to an independent counsel they have appointed, 28 U.S.C. §49(f), we do not think that appointment of the independent counsels by the court runs afoul of the constitutional limitation on "incongruous" interbranch appointments. . . .

<h1 style="text-align:center">V</h1>

We now turn to consider whether the Act is invalid under the constitutional principle of separation of powers. . . .

Unlike both [Bowsher v. Synar, 478 U.S. 714 (1986), and Myers v. United States, 272 U.S. 52 (1926),] this case does not involve an attempt by Congress itself to gain a role in the removal of executive officials other than its established powers of impeachment and conviction. The Act instead puts the removal power squarely in the hands of the Executive Branch. . . . In our view, the removal provisions of the Act make this case more analogous to Humphrey's Executor v. United States, 295 U.S. 602 (1935), and Wiener v. United States, 357 U.S. 349 (1958), than to Myers or Bowsher. . . .

Appellees contend that Humphrey's Executor and Wiener are distinguishable from this case because they did not involve officials who performed a "core executive function." They argue that our decision in Humphrey's Executor rests on a distinction between "purely executive" officials and officials who exercise "quasi-legislative" and "quasi-judicial" powers. In their view, when a "purely executive" official is involved, the governing precedent is Myers, not Humphrey's Executor. . . .

We undoubtedly did rely on the terms "quasi-legislative" and "quasi-judicial" to distinguish the officials involved in Humphrey's Executor and Wiener from those in Myers, but our present considered view is that the determination of whether the Constitution allows Congress to impose a "good cause"-type restriction on the President's power to remove an official cannot be made to turn on whether or not that official is classified as "purely executive." The analysis contained in our removal cases is designed not to define rigid categories of those officials who may or may not be removed at will by the President,[28] but to ensure that Congress does not interfere with the President's exercise of the "executive power" and his constitutionally appointed duty to "take care that the laws be faithfully executed" under Article II. *Myers* was undoubtedly correct in its holding, and in its broader suggestion that there are some "purely executive" officials who must be removable by the President at will if he is to be able to accomplish his constitutional role.[29] *See* 272 U.S. at 132-134. . . .

At the other end of the spectrum from *Myers,* the characterization of the agencies in *Humphrey's Executor* and *Wiener* as "quasi-legislative" or "quasi-judicial" in large part reflected our judgment that it was not essential to the President's proper execution of his Article II powers that these agencies be headed up by individuals who were removable at will. We do not mean to suggest that an analysis of the functions served by the officials at issue is irrelevant. But the real question is whether the removal restrictions are of such a nature that they impede the President's ability to perform his constitutional duty, and the functions of the officials in question must be analyzed in that light.

Considering for the moment the "good cause" removal provision in isolation from the other parts of the Act at issue in this case, we cannot say that the imposition of a "good cause" standard for removal by itself unduly trammels on executive authority. There is no real dispute that the functions performed by the independent counsel are "executive" in the sense that they are law enforcement functions that typically have been undertaken by officials within the Executive Branch. . . . [W]e simply do not see how the President's need to control the exercise of that discretion is so central to the functioning of the Executive

---

28. The difficulty of defining such categories of "executive" or "quasi-legislative" officials is illustrated by a comparison of our decisions in cases such as *Humphrey's Executor,* Buckley v. Valeo, 424 U.S. 1, 140-141 (1976), and *Bowsher, supra.* In *Buckley,* we indicated that the functions of the Federal Election Commission are "administrative," and "more legislative and judicial in nature," and are "of kinds usually performed by independent regulatory agencies or by some department in the Executive Branch under the direction of an Act of Congress." 424 U.S. at 140-141.

In *Bowsher,* we found that the functions of the Comptroller General were "executive" in nature, in that he was required to "exercise judgment concerning facts that affect the application of the Act," and he must "interpret the provisions of the Act to determine precisely what budgetary calculations are required." 478 U.S. at 733. Compare this with the description of the FTC's powers in *Humphrey's Executor,* which we stated "occupie[d] no place in the executive department": "The [FTC] is an administrative body created by Congress to carry into effect legislative policies embodied in the statute in accordance with the legislative standard therein prescribed, and to perform other specified duties as a legislative or as a judicial aid." 295 U.S. at 628. As Justice White noted in his dissent in *Bowsher,* it is hard to dispute that the powers of the FTC at the time of *Humphrey's Executor* would at the present time be considered "executive," at least to some degree. *See* 478 U.S. at 761 n.3.

29. The dissent says that the language of Article II vesting the executive power of the United States in the President requires that every officer of the United States exercising any part of that power must serve at the pleasure of the President and be removable by him at will. This rigid demarcation—a demarcation incapable of being altered by law in the slightest degree, and applicable to tens of thousands of holders of offices neither known nor foreseen by the framers—depends upon an extrapolation from general constitutional language which we think is more than the text will bear. It is also contrary to our holding in United States v. Perkins, 116 U.S. 483 (1886), decided more than a century ago.

Branch as to require as a matter of constitutional law that the counsel be terminable at will by the President.[31]

Nor do we think that the "good cause" removal provision at issue here impermissibly burdens the President's power to control or supervise the independent counsel, as an executive official, in the execution of her duties under the Act. This is not a case in which the power to remove an executive official has been completely stripped from the President, thus providing no means for the President to ensure the "faithful execution" of the laws. Rather, because the independent counsel may be terminated for "good cause," the Executive, through the Attorney General, retains ample authority to assure that the counsel is competently performing her statutory responsibilities in a manner that comports with the provisions of the Act. . . .

B

The final question to be addressed is whether the Act, taken as a whole, violates the principle of separation of powers by unduly interfering with the role of the Executive Branch.

. . . Unlike some of our previous cases, most recently Bowsher v. Synar, this case simply does not pose a "dange[r] of congressional usurpation of Executive Branch functions." 478 U.S. at 727; *see also* INS v. Chadha, 462 U.S. 919, 958 (1983). Indeed, with the exception of the power of impeachment—which applies to all officers of the United States—Congress retained for itself no powers of control or supervision over an independent counsel. . . .

Similarly, we do not think that the Act works any *judicial* usurpation of properly executive functions. As should be apparent from our discussion of the Appointments Clause above, the power to appoint inferior officers such as independent counsels is not in itself an "executive" function in the constitutional sense, at least when Congress has exercised its power to vest the appointment of an inferior office[r] in the "Courts of Law." . . .

Finally, we do not think that the Act "impermissibly undermine[s]" the powers of the Executive Branch[, Commodity Futures Trading Commn. v. Schor, 478 U.S. 833, 856 (1983)], or "disrupts the proper balance between the coordinate branches [by] prevent[ing] the Executive Branch from accomplishing its constitutionally assigned functions," Nixon v. Administrator of General Services, [433 U.S. 425, 443 (1977)]. It is undeniable that the Act reduces the amount of control or supervision that the Attorney General and, through him, the President exercises over the investigation and prosecution of a certain class of alleged criminal activity. The Attorney General is not allowed to appoint the individual of his choice; he does not determine the counsel's jurisdiction; and his power to remove a counsel is limited. Nonetheless, the Act does give the Attorney General several means of supervising or controlling the prosecutorial

---

31. We note by way of comparison that various federal agencies whose officers are covered by "good cause" removal restrictions exercise civil enforcement powers that are analogous to the prosecutorial powers wielded by an independent counsel. *See, e.g.,* 15 U.S.C. §45(m) (giving the FTC the authority to bring civil actions to recover civil penalties for the violations of rules respecting unfair competition); 15 U.S.C. §§2061, 2071, 2076(b)(7)(A) (giving the Consumer Product Safety Commission the authority to obtain injunctions and apply for seizure of hazardous products).

powers that may be wielded by an independent counsel. Most importantly, the Attorney General retains the power to remove the counsel for "good cause," a power that we have already concluded provides the Executive with substantial ability to ensure that the laws are "faithfully executed" by an independent counsel. . . .

The decision of the Court of Appeals is therefore reversed.

JUSTICE KENNEDY took no part in the consideration or decision of this case.

JUSTICE SCALIA, dissenting.

It is the proud boast of our democracy that we have "a government of laws and not of men." Many Americans are familiar with that phrase; not many know its derivation. It comes from Part the First, Article XXX of the Massachusetts Constitution of 1780, which reads in full as follows:

> In the government of this commonwealth, the legislative department shall never exercise the executive and judicial powers, or either of them; the executive shall never exercise the legislative and judicial powers, or either of them; the judicial shall never exercise the legislative and executive powers, or either of them; to the end it may be a government of laws, and not of men.

The framers of the Federal Constitution similarly viewed the principle of separation of powers as the absolutely central guarantee of a just government. In No. 47 of The Federalist, Madison wrote that "[n]o political truth is certainly of greater intrinsic value, or is stamped with the authority of more enlightened patrons of liberty." The Federalist No. 47, p. 301 (C. Rossiter ed. 1961) (hereinafter Federalist). Without a secure structure of separated powers, our Bill of Rights would be worthless, as are the bills of rights of many nations of the world that have adopted, or even improved upon, the mere words of ours. . . .

But just as the mere words of a Bill of Rights are not self-effectuating, the framers recognized "[t]he insufficiency of a mere parchment delineation of the boundaries" to achieve the separation of powers. Federalist No. 73, p. 442 (Hamilton). "[T]he great security," wrote Madison, "against a gradual concentration of the several powers in the same department consists in giving to those who administer each department the necessary constitutional means and personal motives to resist encroachments of the others. The provision for defense must in this, as in all other cases, be made commensurate to the danger of attack." Federalist No. 51, pp. 321-322. Madison continued:

> But it is not possible to give to each department an equal power of self-defense. In republican government, the legislative authority necessarily predominates. The remedy for this inconveniency is to divide the legislature into different branches; and to render them, by different modes of election and different principles of action, as little connected with each other as the nature of their common functions and their common dependence on the society will admit. . . . As the weight of the legislative authority requires that it should be thus divided, the weakness of the executive may require, on the other hand, that it should be fortified. (*Id.* at 322-323.)

The major "fortification" provided, of course, was the veto power. But in addition to providing fortification, the founders conspicuously and very consciously declined to sap the executive's strength in the same way they had weakened the legislature: by dividing the executive power. Proposals to have multiple executives, or a council of advisors with separate authority were rejected. . . .

That is what this suit is about. Power. The allocation of power among Congress, the President and the courts in such fashion as to preserve the equilibrium the Constitution sought to establish—so that "a gradual concentration of the several powers in the same department," Federalist No. 51, p. 321 (J. Madison), can effectively be resisted. Frequently an issue of this sort will come before the Court clad, so to speak, in sheep's clothing: the potential of the asserted principle to effect important change in the equilibrium of power is not immediately evident, and must be discerned by a careful and perceptive analysis. But this wolf comes as a wolf. . . .

II

. . . To repeat, Art. II, §1, cl. 1 of the Constitution provides:

The executive Power shall be vested in a President of the United States.

As I described at the outset of this opinion, this does not mean *some of* the executive power, but *all of* the executive power. It seems to me, therefore, that the decision of the Court of Appeals invalidating the present statute must be upheld on fundamental separation-of-powers principles if the following two questions are answered affirmatively: (1) Is the conduct of a criminal prosecution (and of an investigation to decide whether to prosecute) the exercise of purely executive power? (2) Does the statute deprive the President of the United States of exclusive control over the exercise of that power? Surprising to say, the Court appears to concede an affirmative answer to both questions, but seeks to avoid the inevitable conclusion that since the statute vests some purely executive power in a person who is not the President of the United States it is void.

The Court concedes that "[t]here is no real dispute that the functions performed by the independent counsel are 'executive.'" . . .

As for the second question, whether the statute before us deprives the President of exclusive control over that quintessentially executive activity: The Court does not, and could not possibly, assert that it does not. That is indeed the whole object of the statute. Instead, the Court points out that the President, through his Attorney General, has at least *some* control. That concession is alone enough to invalidate the statute, but I cannot refrain from pointing out that the Court greatly exaggerates the extent of that "some" presidential control. "Most importan[t]" among these controls, the Court asserts, is the Attorney General's "power to remove the counsel for 'good cause.'" . . . This is somewhat like referring to shackles as an effective means of locomotion. . . .

Moving on to the presumably "less important" controls that the President retains, the Court notes that no independent counsel may be appointed without a specific request from the Attorney General. . . . [T]he limited power over referral is irrelevant to the question whether, *once appointed*, the independent counsel exercises executive power free from the President's control. Finally, the Court points out that the Act directs the independent counsel to abide by general Justice Department policy, except when not "possible." *See* 28 U.S.C. §594(f). The exception alone shows this to be an empty promise.

[H]owever, it is ultimately irrelevant *how much* the statute reduces presidential control. . . . It is not for us to determine, and we have never presumed to determine, how much of the purely executive powers of government must be within the full control of the President. The Constitution prescribes that they *all* are. . . .

Is it unthinkable that the President should have . . . exclusive power, even when alleged crimes by him or his close associate are at issue? No more so than that Congress should have the exclusive power of legislation, even when what is at issue is its own exemption from the burdens of certain laws. *See* Civil Rights Act of 1964, Title VII, 42 U.S.C. §2000e *et seq.* (prohibiting "employers," not defined to include the United States, from discriminating on the basis of race, color, religion, sex or national origin). No more so than that this Court should have the exclusive power to pronounce the final decision on justiciable cases and controversies, even those pertaining to the constitutionality of a statute reducing the salaries of the Justices. *See* United States v. Will, 449 U.S. 200, 211-217 (1980). A system of separate and coordinate powers necessarily involves an acceptance of exclusive power that can theoretically be abused. As we reiterate this very day, "[i]t is a truism that constitutional protections have costs." Coy v. Iowa, [487 U.S. 1012, 1020 (1988)]. While the separation of powers may prevent us from righting every wrong, it does so in order to ensure that we do not lose liberty. . . .

The Court has, nonetheless, replaced the clear constitutional prescription that the executive power belongs to the President with a "balancing test." What are the standards to determine how the balance is to be struck, that is, how much removal of presidential power is too much? . . . Once we depart from the text of the Constitution, just where short of that do we stop? The most amazing feature of the Court's opinion is that it does not even purport to give an answer. It simply *announces*, with no analysis, that the ability to control the decision whether to investigate and prosecute the President's closest advisors, and indeed the President himself, is not "so central to the functioning of the Executive Branch" as to be constitutionally required to be within the President's control. Apparently that is so because we say it is so. . . .

In my view, moreover, even as an ad hoc, standardless judgment the Court's conclusion must be wrong. Before this statute was passed, the President, in taking action disagreeable to the Congress, or an executive officer giving advice to the President or testifying before Congress concerning one of those many matters on which the two branches are from time to time at odds, could be assured that his acts and motives would be adjudged—insofar as the decision whether to conduct a criminal investigation and to prosecute is concerned—in the Executive Branch, that is, in a forum attuned to the interests and the policies of the Presidency. That was one of the natural advantages the Constitution gave to the Presidency, just as it gave Members of Congress (and their staffs) the advantage of not being prosecutable for anything said or done in their legislative capacities. *See* U.S. Const., Art. I, §6, cl. 1; Gravel v. United States, 408 U.S. 606 (1972). It is the very object of this legislation to eliminate that assurance of a sympathetic forum. . . .

III

. . . Because appellant (who all parties and the Court agree is an officer of the United States . . .) was not appointed by the President with the advice and consent of the Senate, but rather by the Special Division of the United States Court of Appeals, her appointment is constitutional only if . . . she is an "inferior" officer within the meaning of the above clause.

[T]he Court . . . gives three reasons [why the appellant is an "inferior" officer]: *First*, she "is subject to removal by a higher Executive branch official," namely the Attorney General. . . . *Second*, she is "empowered by the Act to perform only certain, limited duties." . . . *Third*, her office is "limited in jurisdiction" and "limited in tenure."

[I]t is not clear from the Court's opinion why the factors it discusses—even if applied correctly to the facts of this case—are determinative of the question of inferior officer status. . . . I think it preferable to look to the text of the Constitution and the division of power that it establishes. These demonstrate, I think, that the independent counsel is not an inferior officer because she is not *subordinate* to any officer in the Executive Branch (indeed, not even to the President). . . .

That "inferior" means "subordinate" is also consistent with what little we know about the evolution of the Appointments Clause. . . . [I]t was intended merely to make clear (what Madison thought already was clear), that those officers appointed by the President with Senate approval could on their own appoint their subordinates, who would, of course, by chain of command still be under the direct control of the President. . . .

To be sure, it is not a *sufficient* condition for "inferior" officer status that one be subordinate to a principal officer. Even an officer who is subordinate to a department head can be a principal officer. . . . But it is surely a *necessary* condition for inferior officer status that the officer be subordinate to another officer. . . .

Because appellant is not subordinate to another officer, she is not an "inferior" officer and her appointment other than by the President with the advice and consent of the Senate is unconstitutional. . . .

IV . . .

Since our 1935 decision in Humphrey's Executor v. United States, 295 U.S. 602—which was considered by many at the time the product of an activist, anti-New Deal court bent on reducing the power of President Franklin Roosevelt—it has been established that the line of permissible restriction upon removal of principal officers lies at the point at which the powers exercised by those officers are no longer purely executive. . . . Today, however, *Humphrey's Executor* is swept into the dustbin of repudiated constitutional principles. . . .

One can hardly grieve for the shoddy treatment given today to *Humphrey's Executor,* which, after all, accorded the same indignity (with much less justification) to Chief Justice Taft's opinion 10 years earlier in Myers v. United States. . . . It is in fact comforting to witness the reality that he who lives by the ipse dixit dies by the ipse dixit. But one must grieve for the Constitution. *Humphrey's Executor* at least had the decency formally to observe the constitutional principle that the President had to be the repository of *all* executive power, *see* 295 U.S. at

627-628, which, as *Myers* carefully explained, necessarily means that he must be able to discharge those who do not perform executive functions according to his liking. . . . There are now no lines. If the removal of a prosecutor, the virtual embodiment of the power to "take care that the laws be faithfully executed," can be restricted, what officer's removal cannot? This is an open invitation for Congress to experiment. . . . As far as I can discern from the Court's opinion, it is now open season upon the President's removal power for all executive officers, with not even the superficially principled restriction of *Humphrey's Executor* as cover. The Court essentially says to the President: "Trust us. We will make sure that you are able to accomplish your constitutional role." I think the Constitution gives the President—and the people—more protection than that.

V

The purpose of the separation and equilibration of powers in general, and of the unitary Executive in particular, was not merely to assure effective government but to preserve individual freedom. Those who hold or have held offices covered by the Ethics in Government Act are entitled to that protection as much as the rest of us. . . . The mini-Executive that is the independent counsel, . . . operating in an area where so little is law and so much is discretion, is intentionally cut off from the unifying influence of the Justice Department, and from the perspective that multiple responsibilities provide. . . . How frightening it must be to have your own independent counsel and staff appointed, with nothing else to do but to investigate you until investigation is no longer worthwhile—with whether it is worthwhile or not depending upon what such judgments usually hinge on, competing responsibilities. And to have that counsel and staff decide, with no basis for comparison, whether what you have done is bad enough, willful enough, and provable enough, to warrant an indictment. . . .

Worse than what it has done, however, is the manner in which it has done it. A government of laws means a government of rules. Today's decision on the basic issue of fragmentation of executive power is ungoverned by rule, and hence ungoverned by law. It extends into the very heart of our most significant constitutional function the "totality of the circumstances" mode of analysis that this Court has in recent years become fond of. . . .

The ad hoc approach to constitutional adjudication has real attraction, even apart from its work-saving potential. It is guaranteed to produce a result, in every case, that will make a majority of the Court happy with the law. The law is, by definition, precisely what the majority thinks, taking all things into account, it *ought* to be. I prefer to rely upon the judgment of the wise men who constructed our system, and of the people who approved it, and of two centuries of history that have shown it to be sound. Like it or not, that judgment says, quite plainly, that "[t]he executive Power shall be vested in a President of the United States."

NOTES AND QUESTIONS

1. *The unitary executive.* Justice Scalia's dissent makes a powerful argument for the "unitary executive" theory of the Constitution. As textual support, he cites the vesting clause of Article II, §1, of the Constitution. How must Scalia be interpreting

the phrase "executive Power"? Is there an equally plausible alternative definition that argues in favor of the majority position in *Morrison*? Does the enumeration of powers in the rest of Article II support or weaken Scalia's argument? Scalia also cites Article XXX of the Massachusetts Constitution. This language was well known to the Framers of the U.S. Constitution. Does the fact that the Framers used different language to describe the relationship among the three branches undercut Scalia's textual argument? Or do the three vesting clauses in Articles I, II, and III of the Constitution essentially convey the same message?

For functional (and historical) support, Scalia cites a passage from Federalist No. 51 in which Madison talks about the need to fortify the Executive against a potentially overbearing Legislature. In what sense was that true in 1787? Is it still true today? Is Scalia correct that concentrating executive power in the President is necessary to protect liberty? Even if Scalia is right as a general matter that the President should have complete supervisory control over "executive" officers, should there be an exception in cases like this, where the potential for conflict of interest is so apparent? The debate over presidential power in this context focuses mostly on the potential conflict that arises when the same officers accused of wrongdoing, or those associated with them, are empowered to investigate the alleged wrongdoing and enforce the law. Is there an equally strong potential conflict in allowing an administration's political opponents to trigger such investigations and prosecutions? Is this the crux of Scalia's argument that *Morrison* is about power, and that the threat to executive independence in this instance isn't a wolf in sheep's clothing but a bold assault on separation of powers ("this wolf comes as a wolf")?

2. *Inferior versus principal officers.* Is the independent counsel a principal officer or an inferior officer? Who makes the more persuasive argument, Justice Rehnquist or Justice Scalia? In Edmond v. United States, 520 U.S. 651 (1997), the Court ruled that members of the Coast Guard Court of Criminal Appeals (CCA), an intermediate court within the system of military justice, were "inferior" officers who could be appointed by the head of a department. Arguing that *Morrison* "did not purport to set forth a definitive test for whether an office is 'inferior' under the Appointments Clause," Justice Scalia said:

> Generally speaking, the term "inferior officer" connotes a relationship with some higher ranking officer or officers below the President: whether one is an "inferior" officer depends on whether he has a superior. . . . [W]e think it evident that "inferior officers" are officers whose work is directed and supervised at some level by others who were appointed by presidential nomination with the advice and consent of the Senate.

520 U.S. at 662-663. Does this ruling signal the triumph of Justice Scalia's position in *Morrison*?

3. *The history and fate of the independent counsel statute.* Between 1978 and 2001, ICs were appointed to conduct 20 different investigations. By far the most celebrated IC was Kenneth Starr, a former D.C. Circuit Judge and Solicitor General of the United States whose investigation of various allegations against President Bill Clinton culminated in a report to the House of Representatives that there was sufficiently credible evidence of wrongdoing to support a charge of impeachment. The House did in fact impeach Clinton, but the Senate failed to convict. The upshot of the Starr-Clinton episode was that, while Clinton's presidency

survived, the Office of Independent Counsel took a mortal blow. Throughout its lifetime, the independent counsel legislation had contained a sunset provision. When the Act came up for reauthorization in 1999, many observers and participants in the Clinton episode, including Starr himself, argued that the Act should not be reauthorized. Its supporters in Congress could muster so few votes that the Act was allowed to die a quiet death.

Following the demise of the independent counsel statute, Attorney General Janet Reno promulgated regulations providing for the appointment of a "Special Counsel" in cases in which investigation or prosecution by regular Justice Department personnel "would present a conflict of interest for the Department." 28 C.F.R. §600.1(a)(1999). But the Attorney General retained authority to define the scope of a Special Counsel's jurisdiction, to order a Special Counsel not to take a particular "investigative or prosecutorial step" that is "so inappropriate or unwarranted under established Departmental practices that it should not be pursued," and to remove a Special Counsel from office for "misconduct, dereliction of duty, incapacity, conflict of interest, or for other good cause." *Id.* §600.7.

FREE ENTERPRISE FUND v. PUBLIC COMPANY ACCOUNTING OVERSIGHT BOARD
561 U.S. 477 (2010)

CHIEF JUSTICE ROBERTS delivered the opinion of the Court. . . .

Our Constitution divided the "powers of the new Federal Government into three defined categories, Legislative, Executive, and Judicial." INS v. Chadha, 462 U.S. 919, 951 (1983). Article II vests "[t]he executive Power . . . in a President of the United States of America," who must "take Care that the Laws be faithfully executed." Art. II, §1, cl. 1; *id.*, §3. In light of "[t]he impossibility that one man should be able to perform all the great business of the State," the Constitution provides for executive officers to "assist the supreme Magistrate in discharging the duties of his trust." 30 Writings of George Washington 334 (J. Fitzpatrick ed. 1939). . . .

We are asked [in this case] to consider a new situation not yet encountered by the Court. . . . May the President be restricted in his ability to remove a principal officer, who is in turn restricted in his ability to remove an inferior officer, even though that inferior officer determines the policy and enforces the laws of the United States?

We hold that such multilevel protection from removal is contrary to Article II's vesting of the executive power in the President. The President cannot "take Care that the Laws be faithfully executed" if he cannot oversee the faithfulness of the officers who execute them. . . .

I

A

After a series of celebrated accounting debacles, Congress enacted the Sarbanes-Oxley Act of 2002 (or Act), 116 Stat. 745. Among other measures, the Act introduced tighter regulation of the accounting industry under a new Public

Company Accounting Oversight Board. The Board is composed of five members, appointed to staggered 5-year terms by the Securities and Exchange Commission. It was modeled on private self-regulatory organizations in the securities industry—such as the New York Stock Exchange—that investigate and discipline their own members subject to Commission oversight. . . .

Unlike the self-regulatory organizations, however, the Board is a Government-created, Government-appointed entity, with expansive powers to govern an entire industry. Every accounting firm—both foreign and domestic—that participates in auditing public companies under the securities laws must register with the Board, pay it an annual fee, and comply with its rules and oversight. The Board is charged with enforcing the Sarbanes-Oxley Act, the securities laws, the Commission's rules, its own rules, and professional accounting standards. To this end, the Board may regulate every detail of an accounting firm's practice, including hiring and professional development, promotion, supervision of audit work, the acceptance of new business and the continuation of old, internal inspection procedures, professional ethics rules, and "such other requirements as the Board may prescribe."

The Board promulgates auditing and ethics standards, performs routine inspections of all accounting firms, demands documents and testimony, and initiates formal investigations and disciplinary proceedings. The willful violation of any Board rule is [a crime and] the Board itself can issue severe sanctions in its disciplinary proceedings. . . . Despite the . . . provisions specifying that Board members are not Government officials for statutory purposes, the parties agree that the Board is "part of the Government" for constitutional purposes, Lebron v. National Railroad Passenger Corporation, 513 U.S. 374, 397 (1995), and that its members are "'Officers of the United States'" who "exercis[e] significant authority pursuant to the laws of the United States," Buckley v. Valeo, 424 U.S. 1, 125-126 (1976) (per curiam) (quoting Art. II, §2, cl. 2). . . .

The Act places the Board under the SEC's oversight, particularly with respect to the issuance of rules or the imposition of sanctions (both of which are subject to Commission approval and alteration). But the individual members of the Board—like the officers and directors of the self-regulatory organizations—are substantially insulated from the Commission's control. The Commission cannot remove Board members at will, but only "for good cause shown," "in accordance with" certain procedures.

Those procedures require a Commission finding, "on the record" and "after notice and opportunity for a hearing," that the Board member

(A) has willfully violated any provision of th[e] Act, the rules of the Board, or the securities laws;
(B) has willfully abused the authority of that member; or
(C) without reasonable justification or excuse, has failed to enforce compliance with any such provision or rule, or any professional standard by any registered public accounting firm or any associated person thereof.

Removal of a Board member requires a formal Commission order and is subject to judicial review. Similar procedures govern the Commission's removal of officers and directors of the private self-regulatory organizations. The parties agree that the Commissioners cannot themselves be removed by the President except under the *Humphrey's Executor* standard of "inefficiency, neglect of duty, or mal-feasance in office," and we decide the case with that understanding.

B

Beckstead and Watts, LLP, is a Nevada accounting firm registered with the Board. The Board inspected the firm, released a report critical of its auditing procedures, and began a formal investigation. Beckstead and Watts and the Free Enterprise Fund, a nonprofit organization of which the firm is a member, then sued the Board and its members, seeking (among other things) a declaratory judgment that the Board is unconstitutional and an injunction preventing the Board from exercising its powers. [The lower courts rejected the petitioners' claims.]

III

We hold that the dual for-cause limitations on the removal of Board members contravene the Constitution's separation of powers. . . .

B

[In *Humphrey's Executor* and *Morrison*], we have previously upheld limited restrictions on the President's removal power. In those cases, however, only one level of protected tenure separated the President from an officer exercising executive power. It was the President—or a subordinate he could remove at will—who decided whether the officer's conduct merited removal under the good-cause standard.

The Act before us does something quite different. It not only protects Board members from removal except for good cause, but withdraws from the President any decision on whether that good cause exists. That decision is vested instead in other tenured officers—the Commissioners—none of whom is subject to the President's direct control. The result is a Board that is not accountable to the President, and a President who is not responsible for the Board.

The added layer of tenure protection makes a difference. Without a layer of insulation between the Commission and the Board, the Commission could remove a Board member at any time, and therefore would be fully responsible for what the Board does. The President could then hold the Commission to account for its supervision of the Board, to the same extent that he may hold the Commission to account for everything else it does.

A second level of tenure protection changes the nature of the President's review. Now the Commission cannot remove a Board member at will. The President therefore cannot hold the Commission fully accountable for the Board's conduct, to the same extent that he may hold the Commission accountable for everything else that it does. The Commissioners are not responsible for the Board's actions. They are only responsible for their own determination of whether the Act's rigorous good-cause standard is met. And even if the President disagrees with their determination, he is powerless to intervene—unless that determination is so unreasonable as to constitute "inefficiency, neglect of duty, or malfeasance in office." . . .

The diffusion of power carries with it a diffusion of accountability. The people do not vote for the "Officers of the United States." Art. II, §2, cl. 2. They instead look to the President to guide the "assistants or deputies . . . subject to his superintendence." The Federalist No. 72, p. 487 (J. Cooke ed. 1961) (A. Hamilton). Without a clear and effective chain of command, the public cannot "determine on whom the blame or the punishment of a pernicious measure, or series of pernicious measures ought really to fall." *Id.*, No. 70, at 476 (same). . . .

C

Respondents and the dissent resist this conclusion, portraying the Board as [a] practical accommodation between the Legislature and the Executive. . . . According to the dissent, Congress may impose multiple levels of for-cause tenure between the President and his subordinates when it "rests agency independence upon the need for technical expertise." . . . No one doubts Congress's power to create a vast and varied federal bureaucracy. But where, in all this, is the role for oversight by an elected President? The Constitution requires that a President chosen by the entire Nation oversee the execution of the laws. . . .

One can have a government that functions without being ruled by functionaries, and a government that benefits from expertise without being ruled by experts. Our Constitution was adopted to enable the people to govern themselves, through their elected leaders. The growth of the Executive Branch, which now wields vast power and touches almost every aspect of daily life, heightens the concern that it may slip from the Executive's control, and thus from that of the people. This concern is largely absent from the dissent's paean to the administrative state. . . .

D

The United States . . . argues that the Commission's removal power over the Board is "broad," and could be construed as broader still, if necessary to avoid invalidation. But the Government does not contend that simple disagreement with the Board's policies or priorities could constitute "good cause" for its removal. Nor do our precedents suggest as much. . . . Indeed, this case presents an even more serious threat to executive control than an "ordinary" dual for-cause standard. Congress enacted an unusually high standard that must be met before Board members may be removed. A Board member cannot be removed except for willful violations of the Act, Board rules, or the securities laws; willful abuse of authority; or unreasonable failure to enforce compliance—as determined in a formal Commission order, rendered on the record and after notice and an opportunity for a hearing. The Act does not even give the Commission power to fire Board members for violations of other laws that do not relate to the Act, the securities laws, or the Board's authority. The President might have less than full confidence in, say, a Board member who cheats on his taxes; but that discovery is not listed among the grounds for removal under [the Act].

The rigorous standard that must be met before a Board member may be removed was drawn from statutes concerning private organizations like the New York Stock Exchange. While we need not decide the question here, a removal standard appropriate for limiting Government control over private bodies may be inappropriate for officers wielding the executive power of the United States.

Alternatively, respondents portray the Act's limitations on removal as irrelevant, because — as the Court of Appeals held — the Commission wields "at-will removal power over Board functions if not Board members." 537 F.3d, at 683. . . . Broad power over Board functions is not equivalent to the power to remove Board members. The Commission may, for example, approve the Board's budget, issue binding regulations, relieve the Board of authority, amend Board sanctions, or enforce Board rules on its own. But altering the budget or powers of an agency as a whole is a problematic way to control an inferior officer. The Commission cannot wield a free hand to supervise individual members if it must destroy the Board in order to fix it.

Even if Commission power over Board activities could substitute for authority over its members, we would still reject respondents' premise that the Commission's power in this regard is plenary. As described above, the Board is empowered to take significant enforcement actions, and does so largely independently of the Commission. Its powers are, of course, subject to some latent Commission control. But the Act nowhere gives the Commission effective power to start, stop, or alter individual Board investigations, executive activities typically carried out by officials within the Executive Branch. . . .

The parties have identified only a handful of isolated positions in which inferior officers might be protected by two levels of good-cause tenure. . . . [T]he dissent fails to support its premonitions of doom; none of the positions it identifies are similarly situated to the Board. For example, many civil servants within independent agencies would not qualify as "Officers of the United States." . . . Nor do the employees referenced by the dissent enjoy the same significant and unusual protections from Presidential oversight as members of the Board. Senior or policymaking positions in government may be excepted from the competitive service to ensure Presidential control, and members of the Senior Executive Service may be reassigned or reviewed by agency heads (and entire agencies may be excluded from that Service by the President). While the full extent of that authority is not before us, any such authority is of course wholly absent with respect to the Board. Nothing in our opinion, therefore, should be read to cast doubt on the use of what is colloquially known as the civil service system within independent agencies.[10] . . .

IV

Petitioners' complaint argued that the Board's "freedom from Presidential oversight and control" rendered it "and all power and authority exercised by it" in violation of the Constitution. We reject such a broad holding. Instead, we agree with the Government that the unconstitutional tenure provisions are

---

10. For similar reasons, our holding also does not address that subset of independent agency employees who serve as administrative law judges. Whether administrative law judges are necessarily "Officers of the United States" is disputed. See, e.g., Landry v. FDIC, 204 F.3d 1125 (D.C. Cir. 2000). And unlike members of the Board, many administrative law judges of course perform adjudicative rather than enforcement or policymaking functions, or possess purely recommendatory powers. . . .

severable from the remainder of the statute. . . . Concluding that the removal restrictions are invalid leaves the Board removable by the Commission at will, and leaves the President separated from Board members by only a single level of good-cause tenure. The Commission is then fully responsible for the Board's actions, which are no less subject than the Commission's own functions to Presidential oversight. . . .

V

Petitioners raise three more challenges to the Board under the Appointments Clause. None has merit.

First, petitioners argue that Board members are principal officers requiring Presidential appointment with the Senate's advice and consent. We held in *Edmond v. United States*, 520 U.S. 651, 662-663 (1997), that "[w]hether one is an 'inferior' officer depends on whether he has a superior," and that "'inferior officers' are officers whose work is directed and supervised at some level" by other officers appointed by the President with the Senate's consent. . . . Given that the Commission is properly viewed, under the Constitution, as possessing the power to remove Board members at will, and given the Commission's other oversight authority, we have no hesitation in concluding that under *Edmond* the Board members are inferior officers whose appointment Congress may permissibly vest in a "Hea[d] of Departmen[t]."

But, petitioners argue, the Commission is not a "Departmen[t]" like the "Executive departments" (e.g., State, Treasury, Defense) listed in 5 U.S.C. §101. [We disagree.] Because the Commission is a freestanding component of the Executive Branch, not subordinate to or contained within any other such component, it constitutes a "Departmen[t]" for the purposes of the Appointments Clause.

But petitioners are not done yet. They argue that the full Commission cannot constitutionally appoint Board members, because only the Chairman of the Commission is the Commission's "Hea[d]." The Commission's powers, however, are generally vested in the Commissioners jointly, not the Chairman alone. The Commissioners do not report to the Chairman, who exercises administrative and executive functions subject to the full Commission's policies. . . . As a constitutional matter, we see no reason why a multimember body may not be the "Hea[d]" of a "Departmen[t]" that it governs. The Appointments Clause necessarily contemplates collective appointments by the "Courts of Law," Art. II, §2, cl. 2, and each House of Congress, too, appoints its officers collectively, see Art. I, §2, cl. 5; *id.*, §3, cl. 5. Petitioners argue that the Framers vested the nomination of principal officers in the President to avoid the perceived evils of collective appointments, but they reveal no similar concern with respect to inferior officers, whose appointments may be vested elsewhere, including in multimember bodies. . . .

The judgment of the United States Court of Appeals for the District of Columbia Circuit is affirmed in part and reversed in part, and the case is remanded for further proceedings consistent with this opinion.

It is so ordered.

JUSTICE BREYER, with whom JUSTICE STEVENS, JUSTICE GINSBURG, and JUSTICE SOTOMAYOR join, dissenting. . . .

In answering the question presented [in this case], we cannot look to more specific constitutional text, such as the text of the Appointments Clause, . . . because . . . the Constitution is completely "silent with respect to the power of removal from office." Ex parte Hennen, 38 U.S. (13 Pet.) 230, 259 (1839). . . . When previously deciding this kind of nontextual question, the Court has emphasized the importance of examining how a particular provision, taken in context, is likely to function. . . . [A] functional approach permits Congress and the President the flexibility needed to adapt statutory law to changing circumstances.

[T]oday vast numbers of statutes governing vast numbers of subjects, concerned with vast numbers of different problems, provide for, or foresee, their execution or administration through the work of administrators organized within many different kinds of administrative structures, exercising different kinds of administrative authority, to achieve their legislatively mandated objectives. And, given the nature of the Government's work, it is not surprising that administrative units come in many different shapes and sizes.

The functional approach required by our precedents recognizes this administrative complexity and, more importantly, recognizes the various ways presidential power operates within this context—and the various ways in which a removal provision might affect that power. As human beings have known ever since Ulysses tied himself to the mast so as safely to hear the Sirens' song, sometimes it is necessary to disable oneself in order to achieve a broader objective. Thus, legally enforceable commitments—such as contracts, statutes that cannot instantly be changed, and, as in the case before us, the establishment of independent administrative institutions—hold the potential to empower precisely because of their ability to constrain. If the President seeks to regulate through impartial adjudication, then insulation of the adjudicator from removal at will can help him achieve that goal. And to free a technical decisionmaker from the fear of removal without cause can similarly help create legitimacy with respect to that official's regulatory actions by helping to insulate his technical decisions from nontechnical political pressure. . . .

Congress and the President had good reason for enacting the challenged "for cause" provision. First and foremost, the Board adjudicates cases. This Court has long recognized the appropriateness of using "for cause" provisions to protect the personal independence of those who even only sometimes engage in adjudicatory functions. . . . Moreover, in addition to their adjudicative functions, the Accounting Board members supervise, and are themselves, technical professional experts. . . . Here, the justification for insulating the "technical experts" on the Board from fear of losing their jobs due to political influence is particularly strong. . . . [H]istorically, this regulatory subject matter—financial regulation—has been thought to exhibit a particular need for independence. And Congress, by, for example, providing the Board with a revenue stream independent of the congressional appropriations process, helped insulate the Board from congressional, as well as other, political influences. . . .

The Court begins to reveal the practical problems inherent in its double for-cause rule when it suggests that its rule may not apply to "the civil service."

. . . The civil service . . . includes many officers indistinguishable from the members of both the Commission and the Accounting Board. . . . But even if I assume that the majority categorically excludes [most members of the civil service] from the scope of its new rule, the exclusion would be insufficient. This is because the Court's "double for-cause" rule applies to appointees who are "inferior officer[s]." And who are they? Courts and scholars have struggled for more than a century to define the constitutional term "inferior officers," without much success. . . . [Even reading the criteria suggested by courts and scholars] as stringently as possible, I still see no way to avoid sweeping hundreds, perhaps thousands of high level government officials within the scope of the Court's holding, putting their job security and their administrative actions and decisions constitutionally at risk. To make even a conservative estimate, one would have to begin by listing federal departments, offices, bureaus and other agencies whose heads are by statute removable only "for cause." I have found 48 such agencies. . . . Then it would be necessary to identify the senior officials in those agencies (just below the top) who themselves are removable only "for cause." I have identified 573 such high-ranking officials. . . . The potential list of those whom today's decision affects is yet larger. As Justice Scalia has observed, administrative law judges (ALJs) "are all executive officers." *Freytag*, 501 U.S. at 910 (opinion concurring in part and concurring in judgment). My research reflects that the Federal Government relies on 1,584 ALJs to adjudicate administrative matters in over 25 agencies. . . .

Thus, notwithstanding the majority's assertions to the contrary, the potential consequences of today's holding are worrying. The upshot, I believe, is a legal dilemma. To interpret the Court's decision as applicable only in a few circumstances will make the rule less harmful but arbitrary. To interpret the rule more broadly will make the rule more rational, but destructive.

One last question: How can the Court simply assume without deciding that the SEC Commissioners themselves are removable only "for cause"? . . . [T]he statute that established the Commission says nothing about removal. It is silent on the question. . . . Nor is the absence of a "for cause" provision in the statute that created the Commission likely to have been inadvertent. Congress created the Commission during the 9-year period after this Court decided *Myers*, and thereby cast serious doubt on the constitutionality of all "for cause" removal provisions, but before it decided *Humphrey's Executor*, which removed any doubt in respect to the constitutionality of making commissioners of independent agencies removable only for cause. . . .

The Court then, by assumption, reads into the statute books a "for cause removal" phrase that does not appear in the relevant statute and which Congress probably did not intend to write. And it does so in order to strike down, not to uphold, another statute. This is not a statutory construction that seeks to avoid a constitutional question, but its opposite. . . . I do not need to decide whether the Commissioners are in fact removable only "for cause" because I would uphold the Accounting Board's removal provision as constitutional regardless. But were that not so, a determination that the silent SEC statute means no more than it says would properly avoid the determination of unconstitutionality that the Court now makes.

With respect I dissent.

NOTES AND QUESTIONS

1. *Two levels of for-cause restrictions and the unitary executive theory.* Are you persuaded by Chief Justice Roberts's argument that a double-layer system of for-cause insulation violates the Constitution, even in a context in which a single-layer system would not? If he is correct, why isn't the obvious corrective to make the SEC commissioners removable at will, given the fact that there is no statutory restriction on removal of SEC commissioners? Does *Free Enterprise* signal the triumph of the unitary executive theory advanced by Justice Scalia in his *Morrison* dissent? If so, can *Humphrey's Executor* long survive?

2. *Formalism versus functionalism III.* Notice that Justice Breyer makes a plea to use functionalist reasoning to resolve the issue presented by *Free Enterprise.* Does the Chief Justice use a different methodology? Most commentators characterize the reasoning of the majorities in cases like *Bowsher* and *Morrison* as functionalist, in contrast to the apparent formalism of cases like *Chadha* and *Clinton.* Why the difference? Do cases about the scope of the "executive" power call for a different interpretive methodology than cases about the scope of the "legislative" power?

3. Free Enterprise *and the federal civil service system.* Chief Justice Roberts takes pains to reassure his audience that the *Free Enterprise* ruling does not threaten the federal civil service system, which provides extensive "for cause" protections to most federal workers. For the first century following the Founding, the President and his subordinates enjoyed almost unlimited latitude to hire and fire federal workers. While this system had the virtue of enabling executives to remove ineffective employees, it brought with it a concomitant temptation to dispense government jobs as rewards for political support. Appalled by the abuses of the dominant political patronage system, reformers made growing calls to professionalize the federal service, culminating with enactment of the Pendleton Act in 1883, 22 Stat. 403. The Act did not abolish the patronage system wholesale, but it provided modest protection to a fairly narrow range of employees. But the scope of civil service protection and the range of covered employees increased steadily in the subsequent decades, to the point that civil service covered 80 percent of federal civilian employees by 1940.

With the victory of civil service over the patronage system, the focus for criticism shifted to the alleged difficulty of motivating and dismissing ineffective tenured employees. Responding to these criticisms, Congress passed the Civil Service Reform Act of 1978, 92 Stat. 1119, Pub. L. No. 95-454. The Act increased management control over the highest-ranking civil servants, who were identified as the Senior Executive Service. The Act also replaced the old Civil Service Commission with two agencies: the Office of Personnel Management (OPM), which classifies jobs and evaluates applicants' qualifications, and the Merit Systems Protection Board (MSPB), which decides disputed cases involving adverse actions against protected personnel. Although designed to steer a middle course between patronage and civil service, the 1978 Reform Act has not eliminated complaints that the civil service system unduly restricts executive control. Can such a system be reconciled with the logic of *Free Enterprise?*

In addition to civil service statutes, the First Amendment has been invoked to curtail the use of patronage in public employment. In 1976, the Supreme

Court held that dismissal of an official, even a non-"tenured" employee, because of his party affiliation violates the First Amendment. Elrod v. Burns, 427 U.S. 347 (1976). Writing for a three-Justice plurality, Justice William Brennan declared that patronage systems interfere with employees' constitutionally protected freedoms of belief and association and undermine the "free functioning of the electoral process." Brennan wrote that concerns about disloyal employees disrupting government operation were properly limited to employees in policymaking or confidential positions, a sentiment emphasized by concurring Justices Stewart and Blackmun. In Branti v. Finkel, 445 U.S. 507 (1980), the Court focused on the dimensions of the policymaking exception. Justice John Paul Stevens wrote for the six-member majority that "the question is whether the hiring authority can demonstrate that party affiliation is an appropriate requirement for the effective performance of the public office involved." Id. at 518. The Court held that party affiliation was not an appropriate qualification for public defenders, whose decisions properly are informed by "the needs of individual clients and not [by] any partisan political interests." Id. at 519. In Rutan v. Republican Party of Illinois, 497 U.S. 62 (1990), the Supreme Court extended Elrod and Branti to cover hiring, promotion, recall, and transfer decisions, effectively prohibiting state and local governments from basing lower-level employment decisions on political affiliation.

3.   Allocation of Executive Authority: Subdelegation

As we have seen, the first three articles of the Constitution "vest" legislative, executive, and judicial power, respectively, in the three branches. We know from *Chadha* that Congress may not delegate its "legislative" powers to an entity within Congress, such as a single house or legislative committee. Likewise, the Supreme Court may not delegate its "judicial" power to decide "cases or controversies" to a panel of three Justices or a panel of law clerks.

In a similar vein, it seems highly doubtful that the President could delegate to another official, such as the Attorney General, the power to veto legislation or nominate Supreme Court Justices. But may the President subdelegate his statutory powers and duties? Early cases involving presidential authority to delegate duties suggested that while "necessity" dictated some authority to subdelegate, there were official acts that "undoubtedly" were nondelegable. *See, e.g.,* McElrath v. United States, 12 Ct. Cl. 201 (1876). In Runkle v. United States, 122 U.S. 543 (1887), the Supreme Court invalidated a presidential subdelegation, finding that the particular statute at issue (concerning executive confirmation or disapproval of certain court-martial decisions) required an exercise of "personal judgment" by the President. In subdelegation cases following *Runkle,* however, the Court was reluctant to police the required presidential exercise of personal judgment, and in United States v. Chemical Foundation, 272 U.S. 1, 16 (1926), the Court effectively abandoned the requirement. Congress ratified this approach to presidential subdelegation in 1950 in Pub. L. No. 673, 64 Stat. 419, as amended in 1951 and codified at 3 U.S.C. §§301-303. This Act allows the President to empower any executive official appointed with the advice and consent of the Senate to perform any action delegated to presidential authority unless clearly forbidden by the governing statute. *Id.*

As with the President, there was at one time an effort to fashion effective constraints on subdelegation by other executive officers. *See, e.g.,* Cudahy Packing Co. v. Holland, 315 U.S. 356 (1942). The effort necessarily raised the practical problem of finding ways to ensure the desired level of personal involvement from busy executives who consider the matter at issue less significant than other matters competing for their attention. In some instances, courts still attempt to enforce requirements of personal attention. *See, e.g.,* United States v. Giordano, 416 U.S. 505, 513 (1974); Halverson v. Slater, 129 F.3d 180, 185 (D.C. Cir. 1997). But the general approach is acquiescence in subdelegation. *See, e.g.,* Touby v. United States, discussed in section B.1., *supra,* where the Supreme Court summarily rebuffed a challenge to a delegation, from the Attorney General to the Drug Enforcement Agency, of authority to designate certain drugs as controlled substances even though the Court took quite seriously the related arguments concerning delegation of legislative authority to the Attorney General.

Despite their tolerance of internal subdelegation, courts look with a very jaundiced eye on officials' attempts to delegate authority to parties outside the agency, as the following case illustrates.

UNITED STATES TELECOM ASSN. v. FEDERAL COMMUNICATIONS COMMISSION, 359 F.3d 554 (D.C. Cir. 2004) (*USTA II*): At one time the telecommunications industry was characterized by monopolistic local telephone companies, regulated by state public utility commissions, and monopolistic national long-distance providers, regulated by the Federal Communications Commission. Over time the long-distance market became much more competitive. In the Telecommunications Act of 1996, Congress charged the Federal Communications Commission with fostering a competitive market for local telephone service by requiring established local carriers to make their networks available to new competitors. In specifying the terms on which carriers must make their networks available, the FCC must consider whether lack of access would "impair" the ability of the entrant to provide service. The FCC twice issued rules defining "impairment," only to have the rules struck down by the courts. AT&T Corp. v. Iowa Utilities Bd., 525 U.S. 366 (1999); United States Telecom Assn. v. FCC, 290 F.3d 415 (D.C. Cir. 2002) (*USTA I*). In *USTA I* the D.C. Circuit held that the FCC rules were too categorical, and not sufficiently sensitive to varying local economic conditions. In an attempt to respond to this criticism, the FCC on its third try came up with a more "granular" approach that took into consideration a host of local conditions. For those cases in which it lacked sufficient information to apply its "granular" rule, however, the FCC adopted a provisional nationwide rule, subject to the possibility of local exceptions. The commission's rule delegated to state public utility commissions the power to determine whether such a local exception was warranted in any particular case. On review, the D.C. Circuit once again threw out the rules. Among other reasons, the court found that the FCC lacked authority to subdelegate to entities outside the commission its power to determine "impairments." The court said:

> [T]he cases recognize an important distinction between subdelegation to a *subordinate* and subdelegation to an *outside party*. The presumptions that subdelegations are valid absent a showing of contrary congressional intent applies only to the former. There is no such presumption covering subdelegations to outside parties.

Indeed, if anything, the case law strongly suggests that subdelegations to outside parties are assumed to be improper absent an affirmative showing of congressional authorization. . . . This distinction is entirely sensible. When an agency delegates authority to its subordinate, responsibility—and thus accountability—clearly remain with the federal agency. But when an agency delegates power to outside parties, lines of accountability may blur, undermining an important democratic check on government decision-making. Also, delegation to outside entities increases the risk that these parties will not share the agency's "national vision and perspective" [National Park & Conservation Assn. v. Stanton, 54 F. Supp. 2d 7, 20 (D.D.C. 1999)], and thus may pursue goals inconsistent with those of the agency and the underlying statutory scheme. In short, subdelegation to outside entities aggravates the risk of policy drift inherent in any principal-agent relationship.

359 F.3d at 565-566 (emphasis in original). The court distinguished subdelegations of decisionmaking power from cases permitting agencies to use outsiders for "(1) establishing a reasonable condition for granting federal approval; (2) fact gathering; and (3) advice giving." *Id.* at 566.

QUESTIONS

Recall that in the *Carter Coal* case, discussed in notes following *Schechter Poultry, supra*, the Supreme Court struck down a statute that effectively delegated authority to set nationwide maximum hours for coal miners to a subset of the nation's unions and coal producers, citing the obvious conflict of interest. Is there a comparable conflict of interest in *USTA II*? Should the court have given greater weight to the fact that the delegates in this case were agencies of sovereign state governments, which had historically been entrusted with regulating the local telecommunication industry? Is the court's concern about lack of "national vision and perspective" convincing, given the fact that the task delegated was to determine whether local conditions justified variances from uniform national rules?

CHAPTER II

JUDICIAL REVIEW OF
ADMINISTRATIVE DECISIONS

The dominant concern of administrative law is the legal control of administration. Given the centrality of courts in our legal system, that concern quickly translates into the issue of "judicial review," which is the focus of this and the next chapter. Chapter II asks the question: What standard should courts apply when they review administrative decisions? Chapter III asks the related question: Under what circumstances should courts review agency actions? Before examining those issues, however, it is worth pausing to ask why our system of government relies so heavily on the "nonpolitical" judicial branch to supervise the actions of "political" entities such as administrative agencies.

That question was discussed in an article by Professor William Landes and Judge Richard Posner, entitled The Independent Judiciary in an Interest Group Perspective, 18 J.L. & Econ. 875 (1975). Landes and Posner were struck by the general inclination of legislatures to authorize review of administrators' actions by judges, who are far more insulated from legislative influence. Looking from a public choice perspective, Landes and Posner asked, what do legislators gain from review by an independent judiciary? Their answer was that review functions as a sort of contract enforcement mechanism. The initial "deal" struck among legislators and interest groups is more valuable if there is a reliable means for enforcing its terms. Changed circumstances may make future legislators and administrators unwilling to respect the earlier agreement embodied in an agency's legislative mandate. Judges, with life tenure, irreducible salary, and insulation from political influence, should be far better guarantors of the original parties' intent.

As is evident in the materials that follow, most discussion of judicial review focuses on particular aspects of review: the "scope" of review (the standard applied by the reviewing court to an administrative decision), the timing of review, or its availability to specific parties. The general availability of review is now an accepted fact; there is little cause to question it, save in rare instances where that general assumption is re-examined.

To say that judges are more insulated from political pressure does not, of course, mean that they are nonpolitical. It is commonplace in the popular media to identify judges by their political party affiliation or their presumed position on an ideological spectrum from liberal to conservative. Political scientists and legal scholars have long studied judicial voting to discern ideological patterns. In the field of administrative law, this kind of scholarship has tended to focus particularly on the Court of Appeals for the D.C. Circuit, which is the federal court that handles most of the high-profile administrative law business in the federal judicial system. Several studies have purported to find that judges appointed by a Republican President are much more likely to side with the regulated industry and against the regulatory agency in challenges to agency decisions. *See, e.g.,* Frank B. Cross & Emerson H. Tiller, Judicial Partisanship and Obedience to Legal Doctrine: Whistleblowing on the Federal Courts of Appeals, 107 Yale L.J. 2155 (1998). Not surprisingly, members of the D.C. Circuit have strenuously resisted the implications of these findings, *see, e.g.,* Harry T. Edwards, Collegiality and Decision Making on the D.C. Circuit, 83 Va. L. Rev. 1335 (1998), and others have disputed the accuracy of the findings, *see, e.g.,* The District of Columbia Circuit: The Importance of Balance on the Nation's Second Highest Court, S. Hrg. 107-972 before S. Judic. Comm., Subcomm. on Admin. Oversight of the Courts, 107th Cong., 2d Sess., 45, 46-49 (2002) (statement of Ronald A. Cass).

In addition to empirical debates about the actual behavior of judges, the literature is rife with normative debates over the principles that judges *ought* to apply when reviewing administrative decisions. To a large extent, this literature overlaps the general literature on statutory interpretation. One school, inspired by the Landes and Posner "legislation-as-deal" theory, argues that judges ought to enforce legislative deals, no matter how unseemly the deals may be. *See, e.g.,* Frank Easterbrook, The Supreme Court, 1983 Term—Foreword: The Court and the Economic System, 98 Harv. L. Rev. 4 (1984). This approach encompasses arguments for enforcing statutes according to the evident meaning of their text, leaving Congress to fix any practical or political problems that may result. *See, e.g.,* Antonin Scalia, A Matter of Interpretation: Federal Courts and the Law 6-25 (1997). Other commentators have argued that reviewing courts should apply judicially created interpretive "canons" or "norms" that seek to assure that statutes will be given a "public-interest" or "public-regarding" interpretation. *See, e.g.,* William N. Eskridge, Jr., Dynamic Statutory Interpretation, 135 U. Pa. L. Rev. 1479 (1987).

As you read the materials that follow, you should ask yourself what the courts seem to be doing when they review administrative decisions. Are they conscientiously trying to enforce an original legislative "deal," voting their personal political ideologies, or fashioning supra-legislative principles to achieve some conception of the public interest?

A. STANDARDS OF JUDICIAL REVIEW UNDER THE ADMINISTRATIVE PROCEDURE ACT

1. Standards of Review and the Overton Park *Saga*

As is explained more fully at the beginning of Chapter III, *infra*, the authority of American courts to review the actions of administrative agencies developed historically from a patchwork of common law writs and special statutes. That patchwork became unwieldy over time, providing part of the impetus for efforts in the 1930s and 1940s to establish a uniform body of rules to govern the judicial review of federal administrative agencies. The product of that effort was §10 of the Administrative Procedure Act of 1946 (now found at 5 U.S.C. §§701-706 and reproduced in the Appendix at the end of this book). In §10(e) (now §706) Congress attempted to codify the various standards then applied by reviewing courts in determining the lawfulness of administrative action. As would be expected to result from an effort to codify a messy reality, §706 is not a model of linguistic clarity or coherence. Thus, while it is the logical starting point from which to explore the allocation of power between courts and agencies, it is rarely the ending place, as the celebrated case of *Overton Park* makes clear.

Section 706 instructs reviewing courts to "decide all relevant questions of law, interpret constitutional and statutory provisions, and determine the meaning or applicability of the terms of an agency action." It goes on to provide that the reviewing court shall hold agency action unlawful, and set it aside, if the court finds the action to be:

(A) arbitrary, capricious, an abuse of discretion, or otherwise not in accordance with law;

(B) contrary to constitutional right, power, privilege, or immunity;

(C) in excess of statutory jurisdiction, authority, or limitations, or short of statutory right;

(D) without observance of procedure required by law;

(E) unsupported by substantial evidence in a case subject to sections 556 and 557 [of the APA] or otherwise reviewed on the record of an agency hearing provided by statute; or

(F) unwarranted by the facts to the extent that the facts are subject to trial de novo by the reviewing court.

A quick review of these clauses reveals some of the many interpretive problems they present. One is the issue of applicability. The standards set forth in Clauses (E) and (F) are explicitly limited to certain kinds of administrative proceedings. Does the absence of limiting language in the other clauses mean that the standards set forth therein are universally applicable or do these clauses apply only in particular settings? A second problem is the issue of overlap. For example, does the word "law" as used in the prefatory language of §706 and in Clauses (A) and (D) refer to some source of law other than the sources specifically mentioned in Clauses (B) (the Constitution) and (C) (statutes)? Does the instruction to "determine the meaning or applicability of the terms of an agency action" count also as an interpretation of "law" in cases where the agency action expressly is given the "force of law"? A third problem is the precise meaning of the various terms. For example, how much evidence is "substantial"? What does "arbitrary" mean in this context? What is "on the record" review? These are issues addressed in the cases and materials that follow. We begin with the background for one of the signal cases on scope of review, Citizens to Preserve Overton Park v. Volpe, 401 U.S. 402 (1971) (excerpted below).

Most of the nation's network of interstate highways has been built under the auspices of the federal-aid highway program. This program, dating from 1916, allocates federal funds to the states on a formula basis for the construction of highways. Although the federal government pays 90 percent of the cost of these roads, the states historically exercised almost total control over route selection, design, and layout.

That situation began to change in the 1960s, however, as Congress reacted unfavorably to the destruction of urban and scenic areas by state highway planners. In 1966 Senator Ralph Yarborough of Texas introduced an amendment to the proposed Federal-Aid Highway Act of 1966 that would forbid the taking of parkland or historic sites unless: (1) "there is no feasible alternative to the use of such land," and (2) the highway project "includes all possible planning to minimize any harm to such park or site resulting from such use." 112 Cong. Rec. 14,074 (1966). Although the Senate approved the bill, the House-Senate Conference Committee managed to water it down by dropping the first condition. The Amendment, as adopted, was codified at 23 U.S.C. §138 (1982).

Meanwhile, a Senate committee had included language based on the original Yarborough amendment in a pending bill to create a new federal Department of Transportation. This provision (inserted as §4(f) of the bill) again passed the Senate and again was amended by the conference committee. This time, though, instead of striking out the "feasibility" clause altogether, the conference committee inserted the phrase "and prudent" after the word "feasible." The conference committee report provides no explanation for the insertion. Conference Report 2236 on Department of Transportation Act of 1966, 89th Cong., 2d Sess. (1966). But in floor debate prior to adoption of the conference report, Congressman John Kluczynski of the House Public Works Committee remarked:

> Mr. Speaker, I am pleased to see section 4(f) appear in this bill . . . but I would like to sound a word of caution in interpreting section 4(f). There is no question in my mind that the protection of our parks, open spaces, historic sites, fish and game habitats, and the other natural resources with which our Nation is richly endowed, is of the utmost importance and urgency, but not to the total exclusion of other considerations. To do so would result in as many inequities as justifying transportation plans merely on the basis of economy or efficiency. Other considerations would include the integrity of neighborhoods, the displacement of people and businesses, and the protection of schools, and churches and the myriad of other social and human values we find in our communities. Attempting to define "feasible alternative" in light of all of these considerations is virtually impossible

and may result in hampering and otherwise unnecessarily delaying transportation progress. . . . I am glad to see the words "and prudent" added to this section by the conference committee. With this inclusion, and with "prudent" as the operable word, this section now becomes workable and effective and I fully support and intend to vote for the bill as written.

112 Cong. Rec. 26,651 (1966).

When the federal-aid highway program came up for its biennial reauthorization in 1968, pro-highway forces mounted a campaign to dilute §4(f) by "harmonizing" it with the weaker language of §138. The effort provoked a strong response from conservationist groups, however, and when the dust had cleared, precisely the opposite had occurred. The two sections were "harmonized," all right, but the language adopted (and incorporated into both sections) included the "feasible and prudent" clause previously contained only in §4(f). The 1968 version of the statute provided:

> [T]he Secretary shall not approve any program or project which requires the use of any publicly owned land from a public park, recreation area, or wildlife and waterfowl refuge of national, State, or local significance . . . unless (1) there is no feasible and prudent alternative to the use of such land, and (2) such program includes all possible planning to minimize harm to such park, recreational area, wildlife and waterfowl refuge, or historic site resulting from such use.

82 Stat. 824, 49 U.S.C. §1653(f) (1964 ed., Supp. V).

The exact significance of the amendment was clouded, however, by conflicting House and Senate conference reports. A "Statement of the Managers on the Part of the House" signed by the House conferees declared:

> This amendment of both relevant sections of law is intended to make it unmistakably clear that neither section constitutes a mandatory provision against the use of the enumerated lands, but rather, is a discretionary authority which must be used with both wisdom and reason. The Congress does not believe, for example, that substantial numbers of people should be required to move in order to preserve these lands, or that clearly enunciated local preferences should be overruled on the basis of this authority.

Conference Report to Accompany S. 3418, Federal-Aid Highway Act of 1968, H.R. Rep. No. 1799, 90th Cong., 2d Sess. 32 (1968).

The Senate conferees, on the other hand, denied that the amendment conferred any such broad discretion on the Secretary of Transportation. As Senator John Cooper stated during floor debate:

> [T]he language of the [two] section[s] gives no discretion. If a local official, a State official, or a Federal official having jurisdiction finds one of these areas or sites to be of significance, there is no discretion given to the Secretary of Transportation to permit its use for a highway. . . . The legislative language . . . prohibits any intrusion upon or invasion of these lands or areas if one of these bodies finds it is of National, State, or local significance, and the highway cannot be built, unless there is no feasible and prudent alternative to doing so.

114 Cong. Rec. 24,033 (1968).

There the matter stood when Secretary of Transportation John Volpe was called upon to approve a controversial highway project (Interstate 40) in Memphis, Tennessee. Like most interstate highway projects, by the time it reached the Secretary's desk, it had acquired a lengthy history. Planning for the Memphis project had begun early in the 1950s. Expansion of the city's residential area to the east, coupled with the fact that most employers were located on the city's western edge, created pressure for a major east-west highway to relieve congestion on city streets. In 1956, the Federal Bureau of Public Roads (predecessor of the Secretary of Transportation for this purpose) approved a proposed route that would carry I-40 through the northern part of Overton Park, a 342-acre park in the center of Memphis. The Bureau rejected two alternative routes around the park, one just to the north, and the other to the south. According to the Bureau's Deputy Director, these alternatives would have involved excessive dislocation of people and higher costs:

> For instance, the route immediately north of the park would have involved the taking of three schools, including Southwest University and the largest high school in Memphis, plus churches attended by 4,000 people, industries, and the residences of more than 1,500 people. The route south of the park would have involved taking two schools, three churches attended by 7,500 people, 46 commercial establishments, residential units being occupied by over 3,000 persons, and a hospital and home for the aged. Incidentally, the construction and right-of-way costs of the least expensive of these alternate routes would exceed the cost of the chosen route by many millions of dollars.

Affidavit of Edgar H. Swick, quoted in Reply Brief of Respondent, Charles W. Speight, Commissioner, Tennessee Department of Highways, at 9, Citizens to Preserve Overton Park v. Volpe, 401 U.S. 402 (1971).

Following reassignment of highway-approval authority to the newly created Department of Transportation, its first Secretary of Transportation directed a re-examination of the Overton Park project in light of the statute. In February 1968, department officials conducted a public hearing in Memphis on the proposed location. On March 5, the Memphis City Council passed a resolution opposing the location, but after an April 3 meeting with the Federal Highway Administrator, reversed its position and approved the route through the park as "the feasible and prudent location." Two weeks later, the Secretary of Transportation reaffirmed the department's approval for the route. The State Highway Department thereupon proceeded to the design stage.

Meanwhile the state was proceeding to acquire the right-of-way. In 1967 it acquired most of the right-of-way to the west and east of the park, and in September 1969, acquired the 26-acre right-of-way through the park for $2 million. A local ordinance required the city to reinvest this sum in other parkland. By the time of the litigation, it had used half of it to acquire a 160-acre park and golf course.

On November 5, 1969, Secretary of Transportation Volpe approved the design after the state agreed to depress the highway below ground level except where it crossed a small creek. The only public explanation issued by the Secretary for his approval was this press release:

> Secretary of Transportation John A. Volpe today announced he has approved, with significant qualifications, a proposal submitted by the Tennessee Department of Highways to construct a segment of Interstate route 40 through Overton Park in Memphis, Tennessee.

Secretary Volpe said a "hold" on the project had been lifted after the state agreed to adjust the grade line of the depressed freeway to a point as low as possible. This grade line would still permit natural drainage in the area of Lick Creek, a small stream that flows through the 360 acre park near downtown Memphis.

J. D. Braman, Assistant Secretary of Transportation for Environment and Urban Systems, and one of Secretary Volpe's key advisors on environment and downtown highway systems, said, "The plan for Overton Park is the most reasonable now open to use and is designed to do minimum damage to the park. The options of this Administration were few, mainly because the route of the highway had previously been determined."

Quoted in Citizens to Preserve Overton Park v. Volpe, 335 F. Supp. 873, 878-879 (W.D. Tenn. 1972).

As approved, the highway would cut a swath through the park 250 feet wide at its eastern end and gradually widening to 450 feet at its western end. It would follow an existing nonaccess bus road some 40 to 50 feet wide that carried occasional bus traffic through the park. The highway (like the bus route) would separate a zoo at the northern edge of the park from the park's other features (a nine-hole municipal golf course, an outdoor theater, nature trails, a bridle path, an art academy, a lake, picnic areas, and 170 acres of woods). The highway would destroy some 12 acres of trees, but none of the other features described. A pedestrian overpass would be built between the two sections.

Citizens to Preserve Overton Park, a local group of private citizens, supported by national conservation organizations, brought suit in District Court for the Western District of Tennessee to enjoin the release of federal funds for the project on the ground that Secretary Volpe had not complied with §4(f) of the Department of Transportation Act and §138 of the Federal-Aid Highway Act. The district court granted the Secretary's motion for summary judgment and the Sixth Circuit affirmed.

CITIZENS TO PRESERVE OVERTON
PARK v. VOLPE
401 U.S. 402 (1971)

Opinion of the Court by MR. JUSTICE MARSHALL, announced by MR. JUSTICE STEWART.

Petitioners contend that the Secretary's action is invalid without . . . formal findings and that the Secretary did not make an independent determination but merely relied on the judgment of the Memphis City Council. They also contend that it would be "feasible and prudent" to route I-40 around Overton Park either to the north or to the south. And they argue that if these alternative routes are not "feasible and prudent," the present plan does not include "all possible" methods for reducing harm to the park. Petitioners claim that I-40 could be built under the park by using either of two possible tunneling methods,[18] and they

---

18. Petitioners argue that either a bored tunnel or a cut-and-cover tunnel, which is a fully depressed route covered after construction, could be built. Respondents contend that the construction of a tunnel by either method would greatly increase the cost of the project, would create safety hazards, and because of increases in air pollution would not reduce harm to the park.

claim that, at a minimum, by using advanced drainage techniques[19] the express-way could be depressed below ground level along the entire route through the park including the section that crosses the small creek.

Respondents argue that it was unnecessary for the Secretary to make formal findings, and that he did, in fact, exercise his own independent judgment which was supported by the facts. In the District Court, respondents introduced affidavits, prepared specifically for this litigation, which indicated that the Secretary had made the decision and that the decision was supportable. These affidavits were contradicted by affidavits introduced by petitioners, who also sought to take the deposition of a former Federal Highway Administrator who had participated in the decision to route I-40 through Overton Park.

The District Court and the Court of Appeals found that formal findings by the Secretary were not necessary and refused to order the deposition of the former Federal Highway Administrator because those courts believed that probing of the mental processes of an administrative decisionmaker was prohibited. And, believing that the Secretary's authority was wide and reviewing courts' authority narrow in the approval of highway routes, the lower courts held that the affidavits contained no basis for a determination that the Secretary had exceeded his authority.

We agree that formal findings were not required. But we do not believe that in this case judicial review based solely on litigation affidavits was adequate.

A threshold question—whether petitioners are entitled to any judicial review—is easily answered. Section 701 of the Administrative Procedure Act, 5 U.S.C. §701 (1964 ed., Supp. V), provides that the action of "each authority of the Government of the United States," which includes the Department of Transportation, is subject to judicial review except where there is a statutory prohibition on review or where "agency action is committed to agency discretion by law." In this case, there is no indication that Congress sought to prohibit judicial review and there is most certainly no "showing of 'clear and convincing evidence' of a . . . legislative intent" to restrict access to judicial review. Abbott Laboratories v. Gardner, 387 U.S. 136, 141 (1967). Similarly, the Secretary's decision here does not fall within the exception for action "committed to agency discretion." This is a very narrow exception. Berger, Administrative Arbitrariness and Judicial Review, 65 Col. L. Rev. 55 (1965). The legislative history of the Administrative Procedure Act indicates that it is applicable in those rare instances where "statutes are drawn in such broad terms that in a given case there is no law to apply." S. Rep. No. 752, 79th Cong., 1st Sess., 26 (1945).

Section 4(f) of the Department of Transportation Act and §138 of the Federal-Aid Highway Act are clear and specific directives. Both the Department of Transportation Act and the Federal-Aid Highway Act provide that the Secretary "shall not approve any program or project" that requires the use of any public parkland "unless (1) there is no feasible and prudent alternative to the use of such land, and (2) such program includes all possible planning to minimize harm to such park. . . ." 23 U.S.C. §138 (1964 ed., Supp. V); 49 U.S.C. §1653(f) (1964 ed., Supp. V). This language is a plain and explicit bar to the

---

19. Petitioners contend that adequate drainage could be provided by using mechanical pumps or some form of inverted siphon. They claim that such devices are often used in expressway construction.

use of federal funds for construction of highways through parks—only the most unusual situations are exempted.

Despite the clarity of the statutory language, respondents argue that the Secretary has wide discretion. They recognize that the requirement that there be no "feasible" alternative route admits of little administrative discretion. For this exemption to apply the Secretary must find that as a matter of sound engineering it would not be feasible to build the highway along any other route. Respondents argue, however, that the requirement that there be no other "prudent" route requires the Secretary to engage in a wide-ranging balancing of competing interests. They contend that the Secretary should weigh the detriment resulting from the destruction of parkland against the cost of other routes, safety considerations, and other factors, and determine on the basis of the importance that he attaches to these other factors whether, on balance, alternative feasible routes would be "prudent."

But no such wide-ranging endeavor was intended. It is obvious that in most cases considerations of cost, directness of route, and community disruption will indicate that parkland should be used for highway construction whenever possible. Although it may be necessary to transfer funds from one jurisdiction to another, there will always be a smaller outlay required from the public purse when parkland is used since the public already owns the land and there will be no need to pay for right-of-way. And since people do not live or work in parks, if a highway is built on parkland no one will have to leave his home or give up his business. Such factors are common to substantially all highway construction. Thus, if Congress intended these factors to be on an equal footing with preservation of parkland there would have been no need for the statutes.

Congress clearly did not intend that cost and disruption of the community were to be ignored by the Secretary. But the very existence of the statutes indicates that protection of parkland was to be given paramount importance. The few green havens that are public parks were not to be lost unless there were truly unusual factors present in a particular case or the cost or community disruption resulting from alternative routes reached extraordinary magnitudes. If the statutes are to have any meaning, the Secretary cannot approve the destruction of parkland unless he finds that alternative routes present unique problems.

Plainly, there is "law to apply" and thus the exemption for action "committed to agency discretion" is inapplicable. But the existence of judicial review is only the start: the standard for review must also be determined. For that we must look to §706 of the Administrative Procedure Act, 5 U.S.C. §706 (1964 ed., Supp. V), which provides that a "reviewing court shall . . . hold unlawful and set aside agency action, findings, and conclusions found" not to meet six separate standards. . . .

Petitioners argue that the . . . "substantial evidence" standard of §706(2)(E) must be applied. In the alternative, they claim that §706(2)(F) applies and that there must be a de novo review to determine if the Secretary's action was "unwarranted by the facts." Neither of these standards is, however, applicable.

Review under the substantial-evidence test is authorized only when the agency action is taken pursuant to a rulemaking provision of the Administrative Procedure Act itself, 5 U.S.C. §553 (1964 ed., Supp. V), or when the agency action is based on a public adjudicatory hearing. *See* 5 U.S.C. §§556, 557 (1964 ed., Supp. V).* The Secretary's decision to allow the expenditure of federal funds to build I-40 through Overton Park was plainly not an exercise of a rule-making function. *See* 1 K. Davis, Administrative Law Treatise §5.01 (1958). And the only hearing that is required by either the Administrative Procedure Act or the statutes regulating the distribution of federal funds for highway construction is a public hearing conducted by local officials for the purpose of informing the community about the proposed project and eliciting community views on the design and route. 23 U.S.C. §128 (1964 ed., Supp. V). The hearing is non-adjudicatory, quasi-legislative in nature. It is not designed to produce a record that is to be the basis of agency action—the basic requirement for substantial-evidence review. *See* H.R. Rep. No. 1980, 79th Cong., 2d Sess.

Petitioners' alternative argument also fails. De novo review of whether the Secretary's decision was "unwarranted by the facts" is authorized by §706(2)(F) in only two circumstances. First, such de novo review is authorized when the action is adjudicatory in nature and the agency factfinding procedures are inadequate. And, there may be independent judicial factfinding when issues that were not before the agency are raised in a proceeding to enforce nonadjudicatory agency action. H.R. Rep. No. 1980, 79th Cong., 2d Sess. Neither situation exists here.

Even though there is no de novo review in this case and the Secretary's approval of the route of I-40 does not have ultimately to meet the substantial-evidence test, the generally applicable standards of §706 require the reviewing court to engage in a substantial inquiry. Certainly, the Secretary's decision is entitled to a presumption of regularity. *See, e.g.,* Pacific States Box & Basket Co. v. White, 296 U.S. 176, 185 (1935). But that presumption is not to shield his action from a thorough, probing, in-depth review.

The court is first required to decide whether the Secretary acted within the scope of his authority. Schilling v. Rogers, 363 U.S. 666, 676-677 (1960). This determination naturally begins with a delineation of the scope of the Secretary's authority and discretion. As has been shown, Congress has specified only a small range of choices that the Secretary can make. Also involved in this initial inquiry is a determination of whether on the facts the Secretary's decision can reasonably be said to be within that range. The reviewing court must consider whether the Secretary properly construed his authority to approve the use of parkland as limited to situations where there are no feasible alternative routes or where feasible alternative routes involve uniquely difficult problems. And the reviewing court must be able to find that the Secretary could have reasonably believed that in this case there are no feasible alternatives or that alternatives do involve unique problems.

Scrutiny of the facts does not end, however, with the determination that the Secretary has acted within the scope of his statutory authority. Section 706(2)(A) requires a finding that the actual choice made was not "arbitrary, capricious, an abuse of discretion, or otherwise not in accordance with law." 5 U.S.C. §706(2)(A)

---

* [The Court's dictum is incorrect. As the Court later acknowledged in the case of FCC v. National Citizens Comm. for Broadcasting, 436 U.S. 775, 803 (1978), the substantial evidence test is *not* applicable to *informal* rulemaking under §553. It is applicable, however, to *formal* (on-the-record) rulemaking, under §§556-557. On the distinction between the two, *see* Chapter IV.A., *infra.*—Eds.]

(1964 ed., Supp. V). To make this finding the court must consider whether the decision was based on a consideration of the relevant factors and whether there has been a clear error of judgment. . . . Although this inquiry into the facts is to be searching and careful, the ultimate standard of review is a narrow one. The court is not empowered to substitute its judgment for that of the agency.

The final inquiry is whether the Secretary's action followed the necessary procedural requirements. Here the only procedural error alleged is the failure of the Secretary to make formal findings and state his reason for allowing the highway to be built through the park.

Undoubtedly, review of the Secretary's action is hampered by his failure to make such findings, but the absence of formal findings does not necessarily require that the case be remanded to the Secretary. Neither the Department of Transportation Act nor the Federal-Aid Highway Act requires such formal findings. Moreover, the Administrative Procedure Act requirements that there be formal findings in certain rulemaking and adjudicatory proceedings do not apply to the Secretary's action here. *See* 5 U.S.C. §§553(a)(2), 554(a) (1964 ed., Supp. V). And, although formal findings may be required in some cases in the absence of statutory directives when the nature of the agency action is ambiguous, those situations are rare. Plainly, there is no ambiguity here; the Secretary has approved the construction of I-40 through Overton Park and has approved a specific design for the project. . . .

Moreover, there is an administrative record that allows the full, prompt review of the Secretary's action that is sought without additional delay which would result from having a remand to the Secretary.

That administrative record is not, however, before us. The lower courts based their review on the litigation affidavits that were presented. These affidavits were merely "post hoc" rationalizations, Burlington Truck Lines v. United States, 371 U.S. 156, 168-169 (1962), which have traditionally been found to be an inadequate basis for review. Burlington Truck Lines v. United States, *supra*; SEC v. Chenery Corp., 318 U.S. 80, 87 (1943). And they clearly do not constitute the "whole record" compiled by the agency: the basis for review required by §706 of the Administrative Procedure Act.

Thus it is necessary to remand this case to the District Court for plenary review of the Secretary's decision. That review is to be based on the full administrative record that was before the Secretary at the time he made his decision. But since the bare record may not disclose the factors that were considered or the Secretary's construction of the evidence it may be necessary for the District Court to require some explanation in order to determine if the Secretary acted within the scope of his authority and if the Secretary's action was justifiable under the applicable standard.

The court may require the administrative officials who participated in the decision to give testimony explaining their action. Of course, such inquiry into the mental processes of administrative decisionmakers is usually to be avoided. United States v. Morgan, 313 U.S. 409, 422 (1941). And where there are administrative findings that were made at the same time as the decision, as was the case in *Morgan*, there must be a strong showing of bad faith or improper behavior before such inquiry may be made. But here there are no such formal findings and it may be that the only way there can be effective judicial review is by examining the decisionmakers themselves. The District Court is not, however, required to make such an inquiry. It may be that the Secretary can prepare formal findings . . . that will provide an adequate explanation for his action. Such an explanation will, to some extent, be a "post hoc rationalization" and thus must be viewed critically. If the District Court decides that additional explanation is necessary, that court should consider which method will prove the most expeditious so that full review may be had as soon as possible.

Reversed and remanded.

MR. JUSTICE DOUGLAS took no part in the consideration or decision of this case.

[Separate opinions of JUSTICES BLACK and BLACKMUN omitted.]

NOTES AND QUESTIONS

1. *Should courts review highway location decisions?* Congress did not specifically provide for judicial review of highway location decisions by the Secretary of Transportation under the Federal-Aid Highway Act. Why do you suppose it did not? Why doesn't the Court infer from that congressional silence an intention not to permit judicial review?

What are the advantages and disadvantages of permitting courts to review decisions about the design and location of interstate highways? Notice the impressive list of I-40's supporters: the Memphis City Council, the Tennessee Highway Department, and the U.S. Department of Transportation. Should the courts be available to revisit a decision with that kind of backing, at the behest of a group of disgruntled local citizens?

On remand the district judge conducted a 27-day hearing in an attempt to determine the basis for Secretary Volpe's decision. Following the hearing, the court remanded the case to Volpe to decide whether a "feasible and prudent" alternative existed, as those statutory terms had been interpreted by the Supreme Court. Eventually, Volpe found that at least one such alternative existed, forcing the Tennessee Highway Department to redesign the highway. After years of wrangling between the state and federal highway agencies over various proposals to tunnel under Overton Park, the State finally threw in the towel in 1981, and asked that the proposed segment of I-40 through Memphis be dropped from the interstate highway system. The State returned to the City the 26 acres of Overton Park that it had taken anticipating the building of I-40 and converted to parkland acres of land in adjoining neighborhoods that had been cleared along the highway's proposed right of way. The strips of green space stand as mute testimony to the power of judicial review to stop a highway.

2. *Adjudication of "polycentric" issues.* The Secretary of Transportation had argued that the approval of a highway route was so "discretionary" as to be inappropriate for judicial review. His argument echoes a sentiment expressed by Professor Lon Fuller in a famous 1957 article, published posthumously in 1978. Lon L. Fuller, The Forms and Limits of Adjudication, 92 Harv. L. Rev. 353 (1978). Fuller argued that adjudication is inherently ill-equipped to settle "polycentric" problems. A polycentric problem, he said, is like a spider's web:

A pull on one strand will distribute tensions after a complicated pattern through-out the web as a whole. Doubling the original pull will, in all likelihood, not simply double each of the resulting tensions but will rather create a different complicated pattern of tensions.

Id. at 395. Examples of polycentric problems offered by Fuller include the division of a single collection of masterpieces bequeathed to two museums "in equal shares," the distribution of a fund of money for salary increases among all the workers in a textile mill, or the assignment of players to positions on a football team. These problems, Fuller maintained, can be solved only by either "managerial direction" or "reciprocal adjustment." They cannot be settled by "adjudication" ("presentation of proofs and reasoned arguments"), he claimed, because the adjudicator lacks both an intelligible principle to justify any particular outcome and sufficient breadth of vision or continuity of involvement to deal with secondary and tertiary impacts. *Id.* at 394-404.

In what sense was Secretary Volpe's decision "polycentric"? In what sense was it not? Is there a manageable role for courts to play in that decision?

In a retrospective look at the Overton Park controversy, Professor Peter Strauss offers a related critique. He is sharply critical of the Supreme Court for seeing its role as "a form of substantive politics," a role that it is ill-equipped to play and was not called for in the particular circumstances in the case. "Inviting judges to interfere with particular outcomes in the absence of constitutional or like instructions, simply on the grounds that political processes may have been inadequate, is inviting the whirlwind." Peter L. Strauss, Revisiting *Overton Park: Political and Judicial Controls over Administrative Actions Affecting the Community,* 39 UCLA L. Rev. 1251 (1992).

3. *The APA's "recipe" for judicial review.* Section 706 of the APA is Congress's most exhaustive pronouncement on "scope of review" — that is, the standards to be applied by courts upon reviewing administrative action. Section 706 contains a number of catchphrases describing either a judicial function (e.g., "decide all relevant questions of law") or the basis upon which a reviewing court may overturn agency action (e.g., "arbitrary" or "capricious"). The statutory language raises two questions. The first concerns applicability. Under what circumstances does each of these catchphrases apply? As Justice Marshall's opinion in *Overton Park* explains, the various catchphrases in §706 are not interchangeable: each has a distinct function. You should become intimately familiar with both §706 and the Supreme Court's interpretation of it, since legal battles over administrative action are waged over the meaning of its terms.

The second and more interesting question is whether the choice of standard really affects the outcome of such battles. When applying different standards of review, do courts examine different kinds of evidence, apply different criteria, or use different methods of "reasonableness"? Do different verbal formulations of the standard of review correspond with different degrees of judicial "deference" to the agency's judgment? Or, in the end, do all standards of review devolve into a judgment of "reasonableness"?

In attempting to answer these questions, it has long been customary to rely on the familiar distinction between questions of "fact" and "law" developed over the centuries by appellate courts in the context of reviewing trial court decisions. As a general matter, appellate courts are highly deferential to a jury's or trial judge's findings of fact—overturning those findings only if "clearly errone-ous"—while extending little or no deference to a trial judge's conclusions of law. In the context of judicial review of administrative agencies, however, the distinction between "fact" and "law" often proves especially difficult to make. Agencies are expected not only to find "facts" and interpret questions of "law," but also to make "policy" decisions that will have general, prospective applica-tion. Although the lines between fact and policy and between policy and law can be difficult to draw, the courts still find the distinctions among these catego-ries important. As you read the materials in this chapter, ask yourself whether the court's decision to frame agency action as "fact," "law," or "policy" actually dictates how intensive (or how deferential) review will be, and whether courts are consistent in making those judgments. Does the framing determine the out-come or the other way around?

2.   *The Basis for Judicial Review: Records and Reasons*

As we know from everyday experience, it is difficult, and often impossible, to "review" someone else's decision without knowing the basis and reasons for that decision. In *Overton Park*, for example, the Court observed that it would be difficult to determine whether Secretary Volpe's decision was "arbitrary or capri-cious" or whether the Overton Park route was the only "prudent" route, because, due to the lack of formal findings, it was difficult to determine what evidence or other considerations he had relied upon, or whether he had ignored crucial evidence tending to support an alternative decision.

Section 706 directs the court to "review the whole record or those parts of it cited by a party." What is the "record" in a case like *Overton Park*? By refusing Citizens' request for either formal administrative findings or de novo review, the Court effectively closed off the possibility of requiring a formal record at either the administrative or the judicial level. The Court noted that there is no legal requirement for such a record, as there would be in a "formal" adjudica-tion subject to §§556 and 557 of the APA. Would a formal record be helpful apart from court review? What is the difference between a formal record and the "whole record" that the Court directs the lower court to review? Without a formal record, the record consists of whatever information formed the basis for the decision. What are the bounds of that record? How is the reviewing court to determine that? What guidance does the Court give the district court on remand? If you were the district court judge, what would you do?

One possibility would be to ask Secretary Volpe, by written interrogatory or oral testimony, to give a more detailed explanation of his reasoning, per-haps coupled with production of the evidence and documents upon which he claimed to have relied. But Justice Marshall seems to discourage this option by noting that reviewing courts dislike "post hoc rationalizations" or probing the "mental processes" of decisionmakers. The authorities most often cited for those propositions are the *Chenery* and *Morgan* cases excerpted below.

SEC v. CHENERY CORP., 318 U.S. 80 (1943) (*CHENERY I*):   The SEC had ruled that the management of a public utility holding company undergoing restructuring could not convert (into voting shares of the new company) shares of the old company that they had purchased in anticipation of the reorganization. The only justification offered by the SEC for this ruling at the time of its order was an alleged principle of fiduciary duty applied by courts of equity. Later (at the time of litigation challenging its order), the Commission offered an additional justification for its order, this time based on the Public Utility Holding Company Act of 1935. The Supreme Court reversed and vacated the SEC's order. The Court said that the SEC's "fiduciary duty" argument misread the judicial precedents, and the Court refused to consider other justifications offered by the SEC based on the statute:

> The grounds upon which an administrative order must be judged are those upon which the record discloses that its action was based. . . . [W]here the correctness of [a] lower court's decision depends upon a determination of fact which only a jury could make but which has not been made, the appellate court cannot take the place of the jury. Like considerations govern review of administrative orders. If an order is valid only as a determination of policy or judgment which the agency alone is authorized to make and which it has not made, a judicial judgment cannot be made to do service for an administrative judgment.

UNITED STATES v. MORGAN, 313 U.S. 409 (1941) (*MORGAN IV*): The *Morgan* case was the fourth and final Supreme Court opinion in a saga worthy of Charles Dickens's Bleak House. The case grew out of a challenge to an order of the Secretary of Agriculture fixing the maximum rates for buying and selling livestock at the Kansas City stockyards. The order followed a lengthy hearing presided over by the Assistant Secretary. Petitioner Morgan challenged the Secretary's order, alleging that, according to "information and belief," the Secretary had never personally heard or examined any of the evidence or arguments. The district court struck the allegation as not stating a claim upon which relief could be granted. But the Supreme Court reversed, finding that the allegation, if it could be proved, would show a violation of the statutory right to a "full hearing." In the context of such a statute, Chief Justice Charles Evans Hughes decreed, "The one who decides must hear." Morgan v. United States, 298 U.S. 468, 481 (1936). Hughes made it clear, however, that "hear" merely means "consider [the] evidence and arguments," not literally "preside at the hearing," and that staff assistants may help the decisionmaker by digesting the voluminous record.

On remand from *Morgan I,* the district court allowed the Secretary to be interrogated about his personal role in the decision. Based on his testimony, the district court affirmed his order. On appeal, the Supreme Court reversed on unrelated grounds, but in the process uttered the famous dictum that "it was not the function of the court to probe the mental processes of the Secretary." Morgan v. United States, 304 U.S. 1, 18 (1938). After a third appeal, the Secretary issued a new rate order. Once again the order was challenged and once again he was personally interrogated, by deposition and at trial. This time, the Supreme Court made its disapproval emphatic:

> Over the Government's objection the district court authorized the market agencies to take the deposition of the Secretary. The Secretary thereupon appeared in person at the trial. He was questioned at length regarding the process by which he reached the conclusions of his order, including the manner and extent of his

study of the record and his consultation with subordinates. . . . [T]he Secretary should never have been subjected to this examination. The proceeding before the Secretary 'has a quality resembling that of a judicial proceeding'. Morgan v. United States, 298 U.S. 468, 480. . . . Just as a judge cannot be subjected to such a scrutiny . . . so the integrity of the administrative process must be equally respected.

NOTES AND QUESTIONS

1. *"Post hoc rationalizations."* Does the *Chenery* Court give an adequate justification for the doctrine disfavoring post hoc rationalizations? Is the analogy to appellate review of a jury finding apt? So long as it is the *agency* offering the post hoc rationalization, what is the problem?

Professor Kevin Stack has offered a constitutional justification for the *Chenery* rule. *See* Kevin M. Stack, The Constitutional Foundations of *Chenery*, 116 Yale L.J. 952 (2007). According to Professor Stack, *Chenery* supports a now-forgotten aspect of the nondelegation doctrine, that Congress must "condition[] the exercise of authority upon an agency's stating the grounds for its invocation of the statutory authority," *Id.* at 958. To Stack, "the nondelegation doctrine operates not merely to constrain the scope of discretion Congress may vest in others, but also to impede Congress from giving away its own prerogative to establish binding norms without providing justification for them." *Id.* Do you agree that the *Chenery* principle promotes values underlying the nondelegation doctrine? (For discussion of subsequent developments in the *Chenery* litigation, *see* Chapter IV, *infra*.) In looking at the contemporaneous (not "post hoc") reasons for administrative action, what sources may a court consult? What inquiries can be made?

2. *"Probing the mental processes" of administrative decisionmakers.* For 75 years after the *Morgan IV* decision, federal courts did not sanction "probing the mental processes" of an administrative decisionmaker "short of flagrant extremes." Florida Econ. Advisory Council v. FPC, 251 F.2d 643, 651-652 (D.C. Cir. 1957), *cert. denied*, 356 U.S. 959 (1958). Why not? What's wrong with "probing the mental processes" of administrative decisionmakers? Isn't that the best way to determine substantive compliance with the statutory mandate, at least when the statute expressly directs attention to certain factors? What are the risks of such inquiries? Will they discourage some types of beneficial decisions, allow delays inappropriately sought for strategic reasons, or interfere with efficient administration by distracting high-ranking officials from more important tasks? The deeply-ingrained judicial reluctance to inquire into official motivations has shown signs of fraying, with several district judges approving inquiries into official motivation. The Supreme Court responded to one such instance in Department of Commerce v. New York, 139 S. Ct. 2551 (2019), excerpted following the *State Farm* case, *infra*.

3. *The* Overton Park *remand.* Take another look at Justice Marshall's instructions to the district court on remand from the Court's ruling in *Overton Park*. Are they consistent with *Chenery* and *Morgan*? Should the decisions in those cases apply to the situation in *Overton Park*? Why? Does the aftermath of *Overton Park* (discussed in note 1 following the case) shed light on that question?

4. *The Court revisits the issue.* In Camp v. Pitts, 411 U.S. 138 (1973), the Supreme Court attempted to clarify the ambiguities left by its remand in *Overton Park*. At

issue in *Pitts* was the legal adequacy of a decision by the Comptroller of the Currency denying a national bank charter to the respondents. Finding the Comptroller's brief explanation for his decision "unacceptable," the court of appeals remanded the case with instructions for a trial de novo in which all parties could introduce evidence to supplement the administrative record. The Supreme Court reversed, holding that the failure to explain adequately the administrative decision did not warrant a de novo hearing. Instead, the proper "remedy was . . . as contemplated by *Overton Park*, to obtain from the agency, either through affidavits or testimony, such additional explanation of the reasons for the agency decision as may prove necessary." The Court added a "caveat," however:

> Unlike *Overton Park*, in the present case there was contemporaneous explanation of the agency decision. The explanation may have been curt, but it surely indicated the determinative reason for the final action taken: the finding that a new bank was an uneconomic venture in light of the banking needs and the banking services already available in the surrounding community. The validity of the Comptroller's action must, therefore, stand or fall on the propriety of that finding, judged, of course, by the appropriate standard of review. If that finding is not sustainable on the administrative record made, then the Comptroller's decision must be vacated and the matter remanded to him for further consideration.

411 U.S. at 143.

5. *De novo trial.* As the Supreme Court suggested in *Overton Park*, agency determinations of fact or policy are rarely subject to review by de novo judicial trial. You will recall that the Court listed two circumstances in which reviewing courts may engage in de novo trial: "when the action is adjudicatory in nature and the agency factfinding procedures are inadequate" and "when issues that were not before the agency are raised in a proceeding to enforce nonadjudicatory agency action."

The latter category is the most common. In a sense, all criminal statutes fall within this category. Because of the constitutional guarantee of a jury trial in criminal cases, we think of "de novo" judicial trial as the exclusive mode of "finding facts" in criminal cases. Prosecutorial agencies like the Justice Department do, of course, make determinations of "fact" or "policy" in the course of investigating an alleged criminal violation and deciding whether to initiate a formal prosecution. But those determinations *as such* receive absolutely no weight or deference at the subsequent criminal trial. Indeed, the notion of jury trial in criminal cases is so deeply ingrained in our legal consciousness, we do not think of a criminal trial as a form of judicial "review" of an administrative action at all. Yet, in a sense, that is exactly what it is.

Similarly, Congress sometimes expressly provides for de novo judicial enforcement of "civil" regulatory statutes. A conspicuous example is the Equal Employment Opportunity Act, 42 U.S.C. §2000e-5. If the Equal Employment Opportunity Commission (EEOC) concludes that an employment discrimination complaint has merit and is unable to secure consensual conciliation, it may bring a civil action in federal district court against the offending party. The district court conducts a trial de novo. As in the criminal context, both the agency and the respondent introduce evidence and make arguments before the court, and the court finds the "facts" based exclusively on the testimonial and documentary record developed at trial. Again, we are accustomed to think of this merely as direct judicial enforcement, not "review" of the agency's pre-enforcement actions.

Cases falling within the first of the Supreme Court's two categories in *Overton Park,* by contrast, are now extremely rare. At one time, the Supreme Court suggested that the Constitution itself might require courts to re-determine de novo certain findings of "jurisdictional" or "constitutional" fact made by administrative agencies. Crowell v. Benson, 285 U.S. 22 (1932) (discussed in Chapter VI, *infra*); Ohio Valley Water Co. v. Ben Avon Borough, 253 U.S. 287 (1920); Ng Fung Ho v. White, 259 U.S. 276 (1922). Recognizing that this doctrine could destroy the putative advantages of administrative adjudication, however, the Supreme Court quietly abandoned the doctrine in the 1930s. *See* St. Joseph Stock Yards Co. v. United States, 298 U.S. 38 (1936); Henry P. Monaghan, Constitutional Fact Review, 85 Colum. L. Rev. 229, 247-263 (1985).

The Supreme Court has not interpreted the Seventh Amendment's guarantee of jury trial in "suits at common law" to apply to civil regulatory statutes (*see, e.g.,* Atlas Roofing Co. v. Occupational Safety & Health Review Commn., 430 U.S. 442 (1977), discussed *infra*. Therefore, the courts have been reluctant to interpret congressional ambiguity or silence in civil regulatory statutes as calling for trial de novo. As *Overton Park* itself illustrates, reviewing courts go to great lengths to remand to the agency to augment the administrative "record," rather than engage in factfinding at the judicial level.

B.   ARBITRARY AND CAPRICIOUS REVIEW OF QUESTIONS OF FACT OR POLICY

The principal standard for reviewing administrative determinations of fact or policy is the so-called "arbitrary and capricious" standard codified in APA §706(2)(A). As then-Judge Scalia once said: "Paragraph (A) of subsection 706(2) . . . is a catch-all, picking up administrative misconduct not covered by the other more specific paragraphs." Association of Data Processing Serv. Orgs., Inc. v. Board of Governors, 745 F.2d 677 (D.C. Cir. 1984). Although §706(2)(A) actually contains four separate verbal components—"arbitrary," "capricious," "abuse of discretion," and "otherwise not in accordance with law"—the courts have not struggled very hard to give separate content to these four expressions. Just about everyone understands §706(2)(A) to embrace a single test of "arbitrariness." Unlike the "substantial evidence" and "unwarranted by the facts" tests, the "arbitrary and capricious" test may be applied to *any* agency action. As a practical matter, however, it has been applied almost exclusively to determinations *not* subject to "substantial evidence" review, such as informal rulemakings and informal adjudications.

1.   *The Evolving Understanding: From "No Reasonable Ground" to "Hard Look" Review*

At one time most commentators regarded the "arbitrary and capricious" standard of review as highly deferential. One basis for this view was the famous case of Pacific States Box & Basket Co. v. White, 296 U.S. 176 (1935). The case involved a challenge to a rule promulgated by the Oregon Division of Plant Industry setting standards for raspberry and strawberry boxes. The manufacturer of the nonconforming boxes claimed that the rule violated its right of substantive due process because the rule's insistence on a single, uniform standard was irrational. Although the agency made no specific factual findings about the need for a uniform standard, the Supreme Court upheld the rule: "Where the regulation is within the scope of authority legally delegated, the presumption of the existence of facts justifying its specific exercise attaches alike to statutes . . . and to orders of administrative bodies." Similarly, in American Trucking Assns. v. United States, 344 U.S. 298, 314-315 (1953), the Court stated that a claim of arbitrariness must mean that the agency "had no reasonable ground for the exercise of judgment." As recently as 1967, the Court declared that the substantial evidence test affords "a considerably more generous review than the arbitrary and capricious test." Abbott Laboratories v. Gardner, 387 U.S. 136, 143 (1967).

This relaxed view of "arbitrary and capricious" review reflects a permissive judicial attitude toward administrative policymakers. The proliferation of administrative agencies emerging from the New Deal reflected a faith that modern social and economic problems required an expert's attention: "Those who rationalized the New Deal's regulatory initiatives regarded expertise and specialization as the particular strengths of the administrative process." James O. Freedman, Expertise and the Administrative Process, 28 Admin. L. Rev. 363, 364 (1976). That expertise was not shared by judges, since it "springs only from that continuity of interest, that ability and desire to devote fifty-two weeks a year, year after year, to a particular problem." *Id., quoting* James M. Landis, The Administrative Process 23 (1933). The same point was made more memorably by Judge Harold Leventhal in a decision rejecting a challenge to a Civil Aeronautics Board policy restricting a particular type of shipment to cargo-only carriers: "It is the kind of issue where a month of experience will be worth a year of hearings." American Airlines, Inc. v. Civil Aeronautics Bd., 359 F.2d 624, 632-633 (D.C. Cir.), *cert. denied,* 385 U.S. 843 (1966).

While one continues to encounter similar statements in judicial opinions, the faith in administrative expertise described by Freedman began to wane in the late 1960s. Disaffection with the performance of administrative agencies led many observers to become increasingly skeptical of their claims of expertise. All too often, these critics claimed, agencies failed to adopt any coherent "policy" at all, merely waffling back and forth in response to shifting political winds. Or, if they did adopt a coherent policy, it was as likely to make things worse as better. Naturally, the diagnoses differed from critic to critic. To Marver Bernstein the explanation was age: as agencies age, he said, they atrophy and become "captured" by the industries they regulate. Marver Bernstein, Regulating Business by Independent Commission (1955). To Theodore Lowi, the fault lay at Congress's doorstep for failing to give agencies clear legislative guidance. Theodore Lowi, The End of Liberalism (1969). To Ralph Nader, the cause was, at least in large part, bureaucratic incompetence and venality. Mark Green & Ralph Nader, Economic Regulation vs. Competition: Uncle Sam the Monopoly Man, 82 Yale L.J. 871 (1973). In contemporary debates over the appropriate size and scope of government, one often hears complaints about imperial bureaucracies run amok and the need to rein in administrative power.

For all of these reasons, rising disaffection with administrative policymaking has affected judicial attitudes over time. In contrast to the diffident prose of cases like *Pacific States,* courts began flexing their rhetorical muscles. A particularly famous example is the following passage from Greater Boston Television Corp. v. FCC, 444 F.2d 841, 851-852 (D.C. Cir. 1970), *cert. denied,* 403 U.S. 923 (1971), an opinion by the same Judge Leventhal who four years earlier had waxed so eloquent on agency expertise:

> The function of the court is to assure that the agency has given reasoned consideration to all the material facts and issues. This calls for insistence that the agency articulate with reasonable clarity its reasons for decision, and identify the significance of the crucial facts, a course that tends to assure that the agency's policies effectuate general standards, applied without unreasonable discrimination. . . .
>
> Its supervisory function calls on the court to intervene not merely in case of procedural inadequacies, or bypassing of the mandate in the legislative charter, but more broadly if the court becomes aware, especially from a combination of danger signals, that the agency has not really taken a "hard look" at the salient problems, and has not genuinely engaged in reasoned decision-making. . . . If satisfied that the agency has taken a hard look at the issues with the use of reasons and standards, the court will uphold its findings, though of less than ideal clarity, if the agency's path may reasonably be discerned, though of course the court must not be left to guess as to the agency's findings or reasons.
>
> The process thus combines judicial supervision with a salutary principle of judicial restraint, an awareness that agencies and courts together constitute a "partnership" in furtherance of the public interest, and are "collaborative instrumentalities of justice." The court is in a real sense part of the total administrative process, and not a hostile stranger to the office of first instance. This collaborative spirit does not undercut, it rather underlines the court's rigorous insistence on the need for conjunction of articulated standards and reflective findings, in furtherance of even-handed application of law, rather than impermissible whim, improper influence, or misplaced zeal. Reasoned decision promotes results in the public interest by requiring the agency to focus on the values served by its decision, and hence releasing the clutch of unconscious preference and irrelevant prejudice. It furthers the broad public interest of enabling the public to repose confidence in the process as well as the judgments of its decision-makers.

Thus, a "new era" of aggressive judicial review was supposedly launched. *See* Environmental Defense Fund v. Ruckelshaus, 439 F.2d 584, 597 (D.C. Cir. 1971) (Bazelon, C.J.).

"Hard look" rhetoric continues to pervade judicial decisions. *See, e.g.,* Morris Communications, Inc. v. FCC, 566 F.3d 184, 190 (D.C. Cir. 2009). While "hard look" usually refers to the agency's obligation to consider a matter carefully before acting, the D.C. Circuit has occasionally signaled that reviewing courts should take a "hard look" at what agencies do:

> As originally articulated the words 'hard look' described the agency's responsibility and not the court's. However, the phrase subsequently evolved to connote the rigorous standard of judicial review applied to increasingly utilized informal rulemaking proceedings or to other decisions made upon less than a full trial-type record.

National Lime Assn. v. EPA, 627 F.2d 416, 451 n.126 (D.C. Cir. 1980) (footnote omitted).

"Hard look" review has been blamed for many of administrative agencies' ills including the general ineffectiveness of regulation, and the reluctance of agencies to engage in informal rulemaking, lest their handiwork be struck down under "hard look" review. It has also been attacked as inconsistent with the level of deference that courts should pay to agency policy decisions, especially when technical expertise or political considerations are involved.

If the D.C. Circuit led the "hard look" revolution, did the Supreme Court follow? In *Overton Park,* the Supreme Court seemed to signal its intent to join the bandwagon. Although the Court did not use the words "hard look," and conceded that the standard of review under the "arbitrary and capricious" test is "a narrow one," the Court stated that the judicial "inquiry into the facts is to be searching and careful." Because the Court found that the Secretary of Transportation had misinterpreted the statute, the Court did not have occasion to demonstrate what it meant by a "searching and careful" review. That occasion did arise, however, a few years later in yet another celebrated case arising from the U.S. Department of Transportation.

MOTOR VEHICLE MANUFACTURERS ASSN. v. STATE FARM MUTUAL AUTOMOBILE INSURANCE CO.
463 U.S. 29 (1983)

JUSTICE WHITE delivered the opinion of the Court.

[T]he National Traffic and Motor Vehicle Safety Act of 1966 (Act), 80 Stat. 718, as amended, 15 U.S.C. §1381 *et seq.* (1976 ed. and Supp. V) . . . , created for the purpose of "reduc[ing] traffic accidents and deaths and injuries to persons resulting from traffic accidents," 15 U.S.C. §1381, directs the Secretary of Transportation or his delegate to issue motor vehicle safety standards that "shall be practicable, shall meet the need for motor vehicle safety, and shall be stated in objective terms." 15 U.S.C. §1392(a) (1976 ed., Supp. V). In issuing these standards, the Secretary is directed to consider "relevant available motor vehicle safety data," whether the proposed standard "is reasonable, practicable and appropriate" for the particular type of motor vehicle, and the "extent to which such standards will contribute to carrying out the purposes" of the Act. 15 U.S.C. §§1392(f)(1), (3), (4).[3]

The Act also authorizes judicial review under the provisions of the Administrative Procedure Act (APA), 5 U.S.C. §706, of all "orders establishing, amending, or revoking a Federal motor vehicle safety standard," 15 U.S.C. §1392(b). Under this authority, we review today whether NHTSA acted arbitrarily and capriciously in revoking the requirement in Motor Vehicle Safety Standard 208 that new motor vehicles produced after September 1982 be equipped with passive restraints to protect the safety of the occupants of the vehicle in the event of a collision. . . .

---

3. The Secretary's general authority to promulgate safety standards under the Act has been delegated to the Administrator of the National Highway Traffic Safety Administration (NHTSA). 49 CFR §1.50(a) (1982). This opinion will use the terms NHTSA and agency interchangeably when referring to the National Highway Traffic Safety Administration, the Department of Transportation, and the Secretary of Transportation.

I

The regulation whose rescission is at issue bears a complex and convoluted history. Over the course of approximately 60 rulemaking notices, the requirement has been imposed, amended, rescinded, reimposed, and now rescinded again.

As originally issued by the Department of Transportation in 1967, Standard 208 simply required the installation of seatbelts in all automobiles. 32 Fed. Reg. 2415. It soon became apparent that the level of seatbelt use was too low to reduce traffic injuries to an acceptable level. The Department therefore began consideration of "passive occupant restraint systems"—devices that do not depend for their effectiveness upon any action taken by the occupant except that necessary to operate the vehicle. Two types of automatic crash protection emerged: automatic seatbelts and airbags. . . . The lifesaving potential of these devices was immediately recognized, and in 1977, after substantial on-the-road experience with both devices, it was estimated by NHTSA that passive restraints could prevent approximately 12,000 deaths and over 100,000 serious injuries annually. 42 Fed. Reg. 34298.

In 1969, the Department formally proposed a standard requiring the installation of passive restraints, 34 Fed. Reg. 11148, thereby commencing a lengthy series of proceedings. . . .

[After protracted administrative and legislative proceedings, in 1977 Transportation Secretary Brock Adams] issued a new mandatory passive restraint regulation, known as Modified Standard 208. 42 Fed. Reg. 34289 (1977); 49 CFR §571.208 (1978). The Modified Standard mandated the phasing in of passive restraints beginning with large cars in model year 1982 and extending to all cars by model year 1984. The two principal systems that would satisfy the Standard were airbags and passive belts; the choice of which system to install was left to the manufacturers. In Pacific Legal Foundation v. Department of Transportation, 593 F.2d 1338 [D.C. Cir.], *cert. denied,* 444 U.S. 830 (1979), the Court of Appeals upheld Modified Standard 208 as a rational, nonarbitrary regulation consistent with the agency's mandate under the Act. The Standard also survived scrutiny by Congress, which did not exercise its authority under the legislative veto provision of the 1974 Amendments [to the Act].

Over the next several years, the automobile industry geared up to comply with Modified Standard 208. . . . In February 1981, however, Secretary of Transportation Andrew Lewis reopened the rulemaking due to changed economic circumstances and, in particular, the difficulties of the automobile industry. . . . After receiving written comments and holding public hearings, NHTSA issued a final rule (Notice 25) that rescinded the passive restraint requirement contained in Modified Standard 208.

II

In a statement explaining the rescission, NHTSA maintained that it was no longer able to find, as it had in 1977, that the automatic restraint requirement would produce significant safety benefits. Notice 25, *id.,* at 53419. This judgment reflected not a change of opinion on the effectiveness of the technology, but a change in plans by the automobile industry. In 1977, the agency had assumed that airbags would be installed in 60% of all new cars and automatic seatbelts in 40%. By 1981 it became apparent that automobile manufacturers planned to install the automatic seatbelts in approximately 99% of the new cars. For this reason, the lifesaving potential of airbags would not be realized. Moreover, it now appeared that the overwhelming majority of passive belts planned to be installed by manufacturers could be detached easily and left that way permanently. Passive belts, once detached, then required "the same type of affirmative action that is the stumbling block to obtaining high usage levels of manual belts." *Id.*, at 53421. For this reason, the agency concluded that there was no longer a basis for reliably predicting that the Standard would lead to any significant increased usage of restraints at all.

In view of the possibly minimal safety benefits, the automatic restraint requirement no longer was reasonable or practicable in the agency's view. The requirement would require approximately $1 billion to implement and the agency did not believe it would be reasonable to impose such substantial costs on manufacturers and consumers without more adequate assurance that sufficient safety benefits would accrue. In addition, NHTSA concluded that automatic restraints might have an adverse effect on the public's attitude toward safety. Given the high expense and limited benefits of detachable belts, NHTSA feared that many consumers would regard the Standard as an instance of ineffective regulation, adversely affecting the public's view of safety regulation and, in particular, "poisoning . . . popular sentiment toward efforts to improve occupant restraint systems in the future." *Id.*, at 53424.

State Farm Mutual Automobile Insurance Co. and the National Association of Independent Insurers filed petitions for review of NHTSA's rescission of the passive restraint Standard. The United States Court of Appeals for the District of Columbia Circuit held that the agency's rescission of the passive restraint requirement was arbitrary and capricious. 680 F.2d 206 [D.C. Cir. 1982]. . . .

On November 8, 1982, we granted certiorari, 459 U.S. 987. . . .

III

Unlike the Court of Appeals, we do not find the appropriate scope of judicial review to be the "most troublesome question" in these cases. Both the Act and the 1974 Amendments concerning occupant crash protection standards indicate that motor vehicle safety standards are to be promulgated under the informal rulemaking procedures of the Administrative Procedure Act. 5 U.S.C. §553. The agency's action in promulgating such standards therefore may be set aside if found to be "arbitrary, capricious, an abuse of discretion, or otherwise not in accordance with law." . . .

We believe that the rescission or modification of an occupant-protection standard is subject to the same test.

Petitioner Motor Vehicle Manufacturers Association (MVMA) disagrees, contending that the rescission of an agency rule should be judged by the same standard a court would use to judge an agency's refusal to promulgate a rule in the first place—a standard petitioner believes considerably narrower than the traditional arbitrary-and-capricious test. We reject this view. The Act expressly equates orders "revoking" and "establishing" safety standards; neither that Act nor the APA suggests that revocations are to be treated as refusals to promulgate standards. Petitioner's view would render meaningless Congress' authorization for judicial review of orders revoking safety rules. Moreover, the revocation of an extant regulation is substantially different than a failure to act. Revocation constitutes a reversal of the agency's former views as to the proper course. . . . Accordingly, an agency changing its course by rescinding a rule is obligated to supply a reasoned analysis for the change beyond that which may be required when an agency does not act in the first instance.

In so holding, we fully recognize that "[r]egulatory agencies do not establish rules of conduct to last forever," American Trucking Assns., Inc. v. Atchison, T. & S.F.R. Co., 387 U.S. 397, 416 (1967), and that an agency must be given ample latitude to "adapt their rules and policies to the demands of changing circumstances." Permian Basin Area Rate Cases, 390 U.S. 747, 784 (1968). But the forces of change do not always or necessarily point in the direction of deregulation. In the abstract, there is no more reason to presume that changing circumstances require the rescission of prior action, instead of a revision in or even the extension of current regulation. . . . While the removal of a regulation may not entail the monetary expenditures and other costs of enacting a new standard, and, accordingly, it may be easier for an agency to justify a deregulatory action, the direction in which an agency chooses to move does not alter the standard of judicial review established by law. . . .

The scope of review under the "arbitrary and capricious" standard is narrow and a court is not to substitute its judgment for that of the agency. Nevertheless, the agency must examine the relevant data and articulate a satisfactory explanation for its action including a "rational connection between the facts found and the choice made." Burlington Truck Lines, Inc. v. U.S., 371 U.S. 156, 168 (1962). . . . Normally, an agency rule would be arbitrary and capricious if the agency has relied on factors which Congress has not intended it to consider, entirely failed to consider an important aspect of the problem, offered an explanation for its decision that runs counter to the evidence before the agency, or is so implausible that it could not be ascribed to a difference in view or the product of agency expertise. . . .

V

The ultimate question before us is whether NHTSA's rescission of the passive restraint requirement of Standard 208 was arbitrary and capricious. We conclude, as did the Court of Appeals, that it was. We also conclude, but for somewhat different reasons, that further consideration of the issue by the agency is therefore required. We deal separately with the rescission as it applies to airbags and as it applies to seatbelts.

A

The first and most obvious reason for finding the rescission arbitrary and capricious is that NHTSA apparently gave no consideration whatever to modifying the Standard to require that airbag technology be utilized. Standard 208 sought to achieve automatic crash protection by requiring automobile manufacturers to install either of two passive restraint devices: airbags or automatic seatbelts. There was no suggestion in the long rulemaking process that led to Standard 208 that if only one of these options were feasible, no passive restraint standard should be promulgated. . . .

The agency has now determined that the detachable automatic belts will not attain anticipated safety benefits because so many individuals will detach the mechanism. Even if this conclusion were acceptable in its entirety, . . . standing alone it would not justify any more than an amendment of Standard 208 to disallow compliance by means of the one technology which will not provide effective passenger protection. It does not cast doubt on the need for a passive restraint standard or upon the efficacy of airbag technology. . . .

At the very least this alternative way of achieving the objectives of the Act should have been addressed and adequate reasons given for its abandonment. . . .

Although the agency did not address the mandatory airbags option and the Court of Appeals noted that "airbags seem to have none of the problems that NHTSA identified in passive seatbelts," 680 F.2d, at 237, petitioners recite a number of difficulties that they believe would be posed by a mandatory airbag standard. These range from questions concerning the installation of airbags in small cars to that of adverse public reaction. But these are not the agency's reasons for rejecting a mandatory airbag standard. Not having discussed the possibility, the agency submitted no reasons at all. The short—and sufficient—answer to petitioners' submission is that the courts may not accept appellate counsel's post hoc rationalizations for agency action. . . .

B

Although the issue is closer, we also find that the agency was too quick to dismiss the safety benefits of automatic seatbelts. NHTSA's critical finding was that, in light of the industry's plans to install readily detachable passive belts, it could not reliably predict "even a 5 percentage point increase as the minimum level of expected usage increase." 46 Fed. Reg. 53423 (1981). The Court of Appeals rejected this finding because there is "not one iota" of evidence that Modified Standard 208 will fail to increase nationwide seatbelt use by at least 13 percentage points, the level of increased usage necessary for the Standard to justify its cost. . . .

We start with the accepted ground that if used, seatbelts unquestionably would save many thousands of lives and would prevent tens of thousands of crippling injuries. . . .

We move next to the fact that there is no direct evidence in support of the agency's finding that detachable automatic belts cannot be predicted to yield a substantial increase in usage. The empirical evidence on the record, consisting of surveys of drivers of automobiles equipped with passive belts, reveals more than a doubling of the usage rate experienced with manual belts.[16] Much

---

16. Between 1975 and 1980, Volkswagen sold approximately 350,000 Rabbits equipped with detachable passive seatbelts that were guarded by an ignition interlock. General Motors sold 8,000 1978 and 1979 Chevettes with a similar system, but it eliminated the ignition interlock on the 13,000 Chevettes sold in 1980. NHTSA found that belt usage in the Rabbits averaged 34% for manual belts and 84% for passive belts. RIA, at IV-52, App. 108. For the 1978-1979 Chevettes, NHTSA calculated 34% usage for manual belts and 72% for passive belts. On 1980 Chevettes, the agency found these figures to be 31% for manual belts and 70% for passive belts. *Ibid.*

of the agency's rulemaking statement—and much of the controversy in this case—centers on the conclusions that should be drawn from these studies. The agency maintained that the doubling of seatbelt usage in these studies could not be extrapolated to an across-the-board mandatory standard because the passive seatbelts were guarded by ignition interlocks and purchasers of the tested cars are somewhat atypical. Respondents insist these studies demonstrate that Modified Standard 208 will substantially increase seatbelt usage. We believe that it is within the agency's discretion to pass upon the generalizability of these field studies. This is precisely the type of issue which rests within the expertise of NHTSA, and upon which a reviewing court must be most hesitant to intrude.

But accepting the agency's view of the field tests on passive restraints indicates only that there is no reliable real-world experience that usage rates will substantially increase. To be sure, NHTSA opines that "it cannot reliably predict even a 5 percentage point increase as the minimum level of expected increased usage." Notice 25, 46 Fed. Reg. 53423 (1981). But this and other statements that passive belts will not yield substantial increases in seatbelt usage apparently take no account of the critical difference between detachable automatic belts and current manual belts. A detached passive belt does require an affirmative act to reconnect it, but—unlike a manual seatbelt—the passive belt, once reattached, will continue to function automatically unless again disconnected. Thus, inertia—a factor which the agency's own studies have found significant in explaining the current low usage rates for seatbelts—works in *favor* of, not *against*, use of the protective device. Since 20% to 50% of motorists currently wear seatbelts on some occasions, there would seem to be grounds to believe that seatbelt use by occasional users will be substantially increased by the detachable passive belts. Whether this is in fact the case is a matter for the agency to decide, but it must bring its expertise to bear on the question. . . .

The agency also failed to articulate a basis for not requiring nondetachable belts under Standard 208. It is argued that the concern of the agency with the easy detachability of the currently favored design would be readily solved by a continuous passive belt, which allows the occupant to "spool out" the belt and create the necessary slack for easy extrication from the vehicle. The agency did not separately consider the continuous belt option, but treated it together with the ignition interlock device in a category it titled "Option of Adopting Use-Compelling Features." 46 Fed. Reg. 53424 (1981). The agency was concerned that use-compelling devices would "complicate the extrication of [an] occupant from his or her car." *Ibid.* "[T]o require that passive belts contain use-compelling features," the agency observed, "could be counterproductive [given] widespread, latent and irrational fear in many members of the public that they could be trapped by the seat belt after a crash." *Ibid.* . . .

By failing to analyze the continuous seatbelts option in its own right, the agency has failed to offer the rational connection between facts and judgment required to pass muster under the arbitrary-and-capricious standard. We agree with the Court of Appeals that NHTSA did not suggest that the emergency release mechanisms used in nondetachable belts are any less effective for emergency egress than the buckle release system used in detachable belts. In 1978, when General Motors obtained the agency's approval to install a continuous passive belt, it assured the agency that nondetachable belts with spool releases were as safe as detachable belts with buckle releases. . . . While the agency is entitled to change its view on the acceptability of continuous passive belts, it is obligated to explain its reasons for doing so. . . .

VI

"An agency's view of what is in the public interest may change, either with or without a change in circumstances. But an agency changing its course must supply a reasoned analysis. . . ." Greater Boston Television Corp. v. FCC, 444 F.2d 841, 852 [D.C. Cir. 1970] (footnote omitted), *cert. denied*, 403 U.S. 923 (1971). We do not accept all of the reasoning of the Court of Appeals but we do conclude that the agency has failed to supply the requisite "reasoned analysis" in this case. Accordingly, we vacate the judgment of the Court of Appeals and remand the cases to that court with directions to remand the matter to the NHTSA. . . .

JUSTICE REHNQUIST, with whom THE CHIEF JUSTICE, JUSTICE POWELL, and JUSTICE O'CONNOR join, concurring in part and dissenting in part. . . .

I agree that, since the airbag and continuous spool automatic seatbelt were explicitly approved in the Standard the agency was rescinding, the agency should explain why it declined to leave those requirements intact. In this case, the agency gave no explanation at all. Of course, if the agency can provide a rational explanation, it may adhere to its decision to rescind the entire Standard.

I do not believe, however, that NHTSA's view of detachable automatic seatbelts was arbitrary and capricious. The agency adequately explained its decision to rescind the Standard insofar as it was satisfied by detachable belts. . . .

The agency acknowledged that there would probably be some increase in belt usage, but concluded that the increase would be small and not worth the cost of mandatory detachable automatic belts. 46 Fed. Reg. 53421-53423 (1981). The agency's obligation is to articulate a "'rational connection between the facts found and the choice made.'" . . . I believe it has met this standard.

The agency explicitly stated that it will increase its educational efforts in an attempt to promote public understanding, acceptance, and use of passenger restraint systems. 46 Fed. Reg. 53425 (1981). It also stated that it will "initiate efforts with automobile manufacturers to ensure that the public will have [automatic crash protection] technology available. If this does not succeed, the agency will consider regulatory action to assure that the last decade's enormous advances in crash protection technology will not be lost." *Id.*, at 53426.

The agency's changed view of the standard seems to be related to the election of a new President of a different political party. It is readily apparent that the responsible members of one administration may consider public resistance and uncertainties to be more important than do their counterparts in a previous administration. A change in administration brought about by the people casting their votes is a perfectly reasonable basis for an executive agency's reappraisal of the costs and benefits of its programs and regulations. As long as the agency remains within the bounds established by Congress,* it is entitled to

---

* Of course, a new administration may not refuse to enforce laws of which it does not approve, or to ignore statutory standards in carrying out its regulatory functions. But in this case, as the Court correctly concludes, . . . Congress has not required the agency to require passive restraints.

assess administrative records and evaluate priorities in light of the philosophy of the administration.

NOTES AND QUESTIONS

1. *The test for "arbitrariness."* Recall that in *Overton Park*, the Court said that, in applying the arbitrary-capricious standard of review, the reviewing court "must consider whether the decision was based on a consideration of the relevant factors and whether there was clear error of judgment." Notice how Justice White, at the end of Part III of his opinion, has elaborated the test for arbitrariness from those two questions into four questions. Is this just a rhetorical change, or a substantive one, in the test for arbitrariness? Which components of White's four-part test did NHTSA flunk?

2. *Consideration of alternative regulatory approaches.* The Court faults NHTSA for failing to consider an all-airbag option. In its published statement accompanying the order rescinding Modified Standard 208, NHTSA stated that air bags were "inadequately understood" by the public, that the cost of air bags would be "substantially higher" than the estimated $89 per-car incremental cost of automatic belts, that "some large insurance companies do not now offer discounts" on automobile insurance premiums to owners of cars equipped with air bags, and that making current users of manual belts pay for passive restraints that afford them "no additional safety protection" would be inequitable. In view of these statements, is the Court being fair to the agency on this point?

The Court also criticizes NHTSA for "failing to analyze the continuous seatbelts option in its own right." Is that a fair criticism?

Why must the agency consider the all-airbag and continuous seatbelt options? There are presumably hundreds of "options" for reducing the number of automobile collisions or the severity of injuries to occupants in the event of a collision. Does the Court provide the agency with any guidance on which of these options the agency must consider?

3. *How relevant is the regulatory philosophy of a new administration?* Justice Rehnquist states that the agency's "changed view of the standard seems to be related to the election of a new President." Indeed, Modified Standard 208 had been issued during the Carter Administration. During his campaign against Jimmy Carter, Ronald Reagan had criticized the Carter Administration for adopting various macroeconomic, trade, and regulatory policies that had severely injured the American automobile industry. Promptly after taking office in January 1981, President Reagan appointed a cabinet-level task force to examine the problems of the industry, chaired by Vice President George H.W. Bush. Based on the task force report, Reagan issued a 67-page booklet entitled "Actions to Help the U.S. Auto Industry." The booklet contained proposals for the rescission, revision, or re-examination of 34 NHTSA and EPA regulations. The booklet claimed that adoption of the proposals would save the industry $1.3 billion over five years. Re-examination of Modified Standard 208 led NHTSA's list. Three days after the White House issued the booklet, NHTSA published a notice announcing 17 proposed rulemaking actions, including modification of the passive restraint standard. Does this history have any relevance to the question of whether the rescission of Standard 208 was "arbitrary or capricious"? Is

it evidence of "public resistance" to passive restraints? Is it evidence of the relative weights that the agency should assign to the costs and benefits of passive restraints?

Every new administration tries to implement its policy prerogatives; indeed, some might argue that this is both natural and defensible: elections have consequences. But does the deregulatory "philosophy" of the new administration provide a legally relevant justification for the rescission? Professor Kathryn Watts apparently thinks it should. She argues that "what count as 'valid' reasons under arbitrary and capricious review should be expanded to include certain political influences from the President, other executive officials, and members of Congress, so long as the political influences are openly and transparently disclosed in the agency's rulemaking record." Kathryn A. Watts, Proposing a Place for Politics in Arbitrary and Capricious Review, 119 Yale L.J. 2, 8 (2009). How would courts operationalize this idea? By requiring agencies to include in their rulemaking dockets their conversations with various officials? And how should a court determine an administration's regulatory "philosophy"? By reference to the President's executive orders, speeches, or tweets?

In *State Farm*, was Justice Rehnquist arguing in favor of more deregulation? More specifically, had Justice Rehnquist's view prevailed, would automakers have had more or fewer options for meeting the passive restraint requirement?

4. *The evolution of the passive restraint standard.* Following the Supreme Court's decision in *State Farm*, NHTSA adopted a rule requiring the installation of passive restraints, beginning in April 1989, unless states representing at least two-thirds of the American population had adopted laws requiring the use of seat belts. Many states adopted such laws. In 1991, however, Congress mooted the issue by enacting legislation making air bags mandatory beginning with 1996 models. Pub. L. No. 102-240 §2508.

5. *Arbitrary and capricious review of decisions resting on "prediction" and "judgment."* According to one observer, *State Farm* signals a wholehearted embrace of "hard look" review by the Supreme Court. Cass R. Sunstein, Deregulation and the Hard-Look Doctrine, 1983 Sup. Ct. Rev. 177. Do you agree? Before answering, consider two roughly contemporaneous decisions by the Court: Federal Communications Commission v. National Citizens Comm. for Broadcasting, 436 U.S. 775 (1978) (*NCCB*), and Baltimore Gas & Elec. Co. v. NRDC, 462 U.S. 87 (1983). *NCCB* involved a challenge to an FCC rule prospectively prohibiting daily newspapers from obtaining licenses to operate radio or television stations in the market area served by the newspaper. The FCC issued the rule under its statutory authority to license broadcasters in "the public interest, convenience, and necessity." In its rule, the FCC expressly refused, however, to apply its new policy to require divestiture of most existing newspaper-broadcast combinations. The NCCB and the Justice Department challenged the decision to "grandfather" existing combinations as arbitrary and capricious. In upholding this aspect of the rule, the Supreme Court had this to say:

> The Court of Appeals' final basis for concluding that the Commission acted arbitrarily in not giving controlling weight to its divestiture policy was the Court's finding that the rulemaking record did not adequately "disclose the extent to which divestiture would actually threaten" the [Commission's policy of achieving "the

best practicable service to the public"]. . . . However, to the extent that factual determinations were involved in the Commission's decision to "grandfather" most existing combinations, they were primarily of a judgmental or predictive nature—e.g.,
whether a divestiture requirement would result in trading of stations with out-of-
town owners; whether new owners would perform as well as existing cross-owners,
either in the short run or in the long run; whether losses to existing owners would
result from forced sales; whether such losses would discourage future investment
in quality programming; and whether new owners would have sufficient working
capital to finance local programming. In such circumstances complete factual support in the record for the Commission's judgment or prediction is not possible or
required; "a forecast of the direction in which future public interest lies necessarily
involves deductions based on the expert knowledge of the agency."

436 U.S. at 813-814, *quoting* FPC v. Transcontinental Gas Pipe Line Corp., 365
U.S. 1, 29 (1961).

   Baltimore Gas involved a Nuclear Regulatory Commission rule stating that,
in conducting cost-benefit analyses for determining the environmental impact
of future nuclear power plants, it would assume "zero release" of spent nuclear
fuel. Even though no such "zero-release" method of waste storage was then in
use, the commission predicted that a safe method would be found before the
need arose to store spent radioactive fuel from any plant to be licensed in the
future. The commission made this finding on the strength of scientific estimates
of the suitability of deep salt beds as long-term repositories for radioactive waste.
In upholding the rule against attack as "arbitrary and capricious," the Court said:
"[A] reviewing court must remember that the Commission is making predictions, within its area of special expertise, at the frontiers of science. When examining this kind of scientific determination, as opposed to simple findings of fact,
a reviewing court must generally be at its most deferential." 462 U.S. at 103.

   Are the factual determinations in *State Farm* any less "judgmental" or "predictive" than those made in *NCCB* or *Baltimore Gas*? Are there other factors that
might explain the more searching review in *State Farm*?

   6. *Adoption and rescission of rules.* The Court holds that the same standard
of judicial review should apply to rescission of a motor vehicle safety standard
as to its original promulgation. Why? Should the burden of explanation be as
heavy when an agency is deregulating as when it is regulating? One anonymous
commentator (generally known to have been then-Professor Antonin Scalia)
suggested otherwise:

> Granted that a rulemaking proceeding must be conducted to impose regulation
> and to eliminate regulation alike, it does not necessarily follow that in both types
> of proceeding the burden of justification rests on the proponent of change. As far
> as the *substantive* inertia of our laws is concerned, that favors not the status quo
> but private autonomy, whether or not that is what the status quo prescribes. That
> is to say, private freedom can neither be constrained *nor continue to be constrained*
> without good reason.

Active Judges and Passive Restraints, Regulation, July/Aug. 1982, at 10, 13. Do
you agree? If so, does that mean that rescission of a rule should be judged by
the same standard that would apply to review of a decision not to adopt a rule?
Should rescission of a rule be treated the same as not acting at all? Should

agency inaction receive greater deference than agency action? *See Massachusetts v. EPA*, excerpted *infra*, and the discussion of agency action in Chapter III.

7. *"Hard look" review and "ossification" of rulemaking.* In their study of the history of automobile safety regulation by the NHTSA, Professor Jerry Mashaw and David Harfst point to the passive restraint saga as a leading example of how "judicial review . . . burdened, dislocated, and ultimately paralyzed [NHTSA's] rule making efforts." Jerry L. Mashaw & David L. Harfst, Inside the NHTSA: Legal Determinants of Bureaucratic Organization and Performance, 57 U. Chi. L. Rev. 443 (1990). As a consequence, they claim, the agency virtually abandoned the use of rulemaking as a regulatory device, switching instead to an increasing use of safety recalls, a story similar to other complaints that "hard look" judicial review tends to discourage agency use of rulemaking. *See, e.g.,* Stephen Breyer, Judicial Review of Questions of Law and Policy, 38 Admin. L. Rev. 363, 391-393 (1986). (If agencies find the rulemaking process too cumbersome, they may turn to informal policy making instruments like guidance documents or rely more on using enforcement discretion. However, substituting other instruments for legislative rulemaking has significant implications for accountability and, as we shall see *infra*, for judicial review.) For a more supportive view of "hard look" review by courts, *see* William S. Jordan, III, Ossification Revisited: Does Arbitrary and Capricious Review Significantly Interfere with Agency Ability to Achieve Regulatory Goals Through Informal Rulemaking?, 94 Nw. U. L. Rev. 393, 395 (2000).

In any event, *State Farm* is alive and well. In the case excerpted below, the Supreme Court applied arbitrary and capricious review to a significant policy change adopted by the Trump administration.

DEPARTMENT OF COMMERCE v. NEW YORK
139 S. Ct. 2551 (2019)

CHIEF JUSTICE ROBERTS delivered the opinion of the Court.

The Secretary of Commerce decided to reinstate a question about citizenship on the 2020 census questionnaire. A group of plaintiffs challenged that decision on constitutional and statutory grounds. We now decide whether the Secretary violated the Enumeration Clause of the Constitution, the Census Act, or otherwise abused his discretion.

I

A

In order to apportion Members of the House of Representatives among the States, the Constitution requires an "Enumeration" of the population every 10 years, to be made "in such Manner" as Congress "shall by Law direct." Art. I, §2, cl. 3; Amdt. 14, §2. In the Census Act, Congress delegated to the Secretary of Commerce the task of conducting the decennial census "in such form and content as he may determine." 13 U.S.C. §141(a). The Secretary is aided in that task by the Census Bureau, a statistical agency housed within the Department of Commerce. See §§2, 21.

The population count derived from the census is used not only to apportion representatives but also to allocate federal funds to the States and to draw electoral districts. The census additionally serves as a means of collecting demographic information, which "is used for such varied purposes as computing federal grant-in-aid benefits, drafting of legislation, urban and regional planning, business planning, and academic and social studies." Baldrige v. Shapiro, 455 U.S. 345, 353-354 n.9 (1982). Over the years, the census has asked questions about (for example) race, sex, age, health, education, occupation, housing, and military service. It has also asked about radio ownership, age at first marriage, and native tongue. The Census Act obliges everyone to answer census questions truthfully and requires the Secretary to keep individual answers confidential, including from other Government agencies. §§221, 8(b), 9(a). . . .

Every census between 1820 and 2000 (with the exception of 1840) asked at least some of the population about their citizenship or place of birth. Between 1820 and 1950, the question was asked of all households. Between 1960 and 2000, it was asked of about one-fourth to one-sixth of the population. That change was part of a larger effort to simplify the census by asking most people a few basic demographic questions (such as sex, age, race, and marital status) on a short-form questionnaire, while asking a sample of the population more detailed demographic questions on a long-form questionnaire. . . .

In 2010, the year of the latest census, the format changed again. All households received the same questionnaire, which asked about sex, age, race, Hispanic origin, and living arrangements. The more detailed demographic questions previously asked on the long-form questionnaire, including the question about citizenship, were instead asked in the American Community Survey (or ACS), which is sent each year to a rotating sample of about 2.6% of households. . . .

B

In March 2018, Secretary of Commerce Wilbur Ross announced in a memo that he had decided to reinstate a question about citizenship on the 2020 decennial census questionnaire. The Secretary stated that he was acting at the request of the Department of Justice (DOJ), which sought improved data about citizen voting-age population for purposes of enforcing the Voting Rights Act (or VRA) — specifically the Act's ban on diluting the influence of minority voters by depriving them of single-member districts in which they can elect their preferred candidates. . . .

C

[Litigation challenging the Secretary's decision was initiated by several groups of plaintiffs. After issuing several orders to the Secretary to supplement the administrative record, described in Part V of the Court's opinion, *infra*, and after a bench trial, the District Court] ruled that the Secretary's action was arbitrary and capricious [and was] based on a pretextual rationale . . . .

IV

The District Court set aside the Secretary's decision to reinstate a citizenship question on the grounds that the Secretary acted arbitrarily. . . .

At the heart of this suit is respondents' claim that the Secretary abused his discretion in deciding to reinstate a citizenship question. We review the Secretary's exercise of discretion under the deferential "arbitrary and capricious" standard. Our scope of review is "narrow": we determine only whether the Secretary examined "the relevant data" and articulated "a satisfactory explanation" for his decision, "including a rational connection between the facts found and the choice made." [*State Farm*, 463 U.S. at 43.] We may not substitute our judgment for that of the Secretary, but instead must confine ourselves to ensuring that he remained "within the bounds of reasoned decisionmaking." . . .

The Secretary examined the Bureau's analysis of various ways to collect improved citizenship data and explained why he thought the best course was to both reinstate a citizenship question and use citizenship data from administrative records to fill in the gaps. He considered but rejected the Bureau's recommendation to use administrative records alone. As he explained, records are lacking for about 10% of the population, so the Bureau would still need to estimate citizenship for millions of voting-age people. Asking a citizenship question of everyone, the Secretary reasoned, would eliminate the need to estimate citizenship for many of those people. And supplementing census responses with administrative record data would help complete the picture and allow the Bureau to better estimate citizenship for the smaller set of cases where it was still necessary to do so.

The evidence before the Secretary supported that decision. As the Bureau acknowledged, each approach—using administrative records alone, or asking about citizenship and using records to fill in the gaps—entailed tradeoffs between accuracy and completeness. Without a citizenship question, the Bureau would need to estimate the citizenship of about 35 million people; with a citizenship question, it would need to estimate the citizenship of only 13.8 million. Under either approach, there would be some errors in both the administrative records and the Bureau's estimates. With a citizenship question, there would also be some erroneous self-responses (about 500,000) and some conflicts between responses and administrative record data (about 9.5 million).

The Bureau explained that the "relative quality" of the citizenship data generated by each approach would depend on the "relative importance of the errors" in each, but it was not able to "quantify the relative magnitude of the errors across the alternatives." The Bureau nonetheless recommended using administrative records alone because it had "high confidence" that it could develop an accurate model for estimating the citizenship of the 35 million people for whom administrative records were not available, and it thought the resulting citizenship data would be of superior quality. But when the time came for the Secretary to make a decision, the model did not yet exist, and even if it had, there was no way to gauge its relative accuracy. As the Bureau put it, "we will most likely never possess a fully adequate truth deck to benchmark" the model—which appears to be bureaucratese for "maybe, maybe not." The Secretary opted instead for the approach that would yield a more complete set of data at an acceptable rate of accuracy, and would require estimating the citizenship of fewer people.

The District Court overruled that choice, agreeing with the Bureau's assessment that its recommended approach would yield higher quality citizenship data on the whole. But the choice between reasonable policy alternatives in the face of uncertainty was the Secretary's to make. He considered the relevant factors, weighed risks and benefits, and articulated a satisfactory explanation for his decision. In overriding that reasonable exercise of discretion, the court improperly substituted its judgment for that of the agency.

The Secretary then weighed the benefit of collecting more complete and accurate citizenship data against the risk that inquiring about citizenship would depress census response rates, particularly among noncitizen households. In the Secretary's view, that risk was difficult to assess. The Bureau predicted a 5.1% decline in response rates among noncitizen households if the citizenship question were reinstated. It relied for that prediction primarily on studies showing that, while noncitizens had responded at lower rates than citizens to the 2000 short-form and 2010 censuses, which did not ask about citizenship, they responded at even lower rates than citizens to the 2000 longform census and the 2010 American Community Survey [ACS], which did ask about citizenship. The Bureau thought it was reasonable to infer that the citizenship question accounted for the differential decline in noncitizen responses. But, the Secretary explained, the Bureau was unable to rule out other causes. For one thing, the evidence before the Secretary suggested that noncitizen households tend to be more distrustful of, and less likely to respond to, any government effort to collect information. For another, both the 2000 long-form census and 2010 ACS asked over 45 questions on a range of topics, including employment, income, and housing characteristics. Noncitizen households might disproportionately fail to respond to a lengthy and intrusive Government questionnaire for a number of reasons besides reluctance to answer a citizenship question—reasons relating to education level, socioeconomic status, and less exposure to Government outreach efforts.

The Secretary justifiably found the Bureau's analysis inconclusive. Weighing that uncertainty against the value of obtaining more complete and accurate citizenship data, he determined that reinstating a citizenship question was worth the risk of a potentially lower response rate. That decision was reasonable and reasonably explained, particularly in light of the long history of the citizenship question on the census. . . .

V

We now consider the District Court's determination that the Secretary's decision must be set aside because it rested on a pretextual basis, which the Government conceded below would warrant a remand to the agency. We start with settled propositions. First, in order to permit meaningful judicial review, an agency must "disclose the basis" of its action. Second, in reviewing agency action, a court is ordinarily limited to evaluating the agency's contemporaneous explanation in light of the existing administrative record. That principle reflects the recognition that further judicial inquiry into "executive motivation" represents "a substantial intrusion" into the workings of another branch of Government and should normally be avoided.

Third, a court may not reject an agency's stated reasons for acting simply because the agency might also have had other unstated reasons. Relatedly, a court may not set aside an agency's policymaking decision solely because it might have been influenced by political considerations or prompted by an Administration's priorities. Agency policymaking is not a "rarified technocratic process, unaffected by political considerations or the presence of Presidential power." Such decisions are routinely informed by unstated considerations of politics, the legislative process, public relations, interest group relations, foreign relations, and national security concerns (among others).

Finally, we have recognized a narrow exception to the general rule against inquiring into "the mental processes of administrative decisionmakers." *Overton Park*, 401 U.S. at 420. On a "strong showing of bad faith or improper behavior," such an inquiry may be warranted and may justify extra-record discovery.

The District Court invoked that exception in ordering extra-record discovery here. . . . [S]hortly after this litigation began, the Secretary, prodded by DOJ, filed a supplemental memo that added new, pertinent information to the administrative record. The memo disclosed that the Secretary had been considering the citizenship question for some time and that Commerce had inquired whether DOJ would formally request reinstatement of the question. [R]espondents . . . move[d] for both completion of the administrative record and extra-record discovery [and the] District Court granted both requests . . . , agreeing with respondents that the Government had submitted an incomplete administrative record and that the existing evidence supported a prima facie showing that the VRA rationale was pretextual.

The Government did not challenge the court's conclusion that the administrative record was incomplete, and the parties stipulated to the inclusion of more than 12,000 pages of internal deliberative materials as part of the administrative record, materials that the court later held were sufficient on their own to demonstrate pretext. The Government did, however, challenge the District Court's order authorizing extra-record discovery, as well as the court's later orders compelling depositions of the Secretary and of the Acting Assistant Attorney General for DOJ's Civil Rights Division.

We agree with the Government that the District Court should not have ordered extra-record discovery when it did. At that time, the most that was warranted was the order to complete the administrative record. But the new material that the parties stipulated should have been part of the administrative record—which showed, among other things, that the VRA played an insignificant role in the decisionmaking process—largely justified such extra-record discovery as occurred . . . .

We accordingly review the District Court's ruling on pretext in light of all the evidence in the record before the court, including the extra-record discovery. That evidence showed that the Secretary was determined to reinstate a citizenship question from the time he entered office; instructed his staff to make it happen; waited while Commerce officials explored whether another agency would request census-based citizenship data; subsequently contacted the Attorney General himself to ask if DOJ would make the request; and adopted the Voting Rights Act rationale late in the process. . . .

. . . [V]iewing the evidence as a whole, we share the District Court's conviction that the decision to reinstate a citizenship question cannot be adequately explained in terms of DOJ's request for improved citizenship data to better enforce the VRA. Several points, considered together, reveal a significant mismatch between the decision the Secretary made and the rationale he provided.

The record shows that the Secretary began taking steps to reinstate a citizenship question about a week into his tenure, but it contains no hint that he was considering VRA enforcement in connection with that project. The Secretary's Director of Policy did not know why the Secretary wished to reinstate the question, but saw it as his task to "find the best rationale." . . .

. . . [I]t was not until the Secretary contacted the Attorney General directly that DOJ's Civil Rights Division expressed interest in acquiring census-based citizenship data to better enforce the VRA. And even then, the record suggests that DOJ's interest was directed more to helping the Commerce Department than to securing the data. . . . Finally, after sending the letter, DOJ declined the Census Bureau's offer to discuss alternative ways to meet DOJ's stated need for improved citizenship data, further suggesting a lack of interest on DOJ's part.

Altogether, the evidence tells a story that does not match the explanation the Secretary gave for his decision. In the Secretary's telling, Commerce was simply acting on a routine data request from another agency. Yet the materials before us indicate that Commerce went to great lengths to elicit the request from DOJ (or any other willing agency). And unlike a typical case in which an agency may have both stated and unstated reasons for a decision, here the VRA enforcement rationale—the sole stated reason—seems to have been contrived.

. . . Our review is deferential, but we are "not required to exhibit a naiveté from which ordinary citizens are free." United States v. Stanchich, 550 F.2d 1294, 1300 (CA2 1977) (Friendly, J.). The reasoned explanation requirement of administrative law, after all, is meant to ensure that agencies offer genuine justifications for important decisions, reasons that can be scrutinized by courts and the interested public. Accepting contrived reasons would defeat the purpose of the enterprise. If judicial review is to be more than an empty ritual, it must demand something better than the explanation offered for the action taken in this case.

In these unusual circumstances, the District Court was warranted in remanding to the agency, and we affirm that disposition. We do not hold that the agency decision here was substantively invalid. But agencies must pursue their goals reasonably. Reasoned decisionmaking under the Administrative Procedure Act calls for an explanation for agency action. What was provided here was more of a distraction.

The judgment of the United States District Court for the Southern District of New York is affirmed in part and reversed in part, and the case is remanded for further proceedings consistent with this opinion.

JUSTICE THOMAS, with whom JUSTICE GORSUCH and JUSTICE KAVANAUGH join, concurring in part and dissenting in part.

In March 2018, the Secretary of Commerce exercised his broad discretion over the administration of the decennial census to resume a nearly unbroken practice of asking a question relating to citizenship. Our only role in this case is to decide whether the Secretary complied with the law and gave a reasoned explanation for his decision. The Court correctly answers these questions in the affirmative. That ought to end our inquiry.

The Court, however, goes further. For the first time ever, the Court invalidates an agency action solely because it questions the sincerity of the agency's otherwise adequate rationale. Echoing the din of suspicion and distrust that seems to typify modern discourse, the Court declares the Secretary's memorandum "pretextual" because, "viewing the evidence as a whole," his explanation that including a citizenship question on the census would help enforce the Voting Rights Act (VRA) "seems to have been contrived." The Court does not hold that the Secretary merely had additional, unstated reasons for reinstating the citizenship question. Rather, it holds that the Secretary's stated rationale did not factor at all into his decision.

The Court's holding reflects an unprecedented departure from our deferential review of discretionary agency decisions. And, if taken seriously as a rule of decision, this holding would transform administrative law. It is not difficult for political opponents of executive actions to generate controversy with accusations of pretext, deceit, and illicit motives. Significant policy decisions are regularly criticized as products of partisan influence, interest group pressure, corruption, and animus. Crediting these accusations on evidence as thin as the evidence here could lead judicial review of administrative proceedings to devolve into an endless morass of discovery and policy disputes not contemplated by the Administrative Procedure Act (APA). . . . The Court, I fear, will come to regret inventing the principles it uses to achieve today's result. I respectfully dissent from Part V of the opinion of the Court.[1]

II

As relevant here, the APA requires courts to "hold unlawful and set aside" agency action that is "arbitrary, capricious, an abuse of discretion, or otherwise not in accordance with law." §706(2)(A). . . .

A

Section 706(2) of the APA contemplates review of the administrative "record" to determine whether an agency's "action, findings, and conclusions" satisfy six specified standards. See §§706(2)(A)-(F). None instructs the Court to inquire into pretext. Consistent with this statutory text, we have held that a court is "ordinarily limited to evaluating the agency's contemporaneous explanation in light of the existing administrative record." If an agency's stated findings and conclusions withstand scrutiny, the APA does not permit a court to set aside the decision solely because the agency had "other unstated reasons" for its decision, such as "political considerations" or the "Administration's priorities."

Unsurprisingly, then, this Court has never held an agency decision arbitrary and capricious on the ground that its supporting rationale was "pretextual."

---

1. Justice Kavanaugh and I join Parts I, II, III, and IV of the opinion of the Court. Justice Gorsuch joins Parts I, II, III, IV-B, and IV-C.

Nor has it previously suggested that this was even a possibility. Under "settled propositions" of administrative law, pretext is virtually never an appropriate or relevant inquiry for a reviewing court to undertake.

Respondents conceptualize pretext as a subset of "arbitrary and capricious" review. It is far from clear that they are correct. But even if they were, an agency action is not arbitrary or capricious merely because the decisionmaker has other, unstated reasons for the decision. Nor is an agency action arbitrary and capricious merely because the decisionmaker was "inclined" to accomplish it before confirming that the law and facts supported that inclination.

Accordingly, even under respondents' approach, a showing of pretext could render an agency action arbitrary and capricious only in the infinitesimally small number of cases in which the administrative record establishes that an agency's stated rationale did not factor at all into the decision, thereby depriving the action of an adequate supporting rationale.[4] This showing is extremely difficult to make because the administrative record will rarely, if ever, contain evidence sufficient to show that an agency's stated rationale did not actually factor into its decision. And we have stated that a "strong showing of bad faith or improper behavior" is necessary to venture beyond the agency's "administrative findings" and inquire into "the mental processes of administrative decisionmakers." *Overton Park*, 401 U.S. at 420. We have never before found *Overton Park*'s exception satisfied, much less invalidated an agency action based on "pretext."

Undergirding our arbitrary-and-capricious analysis is our longstanding precedent affording the Executive a "presumption of regularity." This presumption reflects respect for a coordinate branch of government whose officers not only take an oath to support the Constitution, as we do, Art. VI, but also are charged with "faithfully execut[ing]" our laws, Art. II, §3. In practice, then, we give the benefit of the doubt to the agency. . . .

C

Even if it were appropriate for the Court to rely on evidence outside the administrative record, that evidence still fails to establish pretext. None of the evidence cited by the Court or the District Court comes close to showing that the Secretary's stated rationale—that adding a citizenship question to the 2020 census questionnaire would "provide . . . data that are not currently available" and "permit more effective enforcement of the [VRA]"—did not factor *at all* into his decision. . . .

The Court emphasizes that the VRA rationale for the citizenship question originated in the Department of Commerce, and suggests that DOJ officials unthinkingly fell in line after the Attorney General was looped into the process. But the Court ignores that the letter was drafted by the then-Acting Assistant Attorney General for Civil Rights and reviewed by five other DOJ

---

4. We do not have before us a claim that information outside the administrative record calls into question the legality of an agency action based on an unstated, unlawful bias or motivation (*e.g.*, a claim of religious discrimination under the Free Exercise Clause). But to the extent such a claim is viable, the analysis would have nothing to do with the arbitrary-and-capricious review pressed by respondents. *See* §§706(2)(A)-(C) (addressing agency actions that violate "constitutional" or "statutory" requirements, or that "otherwise [are] not in accordance with law").

attorneys, including the Chief of the DOJ's Voting Section. Given the DOJ's multilayer review process and its explanation for requesting citizenship data, the Court's suggestion that the DOJ's letter was inadequately vetted or improperly "influence[d]" by the Department of Commerce is entirely unsupported. In any event, none of this suggests, much less proves, that the Secretary harbored an unstated belief that adding the citizenship question would not help enforce the VRA, or that the VRA rationale otherwise did not factor at all into his decision. It simply suggests that a number of executive officials agreed that adding a citizenship question would support VRA enforcement.

The Court's other evidence is even further afield. [T]he evidence cited by the Court establishes, at most, that leadership at both the Department of Commerce and the DOJ believed it important—for a variety of reasons—to include a citizenship question on the census. . . .

III

. . . Today's decision marks the first time the Court has ever invalidated an agency action as "pretextual." Having taken that step, one thing is certain: This will not be the last time it is asked to do so. Virtually every significant agency action is vulnerable to the kinds of allegations the Court credits today. . . .

. . . [O]pponents of executive actions have strong incentives to craft narratives that would derail them. Moreover, even if the effort to invalidate the action is ultimately unsuccessful, the Court's decision enables partisans to use the courts to harangue executive officers through depositions, discovery, delay, and distraction. . . .

. . . [T]oday's decision is a departure from traditional principles of administrative law. Hopefully it comes to be understood as an aberration—a ticket good for this day and this train only.

Because the Secretary's decision to reinstate a citizenship question on the 2020 census was legally sound and a reasoned exercise of his broad discretion, I respectfully dissent from Part V of the opinion of the Court.

JUSTICE BREYER, with whom JUSTICE GINSBURG, JUSTICE SOTOMAYOR, and JUSTICE KAGAN join, concurring in part and dissenting in part. . . .

I agree with the Court that the Secretary of Commerce provided a pretextual reason for placing a question about citizenship on the short-form census questionnaire and that a remand to the agency is appropriate on that ground. But I write separately because I also believe that the Secretary's decision to add the citizenship question was arbitrary and capricious and therefore violated the Administrative Procedure Act (APA). . . .

I

. . . Courts do not apply [the arbitrary, capricious standard of review, as articulated in *Overton Park* and *State Farm*] mechanically. Rather, they take into account, for example, the nature and importance of the particular decision, the relevance and importance of missing information, and the inadequacies of a particular explanation in light of their importance. The Federal Government makes tens of thousands, perhaps millions, of administrative decisions each year. And courts would be wrong to expect or insist upon administrative perfection. But here, the Enumeration Clause, the Census Act, and the nature of the risks created by the agency's decision all make clear that the decision before us is highly important to the proper functioning of our democratic system. It is therefore particularly important that courts here not overlook an agency's . . . failure to consider serious risks of harm . . . .

II

. . .

A

. . . [T]he Secretary [concluded] that he was "not able to determine definitively how inclusion of a citizenship question on the decennial census will impact responsiveness." Insofar as this statement implies that adding the citizenship question is unlikely to affect "responsiveness" very much (or perhaps at all), the evidence in the record indicates the contrary.

The administrative record includes repeated Census Bureau statements that adding the question would produce a less accurate count because noncitizens and Hispanics would be less likely to respond to the questionnaire. The Census Bureau's chief scientist said specifically that adding the question would have "an adverse impact on self-response and, as a result, on the accuracy and quality of the 2020 Census." . . .

The Secretary's decision memorandum reached a quite different conclusion from the Census Bureau. The memorandum conceded that "a lower response rate would lead to . . . less accurate responses." But it concluded that neither the Census Bureau nor any stakeholders had provided "definitive, empirical support" for the proposition that the citizenship question would reduce response rates. The memorandum relied for that conclusion upon a number of considerations, but each is contradicted by the record.

The memorandum first pointed to perceived shortcomings in the Census Bureau's analysis of nonresponse rates. It noted that response rates are generally lower overall for the long form and ACS than they are for the short form. But the Bureau explained that its analysis accounted for this consideration, and no one has given us reason to think the contrary. The Secretary also noted that the Bureau "was not able to isolate what percentage of [the] decline was caused by the inclusion of a citizenship question rather than some other aspect of the long form survey." But the Bureau said attributing the decline to the citizenship question was a "reasonable inference," and again, nothing in the record contradicted the Bureau's judgment. And later analyses have borne out the Bureau's judgment that the citizenship question contributes to the decline in self-response.

The memorandum next cast doubt on the Census Bureau's analysis of the rate at which people responded to particular questions on the ACS. It noted that the "no answer" rate to the citizenship question was comparable to the "no answer" rate for other questions on the ACS, including educational attainment, income, and property insurance. But as discussed above, the Bureau found it significant that the "no answer" rate for the citizenship question was "much greater" than the "no answer" rate for the other questions that appear on the short form—that is, the form on which the citizenship question would appear. The Secretary offered no reason why the demographic variables to which he pointed provided a better point of comparison.

Finally, the memorandum relied on information provided by two outside stakeholders. The first was a study conducted by the private survey company Nielsen, in which questions about place of birth and time of arrival had not led to any appreciable decrease in the response rate. But Nielsen, which in fact urged the Secretary not to add the question, stated that its respondents (unlike census respondents) were paid to respond, and it is consequently not surprising that they did so. The memorandum also cited statements by former Census Bureau officials suggesting that empirical evidence about the question's potential impact on response rates was "limited." But there was no reason to expect the former officials to provide more extensive empirical evidence as to a citizenship question when they were not privy to the internal Bureau analyses on this question. And, like Nielsen, the former officials strongly urged the Secretary not to ask the question.

The upshot is that the Secretary received evidence of a likely drop in census accuracy by a number somewhere in the hundreds of thousands, and he received nothing significant to the contrary. The Secretary pointed out that the Census Bureau's information was uncertain, *i.e.*, not "definitive." But that is not a satisfactory answer. Few public-policy-related statistical studies of risks (say, of many health or safety matters) are definitive. As the Court explained in *State Farm*, "[i]t is not infrequent that the available data do not settle a regulatory issue, and the agency must then exercise its judgment in moving from the facts and probabilities on the record to a policy conclusion." 463 U.S. at 52. But an agency confronted with this situation cannot "merely recite the terms 'substantial uncertainty' as a justification for its actions." *Ibid.* Instead, it "must explain the evidence which is available" and typically must offer a reasoned explanation for taking action without "engaging in a search for further evidence." *Ibid.*

The Secretary did not do so here. He did not explain why he made the decision to add the question without following the Bureau's ordinary practice of extensively testing proposed changes to the census questionnaire. Without that testing, the Secretary could not treat the Bureau's expert opinions and its experience with the relevant surveys as worthless merely because its conclusions were not precise. The Bureau's opinions were properly considered as evidence of likelihoods, probabilities, or risks. . . .

In my view, the Secretary's decision—whether pretextual or not—was arbitrary, capricious, and an abuse of his lawfully delegated discretion. I consequently concur in the Court's judgment to the extent that it affirms the judgment of the District Court.

Justice Alito, concurring in part and dissenting in part [excerpted in Chapter III, *infra*].

an administrative enforcement proceeding against Fox, the FCC found that Fox had not taken sufficient precautions to prevent Cher's impromptu comment and had permitted the scripted interchange between Ms. Richie and Ms. Hilton. Although the FCC did not impose a forfeiture or other penalty on Fox, its formal finding of a violation prompted Fox to seek judicial review of the order. Fox argued that the FCC had not provided adequate justification for its admitted change in policy. The U.S. Court of Appeals for the Second Circuit agreed.]

III.   ANALYSIS

A.   GOVERNING PRINCIPLES . . .

In overturning the Commission's judgment, the Court of Appeals here relied in part on Circuit precedent requiring a more substantial explanation for agency action that changes prior policy. . . . We find no basis in the Administrative Procedure Act or in our opinions for a requirement that all agency change be subjected to more searching review. The Act mentions no such heightened standard. And our opinion in *State Farm* neither held nor implied that every agency action representing a policy change must be justified by reasons more substantial than those required to adopt a policy in the first instance. That case, which involved the rescission of a prior regulation, said only that such action requires "a reasoned analysis for the change beyond that which may be required when an agency *does not act* in the first instance." 463 U.S. at 42 (emphasis added).[2] Treating failures to act and rescissions of prior action differently for purposes of the standard of review makes good sense, and has basis in the text of the statute, which likewise treats the two separately. It instructs a reviewing court to "compel agency action unlawfully withheld or unreasonably delayed," 5 U.S.C. §706(1), and to "hold unlawful and set aside agency action, findings, and conclusions found to be [among other things] . . . arbitrary [or] capricious," §706(2)(A). The statute makes no distinction, however, between initial agency action and subsequent agency action undoing or revising that action.

To be sure, the requirement that an agency provide reasoned explanation for its action would ordinarily demand that it display awareness that it *is* changing position. . . . And of course the agency must show that there are good reasons for the new policy. But it need not demonstrate to a court's satisfaction that the reasons for the new policy are *better* than the reasons for the old one; it suffices that the new policy is permissible under the statute, that there are good reasons for it, and that the agency *believes* it to be better, which the conscious change of course adequately indicates. This means that the agency need not always provide a more detailed justification than what would suffice for a new

---

2. Justice Breyer's contention that *State Farm* did anything more rests upon his failure to observe the italicized phrase and upon a passage quoted in *State Farm* from a plurality opinion in Atchison, T. & S.F. Co. v. Wichita Bd. of Trade, 412 U.S. 800 (1973). That passage referred to "a presumption that [congressional] policies will be carried out best if the settled rule is adhered to." *Id.* at 807-808 (opinion of Marshall, J.). But the *Atchison* plurality made this statement in the context of requiring the agency to provide *some* explanation for a change, "so that the reviewing court may understand the basis of the agency's action and so may judge the consistency of that action with the agency's mandate," *id.* at 808. The opinion did not assert the authority of a court to demand explanation sufficient to enable it to weigh (by its own lights) the merits of the agency's change. Nor did our opinion in *State Farm.*

policy created on a blank slate. Sometimes it must—when, for example, its new policy rests upon factual findings that contradict those which underlay its prior policy; or when its prior policy has engendered serious reliance interests that must be taken into account. Smiley v. Citibank (South Dakota), N.A., 517 U.S. 735, 742 (1996). It would be arbitrary or capricious to ignore such matters. In such cases it is not that further justification is demanded by the mere fact of policy change; but that a reasoned explanation is needed for disregarding facts and circumstances that underlay or were engendered by the prior policy. . . .

B. APPLICATION TO THIS CASE

Judged under the above described standards, the Commission's new enforcement policy and its order finding the broadcasts actionably indecent were neither arbitrary nor capricious. First, the Commission forthrightly acknowledged that its recent actions have broken new ground, taking account of inconsistent "prior Commission and staff action" and explicitly disavowing them as "no longer good law." *Golden Globes Order,* 19 FCC Rcd., at 4980, ¶12. . . . There is no doubt that the Commission knew it was making a change. That is why it declined to assess penalties; and it relied on the *Golden Globes Order* as removing any lingering doubt. . . .

Moreover, the agency's reasons for expanding the scope of its enforcement activity were entirely rational. It was certainly reasonable to determine that it made no sense to distinguish between literal and nonliteral uses of offensive words, requiring repetitive use to render only the latter indecent. . . .

The fact that technological advances have made it easier for broadcasters to bleep out offending words further supports the Commission's stepped-up enforcement policy. And the agency's decision not to impose any forfeiture or other sanction precludes any argument that it is arbitrarily punishing parties without notice of the potential consequences of their action. . . .

* * *

The Commission could reasonably conclude that the pervasiveness of foul language, and the coarsening of public entertainment in other media such as cable, justify more stringent regulation of broadcast programs so as to give conscientious parents a relatively safe haven for their children. In the end, the Second Circuit and the broadcasters quibble with the Commission's policy choices and not with the explanation it has given. We decline to "substitute [our] judgment for that of the agency," *State Farm,* 463 U.S. at 43, and we find the Commission's orders neither arbitrary nor capricious.

The judgment of the United States Court of Appeals for the Second Circuit is reversed, and the case is remanded for further proceedings consistent with this opinion.

It is so ordered.

JUSTICE THOMAS, concurring. [Omitted.]

JUSTICE KENNEDY, concurring in part and concurring in the judgment. . . .

The question whether a change in policy requires an agency to provide a more-reasoned explanation than when the original policy was first announced is not susceptible, in my view, to an answer that applies in all cases. There may be instances when it becomes apparent to an agency that the reasons for a long-standing policy have been altered by discoveries in science, advances in technology, or by any of the other forces at work in a dynamic society. If an agency seeks to respond to new circumstances by modifying its earlier policy, the agency may have a substantial body of data and experience that can shape and inform the new rule. In other cases the altered circumstances may be so new that the agency must make predictive judgments that are as difficult now as when the agency's earlier policy was first announced. Reliance interests in the prior policy may also have weight in the analysis.

The question in each case is whether the agency's reasons for the change, when viewed in light of the data available to it, and when informed by the experience and expertise of the agency, suffice to demonstrate that the new policy rests upon principles that are rational, neutral, and in accord with the agency's proper understanding of its authority. That showing may be required if the agency is to demonstrate that its action is not "arbitrary, capricious, an abuse of discretion, or otherwise not in accordance with law." 5 U.S.C. §706(2)(A). And, of course, the agency action must not be "in excess of statutory jurisdiction, authority, or limitations, or short of statutory right." §706(2)(C).

These requirements stem from the administrative agency's unique constitutional position. The dynamics of the three branches of Government are well understood as a general matter. But the role and position of the agency, and the exact locus of its powers, present questions that are delicate, subtle, and complex. The Federal Government could not perform its duties in a responsible and effective way without administrative agencies. Yet the amorphous character of the administrative agency in the constitutional system escapes simple explanation. . . .

JUSTICE STEVENS, dissenting. [Omitted.]

JUSTICE GINSBURG, dissenting. [Omitted.]

JUSTICE BREYER, with whom JUSTICE STEVENS, JUSTICE SOUTER, and JUSTICE GINSBURG join, dissenting.

In my view, the Federal Communications Commission failed adequately to explain *why* it *changed* its indecency policy from a policy permitting a single "fleeting use" of an expletive, to a policy that made no such exception. Its explanation fails to discuss two critical factors, at least one of which directly underlay its original policy decision. Its explanation instead discussed several factors well known to it the first time around, which by themselves provide no significant justification for a *change* of policy. Consequently, the FCC decision is "arbitrary, capricious, an abuse of discretion." . . . I would affirm the Second Circuit's similar determination.

I

[A]gencies must follow a "logical and rational" decisionmaking "process." Allentown Mack Sales & Service, Inc. v. NLRB, 522 U.S. 359, 374 (1998). An agency's policy decisions must reflect the reasoned exercise of expert judgment.

See [Burlington Truck Lines, Inc. v. United States, 371 U.S. 156, 167 (1962)] (decision must reflect basis on which agency "exercised its expert discretion"). . . . And, as this Court has specified, in determining whether an agency's policy choice was "arbitrary," a reviewing court "must consider whether the decision was based on a consideration of the relevant factors and whether there has been a clear error of judgment." *Overton Park, supra,* at 416.

Moreover, an agency must act consistently. The agency must follow its own rules. And when an agency seeks to change those rules, it must focus on the fact of change and explain the basis for that change. *See, e.g.,* National Cable & Telecommunications Assn. v. Brand X Internet Services, 545 U.S. 967, 981 (2005) ("*Unexplained* inconsistency is" a "reason for holding an interpretation to be an arbitrary and capricious change from agency practice" (emphasis added)).

To explain a change requires more than setting forth reasons why the new policy is a good one. It also requires the agency to answer the question, "Why did you change?" And a rational answer to this question typically requires a more complete explanation than would prove satisfactory were change itself not at issue. . . .

It requires the agency here to focus upon the reasons that led the agency to adopt the initial policy, and to explain why it now comes to a new judgment.

I recognize that *sometimes* the ultimate explanation for a change may have to be, "We now weigh the relevant considerations differently." But at other times, an agency can and should say more. Where, for example, the agency rested its previous policy on particular factual findings . . . or where an agency rested its prior policy on its view of the governing law, . . . or where an agency rested its previous policy on, say, a special need to coordinate with another agency, one would normally expect the agency to focus upon those earlier views of fact, of law, or of policy and explain why they are no longer controlling. Regardless, to say that the agency here must answer the question "why change" is not to require the agency to provide a justification that is "*better* than the reasons for the old [policy]." . . . It is only to recognize the obvious fact that *change* is sometimes (not always) a relevant background feature that sometimes (not always) requires focus (upon prior justifications) and explanation lest the adoption of the new policy (in that circumstance) be "arbitrary, capricious, an abuse of discretion." . . .

III

The three reasons the FCC did set forth in support of its change of policy cannot make up for the failures I have discussed. Consider each of them. First, . . . the FCC based its decision in part upon the fact that "bleeping/delay systems" technology has advanced. I have already set forth my reasons for believing that that fact, without more, cannot provide a sufficient justification for its policy change. [Justice Breyer here cites an earlier portion of his opinion in which he claims that the FCC failed to address arguments by small independent broadcasters that modern bleeping/delay systems are too expensive and will thus discourage them from providing live coverage of local events.]

Second, the FCC says that the expletives here in question always invoke a coarse excretory or sexual image; hence it makes no sense to distinguish between whether one uses the relevant terms as an expletive or as a literal description. The problem with this answer is that it does not help to justify the *change* in policy. The FCC was aware of the coarseness of the "image" the first time around. . . .

Third, the FCC said that "perhaps" its "most importan[t]" justification for the new policy lay in the fact that its new "contextual" approach to fleeting expletives is better and more "[c]onsistent with" the agency's "general approach to indecency" than was its previous "categorica[l]" approach, which offered broadcasters virtual immunity for the broadcast of fleeting expletives. . . . This justification, however, offers no support for the change without an understanding of *why, i.e., in what way,* the FCC considered the new approach better or more consistent with the agency's general approach. . . .

V

In sum, the FCC's . . . answer to the question, "Why change?" is, "We like the new policy better." This kind of answer, might be perfectly satisfactory were it given by an elected official. But when given by an agency, in respect to a major change of an important policy where much more might be said, it is not sufficient. *State Farm,* 463 U.S., at 41-42.

For these reasons I would find the FCC's decision "arbitrary, capricious, an abuse of discretion," 5 U.S.C. §706(2)(A), requiring remand of this case to the FCC. And I would affirm the Second Circuit's similar determination.

With respect, I dissent.

NOTES AND QUESTIONS

1. *Awareness of change.* The Court allows that an agency must "display awareness that it *is* changing position." Why? If the new policy has adequate support in the record and would have been upheld if the repudiated policy had never been adopted, why require an agency to exhibit awareness that its policy has evolved? The answer may lie in a norm of consistency. When agency decisions appear to be inconsistent, something may be amiss. The agency can try to explain away the appearance of inconsistency or forthrightly admit that its views have changed. If it chooses neither of these paths, the reviewing court is likely to invalidate the agency's action. A background question is why the FCC's policy is reviewed under the arbitrary and capricious standard, rather than asking whether the agency's decision is an interpretation of the statutory ban on "any . . . indecent . . . language" that merits *Chevron* deference. Does the change in enforcement policy follow from a change in the FCC's reading of what constitutes "indecent language" or from a change in policy preferences respecting which instances of indecent language to pursue? How would you characterize the difference between those two sources of FCC policy pronouncements?

2. *Reasons for change.* What sorts of reasons must agencies offer in support of policy changes? Under *Fox Television,* must the agency establish that the prior policy has failed or that the new policy is superior to the old one? May an agency change policies simply because it disagrees with prior agency policy, or must it offer reasons that would not have been apparent at the time the prior policy was

adopted? Is it sufficient that the new policy would have survived judicial review had it been adopted in the first instance? Consider the following case:

ENCINO MOTORCARS, LLC V. NAVARRO, 136 S. Ct. 2117 (2016): At issue was whether a category of automobile dealership employees known as "service advisors" was subject to the overtime pay requirements of the Fair Labor Standards Act (FLSA). Service advisors interact with dealership customers to provide advice about servicing their vehicles. They do not sell vehicles or parts and do not service or repair the vehicles, but they may be understood to sell mechanical services. The FLSA had originally exempted all dealership employees from eligibility for overtime pay, but a 1966 amendment limited the exemption to "any salesman, partsman, or mechanic," and authorized the Department of Labor (DOL) to "promulgate necessary rules, regulations or orders" to implement that new provision. In response, DOL adopted an interpretive rule (not using the notice-and-comment procedure required by APA §553 for "legislative" rules) that excluded service advisors from the overtime exemption—meaning they would be eligible for overtime pay. After several lower courts struck down that interpretation, however, DOL issued an opinion letter in 1978 reversing ground, stating that it would henceforth treat service advisors as exempt. It promised to issue a new rule to that effect, but it was not until 2008 that it issued a notice of proposed rulemaking proposing to declare service advisors exempt from the overtime requirements. In the final version of the rule, adopted in 2011, DOL reversed itself once again, declaring that service advisors are not exempt and therefore are eligible for overtime pay.

Invoking the 2011 rule, a group of service advisors employed by Encino Motorcars sued their employer for failing to pay them overtime. Encino defended by arguing that the rule was not a valid interpretation of the FLSA. The Ninth Circuit upheld the rule, giving deference to the agency's interpretation of the statute under the *Chevron* doctrine (discussed in Part C of Chapter II, *infra*). The Supreme Court, in an opinion by Justice Kennedy, reversed. Justice Kennedy had this to say about whether the agency's change of policy was "arbitrary and capricious":

> Agencies are free to change their existing policies as long as they provide a reasoned explanation for the change. When an agency changes its existing position, it "need not always provide a more detailed justification than what would suffice for a new policy created on a blank slate." *Fox Television*, 556 U.S. at 515. But the agency must at least "display awareness that it is changing position" and "show that there are good reasons for the new policy." *Ibid.* (emphasis deleted). In explaining its changed position, an agency must also be cognizant that longstanding policies may have "engendered serious reliance interests that must be taken into account." *Ibid.* . . . It follows that an "[u]nexplained inconsistency" in agency policy is "a reason for holding an interpretation to be an arbitrary and capricious change from agency practice." [National Cable & Telecommunications Ass'n v. Brand X Internet Services, 545 U.S. 967, 981 (2005).] . . .
>
> Applying those principles here, the unavoidable conclusion is that the 2011 regulation was issued without the reasoned explanation that was required in light of the Department's change in position and the significant reliance interests involved. In promulgating the 2011 regulation, the Department offered barely any explanation. A summary discussion may suffice in other circumstances, but

here—in particular because of decades of industry reliance on the Department's prior policy—the explanation fell short of the agency's duty to explain why it deemed it necessary to overrule its previous position.

The retail automobile and truck dealership industry had relied since 1978 on the Department's position that service advisors are exempt from the FLSA's overtime pay requirements. Dealerships and service advisors negotiated and structured their compensation plans against this background understanding. Requiring dealerships to adapt to the Department's new position could necessitate systemic, significant changes to the dealerships' compensation arrangements. Dealerships whose service advisors are not compensated in accordance with the Department's new views could also face substantial FLSA liability, even if this risk of liability may be diminished in some cases by the existence of a separate FLSA exemption for certain employees paid on a commission basis, and even if a dealership could defend against retroactive liability by showing it relied in good faith on the prior agency position. In light of this background, the Department needed a more reasoned explanation for its decision to depart from its existing enforcement policy.

The Department said that, in reaching its decision, it had "carefully considered all of the comments, analyses, and arguments made for and against the proposed changes." 76 Fed. Reg. 18832. It also noted that, since 1978, it had treated service advisors as exempt in certain circumstances. It also noted the comment from the National Automobile Dealers Association stating that the industry had relied on that interpretation. But when it came to explaining the "good reasons for the new policy," *Fox Television, supra*, at 515, the Department said almost nothing. It stated only that it would not treat service advisors as exempt because "the statute does not include such positions and the Department recognizes that there are circumstances under which the requirements for the exemption would not be met." 76 Fed. Reg. 18838. It continued that it "believes that this interpretation is reasonable" and "sets forth the appropriate approach." *Ibid.* Although an agency may justify its policy choice by explaining why that policy "is more consistent with statutory language" than alternative policies, [Long Island Care at Home, Ltd. v. Coke, 551 U.S. 158, 175 (2007)], the Department did not analyze or explain why the statute should be interpreted to exempt dealership employees who sell vehicles but not dealership employees who sell services (that is, service advisors). And though several public comments supported the Department's reading of the statute, the Department did not explain what (if anything) it found persuasive in those comments beyond the few statements above.

It is not the role of the courts to speculate on reasons that might have supported an agency's decision. "[W]e may not supply a reasoned basis for the agency's action that the agency itself has not given." *State Farm*, 463 U.S., at 43 (citing SEC v. Chenery Corp., 332 U.S. 194, 196 (1947)). Whatever potential reasons the Department might have given, the agency in fact gave almost no reasons at all. In light of the serious reliance interests at stake, the Department's conclusory statements do not suffice to explain its decision. . . .

Does *Encino Motorcars* move the Court's treatment of changed policies backward from *Fox Television* and *State Farm*? Does it simply underscore that there is a greater burden on agencies to justify policy changes that harm those who relied on earlier policies? Or does it deal with rare situations in which the agency makes a change without giving much in the way of explanation? Is the "almost no reasons at all" language likely to be apt as a matter of fact or more of a qualitative assessment of the reasons given? How does *Encino Motorcars* fit with the discussion of the reasons given in *Department of Commerce*?

3.   *Arbitrary and Capricious Review of Agency Decisions Not to Act*

The Clean Air Act of 1970 (CAA), described in the introduction to the *Whitman* case in Chapter I, *supra,* authorizes the EPA to set national air quality standards for several pervasive air pollutants that adversely affect the health and welfare of Americans. States must establish plans to implement and enforce these standards within their jurisdiction, or face sanctions. This and other CAA programs are the primary mechanism for regulating pollution from stationary sources like coal-fired utilities, oil and gas refineries, factories, and plants. The CAA also authorizes EPA to directly regulate mobile sources such as cars and trucks by setting vehicle emission standards. Section 202(a) (codified at 42 U.S.C. §7521(2)) states, in part:

> (a)   Authority of Administrator to prescribe by regulation
>   Except as otherwise provided in subsection (b) of this section —
>   (1)   The Administrator shall by regulation prescribe (and from time to time revise) in accordance with the provisions of this section, standards applicable to the emission of any air pollutant from any class or classes of new motor vehicles or new motor vehicle engines, which in his judgment cause, or contribute to, air pollution which may reasonably be anticipated to endanger public health or welfare. . . .
>   (2)   Any regulation prescribed under paragraph (1) of this subsection (and any revision thereof) shall take effect after such period as the Administrator finds necessary to permit the development and application of the requisite technology, giving appropriate consideration to the cost of compliance within such period.

The section contains additional instructions for regulation of heavy-duty trucks and motorcycles, although the EPA (under the authority of §202(a)(1)) has promulgated separate standards for different classes of vehicles not separately identified in the statute, including passenger vehicles and light-duty trucks. The EPA historically has set vehicle emission standards for ground-level pollutants, such as those that contribute to smog.

Section 302(g) (codified at 42 U.S.C. §7602) defines "air pollutant" broadly as:

> any air pollution agent or combination of such agents, including any physical, chemical, biological, radioactive (including source material, special nuclear material, and byproduct material) substance or matter which is emitted into or otherwise enters the ambient air.

When Congress enacted the Clean Air Act in 1970, no federal statute explicitly addressed the problem of global climate change. During the late 1970s and 1980s, Congress enacted a number of laws related to the topic (see, e.g., the National Climate Program Act of 1978, requiring the President to establish a program to study the phenomenon, and the Global Climate Protection Act of 1987, directing the EPA to propose a national policy on global climate change). Yet no statute explicitly called for regulation of greenhouse gases.

In 1990, the Intergovernmental Panel on Climate Change (IPCC), a multinational scientific body established by the United Nations Environmental Program and the World Meteorological Association, issued its first comprehensive report on global climate change, concluding that emissions from human activities were increasing atmospheric greenhouse gas concentrations, which would lead to an increase in average global temperatures. In 1992, the United States and 153 other nations signed the United Nations Framework Convention on Climate Change (UNFCCC), a nonbinding agreement to reduce atmospheric concentrations of greenhouse gases to "prevent dangerous anthropogenic interference with the climate system." The U.S. Senate unanimously ratified the treaty.

The IPCC issued a second report in 1995, reinforcing the view that there is a linkage between human activities, greenhouse gas emissions, and rising global temperatures. Soon after, the UNFCCC signatories adopted the Kyoto protocol, which assigned mandatory greenhouse gas reduction targets to industrialized nations. The U.S. Senate formally expressed its opposition to the treaty, and President Clinton did not submit it to the Senate for ratification.

Frustrated at the relative inaction on the part of the federal government in the face of an increasingly strong scientific consensus about the likely consequences of climate change, a group of non-governmental organizations petitioned the EPA in 1999 to set vehicle emission standards for greenhouse gases. They argued that greenhouse gases fall under the CAA definition of pollutants that "may reasonably be anticipated to endanger public health or welfare" and that emissions from new motor vehicles in particular constituted a sufficiently significant source of those emissions to require regulation under the Act.

After four years, the EPA denied the petition. The original petitioners, now joined by intervenor states, local governments, and additional non-governmental organizations, challenged the EPA's order in the U.S. Court of Appeals for the D.C. Circuit. A divided panel of the D.C. Circuit ruled against petitioners, who turned next to the Supreme Court.

MASSACHUSETTS v. ENVIRONMENTAL PROTECTION AGENCY
549 U.S. 497 (2007)

JUSTICE STEVENS delivered the opinion of the Court. . . .

II

On October 20, 1999, a group of 19 private organizations filed a rulemaking petition asking EPA to regulate "greenhouse gas emissions from new motor vehicles under §202 of the Clean Air Act." . . . In 1998, Jonathan Z. Cannon, then EPA's General Counsel, prepared a legal opinion concluding that "CO_2 emissions are within the scope of EPA's authority to regulate," even as he recognized that EPA had so far declined to exercise that authority. Cannon's successor, Gary S. Guzy, reiterated that opinion before a congressional committee just two weeks before the rulemaking petition was filed.

Fifteen months after the petition's submission, EPA requested public comment on "all the issues raised in [the] petition," adding a "particular" request for comments on "any scientific, technical, legal, economic or other aspect of these issues that may be relevant to EPA's consideration of this petition." EPA received more than 50,000 comments over the next five months.

Before the close of the comment period, the White House sought "assistance in identifying the areas in the science of climate change where there are the greatest certainties and uncertainties" from the National Research Council, asking for a response "as soon as possible." The result was a 2001 report titled Climate Change: An Analysis of Some Key Questions (NRC Report), which, drawing heavily on the 1995 IPCC report, concluded that "[g]reenhouse gases are accumulating in Earth's atmosphere as a result of human activities, causing surface air temperatures and subsurface ocean temperatures to rise. Temperatures are, in fact, rising." On September 8, 2003, EPA entered an order denying the rulemaking petition. The agency gave two reasons for its decision: (1) that contrary to the opinions of its former general counsels, the Clean Air Act does not authorize EPA to issue mandatory regulations to address global climate change; and (2) that even if the agency had the authority to set greenhouse gas emission standards, it would be unwise to do so at this time.

[In a portion of the opinion excerpted later in this chapter, the Court first decided that the EPA possesses statutory authority to regulate greenhouse gas emissions. The majority explained that, even though at the time it enacted the CAA, Congress evidently had not thought about the possibility that greenhouse gases could cause global warming or intended specifically to bring greenhouse gases within the scope of its definition of "air pollutants," the law was written broadly enough to give authority to the EPA to regulate these gases, among other things as shown by the CAA's capacious definition of what constitutes a "pollutant." It then addressed the question whether the EPA administrator properly had declined to say that the gases "in his judgment cause, or contribute to, air pollution which may reasonably be anticipated to endanger public health or welfare," finding a negative judgment on that score would contravene the CAA.]

Even assuming that it had authority over greenhouse gases, EPA explained in detail why it would refuse to exercise that authority. The agency began by recognizing that the concentration of greenhouse gases has dramatically increased as a result of human activities, and acknowledged the attendant increase in global surface air temperatures. EPA nevertheless gave controlling importance to the NRC Report's statement that a causal link between the two "'cannot be unequivocally established.'" Given that residual uncertainty, EPA concluded that regulating greenhouse gas emissions would be unwise.

The agency furthermore characterized any EPA regulation of motor-vehicle emissions as a "piecemeal approach" to climate change, and stated that such regulation would conflict with the President's "comprehensive approach" to the problem. That approach involves additional support for technological innovation, the creation of nonregulatory programs to encourage voluntary private-sector reductions in greenhouse gas emissions, and further research on climate change—not actual regulation. According to EPA, unilateral EPA regulation of motor-vehicle greenhouse gas emissions might also hamper the President's ability to persuade key developing countries to reduce greenhouse gas emissions. . . .

V

The scope of our review of the merits of the statutory issues is narrow. As we have repeated time and again, an agency has broad discretion to choose how best to marshal its limited resources and personnel to carry out its delegated responsibilities. That discretion is at its height when the agency decides not to bring an enforcement action. Therefore, in Heckler v. Chaney, [470 U.S. 821 (1985)], we held that an agency's refusal to initiate enforcement proceedings is not ordinarily subject to judicial review. Some debate remains, however, as to the rigor with which we review an agency's denial of a petition for rulemaking.

There are key differences between a denial of a petition for rulemaking and an agency's decision not to initiate an enforcement action. See American Horse Protection Assn., Inc. v. Lyng, 812 F.2d 1, 3-4 (D.C. Cir. 1987). In contrast to nonenforcement decisions, agency refusals to initiate rulemaking "are less frequent, more apt to involve legal as opposed to factual analysis, and subject to special formalities, including a public explanation." *Id.* at 4; *see also* 5 U.S.C. §555(e). They moreover arise out of denials of petitions for rulemaking which (at least in the circumstances here) the affected party had an undoubted procedural right to file in the first instance. Refusals to promulgate rules are thus susceptible to judicial review, though such review is "extremely limited" and "highly deferential." . . .

As discussed earlier, the Clean Air Act expressly permits review of such an action. §7607(b)(1). We therefore "may reverse any such action found to be . . . arbitrary, capricious, an abuse of discretion, or otherwise not in accordance with law." §7607(d)(9). . . .

VII

The alternative basis for EPA's decision—that even if it does have statutory authority to regulate greenhouse gases, it would be unwise to do so at this time—rests on reasoning divorced from the statutory text. While the statute does condition the exercise of EPA's authority on its formation of a "judgment," 42 U.S.C. §7521(a)(1), that judgment must relate to whether an air pollutant "cause[s], or contribute[s] to, air pollution which may reasonably be anticipated to endanger public health or welfare." Put another way, the use of the word "judgment" is not a roving license to ignore the statutory text. It is but a direction to exercise discretion within defined statutory limits.

If EPA makes a finding of endangerment, the Clean Air Act requires the agency to regulate emissions of the deleterious pollutant from new motor vehicles. EPA no doubt has significant latitude as to the manner, timing, content, and coordination of its regulations with those of other agencies. But once EPA has responded to a petition for rulemaking, its reasons for action or inaction must conform to the authorizing statute. Under the clear terms of the Clean Air Act, EPA can avoid taking further action only if it determines that greenhouse gases do not contribute to climate change or if it provides some reasonable explanation as to why it cannot or will not exercise its discretion to determine whether they do. To the extent that this constrains agency discretion to pursue other priorities of the Administrator or the President, this is the congressional design.

EPA has refused to comply with this clear statutory command. Instead, it has offered a laundry list of reasons not to regulate. For example, EPA said that a number of voluntary executive branch programs already provide an effective response to the threat of global warming, that regulating greenhouse gases might impair the President's ability to negotiate with "key developing nations" to reduce emissions, and that curtailing motor-vehicle emissions would reflect "an inefficient, piecemeal approach to address the climate change issue."

Although we have neither the expertise nor the authority to evaluate these policy judgments, it is evident they have nothing to do with whether greenhouse gas emissions contribute to climate change. Still less do they amount to a reasoned justification for declining to form a scientific judgment. . . .

Nor can EPA avoid its statutory obligation by noting the uncertainty surrounding various features of climate change and concluding that it would therefore be better not to regulate at this time. If the scientific uncertainty is so profound that it precludes EPA from making a reasoned judgment as to whether greenhouse gases contribute to global warming, EPA must say so. That EPA would prefer not to regulate greenhouse gases because of some residual uncertainty — which, contrary to Justice Scalia's apparent belief, is in fact all that it said, see 68 Fed. Reg. 52929 ("We do not believe . . . that it would be either effective or appropriate for EPA *to establish [greenhouse gas] standards for motor vehicles at this time*" (emphasis added)) — is irrelevant. The statutory question is whether sufficient information exists to make an endangerment finding.

In short, EPA has offered no reasoned explanation for its refusal to decide whether greenhouse gases cause or contribute to climate change. Its action was therefore "arbitrary, capricious, . . . or otherwise not in accordance with law." 42 U.S.C. §7607(d)(9)(A). We need not and do not reach the question whether on remand EPA must make an endangerment finding, or whether policy concerns can inform EPA's actions in the event that it makes such a finding. We hold only that EPA must ground its reasons for action or inaction in the statute. . . .

JUSTICE SCALIA, with whom THE CHIEF JUSTICE, JUSTICE THOMAS, and JUSTICE ALITO join, dissenting. . . .

I

A

The provision of law at the heart of this case is §202(a)(1) of the Clean Air Act (CAA), which provides that the Administrator of the Environmental Protection Agency (EPA) "shall by regulation prescribe . . . standards applicable to the emission of any air pollutant from any class or classes of new motor vehicles or new motor vehicle engines, which *in his judgment* cause, or contribute to, air pollution which may reasonably be anticipated to endanger public health or welfare." 42 U.S.C. §7521(a)(1) (emphasis added). As the Court recognizes, the statute "condition[s] the exercise of EPA's authority on its formation of a 'judgment.'" There is no dispute that the Administrator has made no such judgment in this case.

The question thus arises: Does anything *require* the Administrator to make a "judgment" whenever a petition for rulemaking is filed? Without citation of the statute or any other authority, the Court says yes. Why is that so? When Congress wishes to make private action force an agency's hand, it knows how to do so. Where does the CAA say that the EPA Administrator is required to come to a decision on this question whenever a rulemaking petition is filed? The Court points to no such provision because none exists.

Instead, the Court invents a multiple-choice question that the EPA Administrator must answer when a petition for rulemaking is filed. The Administrator must exercise his judgment in one of three ways: (a) by concluding that the pollutant does cause, or contribute to, air pollution that endangers public welfare (in which case EPA is required to regulate); (b) by concluding that the pollutant does not cause, or contribute to, air pollution that endangers public welfare (in which case EPA is not required to regulate); or (c) by "provid[ing] some reasonable explanation as to why it cannot or will not exercise its discretion to determine whether" greenhouse gases endanger public welfare, *ante*, at 30 (in which case EPA is not required to regulate).

I am willing to assume, for the sake of argument, that the Administrator's discretion in this regard is not entirely unbounded—that if he has no reasonable basis for deferring judgment he must grasp the nettle at once. The Court, however, with no basis in text or precedent, rejects all of EPA's stated "policy judgments" as not "amount[ing] to a reasoned justification," effectively narrowing the universe of potential reasonable bases to a single one: Judgment can be delayed *only* if the Administrator concludes that "the scientific uncertainty is [too] profound." The Administrator is precluded from concluding *for other reasons* "that it would . . . be better not to regulate at this time." Such other reasons—perfectly valid reasons—were set forth in the agency's statement.

The Court dismisses [the Administrator's reasons] as "rest[ing] on reasoning divorced from the statutory text." "While the statute does condition the exercise of EPA's authority on its formation of a 'judgment,' . . . that judgment must relate to whether an air pollutant 'cause[s], or contribute[s] to, air pollution which may reasonably be anticipated to endanger public health or welfare.'" True but irrelevant. When the Administrator *makes* a judgment whether to regulate greenhouse gases, that judgment must relate to whether they are air pollutants that "cause, or contribute to, air pollution which may reasonably be anticipated to endanger public health or welfare." 42 U.S.C. §7521(a)(1). But the statute says *nothing at all* about the reasons for which the Administrator may *defer* making a judgment—the permissible reasons for deciding not to grapple with the issue at the present time. Thus, the various "policy" rationales that the Court criticizes are not "divorced from the statutory text," except in the sense that the statutory text is silent, as texts are often silent about permissible reasons for the exercise of agency discretion. The reasons the EPA gave are surely considerations executive agencies *regularly* take into account (and *ought* to take into account) when deciding whether to consider entering a new field: the impact such entry would have on other Executive Branch programs and on foreign policy. There is no basis in law for the Court's imposed limitation.

EPA's interpretation of the discretion conferred by the statutory reference to "its judgment" is not only reasonable, it is the most natural reading of the text. The Court nowhere explains why this interpretation is incorrect, let alone why it is not entitled to deference under [Chevron U.S.A., Inc. v. Natural Resources Defense Council, Inc., 467 U.S. 837 (1984), excerpted *infra*]. As the Administrator acted within the law in declining to make a "judgment" for the policy reasons above set forth, I would uphold the decision to deny the rulemaking petition on that ground alone.

B

Even on the Court's own terms, however, the same conclusion follows. As mentioned above, the Court gives EPA the option of determining that the science is too uncertain to allow it to form a "judgment" as to whether greenhouse gases endanger public welfare. Attached to this option (on what basis is unclear) is an essay requirement: "If," the Court says, "the scientific uncertainty is so profound that it precludes EPA from making a reasoned judgment as to whether greenhouse gases contribute to global warming, EPA must say so." But EPA *has* said precisely that—and at great length, based on information contained in a 2001 report by the National Research Council (NRC) entitled Climate Change Science: An Analysis of Some Key Questions:

> "The science of climate change is extraordinarily complex and still evolving. Although there have been substantial advances in climate change science, there continue to be important uncertainties in our understanding of the factors that may affect future climate change and how it should be addressed. . . ."
> "Reducing the wide range of uncertainty inherent in current model predictions will require major advances in understanding and modeling of the factors that determine atmospheric concentrations of greenhouse gases and aerosols, and the processes that determine the sensitivity of the climate system." [Excerpted from the EPA's petition denial—Eds.]

I simply cannot conceive of what else the Court would like EPA to say.

NOTES AND QUESTIONS

1. *Standard of review.* Justice Stevens's opinion says that agency decisions not to initiate enforcement actions are granted broad discretion, but then goes on to demand that the EPA explain persuasively the reasons for not making the public endangerment finding that would be a threshold judgment for initiating the requested action (adopting a rule that would provide the predicate for other enforcement activity). Does Justice Stevens or Justice Scalia have the better of the argument on the standard that should be used to review decisions like this? Who has the better argument on whether the EPA decision meets that standard?

The Court's statement in *Massachusetts v. EPA* that judicial review of agency decisions not to initiate rulemaking is "extremely limited" and "highly deferential" implies that reversal of such determinations should be infrequent. Recently, the D.C. Circuit decided that the Federal Aviation Administration's explanation for rejecting a petition to make a rule regarding the size of airplane seats flunked even that forgiving standard. *See* Flyers Rights Education Fund, Inc. v. Federal Aviation Administration, 864 F.3d 738 (D.C. Cir. 2017). The Flyers Rights Education Fund, Inc. petitioned the FAA to make a rule on the size of airplane seats, claiming that shrinking seats caused health and safety problems for passengers, including slower evacuations in emergencies. The FAA denied the petition based on studies it characterized as refuting the petitioner's claims. But the court was not satisfied with the agency's explanation:

> In asserting that decreasing seat size and pitch had no effect on emergency egress, the Administration pointed to certain studies and demonstration tests. But the cited studies say nothing about and do not appear to control for seat pitch, width, or any other seat dimension. Nor do they address or control for how increased passenger size interacts with the current seat dimensions to affect emergency egress. Studies cannot corroborate or demonstrate something that they never mention or even indirectly address.

864 F.3d at 744. On the standard of review, the court noted that "when an agency denies a petition for rulemaking, the record can be slim, but it cannot be vacuous. Especially so when, as here, the petition identifies an important issue that falls smack-dab within the agency's regulatory ambit." *Id.* at 747 (no pun intended). The court also faulted the FAA for refusing to disclose the data upon which its decision rested, which the agency claimed was proprietary and thus could not be shared with the public or the court. Does the decision in *Massachusetts* really conform to the statements regarding the limited nature of review? Does the *Flyers Rights* decision?

2. *Decisions not to decide.* Despite the Court's statements in *Massachusetts v, EPA*, it essentially reviews an agency refusal to make a threshold finding that would trigger regulation on the same terms as it would review an affirmative decision to regulate. Is this appropriate? The result is that a category of agency decisionmaking that once enjoyed all the benefits of "inaction" is treated as if it were "action" and subjected to review. On the implications of subjecting "decisions not to decide" to arbitrary and capricious review, *see* Jody Freeman & Adrian Vermeule, *Massachusetts v. EPA*: From Politics to Expertise, 2007 Sup. Ct. Rev. 51 (2008). How does *Massachusetts v. EPA* compare to Norton v. Southern Utah Wilderness Alliance, excerpted in Chapter III, *infra*? Don't both cases involve challenges to agency refusals to act? *See* Lisa Bressman, Judicial Review of Agency Inaction: An Arbitrariness Approach, 79 NYU L. Rev. 1657 (2004) (arguing for revision of the Court's non-reviewability doctrine for inaction cases).

C.   JUDICIAL REVIEW OF QUESTIONS OF LAW

Overton Park, involved, among other things, a dispute over the meaning of a statutory term — the word "prudent," as used in two federal statutes prohibiting the Secretary of Transportation from approving the location of a highway through a public park unless no "feasible and prudent alternative" existed. The Secretary argued that "prudent" meant something akin to "cost-beneficial," requiring (in the words of the Supreme Court) a "wide-ranging balancing of competing interests" such as the "cost of other routes, safety considerations, and other factors" against the "detriment resulting from the destruction of parkland." In challenging the Secretary's decision to approve the design of Highway

I-40, Citizens argued that "prudent" should be interpreted much more narrowly, to mean something more akin to "necessary," giving considerably more weight to the value of protecting parkland than considerations of safety, cost, and directness of route.

When called upon to review the Secretary's decision, the job of the reviewing court clearly included deciding whether the Secretary's suggested reading was legally correct, or whether some other reading (either that offered by Citizens or some third possibility) should have been adopted. As the Supreme Court stated in Marbury v. Madison, 5 U.S. (1 Cranch) 137 (1803): "It is emphatically the province and duty of the judicial department to say what the law is." Surely "saying what the law is" includes settling disputes between administrative agencies and private parties over the proper reading of ambiguous statutory language. If there were any doubt about this, it would seem to be decisively resolved by the enactment in 1946 of APA §706, which begins: "To the extent necessary to decision and when presented, the reviewing court shall decide all relevant questions of law [and] interpret constitutional and statutory provisions. . . ."

While *Marbury* and APA §706 leave no doubt about *who* (court or agency) has the ultimate authority to interpret statutes, they tell us virtually nothing about *how* courts (or agencies, for that matter) should interpret statutes. For the most part, the "law" of statutory interpretation consists of a loose, overlapping, and often internally contradictory collection of "canons," presumptions, principles, and rules articulated over the centuries by courts. The complexity of the legal doctrine reflects the variety and complexity of statutory commands and settings in which legislative directions are contested, but it also reflects different visions of the proper goals and methods of statutory interpretation.

At a theoretical level, there is sharp disagreement among commentators over whether the job of the statutory interpreter is to find the original, contemporaneous understanding of the words used in the law (what a "reasonable" third party would have understood the text to have said), to discover some fixed "intent" of the enacting legislature, to identify a more general "purpose" of the enactment, or to elaborate a more "dynamic" reading responsive to current social realities. At a methodological level, debates rage over the extent to which interpreters should be bound by the "plain meaning" of the statutory language or the extent to which they should look to extrinsic sources such as public statements by legislators, committees, or private parties (either before or after the bill's enactment), information about the social, economic, or political conditions prevailing prior to the bill's enactment, information about the ideologies and private preferences of particular legislators, and so on. For an excellent survey of theories of statutory interpretation, *see* William N. Eskridge, Jr., et al., Cases and Materials on Legislation: Statutes and the Creation of Public Policy (6th ed. 2019).

These perennial questions of interpretive method arise, of course, in private-law as well as public-law litigation, and an analogous (but not entirely identical) set of questions accompanies arguments over the meaning of the Constitution. A full exploration of these issues goes well beyond the scope of a course in administrative law. But there is one aspect of the question of interpretive method that is distinctive to administrative law. Agencies often speak in terms that are similar or identical to those in a governing statue. When a court is reviewing actions by an agency that rely on such statements, to what extent should the court defer to the agency? This inquiry involves identifying whether the agency is engaged in legal interpretation or something else (e.g., a discretionary policy judgment) and determining exactly how the authority given to the agency respecting that decision (or the way the agency exercised its authority) affects the type of judicial review the decision receives. We explore these questions below.

1. The Early Years

During the post–New Deal era a growing tension developed over the allocation of responsibility between agencies and courts. According to the older tradition, "the interpretation of the meaning of statutes . . . is exclusively a judicial function." United States v. American Trucking Assns., Inc., 310 U.S. 534, 544 (1940). This view can be traced to the "private law" origins of judicial review. Just as a court would independently examine the legal authority of a private person to inflict harm upon a plaintiff, so it must independently examine an administrator's claimed legal authority to do so. A similar sentiment supports the nondelegation doctrine discussed in Chapter I, *supra*.

Yet the waning of the nondelegation doctrine after 1935 testifies to the growth of a competing judicial vision of agencies as partners in setting the bounds of liberty and property rights. Regulatory statutes, according to this conception, are as importantly a mandate as a constraint, and courts, in "interpreting" such statutes, must leave ample room for the agency to give shape to that mandate. This notion crept quietly into early judicial decisions. In Norwegian Nitrogen Prods. Co. v. United States, 288 U.S. 294 (1933), for instance, the Court gave "peculiar weight" to "a contemporaneous construction of a statute by the men charged with the responsibility of setting its machinery in motion, of making the parts work efficiently and smoothly while they are yet untried and new." *Id.* at 315. Likewise, in Gray v. Powell, 314 U.S. 402 (1941), the Supreme Court deferred to an interpretation, rendered by the Director of the Interior Department's Bituminous Coal Division, of the word "producer" in a statute granting the Director power to exempt from various marketing restrictions coal "consumed by a producer." The leading authorities on the weight to be given to agency interpretations from the pre-APA era were the *Hearst* and *Skidmore* decisions, rendered in 1943 and 1944, respectively.

NATIONAL LABOR RELATIONS BOARD v. HEARST PUBLICATIONS, INC., 322 U.S. 111 (1944): The NLRB had ordered Hearst to bargain collectively with its "newsboys" (actually, mature men who distributed its newspapers on the streets of Los Angeles), based on a finding that the newsboys were "employees" of Hearst, as that term is used in the National Labor Relations Act. Hearst argued that the statute should be interpreted to incorporate the common law distinction between "employee" and "independent contractor," and that, under that test, the newsboys were independent contractors. The NLRB argued for a different definition, one more tailored to the Act's distinctive purposes of protecting workers in subordinate bargaining positions and promoting labor peace.

The Supreme Court agreed with the Board. It first held that Congress did not intend the Act to import common law standards. While this conclusion corresponded with the NLRB's position, the Court did not claim to "defer" or indeed to rely in any way on the Board's reasoning or result. Rather, the Court appeared to decide the question independently and definitively, by direct reference to the statutory language, purpose, and history.

> The Wagner Act is federal legislation, administered by a national agency, intended to solve a national problem on a national scale. . . . Whether, given the intended national uniformity, the term "employee" includes such workers as these newsboys must be answered primarily from the history, terms and purposes of the legislation. . . . Congress . . . was not thinking solely of the immediate technical relation of employer and employee. It had in mind at least some other persons than those standing in the proximate legal relation of employee to the particular employer involved in the labor dispute. . . .
>
> Congress was not seeking to solve the nationally harassing problems with which the statute deals by solutions only partially effective. It rather sought to find a broad solution, one that would bring industrial peace by substituting, so far as its power could reach, the rights of workers to self-organization and collective bargaining for the industrial strife which prevails where these rights are not effectively established. Yet only partial solutions would be provided if large segments of workers about whose technical legal position . . . local differences exist should be wholly excluded from coverage by reason of such differences. Yet that result could not be avoided, if choice must be made among them and controlled by them in deciding who are "employees" within the Act's meaning. Enmeshed in such distinctions, the administration of the statute soon might become encumbered by the same sort of technical legal refinement as has characterized the long evolution of the employee-independent contractor dichotomy in the courts for other purposes. The consequences would be ultimately to defeat, in part at least, the achievement of the statute's objectives. Congress no more intended to import this mass of technicality as a controlling "standard" for uniform national application than to refer decision of the question outright to the local law.

The Court then turned to the question of what *was* the appropriate definition of "employee" and whether Hearst's newsboys fit within that definition. It said:

> It is not necessary in this case to make a completely definitive limitation around the term "employee." That task has been assigned primarily to the agency created by Congress to administer the Act. Determination of "Where all the conditions of the relation require protection" involves inquiries for the Board charged with this duty. Everyday experience in the administration of the statute gives it familiarity with the circumstances and backgrounds of employment relationships in various industries, with the abilities and needs of the workers for self-organization and collective action, and with the adaptability of collective bargaining for the peaceful settlement of their disputes with their employers. The experience thus acquired must be brought frequently to bear on the question who is an employee under the Act. Resolving that question, like determining whether unfair labor practices have been committed, "belongs to the usual administrative routine" of the Board. Gray v. Powell, 314 U.S. 402, 411. . . . Undoubtedly questions of statutory interpretation, especially when arising in the first instance in judicial proceedings, are for the courts to resolve, giving appropriate weight to the judgment of those whose special duty is to administer the questioned statute. . . . But where the question is one of specific application of a broad statutory term in a proceeding in which the

agency administering the statute must determine it initially, the reviewing court's function is limited. . . . [T]he Board's determination that specified persons are "employees" under this Act is to be accepted if it has "warrant in the record" and a reasonable basis in law.

Justice Roberts dissented, saying:

Clearly . . . Congress did not delegate to the National Labor Relations Board the function of defining the relationship of employment so as to promote what the Board understood to be the underlying purpose of the statute. The question who is an employee, so as to make the statute applicable to him, is a question of the meaning of the Act and, therefore, a judicial and not an administrative question.

SKIDMORE v. SWIFT & CO., 323 U.S. 134 (1944):   Seven persons employed as private firefighters in Swift's meat packing plant sued their employer to recover payment for overtime worked. They claimed that time spent in the company's "fire hall" at night, while on call to respond to alarms, was "working time" under the Fair Labor Standards Act, and thus entitled them to overtime pay. The Administrator of the Wage and Hour Division of the Labor Department had issued an "Interpretive Bulletin" setting forth a flexible standard for determining whether on-duty time should count as working time. During the litigation, the Administrator filed a brief amicus curiae that interpreted the statute to exclude sleeping time, but include waking on-duty time within the definition of working time. The District Court, reading the statute independently, concluded that waiting time could not be working time, and thus denied the employees' claim. The Supreme Court reversed, saying that the District Court should have given at least some modest degree of deference to the Administrator's interpretation:

Congress did not utilize the services of an administrative agency to find facts and to determine in the first instance whether particular cases fall within or without the Act. Instead, it put this responsibility on the courts. But it did create the office of Administrator, impose upon him a variety of duties, endow him with powers to inform himself of conditions in industries and employments subject to the Act, and put on him the duties of bringing injunction actions to restrain violations. Pursuit of his duties has accumulated a considerable experience in the problems of ascertaining working time in employments involving periods of inactivity and a knowledge of the customs prevailing in reference to their solution. From these he is obliged to reach conclusions as to conduct without the law, so that he should seek injunctions to stop it, and that within the law, so that he has no call to interfere. He has set forth his views of the application of the Act under different circumstances in an interpretative bulletin and in informal rulings. They provide a practical guide to employers and employees as to how the office representing the public interest in its enforcement will seek to apply it. . . .

There is no statutory provision as to what, if any, deference courts should pay to the Administrator's conclusions. And, while we have given them notice, we have had no occasion to try to prescribe their influence. The rulings of this Administrator are not reached as a result of hearing adversary proceedings in which he finds facts from evidence and reaches conclusions of law from findings of fact. They are not, of course, conclusive, even in the cases with which they directly deal, much less in those to which they apply only by analogy. They do not constitute an interpretation of the Act or a standard for judging factual situations which binds a district court's processes, as an authoritative pronouncement of a higher court might do. But the Administrator's policies are made in pursuance of official duty, based upon more specialized experience and broader investigations and information than is likely to come to a judge in a particular case. They do determine the policy which will guide applications for enforcement by injunction on behalf of the Government. Good administration of the Act and good judicial administration alike require that the standards of public enforcement and those for determining private rights shall be at variance only where justified by very good reasons. The fact that the Administrator's policies and standards are not reached by trial in adversary form does not mean that they are not entitled to respect. . . .

We consider that the rulings, interpretations and opinions of the Administrator under this Act, while not controlling upon the courts by reason of their authority, do constitute a body of experience and informed judgment to which courts and litigants may properly resort for guidance. The weight of such a judgment in a particular case will depend upon the thoroughness evident in its consideration, the validity of its reasoning, its consistency with earlier and later pronouncements, and all those factors which give it power to persuade, if lacking power to control.

NOTES AND QUESTIONS

1. *Reconciling* Hearst *and* Skidmore. Do *Hearst* and *Skidmore* articulate similar or different rules for consideration of agency decisions on matters of statutory interpretation? Can you formulate a test that incorporates the reasoning of both decisions? Is the different degree of deference accorded by the Court to the agency actions in the two cases a product of express legislative direction or of inferences drawn from the scope and type of authority given to the agency or the kind of function performed by the agency?

2. *The effect of the APA's enactment.* What status do *Hearst* and *Skidmore* have after passage of the APA? Are they merely background or do they help courts understand the APA? Between the enactment of the APA and 1984, the Supreme Court decided dozens of cases involving review of administrative interpretations of law. In some, the Court decided the issue without so much as a nod in the agency's direction. In others it explicitly refused to defer to the agency. And in still others, it expressly deferred to the agency's reading. Collectively, the cases constitute what Thomas Merrill has charitably called "the multiple factors regime." Thomas W. Merrill, Judicial Deference to Executive Precedent, 101 Yale L.J. 969, 972-975 (1992). Whether and to what extent the Court would defer to an agency's interpretation depended on a host of considerations, such as whether the interpretation was contained in a "legislative rule" or an "interpretive rule," whether it fell within the agency's area of "expertise," whether it was "contemporaneous" with enactment of the statute or "longstanding" or "consistent," or whether it was supported by "reasoned analysis." The Court sometimes, but not always, tied its level of deference to indications that the law gave the agency discretion over the particular interpretive decision. Such was the state of affairs when the Supreme Court issued one of the most heavily cited pronouncements of its administrative law jurisprudence, the *Chevron* decision.

2.   *The* Chevron *Decision*

As described in the notes preceding the *Whitman* case in Chapter I, *supra,* and *Massachusetts v. EPA*, above, the Clean Air Act of 1970 set up a framework for reducing air pollution in the United States with oversight from the EPA. The Clean Air Act Amendments of 1977 extended deadlines for states to file compliance plans and tightened requirements for new sources that wished to locate in "non-attainment zones"—areas that do not meet national ambient air quality standards. The Act distinguishes these areas from areas that do attain the national standards (called "PSD" areas because of a court opinion requiring the EPA to "prevent significant deterioration" of their air quality). In nonattainment areas, new or modified sources are subject to "New Source Review," a permitting process that requires them to 1) install state-of-the-art pollution control technology to achieve the "lowest achievable emission rate" possible for that kind of source; and 2) secure offsetting pollution reductions from other sources in the same area. Not surprisingly, to avoid these burdens, firms generally wish to avoid triggering New Source Review.

Even prior to the 1977 Amendments, concerns had been voiced over the mounting costs of pollution control. A portion of the criticism focused on the use of uniform emission control standards under which every boiler or blast furnace within an industrial plant would be required to reduce its emissions of a particular pollutant by the same amount, regardless of relative costs. In any facility with more than one major emissions point, the marginal costs of controlling pollution may vary dramatically from unit to unit. If, instead of requiring an equal percentage reduction from every unit, the EPA allowed facilities to concentrate pollution control efforts on those units with the lowest marginal control costs—by allowing a firm to trade emission increases at one unit for emission reductions at another—the total cost of achieving any given level of emission control could be reduced. Proponents of this concept invited their audience to imagine placing an enormous bubble over an entire facility, with a single hole in the top allowing emissions from the facility's several sources to escape. Hence, the concept came to be known simply as the "bubble."

Advocates of the bubble claimed that it could generate significant cost savings, reduce enforcement costs and enhance pollution reduction. Critics of the bubble concept argued that it weakens emissions reduction incentives and objected that focusing on the total volume of pollutants emitted by a facility ignores dangerous interactions among pollutants.

The EPA initially experimented with the bubble concept in 1975 in connection with its authority to regulate stationary sources under the "New Source Performance Standards" (NSPS) program in Section 111 of the Clean Air Act, which requires the EPA to set emission limits for categories of "stationary sources." For purposes of approving *modifications* to existing sources, the EPA's 1975 rules defined "source" to include entire plants and even combinations of plants, allowing sources to net out their emissions and avoid the permitting requirements. But for new construction, the rules continued to use a narrow definition of "source" as each individual emission point. Industry attached the rules for not going far enough to alleviate permitting burdens while environmentalists challenged them for going too far in compromising air quality. The environmentalists won. In ASARCO Inc. v. EPA, 578 F.2d 319 (D.C. Cir. 1978), the D.C. Circuit ruled that the EPA's bubble was incompatible with §111's mandate to "enhance" air quality.

The EPA used the bubble concept again two years later to implement the new PSD provisions of the 1977 Amendments. These rules, applicable only to modernizing sources in "clean air" regions, used the same definition of "source" as the 1975 rules. Again, industry and environmentalists challenged the rules, but this time the EPA prevailed. Alabama Power Co. v. Costle, 636 F.2d 323 (D.C. Cir. 1979). Although purporting to interpret the same statutory definition of "source" as in *ASARCO,* the Court of Appeals read the legislative history of the 1977 PSD provisions as supporting the bubble concept in *this* context: where the putative statutory goal was simply to prevent air quality from degrading, rather than improving it. Despite the court's effort to distinguish *ASARCO,* the apparent contradiction in the two cases left the legal status of the bubble in considerable doubt when the EPA embarked on its third attempt to use it—this time in non-attainment zones; that is, regions with the country's dirtiest air.

CHEVRON U.S.A., INC. v. NATURAL RESOURCES DEFENSE COUNCIL, INC.
467 U.S. 837 (1984)

JUSTICE STEVENS delivered the opinion of the Court.

In the Clean Air Act Amendments of 1977, Pub. L. 95-95, 91 Stat. 685, Congress enacted certain requirements applicable to States that had not achieved the national air quality standards established by the Environmental Protection Agency (EPA) pursuant to earlier legislation. The amended Clean Air Act required these "nonattainment" States to establish a permit program regulating "new or modified major stationary sources" of air pollution. Generally, a permit may not be issued for a new or modified major stationary source unless several stringent conditions are met.[1] The EPA regulation promulgated to implement this permit requirement allows a State to adopt a plantwide definition of the term "stationary source."[2] Under this definition, an existing plant that contains several pollution-emitting devices may install or modify one piece of equipment without meeting the permit conditions if the alteration will not increase the total emissions from the plant. The question presented by this case is whether EPA's decision to allow States to treat all of the pollution-emitting devices within the same industrial grouping as though they were encased within a single "bubble" is based on a reasonable construction of the statutory term "stationary source."

---

2. 1. Section 172(b)(6), 42 U.S.C. §7502(b)(6), provides:

The plan provisions required by subsection (a) shall . . .

(6) require permits for the construction and operation of new or modified major stationary sources in accordance with section 173 (relating to permit requirements). 91 Stat. 747.

2. "(i) 'Stationary source' means any building, structure, facility, or installation which emits or may emit any air pollutant subject to regulation under the Act.

"(ii) 'Building, structure, facility, or installation' means all of the pollutant-emitting activities which belong to the same industrial grouping, are located on one or more contiguous or adjacent properties, and are under the control of the same person (or persons under common control) except the activities of any vessel." 40 CFR §51.18(j)(1)(i) and (ii) (1983).

I

The EPA regulations containing the plantwide definition of the term stationary source were promulgated on October 14, 1981. 46 Fed. Reg. 50766. Respondents[3] filed a timely petition for review in the United States Court of Appeals for the District of Columbia Circuit pursuant to 42 U.S.C. §7607(b)(1).[4] The Court of Appeals set aside the regulations. . . .

II

When a court reviews an agency's construction of the statute which it administers, it is confronted with two questions. First, always, is the question whether Congress has directly spoken to the precise question at issue. If the intent of Congress is clear, that is the end of the matter; for the court, as well as the agency, must give effect to the unambiguously expressed intent of Congress.[9] If, however, the court determines Congress has not directly addressed the precise question at issue, the court does not simply impose its own construction on the statute, as would be necessary in the absence of an administrative interpretation. Rather, if the statute is silent or ambiguous with respect to the specific issue, the question for the court is whether the agency's answer is based on a permissible construction of the statute.

"The power of an administrative agency to administer a congressionally created . . . program necessarily requires the formulation of policy and the making of rules to fill any gap left, implicitly or explicitly, by Congress." Morton v. Ruiz, 415 U.S. 199, 231 (1974). If Congress has explicitly left a gap for the agency to fill, there is an express delegation of authority to the agency to elucidate a specific provision of the statute by regulation. Such legislative regulations are given controlling weight unless they are arbitrary, capricious, or manifestly contrary to the statute. Sometimes the legislative delegation to an agency on a particular question is implicit rather than explicit. In such a case, a court may not substitute its own construction of a statutory provision for a reasonable interpretation made by the administrator of an agency. . . .

In light of these well-settled principles it is clear that the Court of Appeals misconceived the nature of its role in reviewing the regulations at issue. Once it determined, after its own examination of the legislation, that Congress did not actually have an intent regarding the applicability of the bubble concept to the permit program, the question before it was not whether in its view the concept is "inappropriate" in the general context of a program designed to improve

---

3. National [sic] Resources Defense Council, Inc., Citizens for a Better Environment, Inc., and North Western Ohio Lung Association, Inc.

4. Petitioners, Chevron U.S.A. Inc., American Iron and Steel Institute, American Petroleum Institute, Chemical Manufacturers Association, Inc., General Motors Corporation, and Rubber Manufacturers Association were granted leave to intervene and argue in support of the regulation.

9. The judiciary is the final authority on issues of statutory construction and must reject administrative constructions which are contrary to clear congressional intent. If a court, employing traditional tools of statutory construction, ascertains that Congress had an intention on the precise question at issue, that intention is the law and must be given effect.

air quality, but whether the Administrator's view that it is appropriate in the context of this particular program is a reasonable one. Based on the examination of the legislation and its history which follows, we agree with the Court of Appeals that Congress did not have a specific intention on the applicability of the bubble concept in these cases, and conclude that the EPA's use of that concept here is a reasonable policy choice for the agency to make.

IV

. . . The 1977 Amendments contain no specific reference to the "bubble concept." Nor do they contain a specific definition of the term "stationary source," though they did not disturb the definition of "stationary source" contained in §111(a)(3), applicable by the terms of the Act to the NSPS program.* Section 302(j), however, defines the term "major stationary source" as follows:

> (j) Except as otherwise expressly provided, the terms "major stationary source" and "major emitting facility" mean any stationary facility or source of air pollutants which directly emits, or has the potential to emit, one hundred tons per year or more of any air pollutant (including any major emitting facility or source of fugitive emissions of any such pollutant, as determined by rule by the Administrator).

91 Stat. 770.

V

The legislative history of the portion of the 1977 Amendments dealing with nonattainment areas does not contain any specific comment on the "bubble concept" or the question whether a plantwide definition of a stationary source is permissible under the permit program. It does, however, plainly disclose that in the permit program Congress sought to accommodate the conflict between the economic interest in permitting capital improvements to continue and the environmental interest in improving air quality. . . .

VI

As previously noted, prior to the 1977 Amendments, the EPA had adhered to a plantwide definition of the term "source" under a NSPS program. After adoption of the 1977 Amendments, proposals for a plantwide definition were considered [by the EPA]. . . .

In August 1980, . . . the EPA adopted a regulation that, in essence, applied the basic reasoning of the Court of Appeals in this case. The EPA took particular note of the two then-recent Court of Appeals decisions, which had created the bright-line rule that the bubble concept should be employed in a program

---

* [Section 111(a)(3), enacted in 1970, defined "source," for purposes of the NSPS program, as "any building, structure, facility, or installation which emits or may emit any air pollutant."—Eds.]

designed to maintain air quality but not in one designed to enhance air quality. Relying heavily on those cases,[29] EPA adopted a dual definition of "source" for nonattainment areas that required a permit whenever a change in either the entire plant, or one of its components, would result in a significant increase in emissions even if the increase was completely offset by reductions elsewhere in the plant. The EPA expressed the opinion that this interpretation was "more consistent with congressional intent" than the plantwide definition because it "would bring in more sources or modifications for review," 45 Fed. Reg. 52697 (1980), but its primary legal analysis was predicated on the two Court of Appeals decisions.

In 1981 a new administration took office and initiated a "Government-wide reexamination of regulatory burdens and complexities." 46 Fed. Reg. 16281. In the context of that review, the EPA reevaluated the various arguments that had been advanced in connection with the proper definition of the term "source" and concluded that the term should be given the same definition in both nonattainment areas and PSD areas.

In explaining its conclusion, the EPA first noted that the definitional issue was not squarely addressed in either the statute or its legislative history and therefore that the issue involved an agency "judgment as how to best carry out the Act." *Ibid.* It then set forth several reasons for concluding that the plantwide definition was more appropriate. It pointed out that the dual definition "can act as a disincentive to new investment and modernization by discouraging modifications to existing facilities" and "can actually retard progress in air pollution control by discouraging replacement of older, dirtier processes or pieces of equipment with new, cleaner ones." *Ibid.* Moreover, the new definition "would simplify EPA's rules by using the same definition of 'source' for PSD, nonattainment new source review and the construction moratorium. This reduces confusion and inconsistency." *Ibid.* Finally, the agency explained that additional requirements that remained in place would accomplish the fundamental purposes of achieving attainment with NAAQs's as expeditiously as possible. These conclusions were expressed in a proposed rulemaking in August 1981 that was formally promulgated in October. *See id.* at 50766.

VII

In this Court respondents expressly reject the basic rationale of the Court of Appeals' decision. That court viewed the statutory definition of the term "source" as sufficiently flexible to cover either a plantwide definition, a narrower definition covering each unit within a plant, or a dual definition that could apply to both the entire "bubble" and its components. It interpreted the policies of the statute, however, to mandate the plantwide definition in programs designed to maintain clean air and to forbid it in programs designed to improve air quality. Respondents place a fundamentally different construction on the statute. They contend that the text of the Act requires the EPA to use a

---

29. Alabama Power Co. v. Costle, 636 F.2d 323 [D.C. Cir. 1979]; ASARCO Inc. v. EPA, 578 F.2d 319 [D.C. Cir. 1978].

dual definition—if either a component of a plant, or the plant as a whole, emits over 100 tons of pollutant, it is a major stationary source. They thus contend that the EPA rules adopted in 1980, insofar as they apply to the maintenance of the quality of clean air, as well as the 1981 rules which apply to nonattainment areas, violate the statute. . . .

The definition in §302(j) tells us what the word "major" means—a source must emit at least 100 tons of pollution to qualify—but it sheds virtually no light on the meaning of the term "stationary source." It does equate a source with a facility—a "major emitting facility" and a "major stationary source" are synonymous under §302(j). The ordinary meaning of the term facility is some collection of integrated elements which has been designed and constructed to achieve some purpose. Moreover, it is certainly no affront to common English usage to take a reference to a major facility or a major source to connote an entire plant as opposed to its constituent parts. Basically, however, the language of §302(j) simply does not compel any given interpretation of the term source.

Respondents recognize that, and hence point to §111(a)(3). Although the definition in that section is not literally applicable to the permit program, it sheds as much light on the meaning of the word source as anything in the statute. As respondents point out, use of the words "building, structure, facility, or installation," as the definition of source, could be read to impose the permit conditions on an individual building that is a part of a plant. . . . The language may reasonably be interpreted to impose the requirement on any discrete, but integrated, operation which pollutes. This gives meaning to all of the terms—a single building, not part of a larger operation, would be covered if it emits more than 100 tons of pollution, as would any facility, structure, or installation. Indeed, the language itself implies a bubble concept of sorts: each enumerated item would seem to be treated as if it were encased in a bubble. While respondents insist that each of these terms must be given a discrete meaning, they also argue that §111(a)(3) defines "source" as that term is used in §302(j). The latter section, however, equates a source with a facility, whereas the former defines source as a facility, among other items.

We are not persuaded that parsing of general terms in the text of the statute will reveal an actual intent of Congress. We know full well that this language is not dispositive; the terms are overlapping and the language is not precisely directed to the question of the applicability of a given term in the context of a larger operation. To the extent any congressional "intent" can be discerned from this language, it would appear that the listing of overlapping, illustrative terms was intended to enlarge, rather than to confine, the scope of the agency's power to regulate particular sources in order to effectuate the policies of the Act.

LEGISLATIVE HISTORY

In addition, respondents argue that the legislative history and policies of the Act foreclose the plantwide definition, and that the EPA's interpretation is not entitled to deference because it represents a sharp break with prior interpretations of the Act.

Based on our examination of the legislative history, we agree with the Court of Appeals that it is unilluminating. . . . We find that the legislative history as a whole is silent on the precise issue before us. . . .

Our review of the EPA's varying interpretations of the word "source"—both before and after the 1977 Amendments—convinces us that the agency primarily responsible for administering this important legislation has consistently interpreted it flexibly—not in a sterile textual vacuum, but in the context of implementing policy decisions in a technical and complex arena. The fact that the agency has from time to time changed its interpretation of the term *source* does not, as respondents argue, lead us to conclude that no deference should be accorded the agency's interpretation of the statute. An initial agency interpretation is not instantly carved in stone. On the contrary, the agency, to engage in informed rulemaking, must consider varying interpretations and the wisdom of its policy on a continuing basis. Moreover, the fact that the agency has adopted different definitions in different contexts adds force to the argument that the definition itself is flexible, particularly since Congress has never indicated any disapproval of a flexible reading of the statute. . . .

POLICY

The arguments over policy that are advanced in the parties' briefs create the impression that respondents are now waging in a judicial forum a specific policy battle which they ultimately lost in the agency and in the 32 jurisdictions opting for the bubble concept, but one which was never waged in the Congress. Such policy arguments are more properly addressed to legislators or administrators, not to judges.

In this case, the Administrator's interpretation represents a reasonable accommodation of manifestly competing interests and is entitled to deference: the regulatory scheme is technical and complex, the agency considered the matter in a detailed and reasoned fashion, and the decision involves reconciling conflicting policies. Congress intended to accommodate both interests, but did not do so itself on the level of specificity presented by this case. Perhaps that body consciously desired the Administrator to strike the balance at this level, thinking that those with great expertise and charged with responsibility for administering the provision would be in a better position to do so; perhaps it simply did not consider the question at this level; and perhaps Congress was unable to forge a coalition on either side of the question, and those on each side decided to take their chances with the scheme devised by the agency. For judicial purposes, it matters not which of these things occurred.

Judges are not experts in the field, and are not part of either political branch of the Government. Courts must, in some cases, reconcile competing political interests, but not on the basis of the judges' personal policy preferences. In contrast, an agency to which Congress has delegated policymaking responsibilities may, within the limits of that delegation, properly rely upon the incumbent administration's views of wise policy to inform its judgments. While agencies are not directly accountable to the people, the Chief Executive is, and it is entirely appropriate for this political branch of the Government to make such policy choices—resolving the competing interests which Congress itself either inadvertently did not resolve, or intentionally left to be resolved by the agency charged with the administration of the statute in light of everyday realities.

When a challenge to an agency construction of a statutory provision, fairly conceptualized, really centers on the wisdom of the agency's policy, rather than whether it is a reasonable choice within a gap left open by Congress, the challenge must fail. In such a case, federal judges—who have no constituency—have a duty to respect legitimate policy choices made by those who do. The responsibilities for assessing the wisdom of such policy choices and resolving the struggle between competing views of the public interest are not judicial ones: "Our Constitution vests such responsibilities in the political branches." TVA v. Hill, 437 U.S. 153, 195 (1978).

We hold that the EPA's definition of the term "source" is a permissible construction of the statute which seeks to accommodate progress in reducing air pollution with economic growth. "The Regulations which the Administrator has adopted provide what the agency could allowably view as . . . [an] effective reconciliation of these twofold ends. . . ." United States v. Shimer, 367 U.S. at 383.

The judgment of the Court of Appeals is reversed.

It is so ordered.

JUSTICE MARSHALL and JUSTICE REHNQUIST did not participate in the consideration or decision of these cases.

JUSTICE O'CONNOR did not participate in the decision of these cases.

NOTES AND QUESTIONS

1. Chevron*'s rule.* What, exactly, is the rule laid down in *Chevron?* Does the Court really mean that courts must defer to an agency's interpretation of a statute unless Congress has "unambiguously" spoken "directly" to the "precise" question at issue? What is the "precise" question in *Chevron?* How clearly did Congress "speak" to it? What does the reference in footnote 9 to "traditional methods of statutory construction" add (or subtract)? What does the Court mean by a "permissible" construction of the statute? By a "statute which [the agency] administers"? In the materials that follow, we survey a small slice of the enormous literature that has been devoted to answering those questions. As you consider the more pointed questions in notes and cases below, think about both the actual content of the test in *Chevron* and the question of its legal pedigree (how it connects to APA §706 and other sources of law controlling what courts and agencies do).

2. *Defenses of* Chevron *deference.* Why should a reviewing court *ever* "defer" to an agency's interpretation of a statute? How does Justice Stevens answer that question? How would you? What role do you think the Court gave to agency *interpretations* of law as opposed to agency formulation of *policies* within the authority given by law to the agency? One line in the Court's opinion that did not receive much attention from commentators declared "an agency to which Congress has delegated policymaking responsibilities may, within the limits of that delegation, properly rely upon the incumbent administration's views of

wise policy to inform its judgments." That line is contained in the section of the opinion labeled "Policy." Is that statement consistent with the opinion's other statements respecting the roles of courts and agencies in statutory construction? Put differently, is *Chevron* ultimately about deferring to agency interpretations of law, or is it about deciding how much leeway was given to an agency to act within the law (and whether the agency stayed within the law's limits)?

Commentators have offered a wide variety of justifications for the *Chevron* doctrine. Writing in 1989, Justice Scalia gave this reason:

> An ambiguity in a statute committed to agency implementation can be attributed to either of two congressional desires: (1) Congress intended a particular result, but was not clear about it; or (2) Congress had no particular intent on the subject, but meant to leave its resolution to the agency. When the former is the case, what we have is genuinely a question of law, properly to be resolved by the courts. When the latter is the case, what we have is the conferral of discretion on the agency, and the only question of law presented to the courts is whether the agency has acted within the scope of its discretion — *i.e.*, whether its resolution of the ambiguity is reasonable.

Antonin Scalia, Judicial Deference to Administrative Interpretations of Law, 1989 Duke L.J. 511, 516. Professor Richard Pierce offers a different justification. Where it comes down to a choice between an interpretation favored by an agency and one favored by a court, we should prefer the agency's interpretation, he argues, because the agency is subject to oversight by the politically accountable chief executive. Richard J. Pierce, Jr., *Chevron* and Its Aftermath: Judicial Review of Agency Interpretations of Statutory Provisions, 41 Vand. L. Rev. 301 (1988). Professor Diver bases his defense of judicial deference on an assessment of comparative institutional competence. He claims that agencies are often better at discovering congressional intent and almost always better at making policy than courts. Colin S. Diver, Statutory Interpretation in the Administrative State, 133 U. Pa. L. Rev. 549 (1985). Professor Peter Strauss offers yet another pragmatic explanation. Since the Supreme Court can render only a comparatively small number of decisions each year, he argues, it is increasingly adopting "clear statement" principles of statutory construction, such as the *Chevron* rule, that reduce the likelihood of intercircuit conflict. Peter L. Strauss, One Hundred Fifty Cases per Year: Some Implications of the Supreme Court's Limited Resources for Judicial Review of Agency Action, 87 Colum. L. Rev. 1093 (1987).

Do you agree with the descriptive premises of these hypotheses? Even if they are accurate as a descriptive matter, do they provide a *normative* basis for deference? A *legal* basis for deference?

3. *Criticisms of* Chevron. Many other commentators have criticized the *Chevron* rule on normative grounds. Professor Cass Sunstein, for example, argues that independent judicial review is necessary to safeguard against administrative capitulation to special interest groups. Cass R. Sunstein, Deregulation and the Courts, 5 J. Pol'y Analysis & Mgmt. 517 (1986). Professor Cynthia Farina, by contrast, finds the rule of deference announced in *Chevron* to be incompatible with the nondelegation doctrine. Cynthia R. Farina, Statutory Interpretation

and the Balance of Power in the Administrative State, 89 Colum. L. Rev. 452 (1989). Does the desuetude of the nondelegation doctrine (*see* Chapter I) argue in favor of, or against, judicial deference? *See* Ronald A. Cass, Vive la Deference? Rethinking the Balance Between Administrative and Judicial Expression? 83 Geo. Wash. L. Rev. 1294 (2015). For a broader critique, *see, e.g.,* Jack M. Beermann, End the Failed *Chevron* Experiment Now: How *Chevron* Has Failed and Why It Can and Should Be Overruled, 42 Conn. L. Rev. 779 (2010).

3.   Chevron *Step One*

a.   Modes of Statutory Interpretation

Under *Chevron*'s two-step analysis, a reviewing court must defer to an agency's interpretation (at step two) *only* if it has first decided that Congress has not "directly" spoken to the "precise question at issue" (one formulation of step one) or if the statute "is silent or ambiguous with respect to the specific issue" (a second formulation of step one). The reviewing court presumably conducts its own independent (non-deferential) inquiry at step one, applying, according to footnote 9, "traditional tools of statutory construction." For example, in INS v. Cardoza-Fonseca, 480 U.S. 421 (1987), the Court refused to find ambiguity in a provision of the Refugee Act of 1980, authorizing the INS to grant asylum to an alien because of a "well-founded fear of persecution" in his homeland. The INS interpreted that language co-extensively with another statutory provision requiring a "clear probability" that an asylum applicant's "life or freedom would be threatened." The Court disagreed, interpreting the Act's plain language and legislative history to require a broader, more subjective test. "The question whether Congress intended the two standards to be identical is a pure question of statutory construction for the courts to decide," said the Court. "Employing the traditional tools of statutory construction, we have concluded that Congress did not intend the two standards to be identical." 480 U.S. at 446. Concurring separately, Justice Scalia (who had joined the Court two years after *Chevron*) objected that the Court's reliance on "traditional tools of statutory construction" constituted an "evisceration" of *Chevron* deference. Why would he think so? Do you agree? Does your answer depend on how clear the law is on the interpretive question at issue? Or how consistent judicial resolution of the interpretive question is with the scope of authority delegated to the agency? Is Justice Scalia objecting to courts using traditional tools of construction to decide what a law means or to courts overriding agency decisions when the law is consistent with leaving an agency leeway to choose among a range of policy options?

Justice Scalia is certainly correct that the impact of the *Chevron* rule depends critically on how courts exercise their step-one authority. In the dozens of opinions that apply the *Chevron* doctrine, the Supreme Court has given what might charitably be called mixed signals on this score. Consider the following cases:

MCI TELECOMMUNICATIONS CORP. v. AMERICAN TELEPHONE & TELEGRAPH CO.
512 U.S. 218 (1994)

[This case is excerpted in Chapter VIII, *infra*. Please focus on the *Chevron*-related judicial review issues.]

BABBITT v. SWEET HOME CHAPTER OF COMMUNITIES FOR A GREAT OREGON, 515 U.S. 687 (1995):

The Endangered Species Act of 1973 (16 U.S.C. §§1531 *et seq.*) (ESA) directs the Secretary of the Interior to designate species of fish and wildlife that are "endangered" and to take actions to protect those species. ESA §9(a)(1)(B) makes it unlawful for anyone to "take any such species within the United States or [its] territorial sea. . . ." In §3(19), the Act defines "take" to mean: "harass, harm, pursue, hunt, shoot, wound, kill, trap, capture, or collect. . . ." In 1975, the Secretary issued a regulation defining "harm" to include "significant habitat modification or degradation where it actually kills or injures wildlife by significantly impairing essential behavioral patterns, including breeding, feeding, or sheltering." 50 C.F.R. §17.3.

A group of landowners and loggers in the Pacific Northwest, concerned that their economic activities would subject them to criminal or civil penalties for injury to the habitat of the spotted owl and red-cockaded woodpecker, brought a declaratory judgment action asking for a declaration that the Secretary's regulation was inconsistent with the Act. In an opinion by Justice Stevens, the Supreme Court upheld the validity of the regulation as a permissible interpretation of an ambiguous statute:

> The text of the Act provides three reasons for concluding that the Secretary's interpretation is reasonable. First, an ordinary understanding of the word "harm" supports it. The dictionary definition of the verb form of "harm" is "to cause hurt or damage to: injure." Webster's Third New International Dictionary 1034 (1966). In the context of the ESA, that definition naturally encompasses habitat modification that results in actual injury or death to members of an endangered or threatened species.
>
> Respondents argue that the Secretary should have limited the purview of "harm" to direct applications of force against protected species, but the dictionary definition does not include the word "directly" or suggest in any way that only direct or willful action that leads to injury constitutes "harm."
>
> Second, the broad purpose of the ESA supports the Secretary's decision to extend protection against activities that cause the precise harms Congress enacted the statute to avoid. In TVA v. Hill, 437 U.S. 153 (1978), we described the Act as "the most comprehensive legislation for the preservation of endangered species ever enacted by any nation." . . .
>
> Third, the fact that Congress in 1982 authorized the Secretary to issue permits for takings that §9(a)(1)(B) would otherwise prohibit, "if such taking is incidental to, and not the purpose of, the carrying out of an otherwise lawful activity," [§10(a)(1)(B)], strongly suggests that Congress understood §9(a)(1)(B) to prohibit indirect as well as deliberate takings. . . . No one could seriously request an "incidental" take permit to avert §9 liability for direct, deliberate action against a member of an endangered or threatened species, but respondents would read

"harm" so narrowly that the permit procedure would have little more than that absurd purpose. . . .

We need not decide whether the statutory definition of "take" compels the Secretary's interpretation of "harm," because our conclusions that Congress did not unambiguously manifest its intent to adopt respondents' view and that the Secretary's interpretation is reasonable suffice to decide this case. See generally [*Chevron*] . . .

When it enacted the ESA, Congress delegated broad administrative and interpretive power to the Secretary. . . . The task of defining and listing endangered and threatened species requires an expertise and attention to detail that exceeds the normal province of Congress. Fashioning appropriate standards for issuing permits under §10 for takings that would otherwise violate §9 necessarily requires the exercise of broad discretion. The proper interpretation of a term such as "harm" involves a complex policy choice. When Congress has entrusted the Secretary with broad discretion, we are especially reluctant to substitute our views of wise policy for his.

Justice Scalia, joined by Chief Justice Rehnquist and Justice Thomas, dissented:

If "take" were not elsewhere defined in the Act, none could dispute what it means, for the term is as old as the law itself. To "take," when applied to wild animals, means to reduce those animals, by killing or capturing, to human control. . . . It is obvious that "take"[—as] a term of art deeply embedded in the statutory and common law concerning wildlife—describes a class of acts (not omissions) done directly and intentionally (not indirectly and by accident) to particular animals (not populations of animals).

The Act's definition of "take" does expand the word slightly (and not unusually), so as to make clear that it includes not just a completed taking, but the process of taking, and all of the acts that are customarily identified with or accompany that process ("to harass, harm, pursue, hunt, shoot, wound, kill, trap, capture, or collect"). . . . "Harm" is merely one of ten prohibitory words in [§3(19)], and the other nine fit the ordinary meaning of "take" perfectly. To "harass, pursue, hunt, shoot, wound, kill, trap, capture, or collect" are all affirmative acts . . . which are directed immediately and intentionally against a particular animal—not acts or omissions that indirectly and accidentally cause injury to a population of animals. The Court points out that several of the words ("harass," "pursue," "wound," and "kill") "refer to actions or effects that do not require direct applications of force." That is true enough, but force is not the point. Even "taking" activities in the narrowest sense, activities traditionally engaged in by hunters and trappers, do not all consist of direct applications of force; pursuit and harassment are part of the business of "taking" the prey even before it has been touched. What the nine other words in [§3(19)] have in common—and share with the narrower meaning of "harm" described above, but not with the Secretary's ruthless dilation of the word—is the sense of affirmative conduct intentionally directed against a particular animal or animals. . . .

[T]he Court's contention that "harm" in the narrow sense adds nothing to the other words underestimates the ingenuity of our own species in a way that Congress did not. To feed an animal poison, to spray it with mace, to chop down the very tree in which it is nesting, or even to destroy its entire habitat in order to take it (as by draining a pond to get at a turtle), might neither wound nor kill, but would directly and intentionally harm. . . .

NOTES AND QUESTIONS

1. *Text, meaning, purpose, intent.* What methods of statutory interpretation do the Justices use at step one in *Chevron, MCI,* and *Sweet Home?* What sources of instruction do the Justices consult? Does *Chevron* signal a change in the methods of statutory interpretation that courts should utilize? Would any of these cases be decided differently if the litigation were between two private parties, each of whom advocated for a different reading of the statute?

2. *"Traditional tools."* *Chevron* footnote 9's reference to the "traditional tools of statutory construction" has been expressly invoked in numerous cases involving agency statutory interpretation, but most often by dissenters complaining about an overly deferential majority. *See, e.g.,* Scialabba v. Cuellar de Osorio, 134 S. Ct. 2191, 2220 (2014) (Sotomayor, J., joined by Breyer, J., and Alito, J., dissenting). Justice Stevens, the author of *Chevron,* in one of his last opinions as a member of the Court, invoked the traditional tools of statutory interpretation and argued, in dissent, that the issue before the Court was "the kind of 'pure question of statutory construction for the courts to decide'" and thus *Chevron* deference was inappropriate. Negusie v. Holder, 555 U.S. 511, 534 (2009) (Stevens, J., dissenting), citing INS v. Cardoza-Fonseca, 480 U.S. 421, 446 (1987). Is this surprising? Note that this does not mean that the Court does not *apply* traditional tools of statutory interpretation in its *Chevron* decisions. Many of Justice Scalia's majority opinions, for example, can be characterized as applying the plain meaning rule, and Justice Stevens's majority opinion in *Sweet Home* refers to dictionary definitions and statutory purposes, both of which are traditional tools of interpretation. Perhaps the best example of a majority using traditional tools to reject an agency's statutory interpretation is Dole v. United Steelworkers of America, 494 U.S. 26, 35-36 (1990).

b.   "Extraordinary Cases"?

FOOD AND DRUG ADMINISTRATION v. BROWN & WILLIAMSON TOBACCO CORP.
529 U.S. 120 (2000)

JUSTICE O'CONNOR delivered the opinion of the Court.

[In 1996, the FDA issued a rule designed to prevent the marketing of tobacco products to young people. The FDA claimed that it had legal authority to regulate tobacco products because nicotine was a "drug" and cigarettes were "drug delivery devices," as those terms are used in the Food, Drug, and Cosmetic Act (FDCA). The FDCA defines "drug" to include "articles (other than food) intended to affect the structure or any function of the body," and "device" as "an instrument, apparatus, implement, machine, contrivance . . . intended to affect the structure or any function of the body." The tobacco industry challenged the rules on the grounds that the structure and history of the Act precluded an interpretation that it authorized the FDA to regulate tobacco products. By a 5-4 vote, a majority of the Supreme Court agreed:]

Because this case involves an administrative agency's construction of a statute that it administers, our analysis is governed by *Chevron*. . . . In determining whether Congress has specifically addressed the question at issue, a reviewing court should not confine itself to examining a particular statutory provision in isolation. The meaning—or ambiguity—of certain words or phrases may only become evident when placed in context. . . . It is a "fundamental canon of statutory construction that the words of a statute must be read in their context and with a view to their place in the overall statutory scheme." Davis v. Michigan Dept. of Treasury, 489 U.S. 803, 809 (1989). . . . Similarly, the meaning of one statute may be affected by other Acts, particularly where Congress has spoken subsequently and more specifically to the topic at hand. . . . In addition, we must be guided to a degree by common sense as to the manner in which Congress is likely to delegate a policy decision of such economic and political magnitude to an administrative agency. . . .

With these principles in mind, we find that Congress has directly spoken to the issue here and precluded the FDA's jurisdiction to regulate tobacco products.

Viewing the FDCA as a whole, it is evident that one of the Act's core objectives is to ensure that any product regulated by the FDA is "safe" and "effective" for its intended use. . . . In its rulemaking proceeding, the FDA quite exhaustively documented that "tobacco products are unsafe," "dangerous," and "cause great pain and suffering from illness." 61 Fed. Reg. 44412 (1996). . . . These findings logically imply that, if tobacco products were "devices" under the FDCA, the FDA would be required to remove them from the market. . . .

Congress, however, has foreclosed the removal of tobacco products from the market. A provision of the United States Code currently in force states that "[t]he marketing of tobacco constitutes one of the greatest basic industries of the United States with ramifying activities which directly affect interstate and foreign commerce at every point, and stable conditions therein are necessary to the general welfare." 7 U.S.C. §1311(a). More importantly, Congress has directly addressed the problem of tobacco and health through legislation on six occasions since 1965. . . . Nonetheless, Congress stopped well short of ordering a ban. Instead, it has generally regulated the labeling and advertisement of tobacco products, expressly providing that it is the policy of Congress that "commerce and the national economy may be . . . protected to the maximum extent consistent with" consumers "be[ing] adequately informed about any adverse health effects." 15 U.S.C. §1331. . . . A ban of tobacco products by the FDA would therefore plainly contradict congressional policy. . . .

In determining whether Congress has spoken directly to the FDA's authority to regulate tobacco, we must also consider in greater detail the tobacco-specific legislation that Congress has enacted over the past 35 years. At the time a statute is enacted, it may have a range of plausible meanings. Over time, however, subsequent acts can shape or focus those meanings. . . .

Congress has enacted six separate pieces of legislation since 1965 addressing the problem of tobacco use and human health. Those statutes, among other things, require that health warnings appear on all packaging and in all print and outdoor advertisements [and] prohibit the advertisement of tobacco products through "any medium of electronic communication" subject to regulation by the Federal Communications Commission (FCC). . . .

In adopting each statute, Congress has acted against the backdrop of the FDA's consistent and repeated statements that it lacked authority under the FDCA to regulate tobacco absent claims of therapeutic benefit by the manufacturer. In fact, on several occasions over this period, and after the health consequences of tobacco use and nicotine's pharmacological effects had become well known, Congress considered and rejected bills that would have granted the FDA such jurisdiction. Under these circumstances, it is evident that Congress' tobacco-specific statutes have effectively ratified the FDA's long-held position that it lacks jurisdiction under the FDCA to regulate tobacco products. . . .

Our conclusion does not rely on the fact that the FDA's assertion of jurisdiction represents a sharp break with its prior interpretation of the FDCA. Certainly, an agency's initial interpretation of a statute that it is charged with administering is not "carved in stone." . . . The consistency of the FDA's prior position is significant in this case for a different reason: it provides important context to Congress' enactment of its tobacco-specific legislation. The consistency of the FDA's prior position bolsters the conclusion that when Congress created a distinct regulatory scheme addressing the subject of tobacco and health, it understood that the FDA is without jurisdiction to regulate tobacco products and ratified that position. . . .

Finally, our inquiry into whether Congress has directly spoken to the precise question at issue is shaped, at least in some measure, by the nature of the question presented. Deference under *Chevron* to an agency's construction of a statute that it administers is premised on the theory that a statute's ambiguity constitutes an implicit delegation from Congress to the agency to fill in the statutory gaps. . . . In extraordinary cases, however, there may be reason to hesitate before concluding that Congress has intended such an implicit delegation. . . .

This is hardly an ordinary case. Contrary to its representations to Congress since 1914, the FDA has now asserted jurisdiction to regulate an industry constituting a significant portion of the American economy. . . . Owing to its unique place in American history and society, tobacco has its own unique political history. Congress, for better or for worse, has created a distinct regulatory scheme for tobacco products, squarely rejected proposals to give the FDA jurisdiction over tobacco, and repeatedly acted to preclude any agency from exercising significant policymaking authority in the area. Given this history and the breadth of the authority that the FDA has asserted, we are obliged to defer not to the agency's expansive construction of the statute, but to Congress' consistent judgment to deny the FDA this power. . . .

JUSTICE BREYER, dissenting: . . .

I believe that the most important indicia of statutory meaning—language and purpose—along with the FDCA's legislative history are sufficient to establish that the FDA has authority to regulate tobacco. The statute-specific arguments against jurisdiction that the tobacco companies and the majority rely upon are based on erroneous assumptions and, thus, do not defeat the jurisdiction-supporting thrust of the FDCA's language and purpose. The inferences that the majority draws from later legislative history are not persuasive, since one can just as easily infer from the later laws that Congress did not intend to affect the FDA's tobacco-related authority at all. And the fact that the FDA changed its mind about the scope of its own jurisdiction is legally insignificant because the agency's reasons for changing course are fully justified. Finally, the degree of accountability that likely will attach to the FDA's action in this case should alleviate any concern that Congress, rather than an administrative agency, ought to make this important regulatory decision.

[T]he statute plainly allows the FDA to consider the relative, overall "safety" of a device in light of its regulatory alternatives, and where the FDA has chosen the least dangerous path, i.e., the safest path, then it can—and does—provide a "reasonable assurance" of "safety" within the meaning of the statute. A good football helmet provides a reasonable assurance of safety for the player even if the sport itself is still dangerous. And the safest regulatory choice by definition offers a "reasonable" assurance of safety in a world where the other alternatives are yet more dangerous.

In the majority's view, laws enacted since 1965 require us to deny jurisdiction, whatever the FDCA might mean in their absence. But why? Do those laws contain language barring FDA jurisdiction? The majority must concede that they do not. Do they contain provisions that are inconsistent with the FDA's exercise of jurisdiction? With one exception, the majority points to no such provision. This Court has warned against using the views of a later Congress to construe a statute enacted many years before.

[Finally,] the FDA's change of policy, like the subsequent statutes themselves, does nothing to advance the majority's position. . . . What changed? For one thing, the FDA obtained evidence sufficient [in the 1990s] to prove . . . that the tobacco companies knew nicotine achieved appetite-suppressing, mood-stabilizing, and habituating effects through chemical (not psychological) means, even at a time when the companies were publicly denying such knowledge.

Moreover, scientific evidence of adverse health effects mounted, until, in the late 1980's, a consensus on the seriousness of the matter became firm. . . . Finally, administration policy changed. Earlier administrations may have hesitated to assert jurisdiction for the reasons prior Commissioners expressed. Commissioners of the current administration simply took a different regulatory attitude. . . .

NOTES AND QUESTIONS

1. *"Extraordinary cases."* Justice O'Connor seems to concede that the FDCA is "ambiguous" about the "precise" issue presented. If so, why isn't that the end of the matter under step one of the *Chevron* analysis? What makes this an "extraordinary case" in Justice O'Connor's phrase? Should the Court treat extraordinary cases any differently than ordinary cases? Some scholars have referred to this principle as "democracy-forcing" because it sends matters of large public importance back to democratically elected officials for resolution or clearer statement. *See* Jody Freeman & Adrian Vermeule, Massachusetts v. EPA: From Politics to Expertise, 2007 Sup. Ct. Rev. 51 (2008). In fact, as described in Chapter I, *supra*, Congress eventually did give the FDA explicit statutory authority to do what the Court said in *Brown & Williamson* it had no power to do.

2. *Post-enactment "legislative history."* Why does the Court give interpretive weight to congressional actions (and inactions) that occurred after enactment of the Food, Drug, and Cosmetic Act? Doesn't that effectively give Congress the power authoritatively to "interpret" the handiwork of an earlier Congress? Isn't that precisely the job of the judiciary, not the legislature? Note that Justice Scalia joined the *Brown & Williamson* majority. He was famously opposed to using "legislative history" (committee reports, statements of members in floor debates, etc.) as evidence of statutory meaning. Could he reconcile that position with joining Justice O'Connor's opinion?

3. *Using the extraordinary case principle as sword and shield.* In *Brown & Williamson*, the Court invoked the extraordinary case principle to defeat a claim of statutory authority to regulate, even in the face of apparent statutory ambiguity. Can it also be used, conversely, to justify an agency's decision not to act, even in the face of apparent statutory authorization (or possibly even a mandate) to act? Consider the following case.

MASSACHUSETTS v. ENVIRONMENTAL PROTECTION AGENCY
549 U.S. 497 (2007)

JUSTICE STEVENS delivered the opinion of the Court. . . .

[In the portion of the opinion excerpted earlier in this chapter, the Court held that the EPA's decision not to regulate greenhouse gases was arbitrary and capricious. In this portion of the opinion, the Court addresses the question of whether §202(a)(1) of the Clean Air Act authorizes the agency to regulate greenhouse gases. In declining to take any action, the EPA argued that the statute was sufficiently ambiguous on this point that its decision to exclude greenhouse gases from the category of air pollution agents (and derivatively from the category of air pollutants it was authorized to regulate) was entitled to *Chevron* deference.]

II

. . . In concluding that it lacked statutory authority over greenhouse gases, EPA observed that Congress "was well aware of the global climate change issue when it last comprehensively amended the [Clean Air Act] in 1990," yet it declined to adopt a proposed amendment establishing binding emissions limitations. Congress instead chose to authorize further investigation into climate change. EPA further reasoned that Congress' "specially tailored solutions to global atmospheric issues," — in particular, its 1990 enactment of a comprehensive scheme to regulate pollutants that depleted the ozone layer, — counseled against reading the general authorization of §202(a)(1) to confer regulatory authority over greenhouse gases.

EPA stated that it was "urged on in this view" by this Court's decision in FDA v. Brown & Williamson Tobacco Corp., 529 U.S. 120 (2000). In that case, relying on "tobacco['s] unique political history," *id.,* at 159, we invalidated the Food and Drug Administration's reliance on its general authority to regulate drugs as a basis for asserting jurisdiction over an "industry constituting a significant portion of the American economy."

EPA reasoned that climate change had its own "political history": Congress designed the original Clean Air Act to address *local* air pollutants rather than a substance that "is fairly consistent in its concentration throughout the *world's* atmosphere; declined in 1990 to enact proposed amendments to force EPA to set carbon dioxide emission standards for motor vehicles; and addressed global climate change in other legislation. Because of this political history, and because imposing emission limitations on greenhouse gases would have even greater economic and political repercussions than regulating tobacco, EPA was persuaded that it lacked the power to do so. In essence, EPA concluded that climate change was so important that unless Congress spoke with exacting specificity, it could not have meant the agency to address it.

Having reached that conclusion, EPA believed it followed that greenhouse gases cannot be "air pollutants" within the meaning of the Act. ("It follows from this conclusion, that [greenhouse gases], as such, are not air pollutants under the [Clean Air Act's] regulatory provisions . . .".) The agency bolstered this conclusion by explaining that if carbon dioxide were an air pollutant, the only feasible method of reducing tailpipe emissions would be to improve fuel economy. But because Congress has already created detailed mandatory fuel economy standards subject to Department of Transportation (DOT) administration, the agency concluded that EPA regulation would either conflict with those standards or be superfluous. . . .

VI

On the merits, the first question is whether §202(a)(1) of the Clean Air Act authorizes EPA to regulate greenhouse gas emissions from new motor vehicles in the event that it forms a "judgment" that such emissions contribute to climate change. We have little trouble concluding that it does. In relevant part, §202(a)(1) provides that EPA "shall by regulation prescribe . . . standards applicable to the emission of any air pollutant from any class or classes of new motor vehicles or new motor vehicle engines, which in [the Administrator's] judgment cause, or contribute to, air pollution which may reasonably be anticipated to endanger public health or welfare." Because EPA believes that Congress did not intend it to regulate substances that contribute to climate change, the agency maintains that carbon dioxide is not an "air pollutant" within the meaning of the provision.

The statutory text forecloses EPA's reading. The Clean Air Act's sweeping definition of "air pollutant" includes "*any* air pollution agent or combination of such agents, including *any* physical, chemical . . . substance or matter which is emitted into or otherwise enters the ambient air. . . ." On its face, the definition embraces all airborne compounds of whatever stripe, and underscores that intent through the repeated use of the word "any." Carbon dioxide, methane, nitrous oxide, and hydrofluorocarbons are without a doubt "physical [and] chemical . . . substance[s] which [are] emitted into . . . the ambient air." The statute is unambiguous.[26]

Rather than relying on statutory text, EPA invokes postenactment congressional actions and deliberations it views as tantamount to a congressional command to refrain from regulating greenhouse gas emissions. Even if such post enactment legislative history could shed light on the meaning of an otherwise-unambiguous statute, EPA never identifies any action remotely suggesting that Congress meant to curtail its power to treat greenhouse gases as air pollutants. That subsequent Congresses have eschewed enacting binding emissions limitations to combat global warming tells us nothing about what Congress meant when it amended §202(a)(1) in 1970 and 1977. And unlike EPA, we have no difficulty reconciling Congress' various efforts to promote interagency collaboration and research to better understand climate change with the agency's pre-existing mandate to regulate "any air pollutant" that may endanger the public welfare. Collaboration and research do not conflict with any thoughtful regulatory effort; they complement it.

EPA's reliance on *Brown & Williamson Tobacco Corp.* is similarly misplaced. In holding that tobacco products are not "drugs" or "devices" subject to Food and Drug Administration (FDA) regulation pursuant to the Food, Drug and Cosmetic Act (FDCA), we found critical at least two considerations that have no counterpart in this case.

First, we thought it unlikely that Congress meant to ban tobacco products, which the FDCA would have required had such products been classified as "drugs" or "devices." Here, in contrast, EPA jurisdiction would lead to no such extreme measures. EPA would only *regulate* emissions, and even then, it would have to delay any action "to permit the development and application of the requisite technology, giving appropriate consideration to the cost of compliance," §7521(a)(2). . . .

Second, in *Brown & Williamson* we pointed to an unbroken series of congressional enactments that made sense only if adopted "against the backdrop of the FDA's consistent and repeated statements that it lacked authority under the FDCA to regulate tobacco." We can point to no such enactments here: EPA has not identified any congressional action that conflicts in any way with the regulation of greenhouse gases from new motor vehicles. Even if it had, Congress could not have acted against a regulatory "backdrop" of disclaimers of regulatory authority. Prior to the order that provoked this litigation, EPA had never disavowed the authority to regulate greenhouse gases, and in 1998 it in fact affirmed that it *had* such authority. There is no reason, much less a compelling reason, to accept EPA's invitation to read ambiguity into a clear statute. . . .

---

26. In dissent, Justice Scalia maintains that because greenhouse gases permeate the world's atmosphere rather than a limited area near the earth's surface, EPA's exclusion of greenhouse gases from the category of air pollution "agent[s]" is entitled to deference under *Chevron.* . . . EPA's distinction, however, finds no support in the text of the statute, which uses the phrase "the ambient air" without distinguishing between atmospheric layers. Moreover, it is a plainly unreasonable reading of a sweeping statutory provision designed to capture "any physical, chemical . . . substance or matter which is emitted into or otherwise enters the ambient air." 42 U.S.C. §7602(g). Justice Scalia does not (and cannot) explain why Congress would define "air pollutant" so carefully and so broadly, yet confer on EPA the authority to narrow that definition whenever expedient by asserting that a particular substance is not an "agent." At any rate, no party to this dispute contests that greenhouse gases both "ente[r] the ambient air" and tend to warm the atmosphere. They are therefore unquestionably "agent[s]" of air pollution.

While the Congresses that drafted §202(a)(1) might not have appreciated the possibility that burning fossil fuels could lead to global warming, they did understand that without regulatory flexibility, changing circumstances and scientific developments would soon render the Clean Air Act obsolete. The broad language of §202(a)(1) reflects an intentional effort to confer the flexibility necessary to forestall such obsolescence. Because greenhouse gases fit well within the Clean Air Act's capacious definition of "air pollutant," we hold that EPA has the statutory authority to regulate the emission of such gases from new motor vehicles. . . .

[JUSTICE SCALIA, joined by CHIEF JUSTICE ROBERTS and JUSTICES ALITO and THOMAS, dissented. Using an essentially textualist method of statutory interpretation, Justice Scalia argued that the EPA's reading of the statute was not only "reasonable" but "far more plausible than the Court's alternative," and therefore deserving of *Chevron* deference.]

NOTES AND QUESTIONS

1. *The continued vitality of* Brown & Williamson. Does Justice Stevens fairly characterize the holding in *Brown & Williamson*? At a minimum, Massachusetts v. EPA seems to undercut the "extraordinary cases" principle. After all, if the use of a 1970-vintage air pollution statute to combat global warming in the twenty-first century is not an "extraordinary case," what is? Yet, just eight years later, *Brown & Williamson* sprang back to life in another high-profile case, King v. Burwell, 135 S. Ct. 2489 (2015). *King* involved a crucial provision of the Affordable Care Act that authorizes federal tax subsidies for low-income persons seeking to purchase health insurance on statutorily created health insurance "exchanges." Although the Act provides for both state and federal exchanges, a section of the Act curiously limits eligibility for tax subsidies to persons obtaining insurance on exchanges "established by the State." The Internal Revenue Service interpreted this language to permit tax subsidies for people who purchase health insurance on both federal and state exchanges. While agreeing with that reading of the Act, Chief Justice Roberts, writing for the Court, refused to accord any *Chevron* deference to the IRS's reading, because the case presented a "question of deep 'economic and political significance' that is central to this statutory scheme," 135 S. Ct. 2489, quoting *Brown & Williamson*, 529 U.S. at 160, and also because the IRS "has no expertise in crafting health insurance policy of this sort." *Id.*

2. *Categories of step one interpretations.* In his article, End the Failed *Chevron* Experiment Now: How *Chevron* Has Failed and Why It Can and Should be Overruled, 42 Conn. L. Rev. 779, 817-822 (2010), Professor Beermann identifies four methods of interpretation used by the Court at step one. He labels them "original directly spoken *Chevron*," "traditional tools *Chevron*," "plain meaning *Chevron*," and "extraordinary cases Chevron." Applying "original directly spoken *Chevron*," the Court defers to the agency unless the precise issue has been clearly (unambiguously) resolved by Congress in the language of the statute. Though used in *Chevron* itself, this version rarely, if ever, appears in later cases. More common is "traditional tools *Chevron*," an inclusive mode of statutory construction that resembles the techniques used by the Court to read agency-administered

statutes prior to *Chevron* and non-agency-administered statutes since *Chevron*. The "plain meaning" version of *Chevron,* most enthusiastically championed by Justice Scalia, looks for the meaning of a statute at step one primarily by using the "plain meaning" rule of interpretation. The opinion in MCI v. AT&T is an example of this, as is Justice Scalia's dissenting opinion in the *Sweet Home* case. "Extraordinary cases *Chevron*" connotes presumably rare cases like *Brown & Williamson* and *King,* in which the Court declines to defer to an agency's interpretation of an otherwise ambiguous statute because special factors extrinsic to the statute itself suggest a lack of congressional intent to delegate interpretive authority to the agency.

4.   Chevron *Step Two: "Permissible" or "Reasonable" Constructions*

Application of step two of the *Chevron* test has proved to be no less difficult than step one. What did the Court mean by a "permissible" or "reasonable" interpretation of a statute? That seemingly simple question raises a series of issues. As an initial matter, it is far from clear how this inquiry differs from the inquiry at step one. If the reviewing court has found (step one) that the statute is "silent or ambiguous with respect to the specific issue" (i.e., the legality of the agency's interpretation), has it not already *decided* that the agency's reading is "permissible"? Look back at Justice Stevens's opinion in *Chevron.* Is it clear where the step-one inquiry ends and the step-two inquiry begins? Is review of legislative history appropriate for only one of the two steps? How about questions of "policy"?

UTILITY AIR REGULATORY GROUP v. ENVIRONMENTAL PROTECTION AGENCY
134 S. Ct. 2427 (2014)

Justice Scalia announced the judgment of the Court and delivered the opinion of the Court with respect to Parts I and II.

I.   Background

[After the Supreme Court's decision in *Massachusetts v. EPA,* the EPA issued rules setting standards for greenhouse gas emissions from new motor vehicles under the mobile source provisions of the Act. This case concerns whether, and if so in what way, those rules triggered regulation of greenhouse gas pollution from *stationary* sources like power plants and oil refineries. Under the Clean Air Act's "Prevention of Significant Deterioration (PSD) Program," it is unlawful to construct or modify a "major" stationary source in certain areas of the country (those designated as "in attainment" with at least one national air pollution standard) without first obtaining a permit, and meeting emission standards that reflect the "best available control technology" (BACT) for "each pollutant subject to regulation under" the Act. For this program, the Clean Air Act defines "major" facilities as having the potential to emit either (depending on the type of source) 100 or 250 tons per year ("tpy") of "any air pollutant."

In the EPA's view, once it had set a standard for greenhouse gases under any part of the statute, as it had done for new cars and trucks, the PSD requirements would apply to all stationary sources with the potential to emit greenhouse gases over the 100/250-tpy threshold. However, because greenhouse gases tend to be emitted in amounts that are orders of magnitude greater than conventional pollutants, many thousands of small sources that had never been regulated under the Clean Air Act would be swept into the PSD program and made subject to onerous permitting requirements if the 100/250-tpy threshold were applied. The EPA viewed this as an absurd result, which would radically expand the program and render it "unrecognizable" to the Congress that passed it.

In a rule referred to by the Court as the "Tailoring Rule," 75 Fed. Reg. 31514 (2010), the EPA "tailored" the PSD program by administratively raising the statutory thresholds as they applied to greenhouse gas emissions Under the Tailoring Rule, as a general matter, only sources emitting over 100,000 tpy of greenhouse gases would be considered "major" sources. The Tailoring Rule also specified a lower—75,000 tpy—threshold for so-called "anyway" sources: those sources required to obtain permits "anyway," because of their emission of conventional pollutants.

In deciding a challenge to the legality of the Tailoring Rule, the Supreme Court wrestled with two difficult questions: (1) whether greenhouse gases qualify as "any pollutant" in the PSD program's definition of "major source," and (2) whether the EPA could lawfully "tailor" the program by adjusting the statutory thresholds upward to limit the definition of "major" sources to the largest greenhouse gas emitters.]

II. ANALYSIS

A. THE PSD [TRIGGER]

We first decide whether EPA permissibly interpreted the statute to provide that a source may be required to obtain a PSD . . . permit on the sole basis of its potential greenhouse-gas emissions.

1

EPA thought its conclusion that a source's greenhouse gas emissions may necessitate a PSD . . . permit followed from the Act's unambiguous language. . . . We disagree. . . .

Since 1978, EPA's regulations have interpreted "air pollutant" in the PSD permitting trigger as limited to regulated air pollutants, a class much narrower than *Massachusetts'* "all airborne compounds of whatever stripe," 549 U.S. at 529. [That interpretation was] appropriate: It is plain as day that the Act does not envision an elaborate, burdensome permitting process for major emitters of steam, oxygen, or other harmless airborne substances. It takes some cheek for EPA to insist that it cannot possibly give "air pollutant" a reasonable, context-appropriate meaning in the PSD and Title V contexts when it has been doing precisely that for decades. . . .

Massachusetts does not strip EPA of authority to exclude greenhouse gases from the class of regulable air pollutants under other parts of the Act where their inclusion would be inconsistent with the statutory scheme. The Act-wide definition to which the Court gave a "sweeping" and "capacious" interpretation, *id.* at 528, 532, is not a command to regulate, but a description of the universe of substances EPA may *consider* regulating under the Act's operative provisions. *Massachusetts* does not foreclose the Agency's use of statutory context to infer that certain of the Act's provisions use "air pollutant" to denote not every conceivable airborne substance, but only those that may sensibly be encompassed within the particular regulatory program. . . .

2

Having determined that EPA was mistaken in thinking the Act *compelled* a greenhouse-gas-inclusive interpretation of the PSD and Title V triggers, we next consider the Agency's alternative position that its interpretation was justified as an exercise of its "discretion" to adopt "a reasonable construction of the statute." Tailoring Rule 31517. We conclude that EPA's interpretation is not permissible.

Even under *Chevron*'s deferential framework, agencies must operate "within the bounds of reasonable interpretation." [City of Arlington v. FCC, 133 S. Ct. 1863, 1868 (2013).] And reasonable statutory interpretation must account for both "the specific context in which . . . language is used" and "the broader context of the statute as a whole." Robinson v. Shell Oil Co., 519 U.S. 337, 341 (1997). A statutory "provision that may seem ambiguous in isolation is often clarified by the remainder of the statutory scheme . . . because only one of the permissible meanings produces a substantive effect that is compatible with the rest of the law." United Sav. Assn. of Tex. v. Timbers of Inwood Forest Associates, Ltd., 484 U.S. 365, 371 (1988). Thus, an agency interpretation that is "inconsisten[t] with the design and structure of the statute as a whole," University of Tex. Southwestern Medical Center v. Nassar, 133 S. Ct. 2517, 2529 (2013), does not merit deference.

EPA itself has repeatedly acknowledged that applying the PSD . . . permitting requirements to greenhouse gases would be inconsistent with—in fact, would overthrow—the Act's structure and design. In the Tailoring Rule, EPA described the calamitous consequences of interpreting the Act in that way. Under the PSD program, annual permit applications would jump from about 800 to nearly 82,000; annual administrative costs would swell from $12 million to over $1.5 billion; and decade-long delays in issuing permits would become common, causing construction projects to grind to a halt nationwide. Tailoring Rule 31557. . . . EPA stated that these results would be so "contrary to congressional intent," and would so "severely undermine what Congress sought to accomplish," that they necessitated as much as a 1,000-fold increase in the permitting thresholds set forth in the statute. *Id.* at 31554, 31562.

Like EPA, we think it beyond reasonable debate that requiring permits for sources based solely on their emission of greenhouse gases at the 100- and 250-tons-per-year levels set forth in the statute would be "incompatible" with "the substance of Congress' regulatory scheme." [FDA v. Brown & Williamson Tobacco Corp., 529 U.S. 120, 156 (2000).] . . .

The fact that EPA's greenhouse-gas-inclusive interpretation of the PSD and Title V triggers would place plainly excessive demands on limited governmental resources is alone a good reason for rejecting it; but that is not the only reason. EPA's interpretation is also unreasonable because it would bring about an enormous and transformative expansion in EPA's regulatory authority without clear congressional authorization. When an agency claims to discover in a long-extant statute an unheralded power to regulate "a significant portion of the American economy," *Brown & Williamson*, 529 U.S. at 159, we typically greet its announcement with a measure of skepticism. We expect Congress to speak clearly if it wishes to assign to an agency decisions of vast "economic and political significance." *Id.* at 160. . . . The power to require permits for the construction and modification of tens of thousands, and the operation of millions, of sources nationwide falls comfortably within the class of authorizations that we have been reluctant to read into ambiguous statutory text. Moreover, in EPA's assertion of that authority, we confront a singular situation: an agency laying claim to extravagant statutory power over the national economy while at the same time strenuously asserting that the authority claimed would render the statute "unrecognizable to the Congress that designed" it. Tailoring Rule 31555. . . . [I]t would be patently unreasonable—not to say outrageous—for EPA to insist on seizing expansive power that it admits the statute is not designed to grant.

3

EPA thought that despite the foregoing problems, it could make its interpretation reasonable by adjusting the levels at which a source's greenhouse-gas emissions would oblige it to undergo PSD . . . permitting. Although the Act, in no uncertain terms, requires permits for sources with the potential to emit more than 100 or 250 tons per year of a relevant pollutant, EPA in its Tailoring Rule wrote a new threshold of *100,000* tons per year for greenhouse gases. . . .

We conclude that EPA's rewriting of the statutory thresholds was impermissible and therefore could not validate the Agency's interpretation of the triggering provisions. An agency has no power to "tailor" legislation to bureaucratic policy goals by rewriting unambiguous statutory terms. . . . It is hard to imagine a statutory term less ambiguous than the precise numerical thresholds at which the Act requires PSD . . . permitting. When EPA replaced those numbers with others of its own choosing, it went well beyond the "bounds of its statutory authority." *Arlington*, 133 S. Ct. at 1868 (emphasis deleted). . . .

Were we to recognize the authority claimed by EPA in the Tailoring Rule, we would deal a severe blow to the Constitution's separation of powers. . . . The power of executing the laws necessarily includes both authority and responsibility to resolve some questions left open by Congress that arise during the law's administration. But it does not include a power to revise clear statutory terms that turn out not to work in practice. . . .

In the Tailoring Rule, EPA asserts newfound authority to . . . decide, on an ongoing basis and without regard for the thresholds prescribed by Congress, how many of those sources to regulate. We are not willing to stand on the dock and wave goodbye as EPA embarks on this multiyear voyage of discovery. . . . Instead, the need to rewrite clear provisions of the statute should have alerted EPA that it had taken a wrong interpretive turn. . . . Because the Tailoring Rule cannot save EPA's interpretation of the triggers, that interpretation was impermissible under *Chevron*.[8] . . .

[The Parts of the Court's analysis related to another Clean Air Act permitting program, Title V, are omitted.]

JUSTICE BREYER, with whom JUSTICE GINSBURG, JUSTICE SOTOMAYOR, and JUSTICE KAGAN join, concurring in part and dissenting in part. . . .

I agree with the Court that the word "any," when used in a statute, does not normally mean "any in the universe." . . . But I do not agree with the Court that the only way to avoid an absurd or otherwise impermissible result in these cases is to create an atextual greenhouse gas exception to the phrase "any air pollutant." After all, the word "any" makes an earlier appearance in the definitional provision, which defines "major emitting facility" to mean "*any* . . . source with the potential to emit two hundred and fifty tons per year or more of any air pollutant." [42 U.S.C.] §7479(1) (emphasis added). As a linguistic matter, one can just as easily read an implicit exception for small-scale greenhouse gas emissions into the phrase "any source" as into the phrase "any air pollutant." . . .

JUSTICE ALITO, with whom JUSTICE THOMAS joins, concurring in part and dissenting in part. [Omitted.]

NOTES AND QUESTIONS

1. *Scope of* Chevron *step two.* In *UARG*, the discussion focuses explicitly on the limits of *Chevron* deference in step two, finding that deference ends when it conflicts with judicial construction of the statutory framework. Any administrative decision that cannot be squared with the law, even if the law does not expressly cover other potential exercises of administrative discretion, cannot pass muster under step two. Does this provide a helpful distinction between *Chevron*'s steps? Justice Breyer's dissent in *UARG* would have given both a different reading to the law and greater leeway to the agency to interpret the scope of its authority and to read the law in ways that fit with reasonably broad discretion.

2. *The standard of "reasonableness" at step two.* In Cuozzo Speed Technologies, LLC v. Lee, 136 S. Ct. 2131 (2016), excerpted in Chapter III, *infra,* Justice

---

8. Justice Breyer argues that when the statutory permitting thresholds of 100 or 250 tons per year do not provide a "sensible regulatory line," EPA is entitled to "read an unwritten exception" into "the particular number used by the statute"—by which he apparently means that the Agency is entitled to substitute a dramatically higher number, such as 100,000. We are aware of no principle of administrative law that would allow an agency to rewrite such a clear statutory term, and we shudder to contemplate the effect that such a principle would have on democratic governance.

Justice Breyer, however, claims to perceive no difference between (a) reading the statute to exclude greenhouse gases from the term "any air pollutant" in the permitting triggers, and (b) reading the statute to exclude sources emitting less than 100,000 tons per year from the statutory phrase "any . . . source with the potential to emit two hundred and fifty tons per year or more." The two could scarcely be further apart. As we have explained (and as EPA agrees), statutory context makes plain that the Act's operative provisions use "air pollutant" to denote less than the full range of pollutants covered by the Act-wide definition. It is therefore incumbent on EPA to specify the pollutants encompassed by that term in the context of a particular program, and to do so reasonably in light of that program's overall regulatory scheme. But there is no ambiguity whatsoever in the specific, numerical permitting thresholds, and thus no room for EPA to exercise discretion in selecting a different threshold.

Breyer, writing for the Court, elaborated the "reasonableness" test to be applied at *Chevron* step two. A Patent Office rule required the agency, when conducting an "inter partes review" (one type of internal administrative review) of a previously-granted patent, to give the contested patent claim "its broadest reasonable construction in light of the specification of the patent in which it appears." 37 CFR §42.100(b). Cuozzo had argued that the underlying statute, properly interpreted, required the Patent Office to apply a different standard, namely the "ordinary meaning as understood by a person of skill in the art" standard used in judicial proceedings to determine the legality of a contested patent. After finding, at step one, that the statute "contains a gap," Justice Breyer had this to say about the analysis at step two:

> For one thing, construing a patent claim according to its broadest reasonable construction helps to protect the public. A reasonable, yet unlawfully broad claim might discourage the use of the invention by a member of the public. Because an examiner's (or reexaminer's) use of the broadest reasonable construction standard increases the possibility that the examiner will find the claim too broad (and deny it), use of that standard encourages the applicant to draft narrowly. This helps ensure precision while avoiding overly broad claims, and thereby helps prevent a patent from tying up too much knowledge, while helping members of the public draw useful information from the disclosed invention and better understand the lawful limits of the claim.
>
> For another, past practice supports the Patent Office's regulation. The Patent Office has used this standard for more than 100 years. It has applied that standard in proceedings, which, as here, resemble district court litigation. . . . It also applies that standard in proceedings that may be consolidated with a concurrent inter partes review.
>
> Cuozzo makes two arguments in response. First, Cuozzo says that there is a critical difference between the Patent Office's initial *examination* of an application to determine if a patent should issue, and this proceeding, in which the agency *reviews* an already-issued patent. In an initial examination of an application for a patent the examiner gives the claim its broadest reasonable construction. But if the patent examiner rejects the claim, then . . . the applicant has a right to amend and resubmit the claim. . . . In inter partes review, however, the broadest reasonable construction standard may help protect certain public interests, but there is no absolute right to amend any challenged patent claims. This, Cuozzo says, is unfair to the patent holder.
>
> The process however, is not as unfair as Cuozzo suggests. The patent holder may, at least once in the process, make a motion to do just what he would do in the examination process, namely, amend or narrow the claim. . . .
>
> Second, Cuozzo says that the use of the broadest reasonable construction standard in inter partes review, together with use of an ordinary meaning standard in district court, may produce inconsistent results and cause added confusion. . . . We recognize that that is so. This possibility, however, has long been present in our patent system, which provides different tracks—one in the Patent Office and one in the courts—for the review and adjudication of patent claims. . . . Moreover, the Patent Office uses the broadest reasonable construction standard in other proceedings, including interference proceedings . . . , which may implicate patents that are later reviewed in district court. The statute gives the Patent Office the power to consolidate these other proceedings with inter partes review. To try to create uniformity of standards would consequently prove difficult. And we cannot find unreasonable the Patent Office's decision to prefer a degree of inconsistency in

the standards used between the courts and the agency, rather than among agency proceedings.

Finally, Cuozzo [offers] various policy arguments in favor of the ordinary meaning standard. The Patent Office is legally free to accept or reject such policy arguments on the basis of its own reasoned analysis. Having concluded that the Patent Office's regulation, selecting the broadest reasonable construction standard, is reasonable in light of the rationales described above, we do not decide whether there is a better alternative as a policy matter. That is a question that Congress left to the particular expertise of the Patent Office. . . .

How would you characterize the kinds of arguments that Breyer makes? Are these really distinct from the kinds of arguments one would make to determine whether the statute is "ambiguous," applying "traditional tools of statutory construction"? To determine whether the Patent Office's rule was "arbitrary or capricious"? Are Breyer's arguments qualitatively different from the "policy arguments" that he would leave to the "particular expertise of the Patent Office"?

3. *Does* Chevron *really have two steps?* In light of the cases we have read, this may seem like a silly question. Of course *Chevron* has two steps! Although this seems obvious, a pair of administrative law scholars has argued that in truth there is only one step because if Congress's intent is clear, then only an interpretation consistent with that clear intent can be permissible. Matthew C. Stephenson & Adrian Vermeule, *Chevron* Has Only One Step, 95 Va. L. Rev. 597, 597 (2009). Another pair of scholars responded with the view that step one of *Chevron* is a pinpoint inquiry into whether Congress has compelled resolution of the question at issue, while step two allows the Court to assess the reasonableness of an interpretation arrived at, free from congressional compulsion. Kenneth A. Bamberger & Peter L. Strauss, *Chevron*'s Two Steps, 95 Va. L. Rev. 611, 624-625 (2009). To add fuel to this fire, the Court, in opinions by Justice Scalia relatively late in his tenure on the Court, twice expressed views that seemingly resonate with Stephenson and Vermeule's argument:

> The dissent finds it "puzzling" that we invoke this proposition (that a reasonable agency interpretation prevails) at the "outset," omitting the supposedly prior inquiry of "whether Congress has directly spoken to the precise question at issue." But surely if Congress has directly spoken to an issue then any agency interpretation contradicting what Congress has said would be unreasonable.

Entergy Corp. v. Riverkeeper, Inc., 556 U.S. 208, 218 n.4 (2009) (excerpted in Chapter V, *infra*). *See also* Cuomo v. Clearing House Assn., 557 U.S. 519, 525 (2009). At the same time, however, the Court has continued, in opinions written by others, to apply the familiar two-step formula. *See, e.g.,* Coeur Alaska, Inc. v. Southeast Alaska Conservation Council, 557 U.S. 261, 277-278 (2009) (Kennedy, J.).

4. *Does* Chevron *have a third step?* Some commentators have argued that *Chevron* has a third step, involving application of the arbitrary and capricious standard to test the wisdom of the agency's choice of interpretation from the range of permissible constructions. Some courts have conducted arbitrary, capricious review as a separate inquiry in *Chevron* cases. *See, e.g.,* International Bhd. of Elec. Workers v. ICC, 862 F.2d 330, 338 (D.C. Cir. 1988). While the Supreme Court has not ruled out arbitrary and capricious review in *Chevron* cases, it appears to

view it as subsumed into the question of whether the agency's interpretation is permissible or reasonable. *See* Verizon Communications, Inc. v. FCC, 535 U.S. 467, 527 n.38 (2002).

The Court—albeit briefly—once again addressed the relationship between arbitrary, capricious review and *Chevron* step two in Judulang v. Holder, 132 S. Ct. 476 (2011). The case involved a Board of Immigration Appeals policy for deciding when resident aliens may apply to the Attorney General for relief from deportation. The Court, in an opinion by Justice Kagan, ruled that the policy was arbitrary and capricious. The government had urged the Court to analyze the issue under *Chevron*, but the Court refused on the ground that the policy "is not an interpretation of any statutory language." In a footnote Justice Kagan added:

> Were we to [analyze this case under *Chevron* step two], our analysis would be the same, because under *Chevron* step two, we ask whether an agency interpretation is "'arbitrary or capricious in substance.'" Mayo Foundation for Medical Ed. and Research v. United States, 562 U.S. 44 (2011) (quoting Household Credit Services, Inc. v. Pfennig, 541 U.S. 232, 242 (2004)).

Is Justice Kagan correct that analysis under the arbitrary, capricious standard is the same as review under *Chevron* step two? Is that consistent with the view Justice Scalia expresses in *UARG*?

5. Chevron *Deference to Conflicting or Changing Interpretations?*

If an agency changes its interpretation of its statute, is its new interpretation deserving of deference? Suppose that the first interpretation has been upheld by a reviewing court. Is it then binding on the agency thereafter? Or, to complicate matters further, suppose that a court itself has rendered the first interpretation: May the agency then adopt a different interpretation? That was the issue presented in the following case:

NATIONAL CABLE & TELECOMMUNICATIONS ASSN. v. BRAND X INTERNET SERVS., 545 U.S. 967 (2005):   The interpretive question was how to classify, under the Telecommunications Act of 1996, broadband Internet service provided by cable-modem-based "Internet service providers" (ISPs). Is it a "telecommunications service," subject to mandatory common-carrier-style regulation by the FCC? Or is it an "information service," essentially exempt from regulation? Before the FCC could rule on the matter, the U.S. Court of Appeals for the Ninth Circuit, in a private dispute between a local cable franchising authority and its franchisee, ruled that cable-modem service was a "telecommunications service." AT&T v. City of Portland, 216 F.3d 8712 (9th Cir. 2001). The FCC, alarmed at the implications of the ruling, quickly adopted a rule classifying cable-modem service as an "information service." Challenges to the FCC's rule were consolidated and assigned to the Ninth Circuit, which found the FCC's decision invalid. The Supreme Court reversed the Ninth Circuit. Justice Thomas wrote for the Court:

The Court of Appeals declined to apply *Chevron* because it thought that the Commission's interpretation of the Communications Act was foreclosed by the conflicting construction of the Act [that the Court of Appeals] had adopted in [*Portland*]. It based that holding on the assumption that *Portland*'s construction overrode the Commission's, regardless of whether *Portland* had held the statute to be unambiguous. That reasoning was incorrect.

A court's prior judicial construction of a statute trumps an agency construction otherwise entitled to *Chevron* deference only if the prior court decision holds that its construction follows from the unambiguous terms of the statute and thus leaves no room for agency discretion. This principle follows from *Chevron* itself. . . . *Chevron*'s premise is that it is for agencies, not courts, to fill statutory gaps. The better rule is to hold judicial interpretations contained in precedents to the same demanding *Chevron* step one standard that applies if the court is reviewing the agency's construction on a blank slate: Only a judicial precedent holding that the statute unambiguously forecloses the agency's interpretation, and therefore contains no gap for the agency to fill, displaces a conflicting agency construction.

A contrary rule would produce anomalous results. It would mean that whether an agency's interpretation of an ambiguous statute is entitled to *Chevron* deference would turn on the order in which the interpretations issue: If the court's construction came first, its construction would prevail, whereas if the agency's came first, the agency's construction would command *Chevron* deference. Yet whether Congress has delegated to an agency the authority to interpret a statute does not depend on the order in which the judicial and administrative constructions occur. The Court of Appeals' rule, moreover, would "lead to the ossification of large portions of our statutory law," [United States v. Mead Corp., 533 U.S. 218, 247 (2001)] (Scalia, J., dissenting), by precluding agencies from revising unwise judicial constructions of ambiguous statutes. Neither *Chevron* nor the doctrine of *stare decisis* requires these haphazard results.

The dissent answers that allowing an agency to override what a court believes to be the best interpretation of a statute makes "judicial decisions subject to reversal by Executive officers." It does not. Since *Chevron* teaches that a court's opinion as to the best reading of an ambiguous statute an agency is charged with administering is not authoritative, the agency's decision to construe that statute differently from a court does not say that the court's holding was legally wrong. Instead, the agency may, consistent with the court's holding, choose a different construction, since the agency remains the authoritative interpreter (within the limits of reason) of such statutes. . . .

545 U.S. at 982-983. Justice Scalia, joined by Justices Souter and Ginsburg, dissented, criticizing both the FCC's reading of the law and the majority's deference to it:

Imagine the following sequence of events: FCC action is challenged as ultra vires under the governing statute; the litigation reaches all the way to the Supreme Court of the United States. The Solicitor General sets forth the FCC's official position (approved by the Commission) regarding interpretation of the statute. Applying *Mead,* however, the Court denies the agency position *Chevron* deference, finds that the best interpretation of the statute contradicts the agency's position, and holds the challenged agency action unlawful. The agency promptly conducts a rulemaking, and adopts a rule that comports with its earlier position—in effect disagreeing with the Supreme Court concerning the best interpretation of the statute. According to today's opinion, the agency is thereupon free to take the action that the Supreme Court found unlawful.

This is not only bizarre. It is probably unconstitutional. As we held in Chicago & Southern Air Lines, Inc. v. Waterman S.S. Corp., 333 U.S. 103 (1948), Article III courts do not sit to render decisions that can be reversed or ignored by Executive officers. . . .

A court's interpretation is conclusive, the Court says, only if it holds that interpretation to be "the *only permissible* reading of the statute," and not if it merely holds it to be "the *best reading*." Does this mean that in future statutory-construction cases involving agency-administered statutes courts must specify (presumably in dictum) which of the two they are holding? And what of the many cases decided in the past, before this dictum's requirement was established? Apparently, silence on the point means that the court's decision is subject to agency reversal. . . .

It is indeed a wonderful new world that the Court creates, one full of promise for administrative-law professors in need of tenure articles and, of course, for litigators. I would adhere to what has been the rule in the past: When a court interprets a statute without *Chevron* deference to agency views, its interpretation (whether or not asserted to rest upon an unambiguous text) is the law. . . .

545 U.S. at 1016-1019.

NOTES AND QUESTIONS

1. *Interpretation versus policy judgment.* Justice Scalia, for decades the Court's foremost champion of *Chevron* deference, focuses on the problems the Court's deference could create in the interplay between judicial and administrative readings of the law. Is his complaint really with the concept of judicial deference to agency interpretations of *law*, as opposed to agency determinations of *policy* within the space courts determine was left by the law? Is that same view implicit in Justice Thomas's statement that "*Chevron*'s premise is that it is for agencies, not courts, to fill statutory gaps"? Does the problem come in the confusion between administrative gap-filling through policy decisions (when the law is interpreted to permit that) and agency interpretation of law (when courts decide that Congress has delegated that authority to the agency)? Does the problem of the order of administrative and judicial decisions vanish if the distinction is made between *interpretation of law* for which courts are the deciders and *policy judgments* which are left to agencies subject to the strictures of the governing statutes and the grounds for challenge set out in the APA?

2. *Deference and timing of judicial and administrative decisions.* In looking at the problem of timing and agency changes in interpretation, suppose the first administrative interpretation had been upheld by a reviewing court. In Maislin Industries, U.S., Inc. v. Primary Steel, Inc., 497 U.S. 116 (1990), the Court refused to defer to an ICC interpretation deviating from a prior agency interpretation that had been upheld by the Supreme Court and applied consistently by the agency for many years. The ICC argued that changed competitive conditions justified its reversal. The Supreme Court quickly rejected the idea of according *Chevron* deference to the new interpretation, saying: "Once we have determined a statute's clear meaning, we adhere to that determination under the doctrine of *stare decisis,* and we judge an agency's later interpretation of the statute against our prior determination of the statute's meaning." Is that an adequate analysis of the issue, or should the Court have attempted to determine whether its prior decision (which antedated *Chevron*) applied an independent

or a deferential mode of review? What default rule should the Court adopt if the prior decision is silent on the question? In another case, Lechmere, Inc. v. NLRB, 502 U.S. 527 (1992), the Court held that *Chevron* deference was inappropriate where the agency was attempting to change its interpretation to one that had already been rejected by the Supreme Court decades earlier. Does *Lechmere* make more intuitive sense than *Maislin*? Does your answer depend on the basis for the Supreme Court's earlier rejection?

3. *Age and contemporaneity of interpretation.* Should the judicial obligation of deference depend on whether the agency's interpretation is longstanding or whether the interpretation was rendered contemporaneously with enactment of the statute? The Court has split over the question of how deference changes when an agency has stuck by an interpretation for many years. Writing for the majority in Barnhart v. Walton, 535 U.S. 212 (2002), Justice Breyer declared that "this Court will normally accord particular deference to an agency interpretation of 'longstanding' duration." *Id.* at 220 (quoting North Haven Bd. of Ed. v. Bell, 456 U.S. 512, 522 n.12 (1982)). He noted that the interpretation at issue was of longstanding duration, though he did not say what standard then applied to such interpretations. Justice Scalia, concurring, specifically demurred to the notion that the age of the interpretation matters:

> I do not believe . . . that "particular deference" is owed "to an agency interpretation of 'longstanding' duration." . . . That notion is an anachronism—a relic of the pre-*Chevron* days, when there was thought to be only one "correct" interpretation of a statutory text. A "longstanding" agency interpretation, particularly one that dated back to the very origins of the statute, was more likely to reflect the single correct meaning. But once it is accepted, as it was in *Chevron,* that there is a range of permissible interpretations, and that the agency is free to move from one to another, so long as the most recent interpretation is reasonable its antiquity should make no difference.

535 U.S. at 226. Who has the better argument?

In an earlier decision, Smiley v. Citibank, 517 U.S. 735 (1996), the Court seemed to follow Justice Scalia's view. *Smiley* involved an interpretation of the word "interest" as used in the National Bank Act of 1864. In a rule adopted in 1996, the Comptroller of the Currency interpreted "interest" to include late-payment fees. In attacking the regulation, the petitioner argued that an interpretation rendered over 100 years after enactment of the statute was entitled to no deference. The Court emphatically rejected the argument:

> The 100-year delay makes no difference. To be sure, agency interpretations that are of long standing come before us with a certain credential of reasonableness, since it is rare that error would long persist. But neither antiquity nor contemporaneity with the statute is a condition of validity. We accord deference to agencies under *Chevron,* not because of a presumption that they drafted the provisions in question, or were present at the hearings, or spoke to the principal sponsors; but rather because of a presumption that Congress, when it left ambiguity in a statute meant for implementation by an agency, understood that the ambiguity would be resolved, first and foremost, by the agency, and desired the agency (rather than the courts) to possess whatever degree of discretion the ambiguity allows.

517 U.S. at 740-741.

6. Chevron *"Step Zero": Interpretations Having the "Force of Law" and "Jurisdictional" Questions*

Recall that, according to Justice Stevens, the *Chevron* doctrine applies "[W]hen a court reviews an agency's construction of the statute that it administers." What, exactly, does it mean for an agency to "administer" a statute? In *Chevron*, the answer was pretty obvious: the Clean Air Act had expressly delegated to the EPA authority to issue binding regulations and to take various actions to implement and enforce them. But in other cases, the authority delegated to an agency, or the relationship of the agency to the statute that it purports to interpret, is less clear. In those cases, questions naturally arise whether the *Chevron* doctrine even applies in the first place. This, in the words of one commentator, is the inquiry at *Chevron*'s "step zero." Cass R. Sunstein, *Chevron Step Zero*, 92 Va. L. Rev. 188 (2006). This section examines some of the cases that have addressed these situations.

a. Interpretations Not Having the "Force of Law"

Imports into the United States, as with other nations, are subject to a complex set of rules that dictate the tariff (tax) that must be paid. The rates are set by a combination of international agreements and domestic law, reflecting intense political maneuvering, historical anomalies, and "scientific" assessment of rates that would provide "fair competition," among other considerations. Rates vary greatly across product categories, ranging from no tariff to a substantial percentage of an imported product's value. While broad product categories are subjects for larger political processes, actual rates for particular products are the domain of bureaucratic decisionmaking.

The specific rates for each product are determined by the product's classification, set forth in the Harmonized Tariff Schedule of the United States (HTSUS). The tariff schedule now combines U.S. tariff undertakings with an international classification system for products. HTSUS attempts to line up ground-level decisions that must be made by customs officials (essentially the government's tax assessors for imports) with the 30,000-foot-level decisions on tariff rates that are negotiated and legislated. HTSUS is maintained and published by the United States International Trade Commission (USITC), an independent agency with jurisdiction over certain trade matters and disputes. HTSUS is an enormous document, running to thousands of pages, with a roughly 60-page index and more than 850 pages of general notes. Products are given classification numbers, with the most general categories consisting of 4-digit numbers and subcategories receiving 6-digit or 8-digit classifications. There are more than 17,000 classification categories and subcategories in HTSUS. Determinations of the actual assignment of products to classifications are made not by USITC but by Customs and Border Protection, part of the Department of Homeland Security (formerly—including at the time relevant to the decision in *Mead*—the U.S. Customs Service, which historically was part of the Treasury Department). Firms with questions about the proper classification of a product can ask for a ruling from Customs, which will be published as a "ruling letter" instructing not only the particular firm but also the general public on the classification. These rulings may be issued at the field level, by any of the nearly 500 authorized ports of entry into the United States, or by Customs Headquarters.

Mead Corporation imported a product called "day planners"—three-ring binders that contained pages with calendar information, space for notes on daily schedules, a section for phone numbers and addresses, and in some models other items such as a plastic ruler and plastic pouch. The planners had been treated by the Customs Service as part of a category of products that includes "Registers, account books, notebooks, order books, receipt books, letter pads, memorandum pads, diaries and similar articles." Within that classification, Customs had accepted day planners as falling under the general "other" subcategory, HTSUS 4820.10.40, rather than under the subcategory that includes bound diaries, HTSUS 4820.10.20. The result was that the day planners were subject to a zero duty rate. As the Supreme Court explained in its opinion:

> In January 1993, however, Customs changed its position, and issued a Headquarters ruling letter classifying Mead's day planners as "Diaries . . . , bound" subject to [a 4.0%] tariff under subheading 4820.10.20. That letter was short on explanation . . . but after Mead's protest, Customs Headquarters issued a new letter, carefully reasoned but never published, reaching the same conclusion. This letter considered two definitions of "diary" from the Oxford English Dictionary, the first covering a daily journal of the past day's events, the second a book including "'printed dates for daily memoranda and jottings; also . . . calendars. . . .'" *Id.* (quoting Oxford English Dictionary 321 (Compact ed. 1982)). Customs concluded that "diary" was not confined to the first, in part because the broader definition reflects commercial usage and hence the "commercial identity of these items in the marketplace." As for the definition of "bound," Customs concluded that HTSUS was not referring to "bookbinding," but to a less exact sort of fastening described in the Harmonized Commodity Description and Coding System Explanatory Notes to Heading 4820, which spoke of binding by "'reinforcements or fittings of metal, plastics, etc.'" *Id.* at 45a. . . .

533 U.S. 218, 225 (2001).

Mead brought suit in the Court of International Trade (the specialized district court with jurisdiction over trade matters) to challenge the Customs ruling. The CIT rejected Mead's claim, but on appeal the Federal Circuit reversed, holding that the Customs ruling was based on an improper interpretation of HTSUS.

UNITED STATES v. MEAD CORP.
533 U.S. 218 (2001)

JUSTICE SOUTER delivered the opinion of the Court.

The question is whether a tariff classification ruling by the United States Customs Service deserves judicial deference. The Federal Circuit rejected Customs's invocation of Chevron U.S.A. Inc. v. Natural Resources Defense Council, Inc., in support of such a ruling, to which it gave no deference. We agree that a tariff classification has no claim to judicial deference under *Chevron*, there being no indication that Congress intended such a ruling to carry the force of law, but we hold that under Skidmore v. Swift & Co. [, 323 U.S. 134 (1944)], the ruling is eligible to claim respect according to its persuasiveness.

I

A

Imports are taxed under the Harmonized Tariff Schedule of the United States (HTSUS), 19 U.S.C. §1202.* Title 19 U.S.C. §1500(b) provides that Customs "shall, under rules and regulations prescribed by the Secretary [of the Treasury,] . . . fix the final classification and rate of duty applicable to . . . merchandise" under the HTSUS. . . .

[Customs regulations provide for letter rulings that determine the tariff classification for a particular import.] A ruling letter

> "represents the official position of the Customs Service with respect to the particular transaction or issue described therein and is binding on all Customs Service personnel in accordance with the provisions of this section until modified or revoked. In the absence of a change of practice or other modification or revocation which affects the principle of the ruling set forth in the ruling letter, that principle may be cited as authority in the disposition of transactions involving the same circumstances." [19 C.F.R.] §177.9(a).

[In addition to the transaction addressed in the letter,] a ruling letter is to "be applied only with respect to transactions involving articles identical to the sample submitted with the ruling request or to articles whose description is identical to the description set forth in the ruling letter." §177.9(b)(2). [T]he regulations . . . provide that "no other person should rely on the ruling letter or assume that the principles of that ruling will be applied in connection with any transaction other than the one described in the letter," *ibid.* . . .

B . . .

The Federal Circuit . . . held that Customs classification rulings should not get *Chevron* deference. . . . The appeals court thought classification rulings had a weaker *Chevron* claim even than Internal Revenue Service interpretive rulings, to which that court gives no deference; unlike rulings by the IRS, Customs rulings issue from many locations and need not be published. 185 F.3d at 1307-1308.

The Court of Appeals accordingly gave no deference at all to the ruling classifying the Mead day planners and rejected the agency's reasoning as to both "diary" and "bound." It thought that planners were not diaries because they had no space for "relatively extensive notations about events, observations, feelings, or thoughts" in the past. *Id.* at 1310. And it concluded that diaries "bound" in subheading 4810.10.20 presupposed "unbound" diaries, such that treating ring-fastened diaries as "bound" would leave the "unbound diary" an empty category. *Id.*, at 1311. . . .

---

* [The HTSUS is referenced in 19 U.S.C. §1202, but it is not included in the United States Code. — Eds.]

II

A

When Congress has "explicitly left a gap for an agency to fill, there is an express delegation of authority to the agency to elucidate a specific provision of the statute by regulation," *Chevron,* 467 U.S. at 843-844, and any ensuing regulation is binding in the courts unless procedurally defective, arbitrary or capricious in substance, or manifestly contrary to the statute. But whether or not they enjoy any express delegation of authority on a particular question, agencies charged with applying a statute necessarily make all sorts of interpretive choices, and while not all of those choices bind judges to follow them, they certainly may influence courts facing questions the agencies have already answered. "[T]he well-reasoned views of the agencies implementing a statute 'constitute a body of experience and informed judgment to which courts and litigants may properly resort for guidance,'" Bragdon v. Abbott, 524 U.S. 624, 642 (1998) (quoting *Skidmore,* 323 U.S. at 139-140), and "[w]e have long recognized that considerable weight should be accorded to an executive department's construction of a statutory scheme it is entrusted to administer. . . ." *Chevron, supra,* at 844. . . . The fair measure of deference to an agency administering its own statute has been understood to vary with circumstances, and courts have looked to the degree of the agency's care, its consistency, formality, and relative expertness, and to the persuasiveness of the agency's position, *see Skidmore, supra,* at 139-140. . . .

Since 1984, we have identified a category of interpretive choices distinguished by an additional reason for judicial deference. This Court in *Chevron* recognized that Congress not only engages in express delegation of specific interpretive authority, but that "[s]ometimes the legislative delegation to an agency on a particular question is implicit." 467 U.S. at 844. Congress, that is, may not have expressly delegated authority or responsibility to implement a particular provision or fill a particular gap. Yet it can still be apparent from the agency's generally conferred authority and other statutory circumstances that Congress would expect the agency to be able to speak with the force of law when it addresses ambiguity in the statute or fills a space in the enacted law, even one about which "Congress did not actually have an intent" as to a particular result. *Id.* at 845. When circumstances implying such an expectation exist, a reviewing court . . . is obliged to accept the agency's position if Congress has not previously spoken to the point at issue and the agency's interpretation is reasonable, *see id.* at 842-845; *cf.* 5 U.S.C. §706(2) (a reviewing court shall set aside agency action, findings, and conclusions found to be "arbitrary, capricious, an abuse of discretion, or otherwise not in accordance with law").

We have recognized a very good indicator of delegation meriting *Chevron* treatment in express congressional authorizations to engage in the process of rulemaking or adjudication that produces regulations or rulings for which deference is claimed. . . . It is fair to assume generally that Congress contemplates administrative action with the effect of law when it provides for a relatively formal administrative procedure tending to foster the fairness and deliberation that should underlie a pronouncement of such force. Thus, the overwhelming number of our cases applying *Chevron* deference have reviewed the fruits of notice-and-comment rulemaking or formal adjudication. That said, and as significant as notice-and-comment is in pointing to *Chevron* authority, the want of that procedure here does not decide the case, for we have sometimes found reasons for *Chevron* deference even when no such administrative formality was required and none was afforded. The fact that the tariff classification here was not a product of such formal process does not alone, therefore, bar the application of *Chevron*.

There are, nonetheless, ample reasons to deny *Chevron* deference here. The authorization for classification rulings, and Customs's practice in making them, present a case far removed not only from notice-and-comment process, but from any other circumstances reasonably suggesting that Congress ever thought of classification rulings as deserving the deference claimed for them here.

B

No matter which angle we choose for viewing the Customs ruling letter in this case, it fails to qualify under *Chevron*. On the face of the statute, to begin with, the terms of the congressional delegation give no indication that Congress meant to delegate authority to Customs to issue classification rulings with the force of law. We are not, of course, here making any global statement about Customs's authority, for it is true that the general rulemaking power conferred on Customs, *see* 19 U.S.C. §1624, authorizes some regulation with the force of law. . . . It is true as well that Congress had classification rulings in mind when it explicitly authorized, in a parenthetical, the issuance of "regulations establishing procedures for the issuance of binding rulings prior to the entry of the merchandise concerned," 19 U.S.C. §1502(a). The reference to binding classifications does not, however, bespeak the legislative type of activity that would naturally bind more than the parties to the ruling, once the goods classified are admitted into this country. And though the statute's direction to disseminate "information" necessary to "secure" uniformity, *ibid.*, seems to assume that a ruling may be precedent in later transactions, precedential value alone does not add up to *Chevron* entitlement; interpretive rules may sometimes function as precedents, and they enjoy no *Chevron* status as a class. In any event, any precedential claim of a classification ruling is counterbalanced by the provision for independent review of Customs classifications by the CIT, *see* 28 U.S.C. §§2638-2640; the scheme for CIT review includes a provision that treats classification rulings on par with the Secretary's rulings on "valuation, rate of duty, marking, restricted merchandise, entry requirements, drawbacks, vessel repairs, or similar matters," §1581(h); *see* §2639(b). It is hard to imagine a congressional understanding more at odds with the *Chevron* regime.[16]

It is difficult, in fact, to see in the agency practice itself any indication that Customs ever set out with a lawmaking pretense in mind when it undertook to make classifications like these. Customs does not generally engage in notice-and-comment practice when issuing them, and their treatment by the agency makes it clear that a letter's binding character as a ruling stops short of third parties. . . .

---

16. Although Customs' decision "is presumed to be correct" on review, 28 U.S.C. §2639(a)(1), the CIT "may consider any new ground" even if not raised below, §2638, and "shall make its determinations upon the basis of the record made before the court," rather than that developed by Customs, §2640(a); *see generally* [United States v. Haggar Apparel Co., 526 U.S. 380, 391 (1999)].

Indeed, to claim that classifications have legal force is to ignore the reality that 46 different Customs offices issue 10,000 to 15,000 of them each year. . . . Any suggestion that rulings intended to have the force of law are being churned out at a rate of 10,000 a year at an agency's 46 scattered offices is simply self-refuting. . . .

In sum, classification rulings are best treated like "interpretations contained in policy statements, agency manuals, and enforcement guidelines." Christensen [v. Harris County, 529 U.S. 576, 587 (2000)]. They are beyond the *Chevron* pale.

C

To agree with the Court of Appeals that Customs ruling letters do not fall within *Chevron* is not, however, to place them outside the pale of any deference whatever. *Chevron* did nothing to eliminate *Skidmore*'s holding that an agency's interpretation may merit some deference whatever its form, given the "specialized experience and broader investigations and information" available to the agency, 323 U.S. at 139, and given the value of uniformity in its administrative and judicial understandings of what a national law requires, *id.* . . .

There is room at least to raise a *Skidmore* claim here, where the regulatory scheme is highly detailed, and Customs can bring the benefit of specialized experience to bear on the subtle questions in this case. . . . A classification ruling in this situation may therefore at least seek a respect proportional to its "power to persuade," *Skidmore, supra,* at 140; *see also Christensen,* 529 U.S. at 587. . . . Such a ruling may surely claim the merit of its writer's thoroughness, logic, and expertness, its fit with prior interpretations, and any other sources of weight. . . .

Since the *Skidmore* assessment called for here ought to be made in the first instance by the Court of Appeals for the Federal Circuit or the CIT, we go no further than to vacate the judgment and remand the case for further proceedings consistent with this opinion. . . .

JUSTICE SCALIA, dissenting. . . .

I

Only five years ago, the Court described the *Chevron* doctrine as follows: "We accord deference to agencies under *Chevron* . . . because of a presumption that Congress, when it left ambiguity in a statute meant for implementation by an agency, understood that the ambiguity would be resolved, first and foremost, by the agency, and desired the agency (rather than the courts) to possess whatever degree of discretion the ambiguity allows," Smiley v. Citibank (South Dakota), N. A., 517 U.S. 735, 740-741 (1996). Today the Court collapses this doctrine, announcing instead a presumption that agency discretion does not exist unless the statute, expressly or impliedly, says so. . . . Once it is determined that *Chevron* deference is not in order, the uncertainty is not at an end — and indeed is just beginning. Litigants cannot then assume that the statutory question is one for the courts to determine, according to traditional interpretive principles and by their own judicial lights. No, the Court now resurrects, in full force, the pre-*Chevron* doctrine of *Skidmore* deference, *see Skidmore, supra,* whereby "[t]he fair measure of deference to an agency administering its own statute . . . var[ies] with circumstances," including "the degree of the agency's care, its consistency, formality, and relative expertness, and . . . the persuasiveness of the agency's position," (footnotes omitted). The Court has largely replaced *Chevron,* in other words, with that test most beloved by a court unwilling to be held to rules (and most feared by litigants who want to know what to expect): th' ol' "totality of the circumstances" test.

The Court's new doctrine is neither sound in principle nor sustainable in practice.

A

As to principle: The doctrine of *Chevron*—that all *authoritative* agency interpretations of statutes they are charged with administering deserve deference—was rooted in a legal presumption of congressional intent, important to the division of powers between the Second and Third Branches. When, *Chevron* said, Congress leaves an ambiguity in a statute that is to be administered by an executive agency, it is presumed that Congress meant to give the agency discretion, within the limits of reasonable interpretation, as to how the ambiguity is to be resolved. By committing enforcement of the statute to an agency rather than the courts, Congress committed its initial and primary interpretation to that branch as well.

There is some question whether *Chevron* was faithful to the text of the Administrative Procedure Act (APA), which it did not even bother to cite.[2] But it was in accord with the origins of federal-court judicial review. Judicial control of federal executive officers was principally exercised through the prerogative writ of mandamus. That writ generally would not issue unless the executive officer was acting plainly beyond the scope of his authority. . . .

The basis in principle for today's new doctrine can be described as follows: The background rule is that ambiguity in legislative instructions to agencies is to be resolved not by the agencies but by the judges. Specific congressional intent to depart from this rule must be found—and while there is no single touchstone for such intent it can generally be found when Congress has authorized the agency to act through (what the Court says is) relatively formal procedures such as informal rulemaking and formal (and informal?) adjudication, and when the agency in fact employs such procedures. The Court's background rule is contradicted by the origins of judicial review of administrative action. But in addition, the Court's principal criterion of congressional intent to supplant its background rule seems to me quite implausible. There is no necessary connection between the formality of procedure and the power of the entity

---

2. Title 5 U.S.C. §706 provides that, in reviewing agency action, the court shall "decide all relevant questions of law"—which would seem to mean that all statutory ambiguities are to be resolved judicially. *See* Anthony, The Supreme Court and the APA: Sometimes They Just Don't Get It, 10 Am. U. Admin. L.J. 1, 9-11 (1996). It could be argued, however, that the legal presumption identified by *Chevron* left as the only "questio[n] of law" whether the agency's interpretation had gone beyond the scope of discretion that the statutory ambiguity conferred. Today's opinion, of course, is no more observant of the APA's text than *Chevron* was—and indeed is even more difficult to reconcile with it.

administering the procedure to resolve authoritatively questions of law. The most formal of the procedures the Court refers to — formal adjudication — is modeled after the process used in trial courts, which of course are not generally accorded deference on questions of law. The purpose of such a procedure is to produce a closed record for determination and review of the facts — which implies nothing about the power of the agency subjected to the procedure to resolve authoritatively questions of law. . . .

Some decisions that are neither informal rulemaking nor formal adjudication are required to be made personally by a Cabinet Secretary, without any prescribed procedures. . . . Is it conceivable that decisions specifically committed to these high-level officers are meant to be accorded no deference, while decisions by an administrative law judge . . . are authoritative? This seems to me quite absurd, and not at all in accord with any plausible actual intent of Congress.

B

As for the practical effects of the new rule:

1

The principal effect will be protracted confusion. As noted above, the one test for *Chevron* deference that the Court enunciates is wonderfully imprecise: whether "Congress delegated authority to the agency generally to make rules carrying the force of law, . . . as by . . . adjudication[,] notice-and-comment rulemaking, or . . . some other [procedure] indicati[ng] comparable congressional intent." But even this description does not do justice to the utter flabbiness of the Court's criterion, since, in order to maintain the fiction that the new test is really just the old one, applied consistently throughout our case law, the Court must make a virtually open-ended exception to its already imprecise guidance: In the present case, it tells us, the absence of notice-and-comment rulemaking (and "[who knows?] [of] some other [procedure] indicati[ng] comparable congressional intent") is not enough to decide the question of *Chevron* deference, "for we have sometimes found reasons for *Chevron* deference even when no such administrative formality was required and none was afforded." The opinion then goes on to consider a grab bag of other factors — including the factor that used to be the sole criterion for *Chevron* deference: whether the interpretation represented the *authoritative* position of the agency. It is hard to know what the lower courts are to make of today's guidance.

2

Another practical effect of today's opinion will be an artificially induced increase in informal rulemaking. Buy stock in the [Government Printing Office]. Since informal rulemaking and formal adjudication are the only more-or-less safe harbors from the storm that the Court has unleashed; and since formal adjudication is not an option but must be mandated by statute or constitutional command; informal rulemaking — which the Court was once careful to make voluntary unless required by statute — will now become a virtual necessity. [T]he Court's safe harbor requires not merely that the agency have been given rulemaking authority, but also that the agency have *employed* rulemaking as the means of resolving the statutory ambiguity. . . . Agencies will now have high incentive to rush out barebones, ambiguous rules construing statutory ambiguities, which they can then in turn further clarify through informal rulings entitled to judicial respect.

3

Worst of all, the majority's approach will lead to the ossification of large portions of our statutory law. Where *Chevron* applies, statutory ambiguities remain ambiguities subject to the agency's ongoing clarification. They create a space, so to speak, for the exercise of continuing agency discretion. As *Chevron* itself held, the Environmental Protection Agency can interpret "stationary source" to mean a single smokestack, can later replace that interpretation with the "bubble concept" embracing an entire plant, and if that proves undesirable can return again to the original interpretation. For the indeterminately large number of statutes taken out of *Chevron* by today's decision, however, ambiguity (and hence flexibility) will cease with the first judicial resolution. *Skidmore* deference gives the agency's current position some vague and uncertain amount of respect, but it does not, like *Chevron, leave* the matter within the control of the Executive Branch for the future. Once the court has spoken, it becomes *unlawful* for the agency to take a contradictory position; the statute now *says* what the court has prescribed. . . .

4

And finally, the majority's approach compounds the confusion it creates by breathing new life into the anachronism of *Skidmore*, which sets forth a sliding scale of deference owed an agency's interpretation of a statute. . . . Justice Jackson's eloquence notwithstanding, the rule of *Skidmore* deference is an empty truism and a trifling statement of the obvious: A judge should take into account the well-considered views of expert observers.

It was possible to live with the indeterminacy of *Skidmore* deference in earlier times. But in an era when federal statutory law administered by federal agencies is pervasive, and when the ambiguities (intended or unintended) that those statutes contain are innumerable, totality-of-the-circumstances *Skidmore* deference is a recipe for uncertainty, unpredictability, and endless litigation. To condemn a vast body of agency action to that regime (all except rulemaking, formal (and informal?) adjudication, and whatever else might now and then be included within today's intentionally vague formulation of affirmative congressional intent to "delegate") is irresponsible. . . .

IV

[E]ven were I to accept the Court's revised version of *Chevron* as a correct statement of the law, I would still accord deference to the tariff classification ruling at issue in this case. For the case is indistinguishable, in that regard, from NationsBank of N.C., N.A. v. Variable Annuity Life Ins. Co., 513 U.S. 251

(1995), which the Court acknowledges as an instance in which *Chevron* deference is warranted notwithstanding the absence of formal adjudication, notice-and-comment rulemaking, or comparable "administrative formality." Here, as in *NationsBank*, there is a tradition of great deference to the opinions of the agency head. . . .

For the reasons stated, I respectfully dissent from the Court's judgment. . . . I dissent even more vigorously from the reasoning that produces the Court's judgment, and that makes today's decision one of the most significant opinions ever rendered by the Court dealing with the judicial review of administrative action. Its consequences will be enormous, and almost uniformly bad.

NOTES AND QUESTIONS

1. *"The force of law."* Justice Souter says that the "terms of the congressional delegation give no indication that Congress meant to delegate authority to Customs to issue classification rulings with the force of law." Why not? What factors does the Court look to in making that determination? Do *any* agency rulings have the "force of law" without being dependent on subsequent judicial enforcement? How, in this respect, is Customs' day planner ruling different from, say, the EPA's "bubble" rule (at issue in *Chevron*)?

2. Skidmore *deference*. If Customs rulings do not have the force of law, why should they receive any judicial deference at all? Do any of the justifications for *Chevron* deference, discussed in note 2 following the case, justify some lesser degree of deference in situations like *Skidmore* and *Mead*? Is there a theoretically plausible intermediate position between independent decision and *Chevron* deference? Justice Souter describes this intermediate position as "respect proportional to [the ruling's] 'power to persuade,'" quoting *Skidmore*. How, if at all, is this any different from the way in which a court in purely private litigation should view the legal arguments made by the two parties? Even if this degree of deference is justifiable, does the introduction of a third tier of review create a mischievous level of complexity, as Justice Scalia argues? Justice Souter's majority opinion, in a portion not reproduced above, counters that Justice Scalia's desire for simplicity fails to recognize "the great variety of ways in which the laws invest the Government's administrative arms with discretion, and with procedures for exercising it." Is that a convincing response?

3. *Procedural formality and* Chevron *deference*. Some of the Court's early pronouncements seemed to suggest that an agency's reading of its statute could qualify for *Chevron* deference only if it were embodied in the product of a relatively formal procedure, such as rulemaking or adjudication. For example, in Christensen v. Harris County, 529 U.S. 576 (2000), the Court, in an opinion by Justice Thomas, said that, while *Chevron* deference was due to agency decisions adopted after relatively formal proceedings, that was not the case with less formal agency actions:

> Here, however, we confront an interpretation contained in an opinion letter, not one arrived at after, for example, a formal adjudication or notice-and-comment rulemaking. Interpretations such as those in opinion letters — like interpretations contained in policy statements, agency manuals, and enforcement guidelines,

all of which lack the force of law—do not warrant *Chevron*-style deference. . . . Instead, interpretations in formats such as opinion letters are "entitled to respect" under our decision in Skidmore v. Swift & Co., 323 U.S. 134, 140 (1944), but only to the extent that those interpretations have "the power to persuade," *ibid.*

529 U.S. at 587-588.

Note that the *Mead* Court takes pains to disavow the notion that procedural formality is an absolute precondition to granting *Chevron* deference. Why not? Shouldn't courts be more respectful of interpretations that have undergone at least some adversarial testing before the agency makes a final decision? What, exactly, is the position that Justice Scalia takes on this issue in his *Mead* dissent? On the one hand, he flatly states that there is "no necessary connection" between procedural formality and entitlement to *Chevron* deference. On the other hand, he rather direly predicts that *Mead* will drive agencies to engage in superfluous rulemaking and adjudication, as "more-or-less safe harbors from the storm that the Court has unleashed." Can those two statements be reconciled?

4. "*Procedurally defective*" *decisions and* Chevron *deference.* In Encino Motorcars, LLC v. Navarro, 136 S. Ct. 2117 (2016), summarized *supra*, the Court had to decide whether the Labor Department's interpretation of the statutory terms "salesman, partsman or mechanic" deserved *Chevron* deference. In ruling that it did not, the Court had this to say:

> A premise of *Chevron* is that when Congress grants an agency the authority to administer a statute by issuing regulations with the force of law, it presumes the agency will use that authority to resolve ambiguities in the statutory scheme. When Congress authorizes an agency to proceed through notice-and-comment rulemaking, that "relatively formal administrative procedure" is a "very good indicator" that Congress intended the regulation to carry the force of law, so *Chevron* should apply. *Mead*, [553 U.S.] at 229-230. But *Chevron* deference is not warranted where the regulation is "procedurally defective"—that is, where the agency errs by failing to follow the correct procedures in issuing the regulation. *Id.* at 227. [W]here a proper challenge is raised to the agency procedures, and those procedures are defective, a court should not accord *Chevron* deference to the agency interpretation. . . .
>
> One of the basic procedural requirements of administrative rulemaking is that an agency must give adequate reasons for its decisions. [The Court here discusses the reasons given by DOL for its 2011 rule, concluding that those reasons were not "adequate." This portion of the opinion is excerpted, *supra*.] This lack of reasoned explication for a regulation that is inconsistent with the Department's longstanding earlier position results in a rule that cannot carry the force of law. It follows that this regulation does not receive *Chevron* deference in the interpretation of the relevant statute. . .

The Court invokes a dictum from *Mead* that an interpretation adopted in a "procedurally defective" manner cannot qualify for *Chevron* deference. That seems obvious, but is it? If the underlying statute is ambiguous (*Chevron* step one) and the agency's interpretation is *substantively* reasonable (step two), why should it matter that the interpretation was adopted in a procedurally-defective manner? Justice Kennedy characterizes the defect in DOL's rule as "procedural," but isn't the "adequacy" of an agency's "reasons" a "substantive" matter, rather than a procedural matter? Should it matter? (Note that the *Mead* dictum also says that an interpretation that is "arbitrary and capricious in substance" is ineligible for *Chevron* deference. Is that what the Court is really saying here?) Does *Encino Motorcars* effectively collapse the arbitrary-capricious test with step two of the *Chevron* analysis?

b.   Agency Interpretations of "Jurisdictional" Statutes

Should an agency receive *Chevron* deference when it renders a decision effectively determining that it "administers" a particular statute? The issue arose obliquely in Mississippi Power & Light Co. v. Mississippi, 487 U.S. 354 (1988). The Federal Energy Regulatory Commission (FERC) had expressed the view that a federal statute should be interpreted to pre-empt certain state regulatory actions. The Supreme Court agreed, without discussing *Chevron* or deference. In dissent, however, Justice Brennan argued that no deference should be given to FERC's interpretation, since "agencies do not 'administer' statutes confining the scope of their jurisdiction." In a separate concurring opinion, Justice Scalia debunked the distinction between "jurisdictional" and "nonjurisdictional" statutory provisions. Years later, the issue of deference to "jurisdictional" statutes reared its head once again.

CITY OF ARLINGTON v. FEDERAL COMMUNICATIONS COMMISSION
133 S. Ct. 1863 (2013)

JUSTICE SCALIA delivered the opinion of the Court.

We consider whether an agency's interpretation of a statutory ambiguity that concerns the scope of its regulatory authority (that is, its jurisdiction) is entitled to deference under *Chevron*.

I

Wireless telecommunications networks require towers and antennas; proposed sites for those towers and antennas must be approved by local zoning authorities. In the Telecommunications Act of 1996, Congress "impose[d] specific limitations on the traditional authority of state and local governments to regulate the location, construction, and modification of such facilities," Rancho Palos Verdes v. Abrams, 544 U.S. 113, 115 (2005), and incorporated those limitations into the Communications Act of 1934. Section 201(b) of that Act empowers the Federal Communications Commission to "prescribe such rules and regulations as may be necessary in the public interest to carry out [its] provisions." 47 U.S.C. §201(b). Of course, that rulemaking authority extends to the subsequently added portions of the Act.

The Act imposes five substantive limitations, which are codified in 47 U.S.C. §332(c)(7)(B); only one of them, §332(c)(7)(B)(ii), is at issue here. That provision requires state or local governments to act on wireless siting applications "within a reasonable period of time after the request is duly filed." Two other features of §332(c)(7) are relevant. First, subparagraph (A), known as the "saving clause," provides that nothing in the Act, *except* those limitations provided in §332(c)(7)(B), "shall limit or affect the authority of a State or local government" over siting decisions. Second, §332(c)(7)(B)(v) authorizes a person who believes a state or local government's wireless-siting decision to be inconsistent with any of the limitations in §332(c)(7)(B) to "commence an action in any court of competent jurisdiction."

In theory, §332(c)(7)(B)(ii) requires state and local zoning authorities to take prompt action on siting applications for wireless facilities. But in practice, wireless providers often faced long delays. In July 2008, CTIA, which represents wireless service providers, petitioned the FCC to clarify the meaning of §332(c)(7)(B)(ii)'s requirement that zoning authorities act on siting requests "within a reasonable period of time." In November 2009, the Commission, relying on its broad statutory authority to implement the provisions of the Communications Act, issued a declaratory ruling responding to CTIA's petition. In re Petition for Declaratory Ruling, 24 FCC Rcd. 13994, 14001. The Commission found that the "record evidence demonstrates that unreasonable delays in the personal wireless service facility siting process have obstructed the provision of wireless services" and that such delays "impede the promotion of advanced services and competition that Congress deemed critical in the Telecommunications Act of 1996." *Id.* at 14006, 14008. A "reasonable period of time" under §332(c)(7)(B)(ii), the Commission determined, is presumptively (but rebuttably) 90 days to process a collocation application (that is, an application to place a new antenna on an existing tower) and 150 days to process all other applications.

Some state and local governments opposed adoption of the *Declaratory Ruling* on the ground that the Commission lacked "authority to interpret ambiguous provisions of Section 332(c)(7)." *Id.* at 14000. Specifically, they argued that the saving clause, §332(c)(7)(A), and the judicial review provision, §337(c)(7)(B)(v), together display a congressional intent to withhold from the Commission authority to interpret the limitations in §332(c)(7)(B). Asserting that ground of objection, the cities of Arlington and San Antonio, Texas, petitioned for review of the *Declaratory Ruling* in the Court of Appeals for the Fifth Circuit. [The Fifth Circuit upheld the FCC action, applying *Chevron* deference to the FCC's determination that it had the requisite authority to regulate and to its reading of the statutory term "reasonable period of time."]

We granted certiorari, limited to the [question]: "Whether . . . a court should apply *Chevron* to . . . an agency's determination of its own jurisdiction."

II

A

. . . *Chevron* is rooted in a background presumption of congressional intent: namely, "that Congress, when it left ambiguity in a statute" administered by an agency, "understood that the ambiguity would be resolved, first and foremost, by the agency, and desired the agency (rather than the courts) to possess whatever degree of discretion the ambiguity allows." Smiley v. Citibank (South Dakota), N.A., 517 U.S. 735, 740-741 (1996). *Chevron* thus provides a stable background rule against which Congress can legislate: Statutory ambiguities will be resolved, within the bounds of reasonable interpretation, not by the courts but by the administering agency. *See* [AT&T v. Iowa Utilities Bd., 525 U.S. 366, 397 (1999)]. Congress knows to speak in plain terms when it wishes to circumscribe, and in capacious terms when it wishes to enlarge, agency discretion.

B

The question here is whether a court must defer under *Chevron* to an agency's interpretation of a statutory ambiguity that concerns the scope of the agency's statutory authority (that is, its jurisdiction). The argument against deference rests on the premise that there exist two distinct classes of agency interpretations: Some interpretations—the big, important ones, presumably—define the agency's "jurisdiction." Others—humdrum, run-of-the-mill stuff—are simply applications of jurisdiction the agency plainly has. That premise is false, because the distinction between "jurisdictional" and "nonjurisdictional" interpretations is a mirage. No matter how it is framed, the question a court faces when confronted with an agency's interpretation of a statute it administers is always, simply, *whether the agency has stayed within the bounds of its statutory authority.*

The misconception that there are, for *Chevron* purposes, separate "jurisdictional" questions on which no deference is due derives, perhaps, from a reflexive extension to agencies of the very real division between the jurisdictional and nonjurisdictional that is applicable to courts. In the judicial context, there *is* a meaningful line: Whether the court decided *correctly* is a question that has different consequences from the question whether it had the power to decide *at all.* Congress has the power (within limits) to tell the courts what classes of cases they may decide, but not to prescribe or superintend how they decide those cases. A court's power to decide a case is independent of whether its decision is correct, which is why even an erroneous judgment is entitled to res judicata effect. Put differently, a jurisdictionally proper but substantively incorrect judicial decision is not ultra vires.

That is not so for agencies charged with administering congressional statutes. Both their power to act and how they are to act are authoritatively prescribed by Congress, so that when they act improperly, no less than when they act beyond their jurisdiction, what they do is ultra vires. Because the question—whether framed as an incorrect application of agency authority or an assertion of authority not conferred—is always whether the agency has gone beyond what Congress has permitted it to do, there is no principled basis for carving out some arbitrary subset of such claims as "jurisdictional."

[J]udges should not waste their time in the mental acrobatics needed to decide whether an agency's interpretation of a statutory provision is "jurisdictional" or "nonjurisdictional." Once those labels are sheared away, it becomes clear that the question in every case is, simply, whether the statutory text forecloses the agency's assertion of authority, or not. The federal judge as haruspex, sifting the entrails of vast statutory schemes to divine whether a particular agency interpretation qualifies as "jurisdictional," is not engaged in reasoned decisionmaking.

C

. . . The U.S. Reports are shot through with applications of *Chevron* to agencies' constructions of the scope of their own jurisdiction. And we have applied *Chevron* where concerns about agency self-aggrandizement are at their apogee: in cases where an agency's expansive construction of the extent of its own power would have wrought a fundamental change in the regulatory scheme. In FDA v. Brown & Williamson Tobacco Corp., 529 U.S. 120 (2000), the threshold question was the "appropriate framework for analyzing" the FDA's assertion of "jurisdiction to regulate tobacco products," *id.* at 126, 132—a question of vast "economic and political magnitude," *id.* at 133. "Because this case involves an administrative agency's construction of a statute that it administers," we held, *Chevron* applied. 529 U.S. at 132. . . .

The false dichotomy between "jurisdictional" and "nonjurisdictional" agency interpretations may be no more than a bogeyman, but it is dangerous all the same. Like the Hound of the Baskervilles, it is conjured by those with greater quarry in sight: Make no mistake—the ultimate target here is *Chevron* itself. Savvy challengers of agency action would play the "jurisdictional" card in every case. Some judges would be deceived by the specious, but scary-sounding, "jurisdictional"-"nonjurisdictional" line; others tempted by the prospect of making public policy by prescribing the meaning of ambiguous statutory commands. The effect would be to transfer any number of interpretive decisions—archetypal *Chevron* questions, about how best to construe an ambiguous term in light of competing policy interests—from the agencies that administer the statutes to federal courts. . . . That is precisely what *Chevron* prevents.

III

[T]he dissent proposes that even when general rulemaking authority is clear, *every* agency rule must be subjected to a *de novo* judicial determination of whether *the particular issue* was committed to agency discretion. It offers no standards at all to guide this open-ended hunt for congressional intent (that is to say, for evidence of congressional intent more specific than the conferral of general rulemaking authority). It would simply punt that question back to the Court of Appeals, presumably for application of some sort of totality-of-the-circumstances test—which is really, of course, not a test at all but an invitation to make an ad hoc judgment regarding congressional intent. Thirteen Courts of Appeals applying a totality-of-the-circumstances test would render the binding effect of agency rules unpredictable and destroy the whole stabilizing purpose of *Chevron*. The excessive agency power that the dissent fears would be replaced by chaos. There is no need to wade into these murky waters. It suffices to decide this case that the preconditions to deference under *Chevron* are satisfied because Congress has unambiguously vested the FCC with general authority to administer the Communications Act through rulemaking and adjudication, and the agency interpretation at issue was promulgated in the exercise of that authority.

* * *

Those who assert that applying *Chevron* to "jurisdictional" interpretations "leaves the fox in charge of the henhouse" overlook the reality that a separate category of "jurisdictional" interpretations does not exist. The fox-in-the-henhouse syndrome is to be avoided not by establishing an arbitrary and undefinable category of agency decisionmaking that is accorded no deference, but by taking seriously, and applying rigorously, in all cases, statutory limits on agencies' authority. Where Congress has established a clear line, the agency cannot go beyond it; and where Congress has established an ambiguous line, the agency can go no further than the ambiguity will fairly allow. But in rigorously applying the latter rule, a court need not pause to puzzle over whether the interpretive question presented is "jurisdictional." If "the agency's answer is based on a permissible construction of the statute," that is the end of the matter.

The judgment of the Court of Appeals is affirmed.

It is so ordered.

CHIEF JUSTICE ROBERTS, with whom JUSTICE KENNEDY and JUSTICE ALITO join, dissenting.

My disagreement with the Court is fundamental. It is also easily expressed: A court should not defer to an agency until the court decides, on its own, that the agency is entitled to deference. Courts defer to an agency's interpretation of law when and because Congress has conferred on the agency interpretive authority over the question at issue. An agency cannot exercise interpretive authority until it has it; the question whether an agency enjoys that authority must be decided by a court, without deference to the agency.

One of the principal authors of the Constitution famously wrote that the "accumulation of all powers, legislative, executive, and judiciary, in the same hands, . . . may justly be pronounced the very definition of tyranny." The Federalist No. 47, p. 324 (J. Cooke ed. 1961) (J. Madison). Although modern administrative agencies fit most comfortably within the Executive Branch, as a practical matter they exercise legislative power, by promulgating regulations with the force of law; executive power, by policing compliance with those regulations; and judicial power, by adjudicating enforcement actions and imposing sanctions on those found to have violated their rules. The accumulation of these powers in the same hands is not an occasional or isolated exception to the constitutional plan; it is a central feature of modern American government.

The administrative state "wields vast power and touches almost every aspect of daily life." Free Enterprise Fund v. Public Company Accounting Oversight Bd., 561 U.S. 477 (2010). The Framers could hardly have envisioned today's "vast and varied federal bureaucracy" and the authority administrative agencies now hold over our economic, social, and political activities. . . . And the federal bureaucracy continues to grow; in the last 15 years, Congress has launched more than 50 new agencies. . . . It would be a bit much to describe the result as "the very definition of tyranny," but the danger posed by the growing power of the administrative state cannot be dismissed. . . .

It is against this background that we consider whether the authority of administrative agencies should be augmented even further, to include not only broad power to give definitive answers to questions left to them by Congress, but also the same power to decide when Congress has given them that power.

Before proceeding to answer that question, however, it is necessary to sort through some confusion over what this litigation is about. The source of the confusion is a familiar culprit: the concept of "jurisdiction" . . . which we have repeatedly described as a word with "'many, too many, meanings.'" Union Pacific R. Co. v. Locomotive Engineers, 558 U.S. 67, 81 (2009). . . . The parties, *amici*, and court below too often use the term "jurisdiction" imprecisely, which leads the Court to misunderstand the argument it must confront. That argument is not that "there exist two distinct classes of agency interpretations," some "big, important ones" that "define the agency's 'jurisdiction,'" and other "humdrum, run-of-the-mill" ones that "are simply applications of jurisdiction the agency plainly has." The argument is instead that a court should not defer to an agency on whether Congress has granted the agency interpretive authority over the statutory ambiguity at issue. . . .

"It is emphatically the province and duty of the judicial department to say what the law is." Marbury v. Madison, 1 Cranch 137, 177 (1803). The rise of the modern administrative state has not changed that duty. Indeed, the Administrative Procedure Act, governing judicial review of most agency action, instructs reviewing courts to decide "all relevant questions of law." 5 U.S.C. §706.

We do not ignore that command when we afford an agency's statutory interpretation *Chevron* deference; we respect it. We give binding deference to permissible agency interpretations of statutory ambiguities *because* Congress has delegated to the agency the authority to interpret those ambiguities "with the force of law." . . . But before a court may grant such deference, it must on its own decide whether Congress — the branch vested with lawmaking authority under the Constitution — has in fact delegated to the agency lawmaking power over the ambiguity at issue.

[T]he FCC argues that a court need only locate an agency and a grant of general rulemaking authority over a statute. *Chevron* deference then applies, it contends, to the agency's interpretation of any ambiguity in the Act, including ambiguity in a provision said to carve out specific provisions from the agency's general rulemaking authority. . . . If a congressional delegation of interpretive authority is to support *Chevron* deference, however, that delegation must extend to the specific statutory ambiguity at issue. The appropriate question is whether the delegation covers the "specific provision" and "particular question" before the court. *Chevron*, 467 U.S., at 844. A congressional grant of authority over some portion of a statute does not necessarily mean that Congress granted the agency interpretive authority over all its provisions. . . .

A general delegation to the agency to administer the statute will often suffice to satisfy the court that Congress has delegated interpretive authority over the ambiguity at issue. But if Congress has exempted particular provisions from that authority, that exemption must be respected, and the determination whether Congress has done so is for the courts alone. . . .

The Court sees something nefarious behind the view that courts must decide on their own whether Congress has delegated interpretative authority to an agency, before deferring to that agency's interpretation of law. What is afoot, according to the Court, is a judicial power-grab, with nothing less than "*Chevron* itself" as "the ultimate target." The Court touches on a legitimate concern: *Chevron* importantly guards against the Judiciary arrogating to itself policymaking properly left, under the separation of powers, to the Executive. But there is another concern at play, no less firmly rooted in our constitutional structure. That is the obligation of the Judiciary not only to confine itself to its proper role, but to ensure that the other branches do so as well. . . . Our duty to police the boundary between the Legislature and the Executive is as critical as our duty to respect that between the Judiciary and the Executive.

In these cases, the FCC issued a declaratory ruling interpreting the term "reasonable period of time" in 47 U.S.C. §332(c)(7)(B)(ii). The Fifth Circuit correctly recognized that it could not apply *Chevron* deference to the FCC's interpretation unless the agency "possessed statutory authority to administer §332(c)(7)(B)(ii)," but it erred by granting *Chevron* deference to the FCC's view on that antecedent question. *See* 668 F.3d at 248. Because the court should have determined on its own whether Congress delegated interpretive authority over §332(c)(7)(B)(ii) to the FCC before affording *Chevron* deference, I would vacate the decision below and remand the cases to the Fifth Circuit to perform the proper inquiry in the first instance.

I respectfully dissent.

NOTES AND QUESTIONS

1. *"Jurisdictional" questions.* Is Justice Scalia right that *all* questions of statutory authority are equally "jurisdictional"? Or are there some questions that are more fundamental than others for the purpose of according *Chevron* deference? Is it relevant, in answering that question, that §332(c)(7)(B) of the Communications Act splits enforcement authority between the FCC and state and local zoning authorities and courts? Note that Chief Justice Roberts resists the "jurisdictional-nonjurisdictional" dichotomy. He would require independent judicial review of "whether Congress has delegated interpretative authority to an agency." If one fears the accretion of administrative power, as he clearly does, is his formulation likely to be effective? Administrable?

2. *Statutes "administered" by multiple agencies.* What happens when multiple agencies or government actors are involved in administering a regulatory scheme? In Gonzales v. Oregon, 546 U.S. 243 (2006), the Court denied *Chevron* deference to an interpretive rule issued by the Attorney General that determined that the use of controlled substances in assisted suicide violated the Controlled Substances Act, 21 U.S.C. §801 *et seq.*, in part because key aspects of the Attorney General's authority over the use of controlled substances by the medical profession were shared with the Secretary of Health and Human Services, indicating that Congress did not intend to afford *Chevron* deference to the Attorney General's decisions. Similarly, in Martin v. Occupational Safety & Health Review Commn., 499 U.S. 144 (1991), the division of authority to administer the OSH Act between the Commission and the Department of Labor meant that the OSHRC's adjudicatory decisions concerning the meaning of the Act would not receive *Chevron* deference. The Court appeared to assign policymaking authority to the Secretary of Labor: "Congress intended to delegate to the Commission the type of nonpolicymaking adjudicatory powers typically exercised by a *court* in the agency-review context. [T]he Commission is authorized

to review the Secretary's interpretations only for consistency with the regulatory language and for reasonableness." *Id.* at 154-155. Is this likely to significantly limit the reach of *Chevron* deference? In Epic Systems Corp. v. Lewis, 138 S. Ct. 1612 (2018), in an opinion by Justice Gorsuch, the Court declined to apply *Chevron* deference to the NLRB's interpretation of the National Labor Relations Act, which the agency administers, that would have the effect of limiting the applicability of the Federal Arbitration Act (FAA), which it does not. In general, courts are loath to apply *Chevron* in cases that implicate the interpretation of cross-cutting statutes like the FAA, NEPA, and the APA.

7. *Judicial Deference to an Agency's Interpretations of Its Own Rules*

Should a reviewing court defer to an agency's interpretation of one of its own regulations? The Supreme Court answered that question in the affirmative in the pre-APA case of Bowles v. Seminole Rock & Sand Co., 325 U.S. 410 (1945), and has reflexively repeated the assertion in dozens of subsequent cases, without much discussion of the rationale for such deference. Later cases refer to this as *Seminole Rock* deference or, more commonly, as *Auer* deference, after Auer v. Robbins, 519 U.S. 452, 461 (1997). Many observers assumed that *Auer* deference followed a fortiori from *Chevron* deference. After all, if a court should defer to an agency's interpretation of a statute written by Congress, surely it should defer to an agency's interpretation of a rule that it wrote itself. However, as the following case demonstrates, this attitude has begun to change.

KISOR v. WILKIE
139 S. Ct. 2400 (2019)

JUSTICE KAGAN announced the judgment of the Court and delivered the opinion of the Court with respect to Parts I, II-B, III-B, and IV, in which ROBERTS, C.J., and GINSBURG, BREYER, and SOTOMAYOR, JJ., joined, and an opinion with respect to Parts II-A and III-A, in which GINSBURG, BREYER, and SOTOMAYOR, JJ., joined.

This Court has often deferred to agencies' reasonable readings of genuinely ambiguous regulations. We call that practice *Auer* deference, or sometimes *Seminole Rock* deference, after two cases in which we employed it. *See* Auer v. Robbins, 519 U.S. 452 (1997); Bowles v. Seminole Rock & Sand Co., 325 U.S. 410 (1945). The only question presented here is whether we should overrule those decisions, discarding the deference they give to agencies. We answer that question no. *Auer* deference retains an important role in construing agency regulations. But even as we uphold it, we reinforce its limits. *Auer* deference is sometimes appropriate and sometimes not. Whether to apply it depends on a range of considerations that we have noted now and again, but compile and further develop today. The deference doctrine we describe is potent in its place, but cabined in its scope. On remand, the Court of Appeals should decide whether it applies to the agency interpretation at issue.

I

[James] Kisor is a Vietnam War veteran seeking disability benefits from the Department of Veterans Affairs (VA). He first applied in 1982, alleging that he had developed post-traumatic stress disorder (PTSD) as a result of his participation in a military action called Operation Harvest Moon. The report of the agency's evaluating psychiatrist noted Kisor's involvement in that battle, but found that he "d[id] not suffer from PTSD." The VA thus denied Kisor benefits [in 1983. In] 2006, . . . Kisor moved to reopen his claim. Based on a new psychiatric report, the VA this time agreed that Kisor suffered from PTSD. But it granted him benefits only from the date of his motion to reopen, rather than (as he requested) from the date of his first application.

The Board of Veterans' Appeals—a part of the VA, represented in Kisor's case by a single administrative judge—affirmed . . . , based on its interpretation of an agency rule [stating that] the agency could grant Kisor retroactive benefits if it found there were "relevant official service department records" that it had not considered in its initial denial. The Board acknowledged that Kisor had come up with two new service records, both confirming his participation in Operation Harvest Moon. But according to the Board, those records were not "relevant" because they did not go to the reason for the denial—that Kisor did not have PTSD. . . .

The Court of Appeals for Veterans Claims, an independent Article I court . . . , affirmed for the same reason. The Court of Appeals for the Federal Circuit also affirmed, but it did so based on deference to the Board's interpretation of the VA rule. Kisor had argued to the Federal Circuit that to count as "relevant," a service record need not (as the Board thought) "counter[] the basis of the prior denial"; instead, it could relate to some other criterion for obtaining disability benefits. The Federal Circuit found the regulation "ambiguous" as between the two readings. The rule, said the court, does not specifically address "whether 'relevant' records are those casting doubt on the agency's prior [rationale or] those relating to the veteran's claim more broadly." So how to choose between the two views? The court continued: "Both parties insist that the plain regulatory language supports their case, and neither party's position strikes us as unreasonable." Because that was so, the court believed *Auer* deference appropriate: The agency's construction of its own regulation would govern unless "plainly erroneous or inconsistent with the VA's regulatory framework." Applying that standard, the court upheld the Board's reading—and so approved the denial of retroactive benefits.

We then granted certiorari to decide whether to overrule *Auer* and (its predecessor) *Seminole Rock.*

II

Before addressing that question directly, we spend some time describing what *Auer* deference is, and is not. . .

A

For various reasons, regulations may be genuinely ambiguous. They may not directly or clearly address every issue; when applied to some fact patterns, they may prove susceptible to more than one reasonable reading. Sometimes, this sort of ambiguity arises from careless drafting—the use of a dangling modifier, an awkward word, an opaque construction. But often, ambiguity reflects the well-known limits of expression or knowledge. The subject matter of a rule "may be so specialized and varying in nature as to be impossible"—or at any rate, impracticable—to capture in its every detail. SEC v. Chenery Corp., 332 U.S. 194, 203 (1947). Or a "problem[] may arise" that the agency, when drafting the rule, "could not [have] reasonably foresee[n]." *Id.* at 202. Whichever the case, the result is to create real uncertainties about a regulation's meaning.

Consider these examples:

- In a rule issued to implement the Americans with Disabilities Act (ADA), the Department of Justice requires theaters and stadiums to provide people with disabilities "lines of sight comparable to those for members of the general public." Must the Washington Wizards construct wheelchair seating to offer lines of sight over spectators when they rise to their feet? Or is it enough that the facility offers comparable views so long as everyone remains seated? *See* Paralyzed Veterans of Am. v. D.C. Arena L.P., 117 F.3d 579, 581-582 (CADC 1997).

- The Transportation Security Administration (TSA) requires that liquids, gels, and aerosols in carry-on baggage be packed in containers smaller than 3.4 ounces and carried in a clear plastic bag. Does a traveler have to pack his jar of truffle pâté in that way? *See* Laba v. Copeland, 2016 WL 5958241, *1 (WDNC, Oct. 13, 2016)...

- Or take the facts of *Auer* itself. An agency must decide whether police captains are eligible for overtime under the Fair Labor Standards Act. According to the agency's regulations, employees cannot receive overtime if they are paid on a "salary basis." 29 CFR §541.118(a) (1996). And in deciding whether an employee is salaried, one question is whether his pay is "subject to reduction" based on performance. A police department's manual informs its officers that their pay might be docked if they commit a disciplinary infraction. Does that fact alone make them "subject to" pay deductions? Or must the department have a practice of docking officer pay, so that the possibility of that happening is more than theoretical?

In each case, interpreting the regulation involves a choice between (or among) more than one reasonable reading. To apply the rule to some unanticipated or unresolved situation, the court must make a judgment call. How should it do so?

In answering that question, we have often thought that a court should defer to the agency's construction of its own regulation. For the last 20 or so years, we have referred to that doctrine as *Auer* deference, and applied it often. But the name is something of a misnomer. Before the doctrine was called *Auer* deference, it was called *Seminole Rock* deference—for the 1945 decision in which we declared that when "the meaning of [a regulation] is in doubt," the agency's interpretation "becomes of controlling weight unless it is plainly erroneous or inconsistent with the regulation." 325 U.S. at 414. And *Seminole Rock* itself was not built on sand. Deference to administrative agencies traces back to the late nineteenth century, and perhaps beyond. *See* United States v. Eaton, 169 U.S. 331, 343 (1898) ("The interpretation given to the regulations by the department charged with their execution . . . is entitled to the greatest weight.").

We have explained *Auer* deference (as we now call it) as rooted in a presumption about congressional intent—a presumption that Congress would generally want the agency to play the primary role in resolving regulatory ambiguities. . . . routinely delegates to agencies the power to implement statutes by issuing rules. In doing so, Congress knows (how could it not?) that regulations will sometimes contain ambiguities. But Congress almost never explicitly assigns responsibility to deal with that problem, either to agencies or to courts. . . . We have adopted the presumption—though it is always rebuttable—that "the power authoritatively to interpret its own regulations is a component of the agency's delegated lawmaking powers." [Martin v. Occupational Safety and Health Review Comm'n, 499 U.S. 144, 151 (1991).] Or otherwise said, we have thought that when granting rulemaking power to agencies, Congress usually intends to give them, too, considerable latitude to interpret the ambiguous rules they issue.

In part, that is because the agency that promulgated a rule is in the "better position [to] reconstruct" its original meaning. Consider that if you don't know what some text (say, a memo or an e-mail) means, you would probably want to ask the person who wrote it. [Presumably, this is what Congress generally intends. While there are many valid limitations on this argument,] the point holds good for a significant category of "contemporaneous" readings. Want to know what a rule means? Ask its author.

In still greater measure, the presumption that Congress intended *Auer* deference stems from the awareness that resolving genuine regulatory ambiguities often "entail[s] the exercise of judgment grounded in policy concerns." Thomas Jefferson Univ. v. Shalala, 512 U.S. 504, 512 (1994). Return to our TSA example. In most of their applications, terms like "liquids" and "gels" are clear enough. (Traveler checklist: Pretzels OK; water not.) But resolving the uncertain issues—the truffle pâtés or olive tapenades of the world—requires getting in the weeds of the rule's policy: Why does TSA ban liquids and gels in the first instance? What makes them dangerous? Can a potential hijacker use pâté jars in the same way as soda cans? Or take the less specialized-seeming ADA example. It is easy enough to know what "comparable lines of sight" means in a movie theater—but more complicated when, as in sports arenas, spectators sometimes stand up. How costly is it to insist that the stadium owner take that sporadic behavior into account, and is the viewing value received worth the added expense? That cost-benefit calculation, too, sounds more in policy than in law. . . .

And Congress, we have thought, knows just that: It is attuned to the comparative advantages of agencies over courts in making such policy judgments. Agencies (unlike courts) have "unique expertise," often of a scientific or technical nature, relevant to applying a regulation "to complex or changing circumstances." *Martin*, 499 U.S. at 151. Agencies (unlike courts) can conduct factual investigations, can consult with affected parties, can consider how their experts have handled similar issues over the long course of administering a regulatory program. And agencies (again unlike courts) have political accountability, because they are subject to the supervision of the President, who in turn answers to the public. . . .

Finally, the presumption we use reflects the well-known benefits of uniformity in interpreting genuinely ambiguous rules. We have noted Congress's frequent "preference for resolving interpretive issues by uniform administrative decision, rather than piecemeal by litigation." Ford Motor Credit Co. v. Milhollin, 444 U. S. 555, 568 (1980). . . . *Auer* deference thus serves to ensure consistency in federal regulatory law, for everyone who needs to know what it requires.

B

But all that said, *Auer* deference is not the answer to every question of interpreting an agency's rules. Far from it. . . .

First and foremost, a court should not afford *Auer* deference unless the regulation is genuinely ambiguous. . . . [T]he core theory of *Auer* deference is that sometimes the law runs out, and policy-laden choice is what is left over. But if the law gives an answer—if there is only one reasonable construction of a regulation—then a court has no business deferring to any other reading, no matter how much the agency insists it would make more sense. . . .

And before concluding that a rule is genuinely ambiguous, a court must exhaust all the "traditional tools" of construction. [*Chevron*, 467 U.S. at 843 n.9]. To make that effort, a court must "carefully consider[]" the text, structure, history, and purpose of a regulation, in all the ways it would if it had no agency to fall back on. *Ibid.* . . .

If genuine ambiguity remains, moreover, the agency's reading must still be "reasonable." In other words, it must come within the zone of ambiguity the court has identified after employing all its interpretive tools. (Note that serious application of those tools therefore has use even when a regulation turns out to be truly ambiguous. The text, structure, history, and so forth at least establish the outer bounds of permissible interpretation.) . . . .

Still, we are not done—for not every reasonable agency reading of a genuinely ambiguous rule should receive *Auer* deference. We have recognized in applying *Auer* that a court must make an independent inquiry into whether the character and context of the agency interpretation entitles it to controlling weight. . . . The inquiry on this dimension does not reduce to any exhaustive test. But we have laid out some especially important markers for identifying when *Auer* deference is and is not appropriate.

To begin with, the regulatory interpretation must be one actually made by the agency. In other words, it must be the agency's "authoritative" or "official position," rather than any more ad hoc statement not reflecting the agency's views. *Mead*, 533 U.S. at 257-259 and n.6 (Scalia, J., dissenting). That constraint follows from the logic of *Auer* deference—because Congress has delegated rulemaking power, and all that typically goes with it, to the agency alone. Of course, the requirement of "authoritative" action must recognize a reality of bureaucratic life: Not everything the agency does comes from, or is even in the name of, the Secretary or his chief advisers. . . . The interpretation must at the least emanate from those actors, using those vehicles, understood to make authoritative policy in the relevant context. . . .

Next, the agency's interpretation must in some way implicate its substantive expertise. . . . When the agency has no comparative expertise in resolving a regulatory ambiguity, Congress presumably would not grant it that authority.

Finally, an agency's reading of a rule must reflect "fair and considered judgment" to receive *Auer* deference [*Auer*, 519 U.S. at 462]. That means, we have stated, that a court should decline to defer to a merely "convenient litigating position" or "post hoc rationalizatio[n] advanced" to "defend past agency action against attack." Christopher [v. SmithKline Beecham Corp., 567 U.S. 142], at 155. And a court may not defer to a new interpretation, whether or not introduced in litigation, that creates "unfair surprise" to regulated parties. Long Island Care [at Home, Ltd. v. Coke, 551 U.S. 158, 170 (2007)]. That disruption of expectations may occur when an agency substitutes one view of a rule for another. . . .

III

That brings us to the lone question presented here—whether we should abandon the longstanding doctrine just described. . . .

A

Kisor first attacks *Auer* as inconsistent with the judicial review provision of the Administrative Procedure Act (APA). As Kisor notes, Congress enacted the APA in 1946—the year after *Seminole Rock*—to serve as "the fundamental charter of the administrative state." Section 706 of the Act, governing judicial review of agency action, states (among other things) that reviewing courts shall "determine the meaning or applicability of the terms of an agency action" (including a regulation). According to Kisor, *Auer* violates that edict by thwarting "meaningful judicial review" of agency rules. Courts under *Auer*, he asserts . . . "abdicate their office of determining the meaning" of a regulation. . . .

[T]hat argument ignores the many ways, discussed above, that courts exercise independent review over the meaning of agency rules. . . .

And even when a court defers to a regulatory reading, it acts consistently with Section 706. That provision does not specify the standard of review a court should use in "determin[ing] the meaning" of an ambiguous rule. One possibility, as Kisor says, is to review the issue de novo. But another is to review the agency's reading for reasonableness. To see the point, assume that a regulatory (say, an employment) statute expressly instructed courts to apply *Auer* deference when reviewing an agency's interpretations of its ambiguous rules. Nothing in that statute would conflict with Section 706. [F]or all the reasons spelled out above, we have long presumed (subject always to rebuttal) that the Congress delegating regulatory authority to an agency intends as well to give that agency considerable latitude to construe its ambiguous rules. And that presumption operates just like the hypothesized statute above. . . .

That is especially so given the practice of judicial review at the time of the APA's enactment. Section 706 was understood when enacted to "restate[] the present law as to the scope of judicial review." *See* Dept. of Justice, Attorney General's Manual on the Administrative Procedure Act 108 (1947). . . . That pre-APA common law included *Seminole Rock* itself (decided the year before) along with prior decisions foretelling that ruling. Even assume that the deference regime laid out in those cases had not yet fully taken hold. At a minimum, nothing in the law of that era required all judicial review of agency interpretations to be *de novo*. . . . If Section 706 did not change the law of judicial review (as we have long recognized), then it did not proscribe a deferential standard then known and in use. . . .

To supplement his [APA argument], Kisor turns to policy, leaning on a familiar claim about the incentives *Auer* creates. According to Kisor, *Auer* encourages agencies to issue vague and open-ended regulations, confident that they can later impose whatever interpretation of those rules they prefer. [This] claim has notable weaknesses, empirical and theoretical alike. First, it does not survive an encounter with experience. No real evidence—indeed, scarcely an anecdote—backs up the assertion. As two noted scholars (one of whom reviewed thousands of rules during four years of government service) have written: "[W]e are unaware of, and no one has pointed to, any regulation in American history that, because of *Auer*, was designed vaguely." Sunstein & Vermeule, 84 U. Chi. L. Rev. at 308. And even the argument's theoretical allure dissipates upon reflection. For strong (almost surely stronger) incentives and pressures cut in the opposite direction. "[R]egulators want their regulations to be effective, and clarity promotes compliance." Brief for Administrative Law Scholars as *Amici Curiae* 18-19. Too, regulated parties often push for precision from an agency, so that they know what they can and cannot do. And ambiguities in rules pose risks to the long-run survival of agency policy. Vagueness increases the chance of adverse judicial rulings. And it enables future administrations, with different views, to reinterpret the rules to their own liking. Add all of that up and Kisor's ungrounded theory of incentives contributes nothing to the case against *Auer*.

Finally, Kisor goes big, asserting (though fleetingly) that *Auer* deference violates "separation-of-powers principles." In his view, those principles prohibit "vest[ing]" in a single branch the law-making and law-interpreting functions." If that objection is to agencies' usurping the interpretive role of courts, this opinion has already met it head-on. Properly understood and applied, *Auer* does no such thing. In all the ways we have described, courts retain a firm grip on the interpretive function. If Kisor's objection is instead to the supposed commingling of functions (that is, the legislative and judicial) within an agency, this Court has answered it often before. That sort of mixing is endemic in agencies, and has been "since the beginning of the Republic." *Arlington*, [v. FCC, 569 U.S. 290, 304-305 n.4 (2013)]. It does not violate the separation of powers, we have explained, because even when agency "activities take 'legislative' and 'judicial' forms," they continue to be "exercises of[] the 'executive Power'"—or otherwise said, ways of executing a statutory plan. *Ibid.* . . .

B

[In Part III-B Justice Kagan argued that respect for *stare decisis* should prevent the Court from overruling *Auer*. In Part IV she explained that, because the standard for *Auer* deference articulated by the Court differed from the standard applied by the Federal Circuit, the case should be remanded to the Federal Circuit for further consideration in light of the Court's opinion.]

CHIEF JUSTICE ROBERTS, concurring in part. . . .

I agree that overruling [*Auer*] is not warranted. . . . I write separately to suggest that the distance between the majority and Justice Gorsuch is not as great as it may initially appear. The majority catalogs the prerequisites for, and limitations on, *Auer* deference [and] Justice Gorsuch . . . lists the reasons that a court might be persuaded to adopt an agency's interpretation of its own regulation . . . Accounting for variations in verbal formulation, those lists have much in common.

That is not to say that *Auer* deference is just the same as the power of persuasion discussed in *Skidmore*; there is a difference between holding that a court ought to be persuaded by an agency's interpretation and holding that it should defer to that interpretation under certain conditions. But it is to say that the cases in which *Auer* deference is warranted largely overlap with the cases in which it would be unreasonable for a court not to be persuaded by an agency's interpretation of its own regulation. One further point: Issues surrounding judicial deference to agency interpretations of their own regulations are distinct from those raised in connection with judicial deference to agency interpretations of statutes enacted by Congress. *See Chevron.* I do not regard the Court's decision today to touch upon the latter question.

JUSTICE GORSUCH, with whom JUSTICE THOMAS joins, with whom JUSTICE KAVANAUGH joins as to Parts I, II, III, IV, and V, and with whom JUSTICE ALITO joins as to Parts I, II, and III, concurring in the judgment.

It should have been easy for the Court to say goodbye to *Auer v. Robbins*. In disputes involving the relationship between the government and the people, *Auer* requires judges to accept an executive agency's interpretation of its own regulations even when that interpretation doesn't represent the best and fairest reading. This rule creates a "systematic judicial bias in favor of the federal government, the most powerful of parties, and against everyone else."[2] Nor is *Auer*'s biased rule the product of some congressional mandate we are powerless to correct: This Court invented it, almost by accident and without any meaningful effort to reconcile it with the Administrative Procedure Act or the Constitution. A legion of academics, lower court judges, and Members of this Court—even *Auer*'s author—has called on us to abandon *Auer*. Yet today a bare majority flinches, and *Auer* lives on.

Still, today's decision is more a stay of execution than a pardon. The Court cannot muster even five votes to say that *Auer* is lawful or wise. Instead, a majority retains *Auer* only because of *stare decisis*. And yet, far from standing by that precedent, the majority proceeds to impose so many new and nebulous qualifications and limitations on *Auer* that THE CHIEF JUSTICE claims to see little practical difference between keeping it on life support in this way and overruling it entirely. So the doctrine emerges maimed and enfeebled—in truth, zombified.

---

2. Larkin & Slattery, The World After *Seminole Rock* and *Auer*, 42 Harv. J.L. & Pub. Pol'y 625, 641 (2019) (internal quotation marks omitted).

Respectfully, we owe our colleagues on the lower courts more candid and useful guidance than this. And judges owe the people who come before them nothing less than a fair contest, where every party has an equal chance to persuade the court of its interpretation of the law's demands. One can hope that The Chief Justice is right, and that whether we formally overrule *Auer* or merely neuter it, the results in most cases will prove the same. But means, not just ends, matter, and retaining even this debilitated version of *Auer* threatens to force litigants and lower courts to jump through needless and perplexing new hoops and in the process deny the people the independent judicial decisions they deserve. . . .

I. How We Got Here

Where did *Auer* come from? Not from the Constitution, some ancient common law tradition, or even a modern statute. Instead, it began as an unexplained aside in a decision about emergency price controls at the height of the Second World War. Even then, the dictum sat on the shelf, little noticed, for years. Only in the last few decades of the 20th century did lawyers and courts really begin to dust it off and shape it into the reflexive rule of deference to regulatory agencies we know today. . . . Justice Kagan suggests that *Auer*'s . . . approach to the interpretation of agency regulations was foreshadowed as early as this Court's 1898 decision in *United States v. Eaton*. But this is mistaken. [*Eaton*] simply followed the well-worn path of acknowledging that an agency's interpretation of a regulation can supply evidence of its meaning. Nowhere did the Court even hint that it would have deferred to the State Department's views about the meaning of the law if its own independent textual analysis had not led it to the same conclusion.

All this is borne out by the Court's later teachings in *Skidmore* . . . .

In truth, the seeds of the *Auer* doctrine were first planted only in 1945, in *Bowles v. Seminole Rock & Sand Co.* That case involved regulations issued by the Office of Price Administration (OPA), which Congress had tasked with stabilizing the national economy during the Second World War through the use of emergency price controls. It was in that context that the Court declared—for the first time and without citing any authority—that "if the meaning of [the regulation were] in doubt," the agency's interpretation would merit "controlling weight unless it is plainly erroneous or inconsistent with the regulation." . . .

Yet even then it was far from clear how much weight the Court really placed on the agency's interpretation. As it had in *Eaton*, the Court in *Seminole Rock* began with an extended discussion of "the plain words of the regulation," which led it to conclude that the text "clearly" supported the government's position. Only after reaching that conclusion based on its own independent analysis did the Court proceed to add that "[a]ny doubts . . . are removed by reference to the administrative construction." . . .

[Although the *Seminole Rock* dictum went largely unnoticed until the mid-1960s, it was cited, but not analyzed, increasingly after that, culminating in its reaffirmation in *Auer*.] In the name of what some now call the *Auer* doctrine, courts have in recent years "mechanically applied and reflexively treated" *Seminole Rock*'s dictum "as a constraint upon the careful inquiry that one might ordinarily expect of courts engaged in textual analysis." Under *Auer*, judges are forced to subordinate their own views about what the law means to those of a political actor, one who may even be a party to the litigation before the court. After all, if the court agrees that the agency's reading is the best one, Auer does no real work; the doctrine matters only when a court would conclude that the agency's interpretation is not the best or fairest reading of the regulation. . . .

II. The Administrative Procedure Act

When this Court speaks about the rules governing judicial review of federal agency action, we are not (or shouldn't be) writing on a blank slate or exercising some common-law-making power. We are supposed to be applying the Administrative Procedure Act. . . . Yet, remarkably, until today this Court has never made any serious effort to square the *Auer* doctrine with the APA.

[Section 706] instructs reviewing courts to "decide all relevant questions of law" and "set aside agency action . . . found to be . . . not in accordance with law." Determining the meaning of a statute or regulation, of course, presents a classic legal question. But in case these directives were not clear enough, the APA further directs courts to "determine the meaning" of any relevant "agency action," including any rule issued by the agency. The APA thus requires a reviewing court to resolve for itself any dispute over the proper interpretation of an agency regulation. A court that, in deference to an agency, adopts something other than the best reading of a regulation isn't "decid[ing]" the relevant "questio[n] of law" or "determin[ing] the meaning" of the regulation. Instead, it's allowing the agency to dictate the answer to that question. In doing so, the court is abdicating the duty Congress assigned to it in the APA.

[The APA's] unqualified command requires the court to determine legal questions—including questions about a regulation's meaning—by its own lights, not by those of political appointees or bureaucrats who may even be self-interested litigants in the case at hand. Nor can there be any doubt that, when Congress wrote the APA, it knew perfectly well how to require judicial deference to an agency when it wished—in fact, Congress repeatedly specified deferential standards for judicial review elsewhere in the statute. But when it comes to the business of interpreting regulations, no such command exists; instead, Congress told courts to "determine" those matters for themselves. . . .

Nor does Justice Kagan's reading of §706 offer any logical stopping point. If courts can "determine the meaning" of a regulation by deferring to any "reasonable" agency reading, then why not by deferring to any agency reading? If it were really true that the APA has nothing to say about *how* courts decide what regulations mean, then it would follow that the APA tolerates a rule that "the agency is always right." And if you find yourself in a place as absurd as that, you might want to consider whether you've taken a wrong turn along the way. . . .

If *Auer* cannot be squared with the text of the APA, Justice Kagan suggests it at least conforms to a reasonable "presumption about congressional intent." The theory seems to be that whenever Congress grants an agency "rulemaking power," it also implicitly gives the agency "'the power authoritatively to interpret'" whatever rules the agency chooses to adopt. But against the clear statutory commands Congress gave us in the APA, what sense does it make to "presume" that Congress really, secretly, wanted courts to treat agency interpretations as binding? . . .

III. THE CONSTITUTION

Not only is *Auer* incompatible with the APA; it also sits uneasily with the Constitution. Article III, §1 provides that the "judicial Power of the United States" is vested exclusively in this Court and the lower federal courts. A core component of that judicial power is "'the duty of interpreting [the laws] and applying them in cases properly brought before the courts.'" [Massachusetts v. Mellon, 262 U.S. 447, 488 (1923).] As Chief Justice Marshall put it, "[i]t is emphatically the province and duty of the judicial department to say what the law is." [Marbury v. Madison, 1 Cranch 137, 177 (1803).]

A

[The founders] resisted proposals that would have subjected judicial decisions to review by political actors. And they rejected the British tradition of using the upper house of the legislature as a court of last resort, out of fear that a body with "even a partial agency in passing bad laws" would operate under the "same spirit" in "interpreting them." [Federalist No. 81 (Alexander Hamilton).] Instead, they gave federal judges life tenure, subject only to removal by impeachment; and they guaranteed that the other branches could not reduce judges' compensation so long as they remained in office.

The founders afforded these extraordinary powers and protections not for the comfort of judges, but so that an independent judiciary could better guard the people from the arbitrary use of governmental power. . . .

Auer represents no trivial threat to these foundational principles. Under the APA, substantive rules issued by federal agencies through notice-and-comment procedures bear "the 'force and effect of law'" and are part of the body of federal law, binding on private individuals, that the Constitution charges federal judges with interpreting. Yet *Auer* tells the judge that he must interpret these binding laws to mean not what he thinks they mean, but what an executive agency says they mean. Unlike Article III judges, executive officials are not, nor are they supposed to be, "wholly impartial." They have their own interests, their own constituencies, and their own policy goals . . . *Auer* thus means that, far from being "kept distinct," the powers of making, enforcing, and interpreting laws are united in the same hands—and in the process a cornerstone of the rule of law is compromised. . . .

IV. POLICY ARGUMENTS

Lacking support elsewhere, Justice Kagan is forced to resort to policy arguments to defend *Auer*. But even the most sensible policy argument would not empower us to ignore the plain language of the APA or the demands of the Constitution. And as we've seen, those documents reflect a very different "policy" judgment by the people and their representatives. . . .

Justice Kagan suggests that determining the meaning of a regulation is largely a matter of figuring out what the "person who wrote it . . . intended." In this way, we're told, a legally binding regulation isn't all that different from "a memo or an e-mail." . . . But the federal government's substantive rules are not like memos or e-mails; they are binding edicts that carry the force of law for all citizens. And if the rule of law means anything, it means that we are governed by the public meaning of the words found in statutes and regulations, not by their authors' private intentions. . . . If the best reading of the regulation turns out to be something other than what the agency claims to have intended, the agency is free to rewrite the regulation; but its secret intentions are not the law.

[Further, if] a court's goal in interpreting a regulation really were to determine what its author "intended," *Auer* would be an almost complete mismatch with the goal. Agency personnel change over time, and an agency's policy priorities may shift dramatically from one presidential administration to another. Yet *Auer* tells courts that they must defer to the agency's current view of what the regulation ought to mean, which may or may not correspond to the views of those who actually wrote it. If interpreting a regulation really were just like reading an e-mail, *Auer* would be like seeking guidance about the e-mail's meaning, years or decades later, from the latest user of the computer from which the e-mail was sent. We've repeatedly rejected that approach in the context of statutory interpretation. . . .

Proceeding farther down this doubtful path, Justice Kagan asserts that resolving ambiguities in a regulation "sounds more in policy than in law" and is thus a task more suited to executive officials than judges. But . . . [t]he text of the regulation is treated as the law, and the agency's policy judgment has the force of law only insofar as it is embodied in the regulatory text. If "new issues demanding new policy calls" arise that aren't addressed in existing regulations, the solution is for the agency to promulgate new regulations using the notice-and-comment procedures set forth in the APA. . . .

Pursuing a more modest tack, Justice Kagan next suggests that *Auer* is justified by the respect due agencies' "technical" expertise. [W]hile courts should of course afford respectful consideration to the expert agency's views, they must remain open to competing expert and other evidence supplied in an adversarial setting. Respect for an agency's technical expertise demands no more.

Justice Kagan's final policy argument is that *Auer* promotes "consistency" and "uniformity" in the interpretation of regulations. [But the] judicial process is how we settle disputes about the meaning of written law, and our judicial system is more than capable of producing a single, uniform, and stable interpretation that will last until the regulation is amended or repealed. . . .

* * *

Overruling *Auer* would have taken us directly back to *Skidmore,* liberating courts to decide cases based on their independent judgment and "follow [the] agency's [view] only to the extent it is persuasive." By contrast, the majority's attempt to remodel *Auer*'s rule into a multistep, multi-factor inquiry guarantees more uncertainty and much litigation. Proceeding in this convoluted way burdens our colleagues on the lower courts, who will have to spend time debating deference that they could have spent interpreting disputed regulations. It also continues to deny the people who come before us the neutral forum for their disputes that they rightly expect and deserve.

But this cloud may have a silver lining: The majority leaves *Auer* so riddled with holes that, when all is said and done, courts may find that it does not constrain their independent judgment any more than *Skidmore*. . . .

[W]hatever happens, this case hardly promises to be this Court's last word on *Auer*. If today's opinion ends up reducing *Auer* to the role of a tin god—officious, but ultimately powerless—then a future Court should candidly admit as much and stop requiring litigants and lower courts to pay token homage to it. Alternatively, if *Auer* proves more resilient, this Court should reassert its responsibility to say what the law is and afford the people the neutral forum for their disputes that they expect and deserve.

JUSTICE KAVANAUGH, with whom JUSTICE ALITO joins, concurring in the judgment. [Justice Kavanaugh agreed with JUSTICE GORSUCH that *Auer* should be overruled, but also agreed with CHIEF JUSTICE ROBERTS that the approach set forth in JUSTICE KAGAN's opinion, taken seriously, is not terribly far from directly overruling *Auer*.] . . . If a reviewing court employs all of the traditional tools of construction, the court will almost always reach a conclusion about the best interpretation of the regulation at issue. After doing so, the court then will have no need to adopt or defer to an agency's contrary interpretation.

NOTES AND QUESTIONS

1. *What is left of* Auer*?* Chief Justice Roberts and Justices Kavanaugh and Alito take pains to assert the modesty of the disagreement between Justice Kagan's opinion and Justice Gorsuch's opinion. Do you agree? How would you characterize the disagreement, apart from the formal difference between overruling *Auer* and radically revising the doctrine that bears its name? Would a court relying on the statement that is the essence of the *Auer* doctrine as it was before *Kisor* be affirmed by the Supreme Court? Is there really, as the Chief Justice argues, "a difference between holding that a court ought to be persuaded by an agency's interpretation and holding that it should defer to that interpretation under certain conditions"?

2. *What does* Kisor *portend for* Chevron*?* All of the justices seem keen to emphasize that *Kisor* is about *Auer*, not *Chevron*. Are they being disingenuous? Does the way the justices in *Kisor* categorize the basis for deference to administrators have implications for the way *Chevron* must now be interpreted and applied? Is it significant that only a minority joins the part of Justice Kagan's opinion that appears to predicate deference on the basis of policy considerations long advanced in support of *Chevron*, while a majority supports parts of Justice Kagan's opinion and Justice Gorsuch's opinion that make legislative delegation of discretionary authority the linchpin for deference?

3. *Is deference unconstitutional?* Justice Gorsuch's opinion argues that deference to administrative readings of law violates constitutional assignments of separate functions to the different branches of government, especially treading on the vesting of judicial power in the courts. That argument seems equally to

condemn *Chevron* and *Auer*. In an influential article, written just prior to *Auer's* decision, however, then-Professor John Manning argued that judicial deference in the two contexts of regulatory and statutory interpretations raise different constitutional issues. John F. Manning, Constitutional Structure and Judicial Deference to Agency Interpretations of Agency Rules, 96 Colum. L. Rev. 612 (1996). There are two quasi-constitutional values at work in these doctrines, he argues: political accountability and separation of powers. The former justifies deference in both contexts: policymaking-via-interpretation should be done by politically accountable agencies in preference to politically insulated courts. But the latter principle justifies a different rule in the two contexts, he argues. *Chevron* preserves a separation of lawmaking (by Congress) from law interpretation and application (by administrative agencies). *Seminole Rock–Auer* deference, in contrast, is based on a vision that combines the two functions in one body. This combination is bad, he says, because it encourages agencies to issue vague, incomplete regulations, knowing that they can revise them later by "interpretation." This opens the administrative policymaking process to excessive interest group influence, because interest groups operate more effectively under cover of regulatory obfuscation. Do you agree with these claims? Even if they are correct, do they justify a rule of no-deference in judicial review of an agency's interpretation of its own regulations? For different views on the issues surrounding deference to agency rule interpretations, *see, e.g.,* Aditya Bamzai, The Origins of Judicial Deference to Executive Interpretation, 126 Yale L.J. 908 (2017); Ronald A. Cass, *Auer* Deference: Doubling Down on Delegation's Defects, 87 Fordham L. Rev. 531 (2018); Aaron L. Nielson, Beyond *Seminole Rock*, 105 Geo. L.J. 943 (2017); Kevin M. Stack, Interpreting Regulations, 111 Mich. L. Rev. 355 (2012); Cass R. Sunstein & Adrian Vermeule, The Unbearable Rightness of *Auer*, 84 U. Chi. L. Rev. 297 (2017).

8.   Chevron *Reconsidered: Its Impact, Its Future*

Chevron has been the law of the land since 1984. It has been cited thousands of times by courts and agencies, spawned hundreds of law review articles, and provoked fierce debate in the media and halls of government. Is it a fixture in American law, or has its time come?

One important question is what impact has it actually had on judicial decisionmaking? Scholars have attempted to measure empirically the impact of *Chevron* on the behavior of reviewing courts. *See* Peter H. Schuck & E. Donald Elliott, To the *Chevron* Station: An Empirical Study of Federal Administrative Law, 1990 Duke L.J. 984, and Thomas W. Merrill, Judicial Deference to Executive Precedent, 101 Yale L.J. 969 (1992). In a study of some 2,000 decisions of federal courts of appeals in 1984-1985 and 1988, Schuck and Elliott found that the rate of judicial affirmance of agencies increased from 71 percent (in the six months prior to *Chevron*) to 81 percent (in the six months immediately following *Chevron*), and by 1988 had settled back to 76 percent.

Based on his reading of 135 Supreme Court decisions from 1981 to 1990, Merrill concluded that *Chevron* had had surprisingly little impact on the Supreme Court itself. First, he observed, the Court explicitly applied the *Chevron* framework in only about one-third of the post-*Chevron* cases in which one or more

Justices discerned an issue of deference to an agency interpretation. Second, the rate of agency affirmance was actually *lower* in cases consciously applying the *Chevron* framework than those that did not. Third, he observed that, even after *Chevron*, the Court continued to invoke the variables often invoked in pre-*Chevron* cases to justify giving deference to an agency. But the frequency with which the Court invoked these factors did decline significantly.

A more recent study by William Eskridge and Lauren Baer concludes that *Chevron* is cited in only about one-third of the cases in which it is potentially relevant and that the agency's interpretation is more likely to be rejected in cases citing *Chevron* than in cases in which *Chevron* is not cited. *See* William Eskridge & Lauren Baer, The Continuum of Deference: Supreme Court Treatment of Agency Statutory Interpretations from *Chevron* to *Hamdan*, 96 Geo. L.J. 1083, 1121 (2008). This is probably due to the predominance of cases citing *Chevron* step one in which the Court finds clear congressional intent.

Although Professors Schuck and Elliott concluded in 1990 that *Chevron* had a modest and mostly temporary effect on judicial review, by 2005 Professor Elliott had a very different perspective. He said, "[T]he United States Environmental Protection Agency (EPA) and other agencies gradually internalized and adapted to the additional interpretive discretion (*i.e.*, the expanded power) that *Chevron* provided them. Accordingly, EPA and other agencies are now more adventurous when interpreting and elaborating statutory law." E. Donald Elliott, *Chevron* Matters: How the *Chevron* Doctrine Redefined the Roles of Congress, Courts, and Agencies in Administrative Law, 16 Vill. Envtl. L.J. 1, 3 (2005). Elliott added, "*Chevron* and its progeny created a fundamental change in the rules of the power struggle between the courts and executive agencies. Prior to *Chevron*, the lower federal courts primarily held the power to determine 'what the law is' when a statute was unclear. Post-*Chevron*, a substantial portion of that power shifted from the judiciary to the Executive Branch." Is that how you read the cases?

Another important question concerns doctrinal coherence. Can it fairly be said that there really is a *Chevron* "doctrine," given all of the complications and exceptions that we have surveyed in the preceding materials? Many scholars think not, among them Professor Beermann and Dean Cass. *See* Jack M. Beermann, End the Failed *Chevron* Experiment Now: How *Chevron* Has Failed and Why It Can and Should Be Overruled, 42 Conn. L. Rev. 779 (2010); Ronald A. Cass, Vive la Deference? Rethinking the Balance Between Administrative and Judicial Expression, 83 Geo. Wash. L. Rev. 1294 (2015).

And what about the Justices of the Supreme Court? In one of his last opinions on the Court, Justice Anthony Kennedy took a parting shot at *Chevron*, noting that "it seems necessary and appropriate to reconsider, in an appropriate case, the premises that underlie *Chevron* and how courts have implemented that decision. The proper rules for interpreting statutes and determining agency jurisdiction and substantive agency powers should accord with constitutional separation-of-powers principles and the function and province of the Judiciary." Pereira v. Sessions, 138 S. Ct. 2105, 2121 (2018) (Kennedy, J. concurring). He included a citation to a concurring opinion by then-Judge Gorsuch in which Judge Gorsuch suggested that *Chevron* suffers from irreparable constitutional defects. *See* Gutierrez–Brizuela v. Lynch, 834 F.3d 1142, 1149-1158 (10th Cir. 2016) (Gorsuch, J., concurring). In his first full term on the Court,

Justice Gorsuch declined a party's invitation to abandon *Chevron*, but did not rule it out, stating that "whether *Chevron* should remain is a question we may leave for another day." SAS Institute, Inc. v. Iancu, 138 S. Ct. 1348, 1358 (2018). Then-Judge Brett Kavanaugh, whom President Trump appointed to replace Justice Kennedy, also expressed doubts about *Chevron* before his appointment to the Supreme Court. *See* Brett M. Kavanaugh, Two Challenges for the Judge as Umpire: Statutory Ambiguity and Constitutional Exceptions, 97 Notre Dame L. Rev. 1907, 1912 (2017) ("For *Chevron*, courts would simply determine the best reading of the statute. Courts would no longer defer to agency interpretations of statutes.") Does *Kisor* signal that the time for a frontal confrontation with the *Chevron* doctrine is upon us?

D.   JUDICIAL REVIEW OF QUESTIONS OF FACT OR POLICY UNDER THE SUBSTANTIAL EVIDENCE TEST

In the preceding sections of this chapter, we looked at review under the arbitrary, capricious standard and asked what standard of review a court should apply to an agency's determination of "law." In this section we examine standards of judicial review of agency determinations made in formal adjudication or in rulemaking subject to a specific statute requiring review under the substantial evidence standard. This subsection is devoted to exploring the meaning and illustrating the application of the substantial evidence standard of review.

1.   Formal Adjudication

As the Supreme Court stated not quite correctly in *Overton Park*, APA §706(2)(E) provides for "substantial evidence" review of factual findings made by agencies in *formal proceedings,* that is, proceedings governed by the formal hearing requirements of APA §§556 and 557.[1] In this sense, the "substantial evidence" standard is the administrative-law counterpart of the "clearly erroneous" standard applied by appellate courts to findings of fact by juries or trial judges.

The substantial evidence test was developed in connection with judicial review of Interstate Commerce Commission orders. In ICC v. Union Pacific R.R., 222 U.S. 541, 548 (1912), the Supreme Court stated that lower courts should "examine the facts to determine whether there was substantial evidence to support the order." Over the years, reviewing courts struggled to determine how much evidence, of what kind, would be considered sufficiently "substantial" to sustain an agency's finding of fact. During the late 1930s and 1940s, that struggle occurred primarily in the context of judicial enforcement of orders issued by the National Labor Relations Board. In the Wagner Act of 1935, ch.

---

1. As we describe in subsection 2 of this unit, Congress has occasionally provided in agency enabling acts for substantial evidence review of actions other than formal adjudications, such as rulemakings, notwithstanding the general rule of APA §706(2)(E).

372, §1, 49 Stat. 449, *codified at* 29 U.S.C. §§151 *et seq.,* Congress for the first time created a broad-based federal regulatory system to protect the right of workers to organize and bargain collectively. Section 7 of the Act conferred on all "employees" of businesses in interstate commerce the right:

> to self-organization, to form, join or assist labor organizations, to bargain collectively through representatives of their own choosing, and to engage in concerted activities for the purpose of collective bargaining or other mutual aid for protection.

To enforce its provisions, the Act created a National Labor Relations Board, originally composed of three members, later enlarged to five members, appointed by the President, with the advice and consent of the Senate, for five-year terms. The two primary functions of the NLRB were to ensure the fairness of union representation elections by conducting elections and investigating election controversies, and to prevent "unfair labor practices" by investigating complaints and by issuing orders against violations. Section 8 of the Act defined, as unfair labor practices, various actions or practices by employers or by unions that would interfere with the exercise of rights guaranteed by §7.

Enforcement of the Act's prohibition on unfair labor practices is not in the hands of private parties, but instead rests with the NLRB, in particular its General Counsel. The General Counsel is presidentially appointed and senatorially confirmed to a four-year term and has authority independent of the Board. (*See* discussion in Chapter III, *infra.*) Although the NLRB controls enforcement of the law, cases usually start with a petition from an employee, employer, or union asking the NLRB to investigate and take action. Typically, the allegations are investigated in one of the Board's regional or field offices and reviewed by the Regional Director of the region in which the alleged events occurred, operating under authority delegated from the General Counsel. The investigation may prompt settlement of potential charges or, if the Regional Director finds there is enough merit to the complaint, it may be followed by a formal adjudicatory hearing before a "trial examiner" of the agency (later, designated an "administrative law judge"), who would take evidence and issue an "intermediate report" to the full Board. The full Board would review the trial examiner's report and the record of the hearing, and would issue a final order. If the Board found that an unfair labor practice had occurred, it might order the offending party to cease and desist from its continuation or repetition and, in appropriate cases, to provide compensatory relief to the injured party by such means as reinstatement and back pay.

Orders of the NLRB were not considered self-enforcing. That is, if the respondent refused to comply with such an order, the Board was required to petition an appropriate federal court of appeals to issue an order enforcing the Board's order. In a judicial proceeding to enforce a Board order, the Wagner Act provided that: "The findings of the Board as to the facts, if supported by evidence, shall be conclusive." §10(e).

Assimilating this statutory language to its evolving "common law" jurisprudence of judicial review, the Supreme Court read "evidence" to mean "substantial evidence." Washington, Va. & Md. Coach Co. v. NLRB, 301 U.S. 142 (1937). In two later NLRB cases, the Court made its most famous attempts at giving the lower courts guidance on the meaning of this notoriously slippery phrase. In

Consolidated Edison Co. v. NLRB, 305 U.S. 197, 229 (1938), the Court defined "substantial evidence" as: "more than a mere scintilla. It means such relevant evidence as a reasonable mind might accept as adequate to support a conclusion." In NLRB v. Columbian Enameling & Stamping Co., 306 U.S. 292, 300 (1939), the Court added that, in order to be considered "substantial," evidence "must do more than create a suspicion of the existence of a fact to be established. . . . [I]t must be enough to justify, if the trial were to a jury, a refusal to direct a verdict when the conclusion sought to be drawn from it is one of fact for the jury."

The lower courts should perhaps be forgiven if they found this guidance less than lucid, and their decisions reflected an apparent lack of clarity or agreement on the proper application of the substantial evidence test. A growing chorus of the Board's critics felt that the appeals courts were excessively deferential to the Board, often enforcing orders on the strength of flimsy, speculative evidence. In particular, they claimed that many appeals courts were applying the substantial evidence test in a one-sided manner: that is, by considering only the "substantiality" of the evidence supporting the Board's finding, and disregarding the strength of the competing evidence.

Whatever the underlying truth of such criticisms, they clearly commanded considerable support in Congress during the early to mid-1940s, as Congress debated two bills, one of which was to become the Administrative Procedure Act of 1946, and the other the Taft-Hartley Act of 1947, amending the Wagner Act. Although some members of Congress urged the adoption of the "weight of the evidence" or "clearly erroneous" standards, in the end Congress chose to retain the familiar formulation "substantial evidence" in both acts. But it did provide, in both acts, that, in determining the substantiality of the evidence, the reviewing court was to look at the "whole" record, not merely the evidence supporting an agency's decision. *See, e.g.,* the final sentence of APA §706.

Shortly after the enactment of the APA and the Taft-Hartley Act, the Supreme Court had occasion to reflect on the meaning of the new statutory language. In *Universal Camera, infra,* the Court gave what is still its most authoritative pronouncement on the meaning of the "substantial evidence" test. Before we consider the Court's opinion, however, it is necessary to consider a bit of the background of the case.

In 1946 the NLRB's New York Regional Director brought a proceeding against the Universal Camera Corporation for discharging an employee, named Imre Chairman, in retaliation for exercising his rights under the Labor Act. The company claimed that Chairman was fired for an unrelated act of insubordination.

The case went to hearing before a trial examiner of the Board. At the hearing the evidence indicated the following: Shortly after his appointment as a maintenance engineer, Chairman gave support to a group of Universal Camera's maintenance workers who were seeking representation under the Act. Chairman's support included giving the group advice and assistance. On November 30, 1943, he testified on their behalf, and in opposition to the company's position, at a hearing before the local office of the NLRB. Later that day Chairman's ultimate superior, George Kende, sharply reproved Chairman for having given what Kende claimed was false testimony at the representation hearing. The next day Kende asked Personnel Manager Irving Weintraub to investigate whether Chairman's work was satisfactory and whether there was any irregularity on his job application, including a reference that suggested the possibility that Chairman might be a Communist. Weintraub did so, but evidently found no basis for disciplining or discharging him.

On the evening of December 30, 1943, Chairman and Weintraub got into a heated argument at the plant. When Weintraub observed one of Chairman's maintenance crew standing by idly, he ordered Chairman to send the worker home. Chairman refused, saying that Weintraub was not his supervisor. After further words were exchanged, Chairman accused Weintraub of being drunk. Both principals and several other witnesses gave differing accounts of what happened next. According to Weintraub, he had Chairman ejected from the plant. According to Chairman, the two eventually shook hands and parted amicably.

The next day Weintraub told Chairman's immediate supervisor, Benjamin Politzer, that Chairman should be fired for falsely accusing Weintraub of being drunk and refusing to obey his order. Politzer told Weintraub that he had already discussed the incident with Chairman and that Chairman had offered to resign within "10 to 12" days. In his testimony, Chairman denied ever having offered to resign. A few weeks later, on January 24, 1944, Weintraub noticed that Chairman was still at his post, and demanded once again that Politzer fire him. When Politzer refused, Weintraub took the dispute to Kende, who upheld Weintraub's position. Politzer then filled out a termination slip stating that Chairman was discharged for "misconduct," effective the next day, January 25.

The NLRB's Regional Director argued that the month-long delay between the December 30 incident and Chairman's dismissal showed that that incident was a mere pretext for dismissal, which was really motivated by anger at Chairman for having testified at the prior representation hearing. The trial examiner disagreed, and recommended that the Board dismiss the complaint. In his Intermediate Report, the examiner stated in his Findings of Fact, that: 1. Although Chairman and Weintraub had shaken hands following their argument on December 30, Weintraub continued to be angry at what he regarded as impermissible conduct by Chairman during that incident. 2. Although Chairman never told Politzer that he intended to resign, Politzer did tell Weintraub that Chairman intended to resign. In doing so, he was motivated either "by an honest mistake or by the thought that the quarrel between Weintraub and Chairman might be soon forgotten if action was delayed." 3. The resulting belief that Chairman would voluntarily resign explains the several-week delay between the December 30 incident and the decision by Weintraub to demand that Chairman be fired.

The examiner concluded: "In view of all the facts and circumstances the [examiner] is not persuaded that Kende based his decision on any animus toward Chairman for testifying rather than on an evaluation of Weintraub's request based on its merits."

IN THE MATTER OF UNIVERSAL
CAMERA CORPORATION
79 N.L.R.B. 379 (1948)

On February 18, 1947, Trial Examiner Sidney L. Feiler issued his Intermediate Report in the above-entitled proceeding, finding that the Respondent had not engaged in the unfair labor practices alleged in the complaint and recommending that the complaint be dismissed. . . . Thereafter, the complainant and counsel for the Board filed exceptions and supporting briefs. . . .

The Trial Examiner found that the evidence failed to sustain the allegation of the complaint that Chairman was discharged in violation of Section 8(4) of the Act. We disagree. In our opinion, a preponderance of the evidence shows that Chairman's discharge was due to the Respondent's resentment against Chairman because he had testified for the Union at a representation hearing on November 30, 1943. We believe that the Trial Examiner, in finding otherwise, failed to appreciate the strength of the prima facie case against the Respondent established by the evidence, and erroneously credited certain implausible testimony adduced by the Respondent in explanation of the circumstances leading up to Chairman's discharge. . . .

In the face of [the] clear evidence of the Respondent's animus against Chairman and its desire and intention to discharge him because of his testimony at the Board hearing if a pretext could be found, it was incumbent upon the Respondent to go forward to show convincingly that when Chairman was actually discharged—by Kende himself—8 weeks later, ostensibly because of an episode that was then stale, the real reason was something other than Chairman's appearance as a witness. Contrary to the Trial Examiner, we find the Respondent's explanation of the discharge implausible. . . .

The only testimony offered by the Respondent in explanation of the long delay between Chairman's alleged misconduct and his punishment, is that of Weintraub and Politzer to the effect that Politzer assured Weintraub, within a day or two after December 30, that Chairman intended to resign in about 10 days. The Respondent asserts that Weintraub thereupon lodged no complaint against Chairman until January 24 because he had in the meantime been expecting Chairman to leave, and only noticed, on or about January 24, that Chairman was still at work. The Trial Examiner believed this testimony, although he flatly discredited Politzer's statement, contradicted by Chairman, that Chairman had in fact agreed to resign, and although he also found both Weintraub and Politzer to be unreliable witnesses in many respects. We cannot accept the Trial Examiner's finding that Politzer, in effect, invented the story that Chairman intended to resign in order to appease Weintraub and gain time for Chairman, for this finding is irreconcilable with the other related facts, and all the other evidence bearing on Politzer's behavior and attitudes at that time. We find, then, that the record contains no credible explanation of Weintraub's failure to call for disciplinary action against Chairman, on account of their quarrel on December 30, until about a month after the event. . . . We find, on the entire record, that Chairman was discharged for testifying at the Board hearing, in violation of Section 8(4) of the Act.

[The Board ordered Universal Camera to reinstate Chairman with back pay and to cease and desist from any further similar unfair labor practices.]

NATIONAL LABOR RELATIONS BOARD v. UNIVERSAL CAMERA CORP.
179 F.2d 749 (2d Cir. 1950)

Before L. HAND, Chief Judge, and SWAN and FRANK, Circuit Judges.
L. HAND, Chief Judge.

This case arises upon a petition to enforce an order of the Labor Board, whose only direction that we need consider was to reinstate with back pay a "supervisory employee," named Chairman, whom the respondent discharged on January 24, 1944, avowedly for insubordination. [The Court reviewed the evidence and the Board's findings.]

Whether these findings were justified is the first, and indeed the only important, question of fact; and as a preliminary point arises the extent of our review.

This has been the subject of so much uncertainty that we shall not try to clarify it; but we must decide what change, if any, the [Taft-Hartley] amendment of 1947 has made. Section 10(e) now reads that the findings "shall be conclusive" "if supported by substantial evidence on the record considered as a whole"; and the original was merely that they should be conclusive, "if supported by evidence." . . . It is true that there were efforts, especially in the House, to give to courts of appeal a wider review than before; but the Senate opposed these, and, so far as concerns the adjective, "substantial," it added nothing to the interpretation which the Supreme Court had already put upon the earlier language. The most probable intent in adding the phrase, "on the record considered as a whole," was to overrule what Congress apparently supposed — perhaps rightly — had been the understanding of some courts: i.e. that, if any passage could be found in the testimony to support a finding, the review was to stop, no matter how much other parts of the testimony contradicted, or outweighed, it. That the words throughout section ten were chosen with deliberation and care is evident from the changes in §10(c), apparently intended to confine the Board to the record before it, and in §10(b), restricting it in the admission of evidence to Rule 43(a) of the Federal Rules of Civil Procedure, 28 U.S.C.A. It appears to us that, had it been intended to set up a new measure of review by the courts, the matter would not have been left so at large. We cannot agree that our review has been "broadened"; we hold that no more was done than to make definite what was already implied.

Just what that review was is another and much more difficult matter — particularly, when it comes to deciding how to treat a reversal by the Board of a finding of one of its own examiners. Obviously no printed record preserves all the evidence, on which any judicial officer bases his findings; and it is principally on that account that upon an appeal from the judgment of a district court, a court of appeals will hesitate to reverse. Its position must be: "No matter what you saw of the witnesses and what else you heard than these written words, we are satisfied from them alone that you were clearly wrong. Nothing which could have happened that is not recorded, could have justified your conclusion in the face of what is before us." That gives such findings great immunity, which the Rules[7] extend even to the findings of masters, when reviewed by a district judge. The standing of an examiner's findings under the Labor Relations Act is not plain; but it appears to us at least clear that they were not intended to be as unassailable as a master's. . . .

We hold that, although the Board would be wrong in totally disregarding his findings, it is practically impossible for a court, upon review of those findings which the Board itself substitutes, to consider the Board's reversal as a factor in the court's own decision. This we say, because we cannot find any middle

---

7. Rule 53(e)(2).

ground between doing that and treating such a reversal as error, whenever it would be such, if done by a judge to a master in equity.

[Chief Judge Hand here reviews the evidence supporting the trial examiner's findings that the dismissal was not retaliatory, and the Board's reversal of this finding. He concludes his review by saying:] We should feel obliged in our turn to reverse the reversal of this finding; if we were dealing with the finding of a judge who had reversed the finding of a master, because the reasons given do not seem to us enough to overbear the evidence which the record did not preserve and which may have convinced the examiner. . . .

Nevertheless, in spite of all this we shall direct the Board's order to be enforced. If by special verdict a jury had made either the express finding of the majority that there was an agreement between Kende and Weintraub, or the alternate finding, if there be one, that Kende without Weintraub's concurrence used Weintraub's complaint as an excuse, we should not reverse the verdict; and we understand our function in cases of this kind to be the same. Such a verdict would be within the bounds of rational entertainment. When all is said, Kende had been greatly outraged at Chairman's testimony; he then did propose to get him out of the factory; he still thought at the hearings that he was unfit to remain; and he had told Weintraub to keep watch on him. We cannot say that, with all these circumstances before him, no reasonable person could have concluded that Chairman's testimony was one of the causes of his discharge, little as it would have convinced us, were we free to pass upon the evidence in the first instance. . . .

An enforcement order will issue.

SWAN, Circuit Judge (dissenting).

In National Labor Relations Board v. A. Sartorius & Co., 2 Cir., 140 F.2d 203, 205 we said that "if an administrative agency ignores all the evidence given by one side in a controversy and with studied design gives credence to the testimony of the other side, the findings would be arbitrary and not in accord with the legal requirement." I think that is what the majority of the board has done in the case at bar. I would reverse its findings of motive and deny enforcement of the order.

UNIVERSAL CAMERA CORP. v. NATIONAL LABOR RELATIONS BOARD
340 U.S. 474 (1951)

MR. JUSTICE FRANKFURTER delivered the opinion of the Court.

The essential issue raised by this case . . . is the effect of the Administrative Procedure Act and the legislation colloquially known as the Taft-Hartley Act on the duty of Courts of Appeals when called upon to review orders of the National Labor Relations Board.

The Court of Appeals for the Second Circuit granted enforcement of an order directing, in the main, that petitioner reinstate with back pay an employee found to have been discharged because he gave testimony under the Wagner

Act and cease and desist from discriminating against any employee who files charges or gives testimony under that Act. . . .

I

Want of certainty in judicial review of Labor Board decisions partly reflects the intractability of any formula to furnish definiteness of content for all the impalpable factors involved in judicial review. But in part doubts as to the nature of the reviewing power and uncertainties in its application derive from history, and to that extent an elucidation of this history may clear them away.

The Wagner Act provided: "The findings of the Board as to the facts, if supported by evidence, shall be conclusive." Act of July 5, 1935, §10(e), 49 Stat. 449, 454, 29 U.S.C. §160(e). This Court read "evidence" to mean "substantial evidence," Washington, V. & M. Coach Co. v. Labor Board, 301 U.S. 142, and we said that "substantial evidence is more than a mere scintilla. It means such relevant evidence as a reasonable mind might accept as adequate to support a conclusion." Consolidated Edison Co. v. Labor Board, 305 U.S. 197, 229. Accordingly, it "must do more than create a suspicion of the existence of the fact to be established. . . . [I]t must be enough to justify, if the trial were to a jury, a refusal to direct a verdict when the conclusion sought to be drawn from it is one of fact for the jury." Labor Board v. Columbian Enameling & Stamping Co., 306 U.S. 292, 300.

The very smoothness of the "substantial evidence" formula as the standard for reviewing the evidentiary validity of the Board's findings established its currency. But the inevitably variant applications of the standard to conflicting evidence soon brought contrariety of views and in due course bred criticism. Even though the whole record may have been canvassed in order to determine whether the evidentiary foundation of a determination by the Board was "substantial," the phrasing of this Court's process of review readily lent itself to the notion that it was enough that the evidence supporting the Board's result was "substantial" when considered by itself. It is fair to say that by imperceptible steps regard for the factfinding function of the Board led to the assumption that the requirements of the Wagner Act were met when the reviewing court could find in the record evidence which, when viewed in isolation, substantiated the Board's findings. . . .

[The Court then recounted the history of the enactment of the APA and the Taft-Hartley Act, focusing especially on the provisions for judicial review contained in those acts.]

It is fair to say that in all this Congress expressed a mood. And it expressed its mood not merely by oratory but by legislation. As legislation that mood must be respected, even though it can only serve as a standard for judgment and not as a body of rigid rules assuring sameness of application. Enforcement of such broad standards implies subtlety of mind and solidity of judgment. But it is not for us to question that Congress may assume such qualities in the federal judiciary.

From the legislative story we have summarized, two concrete conclusions do emerge. One is the identity of aim of the Administrative Procedure Act and the Taft-Hartley Act regarding the proof with which the Labor Board must support a decision. The other is that now Congress has left no room for doubt as to the kind of scrutiny which a Court of Appeals must give the record before the Board to satisfy itself that the Board's order rests on adequate proof. . . .

Whether or not it was ever permissible for courts to determine the substantiality of evidence supporting a Labor Board decision merely on the basis of evidence which in and of itself justified it, without taking into account contradictory evidence or evidence from which conflicting inferences could be drawn, the new legislation definitively precludes such a theory of review and bars its practice. The substantiality of evidence must take into account whatever in the record fairly detracts from its weight. This is clearly the significance of the requirement in both statutes that courts consider the whole record. . . .

To be sure, the requirement for canvassing "the whole record" in order to ascertain substantiality does not furnish a calculus of value by which a reviewing court can assess the evidence. Nor was it intended to negative the function of the Labor Board as one of those agencies presumably equipped or informed by experience to deal with a specialized field of knowledge, whose findings within that field carry the authority of an expertness which courts do not possess and therefore must respect. Nor does it mean that even as to matters not requiring expertise a court may displace the Board's choice between two fairly conflicting views, even though the court would justifiably have made a different choice had the matter been before it *de novo*. Congress has merely made it clear that a reviewing court is not barred from setting aside a Board decision when it cannot conscientiously find that the evidence supporting that decision is substantial, when viewed in the light that the record in its entirety furnishes, including the body of evidence opposed to the Board's view. . . .

Whatever changes were made by the Administrative Procedure and Taft-Hartley Acts are clearly within [the] area where precise definition is impossible. Retention of the familiar "substantial evidence" terminology indicates that no drastic reversal of attitude was intended.

But a standard leaving an unavoidable margin for individual judgment does not leave the judicial judgment at large even though the phrasing of the standard does not wholly fence it in. The legislative history of these Acts demonstrates a purpose to impose on courts a responsibility which has not always been recognized. . . .

We conclude, therefore, that the Administrative Procedure Act and the Taft-Hartley Act direct that courts must now assume more responsibility for the reasonableness and fairness of Labor Board decisions than some courts have shown in the past. Reviewing courts must be influenced by a feeling that they are not to abdicate the conventional judicial function. Congress has imposed on them responsibility for assuring that the Board keeps within reasonable grounds. That responsibility is not less real because it is limited to enforcing the requirement that evidence appear substantial when viewed, on the record as a whole, by courts invested with the authority and enjoying the prestige of the Courts of Appeals. The Board's findings are entitled to respect; but they must nonetheless be set aside when the record before a Court of Appeals clearly precludes the Board's decision from being justified by a fair estimate of the worth of the testimony of witnesses or its informed judgment on matters within its special competence or both. . . .

II

The decision of the Court of Appeals is assailed on two grounds. It is said (1) that the court erred in holding that it was barred from taking into account the report of the examiner on questions of fact insofar as that report was rejected by the Board, and (2) that the Board's order was not supported by substantial evidence on the record considered as a whole, even apart from the validity of the court's refusal to consider the rejected portions of the examiner's report.

The latter contention is easily met. . . . [I]t is clear from the court's opinion in this case that it in fact did consider the "record as a whole," and did not deem itself merely the judicial echo of the Board's conclusion. The testimony of the company's witnesses was inconsistent, and there was clear evidence that the complaining employee had been discharged by an officer who was at one time influenced against him because of his appearance at the Board hearing. On such a record we could not say that it would be error to grant enforcement.

The first contention, however, raises serious questions to which we now turn.

III

The Court of Appeals deemed itself bound by the Board's rejection of the examiner's findings because the court considered these findings not "as unassailable as a master's."[24] 179 F.2d at 752. They are not. Section 10(c) of the Labor Management Relations Act provides that "If upon the preponderance of the testimony taken the Board shall be of the opinion that any person named in the complaint has engaged in or is engaging in any such unfair labor practice, then the Board shall state its findings of fact. . . ." 61 Stat. 147, 29 U.S.C. (Supp. III) §160(c). The responsibility for decision thus placed on the Board is wholly inconsistent with the notion that it has power to reverse an examiner's findings only when they are "clearly erroneous." Such a limitation would make so drastic a departure from prior administrative practice that explicitness would be required.

The Court of Appeals concluded from this premise "that, although the Board would be wrong in totally disregarding his findings, it is practically impossible for a court, upon review of those findings which the Board itself substitutes, to consider the Board's reversal as a factor in the court's own decision. This we say, because we cannot find any middle ground between doing that and treating such a reversal as error, whenever it would be such, if done by a judge to a master in equity." 179 F.2d at 753. Much as we respect the logical acumen of the Chief Judge of the Court of Appeals, we do not find ourselves pinioned between the horns of his dilemma.

We are aware that to give the examiner's findings less finality than a master's and yet entitle them to consideration in striking the account, is to introduce another and an unruly factor into the judgmatical process of review. But

---

24. Rule 53(e)(2), Fed. Rules Civ. Proc., gives finality to the findings of a master unless they are clearly erroneous. . . .

we ought not to fashion an exclusionary rule merely to reduce the number of imponderables to be considered by reviewing courts.

The Taft-Hartley Act provides that "The findings of the Board with respect to questions of fact if supported by substantial evidence on the record considered as a whole shall be conclusive." 61 Stat. 148, 29 U.S.C. (Supp. III) §160(e). Surely an examiner's report is as much a part of the record as the complaint or the testimony. According to the Administrative Procedure Act, "All decisions (including initial, recommended, or tentative decisions) shall become a part of the record. . . ." §8(b), 60 Stat. 242, 5 U.S.C. §1007(b). We found that this Act's provision for judicial review has the same meaning as that in the Taft-Hartley Act. The similarity of the two statutes in language and purpose also requires that the definition of "record" found in the Administrative Procedure Act be construed to be applicable as well to the term "record" as used in the Taft-Hartley Act.

It is therefore difficult to escape the conclusion that the plain language of the statutes directs a reviewing court to determine the substantiality of evidence on the record including the examiner's report. . . .

Nothing in the statutes suggests that the Labor Board should not be influenced by the examiner's opportunity to observe the witnesses he hears and sees and the Board does not. Nothing suggests that reviewing courts should not give to the examiner's report such probative force as it intrinsically commands. To the contrary, §11 of the Administrative Procedure Act contains detailed provisions designed to maintain high standards of independence and competence in examiners. Section 10(c) of the Labor Management Relations Act requires that examiners "shall issue . . . a proposed report, together with a recommended order." Both statutes thus evince a purpose to increase the importance of the role of examiners in the administrative process. High standards of public administration counsel that we attribute to the Labor Board's examiners both due regard for the responsibility which Congress imposes on them and the competence to discharge it. . . .

We do not require that the examiner's findings be given more weight than in reason and in the light of judicial experience they deserve. The "substantial evidence" standard is not modified in any way when the Board and its examiner disagree. We intend only to recognize that evidence supporting a conclusion may be less substantial when an impartial, experienced examiner who has observed the witnesses and lived with the case has drawn conclusions different from the Board's than when he has reached the same conclusion. The findings of the examiner are to be considered along with the consistency and inherent probability of testimony. The significance of his report, of course, depends largely on the importance of credibility in the particular case. To give it this significance does not seem to us materially more difficult than to heed the other factors which in sum determine whether evidence is "substantial." . . .

We therefore remand the cause to the Court of Appeals. On reconsideration of the record it should accord the findings of the trial examiner the relevance that they reasonably command in answering the comprehensive question whether the evidence supporting the Board's order is substantial. But the court need not limit its reexamination of the case to the effect of that report on its decision. We leave it free to grant or deny enforcement as it thinks the principles expressed in this opinion dictate.

Judgment vacated and cause remanded.

MR. JUSTICE BLACK and MR. JUSTICE DOUGLAS concur with Parts I and II of this opinion but as to Part III agree with the opinion of the Court below, 179 F.2d 749, 753.

NATIONAL LABOR RELATIONS BOARD v. UNIVERSAL CAMERA CORP.
190 F.2d 429 (2d Cir. 1951)

Before SWAN, Chief Judge, and FRANK and L. HAND, Circuit Judges.

L. HAND, Circuit Judge.

By a divided vote we decided this appeal last year upon the same record that is now before us, holding that the Board's order should be "enforced." The Supreme Court vacated our order and remanded the cause to us for consideration. . . . [The Court held that the Taft-Hartley Amendment] was intended to prescribe an attitude in courts of appeal less complaisant towards the Board's findings than had been proper before; not only were they to look to the record as a whole, but they were to be less ready to yield their personal judgment on the facts; at least less ready than many at times had been. Presumably that does not extend to those issues on which the Board's specialized experience equips it with major premises inaccessible to judges, but as to matters of common knowledge we are to use a somewhat stiffer standard. Just where the Board's specialized experience ends it may no doubt be hard to say; but we are to find the boundary and beyond it to deem ourselves as competent as the Board to pass upon issues of fact. We hold that all the issues at bar are beyond the boundary and for that reason we cannot accept the Board's argument that we are not in as good a position as itself to decide what witnesses were more likely to be telling the truth in this labor dispute. . . .

Perhaps as good a way as any to state the change effected by the amendment is to say that we are not to be reluctant to insist that an examiner's findings on veracity must not be overruled without a very substantial preponderance in the testimony as recorded.

In the case at bar the examiner came to the conclusion that Chairman's discharge on January 24, 1944, was not because of his testimony two months before. He believed that Politzer had told Weintraub, a day or two after Weintraub's quarrel with Chairman at the end of December, that Chairman had said he was going to resign; and, although he did not believe that Chairman had in fact said so, he found that Politzer either thought he had, or told Weintraub that he had in the hope of smoothing over their quarrel. We see nothing improbable in this story. . . .

It is of course true that no one can be sure what may have actuated Kende at least in part; nothing is more difficult than to disentangle the motives of another's conduct—motives frequently unknown even to the actor himself. But for that very reason those parts of the evidence which are lost in print become especially pregnant, and the Board which had no access to them should have hesitated to assume that the examiner was not right to act upon them. A story may indeed be so unreasonable on its face that no plausibility in its telling will make it tenable, but that is seldom true and certainly was not true here. . . . However limited should be the regard which the Board must give to the findings of its examiner, we cannot escape the conclusion that the record in the case at bar was such that the following finding of the examiner should have turned the scale; "the undersigned is not persuaded that Kende based his decision upon any animus against Chairman for testifying rather than on an evaluation of Weintraub's request based upon the merits." . . . [U]pon a reexamination of the record as a whole, and upon giving weight to the examiner's findings—now in compliance with the Court's directions as we understand them—we think that our first disposition of the appeal was wrong, and we hold that the Board should have dismissed the complaint.

Order reversed; complaint to be dismissed.

FRANK, Circuit Judge (concurring).

Recognizing, as only a singularly stupid man would not, Judge Hand's superior wisdom, intelligence and learning, I seldom disagree with him, and then with serious misgivings. In this instance, I have overcome my misgivings because I think that his modesty has moved him to interpret too sweepingly the Supreme Court's criticism of our earlier opinion written by him. I read the Supreme Court's opinion as saying that we had obeyed the new statute with but one exception: We had wholly disregarded the examiner's finding which the Board rejected. . . .

Judge Hand, as I understand him, interprets as follows the Supreme Court's ruling: The Board may never reject an examiner's finding if it rests on his evaluation of the credibility of oral testimony unless (1) that rejection results from the Board's rational use of the Board's specialized knowledge or (2) the examiner has been absurdly naive in believing a witness. This, I think, is somewhat more restrictive of the Board's powers than the Supreme Court suggested. . . .

I would also, by way of caution, add this qualification (to which, judging from his opinions elsewhere, I gather Judge Hand will not demur): An examiner's finding binds the Board only to the extent that it is a "testimonial inference," or "primary inference," *i.e.*, an inference that a fact to which a witness orally testified is an actual fact because that witness so testified and because observation of the witness induces a belief in that testimony. The Board, however, is not bound by the examiner's "secondary inferences," or "derivative inferences," *i.e.*, facts to which no witness orally testified but which the examiner inferred from facts orally testified by witnesses whom the examiner believed. The Board may reach its own "secondary inferences," and we must abide by them unless they are irrational; in that way, the Board differs from a trial judge (in a juryless case) who hears and sees the witnesses, for, although we are usually bound by his "testimonial inferences," we need not accept his "secondary inferences" even if rational, but, where other rational "secondary inferences" are possible, we may substitute our own. Since that is true, it is also true that we must not interfere when the Board adopts either (1) its examiner's "testimonial inferences" and they are not absurd, or (2) his rational "secondary inferences."

Except as noted above, I concur.

NOTES AND QUESTIONS

1. *How "substantial" is "substantial evidence"?* Consider first the trial examiner's finding that the dismissal of Chairman was not motivated by a desire on the part of Kende to punish him for testifying in the representation proceeding. What is the evidence supporting that finding? In what sense can it be said that that evidence is "substantial"? Would that evidence be enough to withstand a motion for a directed verdict or to sustain a jury verdict if this case had been tried to a jury at common law? Is the Supreme Court saying that is the correct standard to apply in this context? On remand, did Chief Judge Hand give a faithful reading of the Supreme Court's instructions on that point?

Now consider the finding rendered by the Board itself, that the discharge *was* retaliatory. If the *trial examiner* had made such a finding, would it be supported by "substantial" evidence? How would Learned Hand have answered that question?

2. *Judicial masters and administrative hearing examiners.* The Supreme Court held that the trial examiner's findings of fact deserved less weight than a court would be required to give to the findings of a master under the Federal Rules of Civil Procedure, but more weight than nothing at all (Hand's original position). Is there an intelligible middle ground? On remand, did Hand comply with the Court's ruling on this point?

Most agencies, like the NLRB, use designated employees to preside at formal adjudicative hearings and to render recommended decisions to the agency's governing body or agency head. APA §557 prescribes general rules for that situation. Is there anything in §557 that speaks to the question of the weight to be accorded to a trial examiner's factfindings? What about the third sentence of §557(b) ("On appeal from or review of the initial decision, the agency has all the powers which it would have in making the initial decision except as it may limit the issues on notice or by rule")? What about §557(c)(3) ("All decisions, including initial, recommended, and tentative decisions, are a part of the record . . .")?

Since the time of the decision in *Universal Camera*, Congress has substantially enhanced the status of administrative trial examiners by re-designating them as "administrative law judges" (ALJs), specifying professional qualifications for their appointment, and increasing their protection against dismissal or discipline. APA §§1305, 3105, 3344, 5372, & 7521. *See* Chapter VI.C.3, *infra.* Do these changes imply that courts should give even greater weight to ALJs' factfindings in cases in which the agency overrules those findings?

3. *Burden of proof in administrative proceedings.* "Standard of review" (in this case, the "substantial evidence" test) is conceptually distinct from "burden of proof" and "burden of persuasion." APA §556(d) (governing formal administrative proceedings) states that "[e]xcept as otherwise provided by statute, the proponent of a rule or order has the burden of proof." In regulatory enforcement proceedings, such as unfair labor practice proceedings, the proponent is usually the agency itself. The APA does not specify a general "burden of persuasion" for administrative adjudications. The normal burden of persuasion is the civil "preponderance of the evidence" standard. Some regulatory statutes specify alternative standards, the most common being "clear and convincing evidence" (considered a somewhat higher standard of proof).

How does the "substantial evidence" standard of judicial review interact with burdens of proof and persuasion? Suppose an agency has the burden of proving X, by a preponderance of the evidence. Then, to be sustainable on judicial review, there must be "substantial evidence" on the administrative record as a whole that X is more likely true than not-X. Note that this does *not* necessarily mean that the *reviewing court* believes that X is more probable than not-X. It merely means that there is enough evidence on the record (more than a "scintilla" but not necessarily a "preponderance") to make it seem reasonable to the reviewing court that the *agency* could have so believed. Hence, there might be "substantial evidence" to support an agency's finding of *either* X or not-X, a point that the Supreme Court has made quite explicit on occasion. *See, e.g.,* Arkansas v. Oklahoma, 503 U.S. 91, 112-113 (1992).

4. *Administrative presumptions.* If a certain factual issue comes up repeatedly in an agency's adjudications, must the agency present evidence on the point at each hearing? The answer is no. The agency may use the device of "presumptions" to economize on the proof of repetitive factual issues. The NLRB has used this device about as often as any agency. Presumptions obviate the necessity for the Board to present primary evidence to support a particular fact in every case and have the effect of shifting the burden of proof to the respondent to show that the presumed "fact" is not true in the particular case. An early example was the Board's presumption against employer rules prohibiting union solicitation activities at the employer's place of business on nonwork time. In several early unfair labor practice cases, the Board had found, as a matter of fact, that the cost of such a rule (by restricting workers' organizational rights) outweighed its benefits (by reducing disruption of the workplace or interference with worker privacy). Based on these repetitive findings, the Board articulated a general presumption that such rules were invalid. In Republic Aviation Corp. v. NLRB, 324 U.S. 793, 803-804 (1945), the Court upheld the presumption. The Board may use presumptions, said the Court, so long as they are based on factual findings and draw "rational" inferences from those findings.

The fact that a presumption is valid does not, of course, relieve the Board from having to adduce specific evidence *if* the respondent adduces evidence to rebut the presumption. An example is NLRB v. Baptist Hosp., Inc., 442 U.S. 773 (1979). Following a 1974 amendment extending the Labor Act to hospitals, the Board adopted a presumption against hospital rules banning union solicitation activity in any areas other than direct patient care areas. The Board brought an unfair labor practice proceeding against Baptist Hospital because its antisolicitation rule applied not only to patient-care areas, but also to corridors and waiting rooms adjacent to patient-care areas. At the administrative hearing, the Hospital presented uncontradicted evidence that solicitation in such adjacent areas would be unduly disruptive of patient care. The Board, relying solely on its general presumption, found the Hospital's rule, insofar as it applied to adjacent areas, to be an unfair labor practice, and ordered the Hospital to cease applying its rule to those areas. The Supreme Court refused to enforce the Board's order, finding that it was not based on substantial evidence on the record.

5. *Experts and substantial evidence.* Many administrative decisions in formal adjudications draw on evidence presented by expert witnesses or drawn from their reports. Issues arise in this context respecting the degree to which agency decisions requiring substantial evidence can rest on expert testimony, especially

when the underlying information that informed the experts' statements is questioned. The greatest volume of formal federal adjudications comes from the Social Security Administration's disposition of challenges to disability determinations. Approximately 1,500 administrative law judges (ALJs) render decisions in 650,000 cases each year. (This process is described further in connection with the *Eldridge* case in Chapter VI, *infra*.) That is the context for the decision below.

BIESTEK v. BERRYHILL
139 S. Ct. 1148 (2019)

JUSTICE KAGAN delivered the opinion of the Court.

The Social Security Administration (SSA) provides benefits to individuals who cannot obtain work because of a physical or mental disability. To determine whether an applicant is entitled to benefits, the agency may hold an informal hearing examining (among other things) the kind and number of jobs available for someone with the applicant's disability and other characteristics. The agency's factual findings on that score are "conclusive" in judicial review of the benefits decision so long as they are supported by "substantial evidence."

This case arises from the SSA's reliance on an expert's testimony about the availability of certain jobs in the economy. The expert largely based her opinion on private market-survey data. The question presented is whether her refusal to provide that data upon the applicant's request categorically precludes her testimony from counting as "substantial evidence." We hold it does not.

I

Petitioner Michael Biestek once worked as a carpenter and general laborer on construction sites. But he stopped working after he developed degenerative disc disease, Hepatitis C, and depression. He then applied for social security disability benefits, claiming eligibility as of October 2009.

After some preliminary proceedings, the SSA assigned an Administrative Law Judge (ALJ) to hold a hearing on Biestek's application. Those hearings, as described in the Social Security Act, are recognizably adjudicative in nature. The ALJ may "receive evidence" and "examine witnesses" about the contested issues in a case. But many of the rules governing such hearings are less rigid than those a court would follow. . . .

To rule on Biestek's application, the ALJ had to determine . . . the types of jobs Biestek could perform . . . [and] . . . whether those kinds of jobs "exist[ed] in significant numbers in the national economy." . . .

At Biestek's hearing, the ALJ asked a vocational expert named Erin O'Callaghan to identify a sampling of "sedentary" jobs that a person with Biestek's disabilities, education, and job history could perform. . . . In response to the ALJ's query, O'Callaghan listed sedentary jobs "such as a bench assembler [or] sorter" that did not require many skills. And she further testified that 240,000 bench assembler jobs and 120,000 sorter jobs existed in the national economy.

On cross-examination, Biestek's attorney asked O'Callaghan "where [she was] getting those [numbers] from." O'Callaghan replied that they came from the Bureau of Labor Statistics and her "own individual labor market surveys." The lawyer then requested that O'Callaghan turn over the private surveys so he could review them. O'Callaghan responded that she wished to keep the surveys confidential because they were "part of [her] client files." . . . [The ALJ stated] that he "would not require" O'Callaghan to produce the files in any form. Biestek's counsel asked no further questions about the basis for O'Callaghan's . . . numbers.

[T]he ALJ issued a decision granting Biestek's application in part and denying it in part. According to the ALJ, Biestek was entitled to benefits beginning in May 2013, when his advancing age (he turned fifty that month) adversely affected his ability to find employment. But before that time, the ALJ held, Biestek's disabilities should not have prevented a "successful adjustment to other work." The ALJ based that conclusion on O'Callaghan's testimony . . . .

Biestek sought review in federal court of the ALJ's denial of benefits for the period between October 2009 and May 2013. On judicial review, an ALJ's factual findings—such as the determination that Biestek could have found sedentary work—"shall be conclusive" if supported by "substantial evidence." 42 U.S.C. §405(g). Biestek contended that O'Callaghan's testimony could not possibly constitute such evidence because she had declined, upon request, to produce her supporting data. . . .

II

The phrase "substantial evidence" is a "term of art" used throughout administrative law to describe how courts are to review agency factfinding. T-Mobile South, LLC v. Roswell, 574 U. S. ___, ___ (2015) (slip op., at 7). Under the substantial-evidence standard, a court looks to an existing administrative record and asks whether it contains "sufficien[t] evidence" to support the agency's factual determinations. Consolidated Edison Co. v. NLRB, 305 U.S. 197, 229 (1938) (emphasis deleted). And whatever the meaning of "substantial" in other contexts, the threshold for such evidentiary sufficiency is not high. Substantial evidence, this Court has said, is "more than a mere scintilla." *Ibid.* It means—and means only—"such relevant evidence as a reasonable mind might accept as adequate to support a conclusion." [*Ibid.*]

Biestek argues that the testimony of a vocational expert who (like O'Callaghan) refuses a request for supporting data about job availability can never clear the substantial-evidence bar. . . .

[W]e begin with the parties' common ground: Assuming no demand, a vocational expert's testimony may count as substantial evidence even when unaccompanied by supporting data. . . . Suppose an expert has top-of-the-line credentials, including professional qualifications and many years' experience; suppose, too, she has a history of giving sound testimony about job availability in similar cases (perhaps before the same ALJ). . . . She answers cogently and thoroughly all questions put to her by the ALJ and the applicant's lawyer. And nothing in the rest of the record conflicts with anything she says. But she never produces her survey data. Still, her testimony would be the kind of evidence—far "more than a mere scintilla"—that "a reasonable mind might accept as adequate to support" a finding about job availability. [*Ibid.*]

But if that is true, why should one additional fact—a refusal to a request for that data—make a vocational expert's testimony categorically inadequate? Assume that an applicant challenges our hypothetical expert to turn over her supporting data; and assume the expert declines because the data reveals private information about her clients and making careful redactions will take a fair bit of time. Nothing in the expert's refusal changes her testimony (as described above) about job availability. Nor does it alter any other material in the record. So if our expert's opinion was sufficient—*i.e.*, qualified as substantial evidence—before the refusal, it is hard to see why the opinion has to be insufficient afterward.

Biestek suggests two reasons for that non-obvious result. First, he contends that the expert's rejection of a request for backup data necessarily "cast[s her testimony] into doubt." Reply Brief 16. And second, he avers that the refusal inevitably "deprives an applicant of the material necessary for an effective cross-examination." *Id.* at 2. But Biestek states his arguments too broadly. . . .

Consider Biestek's claim about how an expert's refusal undercuts her credibility. Biestek here invokes the established idea of an "adverse inference": If an expert declines to back up her testimony with information in her control, then the factfinder has a reason to think she is hiding something. . . . If an ALJ has no other reason to trust the expert, or finds her testimony iffy on its face, her refusal of the applicant's demand for supporting data may properly tip the scales against her opinion. . . . But if . . . the ALJ views the expert and her testimony as otherwise trustworthy, and thinks she has good reason to keep her data private, her rejection of an applicant's demand need not make a difference. . . . In some cases, the refusal to disclose data, considered along with other shortcomings, will prevent a court from finding that "a reasonable mind" could accept the expert's testimony. *Consolidated Edison*, 305 U.S. at 229. But in other cases, that refusal will have no such consequence. . . .

[M]uch the same is true of Biestek's claim that an expert's refusal precludes meaningful cross-examination. . . . Even without specific data, an applicant may probe the strength of testimony by asking an expert about (for example) her sources and methods—where she got the information at issue and how she analyzed it and derived her conclusions. . . .

The [legally required] inquiry, as is usually true in determining the substantiality of evidence, is case-by-case. It takes into account all features of the vocational expert's testimony, as well as the rest of the administrative record. And in so doing, it defers to the presiding ALJ, who has seen the hearing up close. That much is sufficient to decide this case. . . .

JUSTICE SOTOMAYOR, dissenting [omitted].

JUSTICE GORSUCH, with whom JUSTICE GINSBURG joins, dissenting.

Walk for a moment in Michael Biestek's shoes. As part of your application for disability benefits, you've proven that you suffer from serious health problems and can't return to your old construction job. Like many cases, yours turns on whether a significant number of other jobs remain that someone of your age, education, and experience, and with your physical limitations, could perform. When it comes to that question, the Social Security Administration bears the burden of proof. To meet its burden in your case, the agency chooses to rest on the testimony of a vocational expert the agency hired as an independent contractor. The expert asserts there are 120,000 "sorter" and 240,000 "bench assembler" jobs nationwide that you could perform even with your disabilities.

Where did these numbers come from? The expert says she relied on data from the Bureau of Labor Statistics and her own private surveys. But it turns out the Bureau can't be the source; its numbers aren't that specific. The source — if there is a source — must be the expert's private surveys. So you ask to see them. The expert refuses — she says they're part of confidential client files. You reply by pointing out that any confidential client information can be redacted. But rather than ordering the data produced, the hearing examiner, herself a Social Security Administration employee, jumps in to say that won't be necessary. Even without the data, the examiner states in her decision on your disability claim, the expert's say-so warrants "great weight" and is more than enough evidence to deny your application. Case closed.

Would you say this decision was based on "substantial evidence"? . . .

Start with the legal standard. The Social Security Act of 1935 requires the agency to support its conclusions about the number of available jobs with "substantial evidence." Congress borrowed that standard from civil litigation practice, where reviewing courts may overturn a jury verdict when the record lacks "substantial evidence" — that is, evidence sufficient to permit a reasonable jury to reach the verdict it did. Much the same standard governs summary judgment and directed verdict practice today. Next, consider what we know about this standard. Witness testimony that's clearly wrong as a matter of fact cannot be substantial evidence. Falsified evidence isn't substantial evidence. Speculation isn't substantial evidence. And, maybe most pointedly for our purposes, courts have held that a party or expert who supplies only conclusory assertions fails this standard too.

If clearly mistaken evidence, fake evidence, speculative evidence, and conclusory evidence aren't substantial evidence, the evidence here shouldn't be either. . . .

Instead of addressing the realities of this case, the government asks us to imagine a hypothetical one. Assume, it says, that no one had requested the underlying data. In those circumstances, the government points out, even Mr. Biestek appears to accept that the agency's decision could have stood. And if that's true, the government asks, why should it make a difference if we add only one additional fact — the expert's refusal to produce the data? The answer is an old and familiar one. The refusal to supply readily available evidentiary support for a conclusion strongly suggests that the conclusion is, well, unsupported. . . . Meanwhile, a similar inference may not arise if no one's bothered to ask for the evidence, or if the evidence is shown to be unavailable for a good reason. In cases like those, there may be just too many other plausible and innocent excuses for the evidence's absence. Maybe, for example, nobody bothered to seek the underlying data because everyone knew what it would show. . . .

The principle that the government must support its allegations with substantial evidence, not conclusions and secret evidence, guards against arbitrary executive decision making. Without it, people like Mr. Biestek are left to the mercy of a bureaucrat's caprice. . . .

I respectfully dissent.

NOTES AND QUESTIONS

1. *Tests for majority and dissent.* How would you state the tests adopted by the majority and the dissent? Does the dissent define substantial evidence in a way that differentiates between findings favorable to the government and to other parties? Does the majority similarly differentiate the nature of the test? Is the substantial evidence test truly independent of any burden on production or persuasion? Should it be?

2. *How much does context matter?* Biestek is an appeal from an SSA determination on eligibility for disability support. Such decisions are part of a system encompassing a massive caseload of claims, evaluations, contests, and appeals, almost all focused on very specific factual determinations. *See* Chapter VI, *infra.* In this context, should standards of judicial review—particularly for decisions of ALJs—be applied differently than in decisions that are more akin to large-scale policymaking proceedings? If so, how would you characterize the difference? Should courts be more or less demanding in their application of the substantial evidence standard?

3. *The difference between judicial and administrative adjudication.* Section 702 of the Federal Rules of Evidence provides that "a witness qualified as an expert by knowledge, skill, experience, training, or education, may testify thereto in the form of an opinion or otherwise, if (1) the testimony is based upon sufficient facts or data, (2) the testimony is the product of reliable principles and methods, and (3) the witness has applied the principles and methods reliably to the facts of the case." The Social Security Act, by contrast, makes it clear that the Federal Rules of Evidence do not apply to SSA disability proceedings: "Evidence may be received at any hearing before [an SSA ALJ] even though inadmissible under rules of evidence applicable to court procedure." 42 U.S.C. §405(b). Is Justice Gorsuch simply trying to import federal evidentiary rules into such proceedings by the back door?

4. *The Court's reliance on* Con Edison. One of the notable quirks in the majority's decision is its reliance on the Court's 1938 decision in Consolidated Edison v. NLRB, *supra.* As already noted, that decision both led to confusion among the lower courts and was supplanted by the later modifications of the "substantial evidence" review standard in both the field of labor relations (the substantive law giving rise to the *Consolidated Edison* case) and the APA's general rule for review of administrative adjudications. *See* discussion *supra.* Since 1951, courts, including the Supreme Court, have looked to the *Universal Camera* decision as providing the definitive explanation of substantial evidence review of administrative adjudications. Yet the opinions in *Biestek* do not mention *Universal Camera.* In contrast, the majority opinion cites *Consolidated Edison* repeatedly. Why? Do you think that presages a change in the way the Court will treat its *Universal Camera* decision?

5. *Substantial evidence outside formal adjudications.* As noted earlier, the substantial evidence requirement in APA §706(2)(E) applies only to formal proceedings, those required by law to be decided on the record. Some judges, however, have declared this limitation to be largely a formality, finding that other review provisions, such as §706(2)(A)'s provision respecting "arbitrary-capricious" actions. Consider, for example, this statement from then-Judge

Antonin Scalia in Assn. of Data Processing Orgs., Inc. v. Bd. of Governors of Fed. Res. Sys., 745 F.2d 677 (D.C. Cir. 1984):

> [I]n those situations where paragraph (E) has no application (informal rulemaking, for example, which is not governed by §§ 556 and 557 to which paragraph (E) refers), paragraph (A) takes up the slack, so to speak, enabling the courts to strike down, as arbitrary, agency action that is devoid of needed factual support. When the arbitrary or capricious standard is performing that function of assuring factual support, there is no *substantive* difference between what it requires and what would be required by the substantial evidence test, since it is impossible to conceive of a "nonarbitrary" factual judgment supported only by evidence that is not substantial in the APA sense — *i.e.,* not "'enough to justify, if the trial were to a jury, a refusal to direct a verdict when the conclusion sought to be drawn . . . is one of fact for the jury,'" *Illinois Central R.R. v. Norfolk & Western Ry.,* 385 U.S. 57, 66, 87 S.Ct. 255, 260, 17 L.Ed.2d 162 (1966) (*quoting NLRB v. Columbian Enameling & Stamping Co.,* 306 U.S. 292, 300, 59 S.Ct. 501, 505, 83 L.Ed. 660 (1939)).

745 F.2d at 683-684. Is Judge Scalia's statement persuasive? Would it make a difference to know that he was joined on the panel in that case by Judge (also later Justice) Ruth Bader Ginsburg? If you agree, is there really a need for the law to include a separate substantial evidence requirement for formal decisions?

2.   *Informal Rulemaking*

Although, as just discussed, APA §706(2)(E) restricts the applicability of the "substantial evidence" test to formal proceedings, in a few post-APA regulatory statutes Congress has provided for substantial evidence review of informal rulemaking (rulemaking conducted under the procedures outlined in APA §553). Perhaps the leading example is the Occupational Safety and Health Act, 29 U.S.C. §655(f), which provides that health and safety standards promulgated by OSHA shall be upheld by a reviewing court if supported by "substantial evidence on the record considered as a whole." In the *Benzene* case, noted in Chapter I, *supra,* the Supreme Court was presented with its first opportunity to determine how the "substantial evidence" test should apply to OSHA rulemaking.

As you will recall from the discussion of the *Benzene* case, §6(b)(5) of the Occupational Safety and Health Act of 1970 authorized OSHA to set standards for toxic chemicals in the workplace. Since there are literally thousands of toxic substances in the workplace, this mandate presented OSHA with a formidable priority-setting problem. . . .

In 1970 OSHA had adopted as a "national consensus standard" a 10-parts-per-million (ppm) "permissible exposure limit" (PEL) for benzene. This standard had been based on evidence of benzene's acute toxic effects at high concentrations.

In April 1977, a separate agency called the National Institute for Occupational Safety and Health (NIOSH), created to assist OSHA in identifying and listing toxic substances, recommended that OSHA lower the PEL for benzene to 1 ppm. The recommendation was based on an epidemiological study of workers in two Ohio plants conducted by Dr. Peter Infante of the NIOSH staff. The data indicated that workers who had been exposed to benzene had an incidence of leukemia at least five times the expected incidence. NIOSH also cited European clinical observations of the relation between leukemia and benzene, and a canvas of the published literature reporting case histories of leukemia. Another study by Dr. Muzaffer Aksoy in 1972 showed a doubling of leukemia cases among Italian shoemakers exposed to concentrations of between 150 and 200 ppm.

OSHA rejected studies that showed little to no increased risk from exposure levels below 10 ppm. Instead, relying on a "science-policy" judgment reflecting opinions that had been expressed in the scholarly literature and the record of previous OSHA proceedings, OSHA adopted 1 ppm as the lowest "feasible" level for benzene. Thus, despite the lack of direct evidence conclusively linking benzene and leukemia at exposures less than 10 ppm, OSHA lowered the PEL for benzene to 1 ppm.

INDUSTRIAL UNION DEPT., AFL-CIO v. AMERICAN PETROLEUM INSTITUTE (*THE BENZENE CASE*)
448 U.S. 607 (1980)

MR. JUSTICE STEVENS announced the judgment of the Court and delivered an opinion, in which THE CHIEF JUSTICE and MR. JUSTICE STEWART joined and in Parts I, II, III-A, III-B, III-C, and III-E of which MR. JUSTICE POWELL joined. THE CHIEF JUSTICE filed an opinion concurring. MR. JUSTICE POWELL filed an opinion concurring in part and concurring in the judgment. MR. JUSTICE REHNQUIST filed an opinion concurring in the judgment. MR. JUSTICE MARSHALL filed a dissenting opinion, in which MR. JUSTICE BRENNAN, MR. JUSTICE WHITE, and MR. JUSTICE BLACKMUN joined.

The Occupational Safety and Health Act of 1970 (Act), 84 Stat. 1590, 29 U.S.C. §651 *et seq.*, was enacted for the purpose of ensuring safe and healthful working conditions for every working man and woman in the Nation. This litigation concerns a standard promulgated by the Secretary of Labor to regulate occupational exposure to benzene, a substance which has been shown to cause cancer at high exposure levels. The principal question is whether such a showing is a sufficient basis for a standard that places the most stringent limitation on exposure to benzene that is technologically and economically possible.

The Act delegates broad authority to the Secretary to promulgate different kinds of standards. The basic definition of an "occupational safety and health standard" is found in §3(8), which provides: "The term 'occupational safety and health standard' means a standard which requires conditions, or the adoption or use of one or more practices, means, methods, operations, or processes, reasonably necessary or appropriate to provide safe or healthful employment and places of employment." 84 Stat. 1591, 29 U.S.C. §652(8).

Where toxic materials or harmful physical agents are concerned, a standard must also comply with §6(b)(5), which provides:

> The Secretary, in promulgating standards dealing with toxic materials or harmful physical agents under this subsection, shall set the standard which most adequately assures, to the extent feasible, on the basis of the best available evidence, that no employee will suffer material impairment of health or functional capacity even if such employee has regular exposure to the hazard dealt with by

such standard for the period of his working life. Development of standards under this subsection shall be based upon research, demonstrations, experiments, and such other information as may be appropriate. In addition to the attainment of the highest degree of health and safety protection for the employee, other considerations shall be the latest available scientific data in the field, the feasibility of the standards, and experience gained under this and other health and safety laws.

84 Stat. 1594, 29 U.S.C. §655(b)(5).

Wherever the toxic material to be regulated is a carcinogen, the Secretary has taken the position that no safe exposure level can be determined and that §6(b)(5) requires him to set an exposure limit at the lowest technologically feasible level that will not impair the viability of the industries regulated. In this case, after having determined that there is a causal connection between benzene and leukemia (a cancer of the white blood cells), the Secretary set an exposure limit on airborne concentrations of benzene of one part benzene per million parts of air (1 ppm), regulated dermal and eye contact with solutions containing benzene, and imposed complex monitoring and medical testing requirements on employers whose workplaces contain 0.5 ppm or more of benzene. 29 CFR §§1910.1028(c), (e) (1979).

We agree with the Fifth Circuit's holding that §3(8) requires the Secretary to find, as a threshold matter, that the toxic substance in question poses a significant health risk in the workplace and that a new, lower standard is therefore "reasonably necessary or appropriate to provide safe or healthful employment and places of employment." . . .

I

As presently formulated, the benzene standard is an expensive way of providing some additional protection for a relatively small number of employees. According to OSHA's figures, the standard will require capital investments in engineering controls of approximately $266 million, first-year operating costs (for monitoring, medical testing, employee training, and respirators) of $187 million to $205 million and recurring annual costs of approximately $34 million. 43 Fed. Reg. 5934 (1978). The figures outlined in OSHA's explanation of the costs of compliance to various industries indicate that only 35,000 employees would gain any benefit from the regulation in terms of a reduction in their exposure to benzene. Over two-thirds of these workers (24,450) are employed in the rubber-manufacturing industry. Compliance costs in that industry are estimated to be rather low with no capital costs and initial operating expenses estimated at only $34 million ($1,390 per employee); recurring annual costs would also be rather low, totaling less than $1 million. By contrast, the segment of the petroleum refining industry that produces benzene would be required to incur $24 million in capital costs and $600,000 in first-year operating expenses to provide additional protection for 300 workers ($82,000 per employee), while the petrochemical industry would be required to incur $20.9 million in capital costs and $1 million in initial operating expenses for the benefit of 552 employees ($39,675 per employee). . . .

II

The critical issue at this point in the litigation is whether the Court of Appeals was correct in refusing to enforce the 1 ppm exposure limit on the ground that it was not supported by appropriate findings.

Any discussion of the 1 ppm exposure limit must, of course, begin with the Agency's rationale for imposing that limit.[31] The written explanation of the standard fills 184 pages of the printed appendix. Much of it is devoted to a discussion of the voluminous evidence of the adverse effects of exposure to benzene at levels of concentration well above 10 ppm. This discussion demonstrates that there is ample justification for regulating occupational exposure to benzene and that the prior limit of 10 ppm, with a ceiling of 25 ppm (or a peak of 50 ppm) was reasonable. . . .

The evidence in the administrative record of adverse effects of benzene exposure at 10 ppm is sketchy at best. OSHA noted that there was "no dispute" that certain nonmalignant blood disorders, evidenced by a reduction in the level of red or white cells or platelets in the blood, could result from exposures of 25-40 ppm. It then stated that several studies had indicated that relatively slight changes in normal blood values could result from exposures below 25 ppm and perhaps below 10 ppm. OSHA did not attempt to make any estimate based on these studies of how significant the risk of nonmalignant disease would be at exposures of 10 ppm or less. . . .

OSHA also noted some studies indicating an increase in chromosomal aberrations in workers chronically exposed to concentrations of benzene "probably less than 25 ppm." . . .

With respect to leukemia, evidence of an increased risk (*i.e.*, a risk greater than that borne by the general population) due to benzene exposures at or below 10 ppm was even sketchier.

[T]here was only one study that provided any evidence of such an increased risk. That study, conducted by the Dow Chemical Co., uncovered three leukemia deaths, versus 0.2 expected deaths, out of a population of 594 workers; it appeared that the three workers had never been exposed to more than 2 to 9 ppm of benzene. The authors of the study, however, concluded that it could not be viewed as proof of a relationship between low-level benzene exposure and leukemia because all three workers had probably been occupationally exposed to a number of other potentially carcinogenic chemicals at other points in their careers and because no leukemia deaths had been uncovered among workers who had been exposed to much higher levels of benzene. In its explanation of the permanent standard, OSHA stated that the possibility that these three leukemias had been caused by benzene exposure could not be ruled out and that the study, although not evidence of an increased risk of leukemia at 10 ppm, was

---

31. As we have often held, the validity of an agency's determination must be judged on the basis of the agency's stated reasons for making that determination. *See* SEC v. Chenery Corp., 318 U.S. 80, 95 ("[A]n administrative order cannot be upheld unless the grounds upon which the agency acted in exercising its powers were those upon which its action can be sustained"). . . .

therefore "consistent with the findings of many studies that there is an excess leukemia risk among benzene exposed employees." 43 Fed. Reg. 5928 (1978).

In the end OSHA's rationale for lowering the permissible exposure limit to 1 ppm was based, not on any finding that leukemia has ever been caused by exposure to 10 ppm of benzene and that it will *not* be caused by exposure to 1 ppm, but rather on a series of assumptions indicating that some leukemias might result from exposure to 10 ppm and that the number of cases might be reduced by reducing the exposure level to 1 ppm. . . .

III

Our resolution of the issues in these cases turns, to a large extent, on the meaning of and the relationship between §3(8), which defines a health and safety standard as a standard that is "reasonably necessary and appropriate to provide safe or healthful employment," and §6(b)(5), which directs the Secretary in promulgating a health and safety standard for toxic materials to "set the standard which most adequately assures, to the extent feasible, on the basis of the best available evidence, that no employee will suffer material impairment of health or functional capacity. . . ."

[W]e think it is clear that §3(8) does apply to all permanent standards promulgated under the Act and that it requires the Secretary, before issuing any standard, to determine that it is reasonably necessary and appropriate to remedy a significant risk of material health impairment. . . .

The Agency's position is that there is substantial evidence in the record to support its conclusion that there is no absolutely safe level for a carcinogen and that, therefore, the burden is properly on industry to prove, apparently beyond a shadow of a doubt, that there *is* a safe level for benzene exposure. The Agency argues that, because of the uncertainties in this area, any other approach would render it helpless, forcing it to wait for the leukemia deaths that it believes are likely to occur before taking any regulatory action.

We disagree. As we read the statute, the burden was on the Agency to show, on the basis of substantial evidence, that it is at least more likely than not that long-term exposure to 10 ppm of benzene presents a significant risk of material health impairment. Ordinarily, it is the proponent of a rule or order who has the burden of proof in administrative proceedings. See 5 U.S.C. §556(d). In some cases involving toxic substances, Congress has shifted the burden of proving that a particular substance is safe onto the party opposing the proposed rule. The fact that Congress did not follow this course in enacting the Occupational Safety and Health Act indicates that it intended the Agency to bear the normal burden of establishing the need for a proposed standard.

Contrary to the Government's contentions, imposing a burden on the Agency of demonstrating a significant risk of harm will not strip it of its ability to regulate carcinogens, nor will it require the Agency to wait for deaths to occur before taking any action. First, the requirement that a "significant" risk be identified is not a mathematical straitjacket. It is the Agency's responsibility to determine, in the first instance, what it considers to be a "significant" risk. Some risks are plainly acceptable and others are plainly unacceptable. If, for example, the odds are one in a billion that a person will die from cancer by taking a drink of chlorinated water, the risk clearly could not be considered significant. On the other hand, if the odds are one in a thousand that regular inhalation of gasoline vapors that are 2% benzene will be fatal, a reasonable person might well consider the risk significant and take appropriate steps to decrease or eliminate it. Although the Agency has no duty to calculate the exact probability of harm, it does have an obligation to find that a significant risk is present before it can characterize a place of employment as "unsafe."

Second, OSHA is not required to support its finding that a significant risk exists with anything approaching scientific certainty. Although the Agency's findings must be supported by substantial evidence, 29 U.S.C. §655(f), §6(b)(5) specifically allows the Secretary to regulate on the basis of the "best available evidence." . . . Thus, so long as they are supported by a body of reputable scientific thought, the Agency is free to use conservative assumptions in interpreting the data with respect to carcinogens, risking error on the side of overprotection rather than underprotection.

Finally, the record in this case and OSHA's own rulings on other carcinogens indicate that there are a number of ways in which the Agency can make a rational judgment about the relative significance of the risks associated with exposure to a particular carcinogen.[64] . . .

Because our review of these cases has involved a more detailed examination of the record than is customary, it must be emphasized that we have neither made any factual determinations of our own, nor have we rejected any factual findings made by the Secretary. We express no opinion on what factual findings this record might support, either on the basis of empirical evidence or on the basis of expert testimony; nor do we express any opinion on the more difficult question of what factual determinations would warrant a conclusion that significant risks are present which make promulgation of a new standard reasonably necessary or appropriate. The standard must, of course, be supported by the findings actually made by the Secretary, not merely by findings that we believe he might have made.

In this case the record makes it perfectly clear that the Secretary relied squarely on a special policy for carcinogens that imposed the burden on industry of proving the existence of a safe level of exposure, thereby avoiding the Secretary's threshold responsibility of establishing the need for more stringent standards. In so interpreting his statutory authority, the Secretary exceeded his power.

MR. JUSTICE MARSHALL, with whom MR. JUSTICE BRENNAN, MR. JUSTICE WHITE, and MR. JUSTICE BLACKMUN join, dissenting. . . .

---

64. For example, in the coke-oven emissions standard, OSHA had calculated that 21,000 exposed coke-oven workers had an annual excess mortality of over 200 and that the proposed standard might well eliminate the risk entirely. . . .

In other proceedings, the Agency has had a good deal of data from animal experiments on which it could base a conclusion on the significance of the risk. For example, the record on the vinyl chloride standard indicated that a significant number of animals had developed tumors of the liver, lung, and skin when they were exposed to 50 ppm of vinyl chloride over a period of 11 months. . . .

In this case the Agency did not have the benefit of animal studies, because scientists have been unable as yet to induce leukemia in experimental animals as a result of benzene exposure. It did, however, have a fair amount of epidemiological evidence, including both positive and negative studies. Although the Agency stated that this evidence was insufficient to construct a precise correlation between exposure levels and cancer risks, it would at least be helpful in determining whether it is more likely than not that there is a significant risk at 10 ppm.

II

The plurality's discussion of the record in this case is both extraordinarily arrogant and extraordinarily unfair. It is arrogant because the plurality presumes to make its own factual findings with respect to a variety of disputed issues relating to carcinogen regulation. . . . It should not be necessary to remind the Members of this Court that they were not appointed to undertake independent review of adequately supported scientific findings made by a technically expert agency. And the plurality's discussion is unfair because its characterization of the Secretary's report bears practically no resemblance to what the Secretary actually did in this case. Contrary to the plurality's suggestion, the Secretary did not rely blindly on some Draconian carcinogen "policy." . . . If he had, it would have been sufficient for him to have observed that benzene is a carcinogen, a proposition that respondents do not dispute. Instead, the Secretary gathered over 50 volumes of exhibits and testimony and offered a detailed and evenhanded discussion of the relationship between exposure to benzene at all recorded exposure levels and chromosomal damage, aplastic anemia, and leukemia. In that discussion he evaluated, and took seriously, respondents' evidence of a safe exposure level. . . .

III

[T]he Secretary's determinations must be upheld if supported by "substantial evidence in the record considered as a whole." 29 U.S.C. §655(f). This standard represents a legislative judgment that regulatory action should be subject to review more stringent than the traditional "arbitrary and capricious" standard for informal rulemaking. . . . The agency's decision is entitled to the traditional presumption of validity, and the court is not authorized to substitute its judgment for that of the Secretary. If the Secretary has considered the decisional factors and acted in conformance with the statute, his ultimate decision must be given a large measure of respect. . . .

Under this standard of review, the decision to reduce the permissible exposure level to 1 ppm was well within the Secretary's authority. The Court of Appeals upheld the Secretary's conclusions that benzene causes leukemia, blood disorders, and chromosomal damage even at low levels, that an exposure level of 10 ppm is more dangerous than one of 1 ppm, and that benefits will result from the proposed standard. It did not set aside his finding that the number of lives that would be saved was not subject to quantification. Nor did it question his conclusion that the reduction was "feasible."

In these circumstances, the Secretary's decision was reasonable and in full conformance with the statutory language requiring that he "set the standard which most adequately assures, to the extent feasible, on the basis of the best available evidence, that no employee will suffer material impairment of health or functional capacity even if such employee has regular exposure to the hazard dealt with by such standard for the period of his working life." 29 U.S.C. §655(b)(5). . . .

[The concurring opinions of THE CHIEF JUSTICE and JUSTICE POWELL are omitted. The separate opinion of JUSTICE REHNQUIST, who concurred on the ground that the law constituted an unconstitutional delegation of legislative authority (discussed in Chapter I, *supra*), is omitted.]

NOTES AND QUESTIONS

1. *"Substantial evidence" review of policy judgments.* Is a standard of review appropriate for cases like *Universal Camera* also appropriate for cases like *Benzene*? What are the crucial distinctions between the two contexts? Is it the formality of the proceeding or the nature of the inquiry? After enactment of the OSH Act, the lower courts had encountered considerable difficulty in applying a test designed for review of adjudicative factfinding to the review of the mixed fact-policy determinations underlying most OSHA standards. In Industrial Union Dept., AFL-CIO v. Hodgson, 499 F.2d 467 (D.C. Cir. 1974), Judge Carl McGowan offered what has become the leading attempt to reconcile this "anomaly":

> On a record of this mixed nature, when the facts underlying the Secretary's determinations are susceptible of being found in the usual sense, that must be done, and the reviewing court will weigh them by the substantial evidence standard. But, in a statute like OSHA where the decision making vested in the Secretary is legislative in character, there are areas where explicit factual findings are not possible, and the act of decision is essentially a prediction based upon pure legislative judgment, as when a Congressman decides to vote for or against a particular bill. . . .
>
> What we are entitled to at all events is a careful identification by the Secretary, when his proposed standards are challenged, of the reasons why he chooses to follow one course rather than another. Where that choice purports to be based on the existence of certain determinable facts, the Secretary must, in form as well as substance, find those facts from evidence in the record. By the same token, when the Secretary is obliged to make policy judgments where no factual certainties exist or where facts alone do not provide the answer, he should so state and go on to identify the considerations he found persuasive.

Id. at 474-476.

Coming at the question from a different angle, is the standard of review likely to change the outcome of many actual cases? Is there enough of a difference between review under the arbitrary and capricious test and review under the substantial evidence standard that some OSHA rules that would have been upheld under the former will be set aside under the latter? In thinking about this question, consider the following. In *State Farm*, excerpted at p. 137, the Court stated that for a rule to survive review under the arbitrary and capricious test, the agency must "examine the relevant data and articulate a satisfactory explanation for its action including a 'rational connection between the facts found and the choice made.'" 463 U.S. at 43, quoting Burlington Truck Lines, Inc. v. United States, 371 U.S. 156, 168 (1962). *Burlington Truck Lines*, from which the "rational connection" language is quoted, is a decision applying the substantial evidence standard of review to an instance of formal agency adjudication. This suggests that in the hands of the Supreme Court, the two standards, as applied to policy decisions, may tend to converge into a single norm of reasonableness or non-arbitrariness.

2. *Establishing a link between exposure and disease.* If the Secretary of Labor had made a "determination" of "significant risk" on the record described in the *Benzene* opinions, would that determination have been "supported by substantial evidence"?

Did the revised benzene standard "purport to be based on the existence of certain determinable facts"? Or was it based on "policy judgments where no factual certainties exist or where facts alone do not provide the answer"?

In answering those questions, consider the peculiar problems of proving a connection between exposure to a chemical and incidence of cancer. There are three ways to establish a link between exposure to a particular chemical and cancer in human beings: epidemiology, animal bioassays, and short-term studies. Epidemiological studies compare the cancer rate of a population that was exposed to a chemical with the cancer rate of another population that was not exposed to that chemical. Based on the differences between the two rates, the size of the populations, and other factors, epidemiologists can compute the probability of a causal link between exposure and cancer. Because of the long latency period of cancer and the difficulty of controlling for other confounding factors, however, epidemiological studies are not very sensitive to small changes in dosage level.

Animal bioassays involve the administration of a chemical to laboratory animals under closely controlled conditions. While these tests can achieve results with much higher statistical confidence levels, they often take several years to complete and can be quite expensive to conduct, especially if the experimenter wishes to ascertain the response to varying dosage levels. There is also a continuing uncertainty about the extent to which results in laboratory animals can be extrapolated to human beings. Recently developed "short-term tests" solve the former problem by testing chemicals in certain short-lived bacteria or mammalian tissue cells. But, if anything, they exacerbate the second problem. For a more detailed explanation of these techniques, *see* William R. Havender, Assessing and Controlling Risks, in Social Regulation: Strategies for Reform 21, 22-23 (Eugene Bardach & Robert A. Kagan, eds., 1982).

In view of these difficulties, is there "evidence" of a link between low-level exposure to benzene and human cancer? Is the evidence "substantial" enough?

3. *Standard of review and the costs of rulemaking.* Between 1971 and 1988, OSHA managed to establish occupational health standards under §6(b) for only 24 of the hundreds of toxic substances found in workplaces. In 1988, the agency initiated a "generic" proceeding aimed at establishing PELs for over 400 air contaminants in one fell swoop. After a whirlwind process of notice, hearing, post-hearing submissions, and internal review, on January 19, 1989, OSHA promulgated a massive "Air Contaminants Standard," which established PELs for 428 air contaminants, including 164 previously unregulated substances. 54 Fed. Reg. 2332-2983 (1989). In doing so, OSHA relied on a number of existing scientific studies of very uneven quality and utility, as well as a set of "generic" presumptions about the degree of health risks posed by the substances, the level of scientific uncertainty, and the need to establish generous "safety factors." In AFL-CIO v. OSHA, 965 F.2d 962 (11th Cir. 1992), the Eleventh Circuit struck down the standard in its entirety. The court agreed that OSHA could establish standards for more than one substance in a single rulemaking proceeding and that it had adequately established that all 428 substances presented "material

risk" to human health. But it ruled that OSHA had not come close to furnishing the quantum of evidence necessary to establish that the risks posed by any of the substances at their existing concentrations were "significant," or that the specific PELs adopted would be technically and economically "feasible" to implement.

Congress also specified the substantial evidence standard for judicial review of informally promulgated regulations in the Toxic Substance Control Act §6(b), 15 U.S.C. §2618(c)(1)(B)(i), administered by the Environmental Protection Agency. Like OSHA, the EPA has struggled to meet the evidentiary burden imposed on it by reviewing courts. *See, e.g.,* Corrosion Proof Fittings v. EPA, 947 F.2d 1201 (5th Cir. 1995), which invalidated an EPA rule banning the use of asbestos in most products.

Do these cases cast doubt on the wisdom of applying the substantial evidence standard to informal rulemaking in general? To informal rulemaking about toxic substances?

E.   JUDICIAL REMEDIES FOR UNLAWFUL AGENCY ACTION

Once a reviewing court has determined that an administrative agency has made a legal error, the customary recourse is to vacate the administrative action and remand to the agency for further proceedings consistent with the reviewing court's opinion. This is the functional counterpart of an appellate court's treatment of legal errors made by a trial court. The rationale for this form of remedy in the administrative-review context is similar: since an agency may act only on legal authority, an administrative order premised on, or infected by, a legal error has no legal force and should therefore be set aside. Since, however, the agency has primary enforcement responsibility, and presumably possesses the expertise, investigative powers, and staff necessary to fulfill that responsibility, a reviewing court ordinarily should not simply terminate the matter, but instead should remand to the agency to decide what, if any, curative action or other affirmative steps to take next.

Might there be circumstances in which it is appropriate for a reviewing court to vacate *but not remand?* The Supreme Court addressed this question in NLRB v. Food Store Employees Union, Local 347, 417 U.S. 1 (1974). After the NLRB had determined that an employer had committed an unfair labor practice by harassing union organizers, the union asked the Board to order the employer to reimburse the union for its litigation expenses and excessive organizational expenses. The Board refused. The Board brought a proceeding in the court of appeals to enforce its order commanding the employer to cease and desist from the unfair labor practice. In the enforcement proceeding, the union asked the court to review the Board's order denying reimbursement for costs. Citing an intervening decision by the Board in which the Board awarded litigation costs to a union in a case where the employer's position was "patently frivolous," the court of appeals issued the order requested by the union. The Supreme Court reversed, ruling that the court of appeals had exceeded its authority in issuing the order and that, instead, it should remand to the Board for further proceedings consistent with the decision. "This case," said the Court, "does not present the exceptional situation in which crystal-clear Board error renders a remand an unnecessary formality." 417 U.S. at 8.

Are there circumstances other than "crystal-clear errors" in which immediate judicial resolution is appropriate? In Rivera v. Sullivan, 923 F.2d 964 (2d Cir. 1991), the Second Circuit reversed a decision of the Secretary of Health and Human Services that Ms. Rivera was ineligible for Social Security disability benefits. The court found a lack of substantial evidence to support the Secretary's finding that there was work in the national economy for which Rivera was qualified and which she was physically capable of performing. The court then turned to the question of remedy:

> Given th[e] evidence establishing Rivera's inability to perform her prior work . . . , and considering the unskilled nature of [her] earlier work, the failure of HHS to present any evidence to suggest that Rivera possesses other skills . . . and the length of time this litigation has already consumed, reversal and immediate award of benefits is appropriate.

923 F.2d at 970. (However, the court did remand to the agency to calculate the amount of benefits due to Rivera.)

Conversely, might there be circumstances in which it is appropriate for a reviewing court to remand to an agency *but not to vacate its order*? The Supreme Court has not directly answered this question, but the D.C. Circuit has issued "remand only" orders on numerous occasions. One instance provoked an interesting exchange between Judges Silberman and Randolph. In Checkosky v. SEC, 23 F.3d 452 (D.C. Cir. 1994) (*Checkosky I*), the court reviewed an order of the SEC suspending two accountants from practice before the commission for two years for "improper professional conduct." In a brief per curiam opinion, the three-judge panel remanded to the SEC "for a more adequate explanation of its interpretation of [its rule] and its application to this case," but it did not set aside the suspension order. Judge Silberman reasoned that the remand was simply a request for further explanation in an ongoing — and as yet incomplete — process of judicial review rather than a definitive finding by the court that the agency had acted unlawfully. Since the two accountants had not themselves petitioned the SEC to stay their suspensions pending appeal, he thought the court should not take a step (vacating, pending remand) that would have that effect. Judge Randolph argued strenuously that §706 of the APA "flatly prohibits" the court from remanding without vacating. By finding that the SEC explanation was not "adequate," he reasoned, the court had in effect found the SEC's action to be "arbitrary and capricious." Lack of adequate explanation is, after all, one of the principal tests for arbitrariness, as we saw in *Overton Park* and *State Farm*. Under the terms of §706, a reviewing court "*shall* . . . hold unlawful and *set aside* agency action, finding, and conclusions found to be . . . arbitrary [and] capricious . . ." (emphasis added). Can the Silberman position survive Randolph's reading of the statute? How?

Following the remand without vacation in *Checkosky I*, the SEC attempted to offer a better explanation of its action. In Checkosky v. SEC, 139 F.3d 221 (D.C. Cir. 1998) (*Checkosky II*), the D.C. Circuit determined that the SEC had utterly failed to provide an adequate explanation. This time, the court remanded with instructions to the SEC to dismiss the proceeding, an admittedly unusual remedy, but one appropriate, said the court, given the long duration of the proceedings and the agency's failure to make progress toward fashioning an acceptable explanation for its proposed action.

The position taken by Judge Silberman in *Checkosky I* has prevailed, not only in the D.C. Circuit, *see, e.g.,* American Medical Association v. Reno, 57 F.3d 1129 (D.C. Cir. 1995); Pharma v. Shalala, 62 F.3d 1484 (D.C. Cir. 1995), but also in other courts that have spoken to the issue. *See, e.g.,* Idaho Farm Bureau Federation v. Babbitt, 58 F.3d 1392 (9th Cir. 1995).

For discussion of the issues raised by the practice of remands without vacation, *see* Ronald Levin, "Vacation" at Sea: Judicial Remedies and Equitable Discretion in Administrative Law, 53 Duke L.J. 291 (2003), and Frank H. Wu & Denisha S. Williams, Remand without Reversal: An Unfortunate Habit, 30 Envtl. L. Rep. 10193 (2000).

CHAPTER III

AVAILABILITY OF JUDICIAL REVIEW

However useful courts may be in keeping administrators from acting arbitrarily or straying from their statutorily appointed tasks, courts will not entertain all complaints about administrative decisions. Courts have fashioned a collection of doctrines, known by such names as "reviewability," "ripeness," "exhaustion of administrative remedies," "mootness," and "standing" designed to regulate access to the courthouse. These doctrines derive from a variety of constitutional, legislative, and judicial sources. The Constitution provides, at least after Marbury v. Madison, 5 U.S. (1 Cranch) 137 (1803), both the minima and maxima of the Supreme Court's original jurisdiction, and Article III provides additional limits on the scope of the federal judicial power. Subject to these constitutional limitations, Congress can choose the court or courts to which review jurisdiction will be given and define the conditions under which that jurisdiction may be invoked.

The federal courts also may invoke various "prudential" concerns for refusing to hear certain kinds of complaints. It is not entirely clear that a court is free to invoke prudential concerns to avoid deciding a case when its jurisdiction and authority over the matter are plain and the Constitution interposes no obstacles. At the same time, courts manifestly enjoy considerable power to construe statutory grants of jurisdiction, statute-created rights of action, and constitutional mandates. In light of this power, debate over the courts' separate capacity to deny review for purely prudential reasons may be largely academic.

While the relationship among the doctrines governing the availability of judicial review is complex, one can discern four distinct functions that they serve. First, the particular court in which review is sought must be one that has legal authority to resolve the controversy. Second, the complaint must allege the violation of a particular legally enforceable duty by the defendant. Third, the particular complainant must be an appropriate person to present and prosecute such a claim. Fourth, the violation alleged must be one that the court has the practical ability to redress by some appropriate order. These are, of course, universal principles that apply as fully to private-law litigation as to public-law litigation. But, as we shall see in this chapter, the effort to enlist courts in the struggle to discipline administrative agencies can present special difficulties for a judiciary that conscientiously seeks to respect its own institutional limits.

A.   JURISDICTION

The authority of American courts to review the actions of administrators traces back to the common law courts of England. The "King's judges" who presided over early English courts asserted the King's plenary power to supervise the inferior officers of the Crown. They did this primarily in two ways. First, the courts allowed suits for damages against officers alleged to have violated a common law duty under circumstances in which a private defendant could be sued. To escape liability, the officer would have to establish that his action was justified by statute or other higher authority. Beginning in the seventeenth century, the King's Bench gradually developed a group of supplementary remedies, called prerogative writs, by which the authority of officers could be challenged. The most important were the writs of *certiorari* and *mandamus*. Certiorari was used to test the "jurisdiction" of officers or tribunals performing "judicial" or "quasi-judicial" business, while mandamus was available to a petitioner seeking to compel an official to perform a "ministerial" (or "nondiscretionary") duty improperly withheld. Other prerogative writs included *quo warranto* (used to test an incumbent's right to hold office), *habeas corpus* (used to review administrative orders to commit, detain, or deport someone), and *prohibition* (used to prevent a "quasi-judicial" body from acting outside its jurisdiction). Later, the Chancellor's Court of Equity began to apply the general writ of *injunction* to official wrongdoing that threatened "irreparable harm" for which there was no adequate remedy at law. The legality of official action could also be tested in an action brought by an officer seeking judicial enforcement of an order against a private person.

This patchwork system of remedies formed the basis for colonial law and early state law in America. During the nineteenth and early twentieth centuries, however, it was increasingly supplemented by specific statutory provisions for judicial review of administrative action. At the federal level, where the prerogative writs never gained much of a foothold, statutory law has always been the dominant source of judicial authority to supervise administrators. One of the earliest judicial review provisions was contained in the Urgent Deficiencies Act of 1913, 38 Stat. 219, which provided for review of certain agencies' orders by a three-judge district court. The model for most modern judicial review statutes, however, was the Federal Trade Commission Act of 1914, 15 U.S.C. §45(c) (2000), which provides, in pertinent part:

> Any person, partnership, or corporation required by an order of the Commission to cease and desist from using any method of competition or act or practice may obtain a review of such order in the court of appeals of the United States, within any circuit where the method of competition or the act or practice in question was used or where such person, partnership, or corporation resides or carries

on business, by filing in the court, within sixty days from the date of the service of such order, a written petition praying that the order of the Commission be set aside.

The Judicial Review Act of 1950, 64 Stat. 1129, now codified at 28 U.S.C. §2341 *et seq.* (2006), as part of the Administrative Orders Review Act, substituted FTC-type review for all agencies previously subject to review under the Urgent Deficiencies Act except the Interstate Commerce Commission, and that holdout was eliminated in 1975 (*see* 28 U.S.C. §2321). (As discussed in Chapter I, *supra,* the Interstate Commerce Commission has since been abolished.) Although the great majority of specific review statutes confer jurisdiction on the court of appeals, a few statutes provide for review of agency action in the district court. The leading example, because of the enormous volume of cases brought under its authority, is 42 U.S.C. §405(g), which provides for district court review of orders denying or terminating Social Security benefits.

Despite the proliferation of specific review statutes, there remain many types of administrative action for which the agency's organic statute makes no explicit provision for judicial review. A complainant seeking to challenge such an action must ground her complaint in a more general grant of jurisdiction. The source most commonly invoked for this purpose is 28 U.S.C. §1331, which confers on federal district courts "original jurisdiction of all civil actions arising under the Constitution, laws, or treaties of the United States." While most challenges to administrative action easily satisfy the "arising under" test, §1331's $10,000 amount-in-controversy requirement presented a more serious obstacle prior to 1976. Complainants asserting relatively small or nonmaterial claims often had to search for other general sources of jurisdiction, such as 28 U.S.C. §1343 (civil rights actions), §1346 (tax or contract claims against the United States), or §1361 (mandamus actions against officers of the United States). A few petitioners, unable to invoke any other statutory source of jurisdiction, argued that the APA itself (especially §702, *see* the Appendix at the end of this book) conferred jurisdiction on the federal courts. Although seven circuits had expressed agreement with this position, the Supreme Court had not resolved the issue when, in 1976, Congress largely mooted it by eliminating the $10,000 jurisdictional amount in cases seeking nonmonetary relief against officers of the United States. A year later, in Califano v. Sanders, 430 U.S. 99 (1977), the Supreme Court finally settled the question of the APA's jurisdictional status. Relying in part on the recent amendment of §1331, the Court held that the APA did not provide an independent basis for federal court jurisdiction.

Whether a particular court has jurisdiction over a petition for judicial review is a distinct question from whether the challenged agency action is reviewable. The existence of one does not necessarily imply the existence of the other. However, Congress often seems to equate the two. When Congress wishes to preclude judicial review of agency action, rather than legislate in terms of reviewability, it often legislates in terms of jurisdiction, stripping federal courts of jurisdiction to hear a class of claims challenging particular agency actions. For example, a provision of the Illegal Immigration Reform and Immigrant Responsibility Act of 1996, 8 U.S.C. §1252, states that "no court shall have jurisdiction to review" a laundry list of agency actions in the immigration area that Congress exempted from judicial review.

This mix of special and general review statutes ensures that most litigants can find some court with jurisdiction over their claims. But ambiguities in special review statutes often leave litigants guessing which court has jurisdiction — a court of appeals or a district court. The consequence of guessing wrong is not fatal, since the incorrect court can transfer the case directly to the correct court. *See* 28 U.S.C. §1631. There has been considerable litigation over the interpretation of special review statutes, producing a rather inconclusive and messy jurisprudence. Some lower courts have relied on a rule of thumb that appeals courts have jurisdiction when an administrative record exists and district courts have jurisdiction when a record does not exist. The theory is that district courts are better able to cope with the evidentiary problems inherent in reviewing informal actions. *See, e.g.,* United States Steel Corp. v. EPA, 595 F.2d 207 (5th Cir. 1979); Ford Motor Co. v. EPA, 567 F.2d 661 (6th Cir. 1977).

The trend, however, has been to favor appellate review, even of informal administrative actions, in the interest of judicial economy. For example, in Harrison v. PPG Industries, Inc., 446 U.S. 578 (1980), the Supreme Court interpreted the Clean Air Act's provision for direct appellate review of "any other final action" to include review of informal agency actions. The Court rejected the argument that informal agency action provided too scant a record for appellate review: "It may be seriously questioned whether the overall time lost by court of appeals remands to [the agency] of those cases in which the records are inadequate would exceed the time saved by forgoing in every case initial review in a district court." *Id.* at 593-594.

In Florida Power and Light Co. v. Lorion, 470 U.S. 729 (1985), the Court reversed a court of appeals decision that had implicitly relied on the absence of a record to deny appellate-type review. A provision of the Atomic Energy Act provided for review in the court of appeals of any final order of the Nuclear Regulatory Commission made in a proceeding to suspend a license. Respondent Lorion challenged the NRC's refusal to initiate proceedings for the suspension of a nuclear reactor's license. Declining to reach the merits, the court of appeals held that it did not have subject matter jurisdiction. Its interpretation of the review provision allowed for appellate review only if the person who requested the proceeding obtained a hearing in which she could present evidence. Because Lorion was not granted a hearing, the NRC's denial of her request was not reviewable in an appeals court. The Supreme Court reversed, finding that the statutory scheme, legislative history, and policy considerations all supported direct appellate review, regardless of whether a hearing took place. The Court specifically rejected the contention that the district court's factfinding capabilities made it the appropriate forum to review informal agency action in which a hearing had not occurred:

> Perhaps the only plausible justification for linking initial review in the court of appeals to the occurrence of a hearing before the agency would be that, absent a hearing, the reviewing court would lack an adequate agency-compiled factual basis to evaluate the agency action and a district court with factfinding powers could make up that deficiency. Such a justification cannot, however, be squared with fundamental principles of judicial review of agency action. "[T]he focal point for judicial review should be the administrative record already in existence, not some new record made initially in the reviewing court." Camp v. Pitts, 411 U.S. 138, 142 (1973).

470 U.S. at 743. Finding no basis to favor the district courts, the Court relied on considerations of judicial economy to favor court of appeals review. Initial review in the district court would necessarily lead to duplication of effort since both the district court and the court of appeals would review the same record compiled by the agency to determine the legality of the administrative action. Without an explicit command from Congress, the Court refused to adopt an interpretation of the statute that would so needlessly waste time and money.

Does "judicial economy" necessarily favor appellate review rather than district court review? On what empirical assumptions does the Court's assertion rest? Are there factors other than judicial economy and factfinding ability that might favor review by one type of court or the other? *See* David P. Currie & Frank I. Goodman, Judicial Review of Federal Administrative Action: Quest for the Optimum Forum, 75 Colum. L. Rev. 1 (1975), and Thomas O. McGarity, Multi-Party Forum Shopping for Appellate Review of Administrative Action, 129 U. Pa. L. Rev. 302 (1980).

B.   REVIEWABILITY

As the Supreme Court noted in *Overton Park,* excerpted in Chapter II, *supra,* "the threshold question" facing any litigant who seeks judicial redress for alleged administrative wrongs is "whether petitioners are entitled to any judicial review." In the nineteenth century, American courts exhibited an inhospitable attitude toward judicial review of administrative action. As the Supreme Court said in Decatur v. Paulding, 39 U.S. (14 Pet.) 497, 516 (1840): "interference of the courts with the performance of the ordinary duties of the executive departments of the government would be productive of nothing but mischief." While review was theoretically available by way of certain prerogative writs, including certiorari, mandamus, and injunction, technical doctrinal restrictions severely limited their utility. *See* Fredrick P. Lee, The Origins of Judicial Control of Federal Executive Action, 35 Geo. L.J. 287 (1948).

Around the turn of the last century, judicial attitudes began to change. In American School of Magnetic Healing v. McAnnulty, 187 U.S. 94 (1902), for example, the Supreme Court found reviewable an order of the Postmaster General refusing to deliver mail to the petitioner and returning it to the sender marked "fraudulent." "[I]n case an official violates the law," the Court proclaimed, "the courts generally have jurisdiction to grant relief."

It was against this doctrinal background that in 1946 the APA was enacted. The statute specifies the who, what, and when of judicial review. On the what and when, the APA states: "Agency action made reviewable by statute and final agency action for which there is no other adequate remedy in a court are subject to judicial review." 5 U.S.C. §704. The section goes on to provide that preliminary and other non-final agency action is reviewable "on the review of the final agency action." On the who, the APA declares that "A person suffering legal wrong because of agency action, or adversely affected or aggrieved by agency action within the meaning of a relevant statute, is entitled to judicial review thereof." 5 U.S.C. §702. While some doubt surrounds the meaning of phrases like "final agency action," "legal wrong," and "aggrieved . . . within the meaning of a relevant statute," the Supreme Court has read the APA as embodying a "basic presumption of judicial review." Abbott Laboratories v. Gardner, 387 U.S. 136, 140 (1967). *See also* Gutierrez de Martinez v. Lamagno, 515 U.S. 417 (1995).

Because the APA, in §§702, 703, and 704, provides for review of "agency action" as defined in APA §551(13), and nothing else, the presumption in favor of judicial review applies only when "agency action" is the subject of the petition. If what is being challenged is not "agency action," there is no judicial review under the APA. But as the Court and the APA itself recognize, even with regard to agency action, the presumption in favor of judicial review is rebuttable. Section 701(a) specifies that the APA's provisions relating to judicial review apply "except to the extent that—(1) statutes preclude judicial review; or (2) agency action is committed to agency discretion by law."

This section considers each of these provisions in turn. Initially, the section focuses on the requirement of "agency action." Part 2 then turns to the first of §701(a)'s two clauses—statutory "preclusion" of review. Part 3 of the section looks at situations in which agency action is arguably "committed to agency discretion by law."

1. *"Agency Action"*

The APA's judicial review provisions apply to "agency action." There are two ways in which activity of the federal government may not constitute "agency action" within the meaning of the APA. First, the entity taking the action may not be an "agency." APA §551(1)(A)-(F) lists several entities that are not agencies within the meaning of the APA, including Congress, the federal courts, and the government of the District of Columbia. In addition, as noted in Chapter I, *supra*, the Supreme Court has decided that the President is not an "agency." *See* Franklin v. Massachusetts, 505 U.S. 788 (1992). Thus, when Congress delegates authority directly to the President, the President's own actions may not be challenged under the APA.

Second, even if a petition for review successfully identifies an agency, judicial review will not be available if the petitioner does not successfully identify something that constitutes "agency action." This issue comes into play when the petition concerns allegedly improper agency inaction, or challenges an agency's overall modus operandi without identifying a particular improper agency action. As the case study below reveals, the Supreme Court reads the APA as providing for judicial review only of discrete, identifiable agency actions.

Nearly one-third of all land within the United States, totaling more than 700 million acres and located largely in the western part of the country, is owned by the federal government. The majority of federally owned land is administered by three agencies, the Bureau of Land Management (BLM) and National Park Service, both within the Department of the Interior, and the National Forest Service, within the Department of Agriculture. The everyday work of these agencies requires them to balance resource extraction, resource protection, and recreation so as to conserve the public lands for multiple uses. A significant percentage of federal lands are leased to private parties for extractive activities such as forestry, mining, oil and gas drilling, and grazing. Some federal lands are designated as national parks and wilderness areas, where such intensive use is far more constrained. The National Park Service, as the name implies, administers national parks, which include natural wonders such as Yellowstone's geysers, and Yosemite's Half Dome, and historic sites, such as Abraham Lincoln's birthplace. The Forest Service administers 191 million acres of land, including 195 national forests, for recreation, logging, and grazing. BLM manages its 262 million acres of land (almost all in the West) for multiple purposes as well, including mining, grazing, and recreation.

Since 1976, BLM's administration of federal land has been governed by the Federal Land Policy and Management Act of 1976 (FLPMA), 90 Stat. 2744, 43 U.S.C. §1701 *et seq.* The centerpiece of FLPMA is land use planning. The statute requires BLM to produce detailed Resource Management Plans (RMPs) for the areas under its jurisdiction, and to manage those areas in accordance with these plans. An example is the 2008 Resource Management Plan for BLM's Richfield Field Office—a 206-page document that enumerates hundreds of actions and restrictions designed to manage a 2-million-acre area of southern Utah. The list of headings in the plan gives some sense of its breadth: "air quality, soil resources, water resources, vegetation decisions, cultural resources, paleontological resources, visual resources, special status species, fish and wildlife, wild horses and burros, fire and fuels management, forestry and woodland products, livestock grazing, recreation, travel, minerals and energy, wild and scenic rivers, transportation facilities, and health and safety." *See* https://perma.cc/H5WW-Y7PC.

The Bureau also oversees land that has been designated by Congress as a "wilderness area," in which roads and commercial development are forbidden. The statutory process for congressional designation of a wilderness area begins with a finding by the Secretary of the Interior that an area is suitable for wilderness designation. Such areas are designated as "Wilderness Study Areas" (WSAs), and until Congress acts, the statute requires that BLM manage the lands so as not to impair their wilderness values.

Lands designated as WSAs may deteriorate while they await further congressional action, however, because of recreational use. Since the 1990s, off-road vehicle (ORV) use has increased dramatically on public lands. These vehicles are made to traverse mud, sand, and gravel and to access remote areas where standard vehicles cannot go. They produce air pollution and water pollution, disturb wildlife, and degrade habitat, which is why conservationists generally oppose allowing them access to potential wilderness areas. In the case that follows, environmentalists concerned about the prospect that ORV use would impair potential wilderness lands sued to challenge BLM's refusal to ban them from WSAs. In addition to the agency's statutory obligation to manage such areas to prevent impairment, BLM had also committed, under the applicable RMPs, to closely monitor ORV use and close the areas to their use if warranted.

NORTON v. SOUTHERN UTAH WILDERNESS ALLIANCE
542 U.S. 55 (2004)

JUSTICE SCALIA delivered the opinion of the Court.

In this case, we must decide whether the authority of a federal court under the Administrative Procedure Act (APA) to "compel agency action unlawfully withheld or unreasonably delayed," 5 U.S.C. §706(1), extends to the review of the United States Bureau of Land Management's stewardship of public lands under certain statutory provisions and its own planning documents.

I

Almost half the State of Utah, about 23 million acres, is federal land administered by the Bureau of Land Management (BLM), an agency within the Department of Interior. For nearly 30 years, BLM's management of public lands has been governed by the Federal Land Policy and Management Act of 1976 (FLPMA), 90 Stat. 2744, 43 U.S.C. §1701 *et seq.,* which "established a policy in favor of retaining public lands for multiple use management." "Multiple use management" is a deceptively simple term that describes the enormously complicated task of striking a balance among the many competing uses to which land can be put, "including, but not limited to, recreation, range, timber, minerals, watershed, wildlife and fish, and [uses serving] natural scenic, scientific and historical values." 43 U.S.C. §1702(c). . . .

Of course not all uses are compatible. Congress made the judgment that some lands should be set aside as wilderness at the expense of commercial and recreational uses. [T]he Wilderness Act of 1964, 78 Stat. 890, provides that designated wilderness areas, subject to certain exceptions, "shall [have] no commercial enterprise and no permanent road," no motorized vehicles, and no manmade structures. 16 U.S.C. §1133(c). The designation of a wilderness area can be made only by Act of Congress, *see* 43 U.S.C. §1782(b).

Pursuant to §1782, the Secretary of the Interior has identified so-called "wilderness study areas" (WSAs), roadless lands of 5,000 acres or more that possess "wilderness characteristics," as determined in the Secretary's land inventory. §1782(a); *see* 16 U.S.C. §1131(c). As the name suggests, WSAs (as well as certain wild lands identified prior to the passage of FLPMA) have been subjected to further examination and public comment in order to evaluate their suitability for designation as wilderness. . . . Until Congress acts one way or the other, FLPMA provides that "the Secretary shall continue to manage such lands . . . in a manner so as not to impair the suitability of such areas for preservation as wilderness." 43 U.S.C. §1782(c). This nonimpairment mandate applies to all WSAs identified under §1782, including lands considered unsuitable by the Secretary. *See* §1782(a), (b); App. 64 (BLM Interim Management Policy for Lands Under Wilderness Review).

Aside from identification of WSAs, the main tool that BLM employs to balance wilderness protection against other uses is a land use plan—what BLM regulations call a "resource management plan." 43 CFR §1601.0-5(k) (2003). Land use plans, adopted after notice and comment, are "designed to guide and control future management actions," §1601.0-2. *See* 43 U.S.C. §1712; 43 CFR §1610.2 (2003). Generally, a land use plan describes, for a particular area, allowable uses, goals for future condition of the land, and specific next steps. §1601.0-5(k). Under FLPMA, "[t]he Secretary shall manage the public lands under principles of multiple use and sustained yield, in accordance with the land use plans . . . when they are available." 43 U.S.C. §1732(a).

Protection of wilderness has come into increasing conflict with another element of multiple use, recreational use of so-called off-road vehicles (ORVs), which include vehicles primarily designed for off-road use, such as lightweight, four-wheel "all-terrain vehicles," and vehicles capable of such use, such as sport utility vehicles. . . . The use of ORVs on federal land has negative environmental consequences, including soil disruption and compaction, harassment of animals, and annoyance of wilderness lovers. Thus, BLM faces a classic land use dilemma of sharply inconsistent uses, in a context of scarce resources and congressional silence with respect to wilderness designation.

In 1999, respondents Southern Utah Wilderness Alliance and other organizations (collectively SUWA) filed this action in the United States District Court for Utah against petitioners BLM, its Director, and the Secretary. . . . SUWA sought declaratory and injunctive relief for BLM's failure to act to protect public lands in Utah from damage caused by ORV use. SUWA made three claims that are relevant here: (1) that BLM had violated its nonimpairment obligation under §1782(a) by allowing degradation in certain WSAs; (2) that BLM had failed to implement provisions in its land use plans relating to ORV use; (3) that BLM had failed to take a "hard look" at whether, pursuant to the National Environmental Policy Act of 1969 (NEPA), 83 Stat. 852, 42 U.S.C. §4321 *et seq.*, it should undertake supplemental environmental analyses for areas in which ORV use had increased. SUWA contended that it could sue to remedy these three failures to act pursuant to the APA's provision of a cause of action to "compel agency action unlawfully withheld or unreasonably delayed." 5 U.S.C. §706(1). . . .

II

All three claims at issue here involve assertions that BLM failed to take action with respect to ORV use that it was required to take. Failures to act are sometimes remediable under the APA, but not always. We begin by considering what limits the APA places upon judicial review of agency inaction.

The APA authorizes suit by "[a] person suffering legal wrong because of agency action, or adversely affected or aggrieved by agency action within the meaning of a relevant statute." 5 U.S.C. §702. Where no other statute provides a private right of action, the "agency action" complained of must be "*final* agency action." §704 (emphasis added). "Agency action" is defined in §551(13) to include "the whole or a part of an agency rule, order, license, sanction, relief, or the equivalent or denial thereof, *or failure to act.*" (Emphasis added.) The APA provides relief for a failure to act in §706(1): "The reviewing court shall . . . compel agency action unlawfully withheld or unreasonably delayed."

Sections 702, 704, and 706(1) all insist upon an "agency action," either as the action complained of (in §§702 and 704) or as the action to be compelled (in §706(1)). The definition of that term begins with a list of five categories of decisions made or outcomes implemented by an agency—"agency rule, order, license, sanction [or] relief." §551(13). All of those categories involve circumscribed, discrete agency actions[.]

The terms following those five categories of agency action are not defined in the APA: "or the equivalent or denial thereof, or failure to act." §551(13). But an "equivalent . . . thereof" must also be discrete (or it would not be equivalent), and a "denial thereof" must be the denial of a discrete listed action (and perhaps denial of a discrete equivalent).

The final term in the definition, "failure to act," is in our view properly understood as a failure to take an *agency action*—that is, a failure to take one of the agency actions (including their equivalents) earlier defined in §551(13). Moreover, even without this equation of "act" with "agency action" the interpretive canon of *ejusdem generis* would attribute to the last item ("failure to act") the same characteristic of discreteness shared by all the preceding items. A "failure to act" is not the same thing as a "denial." The latter is the agency's act of saying no to a request; the former is simply the omission of an action without formally rejecting a request—for example, the failure to promulgate a rule or take some decision by a statutory deadline. The important point is that a "failure to act" is properly understood to be limited, as are the other items in §551(13), to a *discrete* action.

A second point central to the analysis of the present case is that the only agency action that can be compelled under the APA is action legally *required*. This limitation appears in §706(1)'s authorization for courts to "compel agency action *unlawfully* withheld."[1] . . . As described in the Attorney General's Manual on the APA, a document whose reasoning we have often found persuasive, §706(1) empowers a court only to compel an agency "to perform a ministerial or non-discretionary act," or "to take action upon a matter, without directing *how* it shall act." Attorney General's Manual on the Administrative Procedure Act 108 (1947) (emphasis added).

Thus, a claim under §706(1) can proceed only where a plaintiff asserts that an agency failed to take a *discrete* agency action that it is *required to take*. These limitations rule out several kinds of challenges. The limitation to discrete agency action precludes the kind of broad programmatic attack we rejected in Lujan v. National Wildlife Federation, 497 U.S. 871 (1990). There we considered a challenge to BLM's land withdrawal review program, couched as unlawful agency "action" that the plaintiffs wished to have "set aside" under §706(2). *Id.* at 879. We concluded that the program was not an "agency action":

> "[R]espondent cannot seek *wholesale* improvement of this program by court decree, rather than in the offices of the Department or the halls of Congress, where programmatic improvements are normally made. Under the terms of the APA, respondent must direct its attack against some particular 'agency action' that causes it harm." *Id.* at 891 (emphasis in original).

. . . The limitation to *required* agency action rules out judicial direction of even discrete agency action that is not demanded by law (which includes, of course, agency regulations that have the force of law). Thus, when an agency is compelled by law to act within a certain time period, but the manner of its action is left to the agency's discretion, a court can compel the agency to act,

---

1. Of course §706(1) also authorizes courts to "compel agency action . . . unreasonably delayed"—but a delay cannot be unreasonable with respect to action that is not required.

but has no power to specify what the action must be. For example, 47 U.S.C. §251(d)(1), which required the Federal Communications Commission "to establish regulations to implement" interconnection requirements "[w]ithin 6 months" of the date of enactment of the Telecommunications Act of 1996, would have supported a judicial decree under the APA requiring the prompt issuance of regulations, but not a judicial decree setting forth the content of those regulations.

III

A

With these principles in mind, we turn to SUWA's first claim, that by permitting ORV use in certain WSAs, BLM violated its mandate to "continue to manage [WSAs] . . . in a manner so as not to impair the suitability of such areas for preservation as wilderness," 43 U.S.C. §1782(c). SUWA relies not only upon §1782(c) but also upon a provision of BLM's Interim Management Policy for Lands Under Wilderness Review, which interprets the nonimpairment mandate to require BLM to manage WSAs so as to prevent them from being "degraded so far, compared with the area's values for other purposes, as to significantly constrain the Congress's prerogative to either designate [it] as wilderness or release it for other uses."

Section 1782(c) is mandatory as to the object to be achieved, but it leaves BLM a great deal of discretion in deciding how to achieve it. It assuredly does not mandate, with the clarity necessary to support judicial action under §706(1), the total exclusion of ORV use.

SUWA argues that §1782 *does* contain a categorical imperative, namely the command to comply with the nonimpairment mandate. It contends that a federal court could simply enter a general order compelling compliance with that mandate, without suggesting any particular manner of compliance. It relies upon the language from the Attorney General's Manual quoted earlier, that a court can "take action upon a matter, without directing how [the agency] shall act," and upon language in a case cited by the Manual noting that "mandamus will lie . . . even though the act required involves the exercise of judgment and discretion." Safeway Stores v. Brown, 138 F.2d 278, 280 (Emerg. Ct. App. 1943). The action referred to in these excerpts, however, is *discrete* agency action, as we have discussed above. General deficiencies in compliance, unlike the failure to issue a ruling that was discussed in *Safeway Stores*, lack the specificity requisite for agency action.

The principal purpose of the APA limitations we have discussed—and of the traditional limitations upon mandamus from which they were derived—is to protect agencies from undue judicial interference with their lawful discretion, and to avoid judicial entanglement in abstract policy disagreements which courts lack both expertise and information to resolve. If courts were empowered to enter general orders compelling compliance with broad statutory mandates, they would necessarily be empowered, as well, to determine whether compliance was achieved—which would mean that it would ultimately become the task of the supervising court, rather than the agency, to work out compliance with the broad statutory mandate, injecting the judge into day-to-day agency management. To take just a few examples from federal resources management, a plaintiff might allege that the Secretary had failed to "manage wild free-roaming horses and burros in a manner that is designed to achieve and maintain a thriving natural ecological balance," or to "manage the [New Orleans Jazz National] [H]istorical [P]ark in such a manner as will preserve and perpetuate knowledge and understanding of the history of jazz," or to "manage the [Steens Mountain] Cooperative Management and Protection Area for the benefit of present and future generations." 16 U.S.C. §§1333(a), 410bbb-2(a)(1), 460nnn-12(b). The prospect of pervasive oversight by federal courts over the manner and pace of agency compliance with such congressional directives is not contemplated by the APA.

B

SUWA's second claim is that BLM failed to comply with certain provisions in its land use plans [including a commitment to monitor ORV use in the area], thus contravening the requirement that "[t]he Secretary shall manage the public lands . . . in accordance with the land use plans . . . when they are available." 43 U.S.C. §1732(a); see also 43 CFR §1610.5-3(a) (2003) ("All future resource management authorizations and actions . . . and subsequent more detailed or specific planning, shall conform to the approved plan").

The statutory directive that BLM manage "in accordance with" land use plans, and the regulatory requirement that authorizations and actions "conform to" those plans, prevent BLM from taking actions inconsistent with the provisions of a land use plan. Unless and until the plan is amended, such actions can be set aside as contrary to law pursuant to 5 U.S.C. §706(2). The claim presently under discussion, however, would have us go further, and conclude that a statement in a plan that BLM "will" take this, that, or the other action, is a binding commitment that can be compelled under §706(1). In our view it is not—at least absent clear indication of binding commitment in the terms of the plan.

FLPMA describes land use plans as tools by which "present and future use is *projected*." 43 U.S.C. §1701(a)(2) (emphasis added). The implementing regulations make clear that land use plans are a preliminary step in the overall process of managing public lands—"designed to guide and control future management actions and the development of subsequent, more detailed and limited scope plans for resources and uses." 43 CFR §1601.0-2 (2003). . . .

Quite unlike a specific statutory command requiring an agency to promulgate regulations by a certain date, a land use plan is generally a statement of priorities; it guides and constrains actions, but does not (at least in the usual case) prescribe them. It would be unreasonable to think that either Congress or the agency intended otherwise, since land use plans nationwide would commit the agency to actions far in the future, for which funds have not yet been appropriated. Some plans make explicit that implementation of their programmatic content is subject to budgetary constraints. While the Henry Mountains plan does not contain such a specification, we think it must reasonably be implied. A statement by BLM about what it plans to do, at some point, provided it has the funds and there are not more pressing priorities, cannot be plucked out of context and made a basis for suit under §706(1).

Of course, an action called for in a plan may be compelled when the plan merely reiterates duties the agency is already obligated to perform, or perhaps when language in the plan itself creates a commitment binding on the agency. But allowing general enforcement of plan terms would lead to pervasive interference with BLM's own ordering of priorities. For example, a judicial decree compelling immediate preparation of all of the detailed plans called for in the San Rafael plan would divert BLM's energies from other projects throughout the country that are in fact more pressing. And while such a decree might please the environmental plaintiffs in the present case, it would ultimately operate to the detriment of sound environmental management. Its predictable consequence would be much vaguer plans from BLM in the future—making coordination with other agencies more difficult, and depriving the public of important information concerning the agency's long-range intentions.

We therefore hold that the Henry Mountains plan's statements to the effect that BLM will conduct "use supervision and monitoring" in designated areas—like other "will do" projections of agency action set forth in land use plans—are not a legally binding commitment enforceable under §706(1). That being so, we find it unnecessary to consider whether the action envisioned by the statements is sufficiently discrete to be amenable to compulsion under the APA.

IV

[The Court's discussion of SUWA's contention that BLM failed to fulfill certain obligations under NEPA is omitted.]

The judgment of the Court of Appeals is reversed, and the case is remanded for further proceedings consistent with this opinion.

NOTES AND QUESTIONS

1. *"Discreteness."* Why must agency conduct be "discrete" in order to be reviewable under the APA? Does APA §551(13) provide an answer? Does the Court provide a clear enough guideline to differentiate "discrete" acts from "general" conduct? In subsequent cases, courts have held that general planning documents that identify agency priorities, or provide guidelines for future agency decisions, are not sufficiently "discrete" to constitute "agency actions." *See* Forest Guardians v. Forsgren, 478 F.3d 1149 (10th Cir. 2007). In American Civil Liberties Union v. National Security Agency, 493 F.3d 644 (6th Cir. 2007), the ACLU challenged the NSA's Terrorist Surveillance Program (TSP), through which the agency engaged in warrantless interception of overseas communications. The court held that the NSA's program of warrantless wiretaps was "conduct," not "agency action," and thus was not reviewable.

Although the plaintiffs labeled the NSA's surveillance activities as "the Program," and the district court labeled it the "TSP," the NSA's wiretapping is actually just general conduct given a label for purposes of abbreviated reference. The plaintiffs do not complain of any NSA rule or order, but merely the generalized practice, which—so far as has been admitted or disclosed—was not formally enacted pursuant to the strictures of the APA, but merely authorized by the President (albeit repeatedly, and possibly informally). Nor do the plaintiffs challenge any license, sanction, or relief issued by the NSA.

Id. at 678-679.

2. *Judicial "management" of administrative agencies.* Justice Scalia expresses concern that review of the SUWA claims would "inject" the courts into "day-to-day agency management." Is that necessarily so? Can you imagine an enforceable decree in this case that would not stray beyond the traditional bounds of judicial supervision? What problem does the Court see in ongoing judicial supervision? Federal courts have engaged in ongoing supervision of complex public institutions in the context of "institutional reform litigation," such as cases attacking school segregation or inhumane prison conditions. *See, e.g.*, Brown v. Plata, 563 U.S. 493 (2011) (upholding a judicial decree requiring reduction of the population of California's prisons, and summarizing a long history of federal court supervision of the prison system). What problems does such ongoing involvement of courts in these institutions entail? Are the problems associated with judicial supervision of schools or prisons different (larger, smaller, offering distinct risks to proper judicial roles or to authority of political actors or to federalism considerations) from policing the Interior Department's failures to prevent "impairment" of a wilderness study area? Look back at the discussion of "polycentric" problems and judicial review in the context of the *Overton Park* case, in Chapter II, *supra*. Is BLM's management of WSAs a polycentric problem that is unsuitable for judicial review?

3. *When is "failure to act" an "agency action"?* Is the Court on sound footing in reading the phrase "failure to act" in §551(13) to embody the same sense of "discreteness" as the words that precede it? What about the fact that the failure to issue a rule, order, license, sanction, or relief is already made "agency action" by the inclusion of the words "denial thereof"? What sort of "discrete" agency action would constitute "failure to act" but not amount to a denial of one of the enumerated forms of agency action? What about the power of a reviewing court under APA §706(1) to compel agency action "unreasonably delayed"? Does the "unreasonably delayed" action have to be discrete?

4. *"Legally required."* What is the role of the concept of "legally required" in the Court's analysis? Is it part of the definition of "agency action," and hence a threshold test for whether a legal claim is reviewable in the first place? Or is it merely part of the test for when a court can compel an agency to do something under APA §706(1)? In the *ACLU* case, discussed in note 1, *supra*, the court seemed to read *SUWA* as taking the former position. It found that NSA's warrant procedures contained discretionary considerations, "thus disqualifying them from this definition of "agency action" under the APA." Is this understanding of the APA's definition of agency action consistent with the provision in APA §706(2)(A) that agency action is subject to review for *abuse of discretion*? Also, if "legally required" is part of the definition of "agency action," how can a court decide if something is reviewable, as "agency action," without in fact reviewing its legality on the merits? In this connection, notice that Part III of the Court's opinion in *SUWA* states that §1782(c) "assuredly does not mandate, with the clarity necessary to support judicial action under

§706(1), the total exclusion of ORVs." Does this assume a decision on the legal merits of at least one of the issues that the Court purports not to reach because there is no "agency action" to review?

Perhaps the Court's "legally required" test is a condition for applying APA §706(1): that is, suits to compel agency action wrongfully withheld are available only when the action sought is mandatory and not discretionary. This principle was applied in Bian v. Clinton, 605 F.3d 249 (5th Cir. 2010), *vacated as moot*, 2010 WL 3633770 (5th Cir. 2010), in which a Chinese national sought to compel the United States to adjudicate her application for permanent resident status, which had been pending for three years. The government argued that Congress has left the immigration status adjudicatory process to the Department of Homeland Security's discretion. The court held that since the Immigration and Nationality Act states that an alien's status "*may* be adjusted by the Attorney General, *in his discretion and under such regulations as he may prescribe*," and does not contain a timeline or deadline for adjudication of such applications, the agency's failure to adjudicate her application was unreviewable. Is there any other basis for exempting agency action from review simply because it is discretionary?

5. *Refusal to enforce a rule (or statute) versus refusal to adopt a rule.* How can you square *SUWA* with the Supreme Court's close scrutiny of EPA's refusal to regulate greenhouse gases in Massachusetts v. EPA, in Chapter II, *supra*? In that case, EPA had also chosen not to act. Why wasn't its failure to regulate considered "general" conduct, rather than a "discrete" action? Suppose SUWA had petitioned BLM for a rule banning off-road vehicles from wilderness study areas, or severely restricting their use, and BLM had denied the petition. Would the Court, applying Massachusetts v. EPA, find the denial to be reviewable? If so, isn't the *SUWA* Court merely elevating form over substance, in the sense that BLM is surely aware of SUWA's interest in having it ban ORVs and has decided to take no action? Is there a difference between the statutory provision in SUWA, §1782(c), and the Clean Air Act provision in Massachusetts v. EPA, §202(a), which required EPA to regulate once it made a threshold finding? Or is Massachusetts v. EPA an outlier on what is reviewable?

6. *"Unreasonable delay."* If denial of a rulemaking petition is reviewable, can agencies avoid judicial scrutiny by simply failing to respond to petitions? When does "unlawful withholding" become "unreasonable delay" under §706(1)? Agency rulemakings typically take a year or two, and sometimes longer, but there are also instances of extreme delay. Courts have historically been loath to compel agency action under APA §706(1), as long as the agency can credibly claim to be making progress or can offer plausible reasons for delay, in part for the same reason the Court refused to review the agency's alleged failure to act in *SUWA*: concern about intruding on agency resource allocation and task prioritization. Consider the following example.

PUBLIC CITIZEN HEALTH RESEARCH GROUP v. CHAO, 314 F.3d 143 (3d Cir. 2002): Section 6(b) of the Occupational Safety and Health Act charges OSHA with setting a standard for toxic exposures in the workplace "which most adequately assures, to the extent feasible, on the basis of the best available evidence, that no employee will suffer material impairment of health or functional capacity even if such employee has regular exposure to the hazard dealt with by such standard for the period of his working life." 29 U.S.C. §655(b)(5). In 1971, OSHA promulgated an industry-developed "consensus" standard for workplace exposure to hexavalent chromium. In 1993, Public Citizen Health Research Group ("Public Citizen") petitioned OSHA to adopt a more stringent permissible exposure limit ("PEL"). At the time, OSHA acknowledged that the 1971 consensus standard was inadequate to prevent excess lung cancers and other illnesses, and promised to complete a new rulemaking in 1995. After missing that self-imposed deadline, OSHA repeatedly promised to propose a new PEL at a certain time only to extend the deadline each time. In 1998, the Third Circuit rejected a petition to compel rulemaking, concluding that OSHA's delays were not yet so extreme as to warrant judicial intervention. Oil, Chemical & Atomic Workers Union v. OSHA, 145 F.3d 120 (3d Cir. 1998). In 2001, Public Citizen again petitioned for review, alleging that OSHA's delay in increasing the stringency of its PEL for hexavalent chromium violated the agency's duties under the OSH Act. This time, the Third Circuit announced, it had finally had enough:

> In denying Public Citizen's earlier petition to compel a hexavalent chromium rulemaking, we acknowledged "the quintessential discretion of the Secretary of Labor to allocate OSHA's resources and set its priorities." *Oil Workers*, 145 F.3d at 123. At the same time, however, we recognized that the Secretary's discretion is not unbounded, and noted our obligation under the APA to "compel agency action unlawfully withheld or unreasonably delayed." *Id.* (quoting 5 U.S.C. §706(1)). Our polestar is reasonableness, and while in 1997 we found reasonable OSHA's delay in the face of scientific uncertainty and competing regulatory priorities, we now find ourselves further from a new rule than we were then.
>
> We find extreme OSHA's nine-year (and counting) delay since announcing its intention to begin the rulemaking process, even relative to delays other courts have condemned in comparable cases. Indeed, in no reported case has a court reviewed a delay this long without compelling action. . . .
>
> We agree with OSHA that the evidence may be imperfect, that the feasibility inquiry is formidable, and that premature rulemaking is undesirable. [But despite the fact that the studies do not answer every question and that more research and analysis may still be done,] read fairly, the Act virtually forbids delay in pursuit of certainty—it requires regulation "on the basis of the best *available* evidence," 29 U.S.C. §655(b)(5) (emphasis added), and courts have warned that "OSHA cannot let workers suffer while it awaits the Godot of scientific certainty." United Steelworkers of America v. Marshall, 647 F.2d 1189, 1266 (D.C. Cir. 1980) . . . .
>
> OSHA contends that it simply exercised its discretion to concentrate its resources elsewhere. . . . In 1999 and 2000, OSHA submits that it "focused most of its rulemaking resources on issuing an ergonomics standard before the end of the former Administration's term." . . . OSHA represents that the delays became worse when the Bush administration took office, for it instructed the agencies that any new regulatory actions must be reviewed and approved by a department or agency head appointed after January 20, 2001. As OSHA was not headed by a presidential nominee until August 2001, it alleges that "it could not begin in earnest to set its new regulatory priorities" until that time, and that even then, unforeseen incidents such as the September 11 attacks and anthrax mailings demanded that it "immediately divert[] significant resources to help ensure that the rescue and cleanup efforts did not result in further loss of life." . . .

We do not lightly discount these admittedly significant competing priorities, especially those relating to the events of September 11, but when we view the rulemaking's progress over the past nine years, we reach the ineluctable conclusion that hexavalent chromium has progressively fallen by the wayside. This is unacceptable . . . .

For the foregoing reasons, we hold that OSHA's delay in promulgating a lower permissible exposure limit for hexavalent chromium has exceeded the bounds of reasonableness. We therefore grant Public Citizen's petition to compel OSHA to proceed expeditiously with its hexavalent chromium rulemaking. [The Court ordered the parties to appear before a judge for mandatory mediation following which, if the parties had not agreed on a mutually satisfactory timetable, the Court said it would order its own.]

NOTES AND QUESTIONS

1. *Reasons for delay.* Note the reasons given by OSHA for its delay. Are they illegitimate or inherently implausible? In *SUWA*, the Supreme Court expressed reluctance to interfere with agency decisions concerning the allocation of their scarce resources among competing priorities, a theme reiterated in the *Heckler* and *Lincoln* cases excerpted at pp. 331 and 347, *infra*. In light of that concern, should the Third Circuit have been more sympathetic to OSHA? Or should courts be willing to play a more active role when rules are perpetually delayed?

2. *The effectiveness of a judicial order to regulate.* Does the court's order provide the necessary incentive to impel OSHA to act? Given the limited remedial tools at the courts' disposal, and judicial reluctance to find agency officials in contempt, are orders to regulate necessarily limited in their effectiveness? In fact, the court's decision in *Chao* did not spur OSHA to speedily set a permissible exposure level for hexavalent chromium. The Third Circuit's decision was issued on December 24, 2002. OSHA published a Notice of Proposed Rulemaking on October 4, 2004, and finally published a Final Rule on February 28, 2006, over three years after the Third Circuit decision and thirteen years after Public Citizen's first "emergency petition."

2.   Statutory Preclusion of Review

The Supreme Court has stated that "only upon a showing of clear and convincing evidence of a contrary legislative intent should the courts restrict access to judicial review." Abbott Laboratories v. Gardner, 387 U.S. 136, 141 (1967). However, even when Congress clearly evinces an intent to restrict access to the courts, questions inevitably arise concerning the reach of that restriction. Perhaps the most celebrated example of a statute explicitly precluding review was §211(a) of the Veterans' Administration Act, which was codified at 38 U.S.C. §211(a). (The current version is codified at 38 U.S.C. §511(a).) The Veterans' Administration was created by the Economy Act of 1933 for the purpose of administering veterans' benefits. In 1988, the VA was re-designated the Department of Veterans Affairs, to be headed by the Secretary of Veterans Affairs. *See*

Pub. L. No. 100-527, 102 Stat. 2635 (1988). An explicit no-review provision has been a feature of the agency's statutory mandate since its inception. The version in effect at the time of Johnson v. Robison (excerpted below) read:

> [T]he decisions of the [Veterans'] Administrator on any question of law or fact under any law administered by the Veterans' Administration providing benefits for veterans and their dependents or survivors shall be final and conclusive and no other official or any court of the United States shall have power or jurisdiction to review any such decision by an action in the nature of mandamus or otherwise.

With this provision, the Veterans' Administration stood as a striking example of the only federal administrative agency whose major duties were exempt from judicial review. This sweeping insulation from judicial scrutiny earned mixed reviews from commentators. One critic, arguing that justice ought never take a back seat to administrative illegality for the sake of government efficiency, disparagingly referred to the Veterans' Administration as "Henry VIII in America." Kenneth C. Davis, Veterans' Benefits, Judicial Review, and the Constitutional Problem of "Positive" Government, 39 Ind. L.J. 183, 185 (1964). Another, defending the system with equal fervor, describes it as "the most competent and humane social services agency since King Solomon sat to dispense charity and justice to his adoring subjects." Jerry L. Mashaw, Due Process in the Administrative State 265 (1985).

The courts also gave §211(a) a mixed reception. Although the removal of the Administrator's decisions from judicial scrutiny elicited some early objections on due process grounds, the Supreme Court seemed to lay them to rest with this dictum:

> Pensions, compensation allowances and privileges are gratuities. They involve no agreement of parties; and the grant of them creates no vested right. The benefits conferred by gratuities may be redistributed or withdrawn at any time in the discretion of Congress.

Lynch v. United States, 292 U.S. 571, 577 (1934). Despite this apparent endorsement of the statute's constitutionality, in a series of cases from 1958 to 1967 the D.C. Circuit narrowly interpreted a previous version of §211(a) to limit its effect severely. As it stood at the time, §211(a) insulated from review "decisions of the Administrator on a question of law or fact concerning a claim for benefits or payments." The D.C. Circuit interpreted that language as barring review only of initial claim determinations, not the termination or reduction of existing benefits. Wellman v. Whittier, 259 F.2d 163 (D.C. Cir. 1958); Thompson v. Gleason, 317 F.2d 901 (D.C. Cir. 1962); Tracy v. Gleason, 379 F.2d 469 (D.C. Cir. 1967).

Viewing these decisions as a subversion of its initial intent, Congress amended the Act in 1970. The House Committee on Veterans' Affairs lamented that, since Wellman, "suits in constantly increasing numbers have been filed in U.S. District Courts for the District of Columbia by plaintiffs seeking resumption of terminated benefits." H.R. Rep. No. 91-1166, 91st Cong., 2d Sess. 10 (1970). In addition to the fear of increased litigation, the House Report expressed a desire to keep policy determination within the Veterans' Administration. Id. By eliminating the phrase "concerning a claim for benefits or payments," Congress attempted to close the loophole created by the D.C. Circuit.

JOHNSON v. ROBISON
415 U.S. 361 (1974)

JUSTICE BRENNAN delivered the opinion of the Court.

[Robison, a conscientious objector during the war in Vietnam, made a claim for educational assistance benefits under the Veterans' Readjustment Act of 1966. The administrator denied the claim because Robison had served only two years of alternative service and had not fulfilled the statutory requirement of "active duty." Robison filed suit attacking the constitutionality of the active duty requirement. He claimed the provision violated his rights to equal protection of the law guaranteed by the Fifth Amendment and to religious freedom guaranteed by the First Amendment. In the District Court, the Veterans' Administrator moved to dismiss the suit based on §211(a). The District Court denied the motion, and on the merits rejected Robison's religious freedom claim, but sustained his equal protection claim.]

We consider first appellants' contention that §211(a) bars federal courts from deciding the constitutionality of veterans' benefits legislation. Such a construction would, of course, raise serious questions concerning the constitutionality of §211(a).

Plainly, no explicit provision of §211(a) bars judicial consideration of appellee's constitutional claims. That section provides that "the *decisions* of the Administrator on any question of law or fact *under* any law administered by the Veterans' Administration providing benefits for veterans . . . shall be final and conclusive and no . . . court of the United States shall have power or jurisdiction to review any such decision. . . ." (Emphasis added.) The prohibitions would appear to be aimed at review only of those decisions of law or fact that arise in the *administration* by the Veterans' Administration of a *statute* providing benefits for veterans. A decision of law or fact "under" a statute is made by the Administrator in the interpretation or application of a particular provision of the statute to a particular set of facts. Appellee's constitutional challenge is not to any such decision of the *Administrator,* but rather to a decision of *Congress* to create a statutory class entitled to benefits that does not include conscientious objectors who performed alternative civilian service.

This construction is also supported by the administrative practice of the Veterans' Administration. "When faced with a problem of statutory construction, this Court shows great deference to the interpretation given the statute by the officers or agency charged with its administration." Udall v. Tallman, 380 U.S. 1, 16 (1965). The Board of Veterans' Appeals expressly disclaimed authority to decide constitutional questions in Appeal of *Sly.* C-27 593 725 (May 10, 1972). There the Board denying a claim for educational assistance by a . . . conscientious objector, held that "[t]his decision does not reach the issue of the constitutionality of the pertinent laws as this matter is not within the jurisdiction of this Board." *Sly* thus accepts and follows the principle that "[a]djudication of the constitutionality of congressional enactments has generally been thought beyond the jurisdiction of administrative agencies. . . ."

Nor does the legislative history accompanying the 1970 amendment of §211(a) demonstrate a congressional intention to bar judicial review even of constitutional questions. No-review clauses similar to §211(a) have been a part of veterans' benefits legislation since 1933. While the legislative history accompanying these precursor no-review clauses is almost nonexistent, the Administrator, in a letter written in 1952 in connection with a revision of the clause under consideration by the Subcommittee of the House Committee on Veterans' Affairs, comprehensively explained the policies necessitating the no-review clause and identified two primary purposes: (1) to insure that veterans' benefits claims will not burden the courts and the Veterans' Administration with expensive and time-consuming litigation, and (2) to insure that the technical and complex determinations and applications of Veterans' Administration policy connected with veterans' benefits decisions will be adequately and uniformly made. . . .

Nothing whatever in the legislative history of the 1970 amendment, or predecessor no-review clauses, suggests any congressional intent to preclude judicial cognizance of constitutional challenges to veterans' benefits legislation. Such challenges obviously do not contravene the purposes of the no-review clause, for they cannot be expected to burden the courts by their volume, nor do they involve technical considerations of Veterans' Administration policy. We therefore conclude, in agreement with the District Court, that a construction of §211(a) that does not extend the prohibitions of that section to actions challenging the constitutionality of laws providing benefits for veterans is not only "fairly possible" but is the most reasonable construction, for neither the text nor the scant legislative history of §211(a) provides the "clear and convincing" evidence of congressional intent required by this Court before a statute will be construed to restrict access to judicial review. . . .

[Reaching the merits, the Court found that the statute violated neither the First Amendment nor the Fifth Amendment, and thus reversed the District Court's ruling.]

NOTES AND QUESTIONS

1. *Constitutionality of precluding review of constitutional challenges.* Note the *Robison* Court's concern with the constitutionality of §211(a). Would it be unconstitutional for Congress to preclude constitutional challenges to a statute? Are the considerations that inform whether courts may review statutes for constitutionality different from the factors that inform whether courts may review agency decisions for constitutionality? Before answering these questions, consider that there are judge-made jurisdictional doctrines, such as the political question doctrine, that make it impossible for some constitutional challenges to be brought. If courts can shield some statutes or other government action from constitutional challenges, is there any reason why Congress should not have the same power? For further discussion of this issue, see Justice Scalia's dissent in the *Webster* case, excerpted *infra*.

The Court's reluctance to hold that Congress has precluded judicial review of constitutional questions is reflected in Demore v. Hyung Joon Kim, 538 U.S. 510 (2003), an immigration case in which the Court held that a provision of the Immigration and Nationality Act limiting judicial review of the Attorney General's discretionary judgments regarding detention of aliens during removal proceedings did not deprive the Supreme Court of jurisdiction over a habeas corpus petition alleging that the statute allowing detention without bail was unconstitutional. The Court relied on the presumption in favor of judicial review of constitutional questions and an even stronger presumption in favor of the availability of habeas corpus. *See also* INS v. St. Cyr, 533 U.S. 289, 308-309 (2001) (requiring a particularly clear statement for Congress to preclude habeas corpus).

2. *The reach of preclusion provisions.* Recall that §211(a) barred judicial review of decisions of the Veterans' Administrator "under any law administered by" the VA. Does this include laws of general applicability (as opposed to laws uniquely administered by the VA)? The Supreme Court gave a negative answer to that question in Traynor v. Turnage, 485 U.S. 535 (1988) (declining to find that §211(a) precluded a claim that the VA had violated §504 of the Rehabilitation Act when denying benefits to an alcoholic, because the Rehabilitation Act forbids discrimination against the handicapped by all federal and state agencies).

3. *Preclusion of substantive versus procedural claims.* Does a statute purporting to preclude challenges to substantive agency decisions also preclude challenges to the procedures employed by the agency? If the procedural claim is grounded in the Due Process Clause of the Fifth Amendment, it appears that the answer is no. *See, e.g.,* Maroszan v. United States, 852 F.2d 1469 (7th Cir. 1988) (en banc), *cert. denied,* 520 U.S. 1109 (1997). Suppose, however, that the basis for the alleged procedural violation is statutory. In Gott v. Walters, 756 F.2d 902 (D.C. Cir.), *vacated,* 791 F.2d 172 (D.C. Cir. 1985) (en banc), the court found §211(a) to bar review of a claim that the VA had violated the notice-and-comment requirements of APA §553 when it adopted a policy for determining radiation exposure claims. The court reasoned that, to entertain procedural claims would necessarily entangle courts in day-to-day VA decisionmaking, contrary to congressional intent. *But see* Lindahl v. Office of Personnel Management, 470 U.S. 768 (1985), discussed in the following case.

CUOZZO SPEED TECHNOLOGIES, LLC v. LEE
136 S. Ct. 2131 (2016)

JUSTICE BREYER delivered the opinion of the Court.

The Leahy-Smith America Invents Act, 35 U.S.C. §100 *et seq.,* creates a process called "inter partes review." That review process allows a third party to ask the U.S. Patent and Trademark Office to reexamine the claims in an already-issued patent and to cancel any claim that the agency finds to be unpatentable in light of prior art. See §102 (requiring "novel[ty]"); §103 (disqualifying claims that are "obvious").

We consider two provisions of the Act. The first says: "No Appeal. — The determination by the Director [of the Patent Office] whether to institute an inter partes review under this section shall be final and non-appealable." §314(d). Does this provision bar a court from considering whether the Patent Office wrongly "determin[ed] . . . to institute an inter partes review," when it did so on grounds not specifically mentioned in a third party's review request?

The second provision grants the Patent Office the authority to issue "regulations . . . establishing and governing inter partes review under this chapter." §316(a)(4). Does this provision authorize the Patent Office to issue a regulation stating that the agency, in inter partes review, "shall [construe a patent claim according to] its broadest reasonable construction in light of the specification of the patent in which it appears"? 37 CFR §42.100(b) (2015).

We conclude that the first provision, though it may not bar consideration of a constitutional question, for example, does bar judicial review of the kind of mine-run claim at issue here, involving the Patent Office's decision to institute inter partes review. We also conclude that the second provision authorizes the Patent Office to issue the regulation before us.

I

A

An inventor obtains a patent by applying to the Patent Office. A patent examiner with expertise in the relevant field reviews an applicant's patent claims, considers the prior art, and determines whether each claim meets the applicable patent law requirements. Then, the examiner accepts a claim, or rejects it and explains why.

If the examiner rejects a claim, the applicant can resubmit a narrowed (or otherwise modified) claim, which the examiner will consider anew, measuring the new claim against the same patent law requirements. If the examiner rejects the new claim, the inventor typically has yet another chance to respond with yet another amended claim. Ultimately, the Patent Office makes a final decision allowing or rejecting the application. The applicant may seek judicial review of any final rejection.

For several decades, the Patent Office has also possessed the authority to reexamine—and perhaps cancel—a patent claim that it had previously allowed. In 1980, for example, Congress enacted a statute providing for "ex parte reexamination." Act to Amend the Patent and Trademark Laws, 35 U.S.C. §301 *et seq.* That statute (which remains in effect) gives "[a]ny person at any time" the right to "file a request for reexamination" on the basis of certain prior art "bearing on the patentability" of an already-issued patent. §§301(a)(1), 302. . . . In 1999 and 2002, Congress enacted statutes that established another, similar procedure, known as "inter partes *reexamination.*" Those statutes granted third parties greater opportunities to participate in the Patent Office's reexamination proceedings as well as in any appeal of a Patent Office decision.

In 2011, Congress enacted the statute before us. That statute modifies "inter partes *reexamination,*" which it now calls "inter partes *review.*" Like inter partes reexamination, any third party can ask the agency to initiate inter partes review of a patent claim. But the new statute has changed the standard that governs the Patent Office's institution of the agency's process. Instead of requiring that a request for reexamination raise a "substantial new question of patentability," it now requires that a petition show "a reasonable likelihood that" the challenger "would prevail."

The new statute provides a challenger with broader participation rights. It creates within the Patent Office a Patent Trial and Appeal Board (Board) composed of administrative patent judges, who are patent lawyers and former patent examiners, among others. That Board conducts the proceedings, reaches a conclusion, and sets forth its reasons.

The statute sets forth time limits for completing this review. It grants the Patent Office the authority to issue rules. Like its predecessors, the statute authorizes judicial review of a "final written decision" canceling a patent claim. And, the statute says that the agency's initial decision "whether to institute an inter partes review" is "final and nonappealable." §314(d). . . .

B

In 2002, Giuseppe A. Cuozzo applied for a patent covering a speedometer that will show a driver when he is driving above the speed limit. To understand the basic idea, think of the fact that a white speedometer needle will look red when it passes under a translucent piece of red glass or the equivalent (say, red cellophane). . . . If we attach the red glass to a plate that can itself rotate, if we attach the plate to the speedometer, if we connect the plate to a Global Positioning System (GPS) receiver, and if we enter onto a chip or a disk all the speed limits on all the Nation's roads, then the GPS can signal where the car is, the chip or disk can signal the speed limit at that place, and the plate can rotate to the right number on the speedometer. Thus, if the speed limit is 35 miles per hour, then the white speedometer needle will pass under the red plate at 35, . . . and the driver will know if he is driving too fast.

In 2004, the Patent Office granted the patent. See U.S. Patent No. 6,778,074 (Cuozzo Patent). . . .

C

Petitioner Cuozzo Speed Technologies, LLC (Cuozzo), now holds the rights to the Cuozzo Patent. In 2012, Garmin International, Inc., and Garmin USA, Inc., filed a petition seeking inter partes review of the Cuozzo Patent's 20 claims. Garmin backed up its request by stating, for example, that the invention described in claim 17 was obvious in light of three prior patents. . . .

The Board agreed to reexamine claim 17, as well as claims 10 and 14. The Board recognized that Garmin had not expressly challenged claim 10 and claim 14 on the same obviousness ground. But, believing that "claim 17 depends on claim 14 which depends on claim 10," the Board reasoned that Garmin had "implicitly" challenged claims 10 and 14 on the basis of the same prior inventions, and it consequently decided to review all three claims together.

After proceedings before the Board, it concluded that claims 10, 14, and 17 of the Cuozzo Patent were obvious in light of the earlier patents to which Garmin had referred. . . . The Board also concluded that Cuozzo's proposed amendments would not cure this defect, and it consequently denied Cuozzo's motion to amend its claims. Ultimately, it ordered claims 10, 14, and 17 of the Cuozzo Patent canceled.

Cuozzo appealed to the United States Court of Appeals for the Federal Circuit. Cuozzo argued that the Patent Office improperly instituted inter partes review, at least in respect to claims 10 and 14, because the agency found that Garmin had only *implicitly* challenged those two claims . . . while the statute required petitions to set forth the grounds for challenge "with particularity." §312(a)(3). Cuozzo also argued that the Board, when construing the claims, improperly used the interpretive standard set forth in the Patent Office's regulation (*i.e.*, it gave those claims their "broadest reasonable construction," 37 CFR §42.100(b)), when it should have applied the standard that courts normally use when judging a patent's validity (*i.e.*, it should have given those claims their "ordinary meaning . . . as understood by a person of skill in the art," Phillips v. AWH Corp., 415 F.3d 1303, 1314 (Fed. Cir. 2005) (en banc)).

A divided panel of the Court of Appeals rejected both arguments. First, the panel majority pointed out that 35 U.S.C. §314(d) made the decision to institute inter partes review "nonappealable." Second, the panel majority affirmed the application of the broadest reasonable construction standard on the ground (among others) that the regulation was a reasonable, and hence lawful, exercise of the Patent Office's statutorily granted rulemaking authority.

We granted Cuozzo's petition for certiorari to review these two questions.

II

Like the Court of Appeals, we believe that Cuozzo's contention that the Patent Office unlawfully initiated its agency review is not appealable. For one thing, that is what §314(d) says. It states that the "determination by the [Patent Office] whether to institute an inter partes review under this section shall be *final and nonappealable*." (Emphasis added.)

For another, the legal dispute at issue is an ordinary dispute about the application of certain relevant patent statutes concerning the Patent Office's decision to institute inter partes review. . . . In our view, the "No Appeal" provision's language must, at the least, forbid an appeal that attacks a "determination . . . whether to institute" review by raising this kind of legal question and little more. §314(d).

Moreover, a contrary holding would undercut one important congressional objective, namely, giving the Patent Office significant power to revisit and revise earlier patent grants. We doubt that Congress would have granted the Patent Office this authority, including, for example, the ability to continue proceedings even after the original petitioner settles and drops out, if it had thought that the agency's final decision could be unwound under some minor statutory technicality related to its preliminary decision to institute inter partes review. . . .

The dissent, like the panel dissent in the Court of Appeals, would limit the scope of the "No Appeal" provision to *interlocutory* appeals, leaving a court free to review the initial decision to institute review in the context of the agency's final decision. We cannot accept this interpretation. It reads into the provision a limitation (to interlocutory decisions) that the language nowhere mentions and that is unnecessary. The Administrative Procedure Act already limits review to final agency decisions. 5 U.S.C. §704. The Patent Office's decision to initiate inter partes review is "preliminary," not "final." And the agency's decision to deny a petition is a matter committed to the Patent Office's discretion. See §701(a)(2). So, read as limited to such preliminary and discretionary decisions, the "No Appeal" provision would seem superfluous. The dissent also suggests that its approach is a "familiar practice," consistent with other areas of law. But the kind of initial determination at issue here—that there is a "reasonable likelihood" that the claims are unpatentable on the grounds asserted—is akin to decisions which, in other contexts, we have held to be unreviewable. See Kaley

v. United States, 571 U.S. 320, 328 (2014) ("The grand jury gets to say—without any review, oversight, or second-guessing—whether probable cause exists to think that a person committed a crime").

We recognize the "strong presumption" in favor of judicial review that we apply when we interpret statutes, including statutes that may limit or preclude review. This presumption, however, may be overcome by "clear and convincing" indications, drawn from "specific language," "specific legislative history," and "inferences of intent drawn from the statutory scheme as a whole," that Congress intended to bar review. Block v. Community Nutrition Institute, 467 U. S. 340, 349-350 (1984). That standard is met here. The dissent disagrees, and it points to Lindahl v. Office of Personnel Management, 470 U.S. 768 (1985), to support its view that, in light of this presumption, §314(d) should be read to permit judicial review of any issue bearing on the Patent Office's preliminary decision to institute inter partes review. *Lindahl* is a case about the judicial review of disability determinations for federal employees. We explained that a statute directing the Office of Personnel Management to "determine questions of disability," and making those decisions "final," "conclusive," and "not subject to review," barred a court from revisiting the "factual underpinnings of . . . disability determinations"—though it permitted courts to consider claims alleging, for example, that the Office of Personnel Management "substantial[ly] depart[ed] from important procedural rights." 470 U.S., at 771, 791. Thus, *Lindahl*'s interpretation of that statute preserved the agency's primacy over its core statutory function in accord with Congress' intent. Our interpretation of the "No Appeal" provision here has the same effect. Congress has told the *Patent Office* to determine whether inter partes review should proceed, and it has made the agency's decision "final" and "nonappealable." §314(d). Our conclusion that courts may not revisit this initial determination gives effect to this statutory command. . . .

Nevertheless, in light of §314(d)'s own text and the presumption favoring review, we emphasize that our interpretation applies where the grounds for attacking the decision to institute inter partes review consist of questions that are closely tied to the application and interpretation of statutes related to the Patent Office's decision to initiate inter partes review. This means that we need not, and do not, decide the precise effect of §314(d) on appeals that implicate constitutional questions, that depend on other less closely related statutes, or that present other questions of interpretation that reach, in terms of scope and impact, well beyond "this section." Cf. [Johnson v. Robison; Traynor v. Turnage]. Thus, contrary to the dissent's suggestion, we do not categorically preclude review of a final decision where a petition fails to give "sufficient notice" such that there is a due process problem with the entire proceeding, nor does our interpretation enable the agency to act outside its statutory limits by, for example, canceling a patent claim for "indefiniteness under §112" in inter partes review. Such "shenanigans" may be properly reviewable in the context of §319 and under the Administrative Procedure Act . . . .

[The portion of the Court's opinion upholding the Patent Office's rule is discussed in Chapter II, *supra.*]

For the reasons set forth above, we affirm the judgment of the Court of Appeals for the Federal Circuit.

It is so ordered.

JUSTICE ALITO, with whom JUSTICE SOTOMAYOR joins, concurring in part and dissenting in part. . . .

We have long recognized that "Congress rarely intends to prevent courts from enforcing its directives to federal agencies. For that reason, this Court applies a 'strong presumption' favoring judicial review of administrative action." . . . Our decision in *Lindahl* illustrates the power of this presumption. The statute at issue there provided that agency "'decisions . . . concerning [questions of disability and dependency] are final and conclusive and are not subject to review.'" . . . We acknowledged that the statute "plausibly c[ould] be read as imposing an absolute bar to judicial review," but we concluded that "it also quite naturally c[ould] be read as precluding review only of . . . *factual* determinations" underlying the agency's decision, while permitting review of legal questions. In light of the presumption of reviewability, we adopted the latter reading. We observed that "when Congress intends to bar judicial review altogether, it typically employs language far more unambiguous and comprehensive," giving as an example a statute that made an agency decision "'final and conclusive for all purposes and with respect to all questions of law or fact'" and "'not subject to review by another official of the United States or by a court by mandamus or otherwise.'" [470 U.S.], at 779-780, and n.13.

This is a far easier case than *Lindahl.* There is no question that the statute now before us can naturally — perhaps most naturally — be read to permit judicial review of issues bearing on the Patent Office's institution of inter partes review. . . . Unlike the statutes we addressed in *Lindahl* (including the one we found to permit review), §314(d) does not say that an institution decision is "not subject to review." Instead, it makes the institution decision "nonappealable." This is fairly interpreted to bar only an *appeal* from the institution decision itself, while allowing *review* of institution-related issues in an appeal from the Patent Office's final written decision at the end of the proceeding. Our cases have used the term "nonappealable" in just this way — to refer to matters that are not *immediately* or *independently* appealable, but which are subject to review at a later point. Thus, while the decision to institute inter partes review is "final and nonappealable" in the sense that a court cannot stop the proceeding from going forward, the question whether it was lawful to institute review will not escape judicial scrutiny. This approach is consistent with the normal rule that a party may challenge earlier agency rulings that are themselves "not directly reviewable" when seeking review of a final, appealable decision. 5 U.S.C. §704. And it strikes a sensible balance: The Patent Office may proceed unimpeded with the inter partes review process (which must normally be completed within one year, see §316(a)(11)), but it will be held to account for its compliance with the law at the end of the day.

In rejecting this commonsense interpretation, the Court . . . objects that allowing judicial review "would undercut one important congressional objective, namely, giving the Patent Office significant power to revisit and revise earlier patent grants." I am not sure that the Court appreciates how remarkable this assertion is. It would give us cause to do away with judicial review whenever we think that review makes it harder for an agency to carry out important work. In any event, the majority's logic is flawed. Judicial review enforces the limits that *Congress* has imposed on the agency's power. It thus serves to buttress, not "undercut," Congress's objectives. . . . The inter partes review statute . . . empowers the Patent Office to clean up bad patents, but it expressly forbids the Patent Office to institute inter partes review—or even consider petitions for inter partes review—unless certain conditions are satisfied. Nothing in the statute suggests that Congress wanted to improve patent quality at the cost of fidelity to the law.

The Court also observes that the inter partes review appeal provision, §319, "limit[s] appellate review to the 'final written decision.'" The majority reads too much into this provision. Section 319 provides simply that "[a] party dissatisfied with the final written decision . . . may appeal the decision." The statute does not restrict the issues that may be raised in such an appeal. . . .

The Court next contends that my interpretation renders §314(d) "superfluous." Reading the statute to defer review of institution decisions is "unnecessary," the Court says, because the "Administrative Procedure Act already limits review to final agency decisions" and a "decision to initiate inter partes review is 'preliminary,' not 'final.'" But Congress reasonably may have thought that the matter needed clarifying . . . . Language is not superfluous when it "remove[s] any doubt" about a point that might otherwise be unclear. More important, my reading prevents an appeal from a decision *not* to institute inter partes review, which is plainly final agency action and so—absent §314(d)—might otherwise trigger immediate review. The Court asserts that this too is unnecessary because, in its view, a decision to deny inter partes review is "committed to agency discretion by law" and so unreviewable under normal principles of administrative law. 5 U.S.C. §701(a)(2). I agree that one can infer from the statutory scheme that the Patent Office has discretion to deny inter partes review even if a challenger satisfies the threshold requirements for review. But the law does not say so directly and Congress may not have thought the point self-evident. . . .

NOTES AND QUESTIONS

1. *Intepreting preclusionary statutes.* As Justice Breyer recognizes, the "strong presumption" in favor of judicial review implies that statutes purporting to preclude review must be interpreted narrowly. But how narrowly? Is the evidence that Breyer cites sufficiently "clear and convincing" to overcome that presumption? On the other hand, is Justice Alito demanding too much of Congress, in effect specifying a particular form of words that Congress must use to preclude review?

2. Lindahl *and* Cuozzo. Justices Breyer and Alito spar over the application of the Court's *Lindahl* decision. In that case, the Office of Personal Management (OPM) had denied a disability claim by Lindahl, a federal employee. Lindahl sought judicial review, claiming that OPM imposed the burden of proof on Lindahl to prove that he was disabled, in violation of OPM rules that said the employing agency had the burden to prove non-disability. The Supreme Court ruled that the claim was reviewable, because the statute (quoted in Breyer's and Alito's opinions) barred only review of "factual" disability determinations, not review of "legal and procedural issues." Is Alito correct in saying that *Cuozzo* "is a far easier case than *Lindahl*"? Or is Breyer right in saying, in effect, that *Cuozzo* is just a different case than *Lindahl*?

3. *Precluding versus channeling review.* The dispute between Breyer and Alito is a dispute about whether the statute precludes review altogether or channels review. In taking the latter position, Alito claims that the statute merely precludes interlocutory review of a decision by the Director to institute inter partes review, permitting review of that decision once the Board renders its patentability ruling. Given the general rule against interlocutory review stated in APA §704, is that reading plausible? Is the application of §704 sufficiently ambiguous that Congress might feel the need to clarify its application in this context? Suppose that the Director had *denied* a petition for inter partes review. Would the petitioner have any judicial recourse? If not, how would Alito explain the asymmetrical treatment (no review of denial; review, albeit delayed, of a grant)?

In addition to the general prohibition on interlocutory appeals from preliminary agency actions, many federal statutes channel review by creating a particular review mechanism or by specifying the timing of review. While such statutes are not, strictly speaking, "preclusionary" statutes, they often have the practical effect of precluding judicial review and invariably present interpretive problems of their own. The following case study provides an illustration.

The Immigration and Naturalization Service (INS) was a unit within the Department of Justice with responsibility for many aspects of government authority over immigration, including administration of the various provisions of the Immigration Reform and Control Act of 1986. (After the attacks of September 11, 2001, the INS was abolished. Its former responsibilities are now carried out by U.S. Citizenship and Immigration Services (USCIS), U.S. Immigration and Customs Enforcement (ICE), and U.S. Customs and Border Protection (CBP), all within the Department of Homeland Security.) During the 1980s, undocumented immigration to the United States became a major political issue, and Congress ultimately passed the Act, which, while legalizing certain classes of previously undocumented aliens, was designed to make it more difficult for the remaining undocumented immigrants to work and thus live in the United States. The Act's amnesty provisions for previously illegal immigrants require the INS to make factual determinations regarding applicants' presence in the United States and their work histories. The INS's administration of the Act spawned a great deal of litigation, including the following case regarding the INS's procedures in one program for agricultural workers.

McNARY v. HAITIAN REFUGEE CENTER, INC.
498 U.S. 479 (1991)

JUSTICE STEVENS delivered the opinion of the Court.[*]

The Immigration Reform and Control Act of 1986 (Reform Act)[1] constituted a major statutory response to the vast tide of illegal immigration that had produced a "shadow population" of literally millions of undocumented aliens

---

[*] Justice White joins only Parts I, II, III, and IV of this opinion.

[1] Immigration Reform and Control Act of 1986, Pub. L. 99-603, 100 Stat. 3359.

in the United States. On the one hand, Congress sought to stem the tide by making the plight of the undocumented alien even more onerous in the future than it had been in the past; thus, the Reform Act imposed criminal sanctions on employers who hired undocumented workers and made a number of federally funded welfare benefits unavailable to these aliens. On the other hand, in recognition that a large segment of the shadow population played a useful and constructive role in the American economy, but continued to reside in perpetual fear, the Reform Act established two broad amnesty programs to allow existing undocumented aliens to emerge from the shadows. . . .

The second program required the Attorney General to adjust the status of any alien farmworker who could establish that he or she had resided in the United States and performed at least 90 days of qualifying agricultural work during the 12-month period prior to May 1, 1986, provided that the alien could also establish his or her admissibility in the United States as an immigrant. The Reform Act required the Attorney General first to adjust the status of these aliens to "Special Agricultural Workers" (SAW) lawfully admitted for temporary residence, see 100 Stat. 3417, as amended, 8 U.S.C. §1160(a)(1), and then eventually to aliens lawfully admitted for permanent residence, see §1160(a)(2).

This case relates only to the SAW amnesty program. [T]he only question presented to us is whether §210(e) of the Immigration and Nationality Act (INA), which was added by §302(a) of the Reform Act and sets forth the administrative and judicial review provisions of the SAW program, see 8 U.S.C. §1160(e), precludes a federal district court from exercising general federal question jurisdiction over an action alleging a pattern or practice of procedural due process violations by the Immigration and Naturalization Service (INS) in its administration of the SAW program. We hold that given the absence of clear congressional language mandating preclusion of federal jurisdiction and the nature of respondents' requested relief, the District Court had jurisdiction to hear respondents' constitutional and statutory challenges to INS procedures. Were we to hold otherwise and instead require respondents to avail themselves of the limited judicial review procedures set forth in §210(e) of the INA, meaningful judicial review of their statutory and constitutional claims would be foreclosed.

I . . .

The Reform Act provided that SAW status applications could be filed with a specially created Legalization Office (LO), or with a QDE,* which would forward applications to the appropriate LO, during an 18-month period commencing on June 1, 1987. See §1160(b)(1)(A). Regulations adopted by the INS to administer the program provided for a personal interview of each applicant at an LO. See 8 CFR §210.2(c)(2)(iv)(1990). In the application, the alien had to prove by a preponderance of the evidence that he or she worked the requisite 90 days of qualifying seasonal agricultural services. See §210.3(a), (b)(1). To meet the burden of proof, the applicant was required to present evidence of eligibility

---

* [A "Qualified Designated Entity," which includes qualified farm labor organizations, associations of agricultural employers, and state, local, and community groups. QDEs were not allowed to forward applications for SAW status to the Attorney General unless the applicant consented. —Eds.]

independent of his or her own testimony. *See* §210.3(b)(2). The applicant could meet this burden through production of his or her employer's payroll records, *see* 8 U.S.C. §1160(b)(3)(B)(ii), or through submission of affidavits "by agricultural producers, foremen, farm labor contractors, union officials, fellow employees, or other persons with specific knowledge of the applicant's employment." *See* 8 CFR §210.3(c)(3) (1990). At the conclusion of the interview and of the review of the application materials, the LO could deny the application or make a recommendation to a regional processing facility that the application be either granted or denied. *See id.*, at §210.1(q). A denial, whether at the regional or local level, could be appealed to the legalization appeals unit, which was authorized to make the final administrative decision in each individual case. *See* §103.3(a)(2)(iii).

The Reform Act expressly prohibited judicial review of such a final administrative determination of SAW status except as authorized by §210(e)(3)(A) of the amended INA. That subsection permitted "judicial review of such a denial only in the judicial review of an order of exclusion or deportation."[6] In view of the fact that the courts of appeals constitute the only fora for judicial review of deportation orders, *see* 75 Stat. 651, as amended, 8 U.S.C. §1105a, the statute plainly foreclosed any review in the district courts of individual denials of SAW status applications. Moreover, absent initiation of a deportation proceeding against an unsuccessful applicant, judicial review of such individual determinations was completely foreclosed.

II

This action was filed in the District Court for the Southern District of Florida by the Haitian Refugee Center, the Migration and Refugee Services of the Roman Catholic Diocese of Palm Beach, and 17 unsuccessful individual SAW applicants. The plaintiffs sought relief on behalf of a class of alien farmworkers who either

---

6. The full text of §210(e) of the INA, as set forth in 8 U.S.C. §1160(e), reads as follows:
   "(e) Administrative and judicial review
   "(1) Administrative and judicial review
   "There shall be no administrative or judicial review of a determination respecting an application for adjustment of status under this section except in accordance with this subsection.
      "(2) Administrative review
         "(A) Single level of administrative appellate review
      "The Attorney General shall establish an appellate authority to provide for a single level of administrative appellate review of such a determination.
         "(B) Standard for review
      "Such administrative appellate review shall be based solely upon the administrative record established at the time of the determination on the application and upon such additional or newly discovered evidence as may not have been available at the time of determination.
      "(3) Judicial review
         "(A) Limitation to review of exclusion or deportation
      "There shall be judicial review of such a denial only in the judicial review of an order of exclusion or deportation under section 1105a of this title.
         "(B) Standard for judicial review
      "Such judicial review shall be based solely upon the administrative record established at the time of the review by the appellate authority and the findings of fact and determinations contained in such record shall be conclusive unless the applicant can establish abuse of discretion or that the findings are directly contrary to clear and convincing facts contained in the record considered as a whole."

had been or would be injured by unlawful practices and policies adopted by the INS in its administration of the SAW program. The complaint alleged that the interview process was conducted in an arbitrary fashion that deprived applicants of the due process guaranteed by the Fifth Amendment to the Constitution. Among other charges, the plaintiffs alleged that INS procedures did not allow SAW applicants to be apprised of or to be given opportunity to challenge adverse evidence on which denials were predicated, that applicants were denied the opportunity to present witnesses on their own behalf, that non-English speaking Haitian applicants were unable to communicate effectively with LOs because competent interpreters were not provided, and that no verbatim recording of the interview was made, thus inhibiting even any meaningful administrative review of application denials by LOs or regional processing facilities. . . .

III

At no time in this litigation have petitioners asserted a right to employ arbitrary procedures, or questioned their obligation to afford SAW status applicants due process of law.

Nor, at this stage of the litigation, is there any dispute that the INS routinely and persistently violated the Constitution and statutes in processing SAW applications. . . . The narrow issue, therefore, is whether §210(e), which bars judicial review of individual determinations except in deportation proceedings, also forecloses this general challenge to the INS's unconstitutional practices.

IV

Petitioners' entire jurisdictional argument rests on their view that respondents' constitutional challenge is an action seeking "judicial review of a determination respecting an application for adjustment of status" and that district court jurisdiction over the action is therefore barred by the plain language of §210(e)(1) of the amended INA. *See* 8 U.S.C. §1160(e)(1). The critical words in §210(e)(1), however, describe the provision as referring only to review "of *a determination* respecting *an application*" for SAW status (emphasis added). Significantly, the reference to "a determination" describes a single act rather than a group of decisions or a practice or procedure employed in making decisions. Moreover, when §210(e)(3), *see* 8 U.S.C. §1160 (e)(3), further clarifies that the only judicial review permitted is in the context of a deportation proceeding, it refers to "judicial review of"—again referring to a single act, and again making clear that the earlier reference to "a determination respecting an application" described the denial of an individual application. We therefore agree with the District Court's and the Court of Appeals' reading of this language as describing the process of direct review of individual denials of SAW status, rather than as referring to general collateral challenges to unconstitutional practices and policies used by the agency in processing applications.

This reading of the Reform Act's review provision is supported by the language in §210(e)(3)(B) of the INA, which provides that judicial review "shall be based solely upon the administrative record established at the time of the review by the appellate authority and the findings of fact and determinations contained in such record shall be conclusive unless the applicant can establish abuse of discretion or that the findings are directly contrary to clear and convincing facts contained in the record considered as a whole." 8 U.S.C. §1160 (e)(3)(B). This provision incorporates an assumption that the limited review provisions of §210(e) apply only to claims that have been subjected to administrative consideration and that have resulted in the creation of an adequate administrative record. However, the record created during the SAW administrative review process consists solely of a completed application form, a report of medical examination, any documents or affidavits that evidence an applicant's agricultural employment and residence, and notes, if any, from an LO interview—all relating to a single SAW applicant. Because the administrative appeals process does not address the kind of procedural and constitutional claims respondents bring in this action, limiting judicial review of these claims to the procedures set forth in §210(e) is not contemplated by the language of that provision.

Moreover, the "abuse of discretion" standard of judicial review under §210(e)(3)(B) would make no sense if we were to read the Reform Act as requiring constitutional and statutory challenges to INS procedures to be subject to its specialized review provision. Although the abuse-of-discretion standard is appropriate for judicial review of an administrative adjudication of the facts of an individual application for SAW status, such a standard does not apply to constitutional or statutory claims, which are reviewed de novo by the courts. The language of §210(e)(3)(B) thus lends substantial credence to the conclusion that the Reform Act's review provision does not apply to challenges to INS's practices and procedures in administering the SAW program.

Finally, we note that had Congress intended the limited review provisions of §210(e) of the INA to encompass challenges to INS procedures and practices, it could easily have used broader statutory language. Congress could, for example, have modeled §210(e) on the more expansive language in the general grant of district court jurisdiction under Title II of the INA by channeling into the Reform Act's special review procedures "all causes . . . arising under any of the provisions" of the legalization program. 66 Stat. 230, 8 U.S.C. §1329. It moreover could have modeled §210(e) on 38 U.S.C. §211(a), which governs review of veterans' benefits claims, by referring to review "on all questions of law and fact" under the SAW legalization program.

Given Congress' choice of statutory language, we conclude that challenges to the procedures used by INS do not fall within the scope of §210(e). Rather, we hold that §210(e) applies only to review of denials of individual SAW applications. Because respondents' action does not seek review on the merits of a denial of a particular application, the District Court's general federal question jurisdiction under 28 U.S.C. §1331 to hear this action remains unimpaired by §210(e). . . .

[I]f not allowed to pursue their claims in the District Court, respondents would not as a practical matter be able to obtain meaningful judicial review of their application denials or of their objections to INS procedures notwithstanding the review provisions of §210(e) of the amended INA. It is presumable that Congress legislates with knowledge of our basic rules of statutory construction, and given our well-settled presumption favoring interpretations of statutes that allow judicial review of administrative action . . . coupled with the limited review provisions of §210(e), it is most unlikely that Congress intended to foreclose all forms of meaningful judicial review.

Several aspects of this statutory scheme would preclude review of respondents' application denials if we were to hold that the District Court lacked jurisdiction to hear this challenge. Initially, administrative or judicial review of an agency decision is almost always confined to the record made in the proceeding at the initial decisionmaking level, and one of the central attacks on INS procedures in this litigation is based on the claim that such procedures do not allow applicants to assemble adequate records. . . .

Additionally, because there is no provision for direct judicial review of the denial of SAW status unless the alien is later apprehended and deportation proceedings are initiated, most aliens denied SAW status can ensure themselves review in courts of appeals only if they voluntarily surrender themselves for deportation. Quite obviously, that price is tantamount to a complete denial of judicial review for most undocumented aliens.

Finally, even in the context of a deportation proceeding, it is unlikely that a court of appeals would be in a position to provide meaningful review of the type of claims raised in this litigation. To establish the unfairness of the INS practices, respondents in this case adduced a substantial amount of evidence, most of which would have been irrelevant in the processing of a particular individual application. Not only would a court of appeals reviewing an individual SAW determination therefore most likely not have an adequate record as to the pattern of INS's allegedly unconstitutional practices, but it also would lack the factfinding and record-developing capabilities of a federal district court. . . . It therefore seems plain to us, as it did to the District Court and the Court of Appeals, that restricting judicial review to the courts of appeals as a component of the review of an individual deportation order is the practical equivalent of a total denial of judicial review of generic constitutional and statutory claims. . . .

The strong presumption in favor of judicial review of administrative action is not overcome either by the language or the purpose of the relevant provisions of the Reform Act.

The judgment of the Court of Appeals is affirmed.

It is so ordered.

CHIEF JUSTICE REHNQUIST, with whom JUSTICE SCALIA, joins, dissenting. . . .

The [statute states] as clearly as any language can, that judicial review of a "determination respecting an application for adjustment of status under this section" may not be had except in accordance with the provisions of the subsection. The plain language of subsection (3)(A) provides that judicial review of a denial may be had only in connection with review of an order of exclusion or deportation. The Court chooses to read this language as dealing only with "direct review of individual denials of SAW status, rather than as referring to general collateral challenges to unconstitutional practices and policies used by the agency in processing applications." But the accepted view of judicial review of administrative action generally—even when there is no express preclusion provision as there is in the present statute—is that only "final actions" are reviewable in court. The Administrative Procedure Act provides: "[F]inal agency action for which there is no other adequate remedy in a court [is] subject to judicial review. A preliminary, procedural, or intermediate agency action or ruling not directly reviewable is subject to review on the review of the final agency action." 5 U.S.C. §704.

The Court's reasoning is thus a classic non sequitur. It reasons that because Congress limited judicial review only of what were in effect final administrative decisions, it must not have intended to preclude separate challenges to procedures used by the agency before it issued any final decision. But the type of judicial review of agency action which the Court finds that Congress failed to preclude is a type not generally available even without preclusion. In the light of this settled rule, the natural reading of "determination respecting an application" in §1160(e) encompasses both final decisions and procedures used to reach those decisions. Each of respondents' claims attacks the process used by Immigration and Naturalization Service (INS) to make a determination respecting an application.

We have on several occasions rejected the argument advanced by respondents that individual plaintiffs can bypass restrictions on judicial review by purporting to attack general policies rather than individual results. . . .

It is well settled that when Congress has established a particular review mechanism, courts are not free to fashion alternatives to the specified scheme. . . . In creating the Reform Act and the SAW program, Congress balanced the goals of the unprecedented amnesty programs with the need "to insure reasonably prompt determinations" in light of the incentives and opportunity for ineligible applicants to delay the disposition of their cases and derail the program. The Court's ponderously reasoned gloss on the statute's plain language sanctions an unwarranted intrusion into a carefully drafted congressional program, a program which placed great emphasis on a minimal amount of paperwork and procedure in an effort to speed the process of adjusting the status of those aliens who demonstrated their entitlement to adjustment. "If the balance is to be struck anew, the decision must come from Congress and not from this Court." [Heckler v. Ringer, 466 U.S. 602, 627 (1984).]

The Court bases its conclusion that district courts have jurisdiction to entertain respondents' pattern and practice allegations in part out of "respect [for] the 'strong presumption that Congress intends judicial review of administrative action'" (quoting Bowen v. Michigan Academy of Family Physicians, 476 U.S. 667, 670 (1986)). This presumption, however, comes into play only where there is a genuine ambiguity as to whether Congress intended to preclude judicial review of administrative action. . . . Therefore, since the statute is not ambiguous, the presumption has no force here.

The Court indicates that this presumption of judicial review is particularly applicable in cases raising constitutional challenges to agency action. I believe that Congress intended to preclude judicial review of such claims in this instance, and that in this context it is permissible for it to do so. . . .

Given the structure of the Act, and the status of these alien respondents, it is extremely doubtful that the operation of the administrative process in their cases would give rise to any colorable constitutional claims. "'An alien who seeks political rights as a member of this Nation can rightfully obtain them only upon terms and conditions specified by Congress. Courts are without authority to sanction changes or modifications; their duty is rigidly to enforce the legislative will in respect of a matter so vital to the public welfare.'" INS v. Pangilinan, 486 U.S. 875, 884 (1988) (quoting United States v. Ginsberg, 243 U.S. 472, 474 (1917)).

Respondents are undoubtedly entitled to the benefit of those procedures which Congress has accorded them in the Reform Act. But there is no reason to believe that administrative appeals as provided in the Act—which simply have not been resorted to by these respondents before suing in the District Court—would not have assured them compliance with statutory procedures. The Court never mentions what colorable constitutional claims these aliens, illegally present in the United States, could have had that demand judicial review. The most that can be said for respondents' case in this regard is that it is conceivable, though not likely, that the administrative processing of their claims could be handled in such a way as to deny them some constitutional right, and that the remedy of requesting deportation in order to obtain judicial review is a burdensome one. We have never held, however, that Congress may not, by explicit language, preclude judicial review of constitutional claims, and here, where that body was obviously interested in expeditiously processing an avalanche of claims from noncitizens upon whom it was conferring a substantial benefit, I think it may do so.

NOTES AND QUESTIONS

1. *Interpretation of statutes that "channel" judicial review.* How must Justice Stevens interpret §210(e) in order to avoid its channeling effect? Assume that, in an administrative exclusion or deportation proceeding, the immigrant would be entitled to the full panoply of procedures required by due process and would be able to challenge both the factual and legal basis for the agency's action. Assume also that an administrative expulsion or deportation order is subject to judicial review. Are there any issues raised by the plaintiffs in the *McNary* case that could not have been raised in such a petition for review? Is the key to *McNary* that the plaintiffs were raising constitutional issues? In fact they also made procedural claims based on statute. Should those claims have been barred by §210(e)?

2. *Breadth of channeling provisions and the "effectiveness" of review.* In another channeling case, Shalala v. Illinois Council on Long Term Care, Inc., 529 U.S. 1 (2000), the Court held, unlike *McNary*, that the channeling provision precluded a general challenge to agency regulations and procedures. In *Shalala*, an association of nursing homes brought suit under 28 U.S.C. §1331 (general federal question jurisdiction) to challenge, on substantive and procedural grounds, regulations governing sanctions for noncompliance with the requirements of the Medicare Act and regulations promulgated thereunder. The Medicare Act grants the Secretary of Health and Human Services the power to assess penalties on or terminate the Medicare eligibility of nursing homes that violate the Act or regulations and grants a hearing to any terminated or penalized home. The Act also specifies that a home may seek judicial review, under a provision of the Act, in a federal district court, of "any final decision of the [Secretary] made after a hearing." The Act also precludes any other form of review: "No action against the United States, the Secretary of Health and Human Services, or any officer or employee thereof shall be brought under section 1331 [federal question

jurisdiction] or 1346 [federal defendant jurisdiction] of title 28 to recover on any claim arising under this subchapter." 42 U.S.C. §405(h); 42 U.S.C. §1395ii.

The Illinois Council argued that the channeling provision was limited to "amount determinations" and did not apply to general challenges to the agency's regulations and procedures for enacting regulations. The Court disagreed, holding that the channeling provision applied to general challenges as well as individual amount determinations. The Court reasoned:

> Claims for money, claims for other benefits, claims of program eligibility, and claims that contest a sanction or remedy may all similarly rest upon individual fact determinations, or may all similarly involve the application, interpretation, or constitutionality of interrelated regulations or statutory provisions. There is no reason to distinguish among them in terms of the language or in terms of the purposes of §405(h).

529 U.S. at 14. The Court distinguished *McNary* on the basis that "[*McNary*'s] outcome, however, turned on the different language of that different statute." *Id.* The Court also noted that it had suggested, in its *McNary* opinion, that the Medicare Act's preclusion of review was broader than the statute at issue in that case. Are *Shalala* and *McNary* consistent on the distinction between review of particular decisions and challenges to the overall operation of a program? Should they be?

An issue unique to channeling cases is whether the particular review mechanism allows for effective review of the type of claim being raised. In *McNary*, for example, it was important to the Court that confining the plaintiffs in that case to the specific review procedure would have amounted to the "practical equivalent of a total denial of judicial review." *McNary*, 498 U.S. at 497. In *Shalala*, by contrast, the Court found that meaningful review was available under the specified procedure, and held that the plaintiff in that case could not circumvent the specified procedure by filing suit against the administrator under the general federal question statute, 28 U.S.C. §1331. Should the decision whether review is "channeled" turn, even partly, on whether the specific review provision provides effective review?

3. *Pattern and practice challenges as an "end-run" around preclusion of review.* Is it important in *McNary* that the plaintiffs objected to a "pattern and practice" of alleged procedural violations, rather than procedural violations in an individual case? Was that just a clever litigation ploy to avoid the channeling provision? How can the Court's willingness to review a "pattern and practice" in *McNary* be reconciled with *SUWA*'s holding that only "discrete" actions can be reviewed under the APA?

The use of "pattern and practice" claims to circumvent preclusion-of-review statutes has also arisen in the context of the Comprehensive Environmental Response, Compensation, and Liability Act of 1980 (CERCLA). Section 106 of CERCLA permits EPA to issue "unilateral administrative orders" (UAOs), requiring a property owner or polluter to clean up hazardous wastes if EPA determines that there is "an imminent and substantial endangerment" to public health or the environment. 42 U.S.C. §9606(a). But §113 of CERCLA provides that "[n]o Federal court shall have jurisdiction . . . to review . . . any [UAO]" until either cleanup is complete or EPA brings an enforcement action. *Id.* §9613(h).

In City of Rialto v. West Coast Loading Corp., 581 F.3d 865 (9th Cir. 2009), a corporation that had received a UAO to clean up an industrial site brought a claim alleging that, in administering CERCLA, the EPA followed a "pattern and practice" that violated the Due Process Clause of the Fifth Amendment. More specifically, it alleged that the EPA "routinely" issues emergency orders "where no conceivable emergency exists"; "obstruct[s] judicial review of those orders by delaying its discretionary certification of completion"; and "manipulat[es] the 'Record of Decision' which supports the agency's selection of a response action." 581 F.3d at 869. The Ninth Circuit defined its analysis of a pattern and practice claim as follows: "We first ask whether the claim brings a collateral, procedural challenge to EPA's practices, where no meaningful judicial review is otherwise available. If so, we next ask whether the claim is ripe." *Id.* at 875. To both questions, the Court answered no. Because "*McNary* was not meant to oust normal administrative procedures and other prerequisites to judicial review, except in certain exceptional circumstances," and CERCLA grants meaningful judicial review when a claim is ripe and administrative remedies have been exhausted, *McNary* could not be used as an end-run around administrative procedural requirements. *Id.* at 877-878. *But see* General Electric Co. v. Jackson, 610 F.3d 110 (D.C. Cir. 2010) (while CERCLA precludes review of individual agency actions, it does not preclude review of "pattern and practice" challenges to the EPA's administration of the statute).

4. *Statutory versus regulatory preclusion.* May an agency expand the reach of a statutory preclusion provision by regulation? In Kucana v. Holder, 558 U.S. 233 (2010), an Albanian citizen's business visa expired, and the Bureau of Immigration Appeals denied both his plea for asylum and his motion to re-open removal proceedings on grounds of new evidence. The Illegal Immigration Reform and Immigrant Responsibility Act of 1996 (IIRIRA) states that "no court has jurisdiction to review any action of the Attorney General 'the authority for which is specified under this subchapter to be in the discretion of the Attorney General,'" and the Attorney General had promulgated a regulation providing that the decision to reopen an asylum petition is within the BIA's discretion. The government argued that IIRIRA's preclusion of judicial review applied not only to Attorney General determinations made discretionary by statute, but also to determinations that the Attorney General declares to be discretionary through regulations. The Supreme Court, citing *McNary*, held that determinations made discretionary via regulations may be reviewed even where the statute precludes judicial review of determinations made discretionary via statute. Thus, the Court indicated in *Kucana* that an agency may not expand the limitations on judicial review prescribed by Congress in the agency's enabling statute.

3.   Committed to Agency Discretion by Law

The second of §701(a)'s exceptions to the general availability of judicial review of agency action is where "agency action is committed to agency discretion by law." This provision was interpreted in *Overton Park*, excerpted in Chapter II, *supra*, to bar judicial review where there is "no law [for a court] to apply." The materials in this section explore what agencies must show to satisfy this test.

a. General Principles

The Central Intelligence Agency (CIA) was created by the National Security Act of 1947 and operates as the primary foreign intelligence-gathering agency of the U.S. government. The CIA is led by the Director of Central Intelligence who is appointed by the President with the advice and consent of the Senate and reports to the Director of National Intelligence. At the time the following case reached the Supreme Court, there was a widely shared view in military and intelligence agencies that gay employees posed a risk to national security because they might be easily subject to blackmail. Many gay and lesbian federal employees understandably kept their sexuality a secret out of fear that they would be dismissed if this information were revealed. Until the Supreme Court's decision in Romer v. Evans, 517 U.S. 620 (1996), private consensual gay sex was criminal in many American states and was not protected by the constitutional right to privacy or equal protection. And until fairly recently, gay and lesbian employees fired from their public and private sector jobs had little legal recourse in state or federal courts. Federal policies denied security clearances to these employees until the 1980s and subjected them to invasive questioning well into the 1990s. The case that follows concerns the reviewability of statutory and constitutional challenges to a decision by the Director of Central Intelligence to discharge a "covert electronics technician" because he was gay.

WEBSTER v. DOE
486 U.S. 592 (1988)

Chief Justice Rehnquist delivered the opinion of the Court.

Section 102(c) of the National Security Act of 1947, 61 Stat. 498, as amended, provides that:

> [T]he Director of Central Intelligence may, in his discretion, terminate the employment of any officer or employee of the Agency whenever he shall deem such termination necessary or advisable in the interests of the United States. . . . (50 U.S.C. §403(c).)

In this case we decide whether, and to what extent, the termination decisions of the Director under §102(c) are judicially reviewable.

I

Respondent John Doe was first employed by the Central Intelligence Agency (CIA or Agency) in 1973 as a clerk-typist. He received periodic fitness reports that consistently rated him as an excellent or outstanding employee. By 1977, respondent had been promoted to a position as a covert electronics technician.

In January 1982, respondent voluntarily informed a CIA security officer that he was a homosexual. Almost immediately, the Agency placed respondent on paid administrative leave pending an investigation of his sexual orientation and conduct. On February 12 and again on February 17, respondent was extensively questioned by a polygraph officer concerning his homosexuality and possible security violations. Respondent denied having sexual relations with any foreign nationals and maintained that he had not disclosed classified information to any of his sexual partners. After these interviews, the officer told respondent that the polygraph tests indicated that he had truthfully answered all questions. The polygraph officer then prepared a five-page summary of his interviews with respondent, to which respondent was allowed to attach a two-page addendum.

On April 14, 1982, a CIA security agent informed respondent that the Agency's Office of Security had determined that respondent's homosexuality posed a threat to security, but declined to explain the nature of the danger. Respondent was then asked to resign. When he refused to do so, the Office of Security recommended to the CIA Director (petitioner's predecessor) that respondent be dismissed. After reviewing respondent's records and the evaluations of his subordinates, the Director "deemed it necessary and advisable in the interests of the United States to terminate [respondent's] employment with this Agency pursuant to section 102(c) of the National Security Act. . . ." Respondent was also advised that, while the CIA would give him a positive recommendation in any future job search, if he applied for a job requiring a security clearance the Agency would inform the prospective employer that it had concluded that respondent's homosexuality presented a security threat.

Respondent then filed an action against petitioner in United States District Court for the District of Columbia. Respondent's amended complaint asserted a variety of statutory and constitutional claims against the Director. Respondent alleged that petitioner's decision to terminate his employment violated §706 of the Administrative Procedure Act (APA), because it was arbitrary and capricious, represented an abuse of discretion, and was reached without observing the procedures required by law and CIA regulations. He also complained that the Director's termination of his employment deprived him of constitutionally protected rights to property, liberty, and privacy in violation of the First, Fourth, Fifth, and Ninth Amendments. Finally, he asserted that his dismissal transgressed the procedural due process and equal protection of the laws guaranteed by the Fifth Amendment. . . .

Petitioner moved to dismiss respondent's amended complaint on the ground that §102(c) of the National Security Act (NSA) precludes judicial review of the Director's termination decisions under §§701, 702, and 706 of the APA. . . .

The Court of Appeals . . . decided that judicial review under the APA of the Agency's decision to terminate respondent was not precluded by §§701(a)(1) or (a)(2). . . . We granted certiorari to decide the question whether the Director's decision to discharge a CIA employee under §102(c) of the NSA is judicially reviewable under the APA.

II

In Citizens to Preserve Overton Park v. Volpe, 401 U.S. 402 (1971), this Court explained the distinction between §§701(a)(1) and (a)(2). Subsection (a)(1) is concerned with whether Congress expressed an intent to prohibit judicial review; subsection (a)(2) applies "in those rare instances where 'statutes are drawn in such broad terms that in a given case there is no law to apply,'" 401 U.S., at 410 (*citing* S. Rep. No. 752, 79th Cong., 1st Sess., 26 (1945)).

We further explained what it means for an action to be "committed to agency discretion by law" in Heckler v. Chaney, 470 U.S. 821 (1985). *Heckler* required the Court to determine whether the Food and Drug Administration's decision not to undertake an enforcement proceeding against the use of certain drugs in administering the death penalty was subject to judicial review. We noted that, under §701(a)(2), even when Congress has not affirmatively precluded judicial oversight, "review is not to be had if the statute is drawn so that a court would have no meaningful standard against which to judge the agency's exercise of discretion." 470 U.S., at 830. Since the statute conferring power on the Food and Drug Administration to prohibit the unlawful misbranding or misuse of drugs provided no substantive standards on which a court could base its review, we found that enforcement actions were committed to the complete discretion of the FDA to decide when and how they should be pursued.

Both *Overton Park* and *Heckler* emphasized that §701(a)(2) requires careful examination of the statute on which the claim of agency illegality is based (the Federal-Aid Highway Act of 1968 in *Overton Park* and the Federal Food, Drug, and Cosmetic Act in *Heckler*). In the present case, respondent's claims against the CIA arise from the Director's asserted violation of §102(c) of the National Security Act. As an initial matter, it should be noted that §102(c) allows termination of an Agency employee whenever the Director "shall *deem* such termination necessary or advisable in the interests of the United States" (emphasis added), not simply when the dismissal *is* necessary or advisable to those interests. This standard fairly exudes deference to the Director, and appears to us to foreclose the application of any meaningful judicial standard of review. Short of permitting cross-examination of the Director concerning his views of the Nation's security and whether the discharged employee was inimical to those interests, we see no basis on which a reviewing court could properly assess an Agency termination decision. The language of §102(c) thus strongly suggests that its implementation was "committed to agency discretion by law."

So too does the overall structure of the National Security Act. Passed shortly after the close of the Second World War, the NSA created the CIA and gave its Director the responsibility "for protecting intelligence sources and methods from unauthorized disclosure." *See* 50 U.S.C. §403(d)(3); S. Rep. No. 239, 80th Cong., 1st Sess., 2 (1947); H.R. Rep. No. 961, 80th Cong., 1st Sess., 3-4 (1947). Section 102(c) is an integral part of that statute, because the Agency's efficacy, and the Nation's security, depend in large measure on the reliability and trustworthiness of the Agency's employees. . . .

Th[e] overriding need for ensuring integrity in the Agency led us to uphold the Director's use of §102(d)(3) of the NSA to withhold the identities of protected intelligence sources in CIA v. Sims, 471 U.S. 159 (1985). In denying respondent's Freedom of Information Act requests in *Sims* to produce certain CIA records, we stated that "[t]he plain meaning of the statutory language, as well as the legislative history of the National Security Act, . . . indicates that Congress vested in the Director of Central Intelligence very broad authority to protect all sources of intelligence information from disclosure."

Id., at 168-169. Section 102(c), that portion of the NSA under consideration in the present case, is part and parcel of the entire Act, and likewise exhibits the Act's extraordinary deference to the Director in his decision to terminate individual employees.

We thus find that the language and structure of §102(c) indicate that Congress meant to commit individual employee discharges to the Director's discretion, and that §701(a)(2) accordingly precludes judicial review of these decisions under the APA. We reverse the Court of Appeals to the extent that it found such terminations reviewable by the courts.

III

In addition to his claim that the Director failed to abide by the statutory dictates of §102(c), respondent also alleged a number of constitutional violations in his amended complaint. Respondent charged that petitioner's termination of his employment deprived him of property and liberty interests under the Due Process Clause, denied him equal protection of the laws, and unjustifiably burdened his right to privacy. Respondent asserts that he is entitled, under the APA, to judicial consideration of these claimed violations. . . .

Petitioner maintains that, no matter what the nature of respondent's constitutional claim, judicial review is precluded by the language and intent of §102(c). In petitioner's view, all Agency employment termination decisions, even those based on policies normally repugnant to the Constitution, are given over to the absolute discretion of the Director, and are hence unreviewable under the APA. We do not think §102(c) may be read to exclude review of constitutional claims. We emphasized in Johnson v. Robison, 415 U.S. 361 (1974), that where Congress intends to preclude judicial review of constitutional claims its intent to do so must be clear. *Id.,* at 373-374. . . . We require this heightened showing in part to avoid the "serious constitutional question" that would arise if a federal statute were construed to deny any judicial forum for a colorable constitutional claim. . . .

Our review of §102(c) convinces us that it cannot bear the preclusive weight petitioner would have it support. As detailed above, the section does commit employment termination decisions to the Director's discretion, and precludes challenges to these decisions based upon the statutory language of §102(c). . . . Subsections (a)(1) and (a)(2) of §701, however, remove from judicial review only those determinations specifically identified by Congress or "committed to agency discretion by law." Nothing in §102(c) persuades us that Congress meant to preclude consideration of colorable constitutional claims arising out of the actions of the Director pursuant to that section.

Petitioner complains that judicial review even of constitutional claims will entail extensive "rummaging around" in the Agency's affairs to the detriment of national security. *See* Tr. of Oral Arg. 8-13. But petitioner acknowledges that Title VII claims attacking the hiring and promotion policies of the Agency are routinely entertained in federal court, *see* Reply Brief for Petitioner 13-14; Tr. of Oral Arg. 9, and the inquiry and discovery associated with those proceedings would seem to involve some of the same sort of rummaging. Furthermore, the District Court has the latitude to control any discovery process which may be instituted so as to balance respondent's need for access to proof which would support a colorable constitutional claim against the extraordinary needs of the CIA for confidentiality and the protection of its methods, sources, and mission. . . .

Petitioner also contends that even if respondent has raised a colorable constitutional claim arising out of his discharge, Congress in the interest of national security may deny the courts the authority to decide the claim and to order respondent's reinstatement if the claim is upheld. For the reason previously stated, we do not think Congress meant to impose such restrictions when it enacted §102(c) of the NSA. Even without such prohibitory legislation from Congress, of course, traditional equitable principles requiring the balancing of public and private interests control the grant of declaratory or injunctive relief in the federal courts. . . . On remand, the District Court should thus address respondent's constitutional claims and the propriety of the equitable remedies sought.

The judgment of the Court of Appeals is affirmed in part, reversed in part, and the case is remanded for further proceedings consistent with this opinion.

It is so ordered.

JUSTICE KENNEDY took no part in the consideration or decision of this case.

JUSTICE O'CONNOR, concurring in part and dissenting in part.

I agree that the Administrative Procedure Act (APA) does not authorize judicial review of the employment decisions referred to in §102(c) of the National Security Act. Because §102(c) does not provide a meaningful standard for judicial review, such decisions are clearly "committed to agency discretion by law" within the meaning of §701(a)(2) of the APA. I do not understand the Court to say that the exception in §701(a)(2) is necessarily or fully defined by reference to statutes "drawn in such broad terms that in a given case there is no law to apply." *See* Citizens to Preserve Overton Park v. Volpe, 401 U.S. 402, 410 (1971). Accordingly, I join Parts I and II of the Court's opinion.

I disagree, however, with the Court's conclusion that a constitutional claim challenging the validity of an employment decision covered by §102(c) may nonetheless be brought in a Federal District Court. Whatever may be the exact scope of Congress' power to close the lower federal courts to constitutional claims in other contexts, I have no doubt about its authority to do so here. The functions performed by the Central Intelligence Agency and the Director of Central Intelligence lie at the core of "the very delicate, plenary and exclusive power of the President as the sole organ of the federal government in the field of international relations." United States v. Curtiss-Wright Export Co., 299 U.S. 304 (1936). The authority of the Director of Central Intelligence to control access to sensitive national security information by discharging employees deemed to be untrustworthy flows primarily from this constitutional power of the President, and Congress may surely provide that the inferior federal courts are not used to infringe on the President's constitutional authority. *See, e.g.,* Department of the Navy v. Egan, 484 U.S. 518, 526-530 (1988); Totten v. United States, 92 U.S. (2 Otto) 105 (1875). Section §102(c) plainly indicates that

Congress has done exactly that, and the Court points to nothing in the structure, purpose, or legislative history of the National Security Act that would suggest a different conclusion. Accordingly, I respectfully dissent from the Court's decision to allow this lawsuit to go forward.

JUSTICE SCALIA, dissenting.

I agree with the Court's apparent holding in Part II of its opinion, . . . that the Director's decision to terminate a CIA employee is "committed to agency discretion by law" within the meaning of 5 U.S.C. §701(a)(2). But because I do not see how a decision can, either practically or legally, be both unreviewable and yet reviewable for constitutional defect, I regard Part III of the opinion as essentially undoing Part II. I therefore respectfully dissent from the judgment of the Court.

I

Before proceeding to address Part III of the Court's opinion, which I think to be in error, I must discuss one significant element of the analysis in Part II. Though I subscribe to most of that analysis, I disagree with the Court's description of what is required to come within the second paragraph of §701(a), which provides that judicial review is unavailable "to the extent that . . . agency action is committed to agency discretion by law."* The Court's discussion . . . suggests that the Court of Appeals below was correct in holding that this provision is triggered only when there is "no law to apply." . . . Our precedents amply show that "commit[ment] to agency discretion by law" includes, but is not limited to, situations in which there is "no law to apply." . . .

The "no law to apply" test can account for the nonreviewability of certain issues, but falls far short of explaining the full scope of the areas from which the courts are excluded. For the fact is that there is no governmental decision that is not subject to a fair number of legal constraints precise enough to be susceptible of judicial application—beginning with the fundamental constraint that the decision must be taken in order to further a public purpose rather than a purely private interest; yet there are many governmental decisions that are not at all subject to judicial review. A United States Attorney's decision to prosecute, for example, will not be reviewed on the claim that it is prompted by personal animosity. Thus, "no law to apply" provides much less than the full answer to whether §701(a)(2) applies.

---

* Technically, this provision merely precludes judicial review under the judicial review provisions of the Administrative Procedure Act (APA), that is, under Chapter 7 of Title 5. However, at least with respect to all entities that come within the Chapter's definition of "agency," see 5 U.S.C. §701(b), if review is not available under the APA it is not available at all. Chapter 7 of Title 5 of the United States Code (enacted as §10 of the APA) is an umbrella statute governing judicial review of all federal agency action. While a right to judicial review of agency action may be created by a separate statutory or constitutional provision, once created it becomes subject to the judicial review provisions of the APA unless *specifically* excluded, see U.S.C. §559. To my knowledge, no specific exclusion exists.

The key to understanding the "committed to agency discretion *by law*" provision of §701(a)(2) lies in contrasting it with the "*statutes* preclude judicial review" provision of §701(a)(1). Why "statutes" for preclusion, but the much more general term "law" for commission to agency discretion? The answer is, as we implied in [Heckler v.] *Chaney*, that the latter was intended to refer to "the 'common law' of judicial review of agency action," 470 U.S., at 832—a body of jurisprudence that had marked out, with more or less precision, certain issues and certain areas that were beyond the range of judicial review. That jurisprudence included principles ranging from the "political question" doctrine, to sovereign immunity (including doctrines determining when a suit against an officer would be deemed to be a suit against the sovereign), to official immunity, to prudential limitations upon the courts' equitable powers, to what can be described no more precisely than a traditional respect for the functions of the other branches reflected in the statement in Marbury v. Madison, 1 Cranch 137, 170-171 (1803), that "[w]here the head of a department acts in a case, in which executive discretion is to be exercised; in which he is the mere organ of executive will; it is again repeated, that any application to a court to control, in any respect, his conduct, would be rejected without hesitation." . . . This explains the seeming contradiction between §701(a)(2)'s disallowance of review to the extent that action is "committed to agency discretion," and §706's injunction that a court shall set aside agency action that constitutes "an abuse of discretion." Since, in the former provision, "committed to agency discretion by law" means "of the sort that is traditionally unreviewable," it operates to keep certain categories of agency action out of the courts; but when agency action is appropriately in the courts, abuse of discretion is of course grounds for reversal. . . .

II

Before taking the reader through the terrain of the Court's holding that respondent may assert constitutional claims in this suit, I would like to try to clear some of the underbrush, consisting primarily of the Court's ominous warning that "[a] 'serious constitutional question' . . . would arise if a federal statute were construed to deny any judicial forum for a colorable constitutional claim." . . . What could possibly be the basis for this fear? Surely not some general principle that *all* constitutional violations must be remediable in the courts. The very text of the Constitution refutes that principle, since it provides that "[e]ach House shall be the Judge of the Elections, Returns and Qualifications of its own Members," Art. I, §5, and that "for any Speech or Debate in either House, [the Senators and Representatives] shall not be questioned in any other Place," Art. I, §6. Claims concerning constitutional violations committed in these contexts—for example, the rather grave constitutional claim that an election has been stolen—cannot be addressed to the courts. *See, e.g.,* Morgan v. United States, 801 F.2d 445 (1986). Even apart from the strict text of the Constitution, we have found some constitutional claims to be beyond judicial review because they involve "political questions." . . . The doctrine of sovereign immunity—not repealed by the Constitution, but to the contrary at least partly reaffirmed as to the States by the Eleventh Amendment—is a monument to the principle that some constitutional claims can go unheard. . . . And finally, the doctrine of equitable discretion, which permits a court to refuse relief, even where no relief at law is available, when that would unduly impair the public interest, does not stand aside simply because the basis for the relief is a constitutional claim. In sum, it is simply untenable that there must be a judicial remedy for every constitutional violation. Members of Congress and the supervising officers of the Executive Branch take the same oath to uphold the Constitution that we do, and sometimes they are left to perform that oath unreviewed, as we always are.

Perhaps, then, the Court means to appeal to a more limited principle, that although there may be areas where judicial review of a constitutional claim will be denied, the scope of those areas is fixed by the Constitution and judicial tradition, and cannot be affected by *Congress,* through the enactment of a statute such as §102(c). That would be a rather counter-intuitive principle, especially since Congress has in reality been the principal determiner of the scope of review, for constitutional claims as well as all other claims, through its waiver of the pre-existing doctrine of sovereign immunity. On the merits of the point, however: It seems to me clear that courts would not entertain, for example, an action for backpay by a dismissed Secretary of State claiming that the reason he lost his Government job was that the President did not like his religious views — surely a colorable violation of the First Amendment. I am confident we would hold that the President's choice of his Secretary of State is a "political question." But what about a similar suit by the Deputy Secretary of State? Or one of the Under Secretaries? Or an Assistant Secretary? Or the head of the European Desk? Is there really a constitutional line that falls at some immutable point between one and another of these offices at which the principle of unreviewability cuts in, and which cannot be altered by congressional prescription? I think not. I think Congress can prescribe, at least within broad limits, that for certain jobs the dismissal decision will be unreviewable — that is, will be "committed to agency discretion by law."

Once it is acknowledged, as I think it must be, (1) that not all constitutional claims require a judicial remedy, and (2) that the identification of those that do not can, even if only within narrow limits, be determined by Congress, then it is clear that the "serious constitutional question" feared by the Court is an illusion. . . .

III

I turn, then, to whether the executive action is, within the meaning of §701(a)(2), "committed to agency discretion by law." . . . It seems to me the Court is attempting the impossible feat of having its cake and eating it too. The opinion states that "[a] discharged employee . . . cannot complain that his termination was not 'necessary or advisable in the interests of the United States,' *since that assessment is the Director's alone*" (emphasis added). But two sentences later it says that "[n]othing in §102(c) persuades us that Congress meant to preclude consideration of colorable constitutional claims arising out of the actions of the Director pursuant to that section." . . .

Since the Court's disposition contradicts its fair assurances, I must assume that the §102(c) judgment is no longer "the Director's alone," but rather only "the Director's alone except to the extent it is colorably claimed that his judgment is unconstitutional." I turn, then, to the question of where this exception comes from. . . .

Perhaps . . . a constitutional right is by its nature so much more important to the claimant than a statutory right that a statute which plainly excludes the latter should not be read to exclude the former unless it says so. That principle has never been announced — and with good reason, because its premise is not true. An individual's contention that the government has reneged upon a $100,000 debt owing under a contract is much more important to him — both financially and, I suspect, in the sense of injustice that he feels — than the same individual's claim that a particular federal licensing provision requiring a $100 license denies him equal protection to the laws, or that a particular state tax violates the Commerce Clause. A citizen would much rather have his statutory entitlement correctly acknowledged after a constitutionally inadequate hearing, than have it incorrectly denied after a proceeding that fulfills all the requirements of the Due Process Clause. The *only* respect in which a constitutional claim is necessarily more significant than any other kind of claim is that, regardless of how trivial its real-life importance may be in the case at hand, it can be asserted against the action of the legislature itself, whereas a nonconstitutional claim (no matter how significant) cannot. That is an important distinction, and one relevant to the constitutional analysis that I conducted above. But it has no relevance to the question whether, as between executive violations of statute and executive violations of the Constitution — both of which are equally unlawful, and neither of which can be said, a priori, to be more harmful or more unfair to the plaintiff — one or the other category should be favored by a presumption against exclusion of judicial review.

Even if we were to assume, however, contrary to all reason, that every constitutional claim is ipso facto more worthy, and every statutory claim less worthy, of judicial review, there would be no basis for writing that preference into a statute that makes no distinction between the two. . . . In Johnson v. Robison, 415 U.S. 361 (1974), we considered a statute precluding judicial review of " 'the *decisions* of the Administrator on any question of law or fact *under* any law administered by the Veterans' Administration.' " *Id.*, at 367 (*quoting* 38 U.S.C. §211(a)). We concluded that this statute did not bar judicial review of a challenge to the constitutionality of the statute itself, since that was a challenge not to a decision of the Administrator but to a decision of Congress. Our holding was based upon the text, and not upon some judicial power to read in a "constitutional claims" exception. . . .

The Court seeks to downplay the harm produced by today's decision by observing that "petitioner acknowledges that Title VII claims attacking the hiring and promotion policies of the Agency are routinely entertained in federal court." . . . [C]iting Reply Brief for Petitioner 13-14; Tr. of Oral Arg. 9. Assuming that those suits are statutorily authorized, I am willing to accept the Director's assertion that, while suits regarding hiring or promotion are tolerable, a suit regarding dismissal is not. . . .

The harm done by today's decision is that, contrary to what Congress knows is preferable, it brings a significant decisionmaking process of our intelligence services into a forum where it does not belong. Neither the

Constitution, nor our laws, nor common sense gives an individual a right to come into court to litigate the reasons for his dismissal as an intelligence agent. It is of course not just *valid* constitutional claims that today's decision makes the basis for judicial review of the Director's action, but all *colorable* constitutional claims, whether meritorious or not. And in determining whether what is colorable is in fact meritorious, a court will necessarily have to review the entire decision. If the Director denies, for example, respondent's contention in the present case that he was dismissed because he was a homosexual, how can a court possibly resolve the dispute without knowing what other good, intelligence-related reasons there might have been? I do not see how any "latitude to control any discovery process," . . . could justify the refusal to permit such an inquiry, at least in camera. Presumably the court would be expected to evaluate whether the agent really did fail in this or that secret mission. The documents needed will make interesting reading for district judges (and perhaps others) throughout the country. Of course the Agency can seek to protect itself, ultimately, by an authorized assertion of executive privilege, United States v. Nixon, 418 U.S. 683 (1974), but that is a power to be invoked only in extremis, and any scheme of judicial review of which it is a central feature is extreme. I would, in any event, not like to be the agent who has to explain to the intelligence services of other nations with which we sometimes cooperate, that they need have no worry that the secret information they give us will be subjected to the notoriously broad discovery powers of our courts, because, although we have to litigate the dismissal of our spies, we have available a protection of somewhat uncertain scope known as executive privilege, which the President can invoke if he is willing to take the political damage that it often entails.

Today's result, however, will have ramifications far beyond creation of the world's only secret intelligence agency that must litigate the dismissal of its agents. If constitutional claims can be raised in this highly sensitive context, it is hard to imagine where they cannot. The assumption that there are any executive decisions that cannot be hauled into the courts may no longer be valid. Also obsolete may be the assumption that we are capable of preserving a sensible common law of judicial review.

I respectfully dissent.

NOTES AND QUESTIONS

1. *"No law to apply."* The Court in *Webster* concludes that §102(c) fails to provide a meaningful legal standard against which to assess the Director's decision, but why? Are the words "discretion" and "deem" enough to deprive the court of an applicable legal standard, or is it the vagueness of the "necessary or advisable in the interests of the United States" language? Why would Congress require termination decisions to be "necessary or advisable" unless it meant there to be some underlying justification for the firing rendering it actually necessary or genuinely advisable? Doesn't the inclusion of a statutory standard (even an admittedly vague one) imply that the "deeming" and exercise of "discretion" be supported by reason? If Congress wished to confer absolute power on the

Secretary, couldn't it have authorized the Secretary to, for example, "terminate anyone for any reason, or even without a reason, at any time"?

2. *The distinction between APA §§701(a)(1) and (a)(2).* Does the Court satisfactorily explain the distinction between statutory preclusion of review (§701(a)(1)) and "committed to agency discretion by law" (§701(a)(2))? Does Justice Scalia's discussion, in his separate opinion, of areas traditionally held to be within agency discretion provide a better answer? From what sources would Justice Scalia derive principles to determine whether a matter is "committed to agency discretion by law"?

3. *Separation of powers concerns.* Justice Scalia's analysis is obviously colored by his concern with judicial meddling in affairs that should be entrusted to the discretion of the Executive Branch, and thus ultimately to the President. There is a strong tradition of reluctance to review presidential action, especially for statutory, as opposed to constitutional, legality. *See* Dalton v. Specter, 511 U.S. 462 (1994) (no review of President's decision to approve Base Closure Commission's recommendations regarding which military bases should be closed); Chicago & Southern Air Lines, Inc. v. Waterman S.S. Corp., 333 U.S. 103 (1948) (no review of President's approval of administrative decision to deny airline a certificate to operate an international route). The principle of these cases is that the President's discretionary decisions are political in nature and thus should not be subjected to judicial review.

4. *National security.* Is Justice Scalia correct that constitutional challenges to firings by the Director of Central Intelligence pose the same dangers to national security as challenges based on the statute? Even if he is correct, is the principle in favor of review of constitutional challenges strong enough to justify overlooking those dangers? Could Congress solve the Court's problem by specifying when constitutional challenges should be barred?

Since *Webster,* lower courts have similarly treated hiring and firing decisions related to national security as committed to agency discretion. In Conyers v. Rossides, 558 F.3d 137 (2d Cir. 2009), the Transportation Safety Administration's refusal to hire the plaintiff as an airport security screener was deemed committed to agency discretion because the relevant statute, the Aviation and Transportation Security Act, gave the agency broad authority and was passed in a similar context to the *Webster* statute: "shortly after a cataclysmic event that Congress believed required it to take action to change the way in which the nation protected itself." *Id.* at 147.

5. *Constitutionality of precluding review of constitutional challenges (II).* Once again, citing *Robison,* the *Webster* Court invoked the "'serious constitutional question' that would arise if a federal statute were construed to deny any judicial forum for a colorable constitutional claim." Does Justice Scalia provide a convincing rebuttal to this assertion? Are constitutional claims more important than statutory claims in ways that the amount in controversy cannot fully capture? Does Chief Justice Rehnquist adequately respond to Justice Scalia's argument that allowing review of Doe's constitutional claim will involve just as much "rummaging around" in CIA business as allowing review of his statutory claims? Suppose, for example, that in response to Doe's constitutional claims, Director Webster replied that Doe was in fact fired because he was a security risk (because the agency believed him to be more vulnerable to blackmail than other

employees), and because he had several run-ins with colleagues that proved him "difficult" to work with and untrustworthy. How would the court determine the true reason for his discharge?

6. *Presidential discretion to suspend entry of aliens.* The Immigration and Nationality Act, 8 U.S.C. §1182(f), provides that "Whenever the President finds that the entry of any aliens or of any class of aliens into the United States would be detrimental to the interests of the United States," the President may "suspend the entry of all aliens or any class of aliens as immigrants or nonimmigrants, or impose on the entry of aliens any restrictions he may deem to be appropriate." Is the President's decision to invoke this authority subject to judicial review or is it "committed to agency discretion by law"? In Trump v. Hawaii, 138 U.S. 2392 (2018), the Supreme Court suggested that President Trump's suspension of entry of aliens from several majority-Muslim countries (under the so-called "Travel Ban") might not be reviewable under *Webster v. Doe,* but went on to decide the merits anyway, stating that "even assuming that some form of review is appropriate, plaintiffs' attacks on the sufficiency of the President's findings cannot be sustained." Why didn't the Court rest its decision on reviewability? If the action is exempt from review under the APA, is it appropriate for the Court to reach the merits?

7. *"Routine" disputes under statutory standards.* In Weyerhaeuser Co. v. U.S. Fish and Wildlife Service, 139 S. Ct. 361 (2018), the Court had occasion to reconsider its longstanding approach to the "committed to agency discretion" exception to judicial review. Petitioner challenged the U.S. Fish and Wildlife Service's (FWS) designation of part of their property as "critical habitat" under §4(b)(2) of the Endangered Species Act, arguing that the agency had improperly weighed costs and benefits. Section 4(b)(2) directs the agency to designate critical habitat "after taking into consideration the economic impact, the impact on national security, and any other relevant impact . . . [FWS] may exclude any area from critical habitat if [it] determines that the benefits of such exclusion outweigh the benefits of specifying such an area . . . unless he determines . . . that the failure to designate such area as critical habitat will result in the extinction of the species concerned." The Court rejected FWS's argument that the designation was committed to agency discretion by law, reiterating that the exception in §701(a)(2) is narrow and does not encompass the kinds of "routine dispute[s]" at issue in the case, where "an agency issues an order affecting the rights of a private party, and the party objects that the agency did not properly justify its determination under a standard set forth in the statute."

The Court had another opportunity to address the "committed to agency discretion" exception to judicial review in the "Census" case excerpted below.

DEPARTMENT OF COMMERCE v. NEW YORK
139 S. Ct. 2551 (2019)

CHIEF JUSTICE ROBERTS delivered the opinion of the Court.

[For the facts and the Court's discussion of the merits, see the excerpt in Chapter II, *supra.*]

IV

The District Court set aside the Secretary's decision to reinstate a citizenship question [on the 2020 Census] on the grounds that the Secretary acted arbitrarily. . . . The Government . . . argues that the Secretary's decision was not judicially reviewable under the Administrative Procedure Act in the first place. . . .

We disagree. To be sure, the Act confers broad authority on the Secretary. Section 141(a) instructs him to take "a decennial census of population" in "such form and content as he may determine, including the use of sampling procedures and special surveys." 13 U.S.C. §141. The Act defines "census of population" to mean "a census of population, housing, and matters relating to population and housing," §141(g), and it authorizes the Secretary, in "connection with any such census," to "obtain such other census information as necessary," §141(a). It also states that the "Secretary shall prepare questionnaires, and shall determine the inquiries, and the number, form, and subdivisions thereof, for the statistics, surveys, and censuses provided for in this title." §5. And it authorizes him to acquire materials, such as administrative records, from other federal, state, and local agencies in aid of conducting the census. §6. Those provisions leave much to the Secretary's discretion.

But they do not leave his discretion unbounded. In order to give effect to the command that courts set aside agency action that is an abuse of discretion, and to honor the presumption of judicial review, we have read the §701(a)(2) exception for action committed to agency discretion "quite narrowly, restricting it to 'those rare circumstances where the relevant statute is drawn so that a court would have no meaningful standard against which to judge the agency's exercise of discretion.'" Weyerhaeuser Co. v. United States Fish and Wildlife Serv., 139 S. Ct. 2551, 2568 (2018) (quoting Lincoln v. Vigil, 508 U.S. 182, 191 (1993)). And we have generally limited the exception to "certain categories of administrative decisions that courts traditionally have regarded as 'committed to agency discretion,'" id., at 191, such as a decision not to institute enforcement proceedings, Heckler v. Chaney, 470 U.S. 821, 831-832 (1985), or a decision by an intelligence agency to terminate an employee in the interest of national security, Webster v. Doe, 486 U.S. 592, 600-601 (1988).

The taking of the census is not one of those areas traditionally committed to agency discretion. We and other courts have entertained both constitutional and statutory challenges to census-related decisionmaking. . . .

Nor is the statute here drawn so that it furnishes no meaningful standard by which to judge the Secretary's action. In contrast to the National Security Act in *Webster*, which gave the Director of Central Intelligence discretion to terminate employees whenever he "deem[ed]" it "advisable," 486 U.S. at 594, the Census Act constrains the Secretary's authority to determine the form and content of the census in a number of ways. Section 195, for example, governs the extent to which he can use statistical sampling. Section 6(c) . . . circumscribes his power in certain circumstances to collect information through direct inquiries when administrative records are available. More generally, by mandating a population count that will be used to apportion representatives, see §141(b), 2 U.S.C. §2a, the Act imposes "a duty to conduct a census that is accurate and that fairly accounts for the crucial representational rights that depend on the census and the apportionment." *Franklin* [v. Massachusetts], 505 U.S. 788, 819-820 (1992) (Stevens, J., concurring in part and concurring in judgment).

The Secretary's decision to reinstate a citizenship question is amenable to review for compliance with those and other provisions of the Census Act, according to the general requirements of reasoned agency decisionmaking. Because this is not a case in which there is "no law to apply," *Overton Park*, 401 U.S. at 410, the Secretary's decision is subject to judicial review. . . .

JUSTICE ALITO, concurring in part and dissenting in part. . . .

To put the point bluntly, the Federal Judiciary has no authority to stick its nose into the question whether it is good policy to include a citizenship question on the census or whether the reasons given by Secretary Ross for that decision were his only reasons or his real reasons. Of course, we may determine whether the decision is constitutional. But under the considerations that typically guide this Court in the exercise of its power of judicial review of agency action, we have no authority to decide whether the Secretary's decision was rendered in compliance with the Administrative Procedure Act (APA).

II

A

[T]he statute that vests the Secretary with authority to administer the decennial census [13 U.S.C. §141(a)] gives the Secretary unfettered discretion to include on the census questions about basic demographic characteristics like citizenship. It begins by providing that the Secretary "shall, in the year 1980 and every 10 years thereafter, take a decennial *census of population . . . in such form and content as he may determine,* including the use of sampling procedures and special surveys." *Ibid.* (emphasis added).

The two phrases I have highlighted—"census of population" and "in such form and content as he may determine"—are of immediate importance. A "census of population" is broader than a mere head count. The term is defined as "a census of population . . . *and matters relating to population.*" §141(g) (emphasis added). Because this definition refers to both "a census of population" and "matters relating to population," the latter concept must include more than a "census of population" in the strict sense of a head count. And it seems obvious that what this additional information must include is the sort of basic demographic information that has long been sought in the census. So the statute clearly authorizes the Secretary to gather such information.

The second phrase, "in such form and content as he may determine," specifies how this information is to be gathered, namely, by a method having the "form and content" that the Secretary "may determine." In other words, this is left purely to the Secretary's discretion. A clearer and less restricted conferral of discretion is hard to imagine. . . .

The §141(a) language discussed above is even more sweeping than that of the statute in *Webster.* Unlike the Census Act, the statute in *Webster* placed a condition on the Director's action—in particular, the requirement that he terminate an employee only after concluding that doing so would further the "interests of the United States." No such condition applies to the Secretary's determination about the form and content of the decennial census, a fact that distinguishes the statute at issue here from others this Court has found to fall outside § 701(a)(2) and thus within courts' power to review. . . .

E

[Contrary to respondents' argument] §141(f) [requiring the Commerce Secretary to report to Congress] actually cuts against judicial review. The Constitution gives Congress the authority to "direct" the "Manner" in which the census is conducted, and by imposing the §141(f) reporting requirements, Congress retained some of that supervisory authority. It did not transfer it to the courts.

Respondents protest that congressional review may not be enough to guard against a Secretary's abuses, especially when the party in control of Congress stands to benefit. But that complaint simply expresses disagreement with the Framers' choice to vest power over the census in a political body, and the manner in which Congress has chosen to exercise that power. In any event, the ability to press constitutional challenges to the Secretary's decisions answers many of the examples in respondents' parade of horribles.

In short, the relevant text of §141(a) "fairly exudes deference" to the Secretary. *Webster*, 486 U.S. at 600. And no other provision of law cited by respondents or my colleagues provides any "meaningful judicial standard" for reviewing the Secretary's selection of demographic questions for inclusion on the census. *Ibid.* . . .

III

In addition to requiring an examination of the text and structure of the relevant statutes, our APA §701(a)(2) cases look to whether the agency action in question is a type that has traditionally been viewed as committed to agency discretion or whether it is instead one that "federal courts regularly review." Weyerhaeuser Co., 139 S. Ct. at 370. In cases where the Court has found that agency action is committed to agency discretion by law, an important factor has been the absence of an established record of judicial review prior to the adoption of the APA.

Here, there is no relevant record of judicial review. We are confronted with a practice that reaches back two centuries. The very first census went beyond a mere head count and gathered additional demographic information, and during virtually the entire period prior to the enactment of the APA, a citizenship question was asked of everyone. Notably absent from that long record is any practice of judicial review of the content of the census. Indeed, this Court has never before encountered a direct challenge to a census question. And litigation in the lower courts about the census is sparse and generally of relatively recent vintage. . . .

IV

Respondents [and Justice Breyer] protest that the importance of the census provides a compelling reason to allow APA review. But this argument overlooks the fact that the Secretary is accountable in other ways for census-related decisionmaking. If the Secretary violates the Constitution or any applicable statutory provision related to the census, his action is reviewable. The Secretary is also accountable to Congress with respect to the administration of the census since he has that power only because Congress has found it appropriate to entrust it to him. And the Secretary is always answerable to the President, who is, in turn, accountable to the people. . . .

NOTES AND QUESTIONS

1. Department of Commerce *and* Webster. Notice how the Chief Justice and Justice Alito differ in their treatment of *Webster*. The Chief Justice reads the statute in *Webster* as conferring *more* discretion on the agency than the statute in *Department of Commerce*, and Justice Alito reads the statutes in exactly the opposite way. Who is right? Which reading is more consistent with the text of the APA? What are the implications of each reading for the separation of powers?

2. *Reviewability, delegation,* Chevron, *and* Auer. What, if anything, is the relationship between one's views on how broadly or narrowly to apply the delegation doctrine, the *Chevron* and *Auer* doctrines, and reviewability? Can you line up the positions taken by the various Justices in recent cases such as *Gundy,* discussed in Chapter I, *supra,* and *Department of Commerce* and *Kisor,* both discussed in Chapter II, *supra?*

b. Prosecutorial Discretion

In the context of criminal law enforcement, prosecutors exercise wide discretion whether to investigate allegations of criminal violations and whether to bring charges against those whom they believe to have committed crimes. A decision not to investigate or bring charges is traditionally considered immune from judicial review. For example, a crime victim, or a law-abiding competitor of a criminal enterprise, cannot normally go to court to force the prosecutor to bring charges against someone alleged to have violated or be in violation of the criminal law.

Administrative agencies with civil enforcement responsibilities are often called upon to make similar decisions. The Mine Safety and Health Administration, for example, issues safety citations to owner-operators for safety violations. When the agency's decision to issue a citation was challenged, the Fourth Circuit found that the Secretary's discretion to issue these citations was "not dissimilar from the considerations that guide a prosecutor's exercise of his discretion." Speed Mining, Inc. v. Federal Mine Safety & Health Review Commission, 528 F.3d 310 (4th Cir. 2008). Such agencies may lack sufficient resources to bring enforcement actions against every violator of the statutes they are charged with enforcing. Further, enforcement against some violations may be inconsistent with agency policy. Courts are generally very deferential toward agency prosecutorial decisions, holding them exempt from judicial review except in certain narrow circumstances. For example, under the National Labor Relations Act, the General Counsel, who is independent of the NLRB, has "final authority . . . in respect of the investigation of charges and issuance of complaints . . . and in respect of the prosecution of such complaints before the Board." 29 U.S.C. §153(d) (1982). The Supreme Court has repeatedly refused to review decisions of the General Counsel not to issue a complaint or to withdraw a complaint. *See* NLRB v. Sears, Roebuck & Co., 421 U.S. 132 (1975); NLRB v. United Food & Commercial Workers Union, 484 U.S. 112 (1987).

The Court has, however, recognized exceptions to the general rule that agency prosecutorial decisions are unreviewable. One such exception, for when an agency acts in clear violation of its governing statute or clearly in excess of its statutory authority, is illustrated by Leedom v. Kyne, 358 U.S. 184 (1958). Another exception, also arising in the labor law context, was recognized in Dunlop v. Bachowski, 421 U.S. 560 (1975). *Bachowski* arose under the Labor-Management Reporting and Disclosure Act of 1959. Under that Act, the Secretary of Labor is required to investigate complaints of violations of the rules that govern union elections. The statute provides that "if [the Secretary] finds probable cause to believe that a violation . . . has occurred and has not been remedied, he *shall*, within sixty days, after the filing of such complaint, bring a civil action against the labor organization . . . to set aside the invalid election." 29 U.S.C. §482(b) (emphasis added). Congress's use of the word "shall" in this provision appears mandatory—if the Secretary finds probable cause, it appears that he must bring suit.

The Supreme Court decided that, based on the statute's mandatory language, Bachowski was entitled to judicial review of the Secretary's decision not to bring suit. However, the Court prescribed an exceedingly narrow scope of review. Rather than a wide-ranging factual inquiry into the propriety of the Secretary's decision, the Supreme Court held that the district court should order the Secretary to provide a statement of reasons for the decision not to bring suit, and, in the usual case, should base its review only on that statement. The Court stated that "clearly, the reviewing court is not authorized to substitute its judgment for the decision of the Secretary not to bring suit" and should reject the Secretary's decision only if the statement "evinces that the Secretary's decision is so irrational as to constitute the decision arbitrary and capricious." The Court left open the question whether, if the Secretary's decision is found to be arbitrary and capricious, the district court has the power to order the Secretary to bring suit to set aside the election.

In view of the narrow standard of review adopted by the Court, did Bachowski win only a Pyrrhic victory? While the appeal was pending, the Secretary did in fact supply the district court with a statement of his reasons for deciding to drop Bachowski's case. In that statement, which was appended to the opinion of the Supreme Court, the Secretary concluded that suit was not warranted because the outcome of the election would have been the same even if the violations had not occurred. (The Supreme Court had previously held that the Secretary is not required to bring suit if the violations alleged did not affect the outcome of the election. *See* Wirtz v. Bottle Blowers Assn., 389 U.S. 463 (1968).) In *Bachowski*, a maximum of 884 votes were affected by improper election practices, and

Bachowski lost the election by 907 votes. The Secretary thus concluded that the violations could not have affected the outcome of the election.

Bachowski was greeted by some observers as a signal that the Supreme Court had joined a growing movement to accord regulatory beneficiaries broad "rights of initiation." *See* Richard B. Stewart & Cass R. Sunstein, Public Programs and Private Rights, 95 Harv. L. Rev. 1193, 1205 (1982). In this view, *Bachowski* was not simply an isolated exception to the doctrine of prosecutorial discretion, but a nail in its coffin. But, as the following case indicates, reports of the doctrine's demise were decidedly premature.

HECKLER v. CHANEY
470 U.S. 821 (1985)

JUSTICE REHNQUIST delivered the opinion of the Court.

This case presents the question of the extent to which a decision of an administrative agency to exercise its "discretion" not to undertake certain enforcement actions is subject to judicial review under the Administrative Procedure Act. . . . Respondents are several prison inmates convicted of capital offenses and sentenced to death by lethal injection of drugs. They petitioned the Food and Drug Administration (FDA), alleging that under the circumstances the use of these drugs for capital punishment violated the Federal Food, Drug, and Cosmetic Act, 21 U.S.C. §301 *et seq.* (FDCA), and requesting that the FDA take various enforcement actions to prevent these violations. The FDA refused their request. We review here a decision of the Court of Appeals for the District of Columbia Circuit, which held the FDA's refusal to take enforcement actions both reviewable and an abuse of discretion, and remanded the case with directions that the agency be required "to fulfill its statutory function." . . .

I

Respondents have been sentenced to death by lethal injection of drugs under the laws of the States of Oklahoma and Texas. Those States, and several others, have recently adopted this method for carrying out the capital sentence. Respondents first petitioned the FDA, claiming that the drugs used by the States for this purpose, although approved by the FDA for the medical purposes stated on their labels, were not approved for use in human executions. They alleged that the drugs had not been tested for the purpose they were to be used, and that, given that the drugs would likely be administered by untrained personnel, it was also likely that the drugs would not induce the quick and painless death intended. They urged that use of these drugs for human execution was the "unapproved use of an approved drug" and constituted a violation of the Act's prohibitions against "misbranding."[1] They also suggested that the FDCA's requirements for approval of "new drugs" applied, since these drugs were now being used for a new purpose. Accordingly, respondents claimed that the FDA

---

1. See 21 U.S.C. §352(f): "A drug or device shall be deemed to be misbranded . . . [u]nless its labeling bears (1) adequate directions for use. . . ."

was required to approve the drugs as "safe and effective" for human execution before they could be distributed in interstate commerce. *See* 21 U.S.C. §355. They therefore requested the FDA to take various investigatory and enforcement actions to prevent these perceived violations; they requested the FDA to affix warnings to the labels of all the drugs stating that they were unapproved and unsafe for human execution, to send statements to the drug manufacturers and prison administrators stating that the drugs should not be so used, and to adopt procedures for seizing the drugs from state prisons and to recommend the prosecution of all those in the chain of distribution who knowingly distribute or purchase the drugs with intent to use them for human execution.

The FDA Commissioner responded, refusing to take the requested actions. The Commissioner first detailed his disagreement with respondents' understanding of the scope of FDA jurisdiction over the unapproved use of approved drugs for human execution, concluding that FDA jurisdiction in the area was generally unclear but in any event should not be exercised to interfere with this particular aspect of state criminal justice systems. He went on to state:

> Were FDA clearly to have jurisdiction in the area, moreover, we believe we would be authorized to decline to exercise it under our inherent discretion to decline to pursue certain enforcement matters. The unapproved use of approved drugs is an area in which the case law is far from uniform. Generally, enforcement proceedings in this area are initiated only when there is a serious danger to the public health or a blatant scheme to defraud. We cannot conclude that those dangers are present under State lethal injection laws, which are duly authorized statutory enactments in furtherance of proper State functions. . . .

Respondents then filed the instant suit in the United States District Court for the District of Columbia, claiming the same violations of the FDCA and asking that the FDA be required to take the same enforcement actions requested in the prior petition. Jurisdiction was grounded in the general federal-question jurisdiction statute, 28 U.S.C. §1331, and review of the agency action was sought under the judicial review provisions of the Administrative Procedure Act, 5 U.S.C. §§701-706. The District Court granted summary judgment for petitioner. . . .

A divided panel of the Court of Appeals for the District of Columbia Circuit reversed. . . . Citing this Court's opinions in Dunlop v. Bachowski, 421 U.S. 560 (1975), and Citizens to Preserve Overton Park v. Volpe, 401 U.S. 402 (1971), the court held that the "committed to agency discretion by law" exception of §701(a)(2) should be invoked only where the substantive statute left the courts with "no law to apply." . . .

The court found "law to apply" in the form of a FDA policy statement which indicated that the agency was "obligated" to investigate the unapproved use of an approved drug when such use became "widespread" or "endanger[ed] the public health." . . . The court held that this policy statement constituted a "rule" and was considered binding by the FDA. Given the policy statement indicating that the FDA should take enforcement action in this area, and the strong presumption that all agency action is subject to judicial review, the court concluded that review of the agency's refusal was not foreclosed. It then proceeded to assess whether the agency's decision not to act was "arbitrary, capricious, or an abuse of discretion." Citing evidence that the FDA assumed jurisdiction over drugs used to put animals to sleep and the unapproved uses of drugs on prisoners in clinical experiments, the court found that the FDA's refusal, for the reasons given, was irrational, and that respondents' evidence that use of the drugs could lead to a cruel and protracted death was entitled to more searching consideration. The court therefore remanded the case to the District Court, to order the FDA "to fulfill its statutory function." . . .

We granted certiorari to review the implausible result that the FDA is required to exercise its enforcement power to ensure that States only use drugs that are "safe and effective" for human execution. . . .

We reverse.

II

The Court of Appeals' decision addressed three questions: (1) whether the FDA had jurisdiction to undertake the enforcement actions requested, (2) whether if it did have jurisdiction its refusal to take those actions was subject to judicial review, and (3) whether if reviewable its refusal was arbitrary, capricious, or an abuse of discretion. In reaching our conclusion that the Court of Appeals was wrong, however, we need not and do not address the thorny question of the FDA's jurisdiction. For us, this case turns on the important question of the extent to which determinations by the FDA *not to exercise* its enforcement authority over the use of drugs in interstate commerce may be judicially reviewed. . . . Petitioner urges that the decision of the FDA to refuse enforcement is an action "committed to agency discretion by law" under §701(a)(2).

This Court has not had occasion to interpret this second exception in §701(a) in any great detail. On its face, the section does not obviously lend itself to any particular construction; indeed, one might wonder what difference exists between §(a)(1) and §(a)(2). The former section seems easy in application; it requires construction of the substantive statute involved to determine whether Congress intended to preclude judicial review of certain decisions. . . . But one could read the language "committed to agency discretion *by law*" in §(a)(2) to require a similar inquiry. In addition, commentators have pointed out that construction of §(a)(2) is further complicated by the tension between a literal reading of §(a)(2), which exempts from judicial review those decisions committed to agency "discretion," and the primary scope of review prescribed by §706(2)(A) — whether the agency's action was "arbitrary, capricious, or an *abuse of discretion*." How is it, they ask, that an action committed to agency discretion can be unreviewable and yet courts still can review agency actions for abuse of that discretion? *See* 5 K. Davis, Administrative Law §28.6 (1984); Berger, Administrative Arbitrariness and Judicial Review, 65 Colum. L. Rev. 55, 58 (1965). . . .

This Court first discussed §(a)(2) in Citizens to Preserve Overton Park v. Volpe. That case . . . clearly separates the exception provided by §(a)(1) from the §(a)(2) exception. The former applies when Congress has expressed an intent to preclude judicial review. The latter applies in different circumstances; even where Congress has not affirmatively precluded review, review is not to be had if the statute is drawn so that a court would have no meaningful standard against which to judge the agency's exercise of discretion. In such a case, the statute ("law") can be taken to have "committed" the decisionmaking to the agency's judgment absolutely. This construction avoids conflict with the "abuse of discretion" standard of review in §706—if no judicially manageable standards are available for judging how and when an agency should exercise its discretion then it is impossible to evaluate agency action for "abuse of discretion." . . . To this point our analysis does not differ significantly from that of the Court of Appeals. That court purported to apply the "no law to apply" standard of *Overton Park*. We disagree, however, with that court's insistence that the "narrow construction" of §(a)(2) required application of a presumption of reviewability even to an agency's decision not to undertake certain enforcement actions. Here we think the Court of Appeals broke with tradition, case law, and sound reasoning.

Overton Park did not involve an agency's refusal to take requested enforcement action. It involved an affirmative act of approval under a statute that set clear guidelines for determining when such approval should be given. Refusals to take enforcement steps generally involve precisely the opposite situation, and in that situation we think the presumption is that judicial review is not available. This Court has recognized on several occasions over many years that an agency's decision not to prosecute or enforce, whether through civil or criminal process, is a decision generally committed to an agency's absolute discretion. *See* United States v. Batchelder, 442 U.S. 114, 123-124 (1979); United States v. Nixon, 418 U.S. 683, 693 (1974); Vaca v. Sipes, 386 U.S. 171, 182 (1967); Confiscation Cases, 7 Wall. 454 (1869). This recognition of the existence of discretion is attributable in no small part to the general unsuitability for judicial review of agency decisions to refuse enforcement.

The reasons for this general unsuitability are many. First, an agency decision not to enforce often involves a complicated balancing of a number of factors which are peculiarly within its expertise. Thus, the agency must not only assess whether a violation has occurred, but whether agency resources are best spent on this violation or another, whether the agency is likely to succeed if it acts, whether the particular enforcement action requested best fits the agency's overall policies, and indeed, whether the agency has enough resources to undertake the action at all. An agency generally cannot act against each technical violation of the statute it is charged with enforcing. The agency is far better equipped than the courts to deal with the many variables involved in the proper ordering of its priorities. Similar concerns animate the principles of administrative law that courts generally will defer to an agency's construction of the statute it is charged with implementing, and to the procedures it adopts for implementing that statute. . . .

In addition to these administrative concerns, we note that when an agency refuses to act it generally does not exercise its *coercive* power over an individual's liberty or property rights, and thus does not infringe upon areas that courts often are called upon to protect. Similarly, when an agency *does* act to enforce, that action itself provides a focus for judicial review, inasmuch as the agency must have exercised its power in some manner. The action at least can be reviewed to determine whether the agency exceeded its statutory powers. . . . Finally, we recognize that an agency's refusal to institute proceedings shares to some extent the characteristics of the decision of a prosecutor in the Executive Branch not to indict—a decision which has long been regarded as the special province of the Executive Branch, inasmuch as it is the executive who is charged by the Constitution to "take Care that the Laws be faithfully executed." U.S. Const., Art. II, §3.

We of course only list the above concerns to facilitate understanding of our conclusion that an agency's decision not to take enforcement action should be presumed immune from judicial review under §701(a)(2) . . . .

In so stating, we emphasize that the decision is only presumptively unreviewable; the presumption may be rebutted where the substantive statute has provided guidelines for the agency to follow in exercising its enforcement powers.[4] . . . Dunlop v. Bachowski . . . presents an example of statutory language which supplied sufficient standards to rebut the presumption of unreviewability. . . .

The statute being administered quite clearly withdrew discretion from the agency and provided guidelines for exercise of its enforcement power. . . . The danger that agencies may not carry out their delegated powers with sufficient vigor does not necessarily lead to the conclusion that courts are the most appropriate body to police this aspect of their performance. That decision is in the first instance for Congress, and we therefore turn to the FDCA to determine whether in this case Congress has provided us with "law to apply." . . .

III

To enforce the various substantive prohibitions contained in the FDCA, the Act provides for injunctions, 21 U.S.C. §332, criminal sanctions, §§333 and 335, and seizure of any offending food, drug, or cosmetic article, §334. The Act's general provision for enforcement, §372, provides only that "[t]he Secretary is *authorized* to conduct examinations and investigations. . . ." Unlike the statute at issue in [*Bachowski*], §332 gives no indication of when an injunction should be sought, and §334, providing for seizures, is framed in the permissive—the offending food, drug or cosmetic "shall be liable to be proceeded against." The section on criminal sanctions states baldly that any person who violates the Act's substantive prohibitions "shall be imprisoned . . . or fined." Respondents argue that this statement mandates criminal prosecution of every violator of the Act but they adduce no indication in case law or legislative history that such was Congress' intention in using this language, which is commonly found in the criminal provisions of Title 18 of the United States Code. *See, e.g.,* 18 U.S.C. §471 (counterfeiting); 18 U.S.C. §1001 (false statements to Government officials); 18 U.S.C. §1341 (mail fraud). We are unwilling to attribute such a sweeping meaning to this language, particularly since the Act charges the Secretary only with recommending prosecution; any criminal prosecutions must be instituted by the Attorney General. The Act's enforcement provisions thus commit complete discretion to the Secretary to decide how and when they should be exercised. . . .

---

4. We do not have in this case a refusal by the agency to institute proceedings based solely on the belief that it lacks jurisdiction. Nor do we have a situation where it could justifiably be found that the agency has "consciously and expressly adopted a general policy" that is so extreme as to amount to an abdication of its statutory responsibilities. *See, e.g.,* Adams v. Richardson, 156 U.S. App. D.C. 267, 480 F.2d 1159 (1973) (en banc). Although we express no opinion on whether such decisions would be unreviewable under §701(a)(2), we note that in those situations the statute conferring authority on the agency might indicate that such decisions were not "committed to agency discretion."

   We also find singularly unhelpful the agency "policy statement" on which the Court of Appeals placed great reliance. We would have difficulty with this statement's vague language even if it were a properly adopted agency rule. Although the statement indicates that the agency considered itself "obligated" to take certain investigative actions, that language did not arise in the course of discussing the agency's discretion to exercise its enforcement power, but rather in the context of describing agency policy with respect to unapproved uses of approved drugs by physicians. In addition, if read to circumscribe agency enforcement discretion, the statement conflicts with the agency rule on judicial review, 21 CFR §10.45(d)(2) (1984), which states that "[t]he Commissioner shall object to judicial review . . . if (i) [t]he matter is committed by law to the discretion of the Commissioner, e.g., a decision to recommend or not to recommend civil or criminal enforcement action. . . ." But in any event the policy statement was attached to a rule that was never adopted. Whatever force such a statement might have, and leaving to one side the problem of whether an agency's rules might under certain circumstances provide courts with adequate guidelines for informed judicial review of decisions not to enforce, we do not think the language of the agency's "policy statement" can plausibly be read to override the agency's express assertion of unreviewable discretion contained in the above rule.

   Respondents' . . . argument based upon §306 of the FDCA merits only slightly more consideration. That section provides:

> Nothing in this chapter shall be construed as requiring the Secretary to report for prosecution, or for the institution of libel or injunction proceedings, minor violations of this chapter whenever he believes that the public interest will be adequately served by a suitable written notice or ruling.

21 U.S.C. §336.

   Respondents seek to draw from this section the negative implication that the Secretary is *required* to report for prosecution all "major" violations of the Act, however those might be defined, and that it therefore supplies the needed indication of an intent to limit agency enforcement discretion. We think that this section simply does not give rise to the negative implication which respondents seek to draw from it. The section is not addressed to agency proceedings designed to discover the existence of violations, but applies only to a situation where a violation has already been established to the satisfaction of the agency. We do not believe the section speaks to the criteria which shall be used by the agency for investigating *possible* violations of the Act.

                                                IV

   We therefore conclude that the presumption that agency decisions not to institute proceedings are unreviewable under §701(a)(2) of the APA is not overcome by the enforcement provisions of the FDCA. . . . No colorable claim is made in this case that the agency's refusal to institute proceedings violated any constitutional rights of respondents, and we do not address the issue that would be raised in such a case. *Cf.* Johnson v. Robison, 415 U.S. 361, 366 (1974); Yick

Wo v. Hopkins, 118 U.S. 356, 372-374 (1886). The fact that the drugs involved in this case are ultimately to be used in imposing the death penalty must not lead this Court or other courts to import profound differences of opinion over the meaning of the Eighth Amendment to the United States Constitution into the domain of administrative law.

The judgment of the Court of Appeals is reversed.

JUSTICE BRENNAN, concurring. [Omitted.]

JUSTICE MARSHALL, concurring in the judgment. . . .

In my view, the "presumption of unreviewability" announced today is a product of that lack of discipline that easy cases make all too easy. . . .

I write separately to argue for a different basis of decision: that refusals to enforce, like other agency actions, are reviewable in the absence of a "clear and convincing" congressional intent to the contrary, but that such refusals warrant deference when, as in this case, there is nothing to suggest that an agency with enforcement discretion has abused that discretion.

I

In response to respondents' petition, the FDA Commissioner stated that it would not pursue the complaint. . . . The FDA may well have been legally required to provide this statement of basis and purpose for its decision not to take the action requested. Under the Administrative Procedure Act, such a statement is required when an agency denies a "written application, petition, or other request of an interested person made in connection with any agency proceedings."[1] 5 U.S.C. §555(e). Whether this written explanation was legally required or not, however, it does provide a sufficient basis for holding, *on the merits,* that the FDA's refusal to grant the relief requested was within its discretion. . . .

As long as the agency is choosing how to allocate finite enforcement resources, the agency's choice will be entitled to substantial deference, for the choice among valid alternative enforcement policies is precisely the sort of choice over which agencies generally have been left substantial discretion by their enabling statutes. *On the merits,* then, a decision not to enforce that is based on valid resource-allocation decisions will generally not be "arbitrary, capricious, an abuse of discretion, or otherwise not in accordance with law," 5 U.S.C. §706(2)(A). The decision in this case is no exception to this principle.

---

1. All Members of the Court in Dunlop v. Bachowski, 421 U.S. 560 (1975), agreed that a statement of basis and purpose was required for the denial of the enforcement request at issue there. *See id.,* at 571-575; *id.,* at 594 (Rehnquist, J., concurring in result in part and dissenting in part). Given the revisionist view the Court takes today of [*Bachowski*], perhaps these statements too are to be limited to the specific facts out of which they emerged. Yet the Court's suggestion that review is proper when the agency asserts a lack of jurisdiction to act, *see ante* . . . n.4, or some other basis inconsistent with congressional intent, would seem to presuppose the existence of a statement of basis and purpose explaining the basis for denial of enforcement action.

The Court, however, is not content to rest on this ground. Instead, the Court transforms the arguments for deferential review on the merits into the wholly different notion that "enforcement" decisions are presumptively unreviewable altogether—unreviewable whether the resource-allocation rationale is a sham, unreviewable whether enforcement is declined out of vindictive or personal motives, and unreviewable whether the agency has simply ignored the request for enforcement. *But cf.* Logan v. Zimmerman Brush Co., 455 U.S. 422 (1982) (due process and equal protection may prevent agency from ignoring complaint) . . . .

This "presumption of unreviewability" is also a far cry from prior understandings of the Administrative Procedure Act. [Here Justice Marshall quotes from Abbott Laboratories v. Gardner, 387 U.S. 136 (1967).]

Rather than confront *Abbott Labs*, perhaps the seminal case on judicial review under the APA, the Court chooses simply to ignore it. Instead, to support its newfound "presumption of unreviewability," the Court resorts to completely undefined and unsubstantiated references to "tradition" . . . and to citation of four cases. . . .

Yet these cases hardly support such a broad presumption with respect to agency refusal to take enforcement action. The only one of these cases to involve administrative action, Vaca v. Sipes, suggests, in dictum, that the General Counsel of the National Labor Relations Board has unreviewable discretion to refuse to initiate an unfair labor practice complaint. To the extent this dictum is sound, later cases indicate that unreviewability results from the particular structure of the National Labor Relations Act and the explicit statutory intent to withdraw review found in 29 U.S.C. §153(d), rather than from some general "presumption of unreviewability" of enforcement decisions. *See* NLRB v. Sears, Roebuck & Co., 421 U.S. 132, 138 (1975). Neither *Vaca* nor *Sears, Roebuck* discuss the APA. The other three cases—*Batchelder, Nixon,* and the *Confiscation Cases*—all involve prosecutorial discretion to enforce the criminal law.

[F]or at least two reasons it is inappropriate to rely on notions of prosecutorial discretion to hold agency inaction unreviewable. First, since *Nixon*, the Court has made clear that prosecutorial discretion is not as unfettered or unreviewable as the half-sentence in *Nixon* suggests. . . . In Blackledge v. Perry, 417 U.S. 21, 28 (1974), instead of invoking notions of "absolute" prosecutorial discretion, we held that certain potentially vindictive exercises of prosecutorial discretion were both reviewable and impermissible. The "retaliatory use" of prosecutorial power is no longer tolerated. Thigpen v. Roberts, 468 U.S. 27, 30 (1984). Nor do prosecutors have the discretion to induce guilty pleas through promises that are not kept. Blackledge v. Allison, 431 U.S. 63 (1977); Santobello v. New York, 404 U.S. 257, 262 (1971) . . . .

Second, arguments about prosecutorial discretion do not necessarily translate into the context of agency refusals to act. . . . Criminal prosecutorial decisions vindicate only intangible interests, common to society as a whole, in the enforcement of the criminal law. The conduct at issue has already occurred; all that remains is society's general interest in assuring that the guilty are punished. . . . In contrast, requests for administrative enforcement typically seek to prevent concrete and future injuries that Congress has made cognizable—injuries that result, for example, from misbranded drugs, such as alleged in this case, or unsafe nuclear power plants . . .—or to obtain palpable benefits that Congress has intended to bestow—such as labor union elections free of corruption. . . . Entitlements to receive these benefits or to be free of these injuries often run to specific classes of individuals whom Congress has singled out as statutory beneficiaries. The interests at stake in review of administrative enforcement decisions are thus more focused and in many circumstances more pressing than those at stake in criminal prosecutorial decisions. . . .

Since passage of the APA, the sustained effort of administrative law has been to "continuously narro[w] the category of actions considered to be so discretionary as to be exempted from review." Shapiro, Administrative Discretion: The Next Stage, 92 Yale L.J. 1487, 1489, n.11 (1983). Discretion may well be necessary to carry out a variety of important administrative functions, but discretion can be a veil for laziness, corruption, incompetency, lack of will, or other motives, and for that reason *"the presence of discretion should not bar a court from considering a claim of illegal or arbitrary use of discretion."* L. Jaffe, Judicial Control of Administrative Action 375 (1965). . . .

NOTES AND QUESTIONS

1. *Presumption against review of nonenforcement decisions.* Does the Court provide a convincing justification for its "presumption" against judicial review of decisions to refuse enforcement? Do FDA nonenforcement decisions require any greater or different "expertise" than, say, adjudicating whether a particular drug is "safe" and "effective," or issuing a rule specifying the tests that must be done prior to marketing a drug? Is it true that nonenforcement can be distinguished from enforcement because only the latter involves the exercise of "coercive power" over liberty or property? Why should that matter? Is the Court's "coercive power" argument consistent with the congressional decision to regulate drug safety and effectiveness in the first place? Are you persuaded by the Court's reliance on the tradition of prosecutorial discretion in the criminal law? As Justice Marshall points out in his dissent, that tradition is founded more on folklore and dicta than hard precedent. Even so, he argues, it is not an appropriate analogy for administrative nonenforcement. Why not? For a point-by-point rebuttal of the majority's reasoning, *see* Cass R. Sunstein, Reviewing Agency Inaction after *Heckler v. Chaney*, 52 U. Chi. L. Rev. 653 (1985).

2. *Role of §555(e).* What is the role of APA §555(e) after *Heckler*? If the FDA had not provided the prisoners with an explanation for rejecting their petition, could they have obtained a judicial order compelling an "adequate" or "meaningful" explanation? Could petitioners have argued that §555(e) provides the "law to apply" necessary to overcome §701(a)(2)?

3. *Noneforcement, at the retail level, and the wholesale level.* How important in this context is the distinction between failures to institute enforcement proceedings based on considerations pertinent to the *particular* circumstances of the individual case and decisions not to institute enforcement proceedings for some *class* of cases? Is there a meaningful difference, for example, between a decision of a single U.S. Attorney not to enforce the federal criminal prohibition on possession of marijuana against a particular possessor, and a decision

of the Attorney General directing all U.S. Attorneys not to prosecute marijuana possession? Consider that question in the context of the following celebrated instance of "wholesale" nonenforcement.

TEXAS v. UNITED STATES
787 F.3d 733
aff'd by an equally divided court
136 S. Ct. 2271 (2016)

JERRY E. SMITH, Circuit Judge:

The United States appeals a preliminary injunction, pending trial, forbidding implementation of the Deferred Action for Parents of Americans and Lawful Permanent Residents program ("DAPA"). Twenty-six states (the "states") challenged DAPA under the Administrative Procedure Act ("APA") and the Take Care Clause of the Constitution; in an impressive and thorough Memorandum Opinion and Order issued February 16, 2015, the district court enjoined the program on the ground that the states are likely to succeed on their claim that DAPA is subject to the APA's procedural requirements. Texas v. United States, 86 F. Supp. 3d 591, 677 (S.D. Tex. 2015). . . .

I.

A.

In June 2012, the Department of Homeland Security ("DHS") implemented the Deferred Action for Childhood Arrivals program ("DACA"). In the DACA Memo to agency heads, the DHS Secretary "set[] forth how, in the exercise of . . . prosecutorial discretion, [DHS] should enforce the Nation's immigration laws against certain young people" and listed five "criteria [that] should be satisfied before an individual is considered for an exercise of prosecutorial discretion." The Secretary further instructed that "[n]o individual should receive deferred action . . . unless they [*sic*] first pass a background check and requests for relief . . . are to be decided on a case by case basis." Although stating that "[f]or individuals who are granted deferred action . . . [U.S. Citizenship and Immigration Services ("USCIS")] shall accept applications to determine whether these individuals qualify for work authorization," the DACA Memo purported to "confer[] no substantive right, immigration status or pathway to citizenship." At least 1.2 million persons qualify for DACA, and approximately 636,000 applications were approved through 2014.

In November 2014, by what is termed the "DAPA Memo," DHS expanded DACA by making millions more persons eligible for the program and extending "[t]he period for which DACA and the accompanying employment authorization is granted . . . to three-year increments, rather than the current two-year increments." The Secretary also "direct[ed] USCIS to establish a process, similar to DACA," known as DAPA, which applies to "individuals who . . . have, [as of November 20, 2014], a son or daughter who is a U.S. citizen or lawful permanent resident" and meet five additional criteria. The Secretary stated that, although "[d]eferred action does not confer any form of legal status in this country, much less citizenship[,] it [does] mean[] that, for a specified period of time, an individual is permitted to be *lawfully present* in the United States." Of the approximately 11.3 million illegal aliens in the United States, 4.3 million would be eligible for lawful presence pursuant to DAPA.

"Lawful presence" is not an enforceable right to remain in the United States and can be revoked at any time, but that classification nevertheless has significant legal consequences. Unlawfully present aliens are generally not eligible to receive federal public benefits, or state and local public benefits unless the state otherwise provides. But as the government admits in its opening brief, persons granted lawful presence pursuant to DAPA are no longer "bar[red] . . . from receiving social security retirement benefits, social security disability benefits, or health insurance under Part A of the Medicare program." That follows from §1611(b)(2)–(3), which provides that the exclusion of benefits in §1611(a) "shall not apply to any benefit[s] payable under title[s] II [and XVIII] of the Social Security Act . . . to an alien who is *lawfully present* in the United States as determined by the Attorney General. . . ." (emphasis added). A lawfully present alien is still required to satisfy independent qualification criteria before receiving those benefits, but the grant of lawful presence removes the categorical bar and thereby makes otherwise ineligible persons eligible to qualify.

"Each person who applies for deferred action pursuant to the [DAPA] criteria . . . shall also be eligible to apply for work authorization for the [renewable three-year] period of deferred action." DAPA Memo at 4. The United States concedes that "[a]n alien with work authorization may obtain a Social Security Number," "accrue quarters of covered employment," and "correct wage records to add prior covered employment within approximately three years of the year in which the wages were earned or in limited circumstances thereafter." . . . The district court determined—and the government does not dispute—"that DAPA recipients would be eligible for earned income tax credits once they received a Social Security number."

As for state benefits, although "[a] State may provide that an alien who is *not lawfully present* in the United States is eligible for any State or local public benefit for which such alien would otherwise be ineligible under subsection (a)," §1621(d), Texas has chosen not to issue driver's licenses to unlawfully present aliens. Texas maintains that documentation confirming lawful presence pursuant to DAPA would allow otherwise ineligible aliens to become eligible for state-subsidized driver's licenses. Likewise, certain unemployment compensation "[b]enefits are not payable based on services performed by an alien unless the alien . . . was *lawfully present* for purposes of performing the services. . . ." Texas contends that DAPA recipients would also become eligible for unemployment insurance.

B.

The states sued to prevent DAPA's implementation on three grounds. First, they asserted that DAPA violated the procedural requirements of the APA as a substantive rule that did not undergo the requisite notice-and-comment rulemaking. *See* 5 U.S.C. §553. Second, the states claimed that DHS lacked the authority to implement the program even if it followed the correct rulemaking process, such that DAPA was substantively unlawful under the APA. Third, the states urged that DAPA was an abrogation of the President's constitutional duty to "take Care that the Laws be faithfully executed." U.S. Const. Art. II, §3. . . .

The district court temporarily enjoined DAPA's implementation after determining that Texas had [standing to sue and had] shown a substantial likelihood of success on its claim that the program must undergo notice and comment. Despite full briefing, the court did not rule on the "Plaintiffs' likelihood of success on their *substantive* APA claim or their constitutional claims under the Take Care Clause/separation of powers doctrine." On appeal, the United States maintains [inter alia, that the DAPA memorandum is not subject to judicial review under APA §701(a)(2) as an exercise of prosecutorial discretion]. . . .

V.

The government maintains that judicial review is precluded [under APA §701(a)(2), which precludes] judicial review of certain categories of administrative decisions that courts traditionally have regarded as "committed to agency discretion." . . . The Secretary has broad discretion to "decide whether it makes sense to pursue removal at all" and urges that deferred action—a grant of "lawful presence" and subsequent eligibility for otherwise unavailable benefits—is a presumptively unreviewable exercise of prosecutorial discretion. . . .

Part of DAPA involves the Secretary's decision—at least temporarily—not to enforce the immigration laws as to a class of what he deems to be low-priority illegal aliens. But importantly, the states have not challenged the priority levels he has established, and neither the preliminary injunction nor compliance with the APA requires the Secretary to remove any alien or to alter his enforcement priorities.

Deferred action, however, is much more than nonenforcement: It would affirmatively confer "lawful presence" and associated benefits on a class of unlawfully present aliens. Though revocable, that change in designation would trigger (as we have already explained) eligibility for federal benefits—for example, under title II and XVIII of the Social Security Act—and state benefits—for example, driver's licenses and unemployment insurance—that would not otherwise be available to illegal aliens.

The United States maintains that DAPA is presumptively unreviewable prosecutorial discretion because "'lawful presence' is not a status and is not something that the alien can legally enforce; the agency can alter or revoke it at any time." The government further contends that "[e]very decision under [DAPA] to defer enforcement action against an alien necessarily entails allowing the individual to be lawfully present. . . . Deferred action under DAPA and 'lawful presence' during that limited period are thus two sides of the same coin."

Revocability, however, is not the touchstone for whether agency is action is reviewable. Likewise, to be reviewable agency action, DAPA need not directly confer public benefits—removing a categorical bar on receipt of those benefits and thereby making a class of persons newly eligible for them "provides a focus for judicial review." Moreover, if deferred action meant only nonprosecution, it would not necessarily result in lawful presence. "[A]lthough prosecutorial discretion is broad, it is not 'unfettered.'" Declining to prosecute does not transform presence deemed unlawful by Congress into lawful presence and confer eligibility for otherwise unavailable benefits based on that change. Regardless of whether the Secretary has the authority to offer lawful presence and employment authorization in exchange for participation in DAPA, his doing so is not shielded from judicial review as an act of prosecutorial discretion. . . .

[I]n invoking our jurisdiction, the states do not demand that the federal government "control immigration and . . . pay for the consequences of federal immigration policy" or "prevent illegal immigration." Neither the preliminary injunction nor compliance with the APA requires the Secretary to enforce the immigration laws or change his priorities for removal, which have expressly not been challenged. . . . At its core, this case is about the Secretary's decision to change the immigration classification of millions of illegal aliens on a class-wide basis. The states properly maintain that DAPA's grant of lawful presence and accompanying eligibility for benefits is a substantive rule that must go through notice and comment, before it imposes substantial costs on them, and that DAPA is substantively contrary to law. The federal courts are fully capable of adjudicating those disputes. . . .

KING, Circuit Judge, dissenting:

Although there are approximately 11.3 million removable aliens in this country today, for the last several years Congress has provided the Department of Homeland Security (DHS) with only enough resources to remove approximately 400,000 of those aliens per year. Recognizing DHS's congressionally granted prosecutorial discretion to set removal enforcement priorities, Congress has exhorted DHS to use those resources to "mak[e] our country safer." In response, DHS has focused on removing "those who represent threats to national security, public safety, and border security." The DAPA Memorandum at issue here focuses on a subset of removable aliens who are unlikely to be removed unless and until more resources are made available by Congress: those who are the parents of United States citizens or legal permanent residents, who have resided in the United States for at least the last five years, who lack a criminal record, and who are not otherwise removal priorities as determined by DHS. The DAPA Memorandum has three primary objectives for these aliens: (1) to permit them to be lawfully employed and thereby enhance their ability to be self-sufficient, a goal of United States immigration law since this country's earliest immigration statutes; (2) to encourage them to come out of the shadows and to identify themselves and where they live, DHS's prime law enforcement objective; and (3) to maintain flexibility so that if Congress is able to make more resources for removal available, DHS will be able to respond.

Plaintiffs do not challenge DHS's ability to allow the aliens subject to the DAPA Memorandum—up to 4.3 million, some estimate—to remain in this country indefinitely. Indeed, Plaintiffs admit that such removal decisions are well within DHS's prosecutorial discretion. Rather, Plaintiffs complain of the consequences of DHS's decision to use its decades-long practice of granting "deferred action" to these individuals, specifically that these "illegal aliens" may temporarily work lawfully for a living and may also eventually become eligible for some public benefits. Plaintiffs contend that these consequences and benefits must be struck down even while the decision to allow the "illegal aliens" to remain stands. But Plaintiffs' challenge cannot be so easily bifurcated. For the benefits of which Plaintiffs complain are not conferred by the DAPA Memorandum—the only policy being challenged in this case—but are inexorably tied to DHS's deferred action decisions by a host of unchallenged, preexisting statutes and notice-and-comment regulations enacted by Congresses and administrations long past. Deferred action decisions, such as those contemplated by the DAPA Memorandum, are quintessential exercises of prosecutorial discretion. . . .

Plaintiffs concede that if the DAPA Memorandum is only an exercise in enforcement discretion—without granting any "additional benefits"—it is unreviewable under 5 U.S.C. §701(a). . . . Even the district court concluded that "decisions as to how to marshal DHS resources, how to best utilize DHS manpower, and where to concentrate its activities are discretionary decisions solely within the purview of the Executive Branch." But those are exactly the type of decisions the DAPA Memorandum contemplates. The Memorandum is a statement embodying the Secretary's tentative decision, based on an assessment of the best uses of DHS's limited resources and under his congressionally delegated authority to "[e]stablish[] national immigration enforcement policies and priorities," 6 U.S.C. §202(5), not to remove qualifying applicants for a certain period of time. . . .

To the extent the exercise of deferred action "trigger[s]" other benefits, those are not new or "associated" benefits contained within the DAPA Memorandum itself. Rather, those benefits are a function of statutes and regulations that were enacted by Congresses and administrations long past—statutes and regulations which, vitally, *Plaintiffs do not challenge in this action*. The ability to apply for work authorization, the benefit on which the district court most heavily relied, has been tied to deferred action by a federal regulation since the early 1980s. The most current such regulation, promulgated in 1987, states that "[a]n alien who has been granted deferred action, an act of administrative convenience to the government which gives some cases lower priority," may apply for work authorization "if the alien establishes an economic necessity for employment." 8 C.F.R. §274a.12(c)(14). It is this regulation, not the DAPA Memorandum, which affords those granted deferred action the ability to apply for work authorization. Plaintiffs did not challenge the validity of this regulation, and for good reason—it was promulgated via the notice-and-comment process. . . .

Like work authorization, [access to certain federal] benefits [is] conferred not by the DAPA Memorandum, but by federal statutes or notice-and-comment regulations that are not being directly challenged in this case. And to the extent there are "state benefits," to individuals granted deferred action, those benefits stem from *state* statutes or regulations, none of which is being challenged here. Accordingly, DAPA itself grants no new rights or benefits. It merely announces guidelines for the granting of deferred action (which may trigger benefits under this framework of preexisting law). . . .

Because the DAPA Memorandum contains only guidelines for the exercise of prosecutorial discretion and does not itself confer any benefits to DAPA recipients, I would deem this case non-justiciable. The policy decisions at issue in this case are best resolved not by judicial fiat, but via the political process. . . .

NOTES AND QUESTIONS

1. *Is this a case about "prosecutorial discretion" or something else?* In Judge Smith's view, what distinguishes this case from the no-review rule of *Heckler?* The fact that DHS had codified its "deferred action" policy in a rule-like document (the "DAPA Memo")? The sheer number of people affected? The fact that deferred action enabled beneficiaries to obtain lawful employment? An assumption that the supposed "individualized" determinations of eligibility will in fact be made mechanistically? Does Judge King have a persuasive answer to Smith's arguments?

2. *The aftermath.* The Supreme Court, comprised of eight members following Justice Scalia's death, affirmed the Fifth Circuit, by a vote of 4 to 4, without opinion, thus leaving the nationwide preliminary injunction against DAPA in place, and leaving the legal issues presented in the case without authoritative resolution. The Trump administration has declined to revive the DAPA program, thus making it unlikely that the case will return to the Supreme Court. If a new administration did revive DAPA, how do you predict that the Court, now fully staffed, would rule on the issue of reviewability?

3. *"Regulatory discretion"?* Should an agency's decision not to initiate rulemaking fall within the *Heckler* presumption? As we saw in Massachusetts v. EPA, excerpted *supra*, the Supreme Court granted judicial review of a decision by the EPA refusing to regulate greenhouse gases. In so doing, the Court rejected an argument that *Heckler* applied:

> There are key differences between a denial of a petition for rulemaking and an agency's decision not to initiate an enforcement action. *See* American Horse Protection Assn., Inc. v. Lyng, 812 F.2d 1, 3-4 (D.C. Cir. 1987). In contrast to non-enforcement decisions, agency refusals to initiate rulemaking "are less frequent, more apt to involve legal as opposed to factual analysis, and subject to special formalities, including a public explanation." *Id.*, at 4; *see also* 5 U.S.C. §555(e). They moreover arise out of denials of petitions for rulemaking which (at least in the circumstances here) the affected party had an undoubted procedural right to file in the first instance. Refusals to promulgate rules are thus susceptible to judicial review, though such review is "extremely limited" and "highly deferential."

549 U.S. at 527-528. Are the Court's bases for distinguishing *Heckler* persuasive? Doesn't the decision whether to promulgate a rule regulating a previously unregulated pollutant like greenhouse gases have potentially huge implications for the agency's future enforcement efforts and resources?

4. *Are negotiated settlements of enforcement actions reviewable?* In the exercise of their enforcement discretion, agencies sometimes negotiate settlements with individual parties that seem to establish a new regulatory regime. Should such settlements presumptively be unreviewable? On the one hand, settlement agreements can be opportunities for creativity and cooperation between agencies and those they regulate; on the other hand, they might allow agencies to avoid procedures designed to ensure transparency and accountability. In Association of Irritated Residents v. EPA, 494 F.3d 1027 (D.C. Cir. 2007), the EPA entered into agreements with several animal feeding operations whose emissions historically had proven difficult for the EPA to estimate. Under the agreements, the operations would develop an emissions estimation method and, in exchange,

the EPA would not pursue administrative actions against them for a defined period. Tired of odors emitted by the feedlots, environmental and community groups sued, arguing that the EPA had no authority to induce compliance—the goal of these agreements—in this manner, and that the procedures constituted rulemaking without allowing notice and comment. Citing *Heckler*, the D.C. Circuit held that the EPA has discretion about whether and when to enforce the relevant emissions laws, and that the agreements constitute enforcement decisions that are committed to the discretion of the agency. In dissent, Judge Rogers objected that the EPA was allowing the regulated community to "buy its way out of compliance with the statutes." *Id.* at 1037. While, under *Heckler*, "EPA could opt to forego bringing enforcement actions entirely, and its decision might be unreviewable," the agency could not "adopt[] a new generalized approach toward enforcing three environmental statutes in the future by means of an enforcement protocol unrelated to particularized findings of past or ongoing statutory violations and untethered to the enforcement regimes established by Congress" while remaining immune from judicial review. *Id.* at 1040.

In some instances, agencies can insulate certain settlements from judicial review. The National Labor Relations Board promulgated a rule stating that an "informal" settlement between an NLRB regional director and a party charged with unfair labor practices can only be appealed to the Board's General Counsel but not to the Board itself (unlike "formal" settlement agreements, which are akin to Board-approved consent decrees). As a result, because informal agreements do not result in a Board order, they are not reviewable by courts of appeals. The rule was upheld by the Supreme Court in NLRB v. United Food & Commercial Workers, 484 U.S. 112 (1987).

5. *Can an agency's failure to attempt to mediate a dispute be reviewable?* In Mach Mining, LLC v. EEOC, 135 S. Ct. 1645 (2015), the Supreme Court ruled that an alleged failure of the EEOC to try to resolve an employment discrimination claim by mediation was judicially reviewable. Title VII of the Civil Rights Act of 1964, 42 U.S.C. §2000e-5(b), requires that, before it may bring suit in federal court for an alleged "unlawful employment practice," the EEOC must first "endeavor to eliminate" the practice by "informal methods of conference, conciliation, and persuasion." After receiving a sex discrimination complaint against Mach Mining, the EEOC sent a letter inviting the employer to participate in informal conciliation. A year later the commission sent a letter stating that conciliation had been unsuccessful, and then brought suit against Mach. Mach defended, in part, by alleging that the EEOC had not attempted to conciliate in good faith. The EEOC argued that its conciliation efforts were not reviewable because there were "no standards by which to judge" the performance of that duty. A unanimous Supreme Court, in an opinion by Justice Kagan, disagreed. Conceding that "the statute provides the EEOC with wide latitude over the conciliation process," the Court nonetheless found that "the statute provides certain concrete standards pertaining to what [the conciliation] endeavor must entail," and therefore provided the basis for a "narrow" scope of review of conciliation efforts:

> The statute demands . . . that the EEOC communicate in some way (through "conference, conciliation, and persuasion") about an "alleged unlawful employment practice" in an "endeavor" to achieve an employer's voluntary compliance. That means the EEOC must inform the employer about the specific allegation, as

the Commission typically does in a letter announcing its determination of "reasonable cause." Such notice properly describes both what the employer has done and which employees (or what class of employees) have suffered as a result. And the EEOC must try to engage the employer in some form of discussion (whether written or oral), so as to give the employer an opportunity to remedy the allegedly discriminatory practice. Judicial review of those requirements (and nothing else) ensures that the Commission complies with the statute. At the same time, that relatively barebones review allows the EEOC to exercise all the expansive discretion Title VII gives it to decide how to conduct conciliation efforts and when to end them. And such review can occur consistent with the statute's non-disclosure provision, because a court looks only to whether the EEOC attempted to confer about a charge, and not to what happened (i.e., statements made or positions taken) during those discussions.

A sworn affidavit from the EEOC stating that it has performed the obligations noted above but that its efforts have failed will usually suffice to show that it has met the conciliation requirement. If, however, the employer provides credible evidence of its own, in the form of an affidavit or otherwise, indicating that the EEOC did not provide the requisite information about the charge or attempt to engage in a discussion about conciliating the claim, a court must conduct the factfinding necessary to decide that limited dispute. Should the court find in favor of the employer, the appropriate remedy is to order the EEOC to undertake the mandated efforts to obtain voluntary compliance. . . .

Can *Mach Mining* be squared with *Heckler?* Doesn't a decision about whether and how to settle a case involve just the same range of factors as a decision about whether and how to initiate enforcement action in the first place? Does the Court's "narrow" scope of review accomplish anything substantive, other than making the EEOC run through a mechanical checklist of steps?

c. Resource Allocation and Appropriations

LINCOLN v. VIGIL
508 U.S. 182 (1993)

JUSTICE SOUTER delivered the opinion of the Court.

For several years in the late 1970s and early 1980s, the Indian Health Service provided diagnostic and treatment services, referred to collectively as the Indian Children's Program, to handicapped Indian children in the Southwest. In 1985, the Service decided to reallocate the Program's resources to a nationwide effort to assist such children. We hold that the Service's decision to discontinue the Program was "committed to agency discretion by law" and therefore not subject to judicial review under the Administrative Procedure Act, 5 U.S.C. §701(a)(2). . . .

I

The Indian Health Service, an agency within the Public Health Service of the Department of Health and Human Services, provides health care for some 1.5 million American Indian and Alaska Native people. . . . The Service receives yearly lump-sum appropriations from Congress and expends the funds under authority of the Snyder Act, 25 U.S.C. §13, and the Indian Health Care Improvement Act, 25 U.S.C. §1601 *et seq.* So far as it concerns us here, the Snyder Act authorizes the Service to "expend such moneys as Congress may from time to time appropriate, for the benefit, care, and assistance of the Indians," for the "relief of distress and conservation of health." . . . The Improvement Act authorizes expenditures for, inter alia, Indian mental-health care, and specifically for "therapeutic and residential treatment centers." . . .

This case concerns a collection of related services, commonly known as the Indian Children's Program, that the Service provided from 1978 to 1985. In the words of the Court of Appeals, a "cloud [of] bureaucratic haze" obscures the history of the Program, Vigil v. Rhoades, 953 F.2d 1225, 1226 (10th Cir. 1992), which seems to have grown out of a plan "to establish therapeutic and residential treatment centers for disturbed Indian children." H.R. Rep. No. 94-1026, pt. 1, p. 80 (1976) (prepared in conjunction with enactment of the Improvement Act). These centers were to be established under a "major cooperative care agreement" between the Service and the Bureau of Indian Affairs, *id.*, at 81, and would have provided such children "with intensive care in a residential setting." *Id.*, at 80.

Congress never expressly appropriated funds for these centers. In 1978, however, the Service allocated approximately $292,000 from its fiscal year 1978 appropriation to its office in Albuquerque, New Mexico, for the planning and development of a pilot project for handicapped Indian children, which became known as the Indian Children's Program. . . . The pilot project apparently convinced the Service that a building was needed, and, in 1979, the Service requested $3.5 million from Congress to construct a diagnostic and treatment center for handicapped Indian children. . . . The appropriation for fiscal year 1980 did not expressly provide the requested funds, however, and legislative reports indicated only that Congress had increased the Service's funding by $300,000 for nationwide expansion and development of the Program in coordination with the Bureau. . . .

Plans for a national program to be managed jointly by the Service and the Bureau were never fulfilled, however, and the Program continued simply as an offering of the Service's Albuquerque office, from which the Program's staff of 11 to 16 employees would make monthly visits to Indian communities in New Mexico and Southern Colorado and on the Navajo and Hopi Reservations. . . . The Program's staff provided "diagnostic, evaluation, treatment planning and followup services" for Indian children with emotional, educational, physical, or mental handicaps. . . . Congress never authorized or appropriated monies expressly for the Program, and the Service continued to pay for its regional activities out of annual lump-sum appropriations from 1980 to 1985, during which period the Service repeatedly apprised Congress of the Program's continuing operation. . . .

Nevertheless, the Service had not abandoned the proposal for a nationwide treatment program, and in June 1985 it notified those who referred patients to the Program that it was "re-evaluating [the Program's] purpose . . . as a national mental health program for Indian children and adolescents." . . . In August 1985, the Service determined that Program staff hitherto assigned to provide direct clinical services should be reassigned as consultants to other nationwide

Service programs, . . . and discontinued the direct clinical services to Indian children in the Southwest. . . .

Respondents, handicapped Indian children eligible to receive services through the Program, subsequently brought this action for declaratory and injunctive relief against petitioners, the Director of the Service and others (collectively, the Service), in the United States District Court for the District of New Mexico. Respondents alleged, inter alia, that the Service's decision to discontinue direct clinical services violated the federal trust responsibility to Indians, the Snyder Act, the Improvement Act, the Administrative Procedure Act, various agency regulations, and the Fifth Amendment's Due Process Clause. . . .

II

First is the question whether it was error for the Court of Appeals to hold the substance of the Service's decision to terminate the Program reviewable under the APA. The Act provides that "[a] person suffering legal wrong because of agency action, or adversely affected or aggrieved by agency action within the meaning of a relevant statute, is entitled to judicial review thereof," 5 U.S.C. §702, and we have read the Act as embodying a "basic presumption of judicial review." Abbott Laboratories v. Gardner, 387 U.S. 136, 140 (1967). This is "just" a presumption, however, Block v. Community Nutrition Institute, 467 U.S. 340, 349 (1984), and under §701(a)(2) agency action is not subject to judicial review "to the extent that" such action "is committed to agency discretion by law." As we explained in Heckler v. Chaney, 470 U.S. 821, 830 (1985), §701(a)(2) makes it clear that "review is not to be had" in those rare circumstances where the relevant statute "is drawn so that a court would have no meaningful standard against which to judge the agency's exercise of discretion." . . . "In such a case, the statute ('law') can be taken to have 'committed' the decisionmaking to the agency's judgment absolutely." Heckler, supra, at p. 830.

Over the years, we have read §701(a)(2) to preclude judicial review of certain categories of administrative decisions that courts traditionally have regarded as "committed to agency discretion." See Franklin v. Massachusetts, 505 U.S. 788, 816 (1992) (Stevens, J., concurring in part and concurring in judgment); [Webster v. Doe, 486 U.S. 592, 609 (1988) (Scalia, J., dissenting)].

The allocation of funds from a lump-sum appropriation is another administrative decision traditionally regarded as committed to agency discretion. After all, the very point of a lump-sum appropriation is to give an agency the capacity to adapt to changing circumstances and meet its statutory responsibilities in what it sees as the most effective or desirable way. . . . For this reason, a fundamental principle of appropriations law is that where "Congress merely appropriates lump-sum amounts without statutorily restricting what can be done with those funds, a clear inference arises that it does not intend to impose legally binding restrictions, and indicia in committee reports and other legislative history as to how the funds should or are expected to be spent do not establish any legal requirements on" the agency. LTV Aerospace Corp., 55 Comp. Gen. 307, 319 (1975). . . . Put another way, a lump-sum appropriation reflects a congressional recognition that an agency must be allowed "flexibility to shift . . . funds within a particular . . . appropriation account so that" the agency "can make necessary adjustments for 'unforeseen developments'" and "'changing requirements'" LTV Aerospace Corp., *supra,* at p. 318 (citation omitted).

Like the decision against instituting enforcement proceedings, then, an agency's allocation of funds from a lump-sum appropriation requires "a complicated balancing of a number of factors which are peculiarly within its expertise": whether its "resources are best spent" on one program or another; whether it "is likely to succeed" in fulfilling its statutory mandate; whether a particular program "best fits the agency's overall policies"; and, "indeed, whether the agency has enough resources" to fund a program "at all." *Heckler,* 470 U.S., at 831. As in *Heckler,* so here, the "agency is far better equipped than the courts to deal with the many variables involved in the proper ordering of its priorities." *Id.,* at 831-832. Of course, an agency is not free simply to disregard statutory responsibilities: Congress may always circumscribe agency discretion to allocate resources by putting restrictions in the operative statutes (though not, as we have seen, just in the legislative history). *See id.,* at 833. And, of course, we hardly need to note that an agency's decision to ignore congressional expectations may expose it to grave political consequences. But as long as the agency allocates funds from a lump-sum appropriation to meet permissible statutory objectives, §701(a)(2) gives the courts no leave to intrude. "[T]o [that] extent," the decision to allocate funds "is committed to agency discretion by law." §701(a)(2).

The Service's decision to discontinue the Program is accordingly unreviewable under §701(a)(2). . . . It is true that the Service repeatedly apprised Congress of the Program's continued operation, but, as we have explained, these representations do not translate through the medium of legislative history into legally binding obligations. The reallocation of agency resources to assist handicapped Indian children nationwide clearly falls within the Service's statutory mandate to provide health care to Indian people, *see supra,* and respondents, indeed, do not seriously contend otherwise. The decision to terminate the Program was committed to the Service's discretion. . . .

IV

The judgment of the Court of Appeals is reversed, and the case is remanded for further proceedings consistent with this opinion.

It is so ordered.

NOTES AND QUESTIONS

1. *The basis for the Court's ruling.* Is the Court's understanding of "committed to agency discretion by law" the same as, or different from, the formulation stated in *Overton Park,* excerpted in Chapter II, *supra?* The *Heckler* formulation, *supra?* Justice Scalia's formulation in his *Webster* dissent, *supra?* What authority does Justice Souter cite for the existence of a "tradition" of denying review of agency decisions allocating funds from a lump-sum appropriation? If *Lincoln* had reached the Court after its *SUWA* decision, would the latter case's "discreteness" test for reviewable agency action provide a better rationale for denying review?

2. *Review of procedural challenges.* The *Lincoln* Court entertained and rejected a challenge to the procedures employed by the Service in deciding to terminate the Indian Children's Program. In addition to their substantive arguments, the challengers also claimed that the Service should have engaged in notice and comment rulemaking under APA §553 before terminating the program. Should judicial review of the procedures be available even if the Court decides that the substantive decision is committed to agency discretion by law? The Court apparently thought so, since it decided the procedural issues, albeit in the agency's favor.

3. *Distributing scarce resources.* Consider the following situation in light of *Lincoln*'s holding that lump-sum funding allocations are "committed to agency discretion by law." The Indian Self-Determination Act (ISDA) provides that Indian tribes may themselves operate their federal Indian programs, and if they submit a plan to do so, they receive "contract support funds" to pay the administrative costs of program operation. In 1995, Congress appropriated approximately $10 million less than necessary to fully fund the program. The Secretary of the Interior published a policy stating that plans under the program must be submitted before June 30, and any tribe missing the deadline would receive no more than half the funds to which they would otherwise have been entitled under the program. Tribes that missed the deadline sued, claiming that the Secretary should have allocated the funds under statutory standards, funding all tribes as close to fully as possible, rather than imposing the deadline-induced, half-funding policy. The Secretary argued that *Lincoln* barred review of the claim since the tribes were, in effect, challenging decisions regarding the allocation of funds. What result? *See* Ramah Navajo School Board, Inc. v. Babbitt, 87 F.3d 1338 (D.C. Cir. 1996).

C. STANDING TO SECURE JUDICIAL REVIEW

Closely related to the question whether a particular claim is subject to judicial review is the question whether that claim may be asserted by the particular party before the court. Who may obtain review of agency action generally is referred to as a question of "standing." Courts have identified three different sources of standing limitations. First, there is a constitutionally based limitation of the federal courts' "judicial power" to "cases or controversies" in Article III (see the Appendix, *infra*). Implicit in that concept, the courts have declared, is a requirement that persons presenting a claim for judicial resolution have a sufficiently direct or concrete interest that can be vindicated by its resolution in their favor. As the Court put it in Warth v. Seldin, 422 U.S. 490, 498-499 (1975):

> In its constitutional dimension, standing imports justiciability: whether the plaintiff has made out a "case or controversy" between himself and the defendant within the meaning of Article III. This is the threshold question in every federal case, determining the power of the court to entertain the suit. As an aspect of justiciability, the standing question is whether the plaintiff has "alleged such a personal stake in the outcome of the controversy" as to warrant his invocation of federal-court jurisdiction and to justify exercise of the court's remedial powers on his behalf.

Second, standing to sue may be further restricted by judge-made rules of judicial administration. In a series of cases, mostly involving constitutional attacks on legislative acts, the Supreme Court has fashioned a group of "prudential" principles that limit access to federal courts more severely than the case or controversy constraint in Article III. The Court summarized these principles, too, in Warth v. Seldin:

> Apart from this minimum constitutional mandate, this Court has recognized other limits on the class of persons who may invoke the courts' decisional and remedial powers. First, the Court has held that when the asserted harm is a "generalized grievance" shared in substantially equal measure by all or a large class of citizens, that harm alone normally does not warrant exercise of jurisdiction. . . . Second, even when the plaintiff has alleged injury sufficient to meet the "case or controversy" requirement, this Court has held that the plaintiff generally must assert his own legal rights and interests, and cannot rest his claim to relief on the legal rights or interests of third parties. . . . Without such limitations—closely related to Article III concerns but essentially matters of judicial self-governance—the courts would be called upon to decide abstract questions of wide public significance even though other governmental institutions may be more competent to address the questions and even though judicial intervention may be unnecessary to protect individual rights.

Id. at 499-500.

A third source-of-standing doctrine is legislative enactment. Congress sometimes expressly defines the class of potential plaintiffs by specifying who may petition a court to review a particular administrative action. The Medicare statute provides, for example, that certain actions of the Secretary of Health and Human Services may be challenged only by the program's beneficiaries and not by health care providers or private insurers incidentally injured by such actions. *See* Alabama Hosp. Assn. v. United States, 656 F.2d 606 (Ct. Cl. 1981), *cert. denied,* 456 U.S. 943 (1982).

While these three sources of standing limitations are readily identified, what each source contributes to the doctrine of standing itself and the relation of the differing principles derived from each limitation are less clear. Plainly, courts cannot entertain suits that do not satisfy Article III's case or controversy constraint, no matter what the current judicial inclination or legislative directive. But can Congress *create* Article III standing by granting a right to any person or class it chooses? If it can do so by granting substantive rights, can it also do so by granting the right to review? Can Congress override the court's prudential concerns by a clear command to hear a particular type of dispute? If so, is it sufficient that Congress created a right of action and conferred jurisdiction?

What would be the implication of a negative answer to any of these questions? An affirmative answer to each question makes standing, in effect, wholly subsidiary to the statutory process: standing reduces to interpretation of statute-created rights of action. The constitutional restriction, then, would apply only where an action is purely collusive; it would have no other application where Congress has created a right to be in court. Further, prudential concerns are, in this view, only aids for interpreting ambiguous congressional authorizations. Is this view sound? If not, how would you qualify it? How significant, then, are the standing limits outside Congress's control?

1.   *The Legal Right Test*

Emphasizing the role of statutorily created rights of action helps one to understand why problems of standing are largely confined to suits challenging government conduct. The ordinary lawsuit involving individual persons or entities is based on a claim that the defendant breached a duty owed to the plaintiff, usually coupled with an allegation that the breach caused harm to the plaintiff. To prevail, the plaintiff must establish the elements of his right of action — the nature of the duty, that it ran from defendant to plaintiff, that it was breached, and (where required) that harm of some specified type and magnitude did (or will) flow from the breach. There has been some expansion in the notion of duty and the parties to whom it runs, of what evidence is satisfactory to prove a breach, and of what constitutes harm. The famous "fall of the citadel" of privity of contract and the rise of the "market share" concept of liability for "generic" torts are two examples. Procedural devices, such as the class action, also have enlarged the opportunity for litigation by representatives whose personal injury may be open to question. By and large, however, private rights of action have boundaries that are confining: the universe of potential plaintiffs usually is both small and reasonably well defined. Standing, thus, has been subsumed under arguments concerning duty, breach, and causation.

In the administrative arena, the link between individual complaints and the action complained of is more problematic. Admittedly, the right to sue agencies for misconduct sometimes is granted in terms that look much like a private suit. For instance, some rights of action decree that damages are recoverable for harm suffered by some particular class of persons as a consequence of specific sorts of government misconduct. Although standing may be raised as an issue in such suits, its resolution looks like a decision of the suits' merits. In this context, it makes little sense to ask who can sue; the relevant question is who can recover. This, however, is not the usual context for challenges to administrative conduct. Indeed, the problem of standing in regard to administrative law arises largely because damage suits are not the principal vehicle for challenging agency action and because the contours of nondamage rights of action are often unclear. Statutes frequently provide authority for agencies to act, but only in a specified manner. Rights of action, either general or particular to the agency, allow judicial review to ensure that the limits of agency power are not transcended. But what, absent statutory specification, should dictate who may bring the suit?

A major issue in standing is whether a third party, such as a competitor, should be able to challenge an agency's treatment of someone else. In the first half of the twentieth century, courts faced with ambiguous language respecting the nature of the right to review of agency action frequently analogized suits against agencies to private lawsuits. Even where nondamage remedies were sought, the courts sought to constrain the right of action in the same way that duty rules, causation, and injury requirements do in private civil actions. The test that emerged from this effort became known as the "legal wrong" or "legal right" standard. To establish standing, said the courts, a litigant had to allege injury to a "legally protected interest" — that is, violation of a right conferred upon the litigant by positive (statutory or common) law. This test severely limits the ability of third parties, including competitors, to challenge agency action, because only the subject of the agency action had legal rights at stake.

This test was applied to limit competitors' standing by the Supreme Court in Alexander Sprunt & Son, Inc. v. United States, 281 U.S. 249 (1930). In *Sprunt,* several shippers attacked as unlawful an ICC order that required certain railroads to reduce freight rates charged to their competitors. The ICC had found the rates to be "unduly prejudicial" to those competitors and therefore unlawful. The Court held that the petitioner-shippers lacked standing because, while they would lose their previous competitive advantage, they had not suffered injury to any legal interest granted by the statute. The shippers had a right only to be charged reasonable rates by the railroads, a right unaffected by an order addressed to the lawfulness of rates charged to someone else.

Similarly, in Tennessee Electric Power Co. v. Tennessee Valley Authority, 306 U.S. 118 (1939), the Court refused to allow competing private utilities to challenge the constitutionality of the Act creating the TVA. The utilities could rely on state law to show the legal right that would provide standing for their federal claim, the Court said. But since the states involved had no law barring competition among utilities, the plaintiffs had suffered no legal wrong.

In contrast to *Sprunt* and *Tennessee Electric,* the Court did find standing for railroads to challenge an ICC order approving a merger among competitors. The legal right asserted was access to terminals, guaranteed by the Transportation Act of 1920. The ICC order in approving the merger effectively authorized petitioner's exclusion from the terminal facilities. Concern over this aspect of the ICC approval might not have been the real motivation for suit; it nonetheless was a clearly cognizable legal claim, according to the Court. The Chicago Junction Case, 264 U.S. 258 (1924).

The legal right test was criticized as difficult to apply, as requiring that a determination essentially on the merits of a case precede a full consideration of the merits, and as unfair, denying relief to parties in fact injured by wrongful government action. *See, e.g.,* Lee A. Albert, Standing to Challenge Administrative Action: An Inadequate Surrogate for Claim for Relief, 83 Yale L.J. 425 (1974); Kenneth C. Davis, The Liberalized Law of Standing, 37 U. Chi. L. Rev. 450 (1970).

Aside from the test's desirability, the Court's early decisions did not make plain from what sources the legal right test derived. The Supreme Court clarified this in 1940. Two decisions from the 1939 term, read together, left no doubt that the requirement for a legal wrong was merely a presumptive element of plaintiff's right of action — Congress could eliminate that element if it so chose.

The first decision was Federal Communications Commission v. Sanders Bros. Radio Station, 309 U.S. 470 (1940). Sanders sought review of an FCC order granting a radio station license to a competitor. The Communications Act conferred upon Sanders no legal interest in freedom from competition, but it did authorize "any . . . person aggrieved or whose interests are adversely affected by any decision of the Commission" to petition the Court of Appeals for review of that decision. That provision, the Supreme Court held, gave Sanders standing to challenge the lawfulness of the license award. To use a phrase later coined by Judge Jerome Frank of the Second Circuit, Congress had, in effect, deputized competitors to act as "private attorneys general" to vindicate the "public interest." Associated Industries v. Ickes, 134 F.2d 694 (2d Cir. 1943).

The Court's decision a few months later in Perkins v. Lukens Steel Co., 310 U.S. 113 (1940), underscored that the particular language in the Communications Act was decisive in *Sanders Bros.* In *Perkins,* the Court refused to hear a challenge to an order of the Secretary of Labor setting minimum pay rates for the steel industry under the Walsh-Healey Public Contracts Act of 1936, 49 Stat. 2036, 41 U.S.C. §§35-45. The Secretary, Frances Perkins, had divided the country into six regions, setting a minimum rate for each, and any company that wished to be eligible for federal contracts was required to pay (at least) the wage applicable in its region. The plaintiff companies argued that Congress, in mandating determination of minimum pay by "locality," had intended that rates be set for smaller jurisdictions. Declining to pass on that claim, the Court observed:

> We are of the opinion that no legal rights of [the plaintiff's] were shown to have been invaded or threatened. . . . It is by now clear that neither damage nor loss of income in consequence of the action of Government, which is not an invasion of recognized legal rights, is in itself a source of legal rights in the absence of constitutional legislation recognizing it as such.

310 U.S. at 125. The Court did not think it necessary to discuss or distinguish *Sanders Bros.*

2. *Standing Under the Administrative Procedure Act*

The statute-by-statute analysis exemplified by *Sanders Bros.* and *Perkins* was complicated by the passage of the APA in 1946. An APA provision, now codified at §702 of Title 5, states: "A person suffering legal wrong because of agency action, or adversely affected or aggrieved by agency action within the meaning of a relevant statute, is entitled to judicial review thereof."

Does the APA's "adversely affected or aggrieved" language adopt the broadened view of standing adopted by the Court in *Sanders Bros.* as the pattern for all review of agency conduct? Or does the qualifying phrase "within the meaning of a relevant statute" mean that standing is limited to those suffering legal wrongs *unless* some other statute specifically provides for review at the behest of any "person aggrieved"?

The Supreme Court addressed the issue in 1970, when the Justices decided their first major standing case in three decades:

ASSOCIATION OF DATA PROCESSING SERVICE ORGANIZATIONS, INC. v. CAMP
397 U.S. 150 (1970)

JUSTICE DOUGLAS delivered the opinion of the Court.

[Suit was brought against the Comptroller of the Currency by companies that performed data processing services for other businesses. The Comptroller had ruled that national banks could sell certain data processing services to their customers and to other banks, thus competing with the plaintiff companies. The District Court dismissed the suit on the ground that petitioners lacked standing to obtain judicial review of the Comptroller's ruling. The Court of Appeals affirmed.]

The first question is whether the plaintiff alleges that the challenged action has caused him injury in fact, economic or otherwise. There can be no doubt but that petitioners have satisfied this test. The petitioners not only allege that competition by national banks in the business of providing data processing services might entail some future loss of profits for the petitioners, they also allege that respondent American National Bank & Trust Company was performing or preparing to perform such services for two customers for whom petitioner Data Systems, Inc., had previously agreed or negotiated to perform such services. The petitioners' suit was brought not only against the American National Bank & Trust Company, but also against the Comptroller of the Currency. The Comptroller was alleged to have caused petitioners injury in fact by his 1966 ruling which stated: "Incidental to its banking services, a national bank may make available its data processing equipment or perform data processing services on such equipment for other banks and bank customers." Comptroller's Manual for National Banks ¶3500 (October 15, 1966).

The Court of Appeals viewed the matter differently, stating:

> [A] plaintiff may challenge alleged illegal competition when as complainant it pursues (1) a legal interest by reason of public charter or contract, . . . (2) a legal interest by reason of statutory protection, . . . or (3) a "public interest" in which Congress has recognized the need for review of administrative action and plaintiff is significantly involved to have standing to represent the public. . . .

406 F.2d, at 842-843.[1] . . .

The "legal interest" test goes to the merits. The question of standing is different. It concerns, apart from the "case" or "controversy" test, the question whether the interest sought to be protected by the complainant is arguably within the zone of interests to be protected or regulated by the statute or constitutional guarantee in question. Thus the Administrative Procedure Act grants standing to a person "aggrieved by agency action within the meaning of a relevant statute." 5 U.S.C. §702 (1964 ed., Supp. IV). That interest, at times, may reflect "aesthetic, conservational, and recreational" as well as economic values. Scenic Hudson Preservation Conf. v. FPC, 354 F.2d 608, 616; Office of Communication of United Church of Christ v. FCC, 359 F.2d 994, 1000-1006. A person or a family may have a spiritual stake in First Amendment values sufficient to give standing to raise issues concerning the Establishment Clause and the Free Exercise Clause. Abington School District v. Schempp, 374 U.S. 203. We mention these noneconomic values to emphasize that standing may stem from them as well as from the economic injury on which petitioners rely here. Certainly he who is "likely to be financially" injured, FCC v. Sanders Bros. Radio

---

1. . . . The third test mentioned by the Court of Appeals, which rests on an explicit provision in a regulatory statute conferring standing and is commonly referred to in terms of allowing suits by "private attorneys general," is inapplicable to the present case. *See* FCC v. Sanders Bros. Radio Station, 309 U.S. 470; Associated Industries v. Ickes, 134 F.2d 694, *vacated on suggestion of mootness*, 320 U.S. 707.

Station, 309 U.S. 470, 477, may be a reliable private attorney general to litigate the issues of the public interest in the present case. . . .

Where statutes are concerned, the trend is toward enlargement of the class of people who may protest administrative action. . . .

We find no evidence that Congress in either the Bank Service Corporation Act or the National Bank Act sought to preclude judicial review of administrative rulings by the Comptroller as to the legitimate scope of activities available to national banks under those statutes. Both Acts are clearly "relevant" statutes within the meaning of §702. The Acts do not in terms protect a specified group. But their general policy is apparent; and those whose interests are directly affected by a broad or narrow interpretation of the Acts are easily identifiable. It is clear that petitioners, as competitors of national banks which are engaging in data processing services, are within that class of "aggrieved" persons who, under §702, are entitled to judicial review of "agency action."

Whether anything in the Bank Service Corporation Act or the National Bank Act gives petitioners a "legal interest" that protects them against violations of those Acts, and whether the actions of respondents did in fact violate either of those Acts, are questions which go to the merits and remain to be decided below.

We hold that petitioners have standing to sue and that the case should be remanded for a hearing on the merits. Reversed and remanded.

NOTES AND QUESTIONS

1. *Source of the zone-of-interests test.* Is the "zone of interests" test simply an interpretation of §702's second clause ("adversely affected or aggrieved by agency action within the meaning of a relevant statute")? If so, does it read the statute correctly? Or is the requirement derived from judicially imposed prudential principles with which §702 may be consistent? Alternatively, does the test come from the relevant statute, which Congress designed to encompass certain plaintiffs' interests?

2. *Peeking at the merits?* Justice Douglas asserts that, unlike the legal right test, the harm-plus-zone-of-interests test does not implicate the merits of the case. Is that right? Can you tell whether an interest is "arguably within the zone of interests to be protected or regulated by the statute" without examining the merits of the claim? Look at how Justice Douglas answered that question in the affirmative. Did he successfully distinguish this inquiry from an analysis of the merits?

3. *Whose "interests"?* In Clarke v. Securities Industry Assn., 479 U.S. 388 (1987), the Court held that an association of nonbank securities brokers had standing to challenge the Comptroller of the Currency's decision that allowed a national bank to offer brokerage services at numerous locations. The Comptroller's decision allegedly violated a statutory restriction on the place in which bank services could be performed. The majority concluded that the association's interest in constraining national banks "has a plausible relationship to the policies underlying [the relevant sections] of the National Bank Act." The majority declared that the zone-of-interests test was not "especially demanding" and did not require an indication of congressional intent to benefit the

plaintiff. Subsequently, a new majority adopted what might be viewed as a more restrictive version of the zone-of-interests test. In Air Courier Conference of America v. American Postal Workers Union, 498 U.S. 517 (1991), the Supreme Court unanimously rebuffed an attempt by postal workers' unions to challenge the Postal Service's suspension of its monopoly over international remailing services, under which international air mail is bypassed by sending letters by courier to foreign countries and depositing them directly into the foreign postal systems. In an opinion written on behalf of six Justices by Chief Justice Rehnquist, the Court assumed that the union's members had suffered injury in fact, but held that they lacked standing because statutes granting the Postal Service's monopoly and allowing the Service to make exceptions to that monopoly were written with the public interest in an efficient mail service, and not the interests of postal workers, in mind.

The Supreme Court, without altering or elaborating on the zone-of-interests test, has not denied anyone standing based on the zone-of-interests test since *Air Courier. See, e.g.,* Devlin v. Scardelletti, 536 U.S. 1 (2002) (class members are within the zone of interests of Federal Rule of Civil Procedure requiring that class action settlements be fair to class members); Federal Election Commn. v. Akins, 524 U.S. 11 (1998) (voters are within the zone of interests of election laws requiring political committees to disclose information); National Credit Union Admin. v. First Nat. Bank & Trust Co., 522 U.S. 479 (1998) (competing financial institutions are within the zone of interests of statute regulating the scope of credit unions' business); Monsanto v. Geertson Seed Farms, 561 U.S. 139 (2010) (alfalfa growers and environmental groups claiming economic injury due to deregulation of genetically altered alfalfa are within the zone of interests of the National Environmental Policy Act).

4. *Organizational standing.* Notice that the named petitioner in the *Data Processing* case is an organization of data processing service companies who claim to have been injured by the Comptroller's action. On what basis can an association (as opposed to its members) have standing to sue? In Warth v. Seldin, 422 U.S. 490 (1975), discussed *supra*, the Court declared:

> There is no question that an association may have standing in its own right to seek judicial relief from injury to itself and to vindicate whatever rights and immunities the association itself may enjoy. Moreover, in attempting to secure relief from injury to itself the association may assert the rights of its members, at least so long as the challenged infractions adversely affect its members' associational ties.

Id. at 511. Later cases established that an association may have standing to represent the interests of its members, even when the association has not itself suffered any injury. In Hunt v. Washington Apple Advertising Commission, 432 U.S. 333 (1977), the Court announced a three-part test for this kind of "associational standing":

> [A]n association has standing to bring suit on behalf of its members when: (a) its members would otherwise have standing to sue in their own right; (b) the interests it seeks to protect are germane to the organization's purpose; and (c) neither the claim asserted nor the relief requested requires the participation of individual members in the lawsuit.

Id. at 343.

5. *The effect of "citizen suit" statutes on standing.* In the latter half of the twentieth century, Congress began including "citizen suit provisions" in certain statutes, particularly civil rights and environmental legislation. A typical example is found in the Endangered Species Act (ESA), 16 U.S.C. §1540(g), which provides that "any person may commence a civil suit on his own behalf" to enjoin certain alleged violations of the Act by either the Secretary of the Interior or by other public or private actors. In Bennett v. Spear, 520 U.S. 154 (1997), the Court confronted the question of what effect the ESA's citizen suit provision had on the application of the "zone of interests" test for standing. The Fish and Wildlife Service in the Department of the Interior had issued a "biological opinion" to the Bureau of Reclamation (which operates federal water projects) recommending maintenance of minimum water levels in reservoirs in order to avoid harming the fish. Plaintiff irrigation districts and ranchers, who stood to lose their water allocations, claimed that the biological opinion violated various provisions of the ESA and the APA. One of the plaintiffs' claims was governed by the citizen suit provision. The Ninth Circuit held that, notwithstanding that provision, the plaintiffs lacked standing because their economic interests did not lie within the "zone of interests" protected by the ESA. In an opinion by Justice Scalia, the Court held for the ranchers:

> The first question in the present case is whether the ESA's citizen-suit provision . . . negates the zone-of-interests test (or, perhaps more accurately, expands the zone of interests). We think it does. The first operative portion of the provision says that "any person may commence a civil suit"—an authorization of remarkable breadth when compared with the language Congress ordinarily uses. Even in some other environmental statutes, Congress has used more restrictive formulations, such as "[any person] having an interest which is or may be adversely affected," . . . or "any person having a valid legal interest which is or may be adversely affected . . . whenever such action constitutes a case or controversy," 42 U.S.C. §9124(a) (Ocean Thermal Energy Conversion Act). And in contexts other than the environment, Congress has often been even more restrictive. . . .
>
> Our readiness to take the term "any person" at face value is greatly augmented by two interrelated considerations: that the overall subject matter of this legislation is the environment (a matter in which it is common to think all persons have an interest) and that the obvious purpose of the particular provision in question is to encourage enforcement by so-called "private attorneys general"—evidenced by its elimination of the usual amount-in-controversy and diversity-of-citizenship requirements, its provision for recovery of the costs of litigation (including even expert witness fees), and its reservation to the Government of a right of first refusal to pursue the action initially and a right to intervene later.
>
> It is true that the plaintiffs here are seeking to prevent application of environmental restrictions rather than to implement them. But the "any person" formulation applies to all the causes of action . . . not only to actions against private violators of environmental restrictions, and not only to actions against the Secretary asserting underenforcement . . . , but also to actions against the Secretary asserting overenforcement. . . . [T]here is no textual basis for saying that its expansion of standing requirements applies to environmentalists alone.

520 U.S. at 164-166.

3.   *Constitutional Standing Requirements: Injury, Causation, Redressability*

Although the *Data Processing* opinion apparently laid to rest the legal interest test, long a source of confusion, the Court's decisions generated considerable confusion of their own. One question was how concrete the "injury" had to be in order to confer standing. The Court addressed this issue two years after *Data Processing,* in Sierra Club v. Morton, 405 U.S. 727 (1972). The plaintiffs in *Sierra Club* contested the U.S. Forest Service's approval of a Walt Disney Enterprises plan to develop an extensive resort complex in California's Mineral King Valley. The Sierra Club obtained a preliminary injunction against the development, which was subsequently reversed on a finding that the environmental group lacked standing. The Supreme Court affirmed the court of appeals' holding because of the Sierra Club's failure to assert that any member actually used Mineral King:

> We do not question that [land development that destroys scenery and wildlife and enjoyment of the park is the type of harm that] may amount to an "injury in fact" sufficient to lay the basis for standing under §10 of the APA [5 U.S.C. §702]. . . . But the "injury in fact" test requires more than an injury to a cognizable interest. It requires that the party seeking review be himself among the injured.
>
> . . . The Sierra Club failed to allege that it or its members would be affected in any of their activities or pastimes by the Disney development. Nowhere in the pleadings or affidavits did the Club state that its members use Mineral King for any purpose, much less that they use it in any way that would be significantly affected by the proposed actions of the respondents.

405 U.S. at 734-735.

A second source of confusion bred by *Data Processing* concerned the linkage between the challenged agency action and the petitioner's alleged injury. The "linkage" issue involved two subsidiary issues: causation and redressability. In order to establish standing to sue, petitioners had to allege, with sufficient plausibility, that the challenged agency action was a *cause* of the injury of which they complained and also that a court's decision granting the relief they sought was likely to provide *redress* for that injury. But how plausible did the allegation have to be? A pair of cases decided by the Supreme Court shortly on the heels of *Sierra Club* illustrated the difficulty of applying those tests.

United States v. Students Challenging Regulatory Agency Procedures (SCRAP), 412 U.S. 669 (1973), involved a challenge to a decision of the ICC to approve across-the-board increases in railroad shipping rates. A group of Washington, D.C. law students (SCRAP) alleged that the ICC had unlawfully failed to prepare an environmental impact statement assessing the impact of the rate hike on air pollution and solid waste. They claimed that they would be injured in their use of local parks. By increasing the cost of shipping trash for recycling, they alleged, the rate hikes would reduce the amount of recycling, resulting in more air pollution and more litter. Somewhat surprisingly, given its recent decision in *Sierra Club,* the Supreme Court held these allegations sufficient to confer standing. The Court distinguished *Sierra Club* on the ground that the SCRAP petitioners "claimed that the specific and allegedly illegal action of the

Commission would directly harm them in their use of the natural resources of the Washington Metropolitan Area." On the merits, however, the Court ruled against the petitioners, holding that the District Court lacked jurisdiction to issue the preliminary injunction from which the government had appealed.

Two years later, in Simon v. Eastern Kentucky Welfare Rights Organization, Inc. (EKWRO), 426 U.S. 26 (1975), the Court seemed to reverse ground, rebuffing a challenge to an IRS Revenue Ruling brought by a group of indigent people and organizations representing their interests. The Revenue Ruling at issue had the effect of reducing the amount of free health care to the indigent that a hospital had to provide in order to retain its tax-exempt status. The individual plaintiffs alleged that, following the Ruling, they had been denied free care at tax-exempt hospitals, and that the IRS Ruling had "encouraged" the hospitals to refuse them treatment. The Supreme Court held that the plaintiffs lacked standing to challenge the legality of the Ruling. Although acknowledging that denial of treatment constitutes an "injury in fact," the Court said that "it does not follow from the allegation . . . that the denial of access to hospital services in fact results from [the] Ruling." The Court further expressed doubt that granting petitioners the relief they sought would redress the injury that they alleged. It is "equally speculative," said the Court, "whether the desired exercise of the court's remedial powers in this suit would result in the availability to respondents" of the medical care they sought.

Cases like *Sierra Club*, *SCRAP*, and *EKWRO* left standing jurisprudence in a state of uncertainty that the Supreme Court attempted to resolve in a 1992 case involving the application of the Endangered Species Act to overseas activities of federal agencies.

━━━━━━━━━━━━━━━━

The Endangered Species Act of 1973 (ESA) empowers the Secretary of the Interior to designate species as either endangered or threatened. The first step in protecting a species is "listing." "[A]ny subspecies of fish or wildlife or plants, and any distinct population segment of any species of vertebrate fish or wildlife which interbreeds when mature," 16 U.S.C. §1532(16), may be listed as either threatened or endangered, 16 U.S.C. §1533(a). A species is "threatened" when it is "likely to become an endangered species within the foreseeable future." 16 U.S.C. §1532(20). A species is "endangered" when it is "in danger of extinction throughout all or a significant portion of its range." 16 U.S.C. §1532(6).

The ESA requires that listing decisions be made based on the "best scientific and commercial data available." 16 U.S.C. §1533(b)(1)(A). The Secretary is required to consider numerous factors in making listing decisions, including the adequacy of other efforts to protect the species, whether the species' habitat is threatened with destruction or modification, whether the species is overutilized for commercial purposes, and whether it is subject to disease or predation. 16 U.S.C. §1533(a).

The ESA contains many mechanisms designed to protect listed species. One key provision prohibits any person subject to the jurisdiction of the United States to "take" an endangered species inside the United States or on the high seas. 16 U.S.C. §1532(a)(1). As discussed in *Sweet Home*, excerpted in Chapter II, *supra*, "take" is broadly defined to include both direct and indirect injury, including habitat modification. In addition, the ESA requires every federal agency to consult with the Secretary of the Interior (or for certain fish and marine species, the Secretary of Commerce) to ensure that "any action authorized, funded, or carried out by the agency . . . is not likely to jeopardize the continued existence of any endangered species or threatened species or result in the destruction or adverse modification of habitat of such species which is determined by the Secretary, after consultation as appropriate with affected States, to be critical, unless such agency has been granted an exemption for such action." 16 U.S.C. §1536(a)(2). The Secretary is also empowered to promulgate guidelines to establish when such consultation must take place. 16 U.S.C. §1536(a)(3). Following such consultation, the Secretary is authorized to recommend certain "reasonable and prudent" mitigation measures to avoid jeopardizing the species, or, in some instances, may determine that if the action went forward it would violate the Act and is thus prohibited. 16 U.S.C. §1536 (b), (c).

The case that follows arose out of a dispute over the geographical extent of the Secretary's power to require consultation.

LUJAN v. DEFENDERS OF WILDLIFE
504 U.S. 555 (1992)

JUSTICE SCALIA delivered the opinion of the Court with respect to Parts I, II, III-A, and IV. . . .

This case involves a challenge to a rule promulgated by the Secretary of the Interior interpreting §7 of the Endangered Species Act of 1973 (ESA) . . . as amended, 16 U.S.C. §1536, in such fashion as to render it applicable only to actions within the United States or on the high seas. The preliminary issue, and the only one we reach, is whether the respondents here, plaintiffs below, have standing to seek judicial review of the rule.

I

The ESA . . . instructs the Secretary of the Interior to promulgate by regulation a list of those species which are either endangered or threatened under enumerated criteria, and to define the critical habitat of these species. 16 U.S.C. §§1533, 1536. Section 7(a)(2) of the Act then provides, in pertinent part: "Each Federal agency shall, in consultation with and with the assistance of the Secretary [of the Interior], insure that any action authorized, funded, or carried out by such agency . . . is not likely to jeopardize the continued existence of any endangered species or threatened species or result in the destruction or adverse modification of habitat of such species which is determined by the Secretary, after consultation as appropriate with affected States, to be critical." 16 U.S.C. §1536(a)(2).

In 1978, the Fish and Wildlife Service (FWS) and the National Marine Fisheries Service (NMFS), on behalf of the Secretary of the Interior and the Secretary of Commerce respectively, promulgated a joint regulation stating that the obligations imposed by §7(a)(2) extend to actions taken in foreign nations. . . . The next year, however, the Interior Department began to reexamine its position. . . . A revised joint regulation, reinterpreting §7(a)(2) to require consultation only for actions taken in the United States or on the high seas, was proposed in 1983, . . . and promulgated in 1986. . . .

Shortly thereafter, respondents, organizations dedicated to wildlife conservation and other environmental causes, filed this action against the Secretary of the Interior, seeking a declaratory judgment that the new regulation is in error as to the geographic scope of §7(a)(2), and an injunction requiring the Secretary to promulgate a new regulation restoring the initial interpretation. . . .

II

Over the years, our cases have established that the irreducible constitutional minimum of standing contains three elements: First, the plaintiff must have suffered an "injury in fact"—an invasion of a legally-protected interest which is (a) concrete and particularized, *see* [Allen v. Wright, 468 U.S. 737, 756 (1984)] . . .[1] and (b) "actual or imminent, not 'conjectural' or 'hypothetical,'" Whitmore [v. Arkansas, 495 U.S. 149, 155 (1990)] (quoting Los Angeles v. Lyons, 461 U.S. 95, 102 (1983)). Second, there must be a causal connection between the injury and the conduct complained of—the injury has to be "fairly . . . trace[able] to the challenged action of the defendant, and not . . . th[e] result [of] the independent action of some third party not before the court." Simon v. Eastern Kentucky Welfare Rights Org., 426 U.S. 26, 41-42 (1976). Third, it must be "likely," as opposed to merely "speculative," that the injury will be "redressed by a favorable decision." *Id.*, at 38.

The party invoking federal jurisdiction bears the burden of establishing these elements. *See* FW/PBS, Inc. v. Dallas, 493 U.S. 215, 231 (1990). . . . Since they are not mere pleading requirements but rather an indispensable part of the plaintiff's case, each element must be supported in the same way as any other matter on which the plaintiff bears the burden of proof, *i.e.*, with the manner and degree of evidence required at the successive stages of the litigation. *See* Lujan v. National Wildlife Federation, 497 U.S. 871, 883-889 (1990). . . .

When the suit is one challenging the legality of government action or inaction, the nature and extent of facts that must be averred (at the summary judgment stage) or proved (at the trial stage) in order to establish standing depends considerably upon whether the plaintiff is himself an object of the action (or forgone action) at issue. If he is, there is ordinarily little question that the action or inaction has caused him injury, and that a judgment preventing or requiring the action will redress it. When, however, as in this case, a plaintiff's asserted injury arises from the government's allegedly unlawful regulation (or lack of regulation) of someone else, much more is needed. In that circumstance, causation and redressability ordinarily hinge on the response of the regulated (or regulable) third party to the government action or inaction—and perhaps on the response of others as well. The existence of one or more of the essential elements of standing "depends on the unfettered choices made by independent actors not before the courts and whose exercise of broad and legitimate discretion the courts cannot presume either to control or to predict," ASARCO

---

1. By particularized, we mean that the injury must affect the plaintiff in a personal and individual way.

Inc. v. Kadish, 490 U.S. 605, 615 (1989) (opinion of Kennedy, J.) . . . ; and it becomes the burden of the plaintiff to adduce facts showing that those choices have been or will be made in such manner as to produce causation and permit redressability of injury. . . . Thus, when the plaintiff is not himself the object of the government action or inaction he challenges, standing is not precluded, but it is ordinarily "substantially more difficult" to establish. *Allen, supra,* 468 U.S., at 758. . . .

III

We think the Court of Appeals failed to apply the foregoing principles in denying the Secretary's motion for summary judgment. Respondents had not made the requisite demonstration of (at least) injury. . . .

A

Respondents' claim to injury is that the lack of consultation with respect to certain funded activities abroad "increas[es] the rate of extinction of endangered and threatened species." Complaint, P. 5. Of course, the desire to use or observe an animal species, even for purely aesthetic purposes, is undeniably a cognizable interest for purpose of standing. *See, e.g.,* Sierra Club v. Morton, 405 U.S. [727, 734 (1972)]. "But the 'injury in fact' test requires more than an injury to a cognizable interest. It requires that the party seeking review be himself among the injured." *Id.,* at 734-735. To survive the Secretary's summary judgment motion, respondents had to submit affidavits or other evidence showing, through specific facts, not only that listed species were in fact being threatened by funded activities abroad, but also that one or more of respondent's members would thereby be "directly" affected apart from their " 'special interest' in th[e] subject." *Id.,* at 735, 739. . . .

With respect to this aspect of the case, the Court of Appeals focused on the affidavits of two Defenders' members—Joyce Kelly and Amy Skilbred. Ms. Kelly stated that she traveled to Egypt in 1986 and "observed the traditional habitat of the endangered nile crocodile there and intend[s] to do so again, and hope[s] to observe the crocodile directly," and that she "will suffer harm in fact as a result of [the] American . . . role . . . in overseeing the rehabilitation of the Aswan High Dam on the Nile . . . and [in] develop[ing] . . . Egypt's . . . Master Water Plan." App. 101. Ms. Skilbred averred that she traveled to Sri Lanka in 1981 and "observed th[e] habitat" of "endangered species such as the Asian elephant and the leopard" at what is now the site of the Mahaweli Project funded by the Agency for International Development (AID), although she "was unable to see any of the endangered species"; "this development project," she continued "will seriously reduce endangered, threatened, and endemic species habitat including areas that I visited . . . [, which] may severely shorten the future of these species"; that threat, she concluded, harmed her because she "intend[s] to return to Sri Lanka in the future and hope[s] to be more fortunate in spotting at least the endangered elephant and leopard." *Id.,* at 145-146. When Ms. Skilbred was asked at a subsequent deposition if and when she had any plans to return to Sri Lanka, she reiterated that "I intend to go back to Sri

Lanka," but confessed that she had no current plans: "I don't know [when]. There is a civil war going on right now. I don't know. Not next year, I will say. In the future." *Id.,* at 318.

We shall assume for the sake of argument that these affidavits contain facts showing that certain agency-funded projects threaten listed species—though that is questionable. They plainly contain no facts, however, showing how damage to the species will produce "imminent" injury to Mses. Kelly and Skilbred. That the women "had visited" the areas of the projects before the projects commenced proves nothing. As we have said in a related context, "'[p]ast exposure to illegal conduct does not in itself show a present case or controversy regarding injunctive relief . . . if unaccompanied by any continuing, present adverse effects.'" [Los Angeles v.] Lyons, 461 U.S., at 102 (*quoting* O'Shea v. Littleton, 414 U.S. 488, 495-496 (1974)). And the affiants' profession of an "inten[t]" to return to the places they had visited before—where they will presumably, this time, be deprived of the opportunity to observe animals of the endangered species—is simply not enough. Such "some day" intentions—without any description of concrete plans, or indeed even any specification of when the some day will be—do not support a finding of the "actual or imminent" injury that our cases require. . . .[2]

Besides relying upon the Kelly and Skilbred affidavits, respondents propose a series of novel standing theories. The first, inelegantly styled "ecosystem nexus," proposes that any person who uses any part of a "contiguous ecosystem" adversely affected by a funded activity has standing even if the activity is located a great distance away. This approach, as the Court of Appeals correctly observed, is inconsistent with our opinion in *National Wildlife Federation,* which held that a plaintiff claiming injury from environmental damage must use the area affected by the challenged activity and not an area roughly "in the vicinity" of it. 497 U.S., at 887-889; *see also Sierra Club,* 405 U.S., at 735. It makes no difference that the general-purpose section of the ESA states that the Act was intended in part "to provide a means whereby the ecosystems upon which endangered species and threatened species depend may be conserved," 16 U.S.C. §1531(b). To say that the Act protects ecosystems is not to say that the Act creates (if it were possible) rights of action in persons who have not been injured in fact, that is, persons who use portions of an ecosystem not perceptibly affected by the unlawful action in question.

---

2. The dissent acknowledges the settled requirement that the injury complained of be, if not actual, then at least *imminent*—but it contends that respondents could get past summary judgment because "a reasonable finder of fact could conclude . . . that . . . Kelly or Skilbred will soon return to the project sites." This analysis suffers either from a factual or from a legal defect, depending on what the "soon" is supposed to mean. If "soon" refers to the standard mandated by our precedents—that the injury be "imminent," Whitmore v. Arkansas, 495 U.S. 149, 155 (1990)—we are at a loss to see how, as a factual matter, the standard can be met by respondents' mere profession of an intent, someday, to return. But if, as we suspect, "soon" means nothing more than "in this lifetime," then the dissent has undertaken quite a departure from our precedents. Although "imminence" is concededly a somewhat elastic concept, it cannot be stretched beyond its purpose, which is to ensure that the alleged injury is not too speculative for Article III purposes—that the injury is "*certainly* impending"; *id.,* at 158 (emphasis added). It has been stretched beyond the breaking point when, as here, the plaintiff alleges only an injury at some indefinite future time, and the acts necessary to make the injury happen are at least partly within the plaintiff's own control. In such circumstances we have insisted that the injury proceed with a high degree of immediacy, so as to reduce the possibility of deciding a case in which no injury would have occurred at all. *See, e.g., id.,* at 156-160; Los Angeles v. Lyons, 461 U.S. 95, 102-106 (1983). . . .

Respondents' other theories are called, alas, the "animal nexus" approach, whereby anyone who has an interest in studying or seeing the endangered animals anywhere on the globe has standing; and the "vocational nexus" approach, under which anyone with a professional interest in such animals can sue. Under these theories, anyone who goes to see Asian elephants in the Bronx Zoo, and anyone who is a keeper of Asian elephants in the Bronx Zoo, has standing to sue because the Director of AID did not consult with the Secretary regarding the AID-funded project in Sri Lanka. This is beyond all reason. Standing is not "an ingenious academic exercise in the conceivable," United States v. Students Challenging Regulatory Agency Procedures (SCRAP), 412 U.S. 669, 688 (1973), but as we have said requires, at the summary judgment stage, a factual showing of perceptible harm. It is clear that the person who observes or works with a particular animal threatened by a federal decision is facing perceptible harm, since the very subject of his interest will no longer exist. It is even plausible — though it goes to the outermost limit of plausibility — to think that a person who observes or works with animals of a particular species in the very area of the world where that species is threatened by a federal decision is facing such harm, since some animals that might have been the subject of his interest will no longer exist, *see* Japan Whaling Assn. v. American Cetacean Soc., 478 U.S. 221, 231, n.4 (1986). It goes beyond the limit, however, and into pure speculation and fantasy, to say that anyone who observes or works with an endangered species, anywhere in the world, is appreciably harmed by a single project affecting some portion of that species with which he has no more specific connection. . . .

B*

Besides failing to show injury, respondents failed to demonstrate redressability. Instead of attacking the separate decisions to fund particular projects allegedly causing them harm, respondents chose to challenge a more generalized level of Government action (rules regarding consultation), the invalidation of which would affect all overseas projects. This programmatic approach has obvious practical advantages, but also obvious difficulties insofar as proof of causation or redressability is concerned. As we have said in another context, "suits challenging, not specifically identifiable Government violations of law, but the particular programs agencies establish to carry out their legal obligations [are], even when premised on allegations of several instances of violations of law, . . . rarely if ever appropriate for federal-court adjudication." *Allen,* 468 U.S. at 759-760.

The most obvious problem in the present case is redressability. Since the agencies funding the projects were not parties to the case, the District Court could accord relief only against the Secretary: He could be ordered to revise his regulation to require consultation for foreign projects. But this would not remedy respondents' alleged injury unless the funding agencies were bound by the Secretary's regulation, which is very much an open question. Whereas in other contexts the ESA is quite explicit as to the Secretary's controlling authority, . . .

---

* [This portion of Justice Scalia's opinion was joined only by Chief Justice Rehnquist and Justices White and Thomas, and thus does not represent the views of the majority of the Court. — Eds.]

with respect to consultation the initiative, and hence arguably the initial responsibility for determining statutory necessity, lies with the agencies, *see* §1536(a)(2) ("Each Federal agency shall, in consultation with and with the assistance of the Secretary, insure that any" funded action is not likely to jeopardize endangered or threatened species). When the Secretary promulgated the regulation at issue here, he thought it was binding on the agencies, *see* 51 Fed. Reg. 19928 (1986). The solicitor General, however, has repudiated that position here, and the agencies themselves apparently deny the Secretary's authority.

Respondents assert that this legal uncertainty did not affect redressability (and hence standing) because the District Court itself could resolve the issue of the Secretary's authority as a necessary part of its standing inquiry. Assuming that it is appropriate to resolve an issue of law such as this in connection with a threshold standing inquiry, resolution by the District Court would not have remedied respondents' alleged injury anyway, because it would not have been binding upon the agencies. They were not parties to the suit, and there is no reason they should be obliged to honor an incidental legal determination the suit produced. The Court of Appeals tried to finesse this problem by simply proclaiming that "[w]e are satisfied that an injunction requiring the Secretary to publish [respondents' desired] regulatio[n] would result in consultation." *Defenders of Wildlife*, 851 F.2d, at 1042, 1043-1044. We do not know what would justify that confidence, particularly when the Justice Department (presumably after consultation with the agencies) has taken the position that the regulation is not binding. The short of the matter is that redress of the only injury in fact respondents complain of requires action (termination of funding until consultation) by the individual funding agencies; and any relief the District Court could have provided in this suit against the Secretary was not likely to produce that action.

A further impediment to redressability is the fact that the agencies generally supply only a fraction of the funding for a foreign project. AID, for example, has provided less than 10% of the funding for the Mahaweli project. Respondents have produced nothing to indicate that the projects they have named will either be suspended, or do less harm to listed species, if that fraction is eliminated. As in *Simon,* 426 U.S., at 43-44, it is entirely conjectural whether the nonagency activity that affects respondents will be altered or affected by the agency activity they seek to achieve. There is no standing.

IV

The Court of Appeals found that respondents had standing for an additional reason: because they had suffered a "procedural injury." The so-called "citizen-suit" provision of the ESA provides, in pertinent part, that "any person may commence a civil suit on his own behalf (A) to enjoin any person, including the United States and any other governmental instrumentality or agency . . . who is alleged to be in violation of any provision of this chapter." 16 U.S.C. §1540(g). The court held that, because §7(a)(2) requires interagency consultation, the citizen-suit provision creates a "procedural righ[t]" to consultation in all "persons"—so that anyone can file suit in federal court to challenge the Secretary's (or presumably any other official's) failure to follow the assertedly correct consultative procedure, notwithstanding their inability to allege any discrete injury flowing from that failure. To understand the remarkable nature of this holding one must be clear about what it does not rest upon: This is not a case where plaintiffs are seeking to enforce a procedural requirement the disregard of which could impair a separate concrete interest of theirs (e.g., the procedural requirement for a hearing prior to denial of their license application, or the procedural requirement for an environmental impact statement before a federal facility is constructed next door to them).[7] Nor is it simply a case where concrete injury has been suffered by many persons, as in mass fraud or mass tort situations. Nor, finally, is it the unusual case in which Congress has created a concrete private interest in the outcome of a suit against a private party for the government's benefit, by providing a cash bounty for the victorious plaintiff. Rather, the court held that the injury-in-fact requirement had been satisfied by congressional conferral upon all persons of an abstract, self-contained, noninstrumental "right" to have the Executive observe the procedures required by law. We reject this view.

We have consistently held that a plaintiff raising only a generally available grievance about government—claiming only harm to his and every citizen's interest in proper application of the Constitution and laws, and seeking relief that no more directly and tangibly benefits him from than it does the public at large—does not state an Article III case or controversy. . . .

To be sure, our generalized-grievance cases have typically involved Government violation of procedures assertedly ordained by the Constitution rather than the Congress. But there is absolutely no basis for making the Article III inquiry turn on the source of the asserted right. Whether the courts were to act on their own, or at the invitation of Congress, in ignoring the concrete injury requirement described in our cases, they would be discarding a principle fundamental to the separate and distinct constitutional role of the Third Branch—one of the essential elements that identifies those "Cases" and "Controversies" that are the business of the courts rather than of the political branches. "The province of the court," as Chief Justice Marshall said in Marbury v. Madison, 5 U.S. (1 Cranch) 137, 170 (1803), "is, solely, to decide on the rights of individuals." Vindicating the public interest (including the public interest in government observance of the Constitution and laws) is the function of Congress and the Chief Executive. The question presented here is whether the public interest in proper administration of the laws (specifically, in agencies' observance of a particular, statutorily prescribed procedure) can be converted into an individual right by a statute that denominates it as such, and that permits all citizens (or, for that matter, a subclass of citizens who suffer no distinctive concrete harm) to sue. If

---

7. There is this much truth to the assertion that "procedural rights" are special: The person who has been accorded a procedural right to protect his concrete interests can assert that right without meeting all the normal standards for redressability and immediacy. Thus, under our case law, one living adjacent to the site for proposed construction of a federally licensed dam has standing to challenge the licensing agency's failure to prepare an Environmental Impact Statement, even though he cannot establish with any certainty that the Statement will cause the license to be withheld or altered, and even though the dam will not be completed for many years. (That is why we do not rely, in the present case, upon the Government's argument that, *even if* the other agencies were obliged to consult with the Secretary, they might not have followed his advice.) What respondents' "procedural rights" argument seeks, however, is quite different from this: standing for persons who have no concrete interests affected—persons who live (and propose to live) at the other end of the country from the dam.

the concrete injury requirement has the separation-of-powers significance we have always said, the answer must be obvious: To permit Congress to convert the undifferentiated public interest in executive officers' compliance with the law into an "individual right" vindicable in the courts is to permit Congress to transfer from the President to the courts the Chief Executive's most important constitutional duty, to "take Care that the Laws be faithfully executed," Art. II, §3. It would enable the courts, with the permission of Congress, "to assume a position of authority over the governmental acts of another and co-equal department," Frothingham v. Mellon, 262 U.S. [447, 489 (1923)], and to become "virtually continuing monitors of the wisdom and soundness of Executive action.'" *Allen,* 468 U.S., at 760 (*quoting* Laird v. Tatum, 408 U.S. 1, 15 (1972)). We have always rejected that vision of our role: "When Congress passes an Act empowering administrative agencies to carry on governmental activities, the power of those agencies is circumscribed by the authority granted. This permits the courts to participate in law enforcement entrusted to administrative bodies only to the extent necessary to protect justiciable individual rights against administrative action fairly beyond the granted powers. . . . This is very far from assuming that the courts are charged more than administrators or legislators with the protection of the rights of the people. Congress and the Executive supervise the acts of administrative agents. . . . But under Article III, Congress established courts to adjudicate cases and controversies as to claims of infringement of individual rights whether by unlawful action of private persons or by the exertion of unauthorized administrative power." Stark v. Wickard, 321 U.S. 288, 309-310 (1944). "Individual rights," within the meaning of this passage, do not mean public rights that have been legislatively pronounced to belong to each individual who forms part of the public. *See also Sierra Club,* 405 U.S., at 740-741, n.16.

Nothing in this contradicts the principle that "[t]he . . . injury required by Art. III may exist solely by virtue of 'statutes creating legal rights, the invasion of which creates standing.'" [Warth v. Seldin, 422 U.S. 490, 500 (1975)] (*quoting* Linda R.S. v. Richard D., 410 U.S. 614, 617, n.3 (1973)). Both of the cases used by *Linda R.S.* as an illustration of that principle involved Congress's elevating to the status of legally cognizable injuries concrete, de facto injuries that were previously inadequate in law (namely, injury to an individual's personal interest in living in a racially integrated community, *see* Trafficante v. Metropolitan Life Ins. Co., 409 U.S. 205, 208-212 (1972), and injury to a company's interest in marketing its product free from competition, *see* Hardin v. Kentucky Utilities Co., 390 U.S. 1, 6 (1968)). As we said in *Sierra Club,* "[Statutory] broadening [of] the categories of injury that may be alleged in support of standing is a different matter from abandoning the requirement that the party seeking review must himself have suffered an injury." 405 U.S., at 738. Whether or not the principle set forth in *Warth* can be extended beyond that distinction, it is clear that in suits against the government, at least, the concrete injury requirement must remain.

We hold that respondents lack standing to bring this action and that the Court of Appeals erred in denying the summary judgment motion filed by the United States. The opinion of the Court of Appeals is hereby reversed, and the cause remanded for proceedings consistent with this opinion.

It is so ordered.

JUSTICE KENNEDY, with whom JUSTICE SOUTER joins, concurring in part and concurring in the judgment. . . .

I agree with the Court's conclusion in Part III-A that, on the record before us, respondents have failed to demonstrate that they themselves are "among the injured." . . .

While it may seem trivial to require that Mses. Kelly and Skilbred acquire airline tickets to the project sites or announce a date certain upon which they will return, this is not a case where it is reasonable to assume that the affiants will be using the sites on a regular basis, *see* Sierra Club v. Morton, *supra*, 405 U.S., at 735, n.8, nor do the affiants claim to have visited the sites since the projects commenced. . . .

In light of the conclusion that respondents have not demonstrated a concrete injury here sufficient to support standing under our precedents, I would not reach the issue of redressability that is discussed by the plurality in Part III-B.

I also join Part IV of the Court's opinion with the following observations. As government programs and policies become more complex and far-reaching, we must be sensitive to the articulation of new rights of action that do not have clear analogs in our common law tradition. Modern litigation has progressed far from the paradigm of Marbury suing Madison to get his commission, Marbury v. Madison, 1 Cranch 137 (1803), or Ogden seeking an injunction to halt Gibbons' steamboat operations. Gibbons v. Ogden, 9 Wheat. 1 (1824). In my view, Congress has the power to define injuries and articulate chains of causation that will give rise to a case or controversy where none existed before, and I do not read the Court's opinion to suggest a contrary view. *See* Warth v. Seldin, 422 U.S. 490, 500 (1975). In exercising this power, however, Congress must, at the very least, identify the injury it seeks to vindicate and relate the injury to the class of persons entitled to bring suit. The citizen-suit provision of the Endangered Species Act does not meet these minimal requirements, because, while the statute purports to confer a right on any person . . . to enjoin . . . the United States and any other governmental instrumentality or agency . . . who is alleged to be in violation of any provision of this chapter, it does not, of its own force, establish that there is an injury in "any person" by virtue of any "violation." 16 U.S.C. §§1540(g)(1)(A).

The Court's holding that there is an outer limit to the power of Congress to confer rights of action is a direct and necessary consequence of the case and controversy limitations found in Article III. I agree that it would exceed those limitations if, at the behest of Congress and in the absence of any showing of concrete injury, we were to entertain citizen-suits to vindicate the public's non-concrete interest in the proper administration of the laws. While it does not matter how many persons have been injured by the challenged action, the party bringing suit must show that the action injures him in a concrete and personal way. This requirement is not just an empty formality. It preserves the vitality of the adversarial process by assuring both that the parties before the court have an actual, as opposed to professed, stake in the outcome, and that "the legal questions presented . . . will be resolved, not in the rarefied atmosphere of a debating society, but in a concrete factual context conducive to a realistic appreciation of the consequences of judicial action." Valley Forge Christian College v. Americans United for Separation of Church and State, Inc., 454 U.S.

464, 472 (1982). In addition, the requirement of concrete injury confines the Judicial Branch to its proper, limited role in the constitutional framework of government. . . .

With these observations, I concur in Parts I, II, III-A, and IV of the Court's opinion and in the judgment of the Court.

JUSTICE STEVENS, concurring in the judgment. [Omitted.]

JUSTICE BLACKMUN, with whom JUSTICE O'CONNOR joins, dissenting.

I part company with the Court in this case in two respects. First, I believe that respondents have raised genuine issues of fact—sufficient to survive summary judgment—both as to injury and as to redressability. Second, I question the Court's breadth of language in rejecting standing for "procedural" injuries. I fear the Court seeks to impose fresh limitations on the constitutional authority of Congress to allow citizen-suits in the federal courts for injuries deemed "procedural" in nature. I dissent.

I

. . . Were the Court to apply the proper standard for summary judgment, I believe it would conclude that the sworn affidavits and deposition testimony of Joyce Kelly and Amy Skilbred advance sufficient facts to create a genuine issue for trial concerning whether one or both would be imminently harmed by the Aswan and Mahaweli projects. In the first instance, as the Court itself concedes, the affidavits contained facts making it at least "questionable" (and therefore within the province of the factfinder) that certain agency-funded projects threaten listed species. The only remaining issue, then, is whether Kelly and Skilbred have shown that they personally would suffer imminent harm.

I think a reasonable finder of fact could conclude from the information in the affidavits and deposition testimony that either Kelly or Skilbred will soon return to the project sites, thereby satisfying the "actual or imminent" injury standard. The Court dismisses Kelly's and Skilbred's general statements that they intended to revisit the project sites as "simply not enough." But those statements did not stand alone. A reasonable finder of fact could conclude, based not only upon their statements of intent to return, but upon their past visits to the project sites, as well as their professional backgrounds, that it was likely that Kelly and Skilbred would make a return trip to the project areas. Contrary to the Court's contention that Kelly's and Skilbred's past visits "proves nothing," the fact of their past visits could demonstrate to a reasonable factfinder that Kelly and Skilbred have the requisite resources and personal interest in the preservation of the species endangered by the Aswan and Mahaweli projects to make good on their intention to return again. . . . Similarly, Kelly's and Skilbred's professional backgrounds in wildlife preservation, also make it likely—at least far more likely than for the average citizen—that they would choose to visit these areas of the world where species are vanishing.

By requiring a "description of concrete plans" or "specification of when the some day [for a return visit] will be," the Court, in my view, demands what is likely an empty formality. No substantial barriers prevent Kelly or Skilbred from simply purchasing plane tickets to return to the Aswan and Mahaweli projects. This case differs from other cases in which the imminence of harm turned largely on the affirmative actions of third parties beyond a plaintiff's control. . . . To be sure, a plaintiff's unilateral control over his or her exposure to harm does not necessarily render the harm nonspeculative. Nevertheless, it suggests that a finder of fact would be far more likely to conclude the harm is actual or imminent, especially if given an opportunity to hear testimony and determine credibility.

I fear the Court's demand for detailed descriptions of future conduct will do little to weed out those who are genuinely harmed from those who are not. More likely, it will resurrect a code-pleading formalism in federal court summary judgment practice, as federal courts, newly doubting their jurisdiction, will demand more and more particularized showings of future harm. Just to survive summary judgment, for example, a property owner claiming a decline in the value of his property from governmental action might have to specify the exact date he intends to sell his property and show that there is a market for the property, lest it be surmised he might not sell again. . . .

A plurality of the Court suggests that respondents have not demonstrated redressability: a likelihood that a court ruling in their favor would remedy their injury. Duke Power Co. v. Carolina Environmental Study Group, Inc., 438 U.S. 59, 74-75, and n.20 (1978) (plaintiff must show "substantial likelihood" that relief requested will redress the injury). The plurality identifies two obstacles. The first is that the "action agencies" (e.g., AID) cannot be required to undertake consultation with petitioner Secretary, because they are not directly bound as parties to the suit and are otherwise not indirectly bound by being subject to petitioner Secretary's regulation. Petitioner, however, officially and publicly has taken the position that his regulations regarding consultation under §7 of the Act are binding on action agencies. And he has previously taken the same position in this very litigation, having stated in his answer to the complaint that petitioner "admits the Fish and Wildlife Service (FWS) was designated the lead agency for the formulation of regulations concerning section 7 of the [Endangered Species Act]." I cannot agree with the plurality that the Secretary (or the Solicitor General) is now free, for the convenience of this appeal, to disavow his prior public and litigation positions. . . .

The second redressability obstacle relied on by the plurality is that "the [action] agencies generally supply only a fraction of the funding for a foreign project." What this Court might "generally" take to be true does not eliminate the existence of a genuine issue of fact to withstand summary judgment. Even if the action agencies supply only a fraction of the funding for a particular foreign project, it remains at least a question for the finder of fact whether threatened withdrawal of that fraction would affect foreign government conduct sufficiently to avoid harm to listed species. . . .

The plurality flatly states: "Respondents have produced nothing to indicate that the projects they have named will . . . do less harm to listed species, if that fraction is eliminated." As an initial matter, the relevant inquiry is not, as the plurality suggests, what will happen if AID or other agencies stop funding projects, but what will happen if AID or other agencies comply with the consultation requirement for projects abroad. Respondents filed suit to require consultation, not a termination of funding. Respondents have raised at least a genuine issue of fact that the projects harm endangered species and that the actions of AID and other United States agencies can mitigate that harm. The plurality overlooks an Interior Department memorandum listing eight endangered or threatened species in the Mahaweli project area and recounting that "[t]he Sri Lankan government has requested the assistance of AID in mitigating the negative impacts to the wildlife involved." . . .

As for the Aswan project, the record again rebuts the plurality's assumption that donor agencies are without any authority to protect listed species. Kelly asserted in her affidavit—and it has not been disputed—that the Bureau of Reclamation was "overseeing" the rehabilitation of the Aswan project. . . .

I find myself unable to agree with the plurality's analysis of redressability, based as it is on its invitation of executive lawlessness, . . . unfounded assumptions about causation, and erroneous conclusions about what the record does not say. In my view, respondents have satisfactorily shown a genuine issue of fact as to whether their injury would likely be redressed by a decision in their favor.

II

The Court concludes that any "procedural injury" suffered by respondents is insufficient to confer standing. It rejects the view that the "injury-in-fact requirement . . . [is] satisfied by congressional conferral upon all persons of an abstract, self-contained, noninstrumental 'right' to have the Executive observe the procedures required by law." Whatever the Court might mean with that very broad language, it cannot be saying that "procedural injuries" as a class are necessarily insufficient for purposes of Article III standing. . . .

Congress legislates in procedural shades of gray not to aggrandize its own power but to allow maximum Executive discretion in the attainment of Congress' legislative goals. Congress could simply impose a substantive prohibition on executive conduct; it could say that no agency action shall result in the loss of more than 5% of any listed species. Instead, Congress sets forth substantive guidelines and allows the Executive, within certain procedural constraints, to decide how best to effectuate the ultimate goal. . . . The Court never has questioned Congress' authority to impose such procedural constraints on executive power. Just as Congress does not violate separation of powers by structuring the procedural manner in which the Executive shall carry out the laws, surely the federal courts do not violate separation of powers when, at the very instruction and command of Congress, they enforce these procedures.

To prevent Congress from conferring standing for "procedural injuries" is another way of saying that Congress may not delegate to the courts authority deemed "executive" in nature. (Congress may not "transfer from the President to the courts the Chief Executive's most important constitutional duty, to 'take Care that the Laws be faithfully executed,' Art. II, sec. 3.") Here Congress seeks not to delegate "executive" power but only to strengthen the procedures it has legislatively mandated. "We have long recognized that the nondelegation doctrine does not prevent Congress from seeking assistance, within proper limits, from its coordinate Branches." Touby v. United States, 500 U.S. 160, 165

(1991). "Congress does not violate the Constitution merely because it legislates in broad terms, leaving a certain degree of discretion to executive *or judicial actors*" (emphasis added). *Ibid.*

Ironically, this Court has previously justified a relaxed view of congressional delegation to the Executive on grounds that Congress, in turn, has subjected the exercise of that power to judicial review. INS v. Chadha, 462 U.S. 919, 953-954, n.16 (1983); American Power & Light Co. v. SEC, 329 U.S. [90, 105-106 (1946)]. The Court's intimation today that procedural injuries are not constitutionally cognizable threatens this understanding upon which Congress has undoubtedly relied. In no sense is the Court's suggestion compelled by our "common understanding of what activities are appropriate to legislatures, to executives, and to courts." In my view, it reflects an unseemly solicitude for an expansion of power of the Executive Branch.

It is to be hoped that over time the Court will acknowledge that some classes of procedural duties are so enmeshed with the prevention of a substantive, concrete harm that an individual plaintiff may be able to demonstrate a sufficient likelihood of injury just through the breach of that procedural duty. For example, in the context of the NEPA requirement of environmental-impact statements, this Court has acknowledged "it is now well settled that NEPA itself does not mandate particular results [and] simply prescribes the necessary process," but "*these procedures are almost certain to affect the agency's substantive decision.*" Robertson v. Methow Valley Citizens Council, 490 U.S. 332, 350 (1989) (emphasis added). *See also* Andrus v. Sierra Club, 442 U.S. 347, 350-351 (1979) ("If environmental concerns are not interwoven into the fabric of agency planning, the 'action-forcing' characteristics of [the environmental-impact statement requirement] would be lost"). This acknowledgment of an inextricable link between procedural and substantive harm does not reflect improper appellate factfinding. It reflects nothing more than the proper deference owed to the judgment of a coordinate branch—Congress—that certain procedures are directly tied to protection against a substantive harm. . . .

III

In conclusion, I cannot join the Court on what amounts to a slash-and-burn expedition through the law of environmental standing. In my view, "[t]he very essence of civil liberty certainly consists in the right of every individual to claim the protection of the laws, whenever he receives an injury." Marbury v. Madison, 1 Cranch 137, 163 (1803).

I dissent.

NOTES AND QUESTIONS

1. *"Cognizable" interests.* Justice Scalia's opinion for the Court defines "injury in fact" as an "invasion of a legally-protected interest." Does this merely resurrect the old "legal right" test, but now as an element of the constitutional minimum of standing? Does the use of the word "interest" instead of "right" indicate that something else is required? Perhaps what Justice Scalia means is

that the injury must fall within a general category that is "cognizable" under the relevant statute (as "the desire to use or observe an animal species, even for purely aesthetic purposes" is "cognizable" under the ESA). If Congress can thus create categories of interests that are "cognizable" for standing, is there any limit on its power to do so? Could Congress declare that the interest of any citizen in assuring that the Executive comply with the law is such an interest? Scalia seems to say that it could not. Why? Professor Cass Sunstein vociferously attacked the *Lujan* decision, arguing that the injury in fact requirement has no legitimate role to play where Congress has specifically provided that all citizens have a right to sue. *See* Cass R. Sunstein, What's Standing After *Lujan*? Of Citizen Suits, "Injuries," and Article III, 91 Mich. L. Rev. 163 (1992). In Sunstein's view, once Congress has granted the plaintiff a cause of action, a Case or Controversy exists for Article III purposes, and no further inquiry is warranted, even where the plaintiff's only interest is in seeing that the government obeys the law. *See also* Elizabeth Magill, Standing for the Public: A Lost History, 95 Va. L. Rev. 1131 (2009) (arguing that the concrete and imminent injury requirements are of relatively recent provenance). Does this mean we should jettison much of standing doctrine? Or simply defer to Congress when it creates injuries and confers rights of action? Does the reading suggested by Professor Sunstein depend on a particular reading of the constitutional terms "Cases" and "Controversies"?

2. *"Particularized" versus "concrete."* In Spokeo, Inc. v. Robins, 135 S. Ct. 1892 (2015), Justice Alito, writing for the Court, attempted to clarify *Lujan's* "injury in fact" requirement. The lower court had premised standing on a finding that plaintiff's harm was "personal and individual." This was enough, said Alito, to satisfy the requirement of a "particularized" injury. But it was not enough, by itself, to establish that the injury was "concrete":

> A "concrete" injury must be "*de facto*"; that is, it must actually exist. . . . When we have used the adjective "concrete," we have meant to convey the usual meaning of the term — "real," and not "abstract."

Justice Alito then continued, providing some guidance to lower courts on what counts as a "real" harm. Acknowledging that "intangible" harms can confer standing, Alito said that one must look to "history" (essentially, the common law) and "the judgment of Congress" in determining whether an intangible harm is "real" enough. A "risk of real harm" can confer standing, he ventured, but a "bare procedural harm" cannot. How clear is the distinction between procedural and concrete (i.e., real) harms? What is the most likely impact on standing doctrine of maintaining the distinction?

3. *"Fairly traceable."* Can you construct the causal chain between the alleged violation of law in *Lujan* and the injury that the plaintiffs claim they will suffer? How does it compare to the causal chain in cases like *SCRAP* and *EKWRO*? Do the causal chains differ in terms of the amount of "independent action of some third party not before the court"?

In this regard, the Court has distinguished "third party" actions from steps remaining to be taken by the government agency itself. In *Bennett*, discussed *supra*, the government claimed that the plaintiffs' claimed injury (the reduction of water allocated for irrigation and ranching) was not "fairly traceable" to the contested government action (issuance of an allegedly procedurally defective biological opinion). Yet the Court found that as a practical matter the biological opinion would have a major, probably decisive influence, on the ultimate decision:

> Petitioners allege, among other things, that they currently receive irrigation water from Clear Lake . . . and that "[t]he restrictions on lake levels imposed in the Biological Opinion adversely affect [petitioners] by substantially reducing the quantity of available irrigation water." The Government contends . . . that these allegations fail to satisfy the "injury in fact" element of Article III standing because they demonstrate only a diminution in the aggregate amount of available water, and do not necessarily establish (absent information concerning . . . water allocation practices) that the petitioners will receive less water. This contention overlooks, however, the proposition that each element of Article III standing "must be supported in the same way as any other matter on which the plaintiff bears the burden of proof, i.e., with the manner and degree of evidence required at the successive stages of the litigation. . . . Given petitioners' allegation that the amount of available water will be reduced and that they will be adversely affected thereby, it is easy to presume specific facts under which petitioners will be injured—for example, . . . distribution of the reduction pro rata among its customers. The complaint alleges the requisite injury in fact."

520 U.S. at 167-168.

In other contexts, the Court has found the causal connection between an alleged violation and alleged injury too remote. *See* Linda R.S. v. Richard D., 410 U.S. 614, 618 (1973) (denying standing to woman claiming injury in her inability to collect child support due to a court ruling failing to criminalize a father's failure to support illegitimate children on reasoning that even if father were prosecuted and jailed, payment of support would remain speculative). Is the ranchers' injury in *Bennett* any less speculative than the injury to the plaintiff in *Linda R.S.*, or *EKWRO*, or *Lujan*? For example, isn't it "easy to presume specific facts under which" a hospital in *EKWRO* would have treated an indigent patient rather than forgo its tax-exempt status?

4. *The impact of third-party actions on standing.* If the chain of causation between alleged administrative wrongful action and petitioner injury runs through the actions of third parties who are not before the court, what effect does that have on standing? Notice what Justice Scalia says about the "unfettered choices made by independent actors" in Part II of his opinion and his comments about federal funding agencies and foreign nations in Part III.B. In Department of Commerce v. New York, 139 S. Ct. 2551 (2019), excerpted earlier in Chapter II and this chapter, the Secretary of Commerce argued that petitioners lacked standing because the link between his inclusion of a question on citizenship in the 2020 census and the petitioners' asserted injuries depended on the "independent action of third parties." The Supreme Court disagreed:

> The District Court concluded that the evidence at trial established a sufficient likelihood that the reinstatement of a citizenship question would result in noncitizen households responding to the census at lower rates than other groups, which in turn would cause them to be undercounted and lead to many of respondents' asserted injuries. For purposes of standing, these findings of fact were not so suspect as to be clearly erroneous.

We therefore agree that at least some respondents have Article III standing. Several state respondents here have shown that if noncitizen households are undercounted by as little as 2% — lower than the District Court's 5.8% prediction — they will lose out on federal funds that are distributed on the basis of state population. That is a sufficiently concrete and imminent injury to satisfy Article III, and there is no dispute that a ruling in favor of respondents would redress that harm.

The Government contends, however, that any harm to respondents is not fairly traceable to the Secretary's decision, because such harm depends on the independent action of third parties choosing to violate their legal duty to respond to the census. The chain of causation is made even more tenuous, the Government argues, by the fact that such intervening, unlawful third-party action would be motivated by unfounded fears that the Federal Government will itself break the law by using noncitizens' answers against them for law enforcement purposes. The Government invokes our steady refusal to "endorse standing theories that rest on speculation about the decisions of independent actors," Clapper v. Amnesty Int'l USA, 568 U.S. 398, 414 (2013), particularly speculation about future unlawful conduct, Los Angeles v. Lyons, 461 U.S. 95, 105 (1983).

But we are satisfied that, in these circumstances, respondents have met their burden of showing that third parties will likely react in predictable ways to the citizenship question, even if they do so unlawfully and despite the requirement that the Government keep individual answers confidential. The evidence at trial established that noncitizen households have historically responded to the census at lower rates than other groups, and the District Court did not clearly err in crediting the Census Bureau's theory that the discrepancy is likely attributable at least in part to noncitizens' reluctance to answer a citizenship question. Respondents' theory of standing thus does not rest on mere speculation about the decisions of third parties; it relies instead on the predictable effect of Government action on the decisions of third parties. *Cf.* Bennett v. Spear, 520 U.S. 154, 169-170 (1997); *Davis,* 554 U.S., at 734-735. Because Article III "requires no more than de facto causality," Block v. Meese, 793 F.2d 1303, 1309 (D.C. Cir. 1986) (Scalia, J.), traceability is satisfied here. We may therefore consider the merits of respondents' claims, at least as far as the Constitution is concerned.

Id. at Part II.

5. *Redressability.* How different is the causation inquiry from the question of whether the plaintiff's injury is redressable? In *Lujan,* a plurality would have denied standing because the plaintiff's injury was not redressable. Does evaluation of redressability require the same kind of speculation about probabilities as is relevant to the causation inquiry? Is there any way of making this inquiry more concrete? Redressability also sometimes overlaps with concerns about mootness in cases involving statutory violations that appear, at the time of the court hearing, to be wholly past. *See, e.g.,* Steel Co. v. Citizens for a Better Environment, 523 U.S. 83 (1998) (holding that an environmental group lacked standing because the alleged violations were "purely historical" and not continuing or likely to recur in the future, injunctive relief sought would not redress the injuries previously suffered). *But see* Friends of the Earth, Inc. v. Laidlaw Environmental Services (TOC), Inc., 528 U.S. 167 (2000) (holding that voluntary compliance was not sufficient to defeat standing and that the civil penalties imposed would have a deterrent effect that would redress the respondent's claimed injuries and discourage future violations).

6. *Procedural injury.* "Procedural injury" allegedly occurs when the government fails to follow statutorily required procedures where the relevant statute is intended to protect the plaintiffs from such an omission. Under the Court's opinion in *Lujan,* is the deprivation of a claimed procedural right enough to establish injury? If not, to what does the word "injury" refer in the term "procedural injury"? In Summers v. Earth Island Institute, 555 U.S. 488 (2009), the Supreme Court rejected a claim of standing based on an assertion that petitioners were wrongfully deprived of the ability to file comments on an agency policy decision. Writing for the Court, Justice Scalia said: "[D]eprivation of a procedural right without some concrete interest that is affected by the deprivation—a procedural right *in vacuo*—is insufficient to create Article III standing. Only a 'person who has been accorded a procedural right to protect *his concrete interests* can assert that right without meeting all the normal standards for redressability and immediacy.'" Since the Court concluded that the petitioners' asserted "concrete interests" (the interest in hiking in some national forests at some time in the future) were too speculative, their claimed procedural injury also failed to establish standing.

7. *Informational injury.* Conceptually akin to "procedural injury" is "informational injury." The courts have repeatedly held that the inability to obtain information can constitute an injury sufficient to confer standing if the underlying statute confers a right to obtain such information on a category of persons that encompasses the petitioner. *See, e.g.,* Federal Election Commission v. Akins, 524 U.S. 11 (1998). A group of voters petitioned for review of a decision of the Federal Election Commission refusing publicly to disclose information on the membership, contributions, or expenditures of a political action group. The Supreme Court held that the group had standing because its members desired the information to help make voting decisions. Is that interest sufficiently "concrete" to distinguish *Akins* from the procedural injuries asserted in *Lujan* and *Earth Island?* But what about the Freedom of Information Act (FOIA), surveyed in Chapter IX, which has been consistently interpreted to give the requester of a federal agency "record" a right to challenge an agency's refusal to disclose the record, regardless of what motivated the request? If unadulterated curiosity is enough to give a FOIA petitioner standing, why isn't an unadulterated desire to "comment" on an agency decision allegedly subject to the APA's rulemaking requirements?

MASSACHUSETTS v. ENVIRONMENTAL
PROTECTION AGENCY
549 U.S. 497 (2007)

JUSTICE STEVENS delivered the opinion of the Court.

[For a description of the factual and regulatory setting of the case, see the excerpts in Chapter II, *supra.* Before reaching the merits of the case—whether the EPA had statutory authority to regulate greenhouse gases and whether the agency's refusal to make a threshold "endangerment" finding was arbitrary or capricious—the Court had to decide whether the petitioners, including the Commonwealth of Massachusetts, had standing.]

IV

. . . EPA maintains that because greenhouse gas emissions inflict widespread harm, the doctrine of standing presents an insuperable jurisdictional obstacle. We do not agree. At bottom, "the gist of the question of standing" is whether petitioners have "such a personal stake in the outcome of the controversy as to assure that concrete adverseness which sharpens the presentation of issues upon which the court so largely depends for illumination."

To ensure the proper adversarial presentation, *Lujan* holds that a litigant must demonstrate that it has suffered a concrete and particularized injury that is either actual or imminent, that the injury is fairly traceable to the defendant, and that it is likely that a favorable decision will redress that injury. However, a litigant to whom Congress has "accorded a procedural right to protect his concrete interests"—here, the right to challenge agency action unlawfully withheld, §7607(b)(1)—"can assert that right without meeting all the normal standards for redressability and immediacy," *ibid.* When a litigant is vested with a procedural right, that litigant has standing if there is some possibility that the requested relief will prompt the injury-causing party to reconsider the decision that allegedly harmed the litigant.

Only one of the petitioners needs to have standing to permit us to consider the petition for review. We stress here, as did Judge Tatel below, the special position and interest of Massachusetts. It is of considerable relevance that the party seeking review here is a sovereign State and not, as it was in *Lujan,* a private individual.

Well before the creation of the modern administrative state, we recognized that States are not normal litigants for the purposes of invoking federal jurisdiction. As Justice Holmes explained in Georgia v. Tennessee Copper Co., 206 U.S. 230, 237 (1907), a case in which Georgia sought to protect its citizens from air pollution originating outside its borders:

> . . . This is a suit by a State for an injury to it in its capacity of *quasi*-sovereign. In that capacity the State has an interest independent of and behind the titles of its citizens, in all the earth and air within its domain. It has the last word as to whether its mountains shall be stripped of their forests and its inhabitants shall breathe pure air.

Just as Georgia's "independent interest . . . in all the earth and air within its domain" supported federal jurisdiction a century ago, so too does Massachusetts' well-founded desire to preserve its sovereign territory today. That Massachusetts does in fact own a great deal of the "territory alleged to be affected" only reinforces the conclusion that its stake in the outcome of this case is sufficiently concrete to warrant the exercise of federal judicial power.

When a State enters the Union, it surrenders certain sovereign prerogatives. Massachusetts cannot invade Rhode Island to force reductions in greenhouse gas emissions, it cannot negotiate an emissions treaty with China or India, and in some circumstances the exercise of its police powers to reduce in-state motor-vehicle emissions might well be pre-empted.

These sovereign prerogatives are now lodged in the Federal Government, and Congress has ordered EPA to protect Massachusetts (among others) by prescribing standards applicable to the "emission of any air pollutant from any class or classes of new motor vehicle engines, which in [the Administrator's] judgment cause, or contribute to, air pollution which may reasonably be anticipated to endanger public health or welfare." 42 U.S.C. §7521(a)(1). Congress has moreover recognized a concomitant procedural right to challenge the rejection of its rulemaking petition as arbitrary and capricious. §7607(b)(1). Given that procedural right and Massachusetts' stake in protecting its quasi-sovereign interests, the Commonwealth is entitled to special solicitude in our standing analysis.

With that in mind, it is clear that petitioners' submissions as they pertain to Massachusetts have satisfied the most demanding standards of the adversarial process. EPA's steadfast refusal to regulate greenhouse gas emissions presents a risk of harm to Massachusetts that is both "actual" and "imminent." There is, moreover, a "substantial likelihood that the judicial relief requested" will prompt EPA to take steps to reduce that risk.

THE INJURY

The harms associated with climate change are serious and well recognized. Indeed, the NRC Report itself—which EPA regards as an "objective and independent assessment of the relevant science"—identifies a number of environmental changes that have already inflicted significant harms, including "the global retreat of mountain glaciers, reduction in snowcover extent, the earlier spring melting of rivers and lakes, [and] the accelerated rate of rise of sea levels during the 20th century relative to the past few thousand years. . . ."

Petitioners allege that this only hints at the environmental damage yet to come. According to the [declaration filed by] climate scientist Michael MacCracken, "qualified scientific experts involved in climate change research" have reached a "strong consensus" that global warming threatens (among other things) a precipitate rise in sea levels by the end of the century, "severe and irreversible changes to natural ecosystems," a "significant reduction in water storage in winter snowpack in mountainous regions with direct and important economic consequences," and an increase in the spread of disease. He also observes that rising ocean temperatures may contribute to the ferocity of hurricanes.

That these climate-change risks are "widely shared" does not minimize Massachusetts' interest in the outcome of this litigation. According to petitioners' unchallenged affidavits, global sea levels rose somewhere between 10 and 20 centimeters over the 20th century as a result of global warming. These rising seas have already begun to swallow Massachusetts' coastal land. Because the Commonwealth "owns a substantial portion of the state's coastal property," it has alleged a particularized injury in its capacity as a landowner. The severity of that injury will only increase over the course of the next century: If sea levels continue to rise as predicted, one Massachusetts official believes that a significant fraction of coastal property will be "either permanently lost through inundation or temporarily lost through periodic storm surge and flooding events." Remediation costs alone, petitioners allege, could run well into the hundreds of millions of dollars.

CAUSATION

EPA does not dispute the existence of a causal connection between man-made greenhouse gas emissions and global warming. . . . At a minimum, therefore, EPA's refusal to regulate such emissions "contributes" to Massachusetts' injuries.

EPA nevertheless maintains that its decision not to regulate greenhouse gas emissions from new motor vehicles contributes so insignificantly to petitioners' injuries that the agency cannot be haled into federal court to answer for them. For the same reason, EPA does not believe that any realistic possibility exists that the relief petitioners seek would mitigate global climate change and remedy their injuries. That is especially so because predicted increases in greenhouse gas emissions from developing nations, particularly China and India, are likely to offset any marginal domestic decrease.

But EPA overstates its case. Its argument rests on the erroneous assumption that a small incremental step, because it is incremental, can never be attacked in a federal judicial forum. Yet accepting that premise would doom most challenges to regulatory action. Agencies, like legislatures, do not generally resolve massive problems in one fell regulatory swoop. They instead whittle away at them over time, refining their preferred approach as circumstances change and as they develop a more-nuanced understanding of how best to proceed. . . .

And reducing domestic automobile emissions is hardly a tentative step. Even leaving aside the other greenhouse gases, the United States transportation sector emits an enormous quantity of carbon dioxide into the atmosphere—according to the MacCracken affidavit, more than 1.7 billion metric tons in 1999 alone. That accounts for more than 6% of worldwide carbon dioxide emissions. . . . Judged by any standard, U.S. motor-vehicle emissions make a meaningful contribution to greenhouse gas concentrations and hence, according to petitioners, to global warming.

THE REMEDY

While it may be true that regulating motor-vehicle emissions will not by itself *reverse* global warming, it by no means follows that we lack jurisdiction to decide whether EPA has a duty to take steps to *slow* or *reduce* it. Because of the enormity of the potential consequences associated with man-made climate change, the fact that the effectiveness of a remedy might be delayed during the (relatively short) time it takes for a new motor-vehicle fleet to replace an older one is essentially irrelevant. Nor is it dispositive that developing countries such as China and India are poised to increase greenhouse gas emissions substantially over the next century: A reduction in domestic emissions would slow the pace of global emissions increases, no matter what happens elsewhere.

In sum—at least according to petitioners' uncontested affidavits—the rise in sea levels associated with global warming has already harmed and will continue to harm Massachusetts. The risk of catastrophic harm, though remote, is nevertheless real. That risk would be reduced to some extent if petitioners received the relief they seek. We therefore hold that petitioners have standing to challenge the EPA's denial of their rulemaking petition. . . .

CHIEF JUSTICE ROBERTS, with whom JUSTICE SCALIA, JUSTICE THOMAS, and JUSTICE ALITO join, dissenting.

Global warming may be a "crisis," even "the most pressing environmental problem of our time." . . . Indeed, it may ultimately affect nearly everyone on the planet in some potentially adverse way, and it may be that governments have done too little to address it. It is not a problem, however, that has escaped the attention of policymakers in the Executive and Legislative Branches of our Government, who continue to consider regulatory, legislative, and treaty-based means of addressing global climate change.

Apparently dissatisfied with the pace of progress on this issue in the elected branches, petitioners have come to the courts claiming broad-ranging injury, and attempting to tie that injury to the Government's alleged failure to comply with a rather narrow statutory provision. I would reject these challenges as non-justiciable. Such a conclusion involves no judgment on whether global warming exists, what causes it, or the extent of the problem. Nor does it render petitioners without recourse. This Court's standing jurisprudence simply recognizes that redress of grievances of the sort at issue here "is the function of Congress and the Chief Executive," not the federal courts. *Lujan.* I would vacate the judgment below and remand for dismissal of the petitions for review.

I

. . . Relaxing Article III standing requirements because asserted injuries are pressed by a State . . . has no basis in our jurisprudence, and support for any such "special solicitude" is conspicuously absent from the Court's opinion. The general judicial review provision cited by the Court affords States no special rights or status. . . . Congress knows how to do that when it wants to, but it has done nothing of the sort here. Under the law on which petitioners rely, Congress treated public and private litigants exactly the same.

Nor does the case law cited by the Court provide any support for the notion that Article III somehow implicitly treats public and private litigants differently. The Court has to go back a full century in an attempt to justify its novel standing rule, but even there it comes up short. The Court's analysis hinges on Georgia v. Tennessee Copper Co., 206 U.S. 230 (1907) — a case that did indeed draw a distinction between a State and private litigants, but solely with respect to available remedies. The case had nothing to do with Article III standing.

In *Tennessee Copper,* the State of Georgia sought to enjoin copper companies in neighboring Tennessee from discharging pollutants that were inflicting "a wholesale destruction of forests, orchards and crops" in bordering Georgia counties. Although the State owned very little of the territory allegedly affected, the Court reasoned that Georgia — in its capacity as a "*quasi*-sovereign" — "has an interest independent of and behind the titles of its citizens, in all the earth and air within its domain." The Court explained that while "[t]he very elements that would be relied upon in a suit between fellow-citizens as a ground for equitable relief [were] wanting," a State "is not lightly to be required to give up *quasi*-sovereign rights for pay." Thus while a complaining private litigant would have to make do with a *legal* remedy — one "for pay" — the State was entitled to *equitable* relief.

In contrast to the present case, there was no question in *Tennessee Copper* about Article III injury. . . . A claim of *parens patriae* standing is distinct from an allegation of direct injury. Far from being a substitute for Article III injury, *parens patriae* actions raise an additional hurdle for a state litigant: the articulation of a "quasi-sovereign interest" "*apart* from the interests of particular private parties." Just as an association suing on behalf of its members must show not only that it represents the members but that at least one satisfies Article III requirements, so too a State asserting quasi-sovereign interests as *parens patriae* must still show that its citizens satisfy Article III. Focusing on Massachusetts's interests as quasi-sovereign makes the required showing here harder, not easier. The Court, in effect, takes what has always been regarded as a *necessary* condition for *parens patriae* standing—a quasi-sovereign interest—and converts it into a *sufficient* showing for purposes of Article III.

What is more, the Court's reasoning falters on its own terms. The Court asserts that Massachusetts is entitled to "special solicitude" due to its "quasi-sovereign interests," but then applies our Article III standing test to the asserted injury of the State's loss of coastal property . . . (concluding that Massachusetts "has alleged a particularized injury *in its capacity as a landowner*" (emphasis added)). In the context of *parens patriae* standing, however, we have characterized state ownership of land as a "nonsovereign interes[t]" because a State "is likely to have the same interests as other similarly situated proprietors."

II

[T]he status of Massachusetts as a State cannot compensate for petitioners' failure to demonstrate injury in fact, causation, and redressability.

When the Court actually applies the three-part test, it focuses on the State's asserted loss of coastal land as the injury in fact. If petitioners rely on loss of land as the Article III injury, however, they must ground the rest of the standing analysis in that specific injury. That alleged injury must be "concrete and particularized," *Lujan,* and "distinct and palpable," *Allen,* 468 U.S. 737, 751 (1984).

The very concept of global warming seems inconsistent with this particularization requirement. Global warming is a phenomenon "harmful to humanity at large," 415 F.3d, at 60 (Sentelle, J., dissenting in part and concurring in judgment), and the redress petitioners seek is focused no more on them than on the public generally—it is literally to change the atmosphere around the world.

If petitioners' particularized injury is loss of coastal land, it is also that injury that must be "actual or imminent, not conjectural or hypothetical," "real and immediate," and "certainly impending."

As to "actual" injury, the Court observes that "global sea levels rose somewhere between 10 and 20 centimeters over the 20th century as a result of global warming" and that "[t]hese rising seas have already begun to swallow Massachusetts' coastal land." . . . But none of petitioners' declarations supports that connection. . . . [A]side from a single conclusory statement, there is nothing in petitioners' 43 standing declarations and accompanying exhibits to support an inference of actual loss of Massachusetts coastal land from 20th century global sea level increases. It is pure conjecture.

The Court's attempts to identify "imminent" or "certainly impending" loss of Massachusetts coastal land fares no better. . . . One of petitioners' declarants predicts global warming will cause sea level to rise by 20 to 70 centimeters *by the year 2100*. Another uses a computer modeling program to map the Commonwealth's coastal land and its current elevation, and calculates that the high-end estimate of sea level rise would result in the loss of significant state-owned coastal land. But the computer modeling program has a conceded average error of about 30 centimeters and a maximum observed error of 70 centimeters. . . . [A]ccepting a century-long time horizon and a series of compounded estimates renders requirements of imminence and immediacy utterly toothless. "Allegations of possible future injury do not satisfy the requirements of Art. III. A threatened injury must be *certainly impending* to constitute injury in fact."

III

Petitioners' reliance on Massachusetts's loss of coastal land as their injury in fact for standing purposes creates insurmountable problems for them with respect to causation and redressability. . . .

According to one of petitioners' declarations, domestic motor vehicles contribute about 6 percent of global carbon dioxide emissions and 4 percent of global greenhouse gas emissions. The amount of global emissions at issue here is smaller still; [the applicable section] of the Clean Air Act covers only *new* motor vehicles and *new* motor vehicle engines, so petitioners' desired emission standards might reduce only a fraction of 4 percent of global emissions. . . .

As EPA explained in its denial of petitioners' request for rulemaking, "predicting future climate change necessarily involves a complex web of economic and physical factors. . . ." Petitioners are never able to trace their alleged injuries back through this complex web to the fractional amount of global emissions that might have been limited with EPA standards. In light of the bit-part domestic new motor vehicle greenhouse gas emissions have played in what petitioners describe as a 150-year global phenomenon, and the myriad additional factors bearing on petitioners' alleged injury—the loss of Massachusetts coastal land—the connection is far too speculative to establish causation.

IV

Redressability is even more problematic. To the tenuous link between petitioners' alleged injury and the indeterminate fractional domestic emissions at issue here, add the fact that petitioners cannot meaningfully predict what will come of the 80 percent of global greenhouse gas emissions that originate outside the United States. . . .

The Court previously has explained that when the existence of an element of standing "depends on the unfettered choices made by independent actors not before the courts and whose exercise of broad and legitimate discretion the courts cannot presume either to control or to predict," a party must present facts supporting an assertion that the actor will proceed in such a manner. The declarations' conclusory (not to say fanciful) statements do not even come close.

No matter, the Court reasons, because *any* decrease in domestic emissions will "slow the pace of global emissions increases, no matter what happens elsewhere." . . . Every little bit helps, so Massachusetts can sue over any little bit.

[E]ven if regulation *does* reduce emissions—to some indeterminate degree, given events elsewhere in the world—the Court never explains why that makes it *likely* that the injury in fact—the loss of land—will be redressed. Schoolchildren know that a kingdom might be lost "all for the want of a horseshoe nail," but "likely" redressability is a different matter. The realities make it pure conjecture to suppose that EPA regulation of new automobile emissions will *likely* prevent the loss of Massachusetts coastal land.

V . . .

Today's decision recalls the previous high-water mark of diluted standing requirements, United States v. Students Challenging Regulatory Agency Procedures (SCRAP*)*, 412 U.S. 669 (1973). . . .

Over time, *SCRAP* became emblematic not of the looseness of Article III standing requirements, but of how utterly manipulable they are if not taken seriously as a matter of judicial self-restraint. *SCRAP* made standing seem a lawyer's game, rather than a fundamental limitation ensuring that courts function as courts and not intrude on the politically accountable branches. Today's decision is *SCRAP* for a new generation. . . .

The good news is that the Court's "special solicitude" for Massachusetts limits the future applicability of the diluted standing requirements applied in this case. The bad news is that the Court's self-professed relaxation of those Article III requirements has caused us to transgress "the proper—and properly limited—role of the courts in a democratic society." *Allen.*

I respectfully dissent.

NOTES AND QUESTIONS

1. *States as plaintiffs.* What, exactly, is the characteristic of the Commonwealth of Massachusetts that makes it a good plaintiff: the fact that it is a "sovereign" government? The fact that it is a very large owner of coastal land? The fact that it represents the interests of a large number of citizens? The fact that it can efficiently aggregate many small claims, as in a class action? Is the holding limited to state-initiated litigation, or has the Court relaxed standing requirements across the board? One result might be to empower states to challenge federal actions that would otherwise be immune from suit by private parties. Is this a healthy reinforcement of the states' role in the federal system, or is it an invitation to litigate questions that are essentially political disagreements?

2. *The impact of special solicitude.* Some commentators have suggested that state standing based on "special solicitude" may be unique to Massachusetts v. EPA—and they may have a point: The Supreme Court has not revisited the phrase since. But special solicitude has been influential in lower courts. In Texas v. United States, 787 F.3d 733, *aff'd by an equally divided court*, 136

S. Ct. 2271 (2016), discussed *supra*, the Fifth Circuit held that Texas had standing based on the special solicitude rationale:

> . . . Like Massachusetts, the instant plaintiffs—the states—"are not normal litigants for the purposes of invoking federal jurisdiction," and the same two additional factors are present. First, "[t]he parties' dispute turns on the proper construction of a congressional statute," the APA, which authorizes challenges to "final agency action for which there is no other adequate remedy in a court." 5 U.S.C. §704. . . .
>
> The Clean Air Act's review provision [involved in *Massachusetts*] is more specific than the APA's, but the latter is easily adequate to justify "special solicitude" here. The procedural right to challenge EPA decisions created by the Clean Air Act provided important support to Massachusetts because the challenge Massachusetts sought to bring—a challenge to an agency's decision *not to act*—is traditionally the type for which it is most difficult to establish standing and a justiciable issue. Texas, by contrast, challenges DHS's affirmative decision to set guidelines for granting lawful presence to a broad class of illegal aliens. Because the states here challenge DHS's decision to act, rather than its decision to remain inactive, a procedural right similar to that created by the Clean Air Act is not necessary to support standing. . . .
>
> Second, DAPA affects the states' "quasi-sovereign" interests by imposing substantial pressure on them to change their laws, which provide for issuing driver's licenses to some aliens and subsidizing those licenses. "[S]tates have a sovereign interest in 'the power to create and enforce a legal code.'" Pursuant to that interest, states may have standing based on (1) federal assertions of authority to regulate matters they believe they control, (2) federal preemption of state law, and (3) federal interference with the enforcement of state law, at least where "the state statute at issue regulate[s] behavior or provide[s] for the administration of a state program" and does not "simply purport[] to immunize [state] citizens from federal law." Those intrusions are analogous to pressure to change state law.
>
> Moreover, these plaintiff states' interests are like Massachusetts's in ways that implicate the same sovereignty concerns. When the states joined the union, they surrendered some of their sovereign prerogatives over immigration. They cannot establish their own classifications of aliens, just as "Massachusetts cannot invade Rhode Island to force reductions in greenhouse gas emissions [and] cannot negotiate an emissions treaty with China or India." The states may not be able to discriminate against subsets of aliens in their driver's license programs without running afoul of preemption or the Equal Protection Clause . . . .
>
> The United States urges that Texas's injury is not cognizable, because the state could avoid injury by not issuing licenses to illegal aliens or by not subsidizing its licenses. Although Texas could avoid financial loss by requiring applicants to pay the full costs of licenses, it could not avoid injury altogether. "[S]tates have a sovereign interest in 'the power to create and enforce a legal code,'" and the possibility that a plaintiff could avoid injury by incurring other costs does not negate standing. Indeed, treating the availability of changing state law as a bar to standing would deprive states of judicial recourse for many *bona fide* harms. For instance, under that theory, federal preemption of state law could never be an injury, because a state could always change its law to avoid preemption. But courts have often held that states have standing based on preemption. And states could offset almost any financial loss by raising taxes or fees. The existence of that alternative does not mean they lack standing. . . .
>
> [The dissent argues that Texas' claimed injury is self-inflicted.] In essence, the dissent would have us issue the following edict to Texas: "You may avoid injury

to the pursuit of your policy goals—injury resulting from a change in federal immigration law—by changing your laws to pursue different goals or eliminating them altogether. Therefore, your injuries are self-inflicted." [We disagree. T]here is no allegation that Texas passed its driver's license law to manufacture standing. The legislature enacted the law one year before DACA and three years before DAPA was announced, and there is no hint that the state anticipated a change in immigration policy—much less a change as sweeping and dramatic as DAPA. Despite the dissent's bold suggestion that Texas's license-plate-cost injury "is entirely manufactured by Plaintiffs for this case," the injury is not self-inflicted.

In addition to its notion that Texas could avoid injury, the government theorizes that Texas's injury is not fairly traceable to DAPA because it is merely an incidental and attenuated consequence of the program. But *Massachusetts v. EPA* establishes that the causal connection is adequate. Texas is entitled to the same "special solicitude" as was Massachusetts, and the causal link is even closer here. . . .

Does Massachusetts v. EPA justify giving "special solicitude" to Texas as a sovereign state? Are Texas's alleged injuries, as the dissent claimed, "self-inflicted" or only "incidental" to the adoption of DAPA? Is "pressure to change state law" an "invasion of a legally-protected interest which is (a) concrete and particularized, . . . and (b) 'actual or imminent. . . .'" as required by *Lujan*? Does the grant of standing to Texas violate the Supreme Court's oft-stated prohibition against adjudicating "generalized grievances"?

3. "SCRAP *for a new generation*"? In the expansiveness of its reasoning and implications, is Massachusetts v. EPA truly a "*SCRAP* for a new generation," or simply an outlier, reflecting special concerns about the underlying issue of climate change? In Summers v. Earth Island Institute, 555 U.S. 488 (2009), the Supreme Court strongly hinted at the latter answer. The case involved a challenge to a decision by the U.S. Forest Service to authorize a salvage sale of timber on fire-damaged national forests. Dismissing the petitioner hiker's asserted basis for standing, Justice Scalia, writing for the Court, said: "Bensman's affidavit . . . asserts that he has visited many National Forests and plans to visit several unnamed National Forests in the future. . . . Accepting an intention to visit the National Forests as adequate to confer standing to challenge any Government action affecting any portion of those forests would be tantamount to eliminating the requirement of concrete, particularized injury in fact. . . ."

4. *Widespread political harms and standing*. For decades, plaintiffs tried unsuccessfully to get the Supreme Court to rule on the constitutionality of partisan gerrymandering, i.e., the intentional drawing of legislative districts to favor the party in power. In 2018, the Supreme Court declined to rule on this issue on standing grounds. In Gill v. Whitford, 138 S. Ct. 1916 (2018), the Court held unanimously that Wisconsin Democrats could not base standing to challenge alleged partisan gerrymandering on statewide harm to the interests of Democratic voters. A year later, however, the Court mooted the standing question by ruling that partisan gerrymandering challenges are nonjusticiable "political questions." Rucho v. Common Cause, 588 U.S. ___ (2019).

5. *Congressional standing*. One manifestation of ongoing partisan discord in Washington is the increasing number of instances in which an agency action is challenged by a member, committee, or even a Chamber of Congress. Do such petitioners have standing to challenge administrative actions? The D.C. Circuit has long recognized congressional standing to sue over alleged defects in the

lawmaking processes. For example, in Moore v. United States House of Representatives, 733 F.2d 946, 952 (D.C. Cir. 1984), *cert. denied*, 469 U.S. 1106 (1985), the court held that members of the House of Representatives had standing to challenge a tax increase that they claimed originated in the Senate, in violation of the Origination Clause of the Constitution, which requires that bills for raising revenue originate in the House of Representatives. (Although the court found standing, it held that proper exercise of equitable discretion precluded any remedy in the case on behalf of the members of Congress.) The Supreme Court finally reached the issue and held that members of Congress lacked standing to challenge the constitutionality of the Line Item Veto Act. *See* Raines v. Byrd, 521 U.S. 811 (1997). The Act, which was later struck down by the Supreme Court at the behest of a different group of plaintiffs (see Clinton v. New York, excerpted in Chapter I, *supra*), granted the President the power to cancel individual spending items and tax benefits within an appropriations bill without vetoing the entire bill. The Act explicitly declared that members of Congress had standing to challenge the Act's constitutionality, but the Court found that "individual members of Congress do not have a sufficient 'personal stake' in [the] dispute and have not alleged a sufficiently concrete injury to have established Article III standing."

D.   THE TIMING OF JUDICIAL REVIEW

The process of administration is continuous. Policies are made and unmade and remade in an unbroken progression of official actions and decisions. But litigation is discrete, focusing on isolated incidents or decisions with identifiable consequences and impacts. Courts, unlike administrators, will not act until an issue has crystallized to the point of forming a cognizable "case or controversy." Nor will they intervene after a dispute has run its course.

In this section we examine a closely linked family of doctrines — "ripeness," "finality," and "exhaustion of remedies" — designed to prevent courts from becoming involved in a controversy too early. Like standing, the timeliness doctrines can be traced in part to the "case or controversy" requirement of Article III and in part to various "prudential" concerns, such as judicial economy and competence. *See* Ticor Title Ins. Co. v. FTC, 814 F.2d 731 (D.C. Cir. 1987). They also arise from the APA, since §704 restricts judicial review to "[a]gency action made reviewable by statute and final agency action for which there is no other adequate remedy in a court."

The distinctions among the doctrines of ripeness, finality, and exhaustion often are quite elusive. Generally, the exhaustion requirement refers to steps that the *petitioner* must take (usually, invoking an administrative appeal mechanism) as a precondition to securing judicial review. Ripeness and finality, by contrast, refer to the further steps that the *agency* must take before its action may be challenged in court. "Finality" usually refers to the requirement that the agency's decisionmaking process have reached a natural resting place: tentative or incomplete decisions may not be reviewed in court. In order for an action to be "ripe," it must not only be "final" in that sense, but it must have an immediate and direct adverse impact on the petitioning party. In the materials that follow, we see how the courts have struggled to apply and to distinguish these three doctrines in three paradigmatic contexts: a pre-enforcement challenge to an agency regulation, an effort to force an agency to initiate regulatory action, and an attempt to stop an agency from proceeding with an enforcement action.

1. Pre-Enforcement Challenges: Ripeness and Finality Requirements

At one time the prevailing opinion was that a person who wished to challenge the authority of an agency to issue a particular rule had to wait until the agency brought an enforcement action against that person for violating the rule. The rule could not be challenged in court immediately upon its issuance. As Justice Louis Brandeis said in explaining the Supreme Court's refusal to review an ICC order setting a value on a railroad's property:

> The so-called order here complained of is one which does not command the carrier to do, or to refrain from doing, any thing; which does not grant or withhold any authority, privilege or license; which does not extend or abridge any power or facility; . . . which does not change the carrier's existing or future status or condition; which does not determine any right or obligation.

United States v. Los Angeles & S.L.R.R., 273 U.S. 299, 309-310 (1927). Although the challenged action was not the issuance of a rule, many observers evidently felt that the same logic would generally bar pre-enforcement challenges to informal rules as well. *See* Nathaniel L. Nathanson, Probing the Mind of the Administrator: Hearing Variations and Standards of Judicial Review Under the Administrative Procedure Act and Other Federal Statutes, 75 Colum. L. Rev. 721, 754-755 (1975).

This understanding was shaken somewhat by the Supreme Court's decision in Columbia Broadcasting System, Inc. v. United States, 316 U.S. 407 (1942). The FCC had issued a rule announcing that henceforth it would refuse to issue a broadcast license to any network affiliate whose affiliation agreement contained certain prohibited provisions. Even though the FCC had not yet applied the rule to deny a license, the Court entertained a challenge to the commission's authority to issue such a rule:

> Such regulations have the force of law before their sanctions are invoked as well as after. When, as here, they are promulgated by order of the Commission and the expected conformity to them causes injury cognizable by a court of equity, they are appropriately the subject of attack.

Two cases decided in 1956 further eroded the presumption against pre-enforcement review. In Frozen Food Express v. United States, 351 U.S. 40 (1956), a carrier claiming immunity from ICC regulation under the statute's "agricultural commodities" exemption challenged a rule issued by the ICC that narrowly defined the scope of that exemption. Finding that the rule imposed an immediate burden on the carrier, the Court entertained the claim even though no enforcement action had yet been initiated by the ICC. In *United States v. Storer Broadcasting Co.,* 351 U.S. 192 (1956) (excerpted *infra*), the Supreme Court reviewed an FCC rule announcing that the agency would not issue a television license to any applicant already owning five or more television licenses. The Court found that Storer, a company owning five stations, was sufficiently "aggrieved" by the rule's promulgation to obtain review of its legality.

While *CBS, Frozen Food,* and *Storer* all permitted pre-enforcement judicial review of agency rules, their scope was unclear. All three arose in the context of licensing schemes administered by agencies that exercised close and ongoing supervision over the petitioners' businesses. It was not until a decade later that the Court had occasion to consider whether pre-enforcement review was available in other contexts as well.

ABBOTT LABORATORIES v. GARDNER
387 U.S. 136 (1967)

MR. JUSTICE HARLAN delivered the opinion of the Court.

In 1962 Congress amended the Federal Food, Drug, and Cosmetic Act (52 Stat. 1040, as amended by the Drug Amendments of 1962, 76 Stat. 780, 21 U.S.C. §301 *et seq.*), to require manufacturers of prescription drugs to print the "established name" of the drug "prominently and in type at least half as large as that used thereon for any proprietary name or designation for such drug," on labels and other printed material, §502(e)(1)(B), 21 U.S.C. §352(e)(1)(B). The "established name" is one designated by the Secretary of Health, Education, and Welfare pursuant to §502(e)(2) of the Act, 21 U.S.C. §352(e)(2); the "proprietary name" is usually a trade name under which a particular drug is marketed. The underlying purpose of the 1962 amendment was to bring to the attention of doctors and patients the fact that many of the drugs sold under familiar trade names are actually identical to drugs sold under their "established" or less familiar trade names at significantly lower prices. The Commissioner of Food and Drugs, exercising authority delegated to him by the Secretary, 22 Fed. Reg. 1051, 25 Fed. Reg. 8625, published proposed regulations designed to implement the statute, 28 Fed. Reg. 1448. After inviting and considering comments submitted by interested parties the Commissioner promulgated the following regulation for the "efficient enforcement" of the Act, §701(a), 21 U.S.C. §371(a):

> If the label or labeling of a prescription drug bears a proprietary name or designation for the drug or any ingredient thereof, the established name, if such there be, corresponding to such proprietary name or designation, shall accompany each appearance of such proprietary name or designation.

21 CFR §1.104(g)(1). A similar rule was made applicable to advertisements for prescription drugs, 21 CFR §1.105(b)(1).

The present action was brought by a group of 37 individual drug manufacturers and by the Pharmaceutical Manufacturers Association, of which all the petitioner companies are members, and which includes manufacturers of more than 90% of the Nation's supply of prescription drugs. They challenged the regulations on the ground that the Commissioner exceeded his authority under the statute by promulgating an order requiring labels, advertisements, and other printed matter relating to prescription drugs to designate the established name of the particular drug involved every time its trade name is used anywhere in such material.

The District Court, on cross motions for summary judgment, granted the declaratory and injunctive relief sought, finding that the statute did not sweep so broadly as to permit the Commissioner's "every time" interpretation. 228 F. Supp. 855. The Court of Appeals for the Third Circuit reversed without reaching the merits of the case. 352 F.2d 286. It held first that under the statutory scheme provided by the Federal Food, Drug, and Cosmetic Act pre-enforcement review of these regulations was unauthorized and therefore beyond the jurisdiction of the District Court. Second, the Court of Appeals held that no "actual case or controversy" existed and, for that reason, that no relief under the Administrative Procedure Act, 5 U.S.C. §§701-704 (1964 ed., Supp. II), or under the Declaratory Judgment Act, 28 U.S.C. §2201, was in any event available.

I

The first question we consider is whether Congress by the Federal Food, Drug, and Cosmetic Act intended to forbid pre-enforcement review of this sort of regulation promulgated by the Commissioner. The question is phrased in terms of "prohibition" rather than "authorization" because a survey of our cases shows that judicial review of a final agency action by an aggrieved person will not be cut off unless there is persuasive reason to believe that such was the purpose of Congress. . . .

We conclude that nothing in the Food, Drug, and Cosmetic Act itself precludes this action.

II

A further inquiry must, however, be made. The injunctive and declaratory judgment remedies are discretionary, and courts traditionally have been reluctant to apply them to administrative determinations unless these arise in the context of a controversy "ripe" for judicial resolution. Without undertaking to survey the intricacies of the ripeness doctrine it is fair to say that its basic rationale is to prevent the courts, through avoidance of premature adjudication, from entangling themselves in abstract disagreements over administrative policies, and also to protect the agencies from judicial interference until an administrative decision has been formalized and its effects felt in a concrete way by the challenging parties. The problem is best seen in a twofold aspect, requiring us to evaluate both the fitness of the issues for judicial decision and the hardship to the parties of withholding court consideration.

As to the former factor, we believe the issues presented are appropriate for judicial resolution at this time. First, all parties agree that the issue tendered is a purely legal one: whether the statute was properly construed by the Commissioner to require the established name of the drug to be used *every time* the proprietary name is employed. Both sides moved for summary judgment in the

District Court, and no claim is made here that further administrative proceedings are contemplated. It is suggested that the justification for this rule might vary with different circumstances, and that the expertise of the Commissioner is relevant to passing upon the validity of the regulation. This of course is true, but the suggestion overlooks the fact that both sides have approached this case as one purely of congressional intent, and that the Government made no effort to justify the regulation in factual terms.

Second, the regulations in issue we find to be "final agency action" within the meaning of §10 of the Administrative Procedure Act, 5 U.S.C. §704, as construed in judicial decisions. An "agency action" includes any "rule," defined by the Act as "an agency statement of general or particular applicability and future effect designed to implement, interpret, or prescribe law or policy," §§2(c), 2(g), 5 U.S.C. §§551(4), 551(13). The cases dealing with judicial review of administrative actions have interpreted the "finality" element in a pragmatic way. [The Court here reviews the *CBS, Frozen Food,* and *Storer* decisions.] . . .

We find decision in the present case following a fortiori from these precedents. The regulation challenged here, promulgated in a formal manner after announcement in the Federal Register and consideration of comments by interested parties is quite clearly definitive. There is no hint that this regulation is informal, *see* Helco Products Co. v. McNutt, 137 F.2d 681, or only the ruling of a subordinate official, *see* Swift & Co. v. Wickham, 230 F. Supp. 398, 409, *aff'd,* 364 F.2d 241, or tentative. It was made effective upon publication, and the Assistant General Counsel for Food and Drugs stated in the District Court that compliance was expected.

The Government argues, however, that the present case can be distinguished from cases like *Frozen Food Express* on the ground that in those instances the agency involved could implement its policy directly, while here the Attorney General must authorize criminal and seizure actions for violations of the statute. In the context of this case, we do not find this argument persuasive. These regulations are not meant to advise the Attorney General, but purport to be directly authorized by the statute. Thus, if within the Commissioner's authority, they have the status of law and violations of them carry heavy criminal and civil sanctions. Also, there is no representation that the Attorney General and the Commissioner disagree in this area; the Justice Department is defending this very suit. It would be adherence to a mere technicality to give any credence to this contention. Moreover, the agency does have direct authority to enforce this regulation in the context of passing upon applications for clearance of new drugs, §505, 21 U.S.C. §355, or certification of certain antibiotics, §507, 21 U.S.C. §357.

This is also a case in which the impact of the regulations upon the petitioners is sufficiently direct and immediate as to render the issue appropriate for judicial review at this stage. These regulations purport to give an authoritative interpretation of a statutory provision that has a direct effect on the day-to-day business of all prescription drug companies; its promulgation puts petitioners in a dilemma that it was the very purpose of the Declaratory Judgment Act to ameliorate. As the District Court found on the basis of uncontested allegations, "Either they must comply with the every time requirement and incur the costs of changing over their promotional material and labeling or they must follow their present course and risk prosecution." 228 F. Supp. 855, 861. The regulations are clear-cut, and were made effective immediately upon publication; as

noted earlier the agency's counsel represented to the District Court that immediate compliance with their terms was expected. If petitioners wish to comply
they must change all their labels, advertisements, and promotional materials;
they must destroy stocks of printed matter; and they must invest heavily in new
printing type and new supplies. The alternative to compliance — continued use
of material which they believe in good faith meets the statutory requirements,
but which clearly does not meet the regulation of the Commissioner — may be
even more costly. That course would risk serious criminal and civil penalties for
the unlawful distribution of "misbranded" drugs.[19]

It is relevant at this juncture to recognize that petitioners deal in a sensitive industry, in which public confidence in their drug products is especially
important. To require them to challenge these regulations only as a defense to
an action brought by the Government might harm them severely and unnecessarily. Where the legal issue presented is fit for judicial resolution, and where a
regulation requires an immediate and significant change in the plaintiffs' conduct of their affairs with serious penalties attached to noncompliance, access to
the courts under the Administrative Procedure Act and the Declaratory Judgment Act must be permitted, absent a statutory bar or some other unusual circumstance, neither of which appears here.

The Government does not dispute the very real dilemma in which petitioners are placed by the regulation, but contends that "mere financial expense" is
not a justification for pre-enforcement judicial review. It is of course true that
cases in this Court dealing with the standing of particular parties to bring an
action have held that a possible financial loss is not by itself a sufficient interest
to sustain a judicial challenge to governmental action. Frothingham v. Mellon,
262 U.S. 447; Perkins v. Lukens Steel Co., 310 U.S. 113. But there is no question
in the present case that petitioners have sufficient standing as plaintiffs: the
regulation is directed at them in particular; it requires them to make significant
changes in their everyday business practices; if they fail to observe the Commissioner's rule they are quite clearly exposed to the imposition of strong sanctions. *Compare* Columbia Broadcasting System v. United States, 316 U.S. 407; 3
Davis, Administrative Law Treatise, c. 21 (1958). This case is, therefore, remote
from the *Mellon* and *Perkins* cases.

The Government further contends that the threat of criminal sanctions for
noncompliance with a judicially untested regulation is unrealistic; the Solicitor General has represented that if court enforcement becomes necessary, "the
Department of Justice will proceed only civilly for an injunction . . . or by condemnation." We cannot accept this argument as a sufficient answer to petitioners'
petition. This action at its inception was properly brought and this subsequent
representation of the Department of Justice should not suffice to defeat it.

Finally, the Government urges that to permit resort to the courts in this type of
case may delay or impede effective enforcement of the Act. We fully recognize the
important public interest served by assuring prompt and unimpeded administration of the Pure Food, Drug, and Cosmetic Act, but we do not find the Government's

---

19. Section 502(e)(1)(B) declares a drug not complying with this labeling requirement to be "misbranded." Section 301, 21 U.S.C. §331, designates as "prohibited acts" the misbranding of drugs in interstate commerce. Such prohibited acts are subject to injunction, §302, 21 U.S.C. §332, criminal penalties,
§303, 21 U.S.C. §333, and seizure, §304(a), 21 U.S.C. §334(a).

argument convincing. First, in this particular case, a pre-enforcement challenge by nearly all prescription drug manufacturers is calculated to speed enforcement. If the Government prevails, a large part of the industry is bound by the decree; if the Government loses, it can more quickly revise its regulation.

The Government contends, however, that if the Court allows this consolidated suit, then nothing will prevent a multiplicity of suits in various jurisdictions challenging other regulations. The short answer to this contention is that the courts are well equipped to deal with such eventualities. The venue transfer provision, 28 U.S.C. §1404(a), may be invoked by the Government to consolidate separate actions. Or, actions in all but one jurisdiction might be stayed pending the conclusion of one proceeding. *See* American Life Ins. Co. v. Stewart, 300 U.S. 203, 215-216. A court may even in its discretion dismiss a declaratory judgment or injunctive suit if the same issue is pending in litigation elsewhere. . . .

Further, the declaratory judgment and injunctive remedies are equitable in nature, and other equitable defenses may be interposed. If a multiplicity of suits are undertaken in order to harass the Government or to delay enforcement, relief can be denied on this ground alone. . . . The defense of laches could be asserted if the Government is prejudiced by a delay. . . . And courts may even refuse declaratory relief for the nonjoinder of interested parties who are not, technically speaking, indispensable. . . .

In addition to all these safeguards against what the Government fears, it is important to note that the institution of this type of action does not by itself stay the effectiveness of the challenged regulation. There is nothing in the record to indicate that petitioners have sought to stay enforcement of the "every time" regulation pending judicial review. *See* 5 U.S.C. §705. If the agency believes that a suit of this type will significantly impede enforcement or will harm the public interest, it need not postpone enforcement of the regulation and may oppose any motion for a judicial stay on the part of those challenging the regulation. *Ibid.* It is scarcely to be doubted that a court would refuse to postpone the effective date of an agency action if the Government could show, as it made no effort to do here, that delay would be detrimental to the public health or safety. . . . Reversed and remanded.

MR. JUSTICE BRENNAN took no part in the consideration or decision of this case.

NOTES

In the companion case of Toilet Goods Association v. Gardner, 387 U.S. 158 (1967) (*Toilet Goods I*), the Court denied pre-enforcement review of the following regulation promulgated by the Commissioner of Food and Drugs:

  (a) When it appears to the Commissioner that a person has: . . .
        (4) Refused to permit duly authorized employees of the Food and Drug Administration free access to all manufacturing facilities, processes, and formulae involved in the manufacture of color additives and intermediates from which such color additives are derived; he may immediately

suspend certification service to such person and may continue such suspension until adequate corrective action has been taken.

28 Fed. Reg. 6445-6446. Under the Color Additive Amendments of 1960 to the
Federal Food, Drug, and Cosmetic Act, all color additives to foods, drugs, or cosmetics must be "certified" as safe by the FDA. 74 Stat. 397, 21 U.S.C. §§321-376.
Any food, drug, or cosmetic containing an uncertified color additive is deemed
"adulterated," and its introduction into commerce is subject to injunction,
criminal penalties, and seizure. The Commissioner declared that conditioning
certification on compliance with FDA inspection was necessary to give effect to
these provisions. An association of cosmetics manufacturers filed suit, claiming
that the regulation was not authorized by the statute.

   While the Court agreed that the regulation was "final agency action" under
APA §704, it found the controversy not yet ripe for judicial resolution. First, the
Court reasoned, the question presented was not fit for judicial resolution:

> The regulation serves notice only that the Commissioner *may* under certain cir-
> cumstances order inspection of certain facilities and data, and that further certifi-
> cation of additives *may* be refused to those who decline to permit a duly authorized
> inspection until they have complied in that regard. At this juncture we have no
> idea whether or when such an inspection will be ordered and what reasons the
> Commissioner will give to justify his order. The statutory authority asserted for the
> regulation is the power to promulgate regulations "for the efficient enforcement"
> of the Act, §701(a). Whether the regulation is justified thus depends not only, as
> petitioners appear to suggest, on whether Congress refused to include a specific
> section of the Act authorizing such inspections, although this factor is to be sure
> a highly relevant one, but also on whether the statutory scheme as a whole justi-
> fied promulgation of the regulation. This will depend not merely on an inquiry
> into statutory purpose, but concurrently on an understanding of what types of
> enforcement problems are encountered by the FDA, the need for various sorts of
> supervision in order to effectuate the goals of the Act, and the safeguards devised
> to protect legitimate trade secrets (*see* 21 CFR §130.14(c)). We believe that judicial
> appraisal of these factors is likely to stand on a much surer footing in the context
> of a specific application of this regulation than could be the case in the framework
> of the generalized challenge made here.

387 U.S. at 163-164. Nor, the Court concluded, did petitioners satisfy the "harm"
prong of the ripeness test:

> This is not a situation in which primary conduct is affected—when contracts must
> be negotiated, ingredients tested or substituted, or special records compiled.
> This regulation merely states that the Commissioner may authorize inspectors to
> examine certain processes or formulae; no advance action is required of cosmet-
> ics manufacturers, who since the enactment of the 1938 Act have been under a
> statutory duty to permit reasonable inspection of a "factory, warehouse, establish-
> ment, or vehicle and all pertinent equipment, finished and unfinished materials;
> containers, and labeling therein." §704(a). Moreover, no irremediable adverse
> consequences flow from requiring a later challenge to this regulation by a manu-
> facturer who refuses to allow this type of inspection. Unlike the other regulations
> challenged in this action, in which seizure of goods, heavy fines, adverse publicity

for distributing "adulterated" goods, and possible criminal liability might penalize failure to comply, *see* Gardner v. Toilet Goods Assn., [387 U.S. 167 (1967)], a refusal to admit an inspector here would at most lead only to a suspension of certification services to the particular party, a determination that can then be promptly challenged through an administrative procedure,[1] which in turn is reviewable by a court. Such review will provide an adequate forum for testing the regulation in a concrete situation.

387 U.S. at 164-165.

A second companion case to *Abbott Labs,* Gardner v. Toilet Goods Association, 387 U.S. 167 (1967) (*Toilet Goods II*) (referred to in the *Toilet Goods I* excerpt), involved three regulations defining the types of substances covered by the Color Additives Amendments. The Court found these regulations subject to pre-enforcement review because they were "self-executing, and have an immediate and substantial impact upon the respondents," and because the rules "appear, prima facie, to be susceptible of reasoned comparison with the statutory mandate without inquiry into factual issues." 387 U.S. at 171.

Justice Fortas, in an opinion joined by Chief Justice Warren and Justice Clark, dissented from the result reached in *Toilet Goods II* as well as in *Abbott Labs.*

GARDNER v. TOILET GOODS ASSN.
387 U.S. 167 (1967)

FORTAS, J., concurring and dissenting. . . . In none of these cases is judicial interference warranted at this stage, in this fashion, and to test—on a gross, free-wheeling basis—whether the content of these regulations is within the statutory intendment. The contrary is dictated by a proper regard for the purpose of the regulatory statute and the requirements of effective administration; and by regard for the salutary rule that courts should pass upon concrete, specific questions in a particularized setting rather than upon a general controversy divorced from particular facts.

The Court, by today's decisions in Nos. 39 and 438, has opened Pandora's box. Federal injunctions will now threaten programs of vast importance to the public welfare. The Court's holding here strikes at programs for the public health. The dangerous precedent goes even further. It is cold comfort—it is little more than delusion—to read in the Court's opinion that "It is scarcely to be doubted that a court would refuse to postpone the effective date of an agency action if the Government could show . . . that delay would be detrimental to the public health or safety." Experience dictates, on the contrary, that it can hardly be hoped that some federal judge somewhere will not be moved as the Court is here, by the cries of anguish and distress of those regulated, to grant a disruptive injunction. . . .

1. *See* 21 CFR §§8.28(b), 130.14-130.26. We recognize that a denial of certification might under certain circumstances cause inconvenience and possibly hardship, depending upon such factors as how large a supply of certified additives the particular manufacturer may have, how rapidly the administrative hearing and judicial review are conducted, and what temporary remedial or protective provisions, such as compliance with a reservation pending litigation, might be available to a manufacturer testing the regulation. In the context of the present case we need only say that such inconvenience is speculative, and we have been provided with no information that would support an assumption that much weight should be attached to this possibility.

I

Since enactment of the Federal Food, Drug, and Cosmetic Act in 1938, the mechanism for judicial review of agency actions under its provisions has been well understood. Except for specific types of agency regulations and actions to which I shall refer, judicial review has been confined to enforcement actions instituted by the Attorney General on recommendation of the agency. . . .

The fact of the matter is that . . . the avenue for attack upon the statute and regulations has been by defense to specific enforcement actions by the agency. Congress has been well aware of this for more than a generation that the statute has been in effect.

Where a remedy is provided by statute, I submit that it is and has been fundamental to our law, to judicial administration, to the principle of separation of powers in our Constitution, that the courts will withhold equitable or discretionary remedies unless they conclude that the statutory remedy is inadequate. . . .

Congress did not intend that the regulations at issue in this case might be challenged in gross, apart from a specific controversy, or in the district courts, or by injunction or declaratory judgment action. On the contrary, the clear intent was that the regulations, being to protect the consumer from unsafe, potentially harmful, and "misbranded" foods, drugs, devices, and cosmetics, were to be subject to challenge only by way of defense to enforcement proceedings. It was Congress' judgment, after much controversy, that the special nature of the Act and its administration required this protection against delay and disruption. We should not arrogate to ourselves the power to override this judgment. . . .

II

I come then to the questions whether the review otherwise available under the statute is "adequate," whether the controversies are "ripe" or appropriate for review in terms of the evaluation of the competing private and public interests. . . .

The regulation in No. 39 relates to a 1962 amendment to the Act requiring manufacturers of prescription drugs to print on the labels or other printed material, the "established name" of the drug "prominently and in type at least half as large as that used thereon for any proprietary name or designation for such drug." §502(e)(1), 76 Stat. 790, 21 U.S.C. §352(e)(1). Obviously, this requires some elucidation, either case-by-case or by general regulation or pronouncement, because the statute does not say that this must be done "every time," or only once on each label or in each pamphlet, or once per panel, etc., or that it must be done differently on labels than on circulars, or doctors' literature than on directions to the patients, etc. This is exactly the traditional purpose and function of an administrative agency. The Commissioner, acting by delegation from the Secretary, took steps to provide for the specification. He invited and considered comments and then issued a regulation requiring that the "established name" appear every time the proprietary name is used. A manufacturer—or other person who violates this regulation—has mislabeled his product. The product may be seized; or injunction may be sought; or the mislabeler may be criminally prosecuted. In any of these actions he may challenge the regulation and obtain a judicial determination.

The Court, however, moved by petitioners' claims as to the expense and inconvenience of compliance and the risks of deferring challenge by noncompliance, decrees that the manufacturers may have their suit for injunction at this time and reverses the Third Circuit. The Court says that this confronts the manufacturer with a "real dilemma." But the fact of the matter is that the dilemma is no more than citizens face in connection with countless statutes and with the rules of the SEC, FTC, FCC, ICC, and other regulatory agencies. This has not heretofore been regarded as a basis for injunctive relief unless Congress has so provided. The overriding fact here is—or should be—that the public interest in avoiding the delay in implementing Congress' program far outweighs the private interest; and that the private interest which has so impressed the Court is no more than that which exists in respect of most regulatory statutes or agency rules. Somehow, the Court has concluded that the damage to petitioners if they have to engage in the required redesign and reprint of their labels and printed materials without threshold review outweighs the damage to the public of deferring during the tedious months and years of litigation a cure for the possible danger and asserted deceit of peddling plain medicine under fancy trademarks and for fancy prices which, rightly or wrongly, impelled the Congress to enact this legislation. I submit that a much stronger showing is necessary than the expense and trouble of compliance and the risk of defiance. . . .

MR. JUSTICE CLARK, dissenting. [Omitted.]

NOTES AND QUESTIONS

1. *"Purely legal" questions.* Why was the issue in *Abbott Labs* "purely legal"? Was the issue in *Toilet Goods I* any less "purely legal"? Suppose the plaintiffs in *Abbott Labs* had argued that the FDA's "every time" rule was arbitrary and capricious. Would that be sufficiently "legal" to be fit for pre-enforcement review? Courts consider a number of factors when determining which questions are "purely legal." Perhaps the simplest explanation is that when a case would benefit from further factual development of the issues, the question is not a purely legal one. *See, e.g.,* Utah v. U.S. Dept. of Interior, 535 F.3d 1184 (10th Cir. 2008) (holding that a settlement between DOI and the state regarding BLM management of state and federal lands that arguably deserved designation as wilderness areas was not ripe for review, despite the urging of intervenors who objected to the settlement on a variety of grounds, because the settlement had not yet been applied to the development of specific land use plans).

2. *Hardship.* Exactly how strong a showing of hardship is required to establish ripeness? Are you convinced that the *Abbott Labs* plaintiffs would suffer genuine hardship if they had to wait until an enforcement action to challenge the rule? Is the "dilemma" they face (comply or risk prosecution) any different than the dilemma most people face when confronting a policy that they think is unlawful or a statute that they think is unconstitutional? In some cases the Court has found the claimed hardship clearly minimal, such as National Park Hospitality Assn. v. Dept. of Interior, 538 U.S. 803 (2003), where petitioner concessionaires claimed they could price their government contract bids more accurately if questions about the applicability of rules governing contract disputes were

resolved earlier rather than later. By comparison, how serious is the hardship in *Earth Island Institute,* discussed earlier?

Courts disagree over whether a finding of hardship is even necessary once the "purely legal" question test is satisfied. *Compare* Cement Kiln Recycling Coalition v. EPA, 493 F.3d 207 (D.C. Cir. 2007) (holding no need to proceed to hardship prong once issue deemed purely legal), *with* Texas v. United States, 497 F.3d 491 (5th Cir. 2007) (requiring hardship to establish ripeness). A typical case of hardship involves a plaintiff alleging an economic disadvantage as a result of regulation. Yet a deprivation of economic *advantage* may also amount to hardship. In Teva Pharmaceuticals USA, Inc. v. Sebelius, 595 F.3d 1303 (D.C. Cir. 2010), the court held that an agency decision preventing a company from enjoying exclusive control over products on the market could satisfy hardship because "[t]he first-mover advantage is a valuable asset." *Id.* at 1311. What assumptions does such a holding make about entitlement to the regulatory status quo? Is it correct that whenever agencies re-adjust the economic burdens and benefits among competitors, it creates a hardship for someone?

3. *Why raise the ripeness issue?* Was it in the Secretary's interest to raise the ripeness defense in *Abbott Labs* and *Toilet Goods?* Why not just settle the question of the rule's validity once and for all, rather than allow it to hang as a cloud over future enforcement efforts? The answer to that question may depend in part on knowing who is bound by a judicial decision in a pre-enforcement challenge, as compared to an enforcement challenge. Suppose the Third Circuit had ruled in the FDA's favor in the *Abbott Labs* litigation. Who would have been bound by that decision (in the sense that they could not later re-litigate the same issue)? Abbott Laboratories? Another pharmaceutical company named as a plaintiff? Another company not named as a plaintiff? Would it matter if the company were a member of the Pharmaceutical Manufacturers Association? Suppose, instead, that the Third Circuit ruled against the FDA on the merits. Could the FDA nonetheless proceed to try to enforce its rule in a different federal circuit against a manufacturer who had not been a party to the pre-enforcement suit? As a general matter, the doctrine of nonmutual collateral estoppel bars a particular party from re-litigating an issue that was authoritatively resolved in a prior lawsuit involving that same party, even if the other party to the two cases is different. But the Supreme Court has ruled that the doctrine does not apply to the federal government. In United States v. Mendoza, 464 U.S. 154 (1984), the Court ruled that the United States was not barred by a prior unappealed adverse decision in a federal district court from re-litigating the same issue in a new case. The Court cited a number of factors in ruling that the government should not be subject to the same preclusion rule applied to private parties, including: the large volume of litigation involving the government, the public importance of legal issues involving the government, the need for the government to set litigation priorities, the need for the government to be able to change its policies over time, and the value of intercircuit conflicts in identifying issues requiring Supreme Court resolution.

4. *Administrative "nonacquiescence."* The *Mendoza* ruling has made it possible for—some would say encouraged—some federal agencies to adopt a policy of "nonacquiescence" with rulings of lower federal courts. "Intercircuit nonacquiescence"—refusal to follow the law of one circuit in other circuits—is a fairly common practice among federal agencies. A few agencies, such as the Social

Security Administration, the IRS, and the NLRB, however, have also frequently followed a policy of *intra*circuit nonacquiescence. The most celebrated, and heavily litigated, instance is the Social Security Administration's policy of refusing to apply certain judicial decisions invalidating the procedures and criteria used to terminate disability insurance (DI) benefits to anyone other than the named parties. After the agency publicly announced its refusal to acquiesce in two Ninth Circuit decisions, a group of DI recipients brought a class action on behalf of all DI recipients living in the Ninth Circuit, seeking to enjoin the Secretary of Health and Human Services from following her announced policy of nonacquiescence. The district court granted a preliminary injunction restraining the Secretary from "failing to follow" the two Ninth Circuit cases and from implementing her nonacquiescence policy throughout the Ninth Circuit. Characterizing the Secretary's action as "deliberately and unequivocally flouting the procedures she is required by law to follow," the appeals court affirmed. Lopez v. Heckler, 725 F.2d 1489, 1503 (9th Cir. 1984).

5. *Pre-enforcement review of administrative orders.* In United States Army Corp of Engineers v. Hawkes Co., Inc., 136 S. Ct. 1807 (2016), the Corps of Engineers had issued an "approved jurisdictional determination" (JD), determining that certain wetlands owned by Hawkes were "waters of the United States" for purposes of the Clean Water Act. This ruling effectively prohibited Hawkes from filling ("discharging any pollutant" into) those wetlands without a permit granted by the Corps. The Corps and the Environmental Protection Agency (EPA) have joint authority to take enforcement action against any non-permitted discharge. Hawkes sought judicial review of the JD, invoking APA §704. The Corps claimed that a JD is not a "final" agency action, and that there were "other adequate remedies" available to Hawkes. The Supreme Court rejected both arguments.

As for "finality," the Court applied the two-pronged test announced in Bennett v. Spear, 520 U.S. 154 (1997): "First, the action must mark the consummation of the agency's decisionmaking process—it must not be of a merely tentative or interlocutory nature. And second, the action must be one by which rights or obligations have been determined, or from which legal consequences will flow." *Id.*, at 177-178. The *Hawkes* Court found that the JD satisfied both prongs of the *Bennett* finality test:

> [An approved JD] is issued after extensive factfinding by the Corps regarding the physical and hydrological characteristics of the property, and is typically not revisited if the permitting process moves forward. Indeed, the Corps itself describes approved JDs as "final agency action," and specifies that an approved JD "will remain valid for a period of five years."
>
> The Corps may revise an approved JD within the five-year period based on "new information." That possibility, however, is a common characteristic of agency action, and does not make an otherwise definitive decision nonfinal. By issuing respondents an approved JD, the Corps for all practical purposes "has ruled definitively" that respondents' property contains jurisdictional waters. [Sackett v. EPA, 566 U.S. 120, 131 (Ginsburg, J., concurring).]
>
> The definitive nature of approved JDs also gives rise to "direct and appreciable legal consequences," thereby satisfying the second prong of *Bennett.* Consider the effect of an approved JD stating that a party's property does *not* contain jurisdictional waters—a "negative" JD, in Corps parlance. As noted, such a JD will generally bind the Corps for five years. Under a longstanding memorandum of

agreement between the Corps and EPA, it will also be "binding on the Government and represent the Government's position in any subsequent Federal action or litigation concerning that final determination." . . . It follows that affirmative JDs have legal consequences as well: They represent the denial of the safe harbor that negative JDs afford. . . .

With regard to the adequacy of alternative remedies, the Court had this to say:

> The Corps contends that respondents have two such alternatives: either discharge fill material without a permit, risking an EPA enforcement action during which they can argue that no permit was required, or apply for a permit and seek judicial review if dissatisfied with the results.
>
> Neither alternative is adequate. As we have long held, parties need not await enforcement proceedings before challenging final agency action where such proceedings carry the risk of "serious criminal and civil penalties." *Abbott*, 387 U.S., at 153. If respondents discharged fill material without a permit, in the mistaken belief that their property did not contain jurisdictional waters, they would expose themselves to civil penalties of up to $37,500 for each day they violated the Act, to say nothing of potential criminal liability. Respondents need not assume such risks while waiting for EPA to "drop the hammer" in order to have their day in court.
>
> Nor is it an adequate alternative to APA review for a landowner to apply for a permit and then seek judicial review in the event of an unfavorable decision. As Corps officials indicated in their discussions with respondents, the permitting process can be arduous, expensive, and long. . . . Respondents estimate that undertaking [the necessary analyses] would cost more than $100,000. And whatever pertinence all this might have to the issuance of a permit, none of it will alter the finality of the approved JD, or affect its suitability for judicial review. The permitting process adds nothing to the JD. . . .
>
> Finally, the Corps emphasizes that seeking review in an enforcement action or at the end of the permitting process would be the only available avenues for obtaining review "[i]f the Corps had never adopted its practice of issuing standalone jurisdictional determinations upon request." True enough. But such a "count your blessings" argument is not an adequate rejoinder to the assertion of a right to judicial review under the APA.

Recall that in *Abbott Labs*, the FDA had argued that a pharmaceutical manufacturer seeking to challenge the legality of the "every time" rule could simply await enforcement action brought by the Justice Department and then defend by arguing that the rule is invalid. The Court plainly did not find this to be an "adequate" alternative to pre-enforcement review. Did that ruling settle the issue in *Hawkes*? Or did the Corps have a convincing basis for distinguishing *Abbott Labs*?

6. Can a stay be final? In Clean Air Council v. Pruitt, 862 F.3d 1 (D.C. Cir. 2017), the D.C. Circuit applied the *Bennett* finality test to rule that an agency's decision to stay the effective date of a previously issued rule was reviewable as "final agency action." In the last year of the Obama administration, the EPA had issued a rule regulating methane emissions from oil and natural gas processing facilities. Industry representatives petitioned the EPA to reconsider the rule, invoking a provision of the Clean Air Act authorizing EPA to reconsider an adopted rule and to stay the rule's operation for up to 30 days if the claimant raised an issue that was "impracticable" to have raised in the original rulemaking proceeding. In June 2017, under its new Administrator, Scott Pruitt, EPA issued an order granting reconsideration and staying the operation of the rule. Environmental groups petitioned a federal court to overturn the grant of reconsideration and the stay, claiming a failure to satisfy the statutory "impracticability" condition for reconsideration. A majority of the D.C. Circuit panel agreed. Before concluding that the EPA's grant of reconsideration was arbitrary and capricious, it ruled that the EPA's grant of reconsideration and stay of the rule was reviewable as "final agency action." In the panel's view, the EPA's June action was the "consummation" of the agency's process for determining whether to grant reconsideration and to suspend operation of the rule pending reconsideration. Further, the stay affected legal rights and duties, because it relieved the industry of reporting requirements imposed by the rule.

7. *Foreclosing post-enforcement review.* If, as in *Toilet Goods I*, pre-enforcement challenges can sometimes be too early, can post-enforcement challenges ever be too late? That was the question presented in PDR Network, LLC v. Carlton & Harris Chiropractic, Inc., 139 S. Ct. 2051 (2019). Carlton & Harris sued PDR, alleging that PDR had violated the Telephone Consumer Protection Act of 1991, 47 U.S.C. §227(b)(1)(C), by transmitting by fax certain "unsolicited advertisements," as defined by a Federal Communications Commission (FCC) rule. PDR defended by claiming that the FCC order was an "interpretive rule" not binding on the federal district court in a private enforcement action. The Fourth Circuit ruled that the Administrative Orders Review Act (the Hobbs Act) gives federal courts of appeals "exclusive jurisdiction to enjoin, set aside, suspend (in whole or in part), or to determine the validity of" certain "final orders of the Federal Communication Commission," 28 U.S.C. §2342(1), and requires that petitions to review final orders be brought within 60 days of the entry of the order (which had not happened in this instance). The Supreme Court remanded the case to the Fourth Circuit, for findings on whether the Hobbs Act's exclusive review provision afforded a "prior" and "adequate" opportunity for review sufficient to foreclose post-enforcement review under §703 of the Administrative Procedure Act. Justice Kavanaugh, writing for four members of the Court, wrote a concurrence expressing his view that the Court should answer the question, and that the proper answer must be no:

> Two categories of statutes allow for facial, pre-enforcement review of agency orders. . . . Statutes in the first category authorize facial, pre-enforcement judicial review and expressly preclude judicial review in subsequent enforcement actions. The Clean Water Act, the Comprehensive Environmental Response, Compensation, and Liability Act of 1980 (CERCLA), and the Clean Air Act are examples. The Clean Water Act [for example] provides for facial, pre-enforcement review of certain agency actions in a court of appeals and requires parties to seek review within 120 days. *See* 33 U.S.C. §1369(b)(1). The Act expressly states that those agency orders "shall not be subject to judicial review in any civil or criminal proceeding for enforcement." §1369(b)(2). . . .
>
> Statutes in the second category authorize facial, pre-enforcement judicial review, but are silent on the question whether a party may argue against the agency's legal interpretation in subsequent enforcement proceedings. The Hobbs Act is an example. . . . For that second category . . . there must be a default rule that applies absent statutory language to the contrary. The question is whether the proper default rule is (1) to preclude review by the district court of whether the agency

interpretation is correct or (2) to allow review by the district court of whether the agency interpretation is correct. In my view, elementary principles of administrative law establish that the proper default rule is to allow review by the district court of whether the agency interpretation is correct. In those enforcement actions, the defendant may argue that the agency's interpretation is wrong. And the district courts are not bound by the agency's interpretation. District courts must determine the meaning of the statute under the usual principles of statutory interpretation, affording appropriate respect to the agency's interpretation. . . .

The strong presumption of judicial review, the tradition of allowing defendants in enforcement actions to argue that the agency's interpretation is wrong, and this Court's landmark decision in *Abbott Labs* all suggest the proper default rule: to allow review by the district court of whether the agency interpretation is correct.

Further supporting that default rule is the fact that Congress knows how to explicitly preclude judicial review in enforcement proceedings. . . .

The practical consequences likewise support a default rule of allowing review. Denying judicial review of an agency's interpretation of the statute in enforcement actions can be grossly inefficient and unfair. It would be wholly impractical—and a huge waste of resources—to expect and require every potentially affected party to bring pre-enforcement Hobbs Act challenges against every agency order that might possibly affect them in the future.

8. *Benefits criteria.* In a case arising out of the INS's handling of its responsibilities under the Immigration Reform and Control Act, the Court held that a challenge to an administrative eligibility criterion for a benefit is not ripe until the plaintiff applies for the benefit and is turned down on the basis of the challenged criterion. *See* Reno v. Catholic Social Services, Inc., 509 U.S. 43 (1993). The Court reasoned that in most cases involving criteria for benefits, the hardship prong of *Abbott Labs* is not met when no application has yet been made and rejected. Interestingly, unlike the Court in *Abbott Labs,* neither the majority nor the concurring or dissenting opinions mentioned APA §704's grant of judicial review of final agency action. Why not? The majority referred to Article III and prudential considerations as sources of the ripeness doctrine. Might the majority have reason to prefer those sources to the APA?

Chamber of Commerce v. Reich, 57 F.3d 1099 (D.C. Cir. 1995) (per curiam), raises questions regarding both the fitness and hardship prongs of the *Abbott Labs* ripeness test. President Clinton issued an executive order authorizing the Secretary of Labor to disqualify companies from federal contracts if they hire permanent replacement workers during strikes. The Chamber of Commerce sued to enjoin the Secretary from enforcing the order. The government argued that neither *Abbott Labs*' prong was met. The dispute was not fit, the government argued, because the Secretary had discretion over whether to disqualify a company, and no clear standards existed regarding how the Secretary would exercise that discretion. The court rejected this argument, holding that the mere existence of the executive order was likely to affect the collective bargaining process by making strikes less risky to workers. The court reasoned that since the harm was caused by the existence of the executive order, it did not matter that the Secretary's discretion rendered the operation of the order uncertain. 57 F.3d at 1100. The government also argued that there was no hardship until the Secretary actually disqualified a federal contractor. The court rejected this argument as well, concluding that the hardship of potentially losing the weapon of hiring permanent replacements was sufficient to meet the *Abbott Labs* test.

Do these conclusions meet the concerns that motivated the fitness and hardship prongs of *Abbott Labs*? Ultimately, the D.C. Circuit held that the executive order was pre-empted by the National Labor Relations Act, which, as interpreted, grants employers the right, under certain circumstances, to hire permanent replacement workers. *See* Chamber of Commerce v. Reich, 74 F.3d 1322 (D.C. Cir. 1996).

9. *Finality of agency-established procedures.* In Smith v. Berryhill, 139 S. Ct. 1765 (2019), the Supreme Court considered whether dismissal of a claim by the Social Security Administration (SSA) Appeals Council after a hearing before an administrative law judge constitutes a "final decision . . . made after a hearing" within the terms of the Social Security Act (Act), entitling the plaintiff to judicial review. The Act, which provides disability benefits to eligible claimants, provides for judicial review of "any final decision of the [SSA] made after a hearing." Congress clarified that review would be available only "as herein provided," suggesting that courts have no authority to hear appeals unless authorized by the Act. Through rulemaking, SSA created an appeals process for denied claims, which included deadlines for filing appeals after an adjudicative hearing. Smith missed the regulatory deadline for filing an appeal, and his claim was dismissed by the Appeals Council for untimeliness. In a unanimous opinion penned by Justice Sotomayor, the Court held that the Appeals Council ruling was final agency action subject to judicial review: "[W]e do not presume that Congress intended for this claimant-protective statute to leave a claimant without recourse to the courts when . . . a mistake does occur—least of all when the claimant may have already expended a significant amount of likely limited resources in a lengthy proceeding. . . . While Congress left it to the SSA to define the procedures that claimants like Smith must first pass through Congress has not suggested that it intended for the SSA to be the unreviewable arbiter of whether claimants have complied with those procedures."

10. *Ripeness of less formal action.* Much agency action is considerably less formal than the issuance of regulations. Some agency action, for example, takes the form of letter rulings. Regulated parties write letters seeking advice on issues within the agency's jurisdiction (for example, the Internal Revenue Service answers many questions regarding the tax laws with letter rulings) or they write seeking agency permission to take certain actions. For example, national banks often ask for letter rulings from the Comptroller of the Currency (a federal official having regulatory authority over national banks) regarding the propriety of proposed actions. In First National Bank of Chicago v. Comptroller of the Currency, 956 F.2d 1360 (7th Cir. 1992), the bank had sought a letter ruling from the Comptroller allowing it to distribute in a particular manner property in a real estate investment fund of which it was trustee. The Comptroller denied the bank's request, and the bank sued. The court, in an opinion by Judge Posner, posed the issue as whether this informal action could be challenged on judicial review or whether in order to receive judicial review the bank would have to go ahead and do what it wanted without permission and then challenge the Comptroller's ruling in defense of an enforcement action. The court held that the letter ruling was a final agency action and thus immediately reviewable. Judge Posner analogized a letter ruling denying permission to an agency denial of a permit or license; he also noted that the bank might face severe consequences if it went ahead with its plan in the face of the negative letter ruling. *Cf.* New York

Stock Exchange v. Bloom, 562 F.2d 736 (D.C. Cir. 1977) (holding Comptroller's letter ruling was not subject to judicial review where the recipient was not in the position of either obeying the ruling or acting at the peril of serious adverse consequences). Is this simply an application of the *Abbott Labs* test in a slightly different context? Can a letter denying permission be final agency action when agency enforcement is still a possibility?

In this regard, consider also Air Brake Systems, Inc. v. Mineta, 357 F.3d 632 (6th Cir. 2004). In this case, NHTSA posted an opinion letter on its website stating that plaintiff's antilock braking system for trucks did not meet NHTSA's safety standards. The plaintiff disagreed and sued to have the letter removed from the website on two bases, first that the opinion letter was wrong and second that the agency did not have the authority to issue and post the opinion letter. The Sixth Circuit held that the opinion letter was not final agency action for several reasons. First, insofar as the opinion letter was based on facts relating to the functioning of the plaintiff's braking system, it was tentative and based on limited information. Second, the conclusions of law embodied in the letter were not reviewable because they lacked legal consequences. Even though it was clear that prospective customers were put off by the possibility that if they installed plaintiff's brakes their vehicles would be subject to recall, the letter itself did not determine anyone's legal rights and duties. Further, the letter, as informal agency action, would not receive *Chevron* deference and thus did not have the force of law. How would these conclusions fit into the fitness and hardship test? With regard to the plaintiff's argument that the agency lacked authority to issue the opinion letter, the court held that the agency had made a final decision that it had such authority and therefore reached the merits of this challenge and ruled in favor of the agency.

Another recent case treated an agency's policy guidance—an instrument with broader application than an opinion letter—in a similar way. In Colwell v. Dept. of Health and Human Services, 558 F.3d 1112 (9th Cir. 2009), doctors and other plaintiffs opposed HHS's issuance of a policy guidance designed to "clarify the legal obligation of recipients of federal funds to provide meaningful access for individuals with limited English proficiency." *Id.* at 1116. The Court found the case not ripe because it could not determine the manner in which the guidance would be concretely used in relation to the plaintiffs. The Court emphasized the speculative nature of the guidance based on the document's use of conditional phrases such as "should," "suggest," and "encouraged," which indicated the guidance was advisory and not mandatory. What is the benefit of waiting in such cases? Clearly the agency meant to alter behavior by issuing a policy guidance, and in most cases regulated parties ignore such "advisories" at their peril. Does this mean guidance documents in general are simply unreviewable before an agency seeks to "enforce" them?

2.   *Exhaustion of Administrative Remedies Prior to Seeking Judicial Review*

The *Abbott Labs* trilogy and *Bennett* illustrate typical "ripeness" and "finality" cases, where private parties challenge administrative actions that have not yet (but might in the future) come to focus *specifically* and *concretely* on those parties.

In the paradigmatic "exhaustion of remedies" case, by contrast, the agency has initiated a specific enforcement proceeding against (or otherwise threatened to visit adverse consequences upon) a particular party, who then seeks to enlist judicial aid prior to completing all available steps for challenging the action at the administrative level.

a.   Exhaustion Outside the APA

The leading case on the exhaustion doctrine (outside the APA context) is Myers v. Bethlehem Shipbuilding Corp., 303 U.S. 41 (1938), which arose before the passage of the APA. The NLRB had charged Bethlehem with engaging in unfair labor practices at its Fore River Plant in Quincy, Massachusetts. Bethlehem had the right—under the then-recently enacted National Labor Relations Act—to demand an administrative hearing before a hearing officer, to appeal an adverse finding to the full board, and to obtain judicial review of a board order in a federal court of appeals (in an enforcement proceeding brought by the board). Instead, Bethlehem brought a bill in equity in a federal district court seeking to enjoin the board from conducting the hearing, on the ground that its plant was not in "interstate commerce" and therefore not governed by the Act. The Supreme Court, in an opinion by Justice Brandeis, reversed the lower court's decision to enjoin the board:

> It is true that the Board has jurisdiction only if the complaint concerns interstate or foreign commerce. Unless the Board finds that it does, the complaint must be dismissed. And if it finds that interstate or foreign commerce is involved, but the Circuit Court of Appeals concludes that such finding was without adequate evidence to support it, or otherwise contrary to law, the Board's petition to enforce it will be dismissed, or the employer's petition to have it set aside will be granted. Since the procedure before the Board is appropriate and the judicial review so provided is adequate, Congress had power to vest exclusive jurisdiction in the Board and the Circuit Court of Appeals. . . .
>
> The Corporation contends that, since it denies that interstate or foreign commerce is involved and claims that a hearing would subject it to irreparable damage, rights guaranteed by the Federal Constitution will be denied unless it be held that the District Court has jurisdiction to enjoin the holding of a hearing by the Board. So to hold would, as the Government insists, in effect substitute the District Court for the Board as the tribunal to hear and determine what Congress declared the Board exclusively should hear and determine in the first instance. The contention is at war with the long-settled rule of judicial administration that no one is entitled to judicial relief for a supposed or threatened injury until the prescribed administrative remedy has been exhausted. That rule has been repeatedly acted on in cases where, as here, the contention is made that the administrative body lacked power over the subject matter.
>
> Obviously, the rule requiring exhaustion of the administrative remedy cannot be circumvented by asserting that the charge on which the complaint rests is groundless and that the mere holding of the prescribed administrative hearing would result in irreparable damage. Lawsuits also often prove to have been groundless; but no way has been discovered of relieving a defendant from the necessity of a trial to establish the fact. . . .

Id. at 49-52. *See also* Hoeft v. Tucson Unified School District, 967 F.2d 1298 (9th Cir. 1992) (requiring parents of disabled children suing over school district's violations of Federal Individuals with Disabilities Education Act to exhaust administrative remedies even though parents challenged general policies, not particular educational placement decisions).

Despite the apparently unqualified tone of Justice Brandeis's argument in *Myers,* courts do not always force litigants to pursue every conceivable avenue of administrative relief before entertaining otherwise justiciable challenges. Courts apply to exhaustion claims the same equitable consider-ations of fairness to litigants and institutional competence that inform the "ripeness" cases. A typical example is West v. Bergland, 611 F.2d 710 (8th Cir. 1979), *cert. denied,* 449 U.S. 821 (1980), in which West, a livestock bro-ker, sought to enjoin the Secretary of Agriculture from proceeding with an administrative action to suspend his license for violation of a regulation that West claimed to be unauthorized by the statute. The court held that West did not need to exhaust his administrative remedies before securing a judi-cial determination of the rule's validity. In reaching that conclusion, it care-fully reviewed several asserted government interests in requiring exhaustion (allowing the agency to perform functions within its special competence, discouraging frequent flouting of the administrative process, developing a better record for judicial review, and allowing the agency to correct its own errors). The court also reviewed the private litigant's asserted interests in securing immediate review (preventing irreparable injury and avoiding the futility of pursuing an inadequate administrative remedy). The interplay of these multiple factors has produced a doctrine that one observer claims "is complex and confusing and fosters needless litigation." Marcia R. Gelpe, Exhaustion of Administrative Remedies: Lessons from Environmental Cases, 53 Geo. Wash. L. Rev. 1, 3 (1985).

Litigants often claim that they should be excused from exhausting admin-istrative remedies when there is no doubt that the agency would decide against them. This is called the "futility" exception to the exhaustion requirement. While the Supreme Court has approved such an exception, the lower courts have been rather strict in excusing exhaustion due to futility. The Seventh Cir-cuit is perhaps the strictest of all, holding that the futility exception requires that it be "certain that the . . . claim will be denied on appeal." Smith v. Blue Cross & Blue Shield United, 959 F.2d 655, 659 (7th Cir. 1992). The First Circuit has been slightly more moderate: "the prospect of a refusal must be certain (or nearly so)." Gilbert v. City of Cambridge, 932 F.2d 51, 61 (1st Cir. 1991). Further, the First Circuit has ruled that courts lack discretion to excuse exhaustion on grounds of judicial economy. *See* Portela-Gonzalez v. Secretary of the Navy, 109 F.3d 74 (1st Cir. 1997). In 2008, the Eleventh Circuit held that the futility excep-tion could apply where there is "no meaningful access to administrative pro-ceedings," drawing on an example in which "exhaustion was futile because plan administrators had . . . repeatedly ignor[ed] requests for documents supporting the denial of benefits." Lanfear v. Home Depot, Inc., 536 F.3d 1217 (11th Cir. 2008). In Metropolitan Life Ins. Co. v. Price, 501 F.3d 271 (3d Cir. 2007), the Court included a discretionary balancing of interests test in the futility inquiry in an ERISA case.

The Supreme Court discussed general principles of exhaustion of administrative remedies in another non-APA case, McCarthy v. Madigan, 503 U.S. 140 (1992). In that case, a federal prisoner sued four prison employees for damages, alleging that they had violated his constitutional right to be free from cruel and unusual punishment. The Court ruled that federal prisoners seeking damages against federal officials for violations of constitutional rights need not exhaust administrative remedies within the prison, mainly because the administrative remedy did not provide for damages. In the course of its opinion, the Court engaged in a lengthy exposition of its exhaustion doctrine:

> The doctrine of exhaustion of administrative remedies is one among related doctrines—including abstention, finality, and ripeness—that govern the timing of federal court decisionmaking. . . . Where Congress specifically mandates, exhaustion is required. . . . But where Congress has not clearly required exhaustion, sound judicial discretion governs. . . .
>
> This Court long has acknowledged the general rule that parties exhaust prescribed administrative remedies before seeking relief from the federal courts. *See, e.g.,* Myers v. Bethlehem Shipbuilding Corp., 303 U.S. 41, 50-51, and n.9 (1938) (discussing cases as far back as 1898). Exhaustion is required because it serves the twin purposes of protecting administrative agency authority and promoting judicial efficiency. . . .
>
> As to the first of these purposes, the exhaustion doctrine recognizes the notion, grounded in deference to Congress' delegation of authority to coordinate branches of government, that agencies, not the courts, ought to have primary responsibility for the programs that Congress has charged them to administer. Exhaustion concerns apply with particular force when the action under review involves exercise of the agency's discretionary power or when the agency proceedings in question allow the agency to apply its special expertise. McKart v. United States, 395 U.S. 185, 194 (1969). *See also* Bowen v. City of New York, 476 U.S. 467, 484 (1986). The exhaustion doctrine also acknowledges the commonsense notion of dispute resolution that an agency ought to have an opportunity to correct its own mistakes with respect to the programs it administers before it is haled into federal court. Correlatively, exhaustion principles apply with special force when "frequent and deliberate flouting of administrative processes" could weaken an agency's effectiveness by encouraging disregard of its procedures. McKart v. United States, 395 U.S. at 195.
>
> [E]xhaustion promotes judicial efficiency in at least two ways. When an agency has the opportunity to correct its own errors, a judicial controversy may well be mooted, or at least piecemeal appeals may be avoided. . . . And even where a controversy survives administrative review, exhaustion of the administrative procedure may produce a useful record for subsequent judicial consideration, especially in a complex or technical factual context.
>
> Notwithstanding these substantial institutional interests, federal courts are vested with a "virtually unflagging obligation" to exercise the jurisdiction given them. Colorado River Water Conservation Dist. v. United States, 424 U.S. 800, 817-818 (1976). . . . Accordingly, this Court has declined to require exhaustion in some circumstances even where administrative and judicial interests would counsel otherwise. In determining whether exhaustion is required, federal courts must balance the interest of the individual in retaining prompt access to a federal judicial forum against countervailing institutional interests favoring exhaustion. "[A]dministrative remedies need not be pursued if the litigant's interests in immediate judicial review outweigh the government's interests in the efficiency or

administrative autonomy that the exhaustion doctrine is designed to further." West v. Bergland, 611 F.2d 710, 715 (8th Cir. 1979), *cert. denied,* 449 U.S. 821 (1980).

This Court's precedents have recognized at least three broad sets of circumstances in which the interests of the individual weigh heavily against requiring administrative exhaustion. First, requiring resort to the administrative remedy may occasion undue prejudice to subsequent assertion of a court action. Such prejudice may result, for example, from an unreasonable or indefinite timeframe for administrative action. *See* Gibson v. Berryhill, 411 U.S. 564, 575, n.14 (1973) (administrative remedy deemed inadequate "[m]ost often . . . because of delay by the agency"). . . . Even where the administrative decisionmaking schedule is otherwise reasonable and definite, a particular plaintiff may suffer irreparable harm if unable to secure immediate judicial consideration of his claim. Bowen v. City of New York, 476 U.S., at 483 (disability-benefit claimants "would be irreparably injured were the exhaustion requirement now enforced against them") . . . . By the same token, exhaustion principles apply with less force when an individual's failure to exhaust may preclude a defense to criminal liability. . . .

Second, an administrative remedy may be inadequate "because of some doubt as to whether the agency was empowered to grant effective relief." Gibson v. Berryhill, 411 U.S., at 575, n.14. For example, an agency, as a preliminary matter, may be unable to consider whether to grant relief because it lacks institutional competence to resolve the particular type of issue presented, such as the constitutionality of a statute. . . . In a similar vein, exhaustion has not been required where the challenge is to the adequacy of the agency procedure itself, such that "the question of the adequacy of the administrative remedy . . . [is] for all practical purposes identical with the merits of [the plaintiff's] lawsuit.'" Barry v. Barchi, 443 U.S. 55, 63 (1979) (quoting Gibson v. Berryhill, 411 U.S., at 575). Alternatively, an agency may be competent to adjudicate the issue presented, but still lack authority to grant the type of relief requested. McNeese v. Board of Education, 373 U.S. 668, 675 (1963) (students seeking to integrate public school need not file complaint with school superintendent because the "Superintendent himself apparently has no power to order corrective action" except to request the Attorney General to bring suit).

Third, an administrative remedy may be inadequate where the administrative body is shown to be biased or has otherwise predetermined the issue before it.

503 U.S. at 144-149.

Chief Justice Rehnquist, joined by Justices Scalia and Thomas, concurred in the judgment. He agreed that the absence of a damages remedy doomed the argument for requiring exhaustion. Because that ground alone provided an adequate basis to rule against exhaustion, he argued that the Court's essay on exhaustion principles was unnecessary, and he therefore refused to join the Court's opinion. (Shortly after the decision, Congress overruled *McCarthy,* requiring in the Prison Litigation Reform Act that prisoners exhaust all available administrative remedies, regardless of whether they provide for damages. *See* Prison Litigation Reform Act of 1995, 110 Stat. 1321, 42 U.S.C. §1997e(a) (1994 ed., Supp. V); Booth v. Churner, 532 U.S. 731 (2001).)

When multiple federal statutes apply to the same situation, as often happens, the question arises whether an exhaustion requirement in one statute precludes a party from seeking immediate relief in federal court under another applicable statute. That was the situation in Fry v. Napoleon Community Schools, 137 S. Ct. 743 (2017). The plaintiffs in *Fry* challenged the school district's refusal to allow their disabled daughter to bring her service dog to school. Although they sued under the Americans with Disabilities Act and the Rehabilitation Act, the school district argued that the Individuals with Disabilities Education Act (IDEA) required them to exhaust available administrative remedies before bringing suit. The Supreme Court held that if the remedy they sought was not available under the IDEA, they were not required to exhaust the remedies available under that statute. (The Court remanded the case to the lower court to determine whether the remedy they were seeking was available under the IDEA.) Does this follow from *McCarthy*'s holding that plaintiffs seeking damages are not required to exhaust administrative remedies where damages are not available?

b.   Exhaustion Under the APA

While the Court's comments in *McCarthy* on the policies underlying the exhaustion doctrine are illuminating, exhaustion in cases arising under the APA is governed by a different set of rules. In Darby v. Cisneros, 509 U.S. 137 (1993), a unanimous Court made clear that no matter how strongly the *McCarthy* considerations point toward a mandate for exhaustion, federal courts may not require exhaustion of administrative remedies prior to APA judicial review unless the relevant statute or agency rules mandate it. Darby had been debarred from receiving contracts from the Department of Housing and Urban Development. After his debarment was affirmed at an ALJ hearing, rather than seek reconsideration from the Secretary of the Department, he brought an action under the APA in federal district court. The Supreme Court reversed the holding of the Court of Appeals that Darby's APA claim was barred because he had failed to exhaust his remedies within the Department. The Court explained the APA's effect on the exhaustion doctrine as follows:

> Under §10(a) of the APA, "[a] person suffering legal wrong because of agency action, or adversely affected or aggrieved by agency action within the meaning of a relevant statute, *is entitled to judicial review thereof.*" 5 U.S.C. §702 (emphasis added). Although §10(a) provides the general right to judicial review of agency actions under the APA, §10(c) [5 U.S.C. 704] establishes when such review is available. When an aggrieved party has exhausted all administrative remedies expressly prescribed by statute or agency rule, the agency action is "final for the purposes of this section" and therefore "subject to judicial review" under the first sentence. . . . [Section] 10(c), by its very terms, has limited the availability of the doctrine of exhaustion of administrative remedies to that which the statute or rule clearly mandates.

509 U.S. at 146. The Court noted that APA §704 (originally §10(c)) provides that "[e]xcept as otherwise expressly required by statute, agency action otherwise final is final for the purposes of this section whether or not there has been presented or determined an application, . . . unless the agency otherwise requires by rule and provides that the action meanwhile is inoperative, for an appeal to superior agency authority." This, the Court held, limited a court's authority to require exhaustion not required by the agency itself:

The purpose of §10(c) was to permit agencies to require an appeal to "superior agency authority" before an examiner's initial decision became final. This was necessary because, under §8(a), initial decisions could become final agency decisions in the absence of an agency appeal. *See* 5 U.S.C. §557(b). Agencies may avoid the finality of an initial decision, first, by adopting a rule that an agency appeal be taken before judicial review is available, and, second, by providing that the initial decision would be "inoperative" pending appeal. Otherwise, the initial decision becomes final and the aggrieved party is entitled to judicial review. . . . We noted just last Term in a non-APA case that "appropriate deference to Congress' power to prescribe the basic procedural scheme under which a claim may be heard in a federal court requires fashioning of exhaustion principles in a manner consistent with congressional intent and any applicable statutory scheme." McCarthy v. Madigan, 503 U.S., at 144.

Appropriate deference in this case requires the recognition that, with respect to actions brought under the APA, Congress effectively codified the doctrine of exhaustion of administrative remedies in §10(c). Of course, the exhaustion doctrine continues to apply as a matter of judicial discretion in cases not governed by the APA. But where the APA applies, an appeal to "superior agency authority" is a prerequisite to judicial review *only* when expressly required by statute or when an agency rule requires appeal before review and the administrative action is made inoperative pending that review. Courts are not free to impose an exhaustion requirement as a rule of judicial administration where the agency action has already become "final" under §10(c) [5 U.S.C. §704].

509 U.S. at 152-153. Do the *McCarthy* considerations have any substantive bite in cases governed by the APA? In light of the Court's analysis in *Darby*, once the *Abbott Labs* Court determined that the agency action challenged in that case was "final," did it have the authority to hold that the claim was not ripe?

In a sense, the APA's statutory finality provisions have displaced the common law of exhaustion of administrative remedies. This statute-based exhaustion regime stands in marked contrast to the court's ripeness jurisprudence under which, notwithstanding the APA's statutory provisions—which support immediate review whenever there is "final" agency action—the Supreme Court has developed an additional hurdle: a common law standard requiring a showing of fitness and hardship before a party may obtain pre-enforcement review. Thus, in the related areas of exhaustion of administrative remedies and ripeness we find radically different methods, with one area governed by statute and the other governed by common law standards. *See* Jack M. Beermann, Common Law and Statute Law in Administrative Law, 63 Admin. L. Rev. 1 (2011).

Sims v. Apfel, 530 U.S. 103 (2000), presented yet another twist in the exhaustion riddle. There, the Court was asked to prohibit Social Security claimants from raising issues on judicial review that they had not presented to the Social Security Administration's Appeals Council prior to judicial review. In effect, the Court was asked to impose an "issue exhaustion" requirement, similar to the rule that prohibits an appellate court from reversing a lower court on grounds not presented to the lower court. In an opinion by Justice Thomas, the Court ruled 5-4 against the issue exhaustion rule on the basis, in line with *Darby*, that no statute or regulation required issue exhaustion. In another part of his opinion, Justice Thomas argued that an issue exhaustion requirement was inappropriate because Social Security appeals are informal, with the Appeals Council and not the claimant responsible for framing the issues. This portion of Justice Thomas's opinion, however, garnered only four votes on the Court (including Thomas's own).

Courts may be especially reluctant to impose an exhaustion requirement in cases that involve a constitutional challenge to the agency's procedures. *See* Bangura v. Hansen, 434 F.3d 487 (6th Cir. 2006) (holding that immigration petitioner alleging due process violation by the INA not required to exhaust administrative remedies).

The most common use of the exhaustion doctrine is to deflect premature judicial claims back to the agency. The result for the litigant is delay, but not necessarily defeat. For example, in FTC v. Standard Oil Co. of California (Socal), 449 U.S. 232 (1980), the Supreme Court refused to allow interlocutory review of the issuance of a complaint by the FTC. The FTC had issued a complaint against Socal, alleging under §5 of the FTC Act that it had "reason to believe" that Socal and seven other oil companies had used unfair business practices to create an artificial oil shortage. After the FTC denied Socal's motion to dismiss the complaint, Socal sought direct judicial review, alleging that the FTC lacked sufficient "reason to believe" the facts alleged. The Supreme Court reversed the court of appeals' decision to allow review, on the ground that Socal had failed to exhaust its administrative remedy—namely, defending itself against the charges at the upcoming administrative hearing. The FTC's complaint, said the Court, was not "final agency action," but merely a "threshold determination that further inquiry is warranted." *Id.* at 238-243. As for Socal's alleged "irreparable harm" of having to defend itself in the hearing, that, said the Court, is "part of the social burden of living under government." *Id.* at 244, *quoting* Petroleum Exploration, Inc. v. Public Service Commission, 304 U.S. 209, 222 (1938).

The exhaustion doctrine is sometimes used, however, to destroy potential legal claims altogether. An example is McGee v. United States, 402 U.S. 479 (1971). During the Vietnam War, McGee had petitioned his local Selective Service board for classification as a conscientious objector. The board denied his application. Although the board informed McGee that he could appeal the decision, he did not avail himself of this option. When he refused to submit to induction, he was convicted for violation of the draft laws. The Supreme Court held that McGee's failure to exhaust administrative remedies barred him from asserting as a defense to his conviction that the board had incorrectly classified him. McGee's deliberate sidestepping of the administrative process of appeal, the Court reasoned, directly frustrated the goal of "ensuring that the Selective Service System have full opportunity to make a 'factual record' and 'apply its expertise' in relation to the registrant's claims." *Id.* at 490. To allow McGee to press his claim would encourage many others similarly situated to circumvent administrative procedures.

The *McGee* Court distinguished McKart v. United States, 395 U.S. 185 (1969), a strikingly similar case in which it had reached precisely the opposite result. Like McGee, McKart had been convicted for refusing induction after failing to seek an administrative appeal of his classification. Unlike McGee, however, he was permitted by the Supreme Court to raise the alleged misclassification as a defense to his criminal prosecution. McKart claimed that he was entitled to an exemption from service as the "sole surviving son" of a father killed in action. Characterizing McKart's claim as involving the interpretation of the statute rather than resolution of a factual dispute, the Court held that requiring exhaustion would serve no essential administrative function. Consequently, the interest of allowing a criminal defendant to present his last available defense outweighed the agency's interest in applying its expertise, correcting its own errors, and preventing circumvention of its processes.

How satisfying is the distinction offered by the Court? Is the Court's willingness to bypass the agency on questions of statutory interpretation consistent with the principle of deference applied in cases like *Chevron*?

PART TWO

ADMINISTRATIVE FUNCTIONS

The administrative agency is an enormously flexible instrument: it is used to carry out almost every imaginable kind of governmental activity, from sweeping the streets to waging war. Yet, for all their bewildering variety, the activities performed by administrative agencies naturally cluster into a handful of functional categories. Each of those generic functions is associated with characteristic patterns of behavior and dangers of abuse. As a result, each has called forth characteristic responses from the legal order that sometimes follow traditional doctrinal categories, but more often cut across those categories. The functional organization of Part Two of this book reflects our conviction that reviewing courts respond to the nature of the administrative action being reviewed more than to the inherent logic of some legal doctrine or rule.

In this part, we examine four generic administrative functions—policy formation, adjudication, enforcement, and licensing—and the kinds of legal controls that have become associated with each. Chapters IV and V explore the processes agencies use when they formulate general, prospective policies. Chapter IV introduces the primary instruments that agencies employ—adjudication, rulemaking, and issuance of informal guidance—to make policy, and the principles that govern an agency's choice among those instruments. In Chapter V, we look more closely at administrative rulemaking, including the procedural devices and substantive standards courts deploy to ensure that agency policymaking is analytically rigorous and democratically accountable. Chapter VI introduces students to the procedural requirements for administrative adjudication, with a special focus on the challenge of distributing (or revoking) government benefits in a manner that is humane, fair, and efficient. Chapter VII explores legal mechanisms for disciplining the agency's exercise of enforcement power, taking into account the risk of selectivity, apathy, and bias in the enforcement process. Finally, in Chapter VIII, we consider the legal dilemmas that can arise from the unique interdependence between regulator and regulated party in the context of licensing.

CHAPTER IV

CHOICE OF POLICYMAKING INSTRUMENTS

With the decline of the nondelegation doctrine as a meaningful constitutional constraint on the breadth of delegated power, the struggle over the legitimacy of administrative policymaking has shifted to other terrain. Must agencies use particular formats to express certain types of policy decisions? What procedures must they follow when issuing prospective rules of general application as opposed to making policy in more informal ways? What standard of analytic rigor should courts require of administrative policy decisions? This chapter focuses on the first question, and the following chapter addresses the other two.

In thinking about the possible forms that administrative policymaking might take, one is naturally drawn to the analogies of statute and precedent. That is, administrative policy decisions could look like "little statutes"—prospective, generic, self-contained prescriptions or prohibitions, complete with preambles, section numbers, and effective dates. Or they could resemble a line of judicial precedents—a series of opinions justifying the disposition of particular described disputes, relying on general principles invoked in previous decisions in factually similar cases.

The twin images of legislature and court have long colored our perception of administration. Courts for many years have used adjectives like "quasi-legislative" and "quasi-adjudicative" to describe the functions performed by agencies. *See, e.g.,* Humphrey's Executor v. United States, 295 U.S. 602, 628 (1935) ("[T]he [FTC] acts in part quasi-legislatively and in part quasi-judicially."). A steady pressure exists to analogize agency action to one or the other of these polar models. *See* Ronald A. Cass, Models of Administrative Action, 72 Va. L. Rev. 363 (1986). The agencies themselves seem drawn to courts and legislatures as patterns for decisionmaking. At times, administrative agencies accompany their orders in individual cases with written opinions that resemble judicial opinions, citing as authority their previous opinions. Other times agencies act more like a legislative body, issuing or amending "rules" or "regulations" that purport to bind all who come within their terms by the sheer force of their formal promulgation.

The administrative law tradition places a great deal of weight on these analogies to judicial and legislative decisionmaking. In contrast to legislatures, courts are assumed or expected to operate apolitically; their decisions come in relatively small increments and build explicitly on prior pronouncements, rather than accomplishing sweeping change; and the range of information permitted to influence the outcome is narrowly circumscribed. All of these features of judicial decisionmaking contrast with the general image of legislative decisionmaking. One final feature of the judicial model is important: courts decide specific cases. Thus, their rules generally have an immediate impact on particular parties. This feature alone makes judicial decisions look more like policy *application* than policy *creation*. Indeed, courts and commentators often juxtapose the legislative and judicial models by noting that only in the former do decisionmakers make new policy; in the latter, they merely apply it. In reality, however, the distinction between these two models is not as stark as it is in theory: agencies do both, and their boundaries can blur. As you read this chapter, consider the value of the court/legislature construct. Is the judicial model appropriate for some administrative decisions? When is it right to use the rules associated with that model to discipline the administrative decision maker's power? When, by contrast, is it more appropriate to imagine the administrative decision maker as acting quasi-legislatively and to use that model's rules? To put a fine point on it: Is it useful when analyzing agency decisions to distinguish between policymaking (quasi-legislative action) versus policy application (quasi-judicial action)? Or are agencies always, to greater or lesser extents, making policy?

A.   LEGAL CONSTRAINTS ON CHOICE OF POLICYMAKING INSTRUMENTS

Legal restrictions on the procedures that administrative agencies may use in formulating policy derive from at least three sources: the Due Process Clauses of the Fifth and Fourteenth Amendments to the U.S. Constitution, the APA, and various enabling acts applicable to specific agencies or federal programs.

1.   Due Process Constraints

In two early cases, both involving the assessment of taxes on property owners by state or local officials in Colorado, the Supreme Court examined the application of the Due Process Clause of the Fourteenth Amendment to administrative policymaking.

LONDONER v. DENVER, 210 U.S. 373 (1908):   A group of Denver property owners brought suit in state court contesting the amounts assessed against them by the Denver Board of Public Works pursuant to a Denver City Council ordinance that established a special assessment district for the paving of their street. The Board assessed the cost against each property owner in an amount commensurate with the benefit conferred on each property, as determined by the board, with no opportunity for an individual hearing. After the Colorado Supreme Court upheld the assessments, the owners appealed to the U.S. Supreme Court, arguing that the procedure used by the city violated the Due Process Clause in two respects. First, they argued that they should have been given an opportunity for a hearing before the city council on the issue of whether, as required by city charter, a majority of property owners had submitted a petition requesting that the street be paved. The Supreme Court rejected this claim, saying:

> The state supreme court held that the determination of the city council was conclusive that a proper petition was filed, and that decision must be accepted by us as the law of the state. The only question for this Court is whether the charter provision authorizing such a finding, without notice to the landowners, denies to them due process of law. We think it does not. The proceedings, from the beginning up to and including the passage of the ordinance authorizing the work, did not include any assessment or necessitate any assessment, although they laid the foundation for an assessment, which might or might not subsequently be made. Clearly all this might validly be done without hearing to the landowners, provided a hearing upon the assessment itself is afforded. The legislature might have authorized the making of improvements by the city council without any petition. If it chose to exact a petition as a security for wise and just action, it could, so far as the federal Constitution is concerned, accompany that condition with a provision that the council, with or without notice, should determine finally whether it had been performed.

The plaintiffs' second argument was that the procedure for contesting the specific assessments imposed on them by the city's board of public works—namely, submission of written complaints to the board—was inadequate. The Supreme Court agreed with this claim:

> In the assessment, apportionment, and collection of taxes upon property within their jurisdiction, the Constitution of the United States imposes few restrictions upon the states. In the enforcement of such restrictions as the Constitution does impose, this Court has regarded substance, and not form. But where the legislature of a state, instead of fixing the tax itself, commits to some subordinate body the duty of determining whether, in what amount, and upon whom it shall be levied, and of making its assessment and apportionment, due process of law requires that at some stage of the proceedings, before the tax becomes irrevocably fixed, the taxpayer shall have an opportunity to be heard, of which he must have notice, either personal, by publication, or by a law fixing the time and place of the hearing.
>
> If . . . an opportunity is given to submit in writing all objections to and complaints of the tax to the board, then there was a hearing afforded in the case at bar [thus satisfying the "hearing" requirement in the city charter]. But we think that something more than that, even in proceedings for taxation, is required by due process of law. Many requirements essential in strictly judicial proceedings may be dispensed with in proceedings of this nature. But even here, a hearing, in its very essence, demands that he who is entitled to it shall have the right to support his allegations by argument, however brief, and, if need be, by proof, however informal.

BI-METALLIC INVESTMENT CO. v. STATE BOARD OF EQUALIZATION, 239 U.S. 441 (1915):

The Colorado Board of Equalization and the Colorado Tax Commission issued orders increasing the valuation of all taxable property in Denver by 40 percent and ordering the city's tax department to assess property taxes based on the higher amounts. No notice or opportunity to be heard was given to individual property owners or, for that matter, any official of the City of Denver. A Denver property tax payer claimed that the state had taken his property without due process of law. The Supreme Court, in a summary opinion by Justice Holmes, disagreed:

> Where a rule of conduct applies to more than a few people it is impracticable that every one should have a direct voice in its adoption. The Constitution does not require all public acts to be done in town meeting or an assembly of the whole. [Individuals'] rights are protected in the only way that they can be in a complex society, by their power, immediate or remote, over those who make the rule. . . . There must be a limit to individual argument in such matters if government is to go on. In Londoner v. Denver, 210 U. S. 373, 385, a local board had to determine 'whether, in what amount, and upon whom' a tax for paving a street should be levied for special benefits. A relatively small number of persons was concerned, who were exceptionally affected, in each case upon individual grounds, and it was held that they had a right to a hearing. But that decision is far from reaching a general determination dealing only with the principle upon which all the assessments in a county had been laid.

NOTES AND QUESTIONS

1. *Legislative and adjudicative facts.* Professor Kenneth C. Davis characterized the *Londoner/Bi-Metallic* distinction as illustrating a dichotomy between "legislative facts" and "adjudicative facts":

> Adjudicative facts are the facts about the parties and their activities, businesses, and properties. Adjudicative facts usually answer the questions of who did what, where, when, how, why, with what motive or intent; adjudicative facts are roughly the kind of facts that go to a jury in a jury case. Legislative facts do not usually concern the immediate parties but are general facts which help the tribunal decide questions of law and policy and discretion.

1 Kenneth C. Davis, Administrative Law Treatise §7.02 (1958). Davis believed that adjudicative facts ought to be determined in a trial-type setting, allowing extensive participation by affected parties, because the parties are likely to know far more about the facts concerning themselves and their activities than anyone else. However, similar participation is not recommended when legislative facts are in issue, since these parties "may often have little or nothing to contribute to the development of legislative facts." *Id.* Other commentators dispute the utility of Davis's distinction, although most continue to seek means for separating decisions of general policy from determinations concerning specific individuals. *See, e.g.,* Glen O. Robinson, The Making of Administrative Policy: Another Look at Rulemaking and Adjudication and Administrative Procedure Reform, 118 U. Pa. L. Rev. 485 (1970); Richard B. Stewart, Regulation, Innovation, and Administrative Law: A Conceptual Framework, 69 Cal. L. Rev. 1256 (1981).

2. *The continuing vitality of* Londoner *and* Bi-Metallic. Though they are a century old, courts continue to look to *Londoner* and *Bi-Metallic* to determine whether regulated parties are entitled to individualized hearings. For example, in Philly's the Original Philadelphia Cheese Steak, Inc. v. Byrne, 732 F.2d 87 (7th Cir. 1984), the court relied on *Bi-Metallic* when it upheld an Illinois law that allowed voters to ban alcohol sales in their precinct, thereby depriving restaurant owners of their liquor licenses. And in Xcaliber Intl. Ltd. LLC v. Attorney Gen. State of Louisiana, 62 F.3d 268 (5th Cir. 2010), the court upheld a Louisiana statute requiring tobacco companies not participating in a nationwide settlement over tobacco-related medical expenses to pay into an escrow account for future medical expenses based on the number of cigarettes sold. Xcaliber claimed that the requirement that it pay into the escrow account was "based on a future, hypothetical finding of judicial liability" and as such must be preceded by an individualized hearing. *Id.* at 381. The Fifth Circuit, applying the *Londoner/Bi-Metallic* dichotomy, rejected this argument, observing that "although the payout of escrowed funds to satisfy a judgment will ultimately depend on an individualized assessment of liability, the initial depositing of funds does not. . . . Louisiana's decision to require . . . escrow deposits is legislative in character." *Id.* at 382.

3. *Right to a hearing on what issues?* Suppose 20 property owners received an assessment from the city's board of public works for the paving of their street. The board had determined to pave the street, put out a bid for the contract and selected a contractor, supervised the work, established an assessment district identifying the benefited properties, and assessed the total cost to the benefited property owners based on their frontage on the paved street. Londoner, one of the assessed property owners, wanted an administrative hearing on the following issues: (a) whether the board of public works failed to award the contract to the low bidder, as required by city ordinance; (b) whether the board should have included in the assessment district several adjacent properties that were also benefited by the project; (c) whether the board should have apportioned the total cost based, not on frontage on the street, but acreage of property fronting on the street; (d) whether the paving was done in a substandard fashion; and (e) whether the computation of Londoner's frontage was correct. On which of these issues, if any, should Londoner have a right to an administrative hearing before the board?

2. Statutory Constraints

Although, as we shall see, many enabling acts contain specific provisions regarding the procedures that agencies must follow when making policy, the primary source of statutory guidance in the federal system is the APA. The APA establishes guidelines agencies must follow when employing the legislative and (formal) adjudicatory models of decisionmaking. APA §551 provides that adjudication is the required procedure for issuing an order, and rulemaking is the required procedure for issuing a rule. APA §554 establishes the basic conditions under which "every case of adjudication required by statute to be determined on the record after opportunity for an agency hearing" must take place. The key provisions, which mirror traditional adjudicatory models, include:

- Notice to parties of the "time, place, and nature of the hearing" and the "matters of fact and law asserted";
- The opportunity, to interested parties, for "the submission and consideration of facts, arguments, offers of settlement, or proposals of adjustment";
- A formal hearing under §§556 and 557 of the APA, if settlement efforts fail; and
- An independent decisionmaker who may not communicate outside the hearing with parties or be under the supervision of agency prosecutorial personnel.

On the rulemaking side, the APA provides for two levels of formality, usually referred to as informal and formal rulemaking. Informal rulemaking is governed by §553 of the Act. Its major procedural requirements are

- Notice of the "legal authority under which the rule is proposed";
- Notice of the "terms or substance of the proposed rule or a description of the subjects and issues involved";
- A comment period during which "interested persons [shall have] an opportunity to participate in the rulemaking through submission of written data, views, or arguments with or without opportunity for oral presentation"; and
- Production, after "consideration of the relevant matter presented, [of a] concise general statement of [the rule's] basis and purpose."

The conditions under which the next level of formality, formal rulemaking, applies are provided also in §553, which provides for formal rulemaking only when rules are statutorily required to be made "on the record after opportunity for agency hearing." Additional procedures for formal rulemakings are contained in §§556 and 557.

The bulk of formal hearing procedures, which apply both to adjudication and formal rulemaking, are contained in APA §§556 and 557. These sections provide for traditional judicial procedures, including:

- Oral presentation of evidence;
- Cross-examination of opposing witnesses; and
- Decision supported by "reliable, probative and substantial evidence" on the record in the case after the parties have had an opportunity to submit proposed findings and to challenge tentative findings proposed by the agency.

Agencies using formal processes are also required to place all tentative decisions on the record, are confined to rulings based on the material in the record, and are required to state "findings and conclusions and the reasons or basis therefor, on all the material issues of fact, law, or discretion presented on the record." The independence of decisionmakers is also protected by allowing for disqualification for bias and through strict bans on ex parte communication with agency decisionmakers.

In addition, agencies make policy in the course of administering regulatory programs that are not conducted under either of the models described above. A great deal of agency action, including decisions to allocate resources, cancel or initiate programs, or provide regulatory guidance to the public via policy documents or letters, is essentially informal, with no clear process prescribed by either the APA or the relevant enabling act. Because the APA appears to divide all agency action between rulemaking and adjudication, this varied mass of informal agency action has been referred to by courts and commentators as "informal adjudication." For a discussion of what little clarity exists regarding informal adjudication procedures, see section C.4, *infra*.

These provisions, taken together, provide a comprehensive procedural framework for agencies to follow when they choose to make policy decisions through either the "common law" adjudicatory method or the "legislative" rule-making method. But before one can apply the APA procedural formulas, one must confront two preliminary questions: (1) how can one determine whether an agency possesses authority to make policy by adjudication or by rulemaking in the first place? And (2) if the agency is found to possess both adjudicatory and rulemaking authority, what are the legal constraints, if any, on the agency's choice between those two policymaking instruments?

To answer both of these questions, one must first look to the agency's enabling act. As creatures of statute, administrative agencies possess only those powers—including the choice of mechanisms for promulgating policy—that are conferred by statute. If the enabling statute is clear, that is the end of the matter. For example, many modern environmental, health, and safety statutes clearly confer upon the implementing agencies the authority—and in some cases, the duty—to establish policy by promulgating rules. But regulatory statutes are often silent or ambiguous, in which case courts must look to other sources for guidance. What considerations should inform the elaboration of interpretive principles in such cases? Applying *Chevron*, should courts defer to agencies' interpretations of their own powers? Or, in the spirit of the nondelegation principle, should the courts adopt a more restrictive reading of agency powers, requiring a clear statement of statutory authority? In the materials that follow, we see how the courts have grappled with these questions in three contexts: (1) an agency that possesses clear authority to make policy by the incremental process of case-by-case adjudication chooses, instead, to accelerate the policymaking process (and foreclose certain issues that would otherwise be contestable in subsequent adjudications) by issuing a binding rule; (2) an agency that possesses clear authority to make policy by rule chooses, instead, to elaborate policy by adjudication; and (3) an agency that possesses clear authority to make policy by adjudication or by rule (or both) chooses, instead, to make policy through issuance of informal guidance.

B.   AGENCY AUTHORITY AND DISCRETION TO MAKE POLICY BY RULE

Many of the earliest challenges to agency authority to make policy by rule arose in the context of broadcast licensing by the Federal Communications Commission. While federal regulation of broadcasting began earlier in the twentieth century, it crystallized into its present form in 1927 and 1934 with the creation of the Federal Radio Commission, in the Radio Act of 1927, and its successor, the Federal Communications Commission, in the Communications Act of 1934, 47 U.S.C. §§151 *et seq.* These statutes provided for licensing of radio (and, later, television) stations in two stages: allocation and license award.

The allocation process maps out the general locations for which stations will be authorized, the frequencies on which they may operate, the areas their signals may cover, and power with which their signals may be emitted. The Communications Act does not specify an allocation procedure. In the early days of radio, the FCC used what was called a "demand allocation" process, simply making allocation decisions in the course of passing on individual applications for station licenses. Later, the FCC, employing its rulemaking authority under the Act (discussed below), adopted comprehensive plans for allocating FM radio stations and television stations.

The license award process involves the selection of the entity that will operate a broadcast station, culminating in the grant of an operating license for a term of years (initially three years, now generally eight years). The Communications Act sets forth detailed procedural requirements the FCC must follow when responding to license applications and making license awards, basically requiring the commission to hold a "full hearing" before denying an application. Section 309 of the Act provides:

> (a) [T]he Commission shall determine . . . whether the public interest, convenience, and necessity will be served by the granting of such application, and, if the Commission, upon examination of such application and upon consideration of such other matters as the Commission may officially notice, shall find that public interest, convenience, and necessity would be served by the granting thereof, it shall grant such application.
>
> (b) [N]o such application . . . shall be granted earlier that thirty days following issuance of public notice by the Commission of acceptance for filing of such application. . . .
>
> (d)
>
> (1) Any party in interest may file with the Commission a petition to deny any application . . . to which subsection (b) of this section applies. . . . The petition shall contain specific allegations of fact sufficient to show that the petitioner is a party in interest and that a grant of the application would be prima facie inconsistent with subsection (a) of this section. Such allegations of fact shall, except for those of which official notice may be taken, be supported by affidavit of a person or persons with personal knowledge thereof. The applicant shall be given the opportunity to file a reply in which allegations of fact or denials thereof shall similarly be supported by affidavit.
>
> (2) If the Commission finds on the basis of the application, the pleadings filed, or other matters which it may officially notice that there are no substantial and material questions of fact and that a grant of the application would be consistent with subsection (a) of this section . . . , it shall make the grant, deny the petition, and issue a concise statement of the reasons for denying the petition, which statement shall dispose of all substantial issues raised by the petition. If a substantial and material question of fact is presented or if the Commission for any reason is unable to find that grant of the application would be consistent with subsection (a) of this section . . . , it shall proceed as provided in subsection (e) of this section.

(e) If, in the case of any application to which subsection (a) of this section applies, a substantial and material question of fact is presented or the Commission for any reason is unable to make the finding specified in such subsection, it shall formally designate the application for hearing on the ground or reasons then obtaining and shall forthwith notify the applicant and all other known parties in interest of such action and the grounds and reasons therefor, specifying with particularity the matters and things in issue but not including issues or requirements phrased generally. When the Commission has so designated an application for hearing, the parties in interest, if any, who are not notified by the Commission of such action may acquire the status of a party to the proceeding thereon by filing a petition for intervention showing the basis for their interest not more than thirty days after publication of the hearing issues or any substantial amendment thereto in the Federal Register. Any hearing subsequently held upon such application shall be a full hearing in which the applicant and all other parties in interest shall be permitted to participate. The burden of proceeding with the introduction of evidence and the burden of proof shall be upon the applicant, except that with respect to any issue presented by a petition to deny or a petition to enlarge the issues, such burdens shall be as determined by the Commission.

An important issue in the administration of this system was whether the FCC, by issuing rules of general application, could establish minimum standards for license eligibility, and thereby to constrain the scope of issues that would otherwise be subject to dispute in a licensing hearing. The basic issue of whether the FCC possessed at least some rulemaking authority was settled fairly early in its history. The 1934 Act gave it statutory authority to "[m]ake such regulations not inconsistent with law as it may deem necessary to prevent interference between stations and to carry out the provisions of this Act," subject, however, to a proviso that the FCC could not make changes in frequencies, authorized power, or times of station operation without the consent of affected stations except "after a public hearing." 47 U.S.C. §303(f). Then in 1937 Congress amended the Act to grant the commission power to "[m]ake such rules and regulations and prescribe such restrictions and conditions, not inconsistent with law, as may be necessary to carry out the provisions of this Act." *Id.* §303(r). Why do you think §303(r) was added to the Act? Does it render the proviso in §303(f) merely precatory? Does the grant of rulemaking authority in §303(r) seem broad enough to support issuance of substantive rules defining standards for license eligibility?

Shortly after the enactment of §303(r), the FCC began an investigation into "chain broadcasting" (networking), which culminated three years later in the adoption of the Chain Broadcasting Rules. *See* FCC Report on Chain Broadcasting (1941). At the time the investigation was launched, radio networks were the dominant force in the broadcast industry. The impetus for the investigation was a concern that some networks put undue pressure on stations affiliated with them to accept programming provided by those networks, to the exclusion of programming from other sources. Because the FCC was uncertain whether it had statutory authority to regulate networks directly, it framed its rules on network operation as a series of limitations on the grant of broadcast licenses. Thus, the rules stated that a broadcast license would not be awarded to any applicant (or renewed for any incumbent licensee) affiliated with a network that engaged in various proscribed practices.

Networks challenged the Chain Broadcasting Rules as beyond the FCC's authority, making three distinct arguments. First, they claimed that the FCC's rulemaking authority was restricted to policing technical aspects of broadcast operations in order to prevent signal interference. Second, they argued that the FCC lacked authority to regulate nonbroadcast entities such as networks. Third, they asserted that the rules regulated speech in a manner that violated the First Amendment. In National Broadcasting Co. v. United States, 319 U.S. 190 (1943), the Supreme Court rejected all three challenges to the rules. Justice Frankfurter's opinion for five of the seven participating Justices has become a traditional reference for expansive interpretation of agency authority.

One of the rules upheld in *National Broadcasting Co.* limited the number of stations a network could own. The FCC's concern over station ownership, however, was not limited to networks. It also promulgated rules governing multiple station ownership by any entity. These rules restricted ownership of multiple outlets of any given "service" (AM, FM, or TV) in a single market area, ownership of multiple services in a single market (subject to various exceptions), and total ownership of multiple outlets in any service across markets. The rules are known respectively as the duopoly, cross-ownership, and multiple ownership rules. The latter set of rules was challenged by the Storer Broadcasting Company. Although *National Broadcasting Co.* had construed the FCC's rulemaking power fairly broadly, Storer argued that subsequent decisions interpreting §309 qualified that holding. The Court answered this argument in the opinion reproduced below.

UNITED STATES v. STORER BROADCASTING CO.
351 U.S. 192 (1956)

MR. JUSTICE REED delivered the opinion of the Court.

The Federal Communications Commission issued, on August 19, 1948, a notice of proposed rulemaking under the authority of 47 U.S.C. §§303(r), 311, 313 and 314 (Communications Act of 1934, as amended, 47 U.S.C. §301 *et seq.*). It was proposed, so far as is pertinent to this case, to amend Rules 3.35, 3.240 and 3.636 relating to Multiple Ownership of standard, FM and television broadcast stations. Those rules provide that licenses for broadcasting stations will not be granted if the applicant, directly or indirectly, has an interest in other stations beyond a limited number. The purpose of the limitations is to avoid overconcentration of broadcasting facilities.

As required by 5 U.S.C. §1003(b), the notice permitted "interested" parties to file statements or briefs. Such parties might also intervene in appeals. 47 U.S.C. §402(d) and (e). Respondent, licensee of a number of radio and television stations, filed a statement objecting to the proposed changes, as did other interested broadcasters. Respondent based its objections largely on the fact that the proposed rules did not allow one person to hold as many FM and television stations as standard stations. Storer argued that such limitations might cause irreparable financial damage to owners of standard stations if an obsolescent standard station could not be augmented by FM and television facilities.

In November 1953 the Commission entered an order amending the Rules in question without significant changes from the proposed forms.[1] A review was sought in due course by respondent in the Court of Appeals for the District of Columbia Circuit under 5 U.S.C. §1034, 47 U.S.C. §402(a), and 5 U.S.C. §1009(a), (c). Respondent alleged it owned or controlled, within the meaning of the Multiple Ownership Rules, seven standard radio, five FM radio and five television broadcast stations. It asserted that the Rules complained of were in conflict with the statutory mandates that applicants should be granted licenses if the public interest would be served and that applicants must have a hearing before denial of an application. 47 U.S.C. §309(a) and (b). . . .

On the day the amendments to the Rules were adopted, a pending application of Storer for an additional television station at Miami was dismissed on the basis of the Rules.

In its petition for review Storer prayed the court to vacate the provisions of the Multiple Ownership Rules insofar as they denied to an applicant already controlling the allowable number of stations a "full and fair hearing" to determine whether additional licenses to the applicant would be in the public interest. The Court of Appeals struck out, as contrary to §309(a) and (b) of the Communications Act . . . , the words italicized in Rule 3.636 (n.1, *supra*) and the similar words in Rules 3.35 and 3.240. The case was remanded to the Commission with directions to eliminate these words. 220 F.2d 204. We granted certiorari.

The Commission asserts that its power to make regulations gives it the authority to limit concentration of stations under a single control. It argues that rules may go beyond the technical aspects of radio, that rules may validly give concreteness to a standard of public interest, and that the right to a hearing does not exist where an applicant admittedly does not meet those standards as there would be no facts to ascertain. The Commission shows that its regulations permit applicants to seek amendments and waivers of or exceptions to its Rules. It adds:

> This does not mean, of course, that the mere filing of an application for a waiver . . . would necessarily require the holding of a hearing, for if that were the case a rule would no longer be a rule. It means only that it might be an abuse of discretion

---

1. Section 3.636 will illustrate the problem:

"§3.636 *Multiple ownership.* (a) No license for a television broadcast station shall be granted to any party (including all parties under common control) if:

"(1) Such party directly or indirectly owns, operates, or controls another television broadcast station which serves substantially the same area; or

"(2) Such party, or any stockholder, officer or director of such party, directly or indirectly owns, operates, controls, or has any interest in, or is an officer or director of any other television broadcast station if the grant of such license would result in a concentration of control of television broadcasting in a manner inconsistent with public interest, convenience, or necessity. In determining whether there is such a concentration of control, consideration will be given to the facts of each case with particular reference to such factors as the size, extent and location of areas served, the number of people served, and the extent of other competitive service to the areas in question. *The Commission, however, will in any event consider that there would be such a concentration of control contrary to the public interest, convenience or necessity for any party or any of its stockholders, officers or directors to have a direct or indirect interest in, or be stockholders, officers, or directors of, more than five television broadcast* stations."* (The italicized material is common to all three Rules.)

* "In applying the provisions of paragraph (a) of this section to the stockholders of a corporation which has more than 50 voting stockholders, only those stockholders need be considered who are officers or directors or who directly or indirectly own 1 per cent or more of the outstanding voting stock." 47 CFR, Rev. 1953.

The standard and FM Rules limited stations to seven.

to fail to hear a request for a waiver which showed, on its face, the existence of circumstances making application of the rule inappropriate.

Respondent defends the position of the Court of Appeals. It urges that an application cannot be rejected under 47 U.S.C. §309 without a "full hearing" to applicant. We agree that a "full hearing" under §309 means that every party shall have the right to present his case or defense by oral or documentary evidence, to submit rebuttal evidence, and to conduct such cross-examination as may be required for a full and true disclosure of the facts. *Cf.* 5 U.S.C. §1006(c).* Such a hearing is essential for wise and just application of the authority of administrative boards and agencies.

We do not read the hearing requirement, however, as withdrawing from the power of the Commission the rulemaking authority necessary for the orderly conduct of its business. As conceded by Storer, "Section 309(b) does not require the Commission to hold a hearing before denying a license to operate a station in ways contrary to those that the Congress has determined are in the public interest." The challenged Rules contain limitations against licensing not specifically authorized by statute. But that is not the limit of the Commission's rulemaking authority. 47 U.S.C. §154(i) and §303(r) grant general rulemaking power not inconsistent with the Act or law.

This Commission, like other agencies, deals with the public interest. Scripps-Howard Radio v. Federal Communications Commission, 316 U.S. 4, 14. Its authority covers new and rapidly developing fields. Congress sought to create regulation for public protection with careful provision to assure fair opportunity for open competition in the use of broadcasting facilities. Accordingly, we cannot interpret §309(b) as barring rules that declare a present intent to limit the number of stations consistent with a permissible "concentration of control." It is but a rule that announces the Commission's attitude on public protection against such concentration. The Communications Act must be read as a whole and with appreciation of the responsibilities of the body charged with its fair and efficient operation. The growing complexity of our economy induced the Congress to place regulation of businesses like communication in specialized agencies with broad powers. Courts are slow to interfere with their conclusions when reconcilable with statutory directions. We think the Multiple Ownership Rules, as adopted, are reconcilable with the Communications Act as a whole. An applicant files his application with knowledge of the Commission's attitude toward concentration of control.

In National Broadcasting Co. v. United States, 319 U.S. 190, similar rules prohibiting certain methods of chain broadcasting were upheld despite a claim that the Rules caused licenses to be denied without "examination of written applications presented . . . as required by §§308 and 309." *Id.*, at 230. The *National Broadcasting* case validated numerous regulations couched in the prohibitory language of the present regulations.

In the *National Broadcasting* case we called attention to the necessity for flexibility in the Rules there involved. . . . That flexibility is here under the present §309(a) and (b) and the FCC's regulations. . . . We read the Act and

---

* [Now, APA §556(d). — Eds.]

Regulations as providing a "full hearing" for applicants who have reached the existing limit of stations, upon their presentation of applications conforming to Rules 1.361(c) and 1.702, that set out adequate reasons why the Rules should be waived or amended. The Act, considered as a whole, requires no more. We agree with the contention of the Commission that a full hearing, such as is required by §309(b) . . . , would not be necessary on all such applications. As the Commission has promulgated its Rules after extensive administrative hearings, it is necessary for the accompanying papers to set forth reasons, sufficient if true, to justify a change or waiver of the Rules. We do not think Congress intended the Commission to waste time on applications that do not state a valid basis for a hearing. If any applicant is aggrieved by a refusal, the way for review is open.

Reversed and remanded.

MR. JUSTICE DOUGLAS concurs in the result.

[The opinion of JUSTICE HARLAN, concurring on the merits but dissenting to the Court's finding of jurisdiction is omitted, as is the opinion of JUSTICE FRANKFURTER, dissenting on other grounds not related to the merits.]

NOTES AND QUESTIONS

1. "*Full hearing.*" Does the Court pay sufficient heed to the statutory requirement that the commission may not deny a license without affording the applicant a "full hearing"? How must the Court be interpreting the word "full"? Think of the counterpart situation in the civil or criminal law. For example, in a negligence suit arising from an automobile accident, a civil court must give the defendant a "full" hearing on the question of whether he violated the standard of "reasonable care." Suppose that the legislature enacts a statute declaring that exceeding the posted speed limit is a per se violation of reasonable care in a negligence case. Must the court give the defendant a hearing on whether his violation of the speed limit is, nonetheless, reasonable care? If not, can one argue that a different principle should be applied in the context of administrative regulation?

2. *Waivers, exceptions, and amendments.* The *Storer* decision noted the presence of a waiver provision in the challenged rule. The applicants, thus, could obtain a hearing if a sufficient showing were made that the rule should not apply to them. How important is the inclusion of such a provision? Does it matter whether waivers are in fact granted and, if so, on what grounds? In this regard, *see* WAIT Radio v. FCC, 418 F.2d 1153 (D.C. Cir. 1969); WAIT Radio v. FCC, 459 F.2d 1203 (D.C. Cir.), *cert. denied,* 409 U.S. 1027 (1972). The importance of a waiver provision to agency authority to make policy by rule is discussed further in the next case study, concerning the Federal Trade Commission's regulatory procedures.

The Federal Trade Commission (FTC), a five-member independent agency, was established pursuant to the Federal Trade Commission Act of

1914, 15 U.S.C. §§41-58, to regulate a wide range of business practices. The FTC shares with the Department of Justice responsibility for enforcing several sections of the Clayton Act, 15 U.S.C. §§12-27, passed contemporaneously with the FTC Act, prohibiting specified types of business practices. Over the years the FTC also has acquired jurisdiction over enforcement of a large number of other statutory restrictions on particular businesses and business activities. The FTC Act itself contains two principal provisions broadly proscribing certain business practices. Section 12 prohibits false advertising in the sale of food, drugs, and cosmetics. 15 U.S.C. §52. Section 5 even more broadly declares unlawful all "[u]nfair methods of competition in or affecting commerce, and unfair or deceptive acts or practices in or affecting commerce." 15 U.S.C. §45(a) (1982). The phrase, "and unfair or deceptive acts or practices in commerce," was added by the Wheeler-Lea Act, 52 Stat. 111 (1938), to make plain the FTC's power to protect consumers, as distinguished from business competitors. This amendment of the FTC Act effectively reversed the Supreme Court's decision in FTC v. Raladam Co., 283 U.S. 643 (1931).

In authorizing the FTC to proceed against these activities, Congress gave the commission a variety of powers, including — in §6 of the FTC Act — a generally phrased authorization for the FTC to investigate business practices and to require businesses to file reports with it. Section 6, 15 U.S.C. §46, provides:

The Commission shall also have power —

Investigation of Persons, Partnerships, or Corporations

a) To gather and compile information concerning, and to investigate from time to time the organization, business, conduct, practices, and management of any person, partnership, or corporation engaged in or whose business affects commerce . . . , and its relation to other persons, partnerships, and corporations.

Reports of Persons, Partnerships, and Corporations

(b) To require, by general or special orders, persons, partnerships, and corporations engaged in or whose business affects commerce, . . . or any class of them, or any of them, respectively, to file with the Commission in such form as the Commission may prescribe annual or special, or both annual and special, reports or answers in writing to specific questions, furnishing to the Commission such information as it may require as to the organization, business, conduct, practices, management, and relation to other corporations, partnerships, and individuals of the respective persons, partnerships, and corporations filing such reports or answers in writing. . . .

Publication of Information; Reports

(f) To make public from time to time such portions of the information obtained by it hereunder as are in the public interest; and to make annual and special reports to the Congress and to submit therewith recommendations for additional legislation; and to provide for the publication of its reports and decisions in such form and manner as may be best adapted for public information and use.

Classification of Corporations; Regulations

(g) From time to time to classify corporations and . . . to make rules and regulations for the purpose of carrying out the provisions of this subchapter. . . .

At least for the first 50 years of its existence, however, the principal tool of FTC enforcement, especially in fleshing out its broad mandate under §5, 15 U.S.C. §45, was the "cease and desist" proceeding pursuant to §5(b). That section declares that when the commission has reason to believe that a person or firm is using an unfair or deceptive practice and the FTC also believes that proceeding against the entity would serve the public's interest, the commission should issue and serve a complaint on the suspected offender. The complaint notifies that party of the charge and sets a date for a hearing at which the party, if he chooses, can "show cause why an order should not be entered by the Commission requiring [him] to cease and desist from the violation of law . . . charged in [the] complaint."

The hearings generally resemble judicial trials. A hearing examiner, called an administrative law judge, presides over the proceeding and issues a decision that may be accepted by the party and the commission staff members who are handling the case or may be appealed by either side to the FTC commissioners. Cease-and-desist orders are reviewable in the U.S. Court of Appeals; the defendant may seek review in court or may refuse to comply, putting on the FTC the burden of seeking to enforce its order through the court. Each case takes a great deal of time, with a typical case taking nearly five years to complete the hearing, decision, and internal appeal process. The volume of these hearings is not great and has appeared to have decreased over time. In 1979, the FTC initiated only 13 cases and completed 11 old cases, issuing final cease-and-desist orders. In 1998, the FTC initiated only five cases with administrative complaints, and issued final orders in only two. The most recent reporting year, 2018, shows an increase in administrative enforcement proceedings: The agency initiated 18 administrative proceedings and obtained 19 administrative orders. https://www.ftc.gov/reports/annual-highlights-2018/stats-and-data. Many more cases are disposed of by consent agreement, negotiated through an informal process, usually without a complaint ever being filed. Eighty-five consent agreements were reached during 1979, while in 1998, 58 cases were resolved by consent. *See* FTC Annual Report (1979) and (1998). In the consumer protection area, the FTC also brings enforcement actions directly in federal court. In 2018, for example, the agency initiated 40 actions in federal court and obtained 93 court orders. The numbers for 2017 are even higher. And some of these cases can be quite large. For example, in 2019 the FTC and Facebook settled on a $5 billion penalty for Facebook's violations of previously issued FTC orders related to Facebook's privacy practice. The settlement also required Facebook to make changes to its privacy practices, its corporate structure and the role of Facebook CEO Mark Zuckerberg. *See* https://www.ftc.gov/news-events/blogs/business-blog/2019/07/ftcs-5-billion-facebook-settlement-record-breaking-history.

This cease-and-desist process was the principal but not the exclusive means by which the FTC examined business practices to determine whether they were unfair or deceptive. The commission also used Trade Practice Rules to propound its views on what conduct fell afoul of §5's proscription. Although §6(g) authorized the agency to "classify corporations and to make rules and regulations for the purpose of carrying out the provisions of" the Act, the FTC did not interpret this language as empowering it formally to decide by rule which practices violated the Act. Consequently, the Trade Practice Rules were treated as advisory; any FTC complaint that certain conduct violated the Act, whether the complaint was premised on violation of a Trade Practice Rule or an ad hoc determination that the Act was violated, triggered the full cease-and-desist process. Additionally, the FTC used "Industry Guides" containing "advice to the business community of the FTC's views of the legality of specific conduct in selected areas," Advisory Opinions "rendered in response to individual inquiries concerning a proposed course of action," and the informal negotiation process noted above. Report of the ABA Commission to Study the Federal Trade Commission 8-9 (1969).

Dissatisfaction with the cease-and-desist hearing process, even as augmented by these other measures, led the commission, in 1962, to create a new class of rules, labeled Trade Regulation Rules. The FTC announced that any conduct proscribed by these "legislative" or "substantive" rules would be deemed unfair or deceptive for purposes of an administrative cease-and-desist hearing. In such situations, the hearing would no longer focus on the validity of the practice but only on whether the respondent had engaged in it. The FTC's claim of authority to make policy outside of cease-and-desist proceedings entails a potentially massive increase in the FTC's ability to regulate. Given its broad jurisdiction over almost the entire national economy, it should not be surprising that, as the materials that follow reveal, FTC rulemaking authority was met with some resistance from industry.

In July 1969, the FTC published a Notice of Proposed Rulemaking, proposing a rule that would require the posting of octane ratings in a clear and conspicuous manner on gasoline pumps. 34 Fed. Reg. 12,449 (1969). The octane number of gasoline with which the rule was concerned "is a measure of the antiknock value of the gasoline or its ability to resist knock during combustion in an engine." 36 Fed. Reg. 23,871 (1971). The Notice expressed concern that consumers were buying gasoline with an octane number that was not appropriate for their automobiles, but the consumers were not aware of this fact, since gasoline retailers customarily did not reveal gasoline octane ratings.

Use of gasoline with either too high or too low octane values has ill effects. Fuels with an octane rating lower than required by the vehicle increase the level of pollutants emitted, and octane-poor gasoline also can cause engine "knocking." Persistent knocking can damage engines, a matter of concern at that time to automobile manufacturers. The chief impact of buying gasoline with more octane than an engine requires is not damage to the car, but overinvestment in gasoline, since gasoline with higher octane generally is more expensive than a lower-octane gasoline of the same brand.

The proposed rulemaking suggested that the use of descriptive grade names such as "regular" or "premium" rather than the posting of octane ratings constituted an unfair method of competition and an unfair or deceptive act or practice, in violation of §5 of the FTC Act. The notice of proposed rulemaking invited all interested parties to submit written arguments and data on the proposed rule and announced the opportunity to present arguments orally at a public hearing held at the Federal Trade Commission Building in Washington, D.C.

The invitation to comment on the proposed rule elicited many responses from private individuals, consumer organizations, oil companies, and their trade associations. The FTC received 195 letters in support of the octane posting rule from private individuals following publication of an article written by Ralph Nader in the April 1970 issue of Popular Science Magazine. The article, "Why They Should Tell You the Octane Rating of the Gasoline You Buy," asked readers to let the FTC know of their concern for information about octane ratings. In the same vein, Senator William Proxmire testified at the hearing that,

> the average consumer does not know how to find out the octane ratings of the various gasoline brands and, thus, is liable to be spending much more money for gasoline than he needs to. This is particularly true for poor people who have to spend a large percentage of their income for gasoline in order to get to work.

36 Fed. Reg. at 23,876. The American Petroleum Institute argued in opposition that the posting of octane numbers "could mislead the motorist into buying a product that may lack essential characteristics of a good gasoline. These characteristics include quick starting, dependable acceleration, cleanliness, and good mileage." Posting octane ratings "could delude the consumer into believing that gasoline with a higher posting would perform better, which may not be the case." *Id.* at 23,877.

The commission decided that the arguments adduced in the proceeding supported a rule mandating the posting of octane ratings on gasoline pumps. The FTC rejected the American Petroleum Institute's argument that greater attention to octane could mislead the consumer. "[I]t is too broad a jump to conclude that the consuming public is so gullible as to assume that octane rating is the sole [criterion] of quality." *Id.* at 23,880.

The "octane posting" rule adopted by the FTC provided:

> In connection with the sale or consignment of motor gasoline for general automotive use, in commerce as "commerce" is defined in the Federal Trade Commission Act, it constitutes an unfair method of competition and an unfair or deceptive act or practice for refiners or others who sell to retailers, when such refiners or other distributors own or lease the pumps through which motor gasoline is dispensed to the consuming public, to fail to disclose clearly and conspicuously in a permanent manner on the pumps the minimum octane number or numbers of the motor gasoline being dispensed. . . . Nothing in this section should be construed as applying to gasoline sold for aviation purposes.
>
> NOTE: For the purposes of this section, "octane number" shall mean the octane number derived from the sum of research (R) and motor (M) octane numbers divided by 2; $(R + M)/2$. The research octane (R) and motor octane number (M) shall be described in the American Society for Testing and Materials (ASTM)

"Standard Specifications for Gasoline" D439-70, and subsequent revisions, and ASTM Test Methods D2699 and D2700.

Id. at 23,871.

An industry trade association challenged the rule as beyond the FTC's authority. The *Petroleum Refiners* case, below, considers that challenge.

NATIONAL PETROLEUM REFINERS ASSN. v. FEDERAL TRADE COMMISSION
482 F.2d 672 (D.C. Cir. 1973)

Before BAZELON, Chief Judge, and WRIGHT and ROBINSON, Circuit Judges.
WRIGHT, Circuit Judge:

This case presents an important question concerning the powers and procedures of the Federal Trade Commission. We are asked to determine whether the Commission, under its governing statute, the Trade Commission Act, 15 U.S.C. §41, *et seq.* (1970), and specifically 15 U.S.C. §46(g), is empowered to promulgate substantive rules of business conduct or, as it terms them, "Trade Regulation Rules." The effect of these rules would be to give greater specificity and clarity to the broad standard of illegality — "unfair methods of competition in commerce, and unfair or deceptive acts or practices in commerce" — which the agency is empowered to prevent. 15 U.S.C. §45(a). Once promulgated, the rules would be used by the agency in adjudicatory proceedings aimed at producing cease and desist orders against violations of the statutory standard. The central question in such adjudicatory proceedings would be whether the particular defendant's conduct violated the rule in question. *See* 16 C.F.R. §1.12(c) (1973).

The case is here on appeal from a District Court ruling that the Commission lacks authority under its governing statute to issue rules of this sort. . . .

As always, we must begin with the words of the statute creating the Commission and delineating its powers. Section 5 directs the Commission to "prevent persons, partnerships, or corporations . . . from using unfair methods of competition in commerce and unfair or deceptive acts or practices in commerce."[1] Section 5(b) of the Trade Commission Act specifies that the Commission is to accomplish this goal by means of issuance of a complaint, a hearing,[2] findings as to the facts, and issuance of a cease and desist order. The Commission's assertion that it is empowered by Section 6(g) to issue substantive rules defining the statutory standard of illegality in advance of specific adjudications does not in any formal sense circumvent this method of enforcement. For after the rules are issued, their mode of enforcement remains what it has always been under Section 5: the sequence of complaint, hearing, findings, and issuance of a cease and desist order. What rule-making does do, functionally, is to narrow the inquiry conducted in proceedings under Section 5(b). It is the legality of this practice which we must judge.

4. 15 U.S.C. §45(a)(6).
5. 15 U.S.C. §45(b).

Appellees argue that since Section 5 mentions only adjudication as the means of enforcing the statutory standard, any supplemental means of putting flesh on that standard, such as rule-making, is contrary to the overt legislative design. But Section 5(b) does not use limiting language suggesting that adjudication alone is the only proper means of elaborating the statutory standard. It merely makes clear that a Commission decision, after complaint and hearing, followed by a cease and desist order, is the way to force an offender to halt his illegal activities.[6] Nor are we persuaded by appellees' argument that, despite the absence of limiting language in Section 5 regarding the role of adjudication in defining the meaning of the statutory standard, we should apply the maxim of statutory construction expressio unius est exclusio alterius and conclude that adjudication is the *only* means of defining the statutory standard. This maxim is increasingly considered unreliable, for it stands on the faulty premise that all possible alternative or supplemental provisions were necessarily considered and rejected by the legislative draftsmen. . . . Here we have particularly good reason on the face of the statute to reject such arguments. For the Trade Commission Act includes a provision which specifically provides for rule-making by the Commission to implement its adjudicatory functions under Section 5 of the Act. Section 6(g) of the Act, 15 U.S.C. §46(g), states that the Commission may "[f]rom time to time . . . classify corporations and . . . make rules and regulations for the purpose of carrying out the provisions of sections 41 to 46 and 47 to 58 of this title."

According to appellees, however, this rule-making power is limited to specifying the details of the Commission's nonadjudicatory, investigative and informative functions spelled out in the other provisions of Section 6 and should not be read to encompass substantive rule-making in implementation of Section 5 adjudications. We disagree for the simple reason that Section 6(g) clearly states that the Commission "may" make rules and regulations for the purpose of carrying out the provisions of Section 5 and it has been so applied. For example, the Commission has issued rules specifying in greater detail than the statute the mode of Commission procedure under Section 5 in matters involving service of process, requirements as to the filing of answers, and other litigation details

---

6. Section 5(b) provides:

Whenever the Commission shall have reason to believe that any . . . person, partnership, or corporation has been or is using any unfair method of competition or unfair or deceptive act or practice in commerce, and if it shall appear to the Commission that a proceeding by it in respect thereof would be to the interest of the public, it shall issue and serve upon such person, partnership, or corporation a complaint stating its charges in that respect and containing a notice of a hearing upon a day and at a place therein fixed at least thirty days after the service of said complaint. The person, partnership, or corporation so complained of shall have the right to appear at the place and time so fixed and show cause why an order should not be entered by the Commission requiring such person, partnership, or corporation to cease and desist from the violation of the law so charged in said complaint. Any person, partnership, or corporation may make application, and upon good cause shown may be allowed by the Commission to intervene and appear in said proceeding by counsel or in person. The testimony in any such proceeding shall be reduced to writing and filed in the office of the Commission. If upon such hearing the Commission shall be of the opinion that the method of competition or the act or practice in question is prohibited by sections 41 to 46 and 47 to 58 of this title, it shall make a report in writing in which it shall state its findings as to the facts and shall issue and cause to be served on such person, partnership, or corporation an order requiring such person, partnership, or corporation to cease and desist from using such method of competition or such act or practice. . . . [Under §5(c), FTC cease-and-desist orders are subject to judicial review "within any circuit where the method of competition or the act or practice in question was used or where such person, partnership, or corporation resides or carries on business." 15 U.S.C. §45(c) — Eds.]

necessarily involved in the Commission's work of prosecuting its complaints under Section 5. Such rulemaking by the Commission has been upheld. . . .

Of course, it is at least arguable that these cases go no farther than to justify utilizing Section 6(g) to promulgate procedural, as opposed to substantive, rules for administration of the Section 5 adjudication and enforcement powers. But we see no reason to import such a restriction on the "rules and regulations" permitted by Section 6(g). On the contrary, as we shall see, judicial precedents concerning rule-making by other agencies and the background and purpose of the Federal Trade Commission Act lead us liberally to construe the term "rules and regulations." The substantive rule here unquestionably implements the statutory plan. Section 5 adjudications—trial type proceedings—will still be necessary to obtain cease and desist orders against offenders, but Section 5 enforcement through adjudication will be expedited, simplified, and thus "carried out" by use of this substantive rule. And the overt language of both Section 5 and Section 6, read together, supports its use in Section 5 proceedings.

II

Our belief that "rules and regulations" in Section 6(g) should be construed to permit the Commission to promulgate binding substantive rules as well as rules of procedure is reinforced by the construction courts have given similar provisions in the authorizing statutes of other administrative agencies. . . . In National Broadcasting Co. v. United States, 319 U.S. 190 (1943), for example, the Supreme Court upheld the Federal Communications Commission's chain broadcasting rules regulating programming arrangements between networks and affiliates, in part on the basis of the FCC's generalized rule-making authority in 47 U.S.C. §303(r) (1970). See 319 U.S. at 217. It rejected arguments similar to those made here, ruling that this authority extended beyond specification of technical and financial qualifications to be used as guides in the administration of the Commission's license-granting power. Id. at 220. . . .

United States v. Storer Broadcasting Co., 351 U.S. 192 (1956), took the FCC's rule-making power a step further, holding that applicants for licenses could be rejected before receiving a hearing specified by statute, see 47 U.S.C. §309(b) (1970), in the event they did not comply with the Commission's rule limiting networks' power to own stock in affiliates and did not give sufficient reasons why the rule should be waived.

[T]here is little question that the availability of substantive rule-making gives any agency an invaluable resource-saving flexibility in carrying out its task of regulating parties subject to its statutory mandate. More than merely expediting the agency's job, use of substantive rule-making is increasingly felt to yield significant benefits to those the agency regulates. Increasingly, courts are recognizing that use of rule-making to make innovations in agency policy may actually be fairer to regulated parties than total reliance on case-by-case adjudication.

[U]tilizing rule-making procedures opens up the process of agency policy innovation to a broad range of criticism, advice and data that is ordinarily less likely to be forthcoming in adjudication. Moreover, the availability of notice before promulgation and wide public participation in rule-making avoids the problem of singling out a single defendant among a group of competitors for initial imposition of a new and inevitably costly legal obligation. . . .

True, the decision to impose a bright-line standard of behavior might have been evolved by the Commission in a single or a succession of adjudicatory proceedings, *see, e.g.,* FTC v. Texaco, Inc., 393 U.S. 223 (1968), much as the Supreme Court has imposed per se rules of business behavior in antitrust cases. . . . But evolution of bright-line rules is often a slow process and may involve the distinct disadvantage of acting without the broad range of data and argument from all those potentially affected that may be flushed out through use of legislative-type rule-making procedures. And utilizing rule-making in advance of adjudication here minimizes the unfairness of using a purely case-by-case approach requiring "compliance by one manufacturer while his competitors [engaging in similar practices] remain free to violate the Act." Weinberger v. Bentex Pharmaceuticals, Inc., [412 U.S. 645, 653 (1973)]. . . .

III

Appellees contend, however, that these cases and the general practice of agencies and courts in underwriting the broad use of rule-making are irrelevant to the FTC. They argue that the Trade Commission is somehow sui generis, that it is best characterized as a prosecuting rather than a regulatory agency, and that substantive rule-making power should be less readily implied from a general grant of rule-making authority where the agency does not stand astride an industry with pervasive license-granting, rate-setting, or clearance functions. . . .

Given the expanse of the Commission's power to define proper business practices, we believe it is but a quibble to differentiate between the potential pervasiveness of the FTC's power and that of the other regulatory agencies merely on the basis of its prosecutorial and adjudicatory mode of proceeding. Like other agencies, wholly apart from the question of rule-making power it exerts a powerfully regulatory effect on those business practices subject to its supervision. . . . And the Commission has this regulatory effect irrespective of whether it chooses to elaborate the vague but comprehensive statutory standards through rule-making or through case-by-case adjudication. Businesses whose practices appear clearly covered by the Trade Commission's adjudicatory decisions against similarly situated parties presumably will comply with the Commission's holding rather than await a Commission action against them individually; we must presume that in many cases where a guideline is laid down in an individual case it is, like many common law rules, generally obeyed by those similarly situated. . . .

IV

. . . There is little disagreement that the Commission will be able to proceed more expeditiously, give greater certainty to businesses subject to the Act, and deploy its internal resources more efficiently with a mixed system of rule-making and adjudication than with adjudication alone. With the issues in Section 5 proceedings reduced by the existence of a rule delineating what is a violation of the statute or what presumptions the Commission proposes to rely upon, proceedings will be speeded up. For example, in an adjudication proceeding based on a violation of the octane rating rule at issue here, the central question to be decided will be whether or not pumps owned by a given refiner are properly marked. . . . Without the rule, the Commission might well be obliged to prove and argue that the absence of the rating markers in each particular case was likely to have injurious and unfair effects on consumers or competition. Since this laborious process might well have to be repeated every time the Commission chose to proceed subsequently against another defendant on the same ground, the difference in administrative efficiency between the two kinds of proceedings is obvious. Furthermore, rules, as contrasted with the holdings reached by case-by-case adjudication, are more specific as to their scope, and industry compliance is more likely simply because each company is on clearer notice whether or not specific rules apply to it.

Moreover, when delay in agency proceedings is minimized by using rules, those violating the statutory standard lose an opportunity to turn litigation into a profitable and lengthy game of postponing the effect of the rule on their current practice. As a result, substantive rules will protect the companies which willingly comply with the law against what amounts to the unfair competition of those who would profit from delayed enforcement as to them. This, too, will minimize useless litigation and is likely to assist the Commission in more effectively allocating its resources. In addition, whatever form rules take, whether bright-line standards or presumptions that are rebuttable, they are likely to decrease the current uncertainty many businesses are said to feel over the current scope and applicability of Section 5. But the important point here is not that rule-making is assuredly going to solve the Commission's problems. It is rather that recognition and use of rule-making by the Commission is convincingly linked to the goals of agency expedition, efficiency, and certainty of regulatory standards that loomed in the background of the 1914 passage of the Federal Trade Commission Act. . . .

V

. . . The rule here does not bypass the Commission's statute-based cease-and-desist proceedings. It merely supplements them. Moreover, in light of the concern evident in the legislative history that the Commission give attention to the special circumstances of individual businesses in proceeding against them . . . , the Commission should administer any rules it might promulgate in much the same way that courts have ordinarily required other agencies to administer rules that operate to modify a regulated party's rights to a full hearing. That is, some opportunity must be given for a defendant in a Section 5 proceeding to demonstrate that the special circumstances of his case warrant waiving the rule's applicability, as where the rationale of the rule does not appear to apply to his own situation or a compelling case of hardship can be made out. . . . Furthermore, under the Administrative Procedure Act the public, including all parties in the industry who might be affected, are given a significant opportunity prior to promulgation of a rule to ventilate the policy and empirical issues at stake through written submissions, at a minimum, *see* 5 U.S.C. §553, or more, as here, where the agency permitted oral argument in a nonadjudicatory setting. Finally, any rules promulgated by the agency are subject to judicial review testing their legality and ensuring that they are within the scope of the broad statutory prohibition they purport to define. . . .

VI

Our conclusion as to the scope of Section 6(g) is not disturbed by the fact that the agency itself did not assert the power to promulgate substantive rules until 1962 and indeed indicated intermittently before that time that it lacked such power. . . . Here, the question is simply one of statutory interpretation concerning the procedures and setting in which the Commission may elaborate its statutory standard. Since this sort of question calls largely for the exercise of historical analysis and logical and analogical reasoning, it is the everyday staple of judges as well as agencies. Thus we feel confident in making our own judgment as to the proper construction of Section 6(g). . . .

So far as we can tell, the earlier assertions of lack of rule-making power were based on an unduly crabbed and cautious analysis of the legislative background, an analysis that we have conducted independently and that has brought us to an opposite but, in our judgment, correct conclusion.

A more troubling obstacle to the Commission's position here is the argument that Congress was made fully aware of the formerly restrictive view of the Commission's power and passed a series of laws granting limited substantive rule-making authority to the Commission in discrete areas allegedly on the premise that the 1914 debate withheld such authority. . . . The view that the Commission lacked substantive rule-making power has been clearly brought to the attention of Congress and, rather than simply failing to act on the question, Congress, in expanding the agency's powers in several discrete areas of marketing regulation, affirmatively enacted limited grants of substantive rule-making authority in the Wool Products Act of 1939, the Fur Products Labeling Act of 1951, the Flammable Fabrics Act of 1953 as amended in 1967, the Textile Fiber Products Identification Act of 1958, and the Fair Packaging and Labeling Act of 1967. Thus it is argued that Congress would not have granted the agency such powers unless it had felt that otherwise the agency lacked rule-making authority. . . . [I]t is equally possible that Congress granted the power out of uncertainty, understandable caution, and a desire to avoid litigation. While this argument, like any theory requiring us to draw inferences from congressional action or inaction, may be speculative, we believe it cannot be ignored here. . . . Where there is solid reason, as there plainly is here, to believe that Congress, in fact, has not wholeheartedly accepted the agency's viewpoint and instead enacted legislation out of caution and to eliminate the kind of disputes that invariably attend statutory ambiguity, we believe that relying on the de facto ratification argument is unwise. In such circumstances, we must perform our customary task of coming to an independent judgment as to the statute's meaning, confident that if Congress believes that its creature, the Commission, thus exercises too much power, it will repeal the grant.[40]

VII

In sum, we must respectfully register our disagreement with the District Court's painstaking opinion. Its result would render the Commission ineffective to do the job assigned it by Congress. . . . Thus we must reverse the District Court's judgment and remand this case for further proceedings.

It is so ordered.

NOTES AND QUESTIONS

1. *Authority to engage in rulemaking.* Do you agree that Congress authorized the FTC to issue substantive (as opposed to procedural) rules? In answering yes, Judge Wright overcame several obstacles: (1) the principle of statutory interpretation that an express declaration of one power generally excludes an inference of other "substitute" powers (summed up in the *expressio unius* maxim); (2) the argument that, where ambiguous, a general power in a list should be viewed as similar in kind to the other, more specific, listed powers (a principle encapsulated in another Latin maxim, *ejusdem generis*); (3) half a century of contrary interpretation by the commission; and (4) considerable evidence that many

40. We are aware, of course, that in both the just concluded 92nd Congress and the current 93rd Congress legislation granting the FTC limited substantive rule-making power in the area of "unfair and deceptive practices" has been under consideration. One such bill, S. 986, 92d Cong., 1st Sess. (1971), was passed by the Senate, 117 Cong. Rec. S. 17887 (daily ed. Nov. 8, 1971), but did not come to a vote in the House. It is also true that in the Senate debate on S. 986 comments were made by various Senators to the effect that the Commission currently lacked the power to issue rules defining either unfair methods of competition or unfair or deceptive acts or practices, which rules would be enforceable in cease and desist proceedings. *See id.* at 17843-17848 (statement of Sen. Hruska); *id.* at 17849 (statement of Sen. Cook); *id.* at 17873 (statement of Sen. Cotton), but no such statement was made by the bill's sponsor, Sen. Magnuson, who pointed out, "For years the argument has been going on about the Federal Trade Commission not having the authority it should have. We tried to fashion a bill. I, myself, had some doubts about the rule-making authority, but I think the bill covers it very well." *Id.* at 17858. The bill that passed the Senate not only gave the FTC power "to issue legislative rules defining with specificity acts or practices which are unfair or deceptive to consumers and which section 5(a)(1) of this Act proscribes," S. 986, *supra*, §206, but it also provided that procedures available in adjudication under the Administrative Procedure Act, 5 U.S.C. §§556, 557 (1970), should be employed and judicial review should employ the substantial evidence rule. *Ibid.* Moreover, such rules would only become effective in the event neither the House of Representatives nor the Senate disapproved them within 60 calendar days while in session. *Ibid.* If this legislation had actually been enacted, of course, the Commission would not have *all* the power it assumes today, since the proposed rulemaking section in S. 986 repealed §6(g), as passed in 1914, and substituted a provision allowing only rules and regulations "as are specifically provided for hereinafter," thus nullifying any argument that rules might be promulgated to define "unfair methods of competition." On the other hand, but for the statements on the Senate floor quoted above, it is possible to interpret S. 986 as an indication of senatorial intent to narrow what the legislators felt was presently an overbroad rule-making power under the current statute. In any event, the legislation did not pass, and we take its reintroduction in the current session in substantially similar form, S. 356, 93d Cong., 1st Sess. (1973), as an indication that the questions of FTC rule-making power, its scope, and the safeguards surrounding the promulgation of such rules, are under close study and nothing more. In the event Congress decides that the scope of rule-making power that we find to be implied in the 1914 Act is too broad or lacks sufficient safeguards, surely it appears in a prime position to make the required changes.

members of Congress viewed the FTC as without general, substantive rulemaking power—evidenced in part by formal legislative grants of limited rulemaking authority and in part by statements of individual members. Does Judge Wright convincingly dispose of these points?

2. *The utility of rulemaking.* If Judge Wright is correct that the Act clearly confers substantive rulemaking authority on the FTC, why does he spend so much space defending the utility of rulemaking? Is he correct in his assessment that, as a means of making regulatory policy, rulemaking is preferable to adjudication as a general matter? With specific reference to the FTC's mission respecting unfair and deceptive practices? From whose vantage point should the benefits and costs of substantive rulemaking be assessed? Professor Glen Robinson has argued that the claims for the superiority of rulemaking to adjudication are greatly overblown. Glen O. Robinson, The Making of Administrative Policy: Another Look at Rulemaking and Adjudication and Administrative Procedure Reform, 118 U. Pa. L. Rev. 485 (1970). In fact, he claims, there are often only marginal differences between the two techniques of policymaking. Is that true in the particular context of regulating the marketing of gasoline? Can you imagine whether the difference might be greater in other contexts, like privacy protection, for example?

3. *Subsequent legislation.* The *Petroleum Refiners* case is in good company in upholding the assertion of rulemaking authority. As Judge Wright indicates, courts generally have approved agency resort to substantive rulemaking to set general policies for future application. In the case of the FTC, however, there might have been particular reason for caution. As the court's footnote 40 indicates, a number of legislative efforts to resolve the issue of FTC rulemaking authority were made around the time of the court's decision. Within a year following the *Petroleum Refiners* decision, Congress amended the Federal Trade Commission Act to place limits on the substantive rulemaking power approved by the court of appeals; within the decade following *Petroleum Refiners,* Congress amended that authority five times.

The amendments placed both subject matter and procedural limitations on FTC rulemaking respecting unfair or deceptive practices. Some amendments were narrowly tailored to curtailing specific FTC initiatives, while others focused more generally on FTC rulemaking. The first and most general amendment was the Federal Trade Commission Improvement Act of 1974 (generally known as the Magnuson-Moss Act), 15 U.S.C. §57a (1976). Magnuson-Moss added a number of procedural requirements for FTC rulemaking identifying unfair or deceptive practices. These procedures, discussed in Chapter V, section B.4, *infra,* make the rulemaking process somewhat slower and more akin to adjudication than the process contemplated by Judge Wright. What implications do these amendments have for the issues posed in *Petroleum Refiners?*

4. *The National Labor Relations Board and rulemaking.* Unlike the FTC, which has eagerly exercised the substantive rulemaking power recognized in the *Petroleum Refiners* case, the NLRB has resisted use of rulemaking even though its governing statute expressly grants such power. *See* Cornelius J. Peck, The Atrophied Rule-Making Powers of the National Labor Relations Board, 70 Yale L.J. 729 (1961). Although this practice has been criticized, the board has consistently employed incremental, case-based decisionmaking through

adjudicatory process rather than rulemaking. Why would an agency like the NLRB behave this way? In 1989, the NLRB finally adopted its first substantive legislative rule, governing the determination of bargaining units in health care facilities. The Supreme Court upheld the rule in a subsequent challenge, American Hosp. Assn. v. NLRB, 499 U.S. 606 (1991). The board's second rulemaking venture did not fare so well, as the following case illustrates.

CHAMBER OF COMMERCE OF THE UNITED STATES v. NATIONAL LABOR RELATIONS BOARD, 721 F.3d 152 (4th Cir. 2013):

Section 6 of the National Labor Relations Act, 28 U.S.C. §156, grants the NRLB broad rulemaking authority:

> The Board shall have authority from time to time to make, amend, and rescind, in the manner prescribed by [§553 of] the Administrative Procedure Act, such rules and regulations as may be necessary to carry out the provisions of this Act.

Purporting to act under the authority conferred by §6, the NLRB adopted a rule requiring all employers subject to the Act to post a notice in the workplace informing their workers of their collective bargaining rights under the Act. 76 Fed. Reg. 54,006 (2011). The rule stated that failure to comply would be considered an unfair labor practice under the Act, and could also lead to finding that the employer had an anti-union bias that would weigh against it in other proceedings before the board. The Chamber of Commerce, representing employers subject to the rule, challenged the rule on substantive grounds as inconsistent with the Act and on procedural grounds as having been adopted in an improper manner. In an opinion that somewhat conflated the two arguments, the Fourth Circuit agreed with the Chamber:

> We, like the Chamber, read the language in Section 6 as requiring that some section of the Act provide the explicit or implicit authority to issue a rule. Because the Board is nowhere charged with informing employees of their rights under the NLRA, we find no indication in the plain language of the Act that Congress intended to grant the Board the authority to promulgate such a requirement. . . .
>
> [T]he substantive provisions of the Act make clear that the Board is a reactive entity, and thus do not imply that Congress intended to allow proactive rulemaking of the sort challenged here through the general rulemaking provision of Section 6. . . .
>
> Reports on early versions of the NLRA indicate that the Board was designed to serve a reactive role, with its "quasi-judicial power" being "restricted to [the enumerated] unfair labor practices and to cases in which the choice of representatives is doubtful." S. Rep. No. 73-1184 (1934). . . . There is no indication in the Act's legislative history of an intent to allow the Board to impose duties upon employers proactively; indeed, if anything, it appears to have been the intent of Congress that the Board not be empowered to play such a role. Cf. H.R. Rep. No. 74-969 (1935) (noting that Section 11 does not grant the Board the powers of a "roving commission"). . . .
>
> The contrast between the roles the NLRA sets forth for the NLRB and those that other federal labor statutes prescribe for those of its sister agencies with notice-posting authority is of particular significance. As we have discussed, the Board's core functions are reactive ones. In contrast, other agencies that have

promulgated notice-posting requirements have proactive mandates. For instance, the EEOC, which is granted the authority to require the posting of notices, has the power to proactively file charges and undertake investigations, regardless of whether a party files a charge. The same is true of the Occupational Safety & Health Administration, as well as the Department of Labor ("DOL") more generally.

Congress's continued exclusion of a notice-posting requirement from the NLRA, concomitant with its granting of such authority to other agencies, can fairly be considered deliberate. *See Brown & Williamson*, 529 U.S. [120, 133] (2000) ("[T]he meaning of one statute may be affected by other Acts, particularly where Congress has spoken subsequently and more specifically to the topic at hand."). Had Congress intended to grant the NLRB the power to require the posting of employee rights notices, it could have amended the NLRA to do so.

QUESTIONS

What do you think of the Fourth Circuit's characterization of the NLRB as a "reactive" agency? What characteristics make the NLRB reactive rather than "proactive"? Is it simply Congress's expectation that the NLRB would function primarily as an adjudicative body, making determinations on individual unfair labor practice charges? If so, couldn't the same be said of the FTC's role in cease-and-desist proceedings? Might this be a matter of degree in some cases? In other words, are there agencies that might be viewed as reactive in some situations and proactive in others? What factors might distinguish the two situations? Is *Chamber of Commerce* consistent with the D.C. Circuit's decision in the *Petroleum Refiners* case? With the Supreme Court's decision in *Storer*?

In addition to more effective policy implementation, the use of bright-line rules can be an effective strategy for combating inconsistency and delay in administrative adjudication. In theory, at least, replacing a general standard with a specific rule will enable more controversies to be resolved on the "pleadings," without recourse to time-consuming and unpredictable evidentiary hearings, and will simplify the factfinding and law-applying process in cases that do go to hearing. Likewise, bright-line rules are thought to make it easier for agencies to correct errors of primary decisionmakers. Not surprisingly, this strategy has appealed particularly to the heads of agencies, such as the Social Security Administration, charged with programs, like disability insurance, that generate huge claim caseloads. Disability determinations are made by the Social Security Administration in a process that lies somewhere between formal adjudication and informal decisionmaking. (Details of the process appear in Chapter VI, section B.2.A, *infra*, in connection with *Mathews v. Eldridge*.) The standard used by the Social Security Administration to define eligibility for Disability Insurance (DI) benefits has become increasingly specific over time. SSA devoted most of its early rulemaking attention to the statute's "physical and mental impairment" factor, gradually developing highly detailed guidelines for measuring impairments and defining several "per se disabling" conditions. Aside from a per se "earnings test," however, the nonmedical criteria for determining "inability to engage in substantial gainful activity" remained clouded in imprecise verbiage. Congress amended the Act in 1968 to require the SSA specifically to consider the applicant's "age, education, and work experience" in making the disability determination. Until 1978, however, the assessment of these "vocational" factors was consigned to the individual judgment of claims-processing officials, with heavy reliance on the professional opinion of vocational experts.

In 1978, SSA adopted the so-called "grid rule," substituting a uniform, mechanical formula for the previous process of individualized synthesis to govern a large subset of disability determinations. 43 Fed. Reg. 55,349 (1978). The grid is a matrix that specifies the relationship among four independent medical-vocational variables (the claimant's "exceptional capabilities," "education," "age," and "previous work experience") and the dependent variable ("disability").

For each combination of these variables, the rule specifies the ultimate decision ("disabled"/"not disabled"). The decisionmaker first classifies the applicant into the appropriate category under each of the four medical-vocational headings. She then selects the table appropriate to the applicant's residual functional capacity, reads down the "age," "education," and "experience" columns to find the appropriate values, and reads the corresponding entry in the "decision" column. The following excerpt from the first table of the medical-vocational guidelines is illustrative.

TABLE 1
Residual Functional Capacity: Maximum Sustained Work
Capability Limited to Sedentary Work as a Result of Severe
Medically Determinable Impairment(s)

Rule	Age	Education	Previous work experience	Decision
201.01	Advanced age	Limited or less	Unskilled or none	Disabled
201.02	. . . . . . do*	. . . . . . do	Skilled or semi-skilled—skills not transferable	Do.*
201.03	. . . . . . do	. . . . . . do	Skilled or semi-skilled—skills transferable	Not disabled
201.04	. . . . . . do	High school graduate or more—does not provide for direct entry into skilled work	Unskilled or none	Disabled
201.05	. . . . . . do	High school graduate or more—provides for direct entry into skilled work	. . . . . . do	Not disabled
201.06	. . . . . . do	High school graduate or more—does not provide for direct entry into skilled work	Skilled or semi-skilled—skills not transferable	Disabled

* [Ditto.—Eds.]

The grid rule also allows claimants to challenge application of the guidelines to their particular circumstances:

> Where the findings of fact made with respect to a particular individual's vocational factors and residual functional capacity coincide with all of the criteria of a particular rule, the rule directs a conclusion as to whether the individual is or is not disabled. However, each of these findings of fact is subject to rebuttal and the individual may present evidence to refute such findings. Where any one of the findings of fact does not coincide with the corresponding criterion of a rule, the rule does not apply in that particular case and, accordingly, does not direct a conclusion of disabled or not disabled. In any instance where a rule does not apply, full consideration must be given to all of the relevant facts of the case in accordance with the definitions and discussions of each factor in the appropriate sections of the regulations.

Appendix 2 to Subpart P of Part 404 — Medical-Vocational Guidelines, §200.00.

HECKLER v. CAMPBELL
461 U.S. 458 (1983)

JUSTICE POWELL delivered the opinion of the Court.

The issue is whether the Secretary of Health and Human Services may rely on published medical-vocational guidelines to determine a claimant's right to Social Security disability benefits. . . .

II

In 1979, Carmen Campbell applied for disability benefits because a back condition and hypertension prevented her from continuing her work as a hotel maid. After her application was denied, she requested a hearing de novo before an Administrative Law Judge. He determined that her back problem was not severe enough to find her disabled without further inquiry, and accordingly considered whether she retained the ability to perform either her past work or some less strenuous job. . . . He concluded that even though Campbell's back condition prevented her from returning to her work as a maid, she retained the physical capacity to do light work. In accordance with the regulations, he found that Campbell was 52 years old, that her previous employment consisted of unskilled jobs, and that she had a limited education. He noted that Campbell, who had been born in Panama, experienced difficulty in speaking and writing English. She was able, however, to understand and read English fairly well. Relying on the medical-vocational guidelines, the Administrative Law Judge found that a significant number of jobs existed that a person of Campbell's qualifications could perform. Accordingly, he concluded that she was not disabled.

This determination was upheld by both the Social Security Appeals Council, and the District Court for the Eastern District of New York. The Court of Appeals for the Second Circuit reversed. Campbell v. Secretary of Dept. of Health and Human Services, 665 F.2d 48 (1981). It accepted the Administrative Law Judge's determination that Campbell retained the ability to do light work.

And it did not suggest that he had classified Campbell's age, education, or work experience incorrectly. The court noted, however, that it

> has consistently required that "the Secretary identify specific alternative occupations available in the national economy that would be suitable for the claimant" and that "these jobs be supported by 'a job description clarifying the nature of the job, [and] demonstrating that the job does not require' exertion or skills not possessed by the claimant."

Id., at 53 (*quoting* Decker v. Harris, 647 F.2d 291, 298 (2d Cir. 1981)). The court found that the medical-vocational guidelines did not provide the specific evidence that it previously had required. It explained that in the absence of such a showing, "the claimant is deprived of any real chance to present evidence showing that she cannot in fact perform the types of jobs that are administratively noticed by the guidelines." 665 F.2d, at 53. The court concluded that because the Secretary had failed to introduce evidence that specific alternative jobs existed, the determination that Campbell was not disabled was not supported by substantial evidence. *Id.,* at 54.

We granted certiorari to resolve a conflict among the Courts of Appeals. . . . We now reverse.

III

The Secretary argues that the Court of Appeals' holding effectively prevents the use of the medical-vocational guidelines. By requiring her to identify specific alternative jobs in every disability hearing, the court has rendered the guidelines useless. An examination of both the language of the Social Security Act and its legislative history clearly demonstrates that the Secretary may proceed by regulation to determine whether substantial gainful work exists in the national economy. Campbell argues in response that the Secretary has misperceived the Court of Appeals' holding. Campbell reads the decision as requiring only that the Secretary give disability claimants concrete examples of the kinds of factual determinations that the administrative law judge will be making. This requirement does not defeat the guidelines' purpose; it ensures that they will be applied only where appropriate. Accordingly, respondent argues that we need not address the guidelines' validity.

The Court of Appeals held that "[i]n failing to show suitable available alternative jobs for Ms. Campbell, the Secretary's finding of 'not disabled' is not supported by substantial evidence." 665 F.2d, at 54. It thus rejected the proposition that "the guidelines provide adequate evidence of a claimant's ability to perform a specific alternative occupation," *id.,* at 53, and remanded for the Secretary to put into evidence "particular types of jobs suitable to the capabilities of Ms. Campbell," *id.,* at 54. The court's requirement that additional evidence be introduced on this issue prevents the Secretary from putting the guidelines to their intended use and implicitly calls their validity into question. Accordingly, we think the decision below requires us to consider whether the Secretary may rely on medical-vocational guidelines in appropriate cases.

The Social Security Act directs the Secretary to "adopt reasonable and proper rules and regulations to regulate and provide for the nature and extent of the proofs and evidence and the method of taking and furnishing the same" in disability cases. 42 U.S.C. §405(a). . . . Where, as here, the statute expressly entrusts the Secretary with the responsibility for implementing a provision by regulation, our review is limited to determining whether the regulations promulgated exceeded the Secretary's statutory authority and whether they are arbitrary and capricious. . . .

We do not think that the Secretary's reliance on medical-vocational guidelines is inconsistent with the Social Security Act. It is true that the statutory scheme contemplates that disability hearings will be individualized determinations based on evidence adduced at a hearing. *See* 42 U.S.C. §423(d)(2)(A) (specifying consideration of each individual's condition); 42 U.S.C. §405(b) (1976 ed., Supp. V) (disability determination to be based on evidence adduced at hearing). But this does not bar the Secretary from relying on rulemaking to resolve certain classes of issues. The Court has recognized that even where an agency's enabling statute expressly requires it to hold a hearing, the agency may rely on its rulemaking authority to determine issues that do not require case-by-case consideration. *See* FPC v. Texaco Inc., 377 U.S. 33, 41-44 (1964); United States v. Storer Broadcasting Co., 351 U.S. 192, 205 (1956). A contrary holding would require the agency continually to relitigate issues that may be established fairly and efficiently in a single rulemaking proceeding. *See* FPC v. Texaco Inc., *supra*, at 44.

The Secretary's decision to rely on medical-vocational guidelines is consistent with *Texaco* and *Storer.* As noted above, in determining whether a claimant can perform less strenuous work, the Secretary must make two determinations. She must assess each claimant's individual abilities and then determine whether jobs exist that a person having the claimant's qualifications could perform. The first inquiry involves a determination of historic facts, and the regulations properly require the Secretary to make these findings on the basis of evidence adduced at a hearing. We note that the regulations afford claimants ample opportunity both to present evidence relating to their own abilities and to offer evidence that the guidelines do not apply to them.[11] The second inquiry requires the Secretary to determine an issue that is not unique to each claimant — the types and numbers of jobs that exist in the national economy. This type of general factual issue may be resolved as fairly through rulemaking as by introducing the testimony of vocational experts at each disability hearing. *See* American Airlines, Inc. v. CAB, 123 U.S. App. D.C. 310, 319, 359 F.2d 624, 633 (1966) (en banc).

As the Secretary has argued, the use of published guidelines brings with it a uniformity that previously had been perceived as lacking. To require the Secretary

---

11. Both FPC v. Texaco Inc., 377 U.S. 33, 40 (1964), and United States v. Storer Broadcasting Co., 351 U.S. 192, 205 (1956), were careful to note that the statutory scheme at issue allowed an individual applicant to show that the rule promulgated should not be applied to him. The regulations here provide a claimant with equal or greater protection since they state that an administrative law judge will not apply the rules contained in the guidelines when they fail to describe a claimant's particular limitations. *See* n.5. [The Court's footnote 5 reads: The regulations recognize that the rules only describe "major functional and vocational patterns." 20 CFR pt. 404, subpt. P, app. 2, §200.00(a) (1982). If an individual's capabilities are not described accurately by a rule, the regulations make clear that the individual's particular limitations must be considered. *See* app. 2, §§200.00(a), (d). Additionally, the regulations declare that the administrative law judge will not apply the age categories "mechanically in a borderline situation," 20 CFR §404.1563(a) (1982), and recognize that some claimants may possess limitations that are not factored into the guidelines, *see* app. 2, §200.00(e). Thus, the regulations provide that the rules will be applied only when they describe a claimant's abilities and limitations accurately.]

to relitigate the existence of jobs in the national economy at each hearing would hinder needlessly an already overburdened agency. We conclude that the Secretary's use of medical-vocational guidelines does not conflict with the statute, nor can we say on the record before us that they are arbitrary and capricious. . . .

IV

The Court of Appeals' decision would require the Secretary to introduce evidence of specific available jobs that respondent could perform. It would limit severely her ability to rely on the medical-vocational guidelines. We think the Secretary reasonably could choose to rely on these guidelines in appropriate cases rather than on the testimony of a vocational expert in each case. Accordingly, the judgment of the Court of Appeals is reversed.

NOTES AND QUESTIONS

1. *Legislative and adjudicative facts revisited.* Is the decision whether there are jobs available in the national economy that Ms. Campbell could perform a question of legislative or adjudicative fact? Does it matter to the outcome? Should it?

2. *Substantive objections to the grid rule.* What exactly is the *legal* basis for objecting to what the Secretary did in *Campbell?* Is it a procedural or a substantive objection? In fact, the court of appeals grounded its decision on a substantive basis: that the Secretary's finding of "not disabled" was not supported by "substantial evidence," since the Secretary had not identified *specific* jobs that Ms. Campbell could perform. Isn't that a bit like saying a conviction for exceeding the 55-mph speed limit lacks "substantial evidence" if the state fails to identify specific persons or property endangered by the speeding driver? Is the use of bright-line rules to determine eligibility for government benefits more or less objectionable than their use to regulate traffic? In this connection, you may want to compare *Campbell* to the *Ruiz* case, *infra*, where the Court criticized a welfare agency for rejecting a claim for benefits on an ad hoc basis without the benefit of formal written eligibility standards.

Some observers believe that the burden of providing individualized hearings required by due process decisions like Goldberg v. Kelly, 397 U.S. 254 (1970) (excerpted in Chapter VI, *infra*) generated pressure on legislatures and administrators to adopt increasingly mechanical rules for determining eligibility for government assistance. *See, e.g.,* William H. Simon, Legality, Bureaucracy, and Class in the Welfare System, 92 Yale L.J. 1198 (1983). By reducing the range of discretion accorded to decisionmakers, bright-line eligibility rules reduce the number and complexity of the factual disputes that arise. As a result, the demand for hearings would be expected to decline. *See* Colin S. Diver, The Optimal Precision of Administrative Rules, 93 Yale L.J. 65 (1983). This tactic is rarely an unmixed blessing, however. The easier a rule is to apply, the more likely it will produce results that deviate from the program's underlying goal. A tyranny of inflexible rules replaces the tyranny of bureaucratic caprice. Should the courts have any role in making the choice between these two tyrannies?

3. *Procedural objections to the grid rule.* Why can't Ms. Campbell make a successful *procedural* claim predicated on a violation of the "hearing" entitlement afforded by §405(b) of the Social Security Act (quoted *infra*) and/or §554 of the APA? The Court cites *Storer* for the proposition that an "agency may rely on its rulemaking authority to determine issues that do not require case-by-case consideration." Does *Storer* necessarily control the outcome in *Campbell*? Why or why not?

Contrast to *Campbell* the case of Sullivan v. Zebley, 493 U.S. 521 (1990). The Secretary had issued a rule obviating the need for individualized determinations of functional capacity of children in disability determinations under the Supplemental Security Income program. The Court struck down the rule, finding no basis for making an exception to a statutory requirement that there be individualized determinations of functionality in all cases.

4. *Success of the grid rule.* According to one commentator's relatively recent assessment, the grid rule has only partially succeeded at rationalizing the process of Social Security disability adjudication. *See* Jon C. Dubin, Overcoming Gridlock: *Campbell* After a Quarter-Century and Bureaucratically Rational Gap-Filling in Mass Justice Adjudication in the Social Security Administration's Disability Programs, 62 Admin. L. Rev. 937 (2010). As the Court noted in *Campbell*, the grid rule "will be applied only when [it] describe[s] a claimant's abilities and limitations accurately," 461 U.S. at 462 n.5. Professor Dubin notes that certain disabilities do not lend themselves to grid rule application. "The broadest and most litigated exception to the grid's direct application is in situations involving claimants with nonexertional or non-strength-related medical limitations." 62 Admin. L. Rev. at 942. In such cases, Dubin concludes that the agency's performance suffers from the same weaknesses that inspired the adoption of the grid rule. "[T]he agency's ad hoc adjudicative methodology where grid exceptions are present has undermined the consistency and bureaucratic rationality the grid system was intended to ensure." *Id.* at 943. Is it surprising that the grid rule would not solve these problems in situations to which it does not apply? Do you think it is possible to eliminate inconsistency and bureaucratic irrationality in a system with the scope and quantity of claims possessed by the Social Security disability system? Or is it more realistic to hope to reduce these problems? Is the difficulty of balancing consistency across claims (comparative fairness) versus accuracy in individualized determinations (individual fairness) different in this context than, for example, in assigning grades to students in school?

C. AGENCY DISCRETION TO MAKE POLICY BY ORDER AFTER ADJUDICATION

The preceding section involved administrative policy decisions made by rulemaking, challenged on the ground that the agencies were required to make policy through the case-by-case method of adjudication. This section involves the converse situation: challenges to policies established through adjudicatory procedures on the ground that the adjudicating agency was required to employ the APA's rulemaking process. The Supreme Court first addressed this issue in an iconic pre-APA decision, during the course of an epic litigation saga involving the Securities and Exchange Commission and a public utility holding company called the Chenery Corporation.

SEC v. CHENERY CORP., 332 U.S. 194 (1947) (*CHENERY II*):   The SEC had ordered officers and directors of Chenery to surrender to the company their shares of the company's preferred stock, acquired while the company was undergoing a voluntary reorganization, in exchange for their cost plus interest. The SEC made approval of the company's reorganization plan contingent on this divestment. In an earlier decision (*Chenery I,* excerpted in Chapter II, *supra*), the Supreme Court had reversed the SEC order as unsupported by the judicial precedents on which the SEC relied. On remand, the SEC changed its rationale and based its action not on judicial precedent but on its own interpretation of the standards implied in the Public Utility Holding Company Act of 1935, 49 Stat. 803. This second SEC decision was challenged as improperly establishing a general rule that officers and directors could not profit from actions during reorganization that formerly were thought lawful. The affected individuals claimed that this decision could only be made through the adoption of a notice-and-comment rule that would have future but not retroactive effect. The Court concluded that the SEC was resolving a particular issue in a concrete case and the absence of a prior rule covering the issue did not preclude the commission from basing its action on its interpretation of the Holding Company Act. The Court went on to say:

> The absence of a general rule or regulation governing management trading during reorganization did not affect the Commission's duties in relation to the particular proposal before it. The Commission was asked to grant or deny effectiveness to a proposed amendment to Federal's reorganization plan whereby the management would be accorded parity treatment on its holdings. It could do that only in the form of an order, entered after a due consideration of the particular facts in light of the relevant and proper standards. That was true regardless of whether those standards previously had been spelled out in a general rule or regulation. Indeed, if the Commission rightly felt that the proposed amendment was inconsistent with those standards, an order giving effect to the amendment merely because there was no general rule or regulation covering the matter would be unjustified.
>
> It is true that our prior decision explicitly recognized the possibility that the Commission might have promulgated a general rule dealing with this problem under its statutory rule-making powers, in which case the issue for our consideration would have been entirely different from that which did confront us. 318 U.S. at pages 92, 93. But we did not mean to imply thereby that the failure of the Commission to anticipate this problem and to promulgate a general rule withdrew all power from that agency to perform its statutory duty in this case. To hold that the Commission had no alternative in this proceeding but to approve the proposed transaction, while formulating any general rules it might desire for use in future cases of this nature, would be to stultify the administrative process. That we refuse to do.

The Court acknowledged that agencies ought to undertake rulemaking when possible, but it declined to impose a requirement that agencies do so, leaving the matter to agency discretion:

Since the Commission, unlike a court, does have the ability to make new law prospectively through the exercise of its rule-making powers, it has less reason to rely upon ad hoc adjudication to formulate new standards of conduct within the framework of the Holding Company Act. The function of filling in the interstices of the Act should be performed, as much as possible, through this quasi-legislative promulgation of rules to be applied in the future. But any rigid requirement to that effect would make the administrative process inflexible and incapable of dealing with many of the specialized problems which arise. *See* Report of the Attorney General's Committee on Administrative Procedure in Government Agencies, S. Doc. No. 8, 77th Cong., 1st Sess., p. 29. Not every principle essential to the effective administration of a statute can or should be cast immediately into the mold of a general rule. Some principles must await their own development, while others must be adjusted to meet particular, unforeseeable situations. In performing its important functions in these respects, therefore, an administrative agency must be equipped to act either by general rule or by individual order. To insist upon one form of action to the exclusion of the other is to exalt form over necessity.

In other words, problems may arise in a case which the administrative agency could not reasonably foresee, problems which must be solved despite the absence of a relevant general rule. Or the agency may not have had sufficient experience with a particular problem to warrant rigidifying its tentative judgment into a hard and fast rule. Or the problem may be so specialized and varying in nature as to be impossible of capture within the boundaries of a general rule. In those situations, the agency must retain power to deal with the problems on a case-to-case basis if the administrative process is to be effective. There is thus a very definite place for the case-by-case evolution of statutory standards. And the choice made between proceeding by general rule or by individual, ad hoc litigation is one that lies primarily in the informed discretion of the administrative agency.

Hence we refuse to say that the Commission, which had not previously been confronted with the problem of management trading during reorganization, was forbidden from utilizing this particular proceeding for announcing and applying a new standard of conduct. That such action might have a retroactive effect was not necessarily fatal to its validity. Every case of first impression has a retroactive effect, whether the new principle is announced by a court or by an administrative agency. But such retroactivity must be balanced against the mischief of producing a result which is contrary to a statutory design or to legal and equitable principles. If that mischief is greater than the ill effect of the retroactive application of a new standard, it is not the type of retroactivity which is condemned by law.

Justices Jackson and Frankfurter dissented, finding the SEC denial of profits to the affected corporate officials unlawful, at least absent commission adoption of a clearly articulated general rule.

Note that the argument the court rejected in *Chenery II* was that the agency's application of the new policy had to be prospective — the claim was that it could not be applied in the formative adjudication. The case study that follows asks a slightly different question — is it permissible to make a new prospective policy in an adjudicatory process, or must prospective rules be made legislatively (by rulemaking)?

One of the National Labor Relations Board's principal responsibilities is to supervise the selection of employee representatives, including procedures that determine whether the employees want to be represented by a labor union. When a dispute arises over whether a majority of employees in an appropriate bargaining unit want a given representative, the NLRB may investigate to determine whether there is sufficient question to put the matter to a vote by the affected employees. Following an NLRB determination that a vote is appropriate, there is a "campaign" period and ultimately an election. The NLRB supervises the campaign and election to ensure that improper employer or union practices do not taint the employees' choice. The election is generally held under the supervision of a regional office of the board. Following the balloting, challenges to the election may be filed with the regional director. If she believes it necessary, she may order a formal hearing on the challenges. Decisions of the regional directors may be appealed to the board.

The National Labor Relations Act does not detail what practices will vitiate an election. It merely commands the board to "direct an election by secret ballot and . . . certify the results." 29 U.S.C. §159(c)(1)(B). The Act also proscribes employer or union actions that "restrain or coerce" employees in the exercise of their rights, including the right to choose a representative. In the election context, the board has asserted that the statute contemplates more than freedom from generally proscribed acts—it requires "laboratory conditions" for certification. In this vein, the NLRB has closely scrutinized the conduct of employers during the period preceding an election, including statements about the effects of unionization, promises of benefits, awards of benefits, or failures to award benefits, for signs of undue influence. Of particular concern in many cases have been limitations on union access to employees during the campaign period. See, for example, cases and discussion in Archibald Cox et al., Labor Law: Cases and Materials 112-51 (14th ed. 2006). The *Excelsior Underwear* case that follows involved such an issue.

EXCELSIOR UNDERWEAR, INC.
156 N.L.R.B. 1236 (1966)

[Two cases were consolidated under this heading. In the principal case, the Amalgamated Clothing Workers sought certification as the bargaining representative of Excelsior Underwear's employees. During the campaign, Excelsior mailed to its employees an eight-page letter discussing the company, the union, and the course of events the company foresaw if the union was selected as the employees' representative. The letter allegedly contained "material misrepresentations" concerning the union and the protections offered by federal labor law. The union also characterized the letter as including dire predictions of violent strikes and plant closings and declaring the company's intention not to bargain with the union. The union asked the company to supply a list of its employees so that it could respond to Excelsior's letter. The company refused. When the secret ballots for the election were tallied, the union had received only 35 of the 246 votes cast. Only one eligible employee failed to vote. The union challenged the result.]

[E]ach of these cases poses the question whether an employer's refusal to provide a union with the names and addresses of employees eligible to vote in a representation election should be grounds on which to set that election aside. The Board has not in the past set elections aside on this ground. For, while the Board has required that an employer, shortly before an election, make available for inspection by the parties and the Regional Director a list of employees claimed by him to be eligible to vote in that election, there has been no requirement that this list contain addresses in addition to names. The rules governing representation elections are not, however, "fixed and immutable. They have been changed and refined, generally in the direction of higher standards."

We are persuaded . . . that higher standards of disclosure than we have heretofore imposed are necessary, and that prompt disclosure of the information here sought by the Petitioners should be required in all representation elections. Accordingly, we now establish a requirement that will be applied in all election cases. That is, within 7 days after the Regional Director has approved a consent-election agreement entered into by the parties . . . , or after the Regional Director or the Board has directed an election . . . , the employer must file with the Regional Director an election eligibility list, containing the names and addresses of all the eligible voters. The Regional Director, in turn, shall make this information available to all parties in the case. Failure to comply with this requirement shall be grounds for setting aside the election whenever proper objections are filed.[5] The considerations that impel us to adopt the foregoing rule are these: "The control of the election proceeding, and the determination of the steps necessary to conduct that election fairly [are] matters which Congress entrusted to the Board alone."[6] In discharging that trust, we regard it as the Board's function to conduct elections in which employees have the opportunity to cast their ballots for or against representation under circumstances that are free not only from interference, restraint, or coercion violative of the Act, but also from other elements that prevent or impede a free and reasoned choice. Among the factors that undoubtedly tend to impede such a choice is a lack of information with respect to one of the choices available. In other words, an employee who has had an effective opportunity to hear the arguments concerning representation is in a better position to make a more fully informed and reasonable choice. Accordingly, we think that it is appropriate for us to remove the impediment to communication to which our new rule is directed.

As a practical matter, an employer, through his possession of employee names and home addresses as well as his ability to communicate with employees on plant

---

5. In the event that the payroll period for eligibility purposes is subsequent to the direction of election or consent-election agreement, the eligibility list shall be filed within 7 days after the close of the determinative payroll period for eligibility purposes. In order to be timely, the eligibility list must be *received* by the Regional Director within the period required. No extension of time shall be granted by the Regional Director except in extraordinary circumstances nor shall [the] filing of a request for review operate to stay the requirement here imposed. . . .

However, the rule we have here announced is to be applied prospectively only. It will not apply in the instant cases but only in those elections that are directed, or consented to, subsequent to 30 days from the date of this Decision. We impose this brief period of delay to insure that all parties to forthcoming representation elections are fully aware of their rights and obligations as here stated.

6. NLRB v. Waterman Steamship Corporation, 309 U.S. 206, 226; *see also* NLRB v. Shirlington Supermarket, Inc., et al., 224 F.2d 649, 651 (4th Cir.).

premises, is assured of the continuing opportunity to inform the entire electorate of his views with respect to union representation. On the other hand, without a list of employee names and addresses, a labor organization, whose organizers normally have no right of access to plant premises, has no method by which it can be certain of reaching all the employees with its arguments in favor of representation, and, as a result, employees are often completely unaware of that point of view. This is not, of course, to deny the existence of various means by which a party *might* be able to communicate with a substantial portion of the electorate even without possessing their names and addresses. It is rather to say what seems to us obvious—that the access of *all* employees to such communications can be insured only if all parties have the names and addresses of all the voters.[10] . . .

Nor are employee names and addresses readily available from sources other than the employer. . . .

The arguments against imposing a requirement of disclosure are of little force especially when weighed against the benefits resulting therefrom. Initially, we are able to perceive no substantial infringement of employer interests that would flow from such a requirement. A list of employee names and addresses is not like a customer list, and an employer would appear to have no significant interest in keeping the names and addresses of his employees secret (other than a desire to prevent the union from communicating with his employees—an interest we see no reason to protect). Such legitimate interest in secrecy as an employer may have is, in any event, plainly outweighed by the substantial public interest in favor of disclosure where, as here, disclosure is a key factor in insuring a fair and free electorate. . . .

The main arguments that have been presented to us by the Employers and the amici curiae supporting the Employers relate not to any infringement of *employer* rights flowing from a disclosure requirement but rather to an asserted infringement of *employee* rights. Thus, it is argued that if employees wished an organizing union to have their names and addresses they would present the union with that information. By compelling the employer to provide the union with information that the employees have chosen not to divulge, the Board, it is asserted, compels employer interference with the Section 7 rights of employees to refrain from union activities. We regard this argument as without merit. . . .

Similarly, we reject the argument that to provide the union with employee names and addresses subjects employees to the dangers of harassment and coercion in their homes. We cannot assume that a union, seeking to obtain employees' votes in a secret ballot election, will engage in conduct of this nature; it if does, we shall provide an appropriate remedy. We do not, in any event, regard the mere possibility that a union will abuse the opportunity to communicate with employees in their homes as sufficient basis for denying this opportunity altogether. . . .

---

10. A union that does not know the names or addresses of some of the voters may seek to communicate with them by distributing literature on sidewalks or street corners adjoining the employer's premises or by utilizing the mass media of communication. The likelihood that *all* employees will be reached by these methods is, however, problematical at best. See NLRB v. United Aircraft Corp., et al., 324 F.2d 128, 130 (2d Cir.), *cert. denied*, 376 U.S. 951. Personal solicitation on plant premises by employee supporters of the union, while vastly more satisfactory than the above methods, suffers from the limited periods of nonworking time available for solicitation (generally and legally forbidden during working time, Peyton Packing Company, Inc., 49 N.L.R.B. 828, 843) and, in a large plant, the sheer physical problems involved in communicating with fellow employees.

Inasmuch as the rule we have here announced is to be applied prospectively only . . . , we reject [the union's] exceptions to the [election and we] certify the results of the election. . . .

NOTES AND QUESTIONS

1. *Is prospective adjudication legal?* Re-read footnote 5 of the Board's decision. Did the Board adequately explain its decision to impose its new requirement (that employers furnish employee lists) prospectively only? If the Excelsior Underwear election was unfair, why did the Board certify its result? Following *Excelsior*, a debate ensued about the legality of the Board's decision in that case. Some questioned the requirement's substantive validity under the National Labor Relations Act. More critical for our purposes were assertions such as those addressed in the *Wyman-Gordon* case, below, that the *Excelsior* requirement was defective due to the board's failure to produce it through rulemaking. Instead, the board provided notice to, and opportunity for participation by, a variety of concerned amici before reaching its decision in *Excelsior*. The decision announces in plain language a general requirement for all future cases. Indeed, notice that the opinion of the board repeatedly refers to the requirement as a "rule." The importance of the holding is clear. In what significant way would rulemaking, such as that used by the FTC in *Petroleum Refiners, supra,* differ? Is the choice really one between case-by-case determination and comprehensive decisionmaking? Would the agency have done anything different? Or is the dispute over form? Do the opinions in *Wyman-Gordon* clarify what is at stake?

NATIONAL LABOR RELATIONS BOARD v. WYMAN-GORDON CO.
394 U.S. 759 (1969)

MR. JUSTICE FORTAS announced the judgment of the Court and delivered an opinion in which THE CHIEF JUSTICE, MR. JUSTICE STEWART, and MR. JUSTICE WHITE join.

On the petition of the International Brotherhood of Boilermakers and pursuant to its powers under §9 of the National Labor Relations Act, 49 Stat. 453, 29 U.S.C. §159, the National Labor Relations Board ordered an election among the production and maintenance employees of the respondent company. At the election, the employees were to select one of two labor unions as their exclusive bargaining representative, or to choose not to be represented by a union at all. In connection with the election, the Board ordered the respondent to furnish a list of the names and addresses of its employees who could vote in the election, so that the unions could use the list for election purposes. The respondent refused to comply with the order, and the election was held without the list. Both unions were defeated in the election.

The Board upheld the unions' objections to the election because the respondent had not furnished the list, and the Board ordered a new election. The respondent again refused to obey a Board order to supply a list of employees, and the Board issued a subpoena ordering the respondent to provide the list or else produce its personnel and payroll records showing the employees' names and addresses. The Board filed an action in the United States District Court for the District of Massachusetts seeking to have its subpoena enforced or to have a mandatory injunction issued to compel the respondent to comply with its order.

The District Court held the Board's order valid and directed the respondent to comply. 270 F. Supp. 280 (1967). The United States Court of Appeals for the First Circuit reversed. 397 F.2d 394 (1968). The Court of Appeals thought that the order in this case was invalid because it was based on a rule laid down in an earlier decision by the Board, Excelsior Underwear Inc., 156 N.L.R.B. 1236 (1966), and the *Excelsior* rule had not been promulgated in accordance with the requirements that the Administrative Procedure Act prescribes for rule making, 5 U.S.C. §553. We granted certiorari to resolve a conflict among the circuits concerning the validity and effect of the *Excelsior* rule. . . .

I

Section 6 of the National Labor Relations Act empowers the Board "to make . . . , in the manner prescribed by the Administrative Procedure Act, such rules and regulations as may be necessary to carry out the provisions of this Act." 29 U.S.C. §156. The Administrative Procedure Act contains specific provisions governing agency rule making, which it defines as "an agency statement of general or particular applicability and future effect," 5 U.S.C. §551(4).[2] The Act requires, among other things, publication in the Federal Register of notice of proposed rule making and of hearing; opportunity to be heard; a statement in the rule of its basis and purposes; and publication in the Federal Register of the rule as adopted. *See* 5 U.S.C. §553. The Board asks us to hold that it has discretion to promulgate new rules in adjudicatory proceedings, without complying with the requirements of the Administrative Procedure Act.

The rulemaking provisions of that Act, which the Board would avoid, were designed to assure fairness and mature consideration of rules of general application. *See* H.R. Rep. No. 1980, 79th Cong., 2d Sess., 21-26 (1946); S. Rep. No. 752, 79th Cong., 1st Sess., 13-16 (1945). They may not be avoided by the process of making rules in the course of adjudicatory proceedings. There is no warrant in law for the Board to replace the statutory scheme with a rule-making procedure of its own invention. Apart from the fact that the device fashioned by the Board does not comply with statutory command, it obviously falls short of the substance of the requirements of the Administrative Procedure Act. The "rule" created in *Excelsior* was not published in the Federal Register, which is the statutory and accepted means of giving notice of a rule as adopted; only selected organizations were given notice of the "hearing," whereas notice in the Federal Register would have been general in character; under the Administrative Procedure Act, the terms or substance of the rule would have to be stated in the notice of hearing, and all interested parties would have an opportunity to participate in the rule making.

---

2. We agree with the opinion of Chief Judge Aldrich below that the *Excelsior* rule involves matters of substance and that it therefore does not fall within any of the Act's exceptions. *See* 5 U.S.C. §553(b)(A).

The Solicitor General does not deny that the Board ignored the rulemaking provisions of the Administrative Procedure Act.[3] But he appears to argue that *Excelsior*'s command is a valid substantive regulation, binding upon this respondent as such, because the Board promulgated it in the *Excelsior* proceeding, in which the requirements for valid adjudication had been met. This argument misses the point. There is no question that, in an adjudicatory hearing, the Board could validly decide the issue whether the employer must furnish a list of employees to the union. But that is not what the Board did in *Excelsior*. The Board did not even apply the rule it made to the parties in the adjudicatory proceeding, the only entities that could properly be subject to the order in that case. Instead, the Board purported to make a rule: i.e., to exercise its quasi-legislative power.

Adjudicated cases may and do, of course, serve as vehicles for the formulation of agency policies, which are applied and announced therein. *See* H. Friendly, The Federal Administrative Agencies 36-52 (1962). They generally provide a guide to action that the agency may be expected to take in future cases. Subject to the qualified role of stare decisis in the administrative process, they may serve as precedents. But this is far from saying, as the Solicitor General suggests, that commands, decisions, or policies announced in adjudication are "rules" in the sense that they must, without more, be obeyed by the affected public.

In the present case, however, the respondent itself was specifically directed by the Board to submit a list of the names and addresses of its employees for use by the unions in connection with the election.[5] This direction, which was part of the order directing that an election be held, is unquestionably valid. *See, e.g.,* NLRB v. Waterman S.S. Co., 309 U.S. 206, 226 (1940). Even though the direction to furnish the list was followed by citation to "*Excelsior Underwear Inc.,* 156 N.L.R.B. No. 111," it is an order in the present case that the respondent was required to obey. Absent this direction by the Board, the respondent was under no compulsion to furnish the list because no statute and no validly adopted rule required it to do so.

Because the Board in an adjudicatory proceeding directed the respondent itself to furnish the list, the decision of the Court of Appeals for the First Circuit must be reversed.

II

The respondent also argues that it need not obey the Board's order because the requirement of disclosure of employees' names and addresses is substantively invalid. This argument lacks merit. The objections that the respondent

---

3. The Board has never utilized the Act's rule-making procedures. It has been criticized for contravening the Act in this manner. *See, e.g.,* 1 K. Davis, Administrative Law Treatise §6.13 (Supp. 1965); Peck, The Atrophied Rule-Making Powers of the National Labor Relations Board, 70 Yale L.J. 729 (1961).

5. In his Decision and Direction of Election, the Regional Director ordered that "(a)n election eligibility list, containing the names and addresses of all the eligible voters, must be filed with the Regional Director within seven (7) days of the date of this Decision and Direction of Election. The Regional Director shall make the list available to all parties to the election. * * *"

raises to the requirement of disclosure were clearly and correctly answered by the Board in its *Excelsior* decision. . . .

We have held in a number of cases that Congress granted the Board a wide discretion to ensure the fair and free choice of bargaining representatives. *See, e.g.,* NLRB v. Waterman S.S. Co., *supra,* at 226; NLRB v. A. J. Tower Co., 329 U.S. 324, 330 (1946). The disclosure requirement furthers this objective by encouraging an informed employee electorate and by allowing unions the right of access to employees that management already possesses. It is for the Board and not for this Court to weigh against this interest the asserted interest of employees in avoiding the problems that union solicitation may present. . . .

III

[Part III of Justice Fortas's opinion upholds NLRB use of its subpoena power to compel production of the list.]

MR. JUSTICE BLACK, with whom MR. JUSTICE BRENNAN and MR. JUSTICE MARSHALL join, concurring in the result.

I agree with Parts II and III of the prevailing opinion of Mr. Justice Fortas, holding that the *Excelsior* requirement[1] that an employer supply the union with the names and addresses of its employees prior to an election is valid on its merits and can be enforced by a subpoena. But I cannot subscribe to the criticism in that opinion of the procedure followed by the Board in adopting that requirement in the *Excelsior* case, 156 N.L.R.B. 1236 (1966). Nor can I accept the novel theory by which the opinion manages to uphold enforcement of the *Excelsior* practice in spite of what it considers to be statutory violations present in the procedure by which the requirement was adopted. Although the opinion is apparently intended to rebuke the Board and encourage it to follow the plurality's conception of proper administrative practice, the result instead is to free the Board from all judicial control whatsoever regarding compliance with procedures specifically required by applicable federal statutes such as the National Labor Relations Act, 29 U.S.C. §151 *et seq.,* and the Administrative Procedure Act, 5 U.S.C. §551 *et seq.* Apparently, under the prevailing opinion, courts must enforce any requirement announced in a purported "adjudication" even if it clearly was not adopted as an incident to the decision of a case before the agency, and must enforce "rules" adopted in a purported "rule making" even if the agency materially violated the specific requirements that Congress has directed for such proceedings in the Administrative Procedure Act. I for one would not give judicial sanction to any such illegal agency action.

In the present case, however, I am convinced that the *Excelsior* practice was adopted by the Board as a legitimate incident to the adjudication of a specific

---

1. This requirement first announced in the *Excelsior* case, 156 N.L.R.B. 1236 (1966), has often been referred to by the Board, the lower courts, and the commentators as "the *Excelsior* rule." I understand the use of the word "rule" in this context to imply simply that the requirement is a rule of law such as would be announced in a court opinion and not necessarily that it is the kind of "rule" required to be promulgated in accordance with the "rulemaking" procedures of the Administrative Procedure Act. For the sake of clarity, however, I have chosen in this opinion to avoid use of the word "rule" when referring to the procedure required by the *Excelsior* decision.

case before it, and for that reason I would hold that the Board properly followed the procedures applicable to "adjudication" rather than "rule making." Since my reasons for joining in reversal of the Court of Appeals differ so substantially from those set forth in the prevailing opinion, I will spell them out at some length.

Most administrative agencies, like the Labor Board here, are granted two functions by the legislation creating them: (1) the power under certain conditions to make rules having the effect of laws, that is, generally speaking, quasi-legislative power; and (2) the power to hear and adjudicate particular controversies, that is quasi-judicial power. The line between these two functions is not always a clear one and in fact the two functions merge at many points. For example, in exercising its quasi-judicial function an agency must frequently decide controversies on the basis of new doctrines, not theretofore applied to a specific problem, though drawn to be sure from broader principles reflecting the purposes of the statutes involved and from the rules invoked in dealing with related problems. If the agency decision reached under the adjudicatory power becomes a precedent, it guides future conduct in much the same way as though it were a new rule promulgated under the rule-making power, and both an adjudicatory order and a formal "rule" are alike subject to judicial review. Congress gave the Labor Board both of these separate but almost inseparably related powers. No language in the National Labor Relations Act requires that the grant or the exercise of one power was intended to exclude the Board's use of the other.

Nor does any language in the Administrative Procedure Act require such a conclusion.

[A]lthough it is true that the adjudicatory approach frees an administrative agency from the procedural requirements specified for rule making, the Act permits this to be done whenever the action involved can satisfy the definition of "adjudication" and then imposes separate procedural requirements that must be met in adjudication. Under these circumstances, so long as the matter involved can be dealt with in a way satisfying the definition of either "rule making" or "adjudication" under the Administrative Procedure Act, that Act, along with the Labor Relations Act, should be read as conferring upon the Board the authority to decide, within its informed discretion, whether to proceed by rule making or adjudication. Our decision in SEC v. Chenery Corp., 332 U.S. 194 (1947), though it did not involve the Labor Board or the Administrative Procedure Act, is nonetheless equally applicable here. As we explained in that case, "the choice made between proceeding by general rule or by individual, ad hoc litigation is one that lies primarily in the informed discretion of the administrative agency." *Id.*, at 203.

In the present case there is no dispute that all the procedural safeguards required for "adjudication" were fully satisfied in connection with the Board's *Excelsior* decision, and it seems plain to me that that decision did constitute "adjudication" within the meaning of the Administrative Procedure Act, even though the requirement was to be prospectively applied. *See* Great Northern R. Co. v. Sunburst Co., 287 U.S. 358 (1932). The Board did not abstractly decide out of the blue to announce a brand new rule of law to govern labor activities in the future, but rather established the procedure as a direct consequence of the proper exercise of its adjudicatory powers. Sections 9(c)(1) and (2) of the Labor Relations Act empower the Board to conduct investigations, hold hearings, and supervise elections to determine the exclusive bargaining representative that the employees wish to represent them. This is a key provision of the plan Congress adopted to settle labor quarrels that might interrupt the free flow of commerce. A controversy arose between the Excelsior Company and its employees as to the bargaining agent the employees desired to act for them. The Board's power to provide the procedures for the election was invoked, an election was held, and the losing unions sought to have that election set aside. Undoubtedly the Board proceeding for determination of whether to confirm or set aside that election was "agency process for the formulation of an order" and thus was "adjudication" within the meaning of the Administrative Procedure Act.

The prevailing opinion seems to hold that the *Excelsior* requirement cannot be considered the result of adjudication because the Board did not apply it to the parties in the *Excelsior* case itself, but rather announced that it would be applied only to elections called 30 days after the date of the *Excelsior* decision. But the *Excelsior* order was nonetheless an inseparable part of the adjudicatory process. The principal issue before the Board in the *Excelsior* case was whether the election should be set aside on the ground, urged by the unions, that the employer had refused to make the employee lists available to them. *See* 156 N.L.R.B., at 1236-38. The Board decided that the election involved there should not be set aside and thus rejected the contention of the unions. In doing so, the Board chose to explain the reasons for its rejection of their claim, and it is this explanation, the Board's written opinion, which is the source of the *Excelsior* requirement. The Board's opinion should not be regarded as any less an appropriate part of the adjudicatory process merely because the reason it gave for rejecting the unions' position was not that the Board disagreed with them as to the merits of the disclosure procedure but rather, *see* 156 N.L.R.B., at 1239, 1240, n.5, that while fully agreeing that disclosure should be required, the Board did not feel that it should upset the Excelsior Company's justified reliance on previous refusals to compel disclosure by setting aside this particular election.

Apart from the fact that the decisions whether to accept a "new" requirement urged by one party and, if so, whether to apply it retroactively to the other party are inherent parts of the adjudicatory process, I think the opposing theory accepted by the Court of Appeals and by the prevailing opinion today is a highly impractical one. In effect, it would require an agency like the Labor Board to proceed by adjudication only when it could decide, *prior* to adjudicating a particular case, that any new practice to be adopted would be applied retroactively. Obviously, this decision cannot properly be made until all the issues relevant to adoption of the practice are fully considered in connection with the final decision of that case. If the Board were to decide, after careful evaluation of all the arguments presented to it in the adjudicatory proceeding, that it might be fairer to apply the practice only prospectively, it would be faced with the unpleasant choice of either starting all over again to evaluate the merits of the question, this time in a "rule-making" proceeding, or overriding the considerations of fairness and applying its order retroactively anyway, in order to preserve the validity of the new practice and avoid duplication of effort. I see no good reason to impose any such inflexible requirement on the administrative agencies. . . .

MR. JUSTICE DOUGLAS, dissenting. . . .

I am willing to assume that, if the Board decided to treat each case on its special facts and perform its adjudicatory function in the conventional way, we should have no difficulty in affirming its action. The difficulty is that it chose a different course in the *Excelsior* case and, having done so, it should be bound to follow the procedures prescribed in the Act as my Brother Harlan has outlined them. When we hold otherwise, we let the Board "have its cake and eat it too. . . ."

The "substantive" rules described by §553(d) may possibly cover "adjudications," even though they represent performance of the "judicial" function. But it is no answer to say that the order under review was "adjudicatory." For as my Brother Harlan says, an agency is not adjudicating when it is making a rule to fit future cases. A rule like the one in *Excelsior* is designed to fit all cases at all times. It is not particularized to special facts. It is a statement of far-reaching policy covering all future representation elections.

It should therefore have been put down for the public hearing prescribed by the Act.

The rule-making procedure performs important functions. It gives notice to an entire segment of society of those controls or regimentation that is forthcoming. It gives an opportunity for persons affected to be heard. Recently the proposed Rules of the Federal Highway Administration governing the location and design of freeways, 33 Fed. Reg. 15663, were put down for a hearing; and the Governor of every State appeared or sent an emissary. The result was a revision of the Rules before they were promulgated. 34 Fed. Reg. 727.

That is not an uncommon experience. Agencies discover that they are not always repositories of ultimate wisdom; they learn from the suggestions of outsiders and often benefit from that advice. *See* H. Friendly, The Federal Administrative Agencies 45 (1962).

This is a healthy process that helps make a society viable. The multiplication of agencies and their growing power make them more and more remote from the people affected by what they do and make more likely the arbitrary exercise of their powers. Public airing of problems through rule making makes the bureaucracy more responsive to public needs and is an important brake on the growth of absolutism in the regime that now governs all of us. . . .

Rule making is no cure-all; but it does force important issues into full public display and in that sense makes for more responsible administrative action.

I would hold the agencies governed by the rule-making procedure strictly to its requirements and not allow them to play fast and loose as the National Labor Relations Board apparently likes to do. . . .

MR. JUSTICE HARLAN, dissenting.

The language of the Administrative Procedure Act does not support the Government's claim that an agency is "adjudicating" when it announces a rule which it refuses to apply in the dispute before it. The Act makes it clear that an agency "adjudicates" only when its procedures result in the "formulation of an *order.*" 5 U.S.C. §551(7). (Emphasis supplied.) An "order" is defined to include "the whole or a *part* of a final disposition . . . of an agency *in a matter other than rule making.* . . ." 5 U.S.C. §551(6). (Emphasis supplied.) This definition makes it apparent that an agency is not adjudicating when it is making a rule, which the Act defines as "an agency statement of general or particular applicability and *future effect. . . ."* 5 U.S.C. §551(4). (Emphasis supplied.) Since the Labor Board's *Excelsior* rule was to be effective only 30 days after its promulgation, it clearly falls within the rule-making requirements of the Act.

Nor can I agree that the natural interpretation of the statute should be rejected because it requires the agency to choose between giving its rules immediate effect or initiating a separate rule-making proceeding. An agency chooses to apply a rule prospectively only because it represents such a departure from pre-existing understandings that it would be unfair to impose the rule upon the parties in pending matters. But it is precisely in these situations, in which established patterns of conduct are revolutionized, that rule-making procedures perform the vital functions that my Brother Douglas describes so well in a dissenting opinion with which I basically agree.

Given the fact that the Labor Board has promulgated a rule in violation of the governing statute, I believe that there is no alternative but to affirm the judgment of the Court of Appeals in this case. If, as the plurality opinion suggests, the NLRB may properly enforce an invalid rule in subsequent adjudications, the rule-making provisions of the Administrative Procedure Act are completely trivialized. Under today's prevailing approach, the agency may evade the commands of the Act whenever it desires and yet coerce the regulated industry into compliance. . . .

NOTES AND QUESTIONS

1. *The "rule" of* Wyman-Gordon. What legal "rule" or holding, if any, can be derived from *Wyman-Gordon*? Put differently, did a majority of the Justices agree on any legal proposition that would support the validity of the order issued in *Wyman-Gordon*? In light of the distribution of votes, does *Wyman-Gordon* have any precedential value?

2. *The language of the APA.* Does a close reading of the APA help resolve the issue posed in *Wyman-Gordon*? Professor William Mayton argued that the APA, properly understood, indicates a congressional preference for rulemaking as the instrument of administrative policymaking. William T. Mayton, The Legislative Resolution of the Rulemaking-versus-Adjudication Problem in Agency Lawmaking, 1980 Duke L.J. 103. This is arguably the reading given the Act by the Justice Department shortly after its passage:

> [T]he entire Act is based on a dichotomy between rule making and adjudication. . . . Rule making is . . . essentially legislative in nature, not only because it operates in the future but also because it is primarily concerned with policy considerations. The object of the rule making proceedings is the implementation or prescription of law or policy for the future, rather than the evaluation of respondent's past conduct. . . . Conversely, adjudication is concerned with the determination of past and present rights and liabilities.

U.S. Department of Justice, Attorney General's Manual on the Administrative Procedure Act 14-15 (1947).

But the APA could just as easily be understood simply to present alternative models for policy development and to leave the agencies unfettered discretion to choose between them. Is there any textual basis in the APA for choosing between these two readings? Read §§553 and 554 carefully (excerpted in the Appendix, *infra*). Does either section indicate *when* an agency must use rule-making or adjudication? Do the definitions of "rulemaking" and "adjudication" in §551 (excerpted in the Appendix, *infra*) help? Was the NLRB engaged in "rulemaking" in *Excelsior*, as that term is defined in the APA?

3. *Reconciling* Wyman-Gordon *and* Chamber of Commerce. Do the Fourth Circuit's reasons for rejecting the NLRB's notice-posting rule in *Chamber of Commerce*, excerpted in section B, *supra*, support the NLRB's position in *Wyman-Gordon*? Would a notice-and-comment rule requiring employers to provide a list of employees and their contact information run afoul of the NLRB's role as a "reactive" agency? Or may the NLRB be more proactive when supervising elections than when helping employees become informed of their statutory rights?

4. *The* Majestic Weaving *decision.* Another case involving NLRB adjudication, decided contemporaneously with *Excelsior*, presents what seems to be a plainer case for invalidating agency policymaking by order. NLRB v. Majestic Weaving Co., 355 F.2d 854 (2d Cir. 1966), arose on the NLRB's petition to enforce an order finding that Majestic Weaving had committed unfair labor practices and implementing remedies for those violations. One of the asserted violations was the company's negotiating an agreement with a union, with the effectiveness of agreement contingent on the union securing the support of a majority of the relevant company employees. The argument against such conditional negotiation was that it implied recognition of the union as the employees' representative during a period when other unions might be trying to gain their support. Here, the Textile Workers Union, which subsequently began to sign up members among Majestic's work force, claimed that conditional negotiations entered into by Majestic and the Teamsters prematurely favored one of the two unions contesting for representation. The NLRB agreed with the Textile Workers and overruled a decision that had allowed such negotiations for the prior 15 years. Judge Henry Friendly, in a widely known dictum, wrote:

> On our part, we would entertain no difficulty if the Board, after appropriate proceedings, should fashion for prospective application a principle along the general lines of that adopted here; rational basis plainly exists for some such specification of the language of §8(a)(2) even in cases like this where no other union was on the scene when the negotiations occurred. The problem arises from the Board's attempt to achieve its desire by a shorter road and in a more summary fashion. . . . Although courts have not generally balked at allowing administrative agencies to apply a rule newly fashioned in an adjudicative proceeding to past conduct, a decision branding as "unfair" conduct stamped "fair" at the time a party acted, raises judicial hackles considerably more than a determination that merely brings within the agency's jurisdiction an employer previously left without, *see* NLRB v. Pease Oil Co., 279 F.2d 135, 137-39 (2d Cir. 1960), or shortens the period in which a collective bargaining agreement may bar a new election, *see* Leedom v. International Bhd. of Elec. Workers, 278 F.2d 237, 243 (1960), or imposes a more severe remedy for conduct already prohibited, *see* NLRB v. A.P.W. Prods. Co., [316 F.2d 899 (2d Cir. 1963)]. And the hackles bristle still more when a financial penalty is assessed for action that might well have been avoided if the agency's changed disposition had been earlier made known, or might even have been taken in express reliance on the standard previously established. . . .

It must be recognized that "every case of first impression has a retroactive effect, whether the new principle is announced by a court or by an administrative agency," and that, generally speaking, "the choice made between proceeding by general rule or by individual, ad hoc litigation is one that lies primarily in the informed discretion of the administrative agency," SEC v. Chenery Corp., 332 U.S. [194, 203 (1947)]. But the problem of retroactive application has a somewhat different aspect in cases not of first but of second impression, where an agency alters an established rule defining permissible conduct which has been generally recognized and relied on throughout the industry that it regulates. As a result of the nature of the task Congress has confided to the agencies and the vagueness of the directions it has given, they are, and ought to be, much likelier to engage both in new departures and in alterations than courts with their more limited "molecular motions," Southern Pac. Co. v. Jensen, 244 U.S. 205 (1917) (dissenting opinion of Mr. Justice Holmes); and this makes it peculiarly important for them to take full advantage of their power to act prospectively, whether by rule-making or adjudication. In this case, we might well conclude that where for fifteen years the Board considered conditional negotiation consistent with the statutory design "the ill effect of the retroactive application of a new standard" so far outweighs any demonstrated need for immediate application to past conduct, SEC v. Chenery Corp., *supra*, 332 U.S. at 203, as to render the action "arbitrary." APA §10(e), 5 U.S.C. §1009(e). . . .

Id. at 859-861. Having made its views on this subject clear, the court rested its denial of enforcement on other grounds. *See also* Bowen v. Georgetown University Hospital, 488 U.S. 204 (1988), in which the Court ruled that the Secretary of Health and Human Services lacked the power to make retroactive rules under a statute regulating Medicare reimbursements and noted that because retroactivity is disfavored in law, there is a rebuttable legal presumption against construing statutes to grant the power to make rules with retroactive effect. Thus, retroactive effects are disfavored in rulemaking as well as in adjudication.

The lack of consensus on the *Wyman-Gordon* Court about why the NLRB was free to make policy via adjudication left the scope of its authority to do so uncertain. The NLRB continued to make major policy decisions in the course of adjudicating individual labor disputes, and five years after *Wyman-Gordon,* the issue reached the Court once again.

NATIONAL LABOR RELATIONS BOARD v. BELL AEROSPACE CO., 416 U.S. 267 (1974):   The NLRB had long interpreted the National Labor Relations Act to exclude "managerial employees" from the Act's coverage. In the early 1970s, the Board reversed itself and held that managerial employees are covered by the Act unless their "participation in a labor organization would create a conflict of interest with their job responsibilities." Under this new understanding of the Act's coverage, the Board determined that buyers working for Bell Aerospace were entitled to the protections of the Act, including the right to organize and engage in collective bargaining. Bell Aerospace petitioned for review of a Board order compelling it to bargain with the union representing the buyers. Bell argued that the NLRB's decision extending the Act's coverage to managerial employees was erroneous and that, even if the Act could be construed to cover the buyers, in light of prior Board decisions excluding buyers from the Act's coverage, the Board should have engaged in rulemaking.

After concluding that the Board applied the incorrect substantive legal standard, the Court addressed whether the Board must engage in rulemaking if it decides, applying the correct legal rule, that the buyers should be covered by the Act:

> [T]he present question is whether on remand the Board must invoke its rulemaking procedures if it determines, in light of our opinion, that these buyers are not "managerial employees" under the Act. The Court of Appeals thought that rulemaking was required because *any* Board finding that the company's buyers are not "managerial" would be contrary to its prior decisions and would presumably be in the nature of a general rule designed "to fit all cases at all times."
>
> The views expressed in *Chenery II* and *Wyman-Gordon* make plain that the Board is not precluded from announcing new principles in an adjudicative proceeding and that the choice between rulemaking and adjudication lies in the first instance within the Board's discretion. Although there may be situations where the Board's reliance on adjudication would amount to an abuse of discretion or a violation of the Act, nothing in the present case would justify such a conclusion. Indeed, there is ample indication that adjudication is especially appropriate in the instant context. As the Court of Appeals noted, "[t]here must be tens of thousands of manufacturing, wholesale and retail units which employ buyers, and hundreds of thousands of the latter." 475 F.2d, at 496. Moreover, duties of buyers vary widely depending on the company or industry. It is doubtful whether any generalized standard could be framed which would have more than marginal utility. The Board thus has reason to proceed with caution, developing its standards in a case-by-case manner with attention to the specific character of the buyers' authority and duties in each company. The Board's judgment that adjudication best serves this purpose is entitled to great weight.
>
> The possible reliance of industry on the Board's past decisions with respect to buyers does not require a different result. It has not been shown that the adverse consequences ensuing from such reliance are so substantial that the Board should be precluded from reconsidering the issue in an adjudicative proceeding. Furthermore, this is not a case in which some new liability is sought to be imposed on individuals for past actions which were taken in good-faith reliance on Board pronouncements. Nor are fines or damages involved here. In any event, concern about such consequences is largely speculative, for the Board has not yet finally determined whether these buyers are "managerial."
>
> It is true, of course, that rulemaking would provide the Board with a forum for soliciting the informed views of those affected in industry and labor before embarking on a new course. But surely the Board has discretion to decide that the adjudicative procedures in this case may also produce the relevant information necessary to mature and fair consideration of the issues. Those most immediately affected, the buyers and the company in the particular case, are accorded a full opportunity to be heard before the Board makes its determination.
>
> The judgment of the Court of Appeals is therefore affirmed in part and reversed in part, and the cause remanded to that court with directions to remand to the Board for further proceedings in conformity with this opinion. It is so ordered.

NOTES AND QUESTIONS

1. *What process must agencies employ?* How does *Bell Aerospace* alter the advice you would give agency policymakers on the process to be used in promulgating

policy decisions? How does the context of the case compare with the setting of the other NLRB cases? In *Bell Aerospace,* as in *Wyman-Gordon,* the NLRB relied on a prior adjudicative decision that dictated new agency policy. Moreover, as in *Majestic Weaving,* the new policy was inconsistent with a long-established prior policy. Like the board's decision in *Majestic Weaving* and unlike its *Excelsior* decision, the NLRB applied the new policy in the case in which it was first announced.

2. *Restrictions on agency discretion?* Are there circumstances in which agencies should not have the discretion to choose between rulemaking and adjudication for policy formation? In Ford Motor Co. v. FTC, 673 F.2d 1008 (9th Cir. 1981), *cert. denied,* 459 U.S. 999 (1982), the court of appeals reversed an adjudicatory decision finding a company to have engaged in unfair trade practices. The agency decision was based in part on its interpretation of a section of the Uniform Commercial Code, the (relatively) uniform state law covering a wide range of commercial transactions. The court declared that the decision had to be promulgated by rulemaking rather than adjudication. Two points supported this determination: (1) the unfair trade practice finding would have general application, given the nationwide coverage of the UCC; and (2) the parties to this proceeding had no warning that their acts were improper. While the FTC had not previously approved their conduct, there was no agency or judicial decision disapproving the practices. Is the agency decision here different from that in *Bell Aerospace? Excelsior? Chenery II?*

D.   AGENCY DISCRETION TO MAKE POLICY BY MANUAL OR INFORMAL GUIDANCE

Despite efforts by academics and judges to confine agencies' substantive policymaking to rules issued in accordance with the relevant APA procedures, agencies plainly make policy via many other instruments. Formal adjudication is the most visible and, not coincidentally, the most discussed alternative means of making policy, but agencies also rely on less formal mechanisms, including internal guidelines and staff manuals, and even the forms used within agencies and by those with whom they deal. In the modern era, perhaps agencies will use texts or tweets to announce policy.

In part, the use of less visible means of policy formation may be a deliberate response to the burdens of making decisions via rulemaking and formal adjudication, which can be costly, time consuming, and difficult to reverse as circumstances change. Less visible policy guides can be produced relatively quickly, and changed more readily, than a comprehensive rule, thus infusing what may be a salutary flexibility into the policymaking process. In large part, however, agency decisionmaking through lower-profile policy instruments, such as manuals and guidelines, may be the inevitable by-product of the fact that, in large bureaucracies, responsibility for many "agency actions" is diffuse and subject to interpretation by numerous, and often fairly low-level, officials. One result of this diffusion is that decisions likely will be less consistent than if they were made by fewer officials and subject to more public procedures. A Supreme

Court decision announced just two months before *Bell Aerospace* illustrates the problems presented by such inconsistency.

MORTON v. RUIZ
415 U.S. 199 (1974)

Mr. Justice Blackmun delivered the opinion of the Court.

This case presents a narrow but important issue in the administration of the federal general assistance program for needy Indians:

> Are general assistance benefits available only to those Indians living *on* reservations in the United States (or in areas regulated by the Bureau of Indian Affairs in Alaska and Oklahoma), and are they thus unavailable to Indians (outside Alaska and Oklahoma) living *off*, although near, a reservation . . . ?

The respondents, Ramon Ruiz and his wife, Anita, are Papago Indians and United States citizens. In 1940 they left the Papago Reservation in Arizona to seek employment 15 miles away at the Phelps-Dodge copper mines at Ajo. Mr. Ruiz found work there, and they settled in a community at Ajo called the "Indian Village" and populated almost entirely by Papagos.[2] Practically all the land and most of the homes in the Village are owned or rented by Phelps-Dodge. The Ruizes have lived in Ajo continuously since 1940 and have been in their present residence since 1947. A minor daughter lives with them. They speak and understand the Papago language but only limited English. Apart from Mr. Ruiz' employment with Phelps-Dodge, they have not been assimilated into the dominant culture, and they appear to have maintained a close tie with the nearby reservation.

In July 1967, 27 years after the Ruizes moved to Ajo, the mine where he worked was shut down by a strike. It remained closed until the following March. While the strike was in progress, Mr. Ruiz' sole income was a $15 per week striker's benefit paid by the union. He sought welfare assistance from the State of Arizona but this was denied because of the State's apparent policy that striking workers are not eligible for general assistance or emergency relief.

On December 11, 1967, Mr. Ruiz applied for general assistance benefits from the Bureau of Indian Affairs (BIA). He was immediately notified by letter that he was ineligible for general assistance because of the provision (in effect since 1952) in 66 Indian Affairs Manual 3.1.4 (1965) that eligibility is limited to Indians living "on reservations" and in jurisdictions under the BIA in Alaska and Oklahoma.[6]

---

2. Ajo is located within the borders of the Papago aboriginal tribal land. The Indian Claims Commission has found that this land was taken from the Papagos by the United States. . . .

6. The Manual provides in pertinent part:

3.1 *General Assistance.*

.1 *Purpose.* The purpose of the general assistance program is to provide necessary financial assistance to needy Indian families and persons living on reservations under the jurisdiction of this Bureau and in jurisdictions under the Bureau of Indian Affairs in Alaska and Oklahoma. . . .

.4 *Eligibility Conditions.*

A. *Residence.* Eligibility for general assistance is limited to Indians living on reservations and in jurisdictions under the Bureau of Indian Affairs in Alaska and Oklahoma.

An appeal to the Superintendent of the Papago Indian Agency was unsuccessful. A further appeal to the Phoenix Area Director of the BIA led to a hearing, but this, too, proved unsuccessful. The sole ground for the denial of general assistance benefits was that the Ruizes resided outside the boundaries of the Papago Reservation.

The respondents then instituted the present purported class action against the Secretary, claiming, as a matter of statutory interpretation, entitlement to the general assistance for which they had applied. . . .

The Court of Appeals' reversal of the District Court's summary judgment for the Secretary was on the ground that the Manual's residency limitation was inconsistent with the broad language of the Snyder Act, 25 U.S.C. §13, "that Congress intended general assistance benefits to be available to all Indians, including those in the position" of the Ruizes, 462 F.2d [818, 821 (9th Cir. 1972)], and that subsequent actions of Congress in appropriating funds for the BIA general assistance program did not serve to ratify the imposed limitation. The dissent took the position that the Secretary's policy was within the broad discretionary authority delegated to the Secretary by Congress with respect to the allocation of limited funds.

II

. . . It is to be noted that neither the language of the Snyder Act nor that of the Appropriations Act imposes any geographical limitation on the availability of general assistance benefits and does not prescribe eligibility requirements or the details of any program. . . .

The general assistance program is designed by the BIA to provide direct financial aid to needy Indians where other channels of relief, federal, state, and tribal, are not available. Benefits generally are paid on a scale equivalent to the State's welfare payments. Any Indian, whether living on a reservation or elsewhere, may be eligible for benefits under the various social security programs in which his State participates and no limitation may be placed on social security benefits because of an Indian claimant's residence on a reservation.

In the formal budget request submitted to Congress by the BIA for fiscal 1968, the program was described as follows: "General assistance will be provided to needy Indians on reservations who are not eligible for public assistance under the Social Security Act . . . and for whom such assistance is not available from established welfare agencies or through tribal resources. . . ."

III

We are confronted, therefore, with the [issue] whether the geographical limitation placed on general assistance eligibility by the BIA is consistent with congressional intent and the meaning of the applicable statutes, or, to phrase it somewhat differently, whether the congressional appropriations are properly limited by the BIA's restrictions.

[T]he Secretary argues, first, that the Snyder Act is merely an enabling act with no definition of the scope of the general assistance program, that the Appropriations Act did not provide for off-reservation Indian welfare (other than in Oklahoma and Alaska), and that Congress did not intend to expand the program beyond that presented to it by the BIA request. Secondly, he points to the "on reservations" limitation in the Manual and suggests that Congress was well acquainted with that limitation, and that, by legislating in the light of the Manual's limiting provision, its appropriation amounted to a ratification of the BIA's definitive practice. He notes that, in recent years, Congress has twice rejected proposals that clearly would have provided off-reservation general assistance for Indians. Thus, it is said, Congress has appropriated no funds for general assistance for off-reservation Indians and, as a practical matter, the Secretary is unable to provide such a program. . . .

We need not approach the issue in terms of whether Congress intended for *all* Indians, regardless of residence and of the degree of assimilation, to be covered by the general assistance program. We need only ascertain the intent of Congress with respect to those Indian claimants in the case before us. The question, so limited, is whether Congress intended to exclude from the general assistance program these respondents and their class, who are full-blooded, unassimilated Indians living in an Indian community near their native reservation, and who maintain close economic and social ties with that reservation. Except for formal residence outside the physical boundaries of the Papago Reservation, the respondents, as has been conceded, meet all other requirements for the general assistance program.

IV

There is, of course, some force in the Secretary's argument and in the facts that the BIA's budget requests consistently contained "on reservations" general assistance language and that there was testimony before successive appropriations subcommittees to the effect that assistance of this kind was customarily so restricted. Nonetheless, our examination of this and other material leads us to a conclusion contrary to that urged by the Secretary.

A. In actual practice, general assistance clearly has not been limited to reservation Indians. Indeed, the Manual's provision, *see* n.6, *supra*, so heavily relied upon by the Secretary, itself provides that general assistance is available to non-reservation Indians in Alaska and Oklahoma. . . .

B. There was testimony in several of the hearings that the BIA, in fact, was not limiting general assistance to those within reservation boundaries and, on more than one occasion, Congress was notified that exceptions were being made where they were deemed appropriate. Notwithstanding the Manual, at least three categories of off-reservation Indians outside Alaska and Oklahoma have been treated as eligible for general assistance. . . .

In addition, although not controlling, it is not irrelevant that the "on reservations" limitation in the budget requests has never appeared in the final appropriation bills.

C. Even more important is the fact that, for many years, to and including the appropriation year at issue, the BIA itself made continual representations to the appropriations subcommittees that nonurban Indians living "near" a reservation were eligible for BIA services. Although, to be sure, several passages in the legislative history and the formal budget requests have defined eligibility in terms of Indians living "on reservations," the BIA, not infrequently, has indicated that living "on or near" a reservation equates with living "on" it. . . .

V

A. Having found that the congressional appropriation was intended to cover welfare services at least to those Indians residing "on or near" the reservation, it does not necessarily follow that the Secretary is without power to create reasonable classifications and eligibility requirements in order to allocate the limited funds available to him for this purpose. *See* Dandridge v. Williams, 397 U.S. 471 (1970); Jefferson v. Hackney, 406 U.S. 535 (1972). Thus, if there were only enough funds appropriated to provide meaningfully for 10,000 needy Indian beneficiaries and the entire class of eligible beneficiaries numbered 20,000, it would be incumbent upon the BIA to develop an eligibility standard to deal with this problem, and the standard, if rational and proper, might leave some of the class otherwise encompassed by the appropriation without benefits. But in such a case the agency must, at a minimum, let the standard be generally known so as to assure that it is being applied consistently and so as to avoid both the reality and the appearance of arbitrary denial of benefits to potential beneficiaries.

Assuming, arguendo, that the Secretary rationally could limit the "on or near" appropriation to include only the smaller class of Indians who lived directly "on" the reservation plus those in Alaska and Oklahoma, the question that remains is whether this has been validly accomplished. The power of an administrative agency to administer a congressionally created and funded program necessarily requires the formulation of policy and the making of rules to fill any gap left, implicitly or explicitly, by Congress. In the area of Indian affairs, the Executive has long been empowered to promulgate rules and policies, and the power has been given explicitly to the Secretary and his delegates at the BIA. This agency power to make rules that affect substantial individual rights and obligations carries with it the responsibility not only to remain consistent with the governing legislation . . . but also to employ procedures that conform to the law. *See* NLRB v. Wyman-Gordon Co., 394 U.S. 759, 764 (1969) (plurality opinion). No matter how rational or consistent with congressional intent a particular decision might be, the determination of eligibility cannot be made on an ad hoc basis by the dispenser of the funds.

The Administrative Procedure Act was adopted to provide, inter alia, that administrative policies affecting individual rights and obligations be promulgated pursuant to certain stated procedures so as to avoid the inherently arbitrary nature of unpublished ad hoc determinations. [The Court here quotes from APA §552(a)(1)(D).] The sanction added in 1967 by Pub. L. 90-23, 81 Stat. 54, provides: "Except to the extent that a person has actual and timely notice of the terms thereof, a person may not in any manner be required to resort to, or be adversely affected by, a matter required to be published in the Federal Register and not so published." *Ibid.*

Unlike numerous other programs authorized by the Snyder Act and funded by the annual appropriations, the BIA has chosen not to publish its eligibility requirements for general assistance in the Federal Register or in the CFR. This continues to the present time. The only official manifestation of this alleged policy of restricting general assistance to those directly on the reservations is the material in the Manual which is, by BIA's own admission, solely an internal-operations brochure intended to cover policies that "do not relate to the public." Indeed, at oral argument the Government conceded that for this to be a "real legislative rule," itself endowed with the force of law, it should be published in the Federal Register. Tr. of Oral Arg. 20.

Where the rights of individuals are affected, it is incumbent upon agencies to follow their own procedures. This is so even where the internal procedures are possibly more rigorous than otherwise would be required. Service v. Dulles, 354 U.S. 363, 388 (1957); Vitarelli v. Seaton, 359 U.S. 535, 539-540 (1959). The BIA, by its Manual, has declared that all directives that "inform the public of privileges and benefits available" and of "eligibility requirements" are among those to be published. The requirement that, in order to receive general assistance, an Indian must reside directly "on" a reservation is clearly an important substantive policy that fits within this class of directives. Before the BIA may extinguish the entitlement of these otherwise eligible beneficiaries, it must comply, at a minimum, with its own internal procedures.

The Secretary has presented no reason why the requirements of the Administrative Procedure Act could not or should not have been met. *Cf.* SEC v. Chenery Corp., 332 U.S. 194, 202 (1947). The BIA itself has not attempted to defend its rule as a valid exercise of its "legislative power," but rather depends on the argument that Congress itself has not appropriated funds for Indians not directly on the reservations. The conscious choice of the Secretary not to treat this extremely significant eligibility requirement, affecting rights of needy Indians, as a legislative-type rule, renders it ineffective so far as extinguishing rights of those otherwise within the class of beneficiaries contemplated by Congress is concerned.

The overriding duty of our Federal Government to deal fairly with Indians wherever located has been recognized by this Court on many occasions. . . . Particularly here, where the BIA has continually represented to Congress, when seeking funds, that Indians living near reservations are within the service area, it is essential that the legitimate expectation of these needy Indians not be extinguished by what amounts to an unpublished ad hoc determination of the agency that was not promulgated in accordance with its own procedures, to say nothing of those of the Administrative Procedure Act. . . . Before benefits may be denied to these otherwise entitled Indians, the BIA must first promulgate eligibility requirements according to established procedures.

B. Even assuming the lack of binding effect of the BIA policy, the Secretary argues that the residential restriction in the Manual is a longstanding interpretation of the Snyder Act by the agency best suited to do this, and that deference is due its interpretation. . . . The thrust of this argument is not that the regulation itself has created the "on" and "near" distinction, but that Congress has intended to provide general assistance only to those directly on reservations, and that the Manual's provision is simply an interpretation of congressional intent. As we have already noted, however, the BIA, through its own practices and representations, has led Congress to believe that these appropriations covered Indians "on or near" the reservations, and it is too late now to argue that the words "on reservations" in the Manual mean something different from "on or near" when, in fact, the two have been continuously equated by the BIA to Congress. . . .

The judgment of the Court of Appeals is affirmed and the case is remanded for further proceedings consistent with this opinion. It is so ordered.

NOTES AND QUESTIONS

1. *Legal basis of the decision.* What does the Court say the BIA did wrong? *Ruiz* does not hold the BIA policy substantively invalid, but instead indicates that the Secretary and the Bureau failed to use a policymaking process appropriate to create such a rule. Can *Ruiz* be reconciled with *Bell Aerospace?* *Bell Aerospace* involved a change of policy arrived at—or at least announced—with the aid of formal procedures, albeit not rulemaking. *Ruiz* involved no such formal procedures: There was no outside participation in drafting the manual. Does this distinction explain the different outcomes? If so, does *Ruiz* mean that agencies may never make policy by informal means? That agency policies made through informal processes may not be binding? Or that they may be binding only after some other process?

2. *Fairness?* Can the concerns expressed by the *Ruiz* Court be read as going beyond formalities to the fairness to the parties affected? In other words, do *Bell Aerospace* and *Ruiz* taken together suggest that the Court will approve policy formulation other than by rulemaking, but only so long as the new policy is not applied to any "unsuspecting" party? If *Ruiz* and *Bell Aerospace* are harmonized in this manner, how can *Wyman-Gordon* survive? Must the Court in effect choose any two of these three decisions?

The APA does require, in §552(a)(2)(C), that administrative staff manuals and other instructions to administrators that affect members of the public be published and that an agency may not rely on unpublished materials to affect adversely members of the public. In Smith v. National Transp. Safety Bd., 981 F.2d 1326 (D.C. Cir. 1993), the court relied on these APA provisions to invalidate the suspension of a commercial pilot's license because the agency relied on an unpublished FAA bulletin. Is this how *Ruiz* should be understood and applied?

The implications of *Ruiz* are explored in Lincoln v. Vigil, excerpted in Chapter V, *infra*. What reading of *Ruiz* did *Lincoln* adopt?

3. *Policymaking via guidance documents, interpretative rules, and policy statements.* Many agencies rely heavily on informal guidance documents, interpretative rules, or general policy statements to elaborate agency policy that is otherwise prescribed via notice-and-comment rulemaking. These documents are widely used and often voluminous. *See* Nina A. Mendelson, Guidance Documents and Regulatory Beneficiaries, Admin. & Reg. L. News, Summer 2006, at 8 (noting that EPA and OSHA issued over 2,000 and 1,600 guidance documents respectively in a three-year period and that these documents "range from routine matters to broad policies on program standards, implementation and enforcement"). APA §553(b)(3)(A) exempts "interpretative rules" and "general statements of

policy" from the procedural requirements governing rulemaking (*see* discussion *infra*), and does not mention guidance documents at all. Do agencies have discretion to use these policy formats whenever they wish, even when they effectively impose substantial burdens on regulated parties?

The volume of such documents can dwarf the number of an agency's promulgated rules. Although guidance documents are not binding on the public, their use to shape behavior has often triggered skeptical scrutiny by the courts. For example, in Appalachian Power Co. v. EPA, 208 F.3d 1015 (D.C. Cir. 2000), the D.C. Circuit overturned a "guidance document" issued by the EPA that purported to explain how certain regulations governing permits under the Clean Air Act should be enforced. The D.C. Circuit held that the guidance document "significantly broadened" the underlying regulations and thus was invalid because it was promulgated without notice and comment. The court offered the following observations concerning agencies' use of the type of document at issue in the case:

> The phenomenon we see in this case is familiar. Congress passes a broadly worded statute. The agency follows with regulations containing broad language, open-ended phrases, ambiguous standards and the like. Then as years pass, the agency issues circulars or guidance or memoranda, explaining, interpreting, defining and often expanding the commands in the regulations. One guidance document may yield another and then another and so on. Several words in a regulation may spawn hundreds of pages of text as the agency offers more and more detail regarding what its regulations demand of regulated entities. Law is made, without notice and comment, without public participation, and without publication in the Federal Register or the Code of Federal Regulations. With the advent of the Internet, the agency does not need these official publications to ensure widespread circulation; it can inform those affected simply by posting its new guidance or memoranda or policy statement on its web site. An agency operating in this way gains a large advantage. "It can issue or amend its real rules, i.e., its interpretative rules and policy statements, quickly and inexpensively without following any statutorily prescribed procedures." Richard J. Pierce, Jr., Seven Ways to Deossify Agency Rulemaking, 47 Admin. L. Rev. 59, 85 (1995). The agency may also think there is another advantage — immunizing its lawmaking from judicial review.

Id. at 1020. The court went on to describe how the guidance document was used during the process of negotiating permits to strong-arm states into including requirements contained in the guidance document but not in the applicable regulations. There is a widespread perception that agencies are overusing their discretion to issue guidance documents and policy statements. The preamble to a 2017 recommendation issued by the Administrative Conference of the United States observed that "members of the public may feel bound by what they perceive as coercive guidance." *See* ACUS Recommendation 2017-5, Agency Guidance Through Policy Statements, Adopted December 14, 2017. The issue was also the subject of a 2018 House Oversight Committee staff report, Shining Light on Dark Regulatory Matter, *available at* https://permanent.fdlp.gov/gpo110748/Guidance-Report-for-Issuance1.pdf. Why do you think agencies behave this way, rather than promulgating more of their requirements through notice-and-comment rulemaking? Might limiting the practice have costs in terms of reducing information about an agency's views on important matters of public policy, such as enforcement priorities, not covered in formally promulgated rules? Isn't there a benefit to hearing from an agency on an informal basis concerning how it is likely to approach or enforce a regulatory requirement, rather than waiting for an enforcement action to find out?

4. *Guidance, interpretation, and deference.* Look back to the clarification of the *Auer* doctrine in Kisor v. Wilkie in Chapter II, *supra.* Do the changes to the *Auer* doctrine in the majority opinion signal support for some change in the degree to which the Supreme Court might view reliance on guidance documents to support future agency actions? On the interplay of concerns respecting judicial deference and choice of process for policy formation, see Aaron Nielson, Beyond *Seminole Rock*, 105 Geo. L.J. 943 (2017).

5. *Even less formal policymaking.* Perhaps the least formal method of agency policymaking (and implementation) is what has sometimes been called "jawboning." Regulators use their influence over regulated parties to nudge their behavior in a certain direction without taking any step toward formal policymaking. Policy is arrived at informally and implemented informally, for example by urging a regulated party to voluntarily adopt a code of good conduct in line with the views of regulators. Jawboning's effectiveness often depends on an implicit threat, which may lie in a regulated party's need for continuing agency cooperation. That may be why the most well-known example of jawboning occurred in the area of broadcast licensing, where the Federal Communications Commission used its authority as a licensing agency to influence television licensees to agree to a family friendly hour of prime-time programming. *See* Writers Guild of America, West, Inc. v. American Broadcasting Cos., 609 F.2d 355 (9th Cir. 1980), excerpted in Chapter VIII, *infra.*

NOTE ON AGENCIES' OBLIGATION TO FOLLOW THEIR OWN PROCEDURAL RULES

The *Ruiz* Court noted that the BIA's action violated the requirement in its own manual that statements affecting eligibility be published. Must agencies follow internal procedural guidelines? Is this an independent ground for the *Ruiz* Court's decision? Should it be?

In an early case, a narrow majority of the Supreme Court appeared to adopt a rule requiring agencies to follow their own procedural rules, at least those that had been formally adopted as regulations after §553 notice-and-comment rulemaking. In United States ex rel. Accardi v. Shaughnessy, 347 U.S. 260 (1954), Accardi filed for habeas corpus after the Board of Immigration Appeals denied his appeal from the denial of his application for discretionary relief from deportation. He alleged that the Attorney General had, in effect, ordered the board to deny his appeal before the board heard his case, an alleged violation of regulations that the majority characterized as requiring the board "to exercise its own judgment when considering appeals." Five members of the Court agreed and ordered the board to reconsider Accardi's appeal free of the taint created by the Attorney General's input. The dissent argued that the majority's decision was inconsistent with the fact that the board operated under authority delegated by the Attorney General and that the Attorney General had full power to overrule the board's decision. In Steenholdt v. FAA, 314 F.3d 633, 639 (D.C. Cir. 2003), in the course of holding that the Federal Aviation Administration's failure to follow its own "gratuitous" procedural rules was harmless error in that particular case, the court stated flatly:

> The *Accardi* doctrine requires federal agencies to follow their own rules, even gratuitous procedural rules that limit otherwise discretionary actions. "Courts, of course, have long required agencies to abide by internal, procedural regulations . . . even when those regulations provide more protection than the Constitution or relevant civil service laws." Doe v. United States Dep't of Justice, 753 F.2d 1092, 1098 (D.C. Cir. 1985) (referring to employment regulations).

See also United States v. Caceres, 440 U.S. 741 (1979) (evidence obtained by IRS in violation of its formally adopted regulation may be admitted at criminal trial of taxpayer). For a critique of the *Accardi* principle as "poorly theorized," *see* Thomas W. Merrill, The *Accardi* Principle, 74 Geo. Wash. L. Rev. 569 (2006), arguing that the Supreme Court has never explained the source of the agency's duty.

One unresolved issue regarding the application of the principle that agencies must adhere to their own regulatory requirements is whether prejudice must be shown for a petitioner to obtain judicial relief. In Leslie v. Attorney General, 611 F.3d 171 (3d Cir. 2012), the court reversed a Board of Immigration Appeals removal order on the ground that the immigration judge failed to advise the immigrant that he was entitled to free legal services, as required by the board's own regulations. The court held that while violations of regulations that do not protect fundamental rights may require a showing of prejudice for the violation to constitute reversible error, "when an agency promulgates a regulation protecting fundamental statutory or constitutional rights of parties appearing before it, the agency must comply with that regulation. Failure to comply will merit invalidation of the challenged agency action without regard to whether the alleged violation has substantially prejudiced the complaining party." *Id.* at 180. The Second Circuit held the same in Picca v. Mukasey, 512 F.3d 75 (2008). In Schaefer v. McHugh, 608 F.3d 851 (D.C. Cir. 2010), an army lawyer, who had been mistakenly granted a discharge request merely for having "bad knees" and was then ordered to return to service, claimed that the army did not follow its own procedures because the wrong entity revoked the discharge. In this case, the court held for the army, stating: "A party claiming harm from an agency's failure to follow its own rules must demonstrate some form of prejudice." *Id.* at 854.

Must agencies also follow their own informally adopted policies? In Oglala Sioux Tribe v. Andrus, 603 F.2d 707 (8th Cir. 1979), the court invalidated a BIA decision re-assigning an "Indian officer" responsible for dealing with the Oglala Sioux tribe, on the ground that the BIA failed to follow its own internal guidelines that suggested tribes "should be consulted on recommendations for selection of employees" to such positions. Not only did the consultation policy create a "justified expectation" on the part of the Indian people, but the agency's failure to comply violated "the distinctive obligation of trust incumbent on the Government in its dealings with these dependent and sometimes exploited people." *Id.* at 721. The D.C. Circuit reached a similar conclusion in a setting not involving a fiduciary relationship, holding that a Justice Department bureau had failed to follow procedures specified in the DOJ manual requiring consultation with an independent agency prior to making final determinations regarding grant programs, and that the unilateral decision of the Administrator was also contrary to the spirit of various memoranda and announcements concerning the program. Massachusetts Fair Share v. Law Enforcement Assistance Administration, 758 F.2d 708 (D.C. Cir. 1985).

Another line of cases casts doubt on whether—or at least when—agencies must follow their informally adopted rules. In Schweiker v. Hansen, 450 U.S. 785 (1981), the Court refused to order the Social Security Administration to give retroactive benefits to an eligible applicant who had been given bad advice by an SSA field representative. The SSA claims manual instructed field representatives to advise applicants who were uncertain about their eligibility to file written applications. When Hansen first contacted her local SSA office to inquire about her eligibility, Connelly, a field representative, erroneously told her that she was ineligible and failed to advise her to file a written application. Eleven months later, after learning that she was (and had been) eligible, Hansen filed an application and began obtaining benefits. Her request that SSA pay her benefits retroactive to the time when she first inquired was denied, however, on the basis of a statutory provision restricting benefits to one who "has filed application." Hansen brought suit, claiming that SSA should be estopped by Connelly's conduct from denying her claim. The Supreme Court rejected her claim, arguing that Connelly's conduct was not sufficiently egregious to "justify the abnegation" of the courts' duty " 'to observe the conditions defined by Congress for charging the public treasury' " (quoting Federal Crop Ins. Corp. v. Merrill, 332 U.S. 380, 385 (1947)). The Court conceded that Connelly had violated an agency policy:

> But the Claims Manual is not a regulation. It has no legal force, and it does not bind the SSA. Rather, it is a 13-volume handbook for internal use by thousands of SSA employees, including the hundreds of employees who receive untold numbers of oral inquiries like respondent's each year. If Connelly's minor breach of such a manual suffices to estop petitioner, then the Government is put "at risk that every alleged failure by an agent to follow instructions to the last detail in one of a thousand cases will deprive it of the benefit of the written application requirement which experience has taught to be essential to the honest and effective administration of the Social Security Laws." [Hansen v. Harris,] 619 F.2d 942, 956 (Friendly, J., dissenting).

450 U.S. at 789-790. Is Hansen distinguishable from Ruiz, Oglala Sioux Tribe, and Fair Share? See also American Farm Lines v. Black Ball Freight Serv., 397 U.S. 532, 539 (1970) (holding that the agency may "relax or modify" its own procedural rules if "the ends of justice" require it and the complainant is not substantially prejudiced). The Court in American Farm Lines also found it relevant that the procedures at issue were not adopted with the intent to benefit the public but rather were designed to aid the agency.

Despite Hansen, some lower courts, in evaluating claims based on agency failure to follow informally adopted internal rules, have found that detrimental reliance by a member of the public and an agency intent to benefit the public points strongly toward requiring the agency to follow its rules. See, e.g., Port of Jacksonville v. U.S. Coast Guard, 788 F.2d 705, 708 (11th Cir. 1986) (relying on American Farm Lines). Some courts have focused on reliance and held that procedural due process is violated when an agency fails to follow a publicly announced (even if not promulgated) rule on which the complainant relied. *See, e.g.,* Hupart v. Board of Higher Educ., 420 F. Supp. 1087 (S.D.N.Y. 1976); United States v. Heffner, 420 F.2d 809 (4th Cir. 1970) (requiring IRS to follow instruction to public contained in press release). The weight of authority, however, appears to hold that *Hansen* stands against holding agencies to their informally issued rules, even when members of the public are prejudiced, as long as the agency "rule" appears to have been intended for internal use only. *See* Fano v. O'Neill, 806 F.2d 1262 (5th Cir. 1987); Gatter v. Nimmo, 672 F.2d 343 (3d Cir. 1982). For an extensive discussion of this knotty issue, *see* Peter Raven-Hansen, Regulatory Estoppel: When Agencies Break Their Own "Laws," 64 Tex. L. Rev. 1 (1985).

CHAPTER V

===========================

RULEMAKING

Rulemaking is the most visible mode of agency policymaking. Agencies use rulemaking procedures to formulate their most important and often most controversial policies. Not surprisingly, the rulemaking process tends to attract substantial attention from interest groups, regulated parties, elected officials, and the general public. Perhaps owing to the deference courts afford to substantive agency decisions, especially in the context of policymaking, legal challenges to agency rules often focus on the procedures used by the agency to promulgate a rule. This chapter looks deeply at the predominant procedural model of agency rulemaking under APA §553 as well as exceptions from and alternatives to that model. The chapter then turns to efforts to strengthen the analytical basis and broaden the policy focus of rulemaking, including cost-benefit analysis, presidential oversight, and impact statements.

A. FORMAL AND INFORMAL MODELS OF RULEMAKING UNDER THE ADMINISTRATIVE PROCEDURE ACT

As discussed in Chapter IV, Part A, *supra*, the APA establishes two procedural models for rulemaking—informal (often called "notice and comment") rulemaking and formal (or "on the record") rulemaking. Although formal rulemaking provides greater opportunity for interested parties to present their views orally before the agency decisionmakers, the process is expensive and time-consuming, a point Professor Robert Hamilton underscored in his discussion of formal rulemaking at the Food and Drug Administration (FDA). In the 1960s the FDA conducted 16 formal rulemaking hearings, varying from "unnecessarily drawn out proceedings to virtual disasters." Robert W. Hamilton, Procedures for the Adoption of Rules of General Applicability: The Need for Procedural Innovation in Administrative Rulemaking, 60 Cal. L. Rev. 1276, 1287-1288 (1972).

In not one instance did the agency complete a rulemaking proceeding involving a hearing in less than two years, and in two instances more than ten years elapsed between the first proposal and the final order. The *average* time lapse was roughly four years. The hearings themselves tended to be drawn out, repetitious and unproductive. The *Foods for Special Dietary Uses* hearing consumed over 200 days of testimony and amassed a transcript of more than 32,000 pages. Most of the hearing was devoted to cross-examination of expert government witnesses. Another proceeding involving the standard of identity for peanut butter developed a transcript of over 7,700 pages, largely directed to the question whether the product peanut butter should consist of 90 percent peanuts or 87 ½ percent peanuts.

Id. Hamilton suggested three possible justifications for formal rulemaking hearings—"(a) to develop information so that the agency may make a reasonable decision, (b) to create a record for judicial review of the agency's determination, and (c) to give persons affected by the proposed rules an opportunity to question the agency's factual premises"—but concluded that formal rulemaking at the FDA "does not effectively serve any of these purposes." *Id.* at 1291. Is it plausible that FDA decisionmaking serves *none* of these purposes?

Relatively few statutes explicitly require use of the APA's formal rulemaking procedures. An example of a statute that does is the provision granting the Commodity Futures Trading Commission the power to make rules outlawing trading in specified options. *See* 7 U.S.C. §6c(e): "[t]he Commission may adopt rules and regulations, *after notice and opportunity for a hearing on the record,* prohibiting the granting, issuance, or sale of options permitted under subsection (d) of this section if the Commission determines that such options are contrary to the public interest" (emphasis supplied). While this statute clearly contemplates formal rulemaking, most statutes granting rulemaking authority clearly do not. Some statutes, however, are ambiguous, granting rulemaking authority in language that *might* be read as contemplating formal processes. The following cases illustrate how the Supreme Court has dealt with such ambiguities.

UNITED STATES v. ALLEGHENY-LUDLUM STEEL CORP., 406 U.S. 742 (1972): In 1969, to address a perceived shortage of railroad cars, the Interstate Commerce Commission promulgated "car service" rules which generally required that unloaded freight cars be returned in the direction of the owning railroad. When freight shifts from one railroad line to another, the original carrier simply transfers its loaded cars to the next company's line to be pulled by its engines. This pooling arrangement leads to some difficulty in making cars available in numbers commensurate with each railroad's investment and, therefore, discourages the optimum level of investment in freight cars. The car service rules were attempts to solve these problems. The rules were challenged by railroads and shippers on both procedural and substantive grounds. The procedural argument was based on §1(14)(a) of the Interstate Commerce Act, which provides that "[t]he Commission may, after hearing . . . establish reasonable rules, regulations, and practices. . . ." The plaintiffs argued that this language required the ICC to employ formal rulemaking procedures, including submission of documentary evidence and cross-examination of witnesses, rather than the informal process it had used.

Justice Rehnquist's opinion for a unanimous Court rejected the argument that the rules were procedurally defective:

Appellees claim that the Commission's procedure here departed from the provisions of 5 U.S.C. §§556 and 557 of the Act. Those sections, however, govern a rulemaking proceeding only when 5 U.S.C. §553 so requires. The latter section, dealing generally with rulemaking, makes applicable the provisions of §§556 and 557 only "(w)hen rules are required by statute to be made on the record after opportunity for an agency hearing. . . ." [Section] 1(14)(a), does not require that such rules "be made on the record." 5 U.S.C. §553. That distinction is determinative for this case. "A good deal of significance lies in the fact that some statutes do expressly require determinations on the record." 2 K. Davis. Administrative Law Treatise §13.08, p. 225 (1958). Sections 556 and 557 need be applied "only where the agency statute, in addition to providing a hearing, prescribes explicitly that it be 'on the record.'" Siegel v. Atomic Energy Comm'n, 400 F.2d 778, 785 (D.C. Cir. 1968). . . . We do not suggest that only the precise words "on the record" in the applicable statute will suffice to make §§556 and 557 applicable to rule-making proceedings, but we do hold that the language of [§1(14)(a)] is insufficient to invoke these sections.

Because the proceedings under review were an exercise of legislative rulemaking power rather than adjudicatory hearings . . . , and because 49 U.S.C. §1(14)(a) does not require a determination "on the record," the provisions of 5 U.S.C. §§556 and 557 were inapplicable.

This proceeding, therefore, was governed by the provisions of 5 U.S.C. §553 of the Administrative Procedure Act, requiring basically that notice of proposed rulemaking shall be published in the Federal Register, that after notice the agency give interested persons an opportunity to participate in the rulemaking through appropriate submissions, and that after consideration of the record so made the agency shall incorporate in the rules adopted a concise general statement of their basis and purpose. The "Findings" and "Conclusions" embodied in the Commission's report fully comply with these requirements, and nothing more was required by the Administrative Procedure Act.

UNITED STATES v. FLORIDA EAST COAST RY. CO., 410 U.S. 224 (1973): A year later, the language of §1(14)(a) again came under scrutiny by the Supreme Court. The ICC had issued a proposed rule establishing industry-wide per diem rates for freight car use and notified affected railroads to file statements of position within 60 days. Both appellee railroads filed statements objecting to the commission's proposed rule and requesting an oral hearing. The commission rejected the request for an oral hearing, modified the proposed rule, and then issued the rule in its final form. Recognizing that *Allegheny-Ludlum* had disposed of the argument that the "after hearing" language of §1(14)(a) triggered the formal rulemaking model of APA §§556 and 557, the railroads nonetheless argued that the term "after hearing" mandated at least somewhat more formal procedures than those specified in APA §553. Justice Rehnquist, again writing for the Court, also turned aside that contention:

> [W]e are convinced that the term 'hearing' as used [in the Interstate Commerce Act] does not necessarily embrace either the right to present evidence orally and to cross-examine opposing witnesses, or the right to present oral argument to the agency's decisionmaker.

The Court was guided in part by its view of the basic distinction between rulemaking and adjudication. After discussing *Londoner* and *Bi-Metallic,* excerpted in Chapter IV, *supra,* the Court observed:

While the line dividing them may not always be a bright one, these decisions represent a recognized distinction in administrative law between proceedings for the purpose of promulgating policy-type rules or standards, on the one hand, and proceedings designed to adjudicate disputed facts in particular cases on the other.

[In this rulemaking] [n]o effort was made to single out any particular railroad for special consideration based on its own peculiar circumstances. . . . The factual inferences were used in the formulation of a basically legislative-type judgment, for prospective application only, rather than in adjudicating a particular set of disputed facts.

Taken together, *Allegheny-Ludlum* and *Florida East Coast* seem to say that rulemaking will presumptively be governed by the APA's informal (§553) model, at least absent clear congressional direction otherwise. Whether the lower federal courts have always applied that principle faithfully is, however, open to question, as the materials in the following sections of this chapter illustrate.

B.   RULEMAKING PROCEDURE UNDER APA §553 AND RELATED STATUTES

Although, as we shall see, Congress has written specific rulemaking procedures into many enabling acts, the informal model of rulemaking under APA §553 is still the dominant model for federal agency rulemaking. It contains three basic ingredients: (1) the public must be given "notice" of the proposed rulemaking; (2) the public must be given an "opportunity" to comment orally or in writing on the proposed rule; and (3) the agency must incorporate in the final rule a "concise general statement" of its "basis and purpose." Bareboned as these provisions may appear, they have generated considerable litigation. In this section, we see how the federal courts have sometimes struggled to put some meat on §553's bones.

1.   Notice

Perhaps the most common source of litigation over informal rulemaking procedures involves the adequacy of the agency's "notice." Section 553 does not require the agency to publish the text of a proposed rule; it is enough to set forth the "substance of the proposed rule" or even just "a description of the subjects and issues involved." §553(b)(3). While that language gives agencies considerable leeway in framing their notices, courts have struggled mightily to fashion principles that distinguish needed flexibility from self-serving obscurity. In the years soon after the passage of the APA, courts stayed pretty close to the statutory language, rejecting challenges to the adequacy of agency notices of proposed rulemaking whenever the notice met the statutory minima by specifying the subjects and issues involved in the rulemaking, as required by the APA. *See, e.g.,* Colorado Interstate Gas Co. v. Fed. Power Commn., 209 F.2d 717, 723-724 (10th Cir. 1953), *rev'd on other grounds,* 348

U.S. 492 (1955); Logansport Broad. Corp. v. United States, 210 F.2d 24, 28 (D.C. Cir. 1954). In *Logansport*, for example, the court rejected the argument that the notice was insufficient because the agency departed from the priorities identified in the notice and decided the matter based on a consideration not previously announced.

As the APA matured, courts became concerned that vague or obscure notices might frustrate interested parties' ability to participate fully in rulemaking proceedings and might allow agency proposals to escape meaningful public scrutiny. In a strong signal that minimal compliance with the text of §553 might not always be adequate, the D.C. Circuit explained that the adequacy of the agency's notice depends on "how well the notice that the agency gave serves the policies underlying the notice requirement." Small Refiner Lead Phase-Down Task Force v. EPA, 705 F.2d 506 (D.C. Cir. 1983) The court identified three purposes:

(1) improving the quality of rulemaking by allowing the rule proposed to be "tested by exposure to diverse public comment";
(2) affording fairness to affected parties by giving them an opportunity to express their views; and
(3) allowing more effective judicial review of the final rule by enabling the rule's critics to "develop evidence in the record to support their objections."

Id. at 547. While this statement of the notice provision's purposes is widely accepted, translating it into a ruling on the adequacy of any particular notice has proved to be troublesome, as the following case illustrates.

CHOCOLATE MANUFACTURERS ASSN. v. BLOCK
755 F.2d 1098 (4th Cir. 1985)

Before RUSSELL and SPROUSE, Circuit Judges, and HARGROVE, District Judge.
SPROUSE, Circuit Judge:

Chocolate Manufacturers Association (CMA) appeals from the decision of the district court denying it relief from a rule promulgated by the Food and Nutrition Service (FNS) of the United States Department of Agriculture (USDA or Department). CMA protests that part of the rule that prohibits the use of chocolate flavored milk in the federally funded Special Supplemental Food Program for Women, Infants and Children (WIC Program). Holding that the Department's proposed rulemaking did not provide adequate notice that the elimination of flavored milk would be considered in the rulemaking procedure, we reverse.

I

. . . The WIC Program was established by Congress in 1972 to assist pregnant, postpartum, and breastfeeding women, infants and young children from families with inadequate income whose physical and mental health is in danger because of inadequate nutrition or health care.[10] Under the program, the Department designs food packages reflecting the different nutritional needs of women, infants, and children and provides cash grants to state or local agencies, which distribute cash or vouchers to qualifying individuals in accordance with Departmental regulations as to the type and quantity of food.

In 1975 Congress revised and extended the WIC Program through fiscal year 1978[11] and, for the first time, defined the "supplemental foods" which the program was established to provide. The term

> shall mean those foods containing nutrients known to be lacking in the diets of populations at nutritional risk and, in particular, those foods and food products containing high-quality protein, iron, calcium, vitamin A, and vitamin C. . . . The contents of the food package shall be made available in such a manner as to provide flexibility, taking into account medical and nutritional objectives and cultural eating patterns.

Pub. L. No. 94-105, §17(g)(3), 89 Stat. 511, 520 (1975) (*codified at* 42 U.S.C. §1786(g)(3) (1976) (*replaced by* 42 U.S.C. §1786(b)(14) (1982)).

Pursuant to this statutory definition, the Department promulgated new regulations specifying the contents of WIC Program food packages. These regulations specified that flavored milk was an acceptable substitute for fluid whole milk in the food packages for women and children, but not infants.[12] This regulation formalized the Department's practice of permitting the substitution of flavored milk, a practice observed in the WIC Program since its inception in 1973 as well as in several of the other food programs administered by the Department.

In 1978 Congress, in extending the WIC Program through fiscal year 1982, redefined the term "supplemental foods" to mean

> those foods containing nutrients determined by nutritional research to be lacking in the diets of pregnant, breastfeeding, and postpartum women, infants, and children, as prescribed by the Secretary. State agencies may, with the approval of the Secretary, substitute different foods providing the nutritional equivalent of foods prescribed by the Secretary, to allow for different cultural eating patterns.

Pub. L. No. 95-627, §17(b)(14), 92 Stat. 3603, 3613 (1978) (*codified at* 42 U.S.C. §1786(b)(14) (1982)). Congress stated further:

> The Secretary shall prescribe by regulation supplemental foods to be made available in the program under this section. To the degree possible, the Secretary shall assure that the fat, sugar, and salt content of the prescribed foods is appropriate.

Id. at §17(f)(12), 92 Stat. at 3616 (*codified at* 42 U.S.C. §1786(f)(12) (1982)). To comply with this statutory redefinition, the Department . . . in November 1979 published for comment the proposed rule at issue in this case. 44 Fed. Reg. 69254 (1979). Along with the proposed rule, the Department published

---

10. 42 U.S.C. §1786(a) (1982).
11. Pub. L. No. 94-105, 89 Stat. 511 (1975) (*codified as amended at* 42 U.S.C. §1786 (1982)).
12. 41 Fed. Reg. 1743, 1744 (1976) (*codified at* 7 C.F.R. §246 and since amended).

a preamble discussing the general purpose of the rule and acknowledging the congressional directive that the Department design food packages containing the requisite nutritional value and appropriate levels of fat, sugar, and salt. *Id.* at 69254. Discussing the issue of sugar at length, it noted, for example, that continued inclusion of high sugar cereals may be "contrary to nutrition education principles and may lead to unsound eating practices." *Id.* at 69263. It also noted that high sugar foods are more expensive than foods with lower sugar content, and that allowing them would be "inconsistent with the goal of teaching participants economical food buying patterns." *Id.*

The rule proposed a maximum sugar content specifically for authorized cereals. The preamble also contained a discussion of the sugar content in juice, but the Department did not propose to reduce the allowable amount of sugar in juice because of technical problems involved in any reduction. Neither the rule nor the preamble discussed sugar in relation to flavoring in milk. Under the proposed rule, the food packages for women and children without special dietary needs included milk that could be "flavored or unflavored." *Id.*

The notice allowed sixty days for comment and specifically invited comment on the entire scope of the proposed rules: "The public is invited to submit written comments in favor of or in objection to the proposed regulations or to make recommendations for alternatives not considered in the proposed regulations." *Id.* at 69255. Over 1,000 comments were received from state and local agencies, congressional offices, interest groups, and WIC Program participants and others. Seventy-eight commenters, mostly local WIC administrators, recommended that the agency delete flavored milk from the list of approved supplemental foods.

In promulgating the final rule, the Department, responding to these public comments, deleted flavored milk from the list, explaining:

> In the previous regulations, women and children were allowed to receive flavored or unflavored milk. No change in this provision was proposed by the Department. However, 78 commenters requested the deletion of flavored milk from the food packages since flavored milk has a higher sugar content than unflavored milk. They indicated that providing flavored milk contradicts nutrition education and the Department's proposal to limit sugar in the food packages. Furthermore, flavored milk is more expensive than unflavored milk. The Department agrees with these concerns. There are significant differences in the sugar content of fluid whole milk and low fat chocolate milk. Fluid whole milk supplies 12.0 grams of carbohydrate per cup compared to 27.3 grams of carbohydrate per cup provided by low fat chocolate milk. If we assume that the major portion of carbohydrate in milk is in the form of simple sugar, fluid whole milk contains 4.9% sugar contrasted with 10.9% sugar in low fat chocolate milk. Therefore, to reinforce nutrition education, for consistency with the Department's philosophy about sugar in the food packages, and to maintain food package costs at economic levels, the Department is deleting flavored milk from the food packages for women and children. Although the deletion of flavored milk was not proposed, the comments and the Department's policy on sugar validate this change.

45 Fed. Reg. 74854, 74865-66 (1980). . . .

On this appeal, CMA contends . . . that the Department did not provide notice that the disallowance of flavored milk would be considered. . . .

II

. . . Section 4 of the Administrative Procedure Act (APA) requires that the notice in the Federal Register of a proposed rulemaking contain "either the terms or substance of the proposed rule or a description of the subjects and issues involved." 5 U.S.C. §553(b)(3) (1982). The purpose of the notice-and-comment procedure is both "to allow the agency to benefit from the experience and input of the parties who file comments . . . and to see to it that the agency maintains a flexible and open-minded attitude towards its own rules." National Tour Brokers Assn. v. United States, 591 F.2d 896, 902 (D.C. Cir. 1978). The notice-and-comment procedure encourages public participation in the administrative process and educates the agency, thereby helping to ensure informed agency decisionmaking. . . .

There is no question that an agency may promulgate a final rule that differs in some particulars from its proposal. Otherwise the agency "can learn from the comments on its proposals only at the peril of starting a new procedural round of commentary." International Harvester Co. v. Ruckelshaus, 478 F.2d 615, 632 n.51 (D.C. Cir. 1973). An agency, however, does not have carte blanche to establish a rule contrary to its original proposal simply because it receives suggestions to alter it during the comment period. An interested party must have been alerted by the notice to the possibility of the changes eventually adopted from the comments. . . .

The test devised by the First Circuit for determining adequacy of notice of a change in a proposed rule occurring after comments appears to us to be sound: notice is adequate if the changes in the original plan "are in character with the original scheme," and the final rule is a "logical outgrowth" of the notice and comments already given. *See, e.g.,* BASF Wyandotte Corp. v. Costle, 598 F.2d 637, 642 (1st Cir. 1979), *cert. denied,* 444 U.S. 1096 (1980); South Terminal Corp. v. EPA, 504 F.2d 646, 659 (1st Cir. 1974). Other circuits also have adopted some form of the "logical outgrowth" test. *See, e.g.,* Sierra Club v. Costle, 657 F.2d 298, 352 (D.C. Cir. 1981) (logical outgrowth of the notice and comments); Taylor Diving & Salvage Co. v. Dept. of Labor, 599 F.2d 622, 626 (5th Cir. 1979) (logical outgrowth of the standard originally proposed). Stated differently, if the final rule materially alters the issues involved in the rulemaking or, as stated in Rowell v. Andrus, 631 F.2d 699, 702 n.2 (10th Cir. 1980), if the final rule "substantially departs from the terms or substance of the proposed rule," the notice is inadequate.

There can be no doubt that the final rule in the instant case was the "outgrowth" of the original rule proposed by the agency, but the question of whether the change in it was in character with the original scheme and whether it was a "*logical* outgrowth" is not easy to answer. . . .

It is apparent that for many years the Department of Agriculture has permitted the use of chocolate in some form in the food distribution programs that it administers. The only time the Department has proposed to remove chocolate in any form from its programs was in April 1978 when it sought to characterize chocolate as a candy and remove it from the School Lunch Program. That proposal was withdrawn after CMA commented, supporting chocolate as a part of the diet. Chocolate flavored milk has been a permissible part of the WIC Program diet since its inception and there have been no proposals for its removal until the present controversy.

The Department sponsored commendable information-gathering proceedings prior to publishing its proposed rule. Together with its own research, the information gathered in the pre-publication information solicitations formed the basis for the proposed rule. Most of the same information was presented to Congress prior to enactment of the 1978 statute that precipitated the 1979 rulemaking here in controversy. The National Advisory Council on Maternal, Infant, and Fetal Nutrition provided information and advice. Regional council meetings were open to the public and held in diverse areas of the country. Department of Agriculture personnel attended a number of regional, state, and local meetings and gathered opinions concerning possible changes in the food packages. The agency also gathered a food package advisory panel of experts seeking their recommendations. Food packages were designed based on the information and advice gleaned from these sources. In all of these activities setting out and discussing food packages, including the proposed rule and its preamble, the Department never suggested that flavored milk be removed from the WIC Program.

The published preamble to the proposed rule consisted of twelve pages in the Federal Register discussing in detail factors that would be considered in making the final rule. Two pages were devoted to a general discussion of nutrients, including protein, iron, calcium, vitamin A, vitamin C, folic acid, zinc, and fiber, and the dangers of overconsumption of sugar, fat, and salt. The preamble discussed some foods containing these ingredients and foods posing specific problems. It did not discuss flavored milk.

In the next eight pages of the preamble, the nutrition content of food packages was discussed—under the general headings of "cereal" and "juice" for infants; and "eggs," "milk," "cheese," "peanut butter and mature dried beans and peas," "juice," "additional foods," "cereals," "iron," "sugar," "whole grain cereals," "highly fortified cereals," and "artificial flavors and colors" for women and children. The only reference to milk concerned the correct quantity to be provided to children, i.e., 24 quarts per month instead of 28 quarts. Although there was considerable discussion of the sugar content of juice and cereal, there was none concerning flavored milk. Likewise, there was considerable discussion of artificial flavor and color in cereal but none concerning flavored milk. The only reference to flavored milk was in the two-page discussion of the individual food packages, which noted that the proposed rule would permit the milk to be flavored or unflavored. The proposed rule which followed the preamble expressly noted that flavored or unflavored milk was permitted in the individual food packages for women and children without special dietary needs.

At the time the proposed rulemaking was published, neither CMA nor the public in general could have had any indication from the history of either the WIC Program or any other food distribution programs that flavored milk was not part of the acceptable diet for women and children without special dietary needs. The discussion in the preamble to the proposed rule was very detailed and identified specific foods which the agency was examining for excess sugar. This specificity, together with total silence concerning any suggestion of eliminating flavored milk, strongly indicated that flavored milk was not at issue. The proposed rule positively and unqualifiedly approved the continued use of flavored milk. Under the specific circumstances of this case, it cannot be said that the ultimate changes in the proposed rule were in character with the original scheme or a logical outgrowth of the notice. We can well accept that, in general, an approval of a practice in a proposed rule may properly alert interested parties that the practice may be disapproved in the final rule in the event of adverse comments. The total effect of the history of the use of flavored milk, the preamble discussion, and the proposed rule, however, could have led interested persons only to conclude that a change in flavored milk would not be considered. Although ultimately their comments may well have been futile, CMA and other interested persons at least should have had the opportunity to make them. We believe that there was insufficient notice that the deletion of flavored milk from the WIC Program would be considered if adverse comments were received and, therefore, that affected parties did not receive a fair opportunity to contribute to the administrative rulemaking process. That process was ill-served by the misleading or inadequate notice concerning the permissibility of chocolate flavored milk in the WIC Program and "does not serve the policy underlying the notice requirement."

The judgment of the district court is therefore reversed, and the case is remanded to the administrative agency with instructions to reopen the comment period and thereby afford interested parties a fair opportunity to comment on the proposed changes in the rule.

Reversed and remanded with instructions.

NOTES AND QUESTIONS

1. *Content of the notice.* In addition to the long preamble on which the court focused, the Secretary's notice also contained the text of the proposed regulation, basically a list of permissible foods, that included flavored milk as an acceptable food in several of the food packages for WIC recipients. Further, the proposed rule invited comments "in favor of or in objection to the proposed regulations" as a whole, not merely on the matters discussed in the preamble. In light of these factors, can CMA fairly claim to have been surprised that flavored milk became an issue in the rulemaking? Isn't chocolate milk an obvious potential target of rulemaking designed to implement the 1978 amendments? To what extent is the result influenced by the court's belief that the Secretary had affirmatively lulled CMA into thinking that flavored milk was safe from regulatory attack? Had he done so?

2. *The language of §553.* Does the court pay adequate heed to the language of §553 in determining whether the Secretary's notice was adequate? Section 553(b)(3) requires notice of "either the terms or substance of the proposed rule or a description of the subjects and issues involved." Didn't the Secretary's notice fulfill both requirements? The notice included the terms of the proposed rule, and even though the Secretary's preamble did not specifically mention flavored milk, did it not adequately describe the "subjects and issues involved"?

3. *Modification and public participation.* The Secretary argued that the purpose of public participation in rulemaking would be defeated if he could not modify the proposed rule in response to public comments. How persuasive is that argument here? How severe a burden does the court's ruling impose upon the agency? Other courts have explained the "logical outgrowth" test as ensuring that agencies make only those changes from proposed rules that the public could have anticipated. *See* Small Refiner Lead Phase-Down Task Force

v. EPA, 705 F.2d 506, 546-549 (D.C. Cir. 1983); Shell Oil Co. v. EPA, 950 F.2d 741 (D.C. Cir. 1991). This ensures an adequate opportunity to participate. Consider whether the Supreme Court's understanding of the notice requirement, embodied in the following case, strikes the proper balance between fairness and agency flexibility.

LONG ISLAND CARE AT HOME, LTD. v. COKE, 551 U.S. 158 (2007):   The Fair Labor Standards Act exempts from its wage and hour requirements "any employee employed in domestic service employment to provide companionship services for individuals who (because of age or infirmity) are unable to care for themselves (as such terms are defined and delimited by regulations of the Secretary [of Labor])." 29 U.S.C. §213(a)(15). The Department of Labor proposed rules exempting companionship workers only if they were employed by the infirm individual's family. After receiving comments, the agency decided to exempt all companionship workers, including those employed by the family and those employed, for example, by an agency that sends companionship workers to its clients. Coke, a companionship worker, brought suit against her former employer, Long Island Care, for failure to pay her the minimum wage and overtime payments guaranteed by FLSA. Long Island defended by invoking the rule. Coke argued that the rule was invalid because its adoption had been procedurally defective. In a unanimous decision authored by Justice Breyer, the Supreme Court ruled that the deviation between the proposed rule and final rule did not violate the APA's notice requirement:

> [T]he FLSA explicitly leaves gaps, for example, as to the scope and definition of statutory terms such as "domestic service employment" and "companionship services." 29 U.S.C. §213(a)(15). It provides the Department with the power to fill these gaps through rules and regulations. *Ibid.*; 1974 Amendments, §29(b), 88 Stat. 76 (authorizing the Secretary of Labor "to prescribe necessary rules, regulations, and orders with regard to the amendments made by this Act"). The subject matter of the regulation in question concerns a matter in respect to which the agency is expert, and it concerns an interstitial matter, *i.e.*, a portion of a broader definition, the details of which, as we said, Congress entrusted the agency to work out.
>
> The Department focused fully upon the matter in question. It gave notice, it proposed regulations, it received public comment, and it issued final regulations in light of that comment. . . . The resulting regulation says that employees who provide "companionship services" fall within the terms of the statutory exemption irrespective of who pays them. Since on its face the regulation seems to fill a statutory gap, one might ask what precisely is it about the regulation that might make it unreasonable or otherwise unlawful? . . .
>
> [Respondent claims] that the 1974 agency notice-and-comment procedure, leading to the promulgation of the third-party regulation, was legally "defective" because notice was inadequate and the Department's explanation also inadequate. Brief for Respondent 45-47. We do not agree. . . .
>
> The Courts of Appeals have generally interpreted [the notice requirement in §553(b)(3)] to mean that the final rule the agency adopts must be "a 'logical outgrowth' of the rule proposed." National Black Media Coalition v. FCC, 791 F.2d 1016, 1022 (2d Cir. 1986). The object, in short, is one of fair notice. . . .
>
> The clear implication of the proposed rule was that companionship workers employed by third-party enterprises that *were not* covered by the FLSA prior to the

1974 Amendments (*e.g.,* most smaller private agencies) *would* be included within the §213(a)(15) exemption [meaning they would not be subject to the FLSA].

Since the proposed rule was simply a proposal, its presence meant that the Department was *considering* the matter; after that consideration the Department might choose to adopt the proposal or to withdraw it. As it turned out, the Department did withdraw the proposal for special treatment of employees of "covered enterprises." The result was a determination that exempted *all* third-party-employed companionship workers from the Act. We do not understand why such a possibility was not reasonably foreseeable.

Note the Court's conclusion that proposals should be understood as just that: proposals that may or may not be adopted. Does this undermine the reasoning in *Chocolate Manufacturers* that the petitioners should not have anticipated that inclusion of flavored milk in the list of approved foods might be reconsidered? Should courts always interpret §553's notice requirement to allow agencies to decide not to adopt any aspect of their proposed rules?

4. *Notice of studies and data: the* Portland Cement *doctrine.* Adequacy-of-notice issues arise not only when a final rule deviates from a proposed rule but also when an agency relies on background information not revealed in its notice. The earliest case in which this issue was decisive is the D.C. Circuit's decision in Portland Cement Assn. v. Ruckelshaus, 486 F.2d 375 (D.C. Cir. 1973), remanding the EPA's Clean Air Act rules governing Portland cement plants, based on the agency's failure to disclose test results on the achievability of the rules' requirements. The Second Circuit elaborated on the *Portland Cement* doctrine in United States v. Nova Scotia Food Prods. Corp., 568 F.2d 240 (2d Cir. 1977), excerpted in the following section of this chapter. In *Nova Scotia* the court struck down a rule issued by the Food and Drug Administration that had been based on undisclosed scientific data in the agency's possession when it issued the notice of proposed rulemaking. The data at issue concerned the "time-temperature-salinity" levels to be used in the process of preparing smoked fish to prevent botulism. The court distinguished scientific data received from outside sources—which must be revealed during the notice stage—from information supplied during the comment stage and inferences drawn from the agency's own "expertise." The agency may rely on the latter two sources without specifically focusing commenters' attention on them. But when "the basis for a proposed rule is a scientific decision, the scientific material which is believed to support the rule should be exposed to the view of interested parties for their comment." 568 F.2d at 252. Can the court's ruling find support in the text of §553(b)?

Note that the Supreme Court's decision in *Vermont Yankee*, excerpted *infra*, casts doubt on the continuing validity of the *Portland Cement* doctrine. *See* the *American Radio Relay League* case, excerpted *infra*, and related discussion.

2.   *Explanation of the Decision: The Concise General Statement*

Section 553 requires agencies to incorporate into their rules "a concise general statement of their basis and purpose." This requirement appears designed to improve the decisionmaking process by requiring agencies to furnish reasons for their rules that will provide guidance to members of the public regulated or benefited by the rules and, perhaps, to help reviewing courts to determine whether the rules are substantively valid. The language of §553, however, provides little guidance on how "concise" the statement must be, or how "general" it may be, or what a statement of "basis and purpose" entails.

UNITED STATES v. NOVA SCOTIA FOOD PRODS. CORP., 568 F.2d 240 (2d Cir. 1977):

The *Nova Scotia* court, already upset at the FDA's failure to expose its research to public comment (as discussed above), was also dissatisfied with the agency's explanation for its regulation, especially with its failure to explain why all fish were treated alike when the record contained evidence that species-by-species treatment might be warranted.

> Appellants additionally attack the "concise general statement" required by APA, 5 U.S.C. §553, as inadequate. We think that, in the circumstances, it was less than adequate. It is not in keeping with the rational process to leave vital questions, raised by comments which are of cogent materiality, completely unanswered. The agencies certainly have a good deal of discretion in expressing the basis of a rule, but the agencies do not have quite the prerogative of obscurantism reserved to legislatures. "Congress did not purport to transfer its legislative power to the unbounded discretion of the regulatory body." FCC v. RCA Communications, Inc., 346 U.S. 86, 90 (1953) (Frankfurter, J.). As was said in Environmental Defense Fund, Inc. v. EPA, 465 F.2d 528, 540-51 (1972): "We cannot discharge our role adequately unless we hold EPA to a high standard of articulation. Kennecott Copper Corp. v. EPA, 462 F.2d 846 (1972)."
>
> The test of adequacy of the "concise general statement" was expressed by Judge McGowan in the following terms:
>
>> We do not expect the agency to discuss every item of fact or opinion included in the submissions made to it in informal rulemaking. We do expect that, if the judicial review which Congress has thought it important to provide is to be meaningful, the "concise general statement of . . . basis and purpose" mandated by [§553] will enable us to see what major issues of policy were ventilated by the informal proceedings and why the agency reacted to them as it did. Automotive Parts & Accessories Assn. v. Boyd, 407 F.2d 330, 338 ([D.C. Cir.] 1968).
>
> And Judge Friendly has noted that "[i]n a case where a proposed standard under OSHA [Occupational Safety and Health Act] has been opposed on grounds as substantial as those presented here, the Department has the burden of offering *some* reasoned explanation." Associated Industries of New York State, Inc. v. U.S. Department of Labor, 487 F.2d 342, 352 (2d Cir. 1973).
>
> The Secretary was squarely faced with the question whether it was necessary to formulate a rule with specific parameters that applied to all species of fish, and particularly whether lower temperatures with the addition of nitrite and salt would not be sufficient. Though this alternative was suggested by an agency of the federal government, its suggestion, though acknowledged, was never answered.
>
> Moreover, the comment that to apply the proposed T-T-S [time-temperature-salinity] requirements to whitefish would destroy the commercial product was neither discussed nor answered. We think that to sanction silence in the face of such

vital questions would be to make the statutory requirement of a "concise general statement" less than an adequate safeguard against arbitrary decision-making.

We cannot improve on the statement of the District of Columbia Circuit in Industrial Union Dept., AFL-CIO v. Hodgson, 499 F.2d 467, 475 (1974).

> What we are entitled to at all events is a careful identification by the Secretary, when his proposed standards are challenged, of the reasons why he chooses to follow one course rather than another. Where that choice purports to be based on the existence of certain determinable facts, the Secretary must, in form as well as in substance, find those facts from evidence in the record. By the same token, when the Secretary is obliged to make policy judgments where no factual certainties exist or where facts alone do not provide the answer, he should so state and go on to identify the considerations he found to be persuasive.

One may recognize that even commercial infeasibility cannot stand in the way of an overwhelming public interest. Yet the administrative process should disclose, at least, whether the proposed regulation is considered to be commercially feasible, or whether other considerations prevail even if commercial infeasibility is acknowledged. This kind of forthright disclosure and basic statement was lacking in the formulation of the T-T-S standard made applicable to whitefish. It is easy enough for an administrator to ban everything. In the regulation of food processing, the worldwide need for food also must be taken into account in formulating measures taken for the protection of health. In the light of the history of smoked whitefish to which we have referred, we find no articulate balancing here sufficient to make the procedure followed less than arbitrary.

After seven years of relative inaction, the FDA has apparently not reviewed the T-T-S regulations in the light of present scientific knowledge and experience. In the absence of a new statutory directive by Congress regarding control of micro-organisms, which we hope will be worthy of its consideration, we think that the T-T-S standards should be reviewed again by the FDA.

We cannot, on this appeal, remand to the agency to allow further comments by interested parties, addressed to the scientific data now disclosed at the trial below. We hold in this enforcement proceeding, therefore, that the regulation, as it affects non-vacuum-packed hot-smoked whitefish, was promulgated in an arbitrary manner and is invalid.

NOTES AND QUESTIONS

1. *The definition of "concise" and "general."* Do you think this is what Congress had in mind when it required the concise general statement? Must agencies respond with specificity to every detail in comments submitted? In this regard, consider the following statement by the D.C. Circuit regarding the concise general statement requirement: "An agency need not address every comment, but it must respond in a reasoned manner to those that raise significant problems." Reytblatt v. U.S. Nuclear Regulatory Commission, 105 F.3d 715 (D.C. Cir. 1997). One reason for requiring an agency to respond to comments is to ensure that the agency has considered the relevant factors. *See, e.g.,* Thompson v. Clark, 741 F.2d 401, 409 (D.C. Cir. 1984). Should there be an independent agency obligation to respond to all significant comments? Might this prove too onerous to be worthwhile?

2. *Concise general statements and hard look review.* Another incentive for agencies to include overwhelming detail in the rulemaking record is to protect themselves against rigorous judicial review under the so-called "hard look" doctrine discussed in Chapter II, Part B, *supra.* As a result, according to Professor Pierce, "the appellate courts . . . ha[ve] replaced the statutory adjectives 'concise' and 'general' with the judicial adjectives 'encyclopedic' and 'detailed.'" Richard J. Pierce, Two Problems in Administrative Law: Political Parity on the District of Columbia Circuit and Judicial Deterrence of Agency Rulemaking, 1988 Duke L.J. 300, 309.

Whatever the justification, the modern tendency is for agencies to develop voluminous records to support their rules, including scientific and technical documents and extremely detailed reasons, often amounting to hundreds of pages. For example, the EPA Endangerment and Cause or Contribute Findings for Greenhouse Gases Under Section 202(a) of the Clean Air Act, 74 Fed. Reg. 66,496 (2009), found that six greenhouse gases, in combination, endanger public health and welfare under the Clean Air Act, a legal predicate to setting standards for greenhouse gas emissions from mobile sources under the statute. The proposed endangerment finding generated over 380,000 public comments, 370,000 of which were determined to be the product of mass mail campaigns (in which groups of comments are identical or very similar in form and content). EPA did not respond to each of the comments individually, but instead summarized and responded to significant arguments and assertions within the totality of comments. The resulting rulemaking record includes 52 pages of findings and legal determinations, 210 pages of supporting technical and scientific analysis, and nearly 600 pages of responses to comments contained in 11 volumes. *See* Docket ID No. EPA-HQ-OAR-2009-0171 at *www.regulations.gov.*

As more rulemaking proceedings allow for online comments, the volume of comments is likely to continue to grow, threatening to overwhelm agencies. Further, in recent years, a new problem has emerged—fake comments. *See* James V. Grimaldi & Paul Overberg, Millions of People Post Comments on Federal Regulations. Many Are Fake, Wall Street Journal Online (Dec. 12, 2017), *available at* https://perma.cc/4DBB-UA8Z. Fake comments include mass emails from Russian email addresses and comments submitted under the name of dead people or people whose identities have been stolen. What effect should the revelation of fake comments have on the rulemaking process? Can you think of precautions agencies might take against them?

3. *Are agencies overreacting?* Some recent judicial decisions indicate that agencies may be overestimating the stringency of the requirement that they answer significant comments. "[The concise general statement requirement] is not meant to be particularly onerous. It is enough if the agency's statement identifies the major policy issues raised in the rulemaking and coherently explains why the agency resolved the issues as it did." National Mining Assn. v. Mine Safety & Health Administration, 512 F.3d 696, 700 (D.C. Cir. 2008). The Second Circuit has held that "the statement of basis and purpose provision does not require the agency to supply specific and detailed findings and conclusions of the kind customarily associated with formal proceedings, but rather requires the agency to publish a statement of reasons that will be sufficiently detailed to permit judicial review." Schiller v. Tower Semiconductor Ltd., 449 F.3d 286, 298 (2d Cir. 2006). The court also noted that it "even upheld a regulation with no statement at all

where the basis and purpose was obvious." *Id.* at 303. In a similar vein, reacting to a challenge to an EPA concise general statement as "general and generic," the D.C. Circuit, after reviewing the EPA's responses to the comments supporting the challenger's favored regulatory approach, stated "[t]his response demonstrates that the agency considered and rejected petitioners' arguments (and cited support) for adopting [its preferred regulatory approach]—an issue the agency had already thoroughly addressed in the rulemaking proceeding. This is all that the APA requires. . . . Accordingly, we reject petitioners' challenge to the adequacy of EPA's responses to their comments." City of Waukesha v. EPA, 320 F.3d 228, 258 (D.C. Cir. 2003).

3.   *Protecting the Integrity of the Rulemaking "Record": Ex Parte Contacts, Political Influence, and Prejudgment*

a.   **Exclusivity of the Rulemaking Record and Ex Parte Contacts**

The APA prohibits ex parte contacts in formal adjudication (*see* §557(d)) because such contacts undermine the integrity of the agency adjudicative process, a trial-type hearing presided over by an impartial decisionmaker modeled on a civil trial. The primary rationale for this ban is fairness and transparency in the adversarial process:

> Ex parte contacts deprive one party of an opportunity to become aware of and contest the assertions that the other party is advancing. To the extent that ex parte contacts serve as the basis for decision, they violate the principle that the decision may refer only to evidence presented as part of a formal record.

Edward Rubin, It's Time to Make the Administrative Procedure Act Administrative, 89 Cornell L. Rev. 95, 119 (2003). Yet the APA does not ban ex parte contacts in informal rulemaking under §553. What explains the difference? Compare administrative agencies to Congress, whose members face no restrictions on communications with outside parties. Indeed, members of Congress consider it their responsibility to consult with individual constituents, interest groups, lobbyists, academics, and government officials, all of whom may have strong interests in legislative outcomes. *See* Alan B. Morrison, Administrative Agencies Are Just Like Legislatures and Courts—Except When They're Not, 59 Admin. L. Rev. 79, 95-96 (2007) (noting the restrictions placed on agencies that are not placed on Congress or the President in the legislative process, and offering rationales for this difference). Is agency rulemaking sufficiently like legislation that it should be free of constraints on communications with outsiders? Or is there some potential for unfairness if certain interest groups have access to agency officials while others do not? The case study below illustrates growing judicial concern, in the 1970s, with behind-the-scenes lobbying of agency decisionmakers during the informal rulemaking process.

With the development of television as a commercially viable medium of communication in the 1940s, the Federal Communications Commission (FCC) had to develop a regulatory policy toward this nascent industry. Because its signals were transmitted by radio waves, everyone conceded that the Communications Act applied to television. In particular, §307 of the Act required the FCC to "make such distribution of licenses, frequencies, hours of operation, and of power among the several States and communities as to provide a fair, efficient, and equitable distribution of radio service to each of the same."

In the early regulation of radio, the FCC had developed a policy of "localism" that favored the licensing of radio stations in as many communities as possible. In so doing, it strictly limited the number and power of "superstations" serving large regional areas. Although the available (VHF) spectrum originally assigned to television service permitted the creation of only about 12 television "channels," the FCC followed the same policy of localism in its original geographical assignment of television frequencies as well. Rather than authorize a small number of powerful regional stations, it divided the available spectrum space into a large number of less powerful local allocations. The objective was to allow each community to have its own "voice." This policy had the unfortunate consequence, however, of severely restricting the number of signals available to most viewers. Unlike the regional plan, which could have made up to six channels available to most viewers, the greater spacing problems inherent in the localism policy effectively limited most markets to three or fewer signals.

The emergence of three major television networks (NBC, CBS, and ABC) was a direct consequence of this policy. The considerable cost of producing and distributing high-quality television programming encouraged stations in different markets to affiliate for the purpose of production and distribution. Networks emerged initially as brokers to facilitate those transactions. Since there were only three (or fewer) stations in most markets, however, only three networks could economically be sustained.

In an effort to compensate for the market concentration that flowed from its localism, the FCC adopted various policies to encourage "diversity." The "Fairness Doctrine" imposed on broadcasters a vague affirmative duty to cover "controversial issues of public importance" and a somewhat more concrete duty to provide "balanced" coverage of such issues. The commission also required license holders and applicants to demonstrate that their programming proposals responded to "community needs, problems, and interests," and it later issued detailed "ascertainment" guidelines outlining procedural steps for meeting that responsibility. The published criteria for selecting among competing license applicants emphasized the need for "diversification of ownership" of local media. And the "Prime Time Access Rule" required network affiliates to set aside an hour of prime time for non-network programming each weekday evening.

None of these policies held as much promise for increasing diversity, however, as expanding the number of outlets. The FCC launched an effort in that direction in the 1950s by opening up additional spectrum space (the UHF band) to television; however, technical limitations on signal quality prevented the development of economically robust UHF competitors to the VHF stations. The search for diversity may also be constrained by the fact that commercial television is financed by the sale of advertising time rather than by charges assessed directly on viewers. Population groups that are not particularly responsive to advertising or that have distinctive programming tastes are therefore likely always to feel unserved or underserved by commercial television.

For that reason, advocates for diversity were cheered by two technological developments that emerged in the 1960s: subscription television (STV) and cable television. Unlike conventional broadcasting, STV and cable TV use techniques that permit the program originator to finance his activities by assessing a charge on those who view the program. This is possible because the two technologies permit the originator to exclude persons who have not paid a fee for access to the signal transmitted. STV uses the device of a scrambled signal that can be decoded only with the aid of a special piece of equipment rented to the viewer. Cable TV uses a coaxial cable connecting the transmitter to the viewer. Purveyors of early STV and cable services charged customers a flat monthly fee for the privilege of being able to view anything transmitted over their systems. But technical refinements gradually made it possible to charge a fee on a per-program basis, so that distributors could charge more for highly valued programs (like feature films or major sporting events) than for more conventional local fare. Cable TV, moreover, had the additional option of putting more highly valued programs on one of its many channels and charging subscribers separately for that channel. Such premium services became known as pay cable channels, and these together with STV were referred to (especially by commercial broadcasters) as pay TV.

This prospect alarmed the commercial television broadcasters (and particularly the three networks), for they feared that STV and cable TV would "siphon" off much desirable programming from "free" TV, much the way that closed-circuit TV had "siphoned" world championship boxing matches. In the rulemaking proceeding that led to the *HBO* case, excerpted *infra*, ABC offered a hypothetical illustration of how a pay cable network could outbid the networks for a blockbuster movie like *Love Story*. It estimated (in 1975) that by 1980 there would be 3 million households with pay cable service (out of 73 million television households). If half of these were willing to pay $2.25 to see *Love Story*, the pay cable distributor would generate enough revenue to outbid a network (expecting an audience of roughly 30 million) for the film's exclusive distribution rights.

The result of siphoning, claimed the networks, would be a diminution in the quality of broadcast TV, a weakening of the financial position of many local stations (especially UHF outlets), a reduction in their ability to provide unremunerative "public service programming" favored by the FCC, and the complete denial of desirable programming to persons too poor or geographically remote to have access to STV or cable.

The FCC responded favorably to these arguments in a series of rulemaking proceedings beginning in the late 1960s. The first proceeding applied only to STV, then viewed as the more serious threat to commercial TV. In late 1968, the commission adopted a rule that forbade STV operators from broadcasting: (1) sports events of the sort regularly carried on commercial TV during the preceding two years; (2) feature films more than two and less than ten years old; (3) series-type programs; and (4) commercial advertising. First Report and Order in Docket 11,279, 15 F.C.C.2d 466 (1968). In addition to relying on the networks' siphoning argument, the FCC argued that STV, as a new type of TV service, should carry types of programming not already available on conventional TV. A challenge to the commission's authority to promulgate the rules was rebuffed by the D.C. Circuit in National Assn. of Theatre Owners v. FCC, 420 F.2d 194 (D.C. Cir. 1969), *cert. denied*, 397 U.S. 92 (1970).

Again at the networks' urging, the FCC extended the STV rules to pay cable in 1970. Memorandum and Opinion Order in Docket 18,397, 23 F.C.C.2d 825

(1970). This action, taken with relatively little advance warning, stirred up a storm of protest from cable television operators, motion picture producers, other program producers, sports interests, theatre owners, and even the Justice Department (objecting to the rule's "anticompetitive" nature). In response, the FCC opened up a new rulemaking proceeding in July 1972 to reconsider the pay cable rules. A brief chronology of the proceeding follows:

(1) July 24, 1972: Notice of Proposed Rulemaking issued and published in the Federal Register
(2) November 1, 1972: Deadline for initial comments
(3) November 29, 1972: Deadline for reply comments
(4) November 5-7, 1973: Oral arguments before the commission sitting en banc
(5) August 12, 1974: Further Notice of Proposed Rulemaking issued (expanding the scope of the proceedings to include the STV rules)
(6) September 23, 1974: Deadline for initial comments on the Further Notice
(7) October 4, 1974: Deadline for reply comments
(8) October 23-25, 1974: Oral arguments before the commission sitting en banc

Public participation in the proceeding was extensive. In response to the initial Notice, 40 persons or organizations filed initial or reply comments, totaling over 800 pages, and 56 persons made oral statements. In response to the Further Notice, over 100 comments were filed, totaling over 1,500 pages, and 82 individuals testified at the public hearing. In addition, the commission and its staff conducted an ongoing series of informal meetings and discussions with representatives of virtually every interest affected, including broadcasting, cable TV, STV, motion pictures, sports, theatres, and viewers.

Throughout the proceeding these interests jockeyed for position to amend the existing rules in ways that would improve their positions. But, despite the intricate variations in the participants' positions, they generally lined up in two principal camps: the broadcasters, favoring retention of regulation to prevent siphoning, and everyone else, favoring relaxation of regulation to encourage diversity. In the end, the FCC reenacted the rules largely in their existing form, but with many technical modifications that modestly relaxed the strictures on STV and pay cable programming. First Report and Order on Regulation of Subscription Cablecasting in Docket 19,554 and 18,893, 52 F.C.C.2d 1 (1975).

HOME BOX OFFICE v. FEDERAL COMMUNICATIONS COMMISSION
567 F.2d 9 (D.C. Cir.), *cert. denied*, 434 U.S. 829 (1977)

Before WRIGHT and MACKINNON, Circuit Judges, and WEIGEL, District Judge.
PER CURIAM:
[In 15 cases, consolidated for purposes of argument and decision, most of the participants in the rulemaking challenged various aspects of the commission's rules. In Parts II, III, and V of the opinion the court reviewed substantive

challenges to the rules, concluding that the STV rules should be upheld, but that the pay cable rules should be set aside as inconsistent with the Communications Act and the First Amendment. In Part IV, it turned to a procedural objection raised by only one participant—Henry Geller, a former general counsel of the FCC and chairperson of a public interest group called Citizens Communication Center.]

IV.   EX PARTE CONTACTS

During the pendency of this proceeding Mr. Henry Geller, a participant before the Commission and an amicus here, filed with the Commission a "Petition for Revision of Procedures or for Issuance of Notice of Inquiry or Proposed Rule Making." Brief amicus curiae of Henry Geller at 1 (hereinafter Geller br.). In this petition amicus Geller sought to call the Commission's attention to what were alleged to be violations in these proceedings of the ex parte communications doctrine set out by this court in Sangamon Valley Television Corp. v. United States, 269 F.2d 221 (1959). The Commission took no action in response to the petition, and amicus now presses us to set aside the orders under review here because of procedural infirmity in their promulgation.

It is apparently uncontested that a number of participants before the Commission sought out individual commissioners or Commission employees for the purpose of discussing ex parte and in confidence the merits of the rules under review here. In fact, the Commission itself solicited such communications in its notices of proposed rulemaking and, without discussing the nature, substance, or importance of what was said, argues before us that we should simply ignore these communications because amicus' petition was untimely, because amicus is estopped from complaining about a course of conduct in which he also participated, or, alternatively, because *Sangamon* does not apply. In an attempt to clarify the facts this court sua sponte ordered the Commission to provide "a list of all of the ex parte presentations, together with the details of each, made to it, or to any of its members or representatives, during the rulemaking proceedings." In response to this order the Commission filed a document over 60 pages long which revealed, albeit imprecisely, widespread ex parte communications involving virtually every party before this court, including amicus Geller.

Unfortunately, the document filed with this court does not allow an assessment of what was said to the Commission by the various persons who engaged in ex parte contacts. To give a flavor of the effect of these contacts, however, we think it useful to quote at length from the brief of amicus Geller:

> [Ex parte] presentations have in fact been made at crucial stages of the proceeding. Thus, in early 1974, then-Chairman Burch sought to complete action in this proceeding. [I]n the final crucial decisional period, the tentative course to be taken by the Commission would leak after each non-public meeting, and industry representatives would rush to make ex parte presentations to the Commissioners and staff. On March 10, 1975, the trade journals state that "word of last week's changes . . . got out during the week, and both broadcast and cable lobbyists rushed to the Commission, unhappy with some facets"—that broadcast representatives ". . . were calling on commissioners on Friday . . ." to oppose the changes. . . .

It is important to note that many contacts occurred in the crucial period between the close of oral argument on October 25, 1974 and the adoption of the First Report and Order on March 20, 1975, when the rulemaking record should have been closed while the Commission was deciding what rules to promulgate. The information submitted to this court by the Commission indicates that during this period broadcast interests met some 18 times with Commission personnel, cable interests some nine times, motion picture and sports interests five times each, and "public interest" intervenors not at all.

Although it is impossible to draw any firm conclusions about the effect of ex parte presentations upon the ultimate shape of the pay cable rules, the evidence is certainly consistent with often-voiced claims of undue industry influence over Commission proceedings, and we are particularly concerned that the final shaping of the rules we are reviewing here may have been by compromise among the contending industry forces, rather than by exercise of the independent discretion in the public interest the Communications Act vests in individual commissioners. . . .

Even the possibility that there is here one administrative record for the public and this court and another for the Commission and those "in the know" is intolerable. Whatever the law may have been in the past, there can now be no doubt that implicit in the decision to treat the promulgation of rules as a "final" event in an ongoing process of administration is an assumption that an act of reasoned judgment has occurred, an assumption which further contemplates the existence of a body of material—documents, comments, transcripts, and statements in various forms declaring agency expertise or policy—with reference to which such judgment was exercised. Against this material, "the full administrative record that was before [an agency official] at the time he made his decision," Citizens to Preserve Overton Park, Inc. v. Volpe, [401 U.S. 402, 420 (1971)], it is the obligation of this court to test the actions of the Commission for arbitrariness or inconsistency with delegated authority. *See id.* at 415-16 . . . . Yet here agency secrecy stands between us and fulfillment of our obligation. As a practical matter, *Overton Park's* mandate means that the public record must reflect what representations were made to an agency so that relevant information supporting or refuting those representations may be brought to the attention of the reviewing courts by persons participating in agency proceedings. This course is obviously foreclosed if communications are made to the agency in secret and the agency itself does not disclose the information presented. Moreover, where, as here, an agency justifies its actions by reference only to information in the public file while failing to disclose the substance of other relevant information that has been presented to it, a reviewing court cannot presume that the agency has acted properly, Citizens to Preserve Overton Park, Inc. v. Volpe, *supra,* 401 U.S. at 415, 419-20; *see* K. Davis, Administrative Law of the Seventies §11.00 at 317 (1976), but must treat the agency's justifications as a fictional account of the actual decisionmaking process and must perforce find its actions arbitrary. . . .

The failure of the public record in this proceeding to disclose all the information made available to the Commission is not the only inadequacy we find here. Even if the Commission had disclosed to this court the substance of what was said to it ex parte, it would still be difficult to judge the truth of what the Commission asserted it knew about the television industry because we would not have the benefit of an adversarial discussion among the parties. The importance of such discussion to the proper functioning of the agency decisionmaking and judicial review processes is evident in our cases. We have insisted, for example, that information in agency files or consultants' reports which the agency has identified as relevant to the proceeding be disclosed to the parties for adversarial comment. Similarly, we have required agencies to set out their thinking in notices of proposed rulemaking. This requirement not only allows adversarial critique of the agency but is perhaps one of the few ways that the public may be apprised of what the agency thinks it knows in its capacity as a repository of expert opinion. From a functional standpoint, we see no difference between assertions of fact and expert opinion tendered by the public, as here, and that generated internally in an agency: each may be biased, inaccurate, or incomplete—failings which adversary comment may illuminate. Indeed, the potential for bias in private presentations in rulemakings which resolve "conflicting private claims to a valuable privilege," Sangamon Valley Television Corp. v. United States, *supra,* 269 F.2d at 224, seems to us greater than in cases where we have reversed agencies for failure to disclose internal studies. . . .

Equally important is the inconsistency of secrecy with fundamental notions of fairness implicit in due process and with the ideal of reasoned decisionmaking on the merits which undergirds all of our administrative law. This inconsistency was recognized in *Sangamon,* and we would have thought that the principles announced there so clearly governed the instant proceeding that there could be no question of the impropriety of ex parte contacts here. Certainly any ambiguity in how *Sangamon* should be interpreted has been removed by recent congressional and presidential actions. In the Government in the Sunshine Act, for example, Congress has declared it to be "the policy of the United States that the public is entitled to the fullest practicable information regarding the decisionmaking processes of the Federal Government," Pub. L. No. 94-409, §2, 90 Stat. 1241 (Sept. 13, 1976), and has taken steps to guard against ex parte contacts in formal agency proceedings. . . .

From what has been said above, it should be clear that information gathered ex parte from the public which becomes relevant to a rulemaking will have to be disclosed at some time. On the other hand, we recognize that informal contacts between agencies and the public are the "bread and butter" of the process of administration and are completely appropriate so long as they do not frustrate judicial review or raise serious questions of fairness. Reconciliation of these considerations in a manner which will reduce procedural uncertainty leads us to conclude that communications which are received prior to issuance of a formal notice of rulemaking do not, in general, have to be put in a public file. Of course, if the information contained in such a communication forms the basis for agency action, then, under well-established principles, that information must be disclosed to the public in some form. Once a notice of proposed rulemaking has been issued, however, any agency official or employee who is or may reasonably be expected to be involved in the decisional process of the rulemaking proceeding, should "refus[e] to discuss matters relating to the disposition of a [rulemaking proceeding] with any interested private party, or an attorney or agent for any such party, prior to the [agency's] decision. . . ." If ex parte contacts nonetheless occur, we think that any written document or a summary of any oral communication must be placed in the public file established for each rulemaking docket immediately after the communication is received so that interested parties may comment thereon. . . .

Therefore, we today remand the record to the Commission for supplementation with instructions "to hold, with the aid of a specially appointed hearing examiner, an evidential hearing to determine the nature and source of all ex parte pleas and other approaches that were made to" the Commission or its employees after the issuance of the first notice of proposed rulemaking in these dockets. 269 F.2d at 225. "All parties to the former proceeding and to the present review may on request participate fully in the evidential hearing," *id.*, and may further participate in any proceedings before the Commission which it may hold for the purpose of evaluating the report of the hearing examiner.

[Concurring opinions of Judges MacKINNON and WEIGEL omitted.]

NOTES AND QUESTIONS

1. *Ex parte contacts in trial-type proceedings.* Does the 1976 Amendment to the APA prohibiting ex parte contacts in formal proceedings strengthen or weaken the court's argument for extending the prohibition to informal rulemaking? *See* William Funk, Public Participation and Transparency in Administrative Law—Three Examples as an Object Lesson, 61 Admin. L. Rev. 171 (2009). Does the logic of prohibiting ex parte contacts apply with equal force to the rulemaking context?

2. *Remedy.* What do you think of the remedy ordered by the court? If informal contacts are indeed the "bread and butter" of administration, does the court not deal too harshly with them? Or will the FCC find it all too easy to circumvent the court's ban on ex parte contacts?

3. *The rulemaking record.* The variety of material that influences agency decisionmakers raises the question of what, precisely, comprises the "rulemaking record." At a minimum, a rulemaking record presumably includes the notices of proposed and final rulemaking, the written comments filed with the agency, and the transcript (if any) of the hearing (if any). We have already seen that technical or scientific studies on which the agency relies must be disclosed either as part of the notice or as part of the "concise general statement of basis and purpose," depending on when the agency took notice of the material. What about other sources of information on which the agency might have relied—staff reports, consultant studies, scholarly writings, newspaper articles, written or oral comments by lobbyists or politicians?

One approach is simply to define the record for judicial review to include any additional information that the agency says it relied on. But unless agencies must disclose this information publicly and invite comment *before* finalizing the rule, it seems unfair to those adversely affected by the rule that it be part of the record for judicial review. Permitting agencies to supplement the public comments with additional information from its files encourages them to shield controversial data from the public during the decisionmaking process and to manufacture a self-vindicating one-sided record for review.

The alternative adopted by the *HBO* court is a rule forbidding agencies to rely on information not contained in a public rulemaking docket. Is that the only possible alternative? Is it, as the court says, "intolerable" that there should be "one administrative record for the public and this court and another for the commission and those 'in the know'"?

4. *The prevailing wisdom.* The *HBO* court's decision came as a surprise to most lawyers and regulators. Indeed, the FCC, like many agencies, had made no attempt to conceal the fact that it held meetings to discuss pending rulemaking proceedings with various interested groups. In only one previous case had a court struck down an agency rule because it was based on off-the-record contacts. Sangamon Valley Television Corp. v. United States, 269 F.2d 221 (D.C. Cir. 1959). That proceeding had involved a rule reallocating a VHF television channel from Springfield, Illinois, to St. Louis, Missouri, and two UHF channels from St. Louis to Springfield. The rule was strongly supported by the St. Louis licensee (whose assigned frequency would be upgraded from UHF to VHF) and opposed by an applicant for the erstwhile superior Springfield frequency. Although the FCC had used the form of rulemaking, said the court, in reality it was resolving "conflicting private claims to a valuable privilege." Hence, the *Sangamon* ruling tended to be viewed as limited to adjudication in the guise of rulemaking.

5. *The aftermath. HBO* appears to be the apotheosis of judicial concern about ex parte contacts in the informal rulemaking process. Only a few months later, another panel of the D.C. Circuit took pains to limit the reach of *HBO,* confining it to rulemaking proceedings that were more akin to adjudications—those involving, as in *Sangamon,* "competing claims to a valuable privilege." Action for Children's Television v. FCC, 564 F.2d 458 (D.C. Cir. 1977). The Court drew this line to cabin the potential for going even beyond *HBO* in pursuit of ensuring there is a "whole record" for the court to review, asking rhetorically:

> Why not go further and require the decisionmaker to summarize and make available for public comment every status inquiry from a Congressman or any germane material—say a newspaper editorial—that he or she reads or their evening-hour ruminations? . . . In the end, why not administer a lie-detector test to ascertain whether the required summary is an accurate and complete one? The problem is obviously a matter of degree, and the appropriate line must be drawn somewhere.

Id. at 477. Is *HBO* really a case involving conflicting claims to a valuable privilege, as in *Sangamon?*

In any event, every court since has rejected the idea of banning ex parte contacts during the pendency of a rulemaking absent a statutory requirement to do so. *See, e.g.,* In re FCC, 753 F.3d 1015 (10th Cir. 2014) (upholding FCC rules despite "hundreds" of ex parte communications with the commission, many at the eleventh hour); District No. 1, Pacific Coast Dist., Marine Engineers' Beneficial Association v. Maritime Administration, 215 F.3d 37, 42-43 (D.C. Cir. 2000) (ex parte contacts permitted unless prohibited by statute).

In the opinion of Edward Rubin, permissiveness about ex parte contacts in informal rulemaking may have gone too far:

> If the agency can consult anyone it chooses at any time, what is the point of the comment process? There is something vaguely troubling, especially to a judge, about the image of all those legally required written comments flowing in, to be

time-stamped and filed by the back-room myrmidons, while interest group representatives whisper into the ears of the agency's top officials over steak and champagne dinners.

Edward Rubin, It's Time to Make the Administrative Procedure Act Administrative, 89 Cornell L. Rev. 95, 120 (2003).

b.   Political Influence on Administrative Policy, Late Comments, and Ex Parte Contacts

Is there a difference between private influence on the agency's informal rulemaking process and the influence of public officials? Is it legitimate, even desirable, for public officials to jawbone the agency? Is there any difference between members of Congress and the President in terms of the legality or desirability of their contacts with agencies? These questions are explored below.

Coal-fired power plants were once the leading source of the electric power produced in the United States, but they are also the single most important source of sulfur dioxide (SO_2), a major air pollutant. SO_2 is released into the air when the sulfur that is physically or chemically bonded to coal is incinerated. *See* Bruce A. Ackerman & William T. Hassler, Clean Coal/Dirty Air (1981). Not only is SO_2 a known cause of many respiratory ailments, it is also the leading cause of "acid rain." When SO_2 combines with oxygen in the atmosphere, it forms acid compounds (sulfates) that lower the pH level of rainwater. In lakes that serve as collectors of the resulting acid rain, many fish species have become extinct. Acid rain could also possibly change the nature of whole ecosystems, leading to reductions in timber and agricultural production.

Before 1970, protection of air quality was entrusted principally to a rather haphazard system of state regulation. Responding to the widely acknowledged inadequacy of state regulation, Congress enacted the Clean Air Amendments of 1970, 42 U.S.C. §§1857b-1857l (1976). The Act required the newly created Environmental Protection Agency (EPA) to establish quantitative standards for the allowable concentration of pollutants in the ambient air, which were to be achieved by 1977. The states had primary responsibility to translate these air quality goals into specific implementation plans for most existing pollution sources. But, for new (post-1970) sources of air pollution, EPA had exclusive responsibility to establish uniform nationwide emission ceilings. Each of these "new source performance standards" (NSPS) was to be based on the "best system of emission reduction which (taking into account the costs of achieving such reduction) the Administrator [of EPA] determines has been adequately demonstrated." Clean Air Amendments of 1970, §111(a)(1), 42 U.S.C. §1857c-6(a)(1)(1976).

As part of this responsibility, the EPA was obliged to establish an NSPS for SO_2 emissions by new coal-fired generating plants. At the time the EPA began regulating SO_2 emissions, there were two primary methods of reducing the amount of sulfur dioxide created by burning coal, "washing" and "scrubbing." The washing process removes most of the sulfur that is physically bonded to the coal, by crushing the coal and separating out the heavier sulfur crystals. "Scrubbing" (also known as flue gas desulfurization, or FGD) involves continuous maintenance of a large-scale chemical reaction by spraying a lime solution on the SO_2 as it rises through the smokestack, and then removing the resulting products (water and sludge). Scrubbing is considerably more expensive than washing, but is capable of removing a much higher percentage (over 90 percent) of the SO_2 produced by burning coal.

The problem of setting an SO_2 emission standard was also complicated by the varying sulfur content of coal found in different parts of the country. Coal mined in the West, primarily in the Northern Great Plains and Mountain regions, has a lower sulfur content than eastern coal, produced mainly in the Midwest and Appalachians. The difference in sulfur content can be large. SO_2 emissions can range from one to ten pounds per MBTU (million BTUs), depending on the coal.

Rather than specify either the type of coal to be burned or the cleaning method to be used, the EPA merely established a simple emission ceiling of 1.2 pounds/MBTU, and left the choice of methods to attain that goal up to the utilities. At one extreme, a utility could simply burn low-sulfur fuel, without employing any cleaning device. Or, it could burn coal with a moderate sulfur content that had been washed. Or it could burn high-sulfur coal and rely on scrubbing to remove sufficient SO_2 to satisfy the standard.

The choice depended on geographical location, since coal is costly to transport. Western utilities would naturally continue to burn low-sulfur western coal, while eastern utilities would find it more economical to continue burning eastern coal, combined with washing or scrubbing or both. The standard created a strong incentive for many midwestern utilities, however, to switch from burning eastern coal to burning western coal, since the added cost of cleaning "dirty" eastern coal tended to exceed the cost of hauling "clean" western coal. Naturally, when eastern coal producers realized the full impact of the EPA's standard, they looked for a way to preserve their midwestern markets.

An opportunity soon presented itself. As 1977 approached, it was apparent that the deadline set for achieving the 1970 Act's goals could not be met and that further congressional action would be necessary. Legislation proposed to the House of Representatives in 1976 contained, among other things, modifications to the original NSPS provisions that would effectively require universal scrubbing. An unusual coalition of environmental groups, eastern coal producers, and the United Mine Workers (whose membership was heavily concentrated in the east) helped steer the universal scrubbing requirement through the House. Although a filibuster by Senator Jake Garn (R-Utah) blocked congressional approval in 1976, legislation was adopted the following year with the support of the Carter Administration. Debate on the scrubbing issue took on a distinctly regional cast, with eastern and southern Democrats narrowly defeating a solid western bloc. The final version of the Act required the EPA to adopt an NSPS for coal-fired power plants that would ensure "the achievement of a percentage reduction in the emissions from power plants from the emissions which would have resulted from the use of fuels which are not subject to treatment prior to combustion." Clean Air Amendments of 1977, §111(a)(A)(ii), 42 U.S.C. §7411(a)(1)(A)(ii) (repealed).

In addition, the Clean Air Amendments of 1977 specified the procedures to be followed by the EPA in setting emission standards. Previously, EPA standard-setting was governed solely by §553 of the APA. In an influential article, an EPA lawyer had criticized this procedure as producing an inadequate record for formulating complex environmental regulations or for supporting effective judicial review. William F. Pedersen, Jr., Formal Records and Informal Rulemaking,

85 Yale L.J. 38 (1975). The 1977 Amendments adopted the "procedural record" model proposed by Pedersen. This model requires the EPA to prepare a rule-making docket, containing the notice of proposed rulemaking, a statement of its basis and purpose, all written comments and documents received, transcripts of any public hearings held, proposed draft rules, intra-agency comments, and all documents "which become available after the proposed rule has been published and which the Administrator determines are of central relevance to the rulemaking." In addition, the EPA must provide an opportunity for hearings involving oral presentations of data, views, or arguments. Although cross-examination is not allowed, the hearing record remains open for 30 days to provide for submission of rebuttal or supplementary information. The promulgated rule must include a second statement of basis and purpose, explaining any changes from the proposed rule and responding to all "significant" comments, criticisms, and new data. The record for judicial review is limited to the proposed and promulgated rules and accompanying material, and certain other information from the administrative docket. 42 U.S.C. §7607(d).

In late fall of 1977, the EPA's Office of Air Quality, Planning, and Standards (OAQPS) prepared a proposed standard that would combine an SO_2 emission limit of 1.2 pounds/MBTU with a requirement that each power plant remove 90 percent of the SO_2 produced by it. This would mean, in effect, mandatory universal scrubbing. After lengthy internal discussion and analysis, the EPA submitted the OAQPS proposal for public comment in its September 19, 1978, Notice of Proposed Rulemaking. 43 Fed. Reg. 42,154 (1978). Meanwhile, however, the EPA's Office of Planning and Management (OPM) was toying with a different approach. Rather than require 90 percent emission reduction for all coal-fired generating plants, OPM suggested a sliding scale, allowing a smaller percentage reduction when cleaner coal was used. At the low end of the scale, a utility would be permitted to remove as little as 33 percent of the SO_2, so long as it produced no more than 0.8 pound/MBTU of SO_2 altogether. At the high end, the utility could produce emissions of 1.2 pounds/MBTU, combined with 90 percent reduction. This proposal would produce favorable environmental results in the East, by encouraging some utilities to achieve the more stringent 0.8 standard. But, since only low-sulfur coal was economically available in the West, the original universal 90 percent scrubbing requirement would have produced better results there. OPM sought to correct this flaw by allowing only eastern utilities to take advantage of the sliding scale approach. But this approach was criticized as blatantly discriminatory. As a result, in late 1978 and early 1979, OPM began to consider a new approach—a flat 0.55 pound/MBTU ceiling with no specified level of reduction. This proposal still required the use of scrubbers, since no coal could meet the ceiling otherwise. However, it would allow most utilities to decide for themselves the mix of coal and reduction percentages. OPM estimated that its proposal would cost less than the OAQPS plan with no increase in SO_2 emissions.

At this point, the Carter Administration intervened. As part of his effort to gain control of the federal bureaucracy, President Carter had issued an executive order requiring agencies to conduct an "economic impact analysis" for all significant regulations, and had created a "Regulatory Analysis Review Group" (RARG) to review the analyses and make comments to agencies. Exec. Order No. 12,044, 43 Fed. Reg. 12,661 (1978). The RARG now intervened in the formulation of the NSPS for coal-fired generating plants. Despite challenging some assumptions used by the EPA in formulating its proposal, it endorsed the idea of universal scrubbing and expressed preference for OPM's latest proposal over the earlier OAQPS plan. RARG submitted its report on the last day for public comments, in January 1979.

Fearing that their high-sulfur coal would be unable to meet this new 0.55 standard, regardless of the degree of scrubbing used, eastern coal producers expressed strong opposition to this latest proposal. Supported by the UMW and some eastern utilities, the producers began an intense lobbying effort to defeat the OPM plan.

With political momentum beginning to shift back to the original 1.2-pound ceiling, the EPA moved to find a compromise. In April of 1979, an internal memorandum promoting a new system known as the "dry scrubber" began to circulate. Preliminary research indicated that a dry scrubber could operate more cheaply than the conventional ("wet") scrubber at levels of sulfur reduction below 70 percent. Based on the promise of this new technology, the EPA proposed a new regulation that would give utilities an alternative to the 1.2 pound–90 percent standard—a 0.6 pound/MBTU ceiling coupled with 70 percent reduction in SO_2 emissions. This alternative approach had two advantages. Although dry scrubbing was as yet an untested technology, the Administrator of EPA concluded that this new "variable standard" (offering utilities a choice of 1.2-pounds-plus-90-percent reduction or 0.6-pounds-plus-70-percent reduction) "would achieve virtually the same emission reductions at a national level as a uniform approach but at substantially lower costs." 44 Fed. Reg. 33,580 (1979). Based on that finding, he adopted the standard as the NSPS for SO_2 emissions from coal-fired generating plants on June 11, 1979.

Concerned that the EPA's final standard was not as protective of air quality as the OPM 0.55-pound proposal, various environmental groups, including the Sierra Club and the Environmental Defense Fund (EDF), petitioned the D.C. Circuit to set aside the standard.

SIERRA CLUB v. COSTLE
657 F.2d 298 (D.C. Cir. 1981)

Before ROBB, WALD, and GINSBURG, Circuit Judges.

WALD, Circuit Judge: . . .

EDF challenges . . . the final NSPS on procedural grounds, contending that although there may be evidence supporting the 1.2 lbs./MBTU standard, EPA should have and would have adopted a stricter standard if it had not engaged in post-comment period irregularities and succumbed to political pressures. . . .

B. EDF's Procedural Attack

EDF alleges that as a result of an "ex parte blitz" by coal industry advocates conducted after the close of the comment period, EPA backed away from adopting the .55 lbs./MBtu limit, and instead adopted the higher 1.2 lbs./MBtu restriction. . . .

EDF's procedural objections stem from either (1) comments filed after the close of the official comment period, or (2) meetings between EPA officials and various government and private parties interested in the outcome of the final rule, all of which took place after the close of the comment period.

1. LATE COMMENTS

The comment period for the NSPS began on September 19, 1978, and closed on January 15, 1979. After January 15, EPA received almost 300 written submissions on the proposed rule from a broad range of interests. EPA accepted these comments and entered them all on its administrative docket. EPA did not, however, officially reopen the comment period, nor did it notify the public through the Federal Register or by other means that it had received and was entering the "late" comments. According to EDF, most of the approximately 300 late comments were received after the "leak" of the new .55 lbs./MBtu proposal. EDF claims that of the 138 late comments from non-government sources, at least 30 were from "representatives of the coal or utility industries," and of the 53 comments from members of Congress, 22 were either forwarded by the Congressmen from industry interests, or else were prepared and submitted by Congressmen as advocates of those interests.

2. MEETINGS

EDF objects to nine different meetings. A chronological list and synopsis of the challenged meetings follows:

1. *March 14, 1979*—This was a one and a half hour briefing at the White House for high-level officials from the Department of Energy (DOE), the Council of Economic Advisers (CEA), the White House staff, the Department of Interior, the Council on Environmental Quality (CEQ), the Office of Management and Budget (OMB), and the National Park Service. The meeting was reported in a May 9, 1979 memorandum from EPA to Senator Muskie's staff, responding to the Senator's request for a monthly report of contacts between EPA staff and other federal officials concerning the NSPS. A summary of the meeting and the materials distributed were docketed on May 30, 1979. EDF also obtained, after promulgation of the final rule, a copy of the memorandum to Senator Muskie in response to its Freedom of Information Act ("FOIA") request.

2. *April 5, 1979*—This . . . meeting was attended by representatives of EPA, DOE, NCA [the National Coal Association], EDF, Congressman Paul Simon's office, ICF, Inc. (who performed the microanalysis), and Hunton & Williams (who represented the Electric Utilities). The participants were notified in advance of the agenda for the meeting. Materials relating to EPA's and NCA's presentations during the meeting were distributed and copies were later put into the docket along with detailed minutes of the meeting. Followup calls and letters between NCA and EPA came on April 20, 23, and 29, commenting or elaborating upon the April 5 data. All of these followup contacts were recorded in the docket.

3. *April 23, 1979*—This was a 30-45 minute meeting held at then Senate Majority Leader Robert Byrd's request, in his office, attended by EPA Administrator Douglas Costle, Chief Presidential Assistant Stuart Eizenstat, and NCA officials. A summary of this meeting was put in the docket on May 1, 1979, and copies of the summary were sent to EDF and to other parties. In its denial of the petition for reconsideration, EPA was adamant that no new information was transmitted to EPA at this meeting.

4. *April 27, 1979*—This was a briefing on dry scrubbing technology conducted by EPA for representatives of the Office of Science and Technology Policy, the Council on Wage and Price Stability, DOE, the President's domestic policy staff, OMB, and various offices within EPA. A description of this briefing and copies of the material distributed were docketed on May 1, 1979.

5. *April 30, 1979*—At 10:00 a.m., a one hour White House briefing was held for the President, the White House staff, and high ranking members of the Executive Branch "concerning the issues and options presented by the rulemaking." This meeting was noted on an EPA official's personal calendar which EDF obtained after promulgation in response to its FOIA request, but was never noted in the rulemaking docket.

6. *April 30, 1979*—At 2:30 p.m., a technical briefing on dry scrubbing technology at the White House was conducted by EPA for the White House staff. A short memorandum describing this briefing was docketed on May 30, 1979.

7. *May 1, 1979*—Another White House briefing was held on the subject of FGD technology. A description of the meeting and materials distributed were docketed on May 30, 1979.

8. *May 1, 1979*—EPA conducted a one hour briefing of staff members of the Senate Committee on Environmental and Public Works concerning EPA's analysis of the effect of alternative emission ceilings on coal reserves. The briefing was "substantially the same as the briefing given to Senator Byrd on May 2, 1980." No persons other than Committee staff members and EPA officials attended the briefing. This meeting, like the one at 10:00 a.m. on April 30, was never entered on the rulemaking docket but was listed on an EPA official's calendar obtained by EDF in response to its FOIA request. This EPA official has since stated that it was an oversight not to have a memorandum of this briefing prepared for the docket.

9. *May 2, 1979*—This was a brief meeting between Senator Byrd, EPA, DOE and NCA officials held ostensibly for Senator Byrd to hear EPA's comments on the NCA data. A 49 word, not very informative, memorandum describing the meeting was entered on the docket on June 1, 1979.

On June 16, 1980, responding to motions filed by EDF, this court ordered EPA to file affidavits providing additional information regarding five of these nine meetings (March 14, April 23, April 27, April 30, and May 2, 1979). After EPA complied with the order, EDF argued that the other meetings held on April 30 and May 1 were still undocumented, whereupon EPA voluntarily filed an affidavit describing them. . . .

E. Validity of EPA's Procedures During the Post-Comment Period

. . . As a general matter, . . . we note at the outset that nothing in the statute prohibits EPA from admitting all post-comment communications into the record; nothing expressly requires it, either. Most likely the drafters envisioned promulgation of a rule soon after the close of the public comment period, and did not envision a months-long hiatus where continued outside communications with the agency would continue unabated. We must therefore attempt to glean the law for this case by inference from the procedural framework provided in the statute.

1. Written Comments Submitted During Post-Comment Period

Although no express authority to admit post-comment documents exists, the statute does provide that: "All documents which become available after the proposed rule has been published and which the Administrator determines are of central relevance to the rulemaking shall be placed in the docket as soon as possible after their availability." This provision, in contrast to others in the same subparagraph, is not limited to the comment period. Apparently it allows EPA not only to put documents into the record after the comment period is over, but also to define which documents are "of central relevance" so as to require that they be placed in the docket. The principal purpose of the drafters was to define in advance, for the benefit of reviewing courts, the record upon which EPA would rely in defending the rule it finally adopted; it was not their purpose to guarantee that every piece of paper or phone call related to the rule which was received by EPA during the post-comment period be included in the docket. EPA thus has authority to place post-comment documents into the docket, but it need not do so in all instances.

Such a reading of the statute accords well with the realities of Washington administrative policymaking, where rumors, leaks, and overreactions by concerned groups abound, particularly as the time for promulgation draws near. In a proceeding such as this, one of vital concern to so many interests—industry, environmental groups, as well as Congress and the Administration—it would be unrealistic to think there would not naturally be attempts on all sides to stay in contact with EPA right up to the moment the final rule is promulgated. The drafters of the 1977 Amendments were practical people, well versed in such activity, and we decline now to infer from their silence that they intended to prohibit the lodging of documents with the agency at any time prior to promulgation. Common sense, after all, must play a part in our interpretation of these statutory procedures. . . .

If, however, documents of central importance upon which EPA intended to rely had been entered on the docket too late for any meaningful public comment prior to promulgation, then both the structure and spirit of section 307 would have been violated. . . .

The case before us, however, does not present an instance where documents vital to EPA's support for its rule were submitted so late as to preclude any effective public comment. The vast majority of the written comments . . . were submitted in ample time to afford an opportunity for response. . . .

EDF makes only one particularized allegation concerning its inability to respond adequately to documents submitted during the post-comment period. It argues that at the April 5 meeting called by EPA, representatives of NCA produced new data purporting to show a significant impact upon available coal reserves of more restrictive emissions ceilings. EDF alleges that additional documents supporting a higher ceiling were thereafter forwarded by NCA to EPA following the April 5 meeting. We find, however, that EDF was not denied an adequate opportunity to respond to this material. EDF was provided with advance notice of the April 5 meeting's time, place, and agenda. At the meeting EDF proceeded to question the assumptions used in the coal industry's studies. After the meeting, on April 19, 1979, it sent a detailed memorandum to EPA asserting that NCA's new claims were "false" and "unsupported by the sheafs of new data the Coal Association has hastened to submit. . . ."

2. MEETINGS HELD WITH INDIVIDUALS OUTSIDE EPA

The statute does not explicitly treat the issue of post-comment period meetings with individuals outside EPA. Oral face-to-face discussions are not prohibited anywhere, anytime, in the Act. The absence of such prohibition may have arisen from the nature of the informal rulemaking procedures Congress had in mind. Where agency action resembles judicial action, where it involves formal rulemaking, adjudication, or quasi-adjudication among "conflicting private claims to a valuable privilege," the insulation of the decisionmaker from ex parte contacts is justified by basic notions of due process to the parties involved. But where agency action involves informal rulemaking of a policymaking sort, the concept of ex parte contacts is of more questionable utility.

Under our system of government, the very legitimacy of general policymaking performed by unelected administrators depends in no small part upon the openness, accessibility, and amenability of these officials to the needs and ideas of the public from whom their ultimate authority derives, and upon whom their commands must fall. As judges we are insulated from these pressures because of the nature of the judicial process in which we participate; but we must refrain from the easy temptation to look askance at all face-to-face lobbying efforts, regardless of the forum in which they occur, merely because we see them as inappropriate in the judicial context. Furthermore, the importance to effective regulation of continuing contact with a regulated industry, other affected groups, and the public cannot be underestimated. Informal contacts may enable the agency to win needed support for its program, reduce future enforcement requirements by helping those regulated to anticipate and shape their plans for the future, and spur the provision of information which the agency needs. The possibility of course exists that in permitting ex parte communications with rulemakers we create the danger of "one administrative record for the public and this court and another for the Commission."[505] Under the Clean Air Act procedures, however, "[t]he promulgated rule may not be based (in part or whole) on any information or data which has not been placed in the docket. . . ." Thus

---

505. Home Box Office, Inc. v. FCC, 567 F.2d 9, 54 (D.C. Cir.), *cert. denied*, 434 U.S. 829 (1977).

EPA must justify its rulemaking solely on the basis of the record it compiles and makes public.

Regardless of this court's views on the need to restrict all postcomment contacts in the informal rulemaking context, however, it is clear to us that Congress has decided not to do so in the statute which controls this case. . . . It still can be argued, however, that if oral communications are to be freely permitted after the close of the comment period, then at least some adequate summary of them must be made in order to preserve the integrity of the rulemaking docket, which under the statute must be the sole repository of material upon which EPA intends to rely. The statute does not require the docketing of all post-comment period conversations and meetings, but we believe that a fair inference can be drawn that in some instances such docketing may be needed in order to give practical effect to section 307(d)(4)(B)(i), which provides that all *documents* "of central relevance to the rulemaking" shall be placed in the docket as soon as possible after their availability. This is so because unless *oral* communications of central relevance to the rulemaking are also docketed in some fashion or other, information central to the justification of the rule could be obtained without ever appearing on the docket, simply by communicating it by voice rather than by pen, thereby frustrating the command of section 307 that the final rule not be "based (in part or whole) on any information or data which has not been placed in the docket. . . ."

EDF is understandably wary of a rule which permits the agency to decide for itself when oral communications are of such central relevance that a docket entry for them is required. Yet the statute itself vests EPA with discretion to decide whether "documents" are of central relevance and therefore must be placed in the docket; surely EPA can be given no less discretion in docketing oral communications, concerning which the statute has no explicit requirements whatsoever. Furthermore, this court has already recognized that the relative significance of various communications to the outcome of the rule is a factor in determining whether their disclosure is required. A judicially imposed blanket requirement that all post-comment period oral communications be docketed would, on the other hand, contravene our limited powers of review, would stifle desirable experimentation in the area by Congress and the agencies, and is unnecessary for achieving the goal of an established, procedure-defined docket, *viz.*, to enable reviewing courts to fully evaluate the stated justification given by the agency for its final rule.

Turning to the particular oral communications in this case, we find that only two of the nine contested meetings were undocketed by EPA. The agency has maintained that, as to the May 1 meeting where Senate staff people were briefed on EPA's analysis concerning the impact of alternative emissions ceilings upon coal reserves, its failure to place a summary of the briefing in the docket was an oversight. We find no evidence that this oversight was anything but an honest inadvertence; furthermore, a briefing of this sort by EPA which simply provides background information about an upcoming rule is not the type of oral communication which would require a docket entry under the statute.

The other undocketed meeting occurred at the White House and involved the President and his White House staff. . . .

(a) Intra-Executive Branch Meetings

... The facts ... present us with a single undocketed meeting held on April 30, 1979, at 10:00 a.m., attended by the President, White House staff, other high ranking members of the Executive Branch, as well as EPA officials, and which concerned the issues and options presented by the rulemaking.

[I]t is hard to believe Congress was unaware that intra-executive meetings and oral comments would occur throughout the rulemaking process. We assume, therefore, that unless expressly forbidden by Congress, such intra-executive contacts may take place, both during and after the public comment period; the only real issue is whether they must be noted and summarized in the docket.

The court recognizes the basic need of the President and his White House staff to monitor the consistency of executive agency regulations with Administration policy. He and his White House advisers surely must be briefed fully and frequently about rules in the making, and their contributions to policymaking considered. The executive power under our Constitution, after all, is not shared — it rests exclusively with the President. The idea of a "plural executive," or a President with a council of state, was considered and rejected by the Constitutional Convention. Instead the Founders chose to risk the potential for tyranny inherent in placing power in one person, in order to gain the advantages of accountability fixed on a single source. To ensure the President's control and supervision over the Executive Branch, the Constitution — and its judicial gloss — vests him with the powers of appointment and removal, the power to demand written opinions from executive officers, and the right to invoke executive privilege to protect consultative privacy. In the particular case of EPA, Presidential authority is clear since it has never been considered an "independent agency," but always part of the Executive Branch.

The authority of the President to control and supervise executive policymaking is derived from the Constitution; the desirability of such control is demonstrable from the practical realities of administrative rulemaking. Regulations such as those involved here demand a careful weighing of cost, environmental, and energy considerations. They also have broad implications for national economic policy. Our form of government simply could not function effectively or rationally if key executive policymakers were isolated from each other and from the Chief Executive. Single mission agencies do not always have the answers to complex regulatory problems. An overworked administrator exposed on a 24-hour basis to a dedicated but zealous staff needs to know the arguments and ideas of policymakers in other agencies as well as in the White House.

We recognize, however, that there may be instances where the docketing of conversations between the President or his staff and other Executive Branch officers or rulemakers may be necessary to ensure due process. This may be true, for example, where such conversations directly concern the outcome of adjudications or quasi-adjudicatory proceedings; there is no inherent executive power to control the rights of individuals in such settings. Docketing may also be necessary in some circumstances where a statute like this one *specifically requires* that essential "information or data" upon which a rule is based be docketed. But in the absence of any further Congressional requirements, we hold that it was not unlawful in this case for EPA not to docket a face-to-face policy session involving the President and EPA officials during the post-comment period, since EPA makes no effort to base the rule on any "information or data" arising from that meeting. . . .

The purposes of full-record review which underlie the need for disclosing ex parte conversations in some settings do not require that courts know the details of every White House contact, including a Presidential one, in this informal rulemaking setting. After all, any rule issued here with or without White House assistance must have the requisite *factual support* in the rulemaking record, and under this particular statute the Administrator may not base the rule in whole or in part on any "information or data" which is not in the record, no matter what the source. The courts will monitor all this, but they need not be omniscient to perform their role effectively. Of course, it is always possible that undisclosed Presidential prodding may direct an outcome that *is* factually based on the record, but different from the outcome that would have obtained in the absence of Presidential involvement. In such a case, it would be true that the political process did affect the outcome in a way the courts could not police. But we do not believe that Congress intended that the courts convert informal rulemaking into a rarified technocratic process, unaffected by political considerations or the presence of Presidential power. In sum, we find that the existence of intra-Executive Branch meetings during the post-comment period, and the failure to docket one such meeting involving the President, violated neither the procedures mandated by the Clean Air Act nor due process.

(b) Meetings Involving Alleged Congressional Pressure

Finally, EDF challenges the rulemaking on the basis of alleged Congressional pressure, citing principally two meetings with Senator Byrd. . . .

Senator Byrd requested a meeting in order to express "strongly" his already well-known views that the SO_2 standards' impact on coal reserves was a matter of concern to him. EPA initiated a second responsive meeting to report its reaction to the reserve data submitted by the NCA. In neither meeting is there any allegation that EPA made any commitments to Senator Byrd. The meetings did underscore Senator Byrd's deep concerns for EPA, but there is no evidence he attempted actively to use "extraneous" pressures to further his position. Americans rightly expect their elected representatives to voice their grievances and preferences concerning the administration of our laws. We believe it entirely proper for Congressional representatives vigorously to represent the interests of their constituents before administrative agencies engaged in informal, general policy rulemaking, so long as individual Congressmen do not frustrate the intent of Congress as a whole as expressed in statute, nor undermine applicable rules of procedure. Where Congressmen keep their comments focused on the substance of the proposed rule—and we have no substantial evidence to cause us to believe Senator Byrd did not do so here—administrative agencies are expected to balance Congressional pressure with the pressures emanating from all other sources. To hold otherwise would deprive the agencies of legitimate sources of information and call into question the validity of nearly every controversial rulemaking.

In sum, we conclude that EPA's adoption of the 1.2 lbs./MBtu emissions ceiling was free from procedural error. The post-comment period contacts here violated neither the statute nor the integrity of the proceeding. . . .

Affirmed.

ROBB, Circuit Judge, concurs in the result.

NOTES AND QUESTIONS

1. *Statutory basis.* What statutory or other legal basis did the *Sierra Club* court have for its holdings? Exactly what did the court hold regarding ex parte contracts between agency officials and representatives of private interests? Between agency officials and other officials within the Executive Branch? Between agency officials and members of Congress? Did the court treat off-the-record contacts by members of Congress or the White House any differently from contacts by the public? Should it have?

2. *The President's privilege.* Does the President have a constitutional privilege to engage in off-the-record discussions about proposed rules with administrative policymakers? Does that privilege extend to the expression of "factual" as well as "political" views? Does it extend to conversations between the President's advisors and rulemakers? Does it extend to the President's conversations with heads of "independent" as well as "executive" agencies?

For an argument that courts should not interfere with "direct Presidential intervention in executive-agency rulemaking," *see* Paul R. Verkuil, Jawboning Administrative Agencies: Ex Parte Contacts by the White House, 80 Colum. L. Rev. 943 (1980). But note that Portland Audubon Soc'y v. Endangered Species Committee, 984 F.2d 1534 (9th Cir. 1993), excerpted in Chapter VI, *infra,* applied the ban on ex parte contacts in agency adjudication to the President and White House staff. Can the President go so far as to order the agency to promulgate the rule as he wishes? If the record evinces an independent rationale for the agency's decision, who is to know? For a strong view of presidential authority to make regulatory decisions that are not explicitly delegated to the agency by Congress, *see* Elena Kagan, Presidential Administration, 114 Harv. L. Rev. 2245 (2001). For a discussion of the phenomenon of "presidential administration," *see* Chapter I, section C, *supra.*

3. *Congressional influence.* On the issue of congressional influence in rulemaking, compare *Sierra Club* to the following case.

DISTRICT OF COLUMBIA FEDERATION OF CIVIC ASSNS. v. VOLPE, 459 F.2d 1231 (D.C. Cir. 1971), *cert. denied,* **405 U.S. 1030 (1972):** The federation attacked a decision by Transportation Secretary Volpe to approve the construction of the controversial "Three Sisters" bridge between the Georgetown waterfront in the District of Columbia and Spout Run, Virginia. The bridge had previously been dropped from the district's highway plan, but was restored after Representative William Natcher, Chairman of the House Appropriations Committee's Subcommittee on the District of Columbia, stated publicly that he would hold up appropriations for the district's proposed subway system unless the bridge plans were revived. Although the court reversed and remanded the Secretary's decision on various other substantive and procedural grounds, Chief Judge Bazelon expressed the view that the "impact of this pressure [from Natcher] is sufficient, standing alone, to invalidate the Secretary's action." In a portion of the opinion joined by a second member of the three-member panel, Judge Bazelon explained the governing standard to be applied to such cases:

> [T]he underlying problem cannot be illuminated by a simplistic effort to force the Secretary's action into a purely judicial or purely legislative mold. His decision was not "judicial" in that he was not required to base it solely on a formal record established at a public hearing. At the same time, it was not purely "legislative" since Congress had already established the boundaries within which his discretion could operate. But even though his action fell between these two conceptual extremes, it is still governed by principles that we had thought elementary and beyond dispute. If, in the course of reaching his decision, Secretary Volpe took into account "considerations that Congress could not have intended to make relevant," his action proceeded from an erroneous premise and his decision cannot stand. The error would be more flagrant, of course, if the Secretary had based his decision solely on the pressures generated by Representative Natcher. But it should be clear that his action would not be immunized merely because he also considered some relevant facts. . . .
>
> So long as the Secretary applies his expertise to considerations Congress intended to make relevant, he acts within his discretion and our role as a reviewing court is constrained. We do not hold, in other words, that the bridge can never be built. Nor do we know or mean to suggest that the information now available to the Secretary is necessarily insufficient to justify construction of the bridge. We hold only that the Secretary must reach his decision strictly on the merits and in the manner prescribed by statute, without reference to irrelevant or extraneous considerations. . . .
>
> To avoid any misconceptions about the nature of our holding, we emphasize that we have not found—nor, for that matter, have we sought—any suggestion of impropriety or illegality in the actions of Representative Natcher and others who strongly advocate the bridge. They are surely entitled to their own views on the need for the Three Sisters Bridge, and we indicate no opinion on their authority to exert pressure on Secretary Volpe. Nor do we mean to suggest that Secretary Volpe acted in bad faith or in deliberate disregard of his statutory responsibilities. He was placed, through the actions of others, in an extremely treacherous position. Our holding is designed, if not to extricate him from that position, at least to enhance his ability to obey the statutory command notwithstanding the difficult position in which he was placed.

If the Secretary's decision were otherwise justifiable on the merits, what is wrong with his taking the position of a key member of Congress into account? Isn't the court living in a dreamland if it thinks that it can control political pressures of this sort?

Is *Sierra Club* distinguishable from *D.C. Federation*?

Not only do members of Congress seek to influence agency rules, they also routinely seek to influence formal adjudications, often through "status" inquiries or letters complaining of delay regarding particular applicants or licensees who happen to be their constituents. Is this lawful?

4. *Late comments.* What did the *Sierra Club* court decide regarding the receipt of late comments? Would the court allow an agency to rely on a comment that arrived on the last day of the comment period? Suppose the agency then refused

to consider any comments submitted in response, on the ground that those comments arrived after the comment period was closed. The Tenth Circuit, at least, seems to think that the APA does not require agencies to allow comments on comments at all: "The APA ensures an opportunity to comment on the notice of proposed rulemaking, but not to reply to the rulemaking record." In re FCC, 753 F.3d 1015, 1138 (10th Cir. 2014). For a counterpoint, *see* Ober v. EPA, 84 F.3d 304 (9th Cir. 1996), in which the court invalidated the EPA's approval of Arizona's plan for implementing the particulate matter provisions of the Clean Air Act. The EPA accepted and considered 300 pages of documents that Arizona submitted after the close of the comment period in a proceeding under §553. The court held that because the documents "were relied on and were critical to the EPA's approval of the Implementation Plan," opposing parties should have been given "notice [and] an opportunity to comment on the post-comment period justifications." 84 F.3d at 314-315. Is the principle that agencies may not rely upon post-comment period submissions without exposing them to a new round of comment a proper reading of §553? Before jumping to a conclusion, consider that as late as 2006, the D.C. Circuit has favorably cited *HBO*'s exhortation that "any written document or a summary of any oral communication must be placed in the public file established for each rulemaking docket . . . so that interested parties may comment thereon." *See* EchoStar Satellite LLC v. FCC, 457 F.3d 31, 39 (D.C. Cir. 2006) (quoting Home Box Office, Inc. v. FCC, 567 F.2d 9, 57 (D.C. Cir. 1977)). Should the rules regarding late comments depend on what material they contain? On how that material relates to other information in the rulemaking record?

5. *Ex parte influence and impartiality.* Is the concern raised by the petitioners in *Sierra Club* less about ex parte contacts per se, and more about the impartiality of the agency decisionmaker? Is there any difference? Is the real concern that politics will wind up determining matters that ought to be decided through the agency's application of "objective" expertise? Consider this issue as you read the following case study.

c. Impartiality of the Rulemaker

In the early 1970s, the Federal Trade Commission (FTC) began to shake off its reputation as a repository for patronage appointments and a friend of business. Several chairmen appointed by Presidents Nixon and Ford began to upgrade the quality of agency personnel and shift the focus of enforcement activities. Prosecutions under protectionist statutes like the Robinson-Patman Act, 15 U.S.C. §§13-13b, 21a, and the Wool and Fur Product Labeling Act, 15 U.S.C. §§68-68j, virtually ceased.

In their place, the FTC began to concentrate on more significant market abuses. It began a vigorous campaign to ensure truth in national advertising campaigns, challenging claims by pharmaceutical manufacturers and other large corporations. Under authority of the Magnuson-Moss Act of 1975, Pub. L. No. 93-637, 88 Stat. 2183, the FTC instituted proceedings to establish "trade regulation rules" for a variety of industry practices. By March 1977, 17 rulemakings were in progress, dealing with such industries as funeral parlors, used car dealers, hearing aids, and vocational schools.

In March 1977, President Carter appointed Michael Pertschuk to the chairmanship of the FTC. As Chief of Staff of the Senate Commerce Committee, Pertschuk had been instrumental in devising many federal consumer laws, including the Magnuson-Moss Act. He seemed to be a natural choice for chairman of the commission. At the time of his appointment, Pertschuk was highly regarded by both his allies and his adversaries. One admirer stated:

> Pertschuk was the single most influential person in this town on consumer issues for the last half of the 1970s. Every significant consumer group in this town recognized that Mike Pertschuk was the accomplished leader in the consumer field. There were always people on the House side and people down at FTC and people here and there but Pertschuk was the eminent leader in the same sense that [Ralph] Nader was St. George the Dragon killer.

John F. Kennedy School of Government, "Mike Pertschuk and the Federal Trade Commission" 1 (1981) [hereinafter cited as the Kennedy School Study].

Pertschuk himself believed that he was on "the side of the angels": "In those early days we saw ourselves as the Scarlet Pimpernels of the Consumer movement: secret, in any event, unsung heroes doing good by doing in corporate abuse." Michael Pertschuk, Revolt Against Regulation 44 (1982).

The method used by the "scarlet pimpernels" of the consumer movement, according to Pertschuk, was what James Q. Wilson described as "entrepreneurial politics":

> [Consumer legislation] requires the efforts of a skilled entrepreneur who can mobilize latent public sentiment (by revealing a scandal or capitalizing on a crisis), put the opponents of the plan publicly on the defensive (by accusing them of deforming babies or killing motorists), and associate the legislation with widely shared values (clean air, pure water, health, and safety). The entrepreneur serves as the vicarious representative of groups not directly part of the legislative process.

James Q. Wilson, The Politics of Regulation 370 (1980).

On his accession to the chairmanship of the FTC, Pertschuk sought to make the agency into an efficient organization for advancing the interests of the consumer. Like his immediate three predecessors, Pertschuk endeavored to recruit outstanding lawyers. But, besides ability, the new chairman wanted lawyers whose prior experience demonstrated a commitment to "public interest" activities. Pertschuk's internal management style strongly emphasized negotiation and consensus building. He initiated a series of weekend retreats for upper-level staff and created a management "team" to replace the internal "warfare" characteristic of his predecessor's administration. Pertschuk was especially eager to insulate FTC commissioners and staff from "improper influence" by the business community and the Washington bar. As a symbolic gesture, he declined an invitation to serve on the governing council of the American Bar Association's antitrust section, a position traditionally filled by FTC chairmen. More important, Pertschuk greatly expanded the scope of an FTC rule against ex parte contacts and enforced it far more strenuously than his predecessors. One Washington attorney stated:

Up until Mike came in, the Commission as a whole used to meet regularly with different industries, sit down, have lunch or something, and discuss what was going on. . . . That was perceived as bad when Mike came in. They closed the door and became largely dependent on information generated by their staff. They controlled all information and the ex parte rule prevented people from going directly to the Commission and saying, hey, there's something wrong here.

Kennedy School Study at 11-12.

The first major policy initiative undertaken by Pertschuk's FTC focused on the effect of television advertising on children. As Pertschuk was well aware, a growing number of parents, psychologists, and politicians had expressed concern about the impact of television on young children's perceptions, beliefs, and behavior. Led by a citizens' group from Massachusetts called Action for Children's Television (ACT), the movement had gained significant attention in the media and in the government. Several congressional committees, including the Consumer Subcommittee of Pertschuk's own Senate Commerce Committee, had held hearings on the subject, as had the FCC. Although none of these proceedings had produced concrete regulatory results, interest in the issue — particularly the issue of "commercial exploitation" of children — continued.

At Pertschuk's confirmation hearing, Senator Warren Magnuson (Chairman of the Commerce Committee during Pertschuk's tenure there), commented:

> Now we've all been interested here in children's advertising; it's a difficult, complex subject. . . . I would hope you would take a good, long look when you talk about advertising [with the FCC]. I hate to narrow this down, but the abuses seem to be in children's advertising, advertising directed at children.

Nominations — March Hearings Before the Sen. Comm. on Commerce, Science, and Transportation, 95th Cong., 1st Sess. 80 (1977). In response to a written question regarding his views of the FTC's shortcomings, moreover, Pertschuk stated: "It is not clear that the Commission has yet developed a sophisticated understanding of the impact of broadcast advertising, particularly upon children. . . . If advertising is in part responsible for conditioning a nation of sugar junkies, it should be held accountable." *Id.* at 72.

Pertschuk quickly decided to make children's television — or "kidvid," as it became known — the centerpiece of his consumer protection policy. As he later explained:

> I had come as the candidate of the consumer groups. And I had to do something early to establish my good faith with them, because they were easily dissatisfied, and I felt it was important to maintain their trust. And that was sort of the strategy but also I wanted it. I basically felt close to them and I felt an identity with them. And so it was important to me not to be dismissed as just another coopted bureaucrat.

Kennedy School Study at 13.

Pertschuk began speaking out with increasing frequency on the subject of children's television. In an appearance on the *Today Show*, October 31, 1977, the following colloquy took place between Pertschuk, a viewer named Susan Lovett, and the interviewer, Robert Abernathy:

Susan Lovett: Mr. Pertschuk, I'd like to know what's being done about advertising on TV for children and all the garbage that's advertised for the kiddies.

Pertschuk: Well, I'm glad you asked the question. It's an area of prime concern to me and to the Commission itself. There's a very basic question in our society, and that is the question to which—the extent to which children are to be treated as commercial objects. One advertiser in New York described advertising directed to children as guided missiles, turning the children into guided missiles through the heart of the parent into its pocketbook.

Abernathy: Is it your personal opinion that no television advertising, for instance, should be directed at children?

Pertschuk: I have some serious doubt as to whether any television advertising should be directed at a three or four or five year old, a preschooler. They're not competent to understand the nature of the message. We've never treated children as commercial objects in our society. And of course, print advertising only reaches those who can read. But television advertising in the home, directed to children, is a new phenomenon in our society, and I think a troublesome one.

Abernathy: Would you like to see the FTC ban it altogether?

Pertschuk: Not necessarily. But we've not excluded the possibility of bans on certain advertising of certain products to children. The Trade Commission has not, as a body—you know, there are four other commissioners who must address this issue for the Commission to act—has not, as a body, yet approached the question of the remedy for the evils we see in children's advertising. We'll do that next month.

A week later (November 8, 1977), in a speech before the ACT Research Conference in Boston, Pertschuk sketched out more fully the basis for his concern:

Commercials do not disclose their nature—that is, the economic interest of the advertiser in convincing the viewer. To the small child it is as if a trusted friend urged the consumption of a particular product, not for personal gain, but solely out of concern for the child. . . . If there is one salient public policy which arises commandingly from centuries of common and statutory law, it is that the commercial exploitation of children is repugnant to a civilized society. Why isn't that principle applicable to television advertising directed at young children? Why shouldn't established legal precedents embodying this public policy be applied to protect children from this form of exploitation? In short, why isn't such advertising unfair within the meaning of the Federal Trade Commission Act and, hence, unlawful? [C]hildren have become the target market for products that promise immediate satisfaction. With food, this often means instant pleasure—and the danger of long-term malnutrition. [C]hildren are not adults in miniature. Instead, they bring to advertising a special perspective and sensibility—a credulousness that comes from inexperience—which advertisers exploit. . . . Children lack the judgment and experience to see that something that looks good to them in the short run can hurt them in the long run. They cannot protect themselves against adults who exploit their present-mindedness. . . . Shouldn't society apply the law's strictures against commercial exploitation of children, and the law's solicitude for the health of children to ads that threaten to cause imminent harm—harm which ranges from increasing tooth decay and malnutrition to injecting unconscionable stress into the parent-child relationship? It may be that only a ban on the advertising of these products on programs directed towards the young child can help remedy their inherent defect.

If the Commission is to reach sound and reasoned judgments, it must also hear from the parents, the teachers, the pediatricians, the dentists, those health and education specialists on whom we rely for the advocacy of our children's best interest. We must be rigorous and open-minded in our analysis of both law and fact. At stake are fundamental questions about the extent to which our society will permit the treatment of children as commercial objects rather than formative human beings entrusted to our care.

The next day, he distributed copies of his speech to various people whose views he considered sympathetic. The following note to FCC Chairman Charles Ferris is typical of the cover memoranda that accompanied the text.

November 9, 1977

MEMORANDUM

TO: Charlie Ferris
FROM: Mike Pertschuk

Now after shooting my mouth off for three months here's our effort at putting some legal underpinnings under our initiatives on children's advertising. I should probably come over in the next couple of days to make sure that we don't cross each other inadvertently. . . .

Shortly thereafter Pertschuk dispatched a letter to FDA Commissioner Donald Kennedy describing the kidvid initiative:

November 17, 1977

Honorable Donald Kennedy
Food and Drug Administration
Parklawn Building
5600 Fishers Lane
Rockville, Maryland 20852

Dear Don:

Setting legal theory aside, the truth is that we've been drawn into this issue because of the conviction, which I know you share, that one of the evils flowing from the unfairness of children's advertising is the resulting distortion of children's perceptions of nutritional values. I see, at this point, our logical process as follows: children's advertising is inherently unfair. As a policy planning agency we have to make judgments as to our priorities. The first area in which we choose to act is an area in which a substantial controversy exists as to the health consequences of encouraging consumption of sugared products (not just cereals). With this formulation we do not have to prove the health consequences of sugared cereals. What we do have to prove is that there is a substantial health controversy regarding the health consequences of sugar—a much lower burden of proof.

I'm convinced that the convergence of public policies regarding the commercial exploitation of children with the health controversy over sugared products give[s] us a stronger base and frankly deal[s] directly with the underlying concerns which prompt our action.

Sincerely yours,

Michael Pertschuk

In February 1978, the FTC staff presented to the commission a report recommending that the FTC issue a rule under §18 of the FTC Act prohibiting all television advertising specifically aimed at children under the age of eight. Section 18, 15 U.S.C. §57a, authorizes the commission, after following certain elaborate procedures, to issue rules defining certain acts or practices in or affecting commerce as "unfair" or "deceptive." Children's advertising, the staff argued, is inherently "unfair" because young children lack the capacity to comprehend its commercial purpose. In addition, the staff argued that advertising of sugared foods aimed at children of any age was unfair because it failed to disclose the health hazards associated with the consumption of sugar.

After lengthy discussion, the five commissioners could not agree on any specific proposal. As a compromise, Pertschuk managed to persuade his fellow commissioners to present three different options for comment by the public. The options, as described in the April 27, 1978, Notice of Proposed Rulemaking, were

(a) Ban all televised advertising for any product which is directed to, or seen by, audiences composed of a significant proportion of children who are too young to understand the selling purpose of or otherwise comprehend or evaluate the advertising;

(b) Ban televised advertising for sugared food products directed to, or seen by, audiences composed of a significant proportion of older children, the consumption of which products poses the most serious dental health risks;

(c) Require televised advertising for sugared food products not included in Paragraph (b), which is directed to, or seen by, audiences composed of a significant proportion of older children, to be balanced by nutritional and/or health disclosures funded by advertisers.

43 Fed. Reg. 17,967, 17,969 (1978).

The notice hit the then-$600 million children's advertising industry like a nuclear blast. Advertisers, manufacturers, and broadcasters leapt to the ramparts. On May 8, 1978, the national trade associations of advertisers, advertising agencies, and toy manufacturers petitioned Pertschuk to remove himself from participation in the rulemaking proceeding, alleging that his many public statements on the kidvid issue evidenced prejudgment and bias. On July 13, Pertschuk declined to remove himself; a decision supported five days later by his four colleagues. The following litigation ensued.

ASSOCIATION OF NATIONAL ADVERTISERS,
INC. v. FEDERAL TRADE COMMISSION
627 F.2d 1151 (D.C. Cir. 1979), *cert. denied*, 447 U.S. 921 (1980)

Before TAMM, LEVENTHAL, and MACKINNON, Circuit Judges.

TAMM, Circuit Judge:

Plaintiffs, appellees here, brought an action in the United States District Court for the District of Columbia to prohibit Michael Pertschuk, Chairman of the Federal Trade Commission (Commission), from participating in a pending rulemaking proceeding concerning children's advertising. The district court, citing this court's decision in Cinderella Career & Finishing Schools, Inc. v. FTC, 425 F.2d 583 (D.C. Cir. 1970), found that Chairman Pertschuk had prejudged issues involved in the rulemaking and ordered him disqualified. . . .

III

The Commission attacks the substance of the district court's decision on two grounds. First, it insists that the standard for disqualification of an administrative decisionmaker in rulemaking differs from the standard in adjudication. The Commission's view rests on the different purposes of rulemaking and adjudication and on the long-standing rule that due process requirements are not the same in the two contexts. Second, the Commission asserts that under any disqualification standard, Chairman Pertschuk cannot be found to have prejudged issues in contravention of due process. . . .

A

. . . In *Cinderella,* we held that the standard for disqualifying an administrator in an adjudicatory proceeding because of prejudgment is whether " 'a disinterested observer may conclude that [the decisionmaker] has in some measure adjudged the facts as well as the law of a particular case in advance of hearing it.' " . . . This standard guarantees that the adjudicative hearing of a person facing administrative prosecution for past behavior is before a decisionmaker who has not prejudged facts concerning the events under review.

B

The district court in the case now before us held that "the standard of conduct delineated in *Cinderella*" governs agency decisionmakers participating in a section 18 proceeding. . . . Section 18 authorizes the Commission to promulgate rules designed to "define with specificity acts or practices which are unfair or deceptive." Basically, it allows the Commission to enforce the broad command of section 5 of the FTC Act, which declares "unfair or deceptive acts or practices in or affecting commerce . . . unlawful." The district court ruled that a section 18 proceeding, notwithstanding the appellation rulemaking, "is neither wholly legislative nor wholly adjudicative." According to the district court, the "adjudicative aspects" of the proceeding render *Cinderella* applicable. . . .

The appellees urge us to uphold the district court's analysis of section 18. They emphasize two allegedly "adjudicatory aspects" of a section 18 proceeding: (1) interested persons are entitled to limited cross-examination of those who testify to disputed issues of material fact, *see* 15 U.S.C. §57a(c)(1)(B) (1976), and (2) a reviewing court must set aside any rule not supported by substantial evidence in the rulemaking record taken as a whole, *see* 15 U.S.C. §57a(e)(3)(A) (1976).[14]

The district court's characterization of section 18 rulemaking as a "hybrid" or quasi-adjudicative proceeding . . . ignores the clear scheme of the APA. Administrative action pursuant to the APA is either adjudication or rulemaking. The two processes differ fundamentally in purpose and focus:

> The object of the rule making proceeding is the implementation or prescription of law or policy for the future, rather than the evaluation of a respondent's past conduct. Typically, the issues relate not to the evidentiary facts, as to which the veracity and demeanor of witnesses would often be important, but rather to the policy-making conclusions to be drawn from the facts. . . . Conversely, adjudication is concerned with the determination of past and present rights and liabilities. Normally, there is involved a decision as to whether past conduct was unlawful, so that the proceeding is characterized by an accusatory flavor and may result in disciplinary action.

Attorney General's Manual on the Administrative Procedure Act 14 (1947). *See* United States v. Florida East Coast Railway, 410 U.S. 224, 244-46 (1973).

Adjudication and rulemaking may be conducted pursuant to either informal or formal procedures. . . .

[The APA sets forth] the basic parameters of administrative action. Congress has, in the Magnuson-Moss Warranty—Federal Trade Commission Improvement (Magnuson-Moss) Act §202(a), 15 U.S.C. §57a (1976), and elsewhere, enacted specific statutory rulemaking provisions that require more procedures than those of section 553 but less than the full procedures required under sections 556 and 557. The presence of procedures not mandated by section 553, however, does not, as the appellees urge, convert rulemaking into quasi-adjudication. The appellees err by focusing on the details of administrative process rather than the nature of administrative action. . . .

[T]he Commission's children's advertising inquiry is designed to determine whether certain acts or practices will, in the future, be considered to contravene the FTC Act. The proceeding is not adjudication or quasi-adjudication. It is a clear exercise of the Commission's rulemaking authority.

---

14. The appellees also argue that "the principal characteristic of adjudicative proceedings which necessitates the *Cinderella* prejudgment standard is the requirement (which traditionally has applied to judges but not to legislators) that the ultimate decision be based upon record evidence. This, of course, is one of the most significant characteristics which the Commission's adjudicative proceedings and its Section 18 trade regulation rulemaking proceedings have in common." Brief of Intervening Plaintiff-Appellee Kellogg Company at 38. The appellees' attempt to equate rulemaking with adjudication on the basis of a record requirement would have more force, however, if §18 demanded rulemaking decisions to be based on a closed record, as are adjudicatory determinations. See 5 U.S.C. §556(e) (1976). Section 18, in fact, provides that for purposes of judicial review the "rulemaking record" includes "any . . . information which the Commission considers relevant to such rule." 15 U.S.C. §57a(e)(1)(B) (1976). Section 18 thus does not prohibit reliance on material not adduced during the rulemaking proceedings; it simply requires the Commission to acknowledge that reliance.

C

The appellees also argue that we must apply *Cinderella* because it involves a factual prejudgment similar to the one now before us. In *Cinderella,* Chairman Dixon made statements that reflected prejudgment that Cinderella Career & Finishing Schools, Inc. had engaged in certain acts. In this case, the appellees accuse Chairman Pertschuk of prejudging issues of material fact in the children's television proceeding. We find that the appellees' argument belies a misunderstanding of the factual basis of rules.

The factual predicate of a rulemaking decision substantially differs in nature and in use from the factual predicate of an adjudicatory decision. The factual predicate of adjudication depends on ascertainment of "facts concerning the immediate parties—who did what, where, when, how and with what motive or intent." 2 K. Davis, Administrative Law Treatise, §15.03, at 353 (1958). By contrast, the nature of legislative fact is ordinarily general, without reference to specific parties. Adjudicative and legislative facts are also used differently:

> [A]djudicative facts are those to which the law is applied in the process of adjudication. They are the facts that normally go to the jury in a jury case. . . . Legislative facts are the facts which help the tribunal determine the content of law and of policy and help the tribunal to exercise its judgment or discretion in determining what course of action to take.

Id. Thus, legislative facts are crucial to the prediction of future events and to the evaluation of certain risks, both of which are inherent in administrative policymaking. . . .

Because legislative facts combine empirical observation with application of administrative expertise to reach generalized conclusions, they need not be developed through evidentiary hearings. . . .

Evidentiary hearings, although not necessary to determine legislative facts, nevertheless may be helpful in certain circumstances. For example, Congress, when it enacted the Magnuson-Moss Act, recognized that special circumstances might warrant the use of evidentiary proceedings in determining legislative facts. Under section 18(c)(1)(B)[25] and section 18(c)(2)(B),[26] the Commission must conduct a hearing, with a limited right of cross-examination, when it resolves disputed issues of material fact. The legislative history of the Magnuson-Moss Act states that "[t]he only disputed issues of material fact to be determined for resolution by the Commission are those issues characterized as issues of specific fact in contrast to legislative fact." H.R. Rep. No. 93-1606, 93d Cong., 2d Sess. 33 (1974) (Conference Report). . . .

---

25. Section 18 (c)(1)(B) provides that "an interested person is entitled . . . if the Commission determines that there are disputed issues of material fact it is necessary to resolve, to present such rebuttal submissions and to conduct (or have conducted under paragraph (2)(B)) such cross-examination of persons as the Commission determines (i) to be appropriate, and (ii) to be required for a full and true disclosure with respect to such issues." 15 U.S.C. §57a(c)(1)(B).

26. Section 18 (c)(2)(B) provides that the Commission may prescribe rules that include "requirements that any cross-examination to which a person may be entitled under paragraph (1) be conducted by the Commission on behalf of that person in such manner as the Commission determines (i) to be appropriate, and (ii) to be required for a full and true disclosure with respect to disputed issues of material fact." 15 U.S.C. §57a(c)(2)(B).

Nothing in the legislative history or background of section 18 suggests, however, that Congress believed that the use of evidentiary hearings transformed the nature of the proceedings from rulemaking to adjudication or altered the factual predicate of rulemaking from legislative to adjudicative fact. Accordingly, the appellees' contention that the *Cinderella* standard must be applied to section 18 rulemaking because it invokes the same type of factual judgments as Commission adjudication is simply incorrect. . . .

In *Cinderella,* the court was able to cleave fact from law in deciding whether Chairman Dixon had prejudged particular factual issues. In the rulemaking context, however, the factual component of the policy decision is not easily assessed in terms of an empirically verifiable condition. Rulemaking involves the kind of issues "where a month of experience will be worth a year of hearings." Application of *Cinderella*'s strict law-fact dichotomy would necessarily limit the ability of administrators to discuss policy questions.

The legitimate functions of a policymaker, unlike an adjudicator, demand interchange and discussion about important issues. We must not impose judicial roles upon administrators when they perform functions very different from those of judges. . . .

The *Cinderella* view of a neutral and detached adjudicator is simply an inapposite role model for an administrator who must translate broad statutory commands into concrete social policies. If an agency official is to be effective he must engage in debate and discussion about the policy matters before him. As this court has recognized before, "informal contacts between agencies and the public are the 'bread and butter' of the process of administration." Home Box Office, Inc. v. FCC, 567 F.2d 9, 57 (D.C. Cir.) (per curiam), *cert. denied,* 434 U.S. 829 (1977). . . .

Accordingly, a Commissioner should be disqualified only when there has been a clear and convincing showing that the agency member has an unalterably closed mind on matters critical to the disposition of the proceeding. The "clear and convincing" test is necessary to rebut the presumption of administrative regularity. *See, e.g.,* Withrow v. Larkin, 421 U.S. 35, 55 (1975); Hercules, Inc. v. EPA, 598 F.2d 91, 123 (D.C. Cir. 1978). The "unalterably closed mind" test is necessary to permit rulemakers to carry out their proper policy-based functions while disqualifying those unable to consider meaningfully a section 18 hearing.

V

We view the statements offered as grounds for disqualification as a whole to discern whether they evidence a clear and convincing showing that Chairman Pertschuk has an unalterably closed mind on matters critical to the children's television proceeding. . . .

Chairman Pertschuk's remarks, considered as a whole, represent discussion, and perhaps advocacy, of the legal theory that might support exercise of the Commission's jurisdiction over children's advertising. The mere discussion of policy or advocacy on a legal question, however, is not sufficient to disqualify an administrator. To present legal and policy arguments, Pertschuk not unnaturally employed the factual assumptions that underlie the rationale for Commission action. The simple fact that the Chairman explored issues based on legal and factual assumptions, however, did not necessarily bind him to them forever. Rather, he remained free, both in theory and in reality, to change his mind upon consideration of the presentations made by those who would be affected. . . .

We also note that Chairman Pertschuk made the challenged comments before the Commission adopted its notice of proposed rulemaking. This court has never suggested that the interchange between rulemaker and the public should be limited prior to the initiation of agency action. The period before the Commission first decides to take action on a perceived problem is, in fact, the best time for a rulemaker to engage in dialogue with concerned citizens. Discussion would be futile, of course, if the administrator could not test his own views on different audiences. Moreover, as we stated earlier, an expression of opinion prior to the issuance of a proposed rulemaking does not, without more, show that an agency member cannot maintain an open mind during the hearing stage of the proceeding. . . .

In sum, we hold that the materials adduced by the appellees are insufficient to rebut the strong presumption of administrative regularity. . . .

Reversed.

LEVENTHAL, Circuit Judge, concurring: . . .

In fulfilling the functions of applying or considering the validity of a statute, or a government program, the judge endeavors to put aside personal views as to the desirability of the law or program, and he is not disqualified because he personally deems the program laudable or objectionable. In the case of agency rulemaking, however, the decisionmaking officials are appointed precisely to implement statutory programs, and with the expectation that they have a personal disposition to enforce them vigilantly and effectively. They work with a combination rather than a separation of functions, in legislative modes, and take action on the basis of information coming from many sources, even though that provides a mindset before a proceeding is begun, subject to reconsideration in the light of the proceeding. . . .

One can hypothesize beginning an adjudicatory proceeding with an open mind, indeed a blank mind, a tabula rasa devoid of any previous knowledge of the matter. In sharp contrast, one cannot even conceive of an agency conducting a rulemaking proceeding unless it had delved into the subject sufficiently to become concerned that there was an evil or abuse that required regulatory response. It would be the height of absurdity, even a kind of abuse of administrative process, for an agency to embroil interested parties in a rulemaking proceeding, without some initial concern that there was an abuse that needed remedying, a concern that would be set forth in the accompanying statement of the purpose of the proposed rule. . . .

It is appropriate and indeed mandatory for agency heads and staff to maintain contacts with industry and consumer groups, trade associations and press, congressmen of various persuasions, and to present views in interviews, speeches, meetings, conventions, and testimony. The agency gathers information and perceptions in a myriad of ways and must use it for a myriad of purposes. With capacity and willingness to reconsider there is no basis for disqualification. . . .

MACKINNON, Circuit Judge (dissenting in part and concurring in part). . . .

In my opinion the "unalterably closed mind," where it exists, in many cases is practically impossible to prove, imposes too high a barrier to the public's obtaining fair decisionmakers and is a higher standard than the Supreme Court has applied in its recent decisions. I would require any Federal Trade Commissioner to recuse himself, or failing that to be disqualified, upon a showing by a preponderance of the evidence that he could not participate fairly in the formulation of the rule because of substantial bias or prejudgment with respect to any critical fact that must be resolved in such formulation.

Also, in my view the majority opinion places too much reliance on the strict rulemaking/adjudication dichotomy, applied in earlier cases under the Administrative Procedure Act. The Magnuson-Moss Act creates a rulemaking procedure that combines elements of *both* rulemaking and adjudication, as those functions are exercised under the Administrative Procedure Act, and this blending of the two procedures makes it impossible to look at Magnuson-Moss rulemaking as anything but a combination of the two. . . .

While it may have been Congress' design to place Commissioners in the dual roles of policymaker and decisionmaker, it was also Congress' intent that parties to Magnuson-Moss Act rulemaking have their evidence considered fairly and impartially. Hence, in disqualifying a decisionmaker who cannot decide with the requisite degree of fairness and impartiality, we would protect the political process, rather than interfere with it. . . .

Notwithstanding that the majority opinion holds that a "fair decisionmaker" is to be guaranteed for this rulemaking, the opinion seeks to obviate such guarantee, if I read the opinion correctly, by holding that Commissioners in their Magnuson-Moss rulemaking are to be considered the same as Congressmen, and the fairness with which they approach their rulemaking cannot be attacked because Congressmen are not subject to similar constraints in enacting legislation. . . .

It is true that legislators are not required to make findings of fact to support their legislation and that they cannot be disqualified by any court for bias, but there are other safeguards in the legislative process that compensate for the absence of such safeguards as are expressly imposed or implicit in the administrative process. First of all, legislators are *elected* by the voters of their district, and those in the House are elected for a relatively short term—only two years. They can be turned out very quickly if any bias they disclose offends their constituents. Secondly, there is a protection in the sheer size of Congress—535 members of the House and Senate—that implicitly diffuses bias and guarantees that impermissible bias of individual members will not control. There is safety in numbers and a biased Congressman soon loses influence among the other members, if he ever acquired any. Also, the two house system and the Presidential veto are tremendous guarantees that legislation will not be the result of individual bias or even the impermissible bias of one house.

Because these legislative safeguards were not applicable to Federal Trade Commissioners, Congress saw fit to impose other safeguards, *i.e.,* (1) confirmation by the Senate, (2) limited terms for FTC Commissioners, (3) public notice and mandatory public hearings when proposing legislative type rules, (4) cross-examination, rebuttal, a public written record, a statement of reasons and purpose, and (5) a requirement that *whatever rule is promulgated be supported by substantial evidence on the record as a whole,* and (6) be subject to judicial review and other safeguards previously noted.

Congress considered these safeguards to be necessary to provide the same degree of protection that exists in Congress with respect to its exercise of legislative power. . . .

Because of the deficiencies pointed out above, I would reject the unalterably closed mind standard as imposing a practically impossible impediment in a great many cases to a showing of bias, even when the decisionmaker has in fact made up his mind in advance of the hearing. It is an unfair method of determining unfairness. . . .

This is not to say that a Commissioner is necessarily to be disqualified if he (or she) has expressed opinions on policy matters that are later involved in Commission rulemaking. Rather, the moving party must show by a preponderance of the evidence that the decisionmaker could not participate fairly in the formulation of the rule because of substantial bias or prejudgment on any critical fact that must be resolved in such formulation. Such proof will be greatly aided where, as here, the decisionmaker's public statements repeatedly reveal fixed conclusions upon the primary issue that the agency proceeding contemplated would only be determined *after* the hearing.

NOTES AND QUESTIONS

1. *The standard for disqualification.* Two arguably distinct questions are presented in *National Advertisers*: First, should the standard for disqualification vary with the type of *issue* presented or the type of *proceeding*? Second, what should be the standard for this case? The court seems to have answered the first question by treating the proceeding, rather than the issue, as the significant determinant. Does the court adequately explain its choice of approach? Is the court's strict rulemaking-adjudication dichotomy consistent with the statutory scheme? With *HBO*? With *Sierra Club*?

The second issue is the nature of the standard. Given the strict bipolar approach used by the court, should *any* restriction be placed on the decisionmaker? Would a member of Congress be disqualified from voting on a bill for having an "unalterably closed mind" on the bill? Why should an administrative "lawmaker" be treated differently? For a defense of the majority's standard, *see* Peter L. Strauss, Disqualifications of Decisional Officials in Rulemaking, 80 Colum. L. Rev. 990 (1980).

2. *Pertschuk's statements.* Examine Pertschuk's statements. Has he in fact prejudged *anything*? Isn't this just so much bold political rhetoric, of the sort you would expect from a crusading regulator? Would Pertschuk's statements even violate the *Cinderella* standard? For fuller discussion of the *Cinderella* case and the topic of adjudicative bias, *see* Chapter VI, *infra*.

3. *"Unalterably closed mind" in practice.* As is probably not surprising, no court applying the unalterably closed mind standard has disqualified an agency official from participating in a rulemaking proceeding. The D.C. Circuit has even denied discovery on the issue without " 'strong' evidence of 'unalterably closed minds.' " Air Transport Assn. of America, Inc. v. National Mediation Bd., 663 F.3d 476, 488 (D.C. Cir. 2011). Why would a court apply such a high threshold for discovery?

Although not arising in the context of rulemaking, strictly speaking, Department of Commerce v. New York, 139 S. Ct. 2551 (2019), excerpted at length in Chapter II, *supra*, contains hints of "disqualifying bias." In finding that the Secretary of Commerce offered a "pretextual" rationale for including a citizenship question in the 2020 census, Chief Justice Roberts noted that:

[The] evidence showed that the Secretary was determined to reinstate a citizenship question from the time he entered office; instructed his staff to make it happen; waited while Commerce officials explored whether another agency would request census-based citizenship data; subsequently contacted the Attorney General himself to ask if DOJ would make the request; and adopted the Voting Rights Act rationale late in the process. . . . We are presented, in other words, with an explanation for agency action that is incongruent with what the record reveals about the agency's priorities and decisionmaking process. [W]e cannot ignore the disconnect between the decision made and the explanation given. Our review is deferential, but we are "not required to exhibit a naiveté from which ordinary citizens are free." *United States* v. *Stanchich*, 550 F.2d 1294, 1300 (1977) (Friendly, J.). The reasoned explanation requirement of administrative law, after all, is meant to ensure that agencies offer genuine justifications for important decisions, reasons that can be scrutinized by courts and the interested public. Accepting contrived reasons would defeat the purpose of the enterprise. If judicial review is to be more than an empty ritual, it must demand something better than the explanation offered for the action taken in this case. 139 S. Ct. at 2574-2576. Is the Secretary of Commerce's predisposition qualitatively different from Chairman Pertschuk's predisposition? Are the statutory and procedural contexts different?

4. *The result of the children's advertising rulemaking.* After the *National Advertisers* decision, the FTC's children's advertising rulemaking proceedings went forward with Michael Pertschuk participating. Hearings were held before an administrative law judge, but in the middle of the process Congress passed the FTC Improvements Act of 1980, which prohibited the commission from issuing trade regulation rules except on a theory of deception and required that any proposed rules be published in advance of adoption. After futile efforts by FTC staff to develop proposed rules based exclusively on a theory of deception, on October 2, 1981, the commission terminated the proceedings, concluding that "resolution of the many factual issues essential to a trade regulation rule would involve lengthy and complex proceedings [and i]t is also apparent that the ultimate definitive resolution of these factual issues . . . is highly speculative." The commission also expressed concern that even if it were able to resolve the factual issues it would be unable to construct an effective remedy and that the effort would be so substantial that it would be required to divert resources "from other pressing enforcement priorities." *See* 46 Fed. Reg. at 48,713.

In the wake of the failure of the FTC's children's advertising rulemaking, the only constraints aimed specifically at children's advertising are voluntary standards developed by industry groups. In the meanwhile, spending on advertising directed at children has grown to a more recent estimate of $15 to $17 billion annually, or nearly 10 times the rate of inflation as compared to the spending at the time of *National Advertisers*. Why do you think such impressive growth has occurred in advertising directed at children?

4. Embellishing the APA Model of Informal Rulemaking Through "Hybrid" Procedures

a. Statutory Hybrids

Congress has, on many occasions, statutorily added to the minimal procedures required by §553 of the APA for informal rulemaking, without going all the way to requiring formal rulemaking. Such statutes typically add, *inter alia,* oral hearings and cross-examination to the rulemaking process, procedures that are usually associated with adjudication. In light of this reality, they have become known as "hybrid" procedures.

The statutes involved in *Sierra Club* and *National Advertisers* are good examples of statutory hybrids. For example, the Clean Air Act contains a number of hybrid rulemaking provisions, going beyond the informal rulemaking requirements of the APA. Elaborating on basic notice-and-comment procedures, 42 U.S.C. §7607(d) requires EPA to:

(1) Create a docket for each proposed rulemaking, which must contain comments, data on which the proposed rule relies, and all documents related to the rule. The docket must be open to public inspection at reasonable times, and available for anyone to copy any of the documents contained therein;

(2) Gather and reference input by the Scientific Review Committee and the National Academy of Science, and explain why the proposed rule differs in any respect from the recommendations of these two groups;

(3) Give interested persons an opportunity to make oral presentations of data or arguments in addition to written submissions, and include the transcript of the presentation in the docket;

(4) Respond, in the promulgated rule, to each of the significant comments, data, or criticisms submitted orally or in written form during the period for comments; and

(5) Not base any part of the promulgated rule on information or data that has not been placed in the docket.

In *Sierra Club,* excerpted *supra,* Judge Wald noted that these requirements (particularly the one requiring all documents that are relevant to the rulemaking to be placed in the docket) were intended to address the problems with ex parte communications that *HBO* identified. *See* Sidney A. Shapiro, Two Cheers for *HBO*: The Problem of the Nonpublic Record, 54 Admin. L. Rev. 853, 859-860 (2002).

The Federal Trade Commission Improvement Act of 1974 (generally known as the Magnuson-Moss Act), 15 U.S.C. §57a (1976), provides that:

(1) Before issuing a legally binding trade regulation rule, the Federal Trade Commission must "publish a notice of proposed rulemaking stating with particularity the reason for the proposed rule."

(2) There is a mandatory minimum time for public comment, and any submission during this period must be made "publicly available."

(3) An informal hearing must be held at which interested parties may argue their positions orally, may, within limits, cross-examine other parties, and may submit rebuttal evidence.

(4) The APA requirement that a final rule be accompanied by "a concise general statement of . . . basis and purpose" is expanded by the Magnuson-Moss Act to include "(A) a statement as to the prevalence of the acts or practices treated by the rule; (B) a statement as to the manner and context in which such acts or practices are unfair or deceptive; and (C) a statement as to the economic effect of the rule, taking into account the effect on small business and consumers."

(5) To survive review in court, a trade regulation rule must be "supported by substantial evidence in the rulemaking record . . . taken as a whole," although the rulemaking record is expansively defined as consisting of the rule, the statement of basis and purpose, the transcript of the oral hearing, written submissions, and "any other information which the Commission considers relevant to such rule."

Other procedures were added to this list as a result of the Federal Trade Commission Improvement Act of 1980, Pub. L. No. 96-252, 94 Stat. 374. The 1980 Act directs the FTC, prior to publication of the notice of proposed rulemaking required by Magnuson-Moss, to publish an advance notice of proposed rulemaking in the Federal Register. This advance notice of proposed rulemaking must "(i) contain a brief description of the area of inquiry under consideration, the objectives which the Commission seeks to achieve, and possible regulatory alternatives under consideration by the Commission; and (ii) invite the response of interested parties with respect to such proposed rulemaking, including any suggestions or alternative methods for achieving such objectives." 15 U.S.C. §57a(b)(2)(A). The FTC now also must submit any notice of proposed rulemaking to the Commerce Committees of the House and Senate 30 days before publication in the Federal Register. 15 U.S.C. §57a(b)(2)(B)-(C).

b. Judicially Fashioned Hybrids

Even in the absence of such statutory hybrids, some courts have been tempted to embellish the rather spare rulemaking framework erected by APA §553. One can perhaps sympathize with their reasons for wanting to do so. Decisions like *Abbott Laboratories*, in Chapter II, *supra*, and *Overton Park*, in Chapter II, *supra*, respectively encouraging pre-enforcement review of informal rules and mandating review of informal proceedings on the "administrative record," present reviewing courts with a dilemma. Forced to conduct "on the record" review of "off the record" rulemaking proceedings, or of informal decisions with little in the way of an identifiable administrative record, lower courts began requiring agencies to utilize trial-like procedural devices, such as oral hearings, cross-examination, written interrogatories, and written rebuttals, designed to improve the quality of the rulemaking "record." The D.C. Circuit led the way in fashioning such procedures, as illustrated by the *Portland Cement* case, discussed in Part B.1., *supra*.

Judicial imposition of hybrid procedures was always plagued by the question of legitimacy—on what authority may courts impose greater than §553 procedures in informal rulemaking? While courts paid little attention to this issue, something of an explanation was provided by the D.C. Circuit in Mobil Oil Corp. v. FPC, 483 F.2d 1238 (D.C. Cir. 1973). After rejecting the argument that the Federal Power Commission was required to make certain complicated rate determinations "on the record" and only after a formal hearing under §557, the court went on to hold that the FPC was nonetheless required to provide something more than the bare minimum of §553. The court found support for its decision in the requirement that reviewing courts consider the "whole record" and the fact that the Natural Gas Act provides for "substantial evidence" review of FPC rules. *See id* at 1257-1258.

The era of procedural creativity by the federal appeals courts reached its peak in the latter half of the 1970s, as illustrated by the D.C. Circuit's *HBO* decision of 1977, excerpted *supra*. Throughout this period, the Supreme Court stood by silently, even declining to grant certiorari in several instances (including *HBO*). Then, finally, in a celebrated controversy over the licensing of nuclear power plants, the Supreme Court weighed in, and weighed in decisively!

Since a 1973 leak of 115,000 gallons of high-level radioactive waste from the Hanford Reservation nuclear facility in Washington, waste disposal has become a major issue in the public debate about nuclear energy. One important aspect of that debate has focused on the role that the waste disposal issue should play in decisions about licensing nuclear power plants. Should the dangers posed by nuclear waste count against a utility company's application for permission to build a new plant? If so, how should that factor be incorporated into the decision? The following case study describes the development of federal regulatory policy on that question, beginning with a celebrated controversy over the licensing of the Vermont Yankee power plant in Vernon, Vermont.

There are two methods of producing nuclear energy: fission and fusion. Fission involves the release of energy when uranium or plutonium atoms are split into smaller atoms. Fusion is the release of energy when hydrogen atoms fuse into larger atoms of hydrogen. As a controlled nuclear fusion process has yet to be perfected, present nuclear power plants depend on fission reactors using enriched uranium fuel.

Energy is produced in a fission reaction by placing unstable uranium atoms in metal tubes and heating those tubes through the emission of neutrons from the radioactive uranium. Water flowing past the hot tubes is converted into steam, which generates electricity. After the uranium and tubes are used, they are discharged from the reactor as "spent fuel." Spent fuel is the largest component of nuclear waste: in 1983 about 10,000 tons of it were stored at reactor sites. Other waste products of the uranium fuel cycle include tailings from uranium mining, by-products of fission reactions, and metals and other materials contaminated by exposure to radioactive material. *See* Too Hot to Handle? Social and Policy Issues in the Management of Radioactive Wastes (Charles A. Walker et al., eds., 1983).

During their decay, these materials emit alpha particles, beta particles, gamma rays, and neutrons. Exposure to large doses of radiation can lead to death, genetic changes, and illnesses such as leukemia and cancer. Many by-products of the nuclear fuel cycle continue to emit harmful levels of radiation for long periods of time. The strontium-90 and cesium-137 contained in spent fuel rods, for example, have half-lives of 30 years. The concentration of these elements in spent fuel is so great that the rods must be isolated from the human and natural environment for 600 to 1,000 years.

The goal of nuclear waste management is thus to develop a way to store these materials until their radioactivity is no longer dangerous. As of 1974, some low-level radioactive wastes were being buried in shallow land sites or held in underground tanks, while most high-level waste material was stored in special water-filled pools at reactor sites. Since many of these storage facilities were reaching maximum design capacity, however, pressure was mounting for a longer range solution. In response, the federal government sponsored research on new methods for dealing with nuclear wastes. Proposed storage locations included ice beds, the ocean floor, outer space, or deep underground repositories. The most promising expedient seemed to be underground burial in salt, granite, or clay mines. It was unclear, however, whether the government could locate sites that would be free of geologic faults and water runoffs, capable of being policed and secured for extended time periods, and acceptable to the surrounding public.

Opponents of nuclear power were quick to seize upon these uncertainties as a basis for opposing the licensing of new plants. Under the Atomic Energy Act of 1954, 68 Stat. 919, utilities wishing to construct and operate nuclear power plants must obtain a construction permit and an operating license from the Atomic Energy Commission (later the Nuclear Regulatory Commission). To obtain a construction license, utilities must file a number of reports, including a safety analysis and environmental impact statement, containing a cost-benefit analysis of the proposed facility. 10 C.F.R. §§2.101, 50.3(f), 50.33(a), 50.34(a) (1977). (The environmental impact statement is necessitated by the National Environmental Policy Act (NEPA), discussed in greater detail *infra*.)

A three-member Atomic Safety and Licensing Board (Licensing Board) conducts a public adjudicatory hearing on the application. The hearing procedures include prehearing conferences, interparty discovery, testimony under oath, and cross-examination of witnesses. 42 U.S.C. §2241, 10 C.F.R. pt. 2, App. A, V. To issue a license, the board must find that the benefits of the proposed plant outweigh its economic, social, and environmental costs, and that the health and safety of the public will not be endangered by the plant's operation. 42 U.S.C. §4332(B), 10 C.F.R. §50.35(c). Any party aggrieved by a Licensing Board decision may appeal to a three-member Atomic Safety and Licensing Appeals Board (Appeals Board) within the agency. The procedures for obtaining an operating license are similar to those for a construction permit except that public hearings are held only in contested cases. 42 U.S.C. §2239(a) (1981).

In 1967, after a hearing, the Licensing Board granted Vermont Yankee Power Corp. a permit to build a nuclear plant in Vernon, Vermont. 4 A.E.C. 36 (1967). Vermont Yankee then applied for an operating license. The Natural Resources Defense Council (NRDC), a public-interest group concerned with environmental protection, objected to the application, and on August 10, 1971, a hearing on the application was held. NRDC requested that the Licensing Board evaluate the environmental effects of the nuclear wastes that would be generated by the facility. The Licensing Board declined to do so and granted Vermont Yankee the operating license. The Appeals Board affirmed the decision. In re Vermont Yankee Nuclear Power Corp., ASLAB-56, 4 A.E.C. 930 (1972).

Meanwhile, the commission had instituted a rulemaking proceeding to consider whether, as a general matter, the environmental effects of the uranium fuel cycle should be considered in individual licensing cases. 37 Fed. Reg. 24,191 (1972). The notice of proposed rulemaking offered two alternative proposals for dealing with the waste issue in the environmental assessment of proposed power plants. The first option was to leave the environmental impact of waste disposal out of the cost-benefit calculation altogether, on the theory that the contribution made by any single power plant was too small to measure. The second alternative consisted of a formula (called Table S-3) for computing the environmental impact values for any particular plant, based on the amounts of chemical and radiological elements that the operating reactor would add to the environment. The basis for these proposals was a commission staff report on the nuclear fuel cycle (called the Environmental Survey), which had concluded that the environmental impact of waste disposal was slight.

The commission held a public hearing on the two proposals. Prior to the hearing, it made the Environmental Survey and other background materials available for public inspection, but it did not allow discovery or cross-examination of any of the witnesses at the hearing. Numerous groups participated in the two-day hearing, including representatives of the nuclear industry and environmental groups like the NRDC. After the hearing, a transcript was made available to the public, and the record remained open for 30 days to allow participants to file supplemental written statements.

In April of 1974, the commission issued a rule adopting the second proposed alternative. The rule provided that use of the values specified by Table S-3 in an applicant's environmental impact study would satisfy the commission's NEPA procedures. 39 Fed. Reg. 14,188 (1974). The commission found that the record of the hearing and the Environmental Survey furnished an adequate evidentiary basis for the rule. Finding the environmental effects of the uranium fuel cycle to be "relatively insignificant," however, the commission declined to apply the regulation retroactively to Vermont Yankee, and granted Vermont Yankee its operating license. 39 Fed. Reg. 14,188, 14,191 (1974).

NATURAL RESOURCES DEFENSE COUNCIL, INC. v. NUCLEAR REGULATORY COMMISSION
547 F.2d 633 (D.C. Cir. 1976)

Before BAZELON, Chief Judge, EDWARDS, Circuit Judge for the Sixth Circuit, and TAMM, Circuit Judge.

BAZELON, Chief Judge:

[NRDC petitioned the Court of Appeals to overturn the commission's decisions to adopt the rule and to grant Vermont Yankee's license. NRDC's main contention was that the commission's refusal to allow cross-examination of participants or submission of interrogatories to the staff members who prepared the Environmental Survey violated NEPA's requirement that adverse environmental effects be investigated to the "fullest extent possible." 42 U.S.C. §4332. Had the commission decided not to use the rulemaking process, NRDC claimed, risks associated with waste disposal would have been evaluated in individual licensing proceedings, which include opportunities for discovery and cross-examination.

NRDC argued that the purpose of NEPA was subverted by permitting the commission to reduce the scope of "its environmental fact-finding inquiry merely by choosing to proceed via a rulemaking proceeding." Brief for Petitioners. The D.C. Circuit began its discussion of the procedural issues by describing the procedures employed by the NRC. It then set forth its understanding of the proper judicial role in cases alleging procedural inadequacy:]

An "informal rulemaking hearing" of the "legislative-type" was scheduled to receive comments in the form of "oral or written statements." By subsequent notice, the Commission designated a three-member hearing board to preside, and reiterated, "The procedural format for the hearing will follow the legislative pattern, and no discovery or cross-examination will be utilized." 38 Fed. Reg. 49 (Jan. 3, 1973).

The primary argument advanced by the public interest intervenors is that the decision to preclude "discovery or cross-examination" denied them a meaningful opportunity to participate in the proceedings as guaranteed by due process. They do not question the Commission's authority to proceed by informal rulemaking, as opposed to adjudication. They rely instead on the line of cases indicating that in particular circumstances procedures in excess of the bare minima prescribed by the Administrative Procedure Act, 5 U.S.C. §553, may be required.

The Government concedes that "basic considerations of fairness may under exceptional circumstances" require additional procedures in "legislative-type proceedings," but contends that the procedures here were more than adequate. [Respondent's brief, at 13-14.] Thus, we are called upon to decide whether the procedures provided by the agency were sufficient to ventilate the issues.

A few general observations are in order concerning the role of a court in this area. Absent extraordinary circumstances, it is not proper for a reviewing court to prescribe the procedural format which an agency must use to explore a given set of issues. Unless there are statutory directives to the contrary, an agency has discretion to select procedures which it deems best to compile a record illuminating the issues. Courts are no more expert at fashioning administrative procedures than they are in the substantive areas of responsibility which are left to agency discretion. What a reviewing court can do, however, is scrutinize the record as a whole to insure that genuine opportunities to participate in a meaningful way were provided, and that the agency has taken a good, hard look at the major questions before it.

We have sometimes suggested that elucidation of certain types of issues, by their very nature, might require particular procedures, including cross-examination. In fact, we have been more concerned with making sure that the record developed by agency procedures discloses a thorough ventilation of the issues than with what devices the agency used to create the dialogue.

Of necessity, assessing agency procedures requires that the reviewing court immerse itself in the record. Abstract characterizations are an unsatisfactory guide for determining what procedures are necessary in particular proceedings. Alternative procedural techniques are usually available, and the absence of one device, such as cross-examination, may be compensated for by the sensitive use of substitutes. If review is to be meaningful, it must focus on the actual operation of the whole range of procedures in a particular setting including "context of fact, statutory framework and nature of action." [Kennecott Copper Corp. v. EPA, 462 F.2d 846, 850 (D.C. Cir. 1972).]

[On the merits, the D.C. Circuit agreed with NRDC, finding the commission's action "capricious and arbitrary." After reviewing the record, the court characterized the evidence on a key point supporting the commission's rule in the following terms:]

The only discussion of high-level waste disposal techniques was supplied by a 20-page statement by Dr. Frank K. Pittman, Director of the AEC's Division of Waste Management and Transportation. This statement, delivered during the oral hearings, was then incorporated, often verbatim, into the revised version of the Environmental Survey published after the comment period. Dr. Pittman began his statement by acknowledging that he was "broadly involved" with the subject of high-level waste management since he heads the division of the AEC charged with "responsibility for the development, construction and operation of facilities for ultimate management of commercial high-level waste."

Dr. Pittman proceeded to describe for the first time in public the "design concepts" for a federal surface repository for retrievable storage of high-level waste. This is essentially a warehouse in which sealed canisters containing cylinders of solidified nuclear wastes can be stored in water-filled basins recessed into the ground on a temporary basis (up to 100 years), until such time as a permanent waste disposal scheme is devised, when they can be removed. While the "intended life" of the facility is only 100 years, some high-level wastes must be isolated for up to 250,000 years. . . . Therefore, the Environmental Survey states, without further explanation, that in the future a "permanent" Federal repository for "geologic storage of high-level wastes" will be established and that the "Federal government will have the obligation to maintain control over the site *in perpetuity*." . . .

Until recently the AEC planned to dispose of wastes by burying them deep inside abandoned salt mines. These plans were postponed indefinitely after a series of technical difficulties, including the discovery the salt mines might be susceptible to underground flooding. . . .

Dr. Pittman's description of the new plan . . . begins:

> . . . I hope I will be able to allay what I feel are unwarranted fears . . . and show that the bugaboo of waste management cannot logically be used as a rationale for delays in the progress of an essential technology for meeting our growing power demands. . . .
>
> [T]here are available today proven methods for managing the high-level waste from the nuclear industry in a way which will assure first that man will not be adversely affected by the radioactivity either by external or internal contact with the waste itself or by exposure to the penetrating radiation which it generates, and second that the environment [sic] effects will be very small.

. . . In less than two pages, he set out a very general description of what the facility is supposed to do, . . . accompanied by several schematic drawings. These show the facility will have a cooling system, a transfer area and storage basins, but do not attempt to describe how they will be built and operated, what materials will be used, where such a facility might be located, or what it might cost to build and operate.

Dr. Pittman then explains that "the major factor in the design of the repository for high-level waste is the technique used to remove the heat from the waste." . . . Decaying radioactive waste spontaneously gives off substantial heat and "[s]hould adequate provisions not be made to remove this heat . . . , the waste and the canister would melt." *Id.* A "meltdown" would result in what Dr. Pittman calls a "situation of considerable concern," which would involve the "loss of some fraction of the isolation of the radioactive material from the environment." . . .

Again, without benefit of details, Dr. Pittman offers conclusory reassurances that the proposed facility will be designed so that the possibility of a "meltdown" can be dismissed as "incredible":

> The probability of this situation occurring is prevented by a combination of engineered features including, (i) redundancy of power supply and other essential cooling systems; (ii) structural strength to withstand credible forces of nature—earthquake, tornado, etc.; (iii) combination of structural strength, plant security, etc., to withstand credible overt forces of man; (iv) modular basin cell construction which limits the number of canisters subject to a single catastrophic event.
>
> . . . The number of sequential failures required of highly reliable systems, combined with the long time periods available for repair and recovery from each, result in the judgment that this is an incredible incident. . . .

Dr. Pittman concludes with the judgments that:

> . . . (1) the program being followed by the industry under AEC regulation and by the AEC offers assurance that the commercial high-level waste will be managed safely from its initial production; (2) the surface storage method, to be used by the AEC, is good for as long as adequate human surveillance and maintenance effort is continued; (3) the probability that work currently under way will demonstrate the use of bedded salt as a safe, acceptable, ultimate disposal method within the next ten to fifteen years is very high; (4) should bedded salt not prove to be acceptable other acceptable geologic disposal concepts offer reasonable probability of reaching a point of acceptability within two or three decades; and (5) the waste in initial storage will be easily retrievable for either near-or far-term disposal methods when they are developed.

[Finding this evidence "an insufficient record to sustain a rule limiting consideration of the environmental effects of nuclear waste disposal," the court vacated the rule and remanded for further proceedings. To provide some guidance for the agency in conducting those further proceedings, the court offered this bit of procedural advice:]

Many procedural devices for creating a genuine dialogue on these issues were available to the agency—including informal conferences between intervenors and staff, document discovery, interrogatories, technical advisory committees comprised of outside experts with differing perspectives, limited cross-examination, funding independent research by intervenors, detailed annotation of technical reports, surveys of existing literature, memoranda explaining methodology. We do not presume to intrude on the agency's province by dictating to it which, if any, of these devices it must adopt to flesh out the record. It may be that no combination of the procedures mentioned above will prove adequate, and the agency will be required to develop new procedures to accomplish the innovative task of implementing NEPA through rulemaking. On the other hand, the procedures the agency adopted in this case, if administered in a more sensitive, deliberate manner, might suffice. Whatever techniques the

Commission adopts, before it promulgates a rule limiting further consideration of waste disposal and reprocessing issues, it must in one way or another generate a record in which the factual issues are fully developed. . . .

VERMONT YANKEE NUCLEAR POWER CORP. v. NATURAL RESOURCES DEFENSE COUNCIL, INC.
435 U.S. 519 (1978)

MR. JUSTICE REHNQUIST delivered the opinion of the Court.

In 1946, Congress enacted the Administrative Procedure Act, which as we have noted elsewhere was not only "a new, basic and comprehensive regulation of procedures in many agencies," *Wong Yang Sung v. McGrath,* 339 U.S. 33 (1950), but was also a legislative enactment which settled "long-continued and hard-fought contentions, and enacts a formula upon which opposing social and political forces have come to rest." *Id.,* at 40. Section 4 of the Act, 5 U.S.C. §553 (1976 ed.), dealing with rulemaking, requires in subsection (b) that "notice of proposed rule making shall be published in the Federal Register . . . ," describes the contents of that notice, and goes on to require in subsection (c) that after the notice the agency

> shall give interested persons an opportunity to participate in the rule making through submission of written data, views, or arguments with or without opportunity for oral presentation. After consideration of the relevant matter presented, the agency shall incorporate in the rules adopted a concise general statement of their basis and purpose.

Interpreting this provision of the Act in *United States v. Allegheny-Ludlum Steel Corp.,* 406 U.S. 742 (1972), and *United States v. Florida East Coast R. Co.,* 410 U.S. 224 (1973), we held that generally speaking this section of the Act established the maximum procedural requirements which Congress was willing to have the courts impose upon agencies in conducting rulemaking procedures. Agencies are free to grant additional procedural rights in the exercise of their discretion, but reviewing courts are generally not free to impose them if the agencies have not chosen to grant them. This is not to say necessarily that there are no circumstances which would ever justify a court in overturning agency action because of a failure to employ procedures beyond those required by the statute. But such circumstances, if they exist, are extremely rare. . . .

It is in the light of this background of statutory and decisional law that we granted certiorari to review [a judgment] of the Court of Appeals for the District of Columbia Circuit because of our concern that they had seriously misread or misapplied this statutory and decisional law cautioning reviewing courts against engrafting their own notions of proper procedures upon agencies entrusted with substantive functions by Congress.

[B]efore determining whether the Court of Appeals reached a permissible result [in invalidating the fuel cycle rule], we must determine exactly what result it did reach, and in this case that is no mean feat. Vermont Yankee argues that the court invalidated the rule because of the inadequacy of the procedures employed in the proceedings. Brief for Petitioner in No. 76-419, pp. 30-38. Respondents, on the other hand, labeling petitioner's view of the decision a "straw man," argue to this Court that the court merely held that the record was inadequate to enable the reviewing court to determine whether the agency had fulfilled its statutory obligation. Brief for Respondents in No. 76-419, pp. 28-30, 40. . . .

After a thorough examination of the opinion itself, we conclude that while the matter is not entirely free from doubt, the majority of the Court of Appeals struck down the rule because of the perceived inadequacies of the procedures employed in the rulemaking proceedings. The court first determined the intervenors' primary argument to be "that the decision to preclude 'discovery or cross-examination' denied them a meaningful opportunity to participate in the proceedings as guaranteed by due process." 547 F.2d [633, 643 (1976)]. The court then went on to frame the issue for decision thus: "Thus, we are called upon to decide whether the procedures provided by the agency were sufficient to ventilate the issues." *Ibid.* at 643. The court conceded that absent extraordinary circumstances it is improper for a reviewing court to prescribe the procedural format an agency must follow, but it likewise clearly thought it entirely appropriate to "scrutinize the record as a whole to insure that genuine opportunities to participate in a meaningful way were provided. . . ." *Id.* at 644. The court also refrained from actually ordering the agency to follow any specific procedures, *id.* at 653-54, but there is little doubt in our minds that the ineluctable mandate of the court's decision is that the procedures afforded during the hearings were inadequate. This conclusion is particularly buttressed by the fact that after the court examined the record, particularly the testimony of Dr. Pittman, and declared it insufficient, the court proceeded to discuss at some length the necessity for further procedural devices or a more "sensitive" application of those devices employed during the proceedings. *Ibid.* The exploration of the record and the statement regarding its insufficiency might initially lead one to conclude that the court was only examining the sufficiency of the evidence, but the remaining portions of the opinion dispel any doubt that this was certainly not the sole or even the principal basis of the decision. Accordingly, we feel compelled to address the opinion on its own terms, and we conclude that it was wrong.

In prior opinions we have intimated that even in a rulemaking proceeding when an agency is making a " 'quasi-judicial' " determination by which a very small number of persons are " 'exceptionally affected, in each case upon individual grounds,' " in some circumstances additional procedures may be required in order to afford the aggrieved individuals due process.[16] United States v. Florida East Coast R. Co., 410 U.S., at 242, 245, *quoting from* Bi-Metallic Investment Co. v. State Board of Equalization, 239 U.S. 441, 446 (1915). It might also be true, although we do not think the issue is presented in this case and accordingly do not decide it, that a totally unjustified departure from well-settled agency procedures of long standing might require judicial correction.

---

16. Respondent NRDC does not now argue that additional procedural devices were required under the Constitution. Since this was clearly a rulemaking proceeding in its purest form, we see nothing to support such a view. *See* United States v. Florida East Coast R. Co., 410 U.S. 224, 244-45 (1973); Bowles v. Willingham, 321 U.S. 503 (1944); Bi-Metallic Investment Co. v. State Board of Equalization, 239 U.S. 441 (1915).

But this much is absolutely clear. Absent constitutional constraints or extremely compelling circumstances the "administrative agencies 'should be free to fashion their own rules of procedure and to pursue methods of inquiry capable of permitting them to discharge their multitudinous duties.'" . . .

Respondent NRDC argues that §4 of the Administrative Procedure Act, 5 U.S.C. §553 (1976 ed.), merely establishes lower procedural bounds and that a court may routinely require more than the minimum when an agency's proposed rule addresses complex or technical factual issues or "Issues of Great Public Import." Brief for Respondents in No. 76-419, p.49. We have, however, previously shown that our decisions reject this view. . . . We also think the legislative history, even the part which it cites, does not bear out its contention. The Senate Report explains what eventually became §4 thus:

> This subsection states . . . the minimum requirements of public rule making procedure short of statutory hearing. Under it agencies might in addition confer with industry advisory committees, consult organizations, hold informal "hearings," and the like. Considerations of practicality, necessity, and public interest . . . will naturally govern the agency's determination of the extent to which public proceedings should go. Matters of great import, or those where the public submission of facts will be either useful to the agency or a protection to the public, should naturally be accorded more elaborate public procedures.

S. Rep. No. 752, 79th Cong., 1st Sess., 14-15 (1945). The House Report is in complete accord:

> "[U]niformity has been found possible and desirable for all classes of both equity and law actions in the courts. . . . It would seem to require no argument to demonstrate that the administrative agencies, exercising but a fraction of the judicial power may likewise operate under uniform rules of practice and procedure and that they may be required to remain within the terms of the law as to the exercise of both quasi-legislative and quasi-judicial power." . . .
>
> The bill is an outline of minimum essential rights and procedures. . . . It affords private parties a means of knowing what their rights are and how they may protect them. . . .
>
> [The bill contains] the essentials of the different forms of administrative proceedings. . . .

H.R. Rep. No. 1980, 79th Cong., 2d Sess., 9, 16-17 (1946). And the Attorney General's Manual on the Administrative Procedure Act 31, 35 (1947), a contemporaneous interpretation previously given some deference by this Court because of the role played by the Department of Justice in drafting the legislation, further confirms that view. In short, all of this leaves little doubt that Congress intended that the discretion of the *agencies* and not that of the courts be exercised in determining when extra procedural devices should be employed.

There are compelling reasons for construing §4 in this manner. In the first place, if courts continually review agency proceedings to determine whether the agency employed procedures which were, in the court's opinion, perfectly tailored to reach what the court perceives to be the "best" or "correct" result, judicial review would be totally unpredictable. And the agencies, operating under this vague injunction to employ the "best" procedures and facing the threat of reversal if they did not, would undoubtedly adopt full adjudicatory procedures in every instance. Not only would this totally disrupt the statutory scheme, through which Congress enacted "a formula upon which opposing social and political forces have come to rest," Wong Yang Sung v. McGrath, 339 U.S., at 40, but all the inherent advantages of informal rulemaking would be totally lost.

Secondly, it is obvious that the court in these cases reviewed the agency's choice of procedures on the basis of the record actually produced at the hearing, 547 F.2d, at 644, and not on the basis of the information available to the agency when it made the decision to structure the proceedings in a certain way. This sort of Monday morning quarterbacking not only encourages but almost compels the agency to conduct all rulemaking proceedings with the full panoply of procedural devices normally associated only with adjudicatory hearings.

Finally, and perhaps most importantly, this sort of review fundamentally misconceives the nature of the standard for judicial review of an agency rule. The court below uncritically assumed that additional procedures will automatically result in a more adequate record because it will give interested parties more of an opportunity to participate in and contribute to the proceedings. But informal rulemaking need not be based solely on the transcript of a hearing held before an agency. Indeed, the agency need not even hold a formal hearing. See 5 U.S.C. §553(c) (1976 ed.). Thus, the adequacy of the "record" in this type of proceeding is not correlated directly to the type of procedural devices employed, but rather turns on whether the agency has followed the statutory mandate of the Administrative Procedure Act or other relevant statutes. If the agency is compelled to support the rule which it ultimately adopts with the type of record produced only after a full adjudicatory hearing, it simply will have no choice but to conduct a full adjudicatory hearing prior to promulgating every rule. In sum, this sort of unwarranted judicial examination of perceived procedural shortcomings of a rulemaking proceeding can do nothing but seriously interfere with that process prescribed by Congress.

Respondent NRDC also argues that the fact that the Commission's inquiry was undertaken in the context of NEPA somehow permits a court to require procedures beyond those specified in §4 of the APA when investigating factual issues through rulemaking. The Court of Appeals was apparently also of this view, indicating that agencies may be required to "develop new procedures to accomplish the innovative task of implementing NEPA through rulemaking." 547 F.2d, at 653. But we search in vain for something in NEPA which would mandate such a result. We have before observed that "NEPA does not repeal by implication any other statute." Aberdeen & Rockfish R. Co. v. SCRAP, 422 U.S. 289, 319 (1975). See also United States v. SCRAP, 412 U.S. 669, 694 (1973). In fact, just two Terms ago, we emphasized that the only procedural requirements imposed by NEPA are those stated in the plain language of the Act. Kleppe v. Sierra Club, 427 U.S. 390, 405-06 (1976). Thus, it is clear NEPA cannot serve as the basis for a substantial revision of the carefully constructed procedural specifications of the APA.

In short, nothing in the APA, NEPA, the circumstances of this case, the nature of the issues being considered, past agency practice, or the statutory mandate under which the Commission operates permitted the court to review and overturn the rulemaking proceeding on the basis of the procedural devices employed (or not employed) by the Commission so long as the Commission employed at least the statutory minima, a matter about which there is no doubt in this case.

There remains, of course, the question of whether the challenged rule finds sufficient justification in the administrative proceedings that it should be upheld by the reviewing court. Judge Tamm, concurring in the result reached by the majority of the Court of Appeals, thought that it did not. There are also intimations in the majority opinion which suggest that the judges who joined it likewise may have thought the administrative proceedings an insufficient basis upon which to predicate the rule in question. We accordingly remand so that the Court of Appeals may review the rule as the Administrative Procedure Act provides. We have made it abundantly clear before that when there is a contemporaneous explanation of the agency decision, the validity of that action must "stand or fall on the propriety of that finding, judged, of course, by the appropriate standard of review. . . ." The court should engage in this kind of review and not stray beyond the judicial province to explore the procedural format or to impose upon the agency its own notion of which procedures are "best" or most likely to further some vague, undefined public good.

NOTES AND QUESTIONS

1. *Licensing versus rulemaking.* It is important to distinguish between the licensing proceeding and the rulemaking proceeding. What is the relationship between the two? To what extent is the nuclear waste issue amenable to a generic rulemaking proceeding, and to what extent must it be considered on a reactor-by-reactor basis?

Whether calculation of site-specific nuclear waste costs is amenable to generic rulemaking arose again in State of New York v. NRC, 824 F.3d 1012 (D.C. Cir. 2016). Recognizing the persistent failure of the United States Government to establish a permanent repository for nuclear waste, the NRC prepared a "Generic Environmental Impact Statement" (GEIS) of the environmental costs of indefinitely continuing to store spent nuclear fuel in pools at individual power plant sites. It then adopted a rule providing that the GEIS findings would be incorporated into all future decisions involving the initial and renewal licensing of nuclear power plants. The rule provided that the findings of the GEIS would not be reconsidered in an individual licensing proceeding absent the grant of a waiver. (The standard for granting a waiver is that "special circumstances with respect to the subject matter of the particular proceeding are such that the application of the rule or regulation (or a provision of it) would not serve the purposes for which the rule or regulation was adopted.")

Several states and environmental groups challenged the rule. One claim was that the data on which NRC relied failed adequately to reflect variations in the safety and risk conditions of individual power plants resulting from such factors as nearby population density and seismic risk. The court disagreed:

> We noted in [New York v. NRC (New York I), 681 F.3d 471, 480-481 (D.C. Cir. 2012),] that . . . the NRC may generically analyze risks that are "essentially common" to all plants so long as that analysis is "thorough and comprehensive." In this case, we are convinced that the NRC has met that standard. True, . . . in assessing the risks of pool fires, the GEIS relies on seismic data that covers "about 70 percent" of reactor sites. . . . For pool leaks, the NRC provides a high-level analysis of

spent fuel discharges but neglects any estimate of the expected errors for its input variables, instead averring to specific "low" values for these parameters. Furthermore, the GEIS attempts to justify its reliance on data from the [two power plants in areas of low population density] by noting that the average risks to individuals are independent of population density. However, the NRC admits that this data covers only "the 90th percentile population density" and that "the accident consequences could be greater at higher population sites," [and the NRC concedes] that values in the GEIS "do not represent worst-case values.". . .

Nonetheless, according deference to the NRC's technical decision-making, we find nothing in the GEIS to undermine the NRC's conclusion that the identified risks are "essentially common" to all reactor sites. The GEIS incorporates research demonstrating how the risk analysis for pool fires is conservative, and analyzes the variance in seismic risks. The NRC also considers "typical hydrologic characteristics at nuclear power plant sites" when assessing the impacts of pool leaks. Furthermore, the GEIS "explain[s] qualitatively the factors that may cause the risk to be lower or higher than" at the [two low-population-density] plants. Regardless, the NRC need not provide a perfect analysis, only one that is "thorough and comprehensive. . . ." We hold that the GEIS meets this requirement. . . .

2. *The value of rulemaking.* Is NRDC placed in a stronger or weaker position by NRC's decision to utilize rulemaking (rather than relying solely on case-by-case decisionmaking)? Notice that in the *Vermont Yankee* licensing case, NRC assigned a value of zero to the proposed plant's nuclear waste "cost." In the rulemaking, by contrast, it adopted the alternative formula that would produce a waste-cost figure greater than zero in future licensing cases. Why, then, is NRDC unhappy? If it was dissatisfied with Dr. Pittman's testimony, should it not have introduced competing evidence of its own?

3. Vermont Yankee *and "hard look" review.* Does non-deferential application of the APA's arbitrary, capricious standard of review create the conditions for judicial imposition of procedures beyond those required by the APA? Justice Rehnquist understood the relationship between procedure and substance when, in *Vermont Yankee*, he observed, "[i]f the agency is compelled to support the rule which it ultimately adopts with the type of record produced only after a full adjudicatory hearing, it simply will have no choice but to conduct a full adjudicatory hearing prior to promulgating every rule." 435 U.S. at 547-548. Is the "hard look" standard of review in tension with *Vermont Yankee*?

4. *The court's view of "best" procedures.* Did the court of appeals really impose its "own notion of which procedures are 'best' or most likely to further some vague, undefined public good"? Were its objections procedural or substantive? To the extent that the lower court's objections were procedural, can they find textual support in §553?

5. *What survives* Vermont Yankee*?* Does judicially imposed hybrid rulemaking survive *Vermont Yankee*? What about decisions like *Chocolate Manufacturers, Nova Scotia Foods, HBO,* and *Sierra Club,* that appear to impose additional procedural requirements on agencies? For example, because the notice in *Chocolate Manufacturers* included "the terms or substance of the proposed rule or a description of the subjects and issues involved" as required by APA §553, does the court's application of the "logical outgrowth" test to require additional notice and comment violate *Vermont Yankee*? What about *Sierra Club*'s requirement that written summaries of important oral comments be placed on the

docket? Similarly, if the APA does not ban ex parte contacts in informal rule-making, does *Vermont Yankee* permit a court, as in *HBO,* to order agencies to refuse ex parte contacts and place any that do occur in the "public file"? Do the courts in these and similar cases have a statutory or other basis for their decisions sufficient to satisfy the *Vermont Yankee* Court's concerns?

At least one panel of the D.C. Circuit apparently does not think so, at least with regard to ex parte contacts. In District No. 1, Pacific Coast Dist., Marine Engineers' Beneficial Assoc. v. Maritime Administration, 215 F.3d 37 (D.C. Cir. 2000), in an opinion written by Judge Douglas Ginsburg, the court rejected an ex parte contacts–based challenge to a decision of the Maritime Administration. The court's opinion indicated that judicial imposition of an ex parte contacts ban would violate *Vermont Yankee*:

> Although the APA prohibits *ex parte* contacts in an adjudication or rulemaking "required by statute to be made on the record after opportunity for an agency hearing," 5 U.S.C. §553(c), *see* 5 U.S.C. §§554(a), 557(d), there is no such requirement applicable to the MarAd's review of an application under § 9. In the absence of such a statutory command, of course, "[a]gencies are free to grant additional procedural rights in the exercise of their discretion, but reviewing courts are generally not free to impose them if the agencies have not chosen to grant them." Vermont Yankee Nuclear Power Corp. v. NRDC, 435 U.S. 519, 524 (1978). Here the agency has not granted anyone the right to be free of *ex parte* communications.

Id. at 42-43. Is there a basis for prohibiting ex parte contacts that would not violate *Vermont Yankee*? What about the logical outgrowth test for notice—can you distinguish the notice decisions from the decisions banning ex parte contacts so that the former might survive even if the latter are doomed?

Is the *Portland Cement* doctrine, discussed *supra,* requiring disclosure of studies and data relied upon by an agency, still good law in light of *Vermont Yankee*? The D.C. Circuit addressed this issue in the following case:

AMERICAN RADIO RELAY LEAGUE, INC. v. FEDERAL COMMUNICATIONS COMMISSION, 524 F.3d 227 (D.C. Cir. 2008):   The FCC promulgated a rule regulating the use of a portion of the radio spectrum. The D.C. Circuit struck down the rule on the ground that, although the agency had placed studies on which they had relied into the rulemaking record, it made these studies available only in redacted form. The court ordered the commission to make the unredacted studies available and part of the rulemaking record:

> The narrowness of our holding under section 553 of the APA is manifest. The redacted studies consist of staff-prepared scientific data that the Commission's partial reliance made "critical factual material." The Commission has chosen to rely on the data in those studies and to place the redacted studies in the rulemaking record. Individual pages relied upon by the Commission reveal that the unredacted portions are likely to contain evidence that could call into question the Commission's decision to promulgate the rule. Under the circumstances, the Commission can point to no authority allowing it to rely on the studies in a rulemaking but hide from the public parts of the studies that may contain contrary evidence, inconvenient qualifications, or relevant explanations of the methodology employed. The Commission has not suggested that any other confidentiality considerations would be implicated were the unredacted studies made public for notice and

comment. . . . Of course, it is within the Commission's prerogative to credit only certain parts of the studies. But what it did here was redact parts of those studies that are inextricably bound to the studies as a whole and thus to the data upon which the Commission has stated it relied, parts that explain the otherwise un-identified methodology underlying data cited by the Commission for its conclusions, and parts that signal caution about that data. This is a critical distinction and no precedent sanctions such a "hide and seek" application of the APA's notice and comment requirements.

As [Judge Kavanaugh] notes, in Vermont Yankee Nuclear Power Corp. v. Natural Resources Defense Council, 435 U.S. 519 (1978), the Supreme Court has limited the extent that a court may order additional agency procedures, but the procedures invalidated in *Vermont Yankee* were not anchored to any statutory provision. By contrast, the court does not impose any new procedures for the regulatory process, but merely applies settled law to the facts. The Commission made the choice to engage in notice-and-comment rulemaking and to rely on parts of its redacted studies as a basis for the rule. The court, consequently, is not imposing new procedures but enforcing the agency's procedural choice by ensuring that it conforms to APA requirements. It is one thing for the Commission to give notice and make available for comment the studies on which it relied in formulating the rule while explaining its non-reliance on certain parts. It is quite another thing to provide notice and an opportunity for comment on only those parts of the studies that the Commission likes best. . . .

In a separate opinion (concurring in the judgment and dissenting in part), Judge Kavanaugh raised questions about the propriety of the requirement that agencies disclose studies and data:

I write separately to underscore that *Portland Cement* stands on a shaky legal foundation (even though it may make sense as a policy matter in some cases). Put bluntly, the *Portland Cement* doctrine cannot be squared with the text of §553 of the APA. And *Portland Cement*'s lack of roots in the statutory text creates a serious jurisprudential problem because the Supreme Court later rejected this kind of freeform interpretation of the APA.

Because there is "nothing in the bare text of §553 that could remotely give rise" to the *Portland Cement* requirement, some commentators argue that *Portland Cement* is "a violation of the basic principle of *Vermont Yankee* that Congress and the agencies, but not the courts, have the power to decide on proper agency procedures." Jack M. Beermann & Gary Lawson, Reprocessing *Vermont Yankee*, 75 Geo. Wash. L. Rev. 856, 894 (2007). At the very least, others say, the Supreme Court's decision in *Vermont Yankee* raises "a question concerning the continuing vitality of the *Portland Cement* requirement that an agency provide public notice of the data on which it proposes to rely in a rulemaking." 1 Richard J. Pierce, Administrative Law Treatise §7.3, at 435 (4th ed. 2002).

Given the continued application of *Portland Cement* by the D.C. Circuit post–*Vermont Yankee*, however, Judge Kavanaugh accepted it as binding precedent.

6. Vermont Yankee *on remand.* On remand, the court of appeals still had to determine whether there was sufficient evidentiary support for Table S-3 in the administrative record as prepared by the NRC. During the pendency of the proceedings, NRC amended Table S-3, but the final rule left unchanged the

commission's "zero-release" assumption: that solidified high-level wastes would have no effect on the environment once sealed and permanently buried. The commission acknowledged the uncertainties of finding a permanent repository site and achieving perfect performance, but refused to incorporate these uncertainties in the final Table. 44 Fed. Reg. 45,362 (1979).

The court of appeals once again struck down the rule, finding that it violated NEPA by failing to allow for consideration of the uncertainties underlying the zero-release assumption during individual licensing proceedings. Natural Resources Defense Council, Inc. v. NRC, 685 F.2d 459 (D.C. Cir. 1982).

The Supreme Court again reversed. Baltimore Gas & Electric Co. v. Natural Resources Defense Council, Inc., 462 U.S. 87 (1983). The Court's only task, it said, was to determine whether the commission had considered all relevant factors and presented a rational connection between the facts it found and its choice of rule. The zero-release assumption, the Court found, was within the bounds of reasoned decisionmaking by the commission.

7. *Aftermath of* Vermont Yankee. The Department of Energy was initially given responsibility in the Nuclear Waste Policy Act for selecting a nuclear waste repository, but Congress short-circuited this process by taking a close examination only at Yucca Mountain and itself selecting that site as the repository. Although Yucca Mountain had several advantages over other potential sites—particularly, that it was not near any population centers—the lack of political clout in Nevada, compared to the relatively stronger influence by members of Congress from other states under consideration, made the decision to select Yucca "a virtual fait accompli." Richard B. Stewart, U.S. Nuclear Waste Law and Policy: Fixing a Bankrupt System, 17 N.Y.U. Envtl. L.J. 783, 796-797 (2008).

In 2009, President Obama announced that his administration would abandon plans for using Yucca Mountain for nuclear waste storage. After further presidentially mandated study of the Yucca Mountain site, the Department of Energy filed a motion with the Atomic Safety and Licensing Board within the Nuclear Regulatory Commission to withdraw its license application for a nuclear waste repository at the site. The board denied the motion, reasoning that the administration lacked the authority to unilaterally abandon the project without congressional approval since Congress in 2002 had designated the Nevada site to hold the nation's spent commercial fuel. U.S. Department of Energy, Docket No. 63-001-HLW (June 29, 2010), https://perma.cc/8TAB-TYPB. After this denial, the Nuclear Regulatory Commission asked for briefing on whether the board should have allowed the DOE's motion. While that process is ongoing, the Department of Energy has stopped working on the Yucca Mountain site. This provoked a challenge from state and local government units and individuals, who argued that the DOE's attempt to withdraw its application and its failure to continue to develop the site violated statutes requiring the use of the Yucca Mountain site. On judicial review, the D.C. Circuit held that the administration's decision to withdraw its license application was not ripe for review and that the DOE's determination to stop working on the Yucca Mountain Repository was not "final agency action" subject to judicial review under the APA. *See* In re Aiken County, 645 F.3d 428 (D.C. Cir. 2011). Judge Brett Kavanaugh filed an interesting concurring opinion, lamenting that the whole controversy arose only because the President lacks the authority, under *Humphrey's Executor*, to force the NRC to act in accordance with his wishes. After the decision, the NRC continued to sit on the DOE's application to withdraw its license application. In August 2013, the D.C. Circuit took the rare step of issuing a writ of mandamus requiring the NRC to move the process forward. In re Aiken County, 725 F.3d 255 (D.C. Cir. 2013). In compliance with the court's order, the NRC completed its safety review of the site in January 2015. In the following month the commission ordered its staff to prepare an Environmental Impact Statement. This process could take years, and in the meanwhile, the adjudicatory hearing on the DOE's application "remains suspended." *See* https://perma.cc/S6U8-U3SZ.

In a related development, operators of nuclear power plants petitioned the Department of Energy to stop requiring them to contribute payments toward the Yucca Mountain Repository since the administration had abandoned plans to build and operate it. Ultimately, the D.C. Circuit agreed, holding that payments must be suspended because after the abandonment of Yucca Mountain, the agency was unable to make an accurate estimate of the cost of operating the waste disposal site, and thus could not fulfill its legal obligation to base payments on credible cost estimates. National Assn. of Regulatory Utility Commrs. v. U.S. Dept. of Energy, 736 F.3d 517 (D.C. Cir. 2013).

5. Exemptions from APA §553

When Congress adopted the APA in 1946, it explicitly exempted several categories of administrative policymaking activity from some or all of the requirements of §553. Subsection (a) categorically exempts from the operation of §553 any rulemaking involving "a military or foreign affairs function" or matters of "agency management or personnel or . . . public property, loans, grants, benefits, or contracts." Likewise, subsection (b) contains exceptions from the notice-and-comment requirements (except "when notice or hearing is required by statute") for "interpretative rules, general statements of policy, or rules of agency organization, procedure, or practice" and for situations in which an agency has "good cause" to dispense with notice and comment.

If *Vermont Yankee* prohibits reviewing courts from interpreting §553 in an expansionary way, how broadly or narrowly should courts interpret these exemptions? If §553 is a presumptive ceiling on rulemaking procedures, is it also a presumptive floor so that the exemptions should be read narrowly? The Supreme Court has not provided much guidance on these questions, leaving the appeals courts to fashion their own jurisprudence of §553 exemptions. By far the most contentious issue has involved drawing the line between rules subject to §553 notice-and-comment requirements (so-called legislative rules), on the one hand, and "interpretive rules" or "statements of policy," on the other. Courts have frequently been asked to invalidate an agency policy adopted without notice and opportunity for comment, on the ground that it should have been promulgated as a legislative rule through notice-and-comment rulemaking. *See* Robert A. Anthony, Interpretive Rules, Policy Statements, Guidances, Manuals and the Like—Should Federal Agencies Use Them to Bind the Public?, 41 Duke L.J. 1311 (1992). The following case, challenging agency directives specifying the manner and extent to which federally subsidized family planning clinics could advise patients on abortion, illustrates the courts' efforts to distinguish interpretive rules from legislative rules.

NATIONAL FAMILY PLANNING &
REPRODUCTIVE HEALTH ASSN., INC. v. SULLIVAN
979 F.2d 227 (D.C. Cir. 1992)

Before: MIKVA, Chief Judge, WALD and EDWARDS, Circuit Judges.

WALD, Circuit Judge:

The central issue presented in this case is whether the Department of Health and Human Services ("HHS"), in announcing that a 1988 regulation which had theretofore been construed to strictly prohibit abortion counseling or referral of any kind in Title X programs, would thereafter be interpreted to permit doctors to counsel on abortion within the context of the doctor-patient relationship, erred in failing to first undertake the notice and comment rulemaking prescribed by the Administrative Procedure Act ("APA"), 5 U.S.C. §553. . . .

I. BACKGROUND

Title X of the Public Health Service Act, 42 U.S.C. §§300-300a-6, provides at section 1008 that: "None of the funds appropriated under this subchapter shall be used in programs where abortion is a method of family planning." 42 U.S.C. §3 00a-6. [During the 1970s and 1980s HHS operated under various interpretations of this provision.]

In 1988, HHS promulgated by notice and comment rulemaking new regulations that established a much broader prohibition on abortion counseling or referrals including a "gag rule" applicable to all Title X project personnel against informing or discussing with clients the availability of abortion as an option for individual planning or treatment needs. . . . The regulations provide that a "title X project may not provide counseling concerning the use of abortion as a method of family planning or provide referral for abortion as a method of family planning." . . .

The Supreme Court upheld both the constitutional and statutory validity of these regulations in Rust v. Sullivan, 500 U.S. 173 (1991), against a specific challenge that they directly interfered with a doctor's professional right and duty to treat his patient as he thought best.

[In November 1991, amidst substantial political controversy about the gag rule, President Bush directed HHS not to apply the regulations in a way that interfered with the doctor-patient relationship. Specifically, he ordered that the regulation not be interpreted "to prevent a woman from receiving complete medical information about her condition from a physician" including information that might result in abortion. Dr. Louis Sullivan, Secretary of HHS, complied with the President's wishes by issuing a memorandum ordering his subordinates to apply the regulations in accordance with the President's directive. Following Sullivan's instructions, Dr. William Archer, the Deputy Assistant Secretary for Population Affairs, issued Directives instructing regional administrators to enforce the existing regulations in line with the President's instructions that doctors be allowed to discuss abortion with their patients.]

The appellees in this case, organizations composed primarily of Title X grantees and family planning nurse practitioners, filed suit on April 16, 1992, challenging the validity of these Directives, asserting that the process by which they were adopted did not comply with the notice and comment provisions of the APA, and that the new policy embodied in the Directives was arbitrary and capricious. . . .

II. ANALYSIS

[APA §553 (b) provides:] "this subsection does not apply— (A) to interpretative rules, general statements of policy, or rules of agency organization, procedure, or practice. . . ." The Directives involved here seem clearly to constitute a "rule" under the APA, which defines that term as "the whole or a part of an agency statement of general or particular applicability and future effect designed to implement, interpret, or prescribe law or policy. . . ." 5 U.S.C. §551(4). . . . The only remaining question then is whether the statutory exception for interpretative rules is applicable so as to excuse notice and comment. . . . The dividing line between legislative and interpretative rules has been deemed "fuzzy" in some cases, Avoyelles Sportsmen's League, Inc. v. Marsh, 715 F.2d 897, 909 (5th Cir. 1983); *see also* Chemical Waste Management, Inc. v. EPA, 869 F.2d 1526, 1534 (D.C. Cir. 1989) (distinction "is admittedly far from crystal-clear"), but in the unique circumstances of this case, we find it relatively easy to make the call that the Directives are legislative rules. Briefly summarized, our reasoning is as follows: When an agency promulgates a legislative regulation by notice and comment directly affecting the conduct of both agency personnel and members of the public, whose meaning the agency announces as clear and definitive to the public and, on challenge, to the Supreme Court, it may not subsequently repudiate that announced meaning and substitute for it a totally different meaning without proceeding through the notice and comment rulemaking normally required for amendments of a rule. To sanction any other course would render the requirements of §553 basically superfluous in legislative rulemaking by permitting agencies to alter their requirements for affected public members at will through the ingenious device of "reinterpreting" their own rule. . . .

A. THE 1988 REGULATIONS PROHIBITED PHYSICIANS FROM COUNSELING ON ABORTION

[In promulgating its 1988 regulations,] HHS believed that "counseling and referral for abortion are prohibited by section 1008," and more specifically that "[c]ounseling in a Title X program, whether directive or nondirective, which results in abortion as a method of family planning simply cannot be squared with the language of section 1008. . . ."

There was no hint in the agency's statement of basis and purpose accompanying the regulation, and certainly not in the regulation itself, to suggest that doctors would be exempt from the Title X abortion counseling ban. The rule was typically described in the broadest terms: "The rules . . . do not prevent a health professional or a provider organization from discussing, promoting, or otherwise encouraging a woman to have an abortion as a general matter; they simply do not permit them to do so within a Title X project." . . .

In arguing the validity of the regulations before the Supreme Court, HHS continued to stress that [they] erected a complete prohibition on abortion counseling. Brief for Respondent, *Rust v. Sullivan*, 500 U.S. 173 (1991). The regulation was described as broadly applying to "health care professionals," "Title X project personnel," "staff," and "employees." Responding to concerns that the regulations improperly manipulated the doctor-patient dialogue, the Secretary answered that "the health care professional's dialogue is restricted in only one limited sense. He is hired to provide only pre-pregnancy family planning and infertility services and must refer the client to *other* qualified health care professionals for post-pregnancy services." The argument continued that the "regulations do not prevent a woman from obtaining abortion information; she simply must seek it from a source other than a Title X project[.]" . . .

Indeed, the Supreme Court, in upholding the regulations, underscored their application to all Title X personnel, including physicians. *Rust,* 500 U.S. at 193-94. . . . The opinion asserted that "a doctor employed by the project may be prohibited in the course of his project duties from counseling abortion or referring for abortion." *Id.* The Court specifically went on to rule that the regulation did not improperly impinge on the doctor-patient relationship[.] . . .

In sum, the history unequivocally shows that HHS expressly based the 1988 regulations on a particular interpretation of the language and purpose of the statute as outlawing any counseling or referral services dealing with abortions, even by doctors. . . . It is also undisputed that the 1988 regulations . . . were intended by HHS to be legislative rules, governing the conduct of Title X grantors and grantees. . . . The agency was exercising its congressionally delegated authority to issue binding regulations to implement the statute, and in so doing necessarily followed the required process of notice and comment rulemaking.

[A]n agency issuing a legislative rule is itself bound by the rule until that rule is amended or revoked. *See* United States v. Nixon, 418 U.S. 683, 695-96 (1974). . . . HHS may not alter, without notice and comment, the 1988 regulations to permit doctors to give abortion counseling, unless such a change can be legitimately characterized as merely a permissible interpretation of the regulation, consistent with its language and original purpose. As we show in the next section, the Directives cannot meet such a test.

B.   THE DIRECTIVES ARE LEGISLATIVE RULES

HHS counsel conceded at oral argument that the agency interpreted its own 1988 regulation prior to the Directives not to permit physicians to counsel patients on abortion. In 1991, the Directives changed that basic understanding. Section 59.8(a)(1) of the 1988 regulations states that a "Title X project may not provide counseling concerning the use of abortion as a method of family planning or provide referral for abortion as a method of family planning." The Directives say that Title X physicians may, pursuant to the same regulations, provide counseling and referrals for abortions when their medical judgment so dictates. According to HHS briefs, "[b]ecause of the 1988 regulations, nurses may not counsel about abortion; under the 1988 regulations, as construed by the [Directives], physicians are not so limited," and more pointedly, physicians are now "free to speak without any constraints about abortion" within the context of the doctor-patient relationship. . . .

It is a maxim of administrative law that: "If a second rule repudiates or is irreconcilable with [a prior legislative rule], the second rule must be an amendment of the first; and, of course, an amendment to a legislative rule must itself be legislative." Michael Asimow, Nonlegislative Rulemaking and Regulatory Reform, 1985 Duke L.J. 381, 396. Judge Easterbrook has lucidly explained why in such circumstances notice and comment rulemaking must be followed:

> A *volte face* . . . may be an attempt to avoid the notice and opportunity for comment that the Administrative Procedure Act requires for the alteration of a rule. When an agency gets out the Dictionary of Newspeak and pronounces that for purposes of its regulation war is peace, it has made a substantive change for which the APA may require procedures. If in the air bags case, Motor Vehicle Manufacturers Assn. v. State Farm Mutual Automobile Insurance Co., 463 U.S. 29 (1983), instead of repealing the rule the agency had proclaimed that an ordinary seat belt is a "passive restraint," the Court would have treated this the same as it treated revocation of the rule. Both require notice, an opportunity for comment, and an adequate record.

Homemakers North Shore, Inc. v. Bowen, 832 F.2d 408, 412 (7th Cir. 1987). In this case, while we do not accuse the Directives of Orwellian overtones, they do represent a nonobvious and unanticipated reading of the 1988 regulation, which has the effect of cutting back significantly on its scope and proscriptions. . . . While an agency's construction of the statute need not always be correct for its rules to be considered interpretative, *see* Fertilizer Inst. v. EPA, 935 F.2d 1303, 1308 (D.C. Cir. 1991), the fact that its subsequent interpretation runs 180 degrees counter to the plain meaning of the regulation gives us at least some cause to believe that the agency may be seeking to constructively amend the regulation. . . .

In this case we have the additional, and somewhat unique circumstance of a direct clash between a Supreme Court reading of the 1988 regulation and the Directives. . . . The fact that the Supreme Court has read the 1988 regulation to prohibit abortion counseling by doctors, is persuasive evidence that HHS' current view that the regulation permits physicians to so counsel is a legislative rule. Obviously, HHS may, for good cause, change the regulation and even its interpretation of the statute through notice and comment rulemaking, but it may not constructively rewrite the regulation, which was expressly based upon a specific interpretation of the statute, through internal memoranda or guidance directives that incorporate a totally different interpretation and effect a totally different result. . . .

A rule that clarifies a statutory term is the classic example of an interpretative rule. . . .

An agency rule that reminds parties of existing statutory duties is also considered interpretative, not legislative. *See* Cabais v. Egger, 690 F.2d 234, 238 (D.C. Cir. 1982) (Secretary's recommendation to state agencies that they pass legislation conforming their unemployment income plans to a federal scheme, as they were required to do under a federal statute, was interpretative); Citizens to Save Spencer County v. EPA, 600 F.2d 844, 876 n.153 (D.C. Cir. 1979). Similarly, a regulation that "merely tracked" the statutory requirements and thus "simply explained something the statute already required," has usually been deemed interpretative. . . .

Conversely, a legislative or substantive rule is one that does more than simply clarify or explain a regulatory term, or confirm a regulatory requirement, or maintain a consistent agency policy. For instance, in *American Hospital Association,* this court shared the view of the district court that requirements in an HHS manual defining procedures governing review functions of Peer Review Organizations were "not interpretations of any explicit statutory provisions," and did "not merely interpret or elucidate HHS' official position." American Hosp. Assn. v. Bowen, 834 F.2d 1037, 1049-50 (D.C. Cir. 1987) (quoting American Hosp. Assn. v. Bowen, 640 F. Supp. 453, 462-63 (D.D.C. 1986)). . . . Thus, a rule is legislative if it attempts "to supplement [a statute], not simply to construe it." Chamber of Commerce v. OSHA, 636 F.2d 464, 469 (D.C. Cir. 1980). . . . Other times, courts have explained that a rule which "effect[s] a change in existing law or policy" is legislative. Powderly v. Schweiker, 704 F.2d 1092, 1098 (9th Cir. 1983).

[W]hile the stated intent of the agency in promulgating the rule merits consideration, *see Chamber of Commerce,* 636 F.2d at 468, "the agency's own label, while relevant, is not dispositive," [General Motors Corp. v. Ruckelshaus, 742 F.2d 1561, 1565 (D.C. Cir. 1984) (en banc)]. . . . Even the Secretary's counsel admitted before the trial court that "[i]t would make it too easy if the Secretary could merely come in and say it's an interpretive rule."

More importantly, the record does not support HHS' argument that the Directives do nothing more than make explicit something that was already implicit in the 1988 regulation. First, as previously mentioned, it is clear that there was never any confusion among HHS policymakers or the public over whether doctors were covered by the gag rule in §59.8.

Second, the Directives themselves suggest that the amendment was motivated not by an interpretation of the regulation's terms, but instead by a previously unacknowledged concern for the special relationship between doctors and their patients. . . . Nowhere in the Directives were interpretations of the regulatory terms "abortion" and "counseling" mentioned as the target of the new policy. . . .

Third, rather than simply interpreting the regulation, HHS clearly intends to "grant rights, impose obligations, or produce other significant effects on private interests," Batterton v. Marshall, 648 F.2d 694, 701-02 (D.C. Cir. 1980)]. . . . As part of the modification of the gag rule, the Directives require that Title X grantees sign an assurance within 30 days of notification . . . that the grantee will adhere to §59.8 as altered by the Directives. . . . If a Title X program is found not to be in compliance with the Directives, "standard grants management procedures will be followed by the Department in seeking a remedy," which presumably means that the program could lose its grant. Moreover, doctors who were previously able to refuse to provide advice on abortion . . . now are expected to answer questions concerning abortion. Clearly, the agency intends the Directives to have present binding effect on Title X programs. HHS counsel explained to the district court that the Secretary's "officials have no latitude at all in this regard. They have to comply with these guidelines." . . .

In sum, the Directives do not simply explain or clarify the 1988 regulation or confirm requirements under that regulation. Instead, based on new concerns about the doctor-patient relationship, HHS is substantially amending and even repudiating part of its original regulation. . . .

III. Conclusion

. . . In sum, the law seems clear that when an agency adopts a new construction of an old rule that repudiates or substantially amends the effect of the previous rule on the public, after the old interpretation of that rule has been advanced as a necessary interpretation of the statute and has been argued to and validated by the Supreme Court, the agency must adhere to the notice and comment requirements of §553 of the APA. . . .

Accordingly, we lift this court's stay and reinstate the district court's injunction to the extent that the new policies encompassed in the Directives may not be enforced until and unless they are adopted in a notice and comment rulemaking.

Affirmed.

NOTES AND QUESTIONS

1. *Why this challenge?* Why did the Title X grantees challenge the Directives? On its face, the change increased grantees' ability to provide advice to their patients, narrowing the scope of the "gag rule" that grantees had found objectionable. Note that the plaintiffs argued for more freedom to provide abortion advice than even the revised rule gave them; they did not oppose a requirement that doctors provide abortion advice in some areas. The court of appeals nonetheless held that plaintiffs had standing because if they violated the Directives they might lose Title X funding. *See* 979 F.2d at 238-239 n.8. Should a party whose regulatory burden is lightened have standing to challenge a new regulation? The court did not rule on the standing of the nurses who were complaining that they were still subject to the gag rule. It was conceded that nurses were in the very same regulatory position before and after the Directives. Should they nevertheless have standing to argue that allowing doctors but not nurses to discuss abortion is arbitrary and capricious?

2. *What legal test?* What is the court's test for determining whether the new agency policy was exempt from §553's notice-and-comment requirements as an interpretive rule? Does the court pay sufficient heed to the agency's own characterization of the rule as interpretive? What about the President's apparent determination that notice-and-comment procedures were not necessary?

3. *The end of the gag rule.* On January 22, 1993, President Clinton ordered HHS to suspend the gag rule and conduct rulemaking to overturn it. On February 5, 1993, the Secretary of HHS suspended the gag rule and issued proposed substitute regulations for public comment. The Secretary found "good cause" for suspending the gag rule without notice and comment. Finally, on July 3, 2000, more than seven years later, HHS replaced the gag rule by re-adopting, with a few minor variations, the regulations that had been in place prior to the gag rule's adoption in 1988. *See* 65 Fed. Reg. 41,270 (2000). The regulations allow Title X grantees to discuss abortion as one among many possible responses to an unplanned pregnancy. In fact, under the rules in effect prior to the gag rule, and under the rules as adopted in 2000, Title X grantees "*must* [o]ffer pregnant women the opportunity to be provided information and counseling regarding [several options including] (C) Pregnancy termination." *See* 65

Fed. Reg. at 41,279 (emphasis supplied). Does the President have the authority to order an agency to engage in rulemaking? To suspend a valid regulation while rulemaking is conducted? Under the approach taken by the D.C. Circuit in *National Family Planning*, should suspension be permissible before notice-and-comment rulemaking?

HOCTOR v. UNITED STATES DEPARTMENT
OF AGRICULTURE
82 F.3d 165 (7th Cir. 1996)

Before POSNER, Chief Judge, and DIANE P. WOOD and EVANS, Circuit Judges.
POSNER, Chief Judge: . . .

The question presented by this appeal from an order of the Department of Agriculture is whether a rule for the secure containment of animals, a rule promulgated by the Department under the Animal Welfare Act, 7 U.S.C. §§2131 et seq., without compliance with the notice and comment requirements of the Administrative Procedure Act, is nevertheless valid because it is merely an interpretive rule. Enacted in 1966, the Animal Welfare Act, as its title implies, is primarily designed to assure the humane treatment of animals. The Act requires the licensing of dealers (with obvious exceptions, for example, retail pet stores) and exhibitors, and authorizes the Department to impose sanctions on licensees who violate either the statute itself or the rules promulgated by the Department under the authority of 7 U.S.C. §2151, which authorizes the Secretary of Agriculture "to promulgate such rules, regulations, and orders as he may deem necessary in order to effectuate the purposes of [the Act]." The Act provides guidance to the exercise of this rulemaking authority by requiring the Department to formulate standards "to govern the humane handling, care, treatment, and transportation of animals by dealers," and these standards must include minimum requirements "for handling, housing, feeding, watering, sanitation," etc. 7 U.S.C. §2143(a).

The Department has employed the notice and comment procedure to promulgate a regulation, the validity of which is not questioned, that is entitled "structural strength" and that provides that "the facility [housing the animals] must be constructed of such material and of such strength as appropriate for the animals involved. The indoor and outdoor housing facilities shall be structurally sound and shall be maintained in good repair to protect the animals from injury and to contain the animals." 9 C.F.R. §3.125(a).

Enter the petitioner, Patrick Hoctor, who in 1982 began dealing in exotic animals on his farm outside of Terre Haute. In a 25-acre compound he raised a variety of animals including "Big Cats"—a typical inventory included three lions, two tigers, seven ligers (a liger is a cross between a male lion and a female tiger, and is thus to be distinguished from a tigon), six cougars, and two snow leopards. . . . At the suggestion of a veterinarian employed by the Agriculture Department who was assigned to inspect the facility when Hoctor started his animal dealership in 1982, Hoctor made the perimeter fence six feet high.

The following year the Department issued an internal memorandum addressed to its force of inspectors in which it said that all "dangerous animals," defined as including, among members of the cat family, lions, tigers, and leopards, must be inside a perimeter fence at least eight feet high. This provision is the so-called interpretive rule, interpreting the housing regulation quoted above. An agency has, of course, the power, indeed the inescapable duty, to interpret its own legislative rules, such as the housing standard, just as it has the power and duty to interpret a statute that it enforces. . . .

On several occasions beginning in 1990, Hoctor was cited by a Department of Agriculture inspector for violating 9 C.F.R. §3.125(a), the housing standard, by failing to have an eight-foot perimeter fence. . . . He is a small dealer and it would cost him many thousands of dollars to replace his six-foot-high fence with an eight-foot-high fence. Indeed, we were told at argument that pending the resolution of his dispute over the fence he has discontinued dealing in Big Cats. The parties agree that unless the rule requiring a perimeter fence at least eight feet high is a valid interpretive rule, the sanction for violating it was improper.

[W]e may . . . assume that the containment of dangerous animals is a proper concern of the Department in the enforcement of the Animal Welfare Act, even though the purpose of the Act is to protect animals from people rather than people from animals. Even Big Cats are not safe outside their compounds, and with a lawyer's ingenuity the Department's able counsel reminded us at argument that if one of those Cats mauled or threatened a human being, the Cat might get into serious trouble and thus it is necessary to protect human beings from Big Cats in order to protect the Cats from human beings, which is the important thing under the Act. In fact Hoctor had shot . . . two lions because they were dangerously close to one of his employees. . . . The internal memorandum also justifies the eight-foot requirement as a means of protecting the animals from animal predators, though one might have supposed the Big Cats able to protect themselves against the native Indiana fauna.

Another issue that we need not resolve besides the issue of the statutory authority for the challenged rule is whether the Department might have cited Hoctor for having a perimeter fence that was in fact, considering the number and type of his animals, the topography of the compound, the design and structure of the protective enclosures and the containment fence, the proximity of highways or inhabited areas, and the design of the perimeter fence itself, too low to be safe, as distinct from merely being lower than eight feet. No regulation is targeted on the problem of containment other than 9 C.F.R. §3.125, which seems to be concerned with the strength of enclosures rather than their height. But maybe there is some implicit statutory duty of containment that Hoctor might have been thought to have violated even if there were no rule requiring an eight-foot-high perimeter fence.

We need not decide. The only ground on which the Department defends sanctioning Hoctor for not having a high enough fence is that requiring an eight-foot-high perimeter fence for dangerous animals is an interpretation of the Department's own structural-strength regulation, and "provided an agency's interpretation of its own regulations does not violate the Constitution or a federal statute, it must be given 'controlling weight unless it is plainly erroneous or inconsistent with the regulation.'" Stinson v. United States, [508 U.S. 36,] 44-46 (1993). The "provided" clause does not announce a demanding standard of judicial review, although the absence of any reference in the housing regulation to fences or height must give us pause. . . .

Our doubts about the scope of the regulation that the eight-foot rule is said to be "interpreting" might seem irrelevant, since even if a rule requiring an eight-foot perimeter fence could not be based on the regulation, it could be based on the statute itself, which in requiring the Department to establish minimum standards for the housing of animals presumably authorizes it to promulgate standards for secure containment. But if the eight-foot rule were deemed one of those minimum standards that the Department is required by statute to create, it could not possibly be thought an interpretive rule. For what would it be interpreting? When Congress authorizes an agency to create standards, it is delegating legislative authority, rather than itself setting forth a standard which the agency might then particularize through interpretation. Put differently, when a statute does not impose a duty on the persons subject to it but instead authorizes (or requires—it makes no difference) an agency to impose a duty, the formulation of that duty becomes a legislative task entrusted to the agency. Provided that a rule promulgated pursuant to such a delegation is intended to bind, and not merely to be a tentative statement of the agency's view, which would make it just a policy statement, and not a rule at all, the rule would be the clearest possible example of a legislative rule, as to which the notice and comment procedure not followed here is mandatory, as distinct from an interpretive rule; for there would be nothing to interpret. That is why the Department must argue that its eight-foot rule is an interpretation of the structural-strength regulation—itself a standard, and therefore interpretable, in order to avoid reversal.

Even if, despite the doubts that we expressed earlier, the eight-foot rule is consistent with, even in some sense authorized by, the structural-strength regulation, it would not necessarily follow that it is an interpretive rule. It is that only if it can be derived from the regulation by a process reasonably described as interpretation. Supposing that the regulation imposes a general duty of secure containment, the question is, then, Can a requirement that the duty be implemented by erecting an eight-foot-high perimeter fence be thought an interpretation of that general duty?

"Interpretation" in the narrow sense is the ascertainment of meaning. It is obvious that eight feet is not part of the meaning of secure containment. But "interpretation" is often used in a much broader sense. A process of "interpretation" has transformed the Constitution into a body of law undreamt of by the framers. . . . But our task in this case is not to plumb the mysteries of legal theory; it is merely to give effect to a distinction that the Administrative Procedure Act makes, and we can do this by referring to the purpose of the distinction. The purpose is to separate the cases in which notice and comment rulemaking is required from the cases in which it is not required. As noted at the outset, unless a statute or regulation is of crystalline transparency, the agency enforcing it cannot avoid interpreting it, and the agency would be stymied in its enforcement duties if every time it brought a case on a new theory it had to pause for a bout, possibly lasting several years, of notice and comment rulemaking. Besides being unavoidably continuous, statutory interpretation normally proceeds without the aid of elaborate factual inquiries. When it is an executive or administrative agency that is doing the interpreting it brings to the task a greater knowledge of the regulated activity than the judicial or legislative branches have, and this knowledge is to some extent a substitute for formal fact-gathering.

At the other extreme from what might be called normal or routine inter-pretation is the making of reasonable but arbitrary (not in the "arbitrary or capricious" sense) rules that are consistent with the statute or regulation under which the rules are promulgated but not derived from it, because they repre-sent an arbitrary choice among methods of implementation. A rule that turns on a number is likely to be arbitrary in this sense. There is no way to reason to an eight-foot perimeter-fence rule as opposed to a seven-and-a-half foot fence or a nine-foot fence or a ten-foot fence. None of these candidates for a rule is uniquely appropriate to, and in that sense derivable from, the duty of secure containment. This point becomes even clearer if we note that the eight-foot rule actually has another component—the fence must be at least three feet from any animal's pen. Why three feet? Why not four? Or two?

The reason courts refuse to create statutes of limitations is precisely the dif-ficulty of reasoning to a number by the methods of reasoning used by courts. . . . The choice is arbitrary and courts are uncomfortable with making arbitrary choices. They see this as a legislative function. . . . When agencies base rules on arbitrary choices they are legislating, and so these rules are legislative or substantive and require notice and comment rulemaking, a procedure that is analogous to the procedure employed by legislatures in making statutes. . . .

The common sense of requiring notice and comment rulemaking for legis-lative rules is well illustrated by the facts of this case. There is no process of clois-tered, appellate-court type reasoning by which the Department of Agriculture could have excogitated the eight-foot rule from the structural-strength regula-tion. The rule is arbitrary in the sense that it could well be different without significant impairment of any regulatory purpose. But this does not make the rule a matter of indifference to the people subject to it. There are thousands of animal dealers, and some unknown fraction of these face the prospect of hav-ing to tear down their existing fences and build new, higher ones at great cost. The concerns of these dealers are legitimate and since, as we are stressing, the rule could well be otherwise, the agency was obliged to listen to them before settling on a final rule and to provide some justification for that rule, though not so tight or logical a justification as a court would be expected to offer for a new judge-made rule. . . . The Department's lawyer speculated that if the notice and comment route had been followed in this case the Department would have received thousands of comments. The greater the public interest in a rule, the greater reason to allow the public to participate in its formation.

We are not saying that an interpretive rule can never have a numerical component. . . . Especially in scientific and other technical areas, where quanti-tative criteria are common, a rule that translates a general norm into a number may be justifiable as interpretation. . . . Even in a nontechnical area the use of a number as a rule of thumb to guide the application of a general norm will often be legitimately interpretive. . . .

The Department's position might seem further undermined by the fact that it has used the notice and comment procedure to promulgate rules prescribing perimeter fences for dogs and monkeys. . . . Why it proceeded differently for dangerous animals is unexplained. But we attach no weight to the Department's inconsistency, not only because it would be unwise to penalize the Department for having at least partially complied with the requirements of the Administra-tive Procedure Act, but also because there is nothing in the Act to forbid an agency to use the notice and comment procedure in cases in which it is not required to do so. . . . The order under review, based as it was on a rule that is invalid because not promulgated in accordance with the required procedure, is therefore

Vacated.

NOTES AND QUESTIONS

1. *Definition of legislative rule.* What is the *Hoctor* court's definition of "legislative rule"? Is it consistent with that of the *National Family Planning* court? Do you agree with Judge Posner that the height requirement is not a legitimate interpretation of the structural strength regulation? Isn't the argument that a fence must have some height to be structurally capable of containing animals, coupled with Judge Posner's concession that even in a nontechnical area, "the use of a number as a rule of thumb" can be "legitimately interpretive," grounds for upholding the interpretive rule?

2. *Tests for distinguishing between legislative and interpretive rules.* The dominant test for differentiating between interpretive and legislative rules is the "legal effects test," under which legislative rules are defined as those directly altering the legal rights of the public, while interpretations and policy statements are defined as merely describing how the agency intends to act in the future in interpreting and applying existing norms. In American Mining Congress v. Mine Safety & Health Administration, 995 F.2d 1106, 1112 (D.C. Cir. 1993), the court articulated the following test to determine whether a rule has a legal effect:

> Accordingly, insofar as our cases can be reconciled at all, we think it almost exclusively on the basis of whether the purported interpretive rule has "legal effect," which in turn is best ascertained by asking (1) whether in the absence of the rule there would not be an adequate legislative basis for enforcement action or other agency action to confer benefits or ensure the performance of duties, (2) whether the agency has published the rule in the Code of Federal Regulations, (3) whether the agency has explicitly invoked its general legislative authority, or (4) whether the rule effectively amends a prior legislative rule. If the answer to any of these questions is affirmative, we have a legislative, not an interpretive rule.

Some courts have used a somewhat different approach, termed the substantial impact test. Applying this test, courts have attempted to determine the statement's practical substantive effect on the public. Thus in Lewis-Mota v. Secretary of Labor, 469 F.2d 478 (2d Cir. 1972), the court invalidated the Secretary of Labor's revocation of a precertification procedure whereby certain aliens could obtain visas for permanent residence. The court stated that the Secretary's actions had a direct "substantive impact" on aliens seeking permanent residence and on their prospective employers. In later years, however, the substantial impact test appears to have fallen out of favor. *See, e.g.,* Rivera v. Becerra, 714 F.2d 887, 890-891 (9th Cir. 1983), *cert. denied,* 465 U.S. 1099 (1984) (holding that the substantial impact test is incompatible with the Supreme Court's ruling in *Vermont Yankee*).

In the case below, plaintiffs argued that an executive branch decision, made informally by memo, not to enforce certain immigration provisions amounted to a legislative rule requiring notice and comment.

TEXAS v. UNITED STATES
787 F.3d 733
aff'd by an equally divided court
136 S. Ct. 2271 (2016)

Jerry E. SMITH, Circuit Judge:

[For the facts, the court's discussion of reviewability, and its treatment of standing, see Chapter III, *supra*.]

The [state plaintiffs] asserted that [the Deferred Action for Parents of Americans and Lawful Permanent Residents (DAPA)] Memo violated the procedural requirements of the APA as a substantive rule that did not undergo the requisite notice-and-comment rulemaking. *See* 5 U.S.C. §553. . . .

The United States urges that DAPA is exempt as [a] general statement[] of policy. . . . We evaluate two criteria to distinguish policy statements from substantive rules: whether the rule (1) "impose[s] any rights and obligations" and (2) "genuinely leaves the agency and its decision-makers free to exercise discretion." . . .

Although the DAPA Memo facially purports to confer discretion, the district court determined that "[n]othing about DAPA '*genuinely* leaves the agency and its [employees] free to exercise discretion,'" a factual finding that we review for clear error. That finding was partly informed by analysis of the implementation of DACA, the precursor to DAPA.

Like the DAPA Memo, the [Deferred Action for Childhood Arrivals] Memo instructed agencies to review applications on a case-by-case basis and exercise discretion, but the district court found that those statements were "merely pretext" because only about 5% of the 723,000 applications accepted for evaluation had been denied, and "[d]espite a request by the [district] [c]ourt, the [g]overnment's counsel did not provide the number, if any, of requests that were denied [for discretionary reasons] even though the applicant met the DACA criteria. . . ." The finding of pretext was also based on a declaration by Kenneth Palinkas, the president of the union representing the USCIS employees processing the DACA applications, that "DHS management has taken multiple steps to ensure that DACA applications are simply rubberstamped if the applicants meet the necessary criteria"; DACA's Operating Procedures, which "contain[] nearly 150 pages of specific instructions for granting or denying deferred action"; and some mandatory language in the DAPA Memo itself. In denying the government's motion for a stay of the injunction, the district court further noted that the President had made public statements suggesting that in reviewing applications pursuant to DAPA, DHS officials who "don't follow the policy" will face "consequences," and "they've got a problem." . . . Reviewing for clear error, we conclude that the states have established a substantial likelihood that DAPA would not genuinely leave the agency and its employees free to exercise discretion. . . .

KING, Circuit Judge, dissenting: . . .

Our precedent is clear: "As long as the agency remains free to consider the individual facts in the various cases that arise, then the agency action in question has not established a binding norm," and thus need not go through the procedures of notice-and-comment. Therefore, in order for Plaintiffs to establish a substantial likelihood of success on the merits . . . Plaintiffs bore the burden of demonstrating that the Memorandum was non-discretionary. As the majority admits, the Memorandum "facially purports to confer discretion." But the district court ignored this clear language, concluding that agency officials implementing DAPA will defy the Memorandum and simply rubberstamp applications. In so doing, the district court disregarded a mountain of highly probative evidence from DHS officials charged with implementing DAPA, relying instead on selected excerpts of the President's public statements, facts relating to a program materially distinguishable from the one at issue here, and improper burden-shifting. The majority now adopts the district court's conclusions wholesale and without question. . . .

In determining whether the DAPA Memorandum constitutes a substantive rule, we must begin with the words of the Memorandum itself. The Memorandum states that it reflects "new policies," and "guidance for case-by-case use of deferred action." Accordingly, the Secretary characterizes the Memorandum as a "general statement[] of policy." . . . The Memorandum also repeatedly references (more than ten times) the discretionary, "case-by-case" determinations to be made by agents in deciding whether to grant deferred action. . . .

Although some of the Memorandum's criteria can be routinely applied, many will require agents to make discretionary judgments as to the application of the respective criteria to the facts of a particular case. For example, agents must determine whether an applicant "pose[s] a danger to national security," whether the applicant is "a threat to . . . border security" or "public safety," and whether the applicant has "significantly abused the visa or visa waiver programs." . . .

The district court erred not only in its analysis of the legal effect of the DAPA Memorandum, but also in its resolution of the facts. By eschewing the plain language of the Memorandum, and concluding that its discretionary aspects are "merely pretext," the district court committed reversible error. . . . I am left with such a conviction for three independent reasons: (1) the record lacks any probative evidence of DAPA's implementation; (2) the district court erroneously equated DAPA with DACA; and (3) even assuming DAPA and DACA can be equated, the evidence of DACA's implementation fails to establish pretext. . . .

NOTES AND QUESTIONS

1. *Discretion versus constraint.* How should courts evaluate whether agencies *genuinely* have discretion to apply a policy case-by-case, or whether the outcome is pre-determined? Is it enough that the head of the employee union says that his members feel constrained to decide one way? That the President makes public speeches making his preferred outcomes clear? Would empirical data help? Could the court's concern be alleviated by a better designed policy?

2. *Interpretive rules and* Auer *deference.* In *Kisor v. Wilkie,* excerpted in Chapter II, *supra,* the Court significantly cabined, but did not strike down *Auer*

deference to agency interpretations to their own rules. Justices Kagan and Gorsuch disagreed over how such deference relates to the distinction between "legislative" and "interpretive rules" in APA §553. Justice Kagan argued that deference to agency interpretations *even of interpretive rules* (which do not go through notice-and-comment and are meant only to "advise" the public), does not transform such rules into binding regulations with the "force and effect of law." They may not, she wrote, be the basis of an enforcement action. Justice Gorsuch objected that *Auer* deference effectively nullifies the distinction between legislative and interpretive rules, since courts must treat agency interpretations of both types of rules as "controlling." What is the crux of Justice Gorsuch's concern? Is he saying that *Auer* deference violates the procedural requirements of §553?

3. *Interpretive change and interpretive rules.* Are agencies free to alter their interpretive rules without notice and comment? The D.C. Circuit thought not, reasoning that when an agency adopts a new interpretive rule that conflicts with a prior interpretation, the change may have a "substantial impact" on parties who had been regulated under the prior interpretation. *See* Paralyzed Veterans of America v. D.C. Arena L. P., 117 F.3d 579, 586-588 (D.C. Cir. 1997). After nearly 20 years of D.C. Circuit decisions in accord with *Paralyzed Veterans*, the Supreme Court, invoking *Vermont Yankee*, unanimously rejected the D.C. Circuit's rule, holding that notice and comment is not required when an agency alters an interpretive rule with a new interpretive rule. *See* Perez v. Mortgage Bankers Assn., 133 S. Ct. 1199 (2015). The Court could not have been clearer: "The *Paralyzed Veterans* doctrine is contrary to the clear text of the APA's rulemaking provisions, and it improperly imposes on agencies an obligation beyond the 'maximum procedural requirements' specified in the APA. Vermont Yankee Nuclear Power Corp. v. Natural Resources Defense Council, Inc., 435 U.S. 519, 524 (1978)." Are there circumstances, such as reliance or unfair surprise, that might lead a court to apply *Paralyzed Veterans* even after *Mortgage Bankers*? The *Mortgage Bankers* Court acknowledged that interpretive change might sometimes be unfair, but it stated that statutory "safe-harbor" provisions and "principles of retroactivity" should take care of the problem. *Mortgage Bankers*, 133 S. Ct. at 1209 & n.5.

4. *Agency reliance on guidance documents.* Agencies frequently use "guidance documents" to elaborate policy without going through the notice-and-comment process. For a discussion of this phenomenon, *see* Chapter IV, section D, *supra*.

5. *Other exceptions to the notice-and-comment requirements of §553.* The courts have provided limited guidance on the meaning of other exceptions from §553's notice-and-comment requirements, such as the exceptions for "rules of agency organization" and "general statements of policy."

LINCOLN v. VIGIL, 508 U.S. 182 (1993): In a portion of the opinion excerpted in Chapter III, *supra*, the Court held that the plaintiffs' *substantive* claim that the Indian Health Service acted unlawfully in deciding to close its clinic in Albuquerque, New Mexico, was committed to agency discretion by law. In a separate claim, the plaintiffs also challenged the closing on the *procedural* ground that the agency should have engaged in notice-and-comment rulemaking before deciding to close the clinic. Justice Souter, speaking for the Court, disagreed:

The Service announced its decision in a memorandum, dated August 21, 1985, addressed to Service offices and Program referral sources: "As you are probably aware, the Indian Children's Program has been involved in planning activities focusing on a national program effort. This process has included the termination of all direct clinical services to children in the Albuquerque, Navajo and Hopi reservation service areas. During the months of August and September, . . . staff will [see] children followed by the program in an effort to update programs, identify alternative resources and facilitate obtaining alternative services. In communities where there are no identified resources, meetings with community service providers will be scheduled to facilitate the networking between agencies to secure or advocate for appropriate services." . . . The Service invited public "input" during this "difficult transition," and explained that the reallocation of resources had been "motivated by our goal of increased mental health services for all Indian [c]hildren." . . .

We next consider the Court of Appeals's holding, quite apart from the matter of substantive reviewability, that before terminating the Program the Service was required to abide by the familiar notice-and-comment rulemaking provisions of the APA, 5 U.S.C. §553. . . . Section 553 has no application, [however], to "a matter relating to agency management or personnel or to public property, loans, grants, benefits, or contracts." §553(a)(2).[5] The notice-and-comment requirements apply, moreover, only to so-called "legislative" or "substantive" rules; they do not apply to "interpretative rules, general statements of policy, or rules of agency organization, procedure, or practice." §553(b). . . .

It is undisputed that the Service did not abide by these notice-and-comment requirements before discontinuing the Program and reallocating its resources. The Service argues that it was free from any such obligation because its decision to terminate the Program did not qualify as a "rule" within the meaning of the APA. . . . Respondents, to the contrary, contend that the Service's action falls well within the Act's broad definition of that term. §551(4). . . . Determining whether an agency's statement is what the APA calls a "rule" can be a difficult exercise. We need not conduct that exercise in this case, however. For even assuming that a statement terminating the Program would qualify as a "rule" within the meaning of the APA, it would be exempt from the notice-and-comment requirements of §553. . . . Termination of the Program might be seen as affecting the Service's organization, but "rules of agency organization" are exempt from notice-and-comment requirements under §553(b)(A). Moreover, §553(b)(A) also exempts "general statements of policy," which we have previously described as " 'statements issued by an agency to advise the public prospectively of the manner in which the agency proposes to exercise a discretionary power.' " Chrysler Corp. [v. Brown, 441 U.S. 281, 302, n.31 (1979)] (quoting Attorney General's Manual on the Administrative Procedure Act 30, n.3 (1947)). Whatever else may be considered a "general statemen[t] of policy," the term surely includes an announcement like the one before us, that an agency will discontinue a discretionary allocation of unrestricted funds from a lump-sum appropriation. . . .

[We also do not] think that the Court of Appeals was on solid ground in holding that Morton v. Ruiz, 415 U.S. 199 (1974), required the Service to abide by the APA's notice-and-comment provisions before terminating the Program. Those provisions were not at issue in *Ruiz*, where respondents challenged a provision, contained in a Bureau of Indian Affairs manual, that restricted eligibility for

---

5. In " 'matter[s] relating to . . . benefits,' " the Secretary of Health and Human Services has determined, as a matter of policy, to abide by the APA's notice-and-comment requirements. . . .

Indian assistance. Although the Bureau's own regulations required it to publish the provision in the Federal Register, the Bureau had failed to do so. *Id.*, at 233-34. We held that the Bureau's failure to abide by its own procedures rendered the provision invalid, stating that, under those circumstances, the denial of benefits would be "inconsistent with 'the distinctive obligation of trust incumbent upon the Government in its dealings with these dependent and sometimes exploited people.' " *Id.*, at 236 (quoting Seminole Nation v. United States, 316 U.S. 286, 296 (1942)). No such circumstances exist here. . . .

The judgment of the Court of Appeals is reversed, and the case is remanded for further proceedings consistent with this opinion.

NOTES AND QUESTIONS

1. *Rule of agency organization?* Is the Court's characterization of the decision to terminate services as one of "agency organization" accurate? Could this reasoning apply to any agency's decision to terminate a benefits program? The D.C. Circuit has stated that the purpose of the exception for rules of agency organization, practice, and procedure is to ensure that "agencies retain wide latitude in organizing their internal operations." Batterton v. Marshall, 648 F.2d 694, 707 (D.C. Cir. 1980).

2. *"Statements of policy."* The APA fails to define statements of policy or explain how, if at all, they differ from interpretive rules. The 1947 Attorney General's Manual attempted to formulate a distinct definition for the two terms. It characterized policy statements as agency statements issued to advise the public prospectively on how the agency proposes to exercise its power, whereas interpretive rules were statements issued to advise the public of the agency's construction of the statutes and rules that it administers. The lower courts, however, tend not to draw fine distinctions between the two labels, using the same general approach to applying either exemption.

3. *"Procedural rules."* In a prominent case, the D.C. Circuit decided that directives issued by the Department of Health and Human Services to govern administration of the Medicare program were procedural in nature and thus not subject to §553 notice and comment. American Hospital Association v. Bowen, 834 F.2d 1037 (D.C. Cir. 1987). The court observed that the test for determining whether a rule is procedural "has gradually shifted focus from asking whether a given procedure has a substantial impact on parties to inquiring more broadly whether the agency action also encodes a value judgment or puts a stamp of approval or disapproval on a given type of behavior." *Id.* at 1047 (internal quotation marks and citation omitted). Does this aid in understanding the exception?

Although the procedural rule exception encompasses agency decisions to change filing deadlines or cut-off dates (*see, e.g.,* Bachow Communications v. FCC, 237 F.3d 683 (D.C. Cir. 2001)), there are limits to the agency's ability to add new layers of review that might adversely affect claimants. In Military Order of the Purple Heart of the USA v. Secretary of Veterans Affairs, 580 F.3d 1293 (Fed. Cir. 2009), the Secretary of Veterans Affairs issued a directive to all VA offices, without notice and comment, that all decisions awarding a lump sum of $250,000 or more be sent to the Director of Compensation and Pension Service for final determination, and that claimants shall not be informed that such review occurred or whether the Director reduced the original award. Without discussing the §553(b)(B) exceptions, the court determined "that the procedural change that is here challenged affects the veteran's substantive as well as procedural rights" and that the change could not be made without "compliance with the requirements of the Administrative Procedure Act" because it was inconsistent with governing regulations that guaranteed an in person hearing and the "opportunity to respond to the concerns of the deciding official. . . ." 580 F.3d at 1296-1297.

4. *Good cause exception.* Another ground frequently invoked by agencies as justification for waiving the requirements of §553 is "good cause." Subsection (b)(B) permits an agency to dispense with rulemaking notice "[w]hen the agency for good cause finds (and incorporates the finding and a brief statement of reasons therefor in the rules issued) that notice and public procedure thereon are impracticable, unnecessary, or contrary to the public interest." Although courts often fail to articulate which of the three exceptions apply, impracticability is the one most often invoked. The test for impracticability is whether the execution of the agency's function would be unavoidably prevented by its undertaking public rulemaking proceedings. In DeRieux v. Five Smiths, 499 F.2d 1321 (Temp. Emer. Ct. App.), *cert. denied,* 419 U.S. 896 (1974), general notice of a proposed rule that would freeze prices was found impracticable on the assumption that there would have been a massive rush to raise prices before the freeze deadline. In Clay Broadcasting Corp. v. United States, 464 F.2d 1313 (5th Cir. 1972), the court upheld an FCC revised schedule of fees published without notice, on the ground that the agency was acting under a congressional directive to cover as much of the current fiscal year as possible.

The other two conditions are not as frequently litigated. The term "unnecessary" applies to minor or merely technical amendments that are not a matter of substantial public concern because they do not substantively alter the existing legal framework or change the rights and duties of the regulated parties. National Helium Corp. v. Federal Energy Admin., 569 F.2d 1137 (Temp. Emer. Ct. App. 1977). If, on the other hand, the governmental action under consideration is substantial or would impose new duties on the regulated parties, the courts are reluctant to find notice and comment unnecessary. In United Airlines, Inc. v. Brien, 588 F.3d 158 (2d Cir. 2009), airlines challenged fines imposed on them for transporting undocumented immigrants. The State Department had, without notice and comment, reversed a prior rule providing that airlines could not be fined when the undocumented immigrant was later granted a waiver. The Department contended that its change was merely technical and therefore good cause existed for dispensing with notice and comment. The Second Circuit disagreed, finding that because the new rule expanded liability for the carriers, it was not merely technical and could not be promulgated without notice and comment. *Id.* at 180.

The "public interest" criterion is found almost exclusively as a component of either the "impracticability" condition or the "unnecessary" condition. Compliance with §553 is considered contrary to the public interest if advance notice and the delay attributable to gathering public input would demonstrably worsen the problem the agency is trying to combat. *See, e.g., DeRieux, supra;* Malek-Marzban v. INS, 653 F.2d 113 (4th Cir. 1981). *See also* Air Transport Assn. of America v. Department of Transp., 900 F.2d 369 (D.C. Cir. 1990), *vacated and remanded on other grounds,* 498 U.S. 1077, *dismissed as moot,* 933 F.2d 1043 (D.C.

Cir. 1991) (rejecting FAA's claim that short, two-year, duration of pilot enforcement program provided ground for "good cause" exemption from §553 rulemaking requirements).

The need for quick action based on national security concerns has become an accepted basis for dispensing with notice and comment. In 2003, the Federal Aviation Administration (FAA) and Transportation Security Administration (TSA) promulgated a pair of rules without notice and comment to implement aviation security measures passed by Congress in the wake of the September 11 terrorist attacks. The first rule requires the FAA to suspend a pilot's airman certificate upon notification from the TSA that the pilot poses a security threat. The second rule establishes the procedure by which the TSA notifies the FAA and the pilot. The agencies justified the lack of advance notice and comment as follows:

> The use of notice and comment prior to issuance of this rule could delay the ability of the [FAA and TSA] to take effective action to keep persons found by the TSA to pose a security threat from holding an airman certificate. Further, the [FAA and TSA find] that good cause exists under 5 U.S.C. 553(d) for making this final rule effective immediately upon publication. This action is necessary to prevent a possible imminent hazard to aircraft, persons, and property within the United States.

Ineligibility for an Airman Certification Based on Security Grounds, 68 Fed. Reg. 3772, 3773 (2003). In Jifry v. FAA, 370 F.3d 1174, 1179-1180 (D.C. Cir. 2004), the court upheld the promulgation of the regulations without notice and comment, concluding that "[g]iven the respondents' legitimate concern over the threat of further terrorist acts involving aircraft in the aftermath of September 11, 2001, *see* Declaration of TSA Deputy Administrator Stephen McHale, the agencies had 'good cause' for not offering advance public participation." Note that, as is common in such cases, both agencies invited comments after the fact and promised to consider changes in the rules based on any comments received.

Although some courts defer to the agency's determination of good cause, most courts hold that a mere invocation of the statutory exemption is not enough and will inquire into the agency's basis for its finding. *See, e.g.,* Detroit Edison v. EPA, 496 F.2d 244 (6th Cir. 1974). In Oregon Trollers Assn. v. Gutierrez, 452 F.3d 1104 (9th Cir. 2006), the National Marine Fisheries Service (NMFS) adopted measures limiting commercial and recreational fishing in the Klamath River without notice and comment. The court held that NMFS sufficiently supported its assertion of the exception:

> The NMFS justified its decision with specific fishery-related reasons, not generic complaints about time pressure and data collection difficulties. It observed that the data on which the management measures are based "are not available until January and February because spawning escapement continues through the fall[.]" The Council does not finish its process until early April, and the season must begin on May 1. The NMFS thus has only a month to finalize the Council's proposals. "Delaying implementation of annual fishing regulations, which are based on the current stock abundance projections, for an additional sixty days would require that fishing regulations for May and June be set in the previous year without knowledge of current stock status."

Id. at 1124-1125. In an earlier case, the court had noted, "Under the APA, notice and comment is not 'impracticable' unless the agency cannot both follow section 553 and execute its statutory duties." NRDC v. Evans, 316 F.3d 904 (9th Cir. 2003). In that case, the agency had failed to offer specific analysis of why notice and comment was impractical in the year at issue, instead making general assertions about timeliness, which the court found to be insufficient. *Id.* at 912.

Section 553(b)(B) specifically requires that the agency incorporate a statement of its reasons for dispensing with notice and comment, but failure to do so need not be fatal to the regulations if, on inquiry, the court can find a sufficiently sound basis for a finding of good cause. In *DeRieux, supra,* the court stated: "We cannot agree that Congress intended to visit some consequence upon a technical violation of §553(b)." 499 F.2d at 1333. The court went on to uphold the rule since both the basis and purpose were obvious from the specific governing legislation.

Once courts have decided that an agency did not have good cause to dispense with notice-and-comment requirements, they find themselves in the midst of a dilemma concerning the appropriate remedy. Most plaintiffs seek complete rescission of the rule. In the absence of bad faith, however, courts are reluctant to take such a drastic step. In *Detroit Edison, supra,* the court held that the improperly promulgated rules would be left in place pending completion of a new administrative proceeding. Other courts have left the challenged rule in effect except as to the named petitioners and the classifications to which they specifically object. *E.g.,* Sharon Steel Corp. v. EPA, 597 F.2d 377, 381-382 (3d Cir. 1979).

For extensive treatment of the good cause exemption, *see* Ellen R. Jordan, The Administrative Procedure Act's "Good Cause" Exemption, 36 Admin. L. Rev. 113 (1984). On the use of statutory deadlines to justify claiming the good cause exception, *see* Jacob C. Gerson & Anne Joseph O'Connell, Deadlines in Administrative Law, 156 U. Pa. L. Rev. 923 (2008).

5. *Categorical exemptions.* The categorical exemptions from APA §553, including, *inter alia,* the exemption for military and foreign affairs functions and matters relating to internal agency management (including personnel matters) and matters regarding public property, differ from the exceptions to notice-and-comment rulemaking discussed above in that they are complete exemptions from the operation of §553, not merely exceptions to §553's notice-and-comment requirements. These exemptions have received comparatively little attention, perhaps because controversies regarding them rarely make their way to the courts. Nevertheless, commentary and what little case law exists provide some clues to understanding these exemptions.

The Attorney General's Manual on the APA states that the military functions exemption should be read broadly to cover all military functions, regardless of whether the function is carried out by a branch of the armed forces. However, courts may not be willing to read the military function exemption so broadly. In Independent Guard Association of Nevada v. O'Leary, 57 F.3d 766 (9th Cir. 1995), the court held that a rule concerning the qualifications of employees of independent contractors that guard nuclear weapons sites for the Department of Energy was not exempt from §553 under the military functions exemption. The court stated that APA exemptions should be read narrowly and that the function of guarding nuclear explosives was not a military function because there was no "evidence that the military has ever exercised any direct [supervisory] control over the activities of [the] civilian contract guards." *Id.* at 770. Is this consistent with the standard advocated by the Attorney General's Manual?

There has been more litigation over the meaning of the exemptions relating to agency management (including personnel matters) and public property. For example, in Stewart v. Smith, 673 F.2d 485 (D.C. Cir. 1982), the court held that a rule setting a maximum age of 34 for applicants to be guards in federal prison was exempt from §553 as a personnel matter. In Laketon Asphalt Refining, Inc. v. U.S. Department of the Interior, 624 F.2d 784 (7th Cir. 1980), the court held that rules allocating oil purchased from the government were exempt either as rules of agency management, or as rules relating to government property or contracts. The plaintiff had argued that the §553 exemptions should be read to cover only mechanical, procedural rules, not rules with substantive content. The court rejected that argument, finding "authority [that the exemption] is aimed . . . also at substantive rules." *Id.* at 790. Can you discern reasons why determinations such as these should be exempt from §553?

6. *Direct final rulemaking.* When an agency expects to receive no adverse comments—for example, because it is making technical corrections to a rule or its rulemaking involves routine promulgation of regulations implementing a statute—should notice-and-comment procedures be required to promulgate legislative rules? While the "good cause" exception might be useful in such situations, some agencies have begun to use a procedural innovation, pioneered at EPA, called "direct final rulemaking" under which an agency publishes a final rule (with a statement of basis and purpose) and specifies that it will go into effect on a certain date unless the agency receives adverse comments. The advantage of the procedure is that it speeds the process of promulgating rules and collapses the notice and decision steps into one step of promulgation of a final rule (unless adverse comments are received). This procedure is used for noncontroversial rules when the agency anticipates that no adverse comments will be filed. If the agency does receive adverse comments, the direct final rulemaking is canceled and the agency conducts a normal notice-and-comment process. For a discussion of this procedural innovation, *see* Ronald Levin, Direct Final Rulemaking, 64 Geo. Wash. L. Rev. 1 (1995). While this procedure has not been tested in the courts, the D.C. Circuit approved an agency decision to dispense with notice-and-comment procedures when the agency rescinded regulations that had become legally obsolete due to the expiration of the program under which the regulations had been promulgated. *See* Hadson Gas Systems, Inc. v. Federal Energy Regulatory Commission, 75 F.3d 680 (1996).

7. *Circumventing notice-and-comment requirements in agency-specific rulemaking statutes.* Several federal statutes contain provisions specifying rulemaking procedures comparable to, but somewhat different from, those found in the APA. When an agency, acting under authority of such a statute, takes an action without following that statute's notice-and-comment requirement, distinct interpretive questions may arise. Azar v. Allina Health Services, 139 S. Ct. 1804 (2019) is an example. The Medicare Act requires the Department of Health and Human

Services (DHHS) to provide public notice and a 60-day comment period for any "rule, requirement, or other statement of policy . . . that establishes or changes a substantive legal standard governing . . . the payment for services," §1395hh(a)(2). Without providing public notice and opportunity for comment, DHHS published on its website a new policy that dramatically—and retroactively—reduced Medicare payments to hospitals serving low-income patients. DHHS argued that its new policy was an "interpretive" rule, as that term is understood in the context of the APA, and that therefore the agency was excused from following the notice-and-comment requirement. Justice Gorsuch, writing for a near-unanimous court, disagreed, finding that the term "substantive," as used in the Medicare Act, had a meaning quite different from its meaning in APA jurisprudence. Because the Medicare Act includes "rule, requirement, or other statement of policy" in the term "substantive legal standard," said Justice Gorsuch, it cannot be interpreted to incorporate the rulemaking exemptions from APA §553(b)(3)(A). Therefore, even if the agency's policy would be found to be an "interpretive rule" under the APA, it is nonetheless a "substantive legal standard" under the Medicare Act because it has the effect of reducing reimbursement amounts.

6.   Agency Authority to Stay Promulgated Rules

During presidential transitions, it is typical for the incoming administration temporarily to freeze and review regulations that the outgoing administration had been rushing to finalize. As one commentator put it, "before President Obama took to the dance floor on the night of his inauguration, his then Chief of Staff, Rahm Emanuel, had already fired off a memorandum to the heads of federal agencies instructing them not to start or finish any regulations without approval of the new Administration." Anne Joseph O'Connell, Agency Rulemaking and Political Transitions, 105 Nw. U. L. Rev. 471, 471-472 (citing Memorandum from Rahm Emanuel, Assistant to the President and Chief of Staff, the White House, to Heads of Executive Departments and Agencies (Jan. 20, 2009), 74 Fed. Reg. 4435 (Jan. 26, 2009)).

Executive Orders, interpretive rules, withdrawals of proposed rulemaking, or extensions of rulemakings can be done without notice and comment as early as inauguration day, but rescinding completed rulemakings requires more time and effort. For promulgated rules, agencies must conform with the APA §553 notice-and-comment requirements. Some administrations have found this delay cumbersome.

The Trump administration used a variety of tools to try to stay rules issued by the Obama administration. In an illustrative case excerpted below, several organizations challenged an action of the National Highway Traffic Safety Administration (NHTSA) indefinitely delaying the effective date of a rule increasing civil penalties for automobile manufacturer violations of federally-mandated fuel efficiency standards, known as "CAFE Standards." NHTSA had adopted the increases through notice-and-comment rulemaking, as required by the Federal Civil Penalties Inflation Adjustment Act Improvements Act of 2015 (the Improvements Act).

NATURAL RESOURCES DEFENSE COUNCIL v. NATIONAL HIGHWAY TRAFFIC SAFETY ADMINISTRATION
894 F.3d 95 (2d Cir. 2018)

Before WINTER, POOLER, and PARKER, Circuit Judges. . . .

POOLER and PARKER, Circuit Judges

Petitioners in this action (the "Petitioners") claim NHTSA exceeded its statutory authority in indefinitely delaying a rule implemented pursuant to the clear Congressional directive in the Improvements Act. Petitioners also claim that the agency violated the requirements of the Administrative Procedure Act ("APA").

We agree with Petitioners on both issues and conclude NHTSA's actions were unlawful. . . .

On January 20, 2017, Reince Priebus (at the time, the Assistant to the President and Chief of Staff), issued a Memorandum for the Heads of Executive Departments and Agencies, regarding a "regulatory freeze pending review." The memo directed that:

> With respect to regulations that have been published in the [Federal Register] but have not taken effect, as permitted by applicable law, [agencies should] temporarily postpone their effective date for 60 days from the date of this memorandum, subject to the exceptions described in paragraph 1 [regarding emergencies and other "urgent circumstances"], for the purpose of reviewing questions of fact, law, and policy they raise. Where appropriate and as permitted by applicable law, you should consider proposing for notice and comment a rule to delay the effective date for regulations beyond that 60-day period.

Id. [NHTSA issued successive rules delaying the effective date of the penalty regulation three separate times, once for 60 days, then for 90 days, and finally for 14 more days.]

On July 12, 2017, NHTSA published a final rule in the Federal Register that is the subject of the current petitions for review. This rule, which we refer to as the "Suspension Rule," stated that, "As of July 7, 2017, the effective date of the final rule published in the Federal Register on December 28, 2016, at 81 FR 95489, is delayed indefinitely pending reconsideration." 82 Fed. Reg. 32,139 (July 12, 2017). NHTSA explained:

> NHTSA is now reconsidering the final rule because the final rule did not give adequate consideration to all of the relevant issues, including the potential economic consequences of increasing CAFE penalties by potentially $1 billion per year, as estimated in the Industry Petition. Thus, in a separate document published in this Federal Register, NHTSA is seeking comment on whether $14 per tenth of an mpg is the appropriate penalty level for civil penalties for violations of CAFE standards given the requirements of the Inflation Adjustment Act and the Energy Policy and Conservation Act (EPCA) of 1975, which authorizes civil penalties for violations of CAFE standards. Because NHTSA is reconsidering the final rule, NHTSA is delaying the effective date pending reconsideration.

Id. at 32,139-40. . . .

NHTSA does not argue that the Improvements Act explicitly granted it authority to indefinitely delay the increase, nor could it plausibly do so given the clear terms of the statute and its purpose. The agency instead advances several other theories regarding its authority to indefinitely delay the Civil Penalties Rule. . . .

The need for delay pending reconsideration is the primary ground advanced by NHTSA in this proceeding, but NHTSA offers no authority—statutory or otherwise—for the proposition that an agency has authority to delay a rule because it is engaged in a separate process of reconsideration. NHTSA instead argues that delay pending reconsideration is authorized because that is what many other agencies do.

. . . NHTSA's argument on this point is essentially that there is a categorical authority for an agency to delay an effective date of an earlier rule pending reconsideration. We disagree. As the D.C. Circuit recently held, a decision to reconsider a rule does not simultaneously convey authority to indefinitely delay the existing rule pending that reconsideration. *See* [Clean Air Council v. Pruitt, 862 F.3d 1, 9 (D.C. Cir. 2017]. . . .

We also conclude that NHTSA violated the APA by announcing the Suspension Rule without having first undertaken notice and comment rulemaking. . . .

NHTSA does not appear to dispute that the Suspension Rule constitutes a final rule that would be subject to the notice and comment requirements of APA §553. Instead, it invokes the APA's "good cause" exception to notice and comment rulemaking. . . . The burden is on the agency to establish that notice and comment need not be provided. The good cause exception "should be narrowly construed and only reluctantly countenanced." [NRDC v. Abraham, 355 F.3d 179, 204 (2d Cir. 2004).]

As noted, the good cause exception applies only in circumstances when notice and comment is "impracticable, unnecessary, or contrary to the public interest." 5 U.S.C. §553(b)(B). . . .

We conclude that NHTSA's action does not meet these exacting standards. . . .

Any imminence was NHTSA's own creation. NHTSA promulgated the Civil Penalties Rule on December 28, 2016, and NHTSA subsequently delayed its implementation of the rule through a trio of successive delays of finite durations. The effective date of the Civil Penalties Rule was imminent only insofar as NHTSA's third finite delay was scheduled to elapse. Good cause cannot arise as a result of the agency's own delay. . . .

NHTSA notes that, simultaneously with the Suspension Rule, it published a rule soliciting comments concerning the appropriate penalty and contends that it was entitled to dispense with notice and comment in promulgating the Suspension Rule because it needed time to consider the responses it anticipated receiving. This rationale fares no better. It does not satisfy the "unnecessary" prong because that prong is limited to circumstances when the rule is "inconsequential to the industry and to the public," [Mack Trucks, Inc. v. EPA, 682 F.3d 87, 94 (D.C. Cir. 2012).] The responses of both sides on this petition unquestionably indicate that the Suspension Rule is anything but inconsequential. . . .

Finally, it was not in the public interest to suspend notice and comment. Notice and comment are not mere formalities. They are basic to our system of administrative law. They serve the public interest by providing a forum for the robust debate of competing and frequently complicated policy considerations having far-reaching implications and, in so doing, foster reasoned decisionmaking. These premises apply with full force to this case. This is not a situation of acute health or safety risk requiring immediate administrative action. And it is not a situation in which surprise to the industry is required to preempt manipulative tactics.

That a regulated entity might prefer different regulations that are easier or less costly to comply with does not justify dispensing with notice and comment. The automobile industry was on notice since 2015, long before the Civil Penalties Rule was promulgated in December 2016, that Congress had established a regime requiring agencies across the federal government to institute mandatory, inflation-linked increases to numerous federal civil penalties, including the CAFE penalties and we are unconvinced the industry was taken by surprise. There was not an emergency or other extraordinary circumstance that would justify forgoing notice and comment.

Accordingly, NHTSA violated the APA in promulgating the Suspension Rule without undertaking notice and comment rulemaking. . . .

NOTES AND QUESTIONS

1. *Other challenges to stays.* Courts have struck down agency attempts to stay duly promulgated rules for a variety of other reasons beyond violating APA procedural requirements. For example, in Air Alliance Houston v. EPA, 906 F.3d 1049 (D.C. Cir. 2018), the EPA had published a rule to delay the implementation of a final chemical safety rule. The EPA argued that it needed more time to consider the public comments. The D.C. Circuit rejected this reason as arbitrary because the agency could simply hold a new notice-and-comment rulemaking to collect more comments. Since there is an easy fix for this problem, what do you think explains the agency's decision to bypass it?

2. *Procedural nitpicking?* The caselaw makes clear that a new administration must live with recently finalized rules from a prior administration until the responsible agency can rescind and replace them (at least if they were issued before the time period in which Congress may disapprove them under the Congressional Review Act, which allows Congress to reach back several months to reject rules before they become legally effective, as discussed in Chapter I, *supra*). Does this strict insistence on following APA procedures make sense? Doesn't it create unnecessary costs for regulated parties who must comply with the final rules in the meantime, or opt not to comply and run the risk that they will be enforced (perhaps by third parties filing citizen suits)? Why should courts insist on procedural regularity and nitpick over the agency's reasons when everyone knows that the administration eventually will rescind the rule?

7.   Alternative Rulemaking Models

a.   Negotiated Rulemaking

Despite its putative advantages as a method of making administrative policy, the APA's model of informal rulemaking has been subject to almost continuous criticism since the late 1970s. Critics have argued that a paper rulemaking process is not well suited to eliciting the type of interactive participation that would help agencies develop truly effective rules. Rather, they claim, notice-and-comment rulemaking fosters an excessively adversarial relationship between the public and the agency, and among the interest groups seeking to influence a rule's content. Rarely satisfied with the outcome of the rulemaking process, participants merely shift the arena for their adversarial advocacy to the courts, where adopted rules are often tied up for years before they can be implemented.

These concerns led Philip Harter, a negotiator, mediator, and (later) law professor, to recommend in a 1981 article the creation of a new procedure for rulemaking, which became known as "regulatory negotiation" (or "reg-neg" for short). *See* Philip J. Harter, Negotiating Regulations: A Cure for the Malaise, 71 Geo. L.J. 1 (1981). The Harter proposal was picked up the following year by the Administrative Conference of the United States (ACUS), a federal advisory commission on administrative procedure. *See* Recommendations of the Administrative Conference, 47 Fed. Reg. 30,701 (1983). Several years later, ACUS's proposal was adopted by Congress as the Negotiated Rulemaking Act, Pub. L. No. 101-648, codified at 5 U.S.C. §§561-570. The Act authorizes agencies to use negotiated rulemaking if they determine it is in the public interest. In making that determination, agencies must consider, among other things, whether there is a need for a rule, whether there are a limited number of significantly affected interests affected by the rule, and whether there is a reasonable likelihood that a negotiating committee can be convened that will be balanced and will negotiate in good faith to reach a consensus in a prescribed time. *Id.* §563(a).

The Act authorizes agencies to appoint a convener to facilitate negotiation and defines consensus as "unanimous concurrence among the interests represented on a negotiated rulemaking committee" but allows individual committees to define the term differently. *Id.* §562. The Act also specifies that negotiated rules must still be published for comment and treated as would any other notice-and-comment rule on judicial review. Negotiated rules may "not be accorded any greater deference by a court than a rule which is the product of other rulemaking procedures." *Id.* §570.

In the 1990s, President Clinton urged agencies to use negotiated rulemaking for at least some of their rules (*see* Executive Order 12,866, *infra*). A number of agencies did so, including the Department of Labor, Department of Transportation, and Department of the Interior, but the main early adopter was the Environmental Protection Agency, which by 1992 already had announced 15 reg-negs. Although early reports were positive, the practice never caught on widely, and the numbers of reg-negs declined precipitously during the Bush Administration, notwithstanding President Bush's retention of Executive Order 12,866. And there have been relatively few reg-negs since.

Commentators have disagreed about the value of negotiated rulemaking, particularly on whether it has succeeded in resolving or ameliorating perceived problems with traditional notice-and-comment rulemaking. Participants in this debate draw different conclusions from two unpublished reports by Cornelius M. Kerwin and Lauri I. Langbein: An Evaluation of Negotiated Rulemaking at the Environmental Protection Agency: Phase I (1995) and Phase II (1997). Analyzing the Part I report, Professor Cary Coglianese concluded that negotiated rulemaking has accomplished neither of its goals of reducing the time it takes to promulgate final rules and reducing the likelihood of post-promulgation litigation challenging final rules. *See* Cary Coglianese, Assessing Consensus: The Promise and Performance of Negotiated Rulemaking, 46 Duke L.J. 1255 (1997). Philip Harter, the father of negotiated rulemaking, interpreted the data differently and asserted that Coglianese's methodology was flawed and his conclusions erroneous. *See* Philip J. Harter, Assessing the Assessors: The Actual Performance of Negotiated Rulemaking, 9 N.Y.U. Envtl. L.J. 32 (2000). Harter argued that negotiated rulemaking shortened the rulemaking process by about one-third and had reduced challenges to rules. In another assessment, Professors Jody Freeman and Laura Langbein found that the data bolster the claims of reg-neg proponents. Among other things, participants report that reg-negs generate more learning, better quality rules, and higher satisfaction compared to conventional rulemaking. Jody Freeman & Laura I. Langbein, Regulatory Negotiation and the Legitimacy Benefit, 9 N.Y.U. Envtl. L.J. 60 (2000).

The debate has not been settled, and negotiated rulemaking seems to have stalled as an alternative regulatory process. But it may be worth considering whether the aims of negotiated rulemaking might be achieved by other reforms, which might help to ameliorate the slow pace, high cost, and intense adversarialism of the notice-and-comment rulemaking process without sacrificing administrative law norms of transparency, accountability, and rationality. At a minimum, the experience with reg-neg has helped to illuminate these tradeoffs.

NOTES AND QUESTIONS

1. *Delegation to private parties?* Does negotiated rulemaking amount to an unconstitutional delegation of power to private groups, under *Carter Coal*, discussed in Chapter I, *supra*? Is there another way to involve interest groups more directly in the rulemaking process without the agency abdicating the decision to them?

2. *Public proceedings.* In its proposal for reg-neg legislation, ACUS had proposed that a negotiating group be permitted to close its meetings to the public "when, in the judgment of the participants, the likelihood of achieving consensus would be significantly enhanced." 47 Fed. Reg. at 30,701. Although it adopted most of ACUS's recommendations, Congress shied away from this proposal because it might have appeared to authorize secret proceedings. To the contrary, Congress specified that the Federal Advisory Committee Act (FACA), 86 Stat. 770 (1972), reproduced at 5 U.S.C. App. 1, applies to the formation and operation of negotiating committees. FACA, discussed in Chapter IX, *infra*, applies open government provisions to groups formed to advise the President or an administrative agency. How should Congress balance the privacy (and even secrecy) necessary to make "deals" with the traditional administrative law norms of openness, inclusiveness, and transparency? Is the balance untenable?

3. *Negotiation mandates.* In addition to authorizing the use of reg-neg in the Negotiated Rulemaking Act, Congress mandated negotiated rulemaking in at least a dozen statutes, including the Higher Education Act Amendments of 1992 (HEA Amendments), Pub. L. No. 102-325, amending the Higher Education Act of 1965, which reauthorized federal financial aid programs and adopted reforms to combat high default rates. Pursuant to the HEA Amendments, the Department of Education conducted several negotiated rulemakings, including one to set standards for recognizing accrediting agencies, and another to establish rules for servicing student loans. Because of short statutory deadlines, many negotiations were conducted simultaneously. What are the downsides of

mandating a process like reg-neg? Doesn't its success depend on the willingness of stakeholders to come to consensus voluntarily? Short statutory deadlines may also pose an obstacle to success.

4. *Are agency commitments in reg-neg enforceable?* In one negotiated rulemaking conducted under the HEA Amendments, the Department of Education eventually promulgated a rule that departed from the agreed consensus. The negotiation concerned fraud and errors that had arisen in the loan servicing process, which had resulted in significant losses of federal money.

In this instance, Congress had authorized the Secretary of Education to promulgate regulations governing performance standards and liability of loan servicers. Along with a representative of the DOE, participants in the reg-neg included representatives of loan servicers, lenders, borrowers, and educational institutions. During the negotiations, the loan servicers sought immunity from damages for their servicing mistakes, and the group reached consensus to allow it. However, the DOE ultimately decided not to honor that agreement, and proposed instead a rule that would cap servicers' liability at the amount of servicing fees they collected. After the servicers rejected this proposal, the Department proposed and promulgated the worst possible regulation for them—no immunity and no cap on liability. The servicers sought judicial review, attempting to overturn the rule based, *inter alia*, on violations of the procedural requirements for negotiated rulemaking.

USA GROUP LOAN SERVICES, INC. v. RILEY
82 F.3d 708 (7th Cir. 1996)

Before POSNER, Chief Judge, and DIANE P. WOOD and EVANS, Circuit Judges.
POSNER, Chief Judge: . . .
Mistakes and outright fraud by servicers, some resulting in large losses of federal money, led Congress in 1992 to amend Title IV of the Higher Education Act to authorize the Secretary of Education to "prescribe . . . regulations applicable to third party servicers (including regulations concerning financial responsibility standards for, and the assessment of liabilities for program violations against, such servicers) to establish minimum standards with respect to sound management and accountability." 20 U.S.C. §1082(a)(1). . . . The Secretary has done this, see 34 C.F.R. Parts 668, 682 (1994); Dept. of Education, Student Assistance General Provisions, 59 Fed. Reg. 22,348 (Apr. 29, 1994), esp. pp. 22,405, 22,408-10, and the servicers have brought this suit to invalidate portions of the regulations on substantive and procedural grounds. The district court rejected the challenge, and the servicers appeal.

The challenged provisions make servicers jointly and severally liable with their customers (lenders, guarantors, and institutions) for violations of the statutes, regulations, or contracts governing the student loan program. To be liable, the servicer must itself have violated a statute, regulation, or contract.

[The court, in portions of the opinion omitted here, rejected several substantive challenges to the rules.]

The remaining arguments are procedural and the main one is that the Secretary adopted the challenged regulation in violation of the conditions of "negotiated rulemaking," a novelty in the administrative process. The 1992 amendment to the Higher Education Act, under which the regulation was promulgated, required that the Secretary submit any draft regulation to a process of negotiated rulemaking, to be conducted in accordance with recommendations made by the Administrative Conference of the United States and codified in 1 C.F.R. §§305.82-4 and 305.85-5 and with "any successor recommendation, regulation, or law." 20 U.S.C. §1098a(b). A "successor law" to the Administrative Conference's recommendations had in fact been enacted in 1990. It is the Negotiated Rulemaking Act, 5 U.S.C §§561 et seq. . . . The 1992 amendment to the Higher Education Act made negotiated rulemaking mandatory in proceedings implementing the amendment, as we have seen.

The servicers argue that the Department negotiated in bad faith with them. Neither the 1992 amendment nor the Negotiated Rulemaking Act specifies a remedy for such a case, and the latter act strongly implies there is none. 5 U.S.C. §570. But even if a regulation could be invalidated because the agency had failed to negotiate in good faith, this would not carry the day for the servicers.

During the negotiations, an official of the Department of Education promised the servicers that the Department would abide by any consensus reached by them unless there were compelling reasons to depart. The propriety of such a promise may be questioned. It sounds like an abdication of regulatory authority to the regulated, the full burgeoning of the interest-group state, and the final confirmation of the "capture" theory of administrative regulation. At all events, although the servicers reached a firm consensus that they should not be liable for their mistakes the Department refused to abide by its official's promise. What is more, the draft regulations that the Department submitted to the negotiating process capped the servicers' liability at the amount of the fees they received from their customers, yet when it came time to propose a regulation as the basis for the notice and comment rulemaking the Department abandoned the cap. The breach of the promise to abide by consensus in the absence of compelling reasons not here suggested, and the unexplained withdrawal of the Department's proposal to cap the servicers' liability, form the basis for the claim that the Department negotiated in bad faith.

We have doubts about the propriety of the official's promise to abide by a consensus of the regulated industry, but we have no doubt that the Negotiated Rulemaking Act did not make the promise enforceable. Natural Resources. Defense Council, Inc. v. EPA, 859 F.2d 156, 194 (D.C. Cir. 1988) (per curiam). The practical effect of enforcing it would be to make the Act extinguish notice and comment rulemaking in all cases in which it was preceded by negotiated rulemaking; the comments would be irrelevant if the agency were already bound by promises that it had made to the industry. There is no textual or other clue that the Act meant to do this. Unlike collective bargaining negotiations, to which the servicers compare negotiated rulemaking, the Act does not envisage that the negotiations will end in a binding contract. The Act simply creates a consultative process in advance of the more formal arms' length procedure of notice and comment rulemaking.

The complaint about the Secretary's refusal to adhere to the proposal to cap the servicers' liability misconceives the nature of negotiation. The Secretary proposed the cap in an effort to be accommodating and deflect the industry's wrath. The industry, in retrospect improvidently, rejected the proposal, holding out for no liability. So, naturally, the Secretary withdrew the proposal. A rule that a rejected offer places a ceiling on the offeror's demands would destroy negotiation. Neither party would dare make an offer, as the other party would be certain to reject it in order to limit the future demands that his opponent could make. . . .

The servicers argue that they should be allowed to conduct discovery to uncover the full perfidy of the Department's conduct in the negotiations. Discovery is rarely proper in the judicial review of administrative action. The court is supposed to make its decision on the basis of the administrative record, not create its own record. There are exceptions, . . . and the main one has some potential applicability here: discovery is proper when it is necessary to create a record without which the challenge to the agency's action cannot be evaluated. . . . The servicers argue that if only they could get access to the notes of certain participants in the negotiating sessions they could demonstrate additional instances of bad faith on the part of the Department.

Their conception of "bad faith" reflects, as we have noted, a misconception of the negotiation process. It is not bad faith to withdraw an offer after the other side has rejected it. If as we doubt the Negotiated Rulemaking Act creates a remedy as well as a right, we suppose that a refusal to negotiate that really was in bad faith, because the agency was determined to stonewall, might invalidate the rule eventually adopted by the agency. But we do not think that the Act was intended to open the door wide to discovery in judicial proceedings challenging regulations issued after the notice and comment proceeding that followed the negotiations. If as in this case the public record discloses no evidence of bad faith on the part of the agency, that should be the end of the inquiry. . . .

Affirmed.

NOTES AND QUESTIONS

1. *Promising to abide by consensus: agency abdication?* Judge Posner says in *USA Loan Services* that an agency promise to abide by a consensus unless there are good reasons to depart is an "abdication of regulatory authority to the regulated." Is this correct? If the consensus is within the bounds of the agency's discretion under the statute, and the agency has participated in the negotiations, why would it be problematic to have a presumption in favor of implementing that consensus? In Natural Resources Defense Council, Inc. v. EPA, 859 F.2d 156, 194 (D.C. Cir. 1988) (per curiam) the court stated, in the context of a rulemaking following a settlement agreement, that "a binding promise to promulgate in the proposed form would seem to defeat Congress's evident intention that agencies proceeding by informal rulemaking should maintain minds open to whatever insights the comments produced by notice under §553 may generate." The court compared this to negotiated rulemaking, in which agencies remain free to reshape proposed rules in response to comments received in the notice-and-comment stage of the rulemaking. *Id.* at 194-195. Perhaps negotiated rulemaking should not be viewed as a radical departure from conventional notice-and-comment rulemaking—it simply moves the input of stakeholders earlier in the process, and forces them to respond to each other more directly than in traditional notice-and-comment rulemaking.

2. *Violations of the Negotiated Rulemaking Act.* Should agency violations of the Negotiated Rulemaking Act or other alleged misconduct during negotiations *ever* be grounds for overturning a final rule, which, as required by the Negotiated Rulemaking Act, is issued only after notice-and-comment rulemaking following the negotiation process? Does it make a difference to your answer if the reg-neg has been mandated by Congress?

3. *Judicial review of negotiated rules.* In addition to *USA Group Loan Services,* the courts of appeals have reviewed several rules promulgated after negotiated rulemaking processes. In Career College Assoc. v. Riley, 74 F.3d 1265 (D.C. Cir. 1996), more rules promulgated under the HEA Amendments survived substantive challenges. Although the court mentioned the negotiated rulemaking process, no issue regarding the process was addressed in the court's opinion. In Safe Buildings Alliance v. EPA, 846 F.2d 79 (D.C. Cir. 1988), the court upheld an EPA rule promulgated after negotiation without mentioning that negotiated rulemaking had taken place. Another EPA rule, based in part on negotiated rulemaking, also withstood review by the D.C. Circuit in Natural Resources Defense Council v. EPA, 907 F.2d 1146 (D.C. Cir. 1990).

b.   Alternatives to Negotiated Rulemaking

With technology, economics, and science all evolving at a rapid pace, the need for efficiency, flexibility, consensus, and experimentalism in the regulatory process has never been more acute. There are a number of alternative approaches to rulemaking that fall short of the processes required under the Negotiated Rulemaking Act yet are still more collaborative than traditional notice-and-comment rulemaking. The Environmental Protection Agency has been a leader in experimenting with these alternatives. For example, the EPA used a variant of the reg-neg process to develop its rule regarding the control of emissions from nonroad diesel engines (those used in industries like agriculture, construction, and mining). *See* EPA Control of Emissions of Air Pollution from Nonroad Diesel Engines and Fuel; Final Rule, 69 Fed. Reg. 38,958 (2004). The process was bound to be contentious, with equipment manufacturers and the oil industry on one side, and environmentalists and state and local governments on the other, but the EPA put enormous effort into the process, taking the time to engage industry stakeholders early in the process and continuing to consult throughout. In contrast to standard practice, the Office of Management and Budget (OMB) was also involved early in the process. EPA successfully employed a shuttle diplomacy approach in which it communicated directly with the broadly represented individual stakeholders rather than convening large groups from disparate sectors. (Large gatherings impeded open communication because stakeholders were concerned about revealing—thus compromising—competitive advantage.) When EPA conducted a study of the process, it concluded that these elements were key to success: the process used a convener of stature (in this case, it was EPA, OMB, and the White House itself); the agency was a committed leader in the collaborative process; the appropriate representatives were present; and the agency had a clearly defined purpose. *See* Philip J. Harter, Collaboration: The Future of Governance, 2009 J. Dispute Res. 411, 437.

Another example of a hybrid approach is EPA's rulemaking on mandatory reporting of greenhouse gases, described in the case study below:

On December 26, 2008, in its 2008 Fiscal Year Consolidated Appropriations Bill, Congress authorized funding for EPA to propose and finalize a rule on mandatory reporting of greenhouse gas emissions. This was a very important step for the federal government because a national approach to mitigating greenhouse gas emissions cannot be effective without first knowing current emissions by sector and then monitoring the decline over time. Congress required EPA to issue the proposed rule under the Clean Air Act by September 26, 2008, and the final rule by June 26, 2009. The proposal was not signed until early in the Obama Administration, on March 10, 2009, and published in the Federal Register on April 10, 2009.

EPA went well beyond the usual public notice and comment requirements for rulemaking contained in Section 307(d) of the Clean Air Act. While no public meetings are required under the Clean Air Act before publication of the proposed rule, EPA conducted extensive outreach and held more than 100 meetings with over 250 stakeholders, including trade associations, potentially affected industries, state, local, and tribal government, environmental groups and non-governmental organizations (NGOs), the Department of Energy (DOE), and the U.S. Department of Agriculture (USDA). At these meetings, EPA shared information about the proposed rule and encouraged input from the stakeholders. EPA also established technical work groups that "followed up with stakeholders on a variety of methodological, technical, and policy issues."

Given the expertise that states and local governments have developed on many aspects of climate change and the experience they have had with implementing climate change programs, it is important that the federal government, in developing climate change regulations and policies, take advantage of the lessons learned. To that end, EPA met with state and regional organizations already involved in greenhouse gas reporting programs, such as the California Air Resources Board, the Climate Registry, and the Western Climate Initiative, and "benefited from the leadership the States have shown in developing these programs and their experiences" and built upon those experiences to develop the proposed Greenhouse Gas Reporting Rule.

EPA held two public meetings on the proposed rule, one in Arlington, Virginia, and the other in Sacramento, California. The Agency also employed live audio web-streaming for remote participants in a novel approach to increase stakeholder access to the public meetings; approximately 150 people took advantage of this option. Even after publication of the proposed rule, EPA continued this very active outreach and by late July 2009, had interacted with several thousands of people through face to face meetings in both EPA's headquarters office in Washington, D.C. and several EPA regional offices throughout the country, and conducted or participated in approximately ten to twenty webinars, conference calls, and trade association meetings. The EPA Administrator signed the final rule on September 22, 2009, and EPA used an "open door policy" for public input all the way through to promulgation of the final rule.

While the full benefits of this collaborative approach cannot yet be measured, this robust form of public participation can be considered as an alternative to negotiated rulemaking when the government decides that it lacks the internal or external political support or time for an agreement-seeking process.

Joseph A. Siegel, Collaborative Decision Making on Climate Change in the Federal Government, 27 Pace Envtl. L. Rev. 257, 285-287 (2009) (Collaborative Decision Making).

In a third example, the EPA and DOT pursued a unique process to set greenhouse gas and fuel efficiency standards for cars and light-duty trucks. The agencies collaborated closely and produced separate but "harmonized" rules. This rulemaking process was highly complicated and controversial because of the long history of contentious litigation over fuel efficiency standards; the fact that EPA would be setting the first federal greenhouse gas standards under the Clean Air Act (which could conflict with fuel economy standards set by the DOT); and because along with these two regulators, California had also historically set its own fuel efficiency standards pursuant to a preemption waiver under the Clean Air Act.

The EPA and DOT ultimately agreed to issue their rules jointly, itself a historic event. Prior to doing so, they consulted closely with domestic and foreign auto companies, officials from the state of California, labor groups, and other stakeholders. All of the parties agreed in "letters of commitment" to support the joint rule if the final version was substantially similar to a "notice of intent" the agencies had published. Critically, the White House led the process, helping to spur collaboration not only among the stakeholders but also, crucially, between the EPA and DOT.

For a detailed description of the unusual process, including the innovative use of joint rulemaking, public "commitment" letters, and the harmonized approach to compliance, see Jody Freeman, The Obama Administration's National Auto Policy, Lessons from the Car Deal, 35 Harv. Envtl. L. Rev. 344 (2011).

The EPA's website includes the commitment letters and terms of the agreements. *See* 2010 Commitment Letters for MY2017-2025 Light-Duty and MY 2014-2018 Heavy-Duty Programs, U.S. EPA (2010), https://perma.cc/E4HE-CRTG. Example letters can be found at: https://perma.cc/RF2K-HTLM (Alliance of Automobile Manufacturers); https://perma.cc/K3DX-SBRW (CA Resources Board); and https://perma.cc/TLM3-PFK3 (GM).

The Car Deal raises a difficult question about how to balance transparency with secrecy when negotiating a complex, highly-contentious agreement among many stakeholders with competing interests. Compared to the other examples of hybrid rulemaking processes noted above, including negotiated rulemaking, this process was more private, although it resulted in publicly promulgated notice and comment rules.

> While no formal explanation was provided by the parties about the rationale for conducting the process in a closed fashion, the complexity of the issues and long-standing nature of the conflict between the parties may have made it difficult to successfully collaborate and reach an agreement using an open process. This suggests that while transparency may be a positive element of successful collaboration in many contexts, there may be occasions, particularly in agreement-seeking settings where the dispute between the parties is already joined, when the primary stakeholders may see transparency as a deterrent to a successful resolution. A broad lesson learned from this example is that there is no one "right" set of tools for each collaborative process along the spectrum. Rather, the design of each collaborative effort must be tailored to the specifics of the situation and needs of the parties.

Siegel, Collaborative Decision Making, *supra* at 294.

In sum, although negotiated rulemaking may not be as popular as its proponents once hoped, it appears to have encouraged experimentation with other collaborative procedures. For an analysis of the benefits of collaborative regulatory approaches generally, see Jody Freeman, Collaborative Governance in the Administrative State, 45 UCLA L. Rev. 1 (1997); Jody Freeman & Jim Rossi, Agency Coordination in Shared Regulatory Space, 125 Harv. L. Rev. 1134 (2012). These innovative approaches can be controversial, however, especially when they appear to compromise the transparency associated with conventional rulemaking, or when they involve increased participation by a limited few.

C.   STRENGTHENING THE ANALYTIC BASIS OF POLICYMAKING

In addition to the trend toward "judicializing" and "democratizing" agency policymaking through additional procedural and substantive requirements, administrative law has also witnessed a discernible effort to render policymaking more analytically rigorous. As Colin Diver has observed, federal administrative law has exhibited a general trend in favor of encouraging agencies to take a more comprehensive or "synoptic" view of policy options and to analyze the alternatives carefully and completely before choosing a course of action. *See* Colin S. Diver, Policymaking Paradigms in Administrative Law, 95 Harv. L. Rev. 393 (1981). In this section, we examine three methods that have been employed to increase the analytical rigor underlying rulemaking: cost-benefit analysis, presidential oversight, and impact statement requirements.

1.   *Cost-Benefit Analysis*

Much of the contemporary debate about increasing the analytic rigor of agency policymaking has focused on the use of cost-benefit analysis (CBA). This should not be surprising in light of the public welfare justifications for most government regulation that we surveyed in Chapter I, *supra*. For example, the creation and regulation of public utility monopolies makes sense only if its economic justifications are true. Likewise, regulation of negative externalities is justified only if the cost of regulation is lower than the magnitude of the negative effects avoided. No economically rational society would knowingly spend $2 to avoid $1 in costs. CBA has been central to presidential oversight of regulatory policymaking and has emerged as an important focus of judicial review. The scholarly literature on CBA is voluminous, and the debate over its strengths and weaknesses vociferous. To understand the controversy, it is helpful to understand that there are different forms of CBA:

> The strong form of CBA is a creature of welfare economics. It is both commensuralist and welfarist—that is, it describes the effects of regulatory options, both pro and con, on a single monetary scale, and its function is to maximize overall well-being. Economists have viewed CBA as a tool for achieving Kaldor-Hicks

efficiency.[1] Recently, however, Matthew Adler and Eric Posner have sought to un-couple CBA from Kaldor-Hicks efficiency and to provide independent justification for CBA as a welfare-maximizing procedure. Procedurally, while some proponents of the strong form of CBA—[Cass] Sunstein among them—acknowledge that it may not be possible to monetize all costs and benefits, complete monetization remains the goal. Substantively, CBA's goal is to increase aggregate welfare. There-fore, there is a presumption against regulatory options whose costs exceed their benefits. Sunstein would allow this presumption to be overcome in some circum-stances—for example, where there are distributional concerns or where rights of those affected may be at issue. Some (but not all) other CBA proponents agree that even a well-conducted CBA, while providing crucial input, is not necessarily decisive and that decision makers may take account of other morally relevant con-siderations, including non-welfarist values.

The weak form of CBA is simply a weighing of all the desirable effects of a proposed action against all the undesirable effects. It shares neither the commen-suralist nor welfarist features of the strong form of CBA. There is no imperative for pros and cons to be converted to a common metric, such as dollars; anticipated benefits of regulation may be considered in their natural units, such as lives saved, acres of habitat protected, or diversity of species restored. This weak form of CBA is not tied to an optimizing goal, such as welfare maximization. It operates instead to weed out regulatory alternatives that may be perceived as absurd, irrational, or otherwise not in accord with common sense, as where an option's costs are grossly disproportionate to its benefits.

Jonathan Cannon, The Sounds of Silence: Cost Benefit Analysis in *Entergy Corp. v. Riverkeeper, Inc.*, 34 Harv. Envtl. L. Rev. 425, 428-429 (2010).

At first glance, the idea of tallying up and considering the costs and benefits of a proposed decision hardly seems objectionable. Who among us does not roughly estimate the costs and benefits of alternative courses of action in daily life (e.g., in deciding whether to read this casebook for another hour or go out with friends)? Yet the use of CBA as an input into government policymaking, let alone as a decision rule, is anything but simple, as a methodological mat-ter, or noncontroversial as a moral matter. It may seem fairly straightforward to calculate the costs of regulation—such as the cost of installing pollution control equipment in factories or safety devices in cars. Yet we may tend to over-estimate such costs by failing to anticipate technological innovation, economies of scale, or other adaptive strategies that can reasonably be expected to bring them down. For example, the original passive restraint standard at issue in the *State Farm* case, excerpted in Chapter II, *supra*, overstated the eventual cost of air bags, once they became universally adopted.

Even if we can estimate costs fairly accurately, it can be comparatively dif-ficult to calculate benefits, especially for values, such as human health or envi-ronmental amenities, that do not trade in the market and thus are not easily monetized. To monetize such values, welfare economists often recommend

1. ["Kaldor-Hicks efficiency" refers to an overall increase in social welfare, such that even if some parties are harmed by a change in circumstances, the gains to others are sufficient so that, theoretically, the winners could compensate the losers for their losses. It is not necessary that compensation actually take place, which means that a change in circumstances may be Kaldor-Hicks efficient even if some par-ties are left worse off after the change.—Eds.]

using methodologies such as "willingness to pay" or "willingness to accept." The former asks how much people would be willing to pay to obtain a desired benefit, such as longer life or greater health or cleaner air. The latter asks how much people would demand as compensation to give up such amenities. One way of measuring "willingness" is simply to ask people, but it is difficult to control for a tendency of survey respondents to dissemble or exaggerate. Instead, most economists try to infer willingness to pay or accept from actual risk-related behavior—for example, what people are willing to pay for life or health insurance, or how fast people drive given the risks and benefits of greater speed. CBA detractors, however, criticize such methodologies as flawed for multiple reasons. For example, they attack these methodologies as ignoring the distribution of wealth (poor people tend to assign a lower value to their lives or health than rich people). In addition, it is not obvious whether a regulator should choose willingness to pay or willingness to accept, given the so-called "endowment effect" (people routinely demand more compensation to give up something that they own than they ask to receive something of equal market value that they do not own). And it may be problematic to use discount rates to calculate the net present value of benefits that will accrue relatively far in the future, both because we may be bad at assessing benefits over long time horizons, and because it is morally questionable to devalue future generations compared to present ones. Such critiques, and others that focus on the indeterminacy inherent in CBA, lead many commentators to conclude that CBA is inappropriate as a decision rule, and of limited value even as an input into decisions. There are some who go so far as to reject it wholesale, on moral grounds. *See* Frank Ackerman & Lisa Heinzerling, Priceless: On Knowing the Price of Everything and the Value of Nothing (2005).

Advocates, on the other hand, believe that CBA is necessary for intelligent decisionmaking. To some, it can help compensate for cognitive problems that lead people and societies to make poor judgments. *See* Cass R. Sunstein, Cognition and Cost-Benefit Analysis, 29 J. Legal Stud. 1059 (2000) (arguing that CBA can be a corrective for "informational and reputational cascades, from thinking processes in which benefits are 'on screen' but costs are not, from ignoring systemic effects of one-shot interventions, from seeing cases in isolation, and from intense emotional reactions"). There are also those who, while deeply critical of how CBA is currently used, insist that its methodological flaws can be fixed, and argue that pro-regulatory forces make a strategic mistake by forgoing its use on moral grounds. *See* Richard L. Revesz & Michael A. Livermore, Retaking Rationality: How Cost-Benefit Analysis Can Better Protect the Environment and Our Health (2008). Indeed, CBA has become so institutionalized in the policymaking process in part because there is no widely accepted alternative methodology. When confronted with its shortcomings, advocates tend to say, "What would you prefer, uninformed decisionmaking?"

The three branches of the federal government have all played important roles in raising the profile of cost-benefit analysis in government decisionmaking over the past half-century. As we shall see in the following section of this chapter, the White House has been the most enthusiastic and consistent source of support for the use of CBA by federal regulatory agencies. By contrast, Congress has been more ambivalent about cost-consciousness, sometimes mandating consideration of costs, sometimes prohibiting it, and often leaving the question ambiguous. A recurrent theme in contemporary administrative law is how courts should interpret regulatory statutes that are unclear about the role of cost. Should courts require agencies to conduct cost-benefit analyses, or at least to consider the costs of their regulations, even where statutes do not clearly require it? The following case studies illustrate how courts have answered that question.

Recall that in the *Benzene* case, excerpted in Chapters I and II, *supra,* the Court held that the OSH Act allows regulation of toxic substances only at a level that poses "a significant risk of harm." The Court declined to address the factual determinations necessary to warrant a finding of significant risk, yet once the agency makes such a finding, §6(b)(5) of the Act appears to require fairly stringent regulation, designed to eliminate the risk "to the extent feasible." Plaintiffs invoked the definitional section of the OSH Act, §3(8), which requires that occupational health standards be "reasonably necessary or appropriate," to imply that feasibility should be understood in terms of a balance of costs and benefits. The Court in the *Benzene* case sidestepped this issue, deciding instead that OSHA had not established that the prevailing standard for benzene exposure in the workplace posed a "significant risk of harm."

A year later, the Court directly confronted the issue of whether the Act required consideration of cost. The case, generally referred to as the *Cotton Dust* case, involved an OSHA standard designed to protect cotton workers against the hazard of byssinosis. Byssinosis (sometimes called "brown lung disease") is a generic term used to describe an acute and chronic respiratory disease that afflicts workers engaged in textile manufacturing. The symptoms were first connected with inhalation of textile dust in the eighteenth century by a scientist named Ramazzini who noted that textile workers were "always covered with dust from the hemp, pasty-faced, coughing, asthmatic, and blear-eyed." British scientists later described the phenomenon of chest tightness experienced on Mondays by textile workers.

Although Great Britain had made byssinosis a compensable disease in 1942, the United States made no effort to reduce cotton workers' exposure to cotton dust until 1964. Under authority of the Walsh-Healey Public Contracts Act of 1936, 49 Stat. 2036, 41 U.S.C. §§35-45, the Labor Department set an exposure limit of 1,000 micrograms per cubic meter ($\mu g/m^3$) for workers employed by government contractors. This standard applied to the total amount of cotton dust in the air.

After enactment of the Occupational Safety and Health Act of 1970, OSHA began work on a new cotton-dust exposure standard to be applied to all textile workers in interstate commerce. In setting the cotton dust standard, OSHA adhered to its historical position of refusing explicitly to perform a cost-benefit analysis. Instead, it purported to select the "most protective" standard that was "technologically and economically feasible" for the industry to adopt. The final standard adopted by OSHA established the following "permissible exposure limits" (PELs) for respirable cotton dust: 200 $\mu g/m^3$ for yarn manufacturing, 750 $\mu g/m^3$ for fabric manufacturing, and 500 $\mu g/m^3$ for cottonseed oil mills, waste processing, and warehousing.

Although OSHA refused to calculate the benefits produced by its standard and compare them to the costs, the President's Council on Wage and Price Stability (COWPS) attempted a crude cost-benefit comparison of the various proposed standards. Using data prepared for OSHA, John Morrall, an economist at

COWPS, calculated the cost of each proposed standard per employee protected and per case of byssinosis avoided. These findings are summarized in the following two tables:

TABLE 1

Annual Cost per Employee (in Dollars)

Industry segment	500 µg/m³	200 µg/m³	100 µg/m³
Cotton warehousing	120	1,306	1,306
Cottonseed oil prod'n	6,550	8,700	8,700
Yarn manufacturing	276	1,078	2,790
Fabric manufacturing	104	1,782	4,872
Waste processing	259	422	686

TABLE 2

Annual Incremental Costs per Case of Byssinosis (All Grades) Avoided (in Dollars)

Industry segment	500µg/m³	200 µg/m³	100 µg/m³
Cotton warehousing	0	20,143	n.a.
Cottonseed oil prod'n	54,469	40,952	n.a.
Yarn manufacturing	0	7,194	34,042
Fabric manufacturing	10,118	261,040	129,113
Waste processing	9,920	3,333	15,596

Note: n.a. = not available

John F. Morrall, III, Cotton Dust: An Economist's View, in The Scientific Basis of Health and Safety Regulation 93, 100-101 (Robert W. Crandall & Lester B. Lave, eds., 1981).

Morrall's study criticized OSHA for failing to consider certain regulatory schemes that he considered more cost-effective than the one finally adopted. By placing its primary emphasis on engineering controls, he argued, the agency made it impossible for different employers to meet the same level of employee health protection with different strategies. OSHA could simply have decreed, for example, that no employer should allow an employee to reach an advanced stage of byssinosis. This would have permitted, in some situations, increased reliance on medical surveillance, monitoring, and respirators (at an estimated total cost of $555 per case avoided), and less emphasis on engineering controls (at $42,767 per case avoided).

AMERICAN TEXTILE MANUFACTURERS INSTITUTE v. DONOVAN (THE *COTTON DUST* CASE), 452 U.S. 490 (1981): OSHA's cotton dust standard was challenged by the American Textile Manufacturers Institute and the American Cotton Council, primarily on the basis that the standard's costs outweighed its purported benefits and that the OSH Act required OSHA to establish that "its Standard reflects a reasonable relationship between the costs and benefits associated with the Standard." The Court began its analysis by examining the statutory language of §6(b)(5), which provides that:

> The Secretary, in promulgating standards dealing with toxic materials or harmful physical agents under this subsection, shall set the standard which most adequately assures, *to the extent feasible*, on the basis of the best available evidence, that no employee will suffer material impairment of health or functional capacity even if such employee has regular exposure to the hazard dealt with by such standard for the period of his working life.

The Court then discussed what a feasibility analysis requires:

> The plain meaning of the word "feasible" supports respondents' interpretation of the statute. According to Webster's Third New International Dictionary of the English Language 831 (1976), "feasible" means "capable of being done, executed, or effected." *Accord,* the Oxford English Dictionary 116 (1933) ("Capable of being done, accomplished or carried out"); Funk & Wagnalls New "Standard" Dictionary of the English Language 903 (1957) ("That may be done, performed or effected"). Thus, §6(b)(5) directs the Secretary to issue the standard that "most adequately assures . . . that no employee will suffer material impairment of health," limited only by the extent to which this is "capable of being done." In effect then, as the Court of Appeals held, Congress itself defined the basic relationship between costs and benefits, by placing the "benefit" of worker health above all other considerations save those making attainment of this "benefit" unachievable. Any standard based on a balancing of costs and benefits by the Secretary that strikes a different balance than that struck by Congress would be inconsistent with the command set forth in §6(b)(5). Thus, cost-benefit analysis by OSHA is not required by the statute because feasibility analysis is.

However, the Court did not rely solely on the language of §6(b)(5) in interpreting the Act to not require the agency to engage in cost-benefit analysis. It also examined whether the Act's definitional section incorporated a cost-benefit requirement:

> Even though the plain language of §6(b)(5) supports this construction, we must still decide whether §3(8), the general definition of an occupational safety and health standard, either alone or in tandem with §6(b)(5), incorporates a cost-benefit requirement for standards dealing with toxic materials or harmful physical agents. Section 3(8) of the Act, 29 U.S.C. §652(8) (emphasis added), provides:
>
>> The term "occupational safety and health standard" means a standard which requires conditions, or the adoption or use of one or more practices, means, methods, operations, or processes, *reasonably necessary or appropriate* to provide safe or healthful employment and places of employment.
>
>> Taken alone, the phrase "reasonably necessary or appropriate" might be construed to contemplate some balancing of the costs and benefits of a standard. Petitioners urge that, so construed, §3(8) engrafts a cost-benefit analysis requirement on the issuance of §6(b)(5) standards, even if §6(b)(5) itself does not authorize such analysis. We need not decide whether §3(8), standing alone, would contemplate some form of cost-benefit analysis. For even if it does, Congress specifically chose in §6(b)(5) to impose separate and additional requirements for

issuance of a subcategory of occupational safety and health standards dealing with toxic materials and harmful physical agents: it required that those standards be issued to prevent material impairment of health *to the extent feasible.* Congress could reasonably have concluded that *health* standards should be subject to different criteria than *safety* standards because of the special problems presented in regulating them.

Agreement with petitioners' argument that §3(8) imposes an additional and overriding requirement of cost-benefit analysis on the issuance of §6(b)(5) standards would eviscerate the "to the extent feasible" requirement. Standards would inevitably be set at the level indicated by cost-benefit analysis, and not at the level specified by §6(b)(5). For example, if cost-benefit analysis indicated a protective standard of 1,000 µg/m³ PEL, while feasibility analysis indicated a 500 µg/m³ PEL, the agency would be forced by the cost-benefit requirement to choose the less stringent point. We cannot believe that Congress intended the general terms of §3(8) to countermand the specific feasibility requirement of §6(b)(5). . . .

Finally, the Court found that the legislative history of OSHA supported the Department of Labor's assertion that cost-benefit analysis was not required.

NOTES AND QUESTIONS

1. *Method of analysis.* Precisely what method of analysis was urged upon OSHA? How is it different from OSHA's approach? Why does OSHA prefer its method? Even if the Act does not require OSHA to consider the cost of a proposed occupational health standard, does OSHA have discretion to do so, if it wishes to? Does OSHA have discretion to use CBA as a decision rule, if it wishes to do so?

2. *Definition of "feasible."* The Court relies on the dictionary definition of "feasible" as "capable of being done." We know that attainment of a cotton-dust exposure level equal to that prevailing in the general atmosphere is "capable of being done" by closing cotton mills. Does the Court's definition, therefore, require OSHA to equate the industrial standard to the atmospheric exposure level?

Around the same time as *Cotton Dust,* the D.C. Circuit confronted the issue of whether the Environmental Protection Agency was required or even allowed to consider costs in establishing National Ambient Air Quality Standards (NAAQS) under the Clean Air Act. As described in Chapter I, *supra,* establishing NAAQS is the first step in a multistep process that includes states filing State Implementation Plans (SIPs), and ultimately issuing permits. In Lead Industries Assn., Inc. v. EPA, 647 F.2d 1130 (D.C. Cir. 1980), the D.C. Circuit held that the Act prohibited the EPA from considering costs when establishing NAAQS. Costs would become relevant only in the later implementation stages.

Despite significant controversy, the D.C. Circuit's prohibition on the consideration of costs in establishing NAAQS remained unreviewed by the Supreme

Court for more than 20 years. In the intervening years, CBA became institutionalized as an instrument of centralized presidential oversight, and was championed in much of the scholarly literature, including Breaking the Vicious Circle (1992), an influential book on the need for rational regulation written by Stephen Breyer, then a Circuit Judge and administrative law professor. Finally, in 2001, in the *Whitman* case, excerpted (for its discussion of the delegation issue) in Chapter I, *supra*, the Supreme Court spoke to the issue, ratifying longstanding D.C. Circuit precedent that the Clean Air Act forbids the EPA from considering cost when setting air standards

WHITMAN v. AMERICAN TRUCKING ASSOCIATIONS, INC.
531 U.S. 457 (2001)

JUSTICE SCALIA delivered the opinion of the Court. . . .

Section 109(a) of the CAA, as added, 84 Stat. 1679, and amended, 42 U.S.C. §7409(a), requires the Administrator of the EPA to promulgate NAAQS for each air pollutant for which "air quality criteria" have been issued under §108, 42 U.S.C. §7408. Once a NAAQS has been promulgated, the Administrator must review the standard (and the criteria on which it is based) "at five-year intervals" and make "such revisions . . . as may be appropriate." CAA §109(d)(1), 42 U.S.C. §7409(d)(1). These cases arose when, on July 18, 1997, the Administrator revised the NAAQS for particulate matter (PM) and ozone. . . .

In Lead Industries Ass'n, Inc. v. EPA, the District of Columbia Circuit held that "economic considerations [may] play no part in the promulgation of ambient air quality standards under Section 109" of the CAA. [647 F.2d at 1148.] In the present cases, the court adhered to that holding . . . as it had done on many other occasions.

Section 109(b)(1) instructs the EPA to set primary ambient air quality standards "the attainment and maintenance of which . . . are requisite to protect the public health" with "an adequate margin of safety." 42 U.S.C. §7409(b)(1). Were it not for the hundreds of pages of briefing respondents have submitted on the issue, one would have thought it fairly clear that this text does not permit the EPA to consider costs in setting the standards. The language, as one scholar has noted, "is absolute." The EPA, "based on" the information about health effects contained in the technical "criteria" documents compiled under §108(a)(2), 42 U.S.C. §7408(a)(2), is to identify the maximum airborne concentration of a pollutant that the public health can tolerate, decrease the concentration to provide an "adequate" margin of safety, and set the standard at that level. Nowhere are the costs of achieving such a standard made part of that initial calculation.

Against this most natural of readings, respondents make a lengthy, spirited, but ultimately unsuccessful attack. They begin with the object of §109(b)(1)'s focus, the "public health." When the term first appeared in federal clean air legislation—in the Act of July 14, 1955 (1955 Act), 69 Stat. 322, which expressed "recognition of the dangers to the public health" from air pollution—its ordinary meaning was "[t]he health of the community." Webster's New International Dictionary 2005 (2d ed. 1950). Respondents argue, however, that §109(b)(1), as added by the Clean Air Amendments of 1970 (1970 Act), 84 Stat. 1676, meant to use the term's secondary meaning: "[t]he ways and means of conserving the health of the members of a community, as by preventive medicine, organized care of the sick, etc." Words that can have more than one meaning are given content, however, by their surroundings, and in the context of §109(b)(1) this second definition makes no sense. Congress could not have meant to instruct the Administrator to set NAAQS at a level "requisite to protect" "the art and science dealing with the protection and improvement of community health." *Webster's Third New International Dictionary* 1836 (1981). We therefore revert to the primary definition of the term: the health of the public.

Even so, respondents argue, many more factors than air pollution affect public health. In particular, the economic cost of implementing a very stringent standard might produce health losses sufficient to offset the health gains achieved in cleaning the air—for example, by closing down whole industries and thereby impoverishing the workers and consumers dependent upon those industries. That is unquestionably true, and Congress was unquestionably aware of it. . . . Section 110(f)(1) of the CAA permitted the Administrator to waive the compliance deadline for stationary sources if, *inter alia*, sufficient control measures were simply unavailable and "the continued operation of such sources is *essential . . . to the public health* or welfare." 84 Stat. 1683 (emphasis added). Other provisions explicitly permitted or required economic costs to be taken into account in implementing the air quality standards. . . . Subsequent Amendments to the CAA have added many more provisions directing, in explicit language, that the Administrator consider costs in performing various duties. We have therefore refused to find implicit in ambiguous sections of the CAA an authorization to consider costs that has elsewhere, and so often, been expressly granted.

Accordingly, to prevail in their present challenge, respondents must show a textual commitment of authority to the EPA to consider costs in setting NAAQS under §109(b)(1). And because §109(b)(1) and the NAAQS for which it provides are the engine that drives nearly all of Title I of the CAA, that textual commitment must be a clear one. Congress, we have held, does not alter the fundamental details of a regulatory scheme in vague terms or ancillary provisions—it does not, one might say, hide elephants in mouseholes. Respondents' textual arguments ultimately founder upon this principle.

Their first claim is that §109(b)(1)'s terms "adequate margin" and "requisite" leave room to pad health effects with cost concerns. [W]e find it implausible that Congress would give to the EPA through these modest words the power to determine whether implementation costs should moderate national air quality standards.

The same defect inheres in respondents' next two arguments: that while the Administrator's judgment about what is requisite to protect the public health must be "based on [the] criteria" documents developed under §108(a)(2), *see* §109(b)(1), it need not be based *solely* on those criteria; and that those criteria themselves, while they must include "effects on public health or welfare which may be expected from the presence of such pollutant in the ambient air," are not necessarily *limited* to those effects. Even if we were to concede those premises, we still would not conclude that one of the unenumerated factors that the agency can consider in developing and applying the criteria is cost of implementation. That factor is *both* so indirectly related to public health *and* so full of potential for canceling the conclusions drawn from direct health effects that it would surely have been expressly mentioned in §§108 and 109 had Congress meant it to be considered. Yet while those provisions describe in detail how the health effects of pollutants in the ambient air are to be calculated and given effect, *see* §108(a)(2), they say not a word about costs.

Respondents point, finally, to a number of provisions in the CAA that *do* require attainment cost data to be generated. Section 108(b)(1), for example, instructs the Administrator to "issue to the States," simultaneously with the criteria documents, "information on air pollution control techniques, which information shall include data relating to the cost of installation and operation." 42 U.S.C. §7408(b)(*l*). And §109(d)(2)(C)(iv) requires the Clean Air Scientific Advisory Committee to "advise the Administrator of any adverse public health, welfare, social, economic, or energy effects which may result from various strategies for attainment and maintenance" of NAAQS. 42 U.S.C. §7409(d)(2)(C)(iv). Respondents argue that these provisions make no sense unless costs are to be considered in setting the NAAQS. That is not so. These provisions enable the Administrator to assist the States in carrying out their statutory role as primary *implementers* of the NAAQS. It is to the States that the Act assigns initial and primary responsibility for deciding what emissions reductions will be required from which sources. It would be impossible to perform that task intelligently without considering which abatement technologies are most efficient, and most economically feasible—which is why we have said that "the most important forum for consideration of claims of economic and technological infeasibility is before the state agency formulating the implementation plan," Union Elec. Co. v. EPA, [427 U.S. 246, 266 (1976)]. Thus, federal clean air legislation has, from the very beginning, directed federal agencies to develop and transmit implementation data, including cost data, to the States. That Congress chose to carry forward this research program to assist States in choosing the means through which they would implement the standards is perfectly sensible, and has no bearing upon whether cost considerations are to be taken into account in formulating the standards.

It should be clear from what we have said that the canon requiring texts to be so construed as to avoid serious constitutional problems has no application here. No matter how severe the constitutional doubt, courts may choose only between reasonably available interpretations of a text. The text of §109(b), interpreted in its statutory and historical context and with appreciation for its importance to the CAA as a whole, unambiguously bars cost considerations from the NAAQS-setting process, and thus ends the matter for us as well as the EPA. We therefore affirm the judgment of the Court of Appeals on this point. . . .

Justice Breyer, concurring in part and concurring in the judgment.

[I agree] that the Clean Air Act does not permit the Environmental Protection Agency to consider the economic costs of implementation when setting national ambient air quality standards under §109(b)(1) of the Act. But I would not rest this conclusion solely upon §109's language or upon a presumption, such as the Court's presumption that any authority the Act grants the EPA to consider costs must flow from a "textual commitment" that is "clear." In order better to achieve regulatory goals—for example, to allocate resources so that they save more lives or produce a cleaner environment—regulators must often take account of all of a proposed regulation's adverse effects, at least where those adverse effects clearly threaten serious and disproportionate public harm. Hence, I believe that, other things being equal, we should read silences or ambiguities in the language of regulatory statutes as permitting, not forbidding, this type of rational regulation.

In this case, however, other things are not equal. Here, legislative history, along with the statute's structure, indicates that §109's language reflects a congressional decision not to delegate to the agency the legal authority to consider economic costs of compliance.

For one thing, the legislative history shows that Congress intended the statute to be "technology forcing." Senator Edmund Muskie, the primary sponsor of the 1970 Amendments to the Act, introduced them by saying that Congress' primary responsibility in drafting the Act was not "to be limited by what is or appears to be technologically or economically feasible," but "to establish what the public interest requires to protect the health of persons," even if that means that "*industries will be asked to do what seems to be impossible at the present time.*"

The Senate directly focused upon the technical feasibility and cost of implementing the Act's mandates. And it made clear that it intended the Administrator to develop air quality standards set independently of either.

Indeed, this Court, after reviewing the entire legislative history, concluded that the 1970 Amendments were "expressly designed to force regulated sources to develop pollution control devices that *might at the time appear to be economically or technologically infeasible.*" Union Elec. Co. v. EPA (emphasis added). And the Court added that the 1970 Amendments were intended to be a "drastic remedy to . . . a serious and otherwise uncheckable problem." Subsequent legislative history confirms that the technology-forcing goals of the 1970 Amendments are still paramount in today's Act.

To read this legislative history as meaning what it says does not impute to Congress an irrational intent. Technology-forcing hopes can prove realistic. Those persons, for example, who opposed the 1970 Act's insistence on a 90% reduction in auto emission pollutants, on the ground of excessive cost, saw the development of catalytic converter technology that helped achieve substantial reductions without the economic catastrophe that some had feared.

At the same time, the statute's technology-forcing objective makes regulatory efforts to determine the costs of implementation both less important and more difficult. It means that the relevant economic costs are speculative, for they include the cost of unknown future technologies. It also means that efforts to take costs into account can breed time-consuming and potentially unresolvable arguments about the accuracy and significance of cost estimates. Congress could have thought such efforts not worth the delays and uncertainties that would accompany them. In any event, that is what the statute's history seems to say. And the matter is one for Congress to decide.

Moreover, the Act does not, on this reading, wholly ignore cost and feasibility. . . . [T]he Act allows regulators to take those concerns into account when they determine how to implement ambient air quality standards. Thus, States may consider economic costs when they select the particular control devices used to meet the standards, and industries experiencing difficulty in reducing their emissions can seek an exemption or variance from the state implementation plan.

The Act also permits the EPA, within certain limits, to consider costs when it sets deadlines by which areas must attain the ambient air quality standards.

And Congress can change those statutory limits if necessary. Given the ambient air quality standards' substantial effects on States, cities, industries, and their suppliers and customers, Congress will hear from those whom compliance deadlines affect adversely, and Congress can consider whether legislative change is warranted.

Finally, contrary to the suggestion of the Court of Appeals and of some parties, this interpretation of §109 does not require the EPA to eliminate every health risk, however slight, at any economic cost, however great, to the point of "hurtling" industry over "the brink of ruin," or even forcing "deindustrialization." The statute, by its express terms, does not compel the elimination of *all* risk; and it grants the Administrator sufficient flexibility to avoid setting ambient air quality standards ruinous to industry.

Section 109(b)(1) directs the Administrator to set standards that are "requisite to protect the public health" with "an adequate margin of safety." But these words do not describe a world that is free of all risk—an impossible and undesirable objective. Nor are the words "requisite" and "public health" to be understood independent of context. We consider football equipment "safe" even if its use entails a level of risk that would make drinking water "unsafe" for consumption. And what counts as "requisite" to protecting the public health will similarly vary with background circumstances, such as the public's ordinary tolerance of the particular health risk in the particular context at issue. The Administrator can consider such background circumstances when "decid[ing] what risks are acceptable in the world in which we live."

The statute also permits the Administrator to take account of comparative health risks. That is to say, she may consider whether a proposed rule promotes safety overall. A rule likely to cause more harm to health than it prevents is not a rule that is "requisite to protect the public health." . . .

The statute ultimately specifies that the standard set must be "requisite to protect the public health . . . *in the judgment of the Administrator,*" §109(b)(1) (emphasis added), a phrase that grants the Administrator considerable discretionary standard-setting authority.

The statute's words, then, authorize the Administrator to consider the severity of a pollutant's potential adverse health effects, the number of those likely to be affected, the distribution of the adverse effects, and the uncertainties surrounding each estimate. They permit the Administrator to take account of comparative health consequences. They allow her to take account of context when determining the acceptability of small risks to health. And they give her considerable discretion when she does so.

This discretion would seem sufficient to avoid the extreme results that some of the industry parties fear. After all, the EPA, in setting standards that "protect the public health" with "an adequate margin of safety," retains discretionary authority to avoid regulating risks that it reasonably concludes are trivial in context. Nor need regulation lead to deindustrialization. Preindustrial society was not a very healthy society; hence a standard demanding the return of the Stone Age would not prove "requisite to protect the public health."

Although I rely more heavily than does the Court upon legislative history and alternative sources of statutory flexibility, I reach the same ultimate conclusion. Section 109 does not delegate to the EPA authority to base the national ambient air quality standards, in whole or in part, upon the economic costs of compliance.

NOTES AND QUESTIONS

1. *CBA as part of reasoned decisionmaking.* Prior to *Whitman,* judges occasionally imposed some form of cost-benefit obligations on the EPA as a requirement of reasoned decisionmaking, despite statutory silence on the issue. *See* Richard G. Stoll, Cost-Benefit Analysis Through the Back Door of "Reasoned Decisionmaking," 31 Envtl. L. Rep. 10,228 (2001) (citing, for example, American Petroleum Institute v. U.S. EPA, 216 F.3d 50 (D.C. Cir. 2000)). Does this more indirect mechanism for forcing cost consideration seem problematic in light of *Vermont Yankee?*

2. *"Best" technology.* In numerous health, safety, and environmental statutes, Congress has explicitly required agencies to consider the costs of regulation. Sometimes an agency is required to consider costs as one among many factors when setting a standard; sometimes it is required to compare costs and benefits when setting a standard; and sometimes it is required to do a "cost-effectiveness" analysis to choose among alternative methods of achieving a given level of stringency. Many statutory provisions are silent about cost, however. May an agency use cost-benefit analysis when a statute does not require it to do so? May it do so when a statute requires it to use the "best" technology? The case below, discussed also in Chapter I, *supra,* addresses these questions.

ENTERGY CORP. v. RIVERKEEPER, INC.
556 U.S. 208 (2009)

JUSTICE SCALIA delivered the opinion of the Court.

These cases concern a set of regulations adopted by the Environmental Protection Agency (EPA or agency) under §316(b) of the Clean Water Act, 33 U.S.C. §1326(b). 69 Fed. Reg. 41576 (2004). Respondents—environmental groups and various States—challenged those regulations, and the Second Circuit set them aside. The issue for our decision is whether, as the Second Circuit held, the EPA is not permitted to use cost-benefit analysis in determining the content of regulations promulgated under §1326(b).

I

Petitioners operate—or represent those who operate—large powerplants. In the course of generating power, those plants also generate large amounts of heat. To cool their facilities, petitioners employ "cooling water intake structures" that extract water from nearby water sources. These structures pose various threats to the environment, chief among them the squashing against intake screens (elegantly called "impingement") or suction into the cooling system ("entrainment") of aquatic organisms that live in the affected water sources.

Accordingly, the facilities are subject to regulation under the Clean Water Act, 33 U.S.C. §1251 *et seq.*, which mandates:

> "Any standard established pursuant to section 1311 of this title or section 1316 of this title and applicable to a point source shall require that the location, design, construction, and capacity of cooling water intake structures reflect the best technology available for minimizing adverse environmental impact." §1326(b).

Sections 1311 and 1316, in turn, employ a variety of "best technology" standards to regulate the discharge of effluents into the Nation's waters.

The §1326(b) regulations at issue here were promulgated by the EPA after nearly three decades in which the determination of the "best technology available for minimizing [cooling water intake structures'] adverse environmental impact" was made by permit-issuing authorities on a case-by-case basis, without benefit of a governing regulation.

In 1995, the EPA entered into a consent decree which, as subsequently amended, set a multiphase timetable for the EPA to promulgate regulations under §1326(b). In the first phase the EPA adopted regulations governing certain new, large cooling water intake structures. These regulations were upheld in large part by the Second Circuit in Riverkeeper, Inc. v. EPA, 358 F.3d 174 (2d Cir. 2004).

The EPA then adopted the so-called "Phase II" rules at issue here. They apply to existing facilities that are point sources, whose primary activity is the generation and transmission (or sale for transmission) of electricity, and whose water-intake flow is more than 50 million gallons of water per day, at least 25 percent of which is used for cooling purposes. Over 500 facilities, accounting for approximately 53 percent of the Nation's electric-power generating capacity, fall within Phase II's ambit.

To address those environmental impacts, the EPA set "national performance standards," requiring Phase II facilities (with some exceptions) to reduce "impingement mortality for all life stages of fish and shellfish by 80 to 95 percent from the calculation baseline"; a subset of facilities must also reduce entrainment of such aquatic organisms by "60 to 90 percent from the calculation baseline." Those targets are based on the environmental improvements achievable through deployment of a mix of remedial technologies, which the EPA determined were "commercially available and economically practicable."

In its Phase II rules, however, the EPA expressly declined to mandate adoption of closed-cycle cooling systems or equivalent reductions in impingement and entrainment, as it had done for new facilities subject to the Phase I rules. It refused to take that step in part because of the "generally high costs" of converting existing facilities to closed-cycle operation, and because "other technologies approach the performance of this option." Thus, while closed-cycle cooling systems could reduce impingement and entrainment mortality by up to 98 percent, (compared to the Phase II targets of 80 to 95 percent impingement reduction), the cost of rendering all Phase II facilities closed-cycle-compliant would be approximately $3.5 billion per year, nine times the estimated cost of compliance with the Phase II performance standards. Moreover, Phase II facilities compelled to convert to closed-cycle cooling systems "would produce 2.4 percent to 4.0 percent less electricity even while burning the same amount of coal," possibly requiring the construction of "20 additional 400-MW plants . . . to replace the generating capacity lost." *Id.*, at 41605. The EPA thus concluded that "[a]lthough not identical, the ranges of impingement and entrainment reduction are similar under both options. . . . [Benefits of compliance with the Phase II rules] can approach those of closed-cycle re-circulating at less cost with fewer implementation problems." . . .

II

In setting the Phase II national performance standards and providing for site-specific cost-benefit variances, the EPA relied on its view that §1326(b)'s "best technology available" standard permits consideration of the technology's costs, and of the relationship between those costs and the environmental benefits produced. That view governs if it is a reasonable interpretation of the statute—not necessarily the only possible interpretation, nor even the interpretation deemed *most* reasonable by the courts. Chevron U.S.A. Inc. v. Natural Resources Defense Council, Inc., 467 U.S. 837, 843-844 (1984).

As we have described, §1326(b) instructs the EPA to set standards for cooling water intake structures that reflect "the best technology available for minimizing adverse environmental impact." The Second Circuit took that language to mean the technology that achieves the greatest reduction in adverse environmental impacts at a cost that can reasonably be borne by the industry. That is certainly a plausible interpretation of the statute. The "best" technology—that which is "most advantageous," Webster's New International Dictionary 258 (2d ed. 1953)—may well be the one that produces the most of some good, here a reduction in adverse environmental impact. But "best technology" may also describe the technology that *most efficiently* produces some good. In common parlance one could certainly use the phrase "best technology" to refer to that which produces a good at the lowest per-unit cost, even if it produces a lesser quantity of that good than other available technologies.

Respondents contend that this latter reading is precluded by the statute's use of the phrase "for minimizing adverse environmental impact." Minimizing, they argue, means reducing to the smallest amount possible, and the "best technology available for minimizing adverse environmental impacts," must be the economically feasible technology that achieves the greatest possible reduction in environmental harm. But "minimize" is a term that admits of degree and is not necessarily used to refer exclusively to the "greatest possible reduction." For example, elsewhere in the Clean Water Act, Congress declared that the procedures implementing the Act "shall encourage the drastic minimization of paperwork and interagency decision procedures." 33 U.S.C. §1251(f). If respondents' definition of the term "minimize" is correct, the statute's use of the modifier "drastic" is superfluous.

Other provisions in the Clean Water Act also suggest the agency's interpretation. When Congress wished to mandate the greatest feasible reduction in water pollution, it did so in plain language: The provision governing the discharge of toxic pollutants into the Nation's waters requires the EPA to set "effluent limitations [which] shall require the *elimination* of discharges of all pollutants if the Administrator finds . . . that such elimination is technologically and economically achievable," §1311(b)(2)(A)(emphasis added). *See also* §1316(a)(1) (mandating "where practicable, a standard [for new point sources] permitting *no discharge* of pollutants" (emphasis added)). Section 1326(b)'s use of the less ambitious goal of "minimizing adverse environmental impact" suggests, we think, that the agency retains some discretion to determine the extent of reduction that is warranted under the circumstances. That determination could plausibly involve a consideration of the benefits derived from reductions and the costs of achieving them. It seems to us, therefore, that the phrase "best technology available," even with the added specification "for minimizing adverse environmental impact," does not unambiguously preclude cost-benefit analysis.

Respondents' alternative (and, alas, also more complex) argument rests upon the structure of the Clean Water Act. The Act provided that during its initial implementation period existing "point sources" — discrete conveyances from which pollutants are or may be discharged, 33 U.S.C. §1362(14) — were subject to "effluent limitations . . . which shall require the application of the *best practicable control technology* currently available." §1311(b)(1)(A) (emphasis added). (We shall call this the "BPT" test.) Following that transition period, the Act initially mandated adoption, by July 1, 1983 (later extended to March 31, 1989), of stricter effluent limitations requiring "application of the *best available technology economically achievable* for such category or class, which will result in reasonable further progress toward the national goal of eliminating the discharge of all pollutants." §1311(b)(2)(A). ([T]he "BATEA" test.) Subsequent amendment limited application of this standard to toxic and nonconventional pollutants, and for the remainder established a (presumably laxer) test of "best conventional-pollutant control technology." §1311(b)(2)(E). (We shall call this "BCT.") Finally, §1316 subjected certain categories of new point sources to "the greatest degree of effluent reduction which the Administrator determines to be achievable through application of the *best available demonstrated control technology*." §1316(a)(1); §1316(b)(1)(B). (We shall call this the "BADT" test.) The provision at issue here, applicable not to effluents but to cooling water intake structures, requires, as we have described, "the *best technology available for minimizing adverse environmental impact*," §1326(b) (emphasis added). (We shall call this the "BTA" test.)

The first four of these tests are elucidated by statutory factor lists that guide their implementation. To take the standards in (presumed) order of increasing stringency: In applying the BPT test the EPA is instructed to consider, among other factors, "the total cost of application of technology in relation to the effluent reduction benefits to be achieved." §1314(b)(1)(B). In applying the BCT test it is instructed to consider "the *reasonableness of the relationship* between the costs of attaining a reduction in effluents and the effluent reduction benefits derived." §1314(b)(4)(B). And in applying the BATEA and BADT tests the EPA is instructed to consider the "cost of achieving such effluent reduction." §§1314(b)(2)(B), 1316(b)(1)(B). There is no such elucidating language applicable to the BTA test at issue here.

The Second Circuit, in rejecting the EPA's use of cost-benefit analysis, relied in part on the propositions that (1) cost-benefit analysis is precluded under the BATEA and BADT tests; and (2) that, insofar as the permissibility of cost-benefit analysis is concerned, the BTA test (the one at issue here) is to be treated the same as those two. It is not obvious to us that the first of these propositions is correct, but we need not pursue that point, since we assuredly do not agree with the second. It is certainly reasonable for the agency to conclude that the BTA test need not be interpreted to permit only what those other two tests permit. Its text is not identical to theirs. It has the relatively modest goal of "minimizing adverse environmental impact" as compared with the BATEA's goal of "eliminating the discharge of all pollutants." And it is unencumbered by specified statutory factors of the sort provided for those other two tests, which omission can reasonably be interpreted to suggest that the EPA is accorded greater discretion in determining its precise content.

This extended consideration of the text of §1326(b), and comparison of that with the text and statutory factors applicable to four parallel provisions of the Clean Water Act, lead us to the conclusion that it was well within the bounds of reasonable interpretation for the EPA to conclude that cost-benefit analysis is not categorically forbidden. Other arguments may be available to preclude such a rigorous form of cost-benefit analysis as that which was prescribed under the statute's former BPT standard, which required weighing "the total cost of application of technology" against "the . . . benefits to be achieved." But that question is not before us.

In the Phase II requirements challenged here the EPA sought only to avoid extreme disparities between costs and benefits. The agency limited variances from the Phase II "national performance standards" to circumstances where the costs are "significantly greater than the benefits" of compliance. In defining the "national performance standards" themselves the EPA assumed the application of technologies whose benefits "approach those estimated" for closed-cycle cooling systems at a fraction of the cost: $389 million per year, as compared with (1) at least $3.5 billion per year to operate compliant closed-cycle cooling systems, (or $1 billion per year to impose similar requirements on a subset of Phase II facilities), (2) significant reduction in the energy output of the altered facilities. And finally, EPA's assessment of the relatively meager financial benefits of the Phase II regulations that it adopted—reduced impingement and entrainment of 1.4 billion aquatic organisms with annualized use benefits of $83 million, and non-use benefits of indeterminate value—when compared to annual costs of $389 million, demonstrates quite clearly that the agency did not select the Phase II regulatory requirements because their benefits equaled their costs.

In the last analysis, even respondents ultimately recognize that some form of cost-benefit analysis is permissible. They acknowledge that the statute's language is "plainly not so constricted as to require EPA to require industry petitioners to spend billions to save one more fish or plankton." This concedes the principle—the permissibility of at least some cost-benefit analysis—and we see no statutory basis for limiting its use to situations where the benefits are *de minimis* rather than significantly disproportionate.

* * *

We conclude that the EPA permissibly relied on cost-benefit analysis in setting the national performance standards and in providing for cost-benefit variances from those standards as part of the Phase II regulations. The judgment of the Court of Appeals is reversed, and the cases are remanded for further proceedings consistent with this opinion.

JUSTICE STEVENS, with whom JUSTICE SOUTER and JUSTICE GINSBURG join, dissenting.

Section 316(b) of the Clean Water Act (CWA), 33 U.S.C. §1326(b), which governs industrial powerplant water intake structures, provides that the Environmental Protection Agency (EPA or Agency) "shall require" that such structures "reflect the best technology available for minimizing adverse environmental impact." The EPA has interpreted that mandate to authorize the use of cost-benefit analysis in promulgating regulations under §316(b). For instance, under the Agency's interpretation, technology that would otherwise qualify as the best available need not be used if its costs are "significantly greater than the benefits" of compliance. 40 CFR §125.94(a)(5)(ii)(2008).

Like the Court of Appeals, I am convinced that the EPA has misinterpreted the plain text of §316(b). Unless costs are so high that the best technology is not "available," Congress has decided that they are outweighed by the benefits of minimizing adverse environmental impact. Section 316(b) neither expressly nor implicitly authorizes the EPA to use cost-benefit analysis when setting regulatory standards; fairly read, it prohibits such use.

As typically performed by the EPA, cost-benefit analysis requires the Agency to first monetize the costs and benefits of a regulation, balance the results, and then choose the regulation with the greatest net benefits. The process is particularly controversial in the environmental context in which a regulation's financial costs are often more obvious and easier to quantify than its environmental benefits. And cost-benefit analysis often, if not always, yields a result that does not maximize environmental protection.

For instance, although the EPA estimated that water intake structures kill 3.4 billion fish and shellfish each year, the Agency struggled to calculate the value of the aquatic life that would be protected under its §316(b) regulations, *id.* To compensate, the EPA took a shortcut: Instead of monetizing all aquatic life, the Agency counted only those species that are commercially or recreationally harvested, a tiny slice (1.8 percent to be precise) of all impacted fish and shellfish. This narrow focus in turn skewed the Agency's calculation of benefits. When the EPA attempted to value all aquatic life, the benefits measured $735 million. But when the EPA decided to give zero value to the 98.2 percent of fish not commercially or recreationally harvested, the benefits calculation dropped dramatically—to $83 million. The Agency acknowledged that its failure to monetize the other 98.2 percent of affected species "could result in serious misallocation of resources," because its "comparison of complete costs and incomplete benefits does not provide an accurate picture of net benefits to society."

Because benefits can be more accurately monetized in some industries than in others, Congress typically decides whether it is appropriate for an agency to use cost-benefit analysis in crafting regulations. Indeed, this Court has recognized that "[w]hen Congress has intended that an agency engage in cost-benefit analysis, it has clearly indicated such intent on the face of the statute." American Textile Mfrs. Inst., Inc. v. Donovan, 452 U.S. 490, 510 (1981). Accordingly, we should not treat a provision's silence as an implicit source of cost-benefit authority, particularly when such authority is elsewhere expressly granted and it has the potential to fundamentally alter an agency's approach to regulation. Congress, we have noted, "does not alter the fundamental details of a regulatory scheme in vague terms or ancillary provisions—it does not, one might say, hide elephants in mouse holes." Whitman v. American Trucking Assns. Inc., 531 U.S. 457, 467-468 (2001). . . .

NOTES AND QUESTIONS

1. *CBA and statutory interpretation.* Why is Congress so often imprecise—or even silent—about whether agencies should weigh regulatory costs against regulatory benefits? In interpreting ambiguous regulatory statutes, should courts employ a general presumption that the statute: (a) requires the agency to consider costs and compare them to benefits?; (b) prohibits the agency from considering costs?; or (c) confers discretion on the agency to consider costs or ignore costs, as it sees fit? Is the upshot of *Entergy* essentially an embrace of Justice Breyer's concurrence in *Whitman, supra*? What are the implications of this decision for Congress? Must it explicitly rule out cost-benefit analysis if it wishes to foreclose its use by agencies?

2. *Costs and the Clean Air Act's "Good Neighbor" provisions.* The EPA considered costs of implementation when it promulgated rules implementing the Clean Air Act's Good Neighbor provisions, which address interstate air pollution. The statute requires that state air pollution plans "contain adequate provisions . . . prohibiting . . . any source or other type of emissions activity within the State from emitting any air pollutant in amounts which will . . . contribute significantly to nonattainment in, or interfere with maintenance by, any other State with respect to any . . . [NAAQS]." 42 U.S.C. §7410(a)(2)(D)(i) (2006). The D.C. Circuit overturned the rules on the basis that this statute did not allow the agency to consider costs, but rather only each state's pro rata contribution to downwind air pollution. The Supreme Court reversed, holding that the EPA's reading of the statute to allow consideration of costs was reasonable and thus entitled to *Chevron* deference. EPA v. EME Homer City Generation, L.P., 134 S. Ct. 1584 (2014). Justice Scalia, joined by Justice Thomas dissented, arguing, colorfully as usual, that language of the Clean Air Act cannot bear the EPA's construction:

> The Agency came forward with a textual justification for its action, relying on a farfetched meaning of the word "significantly" in the statutory text. That justification is so feeble that today's majority does not even recite it, much less defend it. The majority reaches its result ("Look Ma, no hands!") without benefit of text, claiming to have identified a remarkable "gap" in the statute, which it proceeds to fill (contrary to the plain logic of the statute) with cost-benefit analysis—and then, with no pretended textual justification at all, simply extends cost-benefit analysis beyond the scope of the alleged gap.

134 S. Ct. at 1610 (Scalia, J. dissenting.)

3. *Costs and the Clean Air Act's hazardous emission provisions.* In sharp contrast to his dissent in *EME Homer City* was Justice Scalia's opinion for the Court in Michigan v. EPA, 135 S. Ct. 2699 (2015). The case involved a provision of the Clean Air Act, 42 U.S.C. §7412, specifying a multi-stage process for regulating

emission of hazardous substances, such as mercury, by fossil-fuel-fired power plants. The Act requires EPA first to conduct a study to determine whether regulation of power plants under *other* provisions of the Act (many of which control pollution from these plants) adequately protects public health. Based on the results of the study, EPA must adopt supplemental hazardous emission standards "if the Administrator finds such regulation is appropriate and necessary" §7412(n)(1)(A). To implement the standards, the Act requires the EPA to divide emitting units at power plants into categories based on statutory criteria, and then adopt emission standards for each category. In *Michigan*, EPA had made the determination to regulate at stage one considering only public health needs without taking into account the cost of additional emission controls (estimated at $9.6 billion per year) to the electric power industry. The EPA read the language of §7412(n)(1)(A) to allow it make a threshold determination about the need for regulation based only on consideration of residual risk to public health and availability of control technology, on the theory that it would consider regulatory costs later, when setting the standards. The Supreme Court, disagreed, finding that the term "appropriate" required the agency to consider the cost of regulating at the initial stage, as well as at subsequent stages. Although acknowledging the applicability of *Chevron* to the case, and the "capaciousness" of the term "appropriate," Justice Scalia concluded that:

> it is unreasonable to read an instruction to an administrative agency to determine whether "regulation is appropriate and necessary" as an invitation to ignore cost. One would not say that it is even rational, never mind "appropriate," to impose billions of dollars in economic costs in return for a few dollars in health or environmental benefits.

135 S. Ct. at 2707. Interestingly, Justice Scalia began his discussion of the interpretive issue, not with *Chevron*, but with *State Farm*, quoting its holding that agencies must base their actions "on a consideration of the relevant factors." *Id.* at 2706, quoting 463 U.S. at 43. In dissent, Justice Kagan chided the Court for failing to defer to the EPA's reading of the statute and for honoring *Chevron* "only in the breach." She observed that although the EPA did not consider costs when determining whether regulation was "appropriate and necessary," it did consider costs later, when dividing sources into categories and establishing standards for their control. This, she argued, made better sense since "EPA could not have measured costs at the process's initial stage with any accuracy." *Id.* at 2714-2715 (Kagan, J. dissenting).

Recall that in *Whitman* the Court (in an opinion by Justice Scalia for a unanimous Court) ruled that EPA may not consider costs in setting an NAAQS, noting that the agency will (and indeed must) consider costs at subsequent stages of the regulatory process. Can Michigan v. EPA be squared with *Whitman*? Does it rest on different statutory content or signal a shift toward an interpretive presumption favoring cost-benefit analysis? Presumptively favoring consideration of cost would be quite different than the *Entergy* decision, which held that an agency faced with ambiguous language (in that case "best . . . available . . . to minimize") *may*, at its discretion, consider cost.

2. *Presidential Oversight of Rulemaking*

As noted above, one of the most important developments in administrative law over the last several decades has been greater and more direct presidential supervision over agency rulemaking. In part, this is a response to Congress's steady expansion of agency policymaking powers; in part it is a response to the perceived costs imposed by regulation. Early efforts at centralizing oversight were motivated by a concern about inflation. For example, President Gerald Ford required all executive agencies to prepare "inflation impact statements" for major rules. President Jimmy Carter went a step further by requiring agencies to suggest less-inflationary alternatives to certain proposed regulations. In the evolution of presidential regulatory oversight, however, the watershed event was the issuance by President Ronald Reagan of Executive Order 12,291, 46 Fed. Reg. 13,193 (1981), which increased centralized White House control over agency rulemaking by requiring executive agencies to furnish the Director of the Office of Management and Budget with a cost-benefit analysis for all "major" rules (defined as having an annual effect on the economy of $100 million or more) prior to their proposal, prohibiting executive agencies from undertaking regulatory action unless the benefits to society outweigh the costs, and requiring that regulatory objectives maximize the net benefits to society. (Although only OMB is mentioned in Executive Order 12,291, OMB's regulatory review function is actually carried out by the Office of Information and Regulatory Affairs (OIRA) within OMB, which had been created by Congress in 1981 to administer the Paperwork Reduction Act. OIRA today is composed of five subject matter branches, and it is led by the OIRA Administrator who is appointed by the President and confirmed by the United States Senate.)

Executive Order 12,291 provoked considerable controversy. Opponents of "excessive" and "inefficient" government regulation generally praised the order as a vehicle for making overzealous regulators more cost-conscious and achieving greater "coordination" among fragmented agencies. Critics contended that the order subverted legislative goals by entangling needed regulatory initiatives in excessive red tape. *Compare, e.g.,* Alan B. Morrison, OMB Interference with Agency Rulemaking: The Wrong Way to Write a Regulation, 99 Harv. L. Rev. 1059 (1986), *with* Christopher C. DeMuth & Douglas H. Ginsburg, White House Review of Agency Rulemaking, 99 Harv. L. Rev. 1075 (1986). The main thrust of the order was deregulatory, consistent with the platform on which the President had campaigned.

Opinions also differed on the order's legality. While most commentators concluded that the President did not overstep his constitutional authority, at least one commentator vigorously disagreed. *See* Morton Rosenberg, Beyond the Limits of Executive Power: Presidential Control of Agency Rulemaking Under Executive Order 12,291, 80 Mich. L. Rev. 193 (1981). Rosenberg, a legal researcher at the Library of Congress, tested Executive Order 12,291 against the spheres of executive power laid out in Justice Jackson's famous *Youngstown* concurrence, *see* Chapter I, *supra*, and found it wanting. Since, according to Rosenberg, administrative rulemaking is "essentially a legislative function," it falls into the third of Jackson's three spheres—powers constitutionally reserved to Congress that may be exercised by the President only when statutorily delegated to him. "To the extent that the President can control rulemaking," he argued, "he has the unilateral ability to enact fundamental domestic policy, a power that the Constitution entrusts to the legislature." *Id.* at 210. It is far from obvious, however, that Executive Order 12,291 gave the President a "unilateral ability to enact fundamental domestic policy." The order itself was carefully conditioned to apply "to the extent permitted by law." Moreover, isn't the President entitled to demand that executive agencies (headed by officials who serve at the President's pleasure) provide him with analyses to support their regulations? Or that they employ sounder and better articulated methods of evaluating the rules they (and their agencies) adopt? (For a discussion of executive authority generally, see Chapter I, *supra.*)

Critics of Executive Order 12,291 argued that by elevating cost-benefit analysis to an exalted position, the Reagan Executive Order sought to subvert legislative mandates aimed at social, economic, or environmental regulation, which do not envision cost-benefit analysis as the key decision tool. And while OMB review might serve as a rationalizing influence, critics contend that in practice the Reagan order skewed decisions about regulation in the direction of protecting industry rather than the diffuse public. OMB regulatory review has remained controversial as every administration has continued to adhere to the central tenets of the Reagan executive order while putting its own stamp on it.

In addition to the basic methodological and analytical features of Executive Order 12,291, the Reagan Administration contributed another element to more centralized, Executive Branch review of agency rulemaking with the issuance of Executive Order 12,498, 50 Fed. Reg. 1036 (1985). The new order required each executive agency to prepare annually a "regulatory program" describing and justifying all significant regulatory initiatives that it intended to undertake in the coming year. Except where necessary to meet judicial or statutory deadlines or in response to an emergency, agencies were to undertake only those significant regulatory actions that were included in a regulatory program approved by OMB.

An additional impetus for President Reagan's actions was the perception that the President had lost control over the vast federal bureaucracy. This problem is arguably most acute with regard to independent agencies whose members cannot easily be replaced by the President. Yet although President Reagan was advised by the Department of Justice that he had constitutional authority to bring independent agencies within the scope of his executive orders, he declined to do so, likely out of concern for the political ramifications of being seen to interfere with the traditionally more arm's-length relationship between the White House and these agencies. President George H.W. Bush took the plunge, however, with a January 28, 1992, memorandum to department and agency heads entitled "Reducing the Burden of Government Regulation," in which he asked each agency to impose a 90-day freeze on new regulations and conduct an inventory of current regulations, identifying those that unnecessarily slow down U.S. economic growth. While the President addressed his memorandum to independent agency heads as well as executive department heads, both the regulatory freeze and the review and deregulation initiative were qualified by an instruction to implement these steps "[t]o the maximum extent permitted by law." Public relations officers from some of the independent agencies were quick to deny that their agencies were bound to follow the President's directive, even if those agencies generally intended to comply "voluntarily."

Shortly after his election, President Clinton replaced the Reagan executive orders with his own version, Executive Order 12,866, 58 Fed. Reg. 51,735 (1993), which remains in force today. Although considerably longer than its predecessors, the Clinton executive order largely maintained the structure of the prior orders, establishing both a regulatory planning mechanism (which helps to keep the White House informed of major agency rulemakings before they happen) and a procedure for reviewing individual rules (to ensure they are cost justified, and provide an opportunity for other agencies with equities in the matter to weigh in). The executive order's statement of regulatory philosophy softened and expanded the Reagan executive order's quantitative approach:

> Costs and benefits shall be understood to include both quantifiable measures (to the fullest extent that these can be usefully estimated) and the qualitative measures of costs and benefits that are difficult to quantify, but nevertheless essential to consider. Further, in choosing among alternative regulatory approaches, agencies should select those approaches that maximize net benefits (including potential economic, environmental, public health and safety, and other advantages; distributive impacts; and equity), unless a statute requires another regulatory approach.

Id. §1, at 51,735. The Clinton executive order, for the first time, explicitly mentions OIRA as the entity within OMB designated to conduct the regulatory review process and administer the regulatory planning process. The regulatory planning mechanism adopted in the executive order creates a Cabinet-level group of advisors on regulatory policy chaired by the Vice President and requires both Executive Branch and independent agencies to prepare semiannually a comprehensive "Regulatory Agenda" that details regulations they have issued or expect to issue, as well as currently effective regulations that are under agency review for possible amendment. *Id.* §4, at 51,738-51,739. After review and discussion within the Executive Branch, OIRA then prepares a "Unified Regulatory Agenda" for the entire government, listing and describing all regulatory actions at five different stages of review: "pre-rule" stage, proposed rule stage, final rule stage, "long-term actions," and completed actions. Notably, the Clinton executive order makes this planning mechanism applicable to both executive and independent agencies, but requires only executive agencies to submit significant regulatory actions for review.

The review mechanism in §6 of the executive order requires that agencies submit to OIRA all "significant regulatory actions" (the successor term to Executive Order 12,291's "major rule"). "Regulatory actions" are defined as substantive actions that promulgate or are expected to lead to the promulgation of a final rule, including notices of proposed rulemaking. "Significant" is defined expansively to include regulatory actions that "[h]ave an annual effect on the economy of $100 million or more"; have a materially adverse effect on the economy, or on the environment, public health, or safety, or on state, local, or tribal governments or communities; "[c]reate a serious inconsistency or otherwise interfere with an action of another agency; [m]aterially alter the budgetary impact of entitlements, grants, user fees, or loan programs or the rights and obligations of recipients"; or "[r]aise novel legal or policy issues arising out of legal mandates." §3(f), at 51,738. Thus, practically speaking, the only limit on the kinds of regulatory actions reviewable by OIRA is whether the Director finds it sufficiently important to merit the attention of the White House—though, depending on the budget and staff available for review, that could be a very significant constraint.

The Order's prescribed analytic burdens are substantial. Section 6 requires that for each matter identified by the agency or determined by the OIRA Administrator to be a significant regulatory action, the agency provide to OIRA:

> (i) The text of the draft regulatory action, together with a reasonably detailed description of the need for the regulatory action and an explanation of how the regulatory action will meet that need; and
>
> (ii) An assessment of the potential costs and benefits of the regulatory action, including an explanation of the manner in which the regulatory action is consistent with a statutory mandate and, to the extent permitted by law, promotes the President's priorities and avoids undue interference with State, local, and tribal governments in the exercise of their governmental functions.

Id. §6(a)(3)(B), at 51,741.

For those matters identified as, or determined by the Administrator of OIRA to be, *economically* significant regulatory actions, the agency must also provide:

> (i) An assessment, including the underlying analysis, of benefits anticipated from the regulatory action (such as, but not limited to, the promotion of the efficient functioning of the economy and private markets, the enhancement of health and safety, the protection of the natural environment, and the elimination or reduction of discrimination or bias) together with, to the extent feasible, a quantification of those benefits;
>
> (ii) An assessment, including the underlying analysis, of costs anticipated from the regulatory action (such as, but not limited to, the direct cost both to the government in administering the regulation and to businesses and others in complying with the regulation, and any adverse effects on the efficient functioning of the economy, private markets (including productivity, employment, and competitiveness), health, safety, and the natural environment), together with, to the extent feasible, a quantification of those costs; and
>
> (iii) An assessment, including the underlying analysis, of costs and benefits of potentially effective and reasonably feasible alternatives to the planned regulation, identified by the agencies or the public (including improving the current regulation and reasonably viable nonregulatory actions), and an explanation why the planned regulatory action is preferable to the identified potential alternatives.

Id. §6(a)(3)(C), at 51,741.

OIRA's responsibility under the executive order is to ensure that agency regulatory actions are "consistent with applicable law, the President's priorities, and the principles set out in th[e] Executive Order and do not conflict with the policies or actions of another agency." OIRA is authorized to review all significant regulatory actions and within 90 days of submission either approve the action or "return" the action to the agency for further consideration. To ensure that OIRA review does not create inordinate regulatory delay, the time limit may be extended by OIRA only once for 30 days upon the written approval of the

Director. *See* §6(b), at 51,742. To increase the transparency of the review process (which critics argued provides secret access to industry to weaken rules through the back door), the executive order further directs that when the agency finalizes and publishes a regulatory action, it must make available to the public the information it submitted to OIRA and identify for the public the changes between the draft submitted to OIRA and the final action.

The Office of Management and Budget under President George W. Bush further refined the OIRA review process, elaborating on what agencies must provide pursuant to the order by defining "good regulatory analysis" in painstaking detail. *See* OMB Circular A-4 (Office of Mgmt. & Budget, Exec. Office of the President, Circular No. A-4 (Sept. 17, 2003), *https://perma. cc/3MMU-NWW3*).

Agencies have been known to blanch at the significant burden that this level of centralized review imposes on them, which—whatever its benefits—makes the rulemaking process more time-consuming and onerous. Political appointees and career staff alike also sometimes bristle at the extent of White House involvement in what they view as their congressionally assigned domain. Agency heads—many of them members of the Cabinet—often find themselves negotiating with the OIRA administrator, or the Director of OMB, over the costs, benefits, stringency, and design of their proposed rules, a situation that can undermine their influence and which they can find galling. Yet centralized review is now an entrenched part of the regulatory process, embraced by Republican and Democratic administrations alike—a staple of modern "presidential administration."

On January 18, 2011, President Barack Obama issued Executive Order 13,563, 76 Fed. Reg. 3821 (2011), which supplements, but does not replace, Executive Order 12,866. The new order expressly reaffirms the fundamental commitment to cost-benefit principles underlying E.O. 12,866 and exhorts agencies to use the best available techniques to quantify anticipated present and future benefits and costs. The order places a new emphasis on costs and benefits that are difficult to quantify, instructing agencies to consider equity, human dignity, fairness, and distributive impacts. Yet it also addresses the need to eliminate unnecessary regulation, stating that the administrative system "must . . . promot[e] economic growth, innovation, competitiveness, and job creation."

The new order's most concrete directive requires agencies to develop a plan for retrospective analysis of existing regulations "to determine whether any such regulations should be modified, streamlined, expanded, or repealed so as to make the agency's regulatory program more effective or less burdensome in achieving the regulatory objectives."

An additional feature of the Obama order is its exhortation to agencies to consider "regulatory approaches that reduce burdens and maintain flexibility and freedom of choice for the public" such as "warnings, appropriate default rules, and disclosure requirements as well as provision of information to the public in a form that is clear and intelligible." This language suggests the influence of Obama's first OIRA Director, Harvard Law Professor Cass Sunstein, whose scholarly writings advocated for behavioral approaches to nudge people through choice architecture rather than through regulatory mandates. *See* Richard H. Thaler & Cass R. Sunstein, Nudge (2008).

NOTES AND QUESTIONS

1. *Regulatory review and regulatory delay.* Although regulatory review may improve the quality of regulation, it unquestionably slows it down. Delay at OIRA was a significant problem in the Obama Administration—which is perhaps surprising given the administration's reputation as friendly to government regulation. From 2011 on, OIRA increasingly exceeded its allotted 90 days for completing regulatory review. According to a report prepared for the Administrative Conference of the United States, before 2012, the average time for OIRA review was 50 days. "However, in 2012, the average time for OIRA to complete reviews increased to 79 days, and in the first half of 2013, the average review time was 140 days—nearly three times the average for the period from 1994 through 2011." Curtis W. Copeland, *Length of Rule Reviews by the Office of Information and Regulatory Affairs* (December 2, 2013), available at https://perma.cc/RQY9-UEW7. Tables in the appendix to Copeland's report list dozens of rules that took more than a year to review, including some that were still pending after 1,000 days or more. Does this pattern of increasing delay tell us something about the value of OIRA review? Or might it say something about the increasingly polarized political environment during Obama's presidency?

2. *Excessive burden on agencies?* Critics argue that the breadth and internal contradictions of the cumulative regulatory review mandates are difficult to manage and nearly impossible to satisfy, creating virtually infinite opportunities for White House officials (or others in the inter-agency review process) to find fault with an agency's regulatory impact analysis. Advocates of the requirements defend them as "good governance" reforms that, while demanding, impose much-needed analytic discipline on what they view as sometimes careless, frequently myopic, and often overzealous regulatory agencies. Do you think that regulatory review has gone too far? Given the opportunity costs for agencies, should there be limits to the analysis that agencies must provide? Is it realistic, for example, to require agencies to look back and study the effectiveness or need for prior rules when they are often barely able to manage their current regulatory obligations? And what are the implications of all of this analysis for judicial review? Is the additional record evidence—which includes methodologies, assumptions, and vernaculars not necessarily known to non-experts—useful fodder for judges? Can they really assess the validity of these methods?

3. *Centralized review and statutory commands.* Executive orders do not override legislative directives. Agencies must comply with OIRA review, per the regulatory review executive orders, only "to the extent permitted by law." Who has the last word interpreting that proviso? The agency proffering the significant regulation? The OIRA director? The President? Who should have the last word?

On a related matter, should agencies be excused from having to analyze alternatives that are statutorily precluded? Or is there a benefit to analyzing the costs and benefits of those options as well? Currently, even if a statute specifically rules out cost as a consideration (or has been interpreted to preclude it by courts), the executive order nevertheless requires agencies to produce a cost-benefit analysis and satisfy OIRA before finalizing a rule. An example is the NAAQS for ozone established by the EPA in 1997, described in the introduction to the *Whitman* case, in Chapter I, *supra.*

4. *Using cost-benefit analysis as a decision tool.* Another important and unresolved question is whether OIRA can insist that agencies use cost-benefit analysis as the *decision tool* (for example, apply marginal cost analysis to determine where to set the level of stringency, rather than just taking cost into account as one among other considerations in choosing that level) when a statute is ambiguous about the role cost should play. This question brings us full circle to the concept of a unitary executive and the president's appropriate role in the regulatory process. When may the president insist that agencies use CBA as a decision tool? Does it make a difference whether the statute delegates the rulemaking to the head of the agency or the President? *See* Kagan, *Presidential Administration, supra.*

5. *Extending OIRA Review to independent agencies?* As discussed above, there has been tension over the years over whether it is constitutional—and even if it is, whether it is advisable—to extend regulatory planning requirements and centralized regulatory review to independent agencies. In April 2019, the Trump administration OMB Acting Director released a memo that applied a new reading of the Congressional Review Act (CRA) to expand OIRA review of independent agency actions. The CRA requires that agencies submit "major" rules to Congress before they go into effect, along with the "cost-benefit analysis of the rule, if any." 5 U.S.C. §801. Congress may reject such rules through a joint resolution of disapproval under expedited voting procedures, and, once disapproved, the agency may not re-propose the same or a substantially similar rule without congressional authorization. *Id.* OIRA decides what rules qualify as "major" under the law. OMB's new memo requires independent agencies to give OIRA advance notice of coming rules, along with a regulatory impact analysis to help OIRA determine if the rule is major. The memo also expands the definition of "major" rules to include "guidance documents, general statements of policy, and interpretive rules." For the text of the memo, see https://perma.cc/Q88J-4DD3.

EXECUTIVE ORDER 13,771: REDUCING REGULATION AND CONTROLLING REGULATORY COSTS, 82 Fed. Reg. 9339 (2017): Almost immediately following his inauguration in January 2017, President Donald Trump issued a series of Executive Orders designed to fulfill his campaign promises to reduce the regulatory burdens borne by American industries and businesses. Potentially, the most consequential is Executive Order 13,771. Two prominent features of the Order, excerpted below, are its "two-for-one" provision (Section 2(a)) and its requirement that the incremental cost of new regulations "shall be no greater than zero." The Order is excerpted below:

Section 2. Regulatory Cap for Fiscal Year 2017.
    (a) Unless prohibited by law, whenever an executive department or agency (agency) publicly proposes for notice and comment or otherwise promulgates a new regulation, it shall identify at least two existing regulations to be repealed.
    (b) For fiscal year 2017, which is in progress, the heads of all agencies are directed that the total incremental cost of all new regulations, including repealed regulations, to be finalized this year shall be no greater than zero, unless otherwise required by law or consistent

with advice provided in writing by the Director of the Office of Management and Budget (Director).

(c) In furtherance of the requirement of subsection (a) of this section, any new incremental costs associated with new regulations shall, to the extent permitted by law, be offset by the elimination of existing costs associated with at least two prior regulations. Any agency eliminating existing costs associated with prior regulations under this subsection shall do so in accordance with the Administrative Procedure Act and other applicable law. . . .

NOTES AND QUESTIONS

1. *Prior Executive Orders.* What does President Trump's order add to existing Executive Orders (which require "significant" agency rules to go through a rigorous cost-benefit analysis overseen by OMB, and also mandate a "look back" at older rules to consider whether they are still warranted)?

2. *Logic of the Executive Order.* EO 13,771 has been widely criticized as focusing only on the costs of regulation, but not its benefits. Is that a fair criticism? Is it possible, for example, that an agency might identify for elimination two rules with far greater net benefits than the new rule being proposed? Can you think of an alternative way to facilitate the repeal of numerous aging regulations that agencies see as unimportant? One that is equally likely to be implemented?

3. *Procedural legality.* Can agencies comply with the Order and still comply with the procedures mandated by the APA for rulemaking?

4. *Substantive legality.* Can agencies achieve the cost- and regulation-reduction goals of the Order and still comply with their statutory mandates? Suppose, for example, that the EPA repealed two air quality standards in exchange for issuing a new one. Can it invoke the Executive Order to defend a claim that its first two actions are arbitrary and capricious? If EPA says nothing about EO 13,771 in rescinding the standards, can environmentalists successfully claim that those actions were nonetheless arbitrary because they were taken in order to comply with EO 13,771?

5. *Standing to challenge.* In Public Citizen, Inc. v. Trump, 297 F. Supp. 3d 6 (D.D.C. 2018), the district court held that neither Public Citizen nor its members had standing to challenge the "two for one" Executive Order. The plaintiffs claimed standing based on potential harms caused by the inability of agencies to issue new rules if they could not or would not repeal two existing rules, and based on chilling their advocacy for new regulations, since no new regulation could be promulgated without repeal of two other regulations, potentially causing more harm than good. The court essentially found that the plaintiffs could not plausibly allege that they would suffer concrete and particularized harm from the operation of the Executive Order since their claims as to which regulatory actions would be affected were speculative at best. Why didn't the plaintiffs wait for a rule to be eliminated pursuant to the Executive Order and challenge that decision? Is there any harm done in the meantime while agencies work to comply with the Order that cannot be redressed later?

6. *Legislative rulemaking reform proposals.* For several years during the Obama administration, the Republican-controlled House of Representatives was

considering and sometimes passing bills aimed at reforming the rulemaking process. At the time, with the prospects dim for passage in the Senate and a certain presidential veto, these bills did not attract much attention. With the election of Republican Donald Trump as President, the prospects for major regulatory reform brightened. In the Senate, a bill called the Regulatory Accountability Act proposed to ramp up procedural and substantive requirements for regulations by imposing additional notice requirements and rigorous additional cost-benefit analysis for all major rules. It also required formal rulemaking for many significant rules, adding considerable procedural burdens to the rulemaking process. The REINS Act, which had been considered by the House for several years, would have gone even further and required approval of major rules by both Houses of Congress. Another provision would prohibit reviewing courts from deferring to agency legal interpretations, a provision that might be read as purporting to overrule *Chevron, Auer,* and (perhaps) *Skidmore.* Proponents view these proposals as necessary curatives for overly zealous regulators who in their view stifle economic productivity and kill jobs. Critics view these proposals as a back-door way of neutering what they consider to be important health, safety, and financial regulatory statutes, allowing legislators to stifle their enforcement without having to vote to repeal them. It remains to be seen whether any major regulatory reform initiatives will become law.

3.   Impact Statements: The Case of the National Environmental Policy Act

Statutes like §553 of the APA are intended to improve agency policymaking by giving the public an opportunity to participate in the policymaking process and by making agencies articulate the basis for their decisions. Another statutory device to improve the quality of administrative policymaking is the requirement that agencies prepare "impact statements" to accompany, and presumably to inform, their decisionmaking. Probably the leading example is the National Environmental Policy Act of 1969, Pub. L. No. 91-190, 83 Stat. 852 (NEPA). NEPA declared a national commitment to "use all practicable means and measures . . . to create and maintain conditions under which man and nature can exist in productive harmony." Title I of the Act probably contains the greatest collection of mellifluous, hortatory language ever assembled under one statutory title. One particularly nice example is §102(2)(A), which requires all federal agencies to "utilize a systematic, interdisciplinary approach which will ensure the integrated use of the natural and social sciences and the environmental design arts in planning and in decisionmaking which may have an impact on man's environment." Nestled among several exhortations is the one provision of the Act with any apparent bite. Section 102(2)(C) directs all federal agencies to:

> include in every recommendation or report on . . . major Federal actions significantly affecting the quality of the human environment, a detailed statement by the responsible official on—
>
> > (i) the environmental impact of the proposed action,
> > (ii) any adverse environmental effects which cannot be avoided should the proposal be implemented,

(iii) alternatives to the proposed action,

(iv) the relationship between local short-term uses of man's environment and the maintenance and enhancement of long-term productivity, and

(v) any irreversible and irretrievable commitments of resources which would be involved in the proposed action should it be implemented.

Prior to making any detailed statement, the responsible Federal official shall consult with and obtain the comments of any Federal agency that has jurisdiction by law or special expertise with respect to any environmental impact involved. Copies of such statement, and the comments and views of the appropriate Federal, State and local agencies, which are authorized to develop and enforce environmental standards, shall . . . accompany the proposal through the existing agency review processes. . . .

Title II of the Act creates a Council on Environmental Quality (CEQ), which is responsible for advising the President on environmental issues and overseeing agencies' compliance with Title I. By Executive Order 11,514, 35 Fed. Reg. 4247 (1970), President Nixon empowered CEQ to issue advisory rules specifying the form and content of impact statements.

NEPA's enactment came on the crest of a wave of public concern about environmental harms, including water and air pollution, and pesticide contamination of the food supply. In 1969 and 1970, Congress enacted a number of environmental and public health statutes, including the Federal Coal Mine Health and Safety Act of 1969, Pub. L. No. 91-173, 83 Stat. 742, the Occupational Safety and Health Act of 1970, Pub. L. No. 91-596, 84 Stat. 1590, and the Clean Air Act Amendments of 1970, Pub. L. No. 91-604, 84 Stat. 1676. Unlike these other statutes that responded in a more focused fashion to particular environmental and health hazards, NEPA was a sweeping manifesto designed to raise the environmental awareness of the entire federal bureaucracy. It was inspired by a widespread perception that federal agencies viewed their mandates narrowly, and often overlooked the environmental consequences of their actions. This was especially true for resource development agencies (those that issue permits to mine, graze, and drill on public lands), or infrastructure agencies (which build highways and dams, or license nuclear reactors), which tended not to give weight to environmental consequences. A good example is New Hampshire v. Atomic Energy Commission, 406 F.2d 170 (1st Cir. 1969), *cert. denied*, 395 U.S. 962 (1969), in which the AEC had refused when licensing a nuclear power plant to consider the thermal pollution that would be caused by its discharge of cooling water into a river. The agency argued that its statutory mandate required it to consider only radiation hazards. The reviewing court upheld the AEC, noting "with regret that the Congress has not yet established procedures requiring timely and comprehensive consideration of non-radiological pollution effects. . . ." *Id.* at 176.

NEPA was intended to change that. While agencies at first resisted their new mandate, the Circuit courts made clear that NEPA's requirements were not to be ignored.

CALVERT CLIFFS COORDINATING COMMITTEE v. ATOMIC ENERGY COMMISSION, 449 F.2d 1109 (D.C. Cir. 1971): *Calvert Cliffs* involved an attack on rules promulgated by the AEC outlining how it intended to implement

NEPA in connection with licensing of nuclear plants. (The licensing procedure is described in Chapter III, *supra.*) The rules provided that AEC staff would prepare an environmental impact statement (EIS) on each license application prior to the public hearing required by the Atomic Energy Act. This EIS would "accompany" the application through the hearing process, but the licensing board would not consider the environmental issues addressed by the EIS unless affirmatively raised by outside intervenors or the agency's staff. The commission argued that this procedure was consistent with the final sentence of §102(2)(C). In a stinging rebuke authored by Judge Skelly Wright, the D.C. Circuit rejected this pro forma compliance as insufficient:

> We believe that the Commission's crabbed interpretation of NEPA makes a mockery of the Act. What possible purpose could there be in the Section 102(2)(C) requirement (that the "detailed statement" accompany proposals through agency review processes) if "accompany" means no more than physical proximity — mandating no more than the physical act of passing certain folders and papers, unopened, to reviewing officials along with other folders and papers? What possible purpose could there be in requiring the "detailed statement" to be before hearing boards, if the boards are free to ignore entirely the contents of the statement? NEPA was meant to do more than regulate the flow of papers in the federal bureaucracy. The word "accompany" in Section 102(2)(C) must not be read so narrowly as to make the Act ludicrous. It must, rather, be read to indicate a congressional intent that environmental factors, as compiled in the "detailed statement," be considered through agency review processes.
>
> Beyond Section 102(2)(C), NEPA requires that agencies consider the environmental impact of their actions "to the fullest extent possible." The Act is addressed to agencies as a whole, not only to their professional staffs. Compliance to the "*fullest*" possible extent would seem to demand that environmental issues be considered at every important stage in the decision making process concerning a particular action — at every stage where an overall balancing of environmental and nonenvironmental factors is appropriate and where alterations might be made in the proposed action to minimize environmental costs. Of course, consideration which is entirely duplicative is not necessarily required. But independent review of staff proposals by hearing boards is hardly a duplicative function. A truly independent review provides a crucial check on the staff's recommendations. The Commission's hearing boards automatically consider nonenvironmental factors, even though they have been previously studied by the staff. Clearly, the review process is an appropriate stage at which to balance conflicting factors against one another. And, just as clearly, it provides an important opportunity to reject or significantly modify the staff's recommended action. Environmental factors, therefore, should not be singled out and excluded, at this stage, from the proper balance of values envisioned by NEPA. . . .
>
> NEPA establishes environmental protection as an integral part of the Atomic Energy Commission's basic mandate. The primary responsibility for fulfilling that mandate lies with the Commission. Its responsibility is not simply to sit back, like an umpire, and resolve adversary contentions at the hearing stage. Rather, it must itself take the initiative of considering environmental values at every distinctive and comprehensive stage of the process beyond the staff's evaluation and recommendation.

As Judge Wright predicted, NEPA unleashed "a flood of new litigation." *Id.* at 1111. Most of the litigation has focused on the scope and content of

§102(2)(C)'s requirement that agencies prepare a "detailed statement" on a proposed action's environmental impact. There has been extensive dispute about all of the threshold requirements: What is a "major Federal action"? When do such actions "significantly" affect the environment? What is included in "the environment"? And what alternatives must the agency consider? The Supreme Court considered this latter question in the *Vermont Yankee* case, another portion of which is excerpted earlier in this chapter.

VERMONT YANKEE NUCLEAR POWER CORP. v. NATURAL RESOURCES DEFENSE COUNCIL, 435 U.S. 519 (1978): Opponents of licensing a nuclear power plant in Midland, Michigan, argued that the EIS prepared by the Nuclear Regulatory Commission (NRC) failed to consider the alternative of energy conservation. The agency stated that a petition by Saginaw, a coalition of environmental groups, failed to meet a "threshold test" of showing that "reasonably available" energy conservation alternatives would curtail demand for electricity to a level at which the proposed facilities would not be needed. Conceding its obligation to develop evidence on energy conservation alternatives in *future* licensing cases, the NRC criticized Saginaw for failure to present "clear and reasonably specific energy conservation contentions in a timely fashion." The Court deferred to the agency:

> [A]s should be obvious even upon a moment's reflection, the term "alternatives" is not self-defining. To make an impact statement something more than an exercise in frivolous boilerplate the concept of alternatives must be bounded by some notion of feasibility. . . . Time and resources are simply too limited to hold that an impact statement fails because the agency failed to ferret out every possible alternative, regardless of how uncommon or unknown that alternative may have been at the time the project was approved. . . .
>
> Prior to the drastic oil shortages incurred by the United States in 1973, there was little serious thought in most Government circles of energy conservation alternatives. Indeed, the Council on Environmental Quality did not promulgate regulations which even remotely suggested the need to consider energy conservation in impact statements until August 1, 1973. . . . The Federal Power Commission likewise did not require consideration of energy conservation in applications to build hydroelectric facilities until June 19, 1973. . . . All this occurred over a year and a half after the draft environmental statement for Midland had been prepared, and over a year after the final environmental statement had been prepared and the hearings completed.
>
> We think these facts amply demonstrate that the concept of "alternatives" is an evolving one, requiring the agency to explore more or fewer alternatives as they become better known and understood. . . .
>
> We also think the court's criticism of the Commission's "threshold test" displays a lack of understanding of the historical setting within which the agency action took place and of the nature of the test itself. . . . [W]hile it is true that NEPA places upon an agency the obligation to consider every significant aspect of the environmental impact of a proposed action, it is still incumbent upon intervenors who wish to participate to structure their participation so that it is meaningful, so that it alerts the agency to the intervenors' position and contentions. This is especially true when the intervenors are requesting the agency to embark upon an exploration of uncharted territory, as was the question of energy conservation in the late 1960s and early 1970s.

[H]ere the agency continually invited further clarification of Saginaw's contentions. Even without such clarification it indicated a willingness to receive evidence on the matters. But . . . Saginaw decline[d] to further focus its contentions. . . .

We also think the court seriously mischaracterized the Commission's "threshold test" as placing "heavy substantive burdens . . . on intervenors. . . ." 547 F.2d, at 627, and n.11. On the contrary, the Commission explicitly stated: "We do not equate this burden with the civil litigation concept of a prima facie case, an unduly heavy burden in this setting. But the showing should be sufficient to require reasonable minds to inquire further. . . . We think this sort of agency procedure well within the agency's discretion."

NOTES AND QUESTIONS

1. *Energy conservation.* While energy efficiency is a well-known alternative to building new electricity generation today, was it fair for the Court to characterize it as "uncharted territory" in the early 1970s? "Uncharted" by whom? The NRC? The U.S. government? Society at large? Is the Court saying that NRC needs to consider only those alternatives that are suggested by intervenors? That are fully developed by intervenors? Are these restrictions consistent with the spirit of NEPA? Professor William Rodgers argues emphatically that they are not: "*Vermont Yankee*, unfortunately, does support an argument that in a sizable category of 'colorable,' partial, or arguable alternatives, the agency can sit back like an umpire, blind and fat, refusing to look into the matter itself and faulting the litigants before it for not curing this homegrown myopia." William H. Rodgers, Jr., A Hard Look at *Vermont Yankee*: Environmental Law Under Close Scrutiny, 67 Geo. L.J. 699, 722 (1979). On the other hand, in what sense is "energy conservation" an "alternative" to granting a construction permit for the Midland nuclear reactor? Doesn't the answer depend on the purpose behind licensing nuclear plants? The Atomic Energy Act of 1954 contains the following statement of purpose: "to encourage widespread participation in the development and utilization of atomic power for peaceful purposes to the maximum extent consistent with the common defense and security and with the health and safety of the public." Section 3(d), 68 Stat. 922. Is energy conservation relevant to that "purpose"? Does NEPA enlarge the purpose of NRC regulation?

2. *Mitigation of environmental effects under NEPA.* Despite the Supreme Court's apparent unwillingness to require agencies to change course in light of serious environmental impacts revealed by the EIS, challengers to agency action have continued to press claims that NEPA requires actual mitigation of environmental effects or at least preparation of plans allowing for such mitigation. The decision that follows reviews a Court of Appeals decision that required detailed mitigation plans under NEPA.

Perhaps the most important question is whether NEPA is a purely procedural statute satisfied by mere disclosure no matter how severe the effects, or does it require agencies to give more substantive weight to environmental impacts once they are disclosed than they otherwise would have? In the case below, the Supreme Court definitively answered that question.

ROBERTSON v. METHOW VALLEY CITIZENS COUNCIL
490 U.S. 332 (1989)

JUSTICE STEVENS delivered the opinion of the Court.

[The plaintiffs challenged the Forest Service's issuance of special-use permits for a ski resort on national forest land. The EIS (referred to in the Court's opinion as the "Early Winters Study") considered the effect of the resort on wildlife and outlined possible mitigation measures. The Court of Appeals found the EIS inadequate for two reasons. First, the State Department of Game had predicted a 50% loss in the mule deer herd. The EIS adopted a 15% estimate, but admitted that the off-site effects of the resort were uncertain because they depended on the extent of private development. The EIS relied on mitigation measures to reduce the impact, but those measures had not been fully developed or tested. In light of this uncertainty, the Court of Appeals held that the EIS should have included a worst-case analysis. Second, the Court of Appeals held that the EIS was inadequate because it did not contain a complete mitigation plan to protect wildlife.]

Simply by focusing the agency's attention on the environmental consequences of a proposed project, NEPA ensures that important effects will not be overlooked or underestimated only to be discovered after resources have been committed or the die otherwise cast. Moreover, the strong precatory language of §101 of the Act and the requirement that agencies prepare detailed impact statements inevitably bring pressure to bear on agencies "to respond to the needs of environmental quality." 115 Cong. Rec. 40425 (1969) (remarks of Sen. Muskie).

Publication of an EIS, both in draft and final form, also serves a larger informational role. It gives the public the assurance that the agency "has indeed considered environmental concerns in its decisionmaking process," *Baltimore Gas & Electric Co.*, and, perhaps more significantly, provides a springboard for public comment. Thus, in this case the final draft of the Early Winters Study reflects not only the work of the Forest Service itself, but also the critical views of the Washington State Department of Game, the Methow Valley Citizens Council, and Friends of the Earth, as well as many others, to whom copies of the draft Study were circulated. Moreover, with respect to a development such as Sandy Butte, where the adverse effects on air quality and the mule deer herd are primarily attributable to predicted off-site development that will be subject to regulation by other governmental bodies, the EIS serves the function of offering those bodies adequate notice of the expected consequences and the opportunity to plan and implement corrective measures in a timely manner.

The sweeping policy goals announced in §101 of NEPA are thus realized through a set of "action-forcing" procedures that require that agencies take a "'hard look' at environmental consequences," and that provide for broad dissemination of relevant environmental information. Although these procedures are almost certain to affect the agency's substantive decision, it is now well settled that NEPA itself does not mandate particular results, but simply prescribes the necessary process. . . .

If the adverse environmental effects of the proposed action are adequately identified and evaluated, the agency is not constrained by NEPA from deciding that other values outweigh the environmental costs. In this case, for example, it would not have violated NEPA if the Forest Service, after complying with the Act's procedural prerequisites, had decided that the benefits to be derived from downhill skiing at Sandy Butte justified the issuance of a special use permit, notwithstanding the loss of 15 percent, 50 percent, or even 100 percent of the mule deer herd. Other statutes may impose substantive environmental obligations on federal agencies, but NEPA merely prohibits uninformed—rather than unwise—agency action.

To be sure, one important ingredient of an EIS is the discussion of steps that can be taken to mitigate adverse environmental consequences. The requirement that an EIS contain a detailed discussion of possible mitigation measures flows from both the language of the Act and, more expressly, from CEQ's implementing regulations. Implicit in NEPA's demand that an agency prepare a detailed statement on "any adverse environmental effects which cannot be avoided should the proposal be implemented," is an understanding that the EIS will discuss the extent to which adverse effects can be avoided. More generally, omission of a reasonably complete discussion of possible mitigation measures would undermine the "action-forcing" function of NEPA. Without such a discussion, neither the agency nor other interested groups and individuals can properly evaluate the severity of the adverse effects. An adverse effect that can be fully remedied by, for example, an inconsequential public expenditure is certainly not as serious as a similar effect that can only be modestly ameliorated through the commitment of vast public and private resources. Recognizing the importance of such a discussion in guaranteeing that the agency has taken a "hard look" at the environmental consequences of proposed federal action, CEQ regulations require that the agency discuss possible mitigation measures in defining the scope of the EIS, 40 CFR §1508.25(b) in discussing alternatives to the proposed action, §1502.14(f), and consequences of that action, §1502.16(h), and in explaining its ultimate decision, §1505.2(c).

There is a fundamental distinction, however, between a requirement that mitigation be discussed in sufficient detail to ensure that environmental consequences have been fairly evaluated, on the one hand, and a substantive requirement that a complete mitigation plan be actually formulated and adopted, on the other. In this case, the off-site effects on air quality and on the mule deer herd cannot be mitigated unless nonfederal government agencies take appropriate action. Since it is those state and local governmental bodies that have jurisdiction over the area in which the adverse effects need be addressed and since they have the authority to mitigate them, it would be incongruous to conclude that the Forest Service has no power to act until the local agencies have reached a final conclusion on what mitigating measures they consider necessary. Even more significantly, it would be inconsistent with NEPA's reliance on procedural mechanisms—as opposed to substantive, result-based standards—to demand the presence of a fully developed plan that will mitigate environmental harm before an agency can act.

We thus conclude that the Court of Appeals erred, first, in assuming that "NEPA requires that 'action be taken to mitigate the adverse effects of major federal actions,'" and, second, in finding that this substantive requirement entails the further duty to include in every EIS 'a detailed explanation of specific measures which *will* be employed to mitigate the adverse impacts of a proposed action.'"

The Court of Appeals also concluded that the Forest Service had an obligation to make a "worst case analysis" if it could not make a reasoned assessment of the impact of the Early Winters project on the mule deer herd. Such a "worst case analysis" was required at one time by CEQ regulations, but those regulations have since been amended. Moreover, although the prior regulations may well have expressed a permissible application of NEPA, the Act itself does not mandate that uncertainty in predicting environmental harms be addressed exclusively in this manner. Accordingly, we conclude that the Court of Appeals also erred in requiring the "worst case" study. . . .

The amended regulation . . . "retains the duty to describe the consequences of a remote, but potentially severe impact, but grounds the duty in evaluation of scientific opinion rather than in the framework of a conjectural 'worst case analysis.' " 50 Fed. Reg. 32,237 (1985).

[T]he amendment was designed to better serve the twin functions of an EIS—requiring agencies to take a "hard look" at the consequences of the proposed action and providing important information to other groups and individuals. CEQ explained that by requiring that an EIS focus on reasonably foreseeable impacts, the new regulation "will generate information and discussion on those consequences of greatest concern to the public and of greatest relevance to the agency's decision," rather than distorting the decisionmaking process by overemphasizing highly speculative harms. In light of this well-considered basis for the change, the new regulation is entitled to substantial deference. . . .

In sum, we conclude that NEPA does not require a fully developed plan detailing what steps *will* be taken to mitigate adverse environmental impacts and does not require a "worst case analysis." . . . The judgment of the Court of Appeals is accordingly reversed, and the case is remanded for further proceedings consistent with this opinion.

NOTES AND QUESTIONS

1. *Procedural requirements.* There was hope among environmental groups that NEPA might have a substantive, and not just a procedural, impact on agency decisionmaking by making plain that some courses of action would be arbitrary and capricious by virtue of their environmental consequences. It seemed conceivable that judicial enforcement of NEPA might actually *rule out* federal projects that portended severe environmental impacts. Yet as time passed, the courts (and particularly the Supreme Court, as illustrated by its *Vermont Yankee* and *Robertson* decisions) have tended to "domesticate" NEPA by integrating it into the fabric of administrative law and declaring it to have only a procedural effect. Another illustration of NEPA's purely procedural impact came in Strycker's Bay Neighborhood Council v. Karlen, 443 U.S. 223 (1980). In *Strycker's Bay*, a neighborhood association used NEPA to challenge the siting of a large low-income housing development. The EIS prepared in connection with the project conceded that there were alternatives that would mitigate the social effects of a large concentration of low-income residents, but the U.S. Department of Housing and Urban Development concluded that mitigation was not worth the cost of delaying the project to move it to a preferable site. The Supreme Court held that NEPA did not require the agency to adopt the environmentally preferable

alternative: "In the present litigation there is no doubt that HUD considered the environmental consequences of its decision to redesignate the proposed site for low-income housing. NEPA requires no more." 443 U.S. at 228 (per curiam).

If NEPA is an essentially procedural statute—that is, if agencies, having "considered" environmental impacts, can do anything they want—what is its value? In a 1973 article, Professor Joseph Sax, an early proponent of NEPA, predicted that NEPA would do little to change agency decisions without Congress giving them either broader mandates or additional fiscal resources. Joseph L. Sax, The (Unhappy) Truth About NEPA, 26 Okla. L. Rev. 239 (1973).

Critics assert that NEPA results in massive paperwork requirements and has become a boondoggle for lawyers and consultants without providing much in the way of environmental benefits. But advocates say that NEPA has made a huge difference. First, the EIS mandate heightens the agency's normal duty to consider relevant factors in decisionmaking, requiring agencies to advert specifically to environmental effects that might never have occurred to them, and which upon reflection they may be prepared to mitigate. Second, to comply with CEQ regulations, many agencies diversified their staff, which brought new expertise into their decisionmaking processes. Third, agencies may prophylactically eliminate certain projects from consideration in anticipation of NEPA review, decisions that may be invisible to outsiders. *See* Serge Taylor, Making Bureaucracies Think: The Environmental Impact Statement Strategy of Administrative Reform (1984); Dinah Bear, NEPA at 19, 19 Envtl. L. Rep. 10,062 (1989). Fourth, proponents also assert that NEPA's information disclosure requirement has had a "democratizing" impact by making the basis of agency decisions more transparent and equipping the public with information they can use, either in litigation or through the political process, to challenge agency actions. Finally, if imitation is an indication of success, NEPA has been successful: at least 15 states have adopted their own versions of NEPA, and EIS-type requirements have now been adopted in over 30 countries.

2. *The impact statement as a model for disclosure.* Congress has drawn on the NEPA prototype to require agencies to reckon with other kinds of impacts. For example, in the 1990s, as federal laws and regulations increasingly imposed new regulatory burdens on state, local, and tribal governments without providing funding for implementation, Congress passed the Unfunded Mandate Reform Act of 1995, Pub. L. No. 104-4, 109 Stat. 48, codified at 2 U.S.C. §§1501 *et seq.*, which requires agencies to analyze and disclose the costs of their regulations for local governments and the private sector. With some exceptions, the Act requires federal agencies proposing regulations to prepare statements detailing the magnitude of any unfunded mandate in proposed regulations that will impose at least $100 million of yearly costs on local governments and the private sector. The statement must include an estimate of the costs imposed by the regulation, information on whether federal money is available, whether particular regions will be more affected than others, the likely effect on the national economy, and a description of the agency's consultation with local and tribal governments. Agencies are also required to consider regulatory alternatives that would impose fewer costs on local governments, and to provide a special explanation when they do not choose the least burdensome alternative. *See* 2 U.S.C. §§1531 *et seq.* Finally, although parties sometimes include allegations that an agency has violated the Unfunded Mandate Reform Act as a reason to invalidate

a regulation, the Act provides that judicial review of agency compliance with the Act is limited to an order to compel the agency to prepare the statement required by the Act, and that courts may not hold a regulation or other agency action invalid for failure to comply with the Act. *See* 2 U.S.C. §1571; American Trucking Associations, Inc. v. EPA, 175 F.3d 1027, 1043 (D.C. Cir. 1999), *aff'd in part and rev'd in part on other grounds sub nom.*, Whitman v. American Trucking Associations, Inc., 531 U.S. 457 (2001) (recognizing that agency rule may not be invalidated for failure to comply with Unfunded Mandate Reform Act).

Presidents have also been attracted to the impact statement mechanism, as illustrated by the Regulatory Impact Analysis requirement of Executive Order 12,291 and its progeny, discussed above.

3. *The future of NEPA.* Lest it appear that NEPA as a purely procedural statute has become a paper tiger, consider the D.C. Circuit's decision in Sierra Club v. Federal Energy Regulatory Commission, 867 F.3d 1357 (D.C. Cir. 2017). The Sierra Club and others challenged FERC's approval of the construction of three natural gas pipelines because FERC's EIS did not adequately address the greenhouse gas emissions that would result from the pipelines' use, *i.e.* the emissions from the natural gas delivered through the pipeline and burned by the utilities purchasing it. FERC argued that it was not required to address the indirect effects of pipeline construction, but the D.C. Circuit disagreed, concluding that NEPA requires agencies to consider the reasonably foreseeable indirect effects of their actions. FERC objected that it would be difficult if not impossible for it to estimate the emissions resulting from the construction of a new pipeline, but the court brushed this argument aside on the basis that the EIS should have addressed the issue, even if simply to point out the difficulty in making the estimate:

> We conclude that the EIS for the Southeast Market Pipelines Project should have either given a quantitative estimate of the downstream greenhouse emissions that will result from burning the natural gas that the pipelines will transport or explained more specifically why it could not have done so. As we have noted, greenhouse-gas emissions are an indirect effect of authorizing this project, which FERC could reasonably foresee, and which the agency has legal authority to mitigate. *See* 15 U.S.C. §717f(e). The EIS accordingly needed to include a discussion of the "significance" of this indirect effect, see 40 C.F.R. §1502.16(b), as well as "the incremental impact of the action when added to other past, present, and reasonably foreseeable future actions."

Id., 867 F.3d at 1374 (citation omitted). *Cf.* Sierra Club v. United States Department of Energy, 867 F.3d 189, 199 (D.C. Cir. 2017) (approving the DOE's EIS without specific estimates of the environmental impact of natural gas exports, characterizing the challenge as requiring the DOE to "foresee the unforeseeable"). In this case, the court concluded that the agency had provided an adequate explanation for why it could not make more specific estimates of indirect effects.

CHAPTER VI

ADJUDICATION

As we pointed out at the outset of Chapter IV, the other pillar of administrative law's bipolar structure is the judicial model. From earliest times, administrative agencies have performed functions in our system of government akin to those performed by courts of law. In some cases considered earlier in this volume, the "judicial" analogy is quite close: for example, when the National Labor Relations Board determines whether an employer has committed an unfair labor practice by discharging an employee in retaliation for supporting union organizing activity (*see, e.g., Universal Camera,* excerpted in Chapter II, *supra*) or when the Board of Immigration Appeals determines whether to deport an alien (*see, e.g., Chadha,* excerpted in Chapter I, *supra*). In other cases, the judicial analogy is less comfortable, as when the Bureau of Indian Affairs determines whether a Native American is eligible for welfare benefits (*see, e.g., Ruiz,* excerpted in Chapter IV, *supra*) or when the Secretary of Transportation decides whether to approve the design of an interstate highway (*see, e.g., Overton Park,* excerpted in Chapter II, *supra*). All of these cases have in common the core attributes of the judicial model of adjudication: the authoritative resolution of factual and legal disputes, involving the application of general policy to a particular party or action. In each instance, the agency, through one or more of its officials, takes evidence, hears arguments, and renders a disposition that, unless overturned on appeal, is legally binding on the parties involved, including the agency itself.

The delegation of adjudicative authority to administrative agencies raises two generic questions in our legal system. First, are there any limitations on the kinds of matters or issues that may be delegated to administrative agencies to adjudicate? Second, to the extent that adjudicative powers may properly be delegated to agencies, what procedures must they follow when they exercise such powers? This chapter is devoted to an exploration of these issues.

A.   AGENCY AUTHORITY TO ADJUDICATE

Until the twentieth century, courts provided the customary forum for adjudicating public law actions. Administrative officials seeking to compel compliance with a statute or impose a sanction for its violation had to commence a civil or criminal action in a trial court of competent jurisdiction. Many modern statutes continue to separate the prosecutorial and adjudicative functions in this fashion. (*See, e.g.,* the statute involved in the *Abbott Laboratories* case, in Chapter III, *supra.*) But the trend — at least at the federal level — has been otherwise. Dating from the creation of modern "integrated" agencies like the ICC and the FTC, Congress has conferred upon administrative agencies power to adjudicate the liability of persons charged with violating their statutes and to issue orders imposing sanctions upon them. While Congress almost always provides for judicial review of such orders, the administrative role has become dominant.

As it has expanded the adjudicative powers of the administrative branch, Congress has had to contend with several potential constitutional obstacles. One is Article III itself, which vests in the federal courts the "judicial power" to decide "cases and controversies." This provision might have been read as a broad limitation on the power of Congress to delegate adjudicatory powers to administrative tribunals. But in Murray's Lessee v. Hoboken Land & Improvement Co., 59 U.S. (18 How.) 272 (1855), the Court acknowledged that Congress could delegate to executive officials the power to adjudicate matters "involving public rights" such as the determination of liability to the government for taxes owed, contract damages, or forfeitures. The Court did add, however, that Congress cannot "withdraw from judicial cognizance any matter which, from its nature, is the subject of a suit at the common law, or in equity, or admiralty." *Id.* at 284. That dictum provided the basis for a subsequent challenge to a federal statute creating an administrative mechanism to adjudicate workers' compensation awards.

The Longshoremen's and Harbor Workers' Compensation Act, 44 Stat. 1424, established a United States Employees Compensation Commission to adjudicate compensation claims made by workers injured while on the navigable waters of the United States, and thus not protected by any state's workers' compensation law. Compensation decisions of a deputy commissioner could be challenged by a civil action in federal district court, and could be set aside if "not in accordance with law." In such an action, the factual findings of the deputy commissioner were to be treated as binding if supported by "substantial evidence." Benson, an employer, challenged an award under the Act on grounds that, *inter alia,* the Act violated the Article III of the Constitution by authorizing the determination of a "case in admiralty" by a non–Article III tribunal. The Court upheld the Act in Crowell v. Benson, 285 U.S. 22 (1932), but in doing so asserted limits on Congress's power to assign adjudication of disputes between two private parties to non–Article III courts. The Court drew a sharp distinction between cases of public right — matters arising "between the Government and persons subject to its authority in connection with the performance of the constitutional functions of the executive or leg-islative departments"—and cases involving questions of private right—that is, "the liability of one individual to another." *Id.* at 50, 51. Congress could freely delegate responsibility to adjudicate the former to "legislative courts"; but only the "constitutional" courts could adjudicate the latter. *Id.* at 50. This did not mean that administrative agencies could not play any role in cases of "private right," only that their role in such cases must be restricted. The courts may be assisted by an administrative tribunal (which can make fact findings), but courts must decide "jurisdictional" facts (facts whose "existence is a condi-tion precedent to the operation of the statutory scheme"), as well as questions of law. *Id.* at 54.

Crowell's "jurisdictional fact" doctrine was a singular exception to the general proposition that Congress may confer adjudicative powers on administrative tribunals until 1982, when the Court struck down a provision of the Bankruptcy Act that specifically authorized the non–Article III bankruptcy courts to exercise the "powers of a court of equity, law, and admiralty," 28 U.S.C. §1481, in "all civil proceedings arising under [the bankruptcy code] 28 U.S.C. §1471(b)." In Northern Pipeline Constr. Co. v. Marathon Pipeline Co., 458 U.S. 50 (1982), six Justices held that the bankruptcy court could not con-stitutionally adjudicate a state common law breach of contract claim brought by a company undergoing reorganization. "Private-rights disputes," observed Justice Brennan in his plurality opinion, "lie at the core of the historically rec-ognized judicial power." *Id.* at 70.

Three years later the Court had another opportunity to delineate the murky boundaries of Article III in Thomas v. Union Carbide Agric. Prods. Co., 473 U.S. 568 (1985). The case involved a challenge to provisions of the Federal Insecticide, Fungicide, and Rodenticide Act described more fully in the *Monsanto* case, excerpted in Chapter VII, *infra*. A 1978 amendment to the Act required registrants of pesticides to "license" other manufacturers by providing information about the registered pesticides. The Act required that the recipients of this valuable information pay compensation to the provider. Disputes about the amount of compensation were to be submitted to binding arbitration with limited judicial review. The Court rejected a claim that the arbitration procedure violated Article III. The Court began by noting that the "theory that the public rights/private rights dichotomy of *Crowell* and *Mur-ray's Lessee*, . . . provides a bright line test for determining the requirements of Article III did not command a majority of the Court in *Northern Pipeline*. The enduring lesson of *Crowell* is that practical attention to substance rather than doctrinaire reliance on formal categories should inform application of Article III." Applying this functional test, the Court noted that the right of compensation created by the Act "bears many of the characteristics of a 'pub-lic' right" because it promotes the statute's purpose of protecting the public health. The Court also relied on the fact that the Act provided for judicial review, albeit limited, of arbitrators' awards and that registrants, in effect, consented to the arbitration procedure by availing themselves of the statute's regulatory protection.

COMMODITY FUTURES TRADING
COMMISSION v. SCHOR
478 U.S. 833 (1986)

JUSTICE O'CONNOR delivered the opinion of the Court.

The question presented is whether the Commodity Exchange Act (CEA or Act), 7 U.S.C. §1 *et seq.,* empowers the Commodity Futures Trading Commission (CFTC or Commission) to entertain state law counterclaims in reparation proceedings and, if so, whether that grant of authority violates Article III of the Constitution.

I

The CEA broadly prohibits fraudulent and manipulative conduct in connection with commodity futures transactions. In 1974, Congress "overhaul[ed]" the Act in order to institute a more "comprehensive regulatory structure to oversee the volatile and esoteric futures trading complex." H.R. Rep. No. 93-975, p.1 (1974). *See* Pub. L. 93-463, 88 Stat. 1389. Congress also determined that the broad regulatory powers of the CEA were most appropriately vested in an agency which would be relatively immune from the "political winds that sweep Washington." H.R. Rep. No. 93-975, at 44, 70. It therefore created an independent agency, the CFTC, and entrusted to it sweeping authority to implement the CEA.

Among the duties assigned to the CFTC was the administration of a reparations procedure through which disgruntled customers of professional commodity brokers could seek redress for the brokers' violations of the Act or CFTC regulations. Thus, §14 of the CEA, 7 U.S.C. §18 (1976 ed.), provides that any person injured by such violations may apply to the Commission for an order directing the offender to pay reparations to the complainant and may enforce that order in federal district court. Congress intended this administrative procedure to be an "inexpensive and expeditious" alternative to existing fora available to aggrieved customers, namely, the courts and arbitration. . . .

In conformance with the congressional goal of promoting efficient dispute resolution, the CFTC promulgated a regulation in 1976 which allows it to adjudicate counterclaims "aris[ing] out of the transaction or occurrence or series of transactions or occurrences set forth in the complaint." [41 Fed. Reg.] at 3995, 4002 (codified at 17 CFR §12-23(b)(2) (1983)). This permissive counterclaim rule leaves the respondent in a reparations proceeding free to seek relief against the reparations complainant in other fora.

The instant dispute arose in February 1980, when respondents Schor and Mortgage Services of America, Inc., invoked the CFTC's reparations jurisdiction by filing complaints against petitioner ContiCommodity Services, Inc. (Conti), a commodity futures broker, and Richard L. Sandor, a Conti employee. Schor had an account with Conti which contained a debit balance because Schor's net futures trading losses and expenses, such as commissions, exceeded the funds deposited in the account. Schor alleged that this debit balance was the result of Conti's numerous violations of the CEA. . . .

Before receiving notice that Schor had commenced the reparations proceeding, Conti had filed a diversity action in Federal District Court to recover the debit balance. Schor counterclaimed in this action, reiterating his charges that the debit balance was due to Conti's violations of the CEA. Schor also moved on two separate occasions to dismiss or stay the District Court action, arguing that the continuation of the federal action would be a waste of judicial resources and an undue burden on the litigants in view of the fact that "[t]he reparations proceedings . . . will fully . . . resolve and adjudicate all the rights of the parties to this action with respect to the transactions which are the subject matter of this action." . . .

Although the District Court declined to stay or dismiss the suit, Conti voluntarily dismissed the federal court action and presented its debit balance claim by way of a counterclaim in the CFTC reparations proceeding. Conti denied violating the CEA and instead insisted that the debit balance resulted from Schor's trading, and was therefore a simple debt owed by Schor.

After discovery, briefing, and a hearing, the Administrative Law Judge (ALJ) in Schor's reparations proceeding ruled in Conti's favor on both Schor's claims and Conti's counterclaims. After this ruling, Schor for the first time challenged the CFTC's statutory authority to adjudicate Conti's counterclaim. The ALJ rejected Schor's challenge, stating himself "bound by agency regulations and published agency policies." The Commission declined to review the decision and allowed it to become final, at which point Schor filed a petition for review with the Court of Appeals for the District of Columbia Circuit. Prior to oral argument, the Court of Appeals, *sua sponte,* raised the question whether CFTC could constitutionally adjudicate Conti's counterclaims in light of *Northern Pipeline.* . . .

After briefing and argument, the Court of Appeals upheld the CFTC's decision on Schor's claim in most respects, but ordered the dismissal of Conti's counterclaims on the ground that "the CFTC lacks authority (subject matter competence) to adjudicate" common law counterclaims. . . .

We . . . granted certiorari, and now reverse.

II

. . . Assuming that the Court of Appeals correctly discerned a "serious" constitutional problem in the CFTC's adjudication of Conti's counterclaim, we nevertheless believe that the court was mistaken in finding that the CEA could fairly be read to preclude the CFTC's exercise of jurisdiction over that counterclaim. Our examination of the CEA and its legislative history and purpose reveals that Congress plainly intended the CFTC to decide counterclaims asserted by respondents in reparations proceedings, and just as plainly delegated to the CFTC the authority to fashion its counterclaim jurisdiction in the manner the CFTC determined necessary to further the purposes of the reparations program. . . .

We therefore are squarely faced with the question whether the CFTC's assumption of jurisdiction over common law counterclaims violates Article III of the Constitution.

III

Article III, §1, directs that the "judicial Power of the United States shall be vested in one supreme Court and in such inferior Courts as the Congress may from time to time ordain and establish," and provides that these federal courts shall be staffed by judges who hold office during good behavior, and whose compensation shall not be diminished during tenure in office. Schor claims that these provisions prohibit Congress from authorizing the initial adjudication of common law counterclaims by the CFTC, an administrative agency whose adjudicatory officers do not enjoy the tenure and salary protections embodied in Article III.

Although our precedents in this area do not admit of easy synthesis, they do establish that the resolution of claims such as Schor's cannot turn on conclusory reference to the language of Article III. Rather, the constitutionality of a given congressional delegation of adjudicative functions to a non–Article III body must be assessed by reference to the purposes underlying the requirements of Article III. . . .

A

Article III, §1, serves both to protect "the role of the independent judiciary within the constitutional scheme of tripartite government," *Thomas* at 583, and to safeguard litigants' "right to have claims decided before judges who are free from potential domination by other branches of government." United States v. Will, 449 U.S. 200, 218 (1980). Although our cases have provided us with little occasion to discuss the nature or significance of this latter safeguard, our prior discussions of Article III, §1's guarantee of an independent and impartial adjudication by the federal judiciary of matters within the judicial power of the United States intimated that this guarantee serves to protect primarily personal, rather than structural, interests. . . .

Our precedents also demonstrate, however, that Article III does not confer on litigants an absolute right to the plenary consideration of every nature of claim by an Article III court. Moreover, as a personal right, Article III's guarantee of an impartial and independent federal adjudication is subject to waiver, just as are other personal constitutional rights that dictate the procedures by which civil and criminal matters must be tried. . . .

In the instant cases, Schor indisputably waived any right he may have possessed to the full trial of Conti's counterclaim before an Article III court. Schor expressly demanded that Conti proceed on its counterclaim in the reparations proceeding rather than before the District Court, and was content to have the entire dispute settled in the forum he had selected until the ALJ ruled against him on all counts; it was only after the ALJ rendered a decision to which he objected that Schor raised any challenge to the CFTC's consideration of Conti's counterclaim.

Even were there no evidence of an express waiver here, Schor's election to forgo his right to proceed in state or federal court on his claim and his decision to seek relief instead in a CFTC reparations proceeding constituted an effective waiver. Three years before Schor instituted his reparations action, a private right of action under the CEA was explicitly recognized in the Circuit in which Schor and Conti filed suit in District Court. *See* Hirk v. Agri-Research Council, Inc., 561 F.2d 96, 103, n.8 (7th Cir. 1977). . . . Moreover, at the time Schor decided to seek relief before the CFTC rather than in the federal courts, the CFTC's regulations made clear that it was empowered to adjudicate all counterclaims "aris[ing] out of the same transaction or occurrence or series of transactions or occurrences set forth in the complaint." 41 Fed. Reg. 3995 (1976) (codified in 17 CFR §12.23(b)(2) (1983)). Thus, Schor had the option of having the common law counterclaim against him adjudicated in a federal Article III court, but, with full knowledge that the CFTC would exercise jurisdiction over that claim, chose to avail himself of the quicker and less expensive procedure Congress had provided him. In such circumstances, it is clear that Schor effectively agreed to an adjudication by the CFTC of the entire controversy by seeking relief in this alternative forum.

B

As noted above, our precedents establish that Article III, §1, not only preserves to litigants their interest in an impartial and independent federal adjudication of claims within the judicial power of the United States, but also serves as "an inseparable element of the constitutional system of checks and balances." *Northern Pipeline,* 458 U.S., at 58. Article III, §1 safeguards the role of the Judicial Branch in our tripartite system by barring congressional attempts "to transfer jurisdiction [to non–Article III tribunals] for the purpose of emasculating" constitutional courts, National Insurance Co. v. Tidewater Co., 337 U.S. 582, 644 (1949) (Vinson, C.J., dissenting), and thereby preventing "the encroachment or aggrandizement of one branch at the expense of the other." Buckley v. Valeo, 424 U.S. 1, 122 (1976) (per curiam). To the extent that this structural principle is implicated in a given case, the parties cannot by consent cure the constitutional difficulty for the same reason that the parties by consent cannot confer on federal courts subject-matter jurisdiction beyond the limitations imposed by Article III, §2. When these Article III limitations are at issue, notions of consent and waiver cannot be dispositive because the limitations serve institutional interests that the parties cannot be expected to protect.

In determining the extent to which a given congressional decision to authorize the adjudication of Article III business in a non–Article III tribunal impermissibly threatens the institutional integrity of the Judicial Branch, the Court has declined to adopt formalistic and unbending rules. Although such rules might lend a greater degree of coherence to this area of the law, they might also unduly constrict Congress' ability to take needed and innovative action pursuant to its Article I powers. Thus, in reviewing Article III challenges, we have weighed a number of factors, none of which has been deemed determinative, with an eye to the practical effect that the congressional action will have on the constitutionally assigned role of the federal judiciary. Among the factors upon which we have focused are the extent to which the "essential attributes of judicial power" are reserved to Article III courts, and, conversely, the extent to which the non–Article III forum exercises the range of jurisdiction and powers normally vested only in Article III courts, the origins and importance of the right to be adjudicated, and the concerns that drove Congress to depart from the requirements of Article III.

An examination of the relative allocation of powers between the CFTC and Article III courts in light of the considerations given prominence in our precedents demonstrates that the congressional scheme does not impermissibly intrude on the province of the judiciary. The CFTC's adjudicatory powers depart from the traditional agency model in just one respect: the CFTC's juris-diction over common law counterclaims. While wholesale importation of con-cepts of pendent or ancillary jurisdiction into the agency context may create greater constitutional difficulties, we decline to endorse an absolute prohibition on such jurisdiction out of fear of where some hypothetical "slippery slope" may deposit us. . . .

The CFTC, like the agency in *Crowell,* deals only with a "particularized area of law," *Northern Pipeline, supra,* 458 U.S., at 85, whereas the jurisdiction of the bankruptcy courts found unconstitutional in *Northern Pipeline* extended to broadly "all civil proceedings arising under title 11 or arising in or *related to* cases under title 11." 28 U.S.C. §1471(b). . . . CFTC orders, like those of the agency in *Crowell,* but unlike those of the bankruptcy courts under the 1978 Act, are enforceable only by order of the district court. CFTC orders are also reviewed under the same "weight of the evidence" standard sustained in *Crowell,* rather than the more deferential standard found lacking in *Northern Pipeline.* The legal rulings of the CFTC, like the legal determinations of the agency in *Crowell,* are subject to *de novo* review. Finally, the CFTC, unlike the bankruptcy courts under the 1978 Act, does not exercise "all ordinary powers of district courts," and thus may not, for instance, preside over jury trials or issue writs of habeas corpus.

Of course, the nature of the claim has significance in our Article III analysis quite apart from the method prescribed for its adjudication. The counterclaim asserted in this litigation is a "private" right for which state law provides the rule of decision. It is therefore a claim of the kind assumed to be at the "core" of matters normally reserved to Article III courts. Yet this conclusion does not end our inquiry; just as this Court has rejected any attempt to make determinative for Article III purposes the distinction between public rights and private rights, there is no reason inherent in separation of powers principles to accord the state law character of a claim talismanic power in Article III inquiries.

We have explained that "the public rights doctrine reflects simply a prag-matic understanding that when Congress selects a quasi-judicial method of resolving matters that 'could be conclusively determined by the Executive and Legislative Branches,' the danger of encroaching on the judicial powers" is less than when private rights, which are normally within the purview of the judi-ciary, are relegated as an initial matter to administrative adjudication. Similarly, the state law character of a claim is significant for purposes of determining the effect that an initial adjudication of those claims by a non–Article III tribunal will have on the separation of powers for the simple reason that private, com-mon law rights were historically the types of matters subject to resolution by Article III courts. The risk that Congress may improperly have encroached on the federal judiciary is obviously magnified when Congress "withdraw[s] from judicial cognizance any matter which, from its nature, is the subject of a suit at the common law, or in equity, or admiralty" and which therefore had tradition-ally been tried in Article III courts, and allocates the decision of those matters to a non–Article III forum of its own creation. Accordingly, where private, common law rights are at stake, our examination of the congressional attempt to control the manner in which those rights are adjudicated has been searching. In this litigation, however, "[l]ooking beyond form to the substance of what" Congress has done, we are persuaded that the congressional authorization of limited CFTC jurisdiction over a narrow class of common law claims as an incident to the CFTC's primary, and unchallenged, adjudicative function does not create a substantial threat to the separation of powers.

It is clear that Congress has not attempted to "withdraw from judicial cognizance" the determination of Conti's right to the sum represented by the debit balance in Schor's account. Congress gave the CFTC the authority to adjudicate such matters, but the decision to invoke this forum is left entirely to the parties and the power of the federal judiciary to take jurisdiction of these matters is unaffected. In such circumstances, separation of powers concerns are diminished, for it seems self-evident that just as Congress may encourage parties to settle a dispute out of court or resort to arbitration without impermissible incursions on the separation of powers, Congress may make available a quasi-judicial mechanism through which willing parties may, at their option, elect to resolve their differences. This is not to say, of course, that if Congress created a phalanx of non–Article III tribunals equipped to handle the entire business of the Article III courts without any Article III supervision or control and without evidence of valid and specific legislative necessities, the fact that the parties had the election to proceed in their forum of choice would necessarily save the scheme from constitutional attack. But this case obviously bears no resemblance to such a scenario, given the degree of judicial control saved to the federal courts, as well as the congressional purpose behind the jurisdictional delegation, the demonstrated need for the delegation, and the limited nature of the delegation.

When Congress authorized the CFTC to adjudicate counterclaims, its primary focus was on making effective a specific and limited federal regulatory scheme, not on allocating jurisdiction among federal tribunals. Congress intended to create an inexpensive and expeditious alternative forum through which customers could enforce the provisions of the CEA against professional brokers. Its decision to endow the CFTC with jurisdiction over such reparations claims is readily understandable given the perception that the CFTC was relatively immune from political pressures, and the obvious expertise that the Commission possesses in applying the CEA and its own regulations. . . .

It also bears emphasis that the CFTC's assertion of counterclaim jurisdiction is limited to that which is necessary to make the reparations procedure workable. The CFTC adjudication of common law counterclaims is incidental to, and completely dependent upon, adjudication of reparations claims created by federal law, and in actual fact is limited to claims arising out of the same transaction or occurrence as the reparations claim.

In such circumstances, the magnitude of any intrusion on the Judicial Branch can only be termed *de minimis*. . . .

Nor does our decision in Bowsher v. Synar, 478 U.S. 714 (1986), require a contrary result. Unlike *Bowsher*, this case raises no question of the aggrandizement of congressional power at the expense of a coordinate branch. Instead, the separation of powers question presented in this litigation is whether Congress impermissibly undermined, without appreciable expansion of its own power, the role of the Judicial Branch. In any case, we have, consistent with *Bowsher*, looked to a number of factors in evaluating the extent to which the congressional scheme endangers separation of powers principles under the circumstances presented, but have found no genuine threat to those principles to be present in this litigation. . . .

C

. . . The judgment of the Court of Appeals for the District of Columbia Circuit is reversed, and the case is remanded for further proceedings consistent with this opinion.

It is so ordered.

JUSTICE BRENNAN, with whom JUSTICE MARSHALL joins, dissenting. . . .

On its face, Article III, §1, seems to prohibit the vesting of *any* judicial functions in either the Legislative or the Executive Branch. The Court has, however, recognized three narrow exceptions to the otherwise absolute mandate of Article III: territorial courts, courts-martial, and courts that adjudicate certain disputes concerning public rights. Unlike the Court, I would limit the judicial authority of non–Article III federal tribunals to these few, long-established exceptions and would countenance no further erosion of Article III's mandate.

I

The Framers knew that "[t]he accumulation of all powers, Legislative, Executive, and Judiciary, in the same hands, whether of one, a few, or many, and whether hereditary, self-appointed, or elective, may justly be pronounced the very definition of tyranny." The Federalist No. 46, p. 334 (H. Dawson ed. 1876) (J. Madison). . . . The federal judicial power, then, must be exercised by judges who are independent of the Executive and the Legislature in order to maintain the checks and balances that are crucial to our constitutional structure.

The Framers also understood that a principal benefit of the separation of the judicial power from the legislative and executive powers would be the protection of individual litigants from decisionmakers susceptible to majoritarian pressures. . . .

These important functions of Article III are too central to our constitutional scheme to risk their incremental erosion. . . .

II

. . . The Court requires that the legislative interest in convenience and efficiency be weighed against the competing interest in judicial independence. In doing so, the Court pits an interest the benefits of which are immediate, concrete, and easily understood against one, the benefits of which are almost entirely prophylactic, and thus often seem remote and not worth the cost in any single case. Thus, while this balancing creates the illusion of objectivity and ineluctability, in fact the result was foreordained, because the balance is weighted against judicial independence. The danger of the Court's balancing approach is, of course, that as individual cases accumulate in which the Court finds that the short-term benefits of efficiency outweigh the long-term benefits of judicial independence, the protections of Article III will be eviscerated. . . .

III

According to the Court, the intrusion into the province of the Federal Judiciary caused by the CFTC's authority to adjudicate state-law counterclaims is insignificant, both because the CFTC *shares* in, rather than displaces, federal district court jurisdiction over these claims and because only a very narrow class of state-law issues are involved. The "sharing" justification fails under the reasoning used by the Court to support the CFTC's authority. If the administrative reparations proceeding is so much more convenient and efficient than litigation in federal district court that abrogation of Article III's commands is warranted, it seems to me that complainants would rarely, if ever, choose to go to district court in the first instance. Thus, any "sharing" of jurisdiction is more illusory than real.

More importantly, the Court, in emphasizing that *this litigation* will permit solely a narrow class of state-law claims to be decided by a non–Article III court, ignores the fact that it establishes a broad principle. The decision today may authorize the administrative adjudication only of state-law claims that stem from the same transaction or set of facts that allow the customer of a professional commodity broker to initiate reparations proceedings before the CFTC, but the *reasoning* of this decision strongly suggests that, given "legislative necessity" and party consent, any federal agency may decide state-law issues that are ancillary to federal issues within the agency's jurisdiction. . . .

NOTES AND QUESTIONS

1. *Public and private rights.* What is left of *Crowell*'s distinction between "public" and "private" rights after *Northern Pipeline, Thomas,* and *Schor*? Did the distinction ever make any sense? Think of a criminal prosecution as the archetype of a "public rights" dispute, and a tort or contract suit as the archetype of a "private rights" dispute. Which better represents the historical "core" function of the judiciary? In which context is it more important, as a matter of justice, to utilize an independent arbiter?

Note that Conti's counterclaim is about as traditional a "private rights" matter as one is likely to find. Is the key to the Court's decision upholding the CFTC's jurisdiction the fact that Schor waived his right to have the counterclaim tried by an Article III court? Or is it the fact that the counterclaim was ancillary to a "public-law" reparations claim?

2. *The next chapter.* In 2011, the Court again addressed the constitutional limits of delegation of judicial authority. In so doing, it showed signs of reverting back to the public rights/private rights distinction that was seemingly abolished by *Thomas* and *Schor*.

STERN v. MARSHALL, 564 U.S. 462 (2011): Vickie Lynn Marshall—also known as Anna Nicole Smith—filed a bankruptcy petition in a California bankruptcy court. The case was part of a series of suits stemming from the contest over the assets of billionaire oilman J. Howard Marshall, some in state probate court in Texas and others in federal and state courts in California. The 89-year-old Marshall had married then 26-year-old exotic dancer Vickie, made lifetime gifts of several million dollars to her, but had not named her in his will. Marshall died not long after. Vickie petitioned the Texas probate court for a declaration that she was entitled to half of Marshall's assets. She then filed a bankruptcy petition in California asserting that a default judgment against her for sexual harassment (of her personal assistant) rendered her bankrupt. Her stepson (who was Marshall's principal heir and trustee) filed a petition in the bankruptcy proceeding, asking the court to acknowledge that the bankruptcy proceeding would not affect potential state court defamation claims against Vickie. Vickie, in turn, filed a counterclaim against her stepson, contending that he had tortiously interfered with a gift she expected to receive from her late husband. The bankruptcy court granted Vickie summary judgment on the defamation claim and awarded her over $400 million in damages for her tortious interference claim. The question of whether Article III allowed the bankruptcy court to enter judgment on Vickie's counterclaim ultimately reached the Supreme Court. Chief Justice Roberts's majority opinion had this to say:

> Article III could neither serve its purpose in the system of checks and balances nor preserve the integrity of judicial decisionmaking if the other branches of the Federal Government could confer the Government's "judicial Power" on entities outside Article III. That is why we have long recognized that, in general, Congress may not "withdraw from judicial cognizance any matter which, from its nature, is the subject of a suit at the common law, or in equity, or admiralty." Murray's Lessee v. Hoboken Land & Improvement Co., 59 U.S. 272 (1856). When a suit is made of "the stuff of the traditional actions at common law tried by the courts at Westminster in 1789," *Northern Pipeline*, 458 U.S., at 90 (Rehnquist, J., concurring in judgment), and is brought within the bounds of federal jurisdiction, the responsibility for deciding that suit rests with Article III judges in Article III courts. . . .
>
> The plurality in *Northern Pipeline* recognized that there was a category of cases involving "public rights" that Congress could constitutionally assign to "legislative" courts for resolution. That opinion concluded that this "public rights" exception extended "only to matters arising between" individuals and the Government "in connection with the performance of the constitutional functions of the executive or legislative departments . . . that historically could have been determined exclusively by those" branches. *Id.*, at 67-68 (internal quotation marks omitted). A full majority of the Court, while not agreeing on the scope of the exception, concluded that the doctrine did not encompass adjudication of the state law claim at issue in that case. *Id.*, at 69-72. . . .
>
> Vickie and the dissent argue that the Bankruptcy Court's entry of final judgment on her state common law counterclaim was constitutional. . . . We disagree. It is clear that the Bankruptcy Court in this case exercised the "judicial Power of the United States" in purporting to resolve and enter final judgment on a state common law claim, just as the court did in *Northern Pipeline*. No "public right" exception excuses the failure to comply with Article III in doing so, any more than in *Northern Pipeline*. . . .
>
> Vickie's counterclaim cannot be deemed a matter of "public right" that can be decided outside the Judicial Branch. . . . [I]n *Northern Pipeline* we rejected the argument that the public rights doctrine permitted a bankruptcy court to adjudicate a state law suit brought by a debtor against a company that had not filed a claim against the estate. Although our discussion of the public rights exception since that time has not been entirely consistent, and the exception has been the subject of some debate, this case does not fall within any of the various formulations of the concept that appear in this Court's opinions. . . .

Shortly after *Northern Pipeline*, the Court rejected the limitation of the public rights exception to actions involving the Government as a party. The Court has continued, however, to limit the exception to cases in which the claim at issue derives from a federal regulatory scheme, or in which resolution of the claim by an expert government agency is deemed essential to a limited regulatory objective within the agency's authority. In other words, it is still the case that what makes a right "public" rather than private is that the right is integrally related to particular federal government action. *See* United States v. Jicarilla Apache Nation, 564 U.S. 162, 173-74 (2011) ("The distinction between 'public rights' against the Government and 'private rights' between private parties is well established[.]").

Vickie's counterclaim . . . does not fall within any of the varied formulations of the public rights exception in this Court's cases. It is not a matter that can be pursued only by grace of the other branches, as in *Murray's Lessee*, or one that "historically could have been determined exclusively by" those branches, *Northern Pipeline*, at 68. The claim is instead one under state common law between two private parties. . . .

In addition, Vickie's claimed right to relief does not flow from a federal statutory scheme, as in *Thomas*. It is not "completely dependent upon" adjudication of a claim created by federal law, as in *Schor*. And in contrast to the objecting party in *Schor*, [Vickie's brother-in-law] did not truly consent to resolution of Vickie's claim in the bankruptcy court proceedings. He had nowhere else to go if he wished to recover from Vickie's estate.

Furthermore, the asserted authority to decide Vickie's claim is not limited to a "particularized area of the law," as in *Crowell*, *Thomas*, and *Schor*. We deal here not with an agency but with a court, with substantive jurisdiction reaching any area of the *corpus juris*. This is not a situation in which Congress devised an "expert and inexpensive method for dealing with a class of questions of fact which are particularly suited to examination and determination by an administrative agency specially assigned to that task." *Crowell*, 285 U.S., at 46. The "experts" in the federal system at resolving common law counterclaims such as Vickie's are the Article III courts, and it is with those courts that her claim must stay. . . .

We recognize that there may be instances in which the distinction between public and private rights—at least as framed by some of our recent cases—fails to provide concrete guidance as to whether, for example, a particular agency can adjudicate legal issues under a substantive regulatory scheme. Given the extent to which this case is so markedly distinct from the agency cases discussing the public rights exception in the context of such a regime, however, we do not in this opinion express any view on how the doctrine might apply in that different context.

What is plain here is that this case involves the most prototypical exercise of judicial power: the entry of a final, binding judgment *by a court* with broad substantive jurisdiction, on a common law cause of action, when the action neither derives from nor depends upon any agency regulatory regime. If such an exercise of judicial power may nonetheless be taken from the Article III Judiciary simply by deeming it part of some amorphous "public right," "then Article III would be transformed from the guardian of individual liberty and separation of powers we have long recognized into mere wishful thinking." . . .

Article III of the Constitution provides that the judicial power of the United States may be vested only in courts whose judges enjoy the protections set forth in that Article. We conclude today that Congress, in one isolated respect, exceeded that limitation in the Bankruptcy Act of 1984. The Bankruptcy Court below lacked the constitutional authority to enter a final judgment on a state law counterclaim that is not resolved in the process of ruling on a creditor's proof of claim. Accordingly, the judgment of the Court of Appeals is affirmed.

Justice Breyer filed a dissenting opinion, joined by Justices Ginsburg, Sotomayor, and Kagan. The dissent argued that under *Schor*, the Court should have upheld Bankruptcy Court adjudication of counterclaims like the one at issue in *Stern*.

NOTES AND QUESTIONS

1. *Whither (or wither)* Schor*?* The dissent in *Stern* accused the majority of abandoning the pragmatic approach applied in *Schor*—which, as you will recall, examined several factors to determine whether a delegation constitutes an impermissible encroachment on Article III authority—in favor of a formalistic approach grounded in the opaque public rights/private rights distinction. Is the dissent right? Does the majority overemphasize the plurality opinion in *Northern Pipeline*, while underemphasizing *Thomas* and *Schor*, both of which commanded clear majorities? Is the majority signaling its view that *Thomas* and *Schor* are mistakes, out of line with broader doctrines on the authority exercisable by non–Article III officials, that should be de-emphasized or possibly overruled if the right case presented that issue? Or does something else explain the majority's treatment of these cases?

Even if the analysis in *Stern* diverges from that in *Schor*, what effect does this have on administrative agencies' power to adjudicate "private" claims and counterclaims within their regulatory jurisdiction? On its face, *Stern* would seem to leave considerable space for such adjudication by expert agencies because the "public right" exception would apply in a great many circumstances under the majority's reasoning. Notice how the Court makes clear that "agency cases" implicating substantive regulatory expertise (presumably what agencies develop under complex, relatively comprehensive regulatory schemes) are "markedly distinct" from the situation in *Stern*. Nonetheless, doesn't the "mood" of *Stern*, as compared to that in *Schor*, suggest that the Court may make future attempts to cut back on congressional delegations of judicial authority?

The implication that *Stern* signaled an abandonment of *Schor*'s multi-factorial test was undercut by six members of the Court in Wellness International Network, Ltd. v. Sharif, 135 S. Ct. 1932 (2015). The issue was whether a bankruptcy court could constitutionally adjudicate a state-law claim (a so-called "*Stern* claim") so long as the litigant consented. Writing for a five-member majority, Justice Sotomayor declared that: "Applying [the *Schor*] factors, we conclude that allowing bankruptcy litigants to waive the right to Article III adjudication of *Stern* claims does not usurp the constitutional prerogatives of Article III courts." Justice Alito, concurring, agreed that *Schor* provided the correct methodology for resolving the issue, but disagreed with the Court on what constituted "consent" for a waiver. Not surprisingly (given his majority opinion in *Stern*), Chief Justice Roberts dissented, arguing that the structural (separation-of-powers) interests served by Article III could not be waived by a private litigant (nor, indeed, even by the government). Does the majority's decision repudiate the *Schor* Court's decision to reach Schor's Article III challenge to the jurisdiction of the CFTC despite the fact that Schor not only explicitly consented to agency adjudication but insisted that his claim be heard in that forum? Or might Wellness's waiver doctrine apply only in the bankruptcy court context, where a wide variety of non–Article III claims with no connection to federal substantive law are likely to reach federal tribunals?

2. *What are "public rights"?* Was the Chief Justice correct in *Stern* to characterize claims between two private parties that derive "from a federal regulatory scheme" in cases like *Schor* as "public rights"? Did the Court in *Schor* really characterize the broker's counterclaim in that case as a "public right?" Does this reasoning perhaps signal the Chief Justice's preference for a categorical approach over the *Schor* Court's multi-factor test? Which of these approaches does the better job at implementing the lines drawn in the Constitution around judicial and executive powers?

In Oil States Energy Services, LLC v. Greene's Energy Group, LLC, 138 S. Ct. 1365 (2018), the Court, in an opinion by Justice Thomas, decided that the Patent Trial and Appeals Board (PTAB) could constitutionally consider challenges to patents that had been previously granted by the Patent and Trademark Office. Although challenges are brought to the PTAB by a private party against another private party, the Court held that a challenge to the validity of a patent falls into the "public rights" category since the grant of a patent has long been viewed as a public right, running from the government to a private party. The Court noted that "granting patents is one of the constitutional functions that can be carried out by the executive or legislative departments without judicial determination." 138 S. Ct., at 1374. Does this help delineate the scope of the "public rights" doctrine?

3. *Other constitutional limitations on delegation of adjudicative power to agencies.* With the exceptions of cases like *Crowell, Northern Pipeline,* and *Stern,* Article III has not proved to be a serious obstacle to conferring power on administrative agencies to adjudicate claims arising under federal statutes. Nor has the Seventh Amendment, which preserves the right of jury trial in "suits at common law, where the value in controversy shall exceed twenty dollars." To be sure, the Court has held the Seventh Amendment applicable to the enforcement of statutorily created rights. For example, in Tull v. United States, 481 U.S. 412 (1987), the Court held that the Seventh Amendment requires a jury trial in a case brought by the United States in federal district court under the Clean Water Act for injunctive relief and civil money penalties, but the trial judge may assess the penalty once the jury has found a violation. In Granfinanciera, S.A. v. Nordberg, 492 U.S. 33 (1989), the Court found a right to a jury trial for parties to a bankruptcy proceeding who were being sued by the trustee in bankruptcy to recover allegedly fraudulent conveyances. "If a statutory right is not closely intertwined with a federal regulatory program Congress has power to enact, and if that right neither belongs to nor exists against the Federal Government, then it must be adjudicated by an Article III Court. If the right is legal in nature, then it carries with it the Seventh Amendment's guarantee of a jury trial." *Id.* at 55.

Nonetheless, during a stretch of at least four decades (from the 1930s through the 1970s) the Court frequently acquiesced in congressional decisions to confer power to adjudicate statutory claims upon administrative agencies (operating without the aid of juries). *See, e.g.,* NLRB v. Jones & Laughlin Steel Corp., 301 U.S. 1 (1937) (upholding NLRB back-pay award against employer for committing an unfair labor practice); Atlas Roofing Co. v. Occupational Safety & Health Review Commn., 430 U.S. 442 (1977) (upholding OSHRC civil money penalty order against employer for violating safety standard).

Nor was the Sixth Amendment's guarantee of a jury trial in "criminal prosecutions" a serious obstacle to administrative adjudication authority during this time period. Although regulatory enforcement proceedings often resemble criminal prosecutions, modern courts have been reluctant to disturb the legislature's characterization of a regulatory scheme as "civil." Thus, for example, the Supreme Court has upheld the authority of administrative agencies to adjudicate claims for "civil" fines (usually called "civil money penalties"). Helvering v. Mitchell, 303 U.S. 391 (1938); Lloyd Sabaudo S.A. v. Elting, 287 U.S. 329 (1932). The only clear restriction on administrative enforcement power involves the sanction of imprisonment; only the judicial branch may sentence a person to prison. Wong Wing v. United States, 163 U.S. 228 (1896).

In Federal Maritime Commission v. South Carolina State Ports Authority, 535 U.S. 743 (2002), the Supreme Court recognized one, albeit rather minor, constitutional constraint on the adjudicative powers of administrative agencies: namely, that states enjoy the same sovereign immunity from suit in a federal administrative agency as they enjoy in federal court. In *SCSPA,* a cruise line operator brought a complaint in the FMC against a state port authority, alleging that it had denied the operator permission to berth its ships at the authority's terminals, in violation of federal law, and seeking damages and an injunction. The Supreme Court ruled that the SCSPA enjoyed sovereign immunity from such a proceeding, noting the numerous similarities between an FMC adjudication and a civil action in federal court.

Does the fact that the *Granfinanciera, South Carolina State Ports Authority,* and *Stern* decisions all post-date *Thomas* and *Schor,* while many of the cases arguably supporting *Thomas* and *Schor* are from the 1930s, suggest that the trend is toward more reliance on categorical assignments of constitutional authority? Does it indicate that the Court is divided on how to analyze the degree to which non–Article III officials can exercise adjudicative authority and still is groping for an approach that satisfactorily separates the proper from improper assignments? Is bankruptcy a special arena that will be handled under different rules than the run of "ordinary" agency adjudication?

B.   DUE PROCESS HEARING RIGHTS

The more significant and interesting legal questions posed by administrative adjudication concern the procedures that agencies must follow when they engage in adjudication. Administrative agencies lack some of the structural protections against misuse of adjudicative power inherent in the common law jury system or the Article III judiciary. For that reason, procedural protections ought to loom especially large in any system designed to legitimize administrative adjudication. Under federal law there are three primary sources of such procedural protections: (1) the Due Process Clauses of the Fifth and Fourteenth Amendments to the Constitution; (2) the Administrative Procedure Act, especially §§554, 556, and 557; and (3) procedural provisions of specific enabling statutes. Because the Due Process Clauses set a floor on the level of procedural formality for all administrative adjudication, both state and federal, we devote the bulk of this chapter to exploring the elements of administrative due process.

The final section of the chapter examines the regime of additional procedural protections afforded by the APA.

1. The Interests Protected by Due Process

The Due Process Clauses of the Fifth and Fourteenth Amendments prohibit the federal and state governments, respectively, from depriving individuals of "life, liberty, or property, without due process of law." At one time, the Due Process Clauses were thought to protect only those individual interests protected at common law, such as real estate, personal possessions, or bodily integrity. Interests created by the legislature, such as a government license, job, or contract, were classified as "privileges" not protected by due process. In Bailey v. Richardson, 182 F.2d 46 (D.C. Cir. 1950), *aff'd by an equally divided Court,* 341 U.S. 918 (1951), for example, the court turned a deaf ear to the plea of a government worker who had been summarily discharged for "disloyalty," despite her denial of the government's undocumented allegations. The court said, "It has been held repeatedly and consistently that Government employ is not 'property' and that in this particular [instance] it is not a contract. We are unable to perceive how it could be held to be 'liberty.' Certainly, it is not 'life.'"

Over the next two decades, however, the "right-privilege" distinction began to erode as courts found creative ways to afford procedural protection to untraditional interests. In Greene v. McElroy, 360 U.S. 474 (1959), the Supreme Court used a strained interpretation of the applicable statute to require the government to afford a hearing to a worker before withdrawing his security clearance. While denying the relief sought by another employee in Cafeteria & Restaurant Workers Union v. McElroy, 367 U.S. 886 (1961), the Court purported to reject the right-privilege distinction in favor of a test that "balanced" the government's and the individual's interests. Meanwhile, some lower courts had begun explicitly to afford constitutional protection to governmentally conferred interests such as education, Dixon v. Alabama State Bd., 294 F.2d 150 (5th Cir.), *cert. denied,* 368 U.S. 930 (1961), and business licenses, Hornsby v. Allen, 326 F.2d 605 (5th Cir. 1964).

Thus matters stood in 1970, when the Supreme Court faced the question of whether the Due Process Clauses afford procedural rights to recipients of public assistance. Until the early twentieth century, responsibility for assisting the poor fell primarily on private charities. That pattern began to change in 1911 with the enactment (by Illinois) of the first "Mother's Assistance" law, requiring county boards to subsidize the care of any dependent or neglected child whose parents were "poor and unable to properly care for the said child, but are otherwise proper guardians." Within ten years, 40 states had such laws. Although voluntary social service agencies continued to distribute most relief funds, by 1929 nearly three-quarters of those funds came from city and county treasuries. *See* June Axinn & Herman Levin, Social Welfare: A History of the American Response to Need (2d ed. 1982).

These piecemeal partnerships between private charities and local governments were no match for the widespread poverty produced by the Great Depression. In 1931 New York became the first state to appropriate funds to be distributed by local relief agencies. Two years later, in the midst of a legislative frenzy that inaugurated Franklin D. Roosevelt's New Deal, Congress enacted the Federal Emergency Relief Act (FERA), ch. 30, 48 Stat. 55 (1933). During the Act's three-year existence, the federal government distributed over $3 billion to local relief agencies. By requiring that federal funds be administered by "public agencies," FERA effectively transformed public assistance from a publicly aided private activity to a fully governmental activity.

FERA's public assistance program was supplanted by the Social Security Act of 1935, ch. 531, 49 Stat. 620 (1935). In addition to establishing a social insurance program for retired workers, the Act created several "categorical aid" programs for the needy, including Old Age Assistance, Aid to the Blind, and Aid to Dependent Children (ADC). Under each of these categorical aid programs, the federal government made matching grants to the states for the administration and distribution of assistance payments. In return, it demanded that the state-run programs conform to certain minimum standards. ADC was clearly the least popular of the Social Security Act programs, as evidenced by its lower benefit levels and smaller federal matching share. ADC continued to languish in political disfavor in succeeding decades, as many states, responding to a gradual loosening of federal controls, adopted tougher eligibility standards, residency requirements, and (from today's perspective, retrograde) "man-in-the-house" prohibitions, in an effort to hold down welfare costs.

In spite of these efforts, growth in the ADC program continued to accelerate during the 1950s and early 1960s. In an effort to stem the tide, Congress amended the Social Security Act in 1962 to increase the federal subsidy for various "rehabilitative" social services provided by the states to help ADC mothers assume self-sufficiency. The amendments renamed the ADC program "Aid for Families with Dependent Children" (AFDC) and offered assistance for the first time to unemployed fathers. By specifying maximum caseload limits and minimum caseworker qualifications, moreover, Congress attempted to upgrade the quality of services to recipients.

Still, the AFDC caseload kept expanding during the 1960s, largely due to a dramatic increase in the number of deserting fathers and illegitimate children. Congress responded by enacting further amendments in 1967 that: (1) imposed a freeze on the number of children who could receive aid due to parental desertion or illegitimacy, and (2) created a Work Incentive Program (briefly known as "WIP," quickly changed to "WIN") to put employable welfare mothers to work. Representative Martha Griffiths's defense of AFDC mothers fell largely on deaf ears:

> Can you imagine any conditions more demoralizing than those welfare mothers live under? Imagine being confined all day every day in a room with falling plaster, inadequately heated in the winter and sweltering in the summer, without enough beds for the family, and with no sheets, the furniture falling apart, a bare bulb in the center of the room as the only light, with no hot water most of the time, plumbing that often does not work, with only the companionship of small children who are often hungry and always inadequately clothed—and, of course, the ever-present rats. To keep one's sanity under such circumstances is a major achievement, and to give children the love and discipline they need for healthy development is superhuman. If one were designing a system to produce alcoholism, crime, and illegitimacy, he could not do better.

114 Cong. Rec. 21,845 (1968). Although the freeze was delayed and later repealed, the 1967 Amendments represented yet another stage in what Gilbert Steiner has called the "tireless tinkering with dependent families." Gilbert Y. Steiner, The State of Welfare (1971) at 31-74.

The ferment surrounding public welfare in the late 1960s is nowhere better dramatized than in New York City. With 10.8 percent of the national AFDC caseload and 22.4 percent of its deserted mothers, New York was indeed welfare's Big Apple in 1967. During the 1960s, the city's welfare rolls tripled, to the point that by 1969 one New Yorker in ten was receiving benefits from the AFDC program. Accompanying the explosion of welfare cases was a rapid surge in militancy among the city's 6,000 caseworkers and 750,000 recipients. Increasingly overworked, harassed, and frustrated, welfare workers walked off the job for six weeks in the summer of 1967, demanding greater fringe benefits for themselves and improved services to recipients.

Meanwhile, previously submissive recipients joined the trend toward demonstrative action. Born of the civil rights movement and fed by small, local welfare groups, the National Welfare Rights Organization (NWRO) provided the focal point for beneficiary activism in the city. Led by NWRO, 2,000 people picketed New York City Hall in June of 1966, demanding higher benefits, improved day care, and an end to welfare investigations. In the following years, NWRO undertook a successful campaign to educate recipients about their rights, resulting in significantly increased outlays for a program of "special grants" for nonrecurring needs. When, in a desperate effort to turn off the faucet, city officials eliminated the program in favor of a uniform $100 per year "flat grant," NWRO organized massive protests that resulted in extensive property damage and numerous arrests.

The lawsuit was another crucial weapon in welfare activists' arsenal. Aided by a growing cadre of "poverty lawyers" supported by foundations and state and federal governments, recipients increasingly turned to the courts to seek both individual redress and systemic reform. In the space of a few months, welfare recipients scored two impressive victories in the Supreme Court, securing judicial invalidation of "man-in-the-house" rules (King v. Smith, 392 U.S. 309 (1968)) and residency requirements (Shapiro v. Thompson, 394 U.S. 618 (1969)).

Another major test involved a challenge to the procedures used to terminate the eligibility of recipients. As AFDC gradually changed from short-term "relief" for a temporary personal need to a source of subsistence for the chronically dependent, the states had placed increasing emphasis on continuing eligibility determinations. Using the evidence gathered by caseworkers in their regular dealings with clients in their homes or at welfare offices, as well as special investigations, welfare agencies attempted to keep abreast of developments in a recipient's life—such as employment, the addition of an income-earner to the household, or the departure of a dependent child—that would justify a reduction or elimination of benefits. Benefits could also be terminated for a recipient's failure to cooperate in providing such information or for not assisting the state to seek indemnification from an absent spouse.

The Social Security Act had, from the beginning, required states to furnish recipients with a "fair hearing" before an independent administrative officer upon termination of benefits. But in New York, like most states, that hearing occurred only after welfare payments had been terminated. Many welfare activists and reformers

viewed the post-termination hearing as inadequate to protect the rights of terminated recipients. The case that follows represents the judicial reaction to this view.

GOLDBERG v. KELLY
397 U.S. 254 (1970)

MR. JUSTICE BRENNAN delivered the opinion of the Court.

The question for decision is whether a State that terminates public assistance
payments to a particular recipient without affording him the opportunity for an
evidentiary hearing prior to termination denies the recipient procedural due
process in violation of the Due Process Clause of the Fourteenth Amendment.

This action was brought in the District Court for the Southern District of
New York by residents of New York City receiving financial aid under the federally assisted program of Aid to Families with Dependent Children (AFDC) or
under New York State's general Home Relief program.[1] Their complaint alleged
that the New York State and New York City officials administering these programs terminated, or were about to terminate, such aid without prior notice and
hearing, thereby denying them due process of law.[2] At the time the suits were
filed there was no requirement of prior notice or hearing of any kind before
termination of financial aid. However, the State and city adopted procedures
for notice and hearing after the suits were brought, and the plaintiffs, appellees
here, then challenged the constitutional adequacy of those procedures. . . .

Pursuant to [these procedures a] caseworker who has doubts about the
recipient's continued eligibility must first discuss them with the recipient. If the
caseworker concludes that the recipient is no longer eligible, he recommends
termination of aid to a unit supervisor. If the latter concurs, he sends the recipient
a letter stating the reasons for proposing to terminate aid and notifying him that
within seven days he may request that a higher official review the record, and may
support the request with a written statement prepared personally or with the aid
of an attorney or other person. If the reviewing official affirms the determination
of ineligibility, aid is stopped immediately and the recipient is informed by letter
of the reasons for the action. Appellees' challenge to this procedure emphasizes
the absence of any provisions for the personal appearance of the recipient before
the reviewing official, for oral presentation of evidence, and for confrontation
and cross-examination of adverse witnesses. However, the letter does inform the
recipient that he may request a post-termination "fair hearing." This is a proceeding before an independent state hearing officer at which the recipient may
appear personally, offer oral evidence, confront and cross-examine the witnesses
against him, and have a record made of the hearing. If the recipient prevails at
the "fair hearing" he is paid all funds erroneously withheld. HEW Handbook, pt.
IV, §§6200-6500; 18 NYCRR §§84.2-84.23. A recipient whose aid is not restored

1. . . . Home Relief is a general assistance program financed and administered solely by New York
state and local governments. N.Y. Social Welfare Law §§157-165 (1966), since July 1, 1967, Social Services
Law §§157-166. It assists any person unable to support himself or to secure support from other sources.
Id., §158.

2. Two suits were brought and consolidated in the District Court. The named plaintiffs were twenty
in number, including intervenors. Fourteen had been or were about to be cut off from AFDC, and six
from Home Relief.

by a "fair hearing" decision may have judicial review. N.Y. Civil Practice Law and Rules, Art. 78 (1963). The recipient is so notified, 18 NYCRR §84.16.

I

The constitutional issue to be decided, therefore, is the narrow one whether the Due Process Clause requires that the recipient be afforded an evidentiary hearing *before* the termination of benefits. The District Court held that only a pre-termination evidentiary hearing would satisfy the constitutional command, and rejected the argument of the state and city officials that the combination of the post-termination "fair hearing" with the informal pre-termination review disposed of all due process claims. . . .

We affirm.

Appellant does not contend that procedural due process is not applicable to the termination of welfare benefits. Such benefits are a matter of statutory entitlement for persons qualified to receive them.[8] Their termination involves state action that adjudicates important rights. The constitutional challenge cannot be answered by an argument that public assistance benefits are "a 'privilege' and not a 'right.'" Shapiro v. Thompson, 394 U.S. 618, 627 n.6 (1969). Relevant constitutional restraints apply as much to the withdrawal of public assistance benefits as to disqualification for unemployment compensation, Sherbert v. Verner, 374 U.S. 398 (1963); or to denial of a tax exemption, Speiser v. Randall, 357 U.S. 513 (1958); or to discharge from public employment, Slochower v. Board of Higher Education, 350 U.S. 551 (1956). The extent to which procedural due process must be afforded the recipient is influenced by the extent to which he may be "condemned to suffer grievous loss," Joint Anti-Fascist Refugee Committee v. McGrath, 341 U.S. 123, 168 (1951) (Frankfurter, J., concurring), and depends upon whether the recipient's interest in avoiding that loss outweighs the governmental interest in summary adjudication. Accordingly, as we said in Cafeteria & Restaurant Workers Union v. McElroy, 367 U.S. 886, 895 (1961), "consideration of what procedures due process may require under any given set of circumstances must begin with a determination of the precise nature of the government function involved as well as of the private interest that has been affected by governmental action." *See also* Hannah v. Larche, 363 U.S. 420, 440, 442 (1960).

---

8. It may be realistic today to regard welfare benefits as more like "property" than a "gratuity." Much of the existing wealth in this country takes the form of rights that do not fall within traditional common-law concepts of property. It has been aptly noted that

> [s]ociety today is built around entitlement. The automobile dealer has his franchise, the doctor and lawyer their professional licenses, the worker his union membership, contract, and pension rights, the executive his contract and stock options; all are devices to aid security and independence. Many of the most important of these entitlements now flow from government: subsidies to farmers and businessmen, routes for airlines and channels for television stations; long term contracts for defense, space, and education; social security pensions for individuals. Such sources of security, whether private or public, are no longer regarded as luxuries or gratuities; to the recipients they are essentials, fully deserved, and in no sense a form of charity. It is only the poor whose entitlements, although recognized by public policy, have not been effectively enforced.

Reich, Individual Rights and Social Welfare: The Emerging Legal Issues, 74 Yale L.J. 1245, 1255 (1965). *See also* Reich, The New Property, 73 Yale L.J. 733 (1964).

It is true, of course, that some governmental benefits may be administratively terminated without affording the recipient a pre-termination evidentiary hearing. But we agree with the District Court that when welfare is discontinued, only a pre-termination evidentiary hearing provides the recipient with procedural due process. *Cf.* Sniadach v. Family Finance Corp., 395 U.S. 337 (1969). For qualified recipients, welfare provides the means to obtain essential food, clothing, housing, and medical care. *Cf.* Nash v. Florida Industrial Commission, 389 U.S. 235, 239 (1967). Thus the crucial factor in this context—a factor not present in the case of the blacklisted government contractor, the discharged government employee, the taxpayer denied a tax exemption, or virtually anyone else whose governmental entitlements are ended—is that termination of aid pending resolution of a controversy over eligibility may deprive an *eligible* recipient of the very means by which to live while he waits. Since he lacks independent resources, his situation becomes immediately desperate. His need to concentrate upon finding the means for daily subsistence, in turn, adversely affects his ability to seek redress from the welfare bureaucracy.

Moreover, important governmental interests are promoted by affording recipients a pre-termination evidentiary hearing. From its founding the Nation's basic commitment has been to foster the dignity and well-being of all persons within its borders. We have come to recognize that forces not within the control of the poor contribute to their poverty. This perception, against the background of our traditions, has significantly influenced the development of the contemporary public assistance system. Welfare, by meeting the basic demands of subsistence, can help bring within the reach of the poor the same opportunities that are available to others to participate meaningfully in the life of the community. At the same time, welfare guards against the societal malaise that may flow from a widespread sense of unjustified frustration and insecurity. Public assistance, then, is not mere charity, but a means to "promote the general Welfare, and secure the Blessings of Liberty to ourselves and our Posterity." The same governmental interests that counsel the provision of welfare, counsel as well its uninterrupted provision to those eligible to receive it; pre-termination evidentiary hearings are indispensable to that end.

Appellant does not challenge the force of these considerations but argues that they are outweighed by countervailing governmental interests in conserving fiscal and administrative resources. These interests, the argument goes, justify the delay of any evidentiary hearing until after discontinuance of the grants. Summary adjudication protects the public fisc by stopping payments promptly upon discovery of reason to believe that a recipient is no longer eligible. Since most terminations are accepted without challenge, summary adjudication also conserves both the fisc and administrative time and energy by reducing the number of evidentiary hearings actually held.

We agree with the District Court, however, that these governmental interests are not overriding in the welfare context. The requirement of a prior hearing doubtless involves some greater expense, and the benefits paid to ineligible recipients pending decision at the hearing probably cannot be recouped, since these recipients are likely to be judgment-proof. But the State is not without weapons to minimize these increased costs. Much of the drain on fiscal and administrative resources can be reduced by developing procedures for prompt pre-termination hearings and by skillful use of personnel and facilities. Indeed, the very provision for a post-termination evidentiary hearing in New York's Home Relief program is itself cogent evidence that the State recognizes the primacy of the public interest in correct eligibility determinations and therefore in the provision of procedural safeguards. Thus, the interest of the eligible recipient in uninterrupted receipt of public assistance, coupled with the State's interest that his payments not be erroneously terminated, clearly outweighs the State's competing concern to prevent any increase in its fiscal and administrative burdens. As the District Court correctly concluded,

> [t]he stakes are simply too high for the welfare recipient, and the possibility for honest error or irritable misjudgment too great, to allow termination of aid without giving the recipient a chance, if he so desires, to be fully informed of the case against him so that he may contest its basis and produce evidence in rebuttal.

294 F. Supp., at 904-905.

II

We also agree with the District Court, however, that the pre-termination hearing need not take the form of a judicial or quasi-judicial trial. We bear in mind that the statutory "fair hearing" will provide the recipient with a full administrative review.[14] Accordingly, the pre-termination hearing has one function only: to produce an initial determination of the validity of the welfare department's grounds for discontinuance of payments in order to protect a recipient against an erroneous termination of his benefits. *Cf.* Sniadach v. Family Finance Corp., 395 U.S. 337, 343 (1969) (Harlan, J., concurring). Thus, a complete record and a comprehensive opinion, which would serve primarily to facilitate judicial review and to guide future decisions, need not be provided at the pre-termination stage. We recognize, too, that both welfare authorities and recipients have an interest in relatively speedy resolution of questions of eligibility, that they are used to dealing with one another informally, and that some welfare departments have very burdensome caseloads. These considerations justify the limitation of the pre-termination hearing to minimum procedural safeguards, adapted to the particular characteristics of welfare recipients, and to the limited nature of the controversies to be resolved. We wish to add that we, no less than the dissenters, recognize the importance of not imposing upon the States or the Federal Government in this developing field of law any procedural requirements beyond those demanded by rudimentary due process.

"The fundamental requisite of due process of law is the opportunity to be heard." Grannis v. Ordean, 234 U.S. 385, 394 (1914). The hearing must be "at a meaningful time and in a meaningful manner." Armstrong v. Manzo, 380 U.S. 545, 552 (1965). In the present context these principles require that a recipient have timely and adequate notice detailing the reasons for a proposed

---

14. Due process does not, of course, require two hearings. If, for example, a State simply wishes to continue benefits until after a "fair" hearing, there will be no need for a preliminary hearing.

termination, and an effective opportunity to defend by confronting any adverse witnesses and by presenting his own arguments and evidence orally. These rights are important in cases such as those before us, where recipients have challenged proposed terminations as resting on incorrect or misleading factual premises or on misapplication of rules or policies to the facts of particular cases.[15]

We are not prepared to say that the seven-day notice currently provided by New York City is constitutionally insufficient per se, although there may be cases where fairness would require that a longer time be given. Nor do we see any constitutional deficiency in the content or form of the notice. New York employs both a letter and a personal conference with a caseworker to inform a recipient of the precise questions raised about his continued eligibility. Evidently the recipient is told the legal and factual bases for the Department's doubts. This combination is probably the most effective method of communicating with recipients.

The city's procedures presently do not permit recipients to appear personally with or without counsel before the official who finally determines continued eligibility. Thus a recipient is not permitted to present evidence to that official orally, or to confront or cross-examine adverse witnesses. These omissions are fatal to the constitutional adequacy of the procedures.

The opportunity to be heard must be tailored to the capacities and circumstances of those who are to be heard.[16] It is not enough that a welfare recipient may present his position to the decision maker in writing or secondhand through his caseworker. Written submissions are an unrealistic option for most recipients, who lack the educational attainment necessary to write effectively and who cannot obtain professional assistance. Moreover, written submissions do not afford the flexibility of oral presentations; they do not permit the recipient to mold his argument to the issues the decision maker appears to regard as important. Particularly where credibility and veracity are at issue, as they must be in many termination proceedings, written submissions are a wholly unsatisfactory basis for decision. The secondhand presentation to the decisionmaker by the caseworker has its own deficiencies; since the caseworker usually gathers the facts upon which the charge of ineligibility rests, the presentation of the recipient's side of the controversy cannot safely be left to him. Therefore a recipient must be allowed to state his position orally. Informal procedures will suffice; in this context due process does not require a particular order of proof or mode of offering evidence. *Cf.* HEW Handbook, pt. IV, §6400(a).

In almost every setting where important decisions turn on questions of fact, due process requires an opportunity to confront and cross-examine adverse witnesses. e.g., ICC v. Louisville & N.R. Co., 227 U.S. 88, 93-94 (1913); Willner v. Committee on Character & Fitness, 373 U.S. 96, 103-104 (1963). What we said

---

15. This case presents no question requiring our determination whether due process requires only an opportunity for written submission, or an opportunity both for written submission and oral argument, where there are no factual issues in dispute or where the application of the rule of law is not intertwined with factual issues. *See* FCC v. WJR, 337 U.S. 265, 275-277 (1949).

16. "[T]he prosecution of an appeal demands a degree of security, awareness, tenacity, and ability which few dependent people have." Wedemeyer & Moore, The American Welfare System, 54 Calif. L. Rev. 326, 342 (1966).

in Greene v. McElroy, 360 U.S. 474, 496-497 (1959), is particularly pertinent here:

> Certain principles have remained relatively immutable in our jurisprudence. One of these is that where governmental action seriously injures an individual, and the reasonableness of the action depends on fact findings, the evidence used to prove the Government's case must be disclosed to the individual so that he has an opportunity to show that it is untrue. While this is important in the case of documentary evidence, it is even more important where the evidence consists of the testimony of individuals whose memory might be faulty or who, in fact, might be perjurers or persons motivated by malice, vindictiveness, intolerance, prejudice, or jealousy. We have formalized these protections in the requirements of confrontation and cross-examination. They have ancient roots. They find expression in the Sixth Amendment. . . . This Court has been zealous to protect these rights from erosion. It has spoken out not only in criminal cases, . . . but also in all types of cases where administrative . . . actions were under scrutiny.

Welfare recipients must therefore be given an opportunity to confront and cross-examine the witnesses relied on by the department.

"The right to be heard would be, in many cases, of little avail if it did not comprehend the right to be heard by counsel." Powell v. Alabama, 287 U.S. 45, 68-69 (1932). We do not say that counsel must be provided at the pre-termination hearing, but only that the recipient must be allowed to retain an attorney if he so desires. Counsel can help delineate the issues, present the factual contentions in an orderly manner, conduct cross-examination, and generally safeguard the interests of the recipient. We do not anticipate that this assistance will unduly prolong or otherwise encumber the hearing. Evidently HEW has reached the same conclusion. . . .

Finally, the decisionmaker's conclusion as to a recipient's eligibility must rest solely on the legal rules and evidence adduced at the hearing. Ohio Bell Tel. Co. v. PUC, 301 U.S. 292 (1937); United States v. Abilene & S.R. Co., 265 U.S. 274, 288-289 (1924). To demonstrate compliance with this elementary requirement, the decision maker should state the reasons for his determination and indicate the evidence he relied on, *cf.* Wichita R. & Light Co. v. PUC, 260 U.S. 48, 57-59 (1922), though his statement need not amount to a full opinion or even formal findings of fact and conclusions of law. And, of course, an impartial decision maker is essential. *Cf.* In re Murchison, 349 U.S. 133 (1955); Wong Yang Sung v. McGrath, 339 U.S. 33, 45-46 (1950). We agree with the District Court that prior involvement in some aspects of a case will not necessarily bar a welfare official from acting as a decision maker. He should not, however, have participated in making the determination under review. Affirmed.

Mr. Justice Black, dissenting.

In the last half century the United States, along with many, perhaps most, other nations of the world, has moved far toward becoming a welfare state, that is, a nation that for one reason or another taxes its most affluent people to help support, feed, clothe, and shelter its less fortunate citizens. The result is that today more than nine million men, women, and children in the United States receive some kind of state or federally financed public assistance in the form of allowances or gratuities, generally paid them periodically, usually by the week, month, or quarter. Since these gratuities are paid on the basis of need, the list of recipients is not static, and some people go off the lists and others are added from time to time. These ever-changing lists put a constant administrative burden on government and it certainly could not have reasonably anticipated that this burden would include the additional procedural expense imposed by the Court today. . . .

The more than a million names on the relief rolls in New York, and the more than nine million names on the rolls of all the 50 States were not put there at random. The names are there because state welfare officials believed that those people were eligible for assistance. Probably in the officials' haste to make out the lists many names were put there erroneously in order to alleviate immediate suffering, and undoubtedly some people are drawing relief who are not entitled under the law to do so. Doubtless some draw relief checks from time to time who know they are not eligible, either because they are not actually in need or for some other reason. Many of those who thus draw undeserved gratuities are without sufficient property to enable the government to collect back from them any money they wrongfully receive. But the Court today holds that it would violate the Due Process Clause of the Fourteenth Amendment to stop paying those people weekly or monthly allowances unless the government first affords them a full "evidentiary hearing" even though welfare officials are persuaded that the recipients are not rightfully entitled to receive a penny under the law. . . . The Court . . . in effect says that failure of the government to pay a promised charitable instalment to an individual deprives that individual of *his own property,* in violation of the Due Process Clause of the Fourteenth Amendment. It somewhat strains credulity to say that the government's promise of charity to an individual is property belonging to that individual when the government denies that the individual is honestly entitled to receive such a payment.

I would have little, if any, objection to the majority's decision in this case if it were written as the report of the House Committee on Education and Labor, but as an opinion ostensibly resting on the language of the Constitution I find it woefully deficient. Once the verbiage is pared away it is obvious that this Court today adopts the views of the District Court "that to cut off a welfare recipient in the face of . . . 'brutal need' without a prior hearing of some sort is unconscionable," and therefore, says the Court, unconstitutional. The majority reaches this result by a process of weighing "the recipient's interest in avoiding" the termination of welfare benefits against "the governmental interest in summary adjudication." . . . Today's balancing act requires a "pre-termination evidentiary hearing," yet there is nothing that indicates what tomorrow's balance will be. Although the majority attempts to bolster its decision with limited quotations from prior cases, it is obvious that today's result does not depend on the language of the Constitution itself or the principles of other decisions, but solely on the collective judgment of the majority as to what would be a fair and humane procedure in this case. . . .

Reduced to its simplest terms, the problem in this case is similar to that frequently encountered when two parties have an ongoing legal relationship that requires one party to make periodic payments to the other. Often the situation arises where the party "owing" the money stops paying it and justifies his conduct by arguing that the recipient is not legally entitled to payment. The recipient can, of course, disagree and go to court to compel payment. But I know of no situation in our legal system in which the person alleged to owe money to another is required by law to continue making payments to a judgment-proof claimant without the benefit of any security or bond to insure that these payments can be recovered if he wins his legal argument. Yet today's decision in no way obligates the welfare recipient to pay back any benefits wrongfully received during the pre-termination evidentiary hearings or post any bond, and in all "fairness" it could not do so. These recipients are by definition too poor to post a bond or to repay the benefits that, as the majority assumes, must be spent as received to insure survival.

The Court apparently feels that this decision will benefit the poor and needy. In my judgment the eventual result will be just the opposite. While today's decision requires only an administrative, evidentiary hearing, the inevitable logic of the approach taken will lead to constitutionally imposed, time-consuming delays of a full adversary process of administrative and judicial review. In the next case the welfare recipients are bound to argue that cutting off benefits before judicial review of the agency's decision is also a denial of due process. Since, by hypothesis, termination of aid at that point may still "deprive an *eligible* recipient of the very means by which to live while he waits," . . . I would be surprised if the weighing process did not compel the conclusion that termination without full judicial review would be unconscionable. After all, at each step, as the majority seems to feel, the issue is only one of weighing the government's pocketbook against the actual survival of the recipient, and surely that balance must always tip in favor of the individual. Similarly today's decision requires only the opportunity to have the benefit of counsel at the administrative hearing, but it is difficult to believe that the same reasoning process would not require the appointment of counsel, for otherwise the right to counsel is a meaningless one since these people are too poor to hire their own advocates. *Cf.* Gideon v. Wainwright, 372 U.S. 335, 344 (1963). Thus the end result of today's decision may well be that the government, once it decides to give welfare benefits, cannot reverse that decision until the recipient has had the benefits of full administrative and judicial review, including, of course, the opportunity to present his case to this Court. Since this process will usually entail a delay of several years, the inevitable result of such a constitutionally imposed burden will be that the government will not put a claimant on the rolls initially until it has made an exhaustive investigation to determine his eligibility. While this Court will perhaps have insured that no needy person will be taken off the rolls without a full "due process" proceeding, it will also have insured that many will never get on the rolls, or at least that they will remain destitute during the lengthy proceedings followed to determine initial eligibility.

For the foregoing reasons I dissent from the Court's holding. The operation of a welfare state is a new experiment for our Nation. For this reason, among others, I feel that new experiments in carrying out a welfare program should not be frozen into our constitutional structure. They should be left, as are other legislative determinations, to the Congress and the legislatures that the people elect to make our laws.

[Dissenting opinions of CHIEF JUSTICE BURGER, joined by JUSTICE BLACK, and of JUSTICE STEWART, omitted.]

NOTES AND QUESTIONS

1. *Triggering due process rights.* The erosion of the right-privilege distinction left many observers believing that the applicability of due process depended only on whether the claimant had an important or valuable interest at stake in the proceedings. In other words, it was not necessary to dwell on the categorization of the interest as a "property" or "liberty" interest. What, if anything, does *Goldberg* have to say about that issue? Note that the government appellants did not contest whether the Due Process Clause was applicable, focusing instead on whether the procedure used constituted "due" process. Was that a tactical error? Look closely at Justice Brennan's language in the text at n.8 and in n.8 itself. Is he saying that it doesn't matter whether welfare benefits are considered "rights" or "privileges"? Or is he saying that it does matter, and that benefits are "rights"? Does he provide a convincing answer to Justice Black's assertion that welfare is a "gratuity" and that it strains credulity to argue that the government's promise of charity is "property" precisely when the government is denying the claimant's eligibility?

2. *Substance and procedure.* Does *Goldberg* imply that the states have a constitutional obligation to provide public assistance benefits in the first place, or that, having once adopted a public assistance program, the state must maintain it? If the states are free to choose whether to provide benefits and at what level, why are they not free to decide what procedures to use in administering those benefits?

Suppose it turned out that administering a pretermination hearing procedure will cost the city a sum equal to 1 percent of AFDC benefit payments. May the city constitutionally reduce benefit levels 1 percent to pay for the new procedures? May it offer new AFDC recipients a choice between (1) a right to a pretermination hearing, and (2) a 1 percent increment in their monthly benefit? If it did, and 90 percent of recipients chose option two, could the city discontinue offering option one?

3. *Reduction of benefits.* Does *Goldberg* apply to reductions, as well as terminations, of benefits? Would the state be required to give a pretermination hearing to:

(a) A recipient whose food allowance was reduced by $10 per month on the ground that she no longer required a special diet?
(b) A family whose monthly benefit was reduced by $50 on the ground that the eldest child had left home?
(c) A recipient whose benefits were reduced pursuant to an across-the-board benefit reduction of 5 percent?

4. *The impact of* Goldberg. If, as the Court asserts, the typical AFDC recipient is in an especially vulnerable position in dealing with the welfare bureaucracy, will a mere change in the *timing* of hearings make much difference? The answer reached by most students of the AFDC "fair hearing" process was no. *See, e.g.,* Jerry L. Mashaw, The Management Side of Due Process: Some Theoretical and Litigation Notes on the Assurance of Accuracy, Fairness, and Timeliness in the Adjudication of Social Welfare Claims, 59 Cornell L. Rev. 772 (1974); Robert E. Scott, The Reality of Procedural Due Process—A Study of the Implementation of Fair Hearing Requirements by the Welfare Caseworker, 13 Wm. & Mary L. Rev. 725 (1972). Is that conclusion (if accurate) necessarily an indictment of the Court's decision in *Goldberg?*

5. *The demise of Aid for Families with Dependent Children.* Throughout its controversial history, the AFDC program served as a symbol of all that was perceived wrong with the "welfare state." Critics blamed AFDC for a host of asserted social ills, including the dissolution of the two-parent family, an epidemic of teenage pregnancy, and a breakdown of the work ethic among the dependent poor. Critics of AFDC finally succeeded in abolishing the program with the passage of the Personal Responsibility and Work Opportunity Reconciliation Act of 1996, Pub. L. No. 104-193, 110 Stat. 2105, *codified at* 42 U.S.C. §§601 *et seq.* The Act replaced AFDC with a program known as "Temporary Aid to Needy Families," a block-grant program that made funds available to the states to set up their own cash-assistance programs, subject, however, to various stringent federal requirements. States receiving TANF block grants were required to establish programs to collect child welfare payments from absent fathers, combat teenage pregnancy, and provide counseling and job training to recipients. To motivate the intended transition "from welfare to work," the Act required participating states to terminate cash-assistance benefits as soon as a recipient is "ready to engage in work" or at the end of 24 months on the welfare rolls, whichever occurs first.

The 1996 Welfare Act dramatically reduced the size of welfare rolls in the United States with caseloads declining steadily from a historic peak of 14.4 million recipients in 1994 to 4.2 million in 2015—a drop of approximately 70 percent. A 1999 study by the Council of Economic Advisors attributed over one-third of the reduction at that time to welfare reform policy. It also appears that the Act is having the desired effect of moving adult welfare recipients into the workforce. In 1996, only 11 percent of adult AFDC recipients were in the workforce. In 2015, by contrast, 48 percent of adult TANF recipients were working. *See* U.S. Department of Health and Human Services, Temporary Assistance for Needy Families Program (TANF), Twelfth Report to Congress (2015), https://www.acf.hhs.gov/sites/default/files/ofa/12th_annual_tanf_report_to_congress_final.pdf.

BOARD OF REGENTS v. ROTH
408 U.S. 564 (1972)

Mr. Justice Stewart delivered the opinion of the Court.

In 1968 the respondent, David Roth, was hired for his first teaching job as assistant professor of political science at Wisconsin State University-Oshkosh. He was hired for a fixed term of one academic year. The notice of his faculty appointment specified that his employment would begin on September 1, 1968, and would end on June 30, 1969.[1] The respondent completed that term. But he was informed that he would not be rehired for the next academic year.

---

1. The respondent had no contract of employment. Rather, his formal notice of appointment was the equivalent of an employment contract.

The notice of his appointment provided that: "*David F. Roth* is hereby appointed to the faculty of the Wisconsin State University Position number 0262. (Location:) *Oshkosh* as (Rank:) *Assistant Professor* of (Department:) *Political Science* this (Date:) *first* day of (Month:) *September* (Year:) *1968.*" The notice went on to specify that the respondent's "appointment basis" was for the "academic year." And it provided that "[r]egulations governing tenure are in accord with Chapter 37.31, Wisconsin Statutes. The employment of any staff member for an academic year shall not be for a term beyond June 30th of the fiscal year in which the appointment is made." *See* n.2, *infra.*

The respondent had no tenure rights to continued employment. Under Wisconsin statutory law a state university teacher can acquire tenure as a "permanent" employee only after four years of year-to-year employment. Having acquired tenure, a teacher is entitled to continued employment "during efficiency and good behavior." A relatively new teacher without tenure, however, is under Wisconsin law entitled to nothing beyond his one-year appointment.[2] There are no statutory or administrative standards defining eligibility for re-employment. State law thus clearly leaves the decision whether to rehire a nontenured teacher for another year to the unfettered discretion of university officials.

The procedural protection afforded a Wisconsin State University teacher before he is separated from the University corresponds to his job security. As a matter of statutory law, a tenured teacher cannot be "discharged except for cause upon written charges" and pursuant to certain procedures. A nontenured teacher, similarly, is protected to some extent *during* his one-year term. Rules promulgated by the Board of Regents provide that a nontenured teacher "dismissed" before the end of the year may have some opportunity for review of the "dismissal." But the Rules provide no real protection for a nontenured teacher who simply is not re-employed for the next year. He must be informed by February 1 "concerning retention or non-retention for the ensuing year." But "no reason for non-retention need be given. No review or appeal is provided in such case."

In conformance with these Rules, the President of Wisconsin State University-Oshkosh informed the respondent before February 1, 1969, that he would not be rehired for the 1969-1970 academic year. He gave the respondent no reason for the decision and no opportunity to challenge it at any sort of hearing.

The respondent then brought this action in Federal District Court alleging that the decision not to rehire him for the next year infringed his Fourteenth Amendment rights. He attacked the decision both in substance and procedure. First, he alleged that the true reason for the decision was to punish him for certain statements critical of the University administration, and that it therefore violated his right to freedom of speech. Second, he alleged that the failure of University officials to give him notice of any reason for non-retention and an opportunity for a hearing violated his right to procedural due process of law.

The District Court granted summary judgment for the respondent on the procedural issue, ordering the University officials to provide him with reasons and a hearing. 310 F. Supp. 972. The Court of Appeals, with one judge dissenting, affirmed this partial summary judgment. 446 F.2d 806. We granted certiorari. 404 U.S. 909. The only question presented to us at this stage in the case is whether the respondent had a constitutional right to a statement of reasons and a hearing on the University's decision not to rehire him for another year. We hold that he did not.

---

2. Wis. Stat. §37.31(1) (1967), in force at the time, provided in pertinent part that:

"All teachers in any state university shall initially be employed on probation. The employment shall be permanent, during efficiency and good behavior after 4 years of continuous service in the state university system as a teacher."

I

The requirements of procedural due process apply only to the deprivation of interests encompassed by the Fourteenth Amendment's protection of liberty and property. When protected interests are implicated, the right to some kind of prior hearing is paramount. But the range of interests protected by procedural due process is not infinite.

The District Court decided that procedural due process guarantees apply in this case by assessing and balancing the weights of the particular interests involved. . . . But, to determine whether due process requirements apply in the first place, we must look not to the "weight" but to the *nature* of the interest at stake. *See* Morrissey v. Brewer, [408 U.S. 471, 481 (1972)]. We must look to see if the interest is within the Fourteenth Amendment's protection of liberty and property.

"Liberty" and "property" are broad and majestic terms. . . .

For that reason, the Court has fully and finally rejected the wooden distinction between "rights" and "privileges" that once seemed to govern the applicability of procedural due process rights. The Court has also made clear that the property interests protected by procedural due process extend well beyond actual ownership of real estate, chattels, or money. By the same token, the Court has required due process protection for deprivations of liberty beyond the sort of formal constraints imposed by the criminal process.

Yet, while the Court has eschewed rigid or formalistic limitations on the protection of procedural due process, it has at the same time observed certain boundaries. For the words "liberty" and "property" in the Due Process Clause of the Fourteenth Amendment must be given some meaning.

II

"While this Court has not attempted to define with exactness the liberty . . . guaranteed [by the Fourteenth Amendment], the term has received much consideration and some of the included things have been definitely stated. Without doubt, it denotes not merely freedom from bodily restraint but also the right of the individual to contract, to engage in any of the common occupations of life, to acquire useful knowledge, to marry, establish a home and bring up children, to worship God according to the dictates of his own conscience, and generally to enjoy those privileges long recognized . . . as essential to the orderly pursuit of happiness by free men." Meyer v. Nebraska, 262 U.S. 390, 399. In a Constitution for a free people, there can be no doubt that the meaning of "liberty" must be broad indeed.

There might be cases in which a State refused to re-employ a person under such circumstances that interests in liberty would be implicated. But this is not such a case.

The State, in declining to rehire the respondent, did not make any charge against him that might seriously damage his standing and associations in his community. It did not base the nonrenewal of his contract on a charge, for example, that he had been guilty of dishonesty, or immorality. Had it done so, this would be a different case. . . . In such a case, due process would accord an opportunity to refute the charge before University officials.[12] In the present case, however, there is no suggestion whatever that the respondent's "good name, reputation, honor, or integrity" is at stake.

Similarly, there is no suggestion that the State, in declining to reemploy the respondent, imposed on him a stigma or other disability that foreclosed his freedom to take advantage of other employment opportunities. The State, for example, did not invoke any regulations to bar the respondent from all other public employment in state universities. Had it done so, this, again, would be a different case. For "[t]o be deprived not only of present government employment but of future opportunity for it certainly is no small injury. . . ." Joint Anti-Fascist Refugee Committee v. McGrath, [341 U.S. 123, 185 (1951)] (Jackson, J., concurring). . . . In the present case, however, this principle does not come into play.[13]

To be sure, the respondent has alleged that the nonrenewal of his contract was based on his exercise of his right to freedom of speech. But this allegation is not now before us. The District Court stayed proceedings on this issue, and the respondent has yet to prove that the decision not to rehire him was, in fact, based on his free speech activities.[14]

Hence, on the record before us, all that clearly appears is that the respondent was not rehired for one year at one university. It stretches the concept too far to suggest that a person is deprived of "liberty" when he simply is not rehired in one job but remains as free as before to seek another. Cafeteria Workers v. McElroy, [367 U.S. 886, 895-896 (1961)].

12. The purpose of such notice and hearing is to provide the person an opportunity to clear his name. Once a person has cleared his name at a hearing, his employer, of course, may remain free to deny him future employment for other reasons.

13. The District Court made an *assumption* "that nonretention by one university or college creates concrete and practical difficulties for a professor in his subsequent academic career." 310 F. Supp., at 979. And the Court of Appeals based its affirmance of the summary judgment largely on the premise that "the substantial adverse effect non-retention is likely to have upon the career interests of an individual professor" amounts to a limitation on future employment opportunities sufficient to invoke procedural due process guarantees. 446 F.2d, at 809. But even assuming, arguendo, that such a "substantial adverse effect" under these circumstances would constitute a state-imposed restriction on liberty, the record contains no support for these assumptions. There is no suggestion of how nonretention might affect the respondent's future employment prospects. Mere proof, for example, that his record of nonretention in one job, taken alone, might make him somewhat less attractive to some other employers would hardly establish the kind of foreclosure of opportunities amounting to a deprivation of "liberty." *Cf.* Schware v. Board of Bar Examiners, 353 U.S. 232.

14. . . . When a State would directly impinge upon interests in free speech or free press, this Court has on occasion held that opportunity for a fair adversary hearing must precede the action, whether or not the speech or press interest is clearly protected under substantive First Amendment standards. Thus, we have required fair notice and opportunity for an adversary hearing before an injunction is issued against the holding of rallies and public meetings. Carroll v. Princess Anne, 393 U.S. 175. Similarly, we have indicated the necessity of procedural safeguards before a State makes a large-scale seizure of a person's allegedly obscene books, magazines, and so forth. A Quantity of Books v. Kansas, 378 U.S. 205; Marcus v. Search Warrant, 367 U.S. 717. *See* Freedman v. Maryland, 380 U.S. 51; Bantam Books v. Sullivan, 372 U.S. 58. *See generally* Monaghan, First Amendment "Due Process," 83 Harv. L. Rev. 518.

In the respondent's case, however, the State has not directly impinged upon interests in free speech or free press in any way comparable to a seizure of books or an injunction against meetings. Whatever may be a teacher's rights of free speech, the interest in holding a teaching job at a state university, simpliciter, is not itself a free speech interest.

III

The Fourteenth Amendment's procedural protection of property is a safeguard of the security of interests that a person has already acquired in specific benefits. . . . To have a property interest in a benefit, a person clearly must have more than an abstract need or desire for it. He must have more than a unilateral expectation of it. He must, instead, have a legitimate claim of entitlement to it. It is a purpose of the ancient institution of property to protect those claims upon which people rely in their daily lives, reliance that must not be arbitrarily undermined. It is a purpose of the constitutional right to a hearing to provide an opportunity for a person to vindicate those claims.

Property interests, of course, are not created by the Constitution. Rather, they are created and their dimensions are defined by existing rules or understandings that stem from an independent source such as state law—rules or understandings that secure certain benefits and that support claims of entitlement to those benefits. Thus, the welfare recipients in Goldberg v. Kelly, *supra,* had a claim of entitlement to welfare payments that was grounded in the statute defining eligibility for them. The recipients had not yet shown that they were, in fact, within the statutory terms of eligibility. But we held that they had a right to a hearing at which they might attempt to do so.

Just as the welfare recipients' "property" interest in welfare payments was created and defined by statutory terms, so the respondent's "property" interest in employment at Wisconsin State University-Oshkosh was created and defined by the terms of his appointment. Those terms secured his interest in employment up to June 30, 1969. But the important fact in this case is that they specifically provided that the respondent's employment was to terminate on June 30. They did not provide for contract renewal absent "sufficient cause." Indeed, they made no provision for renewal whatsoever.

Thus, the terms of the respondent's appointment secured absolutely no interest in re-employment for the next year. They supported absolutely no possible claim of entitlement to re-employment. Nor, significantly, was there any state statute or University rule or policy that secured his interest in re-employment or that created any legitimate claim to it. In these circumstances, the respondent surely had an abstract concern in being rehired, but he did not have a *property* interest sufficient to require the University authorities to give him a hearing when they declined to renew his contract of employment.

IV

. . . We must conclude that the summary judgment for the respondent should not have been granted, since the respondent has not shown that he was deprived of liberty or property protected by the Fourteenth Amendment. The judgment of the Court of Appeals, accordingly, is reversed and the case is remanded for further proceedings consistent with this opinion. It is so ordered.

MR. JUSTICE MARSHALL, dissenting. . . .

The prior decisions of this Court, discussed at length in the opinion of the Court, establish a principle that is as obvious as it is compelling—i.e., federal and state governments and governmental agencies are restrained by the Constitution from acting arbitrarily with respect to employment opportunities that they either offer or control. Hence, it is now firmly established that whether or not a private employer is free to act capriciously or unreasonably with respect to employment practices, at least absent statutory or contractual controls, a government employer is different. The government may only act fairly and reasonably. . . .

In my view, every citizen who applies for a government job is entitled to it unless the government can establish some reason for denying the employment. This is the "property" right that I believe is protected by the Fourteenth Amendment and that cannot be denied "without due process of law." And it is also liberty—liberty to work—which is the "very essence of the personal freedom and opportunity" secured by the Fourteenth Amendment. . . .

Employment is one of the greatest, if not the greatest, benefits that governments offer in modern-day life. When something as valuable as the opportunity to work is at stake, the government may not reward some citizens and not others without demonstrating that its actions are fair and equitable. And it is procedural due process that is our fundamental guarantee of fairness, our protection against arbitrary, capricious, and unreasonable government action. . . .

Where there are numerous applicants for jobs, it is likely that few will choose to demand reasons for not being hired. But, if the demand for reasons is exceptionally great, summary procedures can be devised that would provide fair and adequate information to all persons. As long as the government has a good reason for its actions it need not fear disclosure. It is only where the government acts improperly that procedural due process is truly burdensome. And that is precisely when it is most necessary. . . .

Accordingly, I dissent.

NOTES AND QUESTIONS

1. *The "right-privilege" distinction.* The Court claims to have rejected the "wooden distinction between 'rights' and 'privileges.'" But has it merely resurrected that distinction in a new vocabulary? *See* Rodney A. Smolla, The Reemergence of the Right-Privilege Distinction in Constitutional Law: The Price of Protesting Too Much, 35 Stan. L. Rev. 69 (1982). Does it matter to Roth whether he has no "property or liberty interest" or no "right"? Is the difference merely that the Court has broadened the scope of "property" to include entitlements that formally fall short of "rights" status?

2. *"Legitimate claim of entitlement."* In Perry v. Sindermann, 408 U.S. 593 (1972), a companion case to *Roth,* the Court reached a different result. In *Perry,* the teacher whose contract had not been renewed alleged that ambiguous assurances of continued employment contained in official college publications created a system of "de facto tenure" on which he had legitimately relied. The Supreme Court found these allegations sufficient to withstand a motion for summary judgment on the ground that plaintiff lacked a "property" interest:

A written contract with an explicit tenure provision clearly is evidence of a formal understanding that supports a teacher's claim of entitlement to continued employment unless sufficient "cause" is shown. Yet absence of such an explicit contractual provision may not always foreclose the possibility that a teacher has a "property" interest in re-employment. For example, the law of contracts in most, if not all, jurisdictions long has employed a process by which agreements, though not formalized in writing, may be "implied." 3 A. Corbin on Contracts §§561-572A (1960). Explicit contractual provisions may be supplemented by other agreements implied from "the promisor's words and conduct in the light of the surrounding circumstances." *Id.* at §562. And, "[t]he meaning of [the promisor's] words and acts is found by relating them to the usage of the past." *Ibid.*

A teacher, like the respondent, who has held his position for a number of years, might be able to show from the circumstances of this service—and from other relevant facts—that he has a legitimate claim of entitlement to job tenure. . . .

In this case, the respondent has alleged the existence of rules and understandings, promulgated and fostered by state officials, that may justify his legitimate claim of entitlement to continued employment absent "sufficient cause." We disagree with the Court of Appeals insofar as it held that a mere subjective "expectancy" is protected by procedural due process, but we agree that the respondent must be given an opportunity to prove the legitimacy of his claim of such entitlement in light of "the policies and practices of the institution." 430 F.2d at 943.

408 U.S. at 601-603.

Would it satisfy the standard for recognizing a property interest announced in *Perry* if virtually every candidate received tenure? In a case challenging the Trump Administration's decision to terminate President Obama's Deferred Action for Childhood Arrivals (DACA) Program, the Ninth Circuit rejected the plaintiffs' argument that a 99 percent success rate supported their claim that they had a property interest in the renewal of the status they had been granted under DACA. *See* Regents of the University of California v. U.S. Department of Homeland Security, 908 F.3d 476, 515 (9th Cir. 2018), *cert. granted*, 139 S. Ct. 2779 (2019). The court of appeals noted that the documents governing the DACA program stated that the government "retains the ultimate discretion to determine whether deferred action is appropriate in any given case even if the [renewal] guidelines are met," that any individual's "deferred action may be terminated at any time, with or without a Notice of Intent to Terminate, at DHS's discretion," and that it "confers no substantive right, immigration status or pathway to citizenship." *Id.* The question, the court stated, is "whether a mutually explicit understanding of presumptive renewal existed," and it concluded that "a 99% renewal rate under DACA provides no evidence that the government shared an understanding that the DACA program would continue existing indefinitely to provide such renewals." *Id.* (The court of appeals invalidated the revocation of DACA on other grounds, and, at this writing, the Supreme Court has granted review of that decision.)

3. *Benefits not yet received.* A related issue is whether someone can have a property right in a claimed entitlement to benefits the person has not yet started to receive. Would the claimants in *Goldberg* have had a property right merely in the expectation of receiving future benefits? Would they have had a right to a hearing before an initial decision that they were not within the class entitled to

receive benefits? The Court of Appeals for the Federal Circuit addressed that issue in the context of veterans' benefits in Cushman v. Shinseki, 576 F.3d 1290 (Fed. Cir. 2009). After reciting the long procedural history of claims filed by Philip Cushman dealing with injuries he suffered during service in a combat infantry battalion in Vietnam, the court confronted the question whether Cushman had a property right at issue:

> To raise a due process question, the claimant must demonstrate a property interest entitled to such protections.
>
> It is well established that disability benefits are a protected property interest and may not be discontinued without due process of law. The Supreme Court has not, however, resolved the specific question of whether applicants for benefits, who have not yet been adjudicated as entitled to them, possess a property interest in those benefits.
>
> The Supreme Court has, however, offered guidance relevant to our resolution of this question by explaining, "'[t]o have a property interest in a benefit, a person clearly must have more than an abstract need or desire' and 'more than a unilateral expectation of it. He must, instead, have a legitimate claim of entitlement to it.'" Town of Castle Rock, Colo. v. Gonzales, 545 U.S. 748, 756 (2005). The Court has also clarified that "a benefit is not a protected entitlement if government officials may grant or deny it in their discretion." Id. . . .
>
> Like the statutorily created right of an eligible recipient to social security benefits, entitlement to veteran's benefits arises from a source that is independent from the [Department of Veterans Affairs] proceedings themselves [citing relevant provisions for wartime and peacetime disability compensation as well as compensation for heirs and dependents]. These statutes provide an absolute right of benefits to qualified individuals. . . .
>
> In response, the government cites three cases in which circuit courts found that an individual did not obtain a protected property interest merely by applying for benefits. See Banks v. Block, 700 F.2d 292 (6th Cir. 1983) (declining to find a property interest in food stamp benefits after expiration of the eligibility period); Holman v. Block, 823 F.2d 56 (4th Cir. 1987) (same); DeJournett v. Block, 799 F.2d 430 (8th Cir. 1986) (finding that an applicant had no protected property interest in a discretionary loan). The cited cases, however, are distinguishable from the present case. Banks and Holman deal with the rights of an applicant who is no longer eligible for benefits. DeJournett deals with the denial of a discretionary benefit. As cited above, the respective circuits of these three cases have found that due process attaches in the context of non-discretionary benefits.
>
> Veteran's disability benefits are nondiscretionary, statutorily mandated benefits. A veteran is entitled to disability benefits upon a showing that he meets the eligibility requirements set forth in the governing statutes and regulations. We conclude that such entitlement to benefits is a property interest protected by the Due Process Clause of the Fifth Amendment to the United States Constitution.

576 F.3d at 1296-1298. Does this mean that any time someone would have a property right in a benefit he or she was receiving, there is a property right in an initial claim for such benefits? Does that mean that this obtains regardless of the weightiness of the claim? Would all the same due process protections apply? Do the answers to these questions depend on exactly what the statutory provisions creating the benefit program say?

4. *Sources and contours of protected interests.* Questions about who has due process rights have arisen in a wide array of contexts. As the cases excerpted below

illustrate, the Supreme Court has struggled to delineate both the permissible legal sources of constitutionally protected property and liberty interests and the scope of such interests, where they are found to exist.

ARNETT v. KENNEDY, 416 U.S. 134 (1974): Kennedy, a "nonprobationary" civil service employee of the Office of Economic Opportunity, was fired for allegedly making defamatory public remarks about his boss. The Civil Service statute (based on the Lloyd-La Follette Act of 1912) and implementing rules entitled employees in his position to a *post-termination* adjudicatory hearing, but only to notice and an opportunity to file a written protest *prior to termination*. Kennedy claimed that he, like the *Goldberg* plaintiffs, was constitutionally entitled to a pretermination hearing. Although the Supreme Court rejected his claim, the Justices split on the justification. In the plurality opinion, Justice Rehnquist, joined by Chief Justice Burger and Justice Stewart, argued that Kennedy had not been deprived of any interest protected by the Due Process Clause:

> The District Court, in its ruling on appellee's procedural contentions, in effect held that the Fifth Amendment to the United States Constitution prohibited Congress, in the Lloyd-La Follette Act, from granting protection against removal without cause and at the same time—indeed, in the same sentence—specifying that the determination of cause should be without the full panoply of rights which attend a trial-type adversary hearing. We do not believe that the Constitution so limits Congress in the manner in which benefits may be extended to federal employees. . . .
>
> Appellee contends that he had a property interest or an expectancy of employment which could not be divested without first affording him a full adversary hearing. . . .
>
> Here appellee did have a statutory expectancy that he not be removed other than for "such cause as will promote the efficiency of [the] service." But the very section of the statute which granted him that right, a right which had previously existed only by virtue of administrative regulation, expressly provided also for the procedure by which "cause" was to be determined, and expressly omitted the procedural guarantees which appellee insists are mandated by the Constitution. Only by bifurcating the very sentence of the Act of Congress which conferred upon appellee the right not to be removed save for cause could it be said that he had an expectancy of that substantive right without the procedural limitations which Congress attached to it. . . .
>
> Congress was obviously intent on according a measure of statutory job security to governmental employees which they had not previously enjoyed, but was likewise intent on excluding more elaborate procedural requirements which it felt would make the operation of the new scheme unnecessarily burdensome in practice. Where the focus of legislation was thus strongly on the procedural mechanism for enforcing the substantive right which was simultaneously conferred, we decline to conclude that the substantive right may be viewed wholly apart from the procedure provided for its enforcement. The employee's statutorily defined right is not a guarantee against removal without cause in the abstract, but such a guarantee as enforced by the procedures which Congress has designated for the determination of cause. . . .
>
> Where the grant of a substantive right is inextricably intertwined with the limitations on the procedures which are to be employed in determining that right, a litigant in the position of appellee must take the bitter with the sweet. . . .

Appellee also contends in this Court that because of the nature of the charges on which his dismissal was based, he was in effect accused of dishonesty, and that therefore a hearing was required before he could be deprived of this element of his "liberty" protected by the Fifth Amendment against deprivation without due process. . . . But that liberty is not offended by dismissal from employment itself, but instead by dismissal based upon an unsupported charge which could wrongfully injure the reputation of an employee. Since the purpose of the hearing in such a case is to provide the person "an opportunity to clear his name," a hearing afforded by administrative appeal procedures after the actual dismissal is a sufficient compliance with the requirements of the Due Process Clause. Here appellee chose not to rely on his administrative appeal, which, if his factual contentions are correct, might well have vindicated his reputation and removed any wrongful stigma from his reputation.

Appellee urges that the delays in processing agency and Civil Service Commission appeals, amounting to more than three months in over 50% of agency appeals, mean that the available administrative appeals do not suffice to protect his liberty interest recognized in *Roth*. During the pendency of his administrative appeals, appellee asserts, a discharged employee suffers from both the stigma and the consequent disadvantage in obtaining a comparable job that result from dismissal for cause from Government employment. We assume that some delay attends vindication of an employee's reputation throughout the hearing procedures provided on appeal, and conclude that at least the delays cited here do not entail any separate deprivation of a liberty interest recognized in *Roth*.

416 U.S. at 151-154, 156-158. Justice Powell, joined by Justice Blackmun, concurred in the result, but not the reasoning:

The plurality opinion evidently reasons that the nature of appellee's interest in continued federal employment is necessarily defined and limited by the statutory procedures for discharge and that the constitutional guarantee of procedural due process accords to appellee no procedural protections against arbitrary or erroneous discharge other than those expressly provided in the statute. The plurality would thus conclude that the statute governing federal employment determines not only the nature of appellee's property interest, but also the extent of the procedural protections to which he may lay claim. It seems to me that this approach is incompatible with the principles laid down in *Roth* and *Sindermann*. Indeed, it would lead directly to the conclusion that whatever the nature of an individual's statutorily created property interest, deprivation of that interest could be accomplished without notice or a hearing at any time. This view misconceives the origin of the right to procedural due process. That right is conferred, not by legislative grace, but by constitutional guarantee. While the legislature may elect not to confer a property interest in federal employment, it may not constitutionally authorize the deprivation of such an interest, once conferred, without appropriate procedural safeguards.

416 U.S. at 166-167. Justice Powell went on to conclude, however, that the statutory procedure was all the "process" that was "due" under the Fifth Amendment. In separate dissenting opinions, Justices White, Douglas, and Marshall joined Justice Powell in rejecting Justice Rehnquist's reasoning, but disagreed with Justice Powell's conclusions concerning the constitutional adequacy of a post-termination hearing. The dissenters would have found both a protected property interest and a violation of due process.

BISHOP v. WOOD, 426 U.S. 341 (1976):   Bishop, a policeman classified as a "permanent employee" of the town of Marion, North Carolina, was dismissed by the City Manager without any hearing, under authority of a city ordinance that provided:

> *Dismissal.* A permanent employee whose work is not satisfactory over a period of time shall be notified in what way his work is deficient and what he must do if his work is to be satisfactory. If a permanent employee fails to perform work up to the standard of the classification held, or continues to be negligent, inefficient, or unfit to perform his duties, he may be dismissed by the City Manager. Any discharged employee shall be given written notice of his discharge setting forth the effective date and reasons for his discharge if he shall request such a notice.

Bishop brought suit against the City Manager and Police Chief, alleging that their decision to dismiss him without a hearing violated his due process rights. The Supreme Court, in an opinion by Justice Stevens joined by four other Justices, disagreed:

> The North Carolina Supreme Court has held that an enforceable expectation of continued public employment in that State can exist only if the employer, by statute or contract, has actually granted some form of guarantee. Still v. Lance, 279 N.C. 254, 182 S.E.2d 403 (1971). Whether such a guarantee has been given can be determined only by an examination of the particular statute or ordinance in question.
>
> On its face the ordinance on which petitioner relies may fairly be read as conferring such a guarantee. However, such a reading is not the only possible interpretation; the ordinance may also be construed as granting no right to continued employment but merely conditioning an employee's removal on compliance with certain specified procedures.[8] We do not have any authoritative interpretation of this ordinance by a North Carolina state court. We do, however, have the opinion of the United States District Judge who, of course, sits in North Carolina and practiced law there for many years. Based on his understanding of state law, he concluded that petitioner "held his position at the will and pleasure of the city."[9] This construction of North Carolina law was upheld by the Court of Appeals for the Fourth Circuit, albeit by an equally divided court. In comparable circumstances,

8. This is not the construction which six Members of this Court placed on the federal regulations involved in *Arnett v. Kennedy*, 416 U.S. 134. In that case the Court concluded that because the employee could only be discharged for cause, he had a property interest which was entitled to constitutional protection. In this case, a holding that as a matter of state law the employee "held his position at the will and pleasure of the city" necessarily establishes that he had *no* property interest. The Court's evaluation of the federal regulations involved in *Arnett* sheds no light on the problem presented by this case.

9. "Under the law in North Carolina, nothing else appearing, a contract of employment which contains no provision for the duration or termination of employment is terminable at the will of either party irrespective of the quality of performance by the other party. By statute, G.S. §115-142(b), a county board of education in North Carolina may terminate the employment of a teacher at the end of the school year without filing charges or giving its reasons for such termination, or granting the teacher an opportunity to be heard. Still v. Lance, 279 N.C. 254, 182 S.E.2d 403 (1971).

"It is clear from Article II, Section 6, of the City's Personnel Ordinance, that the dismissal of an employee does not require a notice or a hearing. Upon request of the discharged employee, he shall be given written notice of his discharge setting forth the effective date and the reasons for the discharge. It thus appears that both the city ordinance and the state law have been complied with.

"It further appears that the plaintiff held his position at the will and pleasure of the city." 377 F. Supp., at 504.

this Court has accepted the interpretation of state law in which the District Court and the Court of Appeals have concurred even if an examination of the state-law issue without such guidance might have justified a different conclusion.

In this case, as the District Court construed the ordinance, the City Manager's determination of the adequacy of the grounds for discharge is not subject to judicial review; the employee is merely given certain procedural rights which the District Court found not to have been violated in this case. The District Court's reading of the ordinance is tenable; it derives some support from a decision of the North Carolina Supreme Court, Still v. Lance, *supra*; and it was accepted by the Court of Appeals for the Fourth Circuit. These reasons are sufficient to foreclose our independent examination of the state-law issue.

426 U.S. at 345-347.

Justice White, dissenting, was wholly unpersuaded by the majority's attempt to distinguish *Arnett*:

I dissent because the decision of the majority rests upon a proposition which was squarely addressed and in my view correctly rejected by six Members of this Court in Arnett v. Kennedy, 416 U.S. 134 (1974)....

The second sentence of [the] ordinance plainly conditions petitioner's dismissal on cause—i.e., failure to perform up to standard, negligence, inefficiency, or unfitness to perform the job. The District Court below did not otherwise construe this portion of the ordinance.... The majority ... implicitly concedes that the ordinance supplies the "grounds" for discharge and that the City Manager must determine them to be "adequate" before he may fire an employee. The majority's holding that petitioner had no property interest in his job in spite of the unequivocal language in the city ordinance that he may be dismissed only for certain kinds of cause rests, then, on the fact that state law provides no *procedures* for assuring that the City Manager dismiss him only for cause. The right to his job apparently given by the first two sentences of the ordinance is thus redefined, according to the majority, by the procedures provided for in the third sentence and as redefined is infringed only if the procedures are not followed.

This is precisely the reasoning which was embraced by only three and expressly rejected by six Members of this Court in Arnett v. Kennedy, *supra*.

426 U.S. at 355-357.

CLEVELAND BOARD OF EDUCATION v. LOUDERMILL, 470 U.S. 532 (1985): Loudermill had been dismissed from his position as a security guard for falsely stating on his job application that he had never been convicted of a felony. As a "classified civil servant" under an Ohio statute, Loudermill could be terminated only for cause and was entitled to a post-termination administrative review of his dismissal. Loudermill claimed that the statute was unconstitutional because it provided no opportunity for a discharged employee to respond to charges prior to dismissal, thus depriving him of a property interest without due process.

The Supreme Court, by an 8-1 majority, agreed:

The . . . Board argues . . . that the property right is defined by, and conditioned on, the legislature's choice of procedures for its deprivation. . . . The Board stresses that in addition to specifying the grounds for termination, the statute sets out procedures by which termination may take place. The procedures were adhered to in these cases. According to petitioner, "[t]o require additional procedures would in effect expand the scope of the property interest itself." . . .

This argument, which was accepted by the District Court, has its genesis in the plurality opinion in Arnett v. Kennedy, 416 U.S. 134 (1974). . . . The plurality reasoned that where the legislation conferring the substantive right also sets out the procedural mechanism for enforcing that right, the two cannot be separated. . . .

This view garnered three votes in *Arnett*, but was specifically rejected by the other six Justices. . . . Since then, this theory has at times seemed to gather some additional support. *See* Bishop v. Wood, 426 U.S. 341, 355-361 (1976) (White, J., dissenting). . . . More recently, however, the Court has clearly rejected it. In Vitek v. Jones, 445 U.S. 480 (1980), we pointed out that "minimum [procedural] requirements [are] a matter of federal law, they are not diminished by the fact that the State may have specified its own procedures that it may deem adequate for determining the preconditions to adverse official action." This conclusion was reiterated in Logan v. Zimmerman Brush Co., 455 U.S. 422 (1982), where we reversed the lower court's holding that because the entitlement arose from a state statute, the legislature had the prerogative to define the procedures to be followed to protect that entitlement.

In light of these holdings, it is settled that the "bitter with the sweet" approach misconceives the constitutional guarantee. If a clearer holding is needed, we provide it today. The point is straightforward: the Due Process Clause provides that certain substantive rights—life, liberty, and property—cannot be deprived except pursuant to constitutionally adequate procedures. The categories of substance and procedure are distinct. Were the rule otherwise, the Clause would be reduced to a mere tautology. "Property" cannot be defined by the procedures provided for its deprivation any more than can life or liberty. The right to due process "is conferred, not by legislative grace, but by constitutional guarantee. . . ."

NOTES AND QUESTIONS

1. *Taking the "bitter with the sweet."* Several commentators view Justice Rehnquist's bitter-sweet analysis as the logical outgrowth of *Roth's* positive-law definition of "property." *See, e.g.,* Jerry L. Mashaw, Administrative Due Process: The Quest for a Dignitary Theory, 61 B.U. L. Rev. 885, 888-891 (1981); William W. Van Alstyne, Cracks in "The New Property": Adjudicative Due Process in the Administrative State, 62 Cornell L. Rev. 445, 462-465 (1977). Do you agree? If property rights are "created and their dimensions are defined" by state law, can the Court logically reject as inadequate the procedures authorized by a state legislature for their protection?

Professor (later Judge) Frank Easterbrook used economic analysis to defend Justice Rehnquist's position. "The procedures one uses determine how much substance is achieved, and by whom. Procedural rules are just a measure of how much the substantive entitlements are worth. . . ." Frank Easterbrook, Substance and Due Process, 1982 Sup. Ct. Rev. 85, 112-113. By that analysis, a promise of a $100 benefit enforceable by a formal procedure (which is, say, 90 percent accurate) is equivalent to a promise of a $150 benefit backed by a less formal process that is 60 percent accurate. If we trust legislatures to set the benefit level, Easterbrook asked rhetorically, why do we not also trust them to specify the procedural "discount rate"?

2. *Dignitary theories of procedure.* Many commentators have argued that this analysis ignores the intrinsic value of process. People value the opportunity to participate in decisions affecting them as an affirmation of their personal dignity and worth, so the argument runs, and not just as a device to increase the reliability of the ultimate decision. *See, e.g.,* Jerry L. Mashaw, Due Process in the Administrative State (1985); Frank I. Michelman, Formal and Associational Aims in Procedural Due Process, in Nomos XVIII: Due Process 126 (J. Roland Pennock & John W. Chapman eds., 1977); Robert L. Rabin, Job Security and Due Process: Monitoring Administrative Discretion Through a Reasons Requirement, 44 U. Chi. L. Rev. 60 (1976); Richard B. Saphire, Specifying Due Process Values: Toward a More Responsive Approach to Procedural Protection, 127 U. Pa. L. Rev. 111 (1978); Robert S. Summers, Evaluating and Improving Legal Process . . . A Plea for "Process Values," 60 Cornell L. Rev. 1 (1974). Conceding that process may have intrinsic value, Easterbrook responded that dignity is implicated as much by substantive as procedural rules. "Without property there is no autonomy and little dignity." Easterbrook, *supra,* at 115. Furthermore, he argued, "There is simply no reason to suppose that process values are slighted by legislatures. . . . Process is not historically disfavored. Statutes overflow with process." *Id.* at 117. Consequently, courts should honor the legislature's valuation of dignitary interests, rather than substitute their own.

Do you agree? Is there greater reason for courts to distrust legislatures' procedural decisions than their substantive decisions? Do courts have greater institutional competence in the realm of procedure?

3. *"Liberty."* In contrast to the *Roth* Court's positive-law definition of property, its definition of liberty makes no reference to non-constitutional law. The quotation from Meyer v. Nebraska strongly suggests that liberty is a purely constitutional concept to be elaborated exclusively by the Court. The Court has adhered to this approach in subsequent decisions. For example, in Ingraham v. Wright, 430 U.S. 651 (1977), the Court found the "right to be free from . . . unjustified intrusions on personal security" (in this case, "paddling" of schoolchildren) was an inherent liberty interest protected by due process. In later cases, the Court has recognized liberty interests in freedom from unnecessary restraint and labeling as mentally ill, Parham v. J.R., 442 U.S. 584 (1978), and confinement "in conditions of reasonable care and safety," Youngberg v. Romeo, 457 U.S. 307, 324 (1982).

Kerry v. Din, 135 S. Ct. 2128 (2015), featured an interesting, if inconclusive, debate among the Justices about the definition of "liberty." Din, a United States citizen, petitioned the State Department to have her husband, an Afghan citizen, classified as an "immediate relative" entitled to immigration priority. A consular officer informed her husband that he was inadmissible for having engaged in unspecified "terrorist activities." Unable to obtain further information, Din filed suit claiming that the denial of admissibility violated her right to procedural due process. She claimed that she had been deprived of the "liberty" of her "constitutional right to live in the United States with her spouse." Writing for a plurality of three, Justice Scalia rejected the claim. He began by arguing that the interests protected by due process should properly be limited to those deducible from Magna Carta, as interpreted in the writings of Coke and Blackstone. Quoting from Blackstone's Commentaries, Scalia observed that: "The Government has not 'taken or imprisoned' Din, nor has it 'confine[d]' her, either by 'keeping

[her] against h[er] will in a private house, putting h[er] in the stocks, arresting or forcibly detaining h[er] in the street.'" While conceding that the Court has on occasion derived from the Due Process Clauses additional implied "fundamental rights," Scalia argued that such rights should be found only if "objectively, deeply rooted in this Nation's history and tradition, and implicit in the concept of ordered liberty, such that neither liberty nor justice would exist if [it was] sacrificed," quoting from Washington v. Glucksberg, 521 U.S. 702, 720-721 (1997). Applying this test, Scalia found no authority for the proposition that marital co-habitation was such a fundamental right. In reaching this conclusion, he dismissed, as so much "grandiloquence," the list of constitutional liberties famously recited in *Meyer v. Nebraska* (and quoted approvingly in *Roth*). Justice Kennedy, joined by Justice Alito, concurred in the judgment. He ducked the issue of whether Din had been deprived of a protected interest by deciding that the notice given to her husband was procedurally adequate to satisfy due process. Justice Breyer, writing for four Justices, dissented, arguing that the Court's "liberty" cases clearly establish that: "the institution of marriage, which encompasses the right of spouses to live together and to raise a family, is central to human life, requires and enjoys community support, and plays a central role in most individuals' 'orderly pursuit of happiness,' *Meyer v. Nebraska*, 262 U.S. 390, 399 (1923)." He went on to conclude that the notice was procedurally defective.

4. *Is there a "liberty" interest in one's reputation?* The Court in *Roth* seemed to imply that one has a protected liberty interest in one's "good name, reputation, honor, or integrity." Yet in Paul v. Davis, 424 U.S. 693 (1976), the Court refused to find a liberty interest in one's reputation. Paul, a city police chief, had circulated to local merchants a flyer identifying (by name and photograph) various "active shoplifters," including Davis. Davis had been arrested and charged with shoplifting, but the charge was still pending at the time. Davis claimed that the stigma imposed by circulation of the flyer deprived him of a protected liberty interest. Writing for a majority of five, Justice Rehnquist ruled that injury to reputation alone, without some accompanying alteration of legal rights, does not constitute a liberty deprivation. The Court strained to distinguish Wisconsin v. Constantineau, 400 U.S. 433 (1971), which found a due process violation when a police chief posted in retail liquor outlets a notice identifying the plaintiff as an "excessive" drinker. Unlike the flyer in *Paul*, said Rehnquist, the posting in *Constantineau* changed the plaintiff's legal status, since it had the effect of prohibiting liquor stores from selling to him. By contrast, in *Paul*, "Kentucky law does not extend to respondent any legal guarantee of present enjoyment of reputation which has been altered as a result of petitioners' actions." Not surprisingly, the *Paul* decision provoked an outcry of protest from the dissent and most commentators, who had thought that constitutional "liberty" included freedom from destruction of one's reputation.

The issue raised in *Paul* and *Constantineau* has arisen more recently in the context of sex-offender registration laws. Many states and the federal government have enacted laws requiring sex offenders to register and update the authorities when they relocate. Connecticut's law is typical: all persons convicted of criminal offenses against a minor, violent and nonviolent sexual offenses, and felonies committed for a sexual purpose must register with the state's Department of Public Safety (DPS), providing personal information, including name, current address, and a current photograph. The law requires DPS to compile the information and publish it on its website. The website states that DPS "made no determination that any individual included in the registry is currently dangerous. Individuals included within the registry are included solely by virtue of their conviction record and state law." The website also says, as required by state law: "Any person who uses information in this registry to injure, harass or commit a criminal act against any person included in the registry . . . is subject to criminal prosecution." A registrant (who was a convicted sex offender) brought suit against DPS, arguing that the public posting violated his "liberty" interest, and that due process required that he be given a hearing to establish that he is not dangerous. In Connecticut Department of Public Safety v. Doe, 538 U.S. 1 (2003), the Supreme Court ruled in favor of DPS. The Supreme Court avoided deciding the liberty deprivation issue on the merits by assuming that, even if the plaintiff had been deprived of a liberty interest, due process would not have required a hearing. If the Court had addressed the liberty deprivation issue on the merits, how should it have ruled?

5. *Deprivation of liberty in prison discipline.* The suggestion in *Paul* that liberty, like property, derives from entitlements conferred by the positive law of the state burst into full flower in a succession of Supreme Court cases involving prison discipline. In Meachum v. Fano, 427 U.S. 215 (1976), the Court held that transferring a prisoner from a medium-security to a maximum-security prison did not infringe upon his liberty interest since there was no state-created right to remain in any particular institution absent misconduct. The applicable statute and rules allowed transfers for any reason or no reason. In subsequent prisoners' rights cases, the Court continued to look to state law as the basis for determining whether a prisoner was deprived of a protected liberty interest. *Compare* Board of Pardons v. Allen, 482 U.S. 369 (1987) (finding a liberty interest in parole release because the relevant state statute said that the Parole Board "shall" grant parole "when in its opinion there is a reasonable probability that the prisoner can be released without detriment to the prisoner or to the community"), *with* Kentucky Dept. of Corrections v. Thompson, 490 U.S. 454 (1989) (no protected liberty interest to receive particular visitors in prison, since the applicable regulation merely listed the types of individuals whose visits "might" be denied by prison officials).

A pair of cases illustrates how difficult it has been for the Court to fashion an acceptable conception of "liberty" in the prison discipline context. In Sandin v. Connor, 515 U.S. 472 (1995), the Court, 5-4, found no liberty deprivation when a prisoner in a maximum-security prison was sentenced to 30 days' solitary confinement for misconduct. The Court stated that changes in conditions of confinement amount to liberty deprivations only when restraints "impose[] atypical and significant hardship on the inmate in relation to the ordinary incidents of prison life" or "inevitably affect the duration of [the] sentence." Applying this standard in Wilkinson v. Austin, 545 U.S. 209 (2005), the Court unanimously found that assignment of a prisoner to an Ohio "supermax" prison constituted a liberty deprivation because of the harsh conditions there, including virtually no human contact, having a light on in their cell all the time, receiving only one hour of exercise outside the cell per day, and being disqualified from parole consideration. Is the disparate treatment by the court of solitary confinement versus assignment to a supermax facility defensible?

6. *Due process and indirect effects.* Third parties are often adversely affected by government actions taken against others. For example, customers may suffer if the authorities revoke the liquor license of their favorite restaurant and tenants may suffer if their apartment building is found to be uninhabitable due to the landlord's lack of maintenance. In O'Bannon v. Town Court Nursing Center, 447 U.S. 773 (1980), a particularly sympathetic group of third parties who were residents in a nursing home claimed that they were entitled to a due process hearing before they could be forced to move because their nursing home was found no longer eligible to accept patients receiving government benefits for their care. They claimed a liberty interest based on studies indicating that they would suffer serious harm if they were forced to relocate, and a property interest based on the regulations concerning the use of benefits at certified homes. The Supreme Court rejected both arguments. On the liberty claim, the Court held that only a government decision to impose harm would amount to a deprivation of liberty; the fact that the patients might be indirectly harmed by the government's decision to decertify their home was insufficient. On the property claim, the Court again relied on the indirectness of the patients' claim, noting that the government was not depriving them of their benefits. The Court held that the patients themselves had a right to use their benefits at a certified home, but that no statute or regulation granted the patients a property interest in asserting that an uncertified home ought to be certified. Justice Brennan dissented, arguing that "[t]he Government's action in withdrawing the home's certification deprives them of the expectation of continued residency created by the statutes and regulations. Under our precedents, they are certainly 'entitled . . . to the benefits of appropriate procedures' in connection with the decertification. Vitek v. Jones, 445 U.S. 480, 490 (1980); Perry v. Sindermann, 408 U.S. 593 (1972)."

Another context in which the question of whether an entitlement can exist regarding government regulation of someone else is the criminal law. Can there be an entitlement to the enforcement of the criminal law? Town of Castle Rock v. Gonzales, 545 U.S. 748 (2005), presented that issue in the heart-rending context of a woman whose violent former husband murdered her three children. She brought a claim against the Colorado municipality in which she lived, on the ground that the failure of its police officers to enforce a judicial restraining order against the former husband deprived her of a "property" interest—namely, the right to have the restraining order strictly enforced. The restraining order, obtained at the plaintiff's behest, stated that the police "shall use every reasonable means to enforce this restraining order." Nonetheless, Justice Scalia, writing for the Court, concluded that the order did not create a "legitimate claim of entitlement" such as to constitute a "property" interest. In his view, the order and the statute authorizing it no more established an enforceable right for the person seeking the order than do other criminal laws specifying that law enforcement officials "shall" take prescribed actions. Justice Scalia observed that a "well established tradition of police discretion has long coexisted with apparently mandatory arrest statutes." 545 U.S. at 760-762. Because the former husband had kidnapped the children and fled—and in fact was not in the state during the critical time period, with his location unknown to the children's mother or law enforcement officers—it was unclear what a right to "enforcement" would have meant in this context. Invoking *O'Bannon* as a case in which the indirect nature of the benefit was "fatal" to the due process claim, Scalia concluded that the benefit in *Castle Rock* was merely indirect and "incidental" to a traditional governmental function (enforcement of the criminal law) rather than a monetizable claim arising directly from an entitlement such as the one asserted in *Goldberg*. *Id.* at 767. Justice Souter, joined by Justice Breyer, offered a different reason for reaching the same result: the state-created "right" invoked by the plaintiff here was purely procedural. In order to qualify as a "property" interest under the Due Process Clause, Souter asserted, the right in question must have a substantive dimension that exists "apart from state procedural protection." *Id.* at 772. Justice Stevens, joined by Justice Ginsburg, dissented, reading the Colorado statute as a domestic violence statute that was intended to impose mandatory duties on the police and create private rights of action by beneficiaries against the police to enforce those duties. Does *Castle Rock* resolve the question whether indirect beneficiaries can assert protected interests?

Tenants living in rent-controlled housing have also raised due process claims related to participation in proceedings between government and their landlords involving rent increases. For example, Hahn v. Gottlieb, 430 F.2d 1243, 1247-1248 (1st Cir. 1970), raised the question of whether tenants in a government-subsidized housing development had a right to be heard on the landlord's request to the Federal Housing Authority (FHA) for approval of a rent increase. The court said no:

> The proceeding in which plaintiffs seek to assert their interests is basically an informal rate-making process. . . . [Procedural] safeguards are not, however, essential in "legislative" proceedings, such as rate-making, where decision depends on broad familiarity with economic conditions. . . . As Professor Davis has pointed out, when decision turns on "legislative" rather than "adjudicative" facts, a formal adversary hearing may contribute little or nothing to the agency's understanding of the issues. 1 K. Davis, Administrative Law §7.02 at 413 (1958).
>
> The distinction between "legislative" and "adjudicative" facts is particularly apt in this case, where it is the tenants rather than the landlord who seek a hearing. The tenants are unlikely to have special familiarity with their landlord's financial condition, the intricacies of project management, or the state of the economy in the surrounding area. Hopefully, the FHA can check the accuracy of the landlord's documentation without their assistance. They may be aware of construction defects in their own living areas, but if . . . a building has been approved which does not conform to applicable standards, there would seem to be limited utility in rehearsing old mistakes each time a rental increase is sought. . . .

Should the indirectness of the benefit to the tenants in *Hahn* make a difference? The First Circuit thought so, stating that "[p]laintiffs are not legally 'entitled' to low rents in the same sense that the welfare recipient in Goldberg v. Kelly . . . was entitled to basic sustenance under a system of categorical assistance." Why is this important for due process purposes?

2.   *The Requirements of Due Process*

In pre-*Roth* cases such as Goldberg v. Kelly, the courts engaged in a one-step due process analysis. They asked, in essence: Given all the circumstances, has the petitioner been treated fairly? In *Roth*, the Supreme Court decreed that the text of the Due Process Clauses commanded a two-step inquiry. First, the court must determine whether the petitioner has been deprived of an interest that falls within the categories of "life, liberty, or property." Having answered that question in the affirmative, the court must then decide what process is "due." In the preceding section, we examined the Supreme Court's effort to clarify the first stage of the due process inquiry. In this section, our attention shifts to the second stage. What procedures must administrators use when they deprive people of protected interests? As we shall see in the case studies that follow, the formula developed by the Court for answering that question leaves considerable room for variation from case to case and context to context.

a.   The *Eldridge* Calculus

The Social Security system was established in the depths of the Great Depression as a compulsory "social insurance" system to provide a dependable source of income to retired persons and their dependents. In 1956, Congress added the Disability Insurance (DI) program, which provides benefits to insured workers who become disabled. DI benefits are paid monthly until termination of the disability, death, or attainment of age 65 (when the Old-Age and Survivors Insurance program takes over). The amount of benefits is determined by factors such as the claimant's age, previous pay rate, and number of dependents. Benefits are subject to a ceiling but are tax exempt and adjusted annually for inflation. In 2010, the average monthly benefit was $1,065 for a disabled individual (up from $131 in 1970) and $1,670 for a family of three (up from $272 in 1970).

The growth in the size of the DI program since its inception has been truly staggering. Between 1957 and 2016 the number of DI recipients grew from 149,850 to 11,832,337, while the cost of the program rose from $59 million to more than $135 billion. The volume of claims that must be processed each year is enormous. In 2016, for example, over 2.3 million claims were filed, of which about one-third were granted.

The threshold criterion for eligibility is that the claimant be insured under the Social Security program. With some exceptions, a claimant must have worked 20 quarters out of the immediately preceding 40 quarters to be eligible for DI. This requirement illustrates the "insurance" aspect of the program, since a beneficiary must have made payments into the system in order to receive benefits from it. In 2016, more than 148 million people met this requirement.

Once this coverage is established, a claimant must prove that he is "disabled." The Social Security Act defines disability as the

> inability to engage in any substantial gainful activity by reason of any medically determinable physical or mental impairment which can be expected to result in death or which has lasted or can be expected to last for a continuous period of not less than 12 months.

42 U.S.C. §423(d)(1)(A) (1982). To satisfy this test the worker must show by means of "medically acceptable clinical and laboratory diagnostic techniques" that he has a physical or mental impairment of such severity that

he is not only unable to do his previous work but cannot, considering his age, education, and work experience, engage in any other kind of substantial gainful work which exists in the national economy, regardless of whether such work exists in the immediate area in which he lives, or whether a specific job vacancy exists for him, or whether he would be hired if he applied for work.

Id. §423(d)(2)(A).

The DI program is administered by the Social Security Administration (SSA) in the Department of Health and Human Services. The application process begins with review of a claim by a state vocational rehabilitation agency designated by the SSA to perform that function. If the state agency recommends denial of the claim, the claimant may invoke a multi-step process of appeal that includes review by the SSA's Bureau of Disability Insurance (BDI), a request for reconsideration by the state agency, an administrative hearing before an administrative law judge (ALJ), and discretionary review by the SSA's Appeals Council. Following an Appeals Council decision to affirm a denial (or deny an appeal), an aggrieved claimant has a right to judicial review in federal district court.

Since the program's inception, SSA has been responsible for periodically reviewing cases of DI recipients to determine whether they continue to be disabled. The actual number of continuing disability investigations (CDIs) performed by SSA fell sharply during the 1970s, from a high of 167,000 (112 per 1,000 DI recipients) in 1970 to a low of 83,651 (29 per 1,000 recipients) in 1978. Alarmed at the low rate of CDIs and high rate (46-47 percent) of terminations ordered as a result of the reviews that were done, Congress in 1980 ordered SSA to increase the annual number of CDIs to 567,000 in 1982 and 806,000 in 1983. Despite these legislative efforts, this problem continues. For example, in 2013, SSA's Inspector General reported to Congress that the agency anticipated a backlog of 1.3 million disability reviews by the end of the fiscal year, resulting in over $400 million in annual benefits payments that would not have been made had the number of reviews been adequate.

The CDI process is similar to that used for determining initial claims. After gathering medical and vocational information about the recipient's current condition, the state agency recommends either "continuance" or "cessation" of benefits. In the latter case, the recipient is notified of the proposed action and its asserted justification, and given an opportunity to review his file and respond in writing. Once the state agency makes its final decision, it is reviewed by the BDI. If the BDI accepts a state agency's cessation decision, it notifies the recipient in writing, stating the reasons for the decision. Benefits are thereupon terminated, effective two months after the "recovery" was found to have occurred. The termination notice also informs the recipient of his right to seek a de novo redetermination from the state agency, followed (if necessary) by a de novo ALJ hearing, discretionary Appeals Council review, and judicial review. If it is determined at any point after termination of benefits that the claimant's disability extended beyond the cessation date, he is entitled to retroactive payments.

In light of *Goldberg*, the question naturally arose whether termination of benefits prior to the ALJ hearing was consistent with due process.

MATHEWS v. ELDRIDGE
424 U.S. 319 (1976)

MR. JUSTICE POWELL delivered the opinion of the Court.

The issue in this case is whether the Due Process Clause of the Fifth Amendment requires that prior to the termination of Social Security disability benefit payments the recipient be afforded an opportunity for an evidentiary hearing. . . .

Respondent Eldridge was first awarded benefits in June 1968. In March 1972, he received a questionnaire from the state agency charged with monitoring his medical condition. Eldridge completed the questionnaire, indicating that his condition had not improved and identifying the medical sources, including physicians, from whom he had received treatment recently. The state agency then obtained reports from his physician and a psychiatric consultant. After considering these reports and other information in his file the agency informed Eldridge by letter that it had made a tentative determination that his disability had ceased in May 1972. The letter included a statement of reasons for the proposed termination of benefits, and advised Eldridge that he might request reasonable time in which to obtain and submit additional information pertaining to his condition.

In his written response, Eldridge disputed one characterization of his medical condition and indicated that the agency already had enough evidence to establish his disability.[2] The state agency then made its final determination that he had ceased to be disabled in May 1972. This determination was accepted by the Social Security Administration (SSA), which notified Eldridge in July that his benefits would terminate after that month. The notification also advised him of his right to seek reconsideration by the state agency of this initial determination within six months.

Instead of requesting reconsideration Eldridge commenced this action challenging the constitutional validity of the administrative procedures established by the Secretary of Health, Education, and Welfare for assessing whether there exists a continuing disability. He sought an immediate reinstatement of benefits pending a hearing on the issue of his disability. . . .

Relying entirely upon the District Court's opinion, the Court of Appeals for the Fourth Circuit affirmed the injunction barring termination of Eldridge's benefits prior to an evidentiary hearing. 493 F.2d 1230 (1974). We reverse. . . .

---

2. Eldridge originally was disabled due to chronic anxiety and back strain. He subsequently was found to have diabetes. The tentative determination letter indicated that aid would be terminated because available medical evidence indicated that his diabetes was under control, that there existed no limitations on his back movements which would impose severe functional restrictions, and that he no longer suffered emotional problems that would preclude him from all work for which he was qualified. . . . In his reply letter he claimed to have arthritis of the spine rather than a strained back.

III

A

. . . The Secretary does not contend that procedural due process is inapplicable to terminations of Social Security disability benefits. . . . Rather, the Secretary contends that the existing administrative procedures . . . provide all the process that is constitutionally due before a recipient can be deprived of that interest. . . .

[I]dentification of the specific dictates of due process generally requires consideration of three distinct factors: First, the private interest that will be affected by the official action; second, the risk of an erroneous deprivation of such interest through the procedures used, and the probable value, if any, of additional or substitute procedural safeguards; and finally, the Government's interest, including the function involved and the fiscal and administrative burdens that the additional or substitute procedural requirement would entail. . . .

C

. . . Since a recipient whose benefits are terminated is awarded full retroactive relief if he ultimately prevails, his sole interest is in the uninterrupted receipt of this source of income pending final administrative decision on his claim. . . .

Only in *Goldberg* has the Court held that due process requires an evidentiary hearing prior to a temporary deprivation. . . . Eligibility for disability benefits, in contrast, is not based upon financial need. Indeed, it is wholly unrelated to the worker's income or support from many other sources, such as earnings of other family members, workmen's compensation awards, tort claims awards, savings, private insurance, public or private pensions, veterans' benefits, food stamps, public assistance, or the "many other important programs, both public and private, which contain provisions for disability payments affecting a substantial portion of the work force. . . ." Richardson v. Belcher, 404 U.S. [78, 85-87 (1971)] (Douglas, J., dissenting). . . .

The Secretary concedes that the delay between a request for a hearing before an administrative law judge and a decision on the claim is currently between 10 and 11 months. Since a terminated recipient must first obtain a reconsideration decision as a prerequisite to invoking his right to an evidentiary hearing, the delay between the actual cutoff of benefits and final decision after a hearing exceeds one year.

In view of the torpidity of this administrative review process, . . . and the typically modest resources of the family unit of the physically disabled worker,[26] the hardship imposed upon the erroneously terminated disability recipient may be significant. Still, the disabled worker's need is likely to be less than that of

---

26. Amici cite statistics compiled by the Secretary which indicate that in 1965 the mean income of the family unit of a disabled worker was $3,803, while the median income for the unit was $2,836. The mean liquid assets—i.e., cash, stocks, bonds—of these family units was $4,862; the median was $940. These statistics do not take into account the family unit's nonliquid assets—i.e., automobile, real estate, and the like.

a welfare recipient. In addition to the possibility of access to private resources, other forms of government assistance will become available where the termination of disability benefits places a worker or his family below the subsistence level.[27] . . .

D

An additional factor to be considered here is the fairness and reliability of the existing pretermination procedures, and the probable value, if any, of additional procedural safeguards.

[T]he decision whether to discontinue disability benefits will turn, in most cases, upon "routine, standard, and unbiased medical reports by physician specialists," Richardson v. Perales, 402 U.S. [389, 404 (1971)], concerning a subject whom they have personally examined.[28] . . . To be sure, credibility and veracity may be a factor in the ultimate disability assessment in some cases. But procedural due process rules are shaped by the risk of error inherent in the truth-finding process as applied to the generality of cases, not the rare exceptions. The potential value of an evidentiary hearing, or even oral presentation to the decisionmaker, is substantially less in this context than in *Goldberg*.

The decision in *Goldberg* also was based on the Court's conclusion that written submissions were an inadequate substitute for oral presentation because they did not provide an effective means for the recipient to communicate his case to the decisionmaker. . . . In the context of the disability-benefits-entitlement assessment the administrative procedures under review here fully answer these objections.

The detailed questionnaire which the state agency periodically sends the recipient identifies with particularity the information relevant to the entitlement decision, and the recipient is invited to obtain assistance from the local SSA office in completing the questionnaire. More important, the information critical to the entitlement decision usually is derived from medical sources, such as the treating physician. Such sources are likely to be able to communicate

---

27. Amici emphasize that because an identical definition of disability is employed in both the Title II Social Security Program and in the companion welfare system for the disabled, Supplemental Security Income (SSI), *compare* 42 U.S.C. §423(d)(1) with §1382c(a)(3) (1970 ed., Supp. III), the terminated disability-benefits recipient will be ineligible for the SSI Program. There exist, however, state and local welfare programs which may supplement the worker's income. In addition, the worker's household unit can qualify for food stamps if it meets the financial need requirements. *See* 7 U.S.C. §§2013(c), 2014(b); 7 CFR §271 (1975). Finally, in 1974 480,000 of the approximately 2,000,000 disabled workers receiving Social Security benefits also received SSI benefits. Since financial need is a criterion for eligibility under the SSI program, those disabled workers who are most in need will in the majority of cases be receiving SSI benefits when disability insurance aid is terminated. And, under the SSI program, a pretermination evidentiary hearing is provided, if requested.

28. The decision is not purely a question of the accuracy of a medical diagnosis since the ultimate issue which the state agency must resolve is whether in light of the particular worker's "age, education, and work experience" he cannot "engage in any . . . substantial gainful work which exists in the national economy. . . ." 42 U.S.C. §423(d)(2)(A). Yet information concerning each of these worker characteristics is amenable to effective written presentation. The value of an evidentiary hearing, or even a limited oral presentation, to an accurate presentation of those factors to the decisionmaker does not appear substantial. Similarly, resolution of the inquiry as to the types of employment opportunities that exist in the national economy for a physically impaired worker with a particular set of skills would not necessarily be advanced by an evidentiary hearing. *Cf.* 1 K. Davis, Administrative Law Treatise §7.06, p.429 (1958). The statistical information relevant to this judgment is more amenable to written than to oral presentation.

more effectively through written documents than are welfare recipients or the lay witnesses supporting their cause. The conclusions of physicians often are supported by X-rays and the results of clinical or laboratory tests, information typically more amenable to written than to oral presentation. . . .

A further safeguard against mistake is the policy of allowing the disability recipient's representative full access to all information relied upon by the state agency. In addition, prior to the cutoff of benefits the agency informs the recipient of its tentative assessment, the reasons therefor, and provides a summary of the evidence that it considers most relevant. Opportunity is then afforded the recipient to submit additional evidence or arguments, enabling him to challenge directly the accuracy of information in his file as well as the correctness of the agency's tentative conclusions. These procedures, again as contrasted with those before the Court in *Goldberg*, enable the recipient to "mold" his argument to respond to the precise issues which the decisionmaker regards as crucial.

Despite these carefully structured procedures, amici point to the significant reversal rate for appealed cases as clear evidence that the current process is inadequate. Depending upon the base selected and the line of analysis followed, the relevant reversal rates urged by the contending parties vary from a high of 58.6% for appealed reconsideration decisions to an overall reversal rate of only 3.3%.[29] Bare statistics rarely provide a satisfactory measure of the fairness of a decisionmaking process. Their adequacy is especially suspect here since the administrative review system is operated on an open-file basis. A recipient may always submit new evidence, and such submissions may result in additional medical examinations. Such fresh examinations were held in approximately 30% to 40% of the appealed cases in fiscal 1973, either at the reconsideration or evidentiary hearing stage of the administrative process. . . . In this context, the value of reversal rate statistics as one means of evaluating the adequacy of the pretermination process is diminished. Thus, although we view such information as relevant, it is certainly not controlling in this case.

E

In striking the appropriate due process balance the final factor to be assessed is the public interest. This includes the administrative burden and other societal costs that would be associated with requiring, as a matter of constitutional right, an evidentiary hearing upon demand in all cases prior to the termination of disability benefits. The most visible burden would be the incremental cost resulting from the increased number of hearings and the expense of providing benefits to ineligible recipients pending decision. No one can predict the extent of the increase, but the fact that full benefits

---

29. By focusing solely on the reversal rate for appealed reconsideration determinations amici overstate the relevant reversal rate. As we indicated last Term in Fusari v. Steinberg, 419 U.S. 379, 383 n.6 (1975), in order fully to assess the reliability and fairness of a system of procedure, one must also consider the overall rate of error for all denials of benefits. Here that overall rate is 12.2%. Moreover, about 75% of these reversals occur at the reconsideration stage of the administrative process. Since the median period between a request for reconsideration review and decision is only two months, Brief for AFL-CIO et al. as Amici Curiae App. 4a, the deprivation is significantly less than that concomitant to the lengthier delay before an evidentiary hearing. Netting out these reconsideration reversals, the overall reversal rate falls to 3.3%.

would continue until after such hearings would assure the exhaustion in most cases of this attractive option. Nor would the theoretical right of the Secretary to recover undeserved benefits result, as a practical matter, in any substantial offset to the added outlay of public funds. The parties submit widely varying estimates of the probable additional financial cost. We only need say that experience with the constitutionalizing of government procedures suggests that the ultimate additional cost in terms of money and administrative burden would not be insubstantial.

Financial cost alone is not a controlling weight in determining whether due process requires a particular procedural safeguard prior to some administrative decision. But the Government's interest, and hence that of the public, in conserving scarce fiscal and administrative resources is a factor that must be weighed. At some point the benefit of an additional safeguard to the individual affected by the administrative action and to society in terms of increased assurance that the action is just, may be outweighed by the cost. Significantly, the cost of protecting those whom the preliminary administrative process has identified as likely to be found undeserving may in the end come out of the pockets of the deserving since resources available for any particular program of social welfare are not unlimited. . . .

We conclude that an evidentiary hearing is not required prior to the termination of disability benefits and that the present administrative procedures fully comport with due process.

The judgment of the Court of Appeals is reversed.

MR. JUSTICE STEVENS took no part in the consideration or decision of this case.

MR. JUSTICE BRENNAN, with whom MR. JUSTICE MARSHALL concurs, dissenting.

[T]he Court's consideration that a discontinuance of disability benefits may cause the recipient to suffer only a limited deprivation is no argument. It is speculative. Moreover, the very legislative determination to provide disability benefits, without any prerequisite determination of need in fact, presumes a need by the recipient which is not this Court's function to denigrate. Indeed, in the present case, it is indicated that because disability benefits were terminated there was a foreclosure upon the Eldridge home and the family's furniture was repossessed, forcing Eldridge, his wife, and their children to sleep in one bed. Finally, it is also no argument that a worker, who has been placed in the untenable position of having been denied disability benefits, may still seek other forms of public assistance.

NOTES AND QUESTIONS

1. *The* Eldridge *balancing test.* Suppose you were a policy analyst for a congressional subcommittee and had been asked to advise the subcommittee whether to recommend legislation requiring the SSA to continue paying DI benefits until after the ALJ hearing. How would you do the analysis? Based on the information about the DI program presented in *Eldridge,* what would you recommend?

Is the Court's method of analysis different from the method you used to answer the previous question? Should it be? What exactly are the interests that the Court is "balancing" and how is it balancing them? Does the Court have a theory for placing relative values on the interests it is balancing? For a negative answer, *see* Jerry L. Mashaw, The Supreme Court's Due Process Calculus for Administrative Adjudication in *Mathews v. Eldridge:* Three Factors in Search of a Theory of Value, 44 U. Chi. L. Rev. 28 (1976); and Jerry L. Mashaw, Administrative Due Process as Social-Cost Accounting, 9 Hofstra L. Rev. 1423 (1981).

2. *Inquisitorial and adversarial hearings.* Does *Eldridge* illustrate the Court's reluctance to convert the "inquisitorial" procedures characteristic of many social programs into the "adversarial" model characteristic of judicial trials? For a clearer illustration, *see* Walters v. National Assn. of Radiation Survivors, 473 U.S. 305 (1985). There, the Supreme Court upheld a statutory $10 limit on the amount that an attorney or other advocate may charge to represent a veteran applying for benefits for service-related disability or death. The statutory limit (enacted in 1864!) was designed to protect Civil War veterans from being overcharged by unscrupulous lawyers for little more than filling out a form. Since then, the process for adjudicating disability and death claims has become more complex, especially in cases involving claims for disease resulting from exposure to toxic substances like Agent Orange. Nonetheless, the Court, applying the *Eldridge* calculus, upheld the restriction. Recognizing that the fee limit effectively deprived most claimants of attorneys' services, the majority concluded that widespread participation of lawyers would excessively increase the formality, complexity, and expense of a nonadversarial system of adjudication that the Court characterized as "designed to function throughout with a high degree of informality and solicitude for the claimant."

3. *"Consultation" prior to deprivation.* In Goss v. Lopez, 419 U.S. 565 (1975), the Supreme Court held that a high school student may not be suspended from school for participating in a disturbance without first being given "oral or written notice of the charges against him and, if he denies them, an explanation of the evidence the authorities have and an opportunity to present his side of the story." *Id.* at 581. The Court was careful to indicate that it was not requiring school officials to conduct a full-scale adversarial hearing. In a 1978 article, Professor Melvin Eisenberg read *Goss* to endorse a "consultative" model of due process, which stood in sharp contrast to the adjudicative model endorsed in *Goldberg.* Melvin Eisenberg, Participation, Responsiveness, and the Consultative Process: An Essay for Lon Fuller, 92 Harv. L. Rev. 410, 414-417 (1978). However, purely consultative hearings may not be sufficient in the school disciplinary process. For example, in Doe v. University of Cincinnati, 872 F.3d 393 (6th Cir. 2017), the court held that a student accused of sexual assault was denied due process when he was not provided with an opportunity to confront and question his accuser. In *Doe,* the accuser did not attend the disciplinary hearing and the accused student was found responsible and suspended from the university for one year. The Sixth Circuit upheld the district court's grant of a preliminary injunction, finding that Doe was likely to prevail on his claim that the procedure followed at the hearing denied him due process.

Although *Goss* antedated *Eldridge,* the Court has in several subsequent cases held that the Due Process Clause requires administrators to conduct informal "consultative" hearings prior to depriving a person of a property or liberty interest. An example is Memphis Light, Gas & Water Div. v. Craft, 436 U.S. 1 (1977). There, a municipal utility terminated a customer's service for nonpayment of bills. The failure to pay was due to an erroneous double-billing by Memphis Light. Despite a bona fide effort by respondent to resolve the problem, she was unable to obtain any information about the billing from Memphis Light's employees, nor was she informed about any procedures for discussing the disputed bills with management. The Supreme Court upheld respondent's due process claim, reasoning that Memphis Light must afford customers an opportunity to discuss a contested bill with a responsible utility official *prior* to the termination of services. Applying the *Eldridge* test, the Court found the consumer's interest in maintaining services and the risk of erroneous termination to outweigh the utility's interests in summary termination. The Court also found the available common law remedies inadequate to compensate for the absence of a pretermination administrative review.

Similarly, in *Loudermill*, excerpted above, the Court ruled that a school board may not summarily discharge a tenured employee without first giving him an "opportunity to present his side of the story," even though he was entitled by state law to demand a post-termination adjudicative hearing:

> [S]ome opportunity for the employee to present his side of the case is recurringly of obvious value in reaching an accurate decision. Dismissals for cause will often involve factual disputes. . . . Even where the facts are clear, the appropriateness or necessity of the discharge may not be; in such cases, the only meaningful opportunity to invoke the discretion of the decisionmaker is likely to be before the termination takes effect. . . .
>
> The essential requirements of due process, and all that respondents seek or the Court of Appeals required, are notice and an opportunity to respond. The opportunity to present reasons, either in person or in writing, why proposed action should not be taken is a fundamental due process requirement.

Id. at 544-546.

Is the informal-hearing requirement of *Goss, Memphis Light,* and *Loudermill* a serious constraint on administrative arbitrariness? Or does it trivialize the Due Process Clause, wielding it, like an admonishing forefinger, to regulate the interpersonal give-and-take of everyday bureaucratic life?

4. *The "emergency" exception.* Despite rather categorical dicta to the contrary, the *Loudermill* Court acknowledged that "there are, of course, some situations in which a postdeprivation hearing will satisfy due process requirements." 470 U.S. at 542, n.7. The Court cited the venerable case of North American Cold Storage Co. v. Chicago, 211 U.S. 306 (1908), in which the Court upheld, against a due process challenge, a city ordinance requiring the seizure and destruction of "putrid, decayed, poisoned and infected food" without prior hearing. At the time *North American* was decided, most people thought "due process of law" referred solely to a trial-like hearing. The recognition in cases like *Loudermill* that "due process" may require (and be satisfied by) an informal "consultative" hearing cast some doubt on the continued vitality of *North American*'s "emergency" doctrine. After all, one could reasonably require health department officials to have at least a "conversation" with a warehouser before destroying allegedly

putrid food. But the Supreme Court has made it clear in at least two subsequent cases that the "emergency" exception to pretermination procedure is still alive and well. In FDIC v. Mallen, 486 U.S. 230 (1988), the Court upheld an order of the FDIC to suspend an officer of an insured bank without prior hearing of any form, under a federal statute authorizing summary suspensions of bank officers charged with "a felony involving dishonesty or breach of trust." Likewise, in Gilbert v. Homar, 520 U.S. 924 (1997), the Court upheld the summary suspension of a state college police officer who had been charged with a felony, so long as he was afforded an opportunity for a timely post-suspension hearing.

5. *Due process in the regulatory context.* In Brock v. Roadway Express, 481 U.S. 252 (1987), the Supreme Court struggled to apply its procedural due process test in the context of a government regulatory program (as opposed to a benefits program). Under a statute designed to encourage "whistleblowers" to report safety violations in the trucking industry, the Secretary of Labor ordered Roadway Express to reinstate a discharged employee with pay pending investigation of the grounds for his dismissal. The statute permits an employer to request an evidentiary hearing on the issue, but the request does not stay a temporary reinstatement order. Prior to the reinstatement order, Roadway was given an opportunity to make a statement to the investigator, but not to know or confront the evidence against it. Justice Marshall, writing for a four-member plurality of the Supreme Court, held that the agency's pre-reinstatement procedures were constitutionally defective:

> [M]inimum due process for the employer in this context requires notice of the employee's allegations, notice of the substance of the relevant supporting evidence, an opportunity to submit a written response, and an opportunity to meet with the investigator and present statements from rebuttal witnesses.

481 U.S. at 264. Justices Brennan and Stevens would have gone further and required that the employer be afforded a right to confront and cross-examine adverse witnesses prior to reinstatement. Justice White, joined by Chief Justice Rehnquist and Justice Scalia, disagreed, concluding that due process required only notice of the charges and an opportunity to respond to them, not access to the underlying evidence.

Regulatory due process issues have also arisen with regard to the EPA's enforcement of the Clean Air Act and other statutes it administers. The Clean Air Act authorizes the EPA Administrator to issue an "administrative compliance order" (ACO) whenever she believes, "on the basis of any information available," that the Act has been violated. In Tennessee Valley Authority v. Whitman, 336 F.3d 1236 (11th Cir. 2003), *cert. denied*, 541 U.S. 1030 (2004), the issue was whether an ACO issued against the TVA had the force of law, such that noncompliance with the order could directly trigger imposition of civil or criminal penalties. The court ruled that ACOs cannot, consistent with the Due Process Clause, have legal effect since they are issued without affording the alleged violator any right to a hearing. Therefore, said the court, the EPA must enforce the ACO in an action in federal district court, where the TVA would have a right to contest the alleged violation. Similar issues have arisen regarding the EPA's enforcement of the Comprehensive Environmental Response, Compensation, and Liability Act (CERCLA). For fuller treatment of this issue, see Chapter VII, *infra*.

b.   The Right to a Neutral Decisionmaker

Recall that in *Goldberg* the Supreme Court listed "an impartial decision-maker" as an "essential" element of procedural due process. The Court cited In re Murchison, 349 U.S. 133, 136 (1955), a case involving a state trial judge who had both charged and tried two defendants for criminal contempt. While the courts purport to apply the same standard of impartiality to administrative adjudicators as to judges, the former raise somewhat distinctive problems. Administrators do not customarily possess the same degree of insulation from extrinsic influences as do judges (at least federal court judges, who are not elected). Prior professional experience, future occupational plans, organizational loyalties, and close personal associations are more apt to intrude into the decision-making process. In this section we explore two contexts in which administrative partiality has been drawn into question: self-interest and prejudgment.

The most obvious basis for disqualifying an adjudicator is self-interest. The maxim "no person shall be a judge in her own cause" is so central to our conception of due process as scarcely to require repetition. What is less clear, however, is the extent of its reach. In two celebrated cases from Ohio, decided 45 years apart, the Supreme Court grappled with that very question.

TUMEY v. OHIO, 273 U.S. 510 (1927):   An Ohio statute empowered village mayors to sit as judges in criminal prosecutions involving possession of intoxicating liquors. A village ordinance provided that, from the fines collected, the mayor "shall receive or retain the amount of his costs in each case, in addition to his regular salary, as compensation for hearing such cases." Tumey, convicted by the mayor and fined $100, sought to dismiss the conviction on the ground that the mayor was disqualified by his self-interest. The Supreme Court agreed:

> [I]t certainly violates the Fourteenth Amendment, and deprives a defendant in a criminal case of due process of law, to subject his liberty or property to the judgment of a court the judge of which has a direct, personal, substantial, pecuniary interest in reaching a conclusion against him in his case.
>
> The Mayor of the Village of North College Hill, Ohio, had a direct, personal, pecuniary interest in convicting the defendant who came before him for trial, in the twelve dollars of costs imposed in his behalf, which he would not have received if the defendant had been acquitted. . . . We can not regard the prospect of receipt or loss of such an emolument in each case as a minute, remote, trifling or insignificant interest. It is certainly not fair to each defendant, brought before the Mayor for the careful and judicial consideration of his guilt or innocence, that the prospect of such a loss by the Mayor should weigh against his acquittal.
>
> These are not cases in which the penalties and the costs are negligible. The field of jurisdiction is not that of a small community engaged in enforcing its own local regulations. The court is a state agency, imposing substantial punishment, and the cases to be considered are gathered from the whole county by the energy of the village marshals, and detectives regularly employed by the village for the purpose. It is not to be treated as a mere village tribunal for village peccadilloes. There are doubtless mayors who would not allow such a consideration as $12 costs in each case to affect their judgment in it; but the requirement of due process of law in judicial procedure is not satisfied by the argument that men of the highest honor and the greatest self-sacrifice could carry it on without danger of injustice. Every procedure which would offer a possible temptation to the average man as a

judge to forget the burden of proof required to convict the defendant, or which might lead him not to hold the balance nice, clear and true between the State and the accused, denies the latter due process of law.

WARD v. VILLAGE OF MONROEVILLE, 409 U.S. 57 (1972):   Another Ohio statute, similar to the one at issue in *Tumey*, empowered village mayors to sit as judges in cases involving certain traffic offenses. The fines collected were deposited in the village treasury. Even though the mayor received no direct compensation, the Supreme Court found sufficient self-interest to require disqualification:

> A major part of village income is derived from the fines, forfeitures, costs, and fees imposed by him in his mayor's court. Thus, in 1964 this income contributed $23,589.50 of total village revenues of $46,355.38; in 1965 it was $18,508.95 of $46,752.60; in 1966 it was $16,085 of $43,585.13; in 1967 it was $20,060.65 of $53,931.43; and in 1968 it was $23,439.42 of $52,995.95. . . .
>
> The issue turns, as the Ohio court acknowledged, on whether the Mayor can be regarded as an impartial judge under the principles laid down by this court in *Tumey*. . . .
>
> The fact that the mayor there shared directly in the fees and costs did not define the limits of the principle. . . . Plainly [a] "possible temptation" may also exist when the mayor's executive responsibilities for village finances may make him partisan to maintain the high level of contribution from the mayor's court. This, too, is a "situation in which an official perforce occupies two practically and seriously inconsistent positions, one partisan and the other judicial, [and] necessarily involves a lack of due process of law in the trial of defendants charged with crimes before him." *Id.*, at 534. . . .
>
> Respondent also argues that any unfairness at the trial level can be corrected on appeal and trial de novo in the County Court of Common Pleas. We disagree. This "procedural safeguard" does not guarantee a fair trial in the mayor's court; there is nothing to suggest that the incentive to convict would be diminished by the possibility of reversal on appeal. Nor, in any event, may the State's trial court procedure be deemed constitutionally acceptable simply because the State eventually offers a defendant an impartial adjudication. Petitioner is entitled to a neutral and detached judge in the first instance.

NOTES AND QUESTIONS

1. *The legal test for impartiality.* In small villages it is often necessary for public officials to perform multiple functions. Should the Court have been more responsive to such an argument? If *Tumey* or *Ward* had arisen after *Eldridge*, would it have been appropriate for the Court to apply that case's three-part balancing test to determine whether due process requires a different hearing officer? In fact the courts have not generally used the *Eldridge* test in evaluating claims of administrative self-interest or bias. Why do you suppose they have not? Is the demand for an impartial factfinder qualitatively different from the demand for, say, counsel or cross-examination?

2. *Initial determinations by biased officials.* As the Court notes in *Ward*, a person convicted in the mayor's court is entitled to a de novo trial in the County Court of Common Pleas. Why does that hearing not cleanse any

impurity in the system? If "petitioner is entitled to a neutral and detached judge in the first instance," must the police officer who serves the citation be "neutral and detached"? In *Goldberg*, the Court concluded that welfare caseworkers were *not* impartial, yet it seemed to concede that they could make initial determinations of ineligibility subject to review, at the recipient's request, by an impartial hearing officer. How can *Ward* be reconciled with *Goldberg*?

3. *Financial incentives and self-interest.* Compare Marshall v. Jerrico, Inc., 446 U.S. 238 (1980) with *Ward.* Section 16 of the Fair Labor Standards Act, 29 U.S.C. §216, empowered the Secretary of Labor to assess a civil money penalty against any person whom he determined, after notice and opportunity for hearing, to have violated the Act's child labor provisions. The Secretary delegated enforcement responsibility to the Employment Standards Administration (ESA), and adjudicatory responsibility to the department's ALJs. Instead of requiring the department to deposit any penalties collected into the general treasury of the United States—as was customary—the statute specifically permitted the department to retain them to help reimburse the cost of enforcing the Act. After being fined $18,500 by an ALJ for several violations, Jerrico claimed that the reimbursement provision violated its due process rights by encouraging agency personnel to seek and impose excessive fines. The Supreme Court disagreed. It rejected claims addressed to the alleged bias of ESA personnel on the ground that *Tumey* and *Ward* were inapplicable to officials performing purely prosecutorial functions. In any event, added the Court, the sums at stake (less than 1 percent of the ESA's budget) were too small to create a condition of financial dependence. Nor was there sufficient reason to doubt the ALJ's impartiality, ruled the Court, since ALJs are on a fixed salary and are organizationally separate from the ESA, which benefits from the proceeds.

GIBSON v. BERRYHILL
411 U.S. 564 (1973)

MR. JUSTICE WHITE delivered the opinion of the Court.

Prior to 1965, the laws of Alabama relating to the practice of optometry permitted any person, including a business firm or corporation, to maintain a department in which "eyes are examined or glasses fitted," provided that such department was in the charge of a duly licensed optometrist. This permission was expressly conferred by §210 of Title 46 of the Alabama Code of 1940, and also inferentially by §211 of the Code which regulates the advertising practices of optometrists, and which, until 1965, appeared to contemplate the existence of commercial stores with optical departments.[1] In 1965,

---

1. Sections 210 and 211 of c.11, Tit. 46, of the Code of Alabama, 1940, provided, prior to 1965, as follows:

"§210. Store where glasses are sold; how department conducted.—Nothing in this chapter shall be so construed as to prevent any person, firm, or corporation from owning or operating a store or business establishment wherein eyes are examined or glasses fitted; provided, that such store, establishment, or optometric department shall be in charge of a duly licensed optometrist, whose name must appear on and in all optometry advertising of whatsoever nature done by said person, firm or corporation.

§210 was repealed in its entirety by the Alabama Legislature, and §211 was amended so as to eliminate any direct reference to optical departments maintained by corporations or other business establishments under the direction of employee optometrists.[2]

Soon after these statutory changes, the Alabama Optometric Association, a professional organization whose membership is limited to independent practitioners of optometry *not* employed by others, filed charges against various named optometrists, all of whom were duly licensed under Alabama law but were the salaried employees of Lee Optical Co. The charges were filed with the Alabama Board of Optometry, the statutory body with authority to issue, suspend, and revoke licenses for the practice of optometry. The gravamen of these charges was that the named optometrists, by accepting employment from Lee Optical, a corporation, had engaged in "unprofessional conduct" within the meaning of §206 of the Alabama optometry statute, and hence were practicing their profession unlawfully.[3] More particularly, the Association charged the named individuals with, among other things, aiding and abetting a corporation in the illegal practice of optometry; practicing optometry under a false name, that is, Lee Optical Co.; unlawfully soliciting the sale of glasses; lending their licenses to Lee Optical Co.; and splitting or dividing fees

---

"§211. False or misleading statements in advertisements or stores having optometry department.—It shall be unlawful for any person, firm or corporation, engaged in the practice of optometry in this state, to print or cause to be printed, or circulate or cause to be circulated, or publish, by any means whatsoever, any advertisement or circular in which appears any untruthful, impossible, or improbable or misleading statement or statements, or anything calculated or intended to mislead or deceive the public. And it shall be unlawful for any individual, firm or corporation, engaged in the sale of goods, wares or merchandise who maintains or operates, or who allows to be maintained and operated in connection with said mercantile business an optometry department; or who rents or subleases to any person or persons for the purpose of engaging in the practice of optometry therein, any portion of or space in said store, premises or establishment in which such person, firm or corporation is engaged in said mercantile business, to publish, or circulate or print or cause to be printed, by any means whatsoever, any advertisement or notice of the optometry department maintained, operated, or conducted in said establishment or place of business, in which said advertisement or notice appear any untruthful, improbable, impossible, or misleading statement or statements, or anything calculated to mislead or deceive the public."

Sections 190-213, regulating the practice of optometry in Alabama, were originally adopted in 1919.

2. Section 211, as amended, reads as follows:

"§211. False or misleading statements in advertisements or circulars.—It shall be unlawful for any person engaged in the practice of optometry in this state to print or cause to be printed, or circulate or cause to be circulated, or published, by any means whatsoever, any advertisement or circular in which appears any untruthful, impossible, or improbable or misleading statement or statements, or anything calculated or intended to mislead or deceive the public."

3. Section 206, insofar as relevant here, provides as follows:

"§206. License may be suspended or revoked.—A license issued to any person may be suspended for a definite period of time, or revoked by the state board of optometry for any of the following reasons; to-wit: . . . For unprofessional conduct. 'Unprofessional conduct' shall be defined to mean any conduct of a character likely to deceive or defraud the public, lending his license by any licensed optometrist to any person, the employment of 'cappers,' or 'steerers' to obtain business, 'splitting' or dividing a fee with any person or persons, the obtaining of any fee or compensation by fraud or misrepresentation, employing directly or indirectly any suspended or unlicensed optometrist to do any optometrical work, by use of any advertising, carrying the advertising of articles not connected with the profession, the employment of any drugs or medicines in his practice unless authorized to do so by the laws covering the practice of medicine of this state, or the doing or performing of any acts in his profession declared by the Alabama Optometric Association to be unethical or contrary to good practice."

The section also provides for a hearing before the Board upon due notice of an accused license holder. At such a hearing the accused is entitled to be represented by counsel, to cross-examine the witnesses against him, and to have all testimony taken down by a stenographer.

with Lee Optical. It was apparently the Association's position that, following the repeal of §210 and the amendment of §211, the practice of optometry by individuals as employees of business corporations was no longer permissible in Alabama, and that, by accepting such employment, the named optometrists had violated the ethics of their profession. It was prayed that the Board revoke the licenses of the individuals charged following due notice and a proper hearing.

Two days after these charges were filed by the Association in October 1965, the Board filed a suit of its own in state court against Lee Optical, seeking to enjoin the company from engaging in the "unlawful practice of optometry." The Board's complaint also named 13 optometrists employed by Lee Optical as parties defendant, charging them with aiding and abetting the company in its illegal activities, as well as with other improper conduct very similar to that charged by the Association in its complaint to the Board.

Proceedings on the Association's charges were held in abeyance by the Board while its own state court suit progressed. The individual defendants in that suit were dismissed on grounds that do not adequately appear in the record before us; and, eventually, on March 17, 1971, the state trial court rendered judgment for the Board, and enjoined Lee Optical both from practicing optometry without a license and from employing licensed optometrists.[5] The company appealed this judgment.

Meanwhile, following its victory in the trial court, the Board reactivated the proceedings pending before it since 1965 against the individual optometrists employed by Lee, noticing them for hearings to be held on May 26 and 27, 1971. Those individuals countered on May 14, 1971, by filing a complaint in the United States District Court naming as defendants the Board of Optometry and its individual members, as well as the Alabama Optometric Association and other individuals. The suit, brought under the Civil Rights Act of 1871, 42 U.S.C. §1983, sought an injunction against the scheduled hearings on the grounds that the statutory scheme regulating the practice of optometry in Alabama was unconstitutional insofar as it permitted the Board to hear the pending charges against the individual plaintiffs in the federal suit.[7] The thrust of the complaint was that the Board was biased and could not provide the plaintiffs with a fair and impartial hearing in conformity with due process of law.

A three-judge court was convened in August 1971, and shortly thereafter entered judgment for plaintiffs, enjoining members of the State Board and their successors "from conducting a hearing on the charges heretofore preferred

---

5. A period of nearly five and one-half years passed between the filing of the Board's complaint against Lee Optical, and the decision of the state trial court. Much of this delay appears to be attributable to certain procedural wranglings in the court concerning whether the Board has the power to bring an injunctive action against those it believed to be practicing optometry unlawfully. During the pendency of the litigation, the Alabama Legislature passed a statute expressly conferring such power, both prospectively and retroactively, on state licensing boards, and the suit appears to have proceeded expeditiously thereafter.

7. More specifically, the plaintiffs attacked §§206 and 192 of the statute which provide, respectively, that the Board shall have the power to entertain delicensing proceedings and that its membership shall be limited to members of the Alabama Optometric Association.

against the Plaintiffs" and from revoking their licenses to practice optometry in the State of Alabama. . . .

The District Court thought the Board to be impermissibly biased for two reasons. First, the Board had filed a complaint in state court alleging that appellees had aided and abetted Lee Optical Co. in the unlawful practice of optometry and also that they had engaged in other forms of "unprofessional conduct" which, if proved, would justify revocation of their licenses. These charges were substantially similar to those pending against appellees before the Board and concerning which the Board had noticed hearings following its successful prosecution of Lee Optical in the state trial court.

Secondly, the District Court determined that the aim of the Board was to revoke the licenses of all optometrists in the State who were employed by business corporations such as Lee Optical, and that these optometrists accounted for nearly half of all the optometrists practicing in Alabama. Because the Board of Optometry was composed solely of optometrists in private practice for their own account, the District Court concluded that success in the Board's efforts would possibly redound to the personal benefit of members of the Board, sufficiently so that in the opinion of the District Court the Board was constitutionally disqualified from hearing the charges filed against the appellees.

The District Court apparently considered either source of possible bias—prejudgment of the facts or personal interest—sufficient to disqualify the members of the Board. Arguably, the District Court was right on both scores, but we need reach, and we affirm, only the latter ground of possible personal interest.

It is sufficiently clear from our cases that those with substantial pecuniary interest in legal proceedings should not adjudicate these disputes. Tumey v. Ohio, 273 U.S. 510 (1927). And Ward v. Village of Monroeville, 409 U.S. 57 (1972), indicates that the financial stake need not be as direct or positive as it appeared to be in *Tumey*. It has also come to be the prevailing view that "[m]ost of the law concerning disqualification because of interest applies with equal force to . . . administrative adjudicators." K. Davis, Administrative Law Text §12.04, p.250 (1972), and cases cited. The District Court proceeded on this basis and, applying the standards taken from our cases, concluded that the pecuniary interest of the members of the Board of Optometry had sufficient substance to disqualify them, given the context in which this case arose. As remote as we are from the local realities underlying this case and it being very likely that the District Court has a firmer grasp of the facts and of their significance to the issues presented, we have no good reason on this record to overturn its conclusion and we affirm it. . . .

[The concurring opinions of CHIEF JUSTICE BURGER and of JUSTICE MARSHALL, joined by JUSTICE BRENNAN, are omitted.]

NOTES AND QUESTIONS

1. *Extent of the Board's self-interest.* Is the situation in *Gibson* distinguishable from the one in *Tumey* and *Ward*? Justice White notes that the district

court had "determined that the aim of the Board was to revoke the licenses of all optometrists in the State who were employed by business corporations such as Lee Optical, and that these optometrists accounted for nearly half of all the optometrists practicing in Alabama." 411 U.S. at 578. How important is the percentage of corporate optometrists? Would the outcome of this case change if they accounted for only one-fifth of the optometrists in Alabama?

2. *The optometrist wars.* The battle between individual and corporate optometrists described in *Gibson* is not peculiar to Alabama. At least 19 states have, at one time or another, ruled that any corporation employing optometrists or leasing space to optometrists was itself engaged in the unlicensed practice of optometry. The state's grant of a license to the consenting optometrist did not shield the corporate employer or lessor. Justice Jackson summarized the common argument against corporate practice in these terms:

> The ethical objection has been that intervention by employer or insurance company makes a tripartite matter of the doctor-patient relation. Since the contract doctor owes his employment and looks for his pay to the employer or the insurance company rather than to the patient, he serves two masters with conflicting interests.

United States v. Oregon State Medical Soc'y, 343 U.S. 326, 329 (1952). The controversy over corporate practice is part of a larger conflict pitting optometrists against two other groups of eye care specialists, ophthalmologists and opticians. The division among these groups is described by Justice Douglas, speaking for the Court in Williamson v. Lee Optical Co., 348 U.S. 483, 486 (1955):

> An ophthalmologist is a duly licensed physician who specializes in the care of the eyes. An optometrist examines eyes for refractive errors, recognizes (but does not treat) diseases of the eye, and fills prescriptions for eyeglasses. The optician is an artisan qualified to grind lenses, fill prescriptions, and fit frames.

As opticians increasingly did business through corporate enterprises, optometrists found association with these firms a more lucrative alternative to individual practice. Optical businesses — by organizing on a large scale, enjoying the advantages of national advertising and bulk contracting for supplies, and with ready access at low rates to capital markets — threatened one side of the optometrists' business. An expanded ophthalmological profession threatened the other. Sole-practice optometrists responded by supporting statutory and regulatory actions against optical companies and their employees.

3. *Occupational self-regulation.* Occupational licensure is widespread, and has been much criticized by academics, for the reasons stated in *Gibson*: because regulators who are themselves members of the regulated occupation have a personal stake in the regulations. *Gibson* is something of a maverick case, however. Most courts have found no due process problem with such arrangement unless there is a much more specific showing of self-interest. *See, e.g., Withrow v. Larkin,* excerpted following the *Cinderella* case, *infra.* Why do you suppose courts have been so reluctant to disturb the practice of occupational self-regulation?

CINDERELLA CAREER AND FINISHING SCHOOLS, INC. v. FEDERAL TRADE COMMISSION
425 F.2d 583 (D.C. Cir. 1970)

Before TAMM, MACKINNON, and ROBB, Circuit Judges.

TAMM, Circuit Judge:

This is a petition to review orders of the Federal Trade Commission which required petitioners Cinderella Career College and Finishing Schools, Inc. (hereinafter Cinderella), Stephen Corporation (the corporate entity which operates Cinderella), and Vincent Melzac (the sole owner of the stock of Cinderella and Stephen Corporation), to cease and desist from engaging in certain practices which were allegedly unfair and deceptive.[1]

After the Commission filed its complaint under section 5 of the Federal Trade Commission Act, 15 U.S.C. §45 (1964), which charged Cinderella with making representations and advertising in a manner which was false, misleading and deceptive, a hearing examiner held a lengthy series of hearings which consumed a total of sixteen days; these proceedings are reported in 1,810 pages of transcript. After the Commission had called twenty-nine witnesses and the petitioners twenty-three, and after the FTC had introduced 157 exhibits and petitioners 90, the hearing examiner ruled in a ninety-three page initial decision that the charges in the complaint should be dismissed.

Complaint counsel appealed the hearing examiner's initial decision to the full Commission; oral argument was heard on the appeal on May 28, 1968, and the Commission's final order was issued on October 10, 1968. The full Commission reversed the hearing examiner as to six of the original thirteen charges and entered a cease and desist order against the petitioners, who then brought this appeal. For the reasons which follow we remand to the Commission for further proceedings. . . .

---

1. The Commission's complaint alleged that advertising used by petitioners contained the following false representations:

1. Petitioners make educational loans to students who register for courses at the Cinderella Career and Finishing School.

2. School Services, Inc. is a government or public nonprofit organization that has officially approved the Cinderella School or its courses.

3. Dianna Batts, "Miss U.S.A. 1965," and Carol Ness, "Miss Cinderella 1965," were graduates of the Cinderella School and owe their success to the courses they took there.

4. and 5. Petitioners offer courses of instruction which qualify students to become airline stewardesses and buyers for retail stores.

6. Petitioners find jobs for their students in almost all cases through their job placement service.

7. Graduates of petitioners' courses are qualified to assume executive positions.

8. Cinderella Career and Finishing School is the official Washington, D.C., headquarters for the Miss Universe Beauty Pageant.

9. Cinderella Career College and Finishing School is a college.

The complaint also alleged that the following practices were deceptive:

10. Prospective students who visit petitioners' school are frequently led to believe that they will be qualified to compete in certain beauty contests if they sign up for courses.

11. Petitioners frequently add that completion of their courses will enable applicants in most cases to obtain better jobs.

12. Prospective students are subjected to constant pressure to persuade them to enroll in petitioners' courses.

13. Petitioners fail to disclose the nature of the commitments the students are expected to assume or to provide them with sufficient time or opportunity to read and consider them.

(App. 5-7.)

[The court first discussed the procedures followed by the commission in reviewing the hearing record and evaluating the evidence. After concluding that the FTC's procedures were incompatible with the Fifth Amendment's Due Process Clause, the court continued.]

An additional ground which requires remand of these proceedings—and which would have required reversal even in the absence of the above-described procedural irregularities—is participation in the proceedings by the then Chairman of the Federal Trade Commission, Paul Rand Dixon.

Notice that the hearing examiner's dismissal of all charges would be appealed was filed by the Commission staff on February 1, 1968. On March 12, 1968, this court's decision was handed down in a prior appeal arising from this same complaint, in which we upheld the Commission's issuance of press releases which called attention to the pending proceedings. Then, on March 15, 1968, while the appeal from the examiner's decision was pending before him, Chairman Dixon made a speech before the Government Relations Workshop of the National Newspaper Association in which he stated:

> What kind of vigor can a reputable newspaper exhibit? The quick answer, of course, pertains to its editorial policy, its willingness to present the news without bias. However, that is only half the coin. How about ethics on the business side of running a paper? What standards are maintained on advertising acceptance? What would be the attitude toward accepting good money for advertising by a merchant who conducts a "going out of business" sale every five months? *What about carrying ads that offer college educations in five weeks,* fortunes by raising mushrooms in the basement, getting rid of pimples with a magic lotion, *or becoming an airline's hostess by attending a charm school?* Or, to raise the target a bit, how many newspapers would hesitate to accept an ad promising an unqualified guarantee for a product when the guarantee is subject to many limitations? Without belaboring the point, I'm sure you're aware that advertising acceptance standards could stand more tightening by many newspapers. *Granted that newspapers are not in the advertising policing business, their advertising managers are savvy enough to smell deception when the odor is strong enough.* And it is in the public interest, as well as their own, that their sensory organs become more discriminating. The Federal Trade Commission, even where it has jurisdiction, could not protect the public as quickly.

(App. 134; emphasis added.) It requires no superior olfactory powers to recognize that the danger of unfairness through prejudgment is not diminished by a cloak of self-righteousness. We have no concern for or interest in the public statements of government officers, but we are charged with the responsibility of making certain that the image of the administrative process is not transformed from a Rubens to a Modigliani.

We indicated in our earlier opinion in this case that "there is in fact and law authority in the Commission, acting in the public interest, to alert the public to *suspected violations* of the law by *factual press releases* whenever the Commission shall have reason to believe that a respondent is engaged in activities made unlawful by the Act . . . ." FTC v. Cinderella Career & Finishing Schools, Inc., 404 F.2d 1308, 1314 (1968) (emphasis added). This does not give individual Commissioners license to prejudge cases or to make speeches which give the appearance that the case has been prejudged.[10] Conduct such as this may have the effect of entrenching a Commissioner in a position which he has publicly stated, making it difficult, if not impossible, for him to reach a different conclusion in the event he deems it necessary to do so after consideration of the record. There is a marked difference between the issuance of a press release which states that the Commission has filed a complaint because it has "reason to believe" that there have been violations, and statements by a Commissioner after an appeal has been filed which give the appearance that he has already prejudged the case and that the ultimate determination of the merits will move in predestined grooves. While these two situations — Commission press releases and a Commissioner's pre-decision public statements — are similar in appearance, they are obviously of a different order of merit.

As we noted in our earlier opinion, Congress has specifically vested the administrative agencies both with the "power to act in an accusatory capacity" and with the "responsibility of ultimately determining the merits of the charges so presented." 404 F.2d at 1315.

Chairman Dixon, sensitive to theory but insensitive to reality, made the following statement in declining to recuse himself from this case after petitioners requested that he withdraw:

> As . . . I have stated . . . this principle "is not a rigid command of the law, compelling disqualification for trifling causes, but a consideration addressed to the discretion and sound judgment of the administrator himself in determining whether, irrespective of the law's requirements, he should disqualify himself."

(App. 143.) To this tenet of self-appraisal we apply Lord Macaulay's evaluation more than 100 years ago of our American government: "It has one drawback — it is all sail and no anchor." We find it hard to believe that former Chairman Dixon is so indifferent to the dictates of the Courts of Appeals that he has chosen once again to put his personal determination of what the law requires ahead of what the courts have time and again told him the law requires. If this is a question of "discretion and judgment," Commissioner Dixon has exercised questionable discretion and very poor judgment indeed, in directing his shafts and squibs at a case awaiting his official action. We can use his own words in telling Commissioner Dixon that he has acted "irrespective of the law's requirements"; we will spell out for him once again, avoiding tired cliche and weary generalization, in no uncertain terms, exactly what those requirements are, in the fervent hope that this will be the last time we have to travel this wearisome road.

The test for disqualification has been succinctly stated as being whether "a disinterested observer may conclude that [the agency] has in some measure adjudged the facts as well as the law of a particular case in advance of hearing it." Gilligan, Will & Co. v. SEC. 267 F.2d 461, 469 (2d Cir.), *cert. denied,* 361 U.S. 896 (1959).

---

10. In its brief the respondent has attempted to demonstrate that Chairman Dixon's speech made reference not to the currently pending case, but rather to two cases which had been decided by the Commission in 1964. In light of the timing of the speech in relation to the proceedings herein, we think the reasonable inference a disinterested observer would give these remarks would connect them inextricably with this case.

That test was cited with approval by this court in Texaco, Inc. v. FTC, 336 F.2d 754 (1964), *vacated and remanded on other grounds,* 381 U.S. 739 (1965). In that case Chairman Dixon made a speech before the National Congress of Petroleum Retailers, Inc. while a case against Texaco was pending before the examiner on remand. After restating the test for disqualification, this court said:

> [A] disinterested reader of Chairman Dixon's speech could hardly fail to conclude that he had in some measure decided in advance that Texaco had violated the Act.

336 F.2d at 760. We further stated that such an administrative hearing "must be attended, not only with every element of fairness but with the very appearance of complete fairness," *citing* Amos Treat & Co. v. SEC, 306 F.2d 260, 267 (1962). We therefore concluded that Chairman Dixon's participation in the *Texaco* case amounted to a denial of due process.

After our decision in *Texaco* the United States Court of Appeals for the Sixth Circuit was required to reverse a decision of the FTC because Chairman Dixon refused to recuse himself from the case *even though he had served as Chief Counsel and Staff Director* to the Senate Subcommittee which made the initial investigation into the production and sale of the "wonder drug" tetracycline. American Cyanamid Co. v. FTC, 363 F.2d 757 (1966). . . . It is appalling to witness such insensitivity to the requirements of due process: it is even more remarkable to find ourselves once again confronted with a situation in which Mr. Dixon, pouncing on the most convenient victim, has determined either to distort the holdings in the cited cases beyond all reasonable interpretation or to ignore them altogether. We are constrained to this harshness of language because of Mr. Dixon's flagrant disregard of prior decisions.

The rationale for remanding the case despite the fact that former Chairman Dixon's vote was not necessary for a majority is well established: "Litigants are entitled to an impartial tribunal whether it consists of one man or twenty and there is no way which we know of whereby the influence of one upon the others can be quantitatively measured." Berkshire Employees Assn. of Berkshire Knitting Mills v. NLRB, 121 F.2d 235, 239 (3d Cir. 1941). . . .

For the reasons set forth above we vacate the order of the Commission and remand with instructions that the Commissioners consider the record and evidence in reviewing the initial decision, without the participation of Commissioner Dixon.

Vacated and remanded.

NOTES AND QUESTIONS

1. *The legal standard for prejudgment.* Do Dixon's statements reveal prejudgment? Is the court concerned solely with prejudgment of facts? Or of the ultimate issue of culpability? Is the court concerned about the *reality* or merely the *appearance* of prejudgment? (See the court's footnote 10.) If, after *Cinderella,* you were asked to advise a client on the standard for disqualification, what would you say?

Look back to the *National Advertisers* case, excerpted in Chapter V, *supra.* What distinguishes that case from *Cinderella?* Is it the nature of the issues prejudged, or is it the nature of the proceeding? Should the disqualification standard vary by issue? By procedure? By both?

2. *The Chairman speaks.* As Judge Tamm's opinion indicates, *Cinderella* was not the first case in which Chairman Dixon's participation had been challenged. In Texaco, Inc. v. FTC, 336 F.2d 754 (D.C. Cir. 1964), *vacated and remanded on other grounds,* 381 U.S. 739 (1965), the D.C. Circuit rebuked him for participating in FTC decisionmaking following another speech. During the pendency of FTC proceedings against Texaco for restraining competition by pressuring its franchisees to purchase tires, batteries, and accessories (referred to as TBA) exclusively from Goodrich (which paid a commission to Texaco on sales by Texaco dealers), Dixon addressed the following remarks to the National Congress of Petroleum Retailers:

> We at the Commission are well aware of the practices which plague you and we have challenged their legality in many important cases. You know the practices—price fixing, price discrimination, and overriding commissions on TBA. You know the companies—Atlantic, Texas, Pure, Shell, Sun, Standard of Indiana, American, Goodyear, Goodrich, and Firestone. . . . Some of these cases are still pending before the Commission; some have been decided and are in the courts for appeal. You may be sure that the Commission will continue and, to the extent that increased funds and efficiency permit, will increase its efforts to promote fair competition in your industry.

336 F.2d at 759. Unlike *Cinderella,* Dixon made these remarks before the hearing examiner rendered his decision, yet the court of appeals still faulted his subsequent participation in the commission's review of the matter: "[A] disinterested reader of Chairman Dixon's speech could hardly fail to conclude that he had in some measure decided that Texaco had violated the Act." *Id.* at 760. What was prejudged in *Texaco?* Does this case raise the same problem as *Cinderella?*

Another case involving Dixon grew out of his work with Senator Estes Kefauver's Antitrust and Monopoly Subcommittee prior to becoming FTC Chairman. As counsel to the subcommittee, Dixon had participated in an investigation of alleged anticompetitive practices in connection with the licensing of the drug tetracycline by several pharmaceutical manufacturers, including Chas. Pfizer & Co. and American Cyanamid Co. A proceeding was subsequently initiated before the FTC, alleging that Pfizer and Cyanamid violated the Sherman and FTC Acts in conjunction with the licensing of tetracycline. In the course of the proceeding, Dixon (now Chairman) and his fellow commissioners denied the companies' motion that Dixon be disqualified from participating because of his prior involvement in the matter. The FTC issued an order finding both companies in violation of the law.

The U.S. Court of Appeals for the Sixth Circuit vacated the FTC decision. American Cyanamid Co. v. FTC, 363 F.2d 757 (6th Cir. 1966). Based largely on questions Dixon had put to witnesses before the subcommittee, the court concluded that, before addressing the case based on the record developed at the FTC, Dixon "had formed the opinion that tetracycline prices . . . were artificially high and collusive," and that Pfizer and Cyanamid behaved improperly in connection with the patenting of tetracycline. "Any opinions so formed were conclusions as to facts, and not merely an 'underlying philosophy' or a 'crystallized point of view on questions of law or policy.'" *Id.* at 765, *quoting*

United States v. Morgan, 313 U.S. 409, 421 (1941), and 2 Kenneth C. Davis, Administrative Law §12.01 (1958). Critical to the court's decision that Dixon should not have participated was its judgment that the prejudged facts were "inseparably a part of the ultimate findings of fact of the Commission in disagreeing with the decision of the trial examiner. . . ." 363 F.2d at 765. The court also rejected the FTC's suggestion that, since his vote was unnecessary to the commission's disposition of the charges, Dixon's participation amounted to harmless error.

WITHROW v. LARKIN, 421 U.S. 35 (1975): The Wisconsin medical licensing board received complaints about a licensed physician, Dr. Duane Larkin, whose practice "consisted of performing abortions," then illegal in the state unless to save the life of the mother. The board investigated, found evidence that Larkin had engaged in proscribed acts, notified the district attorney that there existed "probable cause [for criminal action] and for an action to revoke the license of the licensee for unprofessional conduct," and set the case for a formal hearing. Larkin filed suit, contending that the board members who investigated could not, consistent with due process, decide the outcome of that hearing. He argued, first, that the combination of functions biased board members against him (by assimilating them to the role of prosecutor). The Supreme Court rejected this argument, saying:

> [V]arious situations have been identified in which experience teaches that the probability of actual bias on the part of the judge or decisionmaker is too high to be constitutionally tolerable. Among these cases are those in which the adjudicator has a pecuniary interest in the outcome and in which he has been the target of abuse or criticism from the party before him.
>
> The contention that the combination of investigative and adjudicative functions necessarily creates an unconstitutional risk of bias in administrative adjudication has a much more difficult burden of persuasion to carry. It must overcome a presumption of honesty and integrity in those serving as adjudicators; and it must convince that, under a realistic appraisal of psychological tendencies and human weakness, conferring investigative and adjudicative powers on the same individuals poses such a risk of actual bias or prejudgment that the practice must be forbidden if the guarantee of due process is to be adequately implemented. . . .
>
> The processes utilized by the Board . . . do not in themselves contain an unacceptable risk of bias. The investigative proceeding had been closed to the public, but appellee and his counsel were permitted to be present throughout; counsel actually attended the hearings and knew the facts presented to the Board. No specific foundation has been presented for suspecting that the Board had been prejudiced by its investigation or would be disabled from hearing and deciding on the basis of the evidence to be presented at the contested hearing.

Larkin also argued that the board's prior determination of probable cause revealed prejudgment of the issues critical to the hearing. The Court also rejected this argument:

> Here, the Board stayed within the accepted bounds of due process. Having investigated, it issued findings and conclusions asserting the commission of certain acts and ultimately concluding that there was probable cause to believe that appellee had violated the statutes.

The risk of bias or prejudgment in this sequence of functions has not been considered to be intolerably high or to raise a sufficiently great possibility that the adjudicators would be so psychologically wedded to their complaints that they would consciously or unconsciously avoid the appearance of having erred or changed position. . . . Here, if the Board now proceeded after an adversary hearing to determine that appellee's license to practice should not be temporarily suspended, it would not implicitly be admitting error in its prior finding of probable cause. Its position most probably would merely reflect the benefit of a more complete view of the evidence afforded by an adversary hearing.

The initial charge or determination of probable cause and the ultimate adjudication have different bases and purposes. The fact that the same agency makes them in tandem and that they relate to the same issues does not result in a procedural due process violation. Clearly, if the initial view of the facts based on the evidence derived from nonadversarial processes as a practical or legal matter foreclosed fair and effective consideration at a subsequent adversary hearing leading to ultimate decision, a substantial due process question would be raised. But in our view, that is not this case.

The Court noted, by way of analogy, that due process does not disqualify a trial judge from presiding in a case after having previously made a ruling on a motion for a temporary restraining order or preliminary injunction, or after having issued an arrest warrant or presided at a preliminary probable-cause hearing, or having presided at a previous trial that was later overturned on appeal. Is the analogy to trial judges apt?

In reaching its result in *Withrow,* the Supreme Court drew some inspiration from the way in which Congress had resolved the issues presented in the case when it drafted the APA. As we have seen repeatedly, many federal agencies combine the functions of adjudication and enforcement (and often rulemaking as well) under a single organizational roof. Thus, for example, the five Federal Trade Commissioners all participate in promulgating trade regulation rules, approving complaints against alleged violators of the statute or rules, and issuing cease-and-desist orders. They also exercise direct or indirect supervisory and budgetary authority over the staff who carry out those functions.

This pattern of combining adjudication with enforcement within the same agency has been specifically sanctioned in dozens of federal statutes, and it was generally endorsed by the drafters of the Administrative Procedure Act. The 1941 Report of the Attorney General's Committee on Administrative Procedure concluded that complete separation of adjudicative functions was both unnecessary and, in some cases, undesirable. It was unnecessary, the Report's authors concluded, because most federal regulatory agencies were large enough to permit functional specialization of staff. Separation might be undesirable, they argued, because it would hamper coordination of policymaking and enforcement, discourage informal resolution of cases, and foster turf battles.

Questions have naturally arisen about the impartiality of agency adjudicators because they are employees of one of the parties to most of the disputes that arise in administrative adjudications. In light of this reality, the drafters of the APA were unwilling to permit unrestricted intermingling of adjudicative and enforcement functions. Their compromise solution was to require internal separation of adjudicative activities within an agency by creating a special class of hearing officers (initially called "examiners," then "hearing examiners," and now "administrative law judges") who are insulated from the controls normally exercised over subordinates by high-ranking agency officials. See especially §554(d), which deals with separation of functions in federal administrative agencies. How would §554(d) have applied to the facts of *Withrow*? As you explore more carefully the structure of the APA's adjudicatory procedures in the next section of this chapter, you should ask yourself whether they track, illuminate, or supplement the requirements of due process.

The issues of bias and prejudgment also arise, of course, in litigation before courts. Federal judges are supposed to recuse themselves, or be disqualified, whenever, in the words of 28 U.S.C. §455, their "impartiality might reasonably be questioned."

Friendship with a litigant is not in itself always a ground for disqualification. For example, in Cheney v. United States District Court, 541 U.S. 913 (2004), Justice Scalia refused to recuse himself from hearing a case involving Vice President Richard Cheney after it was revealed that the Justice and the Vice President went on a hunting trip together. In refusing to step aside, Justice Scalia relied in part on the fact that the case was about the Vice President's official duties and not personal matters: "while friendship is a ground for recusal of a Justice where the personal fortune or the personal freedom of the friend is at issue, it has traditionally not been a ground for recusal where official action is at issue, no matter how important the official action was to the ambitions or the reputation of the Government officer." *Id.* at 916.

One risk of bias that has attracted increasing scrutiny is the possible predisposition of elected judges to rule in favor of their campaign supporters. Generally, court rules do not require judges to recuse themselves from any case in which a contributor is a party, but the Supreme Court did find a due process violation when a state supreme court justice failed to recuse himself from a case involving a litigant who had spent over $3 million to support his campaign for the office. *See* Caperton v. A.T. Massey Coal Co., Inc., 556 U.S. 868 (2009). Justice Scalia, along with Justices Thomas and Alito, joined Chief Justice Roberts's dissenting opinion. *See also* Williams v. Pennsylvania, 136 S. Ct. 1899 (2016) (due process violation found where Pennsylvania Supreme Court Chief Justice failed to recuse himself from a post-conviction death penalty appeal in a case in which he had participated, 26 years earlier, as District Attorney of Philadelphia).

C. STATUTORY HEARING REQUIREMENTS

The path of the Supreme Court's due process jurisprudence since the so-called "*Goldberg* Revolution" has driven home at least one undeniable lesson: those who would seek procedural justice in the administrative state must look to the positive law as a principal source of rights. In fact, the state and national legislatures have, on the whole, been rather generous in bestowing procedural protections on those whose rights and interests are subject to administrative adjudication. At the federal level, the primary statutory framework for administrative adjudication is, of course, the APA. At this point, you should read §§554,

556, and 557 carefully to get a sense of the basic framework for formal agency adjudications. The essential procedural protections include:

1. The agency must give the parties notice of the "legal authority under which the hearing is to be held" and "matters of fact and law asserted." §554(b).

2. Either an administrative law judge, the head of the agency, or one of the members of a body that "comprises the agency," must preside over the oral evidentiary hearing, and parties have the right to request disqualification of the presiding officer for "personal bias." §556(b).

3. No "interested person" may make an "ex parte communication relevant to the merits of the proceeding" to any agency employee "who may reasonably be expected to be involved in the decisional process," nor may any such employee make an ex parte communication to any interested person. §557(d)(1); see also §554(d).

4. The "proponent of [an] order" has the burden of proof. §556(d).

5. A party is entitled to present "oral or documentary evidence," and "to conduct such cross-examination as may be required for a full and true disclosure of the facts." §556(d).

6. Orders may not be issued "except on consideration of the whole record or those parts thereof cited by a party and supported by and in accordance with the reliable, probative, and substantial evidence." §556(d).

7. The transcript of testimony and exhibits constitute "the exclusive record for decision . . . and shall be made available to parties." §556(e).

8. The decision must include "findings and conclusions, and the reasons or basis therefor, on all the material issues of fact, law, or discretion presented on the record." §557(c)(3)(A).

See Citizens Awareness Network, Inc. v. United States, 391 F.3d 338, 356 (1st Cir. 2004) (Lipez, J., concurring). A quick survey of these protections evokes the familiar judicial model of adjudication. But a close inspection will reveal some significant departures from that model. For example, in proceedings involving "claims for money or benefits or applications for initial licenses an agency may, when a party will not be prejudiced thereby, adopt procedures for the submission of all or part of the evidence in written form." §556(e). Why this exception to the usual requirement of an oral hearing and right of cross-examination?

In addition to the APA, many substantive federal statutes specify the procedures to be used when adjudicating claims for benefits, or in regulatory enforcement proceedings. For example, the Social Security Act, 42 U.S.C. §405(b), provides:

> Upon request by any . . . individual . . . who makes a showing in writing that his or her rights may be prejudiced by any decision the Secretary has rendered, [the Secretary] shall give such applicant . . . reasonable notice and opportunity for a hearing with respect to such decision, and, if a hearing is held, shall, on the basis of evidence adduced at the hearing, affirm, modify, or reverse his findings of fact and such decision. . . . In the course of any hearing, . . . he may administer oaths and affirmations, examine witnesses, and receive evidence. Evidence may be received at any hearing before the Secretary even though inadmissible under rules of evidence applicable to court procedure.

To the extent that specific statutory procedural provisions conflict with the APA, they take precedence. For the most part, however, statutory procedural provisions are either duplicative of or supplementary to the APA. Indeed, the very first sentence of §554 states that the APA's formal adjudication requirements first must be "triggered" by a hearing requirement in a primary statute. Once that "trigger" is pulled, the APA fills in the procedural blanks, as it were. In this section of Chapter VI, we will examine several issues that have arisen in the interpretation of §§554, 556, and 557, and in their interplay with the procedural provisions of other statutes.

1. *"Triggering" the APA's Formal Adjudication Requirements*

Section 554(a) provides that the procedural protections for formal adjudication afforded by §§554, 556, and 557 apply "in every case of adjudication required by statute to be determined on the record after opportunity for an agency hearing." In other words, the APA's formal adjudication requirements are triggered only if an agency's enabling statute requires them. If APA formal adjudication is not triggered by an agency's enabling statute, the agency is generally free to proceed through informal adjudication, an amorphous category of agency action with far fewer procedural constraints. *See* the discussion, *infra.* Because of the disparity in procedural protections applicable to formal, as opposed to informal, adjudication, whether formal adjudication is triggered by an agency's enabling statute is quite significant.

How do courts know when that has happened? Does the simple mention of a "hearing" automatically mean that §§554, 556, and 557 apply? Recall that in the context of rulemaking, the Supreme Court has said that the APA's formal model of rulemaking is not triggered unless an enabling statute clearly indicates that a rulemaking "hearing" must be "on the record" (by using that precise phrase or language functionally equivalent). *See Allegheny-Ludlum,* excerpted in Chapter V, *supra.* Further, in *Florida East Coast, id.,* the Court said that language in an enabling act requiring a rulemaking "hearing" presumptively required only the notice-and-comment procedures of APA §553, and did not authorize a reviewing court to embellish those procedures. Should an analogous presumption apply in the adjudication context, or are there good reasons to treat rulemaking and adjudication differently for these purposes? The next two cases explore these questions.

SEACOAST ANTI-POLLUTION LEAGUE v. COSTLE
572 F.2d 872 (1st Cir. 1978)

Before COFFIN, Chief Judge, CAMPBELL and BOWNES, Circuit Judges.
COFFIN, Chief Judge:
This case is before us on a petition by the Seacoast Anti-Pollution League and the Audubon Society of New Hampshire (petitioners) to review a decision by the Administrator of the Environmental Protection Agency (EPA). . . . The petition presents several important issues relating to the applicability and effect of the Administrative Procedure Act (APA), and the interpretation of the

Federal Water Pollution Control Act of 1972 (FWPCA). In order to place those issues in context we set forth the procedural and factual background of the case.

The Public Service Company of New Hampshire (PSCO) filed an application with the EPA for permission to discharge heated water into the Hampton-Seabrook Estuary which runs into the Gulf of Maine. The water would be taken from the Gulf of Maine, be run through the condensor of PSCO's proposed nuclear steam electric generating station at Seabrook, and then be directly discharged back into the Gulf at a temperature 39° F higher than at intake. . . . Occasionally, in a process called backflushing, the water will be recirculated through the condensor, and discharged through the intake tunnel at a temperature of 120° F in order to kill whatever organisms may be living in the intake system.

Section 301(a) of the FWPCA prohibits the discharge of any pollutant unless the discharger, the point source operator, has obtained an EPA permit. Heat is a pollutant. Section 301(b) directs the EPA to promulgate effluent limitations. The parties agree that the cooling system PSCO has proposed does not meet the EPA standards because PSCO would utilize a once-through open cycle system the water would not undergo any cooling process before being returned to the sea. Therefore, in August, 1974, PSCO applied not only for a discharge permit under §402 of the FWPCA, but also an exemption from the EPA standards pursuant to §316 of the FWPCA. Under §316(a) a point source operator who "after opportunity for public hearing, can demonstrate to the satisfaction of the Administrator" that the EPA's standards are "more stringent than necessary to assure the [protection] and propagation of a balanced, indigenous population of shellfish, fish, and wildlife in and on the body of water" may be allowed to meet a lower standard. . . .

In January, 1975, the Regional Administrator of the EPA held a non-adjudicatory hearing at Seabrook. He then authorized the once-through system in June, 1975. Later, in October, 1975, he specified the location of the intake structure. The Regional Administrator granted a request by petitioners that public adjudicative hearings on PSCO's application be held. These hearings were held in March and April, 1976, pursuant to the EPA's regulations establishing procedures for deciding applications for permits under §402 of the FWPCA. The hearings were before an administrative law judge who certified a record to the Regional Administrator for decision. The Regional Administrator decided in November, 1976, to reverse his original determinations and deny PSCO's application.

PSCO . . . appealed the decision to the Administrator who agreed to review it. Thereafter, a new Administrator was appointed, and he assembled a panel of six in-house advisors to assist in his technical review. This panel met between February 28 and March 3, 1977, and submitted a report finding that with one exception PSCO had met its burden of proof. With respect to that exception, the effect of backflushing, the Administrator asked PSCO to submit further information, offered other parties the opportunity to comment upon PSCO's submission, and stated that he would hold a hearing on the new information if any party so requested and could satisfy certain threshold conditions. . . . Petitioners did request a hearing, but the Administrator denied the request. The Administrator's final decision followed the technical panel's recommendations and, with the additional information submitted, reversed the Regional

Administrator's decision, finding that PSCO had met its burden under §316. It is this decision that petitioners have brought before us for review.

Petitioners assert that the proceedings by which the EPA decided this case contravened certain provisions of the APA governing adjudicatory hearings, 5 U.S.C. §§554, 556, and 557. Respondents answer that the APA does not apply to proceedings held pursuant to §316 or §402 of the FWPCA. The dispute centers on the meaning of the introductory phrases of §554(a) of the APA: "This section applies . . . in every case of adjudication required by statute to be determined on the record after opportunity for an agency hearing. . . ." Both §316(a) and §402(a)(1) of the FWPCA provide for public hearings, but neither states that the hearing must be "on the record." We are now the third court of appeals to face this issue. The Ninth Circuit and the Seventh Circuit have each found that the APA does apply to proceedings pursuant to §402. Marathon Oil Co. v. EPA, 564 F.2d 1253 (9th Cir. 1977); United States Steel Corp. v. Train, 556 F.2d 822 (7th Cir. 1977). We agree.

At the outset we reject the position of intervenor PSCO that the precise words "on the record" must be used to trigger the APA. The Supreme Court has clearly rejected such an extreme reading even in the context of rule making under §553 of the APA. See United States v. Florida East Coast Ry. Co., 410 U.S. 224, 245 (1973). Rather, we think that the resolution of this issue turns on the substantive nature of the hearing Congress intended to provide.

We begin with the nature of the decision at issue. The EPA Administrator must make specific factual findings about the effects of discharges from a specific point source. On the basis of these findings the Administrator must determine whether to grant a discharge permit to a specific applicant. Though general policy considerations may influence the decision, the decision will not make general policy. Only the rights of the specific applicant will be affected. . . .

This is exactly the kind of quasi-judicial proceeding for which the adjudicatory procedures of the APA were intended. As the Supreme Court has said, "[d]etermination of questions of [the Administrative Procedure Act's] coverage may well be approached through consideration of its purposes as disclosed by its background." Wong Yang Sung v. McGrath, 339 U.S. 33, 36 (1950). One of the developments that prompted the APA was the "[m]ultiplication of federal administrative agencies and expansion of their functions to include adjudications which have serious impact on private rights." Id. at 36-37. This is just such an adjudication. The panoply of procedural protections provided by the APA is necessary not only to protect the rights of an applicant for less stringent pollutant discharge limits, but is also needed to protect the public for whose benefit the very strict limitations have been enacted. If determinations such as the one at issue here are not made on the record, then the fate of the Hampton-Seabrook Estuary could be decided on the basis of evidence that a court would never see or, what is worse, that a court could not be sure existed. We cannot believe that Congress would intend such a result. . . .

We are willing to presume that, unless a statute otherwise specifies, an adjudicatory hearing subject to judicial review must be on the record. The legislative history of the APA and its treatment in the courts bear us out. . . . The presumption in rule making cases is that formal, adjudicatory procedures are not necessary. A hearing serves a very different function in the rule making context. Witnesses may bring in new information or different points of view, but the agency's final decision need not reflect the public input. The witnesses are not the only source of the evidence on which the Administrator may base his factual findings. For these reasons, we place less importance on the absence of the words "on the record" in the adjudicatory context[:]

> It is believed that with respect to adjudication the specific statutory requirement of a hearing, without anything more, carries with it the further requirement of decision on the basis of the evidence adduced at the hearing. With respect to rule making, it was concluded that a statutory provision that rules be issued after a hearing, without more, should not be construed as requiring agency action "on the record," but rather as merely requiring an opportunity for the expression of views. That conclusion was based on the legislative nature of rule making, from which it was inferred, unless a statute requires otherwise, that an agency hearing on proposed rules would be similar to a hearing before a legislative committee, with neither the legislature nor the agency being limited to the material adduced at the hearing. No such rationale applies to administrative adjudication. . . .

Attorney General's Manual, 42-43. Here the statute certainly does not indicate that the determination need not be on the record, and we find no indication of a contrary congressional intent. Therefore, we will judge the proceedings below according to the standards set forth in §§554, 556, and 557 of the APA. . . .

[The court went on to find that the agency violated §556(d) by considering non-record evidence.]

NOTES AND QUESTIONS

1. *Adjudication versus rulemaking.* Is it clear that the determination at issue in *Seacoast* was an "adjudication"? Note that the issue to be determined was whether a lower standard for discharging hot water would "assure the [protection] and propagation of a balanced, indigenous population of shellfish, fish, and wildlife in and on the body of water" (namely, the Hampton-Seabrook Estuary, which feeds the Gulf of Maine). Does this sound like the kind of factual determination classically made by a court? Or does it call for a policy judgment based on science, which might typically be made by a legislature?

As noted in *Seacoast*, the Supreme Court has refused to interpret an unembellished statutory "hearing" requirement to trigger the formal hearing procedures of APA §§554, 556, and 557 in the context of rulemaking. In a line of cases exemplified by *Seacoast*, several appeals courts erected an opposing presumption in the context of adjudication. *See* Marathon Oil v. EPA, 564 F.2d 1253 (9th Cir. 1977); United States Steel Corp. v. Train, 556 F.2d 822 (7th Cir. 1977). Indeed, in 1984, the D.C. Circuit proclaimed: "when a statute calls for a hearing in an adjudication the hearing is presumptively governed by 'on the record' procedures." Union of Concerned Scientists v. NRC, 735 F.2d 1437, 1444 n.12 (D.C. Cir. 1984). The divergent presumptions in rulemaking and adjudication were derived, in part, from the Attorney General's Manual, an authoritative source on APA interpretation. *See Seacoast*, 572 F.2d at 877-878. The Manual explains that the presumptive informality of rulemaking is grounded in its legislative character. According to the Manual, because a legislative decision need not be based on evidence adduced at hearings before legislative committees, an agency rulemaking process generally should not be governed by on-the-record requirements either. By contrast, because adjudications affect individual rights—similar to trials—Congress intended them to be presumptively formal, with any decision based solely on evidence adduced at the hearing. *See* Attorney General's Manual 42-43.

2. *Chevron's effect. Seacoast* was decided before the Supreme Court's decision in the *Chevron* case, discussed in Chapter II, *supra*. What effect does that case have on the issue decided in *Seacoast*? Is the meaning of "public hearing," as used in FWPCA §316(a), sufficiently "ambiguous" to trigger deference to a "reasonable" interpretation of those words by the EPA? Would it be "reasonable" to interpret "public hearing" to mean an informal, nonevidentiary hearing? Since the "trigger" issue decided in *Seacoast* involves the interaction of a general statute (the APA) and a specific enabling statute (FWPCA), is *Chevron* deference even applicable? The First Circuit faced these issues in the following case.

DOMINION ENERGY BRAYTON POINT, LLC v. JOHNSON, 443 F.3d 12 (1st Cir. 2006): Following the Supreme Court's decision in *Chevron*, the EPA adopted a rule eliminating formal adjudicative hearings in Clean Water Act (CWA) permit proceedings. Subsequently, Dominion Energy, the owner of an electric generating plant, filed a petition for a thermal variance authorization as part of its permit renewal petition pursuant to the Act's "National Pollution Discharge Elimination System." Dominion asked the EPA to provide an evidentiary hearing, but the agency refused. The company then brought a citizen suit under the Act, alleging that the EPA had a nondiscretionary duty to provide a formal hearing of the sort required in the earlier *Seacoast* decision. The First Circuit ruled against Dominion, saying:

> *Seacoast* simply does not hold that Congress clearly intended the term "public hearing" in sections 402(a) and 316(a) of the CWA to mean "evidentiary hearing." To the contrary, the *Seacoast* court based its interpretation of the CWA on a presumption derived from the legislative history of the APA—a presumption that would hold sway only in the absence of a showing of a contrary congressional intent. In other words, the court resorted to the presumption only because it could find no sign of a plainly discernible congressional intent. A statutory interpretation constructed on such a negative finding is antithetic to a conclusion that Congress's intent was clear and unambiguous.
>
> The short of it is that the *Seacoast* court, faced with an opaque statute, settled upon what it sensibly thought was the best construction of the CWA's "public hearing" language. Such a holding is appropriate at step two of the *Chevron* pavane, not at step one. Consequently, *Seacoast* must yield to a reasonable agency interpretation of the CWA's "public hearing" requirement. . . .
>
> In this instance, the administrative interpretation took into account the relevant universe of factors. The agency's conclusion that evidentiary hearings are unnecessary and that Congress, in using the phrase "opportunity for public hearing," did not mean to mandate evidentiary hearings seems reasonable. . . .
>
> Dominion exhorts us to find that *Seacoast's* holding is actually an interpretation of the APA, not the CWA (and, therefore, the EPA's regulation is also an interpretation of the APA, not entitled to *Chevron* deference). *See, e.g.,* Metro. Stevedore Co. v. Rambo, 521 U.S. 121, 137 n.9 (1997) (noting that *Chevron* deference is inappropriate vis-à-vis an agency interpretation of the APA's burden-of-proof provision). Such a reading of *Seacoast* is plainly incorrect. While the *Seacoast* court relied on a presumption borrowed from the APA, the court's holding is an inter-

pretation of the CWA and, specifically, of the term "public hearing" contained in sections 402(a) and 316(a). The EPA's regulations are also derived from the CWA. Because those changes implicate the statute that the EPA administers (*i.e.*, the CWA), *Chevron* deference is appropriate. . . .

NOTES AND QUESTIONS

1. Chevron *and agency interpretations of procedural requirements.* Courts have held that *Chevron* deference applies only to an agency's interpretation of its "own" enabling act, not to its interpretation of general statutes like the APA. But is this appropriate? The *Chevron* rule relies, in part, on the premise that agencies are better suited than courts to interpret ambiguous statutory provisions because of their superior technical and policymaking expertise. Hence, ambiguity is read as an "implied delegation" to the agency. This rationale has particular force when applied to the construction of substantive statutory provisions—where an agency is presumed to have greater expertise than courts. But is it equally persuasive when applied to the construction of procedural provisions? Judges are generally thought to be procedural experts, and, as such, are perhaps ideally equipped to make independent decisions about procedural requirements. On the other hand, agencies better understand the realities of administrative caseloads and institutional resource constraints, so perhaps they do deserve deference when seeking to take certain procedural shortcuts. *See* Melissa M. Berry, Beyond *Chevron*'s Domain: Agency Interpretations of Statutory Procedural Provisions, 30 Seattle U. L. Rev. 541 (2007). According to Professor Jordan, however, §554 represents a legislative compromise in which Congress intended to establish relatively stringent procedural protections for formal adjudications, while leaving the decision of *when* to require such protections for later Congresses to determine when passing enabling statutes. *See* William S. Jordan, III, *Chevron* and Hearing Rights: An Unintended Combination, 61 Admin. L. Rev. 249, 288 (2009) (claiming that "the argument for deference is flatly contrary to the history of the APA," *id.* at 320, and that "[u]nless Congress has clearly indicated that the courts are to defer to an agency's interpretation of a statutory hearing requirement . . . that interpretive question is for the courts alone," *id.* at 321).

2. Chevron *deference and agency bias.* The result in *Dominion Energy* might also raise concerns if we think that agencies are systematically biased to prefer less formal procedures. *See* William Funk, The Rise and Purported Demise of *Wong Yang Sung*, 58 Admin. L. Rev. 881, 892 (2006) (arguing that, throughout history, agencies have been averse to formal adjudication because they view it as overly costly and time consuming). Is the risk of systematic bias (say, against formal procedures), greater than the risk of systematic substantive bias (say, in favor of excessively stringent regulation)? Why not entrust both types of decisions to the agency?

2.   *Procedural Issues in Formal Adjudication*

Whatever the propriety of granting *Chevron* deference to agency interpretations of statutory procedural provisions, deference appears to be the trend. As a result, formal adjudications governed by §§554, 556, and 557 are less common now than during the pre-*Chevron* era. *See* Gary J. Edles, An APA-Default Presumption for Administrative Hearings: Some Thoughts on "Ossifying" the Adjudication Process, 55 Admin. L. Rev. 787, 815 (2003) (noting a recent "shift away from formal adjudication, and the emergence of informal hearings as a new category"). Nonetheless, there remain many areas of federal administrative law in which the formal model is operative, thanks either to the precision of the "triggering" language or because Congress has specified formal APA-like procedures in the enabling act. When formal adjudication is triggered, the full panoply of procedural entitlements apply. These provisions pose a number of important interpretive questions, discussed below.

a. Discovery and Cross-Examination

CITIZENS AWARENESS NETWORK, INC. v.
UNITED STATES
391 F.3d 338 (1st Cir. 2004)

Before SELYA, LIPEZ, and HOWARD, Circuit Judges.

SELYA, Circuit Judge:

Disenchanted with its existing procedural framework for the conduct of adjudicatory hearings, the Nuclear Regulatory Commission (NRC or Commission) promulgated new rules designed to make its hearing processes more efficient. These new rules greatly reduce the level of formality in reactor licensing proceedings but, at the same time, place certain unaccustomed restrictions upon the parties. The petitioners and petitioner-intervenors are public interest groups. . . . [T]hey claim that the new rules violate a statutory requirement that all reactor licensing hearings be conducted in accordance with sections 554, 556, and 557 of the Administrative Procedure Act (APA). . . .

I

The NRC is the federal agency charged with regulating the use of nuclear energy, including the licensing of reactors used for power generation. The Atomic Energy Act requires the Commission to hold a hearing "upon the request of any person whose interest may be affected" before granting a new license, a license amendment, or a license renewal. The NRC's predecessor agency, the Atomic Energy Commission (AEC), originally interpreted this provision as requiring on-the-record hearings in accordance with the APA. These hearings closely resembled federal court trials, complete with a full panoply of discovery devices and direct and cross-examination of witnesses by advocates for the parties. Such hearings proved to be very lengthy; some lasted as long as seven years. . . .

In January of 1999, the NRC's general counsel drafted a legal memorandum concluding that the Atomic Energy Act did not require reactor licensing hearings to be on the record and, accordingly, that the Commission had the option of replacing the existing format with a truncated regime. Later that year, the Commission held a widely attended workshop on hearing procedures. Building on this foundation, the Commission published a notice of proposed rulemaking on April 16, 2001 suggesting a major revision of its hearing procedures. In an accompanying statement, the Commission took the position that section 189 of the Atomic Energy Act does not require reactor licensing proceedings to be on the record.

On January 14, 2004, the NRC published a final rule, along with a response to the comments that the proposed rule had generated. With minor exceptions, the final rule replicated the proposed rule. The statement of considerations for the final rule reiterated the Commission's view that reactor licensing hearings may be informal. The new rules took effect on February 13, 2004. . . . In [petitioners'] view, the new rules do not comply with the APA's requirements for on-the-record adjudication and, therefore, cannot stand. . . .

III

The mainstay of the petitioners' challenge is the proposition that the new rules exceed the Commission's statutory authority. The petitioners start with the premise that 42 U.S.C. §2239 requires the NRC to conduct licensing hearings on the record, that is, in strict accordance with the relevant provisions of the APA. In their view, the new rules fail to satisfy that requirement and, therefore, must be pole-axed. . . .

We exercise plenary review over the Commission's compliance with the APA The rulemaking at issue here effected several changes in the Commission's procedures. The petitioners focus their challenge on two aspects of the newly minted process. First, they object to the Commission's decision to eliminate discovery. Second, they complain about the Commission's decision to circumscribe the availability of cross-examination. . . .

We begin with the question of whether the new rules fall below the APA's minimum requirements by eliminating discovery. The Commission points out, and the petitioners do not seriously contest, that the APA does not explicitly require the provision of any discovery devices in formal adjudications. *See* 5 U.S.C. §556. Thus, if the APA requires the Commission to provide any discovery to satisfy the standards for formal adjudications, that discovery must be necessary either to effectuate some other procedural right guaranteed by the APA or to ensure an adequate record for judicial review. The petitioners suggest that discovery is necessary to realize the right of citizen-intervenors to present their case and submit an informed rebuttal. *See* 5 U.S.C. §556. If discovery is unavailable, this thesis runs, citizen-intervenors will be unable to gather the evidence needed to support their contentions and, thus, will be shut out of meaningful participation in licensing hearings.

This thesis is composed of more cry than wool. The petitioners argue as if the new rules have eliminated all access to information from opposing parties—but that is a gross distortion. The new rules provide meaningful access to information from adverse parties in the form of a system of mandatory disclosure. Although there might well be less information available to citizen-intervenors under the new rules, the difference is one of degree. There is simply no principled way that we can say that the difference occasioned by replacing traditional discovery methods with mandatory disclosure is such that citizen-intervenors are left with no means of adequately presenting their case.

Nor do we think that full-dress discovery is essential to ensure a satisfactory record for judicial review. The Commission's final decision in any hearing must survive review based on the evidence adduced in the hearing. 5 U.S.C. §556(e). The applicant bears the burden of proof in any licensing hearing, *id.* §556(d), and it will have every incentive to proffer sufficient information to allow the agency to reach a reasoned decision. That same quantum of information should be adequate for a reviewing court to determine whether the agency's action is supportable. To say more on this point would be to paint the lily. There is simply no discovery-linked conflict between the new rules and the APA's on-the-record adjudication requirement. The petitioners' first line of argument is, therefore, a dead end.

Turning to cross-examination, the petitioners' contentions fare no better: the new rules meet the APA's requirements. To explain this conclusion, we first must strip away the rhetorical flourishes in which the petitioners shroud their reasoning. It is important to understand that, contrary to the petitioners' importunings, the new rules do not extirpate cross-examination. Rather, they restrict its use to situations in which it is "necessary to ensure an adequate record for decision." The legitimacy of this restriction must be weighed in light of the fact that the APA does not provide an absolute right of cross-examination in on-the-record hearings. *Seacoast,* 572 F.2d at 880. The APA affords a right only to such cross-examination as may be necessary for a full and fair adjudication of the facts. Equally to the point, "[t]he party seeking to cross-examine bears the burden of showing that cross-examination is in fact necessary." *Id.* at 880 n.16.

The Commission represents that, despite the difference in language, it interprets the standard for allowing cross-examination under the new rules to be equivalent to the APA standard. When an agency provides a plausible interpretation of its own procedural rules and there is no record or pattern of contrary conduct a court has no right either to slough off that interpretation or to deem it disingenuous. Given the Commission's stated interpretation, the new rules on cross-examination cannot be termed inconsistent with the dictates of the APA. Nor do we see how cross-examination that is not "necessary to ensure an adequate record for decision" could be necessary to ensure appropriate judicial review. Because we find that the new rules meet the APA requirements for on-the-record adjudications, we hold that their promulgation does not exceed the Commission's authority. . . .

[The court went on to hold that the NRC's decision to change its procedural rules was not arbitrary and capricious. NRC satisfactorily justified the change based on a need for greater efficiency. The change was reasonable because the new rules still conformed to the APA's procedural requirements.]

IV

Procedural flexibility is one of the great hallmarks of the administrative process—and it is a feature that courts must be reluctant to curtail. Though the Commission's new rules may approach the outer bounds of what is permissible under the APA, we find the statute sufficiently broad to accommodate them. Similarly, the Commission's judgments as to when its procedures need fine-tuning and how they should be retooled are ones to which we accord great respect. We cannot say that the Commission's desire for more expeditious adjudications is unreasonable, nor can we say that the changes embodied in the new rules are an eccentric or a plainly inadequate means for achieving the Commission's goals. Accordingly, both of the instant petitions must be denied.

LIPEZ, Circuit Judge, concurring. . . .

The terminology for hearings under the APA can be imprecise and confusing. The everyday meaning of terms like "formal" and "informal" sometimes creeps into the discussion, although those terms have specific, functional definitions under the APA. As Judge Selya notes, the terms "formal" and "on-the-record" are generally used as shorthand for hearings that must be conducted pursuant to the requirements of 5 U.S.C. §§554, 556, and 557 of the APA. Other terms, too, are sometimes used to refer to such procedures—"trial-type" and "quasi-judicial." These vague and indefinite terms are particularly mischievous because they evoke images of courtroom trials, and they have contributed to the false impression that the APA's requirement of on-the-record hearings involves procedures more akin to civil trials than is actually the case.

To be specific, §554 requires that, in cases of an "adjudication required by statute to be determined on the record after opportunity for an agency hearing," the agency must follow the procedures outlined in §§556 and 557. . . . Strikingly, [in §§556-557] there is no reference to discovery . . . , and cross-examination is assured only if necessary "for a full and true disclosure of the facts." 5 U.S.C. §556(d). Most . . . provisions [within §§556-557] relate to the conduct and responsibilities of the presiding officer or the basis for agency orders (on the record). Only a few relate to the conduct of the hearing itself. These APA requirements leave agencies with a great deal of flexibility in tailoring on-the-record hearing procedures to suit their perceived needs. . . .

If hearings are not required to be "on the record," the procedures of §§556 and 557 are not triggered; the only section of the APA applicable to the proceedings is §555, titled "Ancillary matters." Section 555(b) entitles a party to be represented by a lawyer, §555(c) entitles people who have submitted data or evidence to retain copies of their submissions, and §555(e) requires agencies to give prompt notice when they deny a petition made in connection with a proceeding, and to give a brief statement of the grounds for denial. Additionally, subsections (c) and (d) require that process, subpoenas, and other investigative demands must be made in accordance with law. Of course, these "informal" hearings must also comply with basic due process requirements.

From the beginning of its proposed rulemaking, the NRC repeatedly referred to the procedures outlined in the new regulations as "informal," as opposed to the outmoded formal procedures of the past. The clear implication was that the new informal procedures would not meet the APA's requirements for formal, on-the-record hearings. Thus, the NRC believed that it first had to establish that its authorizing statute, the Atomic Energy Act (AEA), did not require it to hold on-the-record hearings for reactor licensing. . . .

The NRC's belated recognition that the new licensing procedures might in fact comply with the on-the-record requirements of the APA is all the more surprising because sources contemporaneous with the APA's passage suggest that flexibility has always been a hallmark of the APA, and that agencies have always had considerable discretion to structure on-the-record hearings to suit their particular needs. This flexibility is nowhere more evident than in determining the role of cross-examination in on-the-record hearings.

The Attorney General's Manual on the Administrative Procedure Act (1947) . . . offers a vision of cross-examination entirely consistent with that advanced by the NRC in this rulemaking. The Manual begins by stressing the general importance of cross-examination in on-the-record hearings, cautioning that "it is clear that the 'right to present his case or defense by oral or documentary evidence' does not extend to presenting evidence in affidavit or other written form so as to deprive the agency or opposing parties of opportunity for cross-examination." AG's Manual at 77. . . . The Attorney General's Manual goes on, however, to acknowledge that the general opportunity to cross-examine is subject to restrictions which become more salient as the complexity of the hearing's subject matter increases. On this point, the Manual quotes from the Report of the House Committee on the Judiciary on the APA. The Report cautions that the APA's provision for "such cross-examination as may be required for a full and true disclosure of the facts" does not confer a right of so-called "unlimited" cross-examination. . . .

The Attorney General's Manual and the House Report serve as good indicators that Congress, when it passed the APA, understood that agencies needed a considerable amount of flexibility in fashioning hearing procedures for on-the-record hearings. Despite the frequent use of terms like "trial-type" and "quasi-judicial" over the years to refer to on-the-record hearings, agencies have always been able to adapt their procedures for on-the-record hearings under the APA. . . .

NOTES AND QUESTIONS

1. *How "formal" is formal adjudication?* Initially, the NRC believed that the best way to streamline licensing proceedings would be to argue that the "hearing" requirement in the Atomic Energy Act did not trigger the APA model of formal adjudication. Given the First Circuit's ruling in *Dominion Energy, supra,* would that have been a winning argument? The commission eventually realized, however, that it could achieve its goals by invoking the flexibility furnished by the language of §§554, 556, and 557—and the court agreed. The upshot of *Citizens Awareness* seems to be that, despite its label, "formal" adjudication under the APA is not so formal after all. Instead, the court seems to be saying, the APA lays out only "skeletal" requirements that allow considerable agency flexibility. Do you agree in this case? As a general matter?

2. *Cross-examination.* As discussed in *Citizens Awareness*, the administrative model relaxes the virtually absolute right of cross-examination in civil trials. APA §556(d) confers on parties to administrative adjudications the right to conduct only "such cross-examination as may be required for a full and true disclosure of the facts." Courts have interpreted this provision to give agency hearing officers fairly broad discretion to limit cross-examination. The Supreme Court grappled with the extent to which agencies may limit cross-examination in

Richardson v. Perales, 402 U.S. 389 (1971), discussed in the *Eldridge* case, *supra.* Perales applied to the Social Security Administration for disability insurance benefits, claiming that he was totally and permanently disabled as a result of a back injury. At the hearing, he, his physician, and a former coworker testified in support of his claim. The only adverse evidence were written reports from physicians who had examined him, which contained a number of statements that the Court conceded to be "devastating" to Perales's claim, including this one from an orthopedic surgeon: "it has been a long time since I have been so impressed with the obvious attempt of a patient to exaggerate his difficulties. [H]e has a tremendous psychological overlay to his illness. . . ." Perales argued that such reports could not constitute "substantial evidence" of nondisability, when their preparers were not present to defend them and the only live testimony supported the claimant. The Court rejected Perales's argument on the ground that "routine, standard, and unbiased" reports prepared by examining physicians are sufficiently reliable to constitute "substantial evidence." *Id.* at 404. In addition, said the Court, Perales failed to exercise his right to subpoena the physicians to testify at the hearing.

One of the purported benefits of cross-examination is that it allows parties to explore the basis of conclusory statements that might otherwise go unchallenged. Recall, however, the *Biestek* decision, excerpted in Chapter II, *supra.* In that case, a vocational expert, citing confidentiality concerns, refused to reveal the basis for her testimony that approximately 360,000 jobs existed in the national economy that the applicant for disability benefits could perform. The Court held that the expert's testimony alone, even without the underlying data, was sufficient to constitute substantial evidence to support the conclusion that the applicant did not meet the requirements for disability benefits. Is the Court's faith in experts justified?

3. *Evidence and formal adjudication.* The process of submitting and receiving evidence is also generally somewhat looser in the administrative setting than in the judicial setting. The most notable example is the relaxation in agency hearings of the rules of evidence that customarily apply in judicial trials. APA §556(d) codifies this understanding: "Any oral or documentary evidence may be received, but the agency as a matter of policy shall provide for the exclusion of irrelevant, immaterial, or unduly repetitious evidence." In the *Richardson* case, the Court held that the physician's report may be received as evidence when the claimant has not exercised his right to subpoena and cross-examine the reporting physician. *But see* Wallace v. Bowen, 869 F.2d 187 (3d Cir. 1988) (reports may not be received into evidence when claimant is denied the opportunity to confront the consulting physicians). For further discussion, *see* Richard J. Pierce, Jr., Use of Federal Rules of Evidence in Federal Agency Adjudications, 39 Admin. L. Rev. (1987).

b.   Official Notice

Consistent with relaxed rules of evidence, agency hearing officers have broader discretion than judges to take "official notice" of facts "not appearing in the evidence," under APA §556(e). The Federal Rules of Evidence establish criteria constraining a judge's ability to take notice of adjudicative facts — *i.e.,* facts relating to a particular case, as opposed to facts true across all cases. Specifically, a judge may notice an adjudicative fact when that fact is either generally known within the court's jurisdiction or can be accurately and readily determined by sources whose accuracy cannot reasonably be questioned. *See* Fed. R. Evid. 201. By contrast, §556(e) places no explicit constraints on an agency's power to notice particular facts outside the record, providing only that "[w]hen an agency decision rests on official notice of a material fact not appearing in the evidence in the record, a party is entitled . . . to an opportunity to show the contrary." That said, as we shall see, the Constitution's Due Process Clause does restrict agency power to take official notice.

The more permissive rules governing official notice in the administrative context have been justified on at least two grounds. First, because administrators may be experts in their fields, unlike generalist judges, they should have broader authority to rely on facts within their areas of expertise. *See, e.g.*, Sykes v. Apfel, 228 F.3d 259, 272 (3d Cir. 2000) ("[O]fficial notice is broader than judicial notice insofar as it allows an administrative agency to take notice of technical or scientific facts that are within the agency's area of expertise."); *see also* Ernest L. Gellhorn, Rules of Evidence and Official Notice in Formal Administrative Hearings, 1971 Duke L.J. 1; Daniel B. Rodriguez, Official Notice and the Administrative Process, 10 J. Natl. Assn. Admin. L. Judges 47 (1990). Second, because administrators hear many cases of a similar kind, allowing them to take notice of facts that tend to be true across the run of cases may help them focus their attention on the unique facts of a particular case. *See, e.g.*, Castillo-Villagra v. INS, 972 F.2d 1017, 1027 (9th Cir. 1992) ("Hearings may degenerate into an empty form if the adjudicators cannot focus attention upon what is noteworthy about a particular case. The broader notice available in administrative hearings may, if properly used, facilitate more genuine hearings, as opposed to hearings in which the finder of fact hears, but cannot, because of the repetition, listen."). Yet while administrative hearing officers have broad leeway in determining what extra-record facts to officially notice, §556(e)'s requirement that the officer afford a party the opportunity to rebut those facts is far less flexible.

SOUTHERN CALIFORNIA EDISON CO. v. FEDERAL ENERGY REGULATORY COMMISSION
717 F.3d 177 (D.C. Cir. 2013)

Before ROGERS, Circuit Judge, and GINSBURG and SENTELLE, Senior Circuit Judges.

ROGERS, Circuit Judge:

[The Federal Energy Regulatory Commission (FERC) regulates the rates that transmission owners can charge power generators to wheel their power over their lines. In order to encourage companies to build new transmission lines, FERC established an "incentive" rate program designed to provide a reasonable return on equity (ROE), thus helping utilities to attract the capital necessary to finance their projects. Establishing such ROEs can be highly contentious. Utilities understandably want them to be as high as possible, while the agency wishes to control costs, which will be passed on, ultimately, to electricity consumers. In calculating Southern California Edison's (SoCal Edison's) ROE for one such project, FERC used its established formula, based on the ROEs of a "proxy" group of similar publicly traded utilities, adjusted by such factors as the average yields on ten-year Treasury bonds. SoCal Edison applied for an ROE of 11.5 percent. FERC conducted a "paper hearing" on this request, and, based on the submissions made at that paper hearing, set an ROE of 10.55 percent. Subsequent to the close of the paper hearing (in late 2008), however, FERC announced that because of a recent 1.01 percent reduction in ten-year Treasury bond yields, it was adjusting SoCal Edison's allowed ROE downward, from 10.55 percent to 9.54 percent. SoCal Edison requested a rehearing on whether the adjustment was warranted, but FERC denied the request.]

SoCal Edison . . . contends that, in updating its ROE, the Commission erred by taking official notice of the change in U.S. Treasury bond yields as a proxy for its private cost of capital . . . without affording it an opportunity to show to the contrary. SoCal Edison does not contest the fact of the change in the Treasury bond yields or the Commission's updating policy in general. Instead, because rehearing was its first opportunity to respond to the officially noticed data, SoCal Edison maintains that the Commission erred, to SoCal Edison's prejudice, in refusing to consider proffered expert analysis of the unique conditions of the 2008 market collapse.

Section 556(e) of the Administrative Procedure Act ("APA") provides, "[w]hen an agency decision rests on official notice of a material fact not appearing in the evidence in the record, a party is entitled, on timely request, to an opportunity to show the contrary." In Union Electric Co. v. FERC, 890 F.2d 1193 (D.C. Cir. 1989), the court interpreted §556(e) in light of pre-APA decisions involving challenges to official notice, identifying two prerequisites: "First, the information noticed must be appropriate for official notice. Second, the agency must follow proper procedures in using the information, disclosing it to the parties and affording them a suitable opportunity to contradict it or 'parry its effect.'" Id. at 1202. The court viewed Treasury bond rates to be a type of information that was appropriate for official notice because such information is not typically subject to dispute. Id. at 1202-03. Union Electric, however, had raised "substantial objections" to the Commission's apparent assumption of a linear relationship between the trend for Treasury bond rates and Union Electric's cost of equity capital. Id. at 1203. The court held that, despite Union Electric's "partial opportunity" to oppose the Commission's updating, id., the Commission failed to "either accept[] or appropriately refute[]" the company's evidence and "broader attack on [the Commission's] use of the Treasury bond rates," id. at 1203-04.

[Here, t]he Commission took official notice, after the record had closed, of the average ten-year U.S. Treasury bond yields. . . . In response, SoCal Edison proffered on rehearing an affidavit of its expert stating that those yields were not a rational proxy for its private cost of capital due to the unusual economic conditions in late 2008. In a nutshell, this was so because the spread between the U.S. Treasury bond yields and the rates on corporate bonds increased, as investors fled from riskier corporate investments to less risky Treasury bonds, reaching proportions not seen since April 1933. This analysis could not have been submitted during previous proceedings because the critical economic changes occurred months after SoCal Edison's final Paper Hearing brief was filed in May 2008.

The Commission nonetheless declined to consider the affidavit, noting its general rule that once the record is closed it will not be reopened and that it generally does not allow new evidence to be introduced at the rehearing stage. The Commission explained that its "precedent requiring updating ROEs has been applied over the course of more than 25 years, during which time the U.S. economy has experienced many fluctuations," and that "[r]egardless of whether the ten-year bonds perfectly capture every short-term variation in the costs of equity, we continue to find . . . [that] over time the ten-year bond index continues to be a reliable barometer of overall market conditions." . . .

Application of the updating policy without regard to SoCal Edison's expert affidavit illustrates how material such an officially noticed fact can be. On the basis of the decline of the Treasury bond rates . . . , the Commission reduced SoCal Edison's base ROE by 101 basis points (1.01%), from 10.55% to 9.54%. This makes it somewhat odd that the Commission would turn a blind eye to the information SoCal Edison proffered on rehearing. The Commission does not suggest that it has applied the updating policy in such extreme economic circumstances as occurred in late 2008. SoCal Edison thus made the necessary "good showing" that it could contest the significance of the Commission's officially noticed information based on "a[] flaw in the evidence." Although the Commission responded to SoCal Edison's objections at an abstract level, and noted SoCal's argument that the corporate and Treasury bond "rates were inversely related and, therefore, not rationally related," it never confronted the gravity of the economic downturn or the magnitude of the yield spread as public and private bond rates moved in opposite directions. Under §556(e), the Commission was obligated to consider and appropriately respond to SoCal Edison's effort "to parry the effect" of the officially noticed information. . . .

Accordingly, we grant the petition in part and . . . and remand the case to the Commission for further proceedings.

NOTES AND QUESTIONS

1. *Facts appropriate for official notice.* SoCal Edison illustrates how an agency's failure to comply with §556(e)'s requirements for official notice may lead a court to invalidate the results of a formal adjudication. Recall that §556(e) does not specify what types of facts may be officially noticed by administrators, or when, precisely, taking notice is proper. In *Union Electric*, referenced in *SoCal Edison*, the D.C. Circuit identified as a prerequisite for official notice the requirement that "the information noticed must be appropriate for official notice." Has the D.C. Circuit, in essence, imposed an additional procedural requirement on agencies by inquiring into whether a particular fact is appropriate for official notice due to its indisputability? Does this maneuver violate the rule of *Vermont Yankee*, excerpted in Chapter V, *supra*? Or is the court implicitly observing that an agency taking official notice of a fact that is subject to reasonable dispute would constitute an abuse of discretion and therefore violate APA §706?

2. *Official notice and due process.* Even if the APA places no explicit constraints on the types of facts appropriate for official notice, the Constitution's Due Process Clause does. *See* Ohio Bell Telephone Co. v. Public Utilities Commission

of Ohio, 301 U.S. 292 (1937). The relationship between official notice and due process has been explored in several cases involving asylum claims by citizens of repressive regimes that have undergone a recent political change. Castillo-Villagra v. INS, 972 F.2d 1017 (9th Cir. 1992), is illustrative. Petitioners sought asylum in the United States, claiming that, should they be deported to their homeland of Nicaragua, they would be persecuted by members or supporters of the ruling Sandinista Party. While the case was pending on appeal, Violeta Chamorro, a democrat, was elected President of Nicaragua. The Bureau of Immigration Appeals (BIA) took official notice of this fact and determined that, because the Sandinista Party had lost the election, there was no longer a basis for the petitioners to fear persecution. The Ninth Circuit, applying the Due Process Clause, ruled that while the BIA properly took official notice of the election results, it improperly took official notice of the *impact* of the election on the petitioners' risk of persecution. The latter, said the court, was an adjudicative fact that depended on the residual power of the Sandinistas and the petitioners' relationship to the Sandinistas. By taking notice of that fact and additionally failing to afford petitioners an opportunity to introduce evidence to rebut it, the agency violated petitioners' due process rights.

3. *Exclusive record for decision.* With the exception of facts officially noticed in compliance with §556(e), "[t]he transcript of testimony and exhibits, together with all papers and requests filed in the proceeding, constitutes the exclusive record for decision" in a formal adjudication. 5 U.S.C. §556(e). Recall *Seacoast, supra,* in which the EPA Administrator relied on assistance from a panel of scientists when reviewing a regional Administrator's decision to deny a permit application. Petitioners objected to the Administrator's use of the panel on the ground that the panel's report included information not in the record, upon which the Administrator relied. The court agreed:

> The Administrator is charged with making highly technical decisions in fields far beyond his individual expertise. . . . Therefore, "(e)vidence . . . may be sifted and analyzed by competent subordinates." *Morgan,* 298 U.S. at 481. The decision ultimately reached is no less the Administrator's simply because agency experts helped him to reach it.
>
> A different question is presented, however, if the agency experts do not merely sift and analyze but also add to the evidence properly before the Administrator. . . . To the extent the technical review panel's Report included information not in the record on which the Administrator relied, §556(e) was violated. In effect the agency's staff would have made up for [the permit applicant] PSCO's failure to carry its burden of proof.
>
> Our review of the Report indicates that such violations did occur. The most serious instance is on page 19 of the Report where the technical panel rebuts the Regional Administrator's finding that PSCO had failed to supply enough data on species' thermal tolerances by saying:
>
>> There is little information in the record on the thermal tolerances of marine organisms exposed to the specific temperature fluctuation associated with the Seabrook operation. However, the scientific literature does contain many references to the thermal sensitivity of members of the local biota.

Whether or not these references do exist and whether or not they support the conclusions the panel goes on to draw does not concern us here. What is important is that the record did not support the conclusion until supplemented by the panel. The panel's work found its way directly into the Administrator's decision at page 27 where he discusses the Regional Administrator's concerns about insufficient data but then precipitously concludes, "On the recommendation of the panel, however, I find that . . . local indigenous populations will not be significantly affected." This conclusion depends entirely on what the panel stated about the scientific literature. . . .

The appropriate remedy under these circumstances is to remand the decision to the Administrator because he based his decision on material not part of the record. . . . The Administrator will have the options of trying to reach a new decision not dependent on the panel's supplementation of the record; of holding a hearing at which all parties will have the opportunity to cross-examine the panel members and at which the panel will have an opportunity to amplify its position; or of taking any other action within his power and consistent with this opinion.

572 F.2d at 881-882.

4. *Burden of proof.* APA §556(d) provides that, "[e]xcept as otherwise provided by statute, the proponent of a rule or order has the burden of proof." This thoroughly innocuous provision sparked a strenuous debate among the Justices in Director, Office of Workers' Compensation Programs v. Greenwich Collieries, 512 U.S. 267 (1994). The Department of Labor, under two statutes, adjudicates claims for black lung disease brought by workers against their employers. The claimant clearly bears the burden of producing evidence in these cases. But, under the Department's so-called "true doubt" rule, when the evidence is evenly balanced between the proponent and opponent of a benefits award, the claimant wins (*i.e.,* the burden of persuasion falls on the opponent of the claim). In defending its rule, the Department argued that "burden of proof," as used in §556(d), meant "burden of production," not "burden of persuasion." A majority of the Supreme Court disagreed, concluding that, as of 1946 when the APA was enacted, there was a "settled" meaning among legal authorities that burden of proof meant burden of persuasion. Three Justices dissented, denying that the phrase had such a settled meaning and pointing to evidence in the legislative history to suggest that the drafters meant burden of production.

c.   Statement of Findings

Under APA §557(c), when an agency renders a decision in a formal adjudication, it must include a statement of "findings and conclusions, and the reasons of basis therefor, on all the material issues of fact, law, or discretion presented on the record; and the appropriate rule, order, sanction, relief, or denial thereof." Such a statement of findings is essential to enabling effective appellate review of agency decisions in formal adjudications. The case that follows illustrates judicial application of these requirements.

ARMSTRONG v. COMMODITY FUTURES TRADING COMMISSION
12 F.3d 401 (3d Cir. 1993)

Before GREENBERG, COWEN and SEITZ, Circuit Judges.
SEITZ, Circuit Judge:

I

[In 1983 Martin] Armstrong began accepting and fulfilling paid subscriptions for a commodity market forecast newsletter. His attorneys formed three corporations for the provision of commodity services: Princeton Economic Consultants, Inc. ("PEC"), Economic Consultants of Princeton, Inc. ("ECP"), and Armstrong Report, Inc. These corporations provided consulting services, seminar programs, written reports, telephone and telex newsline messages, and account management services.

In 1985, the [Commodity Futures Trading] Commission filed an administrative complaint against Armstrong, PEC, ECP, and Armstrong Report charging them with failure to register as commodity trading advisors, to deliver required disclosure documents to clients, and to maintain proper records. In 1987, the Commission filed a second administrative complaint charging that ECP failed to disclose a commission-sharing agreement, that PEC misrepresented hypothetical performance results and omitted a required disclaimer in advertisements, and that Armstrong was liable for ECP's and PEC's violations as a controlling person of those corporations. The proceedings were consolidated for hearing and decision.

The administrative law judge ("ALJ") issued an Initial Decision finding Armstrong and all three corporations liable on all counts charged in both dockets and proposing sanctions. After a hearing, the ALJ reaffirmed the findings of fact and conclusions of law contained in his Initial Decision and imposed the tentative sanctions. The sanctions banned the parties from trading for 12 months, revoked their registrations, imposed cease and desist orders, and levied civil penalties totaling $50,000.

Armstrong and the corporations appealed both the liability findings and sanctions to the Commission. They convinced the Commission that the ALJ erred by treating them as a single enterprise rather than as four discrete entities in the first complaint. As a result, the Commission reversed the ALJ's finding that Armstrong was individually liable for the violations alleged in the first complaint. The Commission summarily affirmed the findings under the second complaint, including Armstrong's liability for PEC's and EPC's violations. Armstrong and the corporations petitioned this court for review. . . .

II

Armstrong complains that the Commission did not meet the requirements of the Administrative Procedure Act because it did not provide an adequate "statement of . . . findings and conclusions, and the reasons or basis therefor, on all the material issues of fact, law, or discretion presented on the record." 5 U.S.C. §557(c) (1988). . . .

The purposes of the APA provision requiring specific findings and conclusions are to prevent arbitrary agency decisions, provide parties with a reasoned explanation for those decisions, settle the law for future cases, and furnish a basis for effective judicial review. Third Circuit Court of Appeals precedent emphasizes the need for adequate findings to ensure effective judicial review and eliminate appellate speculation.

An administrative agency need not provide an independent statement if it specifically adopts an ALJ's opinion that sets forth adequate findings and reasoning. . . .

No particular form of adoption is required if the agency's action permits meaningful appellate review. The Seventh Circuit has concluded that an agency order stating that "The initial decision is affirmed and the proceeding is terminated" is sufficient to indicate adoption of an ALJ's entire opinion. City of Frankfort, Ind. v. FERC, 678 F.2d 699, 708 & n.18 (7th Cir. 1982). . . .

In the case before us, however, the Commission has not clearly adopted the ALJ's opinion. The Commission's entire opinion regarding the second complaint stated:

> Our review of the record and the briefs submitted by the parties establishes that the ALJ reached a substantially correct result on all the allegations raised in the Second Complaint. Because we also conclude that the parties have not raised important questions of law or policy concerning the ALJ's findings of fact and conclusions on these allegations, we affirm the Second Complaint without opinion.

Summarily affirming the ALJ's opinion as "substantially correct" is insufficient because it does not permit intelligent appellate review. [While the agency may] adopt[] an entire opinion or specified parts of an opinion[,] . . . the Commission's conclusion that the ALJ reached a "substantially correct" result leaves questions about which specific findings or conclusions by the ALJ were incorrect.

The footnote disclaiming the ALJ's decision as an expression of the Commission's views further undermines the Commission's assertion before us that it adopted the entire opinion. We assume that the Commission has the power to determine which of its decisions may be cited as precedent in future proceedings before it. However, the declaration that the opinion does not represent the Commission's views erodes our confidence that the Commission carefully considered and adopted each of the ALJ's findings and conclusions. . . . We hold that a summary affirmance of all or part of an ALJ's opinion must leave no guesswork regarding what the agency has adopted. A decision by an ALJ that is only "substantially correct" should be fully correct by the time an agency imprints its seal of approval.

Although a remand is warranted based on the adoption issue alone, we proceed to review the Commission's and the ALJ's opinions in order to prevent an immediate return of the case to this court. . . . The only theory under which Armstrong was charged with individual liability in the second complaint was as a controlling person as defined in section 13(b) of the Commodity Exchange Act. This section provides:

Any person who, directly or indirectly, controls any person who has violated . . . any of the rules, regulations, or orders issued pursuant to this chapter may be held liable for such violation in any action brought by the Commission to the same extent as such controlled person. In such action, the Commission has the burden of proving that the controlling person did not act in good faith or knowingly induced, directly or indirectly, the act or acts constituting the violation.

Neither the ALJ's Initial Decision nor the Commission's opinion addressed Section 13(b). [T]he Administrative Procedure Act requires an adequate "statement of . . . findings and conclusions, and the reasons or basis therefor, on all the material issues of fact, law, or discretion presented on the record." 5 U.S.C. §557(e). . . . We do not understand how a statement of conclusion on a material issue of law can be adequate without mentioning the statutory provision or its language.

Section 13(b) requires at least two findings before concluding a respondent is liable as a controlling person: (1) that the respondent controlled a violator; and (2) that the controlling person did not act in good faith or knowingly induced the violation. First, the Commission contends that the ALJ's statement that Armstrong "had and exercised full domination and control over all operations of" ECP and PEC is a sufficient finding that Armstrong controlled the corporations. However, this statement was made as part of the single enterprise discussion that the Commission vacated; its continuing validity is at least subject to question. Second, the Commission's appeal brief recites evidence in the record from which the ALJ could have found that Armstrong knowingly induced the violations. Nevertheless, there is still no finding by the ALJ or the Commission that Armstrong did knowingly induce the violations. Finally, and most importantly, there is no conclusion that Armstrong is liable as a controlling person under Section 13(b). Without a conclusion that Armstrong is liable for violations with which he was charged, Armstrong may not be individually penalized. . . . The decision of the Commission will be vacated and the matter remanded to the Commission for further appropriate proceedings.

NOTES AND QUESTIONS

1. *Level of detail required by §557(c).* In *Armstrong*, the court noted that an agency may be able to satisfy §557(c) by adopting the ALJ's opinion in full. The CFTC erred because it adopted *some* of the ALJ's opinion without specifying which parts it declined to adopt and why. Note that if an agency does fully adopt the ALJ's opinion, an appellate court will simply review the adequacy of the ALJ's opinion under §557(c). *See, e.g.*, Dakota Underground, Inc. v. Secretary of Labor, 200 F.3d 564 (8th Cir. 2000) (invalidating portion of an ALJ's decision because it lacked sufficient findings and explanation to support its determination that an employer's OSHA violation was "willful").

2. *Benefits and costs of requiring a detailed explanation.* As the court in *Armstrong* explained, a detailed explanation creates a better record for judicial review, possibly leads to sounder decisionmaking, and enhances the decision's legitimacy in the eyes of a losing party. But for a resource-strapped agency, producing more detailed decisions could result in fewer adjudications over

time. In certain contexts—provision of disability or welfare benefits, for instance—that result is troublesome because it may mean fewer individuals receive the government support they need. *See* Stephens v. Heckler, 766 F.2d 284 (7th Cir. 1985) (Easterbrook, J.) (explaining, in the context of disability benefits, that when agency decisionmakers "slow down to write better opinions, that holds up the queue and prevents deserving people from receiving benefits"). On the other hand, a carefully crafted decision that explains a principle that might apply in future decisions may conserve agency resources. Commentators typically make such claims without the benefit of empirical evidence, so the point remains debatable. In the end, agencies must strike a delicate balance whereby decisions contain sufficient detail to serve §557(c)'s purposes, while at the same time not so much detail as to impair agency efficiency in a world of limited resources.

d.   Intervention

Besides the direct party to an adjudication—for instance, a license applicant, or an entity facing agency sanctions—what other parties are entitled to participate in adjudicatory proceedings? The APA offers little guidance on the question. Section 551(3) defines "party" as anyone "named or admitted as a party, or properly seeking and entitled as of right to be admitted" or admitted "by an agency as a party for limited purposes." And §555(b) states, "[s]o far as the orderly conduct of public business permits, an interested person may appear before an agency or its responsible employees for the presentation, adjustment, or determination of an issue, request, or controversy. . . ." But these provisions tend to beg the question because they fail to illuminate when a person is "entitled as of right to be admitted," or when someone is an "interested person."

Likewise, agency enabling statutes often fail to clearly specify who is entitled to participate in agency adjudications. This statutory ambiguity has led courts to apply *Chevron* deference to agency interpretations of participation rights. The following case provides an example.

ENVIROCARE OF UTAH, INC. v. NUCLEAR REGULATORY COMMISSION
194 F.3d 72 (D.C. Cir. 1999)

Before EDWARDS, Chief Judge, SENTELLE and RANDOLPH, Circuit Judges.
RANDOLPH, Circuit Judge:
Federal agencies may, and sometimes do, permit persons to intervene in administrative proceedings even though these persons would not have standing to challenge the agency's final action in federal court. Agencies, of course, are not constrained by Article III of the Constitution; nor are they governed by judicially-created standing doctrines restricting access to the federal courts. The criteria for establishing "administrative standing" therefore may permissibly be less demanding than the criteria for "judicial standing." *See, e.g.,* Pittsburgh & W. Va. Ry. v. United States, 281 U.S. 479, 486 (1930).

Is the converse true? May an agency refuse to grant a hearing to persons who would satisfy the criteria for judicial standing and refuse to allow them to intervene in administrative proceedings? This is the ultimate question posed in these consolidated petitions for judicial review of two orders of the Nuclear Regulatory Commission refusing to grant Envirocare of Utah, Inc.'s requests for a hearing and for intervention in licensing proceedings.

I

Envirocare was the first commercial facility in the nation the Commission licensed to dispose of certain radioactive byproduct material from offsite sources. The Commission had licensed other companies to dispose of such radioactive waste, but only if the waste was produced onsite. In the late 1990s, the Commission granted the applications of two such companies for amended licenses to allow them to dispose of radioactive waste received from other sites. International Uranium (USA) Corporation's facility in Utah became licensed to receive and dispose of approximately 25,000 dry tons of waste still remaining from the Manhattan Project and currently stored in New York State. Quivira Mining Company's facility in New Mexico, some 500 miles from Envirocare's operation, also became licensed to dispose of specified amounts of such material from offsite sources.

In both licensing proceedings before the Atomic Safety and Licensing Board, Envirocare requested a hearing and sought leave to intervene to oppose the amendment. Envirocare's basic complaint was "that the license amendment permits [the company] to become a general commercial facility like Envirocare, but that the NRC did not require [the company] to meet the same regulatory standards the agency imposed upon Envirocare when Envirocare sought *its* license to become a commercial disposal facility for" radioactive waste. The Licensing Board rejected Envirocare's requests for a hearing and for leave to intervene in both cases, and in separate opinions several months apart, the Commission affirmed.

[T]he Commission ruled that Envirocare did not come within the following "standing" provision in the Atomic Energy Act: when the Commission institutes a proceeding for the granting or amending of a license, "the Commission shall grant a hearing upon the request of any person whose interest may be affected by the proceeding, and shall admit any such person as a party to such proceeding." 42 U.S.C. §2239(a)(1)(A). In determining whether Envirocare possessed the requisite "interest" under this provision, the Commission looked to "current judicial concepts of standing." Envirocare alleged economic injury, claiming that the less stringent application of regulations to [its competitors] placed Envirocare at a competitive disadvantage. This allegation was sufficient, the Commission held, to meet the injury-in-fact requirements of constitutional standing. On the question of prudential standing, however, the Commission determined that "Envirocare's purely competitive interests, unrelated to any radiological harm to itself, do not bring it within the zone of interests of the AEA for the purpose of policing the license requirements of a competitor." . . .

In addition, the Commission made explicit its view that judicial standing doctrines were not controlling in the administrative context and that its duty was to interpret the "interest[s]" Congress intended to recognize in §2239(a)(1)(A): "Our understanding of the AEA requires us to insist that a competitor's pecuniary aim of imposing additional regulatory restrictions or burdens on fellow market participants does not fall within those 'interests' that trigger a right to hearing and intervention under [§2239(a)(1)(A)]."

II

Envirocare spends all of its time arguing that in light of decisions of the Supreme Court and of this court, its status as a competitor satisfies the "zone of interests" test for standing, as the test was formulated in Association of Data Processing Service Organizations v. Camp, 397 U.S. 150 (1970), and as it was refined in National Credit Union Administration v. First National Bank & Trust Co., 522 U.S. 479 (1998). We shall assume that Envirocare is correct. It does not follow that the Commission erred in refusing the company's motions for a hearing and for leave to intervene. . . . The Commission rightly pointed out . . . that it is not an Article III court and thus is not bound to follow the law of standing derived from the "case or controversy" requirement. Judicially-devised prudential standing requirements, of which the "zone of interests" test is one, are also inapplicable to an administrative agency acting within the jurisdiction Congress assigned to it. The doctrine of prudential standing, like that derived from the Constitution, rests on considerations "about the proper—and properly limited—role of the courts in a democratic society." Warth v. Seldin, 422 U.S. 490, 498 (1975).

Whether the Commission erred in excluding Envirocare from participating in [its competitors'] licensing proceeding[s] therefore turns not on judicial decisions dealing with standing to sue, but on familiar principles of administrative law regarding an agency's interpretation of the statutes it alone administers. *See* Chevron U.S.A. Inc. v. Natural Resources Defense Council, Inc., 467 U.S. 837, 842 (1984). The governing provision—42 U.S.C. §2239(a)(1)(A)—requires the Commission to hold a hearing "on the request of any person whose interest may be affected by the proceeding" and to allow such a person to intervene. The term "interest" is not defined in the Act and it is scarcely self-defining. It could mean merely an academic or organizational interest in a problem or subject, an interest in avoiding economic harm or in gaining an economic benefit from agency action directed at others, an "interest" in "aesthetic, conservational and recreational values," [or] all of these. But whatever the judicial mind thinks of today as an "interest" affected by a proceeding is not necessarily what Congress meant when it enacted this provision in 1954. At the time, judicial notions of standing were considerably more restrictive than they are now. . . .

How agencies were then treating standing questions is unclear. According to one report, they were limiting the right to a hearing "to those directly subject to administrative controls, exactions or sanctions." [T]he FCC did not recognize "economic injury" as "sufficient to secure a hearing or to intervene in a hearing on a competitor's license application." Ronald A. Cass & Colin S. Diver, Administrative Law: Cases and Materials 714 (1987) (citing *Voice of Cullman*, 14 F.C.C. 770 (1950)). It was not until the late 1950s that some decisions of this court began expanding the category of persons entitled to participate in agency proceedings on the theory that anyone who had standing to seek judicial review should have administrative standing. *See, e.g.,* National Welfare Rights Org. v. Finch, 429 F.2d 725, 732-33 (D.C. Cir. 1970); Office of Communication of United Church of Christ v. FCC, 359 F.2d 994, 1000-06 (D.C. Cir. 1966); Virginia Petroleum Jobbers Ass'n v. FPC, 265 F.2d 364 (D.C. Cir. 1959).

Because we cannot be confident of what kinds of interests the 1954 Congress meant to recognize in §2239(a)(1)(A)—because, in other words, the statute is ambiguous—the Commission's interpretation of this provision must be sustained if it is reasonable. *See Chevron,* 467 U.S. at 843. We think it is. For one thing, excluding competitors who allege only economic injury from the class of persons entitled to intervene in licensing proceedings is consistent with the Atomic Energy Act. The Act meant to increase private competition in the industry, not limit it. Before its passage in 1954, the federal government completely controlled nuclear energy. Through the Act, Congress sought to foster a private nuclear industry for peaceful purposes. In order to ensure that private industry would not undermine nuclear safety, the Act created an agency—what is today the Nuclear Regulatory Commission—to regulate the private sector. One of the Commission's statutory duties is authorizing the transfer and receipt of radioactive byproduct material. *See* 42 U.S.C. §2111. The statute describes the Commission's responsibility in this area as follows: "The Commission shall insure that the management of any byproduct material . . . is carried out in such a manner as the Commission deems appropriate to protect the public health and safety and the environment from radiological and nonradiological hazards associated with the processing and with the possession and transfer of such material. . . ." 42 U.S.C. §2114(a)(1).

Nothing in this provision, or in the rest of the Act, indicates that the license requirement was intended to protect market participants from new entrants. Envirocare points to the Act's policy statement which mentions "strengthen[ing] free competition in private enterprise." This statement refers to the Act's goal of creating a private nuclear energy industry. Allowing new competitors to enter the market strengthens competition. Permitting current license holders to initiate hearings for the purpose of imposing burdens on potential competitors does the opposite.

In rendering its interpretation of §2239(a)(1)(A), the Commission also properly took account of regulatory burdens on the agency. It wrote: "Competitors, though, whose only 'interest' is lost business opportunities, could readily burden our adjudicatory process with open-ended allegations designed not to advance public health and safety but as a dilatory tactic to interfere with and impose costs upon a competitor. Such an abuse of our hearing process would significantly divert limited agency resources, which ought to be squarely—genuinely—focused upon health and safety concerns." . . .

For these reasons, the view the Commission expressed . . . —that competitors asserting economic injury do not demonstrate the type of interest necessary under §2239(a)(1)(A)—is a permissible construction of the statute. . . .

We mentioned earlier several decisions of this court indicating that agencies should allow administrative standing to those who can meet judicial standing requirements. None of these cases interpreted the administrative standing provision of the Atomic Energy Act. All were decided before *Chevron* and for that reason alone cannot control our decision today. . . . Judged by current law, none gave sufficient weight to the agency's interpretation of the statute governing intervention in its administrative proceedings. . . .

NOTES AND QUESTIONS

1. *The evolution of intervention rights.* In *Envirocare*, the D.C. Circuit cited three pre-*Chevron* cases in which the court articulated a much broader understanding of administrative intervention rights, as in National Welfare Rights Organization v. Finch, 429 F.2d 725 (D.C. Cir. 1970), which concerned hearings before the Secretary of Health, Education, and Welfare to evaluate states' conformity with federal welfare standards. At stake was continued federal funding for certain welfare programs. Not surprisingly, an association of welfare recipients sought to intervene in the hearings. As an initial matter, the court noted that the Social Security Act, the Department's enabling statute, was silent on the issue of hearing participation by parties other than the Department and the relevant state. For guidance, the court looked to judicially-developed tests for standing, and determined that because the welfare organization would have standing to seek judicial review of the agency's decision, it should also possess a right to participate in the hearing at the agency level. The court pointed out that "[t]he right of judicial review cannot be taken as fully realized . . . if [a party is] excluded from participating in the proceeding to be reviewed." Moreover, unlike the court in *Envirocare*, which emphasized the burdens the agency would have to shoulder if participation rights were read expansively, the court in *National Welfare Rights Organization* downplayed these burdens, noting that "[t]he threat of hundreds of intervenors . . . is more apparent than real."

What accounts for the D.C. Circuit's changed approach to intervention rights between *National Welfare Rights Organization* and *Envirocare*? Is *Chevron* a sufficient explanation? Or is the constriction of standing rights, as illustrated by *Lujan*, excerpted in Chapter III, *supra*, also relevant?

2. *A possible middle ground?* Is there a middle ground between denying interested parties access altogether and providing such parties full participation rights? Could an agency allow an interested party to intervene while circumscribing its procedural rights, so as to reduce the administrative burdens emphasized in *Envirocare*? How might the NRC have permitted Envirocare to participate on a limited basis? Would such an approach be upheld under *Chevron*?

e. Restrictions on Ex Parte Communications in Adjudication

The APA protects the decisional independence of ALJs, or other officers who preside over formal adjudications, through two main provisions. First, §554(d) provides that: (1) the hearing officer may not consult a person or party on a fact in issue, unless on notice and opportunity for all parties to participate; (2) the hearing officer may not be responsible to or subject to the supervision of an agency employee engaged in prosecutorial or investigative functions; and (3) an agency employee engaged in prosecutorial or investigative functions in a particular case may not participate in the decision in that case. Second, §557(d)(1) prohibits any ex parte communications relevant to the merits of a formal adjudication between "interested person[s] outside the agency" and any member of an agency involved in the adjudication. Section 551(14), in turn, defines "ex parte communication" as "an oral or written communication not on the public record with respect to which reasonable prior notice to all parties is not given." The following case presents difficult questions regarding the scope of §557(d)(1)'s ex parte communications ban.

For years, environmentalists and loggers waged a fierce battle over some three million acres of old-growth forest in the Pacific Northwest owned by the federal government and managed for "multiple use" purposes by the Agriculture Department's Forest Service and the Interior Department's Bureau of Land Management. To the environmentalists, these dense stands of towering pine, spruce, and hemlock represented the last preserve of aboriginal forest in the coterminous United States, a unique and fragile ecosystem that should be conserved in its natural state. To loggers and their supporters, the old-growth forests represent an economic treasure—capable of producing thousands of jobs, billions of board feet of timber, and billions of dollars—that should be "prudently managed."

The environmentalists' legal arsenal was strengthened in 1990 when the Secretary of the Interior listed the northern spotted owl as a "threatened" species under the Endangered Species Act. The spotted owl depends on the complex ecology of old-growth forests for its habitat. We have already encountered two of the many legal skirmishes fought in the battle to save the spotted owl from the lumberjack's chainsaw, the *Robertson* case, excerpted in Chapter I, and the *Sweet Home* case, excerpted in Chapter II. The following case represents yet another episode in that struggle.

When an agency action is likely to jeopardize the continued existence or adversely affect the critical habitat of a listed species (and thus would be prohibited under the terms of the statute) the agency may nevertheless apply for an exemption. The exemption process has many steps: the agency must submit an application to the Secretary of the Interior, who submits it to a body called the Endangered Species Committee, which votes on whether to grant it. The Committee consists of six members in addition to the Secretary of the Interior: the Secretaries of Agriculture and the Army, the Chairman of the Council of Economic Advisors, the Administrator of the EPA, the Administrator of the National Oceanic and Atmospheric Administration, and one representative from each affected state, appointed by the President.

If the Secretary finds that an application for exemption meets certain threshold criteria, he must, "in consultation with the Members of the Committee," conduct a formal adjudicative hearing on the application, and prepare a report to the Committee discussing the issues presented. The Committee then has the sole and final authority to determine whether to grant the exemption. According to §1536(h)(1):

> The Committee shall grant an exemption . . . for an agency action if, by a vote of not less than five of its members voting in person —
>> (A) it determines on the record, based on the report of the Secretary, the record of the hearing held [by the Secretary] and on such other testimony or evidence as it may receive, that —

(i) there are not reasonable and prudent alternatives to the agency action;

(ii) the benefits of such action clearly outweigh the benefits of alternative courses of action consistent with conserving the species or its critical habitat, and such action is in the public interest;

(iii) the action is of regional or national significance; and

(iv) neither the Federal agency concerned nor the exemption made any irreversible or irretrievable commitment of resources prohibited by [the Act]; and

(B) it establishes such reasonable mitigation and enhancement measures . . . as are necessary and appropriate to minimize the adverse effects of the agency action upon the endangered species. . . .

Because the Committee, in exercising its exemption power, may have final authority to determine the fate of an entire species, it has been nicknamed the "God Squad."

After the Committee granted an exemption for timber sales that would adversely affect the habitat of the spotted owl, environmental groups opposed to the timber sales brought an action for judicial review of the Committee's order, alleging that its decision was tainted by improper ex parte communications, and requesting discovery to verify the press accounts.

PORTLAND AUDUBON SOCIETY v. ENDANGERED SPECIES COMMITTEE
984 F.2d 1534 (9th Cir. 1993)

Before GOODWIN, D.W. NELSON, and REINHARDT, Circuit Judges.
REINHARDT, Circuit Judge:

I

The Endangered Species Act requires that "[e]ach Federal agency shall . . . insure that any action authorized, funded or carried out by such agency . . . is not likely to jeopardize the continued existence of any endangered species . . . or result in the destruction or adverse modification of [critical] habitat of such species." 16 U.S.C. §1536(a)(2) (1988). However, if the Secretary of the Interior ("Secretary") finds that a proposed agency action would violate §1536(a)(2), an agency may apply to the Committee for an exemption from the Endangered Species Act. §§1536(a)(2), (g)(1)-(2). The Committee was created by the Endangered Species Act for the sole purpose of making final decisions on applications for exemptions from the Act, §1536(e), and it is composed of high level officials. Because it is the ultimate arbiter of the fate of an endangered species, the Committee is known as "The God Squad."

The Secretary must initially consider any exemption application, publish a notice and summary of the application in the Federal Register, and determine whether certain threshold requirements have been met. 16 U.S.C. §§1536(g)(1)-(3). If so, the Secretary shall, in consultation with the other members of the Committee, hold a hearing on the application (which is conducted by an ALJ), and prepare a written report to the Committee. §1536(g)(4). Within thirty days of receiving the Secretary's report, the Committee shall make a final determination whether or not to grant the exemption from the Endangered Species Act based on the report, the record of the Secretary's hearing, and any additional hearings or written submissions for which the Committee itself may call. §1536(h)(1)(A). An exemption requires the approval of five of the seven members of the Committee. §1536(h)(1).

On May 15, 1992, the Committee approved an exemption for the Bureau of Land Management for thirteen of forty-four timber sales. It was only the second exemption ever granted by the Committee. . . . Both in their petition and in this motion the environmental groups contend that improper ex parte contacts between the White House and members of the Committee tainted the decision-making process. They base their charges on two press reports, one by Associated Press ("AP") and one by Reuters, and on the facts stated in the declaration of Victor Sher, lead counsel for the environmental groups. Published on May 6, 1992, the AP and Reuters accounts reported that, according to two anonymous administration sources, at least three Committee members had been "summoned" to the White House and pressured to vote for the exemption. In his declaration filed August 25, 1992, Sher stated that his conversations with "several sources within the Administration," who asked for anonymity, revealed that the media reports were accurate, and further that the pressure exerted by the White House may have changed the vote of at least one Committee member. Sher declared that his sources indicated that, in addition to in-person meetings, at least one Committee member had "substantial on-going contacts with White House staff concerning the substance of his decision on the application for exemption by telephone and facsimile, as well as through staff intermediaries." He also declared that he had learned from his sources that White House staff members had made substantial comments and recommendations on draft versions of the "Endangered Species Committee Amendment," a part of the Committee's final decision. For the purposes of the present motion, the Committee neither admits nor denies that these communications occurred.

The environmental groups request three types of discovery: (1) interrogatories and requests for production of documents identifying and relating to the Committee's "decisional staffs" and communications between those individuals and persons in the White House regarding the Committee decision, (2) subpoenas for documents from the White House on the same subject, and (3) depositions of persons identified in response to (1) and (2). . . . To decide what action to take with respect to the motion, we must first determine whether the ex parte contacts concerning which discovery is sought would be impermissible if they occurred in the manner alleged. If so, we must then decide what relief should be afforded.

II

This case raises two important and closely related questions of statutory construction: 1) Are Committee proceedings subject to the ex parte communications ban of 5 U.S.C. §557(d)(1)?, and 2) are communications from the President and his staff covered by that provision? For the reasons that follow, we answer both questions in the affirmative. . . .

The environmental groups contend that the Endangered Species Act incorporates by reference the ex parte communications ban of the APA and forbids ex parte contacts with members of the Committee regarding an exemption application. . . .

The ex parte prohibition is set forth at 5 U.S.C. §557(d)(1). Section 557(d)(1) is a broad provision that prohibits any ex parte communications relevant to the merits of an agency proceeding between "any member of the body comprising the agency" or any agency employee who "is or may reasonably be expected to be involved in the decisional process" and any "interested person outside the agency." 5 U.S.C. §557(d)(1)(A)-(B). The purpose of the ex parte communications prohibition is to ensure that "'agency decisions required to be made on a public record are not influenced by private, off-the-record communications from those personally interested in the outcome.'" *Raz Inland Navigation Co. v. Interstate Commerce Comm'n*, 625 F.2d 258, 260 (9th Cir. 1980) (quoting legislative history).

It is of no consequence that the sections of the Endangered Species Act governing the operations of the Committee fail to mention the APA. The APA itself mandates that its provisions govern certain administrative proceedings. By its terms, section 554 of the APA, which pertains to formal adjudications, applies to "every case of adjudication required by statute to be determined on the record after [the] opportunity for an agency hearing." 5 U.S.C. §554(a). That section also provides that any hearing conducted and any decision made in connection with such an adjudication shall be "in accordance with sections 556 and 557 of this title." 5 U.S.C. §554(c)(2).

In other words, by virtue of the terms of APA §554, sections 556 and 557 are applicable whenever that section applies. Accordingly, the ex parte communications prohibition applies whenever the three requirements set forth in APA §554(a) are satisfied: The administrative proceeding must be 1) an adjudication; 2) determined on the record; and 3) after the opportunity for an agency hearing. The question is, therefore, are those three conditions met here? We find our answer primarily in the language of section 1536(h)(1)(A) of the Endangered Species Act. . . .

[The court looked to the ESA's text and legislative history and concluded that the Committee's proceeding constituted a formal adjudication subject to §557(d)(1)'s ex parte communications ban.]

The APA prohibits an "interested person outside the agency" from making, or knowingly causing to be made, an ex parte communication relevant to the merits of the proceeding with a member of the body comprising the agency. 5 U.S.C. §557(d)(1)(A). Likewise, agency members are prohibited from engaging in such ex parte communication. §557(d)(1)(B). Although the APA's ban on ex parte communications is absolute and includes no special exemption for White House officials, the government advances three arguments in support of its position that section 557(d)(1) does not apply to the President and his staff.

First, the government argues that because the President is the center of the Executive Branch and does not represent or act on behalf of a particular agency, he does not have an interest in Committee proceedings greater than the interest of the public as a whole. Therefore, the government contends, neither the President nor his staff is an "interested person." Next, the government maintains that the President and his staff do not fall within the terms of section 557(d)(1) because the President's interest as the Chief of the Executive Branch is no different from that of his subordinates on the Committee. Specifically, the government claims that by placing the Chairman of the President's Council of Economic Advisors on the Committee, Congress directly and expressly involved the Executive Office of the President in the decision-making process. In other words, it is the government's position that because the Committee members are Executive Branch officials, communications between them and the White House staff cannot be considered to come from "outside the agency." Finally, the government argues that if the APA's ex parte communications ban encompasses the President and his aides, the provision violates the doctrine of separation of powers. We find all three of the government's arguments to be without merit.

There is little decisional law on the meaning of the term "interested person." Nor is the meaning of the term clear on the face of the statute. A person can be "interested" in at least three different senses. First, an interested person can be someone who has a curiosity or a concern about a matter, although he may be neutral with respect to the outcome. Second, an interested person can have a preference or a bias regarding a matter's outcome but no direct stake in the proceedings. Finally, a person can be "interested" in a matter in the sense of having a legal interest that will be determined or affected by the decision.

Ultimately, the ex parte communication provision must be interpreted in a common sense fashion. Its purposes are to insure open decision-making and the appearance thereof, to preserve the opportunity for effective response, and to prevent improper influences upon agency decision-makers. To achieve these ends we must give the provision a broad scope rather than a constricted interpretation. The essential purposes of the APA require that all communications that might improperly influence an agency be encompassed within the ex parte contacts prohibition or else the public and the parties will be denied indirectly their guaranteed right to meaningful participation in agency decisional processes. The legislative history of the ex parte communication provision confirms the breadth of the ban:

> The term "interested person" is intended to be a wide, inclusive term covering any individual or other person with an interest in the agency proceeding that is greater than the general interest the public as a whole may have. The interest need not be monetary, nor need a person to [sic] be a party to, or intervenor in, the agency proceeding to come under this section. The term includes, but is not limited to, parties, competitors, *public officials,* and nonprofit or public interest organizations and associations with a special interest in the matter regulated. The term does not include a member of the public at large who makes a casual or general expression of opinion about a pending proceeding.

H.R. Rep. No. 880, Pt. I, 94th Cong., 2d Sess. 19-20 (1976) U.S. Code Cong. & Admin. News 1976, pp. 2183, 2201 (emphasis added). The legislative history of APA §557(d) makes clear that the term "interested person" was intended to have a broad scope. PATCO v. FLRA, [685 F.2d 547, 562-563 (D.C. Cir. 1982]. In particular, the provision's history makes it clear that the ex parte communication prohibition was meant to include public officials.

In *PATCO* . . . , the District of Columbia Circuit found that the Secretary of Transportation was an "interested person" within the meaning of APA §557(d)(1) when he telephoned two members of the Federal Labor Relations Authority regarding an unfair labor practice charge made by the Federal Aviation Association against the air traffic controllers union. While the court did not set forth the rationale for its holding, it seems evident that it reasoned that the Secretary of Transportation has a special interest in a major transportation dispute which is beyond that of the general public and that he is, therefore, an interested person.

The government does not contest the validity of *PATCO* . . . as it applies to Cabinet level officials and below. However, it argues that the President's broader policy role places him beyond the reach of the "interested person" language. We strongly disagree. In fact, we believe the proper argument is quite the opposite from the one the government advances. We believe the President's position at the center of the Executive Branch renders him, *ex officio,* an "interested person" for the purposes of APA §557(d)(1). As the head of government and chief executive officer, the President necessarily has an interest in *every* agency proceeding. No ex parte communication is more likely to influence an agency than one from the President or a member of his staff. No communication from any other person is more likely to deprive the parties and the public of their right to effective participation in a key governmental decision at a most crucial time. The essential purposes of the statutory provision compel the conclusion that the President and his staff are "interested persons" within the meaning of 5 U.S.C. §557(d)(1).

The government's next argument—that because the President and the members of the Committee are all members of the executive branch the President is, for all intents and purposes, a "member" of the Committee and may attempt to influence its decisions—amounts to a contention that the President is not "outside the agency" for the purposes of APA §557(d)(1). The Supreme Court soundly rejected the basic logic of this argument in United States ex rel. Accardi v. Shaughnessy, 347 U.S. 260 (1954). The Court held that where legally binding regulations delegated a particular discretionary decision to the Board of Immigration Appeals, the Attorney General could not dictate a decision of the Board, even though the Board was appointed by the Attorney General, its members served at his pleasure, and its decision was subject to his ultimate review. Here, the Endangered Species Act explicitly vests discretion to make exemption decisions in the Committee and does not contemplate that the President or the White House will become involved in Committee deliberations. The President and his aides are not a part of the Committee decision-making process. They are "outside the agency" for the purposes of the ex parte communications ban.

The government then argues that Sierra Club v. Costle, [657 F.2d 298 (D.C. Cir. 1981)], determined that contacts with the White House do not constitute ex parte communications that would contaminate the Committee's decision-making process, and that we should follow that precedent. We disagree. *Costle* is inapplicable because that case did not consider and, indeed, could not have considered, whether the APA's definition of ex parte communications includes White House contacts. The decision in *Costle* that the contacts were not impermissible was based explicitly on the fact that the proceeding involved was *informal* rulemaking to which the APA restrictions on ex parte communications are not applicable. In fact, while the *Costle* court recognized that political pressure from the President may not be inappropriate in *informal* rulemaking proceedings, it acknowledged that the contrary is true in formal adjudications. Because Congress has decided that Committee determinations are formal adjudications, *Costle* supports, rather than contradicts, the conclusion that the President and his staff are subject to the APA's ex parte communication ban.

Accordingly, the President and his staff are covered by section 557's prohibition and are not free to attempt to influence the decision-making processes of the Committee through ex parte communications. The APA's ban on such communications is fully applicable to the President and his White House aides, and ex parte contacts by them relevant to the merits of an agency proceeding would be in violation of that Act.

The government next contends that any construction of APA §557(d)(1) that includes presidential communications within the ban on ex parte contacts would constitute a violation of the separation of powers doctrine. It relies on language in Myers v. United States, [272 U.S. 52 (1926)], that states that the President has the constitutional authority to "supervise and guide" Executive Branch officials in "their construction of the statutes under which they act." The government argues that including the President and his staff within the APA's ex parte communication ban would represent Congressional interference with the President's constitutional duty to provide such supervision and guidance to inferior officials. We reject this argument out of hand.

The Supreme Court established the test for evaluating whether an act of Congress improperly interferes with a presidential prerogative in Nixon v. Administrator of Gen. Services, 433 U.S. 425 (1977). First, a court must determine whether the act prevents the executive branch from accomplishing its constitutional functions. If the potential for such disruption exists, the next question is whether the impact is justified by an overriding need to promote objectives within the constitutional authority of Congress. We conclude that Congress in no way invaded any legitimate constitutional power of the President in providing that he may not attempt to influence the outcome of administrative adjudications through ex parte communications and that Congress' important objectives reflected in the enactment of the APA would, in any event, outweigh any *de minimis* impact on presidential power.

While the government's argument to the contrary arises in the context of Committee decisions regarding Endangered Species Act exemption applications, carried to its logical conclusion the government's position would effectively destroy the integrity of all federal agency adjudications. It is a fundamental precept of administrative law that [when] an agency performs a quasi-judicial (or a quasi-legislative) function its independence must be protected. There is no presidential prerogative to influence quasi-judicial administrative agency proceedings through behind-the-scenes lobbying. . . .

[The court remanded to the Committee to hold, "with the aid of a specially appointed administrative law judge, an evidentiary hearing to determine the nature, content, extent, source, and effect of any ex parte communications that may have transpired between any member of the Committee or its staff and the President or any member of his staff regarding the determination of the exemption application at issue."]

NOTES AND QUESTIONS

1. *The denouement.* Two months after the ruling in the *Portland Audubon* case, the Bureau of Land Management withdrew its exemption application, mooting the court's remand order. Bureau officials said that the newly elected Clinton Administration was "not interested in looking backwards or in resurfacing allegations about the previous administration." Greenwire, April 20, 1993. Any other ideas about what might have motivated the new administration's action? What might that suggest about differences between adjudication in courts and agencies?

2. *Ex parte communications in rulemaking versus adjudication.* You will recall that the *Home Box Office* and *Sierra Club* cases, excerpted in Chapter V, *supra*, wrestled with the applicability of an ex parte communications ban in informal rulemaking proceedings. The court in *Sierra Club* juxtaposed the utility of an ex parte communications ban in the contexts of rulemaking and adjudication:

> Where agency action resembles judicial action, where it involves formal rulemaking, adjudication, or quasi-adjudication among "conflicting private claims to a valuable privilege," the insulation of the decisionmaker from ex parte contacts is justified by basic notions of due process to the parties involved. But where agency action involves informal rulemaking of a policymaking sort, the concept of ex parte contacts is of more questionable utility. Under our system of government, the very legitimacy of general policymaking performed by unelected administrators depends in no small part upon the openness, accessibility, and amenability of these officials to the needs and ideas of the public from whom their ultimate authority derives, and upon whom their commands must fall.

657 F.2d at 400-401. Do you agree with the court's assessment? How does this reasoning apply to a determination of the sort involved in *Portland Audubon*: namely, whether to grant an ESA exemption to allow logging of 44 tracts of old-growth national forest?

3. *"Interested persons."* Why, in drafting §557(d)(1), did Congress apply the ex parte communications ban only to "interested persons"? In the *PATCO* case cited by the *Portland Audubon* court, a panel of the D.C. Circuit held that a labor leader was "interested" in an unfair labor practice proceeding involving a different union. The labor leader, Albert Shanker, President of the American Federation of Teachers, had publicly supported the Professional Air Traffic Controllers Organization in its labor dispute with the Federal Aviation Administration. Does the court in *Portland Audubon* adequately respond to arguments that the President (including his executive staff) occupies a unique position that should exclude him from the category of "interested persons"? Notice the language of §557(d)(2). Is Congress once again giving itself favored status?

4. *"Relevant to the merits."* The ex parte ban applies only to communications "relevant to the merits of the proceeding." 5 U.S.C. §557(d)(1)(A). In Louisiana Assn. of Indep. Producers v. FERC, 958 F.2d 1101 (D.C. Cir. 1992), FERC held an open application process for the right to construct a pipeline extending from upstate New York to Long Island. After FERC awarded the project to two companies, a coalition of environmentalists and fuel oil dealers sued, claiming, *inter alia*, that FERC engaged in improper ex parte communications during the application process. First, they pointed to settlement discussions between the ALJ and

a number of applicants competing for the construction project. The court, however, rejected the notion that such discussions violated §557(d), explaining that in the context of settlement negotiations, there are no issues to be decided on an open record, and there is no judicial review available in any event. Consequently, the ex parte communications ban does not apply. Second, petitioners pointed to informal meetings between FERC administrators and project applicants during the course of the proceedings. Yet because "[t]he meetings focused . . . upon the impact of cases pending at that time before [the D.C. Circuit], upon general problems in the industry, and upon the procedural status of [an] application," the court found they were not "relevant to the merits of the proceeding," 5 U.S.C. §557(d)(1)(A), and therefore were permissible. The court expressly stated that "inquiries into the procedural status of [a] case or general background discussions[] are not prohibited." Compare this view with the one espoused in *PATCO*, where a panel of the same court intimated that "even a procedural inquiry may be a subtle effort to influence an agency decision."

5. *Remedy for a violation of the ex parte communications ban.* If an ex parte communication occurs in violation of §557(d)(1), what is the appropriate remedy? Clause (C) of the statute requires the agency to disclose the communication in the public record of the proceeding, which enables opposing parties to offer rebuttal evidence or arguments. Is that enough? If the improper contact comes from a party, the agency has discretion under clause (D) to take adverse action against the party, such as dismissing its claim. Likewise, a reviewing court has equitable discretion to vacate an agency action infected by an improper ex parte communication. In *PATCO,* the court identified five factors relevant to determining the appropriate remedy, including:

> the gravity of the ex parte communications; whether the contacts may have influenced the agency's ultimate decision; whether the party making the improper contacts benefited from the agency's ultimate decision; whether the contents of the communications were unknown to opposing parties . . . ; and whether vacation of the agency's decision and remand for new proceedings would serve a useful purpose.

685 F.2d at 565. Although the case involved one clearly improper communication and two arguably improper communications, the *PATCO* court refused to vacate the agency's order, finding that the communications at issue did not affect the outcome of the case or disadvantage any party.

3.   *Appointment and Oversight of Administrative Hearing Officers and ALJ Impartiality: Achieving Consistency in a Regime of Mass Administrative Justice*

The federal administrative judiciary consists of approximately 1,900 administrative law judges (ALJs) who serve more than 30 federal agencies throughout the country. Over 80 percent of ALJs work for the Social Security Administration, where they decide appeals of initial denials of claims for Social Security disability benefits. Until recently, ALJs were selected pursuant to rules of the Office of Personnel Management (OPM) through a process that limited the involvement of the agency in which they serve. Over the years, many federal ALJs have been former state judges, former federal magistrate judges or, because of a veterans' preference built into the OPM process, former military judges. However, in Executive Order 13,843, issued on July 10, 2018, in the wake of the *Lucia* decision discussed in Chapter I, *supra*, President Trump abolished the OPM selection process and left it to each agency to design and implement their own processes for selecting ALJs.

The Executive Order recites desirable qualities that ALJs should possess, including commitment to the rule of law, "appropriate temperament, legal acumen, impartiality[,] sound judgment," and the ability to "clearly communicate their decisions to the parties who appear before them, the agencies that oversee them, and the public that entrusts them with authority." The EO's only mandatory criterion, however, is that ALJs be licensed attorneys (or the equivalent for members of the judiciary). Each agency will have to decide for itself what criteria to apply to ALJ hiring going forward. Agencies that have implemented the EO have required seven to ten years' experience as a trial litigator, administrative lawyer, or adjudicator. Indeed, ABA policy favors using prior judicial experience as a factor in selecting ALJs. Agencies have differed, however, on whether ALJs should possess agency-specific knowledge or expertise. The ABA has opposed requiring agency-specific expertise on the grounds that those candidates with substantive expertise "appear to be less qualified to manage conflicts and marshal evidence," and also may appear biased in favor of the agency. *See* Daniel F. Solomon, Fundamental Fairness, Judicial Efficiency and Uniformity: Revisiting the Administrative Procedure Act, 33 J. Natl. Assn. Admin. L. Judges 52, 84-86 (2013). Does that seem to be a factual observation? A necessary corollary of the possession of specialized expertise? Or a potential problem if those with specialized expertise are selected from within the ranks of agency lawyers?

Once hired, ALJs serve during good behavior and are protected against discharge by special procedures and substantive guarantees. *See* 5 U.S.C. §§3105, 7521. Under the pre–Executive Order process, their pay was set by OPM "independently of agency recommendations or ratings," §5372. It is unclear whether this system will survive the elimination of OPM from the hiring process. Their case assignments are not subject to control by the agency head. Moreover, ALJs "may not perform duties inconsistent with their duties and responsibilities as administrative law judges," §3105, may not be supervised by officials who investigate or prosecute agency cases, §554(d), and are prohibited from engaging in various extra-record communications, §§554(d), 557(d)(1).

Most observers agree that these provisions effectively insulate ALJs from influences inside and outside the agency. There is disagreement, however, over the propriety of such insulation. The relative independence of ALJs can present problems for agency heads seeking to achieve coordination and consistency in policymaking and implementation. These difficulties are most pronounced in programs like the SSA's disability insurance program, which is characterized by huge caseloads and a far-flung nationwide network of regional offices. But the same problems might arise in other contexts like immigration, where caseloads are also overwhelming.

Disability insurance hearings — mandated by the Social Security Act — account for a very large share of federal adjudications. Like most administrative hearings, they tend to be quite informal. They are generally held in the vicinity of the claimant's home, often in a small conference room in the ALJ's office or in an available state or federal building. In most hearings, the only people present are the ALJ, the claimant, the claimant's representative, and the claimant's witnesses (such as relatives, former coworkers, friends, or family physicians). Hearings are usually short, averaging half a day in length. Once the participants are gathered, the ALJ makes a short explanatory statement and receives into evidence the pertinent parts of the file, such as medical and hospital reports. The claimant and his witnesses may then make statements. The ALJ swears in and questions each witness (the claimant's representative, if present, may also question them). The ALJ may then call an independent vocational expert or medical advisor to review the record and help "interpret" it for the ALJ. Experts' opinions are not binding, but usually receive considerable weight. The ALJ then retires to consider her decision. The decision must be in writing and contain the findings of fact and the reasons for the decision. A copy must be mailed to the claimant who then has 60 days to request review by the Appeals Council of an adverse decision.

The huge growth in DI caseloads described in the notes preceding the *Eldridge* case, excerpted above, generated a corresponding explosion in the demand for ALJ hearings. By the late 1970s there was mounting evidence of widespread inconsistency and inaccuracy in the decisionmaking process. The rate at which ALJs were reversed on appeal rose steadily from 42 percent in 1970 to 58 percent in 1980. Variations among ALJs were wide: in 1980, over one-third had reversal rates below 40 percent and another third had reversal rates above 60 percent.

In response, Congress directed the SSA in 1980 to strengthen its quality control system. As a preliminary step, the SSA conducted an experiment in which the Appeals Council "redecided" 3,600 randomly selected cases based on the factual records before the ALJs (but without knowing the ALJs' decisions). There was significant variation in the results: the Appeals Council agreed with only 63 percent of the ALJs' allowance decisions and 79 percent of the ALJs' denials. The Appeals Council agreed even less frequently with the ALJs on the *reason* for an allowance or denial. Significantly, the Appeals Council's allowance rate for cases decided by ALJs with high allowance rates was about the same as that for cases decided by ALJs with low allowance rates. This strongly suggested that variations in allowance rates among ALJs were attributable to personal characteristics of the decisionmaker, not variations in case mix.

ASSOCIATION OF ADMINISTRATIVE LAW
JUDGES v. HECKLER
594 F. Supp. 1132 (D.D.C. 1984)

JOYCE HENS GREEN, District Judge:

Plaintiff, the Association of Administrative Law Judges, is a not-for-profit corporation whose members are administrative law judges (ALJs) employed by the Department of Health and Human Services (HHS) and assigned to the Office of Hearings and Appeals (OHA) of the Social Security Administration (SSA). Plaintiff's members adjudicate claims for disability benefits under Titles II and XVI of the Social Security Act, 42 U.S.C. §401 *et seq.* (1982) and 42 U.S.C. §1381 *et seq.*

(1982). Plaintiff brought this lawsuit to challenge the "Bellmon Review Program," which defendants instituted to implement Section 304(g) of the Social Security Disability Amendments of 1980, the "Bellmon Amendment." Plaintiff alleges that this program violates the rights of its members to decisional independence under the Administrative Procedure Act (APA, 5 U.S.C. §551 *et seq.* (1982))....

The Bellmon Amendment directed the Secretary of HHS to resume review of decisions of ALJs on her own motion. Congress expressed concern at that time about the high rate at which ALJs were reversing determinations made at the state level and the variance in these rates among ALJs....

A study performed pursuant to the Bellmon Amendment . . . indicated that the Appeals Council more often would have changed decisions by ALJs allowing benefits made by ALJs with above average allowance rates than allowance decisions made by ALJs with average or below average allowance rates. The Bellmon Review Program, a series of measures designed to improve decisional quality and accuracy, began in October 1981. . . . [The program mandated that] individual ALJs with allowance rates of 70% or higher were to have 100% of their allowance decisions reviewed for accuracy. . . . 106 ALJs, or approximately 13% of all ALJs in SSA, were placed on Bellmon Review because of their high allowance rates. . . .

An overview of the program was communicated to the ALJ corps in a Memorandum . . . explain[ing] that Bellmon Review was being instituted because of Congressional concern about high allowance rates and because only ALJ decisions denying benefits were generally subject to further review. Allowance rates were used as the basis for selecting the initial review group, in part, because studies had shown that decisions in this group would be the most likely to contain errors which would otherwise go uncorrected. . . .

Based upon own-motion rates (the frequency with which the Appeals Council takes action to correct an ALJ's decision, as calculated by the Office of Appraisal) the individual ALJs were divided into four groups: 100% review; 75% review; 50% review and 25% review. In determining whether an ALJ should be removed from review, the Appeals Council considered only decisional accuracy, defined as a 5% own motion rate for three consecutive months. . . .

The Bellmon Review Program has evolved substantially since . . . [its inception]. Significantly, in April 1982, before this lawsuit was filed, defendants stopped using allowance rates to target ALJs for Bellmon Review. . . . The ALJs whose allowance decisions were reviewed were selected for individual review solely on the basis of their own motion rates under the national random sample. . . .

Plaintiff charged that the targeting of individual ALJs under Bellmon Review, based upon allowance rates and then own-motion rates, was in essence an attempt to influence ALJs to reduce their allowance rates and thereby compromise their decisional independence. . . .

Evidence . . . strongly[] suggested that OHA had an ulterior goal to reduce ALJ allowance rates. [The] Associate Commissioner . . . issued a memorandum to the ALJs, in which he noted a perception that ALJ allowance rates were "untenable." Sometime later, he sent a memorandum to SSA, in which he described as "good news" a decline in allowance rates. [He then] received a memorandum from SSA's Office of Management Coordination, which requested a decrease in the variance among allowance rates and a decrease in allowance rates overall. . . .

The APA contains a number of provisions designed to safeguard the decisional independence of ALJs. . . . Although employees of the selecting agency, ALJs are entitled to pay prescribed by the Office of Personnel Management independently of agency recommendations or ratings. 5 U.S.C. §5372 (1982), 5 U.S.C. §554 (1982). They are exempted from the performance appraisals to which other Civil Service employees are subject. 5 U.S.C. §4301(2)(D) (1982). *See also* 5 C.F.R. §930.211 (1984). ALJs do not receive monetary awards or periodic step increases based upon performance. Cases must be assigned whenever possible, in rotation, an ALJ may not be assigned duties inconsistent with his or her responsibilities as an ALJ, and an ALJ may not communicate ex parte with anyone inside or outside the agency about the facts of a particular case. 5 U.S.C. §§3105, 557(d)(1) (1982). . . . While the position of an ALJ is not "constitutionally protected," Ramspeck v. Federal Trial Examiners Conference, 345 U.S. [128, 133 (1953)], in many respects, it is "functionally comparable" to that of a federal judge, Butz v. Economou, [438 U.S. 478, 513 (1978)]. . . .

On matters of law and policy, however, ALJs are entirely subject to the agency. . . . Although an ALJ may dispute the validity of agency policy, the agency may impose its policy through the administrative appeals process. In reviewing an ALJ's decision the agency retains "all the powers which it would have in making the initial decision." 5 U.S.C. §557(b) (1982). If the agency accepts the ALJ's decision, or if that decision is not appealed, it becomes the final decision of the agency. . . . In sum, the ALJ's right to decisional independence is qualified.

The sole issue in this case is whether that qualified right has been violated by the now discontinued individual ALJ portion of the Bellmon Review Program, which targeted individual ALJs initially on the basis of their allowance rates and then on the basis of their own motion rates. . . .

The practice of targeting ALJs on the basis of their own motion rates, once that data became available, did reflect defendants' stated goal of improving the quality and accuracy of ALJ decisions. However, the evidence as a whole, persuasively demonstrated that defendants retained an unjustifiable preoccupation with allowance rates, to the extent that ALJs could reasonably feel pressure to issue fewer allowance decisions in the name of accuracy. While there was no evidence that an ALJ consciously succumbed to such pressure, in close cases, and, in particular, where the determination of disability may have been based largely on subjective factors, as a matter of common sense, that pressure may have intruded upon the factfinding process and may have influenced some outcomes. . . .

In sum, the court concludes, that defendants' unremitting focus on allowance rates in the individual ALJ portion of the Bellmon Review Program created an untenable atmosphere of tension and unfairness which violated the spirit of the APA, if no specific provision thereof. Defendants' insensitivity to that degree of decisional independence the APA affords to administrative law judges and the injudicious use of phrases such as "targeting," "goals" and "behavior modification" could have tended to corrupt the ability of administrative law judges to exercise that independence in the vital cases that they decide. However, defendants appear to have shifted their focus, obviating the need for any injunctive relief or restructuring of the agency at this time. While it is incumbent upon the agency to reexamine the role and function of the Appeals Council and its relationship to the ALJs in light of this litigation, it would be unsuitable for the court to order any affirmative relief under the present circumstances. Plaintiff has achieved considerable success in its valid attempt to reveal and change agency practices. . . .

NOTES AND QUESTIONS

1. *"Decisional independence" and adjudicative quality control.* What, exactly, is objectionable about the SSA's Bellmon Review Program? So long as the SSA does not interfere in individual cases, why is it improper for a fiscally minded administration to lean on its hearing officers to "tighten up" the program's administration? Is "allowance rate" ever an appropriate criterion for evaluating the performance of ALJs? For deciding which ALJ's decisions to review? For assigning ALJs to training programs?

From time to time other organizations and commentators have called for increased agency supervision and control of ALJ decisionmaking, but with little success. An example is a recommendation made in 1992 by the Administrative Conference of the United States (a federal agency established to conduct studies of the federal administrative agencies and make recommendations for improving their effectiveness and efficiency). The ACUS report recommended that Chief Administrative Law Judges be given more power to supervise the ALJs who report to them. *See* ACUS Recommendation 92-7, 1992 ACUS 28-42; Paul Verkuil et al., The Federal Administrative Judiciary, 1992 ACUS 779-1120. Fearing a reduction in their independence, the ALJs, through their professional association, successfully enlisted the support of Congress to defeat the proposals. In the wake of this skirmish, Congress cut the budget of ACUS and later abolished the agency, although it was subsequently revived.

2. *Remedies for adjudicative delay.* Besides inconsistency, a second basis for criticism of the DI adjudication process has been the long delays experienced by many claimants in having their claims heard. A principal cause was the failure of claims-processing resources to keep up with the enormous caseload growth in the early 1970s. As the number of hearing petitions tripled (from 42,600 in 1970 to 155,000 in 1975), for example, the hearing backlog increased eightfold (from 13,700 to 111,200). The mean processing time of cases, from hearing request to posthearing decision, reached a high of 288 days in fiscal year 1976. The problem of adjudicatory delay became a perennial subject of congressional concern. Bills proposing mandatory deadlines were introduced in 1975 and almost every year thereafter, but Congress took no action.

Meanwhile, disgruntled claimants were turning increasingly to the courts, claiming that §205(b) of the Social Security Act (which requires the Secretary to give claimants "reasonable notice and an opportunity for hearing") implicitly required that the hearing be held within a "reasonable" time. In White v. Mathews, 559 F.2d 852 (2d Cir. 1977), *cert. denied,* 435 U.S. 908 (1978), the Second Circuit affirmed a district court order requiring the SSA to process hearing requests made by Connecticut residents within 120 days. There followed a spate of similar decrees in other districts. In Heckler v. Day, 467 U.S. 104 (1984), however, the Supreme Court nipped this development in the bud. While apparently conceding that §205(b) required claims to be decided within a "reasonable" time, the majority ruled that the federal courts lack power to grant the kind of injunctive relief ordered by the district court. Judicial imposition of mandatory statewide deadlines, it said, would conflict with Congress's consistent refusal to adopt statutory deadlines.

Are mandatory deadlines likely to improve the operation of the DI claims-processing system? Who is better suited to impose such deadlines, Congress or the federal courts? Does the failure of Congress to enact deadlines necessarily stay the federal courts' hands?

3. *Agency authority to overturn ALJ decisions.* Section 557(b) of the APA states that, when reviewing an ALJ decision, the agency head "has all the powers which [he] would have in making the initial decision." As we saw in the *Universal Camera* case study, in Chapter II, *supra*, the courts have generally accorded agency heads broad authority to review and reverse decisions of ALJs with which they disagree, so long as they treat the ALJ's findings of fact as themselves part of the "record" for review.

Although agency heads have extensive formal authority to review and overturn ALJ decisions, in practice they tend to use the authority sparingly. On average, agencies review less than 5 percent of ALJs' initial decisions. If the Social Security Administration is excluded, that figure rises to 8 percent. But even this figure exaggerates the influence of political officials in the adjudicative process because many agencies delegate the review function to subordinate officials who themselves share some of the ALJs' insulation from political and organizational influence. About a quarter of non-SSA federal administrative adjudications are reviewed by such personnel.

As an example, consider the immigration context. Immigration judges (employees of the Executive Office for Immigration Review (EOIR), a tribunal within the Department of Justice) are the front-line adjudicators of cases concerning individuals' eligibility to remain in the United States. The judges hold evidentiary hearings, 8 U.S.C. §1229(a)(1), culminating in a formal order either directing the individual's deportation, granting relief through asylum, or otherwise disposing of the case. These decisions are appealable by either party to the Board of Immigration Appeals (BIA), which is also housed within the EOIR. The BIA reviews the immigration judge's legal conclusions de novo, but may not reverse findings of fact unless they are clearly erroneous. BIA adjudicators—who are insulated from politics, just like immigration judges—almost always have the final say in immigration cases. The Attorney General can technically overrule their decisions, but given the staggering number of immigration adjudications (approximately 271,000 a year), that step is unlikely to happen. *See generally* Stephen H. Legomsky, Restructuring Immigration Adjudication, 59 Duke L.J. 1635 (2010). Where political officials cannot adequately control agency adjudicators due to sheer bureaucratic expansiveness, individuals must turn to the federal courts. The courts have played a particularly significant role in correcting erroneous BIA decisions in recent years, as Judge Posner chronicled in Benslimane v. Gonzales, 430 F.3d 828 (7th Cir. 2005):

> In the year ending on the date of the argument, different panels of this court reversed the Board of Immigration Appeals in whole or part in a staggering 40 percent of the 136 petitions to review the Board that were resolved on the merits. The corresponding figure, for the 82 civil cases during this period in which the United States was the appellee, was 18 percent. Our criticisms of the Board and of the immigration judges have frequently been severe. E.g., Dawoud v. Gonzales,

424 F.3d 608, 610 (7th Cir. 2005) ("the [immigration judge's] opinion is riddled with inappropriate and extraneous comments"); Ssali v. Gonzales, 424 F.3d 556, 563 (7th Cir. 2005) ("this very significant mistake suggests that the Board was not aware of the most basic facts of [the petitioner's] case"); Sosnovskaia v. Gonzales, 421 F.3d 589, 594 (7th Cir. 2005) ("the procedure that the [immigration judge] employed in this case is an affront to [petitioner's] right to be heard"); Souma-horo v. Gonzales, 415 F.3d 732, 738 (7th Cir. 2005) (per curiam) (the immigration judge's factual conclusion is "totally unsupported by the record"). Other circuits have been as critical. Wang v. Attorney General, 423 F.3d 260, 269 (3d Cir. 2005) ("the tone, the tenor, the disparagement, and the sarcasm of the [immigration judge] seem more appropriate to a court television show than a federal court proceeding"); Chen v. U.S. Dep't of Justice, 426 F.3d 104, 115 (2d Cir. 2005) (the immigration judge's finding is "grounded solely on speculation and conjecture").

   This tension between judicial and administrative adjudicators is not due to judicial hostility to the nation's immigration policies or to a misconception of the proper standard of judicial review of administrative decisions. It is due to the fact that the adjudication of these cases at the administrative level has fallen below the minimum standards of legal justice. Whether this is due to resource constraints or to other circumstances beyond the Board's and the Immigration Court's control, we do not know, though we note that the problem is not of recent origin. All that is clear is that it cannot be in the interest of the immigration authorities, the tax-payer, the federal judiciary, or citizens concerned with the effective enforcement of the nation's immigration laws for removal orders to be routinely nullified by the courts, and that the power of correction lies in the Department of Homeland Security, which prosecutes removal cases, and the Department of Justice, which adjudicates them in its Immigration Court and Board of Immigration Appeals.

Does this disturbing picture of the immigration system make you reconsider the purported "efficiency" benefits of administrative adjudication? Are the risks of procedural irregularity and arbitrariness worse when hearings concern vulnerable populations? Are there practical ways to address the system's weaknesses?

   4. *Proposals to separate adjudication from enforcement.* The integrated structure of agencies contemplated by the APA, although solidly entrenched in administrative practice, continues to generate argument, reflecting the different views of appropriate forms for administrative decisionmaking. Efforts to split adjudicative functions off from other regulatory activities—which began before the APA existed—continue. As early as 1934 the American Bar Association, expressing concern about the distortions inherent in the integrated model, called for creation of an "administrative court." Special Committee on Administrative Law, Report to the 57th Annual Meeting of the ABA, at 7 (1934). The idea was revived in 1955 by the second "Hoover Commission." U.S. Commission on Organization of the Executive Branch of the Government, Task Force on Legal Service and Procedures (1955). Once again in 1971 a presidential commission, the so-called "Ash Council," proposed establishing an administrative court, responsible only for reviewing the decisions of regulatory agencies. President's Advisory Council on Executive Organization, A New Regulatory Framework: Report on Selected Independent Agencies (1971). *See also* Roger Noll, Reforming Regulation: An Evaluation of the Ash Council Proposals (1971).

   Congress did not adopt the recommendations of any of these committees for a new separated-functions model. On occasion, however, Congress has been willing to create separate tribunals to adjudicate specific kinds of regulatory disputes. As you will recall from Chapter I, *supra,* the OSH Act established the Occupational Safety and Health Review Commission to hear and resolve disputes over contested citations issued by the Department of Labor. Not only are the two agencies organizationally independent but relations between them have on occasion been quite strained, as demonstrated by litigation over their respective jurisdictions. *See, e.g.,* Cuyahoga Valley Railway v. United Transportation Union, 474 U.S. 3 (1985) (Labor Secretary has exclusive authority to withdraw a contested citation despite OSHRC opposition); Donovan v. Amorello & Sons, Inc., 761 F.2d 61 (1st Cir. 1985) (Labor Secretary's interpretation of an occupational safety or health standard entitled to greater judicial deference than conflicting interpretation by OSHRC).

5. *Bright-line rules and adjudicative consistency.* Another plausible strategy for combating inconsistency and delay in administrative adjudication is to adopt bright-line rules that can be applied, more or less mechanically, by hearing officers. A leading example is the "grid rule" adopted by the Social Security Administration to streamline disability insurance determinations, and upheld in the *Heckler v. Campbell,* excerpted in Chapter IV, *supra.* Given the complexity of determining whether someone is "disabled," however, it should come as no surprise that the grid rule has only partially succeeded at rationalizing the process of DI adjudication. *See* Jon C. Dubin, Overcoming Gridlock: *Campbell* After a Quarter-Century and Bureaucratically Rational Gap-Filling in Mass Justice Adjudication in the Social Security Administration's Disability Programs, 62 Admin. L. Rev. 937 (2010). According to Professor Dubin, many disabilities—especially those unrelated to exertion or strength-related medical conditions—do not lend themselves to being resolved under the grid rule.

6. *The "irrebuttable presumption" doctrine.* Is there any hope for a constitutional challenge to the application of the "grid rule" to Ms. Campbell? Cases like *Bi-Metallic,* excerpted in Chapter IV, *supra,* would seem to foreclose the possibility of a successful challenge grounded upon the Due Process Clauses. But, in a brief flurry of "irrebuttable presumption" cases decided in the early 1970s, the Supreme Court toyed with the idea that there might be some constitutional limits on the use of bright-line rules to choke off individualized determinations of people's statutory rights. For example, in Bell v. Burson, 402 U.S. 535 (1971), the Court held that Georgia may not require uninsured drivers involved in automobile accidents, on the pain of suspension of their licenses, to post security to cover the amount of damages claimed in the accident report by other parties to the accident. The Georgia Supreme Court had held that "fault" or "innocence" were irrelevant to whether the license should be suspended, but the U.S. Supreme Court suspected that fault, in the sense of potential liability for damages, was indeed the key to understanding Georgia's scheme, and held that "the State may not, consistently with due process, eliminate consideration of that factor in its prior hearing." 402 U.S. at 541. *See also* Stanley v. Illinois, 405 U. S. 645 (1972) (state may not irrebuttably presume that unwed fathers are unfit parents).

Two years later, in Vlandis v. Kline, 412 U.S. 441, 452 (1973), the Court struck down a Connecticut statute that irrebuttably presumed that nonresident matriculants at state universities remained nonresidents throughout the duration of their enrollment, thus remaining ineligible for lower in-state tuition, holding that "standards of due process require that the State allow such an individual the opportunity to present evidence showing that he is a bona fide resident entitled to the in-state rates." And in Cleveland Bd. of Educ. v. LaFleur, 414 U.S. 632 (1974), the Court struck down a school board regulation requiring pregnant teachers to take an unpaid leave of absence for five months prior to the expected date of childbirth and for at least three months after childbirth on that ground that the rule created an irrebuttable presumption that any teacher who is four months or more pregnant is not fit to continue teaching.

It was not long, however, before the Court became painfully aware of the demon that it had unleashed. In Weinberger v. Salfi, 422 U.S. 749 (1975), the Court rebuffed a challenge to a provision of the Social Security Act excluding survivors' benefits to widows who had been married to the deceased wage-earner less than nine months prior to his death. The stated congressional purpose for the durational requirement was to prevent sham marriages to secure Social Security payments. The Supreme Court rejected the argument that this amounted to an unconstitutional irrebuttable presumption that any marriage shorter than nine months before the death of one of the spouses was such a sham. Writing for the majority, Justice Rehnquist expressed a concern that the doctrine would become a "virtual engine of destruction for countless legislative judgments. . . ." *Id.* at 772. Following the logic of the district court, Rehnquist said, almost any durational classification would be struck down. Rather, he said, the proper standard to test the validity of a classification is "whether Congress . . . could rationally have concluded both that a particular limitation or qualification would protect against its occurrence, and that the expense and other difficulties of individual determinations justified the inherent imprecision of a prophylactic rule. . . ." *Id.* at 777. In other words, the fact that the nine-month requirement might be over-inclusive and disqualify some survivors of non-sham marriages was not sufficient to invalidate the rule.

Salfi is generally regarded as signaling the end of the Supreme Court's brief dalliance with the "irrebuttable presumption" doctrine. Although the doctrine and the cases embodying it continue to be cited in pleadings and law reviews, federal courts generally treat the doctrine as a historical curiosity, not a valid constitutional test. *See, e.g.*, Hamby v. Neel, 368 F.3d 549 (6th Cir. 2004) (affirming a district court decision finding unconstitutional certain aspects of Tennessee's Medicaid demonstration project but expressly declining to adopt the language of the district court that had labeled the Tennessee procedure as (unconstitutionally) creating an irrebuttable presumption); Delong v. Dept. of Health & Human Servs., 264 F.3d 1334 (Fed. Cir. 2001) (accepting use of "bright-line rule"—no one with a criminal record could serve in the Indian Health Service—against challenge that it created an irrebuttable presumption). For different views on the doctrine itself, *see, e.g.*, Note, The Irrebuttable Presumption Doctrine in the Supreme Court, 87 Harv. L. Rev. 1534 (1974); Laurence Tribe, Structural Due Process, 10 Harv. C.R.-C.L. L. Rev. 269 (1975).

4.   *Informal Adjudication*

We saw in Chapter IV, *supra*, that the APA specifies procedural models for both "formal" and "informal" rulemaking. In Section C of this chapter, we have thus far focused solely on the APA model for so-called "formal" adjudication, that is, adjudications that are "required by statute to be determined on the record after opportunity for an agency hearing." §554(a). What does the APA have to say about—presumably "informal"—adjudications that do not meet that test? The surprising answer is: almost nothing. There is no counterpart in the APA to the informal rulemaking model presented in §553.

Informal adjudication is the "dark matter" of administration, a large collection of administrative transactions virtually invisible to all but the immediate participants. Recall that APA §551 defines "adjudication" as "agency process for the formulation of an order" and "order" as a "final disposition . . . of an agency in a matter other than rule making but including licensing." In that sense, presumably, agencies "adjudicate" not only when they impose sanctions for violating a rule, but also when they deny an application for a license or permit, order changes in a license or permit, refuse to award a grant or loan, deny a request for an advisory ruling or opinion, withhold a requested service or privilege, decline to initiate an investigation or prosecution, charge a fee for a service, or perhaps make adverse statements about someone in the press. All of these decisions have a quality of "finality," adversely affect someone, and rest on a particularized inquiry. Yet only relatively rarely do enabling statutes require the agency, when taking such actions, to provide the sort of "hearing" that triggers the APA's formal adjudicative model.

The closest thing to a template for informal adjudication in the APA is §555, an odd section entitled "Ancillary Matters" (ancillary to what?), particularly clause (E), which requires that:

> Prompt notice shall be given of the denial in whole or in part of a written application, petition, or other request of an interested person made in connection with any agency proceeding. Except in affirming a prior denial or when the denial is self-explanatory, the notice shall be accompanied by a brief statement of the grounds for denial.

This statutory provision made a brief and inconsequential appearance in the *Bachowski* case, discussed in Chapter III, *supra*. There the Supreme Court opined that §555(e) "would appear to be applicable" to a decision by the Secretary of Labor to deny a request by a disappointed candidate for union office to bring suit to set aside a union election. Section 555(e) made a slightly more consequential appearance in the following case.

PENSION BENEFIT GUARANTY CORP. v. LTV CORP.
496 U.S. 633 (1990)

JUSTICE BLACKMUN delivered the opinion of the Court.

[When LTV Corp. declared bankruptcy and went into a Chapter 11 reorganization proceeding, responsibility for satisfying obligations to its former employees under the company's pension plan shifted to the Pension Benefit Guaranty Corporation (PBGC), a government corporation created by Congress to insure private pension funds. Later, as LTV's economic position began to improve, the PBGC, anxious to protect its insurance fund from a large potential liability, ordered that LTV's pension plan be reinstated. This had the effect of shifting financial responsibility for the plan back to LTV. PBGC took this action without affording LTV any opportunity to participate in the decisionmaking process.

On a petition to review the reinstatement order, the Second Circuit ruled that PBGC's order was arbitrary and capricious because: "PBGC neither apprised LTV of the material on which it was to base its decision, gave LTV an adequate opportunity to offer contrary evidence, proceeded in accordance with ascertainable standards . . . , nor provided [LTV] a statement showing its reasoning in applying those standards." 875 F.2d 1008, 1021.]

The PBGC argues that [the Second Circuit's] holding conflicts with Vermont Yankee Nuclear Power Corp. v. Natural Resources Defense Council, Inc., 435 U.S. 519 (1978), where, the PBGC contends, this Court made clear that when the Due Process Clause is not implicated and an agency's governing statute contains no specific procedural mandates, the APA establishes the maximum procedural requirements a reviewing court may impose on agencies. Although *Vermont Yankee* concerned additional procedures imposed by the Court of Appeals for the District of Columbia Circuit on the Atomic Energy Commission when the agency was engaging in informal rulemaking, the PBGC argues that the informal adjudication process by which the restoration decision was made should be governed by the same principles.

Respondents counter by arguing that courts, under some circumstances, do require agencies to undertake additional procedures. As support for this proposition, they rely on Citizens to Preserve Overton Park, Inc. v. Volpe, 401 U.S. 402 (1971). In *Overton Park*, the Court concluded that the Secretary of Transportation's "*post hoc* rationalizations" regarding a decision to authorize the construction of a highway did not provide "an [a]dequate basis for [judicial] review" for purposes of the APA. Accordingly, the Court directed the District Court on remand to consider evidence that shed light on the Secretary's reasoning at the time he made the decision. Of particular relevance for present purposes, the Court in *Overton Park* intimated that one recourse for the District Court might be a remand to the agency for a fuller explanation of the agency's reasoning at the time of the agency action. Subsequent cases have made clear that remanding to the agency in fact is the preferred course. See Florida Power & Light Co. v. Lorion, 470 U.S. 729, 744 (1985). Respondents contend that the instant case is controlled by *Overton Park* rather than *Vermont Yankee*, and that the Court of Appeals' ruling was thus correct.

We believe that respondents' argument is wide of the mark. We begin by noting that although one initially might feel that there is some tension between *Vermont Yankee* and *Overton Park*, the two cases are not necessarily inconsistent. *Vermont Yankee* stands for the general proposition that courts are not free to impose upon agencies specific procedural requirements that have no basis in the APA. . . . At most, *Overton Park* suggests that §706(2)(A) of the APA, which directs a court to ensure that an agency action is not arbitrary and capricious or otherwise contrary to law, imposes a general "procedural" requirement of sorts by mandating that an agency take whatever steps it needs to provide an explanation that will enable the court to evaluate the agency's rationale at the time of decision.

Here, unlike in *Overton Park,* the Court of Appeals did not suggest that the administrative record was inadequate to enable the court to fulfill its duties under §706. Rather, to support its ruling, the court focused on "fundamental fairness" to LTV. . . . [T]he procedural inadequacies cited by the court all relate to LTV's role in the PBGC's decisionmaking process. But the court did not point to any provision in [its enabling act] or the APA which gives LTV the procedural rights the court identified. Thus, the court's holding runs afoul of *Vermont Yankee* and finds no support in *Overton Park.* . . .

Nor is [Bowman Transp., Inc. v. Arkansas-Best Freight, 419 U.S. 281 (1974)] to the contrary. The statement relied upon (which was dictum) said: "A party is entitled, of course, to know the issues on which decision will turn and to be apprised of the factual material on which the agency relies for decision so that he may rebut it." 419 U.S., at 288, n.4. That statement was entirely correct in the context of *Arkansas-Best,* which involved a formal adjudication by the Interstate Commerce Commission pursuant to the trial-type procedures set forth in [§§554, 556-557] of the APA which include requirements that parties be given notice of "the matters of fact and law asserted," . . . an opportunity for "the submission and consideration of facts [and] arguments," . . . and an opportunity to submit "proposed findings and conclusions" or "exceptions." The determination in this case, however, was lawfully made by informal adjudication, the minimal requirements for which are set forth in §555 of the APA, and do not include such elements. A failure to provide them where the Due Process Clause itself does not require them (which has not been asserted here) is therefore not unlawful.

NOTES AND QUESTIONS

1. *Section 555(e)'s "brief statement of grounds for denial."* What exactly is entailed in §555(e)'s requirement that the agency produce a "brief statement of the grounds for denial" whenever it denies a "written application, petition, or other request"? Butte County v. Hogen, 613 F.3d 190 (D.C. Cir. 2010), involved an effort by the Mechoopda Indian tribe to obtain federal approval to conduct gaming operations. While federal law generally allows Indian tribes to conduct gaming on Indian lands, it forbids gaming on "newly acquired lands," which are defined as lands the Secretary of the Interior takes into trust for a tribe after 1988. *See* 25 U.S.C. §§2701-2721. An exception applies, however, when the Secretary takes land into trust after 1988 as part of "the restoration of lands for an Indian tribe that is restored to Federal recognition." *Id.* §2719(b).

After the Mechoopda tribe was restored to federal recognition in 1992, it purchased and offered to the Department of the Interior to take into trust for its benefit lands on which it hoped to operate a casino. The casino's legality thus rested on whether the lands qualified as restored lands. Under agency regulations, a tribe must demonstrate a significant historical connection to lands in order for them to qualify as restored. In 2003, the Department concluded in an advisory opinion that the lands purchased by the Mechoopda tribe were indeed restored lands, due to a sufficiently strong historical and cultural nexus. Three years later, Butte County, California, home to the purchased lands, filed a memorandum disputing the Department's finding. The memorandum included a report prepared by an expert consultant that cast doubt on the tribe's historical connection to the lands. The Department responded to the memorandum with a very brief rejection letter. When the Secretary ultimately decided to take the tribe's land into trust and approve the casino, the County sued, claiming, *inter alia*, that the agency's rejection letter failed to provide a "statement of grounds" under §555(e). The D.C. Circuit, 613 F.3d at 194-195, agreed:

> [U]nder §555(e), the agency must provide an interested party—here Butte County—with a "brief statement of the grounds for denial" of the party's request. As this court held in Tourus Records, Inc. v. DEA, 259 F.3d 731, 737 (D.C. Cir. 2001), the agency must explain why it decided to act as it did. The agency's statement must be one of "reasoning"; it must not be just a "conclusion"; it must "articulate a satisfactory explanation" for its action. 259 F.3d at 737. . . .
>
> The Interior Department managed to violate the minimal procedural requirements §555(e) imposed. When Butte County furnished the Interior Secretary's office with a copy of the [expert consultant's report] and gave numerous reasons why the Tribe's land did not constitute "restored land," that issue was still pending before the Secretary. The Secretary's final determination did not come until two years later, on March 14, 2008. Yet the entirety of Interior's response to Butte County was this: "We are not inclined to revisit this decision [the opinion of the Gaming Commission] now because the Office of the Solicitor reviewed this matter in 2003, and concurred in the [National Indian Gaming Commission's] determination of March 14, 2003."
>
> This response violates §555(e) for the same reason the response in *Tourus Records* violated that provision. The response "provides no basis upon which we could conclude that it was the product of reasoned decisionmaking." 259 F.3d at 737. It had all the explanatory power of the reply of Bartelby the Scrivener to his employer: "I would prefer not to." Which is to say, it provided no explanation.

2. *Section 555(b)'s "reasonable time" requirement.* Aside from §555(e)'s brief statement of grounds for denial, the APA imposes only one other procedural requirement on agencies undertaking informal adjudication: an agency must conclude a matter presented to it "within a reasonable time." 5 U.S.C. §555(b). In Friends of the Bow v. Thompson, 124 F.3d 1210 (10th Cir. 1997), the court held that the Forest Service complied with §555(b) even though it delayed for approximately one year in responding to an environmental group's request that the Service conduct a supplemental environmental assessment before completing a timber sale. The court noted that the litigants failed to point to a single case in which a court has invalidated an agency action under §555(b) and reasoned that even if a one-year delay could be unreasonable in some circumstances, it was reasonable in the instant case because of the "lengthy, detailed nature of [the environmental group's] request for action, and the thoroughness of the agency's eventual response." *Id.* at 1221.

3. *Dearth of procedure in informal adjudication.* If the APA is nearly silent on procedures for informal adjudication, and *LTV* and *Vermont Yankee* prevent courts from fashioning such procedures, where can one look for legal procedural constraints on informal administrative action? In some cases, the procedural provisions of enabling statutes or (more likely) agency regulations may fill in the gaps left by the APA. But even these sources are quite spotty, consigning

most informal administrative adjudication to the shadowy world of bureaucratic and interpersonal politics. Like it or not, it is primarily this world that most "administrative lawyers" inhabit.

Why, having specified procedural models for formal rulemaking, formal adjudication, and informal rulemaking, would the drafters of the APA not have specified a procedural model for informal adjudication? Is there a lesser need for national uniformity in informal adjudication? Is there a lower probability of official abuse or error in the informal adjudicatory context, or are the consequences of such abuses less serious? Or is "informal adjudication" such an intrinsically heterogeneous collection of phenomena as to defy any attempt at standardization? Should the APA be amended to provide a procedural template for informal adjudications? To what class of matters should it apply? What procedures should it require agencies to employ? In thinking about this question, you might want to consider the Supreme Court's cases requiring agencies to employ a "consultative" process under due process, discussed above.

CHAPTER VII

ENFORCEMENT AND LIABILITY

In one sense, enforcement is what government is principally about. The power of government to affect the behavior of its citizens rests in good measure on the arsenal of coercive sanctions at its disposal, such as imprisonment, imposition of fines, injunctive orders, termination of benefits, and revocation of licenses. Merely reciting such a list reminds us of the ubiquity of enforcement; it is intertwined with virtually all governmental functions, including benefits administration and licensing (treated separately in Chapters VI and VIII). This chapter treats issues that arise concerning two subsets of enforcement activity: first, what are sometimes called "command-and-control" programs and, second, private litigation, either against violators or against government.

A.   GOVERNMENT ENFORCEMENT

The structure of command-and-control programs is elemental: the government issues behavioral commands, monitors behavior, and imposes sanctions for noncompliance. Unlike programs involving administration of benefits or issuance of licenses, contacts with the enforcement target are usually initiated by the government and are almost invariably unwelcome. Contacts between enforcer and target also tend to be episodic and random, as contrasted with the more frequent and predictable contacts characteristic of other kinds of governmental programs.

The archetype for command-and-control regulation is the criminal law. Indeed, civil regulatory enforcement and traditional criminal enforcement are close cousins, if not twins separated at birth. As we shall see, some legal doctrines developed in the criminal context have been applied to civil enforcement as well. Even where the "civil" label has blocked their application, the concerns motivating criminal law doctrines have often shaped judicial and legislative attitudes toward civil enforcement. The answers may differ, but the questions are the same: How can the demand for individual privacy be reconciled with the government's need to monitor regulated behavior and investigate apparent violations? To what extent may the government conscript private citizens into the role of policing their own or others' behavior? Is it fair to prosecute or punish one wrongdoer while others go free? Is there a limit on the pain that may be inflicted upon one wrongdoer, in order to make him an example to others? To whom do we entrust the awesome task of judging guilt or innocence?

Before we turn to the way courts and legislatures have answered these questions, it is useful to ask what the purposes of an enforcement program are, and how an effective program ideally ought to be operated. While it may seem obvious that the best enforcement program achieves 100 percent compliance with regulatory norms, this is not necessarily the case. In an important article, economists Gary Becker and George Stigler analyzed enforcement, using tools of economic theory. Gary Becker & George Stigler, Law Enforcement, Malfeasance, and Compensation of Enforcers, J. Legal Stud. 1, 2-5 (1974). Becker and Stigler argue that people obey the law when the cost of disobedience is greater than the benefits of disobedience. This suggests that society should set the level of investment in detection and prosecution, and the level of the penalty, so that the probability of being punished, multiplied by the penalty level, just exceeds the benefits of disobedience. Thus, for example, when the likelihood of detection is low, the state should set a high penalty.

In recent years, that simple economic model has been challenged by scholars seeking to enrich the understanding of enforcement by considering other, extra-legal mechanisms of enforcing legal and nonlegal norms. A school of thought known as "norms theory" posits that informal norms play an important role in social behavior, and that enforcement cannot be understood fully without looking at these norms. Social norms are enforced informally, for example, when other members of a social group shame violators, and also through regret felt by violators who have internalized the norm. For example, a norms theorist studying factory safety in a particular industry would look beyond the threat of OSHA inspections and penalties and consider also whether an industry norm prescribes a particular level of safety, and whether that norm is enforced, formally or informally, by business groups, employee representatives, or perhaps the market, in which consumers elect not to purchase products or services from companies that do not comply with applicable norms. For an overview of norms theory with an extensive bibliography, *see* Robert A. Cooter, Models of Morality in Law and Economics: Self-Control and Self-Improvement for the "Bad Man" of Holmes, 78 B.U. L. Rev. 903 (1998). Applying a norms-based approach, what differences might you expect in the operation of programs designed to enforce prohibitions against, say, worker safety hazards, illegal dumping of toxic wastes, consumer fraud, corporate campaign contributions, or shoplifting?

Theory aside, command-and-control forms of regulation have been criticized for a variety of reasons, among them that they can be inflexible and inattentive to relative compliance costs. Regulated industries tend to prefer performance standards (which dictate the regulatory outcome but not the means of achieving it), over engineering or design standards, which dictate precisely how to achieve a regulatory outcome. (A design standard might require all ladders used in a workplace to include rungs of a specific thickness made of a particular material, whereas a performance standard might require the ladder to be capable of supporting a certain weight.) Performance standards provide more flexibility, but they may be more difficult to enforce because compliance may be harder or more costly to verify. Regulated entities often prefer market mechanisms—like cap and trade regimes for controlling pollution—to both performance and design standards, because they offer maximum flexibility for achieving the regulatory goal with the greatest opportunities for controlling cost. Trading schemes are thought to be easier to monitor, too.

For example, instead of requiring each polluter to meet the same standard of emissions reduction, the Clean Air Act's acid rain program, which is designed to reduce the total volume of sulfur dioxide and nitrous oxide emissions, allows firms to buy and sell pollution allowances. Firms for which it is relatively cheap to cut emissions can do so at lower cost and sell their excess allowances to firms that find emissions control more costly. *See* generally, Robert W. Hahn & Robert N. Stavins, Incentive-Based Environmental Regulation: A New Era from an Old Idea? 18 Ecology L.Q. 1 (1991). The EPA's bubble approach, approved by the Supreme Court in *Chevron*, excerpted in Chapter II, *supra*, enabled firms to use a form of trading by letting them "net out" emissions across different units at the same facility.

Another development has been to attempt to improve the overall efficiency of regulatory enforcement by fostering a more cooperative relationship between the government and regulated parties. Professor Freeman has proposed a cooperative model of enforcement under which the adversarial nature of agency enforcement would be replaced with a problem-solving orientation involving greater participation and collaboration between the enforcing agency and regulated parties. *See* Jody Freeman, Collaborative Governance in the Administrative State, 45 UCLA L. Rev. 1 (1997). Key to the success of the model would be fostering a regulatory environment in which the subjects of regulation would be more willing to share information and ideas with the agency and in which the agency would be willing to listen and adjust its approach to the realities of the situation. In Freeman's view, based both on theory and on observation of a number of cooperative regulatory initiatives conducted by the EPA, enforcement would improve as the parties worked together to reach common goals. Innovations such as negotiated rulemaking, and the hybrid approaches that share some of its characteristics, are also, to Freeman, evidence of a trend in this direction.

Any significant movement toward a cooperative model of enforcement raises a host of issues not unlike those implicated by the movement from design to performance standards, but perhaps of even greater magnitude. First and foremost is the basic issue of whether it is in the nature of law to be flexible enough to allow feedback from a regulated party to significantly impact the overall direction of enforcement. Even if legal norms could be made adaptable enough to accommodate the flexibility inherent in the cooperative model, there is the institutional problem of delegating authority to relatively low-level officials within an agency to make the decisions necessary to regulate with a high degree of flexibility. Would the gains from adopting a more cooperative model soon be overwhelmed by the cost of monitoring the performance of officials with discretion and the losses from mismanagement and favoritism? Although these issues may not be raised by the typical legal controversy that erupts over methods of enforcement, it is worth considering them as you make your way through the various enforcement issues in the materials that follow.

1.   *Monitoring and Investigation*

"The surveillance process is the generator of the enforcement machine." Colin S. Diver, A Theory of Regulatory Enforcement, 28 Pub. Poly. 257, 281 (1980). The ability of a regulatory agency to enforce its commands depends entirely on the quality of its mechanism for detecting noncompliance with those commands. Prosecutors and judges, in a sense, are prisoners of inspectors. Only those violations unearthed by the surveillance process can be remedied or punished by the state. On that process, therefore, rests the credibility of the enforcement program.

If surveillance is the generator, information is its fuel. The enforcer's appetite for information is ravenous. In regulatory programs of any scope, the number of facilities, actors, or events to be monitored is immense, the opportunities and incentives for noncompliance vast. Detecting, documenting, and proving the occurrence of even a respectable percentage of all violations require massive amounts of information.

As an initial matter, almost all of the information needed to fuel the enforcement machine is in private hands (what is known to economists as "information asymmetry"). The regulator's task is to find ways to get at it. As we shall see in subsequent sections of this chapter, regulatory enforcers often rely heavily on information volunteered by competitors or customers or neighbors of regulated firms. In most cases, however, regulatory enforcement requires that the government be able to obtain information from the regulated population itself. There are, in essence, three devices for obtaining such information: physical inspections of regulated activities, subpoenas requiring the production of documents or tangible objects, and orders requiring the creation and preservation of records. The growth of regulation during the 1960s and 1970s led to a significant rise of inspectors, examiners, and clerks engaged in these activities. *See* Eugene Bardach & Robert Kagan, Going by the Book: The Problem of Regulatory Unreasonableness (1982). And while their number has waxed and waned over time, as Congress and different administrations have adjusted the budget for agency enforcement, a robust federal enforcement capacity remains. However legitimate may be the justifications for their inquisitive activities, equally plain is the threat they pose to liberty and privacy. The task of legal doctrine in these areas—as in their criminal law counterparts—has been to draw the boundary between justified exploration and excessive intrusion.

a.   Physical Inspections

Many regulations address activities that occur at regular, ascertainable places and times—emitting pollutants from a smokestack, operating a nuclear power plant, butchering meat, or constructing a building. The most obvious way for the regulator to ensure compliance with such rules is to go see for herself—collect samples of the pollution being emitted, test the backup cooling system for the nuclear fuel, examine the sides of beef as they roll into the cutting room, watch the steel frame being assembled. This strategy becomes more problematic, however, when one considers that inspections impose burdens on people, and enforcers have to be very selective in choosing whom to inspect. The operational and legal implications of these two facts are nicely illustrated in the federal occupational safety and health program.

The primary enforcement tool of the Occupational Safety and Health Administration (OSHA) is its power to make unannounced inspections of workplaces and to impose civil money penalties for violations. Section 8(a) of the OSH Act (29 U.S.C. §657(a)) provides:

> In order to carry out the purposes of this Act, the Secretary [of Labor], upon presenting appropriate credentials to the owner, operator, or agent in charge, is authorized—
>
> (1) to enter without delay and at reasonable times any factory, plant, establishment, construction site, or other area, workplace or environment where work is performed by an employee of an employer; and
>
> (2) to inspect and investigate during regular working hours and at other reasonable times, and within reasonable limits and in a reasonable manner, any such place of employment and all pertinent conditions, structures, machines, apparatus, devices, equipment, and materials therein, and to question privately any such employer, owner, operator, agent or employee.

Compliance safety and health officers (CSHOs) assigned to OSHA field offices conduct inspections. A typical inspection consists of the following steps: an opening conference with the employer, examination of the employer's accident records, inspection of the workplace (the walkaround), and a closing conference. During the walkaround, the CSHO makes observations and measurements, performs tests, and speaks with employees. As the CSHO conducts the inspection, he takes written notes of his observations. After completing the inspection, he prepares an inspection report to be submitted to his supervisor. The forms provide a place for narrative description of any violations observed and for computation of a proposed penalty for each. Since proposed penalties must be reviewed at the area office, the employer does not receive formal notice of violation (citation) until after the inspection. The citation describes the alleged violations, sets forth a proposed penalty for each, and sets a date by which the violation must be corrected. The employer must notify the area office when the violation is abated. Otherwise, a follow-up inspection will be conducted.

In 2015, Congress enacted the Federal Civil Penalties Inflation Adjustment Act, Pub. L. 114-74, which requires agencies to adjust their penalties each year for inflation. From 2015 to 2019, the maximum OSHA penalties for "other than serious" violations increased from $7,000 per violation to $13,260. The amount of the fine depends on the "size of the business of the employer being charged, the gravity of the violation, the good faith of the employer and the history of previous violations." Section 17(j), 29 U.S.C. §666(j). OSHA *must* assess the maximum penalty if the violation is "serious," that is, "if there is a substantial probability that death or serious physical harm could result from a condition which exists . . . in such place of employment unless the employer did not, and could not with the exercise of reasonable diligence, know of the presence of the violation." Section 17(k), 29 U.S.C. §666(k). If the violation is "willful" or "repeated," OSHA may assess a penalty up to $132,598, up from $70,000. Section 17(a), 29 U.S.C. §666(a); 29 C.F.R. §1903.15.

Throughout its history, OSHA has struggled to achieve adequate surveillance over its vast domain. In 1980 OSHA employed roughly 1,600 CSHOs to monitor 2.5 million workplaces employing 40 million workers. By fiscal year 2009, the number of OSHA inspectors had declined to approximately 1,100 despite the fact that the number of workers and workplaces had increased substantially during that 30-year period to 8.9 million worksites employing 135 million workers. State inspectors also enforce federal workplace safety requirements, bringing the total number of inspectors up to approximately 2,100. What would you expect as an enforcement strategy for an agency overseeing so many workplaces, occupations, and employees?

OSHA uses three principal methods for detecting violations: "fatality and catastrophe" investigations, complaint inspections, and targeted inspections. OSHA's current system for determining the order in which to conduct these three types of inspection is as follows:

First: reports of "imminent danger" situations
Second: fatality and catastrophe investigations
Third: employee complaints
Fourth: referrals from other government agencies
Fifth: targeted inspections
Sixth: follow-up inspections

Fatality and Catastrophe Investigations. The OSH Act requires employers to notify OSHA of any industrial accidents involving a fatality or hospitalization of at least three workers, regardless of its cause. Whenever OSHA receives such a fatality or catastrophe report, it routinely dispatches an investigator to determine whether a violation of the law was responsible. This category accounts for a relatively small number of inspections.

Complaint Inspections. The OSH Act requires OSHA to investigate any written complaint filed by a current worker or his "representative" (typically, his union) that presents "reasonable grounds" to believe that a violation has occurred. Section 8(f)(1), 29 U.S.C. §657(f)(1). Before 1975, OSHA gave high priority only to complaints that met all three conditions. Unwritten complaints or complaints by nonemployees typically went to the bottom of the list, and most were never reached.

That policy came under sharp attack, however, after the "kepone disaster" of 1975 in which OSHA failed to respond to a nonemployee's tip concerning a toxic chemical that later caused several deaths. In response, OSHA decided to conduct priority inspections in response to all complaints, whether written or oral and regardless of the source. As could be anticipated, the new policy resulted in a dramatic increase in the number of complaint-based inspections conducted—from 13 percent of total inspections in 1973 to 32 percent in 1977. Programmed inspections fell during this same period from 66 percent to 41 percent of all inspections.

In a 1979 report, the General Accounting Office criticized OSHA's revised complaint policy, claiming that:

Complaint inspections provide limited benefits in protecting workers from serious hazards. Most complaints (1) come from the types of businesses that OSHA would not visit on its own initiative and (2) do not appear to address serious hazards or, in some cases, any hazards. Although serious hazards were cited in 18 percent of OSHA's complaint inspections, rarely were the hazards related to the complaints. For 80 percent of the complaints we reviewed, inspectors had found no violation of any OSHA standards that related to the complaints.

Comptroller General of the U.S., How Effective Are OSHA's Complaint Procedures? 9 (1979).

Targeted Inspections. Targeted inspections are "aimed at specific high-hazard industries or individual workplaces that have experienced high rates of injuries and illnesses." The "targeted inspections" category replaced OSHA's former "programmed inspections" category, apparently because programmed inspections were usually targeted at notoriously dangerous industries (such as foundries, trenching operations, or construction) and individual workplaces with high rates of injuries and illnesses.

Lower-priority inspections implement general safety and health programs that allocate inspectors among remaining industries according to their relative hazardousness, as measured by worker-injury rates (for safety) or use of known toxic substances (for health). OSHA selects specific firms within industries randomly or based on a variety of factors, including location, size, and prior inspection history.

OSHA's criteria for measuring the performance of its inspectors and area officers have powerfully influenced its allocation of effort. The management control system the agency used in its early years emphasized numbers of inspections conducted and violations cited. Partially as a result, inspectors tended to inspect large numbers of small businesses, which could be inspected quickly, and to concentrate on safety violations, which could be detected and documented more easily than health violations. In 1976, for example, over one-third of OSHA inspections were conducted in businesses with ten or fewer employees, and only 8 percent of all inspections focused on health standards. *See* W. Kip Viscusi, Risk by Choice: Regulating Health and Safety in the Workplace 16-25 (1983). The average penalty per violation that year was only $33, and barely 2 percent of the violations cited were "serious." Extensive public and congressional criticism of these policies led OSHA to change its performance evaluation criteria so as to emphasize "quality" rather than "quantity." By 1980, 19 percent of OSHA inspections focused on health standards, 34 percent found serious violations, and the average penalty per violation was $193. In 2018, OSHA conducted 32,020 inspections (down from 39,324 in 2007). Statistics on the number of violations found in 2018 are not available, but in 2007 OSHA found 67,176 violations, which amounted to approximately 1.7 serious violations per inspection. The average fine in cases of serious violation was approximately $1,000. Do these figures suggest that problems with OSHA enforcement have been solved? Criticism of OSHA's inspections policy has persisted, much of it coming, of course, from employers, many of whom view OSHA inspections as invasions of their privacy, interference with production, and harassment of their supervisors. Not surprisingly, those charges have found legal, as well as political, expression.

MARSHALL v. BARLOW'S, INC.
436 U.S. 307 (1978)

MR. JUSTICE WHITE delivered the opinion of the Court. . . .

On the morning of September 11, 1975, an OSHA inspector entered the customer service area of Barlow's, Inc., an electrical and plumbing installation business located in Pocatello, Idaho. The president and general manager, Ferrol G. "Bill" Barlow, was on hand; and the OSHA inspector, after showing his credentials, informed Mr. Barlow that he wished to conduct a search of the working areas of the business. Mr. Barlow inquired whether any complaint had been received about his company. The inspector answered no, but that Barlow's, Inc., had simply turned up in the agency's selection process. The inspector again asked to enter the nonpublic area of the business; Mr. Barlow's response was to inquire whether the inspector had a search warrant. The inspector had none. Thereupon, Mr. Barlow refused the inspector admission to the employee area of his business. He said he was relying on his rights as guaranteed by the Fourth Amendment of the United States Constitution.

Three months later, the Secretary petitioned the United States District Court for the District of Idaho to issue an order compelling Mr. Barlow to admit the inspector. The requested order was issued on December 30, 1975, and was presented to Mr. Barlow on January 5, 1976. Mr. Barlow again refused admission, and he sought his own injunctive relief against the warrantless searches assertedly permitted by OSHA. A three-judge court was convened. On December 30, 1976, it ruled in Mr. Barlow's favor. . . . The Secretary appealed, challenging the judgment, and we noted probable jurisdiction. . . .

I

The Secretary urges that warrantless inspections to enforce OSHA are reasonable within the meaning of the Fourth Amendment. Among other things, he relies on §8(a) of the Act, 29 U.S.C. §657(a), which authorizes inspection of business premises without a warrant and which the Secretary urges represents a congressional construction of the Fourth Amendment that the courts should not reject. Regrettably, we are unable to agree.

The Warrant Clause of the Fourth Amendment protects commercial buildings as well as private homes. To hold otherwise would belie the origin of that Amendment, and the American colonial experience. An important forerunner of the first 10 Amendments to the United States Constitution, the Virginia Bill of Rights, specifically opposed "general warrants, whereby an officer or messenger may be commanded to search suspected places without evidence of a fact committed." The general warrant was a recurring point of contention in the Colonies immediately preceding the Revolution. The particular offensiveness it engendered was acutely felt by the merchants and businessmen whose premises and products were inspected for compliance with the several parliamentary revenue measures that most irritated the colonists. "[T]he Fourth Amendment's commands grew in large measure out of the colonists' experience with the writs of assistance . . . [that] granted sweeping power to customs officials and other agents of the King to search at large for smuggled goods." United States

v. Chadwick, 433 U.S. 1, 7-8 (1977). *See also* G.M. Leasing Corp. v. United States, 429 U.S. 338, 355 (1977). Against this background, it is untenable that the ban on warrantless searches was not intended to shield places of business as well as of residence.

This Court has already held that warrantless searches are generally unreasonable, and that this rule applies to commercial premises as well as homes. [Camara v. Municipal Court, 387 U.S. 523 (1967); See v. Seattle, 387 U.S. 541 (1967).]

These . . . cases also held that the Fourth Amendment prohibition against unreasonable searches protects against warrantless intrusions during civil as well as criminal investigations. . . . The reason is found in the "basic purpose of this Amendment [which] is to safeguard the privacy and security of individuals against arbitrary invasions by governmental officials." *Camara, supra,* at 528. If the government intrudes on a person's property, the privacy interest suffers whether the government's motivation is to investigate violations of criminal laws or breaches of other statutory or regulatory standards. It therefore appears that unless some recognized exception to the warrant requirement applies, See v. Seattle would require a warrant to conduct the inspection sought in this case.

The Secretary urges that an exception from the search warrant requirement has been recognized for "pervasively regulated business[es]," United States v. Biswell, 406 U.S. 311, 316 (1972), and for "closely regulated" industries "long subject to close supervision and inspection." Colonnade Catering Corp. v. United States, 397 U.S. 72, 74, 77 (1970). These cases are indeed exceptions, but they represent responses to relatively unique circumstances. Certain industries have such a history of government oversight that no reasonable expectation of privacy, *see* Katz v. United States, 389 U.S. 347, 351-52 (1967), could exist for a proprietor over the stock of such an enterprise. Liquor (*Colonnade*) and firearms (*Biswell*) are industries of this type; when an entrepreneur embarks upon such a business, he has voluntarily chosen to subject himself to a full arsenal of governmental regulation. . . .

The clear import of our cases is that the closely regulated industry of the type involved in *Colonnade* and *Biswell* is the exception. The Secretary would make it the rule. Invoking the Walsh-Healey Act of 1936, 41 U.S.C. §35 *et seq.,* the Secretary attempts to support a conclusion that all businesses involved in interstate commerce have long been subjected to close supervision of employee safety and health conditions. But the degree of federal involvement in employee working circumstances has never been of the order of specificity and pervasiveness that OSHA mandates. It is quite unconvincing to argue that the imposition of minimum wages and maximum hours on employers who contracted with the Government under the Walsh-Healey Act prepared the entirety of American interstate commerce for regulation of working conditions to the minutest detail. . . .

The critical fact in this case is that entry over Mr. Barlow's objection is being sought by a Governmental agent. Employees are not being prohibited from reporting OSHA violations. What they observe in their daily functions is undoubtedly beyond the employer's reasonable expectation of privacy. The Government inspector, however, is not an employee. Without a warrant he stands in no better position than a member of the public. What is observable by the public is observable, without a warrant, by the Government inspector as well. The owner of a business has not, by the necessary utilization of employees in his operation, thrown open the areas where employees alone are permitted to the warrantless scrutiny of Government agents. That an employee is free to report, and the Government is free to use, any evidence of noncompliance with OSHA that the employee observes furnishes no justification for federal agents to enter a place of business from which the public is restricted and to conduct their own warrantless search.

II

The Secretary nevertheless stoutly argues that the enforcement scheme of the Act requires warrantless searches, and that the restrictions on search discretion contained in the Act and its regulations already protect as much privacy as a warrant would. The Secretary thereby asserts the actual reasonableness of OSHA searches, whatever the general rule against warrantless searches might be. Because "reasonableness is still the ultimate standard," Camara v. Municipal Court, 387 U.S., at 539, the Secretary suggests that the Court decide whether a warrant is needed by arriving at a sensible balance between the administrative necessities of OSHA inspections and the incremental protection of privacy of business owners a warrant would afford. He suggests that only a decision exempting OSHA inspections from the Warrant Clause would give "full recognition to the competing public and private interests here at stake." *Ibid.*

The Secretary submits that warrantless inspections are essential to the proper enforcement of OSHA because they afford the opportunity to inspect without prior notice and hence to preserve the advantages of surprise. While the dangerous conditions outlawed by the Act include structural defects that cannot be quickly hidden or remedied, the Act also regulates a myriad of safety details that may be amenable to speedy alteration or disguise. The risk is that during the interval between an inspector's initial request to search a plant and his procuring a warrant following the owner's refusal of permission, violations of this latter type could be corrected and thus escape the inspector's notice. To the suggestion that warrants may be issued ex parte and executed without delay and without prior notice, thereby preserving the element of surprise, the Secretary expresses concern for the administrative strain that would be experienced by the inspection system, and by the courts, should ex parte warrants issued in advance become standard practice.

We are unconvinced, however, that requiring warrants to inspect will impose serious burdens on the inspection system or the courts, will prevent inspections necessary to enforce the statute, or will make them less effective. In the first place, the great majority of businessmen can be expected in normal course to consent to inspection without warrant; the Secretary has not brought to this Court's attention any widespread pattern of refusal.[11] In those cases where an owner does insist on a warrant, the Secretary argues that inspection efficiency will be impeded by the advance notice and delay. The Act's penalty provisions

---

11. We recognize that today's holding itself might have an impact on whether owners choose to resist requested searches; we can only await the development of evidence not present on this record to determine how serious an impediment to effective enforcement this might be.

for giving advance notice of a search, 29 U.S.C. §666(f), and the Secretary's own regulations, 29 CFR §1903.6 (1977), indicate that surprise searches are indeed contemplated. However, [it is not] immediately apparent why the advantages of surprise would be lost if, after being refused entry, procedures were available for the Secretary to seek an ex parte warrant and to reappear at the premises without further notice to the establishment being inspected.

Whether the Secretary proceeds to secure a warrant or other process, with or without prior notice, his entitlement to inspect will not depend on his demonstrating probable cause to believe that conditions in violation of OSHA exist on the premises. Probable cause in the criminal law sense is not required. For purposes of an administrative search such as this, probable cause justifying the issuance of a warrant may be based not only on specific evidence of an existing violation but also on a showing that "reasonable legislative or administrative standards for conducting an . . . inspection are satisfied with respect to a particular [establishment]." Camara v. Municipal Court, 387 U.S., at 538. A warrant showing that a specific business has been chosen for an OSHA search on the basis of a general administrative plan for the enforcement of the Act derived from neutral sources such as, for example, dispersion of employees in various types of industries across a given area, and the desired frequency of searches in any of the lesser divisions of the area, would protect an employer's Fourth Amendment rights. We doubt that the consumption of enforcement energies in the obtaining of such warrants will exceed manageable proportions.

Finally, the Secretary urges that requiring a warrant for OSHA inspectors will mean that, as a practical matter, warrantless-search provisions in other regulatory statutes are also constitutionally infirm. The reasonableness of a warrantless search, however, will depend upon the specific enforcement needs and privacy guarantees of each statute. Some of the statutes cited apply only to a single industry, where regulations might already be so pervasive that a *Colonnade-Biswell* exception to the warrant requirement could apply. Some statutes already envision resort to federal-court enforcement when entry is refused, employing specific language in some cases and general language in others. In short, we base today's opinion on the facts and law concerned with OSHA and do not retreat from a holding appropriate to that statute because of its real or imagined effect on other, different administrative schemes. . . . We conclude that the concerns expressed by the Secretary do not suffice to justify warrantless inspections under OSHA or vitiate the general constitutional requirement that for a search to be reasonable a warrant must be obtained. . . .

Mr. Justice Brennan took no part in the consideration or decision of this case.

Mr. Justice Stevens, with whom Mr. Justice Blackmun and Mr. Justice Rehnquist join, dissenting. . . .

The Fourth Amendment contains two separate Clauses, each flatly prohibiting a category of governmental conduct. The first Clause states that the right to be free from unreasonable searches "shall not be violated"; the second unequivocally prohibits the issuance of warrants except "upon probable cause." In this case the ultimate question is whether the category of warrantless searches authorized by the statute is "unreasonable" within the meaning of the first Clause.

In cases involving the investigation of criminal activity, the Court has held that the reasonableness of a search generally depends upon whether it was conducted pursuant to a valid warrant. *See, e.g.,* Coolidge v. New Hampshire, 403 U.S. 443. There is, however, also a category of searches which are reasonable within the meaning of the first Clause even though the probable-cause requirement of the Warrant Clause cannot be satisfied. *See* United States v. Martinez-Fuerte, 428 U.S. 543; Terry v. Ohio, 392 U.S. 1; South Dakota v. Opperman, 428 U.S. 364; United States v. Biswell, 406 U.S. 311. The regulatory inspection program challenged in this case, in my judgment, falls within this category.

I

The warrant requirement is linked "textually . . . to the probable-cause concept" in the Warrant Clause. South Dakota v. Opperman, *supra,* at 370 n.5. The routine OSHA inspections are, by definition, not based on cause to believe there is a violation on the premises to be inspected. Hence, if the inspections were measured against the requirements of the Warrant Clause, they would be automatically and unequivocally unreasonable.

Because of the acknowledged importance and reasonableness of routine inspections in the enforcement of federal regulatory statutes such as OSHA, the Court recognizes that requiring full compliance with the Warrant Clause would invalidate all such inspection programs. Yet, rather than simply analyzing such programs under the "Reasonableness" Clause of the Fourth Amendment, the Court holds the OSHA program invalid under the Warrant Clause and then avoids a blanket prohibition on all routine, regulatory inspections by relying on the notion that the "probable cause" requirement in the Warrant Clause may be relaxed whenever the Court believes that the governmental need to conduct a category of "searches" outweighs the intrusion on interests protected by the Fourth Amendment.

The Court's approach disregards the plain language of the Warrant Clause and is unfaithful to the balance struck by the Framers of the Fourth Amendment—"the one procedural safeguard in the Constitution that grew directly out of the events which immediately preceded the revolutionary struggle with England." This preconstitutional history includes the controversy in England over the issuance of general warrants to aid enforcement of the seditious libel laws and the colonial experience with writs of assistance issued to facilitate collection of the various import duties imposed by Parliament. The Framers' familiarity with the abuses attending the issuance of such general warrants provided the principal stimulus for the restraints on arbitrary governmental intrusions embodied in the Fourth Amendment. . . .

Since the general warrant, not the warrantless search, was the immediate evil at which the Fourth Amendment was directed, it is not surprising that the Framers placed precise limits on its issuance. The requirement that a warrant only issue on a showing of particularized probable cause was the means adopted to circumscribe the warrant power. While the subsequent course of Fourth Amendment jurisprudence in this Court emphasizes the dangers posed by warrantless searches conducted without probable cause, it is the general reasonableness standard in the first Clause, not the Warrant Clause, that the Framers adopted to limit this category of searches. It is, of course, true that the existence of a valid warrant normally satisfies the reasonableness requirement under the Fourth Amendment. But we should not dilute the requirements of the Warrant Clause in an effort to force every kind of governmental intrusion which satisfies the Fourth Amendment definition of a "search" into a judicially developed, warrant-preference scheme.

Fidelity to the original understanding of the Fourth Amendment, therefore, leads to the conclusion that the Warrant Clause has no application to routine, regulatory inspections of commercial premises. If such inspections are valid, it is because they comport with the ultimate reasonableness standard of the Fourth Amendment. If the Court were correct in its view that such inspections, if undertaken without a warrant, are unreasonable in the constitutional sense, the issuance of a "new-fangled warrant"—to use Mr. Justice Clark's characteristically expressive term—without any true showing of particularized probable cause would not be sufficient to validate them.[5]

II

Even if a warrant issued without probable cause were faithful to the Warrant Clause, I could not accept the Court's holding that the Government's inspection program is constitutionally unreasonable because it fails to require such a warrant procedure. In determining whether a warrant is a necessary safeguard in a given class of cases, "the Court has weighed the public interest against the Fourth Amendment interest of the individual. . . ." United States v. Martinez-Fuerte, 428 U.S., at 555. Several considerations persuade me that this balance should be struck in favor of the routine inspections authorized by Congress.

Congress has determined that regulation and supervision of safety in the workplace furthers an important public interest and that the power to conduct warrantless searches is necessary to accomplish the safety goals of the legislation. . . .

The Court's analysis does not persuade me that Congress' determination that the warrantless-inspection power as a necessary adjunct of the exercise of the regulatory power is unreasonable. It was surely not unreasonable to conclude that the rate at which employers deny entry to inspectors would increase if covered businesses, which may have safety violations on their premises, have a right to deny warrantless entry to a compliance inspector. . . . While the Court's prediction of the effect a warrant requirement would have on the behavior of covered employers may turn out to be accurate, its judgment is essentially empirical. On such an issue, I would defer to Congress' judgment regarding the importance of a warrantless-search power to the OSHA enforcement scheme. . . .

Even if a warrant requirement does not "frustrate" the legislative purpose, the Court has no authority to impose an additional burden on the Secretary unless that burden is required to protect the employer's Fourth Amendment interests. The essential function of the traditional warrant requirement is the interposition of a neutral magistrate between the citizen and the presumably

---

5. See v. Seattle, 387 U.S. 541, 547 (Clark, J., dissenting).

zealous law enforcement officer so that there might be an objective determination of probable cause. But this purpose is not served by the newfangled inspection warrant. . . . The Court plainly accepts the proposition that random health and safety inspections are reasonable. It does not question Congress' determination that the public interest in workplaces free from health and safety hazards outweighs the employer's desire to conduct his business only in the presence of permittees, except in those rare instances when the Government has probable cause to suspect that the premises harbor a violation of the law.

What purposes, then, are served by the administrative warrant procedure? The inspection warrant purports to serve three functions: to inform the employer that the inspection is authorized by the statute, to advise him of the lawful limits of the inspection, and to assure him that the person demanding entry is an authorized inspector. Camara v. Municipal Court, 387 U.S. 523, 532. An examination of these functions in the OSHA context reveals that the inspection warrant adds little to the protections already afforded by the statute and pertinent regulations, and the slight additional benefit it might provide is insufficient to identify a constitutional violation or to justify overriding Congress' judgment that the power to conduct warrantless inspections is essential. . . . Congress has determined that industrial safety is an urgent federal interest requiring regulation and supervision, and further, that warrantless inspections are necessary to accomplish the safety goals of the legislation. While one may question the wisdom of pervasive governmental oversight of industrial life, I decline to question Congress' judgment that the inspection power is a necessary enforcement device in achieving the goals of a valid exercise of regulatory power.

I respectfully dissent.

NOTES AND QUESTIONS

1. *The warrant requirement.* The Fourth Amendment to the Constitution has historically restricted the government's right to conduct searches of private property. Absent consent or exigent circumstances, the government must obtain a warrant to conduct a search or effect an arrest in a private home. *See, e.g.,* Steagald v. United States, 451 U.S. 204 (1981); Payton v. New York, 445 U.S. 573 (1980). The requirement of a warrant protects the citizen's interest in privacy by submitting decisions to inspect in individual cases to review by a disinterested party.

In Franks v. Maryland, 359 U.S. 360 (1959), however, the Supreme Court distinguished between searches to obtain criminal evidence or to effect an arrest and administrative searches to ensure compliance with regulatory statutes. In that case, a residential property owner was convicted for noncompliance with the city health inspector's warrantless search of his rat-infested home. The Court refused to extend the Fourth Amendment's protections to such administrative searches. It reasoned that, because the searches were conducted only in daylight and only if valid grounds for suspicion existed, the warrantless search caused "only the slightest restriction on [the resident's] claims of privacy." *Id.* at 367. The need for public health inspections to ensure the safety of the community outweighed the privacy interest involved.

The Supreme Court overruled *Franks* eight years later in Camara v. Municipal Court, 387 U.S. 523 (1967). As in *Franks,* the defendant refused to comply with the city's warrantless annual inspection of his private apartment. Rejecting the balancing of interests in *Franks,* the *Camara* Court concluded that the interest in privacy applies as fully to health inspections as to searches for evidence of criminal conduct. Thus, it held that municipal administrative officers may not inspect a private home without the owner's consent "unless [the inspection] has been authorized by a valid search warrant." In a companion case, See v. Seattle, 387 U.S. 541 (1967), the Court applied the *Camara* rule to administrative inspections of those portions of commercial premises that are closed to the public. See had been convicted for refusing to allow a fire inspector to enter his locked warehouse without a warrant. The Court overturned the conviction, concluding that the businessperson, like the homeowner, has a right to be free from warrantless searches.

Does *Barlow's* necessarily follow from *Camara* and *See?* Is the employer's privacy interest as strong in *Barlow's* as the homeowner's in *Camara* or the warehouseman's in *See?*

2. *Probable cause and programmed searches.* While subjecting regulatory inspections to the warrant requirement, the *Camara* Court relaxed the "probable cause" requirement in the case of programmed or "areawide" searches. Did the Court thus take away, with one hand, the protection that it had given with the other? What does the Court mean in *Barlow's* by a "general administrative plan . . . derived from neutral sources"?

In 1979, OSHA issued an instruction to its field offices outlining a complex and relatively mechanical method for scheduling programmed inspections (based on such factors as industrywide injury rates, geographic distribution, and number of employees). It provided, however, that area directors may "modify the selection [of targets] otherwise resulting" from use of this method for a variety of reasons, including the experience and qualifications of available inspectors, location of workplace, size of establishment, availability of testing equipment, weather, and inspection history of the firm. OSHA Instruction CPL 2.25, Dec. 6, 1978, CCH Empl. Safety & Health Guide, ¶11560 (1979). Does this "administrative plan" satisfy the Court's test?

3. *"Pervasively regulated" industries.* In *See,* the Court "expressly reserved the question whether warrants should be required where inspectors monitor compliance with the terms of a government-issued license." In Colonnade Catering Corp. v. United States, 397 U.S. 72 (1970), the Court, for the first time, confronted that question. The Court upheld a statute permitting federal inspection of a liquor dealer holding a federal retail liquor dealer's occupational tax stamp, even though it did not require the government to obtain a warrant before demanding entry. Since the liquor industry has "long been subject to close supervision and inspection," the Court reasoned, "Congress has broad authority to fashion standards of reasonableness for searches and seizures." 397 U.S. at 77. Congress first authorized warrantless searches of liquor dealers in 1791, during the same session that the Fourth Amendment was adopted. Consequently, the Court concluded, Congress "did not regard searches and seizures of this kind as 'unreasonable.'" *Id.* at 76, *quoting* Boyd v. United States, 116 U.S. 616, 623 (1886). The Court has subsequently applied the *Colonnade* doctrine to such "pervasively regulated industries" as the sale of firearms, United States

v. Biswell, 406 U.S. 311 (1972); coal mining, Donovan v. Dewey, 452 U.S. 594 (1981); and even junkyards, New York v. Burger, 482 U.S. 691 (1987).

More recently, however, the Court has signaled a reluctance to expand the warrant exception announced in the *Colonnade-Burger* line of cases. In City of Los Angeles v. Patel, 135 S. Ct. 2443 (2015), the Court applied the *Camara-Barlow's* doctrine to strike down a Los Angeles city ordinance requiring operators of hotels to maintain guest registries that "shall be made available to any officer of the Los Angeles Police Department for inspection . . . at a time and in a manner that minimizes any interference with the operation of the business." In a 5-4 decision authored by Justice Sotomayor, the Court ruled that the ordinance was facially invalid under the Fourth Amendment because it did not give hotel operators a procedure for "precompliance review before a neutral decisionmaker." The Court suggested that the ordinance could be salvaged by authorizing police officers to issue an administrative subpoena, which could then be challenged by the hotel operator before an administrative law judge. The Court considered and rejected the argument that hotels are a pervasively regulated industry, and therefore exempt from the warrant requirement under the *Colonnade-Burger* line of cases, a position strenuously argued by Justice Scalia (joined by Chief Justice Roberts and Justice Thomas) in dissent. The Court reasoned that "nothing inherent in the operation of hotels poses a clear and significant risk to the public welfare," 135 S. Ct., at 2455, suggesting that the category of closely regulated businesses should be limited to such circumstances. Without such a limitation, the Court feared that "what has always been a narrow exception [would] swallow the rule" prohibiting warrantless searches. *Id.* at 2456. Do you agree that what firearms dealers, coal mines, alcohol sellers, and junkyards have in common is that they "pose[] a significant risk to the public welfare"? Are many other industries likely to satisfy that requirement?

b.   Compulsory Production of Information

A second common method of obtaining information useful in enforcement is to issue an order (a subpoena) requiring a private party to produce testimonial or documentary evidence within its possession. Today, most federal regulatory statutes contain provisions authorizing agencies to issue subpoenas, enforceable through the courts. The relevant provision of the OSH Act is typical:

> In making his inspections and investigations under this chapter the Secretary may require the attendance and testimony of witnesses and the production of evidence under oath. Witnesses shall be paid the same fees and mileage that are paid witnesses in the courts of the United States. In case of a contumacy, failure, or refusal of any person to obey such an order, any district court of the United States or the United States courts of any territory or possession, within the jurisdiction of which such person is found, or resides or transacts business, upon the application by the Secretary, shall have jurisdiction to issue to such person an order requiring such person to appear to produce evidence if, as, and when so ordered, and to give testimony relating to the matter under investigation or in question, and any failure to obey such order of the court may be punished by said court as a contempt thereof.

29 U.S.C. §657(b) (1982).

Judicial acceptance of administrative authority to compel the production of information developed slowly. See, for example, In re Pacific Railway Commn. 32 F. 241 (C.C.N.D. Cal. 1887), where the court held that an agency, not being a judicial body, had no power to compel the production of evidence. To allow an agency to do so, the court held, would violate constitutionally protected rights of the subpoenaed party. In ICC v. Brimson, 154 U.S. 447 (1894), the Supreme Court upheld the power of the Interstate Commerce Commission to issue subpoenas but only because the statute required that they be enforced in the federal courts where the party subpoenaed was entitled to a de novo determination of the order's validity. Since only the Article III courts can punish for contempt, said the Court, only those courts can enforce a subpoena.

In the following years, the courts exercised their enforcement power rather parsimoniously. An example is the doctrine that administrative subpoenas could issue only where there was probable cause to believe that a violation of a law had occurred. In Harriman v. ICC, 211 U.S. 407 (1908), for example, the Court denied enforcement of an ICC subpoena on grounds that investigatory subpoenas could only issue after a violation of a statute had been alleged. A related limitation was the requirement that a subpoena describe the information to be produced with a high degree of specificity. As the Court said in denying enforcement to a Federal Trade Commission subpoena in FTC v. American Tobacco Co., 264 U.S. 298, 306 (1924), "It is contrary to the first principle of justice to allow a search through all the respondent's records, relevant or irrelevant, in the hope that something will turn up." A further limitation on agencies' use of the subpoena power was the Court's refusal, in Cudahy Packing Co. v. Holland, 315 U.S. 357 (1942), to allow an agency head to delegate his statutory power to issue subpoenas without express legislative authority.

The Court's attitude began to change the next year, however, with its decision in Endicott Johnson Corp. v. Perkins, 317 U.S. 501 (1943). A government contractor resisted a subpoena issued by the Labor Secretary under the Walsh-Healey Public Contracts Act, 49 Stat. 2036, on the ground that it sought information pertaining to plants not engaged in government work and thus outside the Secretary's jurisdiction. The district court agreed, but the Supreme Court reversed, saying that the district court should have deferred to the Secretary's determination of jurisdiction: "The evidence sought by the subpoena was not plainly incompetent or irrelevant to any lawful purpose of the Secretary. . . ." Id. at 509. Three years later, the Court eliminated the requirement of probable cause. Oklahoma Press Publishing Co. v. Walling, 327 U.S. 186 (1946). "The very purpose of the subpoena," said the Court, "is to discover and procure evidence, not to prove a pending charge or complaint, but upon which to make one if, in the Administrator's judgment, the facts thus discovered should justify doing so." Id. at 201.

The bar against subdelegating the subpoena power began to crumble in Fleming v. Mohawk Wrecking & Lumber Co., 331 U.S. 111 (1947), where the Court upheld the authority of the wartime Price Administrator to delegate authority to issue subpoenas to district directors. The enormous workload of the agency made it impossible for the Administrator personally to sign every subpoena. Finally, in United States v. Morton Salt Co., 338 U.S. 632 (1950), the Court significantly relaxed the specificity requirement of American Tobacco:

"Even if one were to regard the request for information in this case as caused by nothing more than official curiosity, nevertheless law-enforcing agencies have a legitimate right to satisfy themselves that corporate behavior is consistent with the law and the public interest." *Id.* at 652.

Modern courts still profess to recognize several sources of limitation on the subpoena power of agencies, but none of them are especially stringent. The Fourth Amendment imposes a general requirement of "reasonableness" on subpoenas. However, as the Court said in an oft-quoted passage from *Morton Salt*, that requirement is satisfied if "the inquiry is within the authority of the agency, the demand is not too indefinite and information sought is reasonably relevant." 338 U.S. at 652. Recent efforts to persuade courts to apply more rigorous Fourth Amendment standards to subpoena enforcement have failed. *See* United States v. Sturm, Ruger & Co., Inc., 84 F.3d 1 (1st Cir.), *cert. denied*, 519 U.S. 991 (1996) (subpoena enforcement is not equivalent to an inspection or other administrative search for purposes of Fourth Amendment analysis). In *Sturm*, the First Circuit also declined to examine closely whether the information requested in the subpoena could lead to action within the agency's power to regulate: "We have repeatedly admonished that questions concerning the agency's substantive authority to regulate are not to be resolved in subpoena enforcement proceedings." 84 F.3d at 5. The court went on to find that the information requested by the subpoena was within the agency's mission, broadly conceived, and thus the subpoena was enforceable.

Only rarely do courts refuse to enforce administrative subpoenas as "unreasonable." An example is Dow Chemical Co. v. Allen, 672 F.2d 1262 (7th Cir. 1982), in which the Court denied enforcement of subpoenas issued by the EPA to compel University of Wisconsin researchers to disclose the results of all of their research relating to the effects of certain herbicides on animals. An administrative law judge had issued the subpoena at the request of the Dow Chemical Company, which was the respondent in a hearing to cancel its registration for the manufacture of herbicides. Requiring the researchers to turn voluminous information over to third parties whose interests were antithetical to theirs would, the court held, substantially impede university research and have a chilling effect on academic freedom. The fact that the subjects of the subpoenas were not parties to the investigation, while not decisive, also weighed against compelling disclosure. *See also* Commodity Futures Trading Commission v. Collins, 997 F.2d 1230 (7th Cir. 1993) (district court abused its discretion by enforcing an agency subpoena of an individual's tax returns because requiring disclosure of tax returns would undercut the policy of voluntary compliance with tax laws); Jack W. Campbell, Note, Revoking the "Fishing License": Recent Decisions Place Unwarranted Restrictions on Administrative Agencies' Power to Subpoena Personal Financial Records, 49 Vand. L. Rev. 395 (1996).

The Supreme Court's decision in University of Pennsylvania v. Equal Employment Opportunity Commission, 493 U.S. 182 (1990), illustrates how unusual the result in *Dow Chemical* was. While investigating charges of discrimination by the University of Pennsylvania, the EEOC had subpoenaed faculty peer review evaluations used in the University's tenure process. The University resisted disclosure of these evaluations, claiming that their availability would make it difficult to secure honest appraisals from faculty members during tenure reviews and would chill academic freedom. Given these considerations, the University argued, the EEOC at a minimum should be required to make a showing of the specific reason for belief that disclosure of this information is necessary, rather than rely on the general assertion of relevance to the administrative inquiry. A unanimous Supreme Court rejected the University's arguments. Justice Harry Blackmun, writing for the Court, stated that where an agency, such as the EEOC, has a general statutory subpoena power in aid of an investigative mission, the courts should ask only if the material requested appears relevant, if the request is sufficiently definite to identify the information to be produced, and if grounds exist for particular distrust of the bona fides of the request.

Like judicial subpoenas, administrative subpoenas may not require disclosure of privileged information, but the principal sources of legal privilege have only limited application in the regulatory context. The attorney-client privilege, for instance, applies only to communications made in confidence, while the attorney was acting in a professional capacity, and for purposes of obtaining legal assistance. The Fifth Amendment's privilege against self-incrimination protects only individuals (not corporations) and only against compelled production of testimonial evidence. *See* Fisher v. United States, 425 U.S. 391 (1976); Bellis v. United States, 417 U.S. 85 (1974).

One vestige of *Brimson* and other early subpoena cases is the requirement that agencies must have explicit statutory authority to issue subpoenas. Agencies have no inherent or implied power to do so. While Congress usually couches its delegations of investigative powers in very broad terms, it does not always confer authority reaching to the constitutional limits. The EEOC, for instance, may issue subpoenas only after a specific "charge" of discrimination has been filed in writing. 42 U.S.C. §2000e-8(a). Yet the courts have been quite generous to the agencies in interpreting more limited grants of authority. *See, e.g.,* EEOC v. Shell Oil Co., 466 U.S. 54 (1984), broadly interpreting the term "charge" in 42 U.S.C. §2000e-8(a). In another case involving an EEOC subpoena, the Supreme Court made clear that district court decisions on whether to enforce an agency subpoena are subject to appellate review only for "abuse of discretion." *See* McLane Co., Inc. v. EEOC, 137 S. Ct. 1159 (2017).

c.   Record-Keeping Requirements

As devices for monitoring regulated behavior, physical inspections and subpoenas *duces tecum* have one obvious limitation: they can be used to obtain access only to information that already exists. One cannot inspect or subpoena information that does not exist or that does not exist in a form that is readily usable. One widely utilized tactic for overcoming this problem is to require regulated parties to maintain certain records concerning their regulated activities. The Internal Revenue Service, for example, requires taxpayers to retain information documenting deductions that they have claimed and requires employers to prepare reports on wages paid to their employees.

While record-keeping requirements impose burdens on their addressees similar to those imposed by inspections and subpoenas, they require regulated parties to participate in policing their own behavior to a greater degree than the other two instruments of surveillance. The regulatory target must, in effect, create and maintain the instruments of his own potential condemnation. Consequently, regulatory record-keeping requirements have sometimes been attacked under the Fifth Amendment's privilege against self-incrimination.

As in the case of investigatory subpoenas, the Supreme Court has held that the Fifth Amendment does not apply to records that organizations are required to keep. Bellis v. United States, 417 U.S. 85 (1974). *But see* Note, Organizational Papers and the Privilege Against Self-Incrimination, 99 Harv. L. Rev. 640 (1986) (criticizing the rule). Although individuals are accorded greater constitutional protection against compelled record-keeping requirements, they still face heavy obstacles, as is illustrated in the leading case of Shapiro v. United States, 335 U.S. 1 (1948). Pursuant to the Emergency Price Control Act of 1942, 56 Stat. 23, the government required dealers in commodities to keep and preserve records of sales and to make those records available for government inspection. Shapiro, the proprietor of an unincorporated grocery business, challenged the requirement on Fifth Amendment grounds. The Supreme Court rejected Shapiro's claim. After finding the requirement to be a reasonable exercise of Congress's undeniable constitutional authority to prescribe commodity prices as a war-time measure, the Court concluded that the requirement did not exceed the limits on compelled record-keeping imposed by the Self-Incrimination Clause: "the privilege which exists as to private papers cannot be maintained in relation to 'records required by law to be kept in order that there may be suitable information of transactions which are the appropriate subjects of governmental regulation and the enforcement of restrictions validly established.'" *Id.* at 33, *quoting* Davis v. United States, 328 U.S. 582, 589-590 (1946).

Marchetti v. United States, 390 U.S. 39 (1968), illustrates the rare case in which a record-keeping requirement has been held to exceed constitutional limits. Marchetti had been prosecuted for failing to register with the IRS and to file reports relating to an occupational tax imposed on those engaged in the business of accepting wagers. The information in these reports, Marchetti claimed, could subject him to prosecution under state and federal gambling laws. The Supreme Court upheld his challenge. The Court distinguished *Shapiro* on grounds that in *Marchetti* the records were not "of the same kind as he has customarily kept" and were required from a "selective group inherently suspect of criminal activities." *Id.* at 57.

Reporting requirements imposed by agencies must, of course, be grounded in some source of statutory authority, but most agencies have explicit statutory authority to require the creation of records, and courts have tended to interpret ambiguous mandates quite generously. Section 6(b) of the Federal Trade Commission Act allows the FTC to "require, by general or special orders, persons, partnerships, and corporations, engaged in or whose business affects commerce, . . . to file with the Commission in such form as the Commission may prescribe annual or special reports or answers in writing to specific questions." 15 U.S.C. §46(b). In In re FTC Line of Business Report Litigation, 595 F.2d 685 (D.C. Cir. 1978), the D.C. Circuit broadly construed the FTC's power under this statute. The FTC had required large business enterprises to report business statistics on a "line of business" basis. This required the conglomerates to break down and segregate the records and reports of each type of business in which they were engaged. These FTC demands were strongly challenged as imposing added expenses without providing useful business information. The D.C.

Circuit upheld the commission's requirements in all respects, holding that the information was relevant to a lawful agency purpose, and that the corporations had failed to establish undue burdens or excessive costs.

So long, then, as a regulatory agency seeks merely to obtain information for determining the extent of compliance with its substantive command, it is unlikely to encounter serious statutory or constitutional obstacles. A different and more difficult question may be presented, however, when the agency seeks to use the information it obtained in ways that go beyond enforcement against the subjects of that information. Such a problem is presented in the following case.

RUCKELSHAUS v. MONSANTO CO.
467 U.S. 986 (1984)

JUSTICE BLACKMUN delivered the opinion of the Court.

In this case, we are asked to review a United States District Court's determination that several provisions of the Federal Insecticide, Fungicide, and Rodenticide Act (FIFRA), 61 Stat. 163, as amended, 7 U.S.C. §136 *et seq.*, are unconstitutional. The provisions at issue authorize the Environmental Protection Agency (EPA) to use data submitted by an applicant for registration of a pesticide in evaluating the application of a subsequent applicant, and to disclose publicly some of the submitted data.

I

... Although the Federal Government has regulated pesticide use for nearly 75 years, FIFRA was first adopted in 1947. 61 Stat. 163.

As first enacted, FIFRA was primarily a licensing and labeling statute. ...

Because of mounting public concern about the safety of pesticides and their effect on the environment and because of a growing perception that the existing legislation was not equal to the task of safeguarding the public interest, ... Congress undertook a comprehensive revision of FIFRA through the adoption of the Federal Environmental Pesticide Control Act of 1972, 86 Stat. 973. The amendments transformed FIFRA from a labeling law into a comprehensive regulatory statute. ... As amended, FIFRA regulated the use, as well as the sale and labeling, of pesticides; regulated pesticides produced and sold in both intrastate and interstate commerce; provided for review, cancellation, and suspension of registration; and gave EPA greater enforcement authority. Congress also added a new criterion for registration: that EPA determine that the pesticide will not cause "unreasonable adverse effects on the environment." §§3(c)(5)(C) and (D), 86 Stat. 980-981.

For purposes of this litigation, the most significant of the 1972 amendments pertained to the pesticide-registration procedure and the public disclosure of information learned through that procedure. Congress added to FIFRA a new section governing public disclosure of data submitted in support of an application for registration. [§10.]

The 1972 amendments also included a provision that allowed EPA to consider data submitted by one applicant for registration in support of another application pertaining to a similar chemical, provided the subsequent applicant offered to compensate the applicant who originally submitted the data. §3(c)(1)(D).

[A]ny data designated as "trade secrets or commercial or financial information" [however, was] exempt from disclosure under §10 [and] could not be considered at all by EPA to support another registration application unless the original submitter consented. . . .

Under FIFRA, as amended in 1978, applicants are granted a 10-year period of exclusive use for data on new active ingredients contained in pesticides registered after September 30, 1978. §3(c)(1)(D)(i). All other data submitted after December 31, 1969, may be cited and considered in support of another application for 15 years after the original submission if the applicant offers to compensate the original submitter. §3(c)(1)(D)(ii). If the parties cannot agree on the amount of compensation, either may initiate a binding arbitration proceeding. The results of the arbitration proceeding are not subject to judicial review, absent fraud or misrepresentation. The same statute provides that an original submitter who refuses to participate in negotiations or in the arbitration proceeding forfeits his claim for compensation. Data that do not qualify for either the 10-year period of exclusive use or the 15-year period of compensation may be considered by EPA without limitation. §3(c)(1)(D)(iii).

Also in 1978, Congress added a new subsection, §10(d), 7 U.S.C. §136h(d), that provides for disclosure of all health, safety, and environmental data to qualified requesters, notwithstanding the prohibition against disclosure of trade secrets contained in §10(b). The provision, however, does not authorize disclosure of information that would reveal "manufacturing or quality control processes" or certain details about deliberately added inert ingredients unless "the Administrator has first determined that the disclosure is necessary to protect against an unreasonable risk of injury to health or the environment." §§10(d)(1)(A) to (C). . . .

II

Appellee Monsanto Company (Monsanto) . . . is one of a relatively small group of companies that invent and develop new active ingredients for pesticides and conduct most of the research and testing with respect to those ingredients.

These active ingredients are sometimes referred to as "manufacturing-use products" because they are not generally sold directly to users of pesticides. Rather, they must first be combined with "inert ingredients"—chemicals that dissolve, dilute, or stabilize the active components. The results of this process are sometimes called "end-use products," and the firms that produce end-use products are called "formulators." . . . Monsanto produces both active ingredients and end-use products. . . .

The District Court found that development of a potential commercial pesticide candidate typically requires the expenditure of $5 million to $15 million annually for several years. The development process may take between 14 and 22 years, and it is usually that long before a company can expect any return on its investment. . . . For every manufacturing-use pesticide the average company finally markets, it will have screened and tested 20,000 others. Monsanto has a significantly better-than-average success rate; it successfully markets one out of every 10,000 chemicals tested. . . .

Monsanto, like any other applicant for registration of a pesticide, must present research and test data supporting its application. The District Court found that Monsanto had incurred costs in excess of $23.6 million in developing the health, safety, and environmental data submitted by it under FIFRA. . . .

Monsanto brought suit in District Court, seeking injunctive and declaratory relief from the operation of the data-consideration provisions of FIFRA's §3(c)(1)(D), and the data-disclosure provisions of FIFRA's §10 and the related §3(c)(2)(A). Monsanto alleged that all of the challenged provisions effected a "taking" of property without just compensation, in violation of the Fifth Amendment. In addition, Monsanto alleged that the data-consideration provisions violated the Amendment because they effected a taking of property for a private, rather than a public, purpose. . . .

After a bench trial, the District Court concluded that . . . operation of the disclosure provisions of FIFRA constituted a taking of Monsanto's property [and] that the compulsory binding-arbitration scheme set forth in §3(c)(1)(D)(ii) did not adequately provide compensation for the property taken. . . . Finally, the court found that a remedy under the Tucker Act was not available for the deprivations of property effected by §§3 and 10.

The District Court therefore declared §§3(c)(1)(D), 3(c)(2)(A), 10(b), and 10(d) of FIFRA, as amended by the Federal Pesticide Act of 1978, to be unconstitutional, and permanently enjoined EPA from implementing or enforcing those sections. . . .

III

In deciding this case, we are faced with four questions: (1) Does Monsanto have a property interest protected by the Fifth Amendment's Taking Clause in the health, safety, and environmental data it has submitted to EPA? (2) If so, does EPA's use of the data to evaluate the applications of others or EPA's disclosure of the data to qualified members of the public effect a taking of that property interest? (3) If there is a taking, is it a taking for a public use? (4) If there is a taking for a public use, does the statute adequately provide for just compensation? . . .

This Court never has squarely addressed the applicability of the protections of the Taking Clause of the Fifth Amendment to commercial data of the kind involved in this case. In answering the question now, we are mindful of the basic axiom that "'[p]roperty interests . . . are not created by the Constitution. Rather, they are created and their dimensions are defined by existing rules or understandings that stem from an independent source such as state law.'" Webb's Fabulous Pharmacies, Inc. v. Beckwith, 449 U.S. 155 (1980), *quoting* Board of Regents v. Roth, 408 U.S. 564, 577 (1972). Monsanto asserts that the health, safety, and environmental data it has submitted to EPA are property under Missouri law, which recognizes trade secrets, as defined in §757, Comment *b*, of the Restatement of Torts, as property. . . . The Restatement defines a trade secret as "any formula, pattern, device or compilation of information which is used in one's business, and which gives him an opportunity to obtain an advantage over competitors who do not know or use it." §757, Comment *b*. And the parties have stipulated that much of the information, research, and test data that Monsanto has submitted under FIFRA to EPA "contains or relates to trade secrets as defined by the Restatement of Torts." . . . Trade secrets have many of the characteristics of more tangible forms of property. A trade secret is assignable. . . . A trade secret can form the res of a trust, . . . and it passes to a trustee in bankruptcy. . . . Even the manner in which Congress referred to trade secrets in the legislative history of FIFRA supports the general perception of their property-like nature. In discussing the 1978 amendments to FIFRA, Congress recognized that data developers like Monsanto have a "proprietary interest" in their data. S. Rep. No. 95-334, at 31. Further, Congress reasoned that submitters of data are "entitled" to "compensation" because they "have legal ownership of their data." H.R. Conf. Rep. No. 95-1560, p.29 (1978), U.S. Code Cong. & Admin. News 1978, pp.1966, 2045. This general perception of trade secrets as property is consonant with a notion of "property" that extends beyond land and tangible goods and includes the products of an individual's "labour and invention." 2 W. Blackstone, Commentaries *405; *see generally* J. Locke, The Second Treatise of Civil Government, ch. 5 (J. Gough ed. 1947). . . .

We therefore hold that to the extent that Monsanto has an interest in its health, safety, and environmental data cognizable as a trade-secret property right under Missouri law, that property right is protected by the Taking Clause of the Fifth Amendment.

IV

Having determined that Monsanto has a property interest in the data it has submitted to EPA, we confront the difficult question whether a "taking" will occur when EPA discloses that data or considers the data in evaluating another application, for registration. . . . The inquiry into whether a taking has occurred is essentially an "ad hoc, factual" inquiry. . . . The Court, however, has identified several factors that should be taken into account when determining whether a governmental action has gone beyond "regulation" and effects a "taking." Among those factors are: "the character of the governmental action, its economic impact, and its interference with reasonable investment-backed expectations." PruneYard Shopping Center v. Robins, 447 U.S. [74, 83 (1980)]. It is to the last of these three factors that we now direct our attention, for we find that the force of this factor is so overwhelming, at least with respect to certain of the data submitted by Monsanto to EPA, that it disposes of the taking question regarding that data.

A

A "reasonable investment-backed expectation" must be more than a "unilateral expectation or an abstract need." *Webb's Fabulous Pharmacies*, 449 U.S., at 161. We find that with respect to any health, safety, and environmental data that Monsanto submitted to EPA after the effective date of the 1978 FIFRA amendments—that is, on or after October 1, 1978—Monsanto could not have had a reasonable, investment-backed expectation that EPA would keep the data confidential beyond the limits prescribed in the amended statute itself. Monsanto was on notice of the manner in which EPA was authorized to use and disclose any data turned over to it by an applicant for registration.

Thus, with respect to any data submitted to EPA on or after October 1, 1978, Monsanto knew that, for a period of 10 years from the date of submission, EPA would not consider that data in evaluating the application of another without Monsanto's permission. §3(c)(1)(D)(i). It was also aware, however, that once the 10-year period had expired, EPA could use the data without Monsanto's permission. §§3(c)(1)(D)(ii) and (iii). Monsanto was further aware that it was entitled to an offer of compensation from the subsequent applicant only until the end of the fifteenth year from the date of submission. §3(c)(1)(D)(iii). In addition, Monsanto was aware that information relating to formulae of products could be revealed by EPA to "any Federal agency consulted and [could] be revealed at a public hearing or in findings of fact" issued by EPA "when necessary to carry out" EPA's duties under FIFRA. §10(b). The statute also gave Monsanto notice that much of the health, safety, and efficacy data provided by it could be disclosed to the general public at any time. §10(d). If, despite the data-consideration and data-disclosure provisions in the statute, Monsanto chose to submit the requisite data in order to receive a registration, it can hardly argue that its reasonable investment-backed expectations are disturbed when EPA acts to use or disclose the data in a manner that was authorized by law at the time of the submission.

Monsanto argues that the statute's requirement that a submitter give up its property interest in the data constitutes placing an unconstitutional condition on the right to a valuable government benefit. *See* Brief for Appellee 29. But Monsanto has not challenged the ability of the Federal Government to regulate the marketing and use of pesticides. Nor could Monsanto successfully make such a challenge . . . in an area, such as pesticide sale and use, that has long been the source of public concern and the subject of government regulation. That Monsanto is willing to bear this burden in exchange for the ability to market pesticides in this country is evidenced by the fact that it has continued to expand its research and development and to submit data to EPA despite the enactment of the 1978 amendments to FIFRA.[11] . . .

B

Prior to the 1972 amendments, FIFRA was silent with respect to EPA's authorized use and disclosure of data submitted to it in connection with an application for registration. Another statute, the Trade Secrets Act, 18 U.S.C. §1905, however, arguably is relevant. That Act is a general criminal statute that provides a penalty for any employee of the United States Government who discloses, in a manner not authorized by law, any trade secret information that is

---

11. Because the market for Monsanto's pesticide products is an international one, Monsanto could decide to forgo registration in the United States and sell a pesticide only in foreign markets. Presumably, it will do so in those situations where it deems the data to be protected from disclosure more valuable than the right to sell in the United States.

revealed to him during the course of his official duties. This Court has determined that §1905 is more than an "anti-leak" statute aimed at deterring government employees from profiting by information they receive in their official capacities. *See* Chrysler Corp. v. Brown, 441 U.S. 281, 298-301 (1979). Rather, §1905 also applies to formal agency action, i.e., action approved by the agency or department head. *Ibid.*

It is true that, prior to the 1972 amendments, neither FIFRA nor any other provision of law gave EPA authority to disclose data obtained from Monsanto. But the Trade Secrets Act is not a guarantee of confidentiality to submitters of data, and, absent an express promise, Monsanto had no reasonable, investment-backed expectation that its information would remain inviolate in the hands of EPA. In an industry that long has been the focus of great public concern and significant government regulation, the possibility was substantial that the Federal Government, which had thus far taken no position on disclosure of health, safety, and environmental data concerning pesticides, upon focusing on the issue, would find disclosure to be in the public interest. Thus, with respect to data submitted to EPA in connection with an application for registration prior to October 22, 1972, the Trade Secrets Act provided no basis for a reasonable investment-backed expectation that data submitted to EPA would remain confidential.

A fortiori, the Trade Secrets Act cannot be construed as any sort of assurance against internal agency use of submitted data during consideration of the application of a subsequent applicant for registration.[13] Indeed, there is some evidence that the practice of using data submitted by one company during consideration of the application of a subsequent applicant was widespread and well known. Thus, with respect to any data that Monsanto submitted to EPA prior to the effective date of the 1972 amendments to FIFRA, we hold that Monsanto could not have had a "reasonable investment-backed expectation" that EPA would maintain that data in strictest confidence and would use it exclusively for the purpose of considering the Monsanto application in connection with which the data were submitted.

C

The situation may be different, however, with respect to data submitted by Monsanto to EPA during the period from October 22, 1972, through September 30, 1978. Under the statutory scheme then in effect, a submitter was given an opportunity to protect its trade secrets from disclosure by designating them as trade secrets at the time of submission. . . . Thus, with respect to trade secrets submitted under the statutory regime in force between the time of the adoption of the 1972 amendments and the adoption of the 1978 amendments, the Federal Government had explicitly guaranteed to Monsanto and other registration applicants an extensive measure of confidentiality and exclusive use. . . .

---

13. The Trade Secrets Act prohibits a government employee from "publish[ing], divulg[ing], disclos[ing] or mak[ing] known confidential information received in his official capacity." 18 U.S.C. §1905. In considering the data of one applicant in connection with the application of another, EPA does not violate any of these prohibitions.

With respect to a trade secret, the right to exclude others is central to the very definition of the property interest. Once the data that constitutes a trade secret is disclosed to others, or others are allowed to use that data, the holder of the trade secret has lost his property interest in the data.[15] That the data retain usefulness for Monsanto even after they are disclosed—for example, as bases from which to develop new products or refine old products, as marketing and advertising tools, or as information necessary to obtain registration in foreign countries—is irrelevant to the determination of the economic impact of the EPA action on Monsanto's property right. The economic value of that property right lies in the competitive advantage over others that Monsanto enjoys by virtue of its exclusive access to the data, and disclosure or use by others of the data would destroy that competitive edge. . . .

If a negotiation or arbitration pursuant to §3(c)(1)(D)(ii) were to yield just compensation to Monsanto for the loss in the market value of its trade-secret data suffered because of EPA's consideration of the data in connection with another application, then Monsanto would have no claim against the Government for a taking. Since no arbitration has yet occurred with respect to any use of Monsanto's data, any finding that there has been an actual taking would be premature. . . .

In summary, we hold that . . . EPA consideration or disclosure of health, safety, and environmental data will constitute a taking if Monsanto submitted the data to EPA between October 22, 1972, and September 30, 1978; the data constituted trade secrets under Missouri law; Monsanto had designated the data as trade secrets at the time of its submission; the use or disclosure conflicts with the explicit assurance of confidentiality or exclusive use contained in the statute during that period; and the operation of the arbitration provision does not adequately compensate for the loss in market value of the data that Monsanto suffers because of EPA's use or disclosure of the trade secrets.

V

We must next consider whether any taking of private property that may occur by operation of the data-disclosure and data-consideration provisions of FIFRA is a taking for a "public use." We have recently stated that the scope of the "public use" requirement of the Taking Clause is "coterminous with the scope of a sovereign's police powers." Hawaii Housing Authority v. Midkiff, 467 U.S. 229, 240 (1984); see Berman v. Parker, 348 U.S. 26 (1954). The role of the courts in second-guessing the legislature's judgment of what constitutes a public use is extremely narrow. . . .

The District Court found that EPA's action pursuant to the data-consideration provisions of FIFRA would effect a taking for a private use, rather than a

---

15. We emphasize that the value of a trade secret lies in the competitive advantage it gives its owner over competitors. Thus, it is the fact that operation of the data-consideration or data-disclosure provisions will allow a competitor to register more easily its product or to use the disclosed data to improve its own technology that may constitute a taking. If, however, a public disclosure of data reveals, for example, the harmful side effects of the submitter's product and causes the submitter to suffer a decline in the potential profits from sales of the product, that decline in profits stems from a decrease in the value of the pesticide to consumers, rather than from the destruction of an edge the submitter had over its competitors, and cannot constitute the taking of a trade secret.

public use, because such action benefits subsequent applicants by forcing original submitters to share their data with later applicants. . . . It is true that the most direct beneficiaries of EPA actions under the data-consideration provisions of FIFRA will be the later applicants who will support their applications by citation to data submitted by Monsanto or some other original submitter. Because of the data-consideration provisions, later applicants will not have to replicate the sometimes intensive and complex research necessary to produce the requisite data. This Court, however, has rejected the notion that a use is a public use only if the property taken is put to use for the general public. . . . Here, the public purpose behind the data-consideration provision is clear from the legislative history. Congress believed that the provisions would eliminate costly duplication of research and streamline the registration process, making new end-use products available to consumers more quickly. Allowing applicants for registration, upon payment of compensation, to use data already accumulated by others, rather than forcing them to go through the time-consuming process of repeating the research, would eliminate a significant barrier to entry into the pesticide market, thereby allowing greater competition among producers of end-use products. . . .

Because the data-disclosure provisions of FIFRA provide for disclosure to the general public, the District Court did not find that those provisions constituted a taking for a private use. Instead, the court found that the data-disclosure provisions served no use. It reasoned that because EPA, before registration, must determine that a product is safe and effective, and because the label on a pesticide, by statute, must set forth the nature, contents, and purpose of the pesticide, the label provided the public with all the assurance it needed that the product is safe and effective. . . . It is enough for us to state that the optimum amount of disclosure to the public is for Congress, not the courts, to decide, and that the statute embodies Congress' judgment on that question. *See* 123 Cong. Rec., at 25756 (remarks of Sen. Leahy). We further observe, however, that public disclosure can provide an effective check on the decisionmaking processes of EPA and allows members of the public to determine the likelihood of individualized risks peculiar to their use of the product. . . .

VI

Equitable relief is not available to enjoin an alleged taking of private property for a public use, duly authorized by law, when a suit for compensation can be brought against the sovereign subsequent to the taking. Larson v. Domestic & Foreign Commerce Corp., 337 U.S. 682, 697, n.18 (1949). The Fifth Amendment does not require that compensation precede the taking. Hurley v. Kincaid, 285 U.S. 95, 104 (1932). Generally, an individual claiming that the United States has taken his property can seek just compensation under the Tucker Act, 28 U.S.C. §1491.[20] . . .

20. The Tucker Act, 28 U.S.C. §1491, reads, in relevant part: "The United States Claims Court shall have jurisdiction to render judgment upon any claim against the United States founded either upon the Constitution, or any Act of Congress, or any regulation of an executive department, or upon any express or implied contract with the United States, or for liquidated or unliquidated damages in cases not sounding in tort."

[The Court found nothing in FIFRA or its legislative history to suggest that the Tucker Act remedy should not be available.]

VII

Because we hold that the Tucker Act is available as a remedy for any uncompensated taking Monsanto may suffer as a result of the operation of the challenged provisions of FIFRA, we conclude that Monsanto's challenges to the constitutionality of the arbitration and compensation scheme are not ripe for our resolution. . . . The judgment of the District Court is therefore vacated and the case is remanded for further proceedings consistent with this opinion.

It is so ordered.

JUSTICE WHITE took no part in the consideration or decision of this case.

JUSTICE O'CONNOR, concurring in part and dissenting in part. [Omitted.]

NOTES AND QUESTIONS

1. *Definition of "property."* Note that, in applying the Takings Clause of the Fifth Amendment, the Court uses the same definition of property as in the due process cases (*Roth* and its progeny, discussed in Chapter VI, *supra*). Since the two Clauses appear in the same amendment, that approach seems unexceptionable. Yet, by doing so, the Court risks falling into the same "positivist trap" that we encountered in those materials; namely, the prospect that a legislature can restrict or even nullify a constitutional right by redefining "property" rights. Is that not precisely what happened when Congress passed the 1978 Amendments to FIFRA? Or does Monsanto have a good Takings Clause claim even after 1978, since Missouri law still recognized trade secrets as a form of property?

2. *Investment-backed expectations.* Does the Court's analysis of Monsanto's claim regarding post-1978 submissions mean that Congress could refuse to provide any compensation for subsequent uses of the data? Is the Court correct in characterizing Monsanto as having been "willing" to surrender its data "in exchange for the ability to market pesticides in this country"? How convincing is the Court's argument that, prior to 1972, the Trade Secrets Act gave Monsanto "no reasonable, investment-backed expectation that its information would remain inviolate in the hands of the EPA"? Is the problem that the Trade Secrets Acts is not specific enough in its protection of pesticide data? Or that the Act provides no private right of action for its enforcement?

3. *Compensation and changes in the law.* Professor Louis Kaplow has argued that the government should not ordinarily provide compensation to persons whose investments are devalued by changes in the law. Louis Kaplow, An Economic Analysis of Legal Transitions, 99 Harv. L. Rev. 509 (1986). His reasoning is that market mechanisms for protecting investors against risk ex ante are more efficient than ex-post government compensation. Thus, for example, flood insurance is preferable to disaster relief because the former discourages uneconomic overdevelopment of flood plains. The same kinds of market mechanisms,

he argues, should be used to protect against losses occasioned by legal changes as those occasioned by, say, acts of God, technological changes, or changes in consumer tastes. Do you agree? Does this analysis apply to the *Monsanto* situation? Could Monsanto have adequately protected itself against losses resulting from the 1972 and 1978 Amendments to FIFRA?

2.   *Prosecution and Selective Enforcement*

Endemic to most forms of administrative enforcement is the discretion to select targets for the initiation of formal enforcement action and to choose the official action to be initiated. The scope of this "prosecutorial" discretion has long been a source of concern, in both criminal and civil enforcement. By deciding whether and whom to prosecute, prosecutors can harass disfavored groups or immunize favored groups; they can distort or even nullify the written law.

a.   Prosecutorial Incentives

According to prevailing wisdom, prosecutors are more likely to abuse this discretion by underenforcing the law's commands than overenforcing them. *See, e.g.,* Gary Becker & George Stigler, Law Enforcement, Malfeasance, and Compensation of Enforcers, 3 J. Legal Stud. 1 (1974); William M. Landes & Richard A. Posner, The Private Enforcement of Law, 4 J. Legal Stud. 1 (1975). Erroneous or malicious prosecution will usually be challenged by the person prosecuted, whereas failures to enforce will rarely be noticed and still less frequently be challenged. What assumptions does this argument make about the motivations of enforcers? Should a distinction be drawn between elected and appointed enforcers? Would it matter whether enforcers are paid a fixed salary or a "commission"?

The police-patrol/fire alarm metaphor discussed in Chapter I, *supra,* may be relevant to understanding agency enforcement incentives. *See* Mathew D. McCubbins & Thomas Schwartz, Congressional Oversight Overlooked: Police Patrols Versus Fire Alarms, 2 Am. J. Pol. Sci. 165 (1984). Agencies may have little incentive to take action to enforce the law if no one is complaining, i.e., when no one has pulled an "alarm." Once someone does complain, agency officials are likely to weigh the benefits of enforcement, including professional advancement and satisfaction of ideological or policy goals, against its potential costs, including distraction from other activities and possible retribution (political, legal, or professional) from the subjects of enforcement. In many situations, inertia may work against vigorous enforcement.

Traditional legal doctrine has reinforced this asserted asymmetry of incentives. Judicial interpretation of the Due Process Clause and the procedural provisions of regulatory statutes give targets of enforcement actions generous procedural protections against ill-considered or ill-motivated prosecution. They can usually demand a full-scale evidentiary hearing prior to the imposition of any serious sanction. To be sure, the cost of exercising those rights undoubtedly discourages their use by some innocent respondents. But the prospect of incurring substantial litigation costs also discourages prosecutors from initiating unfounded actions.

Legal remedies for *failure* to prosecute, by contrast, have been much slower to develop. Until rather recently, specific statutory remedies for nonenforcement were almost unheard of; the typical criminal or regulatory statute provided merely that the appropriate official "may" bring an action to enforce its commands. Even when a grievant could invoke a more concrete limitation on a prosecutor's discretion, the courts often turned a deaf ear. In some cases, they interpreted facially mandatory provisions as permissive. More often, they invoked doctrines of standing, ripeness, immunity, or abstention to dismiss nonenforcement complaints for failing to state a justiciable controversy. In Linda R.S. v. Richard D., 410 U.S. 614 (1973), for example, the Supreme Court held that an unwed mother lacked standing to challenge a local prosecutor's failure to bring a criminal action for nonsupport against her child's absent father. The Justices found "speculative" the argument that criminal prosecution would prompt the father to make payments to the mother. After all, they observed, the penalty to be meted out upon conviction would be time in jail, not compensation to the mother. Similarly, in Rizzo v. Goode, 423 U.S. 362 (1976), the Court dismissed a class action against Philadelphia law enforcement officials brought by blacks alleging a systematic pattern of police harassment. While the courts can remedy concrete infringements of identified persons' constitutional rights, a claim of generalized discriminatory enforcement fails to present a justiciable controversy, said the Court.

Still, the courtroom door was never completely closed, and in recent decades the persistent efforts of litigants to pry it open began to pay off. Their success—limited though it has been—illustrates the willingness of some courts to transform administrative law from a system designed solely to protect the "private" rights of regulated industries to a system designed to protect the "public" rights of regulatory beneficiaries. *See* Richard B. Stewart & Cass R. Sunstein, Public Programs and Private Rights, 95 Harv. L. Rev. 1193 (1982). As discussed *infra*, Congress has also participated in these developments by building citizen suit provisions into some regulatory statutes. These provisions grant limited rights for private parties to bring actions to force regulators to perform nondiscretionary duties, sometimes including mandatory duties to regulate under certain narrow circumstances. In this section we examine discriminatory enforcement, and due process issues that arise when agencies aggressively enforce regulatory requirements.

b. Remedies for Selective Enforcement

The broader an agency's mandate, the more opportunities it has to exercise discretion in the choice of its enforcement targets. Few agencies can match the breadth of the Federal Trade Commission's potential enforcement authority. The FTC, as noted in Chapter IV, *supra*, is instructed to combat "unfair methods of competition" and "unfair or deceptive acts or practices," to police the labeling of furs and textiles, to prevent marketing of highly flammable fabrics, to ensure compliance with truth-in-lending requirements, trademark regulations, credit reporting rules, and federal warranty requirements, and it shares with the Department of Justice responsibility for enforcing the antitrust laws. Virtually all businesses come within the FTC's regulatory jurisdiction; and while the statutory directives may pass muster under the nondelegation doctrine, few are precise.

Given the range of potential enforcement targets, the FTC necessarily exercises considerable discretion in deciding where to look for violations of the various laws it enforces and when to prosecute. Not surprisingly, its enforcement policies have been the subject of a substantial body of critical commentary. *See* Gerald Henderson, The Federal Trade Commission: A Study in Administrative Law and Procedure (1924); Commission on Organization of the Executive Branch of the Government, Report (1955); Carl A. Auerbach, The Federal Trade Commission: Internal Organization and Procedure, 48 Minn. L. Rev. 383 (1964); Edward F. Cox et al., "The Nader Report" on the Federal Trade Commission (1969); The American Bar Association Commission to Study the Federal Trade Commission, Report (1969).

These studies of the agency, despite their wide separation by time and viewpoint, repeatedly cited the same three alleged deficiencies. First, they argued, enforcement was too passive. The FTC did not affirmatively seek out violations, but merely waited to see what complaints arrived in the mail. The "mailbag" generated a distorted sample of consumer problems, according to the Nader Report, because few consumers had an incentive to complain and most business firms preferred to go along with a pattern of deceptive practices rather than blow the whistle on a competitor. Second, the commission was accused of spending too much time on trivial cases. Rather than prosecute major violations by large corporations affecting thousands of consumers, it concentrated on technical offenses committed by small businesses. The Nader Report chastised the commission for devoting too many of its resources on small businesses located in upscale Washington, D.C., neighborhoods and suburbs where FTC staffers and members of Congress lived. The Report also took the FTC to task for worrying too much about protecting domestic producers against foreign competition in the fur and textile industries rather than, say, enforcing fabric flammability standards. Finally, the FTC was repeatedly accused of being too lenient. Instead of "throwing the book" at violators, it all too often accepted consent agreements in which the wrongdoer merely promised to sin no more. In this connection, the Nader Report was particularly critical of the FTC's shift from bringing cease-and-desist proceedings toward promulgating industry-wide trade regulation rules, discussed in connection with the *Petroleum Refiners* case, excerpted in Chapter IV, *supra.* Interestingly, the Nader Report characterized trade regulation rules as efforts to advise businesses on how far they can go without breaking the law, rather than as legitimate attempts by the FTC to combat deceptive practices.

The picture that emerges from this and other descriptions of FTC enforcement activity is that of an ill-trained watchdog, often asleep while the house is burglarized, unwilling to confront any dangerous thief, and perhaps placated by a bone from the fellow who is about to cart off the family jewels. But is that necessarily the only plausible explanation for the behavior described by the Nader Report? Is it possible that the behavior described constitutes a rational response to the limitations of information and resources faced by the agency? *See, e.g.,* Alan Stone, Economic Regulation and the Public Interest: The Federal Trade Commission in Theory and Practice 66-73 (1977), and Richard A. Posner, The Behavior of Administrative Agencies, 1 J. Legal Stud. 305 (1972). This view of the FTC enforcement effort is better captured by the metaphor of the spider at rest in its web rather than the watchdog asleep at its post. Can you spin out this argument? A third view, distinct from prevalent "incompetence" theories and the Stone-Posner efficient-management theories, explains the agency's enforcement pattern as a response to the dominant political forces. *See* Mary C. Mahaney & Adrian E. Tschoegl, The Determinants of FTC Antitrust Activity, 35 Admin. L. Rev. 1 (1983). Consider these criticisms in light of the FTC's recent settlement with Facebook (including imposition of a $5 billion penalty), for having violated a prior agreement to protect the privacy of consumer data. *See generally* https://www.ftc.gov/news-events/blogs/business-blog/2019/07/ftcs-5-billion-facebook-settlement-record-breaking-history.

Whatever the explanation for the FTC's general enforcement posture, discrimination in the selection of particular targets can have serious repercussions for the competitive marketplace that the FTC is supposed to foster. The costs imposed by FTC proceedings—including both the direct costs of contesting a threatened action and the burden of complying with an FTC order—can place a target at a serious disadvantage relative to its competitors. That fact may explain more than one aspect of FTC enforcement. (Look back to the list of criticisms. Do some seem less weighty when competitive impact is considered?) It also explains why complaints about selective prosecution may have a special appeal. The two cases that follow illustrate the judicial response.

MOOG INDUSTRIES, INC. v. FEDERAL TRADE COMMISSION
355 U.S. 411 (1958)

PER CURIAM.

The general question presented by these two cases is whether it is within the scope of the reviewing authority of a Court of Appeals to postpone the operation of a valid cease and desist order of the Federal Trade Commission against a single firm until similar orders have been entered against that firm's competitors. In proceedings arising out of alleged violations of the price discrimination provisions of the Clayton Act, §2, 38 Stat. 730, as amended by the Robinson-Patman Act, 49 Stat. 1526, 15 U.S.C. §13, two Courts of Appeals reached opposed results on this underlying issue. In order to resolve the conflict we granted certiorari, 353 U.S. 908, 982.

In No. 77, petitioner (Moog Industries, Inc.) was found by the Commission to have violated the Act and was ordered to cease and desist from further violation. 51 F.T.C. 931. Petitioner sought review in the United States Court of Appeals for the Eighth Circuit. Upon affirmance of the order, 238 F.2d 43, petitioner moved the court to hold the entry of judgment in abeyance on the ground that petitioner would suffer serious financial loss if prohibited from engaging in pricing practices open to its competitors. The court denied the requested relief.

In No. 110, respondent (C. E. Niehoff & Co.) requested the Commission to hold in abeyance the cease and desist order that had been recommended by the hearing examiner, on the ground that respondent would have to go out of business if compelled to sell at a uniform price while its competitors were not under similar restraint. The Commission found that respondent had violated the Act and, in issuing its order, denied respondent's request. 51 F.T.C. 1114, 1153. On review in the United States Court of Appeals for the Seventh Circuit, the Commission's determination of statutory violation was affirmed; however, the court (one judge dissenting) directed that the cease and desist order should take effect "at such time in the future as the United States Court of Appeals for the Seventh Circuit may direct, sua sponte or upon motion of the Federal Trade Commission." 241 F.2d 37, 43.

In view of the scope of administrative discretion that Congress has given the Federal Trade Commission, it is ordinarily not for courts to modify ancillary features of a valid Commission order. This is but recognition of the fact that in the shaping of its remedies within the framework of regulatory legislation, an agency is called upon to exercise its specialized, experienced judgment. Thus, the decision as to whether or not an order against one firm to cease and desist from engaging in illegal price discrimination should go into effect before others are similarly prohibited depends on a variety of factors peculiarly within the expert understanding of the Commission. Only the Commission, for example, is competent to make an initial determination as to whether and to what extent there is a relevant "industry" within which the particular respondent competes and whether or not the nature of that competition is such as to indicate identical treatment of the entire industry by an enforcement agency. Moreover, although an allegedly illegal practice may appear to be operative throughout an industry, whether such appearances reflect fact and whether all firms in the industry should be dealt with in a single proceeding or should receive individualized treatment are questions that call for discretionary determination by the administrative agency. It is clearly within the special competence of the Commission to appraise the adverse effect on competition that might result from postponing a particular order prohibiting continued violations of the law. Furthermore, the Commission alone is empowered to develop that enforcement policy best calculated to achieve the ends contemplated by Congress and to allocate its available funds and personnel in such a way as to execute its policy efficiently and economically.

The question, then, of whether orders such as those before us should be held in abeyance until the respondents' competitors are proceeded against is for the Commission to decide. If the question has not been raised before the Commission, as was the situation in No. 77, a reviewing court should not in any event entertain it. If the Commission has decided the question, its discretionary determination should not be overturned in the absence of a patent abuse of discretion. Accordingly, the judgment in No. 77 is affirmed, and the judgment in No. 110 is vacated and the cause remanded to the Court of Appeals with directions to affirm the order of the Commission in its entirety.

It is so ordered.

MR. JUSTICE WHITTAKER took no part in the consideration or decision of these cases.

FEDERAL TRADE COMMISSION v. UNIVERSAL-RUNDLE CORP.
387 U.S. 244 (1967)

MR. CHIEF JUSTICE WARREN delivered the opinion of the Court.

The question presented by this case is whether the Court of Appeals exceeded its authority as a reviewing court by postponing the operation of a

Federal Trade Commission cease-and-desist order against respondent until an investigation should be made of alleged industry-wide violations of the price discrimination provisions of the Clayton Act, §2, 38 Stat. 730, as amended by the Robinson-Patman Act, 49 Stat. 1526, 15 U.S.C. §13.

Respondent Universal-Rundle produces a full line of china and cast-iron plumbing fixtures which it sells to customers located throughout the United States. In 1960, the Federal Trade Commission issued a complaint charging that for more than three years Universal-Rundle's sales to some of these customers had been made "at substantially higher prices than the prices at which respondent sells such products of like grade and quality to other purchasers, some of whom are engaged in competition with the less favored purchasers in the resale of such products." The effect of the discriminations, the complaint alleged, "may be substantially to lessen competition" in violation of §2(a) of the Clayton Act, as amended. In its answer, Universal-Rundle denied the essential allegations of the complaint, and, in addition, asserted as affirmative defenses that such price differentials as may have existed were cost justified or were made "in good faith to meet competition."

After evidentiary hearings, in which Universal-Rundle made no effort to sustain its affirmative defenses, the Commission found that during 1957 Universal-Rundle had offered "truckload discounts" averaging approximately 10% to all of its customers. Because some of these customers could not afford to purchase in truckload quantities, and thus were unable to avail themselves of the discounts, the Commission held that the offering of the truckload discounts constituted price discrimination within the meaning of §2(a) of the Clayton Act, as amended. Since some Universal-Rundle customers who were able to purchase in truckload quantities were found to be in competition with customers unable to take advantage of the discounts, the Commission concluded that Universal-Rundle's price discrimination had the anticompetitive effect proscribed by §2(a). Accordingly, it ordered Universal-Rundle to refrain from:

> Discriminating in price by selling "Universal-Rundle" brand or Universal-Rundle manufactured plumbing fixtures . . . of like grade and quality to any purchaser at prices higher than those granted any other purchaser, where such other purchaser competes in fact with the unfavored purchaser in the resale or distribution of such products.

At no time during the four years in which the complaint was pending did Universal-Rundle offer the Commission any information as to its competitors' pricing practices or suggest that industry-wide proceedings might be appropriate. But one month after the issuance of the cease-and-desist order, Universal-Rundle petitioned the Commission to stay its cease-and-desist order for a time sufficient "to investigate and institute whatever proceedings are deemed appropriate by the Commission to correct the industry-wide practice by plumbing fixture manufacturers of granting discounts in prices on truckload shipments." In support of its petition, Universal-Rundle submitted affidavits and documents tending to show:

(1) that its principal competitors were offering truckload discounts averaging approximately 18%;

(2) that Universal-Rundle's share of the plumbing fixture market, exclusive of its sales to Sears, Roebuck and Co., was 5.75% whereas the five leading plumbing manufacturing concerns enjoyed market shares of 6 to 32%;[2]

(3) that each of these five competitors had reported profits within the preceding two years whereas Universal-Rundle had sustained substantial losses during each of the preceding three years.

In addition, Universal-Rundle submitted an affidavit in which its marketing vice president declared on information and belief that some of Universal-Rundle's competitors were selling to customers who "may not purchase in truckload quantities." The vice president further averred:

> That based upon his knowledge of the competitive conditions in this industry, if respondent is not permitted to sell plumbing fixtures with a differential in price as are its competitors on truckload and less than truckload quantities, respondent's sales of plumbing fixtures under the "U/R" brand will be substantially decreased and lost to its competitors, who continue to offer substantial discounts on truckload shipments. And he is of the further belief [that] the Company may suffer further substantial financial losses if it must be the sole plumbing fixture manufacturer under an order to cease and desist.

In a unanimous decision denying the petition for the stay, the Commission held that a general allegation that competitors were offering truckload discounts was not a sufficient basis for instituting industry-wide proceedings or for withholding enforcement of the cease-and-desist order. . . . While the granting of such discounts may result in price discriminations having proscribed anticompetitive effects, "the practice is not necessarily illegal as indicated in respondent's petition." In each case, it must be determined:

> whether the discount creates a price difference, whether the recipient of such a discount is competing at the same functional level with a customer paying a higher price, whether the customer buying in less than truckload quantities is able to avail itself of the truckload discount, and whether the differential is sufficient in the competitive conditions shown to exist to have the requisite anticompetitive effects. . . .

Following denial of its petition for a stay, Universal-Rundle instituted review proceedings in the Court of Appeals for the Seventh Circuit. Without reaching

---

2. According to respondent's petition for a stay, the shares enjoyed by its principal competitors were:

	Percent
American Radiator & Standard Sanitary Corp.	32
Kohler Co.	15
Eljer Division of the Murray Corp. of America	10
Crane Co.	9
Briggs Manufacturing Co.	6
Rheem Manufacturing Co.	5

the merits of the petition to set aside the cease-and-desist order, the court below set aside the Commission's order denying the stay and remanded the cause with instructions that the Commission conduct an industry investigation. 352 F.2d 831 (1965). The court conceded that under Moog Industries v. Federal Trade Commission, 355 U.S. 411 (1958), the Federal Trade Commission's discretionary determination to refuse to stay a cease-and-desist order "should not be overturned in the absence of a patent abuse of discretion." 355 U.S., at 414. But it considered that Universal-Rundle's evidentiary offering was sufficient to demonstrate that the refusal to grant the requested stay constituted a patent abuse of discretion. The premises upon which the court below based its conclusion may be briefly restated:

(1) "[i]t is apparent," the court wrote with reference to the evidentiary offering, "that the Commission has directed its attack against a general practice which is prevalent in the industry";
(2) enforcement would lead to the "sacrifice" of one of the "smallest participants" in the industry; and, consequently,
(3) approval of the enforcement sanctions would be contrary to the purposes of the Clayton Act since "the giants in the field would be the real benefactors—not the public."

In Moog Industries v. Federal Trade Commission, *supra*, we set forth the principles which must govern our review of the action taken by the court below. . . .

Viewed in the light of these principles, the decision below must be reversed. The evidence which Universal-Rundle offered in its petition for a stay is so inconclusive that it cannot be said that the Commission's evaluation of the evidence, and its consequent refusal to grant the stay, constituted a patent abuse of discretion. Indeed, Universal-Rundle's evidence does not even support the improper de novo findings which formed the basis for the Court of Appeals' decision. Universal-Rundle's truckload discounts were held to be illegal only because the corporation sold fixtures to one group of customers who were unable to purchase in truckload quantities while simultaneously selling fixtures at a discount to another group of customers who were in competition with the nonfavored group. Since the evidence presented in the petition for a stay did not tend to show that the discounts offered by Universal-Rundle's competitors had such an anticompetitive effect, there was no basis for a conclusion that the practice held illegal by the Commission was prevalent throughout the plumbing industry. Similarly, the unsupported speculation of Universal-Rundle's vice president as to the pecuniary effect of enforcement of the cease-and-desist order does not provide a sufficient basis for a finding that Universal-Rundle would be "sacrificed" or even that it would suffer substantial financial injury. It follows that Universal-Rundle has failed to demonstrate that enforcement would be contrary to the purposes of the Clayton Act.

We note that even if a petitioner succeeded in demonstrating to the Commission that all of its competitors were engaged in illegal price discrimination practices identical to its own, and that enforcement of a cease-and-desist order might cause it substantial financial injury, the Commission would not necessarily be obliged to withhold enforcement of the order. . . .

On the other hand, as the *Moog Industries* case also indicates, the Federal Trade Commission does not have unbridled power to institute proceedings which will arbitrarily destroy one of many law violators in an industry. This is not such a case. The Commission's refusal to withhold enforcement of the cease-and-desist order against respondent was based upon a reasonable evaluation of the merits of the petition for a stay; thus it was not within the scope of the reviewing authority of the court below to overthrow the Commission's determination. Consequently, we reverse the judgment below, set aside the stay, and remand the cause for further proceedings consistent with this opinion.

It is so ordered.

NOTES AND QUESTIONS

1. *Clayton Act requirements.* The applicable provision of the Clayton Act, as amended by the Robinson-Patman Act, generally prohibits the sale of similar goods at different prices. A Seller who offers grade B tires to Buyer 1 at $50 per tire and to Buyer 2 at $75 per tire violates this proscription, provided two conditions are met: the price discrimination must lessen competition, and it must not merely reflect differential costs. The former condition would be met if, for example, the Seller were offering Buyer 2 a discount in order to prevent it from manufacturing tires on its own. The latter condition would be met if the administrative and transportation costs of supplying Buyer 2 were not sufficiently different from the costs of supplying Buyer 1 to justify the $25 price differential. Is it clear, from the information presented in *Universal-Rundle*, that Universal-Rundle's competitors were also violating the law? What additional information would you need to answer that question?

2. *Agency reaction to price fixing.* Put yourself in the place of the director of the FTC's Bureau of Competition. You have information indicating that all major manufacturers of plumbing fixtures were engaged in price discrimination of the sort described in *Universal-Rundle*. Would you:

(a) Ask the commissioners to institute a rulemaking proceeding to declare this practice unlawful;
(b) Ask that complaints be issued against all seven manufacturers; or
(c) Ask that a complaint be issued against only some subset of manufacturers?

What considerations would influence your choice? If the approach chosen were (c), which manufacturer or manufacturers would you target?

3. *Patent abuse of discretion.* Notice that the Court does not slam the courthouse door completely shut on claims of the sort presented by Moog Industries and Universal-Rundle. Why not? Why should the courts *ever* stay enforcement against a wrongdoer? Does the "patent abuse of discretion" window provide any real solace to businesses singled out for prosecution? What must they show in order to obtain a judicial stay of enforcement? That all of their competitors are engaged in identical violations of the Act? Some of their competitors? Similar violations? Similar conduct (whether illegal or not)?

Regulated parties continue to press claims against what they perceive as unequal treatment at the hands of agencies. In United States v. Undetermined

Quantities of an Article of Drug Labeled as "Exachol," 716 F. Supp. 787 (S.D.N.Y. 1989), the Food and Drug Administration seized the dietary supplement Exachol and sought to have it condemned as a misbranded and unapproved new drug. The promotional material for Exachol made health claims that the FDA argued were improper, and at the time of the seizure the FDA was engaged in numerous enforcement actions and a rulemaking regarding health claims for dietary supplements and food products. U.S. Health Club, Inc., Exachol's distributor, argued that the FDA had offered no legitimate reason for condemning its product when it was regulating, but not banning, similar health claims on fish oil dietary supplements and food products such as cereals and margarine-like spreads. The court agreed with Health Club, stating that "[t]he overriding principle of fairness is always the same: the government must govern with an even hand," and the court denied summary judgment to the FDA on the ground that the FDA "has applied an uneven regulatory policy." 716 F. Supp. at 795-796. The court did not cite either *Moog Industries* or *Universal-Rundle*.

In Marco Sales Co. v. FTC, 453 F.2d 1 (2d Cir. 1971), the court of appeals held that the FTC acted improperly when it failed to explain why it ordered one business to cease and desist from a marketing practice while allowing other businesses to continue the practice, subject to regulation. Marco Sales Co. was engaged in the direct marketing of games of chance known as punch boards. Marco Sales would mail the punch board to its customer who would sell chances to win prizes for 39 cents each. After all chances on the board were sold, the customer would send the money to Marco Sales, and Marco Sales would send the prizes to its customer who would provide them to the winners. Punch boards were also used by gasoline stations and food retailers to lure customers, but with no charge for chances, and the FTC adopted a rule regulating this use of punch boards but allowed it to continue. The court held the FTC's cease-and-desist order against Marco Sales invalid: "The arbitrary character of the Commission's action here consists of its total failure to even advert to, much less explain, its reason for the rigid ad hoc adjudicatory stance it adopted toward the petitioner and the flexible tolerance its industry regulation displayed to those utilizing the same or similar devices." 453 F.2d at 6. The FTC did attempt to distinguish the situations in its brief on the basis that customers lured into gasoline stations and other retail stores did not have to pay for their chances, but the court rejected this distinction as unpersuasive. The FTC also argued that *Universal-Rundle* and *Moog Industries* precluded Marco Sales' argument. The court disagreed, stating that those cases would be on point "if Marco were urging that others, engaged in identical practices competing with him, were not similarly pursued by the Commission. . . . [Marco argues] rather that those engaged in the same activity are regulated while Marco is annihilated." *Id.* Is this a persuasive distinction? If the FTC had stated in its regulation or its decision in *Marco Sales* that it would treat punch cards where chances are sold more harshly than those where chances were given away as a promotion, should the court have upheld the distinction? If so, wasn't the FTC's sin here merely its failure to adequately explain itself?

Unequal treatment claims sometimes shade into issues of reviewability. For example, in Kisser v. Cisneros, 14 F.3d 515 (D.C. Cir. 1994), the court of appeals denied a claim of unequal treatment made by an officer of a suspended HUD lender who was debarred from further HUD lending activity. The debarred officer argued that other company officers should also have been debarred.

The court reviewed the debarment decision under the "arbitrary and capricious" standard and declined to examine whether others should also have been debarred on the ground that HUD's decision of whether to debar additional officers was an unreviewable exercise of prosecutorial discretion. Is that consistent with *Moog Industries'* patent-abuse-of-discretion standard for discriminatory enforcement claims, or is this aspect of *Moog Industries* undermined by the ruling in Heckler v. Chaney, excerpted in Chapter III, *supra,* that decisions not to prosecute are presumptively unreviewable?

c.   Agency Enforcement Orders

Under the criminal law, a penalty is assessed, in the form of a fine or prison sentence, only after the defendant has been afforded the opportunity to contest the charges in a formal adjudicatory hearing. In administrative law, the process is not nearly as uniform as in the criminal law. Depending on governing statutes, agency remedial orders can either initiate or follow adjudicatory proceedings. For example, the National Labor Relations Act contemplates a formal adjudicatory hearing before the NLRB issues an order directing an employer or labor union to cease and desist from unfair labor practices. *See* 29 U.S.C. §160. Conversely, several environmental-protection statutes allow the EPA to issue compliance orders without affording the target of an order the opportunity to contest it in advance, except perhaps via an informal conference. *See, e.g.,* 42 U.S.C. §7413 (Clean Air Act); 33 U.S.C. §1319 (Clean Water Act); 42 U.S.C. §9606 (Comprehensive Environmental Response, Compensation, and Liability Act (CERCLA)).

The CERCLA provision, which deals with hazardous waste cleanups, is particularly broad, granting the agency the power to "issu[e] such orders as may be necessary to protect public health and welfare and the environment." 42 U.S.C. §9606.* As noted in Chapter VI, *supra,* targets of EPA compliance orders have complained of due process violations when the EPA issues such orders and treats them as legally binding without affording subjects an adjudicatory hearing. For example, in Tennessee Valley Authority (TVA) v. Whitman, 336 F.3d 1236 (11th Cir. 2003), TVA complained that the EPA had issued an "Administrative Compliance Order" (ACO) against it without providing an opportunity for a hearing to contest the bases for the order. Governing statutes provide that the violation of an ACO is itself a violation of law and can serve as the basis for significant fines and even imprisonment. The Eleventh Circuit agreed with TVA that this scheme violates due process and accordingly held that ACOs cannot be considered legally binding until the target has an opportunity for an adjudicatory hearing before a neutral tribunal. In the context of EPA enforcement, this meant that EPA must bring an action in federal district court to enforce ACOs.

While orders issued under CERCLA and other similar statutes may not be legally binding before the targets have the opportunity to contest them

---

* CERCLA grants the authority to issue orders to the President. *See* 42 U.S.C. §9606. The President has delegated this authority to the Administrator of the EPA.

in a hearing, noncompliance may be financially risky for the target and even nonfinal orders may have serious negative collateral consequences upon issuance. After years of being subjected to compliance orders under CER-CLA, General Electric brought suit against the EPA, claiming that the statute, both as written and as administered by the EPA, violated its right to due process of law.

GENERAL ELECTRIC CO. v. JACKSON
610 F.3d 110 (D.C. Cir. 2010)

Before ROGERS, TATEL, and GRIFFITH, Circuit Judges.

TATEL, Circuit Judge:

In this case, appellant challenges the constitutionality of a statutory scheme that authorizes the Environmental Protection Agency to issue orders, known as unilateral administrative orders (UAOs), directing companies and others to clean up hazardous waste for which they are responsible. Appellant argues that the statute, as well as the way in which EPA administers it, violates the Due Process Clause because EPA issues UAOs without a hearing before a neutral decisionmaker. We disagree. To the extent the UAO regime implicates constitutionally protected property interests by imposing compliance costs and threatening fines and punitive damages, it satisfies due process because UAO recipients may obtain a pre-deprivation hearing by refusing to comply and forcing EPA to sue in federal court. Appellant insists that the UAO scheme and EPA's implementation of it nonetheless violate due process because the mere issuance of a UAO can inflict immediate, serious, and irreparable damage by depressing the recipient's stock price, harming its brand value, and increasing its cost of financing. But such "consequential" injuries—injuries resulting not from EPA's issuance of the UAO, but from market reactions to it—are insufficient to merit Due Process Clause protection. We therefore affirm the district court's grant of summary judgment to EPA.

I.

Congress enacted the Comprehensive Environmental Response, Compensation, and Liability Act (CERCLA) "in response to the serious environmental and health risks posed by industrial pollution." United States v. Bestfoods, 524 U.S. 51, 55 (1998). CERCLA seeks to promote prompt cleanup of hazardous waste sites and to ensure that responsible parties foot the bill. . . .

When EPA determines that an environmental cleanup is necessary at a contaminated site, CERCLA gives the agency four options: (1) it may negotiate a settlement with potentially responsible parties (PRPs), [42 U.S.C.] §9622; (2) it may conduct the cleanup with "Superfund" money and then seek reimbursement from PRPs by filing suit, id. §§9604(a), 9607(a)(4)(A); (3) it may file an abatement action in federal district court to compel PRPs to conduct the cleanup, id. §9606; or (4) it may issue a UAO instructing PRPs to clean the site, id. This last option, authorized by CERCLA section 106, is the focus of this case. . . .

For remedial actions, the longer-term option, CERCLA requires EPA to "provide for the participation of interested persons, including [PRPs], in the development of the administrative record." *Id.* §9613(k)(2)(B). Specifically, EPA must provide "[n]otice to potentially affected persons and the public," "[a] reasonable opportunity to comment and provide information regarding the [remedial] plan," "[a]n opportunity for a public meeting in the affected area," "[a] response to each of the significant comments, criticisms, and new data submitted in written or oral presentations," and "[a] statement of the basis and purpose of the selected action." *Id.*; *see also* §9617(a)(b) (requiring public notice of all remedial actions). . . .

Once EPA issues a UAO, the recipient PRP has two choices. It may comply and, after completing the cleanup, seek reimbursement from EPA. If EPA refuses reimbursement, the PRP may sue the agency in federal district court to recover its costs on the grounds that (1) it was not liable for the cleanup; or (2) it was liable but EPA's selected response action (or some portion thereof) was "arbitrary and capricious or . . . otherwise not in accordance with law." Alternatively, the PRP may refuse to comply with the UAO, in which case EPA may either bring an action in federal district court to enforce the UAO against the noncomplying PRP, or clean the site itself and then sue the PRP to recover its costs. In either proceeding, if the court concludes that the PRP "willfully" failed to comply with an order "without sufficient cause," it "may" (but need not) impose fines, which are currently set at $37,500 per day . . . , and accumulate until EPA brings a recovery or enforcement action—a period of up to six years. . . . If EPA itself undertakes the cleanup and the district court finds that the PRP "fail[ed] without sufficient cause" to comply with the UAO, the court "may" impose punitive damages of up to "three times [ ] the amount of any costs" the agency incurs. 42 U.S.C. §9607(c)(3).

Central to this case, these two options—comply and seek reimbursement, or refuse to comply and wait for EPA to bring an enforcement or cost recovery action—are exclusive. CERCLA section 113(h) bars PRPs from obtaining immediate judicial review of a UAO. *Id.* §9613(h). That section provides that "No Federal court shall have jurisdiction . . . to review any order issued under section [106]" until the PRP completes the work and seeks reimbursement, *id.* §9613(h)(3), or until EPA brings an enforcement action or seeks to recover fines and damages for noncompliance, *id.* §9613(h)(1)(2).

Over the years, appellant General Electric (GE) has received at least 68 UAOs. . . . In addition, GE "is currently participating in response actions at 79 active CERCLA sites" where UAOs may issue.

In 2000, GE filed suit in the United States District Court for the District of Columbia challenging CERCLA's UAO regime. In its amended complaint, GE alleged that the statute violates the Fifth Amendment to the United States Constitution because it "deprive[s] persons of their fundamental right to liberty and property without . . . constitutionally adequate procedural safeguards." . . . According to GE, "[t]he unilateral orders regime . . . imposes a classic and unconstitutional Hobson's choice": because refusing to comply "risk[s] severe punishment [i.e., fines and treble damages]," UAO recipients' only real option is to "comply . . . before having any opportunity to be heard on the legality and rationality of the underlying order." . . . [The district court rejected all of GE's challenges to the statute and EPA's administration of it.]

II.

We begin with GE's facial challenge. . . . "The first inquiry in every due process challenge is whether the plaintiff has been deprived of a protected interest in 'liberty' or 'property.' Only after finding the deprivation of a protected interest do we look to see if the [government's] procedures comport with due process." Amer. Mfrs. Mut. Ins. Co. v. Sullivan, 526 U.S. 40, 59 (1999) (citations omitted). At this second step, we apply the now-familiar Mathews v. Eldridge balancing test, considering (1) the significance of the private party's protected interest, (2) the government's interest, and (3) the risk of erroneous deprivation and "the probable value, if any, of additional or substitute procedural safeguards." 424 U.S. at 335.

GE asserts that UAOs deprive PRPs of two types of protected property: (1) the money PRPs must spend to comply with a UAO or the daily fines and treble damages they face should they refuse to comply; and (2) the PRPs' stock price, brand value, and cost of financing, all of which, GE contends, are adversely affected by the issuance of a UAO. We address each of these alleged deprivations in turn.

COSTS OF COMPLIANCE, FINES, AND DAMAGES

The parties agree that the costs of compliance and the monetary fines and damages associated with noncompliance qualify as protected property interests. They disagree, however, as to whether judicial review is available before any deprivation occurs. EPA contends that CERCLA gives PRPs the right to pre-deprivation judicial review: by refusing to comply with a UAO, a PRP can force EPA to file suit in federal court, where the PRP can challenge the order's validity before spending a single dollar on compliance costs, damages, or fines. GE responds that noncompliance—and thus pre-deprivation judicial review—is but a theoretical option. According to GE, daily fines and treble damages "are so severe that they . . . intimidate [ ] PRPs from exercising the purported option of electing not to comply with a UAO so as to test an order's validity" via judicial review. . . .

GE's argument hinges on the Supreme Court's decision in Ex Parte Young, 209 U.S. 123 (1908), and its progeny. Under those cases, a statutory scheme violates due process if "the penalties for disobedience are by fines so enormous . . . as to intimidate the [affected party] from resorting to the courts to test the validity of the legislation [because] the result is the same as if the law in terms prohibited the [party] from seeking judicial [review]" at all. *Id.* at 147. The Supreme Court has made clear, however, that statutes imposing fines—even "enormous" fines—on noncomplying parties may satisfy due process if such fines are subject to a "good faith" or "reasonable ground[s]" defense. *See* Reisman v. Caplin, 375 U.S. 440, 446-50 (1964). . . . Courts have also held that "there is no constitutional violation if the imposition of penalties is subject to judicial discretion." Wagner Seed Co. v. Daggett, 800 F.2d 310, 316 (2d Cir. 1986). . . .

CERCLA guarantees these safeguards. Indeed, the statute offers noncomplying PRPs several levels of protection: a PRP faces daily fines and treble damages only if a federal court finds (1) that the UAO was proper; (2) that the PRP "willfully" failed to comply "without sufficient cause"; and (3) that, in the court's discretion, fines and treble damages are appropriate. 42 U.S.C. §§9606(b)(1), 9607(c)(3). As to the first of these findings . . . although the PRP must prove that it is not liable by a preponderance of the evidence, EPA's liability determination warrants no judicial deference. . . . As to the second, CERCLA's "willfulness" and "sufficient cause" requirements are quite similar to the good faith and reasonable grounds defenses the Supreme Court has found sufficient to satisfy due process, and GE does not argue otherwise. . . . Moreover, PRPs receive added protection from the fact that the district court has authority to decide not to impose fines even if it concludes that a recipient "without sufficient cause, willfully violate[d], or fail[ed] or refuse[d] to comply with" a UAO. 42 U.S.C. §9606(b)(1). . . . Given these safeguards, we have no basis for concluding that "[t]he necessary effect and result of [CERCLA] must be to preclude a resort to the courts . . . for the purpose of testing [a UAO's] validity." *Young*, 209 U.S. at 146. Contrary to GE's claim, then, PRPs face no Hobson's choice. . . .

STOCK PRICE, BRAND VALUE, AND COST OF FINANCING

GE contends that, in addition to potential cleanup costs, fines, and damages, issuance of a UAO "immediately tag[s]" a PRP "with a massive contingent liability," . . . which in turn depresses its stock price, harms its brand value, and increases its cost of financing. . . . GE points to no "independent source such as state law," for its purported property interests. . . . GE's case boils down to this: by declaring that a PRP is responsible for cleaning up a hazardous waste site, a UAO harms the PRP's reputation, and the market, in turn, devalues its stock, brand, and credit rating. Viewed this way, GE's argument is foreclosed by Paul v. Davis, 424 U.S. 693 (1976). There the Supreme Court held that a sheriff's inclusion of Davis's name and photograph on a flyer captioned "Active Shoplifters" implicated no due process interest. . . . In so holding, the Court distinguished Wisconsin v. Constantineau, 400 U.S. 433 (1971), which ruled that a law allowing for "posting"—forbidding the sale of alcoholic beverages to persons determined to have become hazards based on their "excessive drinking"—violated due process. As the Court explained in *Davis*, the law at issue in *Constantineau* went beyond mere stigma, depriving the plaintiff "of a right previously held under state law . . . to purchase or obtain liquor in common with the rest of the citizenry." *Davis*, 424 U.S. at 708. "[I]t was that alteration of legal status which, combined with the injury resulting from the defamation, justified the invocation of procedural safeguards" in *Constantineau. Id.* at 708-09. . . .

Our conclusion is unaffected by the fact that GE alleges "property" harm while *Davis* addresses a "liberty" claim. [W]e have applied the stigma-plus framework to property claims, requiring plaintiffs to show that alleged reputational harm completely destroys the value of their property. . . .

GE nonetheless insists that this court has "held that consequential impacts can constitute a deprivation." Here, even assuming UAOs are stigmatizing, their consequences fall far short of completely foreclosing employment [Doe v. United States Department of Justice, 753 F.2d 1092 (D.C. Cir. 1985)], or suspending a government contract [Reeve Aleutian Airways, Inc. v. United States, 982 F.2d 594 (D.C. Cir. 1993)]. . . .

III.

GE contends that even if CERCLA's UAO provisions are facially constitutional, EPA administers the statute in a way that denies PRPs due process.

PATTERN AND PRACTICE CHALLENGE

. . . Although GE's briefs are less than clear, we understand the company to be arguing that the way in which EPA implements CERCLA's UAO provisions increases the frequency of UAOs and decreases their accuracy, thus tipping the Mathews v. Eldridge balance toward a finding that the process is constitutionally defective. For example, GE points to EPA's "enforcement first" policy, by which the agency issues UAOs whenever settlement negotiations fail, as well as to the agency's delegation of authority to subordinate regional employees who allegedly issue UAOs in time to comply with internal agency reporting deadlines. . . . GE argues that by encouraging EPA to issue UAOs more frequently, and by increasing the risk that those UAOs will be erroneous, these and other policies targeted in the company's briefs make it more likely that PRPs will suffer pre-hearing "deprivations" in the form of damage to their stock price, brand value, and credit rating. As GE's counsel conceded at oral argument, however, if such harms are insufficient to trigger due process protection, then this argument must fail. . . . Thus, because we have held that these consequential effects do not qualify as constitutionally protected property interests, we need not—indeed, we may not—apply Mathews v. Eldridge to determine what process is due. In other words, even if GE is correct that EPA's implementation of CERCLA results in more frequent and less accurate UAOs, the company has failed to identify any constitutionally protected property interest that could be adversely affected by such errors. . . .

GE also contends that even if CERCLA is not facially coercive, EPA administers the statute in a way that "intimidate[s] PRPs from exercising the purported option of electing not to comply with a UAO so as to test an order's validity, giving rise to an independent due process violation under Ex Parte Young." . . . To the extent GE makes this argument, it urges us to infer coercion from the fact that the vast majority of PRPs elect to comply with UAOs.

[I]n our view, . . . the pattern and practice claim add[s] little to GE's facial Ex Parte Young challenge: regardless of EPA's policies—for example, GE alleges that the agency coerces PRPs into compliance by threatening to seek multiple penalties for violations at a single UAO site—"a judge ultimately decides what, if any, penalty to impose." [See Gen. Elec. Co. v. Jackson (GE IV), 595 F. Supp. 2d 8, 18 (D.D.C. 2009).] [M]oreover, CERCLA's sufficient cause and willfulness defenses protect PRPs from unwarranted fines and damages. As to GE's argument that the high incidence of UAO compliance evidences coercion, the district court found that "GE's own expert . . . demonstrate[d] that instances of noncompliance are sufficiently numerous to suggest that PRPs are not, in fact, forced to comply." GE IV, 595 F. Supp. 2d at 28-29 (GE's expert found that "of the 1,638 PRPs who have been issued UAOs most recently, there were 75 instances of noncompliance—a rate of 4.6 percent."). And for our part, we observe that in light of the extensive procedures CERCLA requires EPA to follow before issuing a UAO, including notice and comment, recipients may be complying in large numbers not because they feel coerced, but because they believe that UAOs are generally accurate and would withstand judicial review. . . .

IV.

We fully understand, as GE argues, that the financial consequences of UAOs can be substantial. We also understand that other administrative enforcement schemes that address matters of public health and safety may provide greater process than does CERCLA. . . . Such concerns, however, do not implicate the constitutionality of CERCLA or of the policies and practices by which EPA implements it. . . . Because our judicial task is limited to determining whether CERCLA's UAO provisions violate the Fifth Amendment either on their face or as administered by EPA, we affirm the decisions of the district court.

NOTES AND QUESTIONS

1. *Why this procedure?* What policy considerations would lead Congress to create an enforcement scheme like CERCLA's, in which the agency has the power to act first and ask questions later? As we see in the second paragraph of Part I of the opinion, the EPA has four enforcement options under CERCLA. It may negotiate a settlement, conduct the cleanup itself and then seek reimbursement, file suit in federal court to compel a cleanup, or issue an order instructing the responsible party to clean up the site. When it exercises the final option, noncompliance subjects the party to substantial civil penalties. What considerations are likely to motivate the EPA's choice among its four options? As in most legal conflicts, settlement is likely to be a preferred outcome.

The EPA has occasionally provided guidance to agency personnel and regulated parties concerning its enforcement and settlement policies and practices. Among these, issued in 1984, is the EPA's "Interim CERCLA Settlement Policy," available at https://www.epa.gov/enforcement/guidance-cercla-settlement-policy-interim, which provides guidance to agency officials on when and how to negotiate settlements. The goal of settlements, according to the policy, is to "obtain complete cleanup by the responsible parties, or collect 100% of the costs of the cleanup action." *Id.* at 3. The policy notes that "cleanups can be started more quickly when private parties do the work themselves" and thus promises "to create a climate that is receptive to private party cleanup proposals." *Id.* at 4. Human nature being what it is, the policy also recognizes that "[a] strong enforcement program is essential to encourage voluntary action by PRPs" and promises that "the government will vigorously seek all remaining relief, including costs, penalties and treble damages . . . from parties whose recalcitrance made a complete settlement impossible." *Id.* at 3-4. What, if anything, do these statements indicate regarding the EPA's general approach to CERCLA cleanup enforcement?

2. *Was GE deprived of an interest protected by due process?* General Electric relied on several bases for its argument that the issuance of a UAO without first providing an adjudicatory hearing violated due process. Did you find any of

them persuasive? The arguments can be broken down into two categories: first, whether GE has suffered damage to a protected interest and, second, whether any such damage occurred without due process. On the first issue, didn't GE's arguments run afoul of the Supreme Court's requirement in *Board of Regents v. Roth*, excerpted in Chapter VI, *supra*, that property interests be created by an external source such as state law? Consider the Second Circuit's decision in Asbestec Construction Services v. EPA, 849 F.2d 765, 767, 769 (2d Cir. 1988), which arose under the Clean Air Act's provision allowing the EPA to issue compliance orders without first holding a hearing. In *Asbestec*, the target complained that its ability to do business was immediately inhibited when the EPA issued an order against it, thus depriving it of property and liberty without due process. The Second Circuit applied *Paul v. Davis*, discussed in the *General Electric* case, above, and also in Chapter VI, *supra*, and held that without exclusion from "certain benefits," reputational harm was insufficient to constitute a deprivation of property or liberty. Was GE's liberty argument foreclosed by *Paul*?

GE also argued that the issuance of a UAO triggers due process protections because it follows a factfinding, adjudicatory proceeding. Given the description of the pre-UAO process in Judge Tatel's opinion, is GE's characterization of the process as an "adjudicatory proceeding" accurate? Even if GE's characterization of the process is accurate, isn't the alleged creation of a property interest from procedural provisions also inconsistent with the *Roth* test for determining whether a protected interest exists? Further, wouldn't acceptance of this argument give Congress a powerful incentive to provide even less pre-order process in future environmental statutes, something that might be worse for GE in the long run?

3. *What process is due?* Assuming deprivation of a protected interest, the next question is whether GE was denied due process of law. Does the court faithfully apply the Supreme Court's three-part balancing test as set forth in *Matthews v. Eldridge*, excerpted in Chapter VI, *supra*? Would requiring agencies to afford more process than an informal consultation before issuing compliance orders cripple agency enforcement? GE seems to be arguing that the costs of fighting UAOs, including the potential for huge fines and serious reputational harm, are likely in many cases to be greater than the cost of complying. Do you agree with the court that despite these potential costs, UAO targets have a realistic opportunity to challenge the orders ex post? Before jumping to the conclusion that due process should require pre-order process, consider that the accepted procedure for challenging tax assessments by the Internal Revenue Service has always been payment of the tax followed by a suit for a refund. *See* 26 U.S.C. §7422. While taxpayers may not like this procedure, it is not thought to violate due process.

Would GE's due process claim be resolved by immediate judicial review of a UAO? In Sackett v. EPA, 566 U.S. 120 (2012), discussed in Chapter III, *supra*, the Supreme Court held, in an opinion by Justice Scalia for a unanimous Court, that the issuance of an ACO under the Clean Water Act is final agency action subject to immediate judicial review. Suppose that the EPA prevails on judicial review of the order issued against the Sacketts. Would it violate due process for the agency to assess daily fines going all the way back to the date the order was issued, including the time that the judicial review action was pending? If so, does the *Sackett* decision provide any substantial benefit to the subjects of ACOs?

4. *Reviewability.* Courts have disagreed over whether pattern and practice claims like those brought in *General Electric* are reviewable. For a discussion of this issue, see Chapter III, *supra.*

B.   PRIVATE LITIGATION AND REGULATORY ENFORCEMENT

Agency enforcement takes place in an environment constrained by institutional, political, and budgetary concerns. Beneficiaries of regulatory programs, frustrated with the slow pace of agency enforcement and the failure of agencies to address their concerns, may take matters into their own hands in one, or both, of two ways. First, a beneficiary may seek a judicial decree forcing an agency to take an enforcement action that, according to the plaintiff, has been improperly withheld or delayed. Given the tradition of judicial deference to prosecutorial discretion (*see* Chapter III, *supra*), this remedy is available only when the agency's enabling statute explicitly confers the right to such a remedy. In the first part of this subsection we examine so-called "citizen suit" provisions that perform such a function.

Second, beneficiaries of regulatory programs may seek to bypass the enforcement agency altogether by directly suing the regulated person for allegedly violating the regulatory statute. Occasionally, as in many citizen suit statutes, Congress confers an explicit private right of action to obtain damages or injunctive relief for violation of a regulatory statute. More commonly, however, the enabling act is ambiguous or silent about private remedies, leaving to the courts the task of determining whether such remedies should be implied from the language and structure of the statute. That is the focus of the second part of this section. As you read the materials that follow, consider the following questions: Is private litigation a desirable supplement to, or substitute for, public enforcement? Or does private litigation threaten to undercut agency policy or interfere with agency priority-setting? Should courts, faced with statutory uncertainty, create a presumption in favor of, or opposed to, private remedies?

1.   *Citizen Suits to Compel Public Enforcement*

The ancient writ of mandamus recognized a judicial power to compel government officials to fulfill "nondiscretionary" duties, which might include a duty to take a particular enforcement action in a particular situation. In recent years, Congress has inserted citizen suit provisions in many regulatory statutes, primarily in the environmental area, authorizing mandamus-like actions against agency officials. These provisions typically authorize any "citizen" or any "person" to seek an injunction requiring an administrative agency to perform certain specified duties. Section 11(g) of the Endangered Species Act, 16 U.S.C. §1540(g)(1), quoted in connection with the *Lujan* case excerpted in Chapter III, *supra*, is a typical example. As we saw in *Lujan*, citizen suit provisions raise questions about the reach of Congress's constitutional power to confer standing to sue. They also raise questions about the class of administrative actions that are subject to judicial mandate, as the following case illustrates.

BENNETT v. SPEAR
520 U.S. 154 (1997)

JUSTICE SCALIA delivered the opinion of the Court.

This is a challenge to a biological opinion issued by the Fish and Wildlife Service in accordance with the Endangered Species Act of 1973 (ESA), 87 Stat. 884, as amended, 16 U.S.C. §1531 *et seq.*, concerning the operation of the Klamath Irrigation Project by the Bureau of Reclamation, and the project's impact on two varieties of endangered fish. . . .

I

The ESA requires the Secretary of the Interior to promulgate regulations listing those species of animals that are "threatened" or "endangered" under specified criteria, and to designate their "critical habitat." 16 U.S.C. §1533. The ESA further requires each federal agency to "insure that any action authorized, funded, or carried out by such agency . . . is not likely to jeopardize the continued existence of any endangered species or threatened species or result in the destruction or adverse modification of habitat of such species which is determined by the Secretary . . . to be critical." §1536(a)(2). If an agency determines that action it proposes to take may adversely affect a listed species, it must engage in formal consultation with the Fish and Wildlife Service, as delegate of the Secretary, *ibid.*; 50 CFR §402.14 (1995), after which the Service must provide the agency with a written statement (the Biological Opinion) explaining how the proposed action will affect the species or its habitat, 16 U.S.C. §1536(b)(3)(A). If the Service concludes that the proposed action will "jeopardize the continued existence of any [listed] species or threatened species or result in the destruction or adverse modification of [critical habitat]," §1536(a)(2), the Biological Opinion must outline any "reasonable and prudent alternatives" that the Service believes will avoid that consequence, §1536(b)(3)(A). Additionally, if the Biological Opinion concludes that the agency action will not result in jeopardy or adverse habitat modification, or if it offers reasonable and prudent alternatives to avoid that consequence, the Service must provide the agency with a written statement (known as the Incidental Take Statement) specifying the "impact of such incidental taking on the species," any "reasonable and prudent measures that the [Service] considers necessary or appropriate to minimize such impact," and setting forth "the terms and conditions . . . that must be complied with by the Federal agency . . . to implement [those measures]." §1536(b)(4).

The Klamath Project, one of the oldest federal reclamation schemes, is a series of lakes, rivers, dams, and irrigation canals in northern California and southern Oregon. The project was undertaken by the Secretary of the Interior and is administered by the Bureau of Reclamation, which is under the

Secretary's jurisdiction. In 1992, the Bureau notified the Service that operation of the project might affect the Lost River Sucker *(Deltistes luxatus)* and Shortnose Sucker *(Chasmistes brevirostris)*, species of fish that were listed as endangered in 1988. After formal consultation with the Bureau in accordance with 50 CFR §402.14 (1995), the Service issued a Biological Opinion which concluded that the "'long-term operation of the Klamath Project was likely to jeopardize the continued existence of the Lost River and shortnose suckers.'" App. to Pet. for Cert. 3. The Biological Opinion identified "reasonable and prudent alternatives" the Service believed would avoid jeopardy, which included the maintenance of minimum water levels on Clear Lake and Gerber reservoirs. The Bureau later notified the Service that it intended to operate the project in compliance with the Biological Opinion.

Petitioners, two Oregon irrigation districts that receive Klamath Project water and the operators of two ranches within those districts, filed the present action against the director and regional director of the Service and the Secretary of the Interior. Neither the Bureau nor any of its officials is named as defendant. The complaint asserts that the Bureau "has been following essentially the same procedures for storing and releasing water from Clear Lake and Gerber reservoirs throughout the twentieth century," *id.*, at 36; that "[t]here is no scientifically or commercially available evidence indicating that the populations of endangered suckers in Clear Lake and Gerber reservoirs have declined, are declining, or will decline as a result" of the Bureau's operation of the Klamath Project, *id.*, at 37; that "[t]here is no commercially or scientifically available evidence indicating that the restrictions on lake levels imposed in the Biological Opinion will have any beneficial effect on the . . . populations of suckers in Clear Lake and Gerber reservoirs," *id.*, at 39; and that the Bureau nonetheless "will abide by the restrictions imposed by the Biological Opinion," *id.*, at 32.

Petitioners' complaint included three claims for relief that are relevant here. The first and second claims allege that the Service's jeopardy determination with respect to Clear Lake and Gerber reservoirs, and the ensuing imposition of minimum water levels, violated §7 of the ESA, 16 U.S.C. §1536. The third claim is that the imposition of minimum water elevations constituted an implicit determination of critical habitat for the suckers, which violated §4 of the ESA, 16 U.S.C. §1533(b)(2), because it failed to take into consideration the designation's economic impact. Each of the claims also states that the relevant action violated the APA's prohibition of agency action that is "arbitrary, capricious, an abuse of discretion, or otherwise not in accordance with law." 5 U.S.C. §706(2)(A).

The complaint asserts that petitioners' use of the reservoirs and related waterways for "recreational, aesthetic and commercial purposes, as well as for their primary sources of irrigation water," will be "irreparably damaged" by the actions complained of, and that the restrictions on water delivery "recommended" by the Biological Opinion "adversely affect plaintiffs by substantially reducing the quantity of available irrigation water." In essence, petitioners claim a competing interest in the water the Biological Opinion declares necessary for the preservation of the suckers.

[The district court dismissed the complaint for lack of jurisdiction. The Ninth Circuit affirmed. After discussing some standing issues addressed in Chapter III, *supra*, the Court addressed the availability and scope of review under the ESA's citizen suit provision.]

B

[T]he Government contends that the ESA's citizen-suit provision does not authorize judicial review of petitioners' claims. The relevant portions of that provision provide that

> any person may commence a civil suit on his own behalf—
> (A) to enjoin any person, including the United States and any other governmental instrumentality or agency . . . who is alleged to be in violation of any provision of this chapter or regulation issued under the authority thereof; or . . .
> (C) against the Secretary [of Commerce or the Interior] where there is alleged a failure of the Secretary to perform any act or duty under section 1533 of this title which is not discretionary with the Secretary. 16 U.S.C. §1540(g)(1).

The Government argues that judicial review is not available under subsection (A) because the Secretary is not "in violation" of the ESA, and under subsection (C) because the Secretary has not failed to perform any nondiscretionary duty under §1533.

1

Turning first to subsection (C): that it covers only violations of §1533 is clear and unambiguous. Petitioners' first and second claims, which assert that the Secretary has violated §1536, are obviously not reviewable under this provision. However, as described above, the third claim alleges that the Biological Opinion implicitly determines critical habitat without complying with the mandate of §1533(b)(2) that the Secretary "tak[e] into consideration the economic impact, and any other relevant impact, of specifying any particular area as critical habitat." This claim does come within subsection (C).

The Government seeks to avoid this result by appealing to the limitation in subsection (C) that the duty sought to be enforced not be "discretionary with the Secretary." But the terms of §1533(b)(2) are plainly those of obligation rather than discretion: "The Secretary *shall* designate critical habitat, and make revisions thereto, . . . on the basis of the best scientific data available and after taking into consideration the economic impact, and any other relevant impact, of specifying any particular area as critical habitat." (Emphasis added.) It is true that this is followed by the statement that, except where extinction of the species is at issue, "[t]he Secretary *may* exclude any area from critical habitat if he determines that the benefits of such exclusion outweigh the benefits of specifying such area as part of the critical habitat." *Ibid.* (emphasis added). However, the fact that the Secretary's ultimate decision is reviewable only for abuse of discretion does not alter the categorical *requirement* that, in arriving at his decision, he "tak[e] into consideration the economic impact, and any other relevant impact," and use "the best scientific data available." *Ibid.* It is rudimentary administrative law that discretion as to the substance of the ultimate decision does not confer discretion to ignore the required procedures of decisionmaking. *See* SEC v. Chenery Corp., 318 U.S. 80, 94-95 (1943). Since it is the omission of these required procedures that petitioners complain of, their §1533 claim is reviewable under §1540(g)(1)(C).

2

Having concluded that petitioners' §1536 claims are not reviewable under subsection (C), we are left with the question whether they are reviewable under subsection (A), which authorizes injunctive actions against any person "who is alleged to be in violation" of the ESA or its implementing regulations. The Government contends that the Secretary's conduct in implementing or enforcing the ESA is not a "violation" of the ESA within the meaning of this provision. In its view, §1540(g)(1)(A) is a means by which private parties may enforce the substantive provisions of the ESA against regulated parties—both private entities and Government agencies—but is not an alternative avenue for judicial review of the Secretary's implementation of the statute. We agree.

The opposite contention is simply incompatible with the existence of §1540(g)(1)(C), which expressly authorizes suit against the Secretary, but only to compel him to perform a nondiscretionary duty under §1533. That provision would be superfluous—and, worse still, its careful limitation to §1533 would be nullified—if §1540(g)(1)(A) permitted suit against the Secretary for *any* "violation" of the ESA. It is the " 'cardinal principle of statutory construction' . . . [that] [i]t is our duty 'to give effect, if possible, to every clause and word of a statute' . . . rather than to emasculate an entire section." United States v. Menasche, 348 U.S. 528, 538 (1955) (quoting NLRB v. Jones & Laughlin Steel Corp., 301 U.S. 1, 30 (1937), and Montclair v. Ramsdell, 107 U.S. 147, 152 (1883)). Application of that principle here clearly requires us to conclude that the term "violation" does not include the Secretary's failure to perform his duties as administrator of the ESA.

Moreover, the ESA uses the term "violation" elsewhere in contexts in which it is most unlikely to refer to failure by the Secretary or other federal officers and employees to perform their duties in administering the ESA. Section 1540(a), for example, authorizes the Secretary to impose substantial civil penalties on "[a]ny person who knowingly violates . . . any provision of [the ESA]," and entrusts the Secretary with the power to "remi[t] or mitigat[e]" any such penalty. We know of no precedent for applying such a provision against those who administer (as opposed to those who are regulated by) a substantive law. Nor do we think it likely that the statute meant to subject the Secretary and his officers and employees to criminal liability under §1540(b), which makes it a crime for "[a]ny person [to] knowingly violat[e] any provision of [the ESA]," or that §1540(e)(3), which authorizes law enforcement personnel to "make arrests without a warrant for any violation of [the ESA]," was intended to authorize warrantless arrest of the Secretary or his delegates for "knowingly" failing to use the best scientific data available.

Finally, interpreting the term "violation" to include any errors on the part of the Secretary in administering the ESA would effect a wholesale abrogation of the APA's "final agency action" requirement. Any procedural default, even one that had not yet resulted in a final disposition of the matter at issue, would form the basis for a lawsuit. We are loathe to produce such an extraordinary regime without the clearest of statutory direction, which is hardly present here.

Viewed in the context of the entire statute, §1540(g)(1)(A)'s reference to any "violation" of the ESA cannot be interpreted to include the Secretary's maladministration of the ESA. Petitioners' claims are not subject to judicial review under §1540(g)(1)(A).

[In Part IV of its opinion, the Court found that because "the Biological Opinion at issue here has direct and appreciable legal consequences" it was immediately reviewable under the APA.]

* * *

Petitioners' §1533 claim is reviewable under the ESA's citizen-suit provision, and petitioners' remaining claims are reviewable under the APA.

The judgment of the Court of Appeals is reversed, and the case is remanded for further proceedings consistent with this opinion.

NOTES AND QUESTIONS

1. *Nondiscretionary duty.* What exactly was the "nondiscretionary duty" identified by the Court that made the claim under §1533 appropriate for a citizen suit? What sort of analysis should a court apply to determine whether a duty is "nondiscretionary" for the purposes of citizen suit provisions? Consider the Ninth Circuit's view that courts ought to apply a "clear statement rule" and recognize a mandatory duty only when "the nondiscretionary nature of the duty [is] clear-cut—that is readily ascertainable from the statute allegedly giving rise to the duty. . . . We must be able to identify a 'specific, unequivocal command' from the text of the statute at issue using traditional tools of statutory interpretation; it's not enough that such a command could be teased out 'from an amalgamation of disputed statutory provisions and legislative history coupled with the EPA's own earlier interpretation.'" WildEarth Guardians v. McCarthy, 772 F.3d 1179, 1182 (9th Cir. 2014) (finding no mandatory duty under the Clean Air Act for EPA to issue revised ozone regulations), *quoting* Our Children's Earth Found. v. EPA, 527 F.3d 842, 851 (9th Cir. 2008). The D.C. Circuit appears to apply a similar analysis. *See* Sierra Club v. Thomas, 828 F.2d 783, 791 (D.C. Cir. 1987), *cited in* City of Dover v. EPA, 956 F. Supp. 2d 272, 282 (D.D.C. 2013).

Deference may also be relevant to citizen suit allegations. In National Wildlife Federation v. Browner, 127 F.3d 1126 (D.C. Cir. 1997), the court deferred to the agency's interpretation of its own regulation as not creating a nondiscretionary duty enforceable through a citizen suit. Should courts defer to agency views on whether a statute administered by the agency creates a mandatory duty?

2. *"Violation" of the ESA.* What sort of government conduct should be reviewable as a violation of the ESA under §1540(g)(1)(A)?

3. *Citizen suit or APA judicial review?* Does *Bennett* provide the basis for a simple division between agency action reviewable in a citizen suit and agency action that can be reviewed only under the judicial review provisions of the APA? In this regard, consider the following case:

SCOTT v. CITY OF HAMMOND, 741 F.2d 992 (7th Cir. 1984):   Illinois Attorney General William J. Scott brought an action against the EPA for failing to prescribe water quality standards for Lake Michigan that are adequate to "protect the public health and welfare" under the Clean Water Act (CWA), 33 U.S.C. §1313(c)(2), and for failing to prescribe Total Maximum Daily Loads (TMDLs) for pollutants discharged into Lake Michigan. Scott claimed that both failures violated nondiscretionary duties assigned to the Administrator of the EPA and thus were appropriate subjects for suit under the CWA's citizen suit provision, 33 U.S.C. §1365(g), which authorizes any "citizen" (defined as "a person or persons having an interest which is or may be adversely affected") to commence a civil action against the Administrator of the EPA "where there is alleged a failure of the Administrator to perform any act or duty under this chapter which is not discretionary with the Administrator."

With regard to Scott's first claim, the Court of Appeals held that an attack on the adequacy of Lake Michigan's water quality standards was not appropriate for a citizen suit:

> [T]he content of water quality standards cannot ordinarily be challenged through a citizen's suit. An administrator's duty to approve or promulgate some water quality standards might be "nondiscretionary" within the meaning of §1365(a)(2), but the content of the standards is certainly at least somewhat discretionary with the EPA. The only recognized avenue for challenge to the substance of EPA's actions taken with respect to state submissions is a suit for judicial review under the Administrative Procedure Act (the "APA"). . . .
>
> We agree with the defendants and with the district court that this complaint is insufficient to state a claim for judicial review of agency action. A complaint seeking judicial review would allege, for example, that some agency action was arbitrary, capricious or an abuse of discretion or that a factual finding by an agency was erroneous or not supported by substantial evidence. *See* APA, 5 U.S.C. §706(2). The complaint before us does not inform the court or the parties as to what agency action is to be reviewed. We are not told whether a legal or factual error has been made or whether Scott seeks substantial evidence review or perhaps a trial de novo in the district court. The complaint is drafted as a citizen's suit to require performance of a nondiscretionary duty; such a suit cannot be employed to challenge the substance or content of an agency action.

The court reached a different conclusion, however, with regard to Scott's second claim, that the EPA had a duty to prescribe TMDLs for Lake Michigan since the States of Illinois and Indiana had failed to submit proposed TMDLs within the statutory deadline for doing so. The EPA had argued, and the district court had agreed, that even in these circumstances the EPA had no nondiscretionary duty to act until it received a state submission. The Seventh Circuit disagreed:

> We believe that, if a state fails over a long period of time to submit proposed TMDL's, this prolonged failure may amount to the "constructive submission" by that state of no TMDL's. Our view of the case is quite simple, and tracks the statutory scheme set up by Congress. The EPA, in 1978, took the first step by identifying the pollutants for which TMDL's were "suitable." CWA §304(a)(2)(D), 33 U.S.C. §1314(a)(2)(D). The states were then required, within 180 days, to promulgate TMDL's for those waters defined in the statute. CWA §303(d)(2), 33 U.S.C. §1313(d)(2). The allegation of the complaint that no TMDL's are in place, coupled with the EPA's admission that the states have not made their submissions, raises the possibility that the states have determined that TMDL's for Lake Michigan are unnecessary. If the district court agrees with our analysis that in this case the delay by the states may amount to the "constructive submission" of no TMDL's, then the EPA would be under a duty to either approve or disapprove the "submission." If the EPA approves, as Part II of this opinion clearly indicates, the next step

for a dissatisfied party would be to seek judicial review of the EPA's action. If the EPA disapproves, it then presumably would be under a mandatory duty to issue its own TMDL's.

[W]e do not believe that Congress intended that the states by inaction could prevent the implementation of TMDL's. . . . We believe that more than enough time has passed since Congress prescribed promulgation of TMDL's. The statutory time limits demonstrate that Congress anticipated that the entire process would take a relatively short time after the passage of the 1972 amendments. The EPA's inaction appears to be tantamount to approval of state decisions that TMDL's are unneeded. State inaction amounting to a refusal to act should not stand in the way of successfully achieving the goals of federal anti-pollution policy. Thus, the dismissal of the TMDL claim was erroneous.

Does this opinion help distinguish cases appropriate for citizen suit treatment from cases in which judicial review must be had under the APA? Why does the distinction matter?

2.   *Implied Private Rights of Action to Enforce Public Laws*

One alternative to judicial oversight of prosecutorial discretion is to allow persons claiming to be injured by violations of regulatory laws to bring suit directly against the alleged violator. Some regulatory statutes expressly provide for private, as well as public, enforcement. One example is citizen suit statutes, such as the Endangered Species Act provision at issue in *Bennett*; another example is the antitrust laws, which authorize suits by private parties as well as government agencies (the Department of Justice or the Federal Trade Commission). *See, e.g.,* 15 U.S.C. §§4, 15 (1982). Where both public and private suits are permitted, moreover, the statute may define the relationship between them. For example, a judgment of liability in a government-prosecuted antitrust suit can be introduced in evidence in a subsequent private suit to satisfy the plaintiff's burden of proving the existence of the violation. 15 U.S.C. §16(a) (1982).

Most regulatory statutes, however, contain no explicit textual reference to private enforcement. They provide merely that some designated public official is authorized to institute some kind of civil or criminal action to enforce their commands. Determining whether private litigants can "piggyback" on such statutes has proved to be a remarkably durable problem for our legal system. The problem can arise in two different contexts. In the first, the plaintiff asserts a right of action independent of the regulatory statute but attempts to rely on violation of the statute as evidence of the collateral offense charged in her complaint. Thus, in a negligence suit for injuries suffered in an automobile collision, defendant's violation of a vehicular speed limit law enforced by public authorities would be invoked in support of the plaintiff's case. In the second context, the plaintiff asserts a right derived directly from the regulatory statute. Even though the statute explicitly provides only for enforcement by a government agency, a would-be beneficiary of the statutory regime argues that the statute creates an "implied private right of action" to obtain judicial redress for a violation committed by the regulated party. This section of Chapter VII addresses claims of this latter sort, tracing the convoluted path of the Supreme Court's jurisprudence in this area.

a.   Expansion: Policy-Based Justifications for Implying Private Rights of Action

The case usually cited as first finding an implied private right of action under a federal regulatory statute is Texas & Pacific Ry. v. Rigsby, 241 U.S. 33 (1916). *Rigsby* allowed a railroad switchman to sue his employer for damages allegedly resulting from the employer's violation of the Federal Safety Appliance Acts, *formerly codified at* 45 U.S.C. §§1-7, 11-15, *repealed*, Pub. L. No. 103-272, 108 Stat. 1379 (1994). The Court declared that a "disregard of the command of the statute is a wrongful act, and where it results in damage to one of the class for whose especial benefit the statute was enacted, the right to recover the damages from the party in default is implied." 241 U.S. at 39. Despite this language, there is reason to doubt that the Court decided to create a new right of action based on the Safety Appliance Acts rather than to infuse the Acts' substantive standards into extant rights. The lower courts do not seem to have addressed the issue in either form. The arguments to the Supreme Court were preoccupied with the substance of the Acts — did Rigsby have to be engaged in interstate commerce at the time he was injured? — and their constitutionality. And subsequent Supreme Court decisions treat the Safety Appliance Acts as providing, not a right of action, but substantive standards for common law negligence suits. *See* Moore v. Chesapeake & Ohio Ry., 291 U.S. 205 (1934); Jacobson v. New York, N.H. & H.R. Co., 206 F.2d 153 (1st Cir. 1953), *aff'd per curiam*, 347 U.S. 909 (1954). Whatever reading is appropriate to *Rigsby*, the Court later did find rights of action implied in other, similar statutes. *See* International Association of Machinists v. Central Airlines, Inc., 372 U.S. 682 (1963); Tunstall v. Brotherhood of Locomotive Firemen, 323 U.S. 210 (1944). In the 1960s, in the midst of a major expansion of judicial recognition of constitutional rights and federal civil rights jurisdiction, the Supreme Court took a major step in the direction of liberal recognition of private rights of action under federal regulatory statutes:

J.I. CASE CO. v. BORAK, 377 U.S. 426 (1964):   Borak, a shareholder in the J.I. Case Company, brought suit in federal court alleging that the company issued a false and misleading proxy statement to induce shareholders to approve a merger between the company and the American Tractor Corporation. Borak claimed that the company's action violated §14 of the Securities and Exchange Act, which makes it unlawful to solicit a proxy "in contravention of such rules and regulations as the [Securities and Exchange] Commission may prescribe," and also violated the Commission's Rule 14a-9, which prohibited "false or misleading" proxy statements. Section 14 makes no reference to private suits, although another provision (§27) of the Act grants federal courts jurisdiction over "suits in equity and actions at law brought to enforce any liability or duty created by this title or the rules and regulations thereunder." 15 U.S.C. §78aa. In an opinion by Justice Clark, the Court held that a shareholder allegedly victimized by a false or misleading proxy statement may bring a civil action in federal court for damages and injunctive relief:

> The purpose of §14(a) is to prevent management or others from obtaining authorization for corporate action by means of deceptive or inadequate disclosure in proxy solicitation. . . .

Private enforcement of the proxy rules provides a necessary supplement to Commission action. As in antitrust treble damage litigation, the possibility of civil damages or injunctive relief serves as a most effective weapon in the enforcement of the proxy requirements. The Commission advises that it examines over 2,000 proxy statements annually and each of them must necessarily be expedited. Time does not permit an independent examination of the facts set out in the proxy material and this results in the Commission's acceptance of the representations contained therein at their face value, unless contrary to other material on file with it. Indeed, on the allegations of respondent's complaint, the proxy material failed to disclose alleged unlawful market manipulation of the stock of ATC, and this unlawful manipulation would not have been apparent to the Commission until after the merger.

We, therefore, believe that under the circumstances here it is the duty of the courts to be alert to provide such remedies as are necessary to make effective the congressional purpose. . . . It is for the federal courts "to adjust their remedies so as to grant the necessary relief" where federally secured rights are invaded. "And it is also well settled that where legal rights have been invaded, and a federal statute provides for a general right to sue for such invasion, federal courts may use any available remedy to make good the wrong done." Bell v. Hood, 327 U.S. 678, 684 (1946).

NOTES AND QUESTIONS

1. *Statutory basis.* In recognizing a private cause of action under the Securities Exchange Act, the Court relies heavily on §27. Is this reliance justified? Does §27 create a cause of action or merely specify what court will have cognizance of actions otherwise created? Does §14(a) provide any better foundation for a private cause of action?

2. *Congressional purpose.* Is it clear that the congressional "purpose" is better served by allowing suits by shareholders? Why didn't Congress include a private right of action for shareholders in the statute? What, if anything, can be inferred from the following facts?

(1) The SEC, as amicus curiae, supported the implication of a private right of action.
(2) The SEC prescreens all proxy statements, but it lacks sufficient resources (under appropriations made annually by Congress) to investigate the factual basis of all proxy statements.
(3) Prior to the 1934 Act, protection of shareholders was committed almost exclusively to state law. Many states (like Wisconsin) had security-for-expense requirements to protect corporate management from harassment by unfounded shareholder derivative suits.
(4) Section 14's prohibition is not self-activating, but requires the SEC first to issue rules specifying prohibited conduct.

3. *Enforcement incentives.* Two economists have argued that private enforcement of law is presumptively more efficient than public enforcement because "private enforcement agents, unlike government regulators, will possess ongoing economic interests directly related to the costs and benefits of public policy implementation." Mark A. Cohen & Paul H. Rubin, Private Enforcement

of Public Policy, 3 Yale J. on Reg. 167, 169 (1985). Is that true in the context involved in *Borak?* Are there specific settings in which private interests are either more likely or less likely to be congruent with the costs and benefits of policy implementation? Does your answer depend on the private parties' available remedies apart from litigation—and, if so, what does that say about the *Borak* setting?

4. *Borak's aftermath.* Following *Borak,* the federal courts liberally inferred private rights of action from a variety of statutory grants. *See, e.g.,* Wyandotte Co. v. United States, 389 U.S. 191 (1967). Paralleling this expansion of federal statute-based rights of action, the courts also began to find private enforcement implicit in various constitutional commands. For example, in Bivens v. Six Unknown Named Agents of Federal Bureau of Narcotics, 403 U.S. 388 (1971), the Court decided that private rights of action were implied in the Fourth Amendment.

By the mid-1970s, however, the Supreme Court's enthusiasm for expanding private rights of action based on federal regulatory statutes was plainly on the wane. One straw in the wind was National Railroad Passenger Corp. v. National Association of Railroad Passengers, 414 U.S. 453 (1974). In that case, Justice Stewart invoked the Latin maxim "*inclusio unius est exclusio alterius*" to deny a private right of action for Amtrak passengers under the Rail Passenger Service Act of 1970, 45 U.S.C. §§501 *et seq.,* partly because the statute explicitly recognized suits brought by the Attorney General and employees in labor disputes. This decision seemed to portend a general shift of attitude toward implied rights. While the *Amtrak* case was before the Supreme Court, another case that was to provide the occasion for a forthright reconsideration of the *Borak* test for implied private rights of action was making its way through the lower courts.

b. Retrenchment: Reading Legislative Intent to Exclude Private Rights of Action

As you will recall from the discussion of the *Buckley* case, excerpted in Chapter I, *supra,* the financing of political campaigns has proved to be a source of controversy. Since its first effort to regulate campaign financing in the Federal Corrupt Practices Act of 1907, 34 Stat. 864, Congress has exhibited a special concern about the influence of large organizations on the political process. One provision of the 1907 Act, modified and carried forward in the 1925 Corrupt Practices Act, 43 Stat. 1070, and the 1971 Federal Election Campaign Act, 86 Stat. 18, prohibited corporations and unions from either contributing to federal candidates' campaign funds or making direct expenditures to influence the public to vote for or against a federal candidate. This provision was codified in the Federal Criminal Code at 18 U.S.C. §610, which, until its repeal in 1976, was enforced by the Attorney General.

During the 1972 presidential contest between Richard Nixon and George McGovern, Stewart Cort, then Chairman of Bethlehem Steel Corporation, publicly criticized statements made by McGovern, calling them outrageous lies and otherwise unsubtly indicating disagreement with the Democratic Party's candidate. Cort's statements were reprinted in newspaper and news magazine advertisements and in pamphlets. Both the advertisements (carried in more than 20 different publications) and the pamphlets were paid for and distributed by Bethlehem Steel Corporation.

Suit was filed by Ash, a stockholder of Bethlehem Steel, against corporate directors, to stop the expenditure of corporate funds allegedly in aid of the Nixon campaign and to secure the return to the corporate treasury of funds already spent. The court of appeals, in an opinion by Chief Judge Collins Seitz, held that in accordance with the standards announced in *Borak,* a private right of action should be implied under §610. Ash v. Cort, 496 F.2d 416 (3d Cir. 1974). The court noted that while voters were the primary class to be protected by the statute, stockholders were within the class "secondarily protected" by §610. It also held that suits by private parties would effectuate the purposes of §610 by preventing illegal expenditures, especially since stockholders "able to protect their investments by recovering damages on behalf of the corporation, may be expected to be particularly vigilant in detecting violation of §610." The court also observed that this form of private enforcement was particularly appropriate—the allegedly wrongful expenditures were made in behalf of the Nixon campaign, and John Mitchell, who had been Nixon's campaign chairman, at the time of suit was the U.S. Attorney General, charged with enforcement of §610.

Following the Court of Appeals' decision, Congress, moved by the Watergate scandal, substantially amended the 1971 Federal Election Campaign Act. Before the Supreme Court found portions of that Act unconstitutional in *Buckley,* it was called upon to consider whether Ash was properly in federal court with his claim that §610 had been breached.

CORT v. ASH
422 U.S. 66 (1975)

JUSTICE BRENNAN delivered the opinion of the Court.

[T]he principal issue presented for decision is whether a private cause of action for damages against corporate directors is to be implied in favor of a corporate stockholder under 18 U.S.C. §610, a criminal statute prohibiting corporations from making "a contribution or expenditure in connection with any election at which Presidential and Vice Presidential electors . . . are to be voted for." We conclude that implication of such a federal cause of action is not suggested by the legislative context of §610 or required to accomplish Congress' purposes in enacting the statute. . . .

II

We consider first the holding of the Court of Appeals that respondent has "a private cause of action . . . [as] a citizen [or as a stockholder] to secure injunctive relief." The 1972 Presidential election is history, and respondent as citizen or stockholder seeks injunctive relief only as to future elections. In that circumstance, a statute enacted after the decision of the Court of Appeals, the

Federal Election Campaign Act Amendments of 1974, Pub. L. 93-443, 88 Stat.
1263 (Amendments) (amending the Federal Election Campaign Act of 1971, 86
Stat. 3), requires reversal of the holding of the Court of Appeals.

In terms, §610 is only a criminal statute, providing a fine or imprisonment
for its violation. At the time this suit was filed, there was no statutory provision
for civil enforcement of §610, whether by private parties or by a Government
agency. But the Amendments created a Federal Election Commission, 2 U.S.C.
§437c(a)(1) (1970 ed., Supp. IV); established an administrative procedure
for processing complaints of alleged violations of §610 after January 1, 1975,
2 U.S.C. §437g (1970 ed., Supp. IV), and §410, note following 2 U.S.C. §431
(1970 eds., Supp. IV); and provided that "[a]ny person who believes a violation
. . . [of §610] has occurred may file a complaint with the Commission." 2 U.S.C.
§437g(a)(1)(A) (1970 ed., Supp. IV). The Commission must either investigate the complaint or refer the complaint to the Attorney General, 2 U.S.C.
§§437g(a)(2)(A) and (B) (1970 ed., Supp. IV).[8] If the Commission chooses to
investigate the complaint, and after investigation determines that "any person
has engaged or is about to engage in any acts or practices which constitute or
will constitute a violation" of §610, the Commission may request the Attorney
General to "institute a civil action for relief, including a permanent or temporary injunction, restraining order, or any other appropriate order. . . ." 2 U.S.C.
§437g(a)(7) (1970 ed., Supp. IV). And 2 U.S.C. §437c(b) (1970 ed., Supp. IV),
expressly vests the Commission with "primary jurisdiction" over any claimed violation of §610 within its purview.[9] Consequently, a complainant seeking as citizen or stockholder to enjoin alleged violations of §610 in future elections must
henceforth pursue the statutory remedy of a complaint to the Commission, and
invoke its authority to request the Attorney General to seek the injunctive relief.
H.R. Conf. Rep. No. 93-1438, p.94 (1974). Thus, the Amendments constitute
an intervening law that relegates to the Commission's cognizance respondent's
complaint as citizen or stockholder for injunctive relief against any alleged violations of §610 in future elections. In that circumstance, the holding of the
Court of Appeals must be reversed, for our duty is to decide this case according
to the law existing at the time of our decision. . . .

III

Our conclusion in Part II pretermits any occasion for addressing the question of respondent's standing as a citizen and voter to maintain this action, for
respondent seeks damages only derivatively as stockholder. Therefore, we turn

---

8. Other provisions of the Amendments which may have relevance to private parties' complaints of
violations of §610 include 2 U.S.C. §437g(a)(9) (1970 ed., Supp. IV), providing for judicial review at the
behest of "[a]ny party aggrieved" by any order granted in a civil action filed by the Attorney General, and
2 U.S.C. §437h(a)(1970 ed., Supp. IV), permitting "any individual eligible to vote in any election for the
office of President of the United States" to file "such actions . . . as may be appropriate to construe the
constitutionality of . . . [§610]."

9. The parties disagree upon whether this reference to "primary jurisdiction" suggests that a complainant, after filing a complaint with the Commission, may file a civil suit for injunctive relief if the
Commission fails to cause one to be filed. They also dispute whether the exhaustion requirement applies
to a suit for damages. . . .

next to the holding of the Court of Appeals that "a private cause of action . . . by a stockholder to secure . . . derivative damage relief [is] proper to remedy violation of §610." We hold that such relief is not available with regard to a 1972 violation under §610 itself, but rather is available, if at all, under Delaware law governing corporations.

In determining whether a private remedy is implicit in a statute not expressly providing one, several factors are relevant. First, is the plaintiff "one of the class for whose *especial* benefit the statute was enacted," Texas & Pacific R. Co. v. Rigsby, 241 U.S. 33, 39 (1916) (emphasis supplied) — that is, does the statute create a federal right in favor of the plaintiff? Second, is there any indication of legislative intent, explicit or implicit, either to create such a remedy or to deny one? *See, e.g.,* National Railroad Passenger Corp. v. National Assn. of Railroad Passengers, 414 U.S. 453, 458, 460 (1974) *(Amtrak).* Third, is it consistent with the underlying purposes of the legislative scheme to imply such a remedy for the plaintiff? *See, e.g., Amtrak, supra;* Securities Investor Protection Corp. v. Barbour, 421 U.S. 412, 423 (1975); Calhoon v. Harvey, 379 U.S. 134 (1964). And finally, is the cause of action one traditionally relegated to state law, in an area basically the concern of the States, so that it would be inappropriate to infer a cause of action based solely on federal law? *See* Wheeldin v. Wheeler, 373 U.S. 647, 652 (1963); *cf.* J. I. Case Co. v. Borak, 377 U.S. 426, 434 (1964); Bivens v. Six Unknown Federal Narcotics Agents, 403 U.S. 388, 394-395 (1971); *id.,* at 400 (Harlan, J., concurring in judgment).

The dissenting judge in the Court of Appeals and petitioners here suggest that where a statute provides a penal remedy alone, it cannot be regarded as creating a right in any particular class of people. . . .

We need not, however, go so far as to say that in this circumstance a bare criminal statute can *never* be deemed sufficiently protective of some special group so as to give rise to a private cause of action by a member of that group. For the intent to protect corporate shareholders particularly was at best a subsidiary purpose of §610, and the other relevant factors all either are not helpful or militate against implying a private cause of action.

First, §610 is derived from the Act of January 26, 1907, which "seems to have been motivated by two considerations. First, the necessity for destroying the influence over elections which corporations exercised through financial contribution. Second, the feeling that corporate officials had no moral right to use corporate funds for contribution to political parties without the consent of the stockholders." United States v. CIO, 335 U.S. 106, 113 (1948). *See* 40 Cong. Rec. 96 (1905) (Annual Message of President Theodore Roosevelt). Respondent bases his derivative action on the second purpose, claiming that the intent to protect stockholders from use of their invested funds for political purposes demonstrates that the statute set up a federal right in shareholders not to have corporate funds used for this purpose.

However, the legislative history of the 1907 Act, recited at length in United States v. Auto Workers, 352 U.S. 567 (1957), demonstrates that the protection of ordinary stockholders was at best a secondary concern.[13] Rather, the primary

---

13. Section 610 was later expanded to include labor unions within its prohibition. The history of this expansion has been recounted before. United States v. CIO, 335 U.S. 106, 114-16 (1948); United

purpose of the 1907 Act, and of the 1925 Federal Corrupt Practices Act, 43 Stat. 1070, which re-enacted the 1907 provision with some changes as §313 of that Act, *see* United States v. Auto Workers, *supra*, at 577, was to assure that federal elections are " 'free from the power of money,' " 352 U.S., at 574, to eliminate " 'the apparent hold on political parties which business interests . . . seek and sometimes obtain by reason of liberal campaign contributions.' " *Id.*, at 576, *quoting* 65 Cong. Rec. 9507 (1924) (remarks of Sen. Robinson). *See also* 352 U.S., at 571-577. Thus, the legislation was primarily concerned with corporations as a source of aggregated wealth and therefore of possible corrupting influence, and not directly with the internal relations between the corporations and their stockholders. In contrast, in those situations in which we have inferred a federal private cause of action not expressly provided, there has generally been a clearly articulated federal right in the plaintiff, e.g., Bivens v. Six Unknown Federal Narcotics Agents, *supra*, or a pervasive legislative scheme governing the relationship between the plaintiff class and the defendant class in a particular regard, e.g., J. I. Case Co. v. Borak, *supra*.

Second, there is no indication whatever in the legislative history of §610 which suggests a congressional intention to vest in corporate shareholders a federal right to damages for violation of §610. True, in situations in which it is clear that federal law has granted a class of persons certain rights, it is not necessary to show an intention to *create* a private cause of action, although an explicit purpose to *deny* such cause of action would be controlling. But where, as here, it is at least dubious whether Congress intended to vest in the plaintiff class rights broader than those provided by state regulation of corporations, the fact that there is no suggestion at all that §610 may give rise to a suit for damages or, indeed, to any civil cause of action, reinforces the conclusion that the expectation, if any, was that the relationship between corporations and their stockholders would continue to be entrusted entirely to state law.

Third, while "it is the duty of the courts to be alert to provide such remedies as are necessary to make effective the congressional purpose," J. I. Case Co. v. Borak, 377 U.S., at 433, in this instance the remedy sought would not aid the primary congressional goal. Recovery of derivative damages by the corporation for violation of §610 would not cure the influence which the use of corporate funds in the first instance may have had on a federal election. Rather, such a remedy would only permit directors in effect to "borrow" corporate funds for a time; the later compelled repayment might well not deter the initial violation, and would certainly not decrease the impact of the use of such funds upon an election already past.

Fourth, and finally, for reasons already intimated, it is entirely appropriate in this instance to relegate respondent and others in his situation to whatever remedy is created by state law. [T]he use of corporate funds in violation of federal law may, under the law of some States, give rise to a cause of action for breach of

States v. Auto Workers, 352 U.S. 567, 578-584 (1957); Pipefitters v. United States, 407 U.S. 385, 402-09 (1972). We note that Congress did show concern, in permanently expanding §610 to unions, for protecting union members from use of their funds for political purposes. *See* United States v. CIO, *supra*, at 135, 142 (Rutledge, J., concurring). This difference in emphasis may reflect a recognition that, while a stockholder acquires his stock voluntarily and is free to dispose of it, union membership and the payment of union dues is often involuntary because of union security and check-off provisions. *Cf.* Machinists v. Street, 367 U.S. 740 (1961).

fiduciary duty. *See, e.g.,* Miller v. American Telephone & Telegraph Co., 507 F.2d 759 (3d Cir. 1974). Corporations are creatures of state law, and investors commit their funds to corporate directors on the understanding that, except where federal law expressly requires certain responsibilities of directors with respect to stockholders, state law will govern the internal affairs of the corporation. If, for example, state law permits corporations to use corporate funds as contributions in state elections, *see Miller, supra,* at 763 n.4, shareholders are on notice that their funds may be so used and have no recourse under any federal statute. We are necessarily reluctant to imply a federal right to recover funds used in violation of a federal statute where the laws governing the corporation may put a shareholder on notice that there may be no such recovery.

In *Borak, supra,* we said: "[If] the law of the State happened to attach no responsibility to the use of misleading proxy statements, the whole purpose of [§14(a) of the Securities Exchange Act of 1934] might be frustrated." 377 U.S., at 434-35. Here, committing respondent to state-provided remedies would have no such effect. In *Borak,* the statute involved was clearly an intrusion of federal law into the internal affairs of corporations; to the extent that state law differed or impeded suit, the congressional intent could be compromised in state-created causes of action. In this case, Congress was concerned, not with regulating corporations as such, but with dulling their impact upon federal elections. As we have seen, the existence or nonexistence of a derivative cause of action for damages would not aid or hinder this primary goal.

Because injunctive relief is not presently available in light of the Amendments, and because implication of a federal right of damages on behalf of a corporation under §610 would intrude into an area traditionally committed to state law without aiding the main purpose of §610, we reverse.

It is so ordered.

NOTES AND QUESTIONS

1. *A manageable four-part test?* The test announced in *Cort* quickly became the accepted formula for determining whether statutes imply private rights of action. Is it a coherent formula? Why, for example, are legislative "intent" and "purpose" only two parts rather than the whole of the inquiry? If other factors are relevant, why only the two identified by the Court? If the Supreme Court wanted to curb the lower courts' propensity for finding implied rights to sue in federal courts, does its test, taken at face value, serve that goal? The difficulty of establishing a private right of action is compounded by the disjunctive nature of the Court's test. Each of the four hurdles must be cleared, as the Court's decision in Transamerica Mortgage Advisors, Inc. v. Lewis, 444 U.S. 11 (1979), makes plain. In *Transamerica,* the Court found in the Investment Advisors Act of 1940, 15 U.S.C. §§80b-1 *et seq.,* a legislative intent especially to protect the clients of investment advisors. Even so, a 5-4 majority, finding no legislative intent to accord a private remedy to investors injured by Advisors' violation of the Act's antifraud provision, declined to allow private suit.

2. *Application of the* Cort *test.* What do you think of the way the Court applied the test to the facts in *Cort?* Is it plain, for instance, that a private right of action would not promote §610's purpose of deterring corporate political

expenditures because the offending officers would merely be required to pay the money back? Note that in this case more than $500,000 was allegedly "borrowed" from Bethlehem (in 1972 dollars!). If the private remedy sought by Ash would not advance the Act's deterrent purposes, would criminal liability do any better?

3. *Other considerations.* Should the *Cort* decision be read as reflecting, not a desire to limit private enforcement generally, but an inclination to shield putative defendants, such as corporate directors, for whose decisions we have special solicitude? Was *Cort* a case in which, putting aside other judicial remedies (here, state court relief in derivative suits), the private plaintiff has adequate nonlegal remedies? What might those be? For a very different application of very similar guidelines, *see* Justice Brennan's opinion for the Court in Bivens v. Six Unknown Named Agents of Federal Bureau of Narcotics, 403 U.S. 388 (1971).

4. *Election advocacy by corporations and labor unions: the controversy continues.* In the 2002 Bipartisan Campaign Reform Act (known as the McCain-Feingold Act), Pub. L. 107-155, 116 Stat. 81, Congress updated the Federal Election Campaign Act Amendments of 1974 at issue in the *Cort* case. The 2002 act prohibited corporations or labor unions from making any "electioneering communication" within 30 days of a primary election or 60 days of a general election and prohibited such entities from making any expenditure advocating the election or defeat of any candidate for office at any time. In Citizens United v. Federal Election Commission, 558 U.S. 310 (2010), a decision that continues to spark controversy, a divided Supreme Court struck down these provisions as a violation of the Speech Clause of the First Amendment.

5. *Separation of powers.* Although the *Cort* test might have been intended to tighten up on judicial creation of private rights of action, dissatisfaction with its four-part test quickly emerged, as illustrated by Justice Powell's famous dissent in the following case:

CANNON v. UNIVERSITY OF CHICAGO, 441 U.S. 677 (1979): Title IX of the 1972 Education Act Amendments, 20 U.S.C. §1681, prohibits discrimination in educational institutions that receive federal funds, and it provides for enforcement through funding cut-offs. Geraldine Cannon sued two universities after she was denied admission to medical school, claiming sex discrimination. The Court applied *Cort*'s four factors and recognized a private right of action to enforce Title IX. The Court noted that "Title IX explicitly confers a benefit on persons discriminated against on the basis of sex," and further declared that "[t]he language in [this statute]—which expressly identifies the class Congress intended to benefit—contrasts sharply with statutory language customarily found in criminal statutes, such as that construed in *Cort,* and other laws enacted for the protection of the general public." Justice Powell, in dissent, argued that the *Cort* analysis should be scrapped in favor of a focus on legislative intent:

> The "four factor" analysis . . . is an open invitation to federal courts to legislate causes of action not authorized by Congress. It is an analysis not faithful to constitutional principles and should be rejected. Absent the most compelling evidence of affirmative congressional intent, a federal court should not infer a private cause of action. . . .

Of the four factors mentioned in *Cort,* only one refers expressly to legislative intent. The other three invite independent judicial lawmaking. Asking whether a statute creates a right in favor of a private party, for example, begs the question at issue. What is involved is not the mere existence of a legal right, but a particular person's right to invoke the power of the courts to enforce that right. Determining whether a private action would be consistent with the "underlying purposes" of a legislative scheme permits a court to decide for itself what the goals of a scheme should be, and how those goals should be advanced. Finally, looking to state law for parallels to the federal right simply focuses inquiry on a particular policy consideration that Congress already may have weighed in deciding not to create a private action.

That the *Cort* analysis too readily permits courts to override the decision of Congress not to create a private action is demonstrated conclusively by the flood of lower-court decisions applying it. Although from the time *Cort* was decided until today this Court consistently has turned back attempts to create private actions, other federal courts have tended to proceed in exactly the opposite direction. In the four years since we decided *Cort,* no less than 20 decisions by the Courts of Appeals have implied private actions from federal statutes.

Cort allows the Judicial Branch to assume policymaking authority vested by the Constitution in the Legislative Branch. It also invites Congress to avoid resolution of the often controversial question whether a new regulatory statute should be enforced through private litigation. Rather than confronting the hard political choices involved, Congress is encouraged to shirk its constitutional obligation and leave the issue to the courts to decide. When this happens, the legislative process with its public scrutiny and participation has been bypassed, with attendant prejudice to everyone concerned. Because the courts are free to reach a result different from that which the normal play of political forces would have produced, the intended beneficiaries of the legislation are unable to ensure the full measure of protection their needs may warrant. For the same reason, those subject to the legislative constraints are denied the opportunity to forestall through the political process potentially unnecessary and disruptive litigation. Moreover, the public generally is denied the benefits that are derived from the making of important societal choices through the open debate of the democratic process.

Henceforth, we should not condone the implication of any private action from a federal statute absent the most compelling evidence that Congress in fact intended such an action to exist. Where a statutory scheme expressly provides for an alternative mechanism for enforcing the rights and duties created, I would be especially reluctant ever to permit a federal court to volunteer its services for enforcement purposes. Because the Court today is enlisting the federal judiciary in just such an enterprise, I dissent.

Although Justice Powell did not, in *Cannon,* persuade his colleagues to repudiate *Cort,* his arguments substantially affected the analysis of private rights of action. Do you agree with Justice Powell that implying a right of action is inconsistent with the proper role of the judiciary? Is the existence of an alternative enforcement mechanism compelling evidence against congressional intent to allow a private right of action?

Soon after *Cannon,* although decisions concerning implied rights began with a recitation of *Cort*'s four factors, the Court rarely went beyond inquiry into the statutory text and legislative history, focusing almost exclusively on the first two factors, especially the second. As all lawyers know, legislative history often provides an analytic base of quicksand-like firmness. In part, this is because partisans for competing positions seek to pack the legislative record with statements that, they hope, will be conducive to a favorable interpretation of matters not resolved by the text. The Supreme Court remedied this analytic infirmity by creating a strong presumption against implying a private right of action in the absence of a rather clear legislative statement that one was intended. *See, e.g.,* Middlesex County Sewerage Authority v. National Sea Clammers Association, 453 U.S. 1 (1981); California v. Sierra Club, 451 U.S. 287 (1981); Universities Research Association v. Coutu, 450 U.S. 754 (1981); Touche Ross & Co. v. Redington, 442 U.S. 560 (1979); Transamerica Mortgage Advisors, Inc. v. Lewis, 444 U.S. 11, 19-24 (1979).

While reading the following case, ask yourself whether *Cort* is still good law.

KARAHALIOS v. NATIONAL FEDERATION OF FEDERAL EMPLOYEES, LOCAL 1263
489 U.S. 527 (1989)

JUSTICE WHITE delivered the opinion of the Court.

The question before the Court is whether Title VII of the Civil Service Reform Act of 1978 (CSRA or Act), 5 U.S.C. §7101 *et seq.* (1982 ed. and Supp. IV), confers on federal employees a private cause of action against a breach by a union representing federal employees of its statutory duty of fair representation. Because we decide that Congress vested exclusive enforcement authority over this duty in the Federal Labor Relations Authority (FLRA) and its General Counsel, we agree with the Court of Appeals that no private cause of action exists. Hence we affirm.

[Karahalios was a non-Union employee of the Defense Language Institute/ Foreign Language Center, Presidio of Monterey, California ("Institute"), a federal agency subject to the CSRA. Karahalios was awarded a promotion, but later was demoted after another employee, Kuntelos, filed a grievance and ultimately won a promotion to the same position. The Union represented Kuntelos in proceedings related to the grievance and promotion, and then declined to prosecute Karahalios's grievances over his demotion, citing a conflict of interest with its earlier representation of Kuntelos. Karahalios filed unfair labor practice charges with the FLRA against both the Institute and the Union. The General Counsel of the FLRA ruled that the Union had violated its duty of fair representation and filed a formal complaint against the Union. This charge was resolved pursuant to a settlement under which Karahalios received no personal benefit, and as a result, Karahalios filed a damages action in federal District Court against both the Institute and the Union. The District Court ruled in favor of a private right of action against the Union, and after the Court of Appeals reversed this decision, the Supreme Court granted Karahalios's petition for certiorari.]

Prior to 1978, labor relations in the federal sector were governed by a 1962 Executive Order administered by a Federal Labor Relations Council whose decisions were not subject to judicial review. . . . Since 1978, Title VII of the CSRA has been the controlling authority. Of particular relevance here, 5 U.S.C. §7114(a)(1) provides that a labor organization that has been accorded the exclusive right of representing employees in a designated unit "is responsible for representing the interests of all employees in the unit it represents without discrimination and without regard to labor organization membership." This provision is "virtually identical" to that found in the Executive Order and is the source of the collective-bargaining agent's duty of fair representation. . . . This duty also parallels the fair representation obligation of a union in the private sector that has been found implicit in the National Labor Relations Act (NLRA), . . . 29 U.S.C. §151 *et seq.* . . . and the Railway Labor Act (RLA), . . . 45 U.S.C. §151 *et seq.* . . . .

Title VII also makes it clear that a breach of the duty of fair representation is an unfair labor practice, for it provides that it is "an unfair labor practice for a labor organization . . . to otherwise fail or refuse to comply with any provision of this chapter." §7116(b)(8). Under §7118, unfair labor practice complaints are adjudicated by the FLRA, which is authorized to order remedial action appropriate to carry out the purposes of Title VII, including an award of backpay against either the agency or the labor organization that has committed the unfair practice.

There is no express suggestion in Title VII that Congress intended to furnish a parallel remedy in a federal district court to enforce the duty of fair representation. The Title provides recourse to the courts in only three instances: with specified exceptions, persons aggrieved by a final FLRA order may seek review in the appropriate court of appeals, §7123(a); the FLRA may seek judicial enforcement of its orders, §7123(b); and temporary injunctive relief is available to the FLRA to assist it in the discharge of its duties, §7123(d).

Petitioner nevertheless insists that a cause of action to enforce the Union's fair representation duty should be implied. Such a claim poses an issue of statutory construction: the "ultimate issue is whether Congress intended to create a private cause of action," California v. Sierra Club, 451 U.S. 287, 293 (1981) (citations omitted). . . . Unless such "congressional intent can be inferred from the language of the statute, the statutory structure, or some other source, the essential predicate for implication of a private remedy simply does not exist." Thompson v. Thompson, 484 U.S. 174 (1988). It is also an "elemental canon" of statutory construction that where a statute expressly provides a remedy, courts must be especially reluctant to provide additional remedies. Transamerica Mortgage Advisers, Inc. v. Lewis, 444 U.S. 11, 19 (1979). In such cases, "[i]n the absence of strong indicia of contrary congressional intent, we are compelled to conclude that Congress provided precisely the remedies it considered appropriate." Middlesex County Sewerage Authority v. Sea Clammers, 453 U.S. 1, 15 (1981). . . .

These guideposts indicate that the Court of Appeals was quite correct in concluding that neither the language nor the structure of the Act shows any congressional intent to provide a private cause of action to enforce federal employees unions' duty of fair representation. That duty is expressly recognized in the Act, and an administrative remedy for its breach is expressly provided for before the FLRA, a body created by Congress to enforce the duties imposed on agencies and unions by Title VII, including the duty of fair representation. Nothing in the legislative history of Title VII has been called to our attention indicating that Congress contemplated direct judicial enforcement of the union's duty. . . .

Petitioner, however, relies on another source to find the necessary congressional intent to provide him with a cause of action. Petitioner urges that Title VII was modeled after the NLRA and that the authority of the FLRA was meant to be similar to that of the National Labor Relations Board (NLRB). Because this Court found implicit in the NLRA a private cause of action against unions to enforce their fair representation duty even after the NLRB had construed the NLRA to make a breach of the duty an unfair labor practice, petitioner argues that Congress must have intended to preserve this judicial role under Title VII. [Vaca v. Sipes, 386 U.S. 171, 180-183 (1967).]

[The difficulty with this argument is that] Title VII is not a carbon copy of the NLRA, nor is the authority of the FLRA the same as that of the NLRB. The NLRA, like the RLA, did not expressly make a breach of the duty of fair representation an unfair labor practice and did not expressly provide for the enforcement of such a duty by the NLRB. That duty was implied by the Court because members of bargaining units were forced to accept unions as their exclusive bargaining agents. Because employees had no administrative remedy for a breach of the duty, we recognized a judicial cause of action on behalf of the employee. . . . Very dissimilarly, Title VII of the CSRA not only expressly recognizes the fair representation duty but also provides for its administrative enforcement. . . .

We therefore discern no basis for finding congressional intent to provide petitioner with a cause of action against the Union. Congress undoubtedly was aware from our cases such as Cort v. Ash, 422 U.S. 66 (1975), that the Court had departed from its prior standard for resolving a claim urging that an implied statutory cause of action should be recognized, and that such issues were being resolved by a straightforward inquiry into whether Congress intended to provide a private cause of action. Had Congress intended the courts to enforce a federal employees union's duty of fair representation, we would expect to find some evidence of that intent in the statute or its legislative history. We find none. . . . To be sure, courts play a role in CSRA §7116(b)(8) fair representation cases, but only sitting in review of the FLRA. To hold that the district courts must entertain such cases in the first instance would seriously undermine what we deem to be the congressional scheme, namely to leave the enforcement of union and agency duties under the Act to the General Counsel and the FLRA and to confine the courts to the role given them under the Act.

Accordingly the judgment of the Court of Appeals is Affirmed.

NOTES AND QUESTIONS

1. *What is left of* Cort*?* Is the Court's discussion of *Cort* accurate? What is the principle guiding the decision of whether to imply a private right of action? Has the Court accepted Justice Powell's *Cannon* dissent? In Spicer v. Chicago Board of Options Exchange, Inc., 977 F.2d 255, 258 (7th Cir. 1992), the court stated that "[t]he four part test from Cort v. Ash . . . survives but only nominally. In recent years, the focus has shifted to the second *Cort* factor: whether Congress . . . intended to create a private remedy." In Alexander v. Sandoval, 532 U.S. 275, 287 (2001), the Supreme Court stated that "[l]ike substantive federal law itself, private rights of action to enforce federal law must be created by Congress." More recently, the Court relied on the twin peaks of congressional intent and separation of powers to reject aider and abettor liability in implied securities fraud actions. As the Court stated, "[t]he decision to extend the cause of action is for Congress, not for us." Stoneridge Inv. Partners, LLC v. Scientific-Atlanta, 552 U.S. 148, 165 (2008).

For a strong critique of the Court's near-exclusive focus on congressional intent in deciding whether to recognize a private right of action, *see* Susan Stabile, The Role of Congressional Intent in Determining the Existence of Implied Private Rights of Action, 71 Notre Dame L. Rev. 861 (1996).

2. *Standing by another name?* When all is said and done, is "implied private right of action" merely another name for "standing"? Reviewing the materials on standing, in Chapter III, *supra*, do you see any difference between the two? Why do you suppose the Court uses different terminology and different tests?

3. *Remedies.* When a federal court does imply a right of action, at some point in the litigation, the question of remedies arises. In Franklin v. Gwinnett County Public Schools, 503 U.S. 60 (1992), the Court reviewed the Eleventh Circuit's decision not to allow monetary damages in cases brought under Title IX of the 1972 Education Act Amendments, the statute at issue in *Cannon, supra*. The lower court reasoned that relief under a statute enacted under the Spending Clause should be limited to equitable relief so that the recipient of federal funds could avoid serious consequences of liability by choosing to forgo federal funds. The Supreme Court reversed, holding that "if a right of action exists to enforce a federal right and Congress is silent on the question of remedies, a federal court may order any appropriate relief." 503 U.S. at 69. The Court found no congressional intent to disallow damages in claims brought under Title IX. Is this consistent with the approach taken in *Karahalios*? Shouldn't the Court ask whether Congress intended to grant the damages remedy, not whether Congress intended to foreclose it? *See also* Jackson v. Birmingham Board of Education, 544 U.S. 167 (2005) (allowing damages remedy under Title IX based on retaliation against male high school basketball coach who complained about alleged unequal treatment of girls' team).

"Any appropriate relief" apparently does not include punitive damages. In Barnes v. Gorman, 536 U.S. 181 (2002), the Court held that punitive damages may not be awarded in cases arising under Title IX because Title IX is a Spending Clause provision. The Court reasoned that "[a] funding recipient is generally on notice that it is subject not only to those remedies explicitly provided in the relevant legislation, but also to those remedies traditionally available in suits for breach of contract. Thus we have held that under Title IX, which contains no express remedies, a recipient of federal funds is nevertheless subject to suit for compensatory damages, and injunction. . . . But punitive damages, unlike compensatory damages and injunction, are generally not available for breach of contract." 536 U.S. at 187. Query whether punitive damages should be available in actions implied from statutes enacted under other powers, such as the commerce power.

3.   Public-Law Preclusion of Existing Private Remedies: Primary Jurisdiction and Pre-emption

Cases like *Borak* tell us that regulatory statutes may be read to create private rights of action that *would not* otherwise exist. The obverse is also possible. Regulatory statutes may be read to destroy or modify private rights of action that *would* otherwise exist. The legal doctrines under which private remedies may be supplanted or altered are known as "primary jurisdiction" and "pre-emption."

a.   Primary Jurisdiction

Because many agencies regulate in areas that are also covered by traditional common law doctrines, controversy inevitably arises over the distribution of authority between courts and agencies. The primary jurisdiction doctrine regulates the allocation of disputes between agencies and courts. Primary jurisdiction is illustrated by the landmark case of Texas & Pacific Ry. Co. v. Abilene Cotton Oil Co., 204 U.S. 426 (1907). A cotton oil manufacturer brought a common law action against a common carrier for charging what it asserted to be "unreasonable" rates. The carrier defended on the ground that the Interstate Commerce Act effectively superseded the shipper's common law remedies. The Act prohibited carriers from charging unreasonable rates and gave the Interstate Commerce Commission jurisdiction to award reparations to any shipper whom it found to have been overcharged. The Supreme Court ruled that the shipper must bring its claim for overcharge before the ICC. Despite the fact that a section of the Act *explicitly* saved shippers' common law remedies, the Court reasoned that allowing common law actions would destroy the "uniformity" of railroad rates that Congress had charged the ICC to effectuate. 204 U.S. at 441. While the ICC and the courts might apply the same legal standard of reasonableness, the Court observed that allowing actions in various courts could result in conflicting decisions about the same rates. The Act, said the Court, "cannot be held to destroy itself." *Id.* at 447.

Abilene is the first in a long line of decisions that have attempted to articulate criteria for resolving jurisdictional disputes between courts and agencies—for deciding, that is, which institution has "primary" jurisdiction over a matter. Conflicts between shippers and regulated carriers have been a fertile source for such decisions. Great Northern Ry. Co. v. Merchants Elevator Co., 259 U.S. 285 (1922), was another common law action for an overcharge brought by a shipper against a carrier. At issue was the meaning of two provisions in the tariff filed by the railroad with the ICC. The Court refused to refer this dispute to the ICC, however, arguing that courts had competence to decide the "meaning of words of the tariff which were used in their ordinary sense." *Id.* at 294. Had the tariff used words in a "technical" sense, by contrast, the ICC would have had primary jurisdiction to interpret its language. *Id.* at 292. That situation was presented in United States v. Western Pacific R.R. Co., 352 U.S. 59 (1956). The railroad sued the government in the Court of Claims to recover charges allegedly due it for shipping unfused napalm bombs. The railroad demanded payment based on the rate specified in the tariff for "incendiary bombs"; the government offered to pay the (lower) rate for "gasoline in steel drums." The Supreme Court held that the dispute should have been presented to the ICC since the ICC had originally established the tariff categories at issue and would understand far better than a court how its rationale in doing so applied to these facts.

In Nader v. Allegheny Airlines, Inc., 426 U.S. 290 (1976), the Supreme Court rejected an argument for primary jurisdiction in a suit brought in federal district court against Allegheny Airlines by consumer activist (and later presidential candidate) Ralph Nader, after he was "bumped" from an overbooked flight. Allegheny argued that the Civil Aeronautics Board (CAB) had primary jurisdiction over the dispute because its bumping policy was subject to CAB regulation. Because Allegheny's bumping policy was part of the tariff it filed with the CAB, Nader was careful to direct his complaint not at the substance of the policy but rather at Allegheny's failure to disclose its policy in advance, which Nader argued gave rise to a common law action for misrepresentation. At trial, Nader was awarded $10 in compensatory damages (he had been able to make alternate travel arrangements) and $25,000 in punitive damages. In rejecting Allegheny's primary jurisdiction argument, the Court distinguished *Abilene* on the ground that "unlike *Abilene* we are not faced with an irreconcilable conflict between the statutory scheme and the persistence of common-law remedies." 426 U.S. at 299. The Court also noted that the governing statute contained a savings clause preserving alternative remedies. Although the CAB had the power to prohibit airlines from engaging in unfair and deceptive practices, individual consumers had no power to initiate proceedings before the CAB, "a circumstance that indicates that Congress did not intend to require private litigants to obtain [an agency] determination before they could proceed with the common-law remedies preserved [by the statute]." *Id.* at 302.

The NLRB has primary jurisdiction over enforcement of the National Labor Relations Act. Allegations that an employer or a union has violated the NLRA must thus be brought, in the first instance, to the NLRB. Yet, the Supreme Court has held that claims alleging that a union has breached its duty of fair representation may be brought directly in federal court, because such claims do not arise under the NLRA. *See* Vaca v. Sipes, 386 U.S. 171, 177-183 (1967). This has led plaintiffs to attempt to avoid the NLRB's jurisdiction by casting a wide variety of complaints as raising the duty of fair representation, forcing courts to make complicated determinations concerning whether a claim arises under the NLRA or truly states a claim for violation of the duty of fair representation. *See* Marquez v. Screen Actors Guild, Inc., 525 U.S. 33, 49-51 (1998).

The statement that an administrative agency has "primary jurisdiction" may have one of two meanings. Usually, as in *Abilene,* it means that the agency has exclusive authority to dispose of the controverted issue: the courts are ousted of jurisdiction over the claim, although they may ultimately engage in judicial review of the agency's decision. Sometimes, however, it simply means that judicial consideration must be postponed until an agency has an opportunity to pass on one or more questions whose resolution is important to, but not dispositive of, the judicial action. An example of the latter usage is Ricci v. Chicago Mercantile Exchange, 409 U.S. 289 (1973). Ricci, a commodity futures dealer, brought an antitrust action against the exchange and one of its members, alleging that they conspired to deprive him of a seat on the exchange. Defendants argued that their conduct was immunized by the Commodity Exchange Act, 7 U.S.C. §§1 *et seq.,* which requires exchanges to submit their membership rules to the Secretary of Agriculture for approval and empowers the Commodities Exchange Commission, upon petition by any interested person, to compel an exchange to enforce its rules. The Supreme Court affirmed an appeals court order staying the antitrust suit until Ricci sought a commission determination of whether the defendants had violated the exchange's rules. "A prior agency adjudication of this dispute," said the Court, "will be a material aid in ultimately deciding whether the Commodity Exchange Act forecloses this antitrust suit, a matter that seems to depend in the first instance on whether the transfer of Ricci's membership was in violation of the Act for failure to follow Exchange rules." 409 U.S. at 305. An agency "especially familiar with the customs and practices of the industry" is better equipped than a court to decide that issue. *Ibid.* Justice Marshall, joined by three other Justices, dissented, arguing that referral to the commission might prove to be futile since the Act gave Ricci no absolute right to administrative relief and the cost and inconvenience to Ricci would outweigh the marginal benefit of prior administrative determination to the subsequent antitrust action. With *Ricci, compare* Far East Conference v. United States, 342 U.S. 570 (1952) (refusing to order an antitrust case to be retained on the district court docket pending referral to an administrative agency).

The issue not reached in *Ricci*—whether compliance with a regulatory statute implicitly immunizes the conduct from antitrust liability—has received different answers in different contexts. For example, the Court has found an implied antitrust immunity for conduct subject to regulation by the Securities and Exchange Commission (United States v. National Association of Securities Dealers, Inc., 422 U.S. 694 (1975); Gordon v. New York Stock Exchange, 422 U.S. 659 (1975)) and the Civil Aeronautics Board (Hughes Tool Co. v. Trans World Airlines, Inc., 409 U.S. 363 (1973); Pan American World Airways, Inc. v. United States, 371 U.S. 296 (1963)). Yet, the Court has found no implied immunity for conduct regulated by the Federal Communications Commission (United States v. Radio Corporation of America, 358 U.S. 334 (1959)) or the Federal Power Commission (Otter Tail Power Co. v. United States, 410 U.S. 366 (1973); California v. FPC, 369 U.S. 482 (1962)). The test in all these cases, the Court has said repeatedly, is whether allowing antitrust suits would unduly burden or disrupt the other regulatory scheme. But the cases go off in so many directions as to seem incapable of convincing rationalization. For further discussion of this complex subject, *see* Phillip Areeda & Donald F. Turner, Antitrust Law 134-178 (1978); Louis L. Jaffe, Judicial Control of Administrative Action 132-141 (1965); Israel Convisser, Primary Jurisdiction: The Rule and Its Rationalizations, 65 Yale L.J. 315 (1956).

b.   Regulatory Pre-emption

The doctrine of primary jurisdiction mediates "horizontal" conflicts between agencies and courts. Even if courts and agencies would apply the same legal standards to resolve a dispute, the primary jurisdiction doctrine is used to determine where the dispute should be heard, agency or court. The doctrine of pre-emption mediates "vertical" conflicts between federal and state law. Under the doctrine of pre-emption, federal law, including federal regulatory action, may override state regulation or displace state law that would otherwise provide private remedies for conduct violating state law standards. Federal pre-emption relegates plaintiffs to whatever remedies are available under federal law, which means that if federal law provides no remedy, pre-emption may eliminate liability for conduct that would otherwise be actionable under state law.

Congressional power to pre-empt state law is based on the Supremacy Clause of the Constitution, Art. VI, cl. 2:

> This Constitution, and the Laws of the United States which shall be made in Pursuance thereof; and all Treaties made, or which shall be made, under the Authority of the United States, shall be the supreme Law of the Land; and the

Judges in every State shall be bound thereby, any Thing in the Constitution or Laws of any State to the Contrary notwithstanding.

The Supreme Court has stated repeatedly that pre-emption is a matter of congressional intent—federal law pre-empts state law only when Congress intends it to. The Court has explained that federal law pre-empts state law in two broad categories. First, federal law may expressly pre-empt state law (i.e., a federal statute or regulation may explicitly state that certain state laws are pre-empted). Second, federal law may implicitly pre-empt state law (i.e., congressional intent to pre-empt may be found even in the absence of express pre-empting language).

Courts have recognized three forms of implied pre-emption usually referred to as "field," "conflict," and "obstacle" pre-emption. Field pre-emption arises when the federal statutory scheme is so comprehensive that federal law is said to "occupy the field." Congressional intent to pre-empt state law within the field is inferred from the comprehensiveness of the federal legislative program. For example, in Campbell v. Hussey, 368 U.S. 297 (1961), the Supreme Court held that federal regulation of tobacco labeling for auction sales was so pervasive that there was no room for state regulation, even if state law did not conflict with, but only supplemented, federal law. The Court is especially likely to invoke field pre-emption analysis in contexts involving relations with foreign nations or the policing of national boundaries. For example, in Arizona v. United States, 132 S. Ct. 2492 (2012), the Court invalidated most of an Arizona law seeking to regulate undocumented immigrants. The Court said:

> [T]he States are precluded from regulating conduct in a field that Congress, acting within its proper authority, has determined must be regulated by its exclusive governance. The intent to displace state law altogether can be inferred from a framework of regulation "so pervasive . . . that Congress left no room for the States to supplement it" or where there is a "federal interest . . . so dominant that the federal system will be assumed to preclude enforcement of state laws on the same subject." Rice v. Santa Fe Elevator Corp., 331 U.S. 218, 230 (1947).

Id. at 2501. *See also* Hines v. Davidowitz, 312 U.S. 52 (1941) (finding field pre-emption of state laws regarding aliens).

One obvious challenge in applying "field pre-emption" doctrine is defining the boundaries of the "field" occupied by federal regulation. This was the issue in Virginia Uranium, Inc. v. Warren, 139 S. Ct. 1894 (2019). A uranium mining company challenged a Virginia statute prohibiting the mining of uranium ore anywhere within the state as pre-empted by the Atomic Energy Act (administered by the Nuclear Regulatory Commission). A split Supreme Court disagreed based primarily on a provision of the AEA stating that the NRC's "exclusive" jurisdiction began only "after [uranium ore's] removal from its place of deposit in nature." For six members of the Court, that was, essentially the end of the matter and a sufficient basis for finding no pre-emption of a state ban on mining. But Chief Justice Roberts, in dissent, argued that the Act should be interpreted to pre-empt any state regulation whose *purpose* was to interfere with any NRC-regulated activities. That was the case here, he said, pointing to evidence that the state's ban on mining was designed as an indirect method to prevent uranium "milling" and "tailing" operations (refining the ore into fissionable fuel and storing radioactive waste) within the state, activities clearly committed to exclusive NRC regulation by the AEA. In his plurality opinion for the Court, Justice Gorsuch rejected that argument, stating that federal courts should avoid the fraught exercise of inquiring into state legislative "purposes." For that reason, he said, "[T]his Court has generally treated field preemption inquiries like this one as depending on *what* the State did, not *why* it did it."

Conflict pre-emption arises when federal and state law conflict, so that regulated parties cannot comply with one without simultaneously violating the other. For example, if federal law requires that gasoline contain ethanol, and state law prohibits the introduction of ethanol into gasoline, the two provisions conflict and it is presumed that Congress intended the federal standard to prevail. In this kind of situation, the principle of federal supremacy applies most clearly and directly. Obstacle pre-emption, a close cousin of conflict pre-emption, arises when enforcement of state law would arguably prevent the accomplishment of the purposes of the federal law. In such cases, while it is technically possible for regulated parties to comply with both federal and state law, intent to pre-empt state law is inferred from the court's judgment that compliance with state law would undercut the achievement of the federal law's purposes. As we shall see in the materials in this unit, critics attack this form of pre-emption as leaving too much to the judgment of the courts, which may be overly influenced by their views on the substance of the regulation rather than a finding of a true conflict between state law and federal policy.

Perhaps because they involve delicate questions of federalism, express pre-emption provisions tend to present tricky interpretive questions, and claims of implied pre-emption tend to provoke sharp disagreement, as illustrated by the following case study.

━━━━━━━━━━

Conflicts often arise between state tort law and federal safety regulation. Many products, including medicines, medical devices, pesticides, and automobiles are subject to federal safety regulation and can also give rise to state tort claims. When tort claims are brought, the defendant often argues that the federal safety regulation pre-empts state tort liability. Consider the example of automobile safety. We have previously encountered Federal Motor Vehicle Safety Standard 208, the federal regulation requiring passenger-protection devices, such as seat belts or airbags, in automobiles. FMVSS 208 evolved from a 1967 requirement that all new cars be equipped with seat belts in the front seat to a 1977 requirement that all new cars be equipped with passive restraints, either automatic safety belts or airbags. In *State Farm,* excerpted in Chapter II, *supra,* the Supreme Court overturned the Reagan Administration's decision to rescind the passive restraint requirement. That led to a new version of FMVSS 208, adopted in 1984, that did not immediately require all cars to be equipped with passive restraints and allowed automakers to choose between airbags and automatic belts. However, the regulation expressed a preference for airbags by counting each car equipped with an airbag as 1.5 cars toward its required quota of cars equipped with passive restraints. It was not until 1997 that airbags were deemed the only permissible form of passive restraint. A state tort suit premised on Honda's failure to equip a 1987 Accord with a driver's side airbag resulted in the following pre-emption decision by the Supreme Court.

GEIER v. AMERICAN HONDA MOTOR CO., INC.
529 U.S. 861 (2000)

Justice Breyer delivered the opinion of the Court.

This case focuses on the 1984 version of a Federal Motor Vehicle Safety Standard promulgated by the Department of Transportation under the authority of the National Traffic and Motor Vehicle Safety Act of 1966, 80 Stat. 718, 15 U.S.C §1381 *et seq.* (1988 ed.). The standard, FMVSS 208, required auto manufacturers to equip some but not all of their 1987 vehicles with passive restraints. We ask whether the Act pre-empts a state common-law tort action in which the plaintiff claims that the defendant auto manufacturer, who was in compliance with the standard, should nonetheless have equipped a 1987 automobile with airbags. We conclude that the Act, taken together with FMVSS 208, pre-empts the lawsuit.

I

In 1992, petitioner Alexis Geier, driving a 1987 Honda Accord, collided with a tree and was seriously injured. The car was equipped with manual shoulder and lap belts which Geier had buckled up at the time. The car was not equipped with airbags or other passive restraint devices.

Geier and her parents, also petitioners, sued the car's manufacturer, American Honda Motor Company, Inc., and its affiliates (hereinafter American Honda), under District of Columbia tort law. They claimed, among other things, that American Honda had designed its car negligently and defectively because it lacked a driver's side airbag. . . .

We now hold that this kind of "no airbag" lawsuit conflicts with the objectives of FMVSS 208, a standard authorized by the Act, and is therefore pre-empted by the Act. . . .

II

We first ask whether the Safety Act's express pre-emption provision pre-empts this tort action. The provision reads as follows:

> Whenever a Federal motor vehicle safety standard established under this subchapter is in effect, no State or political subdivision of a State shall have any authority either to establish, or to continue in effect, with respect to any motor vehicle or item of motor vehicle equipment[,] any safety standard applicable to the same aspect of performance of such vehicle or item of equipment which is not identical to the Federal standard. 15 U.S.C. §1392(d)(1988 ed.).

American Honda points out that a majority of this Court has said that a somewhat similar statutory provision in a different federal statute — a provision that uses the word "requirements" — may well expressly pre-empt similar tort actions. *See, e.g.,* Medtronic, Inc. v. Lohr, 518 U.S. 470, 502-504 (1996) (plurality opinion); 518 U.S. at 503-505 (Breyer, J., concurring in part and concurring in judgment); 518 U.S. at 509-512 (O'Connor, J., concurring in part and dissenting in part). Petitioners reply that this statute speaks of pre-empting a state-law "safety standard," not a "requirement," and that a tort action does not involve a safety standard. Hence, they conclude, the express pre-emption provision does not apply.

We need not determine the precise significance of the use of the word "standard," rather than "requirement," however, for the Act contains another provision, which resolves the disagreement. That provision, a "saving" clause, says that "compliance with" a federal safety standard "does not exempt any person from any liability under common law." 15 U.S.C. §1397(k) (1988 ed.). The saving clause assumes that there are some significant number of common-law liability cases to save. [I]t is possible to read the pre-emption provision, standing alone, as applying to standards imposed in common-law tort actions, as well as standards contained in state legislation or regulations. And if so, it would pre-empt all nonidentical state standards established in tort actions covering the same aspect of performance as an applicable federal standard, even if the federal standard merely established a minimum standard. On that broad reading of the pre-emption clause little, if any, potential "liability at common law" would remain. And few, if any, state tort actions would remain for the saving clause to save. . . . Hence the broad reading cannot be correct. The language of the pre-emption provision permits a narrow reading that excludes common-law actions. Given the presence of the saving clause, we conclude that the pre-emption clause must be so read.

III

We have just said that the saving clause at least removes tort actions from the scope of the express pre-emption clause. Does it do more? In particular, does it foreclose or limit the operation of ordinary pre-emption principles insofar as those principles instruct us to read statutes as pre-empting state laws (including common-law rules) that "actually conflict" with the statute or federal standards promulgated thereunder? Fidelity Fed. Sav. & Loan Assn. v. De la Cuesta, 458 U.S. 141, 153 (1982). [We] conclude that the saving clause (like the express pre-emption provision) does not bar the ordinary working of conflict pre-emption principles.

Nothing in the language of the saving clause suggests an intent to save state-law tort actions that conflict with federal regulations. . . .

Why . . . would Congress not have wanted ordinary pre-emption principles to apply where an actual conflict with a federal objective is at stake? Some such principle is needed. In its absence, state law could impose legal duties that would conflict directly with federal regulatory mandates, say, by premising liability upon the presence of the very windshield retention requirements that federal law requires. *See, e.g.,* 49 CFR §571.212 (1999). Insofar as petitioners' argument would permit common-law actions that "actually conflict" with federal regulations, it would take from those who would enforce a federal law the very ability to achieve the law's congressionally mandated objectives that the Constitution, through the operation of ordinary pre-emption principles, seeks to protect. To the extent that such an interpretation of the saving provision reads into a particular federal law toleration of a conflict that those principles would otherwise forbid, it permits that law to defeat its own objectives, or potentially, as the Court has put it before, to "destroy itself." [American Telephone & Telegraph Co. v. Central Office Telephone, Inc., 524 U.S. 214, 228 (1998), *quoting* Texas & Pacific R. Co. v. Abilene Cotton Oil Co., 204 U.S. 426, 446 (1907).] We do not claim that Congress lacks the constitutional power to write a statute that mandates such a complex type of state/federal relationship. But there is no reason to believe Congress has done so here. . . .

IV

The basic question, then, is whether a common-law "no airbag" action like the one before us actually conflicts with FMVSS 208. We hold that it does.

In petitioners' and the dissent's view, FMVSS 208 sets a minimum airbag standard. As far as FMVSS 208 is concerned, the more airbags, and the sooner, the better. But that was not the Secretary's view. DOT's comments, which accompanied the promulgation of FMVSS 208, make clear that the standard deliberately provided the manufacturer with a range of choices among different passive restraint devices. Those choices would bring about a mix of different devices introduced gradually over time; and FMVSS 208 would thereby lower costs, overcome technical safety problems, encourage technological development, and win widespread consumer acceptance—all of which would promote FMVSS 208's safety objectives. *See generally* 49 Fed. Reg. 28962 (1984). . . .

B

FMVSS 208 . . . deliberately sought variety—a mix of several different passive restraint systems. It did so by setting a performance requirement for passive restraint devices and allowing manufacturers to choose among different passive restraint mechanisms, such as airbags, automatic belts, or other passive restraint technologies to satisfy that requirement. . . . DOT wrote that it had *rejected* a proposed FMVSS 208 "all airbag" standard because of safety concerns (perceived or real) associated with airbags, which concerns threatened a "backlash" more easily overcome "if airbags" were "not the only way of complying." [49 Fed. Reg.] at 29001. It added that a mix of devices would help develop data on comparative effectiveness, would allow the industry time to overcome the safety problems and the high production costs associated with airbags, and would facilitate the development of alternative, cheaper, and safer passive restraint systems. And it would thereby build public confidence, necessary to avoid another interlock-type fiasco.

The 1984 FMVSS 208 standard also deliberately sought a *gradual* phase-in of passive restraints. It required the manufacturers to equip only 10% of their car fleet manufactured after September 1, 1986, with passive restraints. It then increased the percentage in three annual stages, up to 100% of the new car fleet for cars manufactured after September 1, 1989. And it explained that the phased-in requirement would allow more time for manufacturers to develop airbags or other, better, safe passive restraint systems. It would help develop information about the comparative effectiveness of different systems, would lead to a mix in which airbags and other nonseatbelt passive restraint systems played a more prominent role than would otherwise result, and would promote public acceptance.

Of course, as the dissent points out, FMVSS 208 did not guarantee the mix by setting a ceiling for each different passive restraint device. In fact, it provided a form of extra credit for airbag installation (and other nonbelt passive restraint devices) under which each airbag-installed vehicle counted as 1.5 vehicles for purposes of meeting FMVSS 208's passive restraint requirement. But why should DOT have bothered to impose an airbag ceiling when the practical threat to the mix it desired arose from the likelihood that manufacturers would install, not too many airbags too quickly, but too few or none at all? After all, only a few years earlier, Secretary Dole's predecessor had discovered that manufacturers intended to meet the then-current passive restraint requirement almost entirely (more than 99%) through the installation of more affordable automatic belt systems. The extra credit, as DOT explained, was designed to "encourage manufacturers to equip *at least some* of their cars with airbags." 49 Fed. Reg. 29001 (1984) (emphasis added) (responding to comment that failure to mandate airbags might mean the "end of . . . airbag technology"). . . . The credit provision reinforces the point that FMVSS 208 sought a gradually developing mix of passive restraint devices; it does not show the contrary.

Finally FMVSS 208's passive restraint requirement was conditional. DOT believed that ordinary manual lap and shoulder belts would produce about the same amount of safety as passive restraints, and at significantly lower costs—*if only auto occupants would buckle up.* Thus, FMVSS 208 provided for rescission of its passive restraint requirement if, by September 1, 1989, two-thirds of the States had laws in place that, like those of many other nations, required auto occupants to buckle up (and which met other requirements specified in the standard). The Secretary wrote that "coverage of a large percentage of the American people by seatbelt laws that are enforced would largely negate the incremental increase in safety to be expected from an automatic protection requirement." *Id.*, at 28997. In the event, two-thirds of the States did not enact mandatory buckle-up laws, and the passive restraint requirement remained in effect.

In sum, as DOT now tells us through the Solicitor General, the 1984 version of FMVSS 208 "embodies the Secretary's policy judgment that safety would best be promoted if manufacturers installed *alternative* protection systems in their fleets rather than one particular system in every car." . . .

In effect, petitioners' tort action depends upon its claim that manufacturers had a duty to install an airbag when they manufactured the 1987 Honda Accord. Such a state law—i.e., a rule of state tort law imposing such a duty—by its terms would have required manufacturers of all similar cars to install airbags rather than other passive restraint systems, such as automatic belts or passive interiors. It thereby would have presented an obstacle to the variety and mix of devices that the federal regulation sought. . . . It . . . also would have stood as an obstacle to the gradual passive restraint phase-in that the federal regulation deliberately imposed. In addition, it could have made less likely the adoption of a state mandatory buckle-up law. Because the rule of law for which petitioners contend would have stood "as an obstacle to the accomplishment and execution of" the important means-related federal objectives that we have just discussed, it is pre-empted. Hines [v. Davidowitz, 312 U.S. 52, 67 (1941)].

One final point: We place some weight upon DOT's interpretation of FMVSS 208's objectives and its conclusion, as set forth in the Government's brief, that a tort suit such as this one would " 'stand as an obstacle to the accomplishment and execution'" of those objectives. Brief for United States as *Amicus Curiae* 25-26 (quoting *Hines,* 312 U.S. at 67). Congress has delegated to DOT authority to implement the statute; the subject matter is technical; and the relevant history and background are complex and extensive. The agency is likely to have a thorough understanding of its own regulation and its objectives and is "uniquely qualified" to comprehend the likely impact of state requirements. *Medtronic,* 518 U.S. at 496. . . .

The dissent would require a formal agency statement of pre-emptive intent as a prerequisite to concluding that a conflict exists. [T]hough the Court has looked for a specific statement of pre-emptive intent where it is claimed that the mere "volume and complexity" of agency regulations demonstrate an implicit intent to displace all state law in a particular area — so-called "field pre-emption" — the Court has never before required a specific, formal agency statement identifying conflicts in order to conclude that such a conflict in fact exists. Indeed, one can assume that Congress or an agency ordinarily would not intend to permit a significant conflict. While we certainly accept the dissent's basic position that a court should not find pre-emption too readily in the absence of clear evidence of a conflict, . . . for the reasons set out above we find such evidence here. To insist on a specific expression of agency intent to pre-empt, made after notice-and-comment rulemaking, would be in certain cases to tolerate conflicts that an agency, and therefore Congress, is most unlikely to have intended. . . .

The judgment of the Court of Appeals is affirmed.

JUSTICE STEVENS, with whom JUSTICE SOUTER, JUSTICE THOMAS, and JUSTICE GINSBURG join, dissenting. . . .

I

. . . Although the standard did not require airbags in all cars, it is clear that the Secretary did intend to encourage wider use of airbags. One of her basic conclusions was that "automatic occupant protection systems that do not totally rely upon belts, such as airbags . . . offer significant additional potential for preventing fatalities and injuries, at least in part because the American public is likely to find them less intrusive; their development and availability should be encouraged through appropriate incentives." The Secretary therefore included a phase-in period in order to encourage manufacturers to comply with the standard by installing airbags and other (perhaps more effective) nonbelt technologies that they might develop, rather than by installing less expensive automatic seatbelts. As a further incentive for the use of such technologies, the standard provided that a vehicle equipped with an airbag or other nonbelt system would count as 1.5 vehicles for the purpose of determining compliance with the required 10, 25, or 40% minimum passive restraint requirement during the phase-in period. With one oblique exception,[5] there is no mention, either

---

5. In response to a comment that the manufacturers were likely to use the cheapest system to comply with the new standard, the Secretary stated that she believed "that competition, potential liability for any deficient systems[,] and pride in one's product would prevent this." [49 Fed. Reg. 29000 (1984).]

in the text of the final standard or in the accompanying comments, of the possibility that the risk of potential tort liability would provide an incentive for manufacturers to install airbags. Nor is there any other specific evidence of an intent to preclude common-law tort actions. . . .

III

[T]he Supremacy Clause does not give unelected federal judges *carte blanche* to use federal law as a means of imposing their own ideas of tort reform on the States. Because of the role of States as separate sovereigns in our federal system, we have long presumed that state laws—particularly those, such as the provision of tort remedies to compensate for personal injuries, that are within the scope of the States' historic police powers—are not to be preempted by a federal statute unless it is the clear and manifest purpose of Congress to do so. . . .

The saving clause in the Safety Act unambiguously expresses a decision by Congress that compliance with a federal safety standard does not exempt a manufacturer from any common-law liability. . . .

IV

. . . Honda argues, and the Court now agrees, that the risk of liability presented by common-law claims that vehicles without airbags are negligently and defectively designed would frustrate the policy decision that the Secretary made in promulgating Standard 208. This decision, in their view, was that safety—including a desire to encourage "public acceptance of the airbag technology and experimentation with better passive restraint systems," — would best be promoted through gradual implementation of a passive restraint requirement making airbags only one of a variety of systems that a manufacturer could install in order to comply, rather than through a requirement mandating the use of one particular system in every vehicle. . . .

In light of the inevitable time interval between the eventual filing of a tort action alleging that the failure to install an airbag is a design defect and the possible resolution of such a claim against a manufacturer, as well as the additional interval between such a resolution (if any) and manufacturers' "compliance with the state law duty in question," by modifying their designs to avoid such liability in the future, it is obvious that the phase-in period would have ended long before its purposes could have been frustrated by the specter of tort liability. . . .

[D]espite its acknowledgement that the saving clause "preserves those actions that seek to establish greater safety than the minimum safety achieved by a federal regulation intended to provide a floor," the Court completely ignores the important fact that by definition all of the standards established under the Safety Act—like the British regulations that governed the number and capacity of lifeboats aboard the *Titanic*—impose minimum, rather than fixed or maximum, requirements. 15 U.S.C. §1391(2). . . . The phase-in program authorized by Standard 208 thus set minimum percentage requirements for the installation of passive restraints, increasing in annual stages of 10, 25, 40, and 100%. Those requirements were not ceilings, and it is obvious that the Secretary favored a more rapid increase. The possibility that exposure to potential tort liability might accelerate the rate of increase would actually further the only goal explicitly mentioned in the standard itself: reducing the number of deaths and severity of injuries of vehicle occupants. Had gradualism been independently important as a method of achieving the Secretary's safety goals, presumably the Secretary would have put a ceiling as well as a floor on each annual increase in the required percentage of new passive restraint installations. For similar reasons, it is evident that variety was not a matter of independent importance to the Secretary. Although the standard allowed manufacturers to comply with the minimum percentage requirements by installing passive restraint systems other than airbags (such as automatic seatbelts), it encouraged them to install airbags and other nonbelt systems that might be developed in the future. The Secretary did not act to ensure the use of a variety of passive restraints by placing ceilings on the number of airbags that could be used in complying with the minimum requirements. . . .

V

For these reasons, it is evident that Honda has not crossed the high threshold established by our decisions regarding pre-emption of state laws that allegedly frustrate federal purposes: it has not demonstrated that allowing a common-law no-airbag claim to go forward would impose an obligation on manufacturers that directly and irreconcilably contradicts any primary objective that the Secretary set forth with clarity in Standard 208. . . .

Our presumption against pre-emption is rooted in the concept of federalism. It recognizes that when Congress legislates "in a field which the States have traditionally occupied[,] we start with the assumption that the historic police powers of the States were not to be superseded by the Federal Act unless that was the clear and manifest purpose of Congress." Rice v. Santa Fe Elevator Corp., 331 U.S. at 230. . . . The signal virtues of this presumption are its placement of the power of pre-emption squarely in the hands of Congress, which is far more suited than the Judiciary to strike the appropriate state/federal balance (particularly in areas of traditional state regulation), and its requirement that Congress speak clearly when exercising that power. In this way, the structural safeguards inherent in the normal operation of the legislative process operate to defend state interests from undue infringement. . . .

While the presumption is important in assessing the pre-emptive reach of federal statutes, it becomes crucial when the pre-emptive effect of an administrative regulation is at issue. Unlike Congress, administrative agencies are clearly not designed to represent the interests of States, yet with relative ease they can promulgate comprehensive and detailed regulations that have broad pre-emption ramifications for state law. [E]ven in cases where implied regulatory pre-emption is at issue, we generally "expect an administrative regulation to declare any intention to pre-empt state law with some specificity." California Coastal Comm'n v. Granite Rock Co., 480 U.S. 572, 583 (1987). . . .

When the presumption and its underpinnings are properly understood, it is plain that Honda has not overcome the presumption in this case. Neither Standard 208 nor its accompanying commentary includes the slightest specific indication of an intent to pre-empt common-law no-airbag suits. Indeed, the only mention of such suits in the commentary tends to suggest that they would not be pre-empted. *See* n.5, *supra*. . . .

Given the Secretary's contention that he has the authority to promulgate safety standards that pre-empt state law and the fact that he could promulgate [such] a standard . . . with relative ease, we should be quite reluctant to find pre-emption based only on the Secretary's informal effort to recast the 1984 version of Standard 208 into a pre-emptive mold. . . . Requiring the Secretary to put his pre-emptive position through formal notice-and-comment rulemaking—whether contemporaneously with the promulgation of the allegedly pre-emptive regulation or at any later time that the need for pre-emption becomes apparent—respects both the federalism and nondelegation principles that underlie the presumption against pre-emption in the regulatory context and the APA's requirement of new rulemaking when an agency substantially modifies its interpretation of a regulation. . . .

NOTES AND QUESTIONS

1. *Is state tort liability an "obstacle" to, or in "conflict" with, federal regulation?* In what sense did "no airbag" tort suits conflict with FMVSS 208? Wouldn't a carmaker that installed airbags in every car have been in full compliance with both federal and state law? Do you agree with the Court that the Secretary of Transportation intended to allow carmakers to choose between belts and airbags, and that tort liability for failing to install an airbag would frustrate this purpose? In general, does it make sense to read regulations that phase in their requirements over time and allow choice regarding compliance methods to pre-empt state tort law that might lead to a faster schedule with less choice? Or do you agree with the dissent that the Court has used "federal law as a means of imposing [its] own idea[] of tort reform on the States"?

2. *The Constitution and obstacle pre-emption doctrine.* The Constitution, through its Supremacy Clause, provides the source of the pre-emption doctrine. But does it also impose a limit on its scope? Justice Thomas has been particularly outspoken in offering an affirmative answer. In Wyeth v. Levine, 555 U.S. 555 (2009), the Supreme Court rejected a claim that FDA regulation of prescription drugs pre-empted a state product liability claim. Though agreeing with the result, Justice Thomas took the opportunity in a separate opinion to excoriate the Court's "vague and 'potentially boundless' doctrine of 'purposes and objectives'" pre-emption, citing Justice Stevens's dissent in *Geier*, 529 U.S. at 907:

> The Court's decision in *Geier* to apply "purposes and objectives" pre-emption based on agency comments, regulatory history, and agency litigating positions was especially flawed, given that it conflicted with the plain statutory text of the saving clause within the Safety Act, which explicitly preserved state common-law actions by providing that "[c]ompliance with any Federal motor vehicle safety standard issued under this subchapter does not exempt any person from any liability under common law," 15 U.S.C. §1397(k) (1988 ed.). . . . With text that allowed state actions like the one at issue in *Geier*, the Court had no authority to comb through agency commentaries to find a basis for an alternative conclusion.

Applying "purposes and objectives" pre-emption in *Geier,* as in any case, allowed this Court to vacate a judgment issued by another sovereign based on nothing more than assumptions and goals that were untethered from the constitutionally enacted federal law authorizing the federal regulatory standard that was before the Court. . . . [N]o agency or individual Member of Congress can pre-empt a State's judgment by merely musing about goals or intentions not found within or authorized by the statutory text. . . .

Under the Supremacy Clause, state law is pre-empted only by federal law "made in Pursuance" of the Constitution, Art. VI, cl. 2—not by extratextual considerations of the purposes underlying congressional inaction. . . .

The origins of this Court's "purposes and objectives" pre-emption jurisprudence . . . facilitates freewheeling, extratextual, and broad evaluations of the "purposes and objectives" embodied within federal law. This, in turn, leads to decisions giving improperly broad pre-emptive effect to judicially manufactured policies, rather than to the statutory text enacted by Congress pursuant to the Constitution and the agency actions authorized thereby. Because such a sweeping approach to pre-emption leads to the illegitimate—and thus, unconstitutional—invalidation of state laws, I can no longer assent to a doctrine that pre-empts state laws merely because they "stan[d] as an obstacle to the accomplishment and execution of the full purposes and objectives" of federal law . . . as perceived by this Court. I therefore respectfully concur only in the judgment.

Do you agree? Does the Supremacy Clause implicitly require federal courts, in the context of pre-emption claims, to use a more "originalist" or "textualist" mode of statutory interpretation than they would use in other contexts?

3. *The relationship between express pre-emption clauses and implied pre-emption.* If pre-emption is a matter of congressional intent, and Congress wrote a pre-emption provision that did not cover this particular claim, shouldn't the Court have concluded that Congress did not intend for federal law to pre-empt this sort of claim? At one time, it appears that this was the governing rule. Cipollone v. Liggett Group, Inc., 505 U.S. 504, 517 (1992). The Court subsequently backed away from this language, stating in Freightliner Corp. v. Myrick, 514 U.S. 280, 289 (1995), a case in which arguments for both express and implied pre-emption were rejected, that "[a]t best, *Cipollone* supports an inference that an express pre-emption clause forecloses implied pre-emption; it does not establish a rule." In *Geier* and other recent decisions, the Court has disavowed even its more moderate language in *Myrick,* and now treats express and implied pre-emption as complementary doctrines, coexisting comfortably under the same regulatory regime.

What reasons underlie the Court's change of heart on the interaction between express and implied pre-emption? Apparently, the Court is concerned with the potential that state law could frustrate the purposes of federal law in situations where Congress has drawn its pre-emption provision too narrowly. For example, in *Geier,* the Court stated:

Insofar as petitioners' argument would permit common-law actions that "actually conflict" with federal regulations, it would take from those who would enforce a federal law the very ability to achieve the law's congressionally mandated objectives that the Constitution, through the operation of ordinary pre-emption principles, seeks to protect.

529 U.S. at 872. Isn't Congress's power to expand the pre-emption provision at issue a complete, or nearly complete, answer to this argument? Why should a court infer that Congress intended pre-emption beyond that which Congress took the trouble statutorily to specify? Or is the Court correct that as a matter of common sense, even in the absence of sufficiently broad express pre-emption, Congress would not have intended to allow state law to undercut the operation of federal law?

4. *Interpreting express pre-emption clauses.* How broadly should courts interpret express pre-emption provisions? Sometimes Congress uses language suggesting total pre-emption. For example, in the Federal Cigarette Labeling and Advertising Act (which requires the "Surgeon General's Warning" to be displayed on cigarette packages and advertisements), Congress provided: "No requirement or prohibition based on smoking and health shall be imposed under State law with respect to the advertising or promotion of any cigarettes the packages of which are labeled in conformity with the provisions of this chapter." 15 U.S.C. §1334(b) (1982).

Even such absolute-sounding examples of express pre-emption can present troublesome questions of interpretation. Does the Cigarette Labeling Act bar a tort suit based on a theory of implied warranty or misrepresentation? May a state court judge instruct jurors that they may reject a manufacturer's "assumption-of-the-risk" defense if they conclude that the overall effect of the defendant's advertising (despite the warning) was to downplay health hazards? What if the jury concludes that the plaintiff became addicted to cigarettes before the Labeling Act took effect? For cases resolving difficult questions under the Cigarette Labeling Act, *see* Cipollone v. Liggett Group, Inc., 505 U.S. 504 (1992), and Altria Group, Inc. v. Good, 555 U.S. 70 (2008).

5. *Saving clauses.* Many federal regulatory statutes contain "saving clauses" like the one at issue in *Geier,* specifying that compliance with federal regulatory requirements does not exempt the subject of federal regulation from common law liability. Should the existence of a saving clause completely preclude pre-emption of state common law claims? Justice Thomas may think so. In Williamson v. Mazda Motor Corp., 562 U.S. 323 (2011), a case in which the Court held that FMVSS 208 did not pre-empt a state tort claim over the lack of a shoulder belt in the middle back seat of a minivan, Justice Thomas argued in a concurring opinion that the majority need not have looked beyond the Motor Vehicle Safety Act's saving clause which "explicitly preserv[es] state common law actions." 562 U.S. at 339 (Thomas, J., concurring in the judgment).

6. *Agency power to pre-empt state law.* A related issue is whether federal agencies have the power to expand or contract the pre-emptive scope of federal law. Although the Supremacy Clause refers only to the federal Constitution, treaties, and statutes, the Supreme Court has "held repeatedly that state laws can be pre-empted by federal regulations as well as by federal statutes." Hillsborough Cty., Fla. v. Automated Medical Labs., Inc., 471 U.S. 707, 713 (1985). *See also* Bradford R. Clark, Separation of Powers as a Safeguard of Federalism, 79 Tex. L. Rev. 1321 (2001) (citing cases in which federal regulations were held to pre-empt conflicting state law). Otherwise, states would have the power severely to undercut the effectiveness of federal regulations. In *Geier,* not even actual conflict was necessary for a federal regulation to pre-empt state law since Honda could have complied with both federal and state law by installing airbags in all of its cars. In

fact, the Court has held that it is proper to afford *Chevron* deference to regulations that result in the pre-emption of state law. *See* Smiley v. Citibank (South Dakota), N.A., 517 U.S. 735, 744 (1996). Is there good reason to afford less deference to regulations that pre-empt state law? If so, what if state law post-dates the adoption of the regulation?

Complicating matters further, some federal agencies attempt to define the scope of federal pre-emption, for example by promulgating a regulation specifying what types of state laws, regulations, and common law tort actions are pre-empted by federal law. Should these regulations receive deference? Here, the Court has been less clear about agency power. Recall that in *Geier*, the Court stated that it placed "some weight" on the agency's pro-pre-emption litigation position even though it was not contained in any regulation or other formal agency document. In Medtronic, Inc. v. Lohr, 518 U.S. 470, 495 (1996), although the Court stated only that its pre-emption holding was "substantially informed" by an FDA pre-emption regulation, it did not apply *Chevron* deference to the agency's pre-emption regulation. Should agency statements on the scope of federal pre-emption receive deference? If so, how much? If not, why not?

7. *Pre-emption and the decision not to regulate after* Geier. *Geier* appeared to be a signal that the Court had become much more receptive to regulatory pre-emption of state tort claims. However, the next case involving pre-emption of state tort claims muddied the waters by finding against pre-emption in a situation that was, in some respects, analogous to that presented in *Geier*. In Sprietsma v. Mercury Marine, 537 U.S. 51 (2002), the Court rejected an argument for pre-emption of a state tort claim against the manufacturer of a motorboat. The claim was based on the failure of the manufacturer to include propeller guards. Mercury Marine argued that this tort claim was pre-empted by the Federal Boat Safety Act of 1971 because the United States Coast Guard had studied propeller strike accidents and decided, mainly for technical reasons but also out of cost concerns, not to issue regulations requiring propeller guards. After finding that the claim was not expressly pre-empted, the Court turned to implied pre-emption:

> We first consider, and reject, respondent's reliance on the Coast Guard's decision not to adopt a regulation requiring propeller guards on motorboats. It is quite wrong to view that decision as the functional equivalent of a regulation prohibiting all States and their political subdivisions from adopting such a regulation. The decision in 1990 to accept the subcommittee's recommendation to "take no regulatory action," App. 80, left the law applicable to propeller guards exactly the same as it had been before the subcommittee began its investigation. Of course, if a state common-law claim directly conflicted with a federal regulation promulgated under the Act, or if it were impossible to comply with any such regulation without incurring liability under state common law, pre-emption would occur. This, however, is not such a case.
>
> Indeed, history teaches us that a Coast Guard decision not to regulate a particular aspect of boating safety is fully consistent with an intent to preserve state regulatory authority pending the adoption of specific federal standards. That was the course the Coast Guard followed in 1971 immediately after the Act was passed, and again when it imposed its first regulations in 1972 and 1973. The Coast Guard has never taken the position that the litigation of state common-law claims relating

to an area not yet subject to federal regulation would conflict with "the accomplishment and execution of the full purposes and objectives of Congress." Hines v. Davidowitz, 312 U.S. 52, 67 (1941).

[The Coast Guard's explanation for its decision not to regulate] reveals only a judgment that the available data did not meet the FBSA's "stringent" criteria for federal regulation. The Coast Guard did not take the further step of deciding that, as a matter of policy, the States and their political subdivisions should not impose some version of propeller guard regulation, and it most definitely did not reject propeller guards as unsafe. The Coast Guard's apparent focus was on the lack of any "universally acceptable" propeller guard for "all modes of boat operation." But nothing in its official explanation would be inconsistent with a tort verdict premised on a jury's finding that some type of propeller guard should have been installed on this particular kind of boat equipped with respondent's particular type of motor. Thus, although the Coast Guard's decision not to require propeller guards was undoubtedly intentional and carefully considered, it does not convey an "authoritative" message of a federal policy against propeller guards. And nothing in the Coast Guard's recent regulatory activities alters this conclusion.

537 U.S. at 65. The Court viewed *Geier* as supporting, rather than undercutting, this conclusion:

The Coast Guard's decision *not* to impose a propeller guard requirement presents a sharp contrast to the decision of the Secretary of Transportation that was given pre-emptive effect in Geier v. American Honda Motor Co., 529 U.S. 861 (2000). As the Solicitor General had argued in that case, the promulgation of Federal Motor Vehicle Safety Standard (FMVSS) 208 embodied an affirmative "policy judgment that safety would best be promoted if manufacturers installed *alternative* protection systems in their fleets rather than one particular system in every car." *Id.* at 881. In finding pre-emption, we expressly placed "weight upon the DOT's interpretation of FMVSS 208's objectives and its conclusion, as set forth in the Government's brief, that a tort suit such as this one would 'stan[d] as an obstacle to the accomplishment and execution' of those objectives. . . ." *Id.* at 883. In the case before us today, the Solicitor General, joined by counsel for the Coast Guard, has informed us that the agency does not view the 1990 refusal to regulate or any subsequent regulatory actions by the Coast Guard as having any pre-emptive effect. Our reasoning in *Geier* therefore provides strong support for petitioner's submission.

537 U.S. at 67-68. After *Sprietsma*, will it be simple to distinguish cases of failure to regulate in which pre-emption is warranted from those in which it is not?

C.   LIABILITY OF PUBLIC ENTITIES AND OFFICERS

Judicial supervision of administrative action commonly occurs in the context of a statutorily authorized "appellate-style" review of an agency decision. The petition for review, however, is not the only mechanism by which courts can scrutinize the lawfulness of agency action. An alternative is a civil suit against a government official, or against the government agency itself, for invading some interest of the plaintiff protected by an independent source of law, such as tort or contract law. In principle, such suits would be governed by the same rules and standards as would be applied to a private defendant. In practice, however, government entities occupy very distinct status as defendants. First, government defendants can invoke special defenses — under the rubrics of "sovereign immunity" and "official immunity" — not available to private defendants. Second, the unique status of government actors in our society — deriving from their monopoly of legal coercion and their supposedly democratic pedigree — means that private-law concepts, such as the concept of "duty" in tort law, have a distinctive meaning.

1. Suits Against Sovereigns: Sovereign Immunity and the Federal Tort Claims Act

The traditional rule in American common law, derived, albeit in a somewhat exaggerated form, from English law, was that suits against a sovereign government cannot be maintained without the sovereign's consent. Even in the absence of government consent, however, the principle of sovereign immunity was subject to many qualifications. For example, the principle applied only to government entities, not to their employees who were accused of acting wrongfully. This principle forced courts to answer the difficult question of whether a suit nominally against individual officials is in reality a thinly disguised effort to obtain relief against their employing entity. Another qualification is the distinction between "governmental" and "proprietary" functions. Case law has long held that suit may be maintained against a municipal corporation for harm arising from such "proprietary" activities as management of its property, with immunity attaching only to "governmental" functions. One justification for this distinction is that when a government enters the marketplace to compete with others in the provision of goods or services, it does not exercise the coercive powers it enjoys in exercising regulatory powers.

By far the most important qualification of the doctrine of sovereign immunity, however, is the principle of consent. Over the past century and a half, state and federal governments have increasingly consented to suit in at least broad categories of civil law actions. In most instances, consent has come in the form of legislation, though many state courts have used their common-law making power to abolish or restrict the doctrine of sovereign immunity. At the federal level, constriction of sovereign immunity took place gradually, in three primary stages. In the nineteenth century, Congress addressed the injustice of denying relief to persons injured by the federal government primarily by enacting private bills providing relief to specific named individuals. Responding to the defects of the private bill regime, Congress enacted the Tucker Act, Act of Mar. 3, 1887, 24 Stat. 505, *codified at* 28 U.S.C. §§1346(a), 1491, to provide federal jurisdiction for suits in admiralty, contract actions, and other civil suits "not sounding in tort" against the federal government. Sixty years later, Congress enacted the Federal Tort Claims Act of Aug. 2, 1947, 60 Stat. 812, codified at scattered sections of 28 U.S.C., providing government damage liability for certain tortious acts by the United States or its employees. The FTCA makes the government liable for any "negligent or wrongful act or omission . . . in the same manner and to the same extent as a private individual under like circumstances." 28 U.S.C. §§1346(b), 2674.

The FTCA does not purport to create a basis for liability; in form, it merely waives sovereign immunity for a class of pre-existing common law rights of action. The Act thus requires that suit be for acts analogous to tortious private conduct. The Act broadly incorporates into the statutory action the law of the state where the tort occurred. Although it builds on state common law, however, the FTCA limits the application of state rules and procedures in a number of ways. For example, it allows only bench (not jury) trials, §2402; it precludes imposition of punitive damages, §2674; it requires presentation of claims for possible administrative settlement, and exhaustion of administrative remedies, prior to filing suit, §2675; and it requires that the agency be notified within two years of accrual of the claim and that suit be filed no later than six months after the agency denies the claim, §2401(b).

Most important, the FTCA excepts a range of arguably tortious conduct from its coverage. The exceptions take two forms. First, §2680 contains an explicit list of exceptions that includes such items as:

(a) Any claim based upon an act or omission of an employee of the Government, exercising due care, in the execution of a statute or regulation, whether or not such statute or regulation be valid, or based upon the exercise or performance or the failure to exercise or perform a discretionary function or duty on the part of a federal agency or an employee of the Government, whether or not the discretion involved be abused.

(c) Any claim arising in respect of the assessment or collection of any tax or customs duty, or the detention of any goods or merchandise by any officer of customs or excise or any other law-enforcement officer. . . .

(h) Any claim arising out of assault, battery, false imprisonment, false arrest, malicious prosecution, abuse of process, libel, slander, misrepresentation, deceit or interference with contract rights: *Provided,* That, with regard to acts or omissions of investigative or law enforcement officers of the United States Government, the provisions of this chapter . . . of this title shall apply to any claim arising, on or after the date of the enactment of this proviso, out of assault, battery, false imprisonment, false arrest, abuse of process, or malicious prosecution. For the purpose of the subsection, "investigative or law enforcement officer" means any officer of the United States who is empowered by law to execute searches, to seize evidence, or to make arrests for violations of Federal law.

(i) Any claim for damages caused by the fiscal operations of the Treasury or by the regulation of the monetary system.

(j) Any claim arising out of the combatant activities of the military or naval forces, or the Coast Guard, during time of war. . . .

In addition to this list, courts have found exceptions implicit in the language granting district court jurisdiction over FTCA suits and prescribing the general rule of liability. The jurisdictional grant, 28 U.S.C. §1346(b), authorizes district courts to hear claims against the government for harms "caused by the negligent or wrongful act or omission of any employee of the Government." This language has been read to require proof of fault. *See* Laird v. Nelms, 406 U.S. 797 (1972). Thus, even if the applicable state law adopts strict liability as the standard for recovery based on similar conduct, no liability arises under the FTCA absent proof of at least negligence.

The Act's statement that the government is liable "in the same manner and to the same extent as a private individual under like circumstances" also has been relied on to except acts from the ambit of potential government liability.

What does the "like circumstances" language mean? Does it suggest that plaintiffs must make out elements of a cause of action that would lead to private liability? Or does it require that plaintiffs establish that some private, tortious conduct is analogous to the government conduct at issue, in other words, both that private actors engage in the same sort of conduct and that when they do liability attaches?

The difficulty with the analogy to private conduct is obvious: government conduct can often be analogized to private conduct, but it never will be identical to it. A leading example of this dilemma is the seminal case of *Feres v. United States*, 340 U.S. 135 (1950). *Feres* consolidated three suits by servicemen injured while on active duty, but not in combat: two alleged medical malpractice by military doctors at a base hospital, and the third alleged negligence in quartering soldiers in unsafe barracks. Even though §2680(h), quoted above, expressly exempts only claims "arising out of the combatant activities of the military or naval forces . . . during time of war," the Supreme Court rejected all three suits because there is no counterpart in private life for the compulsory quartering of troops on military bases. By contrast, the Court has held that claims based on injuries not "incident to service" are cognizable under the FTCA. *See* United States v. Brown, 348 U.S. 110 (1954) (*Feres* does not bar malpractice claim for injuries suffered by veteran in VA hospital during surgery to treat injuries suffered while on active duty); Brooks v. United States, 337 U.S. 49 (1949) (FTCA allows recovery based on death of serviceman on active duty whose private car collided with Army truck driven by civilian Army employee; accident not incident to service).

The private action analogy at the heart of the *Feres* doctrine also is intertwined with another important exception, contained in §2680(a), quoted above, excluding from the FTCA those claims based on non-negligent execution of a statute or regulation (regardless of its validity). Because non-negligent private acts honestly based on a statutory command may give rise to liability, as in certain trespass cases, the FTCA separately relieves government from liability for these acts of its employees. That is the meaning of §2680(a)'s first clause. Liability under the FTCA cannot be established simply by showing that the statutory or regulatory basis for official action was invalid. Rather, negligent application or absence of statutory or regulatory command is required.

Because it shields such a broad spectrum of government conduct from liability, the most important exception to FTCA liability, also contained in §2680(a), is the discretionary function exception. Given the fact that every governmental action (or inaction) involves the exercise of at least some degree of discretion, the Supreme Court has struggled mightily to give meaning to this exception. For example, in Dalehite v. United States, 346 U.S. 15 (1953), the Supreme Court ruled that the discretionary function exception protected the U.S. government from liability for a catastrophic explosion of fertilizer being loaded for shipment to boost food production in certain foreign countries. Injured parties had claimed that government employees were negligent in handling, transporting, and storing the fertilizer. In denying liability, the Court suggested at least four different rationales for the result: that the function was uniquely "governmental," with no private analogy; that the acts were part of a program initiated by a high-ranking (here, Cabinet-level) officer; that the acts involved conscious choices; and that the acts implemented decisions made at the planning level, as distinguished from the operational level. Later cases, by contrast, seemed to adopt the "planning"-"operational" distinction. For example, in Indian Towing Co. v. United States, 350 U.S. 61 (1955), the Court refused to bar a suit against the Coast Guard for negligently failing to maintain the light in a lighthouse, with the result that the plaintiff's boat ran aground. The Court found that, although the decision whether to operate a lighthouse was discretionary, the mechanics of its maintenance and repair were decisions at the "operational level."

For our purposes, given the general focus on governmental regulation in a course on administrative law, the most interesting FTCA claims are those that arise in the regulatory context. In theory, such claims could arise in one of two possible ways. In the first, a person who is ordered to alter his or her conduct by a regulatory agency action might bring suit under the FTCA, alleging that the agency negligently misapplied its legal authority, harming the plaintiff's business. In the second, and far more likely, scenario, a putative beneficiary of a regulatory program might bring an FTCA claim against an agency for negligently failing to discharge its regulatory responsibilities or doing so in a way that left the plaintiff unprotected against injury caused by the regulated party. In either case, the question arises whether regulatory enforcement (or lack of enforcement) always involves policy considerations that should be protected by the discretionary function exception, or whether there are at least some instances in which regulatory duties are sufficiently clear-cut that their neglect can trigger governmental tort liability. These are the questions addressed in the following materials.

UNITED STATES v. S.A. EMPRESA DE VIAÇÃO AÉREA RIO-GRANDENSE (VARIG AIRLINES), 467 U.S. 797 (1984):   An airline company and executors for deceased passengers filed suit under the FTCA alleging that the Federal Aviation Administration (FAA), a federal agency charged with regulating air travel safety, negligently certified that a plane, the Boeing 707, met FAA standards. The Court held that the FAA's administration of the certification procedure is a discretionary function and that therefore FTCA damages were barred:

> [T]he FAA . . . has devised a system of compliance review that involves certification of aircraft design and manufacture at several stages of production. The FAA certification process is founded upon a relatively simple notion: the duty to ensure that an aircraft conforms to FAA safety regulations lies with the manufacturer and operator, while the FAA retains the responsibility for policing compliance. Thus, the manufacturer is required to develop the plans and specifications and perform the inspections and tests necessary to establish that an aircraft design comports with the applicable regulations; the FAA then reviews the data for conformity purposes by conducting a "spot check" of the manufacturer's work. . . .
>
> Respondents' contention that the FAA was negligent in failing to inspect certain elements of aircraft design before certificating the Boeing 707 . . . necessarily challenges two aspects of the certification procedure: the FAA's decision to implement the "spot-check" system of compliance review, and the application of that "spot-check" system to the particular aircraft involved in [this case]. In our view, both components of respondents' claim are barred by the discretionary function exception to the Act. . . .
>
> When an agency determines the extent to which it will supervise the safety procedures of private individuals, it is exercising discretionary regulatory authority of the most basic kind. Decisions as to the manner of enforcing regulations directly affect the feasibility and practicality of the Government's regulatory

program; such decisions require the agency to establish priorities for the accomplishment of its policy objectives by balancing the objectives sought to be obtained against such practical considerations as staffing and funding. Here, the FAA has determined that a program of "spot-checking" manufacturers' compliance with minimum safety standards best accommodates the goal of air transportation safety and the reality of finite agency resources. Judicial intervention in such decisionmaking through private tort suits would require the courts to "second-guess" the political, social, and economic judgments of an agency exercising its regulatory function. It was precisely this sort of judicial intervention in policymaking that the discretionary function exception was designed to prevent. . . .

Is this decision consistent with *Indian Towing*'s distinction between operational and planning-level decisionmaking?

Some lower courts read *Varig Airlines* as establishing a "regulatory functions" exception, if not a "governmental functions" exception to FTCA liability, construing the FTCA as precluding federal liability for any decision taken in the course of regulating private conduct. Other courts read the Act and *Varig Airlines* as suggesting a narrower exception from liability for federal regulatory activity. The Supreme Court addressed this "regulatory functions" exception in a case arising out of the government's alleged negligent licensing of a polio vaccine.

BERKOVITZ v. UNITED STATES
486 U.S. 531 (1988)

JUSTICE MARSHALL delivered the opinion of the Court.

The question in this case is whether the discretionary function exception of the Federal Tort Claims Act (FTCA or Act), 28 U.S.C. §2680(a), bars a suit based on the Government's licensing of an oral polio vaccine and on its subsequent approval of the release of a specific lot of that vaccine to the public.

I

On May 10, 1979, Kevan Berkovitz, then a 2-month-old infant, ingested a dose of Orimune, an oral polio vaccine manufactured by Lederle Laboratories. Within one month, he contracted a severe case of polio. The disease left Berkovitz almost completely paralyzed and unable to breathe without the assistance of a respirator. The Communicable Disease Center, an agency of the Federal Government, determined that Berkovitz had contracted polio from the vaccine.

Berkovitz, joined by his parents as guardians, subsequently filed suit against the United States in Federal District Court. The complaint alleged that the United States was liable for his injuries under the FTCA, 28 U.S.C. §§1346(b), 2674, because the Division of Biologic Standards (DBS), then a part of the National Institutes of Health, had acted wrongfully in licensing Lederle Laboratories to produce Orimune and because the Bureau of Biologics of the Food and Drug Administration (FDA) had acted wrongfully in approving release to the public of the particular lot of vaccine containing Berkovitz's dose. According to petitioners, these actions violated federal law and policy regarding the inspection and approval of polio vaccines.

The Government moved to dismiss the suit for lack of subject-matter jurisdiction on the ground that the agency actions fell within the discretionary function exception of the FTCA. The District Court denied this motion. . . . A divided panel of the [Third Circuit] Court of Appeals reversed. . . . We granted certiorari to resolve a conflict in the Circuits. . . . We now reverse the Third Circuit's judgment. . . .

II

The FTCA, 28 U.S.C. §1346(b), generally authorizes suits against the United States for damages for injury or loss of property, or personal injury or death caused by the negligent or wrongful act or omission of any employee of the Government while acting within the scope of his office or employment, under circumstances where the United States, if a private person, would be liable to the claimant in accordance with the law of the place where the act or omission occurred.

The Act includes a number of exceptions to this broad waiver of sovereign immunity. The exception relevant to this case provides that no liability shall lie for

[a]ny claim . . . based upon the exercise or performance or the failure to exercise or perform a discretionary function or duty on the part of a federal agency or an employee of the Government, whether or not the discretion involved be abused. 28 U.S.C. §2680(a).

This exception, as we stated in our most recent opinion on the subject, "marks the boundary between Congress' willingness to impose tort liability upon the United States and its desire to protect certain governmental activities from exposure to suit by private individuals." United States v. Varig Airlines, [467 U.S. at 808].

The determination of whether the discretionary function exception bars a suit against the Government is guided by several established principles. This Court stated in *Varig* that "it is the nature of the conduct, rather than the status of the actor, that governs whether the discretionary function exception applies in a given case." *Id.*, at 813. In examining the nature of the challenged conduct, a court must first consider whether the action is a matter of choice for the acting employee. This inquiry is mandated by the language of the exception; conduct cannot be discretionary unless it involves an element of judgment or choice. . . . Thus, the discretionary function exception will not apply when a federal statute, regulation, or policy specifically prescribes a course of action for an employee to follow. In this event, the employee has no rightful option but to adhere to the directive. And if the employee's conduct cannot appropriately be the product of judgment or choice, then there is no discretion in the conduct for the discretionary function exception to protect. . . .

Moreover, assuming the challenged conduct involves an element of judgment, a court must determine whether that judgment is of the kind that the discretionary function exception was designed to shield. The basis for the discretionary function exception was Congress' desire to "prevent judicial 'second-guessing' of legislative and administrative decisions grounded in social, economic, and political policy through the medium of an action in tort." United States v. Varig Airlines, *supra,* at 814. The exception, properly construed, therefore protects only governmental actions and decisions based on considerations of public policy. . . . In sum, the discretionary function exception insulates the Government from liability if the action challenged in the case involves the permissible exercise of policy judgment. . . .

In restating and clarifying the scope of the discretionary function exception, we intend specifically to reject the Government's argument, pressed both in this Court and the Court of Appeals, that the exception precludes liability for any and all acts arising out of the regulatory programs of federal agencies. That argument is rebutted first by the language of the exception, which protects "discretionary" functions, rather than "regulatory" functions. The significance of Congress' choice of language is supported by the legislative history. As this Court previously has indicated, the relevant legislative materials demonstrate that the exception was designed to cover not all acts of regulatory agencies and their employees, but only such acts as are "discretionary" in nature. . . . This coverage accords with Congress' purpose in enacting the exception: to prevent "[j]udicial intervention in . . . the political, social, and economic judgments" of governmental-including regulatory-agencies. United States v. Varig Airlines, 467 U.S., at 820. . . . To the extent we have not already put the Government's argument to rest, we do so now. The discretionary function exception applies only to conduct that involves the permissible exercise of policy judgment. The question in this case is whether the governmental activities challenged by petitioners are of this discretionary nature.

III

Petitioners' suit raises two broad claims. First, petitioners assert that the DBS violated a federal statute and accompanying regulations in issuing a license to Lederle Laboratories to produce Orimune. Second, petitioners argue that the Bureau of Biologics of the FDA violated federal regulations and policy in approving the release of the particular lot of Orimune that contained Kevan Berkovitz's dose. We examine each of these broad claims by reviewing the applicable regulatory scheme and petitioners' specific allegations of agency wrongdoing. Because the decision we review adjudicated a motion to dismiss, we accept all of the factual allegations in petitioners' complaint as true and ask whether, in these circumstances, dismissal of the complaint was appropriate.

A

Under federal law, a manufacturer must receive a product license prior to marketing a brand of live oral polio vaccine. *See* 42 U.S.C. §262(a). In order to become eligible for such a license, a manufacturer must first make a sample of the vaccine product. *See* 42 CFR §73.3 (Supp. 1964); 21 CFR § 601.2 (1987). . . . Under the regulations, the manufacturer must conduct a variety of tests to measure the safety of the product at each stage of the manufacturing process. . . . Upon completion of the manufacturing process and the required testing, the manufacturer is required to submit an application for a product license to the DBS. . . . In addition to this application, the manufacturer must submit data from the tests performed and a sample of the finished product.

In deciding whether to issue a license, the DBS is required to comply with certain statutory and regulatory provisions. The Public Health Service Act provides:

> Licenses for the maintenance of establishments for the propagation or manufacture and preparation of products [including polio vaccines] may be issued only upon a showing that the establishment and the products for which a license is desired meet standards, designed to insure the continued safety, purity, and potency of such products, prescribed in regulations, and licenses for new products may be issued only upon a showing that they meet such standards. All such licenses shall be issued, suspended, and revoked as prescribed by regulations. . . . 42 U.S.C. §262(d).

A regulation similarly provides that "[a] product license shall be issued only upon examination of the product and upon a determination that the product complies with the standards prescribed in the regulations. . . ." 42 CFR §73.5(a) (Supp. 1964). In addition, a regulation states that "[a]n application for license shall not be considered as filed" until the DBS receives the information and data regarding the product that the manufacturer is required to submit. 42 CFR §73.3 (Supp. 1964). These statutory and regulatory provisions require the DBS, prior to issuing a product license, to receive all data the manufacturer is required to submit, to examine the product, and to make a determination that the product complies with safety standards.

Petitioners' first allegation with regard to the licensing of Orimune is that the DBS issued a product license without first receiving data that the manufacturer must submit showing how the product, at the various stages of the manufacturing process, matched up against regulatory safety standards. . . . The discretionary function exception does not bar a cause of action based on this allegation. . . . The DBS has no discretion to issue a license without first receiving the required test data; to do so would violate a specific statutory and regulatory directive. Accordingly, to the extent that petitioners' licensing claim is based on a decision of the DBS to issue a license without having received the required test data, the discretionary function exception imposes no bar.

Petitioners' other allegation regarding the licensing of Orimune is difficult to describe with precision. Petitioners contend that the DBS licensed Orimune even though the vaccine did not comply with certain regulatory safety standards. . . . This charge may be understood in any of three ways. First, petitioners may mean that the DBS licensed Orimune without first making a determination as to whether the vaccine complied with regulatory standards. Second, petitioners may intend to argue that the DBS specifically found that Orimune failed to comply with certain regulatory standards and nonetheless issued a license for the vaccine's manufacture. Third, petitioners may concede that the DBS made a determination of compliance, but allege that this determination was incorrect. Neither petitioners' complaint nor their briefs and argument before this Court make entirely clear their theory of the case.

If petitioners aver that the DBS licensed Orimune either without determining whether the vaccine complied with regulatory standards or after determining that the vaccine failed to comply, the discretionary function exception does not bar the claim. Under the scheme governing the DBS's regulation of polio vaccines, the DBS may not issue a license except upon an examination of the product and a determination that the product complies with all regulatory standards. . . . The agency has no discretion to deviate from this mandated procedure. Petitioners' claim, if interpreted as alleging that the DBS licensed Orimune in the absence of a determination that the vaccine complied with regulatory standards, therefore does not challenge a discretionary function. Rather, the claim charges a failure on the part of the agency to perform its clear duty under federal law. When a suit charges an agency with failing to act in accord with a specific mandatory directive, the discretionary function exception does not apply.

If petitioners' claim is that the DBS made a determination that Orimune complied with regulatory standards, but that the determination was incorrect, the question of the applicability of the discretionary function exception requires a somewhat different analysis. In that event, the question turns on whether the manner and method of determining compliance with the safety standards at issue involve agency judgment of the kind protected by the discretionary function exception. Petitioners contend that the determination involves the application of objective scientific standards, whereas the Government asserts that the determination incorporates considerable "policy judgment." In making these assertions, the parties have framed the issue appropriately; application of the discretionary function exception to the claim that the determination of compliance was incorrect hinges on whether the agency officials making that determination permissibly exercise policy choice. The parties, however, have not addressed this question in detail, and they have given us no indication of the way in which the DBS interprets and applies the regulations setting forth the criteria for compliance. Given that these regulations are particularly abstruse, we hesitate to decide the question on the scanty record before us. We therefore leave it to the District Court to decide, if petitioners choose to press this claim, whether agency officials appropriately exercise policy judgment in determining that a vaccine product complies with the relevant safety standards.

B

The regulatory scheme governing release of vaccine lots is distinct from that governing the issuance of licenses. The former set of regulations places an obligation on manufacturers to examine all vaccine lots prior to distribution to ensure that they comply with regulatory standards. *See* 21 CFR §610.1 (1978). These regulations, however, do not impose a corresponding duty on the Bureau of Biologics. Although the regulations empower the Bureau to examine any vaccine lot and prevent the distribution of a noncomplying lot, they do not require the Bureau to take such action in all cases. The regulations generally allow the Bureau to determine the appropriate manner in which to regulate the release of vaccine lots, rather than mandating certain kinds of agency action. The regulatory scheme governing the release of vaccine lots is substantially similar in this respect to the scheme discussed in [*Varig Airlines*].

Given this regulatory context, the discretionary function exception bars any claims that challenge the Bureau's formulation of policy as to the appropriate way in which to regulate the release of vaccine lots. *Cf. id.*, at 819-820 (holding that discretionary function exception barred claim challenging FAA's decision to establish a spot-checking program). In addition, if the policies and programs formulated by the Bureau allow room for implementing officials to make independent policy judgments, the discretionary function exception protects the acts taken by those officials in the exercise of this discretion. . . . The discretionary function exception, however, does not apply if the acts complained of do not involve the permissible exercise of policy discretion. Thus, if the Bureau's policy leaves no room for an official to exercise policy judgment in performing a given act, or if the act simply does not involve the exercise of such judgment, the discretionary function exception does not bar a claim that the act was negligent or wrongful. *Cf.* Indian Towing Co. v. United States, [350 U.S. 61, 69 (1955)] (holding that a negligent failure to maintain a lighthouse in good working order subjected the Government to suit under the FTCA even though the initial decision to undertake and maintain lighthouse service was a discretionary policy judgment).

Viewed in light of these principles, petitioners' claim regarding the release of the vaccine lot from which Kevan Berkovitz received his dose survives the Government's motion to dismiss. Petitioners allege that, under the authority granted by the regulations, the Bureau of Biologics has adopted a policy of testing all vaccine lots for compliance with safety standards and preventing the distribution to the public of any lots that fail to comply. Petitioners further allege that notwithstanding this policy, which allegedly leaves no room for implementing officials to exercise independent policy judgment, employees of the Bureau knowingly approved the release of a lot that did not comply with safety standards. Thus, petitioners' complaint is directed at a governmental action that allegedly involved no policy discretion. Petitioners, of course, have not proved their factual allegations, but they are not required to do so on a motion to dismiss. . . .

IV

For the foregoing reasons, the Court of Appeals erred in holding that the discretionary function exception required the dismissal of petitioners' claims respecting the licensing of Orimune and the release of a particular vaccine lot. The judgment of the Court of Appeals is accordingly reversed, and the case is remanded for further proceedings consistent with this opinion.

It is so ordered.

NOTES AND QUESTIONS

1. *Varig Airlines revisited.* Were the regulatory decisions concerning the polio vaccine at issue in *Berkovitz* any less discretionary than the airplane certification decision at issue in *Varig Airlines*? Put another way, is the Court's statement in *Varig Airlines* that "[j]udicial intervention in such decisionmaking through

private tort suits would require the courts to 'second-guess' the political, social, and economic judgments of an agency exercising its regulatory function" any less applicable to the vaccine licensing program challenged in *Berkovitz*?

2. *The making of law or policy.* Professor Kenneth Culp Davis argued that well-reasoned judicial decisions increasingly often interpret the discretionary function exception as limited to the making of law or policy. Kenneth C. Davis, Constitutional Torts §§11-16 (1984). Do *Berkovitz* and *Varig Airlines* adopt or reject this approach?

3. *Failure to follow clear guidelines.* Under *Berkovitz*, strict guidelines in statutes or regulations can turn what might otherwise be a discretionary function into a situation in which government liability is possible. For example, in Faber v. United States, 56 F.3d 1122 (9th Cir. 1995), the plaintiff was injured when he dove off a 20-foot ledge at the top of a waterfall into a pool at the bottom of the falls. He sued, claiming that the failure of the Forest Service to post signs warning of diving dangers was tortious. The government argued that the decision whether to post warning signs was a discretionary function. It had support in the Ninth Circuit's decision in Valdez v. United States, 56 F.3d 1177 (9th Cir. 1995), which held, *inter alia,* that the failure to warn of dangerous conditions and the failure to install guard rails at a waterfall implicated a discretionary function and thus could not give rise to FTCA liability. In *Faber,* however, the court held that the discretionary function exception did not apply because the failure to post signs there violated "unambiguous directives" and thus was not discretionary. The court stated that the discretionary function exception does not apply where the government agency "fail[s] to follow specifically prescribed policies." *Faber,* 56 F.3d at 1126.

4. *Government management decisions.* When financial or economic crisis strikes, the government often steps in to bail out failing firms in large important industries. Following a financial crisis in the savings and loan industry in the 1980s, authority to regulate the industry was given to the Federal Deposit Insurance Corporation and the newly created Office of Thrift Supervision. If the government's management or supervision of a firm makes matters worse for the firm, might the FTCA provide liability in favor of shareholders injured when a government-managed business fails?

UNITED STATES v. GAUBERT, 499 U.S. 315 (1991): Due to perceived financial problems, day-to-day management of the Independent American Savings Association (IASA), a Texas savings and loan institution, was subjected to supervision and oversight by the Federal Home Loan Bank Board (FHLBB) and the Federal Home Loan Bank-Dallas (FHLB-D). Gaubert, IASA's chairman and largest shareholder, brought suit against the United States under the FTCA alleging that negligent management by federal regulators caused him to lose $100 million, including $75 million in stock value and a $25 million loan guarantee he had provided to aid IASA's recovery. In an opinion by Justice White, the Court held that Gaubert's claims were barred by the discretionary function exception to the FTCA:

> In the spring of 1986, the regulators threatened to close IASA unless its management and board of directors were replaced; all of the directors agreed to resign. The new officers and directors, including the chief executive officer who was

a former FHLB-D employee, were recommended by FHLB-D. After the new management took over, FHLB-D officials became more involved in IASA's day-to-day business. They recommended the hiring of a certain consultant to advise IASA on operational and financial matters; they advised IASA concerning whether, when, and how its subsidiaries should be placed into bankruptcy; they mediated salary disputes; they reviewed the draft of a complaint to be used in litigation; they urged IASA to convert from state to federal charter; and they actively intervened when the Texas Savings and Loan Department attempted to install a supervisory agent at IASA. In each instance, FHLB-D's advice was followed. . . .

Where Congress has delegated the authority to an independent agency or to the executive branch to implement the general provisions of a regulatory statute and to issue regulations to that end, there is no doubt that planning-level decisions establishing programs are protected by the discretionary function exception, as is the promulgation of regulations by which the agencies are to carry out the programs. In addition, the actions of Government agents involving the necessary element of choice and grounded in the social, economic, or political goals of the statute and regulations are protected. . . .

In light of our cases and their interpretation of §2680(a), it is clear that the Court of Appeals erred in holding that the exception does not reach decisions made at the operational or management level of the bank involved in this case. A discretionary act is one that involves choice or judgment; there is nothing in that description that refers exclusively to policymaking or planning functions. Day-to-day management of banking affairs, like the management of other businesses, regularly require judgment as to which of a range of permissible courses is the wisest. Discretionary conduct is not confined to the policy or planning level. "[I]t is the nature of the conduct, rather than the status of the actor, that governs whether the discretionary function exception applies in a given case." *Varig Airlines, supra,* at 813.

NOTES AND QUESTIONS

1. *The test in* Gaubert? The key statement in the Court's opinion in *Gaubert* is this: "Day-to-day management of banking affairs, like the management of other businesses, regularly require judgment as to which of a range of permissible courses is the wisest." Is this an accurate statement of the test for a discretionary function? Does it seem closer to *Dalehite* than to *Varig Airlines* and *Berkovitz*? Does the decision in effect eliminate the possibility of liability for government management of distressed businesses during a government bailout?

2. *Government function.* Can *Gaubert* be read as creating a variant of the government function approach that was apparently rejected in *Berkovitz*, in which liability is barred for activities thought to be uniquely appropriate for government while liability is imposed for proprietary functions as that concept is understood in tort law regarding local government immunity? In thinking about this question, reflect on the *Gaubert* Court's reasoning that the day-to-day operation of a bank by federal regulators is designed to further important government policies. Isn't this true of all government activity, even the most routine actions like driving a truck loaded with government office supplies? Do you agree with the suggestion that "*Gaubert's* most lasting value may be implicit rejection of any need for examination of whether government officials actually engaged in reasoned policymaking"? Donald N. Zillman, Protecting Discretion:

Judicial Interpretation of the Discretionary Function Exception to the Federal Tort Claims Act, 47 Me. L. Rev. 365, 387 (1995).

3. *Discretionary function and APA review standards.* The discretionary function cases do not discuss the APA's scope-of-review provisions that would be applied in direct reviews. Should they? In all of the cases discussed above, some decisions respecting the activity at issue would be insulated from review (as committed to agency discretion) or would receive deferential review if challenged directly in court because the governing statute provides room for choice by the administrator. One question in each case is how far into the protected sphere of administrative choice the court goes in scrutinizing a given facet of the activity. Can courts evaluate the care appropriate to FAA inspections without also judging the propriety of decisions respecting the number, training, assignment, and supervision of inspectors? A second question is whether the FTCA dictates greater insulation of administrative judgments from review in damage suits than in direct review actions. Should the standards differ?

4. *Strict liability and intentional torts.* The FTCA, in §§2680(a) and 2680(h) respectively, excludes from its coverage strict liability torts and most intentional torts (other than those discussed in note 5, *infra*). Why? Are the reasons for these exceptions similar? To what extent are these exceptions explicable by the special problems of supervising staff within government agencies?

Lawyers briefing FTCA claims often attempt to avoid subsection (h) by pleading other related torts. One common assertion is that negligent supervision by superiors, allowing the intentional tort by the inferior employee to occur, constitutes a separate actionable tort. How should courts treat this claim? Is the problem raised by this claim distinct from that raised in discretionary function analysis? In other cases, the same employees may be alleged to have committed intentional torts excluded from FTCA liability, and, at the same time, related but nonexcluded torts. *See, e.g., Varig Airlines, supra;* Block v. Neal, 460 U.S. 289 (1983); United States v. Neustadt, 366 U.S. 696 (1961). Given the realm of possible negligence claims, what impact do you think the intentional tort exception has? What information about the rules for calculation of damages for intentional and other torts would you want before answering that question?

5. *FTCA claims in the criminal justice arena.* Congress amended the FTCA in 1974, adding the proviso to §2680(h), quoted earlier in this section. Following the Federal Tort Claims Act Intentional Tort Amendment of 1974, Pub. L. No. 93-253, §2, 88 Stat. 50, the FTCA allows suits against the United States for claims of assault, battery, false imprisonment, false arrest, abuse of process, or malicious prosecution premised on "acts or omissions of investigative or law enforcement officers of the United States Government." The amendment substantially narrows the scope of the exception in subsection (h), as originally enacted. What accounts for alteration of the exception in this fashion? The amendment and the circumstances surrounding its adoption are discussed in Jack Boger et al., The Federal Tort Claims Act Intentional Torts Amendment: An Interpretive Analysis, 54 N.C. L. Rev. 497 (1976). For a spectacularly successful use of the FTCA in the criminal justice arena, *see* Limone v. United States, 579 F.3d 79 (1st Cir. 2009), which affirmed an award of more than $100 million after it was found that the United States government participated in the incarceration of three individuals that were known by the FBI to be innocent of the state law charges for which they were convicted. Because the federal government did

not initiate the criminal charges against the innocent victims, their malicious prosecution claim failed. However, the First Circuit upheld liability based on the tort of intentional infliction of emotional distress. 579 F.3d at 92. The court also rejected the government's discretionary function defense:

> It is elementary that the discretionary function exception does not immunize the government from liability for actions proscribed by federal statute or regulation. . . . Nor does it shield conduct that transgresses the Constitution. . . . In [a prior opinion in this case] we held that the plaintiffs' allegations that FBI agents had participated in framing them and had withheld exculpatory evidence to cover up their malefactions stated a clear violation of due process. . . . The plaintiffs proved the substance of these allegations. . . . Consequently, the conduct was unconstitutional and, therefore, not within the sweep of the discretionary function exception.

579 F.3d at 101-102. Is a rule that unconstitutional conduct is never covered by the discretionary function exception consistent with the language or purposes ascribed to that exception?

    6. *"Sue and be sued" clauses.* Aside from the FTCA, another device Congress often uses to waive sovereign immunity is the so-called "sue and be sued" clause. Beginning well before enactment of the FTCA, Congress inserted such clauses in dozens of statutes creating government corporations. An example is the Federal Housing Administration, whose enabling act stated that the "Administrator [of the FHA] shall, in carrying out the provisions of [the act], be authorized, in his official capacity, to sue and be sued in any court of competent jurisdiction, State or Federal." Although the bare phrase "be sued" in such clauses clearly indicates a Congressional intent to waive the sovereign immunity such corporations would otherwise have enjoyed, a recurring issue has been determining the extent of that waiver. For example, in Federal Housing Admin. v. Burr, 309 U.S. 242 (1940), the Court had to decide whether a state court could garnish the wages of an employee of the FHA. Based on its view that "sue and be sued" clauses should be "liberally construed," the Court answered the question in the affirmative:

> [W]hen Congress establishes such an agency, authorizes it to engage in commercial and business transactions with the public, and permits it to "sue and be sued," it cannot be lightly assumed that restrictions on that authority are to be implied. Rather, if the general authority to "sue and be sued" is to be delimited by implied exceptions, it must be clearly shown that certain types of suits are not consistent with the statutory or constitutional scheme, that an implied restriction of the general authority is necessary to avoid grave interference with the performance of a governmental function, or that, for other reasons, it was plainly the purpose of Congress to use the "sue and be sued" clause in a narrow sense. In the absence of such showing, it must be presumed that, when Congress launched a governmental agency into the commercial world and endowed it with authority to "sue or be sued," that agency is not less amenable to judicial process than a private enterprise under like circumstances would be.

Id. at 245.

    The question of "implied restrictions" arose in Thacker v. TVA, 139 S. Ct. 1435 (2019). The case involved a tort claim by a motorboat operator who was injured when his boat hit an electric cable that had fallen into the Tennessee River while being installed by TVA employees. The Tennessee Valley Authority Act of 1933 established the TVA as a "wholly owned public corporation of the United States" to provide a wide variety of economic development functions in the Tennessee River Valley, including most prominently the generation and sale of electricity. The Act provided that the TVA "[m]ay sue and be sued in its corporate name." 16 U.S.C. §831c(b). Although the FTCA expressly excludes any claim made against the TVA, the TVA argued that a "discretionary functions" exemption, similar to the exemption contained in the FTCA, should be read into the TVA's "sue and be sued" clause. Writing for a unanimous Court, Justice Kagan ruled that, as applied to "commercial" (as opposed to "governmental") activities of the TVA, the "sue and be sued" clause should be interpreted not to contain a "discretionary functions" exemption, but rather should subject the TVA to liability under the same standard and circumstances as would be applied to a purely private electric utility. The Court remanded the case to the lower court to determine whether the allegedly negligent activity was commercial or governmental, and, if the latter, whether immunity was "necessary to avoid grave interference" with that activity, quoting *Burr*.

2.   Suits Against Individual Government Officers

The FTCA displaces suits against individual federal officers. Under the FTCA, if a federal officer is sued for conduct within his or her official duties, the federal government is substituted as defendant and the individual officer is dismissed from the case. Even if the FTCA suit against the government fails, the case against the individual official or officials involved cannot be revived. The only way a federal official can be sued individually is if the plaintiff alleges a violation of constitutional rights. *See* Bivens v. Six Unknown Named Agents of Federal Bureau of Narcotics, 403 U.S. 388 (1971) (implying a right of action against federal officials directly from the Constitution).

At common law, government officials had three special defenses if they were sued in tort. The first of these is tort specific, a privilege for particular officials to commit particular tortious acts in particular circumstances. For example, in many jurisdictions, police officers enjoy a privilege to falsely arrest provided the arrest is made in good faith and there is a reasonable basis for belief that the plaintiff had committed a crime. The second set of defenses is available to both private citizens and government officials but is of special utility to public officials. This group includes the privileges of public interest, fair report, and fair comment (defenses to defamation suits) and is useful to government officials sued over information they may have provided to members of the press or public.

The third sort of defense applicable in suits against individual officers is not tied to particular torts but is rather a generic set of defenses that have evolved over time into what is known today as "absolute" and "qualified" immunity. These defenses are used most often today in *Bivens* cases (and similar cases against state officials under 42 U.S.C. §1983) involving constitutional tort claims. Some officials, such as judges, legislators, and prosecutors, are entitled to absolute immunity from suit as long as the claim arises out of the performance of a judicial, legislative, or prosecutorial function. Other officials, such as police officers, are entitled to qualified immunity, which protects them so long as their actions did not violate a clearly established constitutional right. While at one time the qualified immunity also required the officer to act in subjective good faith, the Supreme Court has broadened the defense to include all actions not violating clearly established law, even if the officer acted in bad faith or maliciously.

The numerous twists and turns of the convoluted jurisprudence under *Bivens* and related areas are beyond the scope of the course on Administrative Law. Two points may help place *Bivens* in proper perspective for present purposes. First, over the decades since *Bivens* was decided, members of the Supreme Court appear to have come to regret it, and its scope has been narrowed significantly. In 2012, the Court noted that "[s]ince [1982], the Court has had to decide in several different instances whether to imply a *Bivens* action. And in each instance it has decided against the existence of such an action." Minneci v. Pollard, 565 U.S. 118, 126 (2012). In 2017, in Ziglar v. Abbasi, 137 S. Ct. 1843 (2017), the Court appears to have tightened up on *Bivens* even further, proclaiming the federal courts should not extend *Bivens* to any new context without engaging in a careful analysis of whether special factors counsel leaving the decision of whether to extend *Bivens* to Congress. And the Court clearly implied that there should be a weighty thumb on the scale against extension. Further, the Court defined "new context" broadly to include cases that differ in "a meaningful way" from prior claims. It stated that meaningful differences include consideration of

> the rank of the officers involved; the constitutional right at issue; the generality or specificity of the official action; the extent of judicial guidance as to how an officer should respond to the problem or emergency to be confronted; the statutory or other legal mandate under which the officer was operating; the risk of disruptive intrusion by the Judiciary into the functioning of other branches; or the presence of potential special factors that previous *Bivens* cases did not consider.

137 S. Ct. at 1860. Under this analysis, it seems highly unlikely that the current Court will extend *Bivens* even slightly beyond contexts in which it has already been recognized. In *Abbasi*, the Court rejected extending *Bivens* to a claim against high- and low-level Justice Department officials, including the Attorney General, by post-9/11 detainees that they were subjected to physical and verbal abuse and arbitrary strip searches during prolonged unjustifiable detention.

Second, perhaps more important for administrative law, the Court has rejected *Bivens* liability for federal agencies. In FDIC v. Meyer, 510 U.S. 471 (1994), the Court rebuffed the plaintiff's attempt to sue a federal agency under *Bivens*. The Court held that a *Bivens* action against a federal agency would be inconsistent with the premise of *Bivens,* that individual liability was necessary because an action against the government was not available. The Court also held that the "potentially enormous financial burden" on the federal government of *Bivens* actions against agencies was a "special factor counselling hesitation" so that no *Bivens* action should be implied. 510 U.S. at 485. This leaves actions under the FTCA and the Tucker Act as the primary avenues for damages against the United States government and preserves the APA's role as the roadmap for attacking the substance of federal agency policy in federal court.

CHAPTER VIII

LICENSING

An enormous array of activities in American life requires prior approval from some government agency. One must typically obtain a license or permit to build an addition to a house, put a sign in front of a business, stage a rally in a public park, discharge pollutants into a waterway, make a living as a beautician, or operate a radio station. We use the term "licensing" to refer to the generic governmental activity involved in granting, denying, suspending, revoking, and renewing such permissions. Because a license is a precondition for engaging in certain desirable or profitable activities, it is a form of governmentally conferred benefit, much like assistance payments or public housing. Licenses are also used as devices to enforce command-and-control regulations. Most licenses contain explicit conditions that are, in effect, tailor-made regulatory commands addressed to the licensee. The suspension, revocation, and nonrenewal of a license, moreover, is a sanction, with the threat of imposition alone serving as a powerful inducement to compliance. And the policies that guide licensing decisions generally must be made through the same process—and address the same sorts of considerations respecting openness, analytical foundation, and articulation—as other administrative policymaking.

For these reasons, licensing raises many of the same legal problems we have seen in preceding chapters. But licensing schemes present special challenges for legal control of administration, as well. First, licensing arrangements often entail close and continuous relationships between the regulator and the regulated. The resulting mutual interdependence can be problematic: regulators may be coopted, or they might coerce the regulated party. Second, because licensing is an enabling activity by nature, it often requires a complex prediction of future market needs and applicant performance that requires the licensor to synthesize a large amount of factual material and predictive judgments. As a cognitive and political process, licensing therefore lies somewhere between a specific enforcement action and a general rulemaking proceeding. Third, licenses are sometimes quite scarce—a fact variously attributed to technical, economic, or political considerations. As a consequence, licensing agencies must sometimes make comparative judgments about the relative merits of competing applicants as well as absolute judgments about their qualifications. The explicitly comparative character of decisions together with extensive opportunity for bias increases concerns over the consistency of administrative decisions. Finally, because licensing systems—and the advantages conferred on particular activities under these systems—lose significance when new, unregulated technologies or industries replace (or threaten to replace) licensed industries, regulators episodically are asked to subject new industries and technologies to the same or similar licensing requirements. Decisions on these requests inevitably raise questions respecting the standards to be used in deciding the boundaries of administrative authority and the extent to which reviewing courts should defer to these regulatory decisions.

This chapter addresses these problems in three contexts—occupational licensing, broadcast licensing, and licensing of utilities. Occupational licensing, as it is customarily practiced in this country, is a form of governmentally sanctioned self-regulation. Most licensed occupations exercise extensive de jure as well as de facto influence over their own regulation. The danger of administrative bias and self-interest, discussed in Chapter VI, *supra,* recurs here with a vengeance. Broadcast licensing, on the other hand, illustrates the challenge, encountered in business licensing programs, of establishing procedural and substantive controls on an activity in which the stakes are enormous and the competition fierce. It also illustrates the way in which technological change alters the business and regulatory landscapes. Utilities—gas, water, electricity, telephones—traditionally were regulated by licensing agencies, at least in part because competition in those industries (at least in key components of each industry) was expected to be virtually nonexistent. Most utility licensing issues concern traditional economic regulation in which agencies set prices for the utilities' products to ensure a reasonable rate of return in lieu of the market doing so (although rate regulation has significant implications for other aspects of a utility's operations, too). If these industries become more competitive over time, regulators face a choice among three options: continuing as usual with their regulation (which may be unnecessary or excessive), loosening the reins on rate regulation (to enable a transition to a market-driven regime), or expanding the reach of their regulations (to encompass new activity). The latter two options may only be available if the governing statute contains sufficient flexibility.

A.   OCCUPATIONAL LICENSING

1.   *Due Process, Equal Protection, and the Problem of Self-Interest*

Occupational licensure is a ubiquitous function of American state governments. Under the typical licensure statute, no person may practice a specified trade or profession in the state without having first obtained a license from a regulatory agency, usually composed primarily or exclusively of members of the licensed occupation. The licensing board prescribes criteria for admission into the occupation, administers examinations to determine competence, establishes standards of practice, and disciplines licensees for violating such standards. The contemporary American system of occupational licensing has its roots in the medieval guild system. The guilds shared several characteristics with today's licensing schemes. Practice of a guild occupation was restricted to guild members, and guild membership itself was restricted. Having eliminated competition from outside the guild, guild rules also restricted competition from within. And the governance of each occupation was entrusted to guild members who practiced that occupation.

The guild system was not imported into colonial America, and most occupations were unregulated until the advent of professional licensing in the late nineteenth and early twentieth century. The prevailing American attitude was captured in Lemuel Shattuck's 1850 Report of the Sanitary Commission of Massachusetts, quoted in J. Young, The Medical Messiah (1967):

> Anyone, male or female, an honest man or a knave, can assume the name physician and "practice" upon any one, to cure or kill, as either may happen, without accountability.

Over time, however, that attitude changed. Now we require licenses for hundreds of occupations, including beekeepers, embalmers, lightning rod salespersons, barbers, septic tank cleaners, taxidermists, tattoo artists, tour guides, aestheticians, florists, ballroom dance instructors, sellers of medical marijuana—and lawyers. See Walter Gellhorn, The Abuse of Occupational Licensing, 44 U. Chi. L. Rev. 6 (1976); Simon Rottenberg, ed., Occupational Licensure and Regulation 2 (1980). In California serious consideration was given to proposed legislation that would have licensed people to mow lawns. See John A. C. Hetherington, State Economic Regulation and Substantive Due Process of Law II, 53 Nw. U. L. Rev. 226, 249 (1958).

The broad sweep of licensure has raised suspicions about the real rationale for state-sanctioned regulation. Those supporting licensure invariably invoke the need to protect the consuming public from deleterious effects of poor quality service. The motivation in reality, however, might be anticompetitive. As one commentator noted: "the pressure on the legislature to license an occupation rarely comes from the members of the public who have been mulcted or in other ways abused by members of the occupation. On the contrary, the pressure invariably comes from members of the occupation itself." Milton Friedman, Capitalism and Freedom 139 (1962). See also Jonathan Rose, Occupational Licensing: A Framework for Analysis, 1979 Ariz. St. L.J. 189.

Critics of occupational licensure stress that its defining feature — restrictions on entry into the licensed service — excludes some would-be customers from access to the service and increases income and status for providers. Economist Milton Friedman notes that there are other ways to protect consumers:

> It is important to distinguish three different levels of control: first, registration; second, certification; third, licensing.

By registration, I mean an arrangement under which individuals are required to list their names in some official register if they engage in certain kinds of activities. There is no provision for denying the right to engage in the activity to anyone who is willing to list his name. He may be charged a fee, either as a registration fee or as a scheme of taxation.

The second level is certification. The governmental agency may certify that an individual has certain skills but may not prevent, in any way, the practice of any occupation using these skills by people who do not have such a certificate. One example is accountancy. In most states, anybody can be an accountant, whether he is a certified public accountant or not, but only those people who have passed a particular test can put the title CPA after their names or can put a sign in their offices saying they are certified public accountants. Certification is frequently only an intermediate state. In many states, there has been a tendency to restrict an increasing range of activities to certified public accountants. With respect to such activities there is licensure, not certification. In some states, "architect" is a title which can be used only by those who have passed a specified examination. This is certification. It does not prevent anyone else from going into the business of advising people for a fee how to build houses.

The third stage is licensing proper. This is an arrangement under which one must obtain a license from a recognized authority in order to engage in the occupation. The license is more than a formality. It requires some demonstration of competence or the meeting of some tests ostensibly designed to insure competence, and anyone who does not have a license is not authorized to practice and is subject to a fine or a jail sentence if he does engage in practice.

Friedman, *supra,* at 144-145. The dominance of the third form, argues Friedman, demonstrates that occupational licensing is designed primarily to benefit the licensed profession, not its customers.

One of the most troubling aspects of occupational licensing is self-regulation: when members of the licensed occupation (usually as licensing "boards") act as their own regulator. Long ago, Walter Gellhorn observed the deference given to practitioners of the licensed professions:

Seventy-five percent of the occupational licensing boards at work in this country today are composed exclusively of licensed practitioners in the respective occupations. These men and women, most of whom are only part-time officials, may have a direct economic interest in many of the decisions they make concerning admission requirements and the definition of standards to be observed by licensees. More importantly, they are as a rule directly representative of organized groups within the occupations. Ordinarily they are nominated by these groups as a step toward a gubernatorial or other appointment that is frequently a mere formality. Often the formality is dispensed with entirely, appointment being made directly by the occupational association—as happens, for example, with the embalmers in North Carolina, the dentists in Alabama, the psychologists in Virginia, the physicians in Maryland, and the attorneys in Washington.

Walter Gellhorn, Individual Freedom and Governmental Restraints 106 (1956). That description remains accurate. While the composition of some licensing boards has been altered to allow greater "outside" participation, licensees still play both roles, fox and guardian of the chicken coop. This is a perception many people have of the legal profession.

GIBSON v. BERRYHILL
411 U.S. 564 (1973)

[This case is excerpted in Chapter VI, *supra*. Please read the case and the notes and questions that follow it.]

━━━━━━━━━

Although the financial interest rationale relied on in *Gibson* may apply to a wide array of occupational licensing decisions, there also are several ways to confine the doctrine. Not long after *Gibson*, the Court considered one proposed limitation.

FRIEDMAN v. ROGERS, 440 U.S. 1 (1979): Two groups of Texas optometrists used different practice models. "Professional" optometrists practiced individually or in small groups, while "commercial" optometrists practiced under trade names, often affiliated with large practice groups or with other enterprises that wanted to offer optometry as an adjunct service. The two groups had different professional organizations and different professional rules. After a period of intense competition between the two, the Texas legislature sided with the professional optometrists represented by the Texas Optometric Association (TOA). The Texas Optometry Act adopted the TOA's ban on practice under trade names into law. Section 2.02 of the Act reconstituted the Texas Optometry Board, the state's regulatory body, to require (in essence) that at least four of the six members be accepted by the TOA. Rogers and other commercial optometrists challenged the Act as unconstitutional, alleging, *inter alia*, that they were deprived of equal protection and due process by being subject to regulation by a board composed of a majority of optometrists hostile to commercial optometrists. The Supreme Court, in an opinion by Justice Powell, upheld the law against those objections:

> We stated the applicable constitutional rule for reviewing equal protection challenges to local economic regulations such as §2.02 in New Orleans v. Dukes, 427 U.S. 297, 303 (1976).
>
> . . . Unless a classification trammels fundamental personal rights or is drawn upon inherently suspect distinctions such as race, religion, or alienage, our decisions presume the constitutionality of the statutory discriminations and require only that the classification challenged be rationally related to a legitimate state interest.
>
> The history of the Act shows that §2.02 is related reasonably to the State's legitimate purpose of securing a Board that will administer the Act faithfully.
>
> Prior to 1967, the TOA dominated the State Board of Examiners; during that period, the State Board adopted various rules for the regulation of the optometrical profession, including the Professional Responsibility Rule. Between 1967 and 1969, the commercial optometrists secured a majority on the State Board and took steps to repeal the Professional Responsibility Rule. . . . [I]n 1969 . . . the legislature enacted . . . the Professional Responsibility Rule long supported by the TOA, and created the Board to administer the Act. In view

of its experience with the commercial and professional optometrists preceding the passage of the Act, it was reasonable for the legislature to require that a majority of the Board be drawn from a professional organization that had demonstrated consistent support for the rules that the Board would be responsible for enforcing. . . .

Although Rogers has no constitutional right to be regulated by a Board that is sympathetic to the commercial practice of optometry, he does have a constitutional right to a fair and impartial hearing in any disciplinary proceeding conducted against him by the Board. Gibson v. Berryhill, 411 U.S. 564 (1973); Wall v. American Optometric Assn., 379 F. Supp. 175 (N.D. Ga.), *summarily aff'd sub nom.* Wall v. Hardwick, 419 U.S. 888 (1974). In both *Gibson* and *Wall,* however, disciplinary proceedings had been instituted against the plaintiffs, and the courts were able to examine in a particular context the possibility that the members of the regulatory board might have personal interests that precluded a fair and impartial hearing of the charges. Finding the presence of such prejudicial interests, it was appropriate for the courts to enjoin further proceedings against the plaintiffs. *E.g., Gibson, supra,* at 570, 578-579. In contrast, Rogers' challenge to the fairness of the Board does not arise from any disciplinary proceeding against him. . . .

[The Court also rejected a First Amendment challenge to the Act's ban on the use of trade names in optometry. *See* discussion in part 3, *infra.*]

NOTES AND QUESTIONS

1. *Procedural due process in occupational licensing.* The Court, without much elaboration, holds that *Gibson* is inapplicable to Rogers' claim because it did not involve a "disciplinary proceeding." Why? Is the Court saying that Rogers' interest in his license is not a "liberty" or "property" interest protected by due process? Reviewing the materials on procedural due process in Chapter VI, *supra,* does that seem plausible? Or is the Court saying that Rogers has not (yet) been "deprived" of such an interest?

In a key passage, the Court states that "[a]lthough Rogers has no constitutional right to be regulated by a Board that is sympathetic to the commercial practice of optometry, he does have a constitutional right to a fair and impartial hearing in any disciplinary proceeding conducted against him by the Board." Recall the distinction that courts have drawn, for purposes of applying due process protections, between policymaking and adjudication, in cases like *Londoner* and *Bi-Metallic,* excerpted in Chapter IV, *supra,* and *National Advertisers* and *Cinderella,* excerpted in Chapter V, *supra.* Does this distinction make sense in the context of occupational licensure? *See, e.g.,* Ernest L. Gellhorn & Glen O. Robinson, Rulemaking "Due Process": An Inconclusive Dialogue, 48 U. Chi. L. Rev. 201 (1981); Hans Linde, Due Process of Lawmaking, 55 Neb. L. Rev. 197 (1976).

2. *Malpractice claims against licensed professionals.* A number of states have required that tort claims alleging medical malpractice be submitted to an administrative tribunal for screening before they may be filed in court. Would the principles underlying *Gibson* and *Friedman* place limits on the composition of these panels?

3. *Separating investigative and adjudicative functions.* Another issue that affects occupational licensing is the degree of separation required between the investigating and adjudicating decisionmakers. Should different rules apply in this context than for the general run of administrative decisions? *See* Withrow v. Larkin, excerpted in Chapter VI, *supra.*

2. Anticompetitive Behavior and Antitrust Restraints

The antitrust laws—principally the Sherman Act, the Clayton Act, and the Federal Trade Commission Act—seek to preserve competition among providers of goods and services. The roots of antitrust are old, but these laws are enjoying something of a resurgence as large technology companies like Google, Facebook, and Amazon have amassed significant power in their respective realms. In recent years, critics have called for these behemoths to be broken up; the FTC and DOJ have intensified their scrutiny of the companies' consumer privacy and other practices; and Congress has held several hearings on whether they are effectively monopolies.

The traditional antitrust concern with competition dovetails nicely with the argument that occupational self-regulation amounts to state-sanctioned restrictions on competition, yet the antitrust laws historically were not applied to occupational licensing. There are two judicially created obstacles to applying antitrust laws to occupational regulation: the "trade or commerce" limitation and the "state action" doctrine.

A series of Supreme Court dicta spanning half a century suggested that professional activity fell outside the definition of "trade or commerce" for the purposes of antitrust law. *See, e.g.,* FTC v. Raladam Co., 283 U.S. 643, 653 (1931) ("medical practitioners . . . follow a profession and not a trade"). Later pronouncements cast doubt on the status of this so-called "learned professions" exception to the antitrust laws, but the Court did not expressly repudiate the earlier dicta. *See* United States v. Oregon State Medical Socy., 343 U.S. 326 (1952).

A second obstacle to applying antitrust law to the operation of state occupational licensing boards is the state action doctrine. Derived from the Supreme Court's decision in Parker v. Brown, 317 U.S. 341 (1943), the doctrine excludes from antitrust scrutiny some anticompetitive practices sanctioned by state law. The vitality of the state action doctrine has ebbed and flowed over time. In Goldfarb v. Virginia State Bar, 421 U.S. 773 (1974), the Court allowed antitrust challenges to anticompetitive activities by the body regulating the practice of law, finding no basis for a general exemption of the learned professions nor for specifically excluding lawyers' work from the definition of commerce or, derivatively, interstate commerce. Other Supreme Court decisions in the 1980s, however, sent mixed signals on the scope of the state action doctrine. As a result, the basis for exempting professional licensing boards from antitrust scrutiny were unclear until the decision below.

NORTH CAROLINA STATE BOARD OF DENTAL EXAMINERS v. FEDERAL TRADE COMMISSION
135 S. Ct. 1101 (2015)

JUSTICE KENNEDY delivered the opinion of the Court. . . .

I

A

In its Dental Practice Act (Act), North Carolina has declared the practice of dentistry to be a matter of public concern requiring regulation. N.C. Gen. Stat. Ann. §90-22(a) (2013). Under the Act, the North Carolina State Board of Dental Examiners (Board) is "the agency of the State for the regulation of the practice of dentistry." §90-22(b).

The Board's principal duty is to create, administer, and enforce a licensing system for dentists. To perform that function it has broad authority over licensees. The Board's authority with respect to unlicensed persons, however, is more restricted: like "any resident citizen," the Board may file suit to "perpetually enjoin any person from . . . unlawfully practicing dentistry." §90-40.1.

The Act provides that six of the Board's eight members must be licensed dentists engaged in the active practice of dentistry. They are elected by other licensed dentists in North Carolina who cast their ballots in elections conducted by the Board. The seventh member must be a licensed and practicing dental hygienist, and he or she is elected by other licensed hygienists. The final member is referred to by the Act as a "consumer" and is appointed by the Governor. . . .

The Board may promulgate rules and regulations governing the practice of dentistry within the State, provided those mandates are not inconsistent with the Act and are approved by the North Carolina Rules Review Commission, whose members are appointed by the state legislature.

B

In the 1990's, dentists in North Carolina started whitening teeth. Many of those who did so, including 8 of the Board's 10 members during the period at issue in this case, earned substantial fees for that service. By 2003, nondentists arrived on the scene. They charged lower prices for their services than the dentists did. Dentists soon began to complain to the Board about their new competitors. Few complaints warned of possible harm to consumers. Most expressed a principal concern with the low prices charged by nondentists.

Responding to these filings, the Board opened an investigation into nondentist teeth whitening. A dentist member was placed in charge of the inquiry. Neither the Board's hygienist member nor its consumer member participated in this undertaking. The Board's chief operations officer remarked that the Board was "going forth to do battle" with nondentists. App. to Pet. for Cert. 103a. The Board's concern did not result in a formal rule or regulation reviewable by the independent Rules Review Commission, even though the Act does not, by its terms, specify that teeth whitening is "the practice of dentistry."

Starting in 2006, the Board issued at least 47 cease-and-desist letters on its official letterhead to nondentist teeth whitening service providers and product manufacturers. Many of those letters directed the recipient to cease "all activity constituting the practice of dentistry"; warned that the unlicensed practice of dentistry is a crime; and strongly implied (or expressly stated) that teeth whitening constitutes "the practice of dentistry." In early 2007, the Board persuaded the North Carolina Board of Cosmetic Art Examiners to warn cosmetologists against providing teeth whitening services. Later that year, the Board sent letters to mall operators, stating that kiosk teeth whiteners were violating the Dental Practice Act and advising that the malls consider expelling violators from their premises.

These actions had the intended result. Nondentists ceased offering teeth whitening services in North Carolina.

C

In 2010, the Federal Trade Commission (FTC) filed an administrative complaint charging the Board with violating §5 of the Federal Trade Commission Act, 38 Stat. 719, as amended, 15 U.S.C. §45.[1] The FTC alleged that the Board's concerted action to exclude nondentists from the market for teeth whitening services in North Carolina constituted an anticompetitive and unfair method of competition. . . .

The FTC ordered the Board to stop sending the cease-and-desist letters or other communications that stated nondentists may not offer teeth whitening services and products. It further ordered the Board to issue notices to all earlier recipients of the Board's cease-and-desist orders advising them of the Board's proper sphere of authority and saying, among other options, that the notice recipients had a right to seek declaratory rulings in state court.

On petition for review, the Court of Appeals for the Fourth Circuit affirmed the FTC in all respects. 717 F.3d 359, 370 (2013). . . .

III

In this case the Board argues its members were invested by North Carolina with the power of the State and that, as a result, the Board's actions are cloaked with . . . immunity [under Parker v. Brown]. This argument fails, however. A nonsovereign actor controlled by active market participants—such as the Board—enjoys *Parker* immunity only if it satisfies two requirements: "first that 'the challenged restraint . . . be one clearly articulated and affirmatively expressed as state policy,' and second that 'the policy . . . be actively supervised by the State.'" FTC v. Phoebe Putney Health System, Inc., 133 S. Ct. 1003, 1010 [(2013)] (*quoting* California Retail Liquor Dealers Assn. v. Midcal Aluminum, Inc., 445 U.S. 97, 105 (1980)). . . . [Even assuming that it satisfied the first requirement,] the Board did not receive active supervision

---

1. [The FTC alleged, and later found, that the Board had engaged in an "unfair method of competition," within the meaning of the FTC Act §5, because it had violated §1 of the Sherman Act—hence, the references to the Sherman Act in the Court's opinion.—Eds.]

by the State when it interpreted the Act as addressing teeth whitening and when it enforced that policy by issuing cease-and-desist letters to nondentist teeth whiteners.

A

An entity may not invoke *Parker* immunity unless the actions in question are an exercise of the State's sovereign power. [W]hile the Sherman Act confers immunity on the States' own anticompetitive policies out of respect for federalism, it does not always confer immunity where, as here, a State delegates control over a market to a nonsovereign actor. For purposes of *Parker*, a nonsovereign actor is one whose conduct does not automatically qualify as that of the sovereign State itself. State agencies are not simply by their governmental character sovereign actors for purposes of state-action immunity. . . .

Limits on state-action immunity are most essential when the State seeks to delegate its regulatory power to active market participants, for established ethical standards may blend with private anticompetitive motives in a way difficult even for market participants to discern. . . . In consequence, active market participants cannot be allowed to regulate their own markets free from antitrust accountability. *See Midcal, supra,* at 106 ("The national policy in favor of competition cannot be thwarted by casting [a] gauzy cloak of state involvement over what is essentially a private price-fixing arrangement"). The question is not whether the challenged conduct is efficient, well-functioning, or wise. Rather, it is "whether anticompetitive conduct engaged in by [nonsovereign actors] should be deemed state action and thus shielded from the antitrust laws." Patrick v. Burget, 486 U.S. 94, 100 (1988).

C

. . . State agencies controlled by active market participants, who possess singularly strong private interests, pose the very risk of self-dealing *Midcal*'s supervision requirement was created to address. This conclusion does not question the good faith of state officers but rather is an assessment of the structural risk of market participants' confusing their own interests with the State's policy goals. *See Patrick,* 486 U.S., at 100-101.

The Court applied this reasoning to a state agency in *Goldfarb*. There the Court denied immunity to a state agency (the Virginia State Bar) controlled by market participants (lawyers) because the agency had "joined in what is essentially a private anticompetitive activity" for "the benefit of its members." 421 U.S., at 791, 792. This emphasis on the Bar's private interests explains why *Goldfarb*, though it predates *Midcal*, considered the lack of supervision by the Virginia Supreme Court to be a principal reason for denying immunity. *See* 421 U.S., at 791; *see also* . . . Bates v. State Bar of Ariz., 433 U.S. 350, 361-362 (1977) (granting the Arizona Bar state-action immunity partly because its "rules are subject to pointed re-examination by the policymaker").

The Court holds today that a state board on which a controlling number of decisionmakers are active market participants in the occupation the board regulates must satisfy *Midcal*'s active supervision requirement in order to invoke state-action antitrust immunity. . . .

The Sherman Act protects competition while also respecting federalism. It does not authorize the States to abandon markets to the unsupervised control of active market participants, whether trade associations or hybrid agencies. If a State wants to rely on active market participants as regulators, it must provide active supervision if state-action immunity under *Parker* is to be invoked.

The judgment of the Court of Appeals for the Fourth Circuit is affirmed.

JUSTICE ALITO, with whom JUSTICE SCALIA and JUSTICE THOMAS join, dissenting.

The Court's decision in this case is based on a serious misunderstanding of the doctrine of state-action antitrust immunity that this Court recognized more than 60 years ago in Parker v. Brown, 317 U.S. 341 (1943). In *Parker*, the Court held that the Sherman Act does not prevent the States from continuing their age-old practice of enacting measures, such as licensing requirements, that are designed to protect the public health and welfare. *Id.*, at 352. The case now before us involves precisely this type of state regulation—North Carolina's laws governing the practice of dentistry, which are administered by the North Carolina Board of Dental Examiners (Board).

Today, however, the Court takes the unprecedented step of holding that *Parker* does not apply to the North Carolina Board because the Board is not structured in a way that merits a good-government seal of approval; that is, it is made up of practicing dentists who have a financial incentive to use the licensing laws to further the financial interests of the State's dentists. There is nothing new about the structure of the North Carolina Board. When the States first created medical and dental boards, well before the Sherman Act was enacted, they began to staff them in this way. Nor is there anything new about the suspicion that the North Carolina Board—in attempting to prevent persons other than dentists from performing teeth-whitening procedures—was serving the interests of dentists and not the public. Professional and occupational licensing requirements have often been used in such a way. But that is not what *Parker* immunity is about. Indeed, the very state program involved in that case was unquestionably designed to benefit the regulated entities, California raisin growers.

The question before us is not whether such programs serve the public interest. The question, instead, is whether this case is controlled by *Parker*, and the answer to that question is clear. Under *Parker*, the Sherman Act (and the Federal Trade Commission Act, *see* FTC v. Ticor Title Ins. Co., 504 U.S. 621, 635 (1992)) do not apply to state agencies; the North Carolina Board of Dental Examiners is a state agency; and that is the end of the matter. By straying from this simple path, the Court has not only distorted *Parker*, it has headed into a morass. Determining whether a state agency is structured in a way that militates against regulatory capture is no easy task, and there is reason to fear that today's decision will spawn confusion. The Court has veered off course, and therefore I cannot go along.

I

. . . In *Parker*, a raisin producer challenged the California Agricultural Prorate Act, an agricultural price support program. The California Act authorized the creation of an Agricultural Prorate Advisory Commission (Commission) to establish marketing plans for certain agricultural commodities within the State. Raisins were among the regulated commodities, and so the Commission established a marketing program that governed many aspects of raisin sales, including the quality and quantity of raisins sold, the timing of sales, and the price at which raisins were sold. The *Parker* Court assumed that this program would have violated "the Sherman Act if it were organized and made effective solely by virtue of a contract, combination or conspiracy of private persons," and the Court also assumed that Congress could have prohibited a State from creating a program like California's if it had chosen to do so. [317 U.S.], at 350. Nevertheless, the Court concluded that the California program did not violate the Sherman Act because the Act did not circumscribe state regulatory power. *Id.*, at 351.

[T]he Court reasoned that "[i]n a dual system of government in which, under the Constitution, the states are sovereign, save only as Congress may constitutionally subtract from their authority, an unexpressed purpose to nullify a state's control over its officers and agents is not lightly to be attributed to Congress." 317 U.S., at 351. For the Congress that enacted the Sherman Act in 1890, it would have been a truly radical and almost certainly futile step to attempt to prevent the States from exercising their traditional regulatory authority, and the *Parker* Court refused to assume that the Act was meant to have such an effect.

When the basis for the *Parker* state-action doctrine is understood, the Court's error in this case is plain. In 1890, the regulation of the practice of medicine and dentistry was regarded as falling squarely within the States' sovereign police power. By that time, many States had established medical and dental boards, often staffed by doctors or dentists, and had given those boards the authority to confer and revoke licenses. This was quintessential police power legislation, and although state laws were often challenged during that era under the doctrine of substantive due process, the licensing of medical professionals easily survived such assaults. Just one year before the enactment of the Sherman Act, in Dent v. West Virginia, 129 U.S. 114, 128 (1889), this Court rejected such a challenge to a state law requiring all physicians to obtain a certificate from the state board of health attesting to their qualifications. And in Hawker v. New York, 170 U.S. 189, 192 (1898), the Court reiterated that a law specifying the qualifications to practice medicine was clearly a proper exercise of the police power. Thus, the North Carolina statutes establishing and specifying the powers of the State Board of Dental Examiners represent precisely the kind of state regulation that the *Parker* exemption was meant to immunize. . . .

II

. . . The Court crafts a test under which state agencies that are "controlled by active market participants," must demonstrate active state supervision in order to be immune from federal antitrust law. The Court thus treats these state agencies like private entities. But in *Parker*, the Court did not examine the structure of the California program to determine if it had been captured by private interests. If the Court had done so, the case would certainly have come out differently, because California conditioned its regulatory measures on the participation and approval of market actors in the relevant industry. . . .

III

Not only is the Court's decision inconsistent with the underlying theory of *Parker*; it will create practical problems and is likely to have far-reaching effects on the States' regulation of professions. As previously noted, state medical and dental boards have been staffed by practitioners since they were first created, and there are obvious advantages to this approach. It is reasonable for States to decide that the individuals best able to regulate technical professions are practitioners with expertise in those very professions. Staffing the State Board of Dental Examiners with certified public accountants would certainly lessen the risk of actions that place the well-being of dentists over those of the public, but this would also compromise the State's interest in sensibly regulating a technical profession in which lay people have little expertise.

As a result of today's decision, States may find it necessary to change the composition of medical, dental, and other boards, but it is not clear what sort of changes are needed to satisfy the test that the Court now adopts. The Court faults the structure of the North Carolina Board because "active market partici-pants" constitute "a controlling number of [the] decisionmakers," but this test raises many questions.

What is a "controlling number"? Is it a majority? And if so, why does the Court eschew that term? Or does the Court mean to leave open the possibility that something less than a majority might suffice in particular circumstances? . . .

Who is an "active market participant"? If Board members withdraw from practice during a short term of service but typically return to practice when their terms end, does that mean that they are not active market participants during their period of service?

What is the scope of the market in which a member may not participate while serving on the board? Must the market be relevant to the particular reg-ulation being challenged or merely to the jurisdiction of the entire agency? Would the result in the present case be different if a majority of the Board members, though practicing dentists, did not provide teeth whitening services? What if they were orthodontists, periodontists, and the like? And how much participation makes a person "active" in the market?

The answers to these questions are not obvious, but the States must predict the answers in order to make informed choices about how to constitute their agencies.

I suppose that all this will be worked out by the lower courts and the Federal Trade Commission (FTC), but the Court's approach raises a more fundamental question, and that is why the Court's inquiry should stop with an examination of the structure of a state licensing board. When the Court asks whether market participants control the North Carolina Board, the Court in essence is asking whether this regulatory body has been captured by the entities that it is sup-posed to regulate. Regulatory capture can occur in many ways.[1] So why ask only whether the members of a board are active market participants? The answer

---

1. *See, e.g.*, R. Noll, Reforming Regulation 40-43, 46 (1971); J. Wilson, The Politics of Regulation 357-394 (1980). Indeed, it has even been charged that the FTC, which brought this case, has been cap-tured by entities over which it has jurisdiction. *See* E. Cox, "The Nader Report" on the Federal Trade Commission vii-xiv (1969); R. Posner, Federal Trade Commission, 37 U. Chi. L. Rev. 47, 82-84 (1969).

may be that determining when regulatory capture has occurred is no simple task. That answer provides a reason for relieving courts from the obligation to make such determinations at all. It does not explain why it is appropriate for the Court to adopt the rather crude test for capture that constitutes the holding of today's decision. . . .

NOTES AND QUESTIONS

1. *Antitrust and state regulation.* What is the underlying rationale of the *Parker* doctrine? Is it based on the view that antitrust is merely one among several equally plausible ways to assure well-functioning markets, and that the courts should therefore defer to the assumed wisdom of state legislatures in choosing an alternative approach? Or is it based on the view that, even though antitrust is superior to regulation, the principle of federalism counsels deference to the judgment of a sovereign state? Can the difference between Justice Alito's dissent and the majority opinion be understood in those terms? Or is it simply a disagreement about the force of history? Or the workability of an "active supervision" standard?

2. *Regulatory capture.* Recall the discussion of regulatory "capture" from Chapter I, *supra.* One of the challenges for administrative law is to fashion workable doctrines to constrain the worst effects of regulatory capture. Perhaps the clearest example is the *Carter Coal* rule forbidding delegation of lawmaking power to private parties, discussed in Chapter I, *supra.* Is the doctrine fashioned by the Court in *North Carolina Dental* another illustration? If so, is it likely to be workable, or will it be too easy to circumvent? What position does Justice Alito take with regard to regulatory capture? Is it, in his view, acceptable, or is it just impossible to prohibit without sacrificing the benefits of expertise?

3. *Are antitrust, due process, and equal protection complements or substitutes?* Does the majority's approach in *North Carolina Dental* make antitrust law a substitute for adjudication of due process and equal protection claims of the sort advanced in *Gibson* and *Friedman?* Look back at the *Friedman* decision. Is the Court's message there essentially the same as the dissent's in *North Carolina Dental?* Does antitrust law's focus on anticompetitive behavior narrow the ambit of interventions possible under those laws, or merely restate the sorts of concerns addressed under other provisions? Should the answer to that question matter for analysis of the questions presented in *North Carolina Dental?*

3.   Other Constraints on Occupational Licensing

Another body of law that can limit occupational licensure requirements is the Free Speech Clause of the First Amendment, made applicable to the states through the Fourteenth Amendment. The First Amendment does not present a direct threat to occupational licensure, but it does threaten one of its historic cornerstones: restraints on advertising. Such restraints have been defended as necessary to protect against fraud and deception and to promote a sense of professionalism. More than a few commentators have observed, however, that advertising restrictions are among the most effective mechanisms for reducing competition among practitioners and, not coincidentally, raising prices for their services. In Virginia Pharmacy Bd. v. Virginia Consumer Council, 425 U.S. 748 (1976), the Supreme Court decided that commercial speech was entitled to First Amendment protection. Balancing speech interests against state regulatory interests, the Court concluded that Virginia could not constitutionally prohibit, as "unprofessional conduct," pharmacists' advertisement of prescription drug prices. The following year in Bates v. State Bar of Arizona, 433 U.S. 350 (1977), after rejecting a Sherman Act claim, the Court struck down a similar ban on lawyer advertising on First Amendment grounds.

In Part II of its opinion in *Friedman v. Rogers*, however, the Supreme Court held that the Texas ban on practicing optometry under a trade name did not violate the First Amendment:

> A trade name is . . . a significantly different form of commercial speech from that considered in *Virginia Pharmacy* and *Bates*. In those cases, the State had proscribed advertising by pharmacists and lawyers that contained statements about the products or services offered and their prices. These statements were self-contained and self-explanatory. Here, we are concerned with a form of commercial speech that has no intrinsic meaning. A trade name conveys no information about the price and nature of the services offered by an optometrist until it acquires meaning over a period of time by associations formed in the minds of the public between the name and some standard of price or quality. Because these ill-defined associations of trade names with price and quality information can be manipulated by the users of trade names, there is a significant possibility that trade names will be used to mislead the public.
>
> The possibilities for deception are numerous. The trade name of an optometrical practice can remain unchanged despite changes in the staff of optometrists upon whose skill and care the public depends when it patronizes the practice. Thus, the public may be attracted by a trade name that reflects the reputation of an optometrist no longer associated with the practice. A trade name frees an optometrist from dependence on his personal reputation to attract clients, and even allows him to assume a new trade name if negligence or misconduct casts a shadow over the old one. By using different trade names at shops under his common ownership, an optometrist can give the public the false impression of competition among the shops. The use of a trade name also facilitates the advertising essential to large-scale commercial practices with numerous branch offices, conduct the State rationally may wish to discourage while not prohibiting commercial optometrical practice altogether.

440 U.S. at 12-13.

Has the Court successfully distinguished the speech and nonspeech interests in *Friedman* from those in *Virginia Pharmacy* and *Bates*? What do you think prompted the Texas legislature to prohibit use of trade names? Pressure from consumers? From professionals? Why might some optometrists want to bar others from using trade names? How different is the regulation at issue in *Gibson* from that in *Friedman*?

Do rules governing different professions merit (or receive) different levels of scrutiny? Compare *Friedman* with Florida Bar v. Went for It, Inc., 515 U.S. 618 (1995) (upholding, 5-4, a Florida prohibition on soliciting accident victims or their relatives within 30 days of an accident). The dissenting Justices saw no difference between the Florida restriction on lawyers and a Florida prohibition on in-person solicitation by certified public accountants struck down by the Court two years earlier. Edenfield v. Fane, 507 U.S. 761 (1993). The majority, observing that the regulation challenged in *Went for It* was intended "to protect the flagging reputations of Florida lawyers," noted that this put the case in a more favorable light than if the Bar were trying to protect the privacy interests of accident victims and their relatives: "There is an obvious difference between situations in which the Government acts in its own interests, or on behalf of entities it regulates, and situations in which the Government is motivated primarily by paternalism." 515 U.S. at 622 n.2. What is that obvious difference? What are the government's *own* interests? Even within a single occupation, courts differ on analysis of claims that occupational licensing rules contravene the First Amendment. *See, e.g.*, Edwards v. District of Columbia, 755 F.3d 996 (D.C. Cir. 2014) (licensing requirements for D.C. tour guides held unconstitutional); Kagan v. City of New Orleans, 753 F.3d 560 (5th Cir. 2014) (upholding similar licensing requirements for New Orleans tour guides).

B.   BUSINESS LICENSING

In a sense, licensing of businesses presents the same issues as licensing of occupations. The regulatory agency must establish and administer criteria for determining eligibility to receive a license, the quality of service that the licensee must provide, and in some cases the rates that the licensee may charge for those services. The main difference from occupational licensing is the size and complexity of the regulated undertaking, and, with it, the complexity of the regulatory regime necessary to oversee that undertaking. Also, business licensing often occurs in a setting in which economic or technological conditions severely limit the number of potential service producers. In such settings, the licensing agency must administer what can be a fiercely competitive process for securing licenses. In our history, perhaps the paradigmatic example of business licensing has been the regulation of the broadcast and telecommunications industries by the Federal Communications Commission (FCC). In this section we survey that history, focusing on two generic issues that the FCC has had to grapple with: how to allocate scarce and very valuable resources (broadcast licenses), and how to regulate rates for (telecommunications) services during times of technological and economic change. Although most of the materials in this section arose before the modern era of high-speed broadband, on-line streaming of video, and ubiquitous mobile access to the Internet, the issues discussed continue to challenge regulators and regulated industries in many contemporary contexts.

1.   *Entry Regulation: The Case of Broadcasting*

As described in the introduction to the *Storer* case, excerpted in Chapter IV, *supra*, the FCC is responsible for allocating radio and television station licenses to such parts of the nation and in such a fashion as is "fair, efficient, and equitable," to license particular individuals or entities to operate those stations when licensing would advance "the public interest, necessity, or convenience," and to prescribe the various details of operation of those stations (power, frequency, hours, location, etc.). Because there are many competing users of radio spectrum (such as commercial broadcasters, the military, police agencies, microwave signal transmitters, and so on), the commission allocated only a certain range of frequencies for radio and television broadcasting. And to prevent interference of signals transmitted by multiple broadcasters, the FCC further restricted the number of potential broadcast licenses that could be awarded in any given market area. This legally enforced scarcity drove up the value of broadcast licenses and thus attracted many potential license applicants. It thus became necessary for the commission to develop procedures for handling competitive applications and standards for making comparative judgments among multiple applicants.

a. Comparative Hearing Procedure

The statutory procedure for processing station license applications is set forth in §309 of the Communications Act, excerpted in the introduction to the *Storer* case, Chapter IV, *supra.* Section 309(b) required the FCC to notify the public when it receives a license application and to withhold grants for 30 days after such notice. Subsection (d) provided that "any party in interest" may petition the commission to deny a license application. Subsection (e) told the commission that if "a substantial and material question of fact is presented or the Commission for any reason is unable to [find that the license grant serves the public interest, convenience, and necessity] . . . it shall formally designate the application for hearing." Subsection (e) also instructed the commission that "[a]ny hearing subsequently held upon such application shall be a full hearing in which the applicant and all other parties in interest shall be permitted to participate."

Early in the FCC's administration of the Act, it confronted the question of how §309 applied to a situation in which there were two mutually exclusive applications pending simultaneously before the commission. Could the commission act on the two applications one at a time, or must it act on both in a consolidated proceeding? That was the question presented to the Supreme Court in the following case.

**ASHBACKER RADIO CORP. v. FEDERAL
COMMUNICATIONS COMMISSION**
326 U.S. 327 (1945)

MR. JUSTICE DOUGLAS delivered the opinion of the Court.

The primary question in this case is whether an applicant for a construction permit under the Federal Communications Act (48 Stat. 1064, 47 U.S.C. §151) is granted the hearing to which he is entitled by §309(a) of the Act,[1] where the Commission, having before it two applications which are mutually exclusive, grants one without a hearing and sets the other for hearing.

In March 1944 the Fetzer Broadcasting Company filed with the Commission an application for authority to construct a new broadcasting station at Grand Rapids, Michigan, to operate on 1230 kc with 250 watts power, unlimited time. In May 1944, before the Fetzer application had been acted upon, petitioner filed an application for authority to change the operating frequency of its station WKBZ of Muskegon, Michigan, from 1490 kc with 250 watts power, unlimited time, to 1230 kc. The Commission, after stating that the simultaneous operation on 1230 kc at Grand Rapids and Muskegon "would result in intolerable interference to both applicants," declared that the two applications were "actually exclusive." The Commission, upon an examination of the Fetzer application and supporting data, granted it in June 1944 without a hearing. On the same day the Commission designated petitioner's application for hearing. Petitioner thereupon filed a petition for hearing, rehearing and other relief directed against the grant of the Fetzer application. The Commission denied this petition, stating,

> The Commission has not denied petitioner's application. It has designated the application for hearing as required by Section 309(a) of the Act. At this hearing, petitioner will have ample opportunity to show that its operation as proposed will better serve the public interest than will the grant of the Fetzer application as authorized June 27, 1944. Such grant does not preclude the Commission, at a later date, from taking any action which it may find will serve the public interest. . . .

Our chief problem is to reconcile two provisions of §309(a) where the Commission has before it mutually exclusive applications. The first authorizes the Commission "upon examination" of an application for a station license to grant it if the Commission determines that "public interest, convenience, or necessity would be served" by the grant.[3] The second provision of §309(a) says that if, upon examination of such an application, the Commission does not reach such a decision, "it shall notify the applicant thereof, shall fix and give notice of a time and place for hearing thereon, and shall afford such applicant an opportunity to be heard under such rules and regulations as it may prescribe."[4] It is thus plain that §309(a) not only gives the Commission authority

---

1. Sec. 319 relates to applications for construction permits. But since such applications are in substance applications for station licenses (Goss v. Federal Radio Commission, 62 App. D.C. 301, 67 F.2d 507, 508), the Commission in such cases uniformly follows the procedure prescribed in §309(a) for station licenses.

3. Sec. 307(a) provides: "The Commission, if public convenience, interest, or necessity will be served thereby, subject to the limitations of this chapter, shall grant to any applicant therefor a station license provided for by this chapter."

4. Sec. 309(a) reads as follows:

"If upon examination of any application for a station license or for the renewal or modification of a station license the Commission shall determine that public interest, convenience, or necessity would be served by the granting thereof, it shall authorize the issuance, renewal, or modification thereof in accordance with said finding. In the event the Commission upon examination of any such application does not reach such decision with respect thereto, it shall notify the applicant thereof, shall fix and give notice of a time and place for hearing thereon, and shall afford such applicant an opportunity to be heard under such rules and regulations as it may prescribe."

to grant licenses without a hearing, but also gives applicants a right to a hearing before their applications are denied. We do not think it is enough to say that the power of the Commission to issue a license on a finding of public interest, convenience or necessity supports its grant of one of two mutually exclusive applications without a hearing of the other. For if the grant of one effectively precludes the other, the statutory right to a hearing which Congress has accorded applicants before denial of their applications becomes an empty thing. We think that is the case here.

The Commission in its notice of hearing on petitioner's application stated that the application "will not be granted by the Commission unless the issues listed above are determined in favor of the applicant on the basis of a record duly and properly made by means of a formal hearing." One of the issues listed was the determination of "the extent of any interference which would result from the simultaneous operation" of petitioner's proposed station and Fetzer's station. Since the Commission itself stated that simultaneous operation of the two stations would result in "intolerable interference" to both, it is apparent that petitioner carries a burden which cannot be met. To place that burden on it is in effect to make its hearing a rehearing on the grant of the competitor's license rather than a hearing on the merits of its own application. That may satisfy the strict letter of the law but certainly not its spirit or intent.

The Fetzer application was not conditionally granted pending consideration of petitioner's application. Indeed a stay of it pending the outcome of this litigation was denied. Of course the Fetzer license, like any other license granted by the Commission, was subject to certain conditions which the Act imposes as a matter of law. We fully recognize that the Commission, as it said, is not precluded "at a later date from taking any action which it may find will serve the public interest." No licensee obtains any vested interest in any frequency. The Commission for specified reasons may revoke any station license pursuant to the procedure prescribed by §312(a) and may suspend the license of any operator on the grounds and in the manner specified by §303(m). It may also modify a station license if in its judgment "such action will promote the public interest, convenience, and necessity, or the provisions of this chapter . . . will be more fully complied with." §312(b). And licenses for broadcasting stations are limited to three years, the renewals being subject to the same considerations and practice which affect the granting of original applications. §307(d). But in all those instances the licensee is given an opportunity to be heard before final action can be taken. What the Commission can do to Fetzer it can do to any licensee. As the Fetzer application has been granted, petitioner, therefore, is presently in the same position as a newcomer who seeks to displace an established broadcaster. By the grant of the Fetzer application petitioner has been placed under a greater burden than if its hearing had been earlier. Legal theory is one thing. But the practicalities are different. . . .

It is suggested that the Commission, by granting the Fetzer application first, concluded that the public interest would be furthered by making Fetzer's service available at the earliest possible date. If so, that conclusion is only an inference from what the Commission did. There is no suggestion, let alone a finding, by the Commission that the demands of the public interest were so urgent as to preclude the delay which would be occasioned by a hearing.

The public, not some private interest, convenience, or necessity governs the issuance of licenses under the Act. But we are not concerned here with the merits. This involves only a matter of procedure. Congress has granted applicants a right to a hearing on their applications for station licenses. Whether that is wise policy or whether the procedure adopted by the Commission in this case is preferable is not for us to decide. We only hold that where two bona fide applications are mutually exclusive the grant of one without a hearing to both deprives the loser of the opportunity which Congress chose to give him. . . .

Reversed.

MR. JUSTICE BLACK and MR. JUSTICE JACKSON took no part in the consideration or decision of this case.

MR. JUSTICE FRANKFURTER, dissenting. . . .

Since [administrative] agencies deal largely with the vindication of public interest and not the enforcement of private rights, this Court ought not to imply hampering restrictions, not imposed by Congress, upon the effectiveness of the administrative process. One reason for the expansion of administrative agencies has been the recognition that procedures appropriate for the adjudication of private rights in the courts may be inappropriate for the kind of determinations which administrative agencies are called upon to make.

The disposition of the present case seems to me to disregard these controlling considerations, if the Court now holds, as I understand it so to do, that whenever conflicting applications are made for a radio license the Communications Commission must hear all the applications together.

In the regulation of broadcasting, Congress moved outside the framework of protected property rights. *See* Commission v. Sanders Radio Station, 309 U.S. 470. Congress could have retained for itself the granting or denial of the use of the air for broadcasting purposes, and it could have granted individual licenses by individual enactments as in the past it gave river and harbor rights to individuals. Instead of making such a crude use of its Constitutional powers, Congress, by the Communications Act of 1934, 48 Stat. 1064, 47 U.S.C. §151, formulated an elaborate licensing scheme and established the Federal Communications Commission as its agency for enforcement. Our task is to give effect to this legislation and to the authority which Congress has seen fit to repose in the Communications Commission. . . .

The Commission is charged with the ascertainment of the public interest. We must assume that an agency which Congress has trusted discharges its trust. On the record before us it must be accepted that the Commission, before having taken action, carefully tested, according to its established practice, the claims both of Fetzer and of petitioner by the touchstone of public interest. *See* Attorney General's Committee on Administrative Procedure, Monograph No. 3, The Federal Communications Commission (1940) 8 *et seq.* On the basis of such inquiry, it found that the Fetzer application was clearly in the public interest; it found that the Ashbacker application did not make a sufficient showing even to stay the Commission's hand in withholding the Fetzer grant long enough to enable Ashbacker to support its application more persuasively. On the contrary, it thought the public interest would be furthered by making Fetzer's service available at the earliest possible date. There is nothing in the Communications

Act that restricts the Commission in translating its duty to further the public interest as it did in the particular situation before it. . . .

In this case, however, the restrictions of the hearing granted to Ashbacker do make of it a mere formality, for the Commission put upon Ashbacker the burden of establishing that the grant of a license to it would not interfere with the simultaneous operations of the proposed Fetzer station. . . .

Ashbacker . . . is entitled to show the superiority of its claim over that of Fetzer, even though the Commission, on the basis of its administrative inquiry, was entitled to grant Fetzer the license in the qualified way in which the statute authorized, and the Commission made, the grant. In my view, therefore, the proper disposition of the case is to return it to the Commission with direction that it modify its order so as to assure an appropriate hearing of the Ashbacker application. . . .

MR. JUSTICE RUTLEDGE joins in this opinion.

NOTES AND QUESTIONS

1. *Ashbacker's reception.* Over the years, the *Ashbacker* decision has drawn scant criticism. Is its appeal the evenhandedness it seems to impose on the licensing process? Or its consistency with the statutory text? Is Justice Douglas's reading of the statute more persuasive than Justice Frankfurter's? Look back to the discussion of *Chevron* and *Mead,* excerpted in Chapter II, *supra.* Under the review standards articulated in those cases, how do you think *Ashbacker* would have been decided today?

2. *Timing problems and defining conflicts.* The FCC had to adopt a time bar to deal with timing problems that might arise under *Ashbacker* if a series of mutually exclusive license applications is filed at varying times. *See* 47 C.F.R. §1.227(b). Beyond timing difficulties, the determination of conflict can be problematic. The *Ashbacker* decision has been applied most often to licensing schemes that involve government distribution of a relatively fixed supply of goods. Nearly all licensing programs, however, retain some flexibility in this regard, and the conflict need not be one of complete exclusivity. Defining the extent of interference among broadcast stations and the degree of restriction on one station's operation necessary to prevent interference with another obviously can present additional questions.

3. *Hearing requirements.* One advantage of the Frankfurter-Rutledge position, dissenting in *Ashbacker,* is that it seems to reduce the questions that remain to be answered. If the agency enjoys latitude to decide when to hold a hearing and on what ground, there is relatively little left for judicial determination. But if the *Ashbacker* majority's view is accepted—that one must have a *meaningful* hearing, not just the formality of a hearing—can the courts avoid further specification of the issues that must be considered or the allocation of burdens of persuasion? Would courts have to decide, not just when there is conflict between putative licensees, but also just how the agency should go about resolving it?

Indeed, since *Ashbacker,* licensing decisions repeatedly have been challenged as incompatible with hearing requirements because the licensing agency treated some issue as foreclosed by prior adjudications. While many challenges arise from contestants for licenses that are, to some degree, mutually exclusive, the same problem can occur with a single potential licensee.

4. *Informal hearings?* The FCC had interpreted the "hearing" provision in §309 to require a formal, adjudicative hearing. Could the FCC soften the impact of *Ashbacker* by giving competitive applicants only an informal (notice-and-comment) "hearing"? In doing so, could it rely on *Allegheny-Ludlum* and *Florida East Coast Railway*, excerpted in Chapter V, *supra?*

What effect, if any, does the APA (enacted after *Ashbacker*) have on the answer to these questions? What procedure does the APA require for licensing? *See, e.g., Seacoast Anti-Pollution League,* excerpted in Chapter VI, *supra.* Also, consider the potential impact of the *Storer* decision. How much does *Storer* moderate *Ashbacker*'s effect on licensing decisions?

b.   Licensing Standards

Until relatively recently, the awarding of broadcast licenses relied in significant measure on the sort of comparative evaluation of multiple applications called for by *Ashbacker*. The typical context, however, was not contests between applicants for two mutually conflicting broadcast licenses, but rather contests for a single station license between two or more competing applicants. During the years when this was a large part of the FCC's broadcast regulation work, criteria for selecting among competing license applicants was a subject of frequent dispute among members of the FCC and between the FCC and its reviewing court, the U.S. Court of Appeals for the D.C. Circuit.

The pattern that emerged varied depending on whether the comparative hearing was being employed to award an initial license between two (or more) non-incumbent applicants, or to resolve a competition between an incumbent licensee and one or more challengers. Prior to 1965, the FCC resisted articulating standards for initial license grants, leaving to potential applicants the task of reading the tea leaves of prior FCC license award decisions. In 1965, the FCC adopted a policy statement that made at least an attempt at providing some guidance about its standards for initial licensing decisions. Policy Statement on Comparative Broadcast Hearings, 1 F.C.C.2d 393 (1965). Assuming that two or more applicants met certain basic technical and ownership qualifications specified in the Act or in FCC rules, said the Statement, the commission would choose among the qualified applicants, based on a comparative assessment of such factors as diversifying ownership of broadcast outlets (having more people own broadcast stations), the moral character of would-be owners, technical efficiency of spectrum use, and integration of ownership and management (having owners who are actually engaged in day-to-day decisionmaking for the station). While the Policy Statement identified the relevant factors, it provided very little guidance on how to assign a comparative "score" on each factor, and even less guidance on how to weight and combine the implicit scores on the individual factors into one overall "score."

The pattern for license renewals was much clearer than for initial license awards. Absent some obvious problem in station operation during its current or prior license term, the licensee could expect to have its license renewed, even in the face of a challenge mounted by an impressive applicant. (Of course, the preference for incumbents tended to discourage many challenges, impressive or otherwise.) The FCC codified this renewal preference in its 1970 Policy Statement Concerning Comparative Hearings Involving Regular Renewal Applicants, 22 F.C.C.2d 424 (1970). The commission justified its policy on the grounds that, because license terms (then, three years) were short, a renewal expectancy was needed to provide station operators the economic incentive to make long-term investments in program quality. The D.C. Circuit was unpersuaded, holding that the policy violated the principle of *Ashbacker,* by limiting the "comparative" hearing to the (non-comparative) question whether the renewal applicant had rendered substantial service during its prior license term. Citizens Communications Center v. FCC, 447 F.2d 1201 (D.C. Cir. 1971). Undaunted, the FCC continued to decide contested renewal proceedings in favor of the incumbent, and the D.C. Circuit continued to reverse the FCC. *See, e.g.,* Central Florida Enterprises, Inc. v. FCC, 598 F.2d 37 (D.C. Cir. 1978), *cert. dismissed,* 441 U.S. 957 (1979).

The use of comparative licensing proceedings, with all of their procedural and substantive complexities, is now a thing of the past in broadcast regulation. The Telecommunications Act of 1996, Pub. L. No. 104-104, 110 Stat. 56 (*codified at* various sections of 47 U.S.C.), essentially eliminated comparative hearings for renewal applicants. For a while, the law retained the comparative hearing for initial broadcast applications, but that changed too, and in 1999 the FCC began making initial license awards through auctions. But the problems illustrated by broadcast licensing persist in other industries and sectors, in which a limited number of valuable franchises are parceled out by government action. Contemporary examples include airline route awards, airport landing rights, cable television franchises, liquor licenses, and casino licenses. Some, but not all, of these decisions are made through *Ashbacker*-type comparative hearing processes. *See, e.g.,* Northwest Airlines, Inc. v. Civil Aeronautics Bd., 194 F.2d 339 (D.C. Cir. 1952); Pollak v. Simonson, 350 F.2d 740 (D.C. Cir. 1965). What determines which decisions use comparative hearings? What process would you expect where comparative hearings are eschewed, as in cable franchise awards? Would you expect the criteria for award to vary with the process?

Two alternatives to the use of comparative hearings, with or without a strong renewal expectancy, are lotteries and auctions. Congress first conferred on the FCC authority to use lotteries to award spectrum licenses in the Omnibus Budget Reconciliation Act of 1981, Pub. L. No. 97-35, 95 Stat. 736-737, *codified, in part, at* 47 U.S.C. §309(i). The commission initially declined to exercise its new authority, but after congressional modification of the lottery statute, revising §309(i) of the Communication Act of 1934, the commission adopted implementing rules. Random Selection Lotteries, 93 F.C.C.2d 952 (1983), *modified,* 95 F.C.C.2d 432 (1984). The rules, adopted initially for low-power television stations but also extended to other types of spectrum licenses, eliminated the costly comparative hearing for initial licenses. By giving applicants extra credit for "minority" ownership and "diversity" of programming, the rules did not put all applicants on an identical footing or completely avoid difficult judgments about which applicant merits preferences. Still, in large measure, those judgments are now restricted to a small number of issues, and, unlike the process criticized so heavily in the courts, the lottery system specifies precisely what weight attaches to a preference.

Congress first authorized use of auctions for broadcast licenses in the early 1990s, then expanded that authorization, leading the commission eventually to utilize auctions broadly. While the use of auctions has raised a number of peculiar issues, *see, e.g.,* FCC v. Nextwave Personal Communications, Inc., 537 U.S. 293 (2003), they have eliminated the cost and uncertainty of comparative licensing hearings at the FCC and also have become a source of considerable profit for the government, raising billions of dollars.

The FCC's turn toward auctions, although notable, is not exceptional. Auctions are used by the government in many circumstances as a means of allocating rights to use public property. Mineral exploration and extraction are two highly visible examples. How different are the allocation problems in these areas from those encountered in broadcast licensing? Whether one views the auction process as good or bad, it is important to recognize that de facto auction systems frequently exist even where the licensing authority has chosen to allocate through some other process. Broadcast licenses long were in effect bought and sold on the open market, although the FCC had to place its imprimatur on such sales and required that the sale be denominated a transfer of the assets or the equity of the licensee, rather than the license itself, with the license then following the transfer "like the night the day." Does the existence of these "gray markets" in licenses argue in favor of government auctions in a broader array of settings?

c. License Removal

Notwithstanding the FCC's general unwillingness to replace an incumbent licensee with a competing applicant, the commission has occasionally found that a licensee is not qualified to continue operating a broadcast outlet. Precisely because broadcast licenses are so valuable, however, the commission bears a heavy burden of demonstrating that its standards for nonrenewal or revocation are sufficiently clear and applied in a consistent manner. *See, e.g.,* RKO General, Inc. (WNAC-TV), 78 F.C.C.2d 1 (1980), *rev'd,* RKO General, Inc. v. FCC, 670 F.2d 215 (D.C. Cir. 1981), *cert. denied,* 456 U.S. 927 (1982); Melody Music, Inc. v. FCC, 345 F.2d 730 (D.C. Cir. 1965). *Melody Music* was an appeal from the FCC's decision not to renew a standard (i.e., AM) radio license for a company whose principals had been engaged in "censurable" conduct unrelated to their station's operation. The two principals of *Melody Music* earlier had produced television quiz programs in which certain contestants secretly were given answers to some questions. Reversing the hearing examiner's decision, the commission found Melody Music disqualified on character grounds. The FCC, however, granted renewals to the National Broadcasting Co., which had broadcast the quiz shows in question and, for a time, had owned rights to them. Melody asked that it receive the same treatment as NBC. The court of appeals remanded to the FCC for an explanation of the difference:

> We think the Commission's refusal at least to explain its different treatment of appellant and NBC was error. Both were connected with the deceptive practices and their renewal applications were considered by the Commission at virtually the same time. Yet one was held disqualified and the other was not. Moreover, while in

other cases the Commission found that criminal violations of antitrust laws were not sufficient character disqualifications to bar license renewals, in the present case it found noncriminal conduct sufficient. . . . Whatever action the Commission takes on remand, it must explain its reasons and do more than enumerate factual differences, if any, between appellant and the other cases; it must explain the relevance of those differences to the purposes of the Federal Communications Act.

Id. at 732-733.

License revocation is the most drastic punishment most regulatory agencies can impose. It is not, however, the only formal means for disciplining licensees. Many agencies also can impose civil fines or "forfeitures" for violation of agency rules. The FCC has exercised this authority from time to time. Under what circumstances would you expect such action? FCC forfeiture procedures have been upheld against constitutional challenge. Action for Children's Television v. FCC, 59 F.3d 1249 (D.C. Cir. 1995). On the permissible magnitude of civil fines, *see* Austin v. United States, 509 U.S. 602 (1993). How are civil fines different from criminal fines? Should different standards apply where the fines are assessed against licensees?

d. Licensee Supervision: The Problem of "Jawboning"

A corollary to concerns over clarity and consistency is the frequent claim that agencies can affect licensees' behavior without engaging in any formal action, such as rulemaking, adjudication, or adoption of a policy statement. Given substantial agency discretion to terminate the stream of benefits the license represents, licensees are thought to be quite responsive to veiled threats by regulators, often referred to as "jawboning" or "regulation by raised eyebrow." This picture of regulatory behavior presents obvious tensions with the "regulatory capture" explanations of agency-client behavior offered by political science and public choice theorists. *Compare* Harry Kalven, Broadcasting, Public Policy, and the First Amendment, 10 J.L. & Econ. 15 (1967), *with* Richard Posner, Theories of Economic Regulation, 5 Bell J. Econ. & Mgmt. Sci. 335 (1974). Most of these latter theories draw on the operation of licensing agencies, which seem to have a symbiotic relationship with the licensee. Empirical observation seems to confirm this view: the infrequency of license revocation and the general perception that licensing regulations seldom truly constrain licensed businesses strongly suggest that, far more often than not, those who administer business licensing share interests with the businesses they regulate.

Virtually every lawyer who represents a licensed business, however, has at least one good anecdote about informal regulation—actions by regulators that alter behavior of licensees without formal adoption of rules or adjudicatory decisions. A well-known example from the FCC's ledger allegedly led to the television networks' decision—long since abandoned in the face of competition from an array of less constrained cable television and direct-from-satellite shows—to air family-oriented entertainment (shows light on sex and violence) during the prime time period of 8 p.m. to 9 p.m. It is the basis for the following case.

WRITERS GUILD OF AMERICA, WEST, INC. v. AMERICAN BROADCAST-ING COS. 609 F.2d 355 (9th Cir.), *cert. denied*, 449 U.S. 824 (1980): In late 1974, a committee of the House of Representatives directed the FCC "to submit a report to the Committee . . . outlining the specific positive actions taken or planned by the Commission to protect children from excessive violence and obscenity." Fearing First Amendment problems if the commission took formal action, FCC Chairman Richard Wiley embarked on what was described as a course of "jawboning," urging the networks to adopt a system of self-regulation to reduce the amount of sex and violence in television programming.

This jawboning campaign included: speeches before broadcasters' organizations; personal lobbying with representatives of the three major television networks at that time (ABC, NBC, and CBS), including meetings with the network presidents and vice-presidents; and meetings between FCC staff members and programming officials at the networks. Chairman Wiley also met with officials from the National Association of Broadcasters (NAB), a private entity that set "voluntary" guidelines for television broadcasting—guidelines that all networks and major broadcast outlets followed. The number of meetings and speeches during the fall and winter of 1974-1975 devoted to the theme that broadcasters needed to present fare suitable for families was extraordinary. The speeches and frequent high-level meetings between the FCC chairman, his associates, and the top network officials left no doubt about the intensity of Chairman Wiley's interest in this subject.

In response to Chairman Wiley's campaign, the networks, together with the NAB, established a rule setting aside the first hour of prime time for programming suitable for general family viewing. After Chairman Wiley reported on these activities to Congress and the NAB formally adopted its family viewing policy, the National Writers Guild and others sued the networks, the FCC, and the NAB in federal court. The district court decided that government pressure had induced adoption of the family viewing policy in violation of both the First Amendment to the Constitution and also of the APA. Speaking through Judge Sneed, the Ninth Circuit vacated the district court's decision and remanded the case:

> The FCC and its Chairman engaged in "serious misconduct" only if the law is as the district court found it. Weaken that foundation and what appeared as "serious misconduct" looks more like, at worst, jawboning of the type often praised as effective leadership by those satisfied with its results and condemned as unprincipled administration by those who disapprove of those results.
>
> Jawboning relates, of course, to the district court's holding that the Commission violated the APA in its use of informal procedures in the manner described above. The technique raises serious issues. It is not surprising that the Commission often seeks to "chart a workable 'middle course' in its quest to preserve a balance between the essential public accountability and the desired private control of the media." CBS v. DNC, 412 U.S. at 120. One such "middle course" has been the tendency of the FCC to rely upon self-regulation by the broadcast industry to promote the public interest, a practice that has possibly had the salutary effect of diminishing the need for formal governmental intervention and regulation. Moreover, reliance upon self-regulation no doubt has relieved both the FCC and the industry of the need to confront the dilemma of delineating the precise extent of the agency's formal regulatory authority in various areas. Hence, informal discussions between

the Commission and members of the industry that lead to self-regulation constitute but one aspect of the ongoing effort by both the government and the licensees to negotiate the regulatory "tightrope" on which they confront one another.

We acknowledge that informal procedures permit the FCC to exercise "wide-ranging and largely uncontrolled administrative discretion in the review of telecommunications programming" which can be used to apply "sub silentio pressure" on broadcast licensees. Bazelon, FCC Regulation of the Telecommunications Press, 1975 Duke L.J. 213, 215. Regulation through "raised eyebrow" techniques or through forceful jawboning is commonplace in the administrative context, and in some instances may fairly be characterized, as it was by the district court in this case, as official action by the agency.

While we agree that the use of these techniques by the FCC presents serious issues involving the Constitution, the Communications Act, and the APA, we nevertheless believe that the district court should not have thrust itself so hastily into the delicately balanced system of broadcast regulation. Because the "line between permissible regulatory activity and impermissible 'raised eyebrow' harassment of vulnerable licensees" is so exceedingly vague, Bazelon, *supra*, 1975 Duke L.J. at 217, it is important that judicial attempts to control these techniques be sensitive to "the particular regulatory context in which it occurs, the interests affected by it, and the potential for abuse." Consolidated Edison Co. v. FPC, 512 F.2d 1332, 1341 (D.C. Cir. 1975) (footnote omitted). The development of standards governing the agency's use of informal methods to influence broadcast industry policy is an issue "that should be dealt with in the first instance by those especially familiar with the customs and practices of the industry." Ricci v. Chicago Mercantile Exchange, 409 U.S. 289, 305 (1973). . . .

Accordingly, we vacate the judgment of the district court and remand with instructions to refer plaintiffs' claims against the government defendants to the FCC, and to hold in abeyance plaintiffs' claims against the private defendants pending resolution and judicial review of the administrative proceedings before the FCC.

NOTES AND QUESTIONS

1. *Rulemaking versus informal action.* The main problem with regulation by raised eyebrow is the absence of formal process. The district court thought Chairman Wiley's conduct substituted private negotiation for the APA-required public rulemaking process:

> The purpose of 5 U.S.C. §553 is obvious. It recognizes that interested members of the public and the regulated industry have the right to participate in the policymaking process and assumes that the quality of policy decisions will be improved if public input is considered before decisions are made. . . .
>
> Here, ironically, the government and the networks, both acting as public trustees, negotiated public policy while refusing to comply with procedural safeguards designed to protect the public they serve. If this process is considered acceptable administrative procedure, the Act's provisions will become meaningless. The government could sit down at a table with the regulated industry, negotiate policy, delegate to the industry the power to enforce the policy, mouth empty words of congratulation about self-regulation, issue cynical denials of government responsibility, and avoid the Act entirely. Such procedures would permit government and industry to seal out the public from the decisionmaking process and to frustrate judicial scrutiny.

Writers Guild of America, West, Inc. v. FCC, 423 F. Supp. 1064, 1151-1152 (C.D. Cal. 1976). Do you agree? Is the district court's opinion consistent with *Wyman-Gordon* and *Bell Aerospace*, excerpted in Chapter IV, *supra*? Look back at §553 of the APA. Does it require the FCC to adopt a policy such as that respecting family viewing through notice-and-comment rulemaking?

Does it affect your view of this episode that Chairman Wiley was widely regarded as having a very balanced approach to his position? Indeed, Chairman Wiley was so well regarded within the communications community that he was sometimes referred to as FCC "Chairman for Life." Does that make his conduct more or less troublesome from an administrative law standpoint?

2. *Informal action after rulemaking.* In *Action for Children's Television*, discussed in Chapter V, *supra*, the petitioner ACT had challenged a decision formally promulgated by the FCC *not* to adopt a rule. After conducting a rulemaking proceeding fully complying with the requirements of §553, the commission issued a published decision opting to encourage licensees voluntarily to carry more programming specifically aimed at children, rather than mandate such programming. ACT argued that the commission had acted unreasonably in failing to adopt specific rules. ACT found the FCC's hortatory approach too weak a response to licensee departures from the public interest as ACT saw it. The complaint, in effect, was the flip-side of the challenge in *Writers Guild*. The Guild argued that raising eyebrows accomplished too much; ACT contended that it accomplished too little.

3. *Informal action and constitutional questions.* Judges commonly scrutinize attempts by government agents to control speech more carefully than other exercises of government authority. However, courts have been more sympathetic to regulation of broadcast speech than to most other speech regulation. *Compare* Red Lion Broadcasting Co. v. FCC, 395 U.S. 367 (1969), *with* Miami Herald Pub. Co. v. Tornillo, 418 U.S. 241 (1974). In FCC v. Pacifica Foundation, 438 U.S. 726 (1978), the Supreme Court upheld the constitutionality of FCC rules regulating broadcast "indecency," and their application to assess sanctions against specific broadcasters. The Court has been less receptive to other attempts to police indecency, for example, finding that the Communications Decency Act's limitations on distribution of indecent material over the Internet violated the First Amendment. Reno v. ACLU, 521 U.S. 844 (1997). Does this difference affect how the court of appeals responded to the FCC's informal actions in *Writers Guild*? Not infrequently, courts find complaints about administrative process more compelling when a serious constitutional question lies immediately behind the process issue.

e.   "The Regulatory Ratchet": Expansion of Regulatory Jurisdiction to Ancillary Activities

As we have seen, licensure dispenses a valuable privilege, which, in turn, gives its recipients an incentive to fight encroachment on their business by unlicensed competitors. Such encroachment may arise from changes in market structures, consumer demand, or technology of production. Whatever the underlying cause, when competition from unlicensed entities occurs, licensees often turn to their licensing authority to protect them from the interlopers.

Not surprisingly, given the parasitic relationship that often develops between licensing authorities and licensees, the authorities frequently oblige. We saw this dynamic in *North Carolina Dental*, excerpted *supra*, as licensed dentists in North Carolina turned to the Board of Dental Examiners to protect them from competition from non-dentist teeth whiteners.

Another classic example is the emergence of cable television in the 1950s as a perceived threat to over-the-air broadcasters. Originally called "community antenna television" (CATV), cable allowed the amplification of broadcast signals to reach customers unable to receive high quality over-the-air signals. The CATV operator would erect a tall tower to receive signals over the air or by microwave and transmit them via coaxial cables to individual customers. The operator would, of course, charge a fee for this service, which most customers otherwise denied good service would happily pay. Initially, broadcasters welcomed the advent of CATV as a way of expanding the audience for their signals and, therefore, a basis for increasing the fees that they could charge to advertisers to support their offerings of "free" radio and television programming. Over time, however, their support turned to opposition, as CATV operators began to "import" distant signals from remote markets, thereby competing with local broadcasters. This led to the regulatory response described in the following classic case.

UNITED STATES v. SOUTHWESTERN CABLE CO.
392 U.S. 157 (1968)

Justice Harlan delivered the opinion of the Court.

These cases stem from proceedings conducted by the Federal Communications Commission after requests by Midwest Television. . . . Midwest averred that respondents' CATV systems transmitted the signals of Los Angeles broadcasting stations into the San Diego area, and thereby had, inconsistently with the public interest, adversely affected Midwest's San Diego station. Midwest sought an appropriate order limiting the carriage of such signals by respondents' systems. After consideration of the petition and of various responsive pleadings, the Commission restricted the expansion of respondents' service in areas in which they had not operated on February 15, 1966, pending hearings to be conducted on the merits of Midwest's complaints.

On petitions for review, the Court of Appeals for the Ninth Circuit held that the Commission lacks authority under the Communications Act of 1934, to issue such an order. We granted certiorari to consider this important question of regulatory authority. For reasons that follow, we reverse.

I

CATV systems receive the signals of television broadcasting stations, amplify them, transmit them by cable or microwave, and ultimately distribute them by wire to the receivers of their subscribers. CATV systems characteristically do not produce their own programming, and do not recompense producers or broadcasters for use of the programming which they receive and redistribute. Unlike ordinary broadcasting stations, CATV systems commonly charge their subscribers installation and other fees.

The CATV industry has grown rapidly since the establishment of the first commercial system in 1950. In the late 1950's, some 50 new systems were established each year; by 1959, there were 550 "nationally known and identified" systems serving a total audience of 1,500,000 to 2,000,000 persons. It has been more recently estimated that "new systems are being founded at the rate of more than one per day, and . . . subscribers . . . signed on at the rate of 15,000 per month." By late 1965, it was reported that there were 1,847 operating CATV systems, that 758 others were franchised but not yet in operation, and that there were 938 applications for additional franchises. . . .

CATV systems perform either or both of two functions. First, they may supplement broadcasting by facilitating satisfactory reception of local stations in adjacent areas in which such reception would not otherwise be possible, and second, they may transmit to subscribers the signals of distant stations entirely beyond the range of local antennae. As the number and size of CATV systems have increased, their principal function has more frequently become the importation of distant signals. . . .

The Commission has on various occasions attempted to assess the relationship between community antenna television systems and its conceded regulatory functions. In 1959, it completed an extended investigation of several auxiliary broadcasting services, including CATV. Although it found that CATV is "related to interstate transmission," the Commission reasoned that CATV systems are neither common carriers nor broadcasters, and therefore are within neither of the principal regulatory categories created by the Communications Act. The Commission declared that it had not been given plenary authority over "any and all enterprises which happen to be connected with one of the many aspects of communications." It refused to premise regulation of CATV upon assertedly adverse consequences for broadcasting, because it could not "determine where the impact takes effect, although we recognize that it may well exist."

The Commission instead declared that it would forthwith seek appropriate legislation "to clarify the situation." Such legislation was introduced in the Senate in 1959, favorably reported, and debated on the Senate floor. The bill was, however, ultimately returned to committee.

Despite its inability to obtain amendatory legislation, the Commission has, since 1960, gradually asserted jurisdiction over CATV. It first placed restrictions upon the activities of common carrier microwave facilities that serve CATV systems. Finally, the Commission, in 1962, conducted a rulemaking proceeding in which it reevaluated the significance of CATV for its regulatory responsibilities. The proceeding was explicitly restricted to those systems that are served by microwave, but the Commission's conclusions plainly were more widely relevant. [Finding that] the importation of distant signals into the service areas of local stations necessarily creates "substantial competition" for local broadcasting [the FCC adopted a rule requiring] CATV systems . . . to transmit to their subscribers the signals of any station into whose service area they have brought competing signals [and forbade CATV systems] to duplicate the programming of such local stations for periods of 15 days before and after a local broadcast. . . .

The Commission in 1965 issued additional . . . rules, applicable both to cable and to microwave CATV systems, [which] forbade the importation by

CATV of distant signals into the 100 largest television markets, except insofar as such service was offered on February 15, 1966, unless the Commission has previously found that it "would be consistent with the public interest." . . . Thirteen days after the Commission's adoption of the Second Report, Midwest initiated these proceedings by the submission of its petition for special relief.

II

. . . The Commission's authority to regulate broadcasting and other communications is derived from the Communications Act of 1934, as amended. The Act's provisions are explicitly applicable to "all interstate and foreign communication by wire or radio. . . ." 47 U.S.C. §152(a). . . . Respondents do not suggest that CATV systems are not within the term "communication by wire or radio." Indeed, such communications are defined by the Act so as to encompass "the transmission of . . . signals, pictures, and sounds of all kinds," whether by radio or cable, "including all instrumentalities, facilities, apparatus, and services (among other things, the receipt, forwarding, and delivery of communications) incidental to such transmission." 47 U.S.C. §§153(a), (b). These very general terms amply suffice to reach respondents' activities. Nor can we doubt that CATV systems are engaged in interstate communication. . . .

Nonetheless, respondents urge that the Communications Act, properly understood, does not permit the regulation of CATV systems. First, they emphasize that the Commission, in 1959 and again in 1966, sought legislation that would have explicitly authorized such regulation, and that its efforts were unsuccessful. In the circumstances here, however, this cannot be dispositive. The Commission's requests for legislation evidently reflected in each instance both its uncertainty as to the proper width of its authority and its understandable preference for more detailed policy guidance than the Communications Act now provides. . . .

Second, respondents urge that §152(a) does not independently confer regulatory authority upon the Commission, but instead merely prescribes the forms of communication to which the Act's other provisions may separately be made applicable. Respondents emphasize that the Commission does not contend either that CATV systems are common carriers, and thus within Title II of the Act, or that they are broadcasters, and thus within Title III. They conclude that CATV, with certain of the characteristics both of broadcasting and of common carriers, but with all of the characteristics of neither, eludes altogether the Act's grasp.

We cannot construe the Act so restrictively. . . . Certainly Congress could not, in 1934, have foreseen the development of community antenna television systems, but it seems to us that it was precisely because Congress wished "to maintain, through appropriate administrative control, a grip on the dynamic aspects of radio transmission," F.C.C. v. Pottsville Broadcasting Co., [134 U.S. 134, 138 (1940)], that it conferred upon the Commission a "unified jurisdiction" and "broad authority." . . .

Moreover, the Commission has reasonably concluded that regulatory authority over CATV is imperative if it is to perform with appropriate effectiveness certain of its other responsibilities. Congress has imposed upon the

Commission the "obligation of providing a widely dispersed radio and television service," with a "fair, efficient, and equitable distribution" of service among the "several States and communities." 47 U.S.C. §307(b). The Commission has, for this and other purposes, been granted authority to allocate broadcasting zones or areas, and to provide regulations "as it may deem necessary" to prevent interference among the various stations. 47 U.S.C. §§303(f), (h). The Commission has concluded, and Congress has agreed, that these obligations require for their satisfaction the creation of a system of local broadcasting stations, such that "all communities of appreciable size [will] have at least one television station as an outlet for local self-expression." In turn, the Commission has held that an appropriate system of local broadcasting may be created only if two subsidiary goals are realized. First, significantly wider use must be made of the available ultra-high-frequency channels. Second, communities must be encouraged "to launch sound and adequate programs to utilize the television channels now reserved for educational purposes." . . .

The Commission has reasonably found that the achievement of each of these purposes is "placed in jeopardy by the unregulated explosive growth of CATV." Although CATV may in some circumstances make possible "the realization of some of the [Commission's] most important goals," its importation of distant signals into the service areas of local stations may also "destroy or seriously degrade the service offered by a television broadcaster," and thus ultimately deprive the public of the various benefits of a system of local broadcasting stations. In particular, the Commission feared that CATV might, by dividing the available audiences and revenues, significantly magnify the characteristically serious financial difficulties of UHF and educational television broadcasters. . . .

There is no need here to determine in detail the limits of the Commission's authority to regulate CATV. It is enough to emphasize that the authority which we recognize today under §152(a) is restricted to that reasonably ancillary to the effective performance of the Commission's various responsibilities for the regulation of television broadcasting. . . .

The judgments of the Court of Appeals are reversed, and the cases are remanded for further proceedings consistent with this opinion.

It is so ordered.

NOTES AND QUESTIONS:

1. *Expansion of regulatory jurisdiction.* The history of broadcast regulation is a classic illustration of the "regulatory ratchet." A regulatory regime originally created to parcel out radio spectrum so as to minimize interference among radio signals gradually morphed into a system of elaborate regulatory controls over not only broadcasters, but also ancillary industries such as radio and television networks and cable television. All of this occurred without any change in the underlying legislation, but simply as a result of policy decisions made by the FCC, especially its policy of "localism," described in greater detail in the notes preceding the *Home Box Office* case in Chapter V, *supra*. Once the FCC had determined that every community should have its own "voice" on the airwaves, it became necessary, in the agency's view, to protect incumbents against domination by national networks or competition from imported distant signals,

so as to enable them to devote at least some of their broadcast time (and advertising-based revenues) to non-remunerative local news and information programming. At each major step along this path, the Supreme Court willingly embraced the FCC's reasoning. Is there any logical stopping point in this progression? Didn't *Southwestern Cable* present a perfect opportunity? CATV, after all, is a distinct industry, neither "broadcasting" nor "common carrier," as those terms were historically understood and defined in the Communications Act's operative provisions (Title III for broadcasting, Title II for common carriers).

In fact, the ratchet took one more turn before the Court finally stopped it. United States v. Midwest Video Corp., 406 U.S. 649 (1972) (*Midwest Video I*), involved an FCC rule requiring large CATV systems to originate programming of their own. The FCC's stated purpose for its cablecasting requirement was to "further the achievement of long-established regulatory goals in the field of television broadcasting by increasing the number of outlets for community self-expression and augmenting the public's choice of programs and types of services." Although no opinion garnered support of a majority, five members of the Court found this policy to fall within the scope of the FCC's "ancillary jurisdiction" to regulate broadcasting, consistent with *Southwestern Cable*.

But in United States v. Midwest Video Corp., 440 U.S. 689 (1979) (*Midwest Video II*), the Court held that the FCC lacked authority to require large CATV systems to make available a portion of their channels for access by public, educational, and leased-access users, and to furnish equipment and facilities for program generation by such users. This requirement, said the six-Justice majority, effectively made CATV systems into "common carriers," in violation of an express provision of the Communications Act that broadcasters could not be regulated as common carriers.

Finally, Congress came to the rescue by enacting the Cable Communications Policy Act of 1984, which inserted a new Title VI of the Communications Act, *codified at* 47 U.S.C. §§521 et seq. The Act required cable companies to carry local television signals and make some channels available for public, educational, and leased-access usage. It also contained various provisions designed to protect consumers and program producers from exploitation by monopolistic cable companies, protect cable franchisees from exploitation by state or local franchising authorities, and promote competition among cable companies.

2. *"Ancillary jurisdiction" and FCC regulation of the Internet.* The regulatory ratchet played out once again in recent decades as the FCC has struggled to decide whether and how to regulate the Internet. This time, however, the ratchet proved to turn both ways. The Internet emerged in the 1980s as a platform for telecommunication that combined features of point-to-point telecommunications and point-to-mass-audience broadcast and cable service, but it was conceptually distinct from both of them. Beginning in the 1970s, the FCC issued a series of rulings dealing with the provision of data transmission and data processing services by telephone companies (under the commission's Title II authority). The rulings distinguished between "basic service" (transmission of voice or data communications without altering the text) and "enhanced service" (transmission of data communications that included capacity to alter "the content, code, protocol, and other aspects of the subscriber's information"). The FCC ruled that it had authority to regulate basic service, but not enhanced service.

The Telecommunications Act of 1996 codified these distinctions, replacing the term "basic service" with the term "telecommunications service," and replacing "enhanced service" with "information service." The Act defined telecommunications service as "the offering of telecommunications for a fee to the public," 47 U.S.C. §153(53), with "telecommunications" defined as "the transmission, between or among points specified by the user, or information of the user's choosing, without change in the form or content of the information," §153(50). "Information service," by contrast, was defined as "the offering of a capability for generating, acquiring, storing, transforming, processing, retrieving, utilizing, or making available information via telecommunications," §153(24).

Shortly after the 1996 Act's enactment, the issue arose how to classify Internet service providers (ISPs) who enable users to connect their computers to the Internet through cable-modem services. Before the FCC took a position on this question, in a private dispute between a cable franchising authority and its franchisee, a court of appeals ruled that cable modem service is a "telecommunications service." AT&T Corp. v. Portland, 216 F.3d 871 (9th Cir. 2000). The ruling caught the FCC flat-footed. Unwilling to impose "common carrier" obligations on ISPs under Title II of the Communications Act, in 2002 the commission promulgated a rule classifying cable-modem service as an "information service" not subject to regulation, rather than as a "telecommunications service."

The Supreme Court upheld the 2002 rule in National Cable & Telecommunications Assn. v. Brand X Internet Services, 545 U.S. 967 (2005). Applying the *Chevron* framework (see Chapter II, *supra*), the majority found ambiguity in the definition of "telecommunications service," particularly in the word "offering." The FCC had argued that, although ISP service makes use of telecommunications facilities (and to that extent could be seen as a telecommunications service), what the ISP "offers" is understood by its consumers as the capacity to manipulate the data (that is, the integrated product of high-speed wire transmission plus information-processing capacity). Employing such home-spun examples as automobiles, dogs with leashes, and home-delivered pizza, Justice Thomas, writing for the Court, and Justice Scalia, in dissent, dueled over what it means to "offer" an integrated product and whether such an offer includes an "offer" of the component parts. Thomas concluded:

> The entire question is whether the products here are functionally integrated (like the components of a car) or functionally separate (like pets and leashes). That question turns not on the language of the Act, but on the factual particulars of how Internet technology works and how it is provided, questions *Chevron* leaves to the Commission to resolve in the first instance.

545 U.S. at 991. Justice Scalia, joined by two colleagues, was unpersuaded:

> [C]able-modem service is popular precisely because of the high-speed access it provides, and that, once connected with the Internet, cable-modem subscribers often use Internet applications and functions from providers other than the cable company. [T]he telecommunications component of cable-modem service retains such ample independent identity that it must be regarded as being on offer. . . .

545 U.S., at 1005, 1014. [The other issue in *Brand X* was whether the fact that a federal court had previously ruled that cable-modem service was a "telecommunications service" should preclude the FCC from later adopting the opposite interpretation of the Act. That issue is addressed in Chapter II, *supra*.]

After its victory in *Brand X*, the FCC soon had second thoughts about its deregulatory approach. A group of influential academics began arguing for something they called "net neutrality"—a policy of assuring that ISPs could not grant preferential treatment to large-scale commercial users such as Netflix or Google at the expense of individuals and small start-ups. Candidate, and then President, Barack Obama picked up the call, and, after he had appointed a majority of commissioners, so did the FCC. Several groups using peer-to-peer services that consumed large amounts of bandwidth complained to the commission that Comcast (a cable company) was blocking (or slowing down) their services. After hearing, the FCC ordered Comcast to cease its alleged discriminatory practices. As legal justification, the commission invoked the "ancillary jurisdiction" doctrine first embraced in *Southwestern Cable*. But, in Comcast Corp. v. FCC, 600 F.3d 642 (D.C. Cir. 2010), the D.C. Circuit overturned the order, concluding that the commission had failed to explain why its specific prohibitions were reasonably necessary to effectuate a directly granted regulatory authority. The FCC responded by initiating a rulemaking proceeding, which culminated in a set of rules prohibiting blocking, slowing, and rate discrimination. Once again, the D.C. Circuit slapped the FCC down, in Verizon v. FCC, 740 F.3d 623 (D.C. Cir. 2014). The court held that the rules effectively imposed "common-carrier-like" obligations on ISPs, and that such treatment was inconsistent with the FCC's earlier ruling that ISPs are not common carriers under the Act.

Undaunted, the FCC went back to the drawing board and adopted yet a new rule reclassifying ISPs as common carriers and once again imposing the anti-blocking and anti-discrimination prohibitions. This time, the D.C. Circuit was persuaded and upheld the rules in U.S. Telecom Association v. FCC, 825 F.3d 674 (D.C. Cir. 2016). By a vote of 2-1, the panel held that the FCC had authority under the Communications Act to reclassify broadband as a "telecommunications service," based on the fact that consumers generally perceived the provision of Internet access as distinct from "add-on applications, content, and services that are generally information services." Purporting to follow *Brand X*, the court ruled that the agency's interpretation was deserving of *Chevron* deference because the statutory terms ("telecommunications service" and "information service") were ambiguous and the commission's new interpretation was reasonable.

The saga might have ended there, but for the election of Donald Trump as President. Following his appointment of a new FCC majority, the commission lost no time in revoking the "net neutrality" regulations, once again classifying ISP service as a largely unregulated "information" service. In the Matter of Restoring Internet Freedom, FCC 17-166, 83 Fed. Reg. 7852 (Feb. 22, 2018). On review, a panel of the D.C. Circuit upheld the most important aspects of the commission's 2018 Order, although the panel (with one dissent) vacated the portion of the Order that purported to pre-empt any state "net neutrality" regulations, as beyond the agency's statutory authority. Mozilla Corp. v. FCC, No. 18-1051 (D.C. Cir. 10-1-2019), *per curiam*. In a separate concurring opinion,

Judge Millett expressed obvious unease at having to adhere to the *Brand X* precedent, noting that the Internet had changed dramatically in the 15 years since *Brand X* was decided. Further litigation on the subject seems inevitable.

2.   *Rate Regulation: The Case of Telephone*

Many of the earliest business licensing regimes, such as the Interstate Commerce Act's regulation of the railroad industry, were focused on policing the rates charged by industries thought to be characterized by natural monopoly or providing a service deemed essential for the public welfare. These industries were typically called "public utilities" or industries "affected with a public interest." Historically, the primary examples have included electricity, natural gas, telephone service, and shipping and transportation by rail, land, air, and water.

The telephone industry provides a paradigmatic example of rate regulation. After Alexander Graham Bell invented the telephone, the company holding his patents, which became known as the American Telephone and Telegraph Company (AT&T), dominated local markets for telephone service. The company provided service by stringing miles of twisted copper wires, mostly on utility poles or occasionally through underground conduits, that connected subscribers' businesses and homes through elaborate switching devices (initially operated by human operators, but later automated). AT&T also quickly dominated interstate telephony by stringing trunk cables that interconnected the local exchanges. After the Bell patents expired, numerous independent companies tried to enter local markets by creating wire-and-switch networks of their own. But the value of their services was severely constrained because AT&T refused to interconnect with the independents, thus denying their customers access to AT&T's customers.

Rather than try to foster competition by requiring AT&T to interconnect with the independents, state and federal regulators opted to impose "common carrier" regulation on telephone. The very high fixed costs of creating a network to interconnect thousands of customers convinced most observers that telephone, like the retail provision of electricity, natural gas, or water, was a natural monopoly and should be regulated as such. This became a self-fulfilling prophesy: denied interconnection, most of the independents either went out of business or were acquired by AT&T. State public utility commissions assumed responsibility for regulating local carriers (mostly subsidiaries of AT&T), and the federal government regulated interstate carriage (exclusively by AT&T). Title II of the Communications Act of 1934 enshrined this system, by conferring exclusive jurisdiction on the states to regulate intrastate telephony and exclusive jurisdiction on the Federal Communications Commission to regulate interstate telephony.

Treatment of telephone companies as "common carriers" entailed three principal elements. Carriers were required to obtain a license in order to operate a telephone service; the rates that they charged to their customers were subject to regulation; and they were required to provide service to all comers (what became known as the "universal service" requirement). The three elements worked in tandem. Licensure presumably assured not only that carriers would be responsible actors (and highly responsive to regulators), but also that they would be protected against competitors who might try to "skim the cream" of their most desirable customers. Rate regulation presumably assured that carriers would not exploit their monopoly position by charging exorbitant rates in general and also made it possible to cross-subsidize service to high-cost customers protected by the "universal service" obligation.

Substantively, the typical statutory standard for approving a regulated entity's rates is that they be "just and reasonable" and not "unduly discriminatory." The former standard implies that the regulated firm should be able to recover its "reasonable" costs of doing business. The latter term implies that the rates charged for different services or to different customers must be cost-justified, except to the extent that cross-subsidization is necessary and appropriate to achieve universal service.

Determining the "reasonableness" of rates has proved to be persistently difficult for regulators charged with that task. Cost-based methods focus on two general categories of cost: cost of operations and cost of capital. The former category can raise issues relating to the wisdom of certain items of expenditure (for example, charitable contributions by a utility) or the excessiveness of certain expenses (for example, executive compensation or no-bid contracts). But most of the controversy in rate proceedings focuses on the costs of capital. Since most regulated monopolies, including wire-based telecommunications, are characterized by a very high fixed investment in equipment and distribution systems, calculating the value of the firm's capital assets (known as the "rate base") and setting the allowable rate of return on that rate base loom very large in the calculus.

Rate-of-return regulation was once policed by the courts as a matter of constitutional law, in an effort to prevent overzealous regulators from confiscating the regulated firm's "property" under the Takings and Due Process Clauses. One of the Supreme Court's early pronouncements on rate regulation declared the test for constitutionality of a governmentally prescribed rate to be whether it allowed "a fair return upon the value of [property employed] for the public convenience." Smyth v. Ames, 169 U.S. 466, 547 (1898). After a half-century of struggling to give greater content to this standard, however, the Supreme Court largely bowed out of the business of supervising the mechanics of rate-setting in FPC v. Hope Natural Gas Co., 320 U.S. 591 (1944). Courts still review rate regulation when parties challenge the rate of return as too low or the rate base as improperly calculated, but the questions invariably involve the reasonableness of economic and accounting judgments, not the constitutionality of the basic approach.

Rate-of-return regulation has been criticized severely. It assertedly undermines incentives to innovate, locks companies into old technologies, and provides incentives to overinvest in capital stock (durable, physical inputs) as these costs provide the base on which allowable returns are calculated. Predictably, regulatory authorities often are suspicious of claims by regulated enterprises, so that disputes over what costs are reasonable or what rate of return is reasonable are common. The story of rate-of-return regulation has been a search for new regulatory tools to combat the initial disincentives of regulation and discovery of new flaws with each tool.

Rate-regulatory statutes, such as those historically governing the telephone industry, typically require firms to file with the regulatory agency a proposed schedule of prices, called a tariff. The agency then has a set period of time to review the tariff and to decide whether to accept it, reject it, or delay its effect pending an investigation. The agency may reject or adjust rates proposed in a tariff only after an adjudicatory hearing. So long as a tariff is in effect, the regulated firm must adhere to the published rates, and most statutes provide that published rates may not be changed for a minimum specified period of time.

Here too, regulatory practice has been criticized. The publication requirement has been faulted both for creating undue rigidity in prices (preventing efficient price reductions) and for failing to constrain inefficient price-cutting. Another concern is that, like automobile sticker prices, as a practical matter, a tariff may only set the *maximum* rate. Concerns about discriminatory discounts cannot be fully allayed by tariff publication unless the tariff itself is nondiscriminatory *and* is effectively binding. At the same time, published rates can facilitate cartel arrangements through "conscious parallelism," where price competition otherwise would occur. In the airline, railroad, and trucking industries, that is exactly the effect many critics observed.

Section 203 of the Communications Act of 1934 required all federally licensed interstate telephone carriers—which, for the next four decades meant AT&T—to comply with its tariffing requirement. Beginning in the 1970s, however, the introduction of microwave relay technology made it possible for independent firms, such as MCI Telecommunications Corp., to compete with AT&T for the lucrative interstate telephone market. The FCC responded, hesitantly at first, but then with increasing enthusiasm for the promotion of competition, by requiring AT&T to interconnect with the independents, and then by gradually relieving the independents of the burden of tariffing, which is expensive and thought by many economists to stifle competition. After several fits and starts, the FCC settled on a policy of "permissive" detariffing" for all "nondominant" interstate carriers (that is, all carriers other than AT&T). AT&T challenged the commission's authority to excuse its competitors from the tariff requirement, and a divided Supreme Court agreed.

MCI TELECOMMUNICATIONS CORP. v. AMERICAN TELEPHONE & TELEGRAPH CO.
512 U.S. 218 (1994)

JUSTICE SCALIA delivered the opinion of the Court.

Section 203(a) of Title 47 of the United States Code requires communications common carriers to file tariffs with the Federal Communications Commission, and §203(b) authorizes the Commission to "modify" any requirement of §203. These cases present the question whether the Commission's decision to make tariff filing optional for all nondominant long-distance carriers is a valid exercise of its modification authority. . . .

II

Section 203 of the Communications Act contains both the filed rate provisions of the Act and the Commission's disputed modification authority. It provides in relevant part:

"(a) Filing; public display.

"Every common carrier, except connecting carriers, shall, within such reasonable time as the Commission shall designate, file with the Commission and print and keep open for public inspection schedules showing all charges . . . , whether such charges are joint or separate, and showing the classifications, practices, and regulations affecting such charges. . . .

"(b) Changes in schedule; discretion of Commission to modify requirements.

"(1) No change shall be made in the charges, classifications, regulations, or practices which have been so filed and published except after one hundred and twenty days notice to the Commission and to the public, which shall be published in such form and contain such information as the Commission may by regulations prescribe.

"(2) The Commission may, in its discretion and for good cause shown, modify any requirement made by or under the authority of this section either in particular instances or by general order applicable to special circumstances or conditions except that the Commission may not require the notice period specified in paragraph (1) to be more than one hundred and twenty days.

"(c) Overcharges and rebates.

"No carrier, unless otherwise provided by or under authority of this chapter, shall engage or participate in such communication unless schedules have been filed and published in accordance with the provisions of this chapter and with the regulations made thereunder; and no carrier shall (1) charge, demand, collect, or receive a greater or less or different compensation for such communication . . . than the charges specified in the schedule then in effect, or (2) refund or remit by any means or device any portion of the charges so specified, or (3) extend to any person any privileges or facilities in such communication, or employ or enforce any classifications, regulations, or practices affecting such charges, except as specified in such schedule."

The dispute between the parties turns on the meaning of the phrase "modify any requirement" in §203(b)(2). Petitioners argue that it gives the Commission authority to make even basic and fundamental changes in the scheme created by that section. We disagree. The word "modify"—like a number of other English words employing the root "mod" ("deriving from the Latin word for "measure"), such as "moderate," "modulate," "modest," and "modicum"—has a connotation of increment or limitation. Virtually every dictionary we are aware of says that "to modify" means to change moderately or in minor fashion. [Justice Scalia here quotes approvingly from four dictionaries that contain such a definition, while dismissing, as self-contradictory and "out of step," a fifth dictionary (cited by MCI) that defines "modify" to mean both "to change in some respects" and "to change fundamentally."]

Since an agency's interpretation of a statute is not entitled to deference when it goes beyond the meaning that the statute can bear, the Commission's permissive detariffing policy can be justified only if it makes a less than radical or fundamental change in the Act's tariff-filing requirement. The Commission's attempt to establish that no more than that is involved greatly understates the extent to which its policy deviates from the filing requirement, and greatly undervalues the importance of the filing requirement itself.

To consider the latter point first: For the body of a law, as for the body of a person, whether a change is minor or major depends to some extent upon the importance of the item changed to the whole. Loss of an entire toenail is insignificant; loss of an entire arm tragic. The tariff-filing requirement is, to pursue this analogy, the heart of the common-carrier section of the Communications Act. In the context of the Interstate Commerce Act, which served as its model, this Court has repeatedly stressed that rate filing was Congress's chosen means of preventing unreasonableness and discrimination in charges: "[T]here is not only a relation, but an indissoluble unity between the provision for the establishment and maintenance of rates until corrected in accordance with the statute and the prohibitions against preferences and discrimination." Texas & Pacific R. Co. v. Abilene Cotton Oil Co., 204 U.S. 426, 440 (1907); *see also* Robinson v. Baltimore & Ohio R. Co., 222 U.S. 506, 508-509 (1912). "The duty to file rates with the Commission, [the analog to §203(a)], and the obligation to charge only those rates, [the analog to §203(c)], have always been considered essential to preventing price discrimination and stabilizing rates." Maislin Industries, U.S., Inc. v. Primary Steel, Inc., 497 U.S. 116, 126 (1990). . . .

Much of the rest of the Communications Act subchapter applicable to Common Carriers . . . [is] premised upon the tariff-filing requirement of §203. For example, §415 defines "overcharges" (which customers are entitled to recover) by reference to the filed rate. *See* §415(g). The provisions allowing customers and competitors to challenge rates as unreasonable or as discriminatory, would not be susceptible of effective enforcement if rates were not publicly filed. . . . Rate filings are, in fact, the essential characteristic of a rate-regulated industry. It is highly unlikely that Congress would leave the determination of whether an industry will be entirely, or even substantially, rate-regulated to agency discretion—and even more unlikely that it would achieve that through such a subtle device as permission to "modify" rate-filing requirements.

Bearing in mind, then, the enormous importance to the statutory scheme of the tariff-filing provision, we turn to whether what has occurred here can be considered a mere "modification." The Commission stresses that its detariffing policy applies only to nondominant carriers, so that the rates charged to over half of all consumers in the long-distance market are on file with the Commission. It is not clear to us that the proportion of customers affected, rather than the proportion of carriers affected, is the proper measure of the extent of the exemption (of course *all* carriers in the long-distance market are exempted, except AT&T). But even assuming it is, we think an elimination of the crucial provision of the statute for 40% of a major sector of the industry is much too extensive to be considered a "modification." What we have here, in reality, is a fundamental revision of the statute, changing it from a scheme of rate regulation in long-distance common-carrier communications to a scheme of rate regulation only where effective competition does not exist. That may be a good idea, but it was not the idea Congress enacted into law in 1934.

Finally, petitioners earnestly urge that their interpretation of §203(b) furthers the Communications Act's broad purpose of promoting efficient telephone service. They claim that although the filing requirement prevented price discrimination and unfair practices while AT&T maintained a monopoly over long-distance service, it frustrates those same goals now that there is greater competition in that market. Specifically, they contend that filing costs raise artificial barriers to entry and that the publication of rates facilitates parallel pricing and stifles price competition. We have considerable sympathy with these arguments (though we doubt it makes sense, if one is concerned about the use of filed tariffs to communicate pricing information, to require filing by the dominant carrier, the firm most likely to be a price leader). . . . But our estimations, and the Commission's estimations, of desirable policy cannot alter the meaning of the federal Communications Act of 1934. For better or worse, the Act establishes a rate-regulation, filed-tariff system for common-carrier communications. . . .

We do not mean to suggest that the tariff-filing requirement is so inviolate that the Commission's existing modification authority does not reach it at all. Certainly the Commission can modify the form, contents, and location of required filings, and can defer filing or perhaps even waive it altogether in limited circumstances. But what we have here goes well beyond that. It is effectively the introduction of a whole new regime of regulation (or of free-market competition), which may well be a better regime but is not the one that Congress established.

The judgment of the Court of Appeals is Affirmed.

JUSTICE O'CONNOR took no part in the consideration or decision of these cases.

JUSTICE STEVENS, with whom JUSTICE BLACKMUN and JUSTICE SOUTER join, dissenting.

The communications industry has an unusually dynamic character. In 1934, Congress authorized the Federal Communications Commission (FCC or Commission) to regulate "a field of enterprise the dominant characteristic of which was the rapid pace of its unfolding." National Broadcasting Co. v. United States, 319 U.S. 190, 219 (1943). The Communications Act of 1934 (Act) gives the FCC unusually broad discretion to meet new and unanticipated problems in order to fulfill its sweeping mandate "to make available, so far as possible, to all the people of the United States, a rapid, efficient, Nation-wide and world-wide wire and radio communication service with adequate facilities at reasonable charges." 47 U.S.C. §151. This Court's consistent interpretation of the Act has afforded the Commission ample leeway to interpret and apply its statutory powers and responsibilities. . . . The Court today abandons that approach in favor of a rigid literalism that deprives the FCC of the flexibility Congress meant it to have in order to implement the core policies of the Act in rapidly changing conditions. . . .

According to the Court, the term "modify," as explicated in all but the most unreliable dictionaries, rules out the Commission's claimed authority to relieve nondominant carriers of the basic obligation to file tariffs. Dictionaries can be useful aides in statutory interpretation, but they are no substitute for close analysis of what words mean as used in a particular statutory context. . . . When §203 is viewed as part of a statute whose aim is to constrain monopoly power, the Commission's decision to exempt nondominant carriers is a rational and "measured" adjustment to novel circumstances—one that remains faithful to the core purpose of the tariff-filing section.

The Court seizes upon a particular sense of the word "modify" at the expense of another, long-established meaning that fully supports the Commission's position. That word is first defined in Webster's Collegiate Dictionary 628 (4th ed. 1934) as meaning "to limit or reduce in extent or degree." The Commission's permissive detariffing policy fits comfortably within this common understanding of the term. The FCC has in effect adopted a general rule stating that "if you are dominant you must file, but if you are nondominant you need not." The Commission's partial detariffing policy—which excuses nondominant carriers from filing *on condition that* they remain nondominant—is simply a relaxation of a costly regulatory requirement that recent developments had rendered pointless and counterproductive in a certain class of cases.

A modification pursuant to §203(b)(1), like any other order issued under the Act, must of course be consistent with the purposes of the statute. On this point, the Court asserts that the Act's prohibition against unreasonable and discriminatory rates "would not be susceptible of effective enforcement if rates were not publicly filed." That determination, of course, is for the Commission to make in the first instance. But the Commission has repeatedly explained that (1) a carrier that lacks market power is entirely unlikely to charge unreasonable or discriminatory rates, (2) the statutory bans on unreasonable charges and price discrimination apply with full force regardless of whether carriers have to file tariffs, (3) any suspected violations by nondominant carriers can be addressed on the Commission's own motion or on a damages complaint . . . and (4) the FCC can reimpose a tariff requirement should violations occur. . . . The Court does not adequately respond to the FCC's explanations, and gives no reason whatsoever to doubt the Commission's considered judgment that tariff filing is altogether unnecessary in the case of competitive carriers. . . . We should sustain its eminently sound, experience-tested, and uncommonly well-explained judgment.

I respectfully dissent.

NOTES AND QUESTIONS

1. *Tariffing.* Why did the Communications Act require regulated carriers to publish tariffs of their rates? Does the answer depend on the underlying reason for imposing rate regulation on the telephone industry; that is, whether Congress viewed telecommunications as inherently monopolistic or as a "public good" of the sort that justified imposition of "common carrier" obligations? In either case, why do you suppose Congress authorized the FCC to "modify any requirement made by or under authority of" §203? Does it strike you as constitutionally troublesome that Congress effectively authorized an agency essentially to "amend" a portion of its governing statute? Might the specter of a nondelegation problem have haunted the Court's view of the Act?

2. *Tariffing and competition.* How serious an impediment to competition is the tariffing requirement? Competitive firms in countless industries publish their prices. What's the big deal? As it turned out, the setback to the FCC's pro-competition policy entailed in *MCI* was only temporary, as two years later Congress enacted the Telecommunications Act of 1996, which ushered in a whole new regime of competition-promoting regulation. In addition to relieving nondominant carriers of tariffing requirements, the Act decreed a new "forward-looking"

methodology of rate regulation, focusing on the cost of efficient contemporary technologies, rather that inefficient historic technologies.

3. Chevron *deference?* What methods of statutory interpretation do the Court and the dissent employ to discern whether the Communications Act is sufficiently "ambiguous" to tolerate the FCC's reading? Is a "battle of dictionaries" helpful? If dictionaries disagree, as was evidently the case here, how should a court decide which ones to credit? Those published contemporaneously with enactment of the statute? (Interestingly, all of the dictionaries cited by Justice Scalia were editions from the 1980s, whereas the dictionary cited by Justice Stevens was a 1934 edition.) Given the regulatory context, what method seems most appropriate? We have seen several cases in which agencies have struggled to apply relatively old regulatory statutes to changed conditions: e.g., *Brown & Williamson* and *Massachusetts v. EPA*, excerpted in Chapter II, *supra.* Do those cases provide useful guidance on how the Court should confront the issue in *MCI?* Should the Court be more willing to find statutory ambiguity when an agency interprets its statute to reduce regulatory barriers (as in *MCI*) than when it seeks to expand regulatory power? On the challenges that old statutes pose for agencies such as the FCC, see Jody Freeman & David B. Spence, *Old Statutes, New Problems,* 163 U. Pa. L. Rev. 1 (2014).

PART THREE

INDIRECT CONTROLS

In Parts One and Two of this book we explored the uses and limitations of law as a form of direct control on administrative action. By "direct control" we mean a set of commands addressed directly and specially to administrators, enforced by courts exercising primarily "appellate-style" review of their actions. Yet law also constrains officials' behavior in countless indirect ways, by defining the general legal and organizational environments in which they operate. In Chapter I we examined several examples. The nondelegation doctrine (as professed, if not applied, by the courts) seeks to limit the range of discretion that may be delegated to an agency. The appointment and removal cases restrict the way in which agency heads may be selected and disciplined. Civil service laws prescribe procedures for the staffing of agencies, appropriations acts establish funding limits, and public finance statutes set conditions for making expenditures.

In this part we examine an additional form of indirect control that has played an increasingly important role in the modern administrative state: public access rights. The materials in Chapter IX explore several types of legal rules that require agencies to create and make available to the public information about their activities. These rules are designed to shape administrative behavior by creating the conditions necessary for normal processes of political control to function. As you read the materials in Chapter IX, you should ask yourself whether such indirect forms of control hold greater promise for constraining administrative discretion than direct judicial supervision, or whether they are helpful complements.

CHAPTER IX

PUBLIC ACCESS

The legal strategy of disciplining administrative discretion by opening bureaucratic processes to the glare of public scrutiny is comparatively new. In recent decades, legislatures and courts have fashioned a variety of legal rules creating rights of public access to information about the activities of government agencies. Records statutes, like the Federal Records Act, 44 U.S.C. chs. 29-33, define the records that agencies must create and maintain. Disclosure statutes, like the Freedom of Information Act, 5 U.S.C. §552, define the circumstances under which members of the public may obtain access to those records. Confidentiality statutes, such as the Privacy Act, 5 U.S.C. §552a, or the Trade Secrets Act, 18 U.S.C. §1905, specifically forbid disclosure of certain kinds of records or information. Finally, open meeting laws, like the picturesquely titled Government in the Sunshine Act, 5 U.S.C. §552b, and the more mundanely titled Federal Advisory Committee Act, 5 U.S.C. app. 2, require certain administrative business to be carried on in public sessions.

Taken together, these various bodies of law help to determine the extent to which administrative activity may be subject to the discipline of public scrutiny. Without judicially enforceable rights to open the "black box" of administrative action, the media, scholars, citizens, and even elected officials would be completely at the mercy of the bureaucrats. In an open, democratic society, the means to hold government officials accountable is essential. Yet, as the materials of this chapter should demonstrate, making good on the promise of "open government" is a formidable task for the judiciary as well.

A. PUBLIC ACCESS TO GOVERNMENT RECORDS

Prior to 1967, members of the public had no means by which to compel federal officials to disclose information not subject to subpoena in the course of litigation. The Federal Register Act of 1935, ch. 417, §5, 49 Stat. 501 (1935), *codified as amended at* 44 U.S.C. §1505, did require publication of all agency regulations of "general applicability and legal effect," and declared that unpublished regulations were unenforceable except against those with actual knowledge of

them. But the Act did not require public disclosure of agency opinions, procedures, policies, delegations of authority, investigative reports, or other information. Although called a public information provision, §3 of the Administrative
Procedure Act, as enacted in 1946, provided little aid to the information seeker.
First, it contained a number of vague exceptions that allowed agencies to withhold information "in the public interest" or "for good cause found." Second,
only those persons "properly and directly concerned" were allowed access to
information. Lastly, §3 failed to provide any judicial remedy for citizens when
the government refused to release information, even if it had absolutely no justification for doing so. *See generally* John E. Moss, Public Information Policies, The
APA, and Executive Privilege, 15 Admin. L. Rev. 111 (1963).

     This, then, was the situation when Congress enacted the Freedom of Infor-
mation Act (FOIA) in 1966. Pub. L. No. 89-487, 80 Stat. 250 (1966), *codified by*
Pub. L. No. 90-23 (1967) *at* 5 U.S.C. §552. The Act became effective on July 4,
1967. Eleven years in the making, FOIA expressed Congress's profound dissatisfaction with the legal remedies available to the public to compel disclosure of public documents. Although not a single federal agency supported
the legislation, it passed both houses of Congress by an overwhelming majority. FOIA totally rewrote §3 of the APA (now, 5 U.S.C. §552). While preserving
largely intact §3(a)'s "publication" requirement (§552(a)(1)), it considerably
expanded §3(b)'s "inspection" requirement (§552(a)(2)), by detailing the
kinds of opinions, interpretations, and staff instructions that agencies must
index and make available for inspection and copying. FOIA's major contribution, however, may be seen in subsections (a)(3)-(5) and (b)-(c), which establish an expansive right of public access to all agency records unless specifically
exempted, enforceable in the federal courts.

     During the years following FOIA's enactment, complaints mounted that
agency recalcitrance was frustrating its original intent. Critics charged agencies with various obstructionist tactics: excessively delaying response to requests,
charging high fees for record searches and copying, insisting on detailed descriptions of records sought, producing illegible copies of records, and interpreting
the Act's exceptions too liberally. Congress has responded to these criticisms
by amending the Act at roughly ten-year intervals, most recently in 2016, in an
ongoing effort to toughen procedures for its implementation and enforcement.
The repeated attention Congress pays to FOIA is striking. The most optimistic
interpretation is that it signals a genuine and enduring bipartisan commitment
to open government. A more cynical view is that members of Congress can support transparency in theory, while knowing that when their party controls the
executive branch, FOIA is fairly easy to evade.

     On its face, FOIA is strong medicine—a statute that bristles with "teeth."
Arguably, strong medicine is needed to redress the obvious inequality between
citizen-requestor and agency-custodian. How can a requestor—usually unsure
about a record's content, location, or even existence—rebut an agency's claim
that the record sought does not exist or is in the possession of another agency
or contains exempt material? When the last of these claims is made, moreover,
the usual adversary process of investigation and argument cannot work, since it
is the very right to inspect the record that is at issue. Courts have responded by
using the device of *in camera* inspection. But, in addition to being extraordinarily
time consuming, *in camera* inspection forces judges to shed their comfortable

role of passive arbiter and adopt the unfamiliar role of inquisitor. Responding to that dilemma, the D.C. Circuit in Vaughn v. Rosen, 484 F.2d 820 (D.C. Cir. 1973), *cert. denied,* 415 U.S. 977 (1974), authorized trial judges to "designate a special master to examine documents and evaluate an agency's claim of exemption." 484 F.2d at 828. In addition, the court suggested that agencies be required to prepare indexes of particularly voluminous records, and present a specific and detailed justification for each exemption claimed.

Not surprisingly, presidential administrations have varied in their degree of enthusiasm for providing the public access to the inner workings of government. A series of advisory memoranda from the Justice Department have taken positions alternating from relatively hostile to disclosure (in the Reagan and George W. Bush Administrations) to much more supportive of disclosure (in the Clinton and Obama Administrations). Although the partisan pedigree of these oscillating positions is unmistakable, one should not lose sight of the deep philosophical differences about the costs and benefits of "open government" upon which they rest. On the one side are arrayed familiar and attractive arguments about the need for a fully informed citizenry in a functioning democracy; on the other, equally familiar and attractive arguments about preserving efficiency of operations and necessary confidentiality. The question is whether it is possible to have enough of both and how best to strike the balance. For a taste of the scholarly debate, *see, e.g.,* Antonin Scalia, The Freedom of Information Act Has No Clothes, Regulation, Mar/Apr. 1982, at 15; Glen O. Robinson, Access to Government Information: The American Experience, 14 Fed. L. Rev. 35 (1983). In the materials that follow, you should ask yourself whether the Act, as interpreted by the courts, strikes an appropriate balance between social costs and benefits. Imagine yourself having to manage FOIA requests from inside the government versus trying to use it as a journalist.

1. Agency Records Under the Freedom of Information Act

The core provision of FOIA is a simple command that federal agencies make their "records promptly available to any person" who requests them. 5 U.S.C. §552(a)(3). To enforce that command, FOIA confers on federal district courts jurisdiction "to order the production of any agency records improperly withheld." §552(a)(4)(B). In reviewing any FOIA request, then, the threshold question is whether the thing requested is an "agency record." As the following materials indicate, the answer to that question is not always self-evident.

KISSINGER v. REPORTERS COMMITTEE FOR FREEDOM OF THE PRESS
445 U.S. 136 (1980)

JUSTICE REHNQUIST delivered the opinion of the Court.

The Freedom of Information Act (FOIA) vests jurisdiction in federal district courts to enjoin an "agency from withholding agency records and to order the production of any agency records improperly withheld from the complainant." 5 U.S.C. §552(a)(4)(B). We hold today that even if a document requested under the FOIA is wrongfully in the possession of a party not an "agency," the agency which received the request does not "improperly withhold" those materials by its refusal to institute a retrieval action. When an agency has demonstrated that it has not "withheld" requested records in violation of the standards established by Congress, the federal courts have no authority to order the production of such records under the FOIA.

I

This litigation arises out of FOIA requests seeking access to various transcriptions of petitioner Kissinger's telephone conversations. The questions presented by the petition necessitate a thorough review of the facts.

A

Henry Kissinger served in the Nixon and Ford administrations for eight years. He assumed the position of Assistant to the President for National Security Affairs in January 1969. In September 1973, Kissinger was appointed to the office of Secretary of State, but retained his National Security Affairs advisory position until November 3, 1975. After his resignation from the latter position, Kissinger continued to serve as Secretary of State until January 20, 1977. Throughout this period of Government service, Kissinger's secretaries generally monitored his telephone conversations and recorded their contents either by shorthand or on tape. The stenographic notes or tapes were used to prepare detailed summaries, and sometimes verbatim transcripts, of Kissinger's conversations.[1] Since Kissinger's secretaries generally monitored all of his conversations, the summaries discussed official business as well as personal matters. The summaries and transcripts prepared from the electronic or stenographic recording of his telephone conversations throughout his entire tenure in Government service were stored in his office at the State Department in personal files.

On October 29, 1976, while still Secretary of State, Kissinger arranged to move the telephone notes from his office in the State Department to the New York estate of Nelson Rockefeller. Before removing the notes, Kissinger did not consult the State Department's Foreign Affairs Document and Reference Center (FADRC), the center responsible for implementing the State Department's record maintenance and disposal program. Nor did he consult the National Archives and Records Service (NARS), a branch of the General Services Administration (GSA) which is responsible for records preservation throughout the Federal Government. Kissinger had obtained an opinion from the Legal Adviser of the Department of State, however, advising him that the telephone summaries were not agency records but were his personal papers which he would be free to take when he left office.[2]

---

1. Tapes and stenographic notes were always destroyed immediately after they were summarized or transcribed.

2. This conclusion was premised on the Adviser's finding that the notes were covered by a Department regulation providing that a retiring official may retain papers "explicitly designated or filed as personal at the time of origin or receipt." 5 FAM §417.1(a) (1974).

After Kissinger effected this physical transfer of the notes, he entered into two agreements with the Library of Congress deeding his private papers. In the first agreement, dated November 12, 1976, Kissinger deeded to the United States, in care of the Library of Congress, one collection of papers. Kissinger's telephone notes were not included in this collection. The agreement established terms obligating Kissinger to comply with certain restrictions on the inclusion of official documents in the collection and obligating the Library to respect restrictions on access. . . .

On December 24, 1976, by a second deed, Kissinger donated a second collection consisting of his telephone notes. This second agreement with the Library of Congress incorporated by reference all of the terms and conditions of the first agreement. It provided in addition, however, that public access to the transcripts would be permitted only with the consent, or upon the death, of the other parties to the telephone conversations in question.

On December 28, 1976, the transcripts were transported directly to the Library from the Rockefeller estate. Thus the transcripts were not reviewed by the Department of State Document and Reference Center with the first collection of donated papers before they were delivered into the possession of the Library of Congress. Several weeks after they were moved to the Library, however, one of Kissinger's personal aides did extract portions of the transcripts for inclusion in the files of the State Department and the National Security Council. Pursuant to the instructions of the State Department Legal Adviser, the aide included in the extracts, "any significant policy decisions or actions not otherwise reflected in the Department's records."

B

Three separate FOIA requests form the basis of this litigation. All three requests were filed while Kissinger was Secretary of State, but only one request was filed prior to the removal of the telephone notes from the premises of the State Department. This first request was filed by William Safire, a New York Times columnist, on January 14, 1976. Safire requested the Department of State to produce any transcripts of Kissinger's telephone conversations between January 21, 1969, and February 12, 1971, in which (1) Safire's name appeared or (2) Kissinger discussed the subject of information "leaks" with certain named White House officials. The Department denied Safire's FOIA request by letter of February 11, 1976. The Department letter reasoned that the requested notes had been made while Kissinger was National Security Adviser and therefore were not agency records subject to FOIA disclosure.[3]

The second FOIA request was filed on December 28 and 29, 1976, by the Military Audit Project (MAP) after Kissinger publicly announced the gift of his telephone notes to the United States and their placement in the Library of Congress. The MAP request, filed with the Department of State, sought records of all Kissinger's conversations made while Secretary of State and National Security Adviser. On January 18, 1977, the Legal Adviser of the Department of State

---

3. Safire filed an administrative appeal from this decision, contending that the notes were agency records by virtue of their relocation to the State Department. The appeal was denied.

denied the request on two grounds. First, he found that the notes were not agency records. Second, the deposit of the notes with the Library of Congress prior to the request terminated the Department's custody and control. The denial was affirmed on administrative appeal.

The third FOIA request was filed on January 13, 1977, by the Reporters Committee for Freedom of the Press (RCFP), the American Historical Association, the American Political Science Association, and a number of other journalists (collectively referred to as the RCFP requesters). This request also sought production of the telephone notes made by Kissinger both while he was National Security Adviser and Secretary of State. The request was denied for the same reasons given to the MAP requesters. . . .

II

We first address the issue presented by Kissinger—whether the District Court possessed the authority to order the transfer of that portion of the deeded collection, including the transcripts of all conversations Kissinger made while Secretary of State, from the Library of Congress to the Department of State at the behest of the named plaintiffs. . . .

The FOIA represents a carefully balanced scheme of public rights and agency obligations designed to foster greater access to agency records than existed prior to its enactment. That statutory scheme authorizes federal courts to ensure private access to requested materials when three requirements have been met. Under 5 U.S.C. §552(a)(4)(B) federal jurisdiction is dependent upon a showing that an agency has (1) "improperly"; (2) "withheld"; (3) "agency records." Judicial authority to devise remedies and enjoin agencies can only be invoked, under the jurisdictional grant conferred by §552, if the agency has contravened all three components of this obligation. We find it unnecessary to decide whether the telephone notes were "agency records" since we conclude that a covered agency—here the State Department—has not "withheld" those documents from the plaintiffs. We also need not decide the full contours of a prohibited "withholding." We do decide, however, that Congress did not mean that an agency improperly withholds a document which has been removed from the possession of the agency prior to the filing of the FOIA request. In such a case, the agency has neither the custody nor control necessary to enable it to withhold.

In looking for congressional intent, we quite naturally start with the usual meaning of the word "withhold" itself. The requesters would have us read the "hold" out of "withhold." The act described by this word presupposes the actor's possession or control of the item withheld. A refusal to resort to legal remedies to obtain possession is simply not conduct subsumed by the verb "withhold."

The Act and its legislative history do not purport to define the word. An examination of the structure and purposes of the Act, however, indicates that Congress used the word in its usual sense. An agency's failure to sue a third party to obtain possession is not a withholding under the Act.

Several sources suggest directly that agency possession or control is prerequisite to triggering any duties under the FOIA. In the debates, the Act was described as ensuring "access to the information *possessed* by [Government] servants." (Emphasis added.) 112 Cong. Rec. 13652 (1966), *reprinted in* Freedom of Information Act Source Book, S. Doc. No. 93-82, p. 69 (1974) (remarks of Rep. Monagan). . . .

The conclusion that possession or control is a prerequisite to FOIA disclosure duties is reinforced by an examination of the purposes of the Act. The Act does not obligate agencies to create or retain documents; it only obligates them to provide access to those which it in fact has created and retained. . . .

If the agency is not required to create or to retain records under the FOIA, it is somewhat difficult to determine why the agency is nevertheless required to retrieve documents which have escaped its possession, but which it has not endeavored to recover. If the document is of so little interest to the agency that it does not believe the retrieval effort to be justified, the effect of this judgment on an FOIA request seems little different from the effect of an agency determination that a record should never be created, or should be discarded.

The procedural provisions of the Act, in particular, reflect the nature of the obligation which Congress intended to impose on agencies in the production of agency records. First, Congress has provided that agencies normally must decide within 10 days whether to comply with an FOIA request unless they can establish "unusual circumstances" as defined in the Act. 5 U.S.C. §§552(a)(6)(A), (B). . . . Either Congress was operating under the assumption that lawsuits could be waged and won in 10 days, or it was operating under the assumption that agencies would not be obligated to file lawsuits in order to comply with FOIA requests.

A similarly strong expression of congressional expectations emerges in 5 U.S.C. §552(a)(4)(A) providing for recovery of certain costs incurred in complying with FOIA requests. This section was included in the Act in order to reduce the burdens imposed on the agencies. The agency is authorized to establish fees for the "direct costs" of "document search and duplication." The costs allowed reflect the congressional judgment as to the nature of the costs which would be incurred. Congress identified these costs, and thus the agency burdens, as consisting of "search" and "duplication." . . . It is doubtful that Congress intended that a "search" include legal efforts to retrieve wrongfully removed documents, since such an intent would authorize agency assessment to the private requester of its litigation costs in such an endeavor. . . .

This construction of "withholding" readily disposes of the RCFP and MAP requests. Both of these requests were filed after Kissinger's telephone notes had been deeded to the Library of Congress.[9] The Government, through the Archivist, has requested return of the documents from Kissinger. The request has been refused. The facts make it apparent that Kissinger, and the Library of Congress as his donee, are holding the documents under a claim of right. Under these circumstances, the State Department cannot be said to have had

---

9. There is no question that a "withholding" must here be gauged by the time at which the request is made since there is no FOIA obligation to retain records prior to that request. This temporal factor has always governed requests under the subpoena power, Jurney v. MacCracken, 294 U.S. 125 (1935), as well as under other access statutes. *See* Fed. Rules Civ. Proc. 34, 45. We need not decide whether this standard might be displaced in the event that it was shown that an agency official purposefully routed a document out of agency possession in order to circumvent a FOIA request. No such issue is presented here. We also express no opinion as to whether an agency withholds documents which have been wrongfully removed by an individual after a request is filed.

possession or control of the documents at the time the requests were received. It did not, therefore, withhold any agency records, an indispensable prerequisite to liability in a suit under the FOIA.

III

The Safire request raises a separate question. At the time when Safire submitted his request for certain notes of Kissinger's telephone conversations, all the notes were still located in Kissinger's office at the State Department. For this reason, we do not rest our resolution of his claim on the grounds that there was no withholding by the State Department. As outlined above, the Act only prohibits the withholding of "agency records." We conclude that the Safire request sought disclosure of documents which were not "agency records" within the meaning of the FOIA.

Safire's request sought only a limited category of documents. He requested the Department to produce all transcripts of telephone conversations made by Kissinger from his White House office between January 21, 1969, and February 12, 1971, in which (1) Safire's name appeared; or (2) in which Kissinger discussed the subject of information "leaks" with General Alexander Haig, Attorney General John Mitchell, President Richard Nixon, J. Edgar Hoover, or any other official of the FBI.

The FOIA does render the "Executive Office of the President" an agency subject to the Act. 5 U.S.C. §552(e).* The legislative history is unambiguous, however, in explaining that the "Executive Office" does not include the Office of the President. The Conference Report for the 1974 FOIA Amendments indicates that "the President's immediate personal staff or units in the Executive Office whose sole function is to advise and assist the President" are not included within the term "agency" under the FOIA. H.R. Conf. Rep. No. 93-1380, p. 15 (1974), reprinted in Source Book II, p. 232. Safire's request was limited to a period of time in which Kissinger was serving as Assistant to the President. Thus these telephone notes were not "agency records" when they were made.

The RCFP requesters have argued that since some of the telephone notes made while Kissinger was adviser to the President may have related to the National Security Council they may have been National Security Council records and therefore subject to the Act. . . . Safire never identified the request as implicating any National Security Council records. The request did not mention the National Security Council or any subject relating to the NSC. To the contrary, he requested to see transcripts Kissinger made from his White House office. Moreover, after the State Department denied the request on the grounds that these were White House records, Safire's appeal argued these were State Department records, again never suggesting they were NSC records. The FOIA requires the requester to adequately identify the records which are sought. 5 U.S.C. §552(a)(3)(A). Safire's request did not describe the records as relating to the NSC or in any way put the agency on notice that it should refer the request to the NSC. *See* 5 U.S.C. §552(a)(6)(B)(iii). Therefore, we

* [Subsequently recodified as §552(f) (*see* Appendix).—Eds.]

also need not address the issue of when an agency violates the Act by refusing to produce records of another agency, or failing to refer a request to the appropriate agency.

The RCFP requesters nevertheless contend that if the transcripts of telephone conversations made while adviser to the President were not then "agency records," they acquired that status under the Act when they were removed from White House files and physically taken to Kissinger's office at the Department of State. We simply decline to hold that the physical location of the notes of telephone conversations renders them "agency records." The papers were not in the control of the State Department at any time. They were not generated in the State Department. They never entered the State Department's files, and they were not used by the Department for any purpose. If mere physical location of papers and materials could confer status as an "agency record" Kissinger's personal books, speeches, and all other memorabilia stored in his office would have been agency records subject to disclosure under the FOIA. . . .

Accordingly, we reverse the order of the Court of Appeals compelling production of the telephone manuscripts made by Kissinger while Secretary of State and affirm the order denying the requests for transcripts produced while Kissinger served as National Security Adviser.

It is so ordered.

JUSTICE MARSHALL took no part in the consideration or decision of these cases.

JUSTICE BLACKMUN took no part in the decision of these cases.

JUSTICE BRENNAN, concurring in part and dissenting in part. [Omitted.]

JUSTICE STEVENS, concurring in part and dissenting in part. . . .

The decision today exempts documents that have been wrongfully removed from the agency's files from any scrutiny whatsoever under FOIA. It thus creates an incentive for outgoing agency officials to remove potentially embarrassing documents from their files in order to frustrate future FOIA requests. It is the creation of such an incentive, which is directly contrary to the purpose of FOIA, rather than the result in this particular case, that prompts me to write in dissent.

In my judgment, a "withholding" occurs within the meaning of FOIA whenever an agency declines to produce agency records which it has a legal right to possess or control. . . .

I

Everyone seems to agree that the summaries of Dr. Kissinger's State Department telephone conversations should be considered "agency records" subject to disclosure under FOIA if they were "agency records" under the definitions set forth in the Federal Records Act (FRA). The parties disagree, however, as to the proper application of that Act to the facts of this case. . . .

I cannot accept Dr. Kissinger's argument that the summaries are private papers. As the District Court noted, they were made in the regular course of conducting the agency's business, were the work product of agency personnel and agency assets, and were maintained in the possession and control of the agency prior to their removal by Dr. Kissinger. They were also regularly circulated to Dr. Kissinger's immediate staff and presumably used by the staff in making day-to-day decisions on behalf of the agency. Finally, Dr. Kissinger himself recognized that the State Department continued to have an interest in the summaries even after they had been removed, since he had a State Department employee review them in order to extract information that was not otherwise in the agency's files. . . .

II

The second question to be considered is whether the State Department continued to have custody or control of the telephone summaries after they were removed from its files so that its refusal to take steps to regain them should be deemed a "withholding" within the meaning of the Freedom of Information Act. As I stated at the outset, I do not agree with the Court that the broad concepts of "custody" and "control" can be equated with the much narrower concept of physical possession. In my view, those concepts should be applied to bring all documents within the *legal* custody or control of the agency within the purview of FOIA. Thus, if an agency has a legal right to regain possession of documents wrongfully removed from its files, it continues to have custody of those documents. If it then refuses to take any steps whatsoever to demand, or even to request, that the documents be returned, then the agency is "withholding" those documents for purposes of FOIA.

In this case, I think it is rather clear that the telephone summaries were wrongfully removed from the State Department's possession. Under these circumstances, the State Department's failure even to request their return constituted a "withholding" for purposes of FOIA.

III

The third and most difficult question is whether the State Department's "withholding" was "improper." In my view, the answer to that question depends on the agency's explanation for its failure to attempt to regain the documents. If the explanation is reasonable, then the withholding is not improper. For example, I would not find an agency's inaction improper in a case in which it simply did not know where the documents were located or had no interest whatsoever in retrieving them. The FOIA does not require federal agencies to engage in prolonged searches for documents or institute legal proceedings that will not yield any appreciable benefits to the agency.

On the other hand, if the agency is unable to advance a reasonable explanation for its failure to act, a presumption arises that the agency is motivated

Navy (Navy or Government) invoked Exemption 2 to deny a FOIA request for data and maps used to help store explosives at a naval base in Washington State. We hold that Exemption 2 does not stretch so far.

I

[I]n Department of Air Force v. Rose [425 U.S. 352 (1976)], we rejected the Government's invocation of Exemption 2 to withhold case summaries of honor and ethics hearings at the United States Air Force Academy. The exemption, we suggested, primarily targets material concerning employee relations or human resources: "use of parking facilities or regulations of lunch hours, statements of policy as to sick leave, and the like." *Id.*, at 363 (quoting S. Rep. No. 813, 89th Cong., 1st Sess., 8 (1965) (hereinafter S. Rep.)). "[T]he general thrust" of Exemption 2, we explained, "is simply to relieve agencies of the burden of assembling and maintaining [such information] for public inspection." *Id.*, at 369. We concluded that the case summaries did not fall within the exemption because they "d[id] not concern only routine matters" of "merely internal significance." *Id.*, at 370. But we stated a possible caveat to our interpretation of Exemption 2: That understanding of the provision's coverage governed, we wrote, "at least where the situation is not one where disclosure may risk circumvention of agency regulation." *Id.*, at 369.

In Crooker v. Bureau of Alcohol, Tobacco & Firearms, 670 F.2d 1051 (1981), the D.C. Circuit converted this caveat into a new definition of Exemption 2's scope. *Crooker* approved the use of Exemption 2 to shield a manual designed to train Government agents in law enforcement surveillance techniques. The D.C. Circuit . . . thought Exemption 2 should . . . cover any "predominantly internal" materials, *Crooker*, 670 F.2d, at 1056-1057, whose disclosure would "significantly ris[k] circumvention of agency regulations or statutes," *id.*, at 1074. . . . In the ensuing years, three Courts of Appeals adopted the D.C. Circuit's interpretation of Exemption 2. And that interpretation spawned a new terminology: Courts applying the *Crooker* approach now refer to the "Low 2" exemption when discussing materials concerning human resources and employee relations, and to the "High 2" exemption when assessing records whose disclosure would risk circumvention of the law. . . .

II

The FOIA request at issue here arises from the Navy's operations at Naval Magazine Indian Island, a base in Puget Sound, Washington. The Navy keeps weapons, ammunition, and explosives on the island. To aid in the storage and transport of these munitions, the Navy uses data known as Explosive Safety Quantity Distance (ESQD) information. ESQD information prescribes "minimum separation distances" for explosives and helps the Navy design and construct storage facilities to prevent chain reactions in case of detonation. The ESQD calculations are often incorporated into specialized maps depicting the effects of hypothetical explosions. In 2003 and 2004, petitioner Glen Milner, a Puget Sound resident, submitted FOIA requests for all ESQD information relating to Indian Island. The Navy refused to release the data, stating that disclosure would threaten the security of the base and surrounding community. In support of its decision to withhold the records, the Navy invoked Exemption 2. The District Court granted summary judgment to the Navy, and the Court of Appeals affirmed, relying on the High 2 interpretation developed in *Crooker.* . . .

We granted certiorari in light of the Circuit split respecting Exemption 2's meaning, and we now reverse.

III

Our consideration of Exemption 2's scope starts with its text. Judicial decisions since FOIA's enactment have analyzed and reanalyzed the meaning of the exemption. But comparatively little attention has focused on the provision's 12 simple words: "related solely to the internal personnel rules and practices of an agency."

The key word in that dozen—the one that most clearly marks the provision's boundaries—is "personnel." When used as an adjective, as it is here to modify "rules and practices," that term refers to human resources matters. "Personnel," in this common parlance, means "the selection, placement, and training of employees and . . . the formulation of policies, procedures, and relations with [or involving] employees or their representatives." Webster's Third New International Dictionary 1687 (1966). . . . As we recognized in *Rose*, "the common and congressional meaning of . . . 'personnel file' " is the file "showing, for example, where [an employee] was born, the names of his parents, where he has lived from time to time, his . . . school records, results of examinations, [and] evaluations of his work performance." 425 U.S., at 377. It is the file typically maintained in the human resources office—otherwise known . . . as the "personnel department." . . . Courts in practice have had little difficulty identifying the records that qualify for withholding under this reading: They are what now commonly fall within the Low 2 exemption. Our construction of the statutory language simply makes clear that Low 2 is all of 2 (and that High 2 is not 2 at all, see *infra*).

The statute's purpose reinforces this understanding of the exemption. We have often noted "the Act's goal of broad disclosure" and insisted that the exemptions be "given a narrow compass." Department of Justice v. Tax Analysts, 492 U.S. 136, 151 (1989). This practice of "constru[ing] FOIA exemptions narrowly," Department of Justice v. Landano, 508 U.S. 165, 181 (1993), stands on especially firm footing with respect to Exemption 2. . . . Congress worded that provision to hem in the prior APA exemption for "any matter relating solely to the internal management of an agency," which agencies had used to prevent access to masses of documents. *See Rose*, 425 U.S., at 362. We would ill-serve Congress's purpose by construing Exemption 2 to reauthorize the expansive withholding that Congress wanted to halt. . . .

Exemption 2, as we have construed it, does not reach the ESQD information at issue here. These data and maps calculate and visually portray the magnitude of hypothetical detonations. By no stretch of imagination do they relate to "personnel rules and practices," as that term is most naturally understood. They concern the physical rules governing explosives, not the workplace rules governing sailors; they address the handling of dangerous materials, not the treatment of employees. The Navy therefore may not use Exemption 2, interpreted in accord with its plain meaning to cover human resources matters, to prevent disclosure of the requested maps and data.

IV

[The Government suggests that we should interpret Exemption 2 to encompass] "records concerning an agency's internal rules and practices for its personnel to follow in the discharge of their governmental functions." According to the Government, this interpretation makes sense because "the phrase 'personnel rules and practices of an agency' is logically understood to mean an agency's rules and practices for its personnel."

But the purported logic in the Government's definition eludes us. We would not say, in ordinary parlance, that a "personnel file" is any file an employee uses, or that a "personnel department" is any department in which an employee serves. No more would we say that a "personnel rule or practice" is any rule or practice that assists an employee in doing her job. The use of the term "personnel" in each of these phrases connotes not that the file or department or practice/rule is for personnel, but rather that the file or department or practice/rule is about personnel—i.e., that it relates to employee relations or human resources. . . .

Many documents an agency generates in some way aid employees in carrying out their responsibilities. If Exemption 2 were to reach all these records, it would tend to engulf other FOIA exemptions, rendering ineffective the limitations Congress placed on their application. Exemption 7, for example, shields records compiled for law enforcement purposes, but only if one of six specified criteria is met. §552(b)(7). Yet on the Government's view, an agency could bypass these restrictions by invoking Exemption 2 whenever law enforcement records guide personnel in performing their duties. Indeed, an agency could use Exemption 2 as an all-purpose back-up provision to withhold sensitive records that do not fall within any of FOIA's more targeted exemptions. . . .

V

Although we cannot interpret Exemption 2 as the Government proposes, we recognize the strength of the Navy's interest in protecting the ESQD data and maps and other similar information. The Government has informed us that "[p]ublicly disclosing the [ESQD] information would significantly risk undermining the Navy's ability to safely and securely store military ordnance," and we have no reason to doubt that representation. . . . Concerns of this kind—a sense that certain sensitive information should be exempt from disclosure—in part led the *Crooker* court to formulate the High 2 standard. And we acknowledge that our decision today upsets three decades of agency practice relying on *Crooker*, and therefore may force considerable adjustments.

We also note, however, that the Government has other tools at hand to shield national security information and other sensitive materials. Most notably,

Exemption 1 of FOIA prevents access to classified documents. The Government generally may classify material even after receiving a FOIA request. Exemption 3 also may mitigate the Government's security concerns. That provision applies to records that any other statute exempts from disclosure, thus offering Congress an established, streamlined method to authorize the withholding of specific records that FOIA would not otherwise protect. And Exemption 7, as already noted, protects "information compiled for law enforcement purposes" that meets one of six criteria, including if its release "could reasonably be expected to endanger the life or physical safety of any individual." §552(b)(7)(F). The Navy argued below that the ESQD data and maps fall within Exemption 7(F), and that claim remains open for the Ninth Circuit to address on remand. . . .

VI

Exemption 2, consistent with the plain meaning of the term "personnel rules and practices," encompasses only records relating to issues of employee relations and human resources. The explosives maps and data requested here do not qualify for withholding under that exemption. We therefore reverse the judgment of the Court of Appeals and remand the case for further proceedings consistent with this opinion.

It is so ordered.

JUSTICE ALITO, concurring. [Omitted.]

JUSTICE BREYER, dissenting.

[The *Crooker* court's interpretation of Exemption 2] reflects this Court's longstanding recognition that it cannot interpret the FOIA (and the Administrative Procedure Act (APA) of which it is a part) with the linguistic literalism fit for interpretations of the tax code. That in large part is because the FOIA (like the APA but unlike the tax code) must govern the affairs of a vast Executive Branch with numerous different agencies, bureaus, and departments, performing numerous tasks of many different kinds. Too narrow an interpretation, while working well in the case of one agency, may seriously interfere with congressional objectives when applied to another. . . . [Thirty] years of experience with *Crooker*'s holding suggests that it has not seriously interfered with the FOIA's informational objectives, while at the same time it has permitted agencies to withhold much information which, in my view, Congress would not have wanted to force into the public realm. To focus only on the case law, courts have held that that information protected by Exemption 2 includes blueprints for Department of Agriculture buildings that store biological agents; documents that would help hackers access National Aeronautics and Space Administration computers; agency credit card numbers; Commodity Futures Trading Commission guidelines for settling cases; "trigger figures" that alert the Department of Education to possible mismanagement of federal funds; security plans for the Supreme Court Building and Supreme Court Justices; vulnerability assessments of Commerce Department computer security plans; Bureau of Prisons guidelines for controlling riots and for storing hazardous chemicals; guidelines for assessing the sensitivity of military programs; and guidelines for processing Medicare reimbursement claims. . . .

The majority acknowledges that "our decision today upsets three decades of agency practice relying on *Crooker*, and therefore may force considerable adjustments." But how are these adjustments to be made? Should the Government rely upon other exemptions to provide the protection it believes necessary? As Justice Alito notes, Exemption 7 applies where the documents consist of "records or information compiled for law enforcement purposes" and release would, e.g., "disclose techniques and procedures for law enforcement investigations," or "could reasonably be expected to endanger the life or physical safety of any individual." 5 U.S.C. §552(b)(7). But what about information that is not compiled for law enforcement purposes, such as building plans, computer passwords, credit card numbers, or safe deposit combinations? . . .

The majority suggests that the Government can classify documents that should remain private. But classification is at best a partial solution. It takes time. It is subject to its own rules. As the Government points out, it would hinder the sharing of information about Government buildings with "first responders," such as local fire and police departments. And both Congress and the President believe the Nation currently faces a problem of too much, not too little, classified material. . . .

That leaves congressional action. As the Court points out, Congress remains free to correct whatever problems it finds in today's narrowing of Exemption 2. But legislative action takes time; Congress has much to do; and other matters, when compared with a FOIA revision, may warrant higher legislative priority. In my view, it is for the courts, through appropriate interpretation, to turn Congress' public information objectives into workable agency practice, and to adhere to such interpretations once they are settled. . . .

For these reasons, with respect, I dissent.

NOTES AND QUESTIONS

1. *Interpretive methodology.* Recognizing that FOIA seeks to strike a balance between open government and effective government, does the canon of narrowly interpreting FOIA exemptions make sense? Should there at least be sufficient room for courts to fill gaps in the FOIA exemptions that might permit disclosure of highly sensitive information like maps of munitions storage facilities? Or is Justice Breyer correct in saying that FOIA should be interpreted expansively, in the same manner as the APA, of which it is a part?

2. *"Internal personnel rules and practices."* Why would Congress have enacted Exemption 2? Is Justice Kagan's explanation convincing? Is it fair to say that agency personnel rules and policies are ever "solely internal," or that there is no legitimate public interest in "the selection, placement, and training of employees and . . . the formulation of policies, procedures, and relations with [or involving] employees or their representatives"?

3. *Enforcement practices.* Recall from cases like *Heckler v. Chaney*, excerpted in Chapter III, *supra*, and *Universal-Rundle*, excerpted in Chapter VII, *supra*,

that the courts have largely insulated enforcement practices from direct judicial oversight. Does it follow that agencies should have discretion to shield information about enforcement priorities and practices from public disclosure? *Crooker* involved a FOIA request for a copy of the BATF's manual entitled "Surveillance of Premises, Vehicles and Persons—New Agent Training." If there were no other applicable FOIA exemption, should Exemption 2 be stretched to prohibit the manual's disclosure, on the grounds that disclosure would, as the BATF Director asserted, "benefit those attempting to violate the law and avoid detection"? Are you persuaded by any of Justice Breyer's parade of horribles?

b.   Deliberation

NATIONAL LABOR RELATIONS BOARD
v. SEARS, ROEBUCK & CO.
421 U.S. 132 (1975)

Mr. Justice White delivered the opinion of the Court.

The National Labor Relations Board (the Board) and its General Counsel seek to set aside an order of the United States District Court directing disclosure to respondent, Sears, Roebuck & Co. (Sears), pursuant to the Freedom of Information Act, 5 U.S.C. §552 (Act), of certain memoranda, known as "Advice Memoranda" and "Appeals Memoranda," and related documents generated by the Office of the General Counsel in the course of deciding whether or not to permit the filing with the Board of unfair labor practice complaints. . . .

I

[Under the National Labor Relations Act, any charge that an employer or union has committed an "unfair labor practice" must originate with a complaint filed by the General Counsel of the NLRB. Congress has specifically delegated to the General Counsel the unreviewable authority to decide whether to file a complaint with the Labor Board. The General Counsel exercises this prosecutorial discretion through a network of 31 regional offices. In order to coordinate policy among these offices, the Office of General Counsel created an elaborate mechanism to provide written advice to Regional Directors. This advice takes two forms: "Appeals Memoranda" and "Advice Memoranda." When a Regional Director decides not to file a complaint, the complainant can appeal to the Office of General Counsel. The disposition of such an appeal (either sustaining the Regional Director's decision not to prosecute or ordering the Regional Director to prosecute) is embodied in an Appeals Memorandum. In addition, Regional Directors are directed to seek the advice of the Office of General Counsel before deciding whether to file complaints dealing with certain types of issues. In response to such a request, the General Counsel sends an Advice Memorandum instructing the Regional Director either to file a complaint or not to file a complaint.]

II

This case arose in the following context. By letter dated July 14, 1971, Sears requested that the General Counsel disclose to it pursuant to the Act all Advice and Appeals Memoranda issued within the previous five years on the subjects of "the propriety of withdrawals by employers or unions from multi-employer bargaining, disputes as to commencement date of negotiations, or conflicting interpretations in any other context of the Board's *Retail Associates* (120 NLRB 388) rule." The letter also sought the subject-matter index or digest of Advice and Appeals Memoranda. The letter urged disclosure on the theory that the Advice and Appeals Memoranda are the only source of agency "law" on some issues. By letter dated July 23, 1971, the General Counsel declined Sears' disclosure request in full. The letter stated that Advice Memoranda are simply "guides for a Regional Director" and are not final; that they are exempt from disclosure under 5 U.S.C. §552(b)(5) as "intra-agency memoranda" which reflect the thought processes of the General Counsel's staff. . . . Sears filed a complaint pursuant to the Act seeking a declaration that the General Counsel's refusal to disclose the Advice and Appeals Memoranda and indices thereof requested by Sears violated the Act, and an injunction enjoining continued violations of the Act. . . .

The District Court granted Sears' motion for summary judgment and denied that of the General Counsel. . . . This decision was affirmed without opinion by the Court of Appeals for the District of Columbia Circuit. . . .

III

. . . We hold for reasons more fully set forth below that those Advice and Appeals Memoranda which explain decisions by the General Counsel not to file a complaint are "final opinions" made in the adjudication of a case and fall outside the scope of Exemption 5; but that those Advice and Appeals Memoranda which explain decisions by the General Counsel to file a complaint and commence litigation before the Board are not "final opinions" made in the adjudication of a case and do fall within the scope of Exemption 5.

A

The parties are in apparent agreement that Exemption 5 withholds from a member of the public documents which a private party could not discover in litigation with the agency. . . . The [discovery] privileges claimed by petitioners to be relevant to this case are (i) . . . "executive privilege" . . . and (ii) the attorney-client and attorney work-product privileges generally available to all litigants.

(i)

That Congress had the Government's executive privilege specifically in mind in adopting Exemption 5 is clear. . . .

Manifestly, the ultimate purpose of this long-recognized privilege is to prevent injury to the quality of agency decisions. The quality of a particular agency decision will clearly be affected by the communications received by the decisionmaker on the subject of the decision prior to the time the decision is made. However, it is difficult to see how the quality of a decision will be affected by communications with respect to the decision occurring after the decision is finally reached; and therefore equally difficult to see how the quality of the decision will be affected by forced disclosure of such communications, as long as prior communications and the ingredients of the decisionmaking process are not disclosed. . . . This distinction is supported not only by the lesser injury to the decisionmaking process flowing from disclosure of postdecisional communications, but also, in the case of those communications which explain the decision, by the increased public interest in knowing the basis for agency policy already adopted. The public is only marginally concerned with reasons supporting a policy which an agency has rejected, or with reasons which might have supplied, but did not supply, the basis for a policy which was actually adopted on a different ground. In contrast, the public is vitally concerned with the reasons which did supply the basis for an agency policy actually adopted. These reasons, if expressed within the agency, constitute the "working law" of the agency and have been held by the lower courts to be outside the protection of Exemption 5. . . . Exemption 5, properly construed, calls for "disclosure of all 'opinions and interpretations' which embody the agency's effective law and policy, and the withholding of all papers which reflect the agency's group thinking in the process of working out its policy and determining what its law shall be." Davis, The Information Act: A Preliminary Analysis, 34 U. Chi. L. Rev. 761, 797 (1967). . . .

This conclusion is powerfully supported by the other provisions of the Act. The affirmative portion of the Act, expressly requiring indexing of "final opinions," "statements of policy and interpretations which have been adopted by the agency," and "instructions to staff that affect a member of the public," 5 U.S.C. §552(a)(2), represents a strong congressional aversion to "secret [agency] law," Davis, *supra*, at 797; and represents an affirmative congressional purpose to require disclosure of documents which have "the force and effect of law." H.R. Rep. No. 1497, p.7. We should be reluctant, therefore, to construe Exemption 5 to apply to the documents described in 5 U.S.C. §552(a)(2); and with respect at least to "final opinions," which not only invariably explain agency action already taken or an agency decision already made, but also constitute "final dispositions" of matters by an agency, . . . we hold that Exemption 5 can never apply.

(ii)

It is equally clear that Congress had the attorney's work-product privilege specifically in mind when it adopted Exemption 5 and that such a privilege had been recognized in the civil discovery context by the prior case law. . . . Whatever the outer boundaries of the attorney's work-product rule are, the rule clearly applies to memoranda prepared by an attorney in contemplation of litigation which set forth the attorney's theory of the case and his litigation strategy. . . .

B

Applying these principles to the memoranda sought by Sears, it becomes clear that Exemption 5 does not apply to those Appeals and Advice Memoranda which conclude that no complaint should be filed and which have the effect of finally denying relief to the charging party; but that Exemption 5 does protect from disclosure those Appeals and Advice Memoranda which direct the filing of a complaint and the commencement of litigation before the Board.

(i)

. . . In the case of decisions *not* to file a complaint, the memoranda effect as "final" a "disposition" . . . as an administrative decision can—representing, as it does, an unreviewable rejection of the charge filed by the private party. Vaca v. Sipes, 386 U.S. 171 (1967). Disclosure of these memoranda would not intrude on predecisional processes, and protecting them would not improve the quality of agency decisions, since when the memoranda are communicated to the Regional Director, the General Counsel has already reached his decision and the Regional Director who receives them has no decision to make—he is bound to dismiss the charge. Moreover, the General Counsel's decisions not to file complaints together with the Advice and Appeals Memoranda explaining them, are precisely the kind of agency law in which the public is so vitally interested and which Congress sought to prevent the agency from keeping secret. . . .

For essentially the same reasons, these memoranda are "final opinions" made in the "adjudication of cases" which must be indexed pursuant to 5 U.S.C. §552(a)(2)(A). The decision to dismiss a charge is a decision in a "case" and constitutes an "adjudication": an "adjudication" is defined under the Administrative Procedure Act, of which 5 U.S.C. §552 is a part, as "agency process for the formulation of an order," 5 U.S.C. §551(7); an "order" is defined as "the whole or a part of a *final disposition,* whether affirmative [or] negative . . . of an agency in a matter . . . ," 5 U.S.C. §551(6) (emphasis added); and the dismissal of a charge, as noted above, is a "final disposition." Since an Advice or Appeals Memorandum explains the reasons for the "final disposition" it plainly qualifies as an "opinion"; and falls within 5 U.S.C. §552(a)(2)(A). . . .

(ii)

Advice and Appeals Memoranda which direct the filing of a complaint, on the other hand, fall within the coverage of Exemption 5. The filing of a complaint does not finally dispose even of the General Counsel's responsibility with respect to the case. The case will be litigated before and decided by the Board; and the General Counsel will have the responsibility of advocating the position of the charging party before the Board. The Memoranda will inexorably contain the General Counsel's theory of the case and may communicate to the Regional Director some litigation strategy or settlement advice. Since the Memoranda will also have been prepared in contemplation of the upcoming litigation, they fall squarely within Exemption 5's protection of an attorney's work product. At the same time, the public's interest in disclosure is substantially reduced by the fact . . . that the basis for the General Counsel's legal decision will come out in the course of litigation before the Board; and that the "law" with respect to these cases will ultimately be made not by the General Counsel but by the Board or the courts. . . .

We recognize that an Advice or Appeals Memorandum directing the filing of a complaint . . . does explain a decision already reached by the General Counsel which has real operative effect—it permits litigation before the Board; and we have indicated a reluctance to construe Exemption 5 to protect such documents. . . . We do so in this case only because the decisionmaker—the General Counsel—must become a litigating party to the case with respect to which he has made his decision. The attorney's work-product policies which Congress clearly incorporated into Exemption 5 thus come into play and lead us to hold that the Advice and Appeals Memoranda directing the filing of a complaint are exempt whether or not they are, as the District Court held, "instructions to staff that affect a member of the public."[26]

C

Petitioners assert that the District Court erred in holding that documents incorporated by reference in nonexempt Advice and Appeals Memoranda lose any exemption they might previously have held as "intra-agency" memoranda. We disagree.

The probability that an agency employee will be inhibited from freely advising a decisionmaker for fear that his advice, *if adopted,* will become public is slight. First, when adopted, the reasoning becomes that of the agency and becomes *its* responsibility to defend. Second, agency employees will generally be encouraged rather than discouraged by public knowledge that their policy suggestions have been adopted by the agency. Moreover, the public interest in knowing the reasons for a policy actually adopted by an agency supports the District Court's decision below. Thus, we hold that, if an agency chooses *expressly* to adopt or incorporate by reference an intra-agency memorandum previously covered by Exemption 5 in what would otherwise be a final opinion, that memorandum may be withheld only on the ground that it falls within the coverage of some exemption other than Exemption 5.

So ordered.

THE CHIEF JUSTICE concurs in the judgment.

MR. JUSTICE POWELL took no part in the consideration or decision of this case.

NOTES AND QUESTIONS

1. *Discovery against the government.* Note that FOIA Exemption 5 applies only to documents that "would not be available by law to a party other than an agency in litigation with the agency." Long before enactment of modern information statutes, litigants attempted to use the discovery process to obtain information from government officials. Under Rule 45 of the Federal Rules of Civil Procedure, for example, courts may order a custodian of records—whether

---

26. It is unnecessary, therefore, to decide whether petitioners are correct in asserting that, properly construed, "instructions to staff" do not in any event include documents prepared in furtherance of the "prosecution" of a specific case.

a private person or government official—to produce documents containing evidence relevant to a pending lawsuit. *See also* Fed. R. Civ. P. 34 (discovery from another party); Fed. R. Crim. P. 16(a)(1)(C) (compelled disclosure to criminal defendant of documents that are "material to the preparation of his defense"); Fed. R. Crim. P. 17(c) (discovery from nonparties to obtain evidence needed in defense).

Using discovery to compel disclosure of government information is limited to information that is not privileged. There are two basic forms of privilege available to government officials: evidentiary privileges and executive immunity. Evidentiary privilege, in this context, means a right to withhold information, such as state, military, or diplomatic secrets, the disclosure of which would be contrary to the public interest. The Supreme Court set out the rules controlling government claims of privilege in United States v. Reynolds, 345 U.S. 1 (1953): "There must be a formal claim of privilege, lodged by the head of the department which has control over the matter, after actual personal consideration by that officer." *Id.* at 7-8. Once a formal claim of privilege had been lodged, a court would evaluate it by balancing the intensity of the litigant's need for the information against the government's need for secrecy. If the court found a "reasonable possibility" that privileged information was involved, it would uphold the claim without even inspecting the documents. If the balance were more favorable to the requestor, the court could inspect the documents *in camera* to aid its decision.

Reynolds was a victory of sorts for private litigants because it made the courts, and not the agencies, the final arbiters of whether information is privileged. Although claims of privilege are usually upheld, agencies no longer have the last word. And, on occasion, litigants do win the balancing test. *See, e.g.,* In re Zuckert, 28 F.R.D. 29 (D.D.C. 1961).

2. *Executive privilege.* The government rarely asserts executive immunity, but it can be a powerful defense to oversight. The scope of this exemption remained in considerable doubt until 1973, when the Watergate scandal (described in Chapter I, *supra*) produced a famous constitutional confrontation. In March 1974, the Special Prosecutor, appointed to investigate alleged criminal violations arising out of the Watergate scandal, secured indictments from a federal grand jury charging top aides of President Nixon with obstruction of justice and naming the President himself as an unindicted co-conspirator. On motion of the Special Prosecutor, the U.S. District Court for the District of Columbia issued a subpoena commanding the President to turn over certain tape recordings, papers, and transcripts relating to various meetings between the President and members of his staff. The President moved to quash the subpoenas, invoking an absolute executive privilege to withhold "confidential conversations between a President and his close advisors." The Supreme Court, in a unanimous opinion authored by Chief Justice Burger, rejected the President's claim:

> The President's need for complete candor and objectivity from advisers calls for great deference from the courts. However, when the privilege depends solely on the broad, undifferentiated claim of public interest in the confidentiality of such conversations, a confrontation with other values arises. Absent a claim of need to protect military, diplomatic, or sensitive national security secrets, we find it difficult to accept the argument that even the very important interest in

confidentiality of Presidential communications is significantly diminished by production of such material for *in camera* inspection with all the protection that a district court will be obliged to provide. . . .

The impediment that an absolute, unqualified privilege would place in the way of the primary constitutional duty of the Judicial Branch to do justice in criminal prosecutions would plainly conflict with the function of the courts under Art. III.

United States v. Nixon, 418 U.S. 683, 706-707 (1974). Has *Nixon* aged well? In the modern era, are there different or stronger arguments for a more robust executive privilege?

3. *The attorney work product privilege.* The Supreme Court explored the "attorney work product" privilege as it relates to Exemption 5 in FTC v. Grolier, Inc., 462 U.S. 19 (1983). A corporation requested FTC documents relating to the commission's investigation of its subsidiary. The agency withheld the documents under Exemption 5. The court of appeals, noting the limited protection of work products under Rule 26(b)(3) of the Federal Rules of Civil Procedure, held that the FRC could not invoke the exemption unless it could show that the investigation had or would lead to litigation. The Supreme Court reversed, holding that attorney work products are exempt from mandatory disclosure regardless of the state of the litigation for which they were prepared. The statutory language of Exemption 5 requires reference to whether discovery could normally be required during litigation with an agency. Since work-product materials are normally immune from discovery unless a party can show "substantial need," they are certainly not "routinely available" to parties in litigation and are, thus, categorically exempt under Exemption 5.

4. *Confidential information.* In addition to the executive privilege and the attorney client and attorney work product privileges, the Court has held the common law privilege for confidential commercial information applicable to Exemption 5. In Federal Open Market Comm. of the Fed. Reserve Sys. v. Merrill, 443 U.S. 340 (1979), the Court held that the Federal Reserve could invoke such a privilege to justify brief delays in releasing directives relating to its open-market monetary transactions if the Fed could show that immediate release would "significantly harm the Government's monetary functions or commercial functions or commercial interests." The Court noted, however, that it would view with skepticism efforts to enlarge the sphere of discovery privileges made applicable to Exemption 5.

5. *"Inter-agency" memoranda.* Department of the Interior v. Klamath Water Users Protective Assn., 532 U.S. 1 (2001), presented the question whether written communications between the DOI and Indian tribes under its protective jurisdiction constitute "inter-agency" memoranda. The communications at issue dealt with tribal interests in water claims subject to federal and state legal proceedings. Acknowledging that Indian tribes are not "agencies" for purposes of FOIA, DOI had invoked a doctrine developed by several courts of appeals, which extends the inter-agency memoranda exemption to communications between federal agencies and government contractors employed by them. Assuming, without deciding, that this doctrine is consistent with the language and intent of FOIA, the Supreme Court unanimously held that the doctrine is not applicable in a case such as *Klamath,* where the external entity is representing its own

interests, rather than the government's interests—all the more so, when the external entity's interests (in this case, claims for scarce water) were in direct conflict with those of other private parties. Likewise, the Court refused to read an "Indian trust" exemption into FOIA. Although DOI serves as trustee for the tribes, FOIA's "general philosophy of full agency disclosure" takes precedence over confidentiality principles of common law trust doctrine.

c.   Law Enforcement

FEDERAL BUREAU OF INVESTIGATION
v. ABRAMSON
456 U.S. 615 (1982)

JUSTICE WHITE delivered the opinion of the Court.

The Freedom of Information Act . . . does not require the disclosure of "investigatory records compiled for law enforcement purposes" when the release of such records would interfere with effective law enforcement, impede the administration of justice, constitute an unwarranted invasion of privacy, or produce certain other specified consequences. §552(b)(7). The sole question presented in this case is whether information contained in records compiled for law enforcement purposes loses that exempt status when it is incorporated into records compiled for purposes other than law enforcement.

I

Respondent Howard Abramson is a professional journalist interested in the extent to which the White House may have used the Federal Bureau of Investigation (FBI) and its files to obtain derogatory information about political opponents. On June 23, 1976, Abramson filed a request pursuant to FOIA for specific documents relating to the transmittal from the FBI to the White House in 1969 of information concerning particular individuals who had criticized the administration.[2] The Bureau denied the request on grounds that the information was exempt from disclosure pursuant to §552(b)(6) (Exemption 6) and §552(b)(7)(C)

---

2. Abramson sought the following documents:

— Copies of any and all information contained in [FBI] files showing or indicating the transmittal of any documents or information from the FBI to the White House, or any White House aides, for the years 1969 and 1970, concerning the following individuals: Lowell P. Weicker, Jr.; Thomas J. Meskill; Joseph Duffey; Thomas J. Dodd; Alphonsus J. Donahue; John Lupton; Wallace C. Barnes; and Emilio Q. Daddario.

— Copies of any and all information so transmitted.

— An uncensored copy of the Oct. 6, 1969 letter from J. Edgar Hoover to John D. Ehrlichman by which Mr. Hoover transmits "memoranda" on several individuals to Mr. Ehrlichman.

— A copy of the original request letter from Mr. Ehrlichman to Mr. Hoover for that data.

— Copies of all data so transmitted by the Oct 6, 1969 letter from Mr. Hoover to Mr. Ehrlichman.

— A copy of the receipt signed by the recipient at the White House of the Oct. 6, 1969, letter.

658 F.2d 806, 808 (1980).

(Exemption 7(C)), both of which protect against unwarranted invasions of personal privacy. . . .

In December 1977, after unsuccessfully appealing both denials within the agency, Abramson filed suit in the United States District Court for the District of Columbia to enjoin the FBI from withholding the requested records. While the suit was pending, the FBI provided Abramson with 84 pages of documents, some intact and some with deletions. . . . In light of the released material and the Bureau's affidavit, Abramson modified his request, seeking only the material withheld from a single document consisting of a one-page memorandum from J. Edgar Hoover to John D. Ehrlichman, together with approximately 63 pages of "name check" summaries and attached documents. The "name check" summaries contained information, culled from existing FBI files, on 11 public figures.

The District Court found that the FBI had failed to show that the information was compiled for law enforcement rather than political purposes, but went on to rule that Exemption 7(C) was validly invoked by the Government because disclosure of the withheld materials would constitute an unwarranted invasion of personal privacy. . . .

The Court of Appeals reversed. . . . We now reverse.

II

[J]udicial review of an asserted Exemption 7 privilege requires a two-part inquiry. First, a requested document must be shown to have been an investigatory record "compiled for law enforcement purposes." If so, the agency must demonstrate that release of the material would have one of the six results specified in the Act.

As the case comes to us, it is agreed that the information withheld by the Bureau was originally compiled for law enforcement purposes. It is also settled that the name check summaries were developed pursuant to a request from the White House for information about certain public personalities and were not compiled for law enforcement purposes. Finally, it is not disputed that if the threshold requirement of Exemption 7 is met—if the documents were compiled for law enforcement purposes—the disclosure of such information would be an unwarranted invasion of privacy. The sole question for decision is whether information originally compiled for law enforcement purposes loses its Exemption 7 protection if summarized in a new document not created for law enforcement purposes.

III

No express answer is provided by the statutory language or by the legislative history. The Court of Appeals resolved the question in favor of Abramson by construing the threshold requirement of Exemption 7 in the following manner. The cover letter to the White House, along with the accompanying summaries and attachments, constituted a "record." Because that "record" was not compiled for law enforcement purposes, the material within it could not qualify for the exemption, regardless of the purpose for which that material was originally gathered and recorded and regardless of the impact that disclosure of such information would produce. The Court of Appeals supported its interpretation by distinguishing between documents and information. "[T]he statutory scheme of the FOIA very clearly indicates that exemptions from disclosure apply only to *documents,* and not to the use of information contained in such documents." 658 F.2d, at 813. A "record" is a "document" and, for the Court of Appeals, the document must be treated as a unit for purposes of deciding whether it was prepared for law enforcement purposes. . . .

The Court of Appeals' view is a tenable construction of Exemption 7, but there is another interpretation, equally plausible on the face of the statute, of the requirement that the record sought to be withheld must have been prepared for law enforcement purposes. If a requested document, such as the one sent to the White House in this case, contains or essentially reproduces all or part of a record that was previously compiled for law enforcement reasons, it is reasonably arguable that the law enforcement record does not lose its exemption by its subsequent inclusion in a document created for a nonexempt purpose. The Court of Appeals itself pointed the way to this alternative construction by indicating that Exemption 7 protected attachments to the name check summaries that were duplicates of original records compiled for law enforcement purposes. . . .

The question is whether FOIA permits the same result where the exempt record is not reproduced verbatim but is accurately reflected in summary form. The Court of Appeals would have it that because the FBI summarized the relevant records rather than reproducing them verbatim, the identical information no longer qualifies for the exemption. The originally compiled record and the derivative summary would be treated completely differently although the content of the information is the same and although the reasons for maintaining its confidentiality remain equally strong. We are of the view, however, that the statutory language is reasonably construable to protect that part of an otherwise nonexempt compilation which essentially reproduces and is substantially the equivalent of all or part of an earlier record made for law enforcement uses. Moreover, that construction of the statute rather than the interpretation embraced by the Court of Appeals, more accurately reflects the intention of Congress, is more consistent with the structure of the Act, and more fully serves the purposes of the statute. . . .

The 1974 amendments modified Exemption 7 in two ways. First, by substituting the word "records" for "files," Congress intended for courts to "consider the nature of the particular document as to which exemption was claimed, in order to avoid the possibility of impermissible 'commingling' by an agency's placing in an investigatory file material that did not legitimately have to be kept confidential." NLRB v. Robbins Tire & Rubber Co., 437 U.S. [214, 229-230 (1978)]. Second, by enumerating six particular objectives of the Exemption, the amendments required reviewing courts to "loo[k] to the reasons" for allowing withholding of information. *Id.,* at 230. The requirement that one of six types of harm must be demonstrated to prevent production of a record compiled for law enforcement purposes was a reaction to a line of cases decided by the Court of Appeals for the District of Columbia Circuit which read the original Exemption 7 as protecting all law enforcement files. The amendment requires that the Government "specify some harm in order to claim the exemption" rather than "affording all law enforcement matters a blanket exemption." 120 Cong. Rec. 36626 (1974), 1975 Source Book 413 (statement of Rep. Reid). The enumeration of these categories of undesirable consequences indicates Congress believed the harm of disclosing this type of information would outweigh its benefits. There is nothing to suggest, and no reason for believing, that Congress would have preferred a different outcome simply because the information is now reproduced in a non-law-enforcement record. . . .

IV

Neither are we persuaded by the several other arguments Abramson submits in support of the decision below.

First, we reject the argument that the legitimate interests in protecting information from disclosure under Exemption 7 are satisfied by other exemptions when a record has been recompiled for a non-law-enforcement purpose. In particular, Abramson submits that Exemption 6 suffices to protect the privacy interest of individuals. Even if this were so with respect to the particular information requested in this case, the threshold inquiry of what constitutes compilation for law enforcement purposes must be considered with regard for all six of the types of harm stemming from disclosure that Congress sought to prevent. Assuming that Exemption 6 provided fully comparable protection against disclosures which would constitute unwarranted invasions of privacy, a questionable proposition itself, no such companion provision in FOIA would halt the disclosure of information that might deprive an individual of a fair trial, interrupt a law enforcement investigation, safeguard confidential law enforcement techniques, or even protect the physical well-being of law enforcement personnel. No other provision of FOIA could compensate for the potential disruption in the flow of information to law enforcement agencies by individuals who might be deterred from speaking because of the prospect of disclosure. It is therefore critical that the compiled-for-law-enforcement requirement be construed to avoid the release of information that would produce the undesirable results specified.

For much the same reason, the result we reach today is fully consistent with our holding in NLRB v. Sears, Roebuck & Co., 421 U.S. 132, 148-154 (1975), that Exemption 5 . . . does not protect internal advisory communications when incorporated in a final agency decision. The purposes behind Exemption 5, protecting the give-and-take of the decisional process, were not violated by disclosure once an agency chooses expressly to adopt a particular text as its official view. As we have explained above, this cannot be said here. The reasons for an Exemption 7 exemption may well remain intact even though information in a law enforcement record is recompiled in another document for a non-law-enforcement function.

The result is also consistent with the oft-repeated caveat that FOIA exemptions are to be narrowly construed, Department of Air Force v. Rose, 425 U.S. 352, 361 (1976). While Congress established that the basic policy of the Act is in favor of disclosure, it recognized the important interests served by the exemptions. We are not asked in this case to expand Exemption 7 to agencies or material not envisioned by Congress: "It is . . . necessary for the very operation of our Government to allow it to keep confidential certain material such as the investigatory files of the Federal Bureau of Investigation." S. Rep. No. 813, 89th Cong., 1st Sess., 3 (1965). Reliance on this principle of narrow construction is particularly unpersuasive in this case where it is conceded that the information as originally compiled is exempt under Exemption 7 and where it is the respondent, not the Government, who urges a formalistic reading of the Act.

We are not persuaded that Congress' undeniable concern with possible misuse of governmental information for partisan political activity is the equivalent of a mandate to release any information which might document such activity. . . . Congress . . . created a scheme of categorical exclusion; it did not invite a judicial weighing of the benefits and evils of disclosure on a case-by-case basis.

V

We therefore find that the construction adopted by the Court of Appeals, while plausible on the face of the statute, lacks support in the legislative history and would frustrate the purposes of Exemption 7. We hold that information initially contained in a record made for law enforcement purposes continues to meet the threshold requirements of Exemption 7 where that recorded information is reproduced or summarized in a new document prepared for a non-law-enforcement purpose. Of course, it is the agency's burden to establish that the requested information originated in a record protected by Exemption 7. The Court of Appeals refused to consider such a showing as a sufficient reason for withholding certain information. The judgment of the Court of Appeals is therefore reversed, and the case is remanded to that court for further proceedings consistent with this opinion.

So ordered.

JUSTICE BLACKMUN, with whom JUSTICE BRENNAN joins, dissenting. [Omitted.]

JUSTICE O'CONNOR, with whom JUSTICE MARSHALL joins, dissenting. . . .

At issue in this case[2] is the meaning of the seven-word phrase Congress used to describe the documents it intended to exempt: "investigatory records compiled for law enforcement purposes." . . .

Since neither of the parties before this Court contends that the District Court erred in finding that the records at issue, though perhaps "investigatory," were "not compiled for law enforcement purposes," . . . the case would, at first blush, seem to be over: the documents withheld by the FBI do not fit within the language of the Exemption and, therefore, must be released to the respondent.

The logic of this straightforward result is all the more compelling in light of the canons of construction peculiar to FOIA cases. As we have emphasized

---

2. The Court rephrases the "sole question for decision" as "whether information originally compiled for law enforcement purposes loses its Exemption 7 protection if summarized in a new document not created for law enforcement purposes." . . . The question presented by this case, however, is simply whether the contested documents are "investigatory records compiled for law enforcement purposes" within the meaning of Exemption 7.

before, the enumerated exemptions to the FOIA "[were] explicitly made exclusive," EPA v. Mink, 410 U.S. 73, 79 (1973), and "must be narrowly construed." Department of Air Force v. Rose, 425 U.S. 352, 361 (1976) (citations omitted). . . .

The Court, however, rejects the plain language of Exemption 7 without identifying any "obvious" evidence of a "clearly expressed" congressional intention to have Exemption 7 mean something other than what it says. In fact, the Court candidly admits that "[n]o express answer is provided . . . by the legislative history," . . . which explains, perhaps, why the Court's opinion is nearly devoid of references to it. . . .

Even without the legislative history on its side, to be sure, the Court might be entitled to reject the plain language of Exemption 7 in order to avoid "patently absurd consequences," United States v. Brown, 333 U.S. 18, 27 (1948), that Congress could not possibly have intended. The Court, however, cannot, and does not, claim that the plain language of Exemption 7 leads to such results, though the Court . . . accuses Congress of having arbitrarily drawn the line between exempt and nonexempt materials.

Congress, however, ordinarily is free to draw lines without cavil from the Court, so long as it respects the constitutional proprieties. We do not, and should not, make it our business to second-guess the Legislature's judgment when it comes to such matters. Line-drawing, after all, frequently requires arbitrary decisions that cannot sensibly be subjected to judicial review. . . .

The particular balance struck by Congress and enshrined in Exemption 7 may be open to attack as ill-advised, but, exactly because it represents a compromise between competing policies, it cannot be said to lead to results so "patently absurd" that a court can only conclude that Congress did not mean what it said.

NOTES AND QUESTIONS

1. *"Compiled for law enforcement purposes."* The Court assumes, because there is no longer any dispute, that the records in question were *originally* "compiled for law enforcement purposes." The Supreme Court had occasion to construe the term "compiled" in the case of John Doe Agency v. John Doe Corp., 493 U.S. 146 (1989). The "John Doe Corporation" was a defense contractor subject to a 1985 grand jury investigation into possible fraudulent practices in connection with the allocation of costs to government contracts. Following receipt of a subpoena for documents relating to a prior contract, the corporation requested the Defense Department's Defense Contract Audit Agency (DCAA) to provide it with records relating to an audit of the corporation conducted by DCAA in 1978. Upon the recommendation of the U.S. Attorney, DCAA refused to disclose the records. Two days later, DCAA transferred the records to the FBI. The corporation requested the records from the FBI, which also refused. In declining the request, DCAA and the FBI both invoked Exemption 7(A). The corporation argued that Exemption 7 did not apply because the records at issue had originally been created as part of a routine financial audit and hence had not been "compiled for law enforcement purposes." The agencies answered that the records had been assembled into a law enforcement file and were therefore exempt.

The Supreme Court agreed with the two agencies:

> A compilation, in its ordinary meaning, is something composed of materials collected and assembled from various sources or other documents. . . . This definition seems readily to cover documents already collected by the Government originally for non-law-enforcement purposes.

493 U.S. at 153. Justice Scalia dissented on the ground that the well-established doctrine of narrowly construing FOIA exemptions required the Court to select the narrower meaning of "compiled" (i.e., "created") rather than the broader meaning ("assembled" or "gathered").

2. *Confidential sources.* As the Court noted in *Abramson,* FOIA's exemption for "investigatory records compiled for law enforcement purposes" applies only if the agency can demonstrate that one of six enumerated harms would result from disclosure. One of these harms is the "disclos[ure of] the identity of a confidential source [or] confidential information furnished only by the confidential source." How does a law enforcement agency show that a source was "confidential"?

In Department of Justice v. Landano, 508 U.S. 165 (1993), the government argued that a presumption of confidentiality should arise whenever "any individual or institutional source supplies information to the [FBI] during a criminal investigation." The Supreme Court refused to recognize such a categorical presumption, given the wide variety of sources on which the FBI relies. But the Court did recognize that confidentiality might be inferred from the circumstances and need not be proven by a particular assurance of confidentiality.

3. *Intelligence and national security.* Another context in which protection of confidential sources looms large is intelligence gathering to protect national security. As originally enacted, FOIA Exemption 1 provided a broad basis to withhold records for this reason. Congress tightened the exemption in 1974 by adding what is now clause (B) and by expressly authorizing courts to conduct *in camera* review under "any" FOIA exemption (including Exemption 1). But the courts remain highly deferential to claims of national security made by intelligence agencies, whether grounded on Exemption 1 or some other statutory source. An example is Central Intelligence Agency v. Sims, 471 U.S. 159 (1985). Between 1953 and 1966, the CIA contracted with various universities and research foundations to conduct research on chemical, biological, and radiological warfare. In 1977, representatives of a public interest group filed a FOIA request with the CIA, seeking information on the research projects. The CIA provided some information on the research projects, but specifically refused to disclose the names of the researchers or their institutional affiliations. In justifying his refusal to disclose the information, the CIA Director invoked §102(d)(3) of the National Security Act, which requires the Director to protect "intelligence sources and methods from unauthorized disclosure." The requesters argued that a particular source of information could not be classified as an "intelligence source" unless the reviewing court found that the source would not have supplied the information without a promise of confidentiality. The Supreme Court, upholding the Director's decision, disagreed:

We seriously doubt whether a potential intelligence source will rest assured knowing that judges, who have little or no background in the delicate business of intelligence gathering, will order his identity revealed only after examining the facts of
the case to determine whether the Agency actually needed to promise confidentiality in order to obtain the information.

471 U.S. at 176. Nor was the Court impressed with the fact that some of the
information sought by the requesters was otherwise publicly available:

Disclosure of the subject matter of the Agency's research efforts and inquiries may
compromise the Agency's ability to gather intelligence as much as disclosure of
the identities of intelligence sources. A foreign government can learn a great deal
about the Agency's activities by knowing the public sources of information that
interest the Agency. [H]ad foreign governments learned the Agency was [conduct-
ing] research of "brainwashing" and certain countermeasures, they might have
been able to infer both the general nature of the project and the general scope
that the Agency's inquiry was taking.

471 U.S. at 176-177.
    The so-called war on terror launched in the wake of September 11, 2001,
significantly strengthened the "national security" rationale for withholding
government records. An example is provided by Center for National Security
Studies v. United States Dept. of Justice, 331 F.3d 918 (D.C. Cir. 2003). Following the terrorist attacks, the government launched a massive investigation of
persons suspected to have ties to or knowledge about al Qaeda or other terrorist organizations. As a result, a large number of persons—estimated to exceed
1,100—were detained for various reasons, including asserted immigration law
violations, criminal conduct, or possession of information relevant to grand jury
investigations. A group of concerned organizations filed a FOIA request with
the Justice Department seeking disclosure of the names of every such detainee
and their lawyers, and other information about their arrest, detention, and status. Rejecting the request, a panel of the D.C. Circuit ruled that the information sought constituted "records or information compiled for law enforcement
purposes" that "could reasonably be expected to interfere with enforcement
proceedings" under Exemption 7(A). Judge Sentelle, writing for a two-judge
majority, found "reasonable" the government's assertion, contained in two official affidavits, that disclosure "would enable al Qaeda or other terrorist groups
to map the course of the investigation and thus develop the means to impede
it," and that "disclosure would deter or hinder cooperation by detainees" by subjecting them to possible intimidation or coercion. 331 F.3d at 928-929. Dissenting, Judge Tatel argued that the court had granted excessive deference to the
government's affidavits. In his view, the government's argument was much too
sweeping and categorical, lumping together all detainees, regardless of whether
they had been charged with crimes or whether they had been found to possess
information relevant to the terrorist attacks. Is there a risk that, on occasions
when the need for transparency is at its highest (in terms of the difficulty of
obtaining the information otherwise and the public interest in accountability),
the tendency for courts to defer to government claims of exemption from FOIA
might also be at its zenith? Or should the balance always tip in favor of the
government when it asserts a national security interest?

d. Privacy

DEPARTMENT OF JUSTICE v. REPORTERS COMMITTEE
FOR FREEDOM OF THE PRESS
489 U.S. 749 (1989)

JUSTICE STEVENS delivered the opinion of the Court.

The Federal Bureau of Investigation (FBI) has accumulated and maintains criminal identification records, sometimes referred to as "rap sheets," on over 24 million persons. The question presented by this case is whether the disclosure of the contents of such a file to a third party "could reasonably be expected to constitute an unwarranted invasion of personal privacy" within the meaning of [FOIA Exemption 7(c)].

I

In 1924 Congress appropriated funds to enable the Department of Justice (Department) to establish a program to collect and preserve fingerprints and other criminal identification records. 43 Stat. 217. That statute authorized the Department to exchange such information with "officials of States, cities and other institutions." *Ibid.* Six years later Congress created the FBI's identification division, and gave it responsibility for "acquiring, collecting, classifying, and preserving criminal identification and other crime records and the exchanging of said criminal identification records with the duly authorized officials of governmental agencies, of States, cities, and penal institutions." Ch. 455, 46 Stat. 554. . . . Rap sheets compiled pursuant to such authority contain certain descriptive information, such as date of birth and physical characteristics, as well as a history of arrests, charges, convictions, and incarcerations of the subject. Normally a rap sheet is preserved until its subject attains age 80. Because of the volume of rap sheets, they are sometimes incorrect or incomplete and sometimes contain information about other persons with similar names.

The local, state, and federal law enforcement agencies throughout the Nation that exchange rap-sheet data with the FBI do so on a voluntary basis. The principal use of the information is to assist in the detection and prosecution of offenders; it is also used by courts and corrections officials in connection with sentencing and parole decisions. As a matter of executive policy, the Department has generally treated rap sheets as confidential and, with certain exceptions, has restricted their use to governmental purposes. [The FBI, as a matter of agency policy, allows the subject of a rap sheet to obtain a copy, and sometimes uses rap-sheet information in preparing publicity designed to assist in the apprehension of wanted persons. In three statutes enacted between 1972 and 1986, Congress explicitly permitted disclosure of rap sheets to authorities responsible for regulating the banking, securities, and nuclear power industries.]

Although much rap-sheet information is a matter of public record, the availability and dissemination of the actual rap sheet to the public is limited. Arrests, indictments, convictions, and sentences are public events that are usually documented in court records. In addition, if a person's entire criminal history transpired in a single jurisdiction, all of the contents of his or her rap sheet may be available upon request in that jurisdiction. That possibility, however, is present in only three States. All of the other 47 States place substantial restrictions on the availability of criminal-history summaries even though individual events in those summaries are matters of public record. Moreover, even in Florida, Wisconsin, and Oklahoma, the publicly available summaries may not include information about out-of-state arrests or convictions. . . .

III

This case arises out of requests made by a CBS news correspondent and the Reporters Committee for Freedom of the Press (respondents) for information concerning the criminal records of four members of the Medico family. The Pennsylvania Crime Commission had identified the family's company, Medico Industries, as a legitimate business dominated by organized crime figures. Moreover, the company allegedly had obtained a number of defense contracts as a result of an improper arrangement with a corrupt Congressman.

The FOIA requests sought disclosure of any arrests, indictments, acquittals, convictions, and sentences of any of the four Medicos. Although the FBI originally denied the requests, it provided the requested data concerning three of the Medicos after their deaths. In their complaint in the District Court, respondents sought the rap sheet for the fourth, Charles Medico (Medico), insofar as it contained "matters of public record." [The District Court granted the Department's motion for summary judgment, and the D.C. Circuit reversed.] We now reverse.

IV

Exemption 7(C) requires us to balance the privacy interest in maintaining, as the government puts it, the "practical obscurity" of the rap sheets against the public interest in their release.

The preliminary question is whether Medico's interest in the nondisclosure of any rap sheet the FBI might have on him is the sort of "personal privacy" interest that Congress intended Exemption 7(C) to protect.[13] As we have pointed out before, "[t]he cases sometimes characterized as protecting 'privacy' have in fact involved at least two different kinds of interests. One is the individual interest in avoiding disclosure of personal matters, and another is the interest in independence in making certain kinds of important decisions." Whalen v. Roe, 429 U.S. 589, 598-600 (1977) (footnotes omitted). Here, the former interest, "in avoiding disclosure of personal matters," is implicated. Because events summarized in a rap sheet have been previously disclosed to the public, respondents contend that Medico's privacy interest in avoiding disclosure of a federal

---

13. The question of the statutory meaning of privacy under the FOIA is, of course, not the same as the question whether a tort action might lie for invasion of privacy or the question whether an individual's interest in privacy is protected by the Constitution. . . .

compilation of these events approaches zero. We reject respondents' cramped notion of personal privacy.

To begin with, both the common law and the literal understandings of privacy encompass the individual's control of information concerning his or her person. In an organized society, there are few facts that are not at one time or another divulged to another. Thus the extent of the protection accorded a privacy right at common law rested in part on the degree of dissemination of the allegedly private fact and the extent to which the passage of time rendered it private. According to Webster's initial definition, information may be classified as "private" if it is "intended for or restricted to the use of a particular person or group or class of persons: not freely available to the public."[16] Recognition of this attribute of a privacy interest supports the distinction, in terms of personal privacy, between scattered disclosure of the bits of information contained in a rap sheet and revelation of the rap sheet as a whole. The very fact that federal funds have been spent to prepare, index, and maintain these criminal-history files demonstrates that the individual items of information in the summaries would not otherwise be "freely available" either to the officials who have access to the underlying files or to the general public. Indeed, if the summaries were "freely available," there would be no reason to invoke the FOIA to obtain access to the information they contain. Granted, in many contexts the fact that information is not freely available is no reason to exempt that information from a statute generally requiring its dissemination. But the issue here is whether the compilation of otherwise hard-to-obtain information alters the privacy interest implicated by disclosure of that information. Plainly there is a vast difference between the public records that might be found after a diligent search of courthouse files, county archives, and local police stations throughout the country and a computerized summary located in a single clearinghouse of information. . . .

Also supporting our conclusion that a strong privacy interest inheres in the nondisclosure of compiled computerized information is the Privacy Act of 1974, *codified at* 5 U.S.C. §552a (1982 ed. and Supp. V). The Privacy Act was passed largely out of concern over "the impact of computer data banks on individual privacy." H.R. Rep. No. 93-1416, p. 7 (1974). The Privacy Act provides generally that "[n]o agency shall disclose any record which is contained in a system of records . . . except pursuant to a written request by, or with the prior written consent of, the individual to whom the record pertains." 5 U.S.C. §552a(b). Although the Privacy Act contains a variety of exceptions to this rule, including an exemption for information required to be disclosed under the FOIA, *see* 5 U.S.C. §552a(b)(2), Congress' basic policy concern regarding the implications of computerized data banks for personal privacy is certainly relevant in our consideration of the privacy interest affected by dissemination of rap sheets from the FBI computer. . . .

[O]ur cases have also recognized the privacy interest inherent in the nondisclosure of certain information even where the information may have been at one time public. Most apposite for present purposes is our decision in Department of Air Force v. Rose, 425 U.S. 352 (1976). New York University law students

---

16. *See* Webster's Third New International Dictionary 1804 (1976). . . .

sought Air Force Academy Honor and Ethics Code case summaries for a law review project on military discipline. The Academy had already publicly posted these summaries on 40 squadron bulletin boards, usually with identifying names redacted (names were posted for cadets who were found guilty and who left the Academy), and with instructions that cadets should read the summaries only if necessary. . . . *Even though the summaries, with only names redacted, had once been public,* we recognized the potential invasion of privacy through later recognition of identifying details, and approved the Court of Appeals' rule permitting the District Court to delete "other identifying information" in order to safeguard this privacy interest. If a cadet has a privacy interest in past discipline that was once public but may have been "wholly forgotten," the ordinary citizen surely has a similar interest in the aspects of his or her criminal history that may have been wholly forgotten. . . .

V

Exemption 7(C), by its terms, permits an agency to withhold a document only when revelation "could reasonably be expected to constitute an unwarranted invasion of personal privacy." We must next address what factors might warrant an invasion of the interest described in Part IV, *supra.*

[W]hether disclosure of a private document under Exemption 7(C) is warranted must turn on the nature of the requested document and its relationship to "the basic purpose of the Freedom of Information Act 'to open agency action to the light of public scrutiny.'" Department of Air Force v. Rose, 425 U.S., at 372, rather than on the particular purpose for which the document is being requested. In our leading case on the FOIA, we declared that the Act was designed to create a broad right of access to "official information." EPA v. Mink, 410 U.S. 73, 80 (1973). In his dissent in that case, Justice Douglas characterized the philosophy of the statute by quoting this comment by Henry Steele Commager:

> "'The generation that made the nation thought secrecy in government one of the instruments of Old World tyranny and committed itself to the principle that a democracy cannot function unless the people are permitted to know what their government is up to.'" *Id.,* at 105 (quoting from The New York Review of Books, Oct. 5, 1972, p. 7) (emphasis added).

This basic policy of "'full agency disclosure unless information is exempted under clearly delineated statutory language,'" Department of Air Force v. Rose, 425 U.S., at 360-361 (quoting S. Rep. No. 813, 89th Cong., 1st Sess., 3 (1965)), indeed focuses on the citizens' right to be informed about "what their government is up to." Official information that sheds light on an agency's performance of its statutory duties falls squarely within that statutory purpose. That purpose, however, is not fostered by disclosure of information about private citizens that is accumulated in various governmental files but that reveals little or nothing about an agency's own conduct. In this case—and presumably in the typical case in which one private citizen is seeking information about another—the requester does not intend to discover anything about the conduct of the agency that has possession of the requested records. Indeed, response to this request would not shed any light on the conduct of any Government agency or official. . . .

Respondents argue that there is a twofold public interest in learning about Medico's past arrests or convictions: He allegedly had improper dealings with a corrupt Congressman, and he is an officer of a corporation with defense contracts. But if Medico has, in fact, been arrested or convicted of certain crimes, that information would neither aggravate nor mitigate his allegedly improper relationship with the Congressman; more specifically, it would tell us nothing directly about the character of the Congressman's behavior. Nor would it tell us anything about the conduct of the Department of Defense (DOD) in awarding one or more contracts to the Medico Company. Arguably a FOIA request to the DOD for records relating to those contracts, or for documents describing the agency's procedures, if any, for determining whether officers of a prospective contractor have criminal records, would constitute an appropriate request for "official information." Conceivably Medico's rap sheet would provide details to include in a news story, but, in itself, this is not the kind of public interest for which Congress enacted the FOIA. In other words, although there is undoubtedly some public interest in anyone's criminal history, especially if the history is in some way related to the subject's dealing with a public official or agency, the FOIA's central purpose is to ensure that the Government's activities be opened to the sharp eye of public scrutiny, not that information about private citizens that happens to be in the warehouse of the Government be so disclosed. Thus, it should come as no surprise that in none of our cases construing the FOIA have we found it appropriate to order a Government agency to honor a FOIA request for information about a particular private citizen.[21] . . .

VI

Both the general requirement that a court "shall determine the matter de novo" and the specific reference to an "unwarranted" invasion of privacy in Exemption 7(C) indicate that a court must balance the public interest in disclosure against the interest Congress intended the Exemption to protect. Although both sides agree that such a balance must be undertaken, how such a balance should be done is in dispute. The Court of Appeals majority expressed concern about assigning federal judges the task of striking a proper case-by-case, or ad hoc, balance between individual privacy interests and the public interest in the disclosure of criminal-history information without providing those judges standards to assist in performing that task. Our cases provide support for the proposition that categorical decisions may be appropriate and individual circumstances disregarded when a case fits into a genus in which the balance characteristically tips in one direction. . . . The privacy interest in maintaining the practical obscurity of rap-sheet information will always be high. When the subject of such a rap sheet is a private citizen and when the information is in

21. In fact, in at least three cases we have specifically *rejected* requests for information about private citizens. *See* CIA v. Sims, 471 U.S. 159 (1985); FBI v. Abramson, 456 U.S. 615 (1982); United States Department of State v. Washington Post Co., 456 U.S. 595 (1982).

the Government's control as a compilation, rather than as a record of "what the Government is up to," the privacy interest protected by Exemption 7(C) is in fact at its apex while the FOIA-based public interest in disclosure is at its nadir. . . . Such a disparity on the scales of justice holds for a class of cases without regard to individual circumstances; the standard virtues of bright-line rules are thus present, and the difficulties attendant to ad hoc adjudication may be avoided. Accordingly, we hold as a categorical matter that a third party's request for law enforcement records or information about a private citizen can reasonably be expected to invade that citizen's privacy, and that when the request seeks no "official information" about a Government agency, but merely records that the Government happens to be storing, the invasion of privacy is "unwarranted." The judgment of the Court of Appeals is reversed.

It is so ordered.

JUSTICE BLACKMUN, with whom JUSTICE BRENNAN joins, concurring in the judgment.

I concur in the result the Court reaches in this case, but I cannot follow the route the Court takes to reach that result. In other words, the Court's use of "categorical balancing" under Exemption 7(C), I think, is not basically sound. Such a bright-line rule obviously has its appeal, but I wonder whether it would not run aground on occasion, such as in a situation where a rap sheet discloses a congressional candidate's conviction of tax fraud five years before. Surely, the FBI's disclosure of that information could not "reasonably be expected" to constitute an invasion of personal privacy, much less an unwarranted invasion, inasmuch as the candidate relinquished any interest in preventing the dissemination of this information when he chose to run for Congress. In short, I do not believe that Exemption 7(C)'s language and its legislative history, or the case law, support interpreting that provision as exempting all rap-sheet information from the FOIA's disclosure requirements. . . .

NOTES AND QUESTIONS

1. *The nature and weight of "privacy" interests.* Do you agree with the Court that Medico has a privacy interest in the nondisclosure of rap-sheet information otherwise available from public records? Given FOIA's strong bias in favor of disclosure, is that the sort of information that ought to be protected from disclosure? How does Medico's privacy interest stack up against that of the Air Force Academy cadets in *Rose*?

2. *"Unwarranted invasion" of privacy.* Protection of personal privacy features explicitly in FOIA Exemptions 6 (relating to personnel and medical files) and 7 (law enforcement files). Both use the language "unwarranted invasion of personal privacy." Although Exemption 6 adds the adverb "clearly," the courts use pretty much the same sort of "balancing test" to interpret and apply both exemptions. Does the Court in *Reporters Committee* do a creditable job of identifying and weighing the competing interests? In determining the "public interest" in favor of disclosure, the Court says that the purpose for which the records are sought is irrelevant. Why? How can you put a value on the disclosure of information without knowing how it will be used? Does the structure of FOIA preclude

courts from inquiring into a requester's motives or purposes? Is the Court's "what the government is up to" test coherent? Is it so clear that releasing the Medico rap sheet would not reveal much about "what the government is up to"?

As Justice Stevens noted, given the Court's rather restrictive definition of "public interest," the courts hardly ever order disclosure of personal private information. For example, in United States Dept. of State v. Ray, 502 U.S. 164 (1991), the Supreme Court refused to compel release of the names of Haitians who had been interviewed by State Department officials following the denial of their claims for asylum and their involuntary return to Haiti. The Court recognized a public interest in knowing whether the "State Department has adequately monitored Haiti's compliance with its promise not to prosecute returnees." But, said the Court, the release of summaries of the interviews with names and addresses of interviewees redacted adequately served that public interest, while protecting the interviewees' privacy interest.

3. *Whose privacy interests are protected?* In National Archives v. Favish, 541 U.S. 157 (2004), the Supreme Court unanimously ruled that Exemption 7(C) permitted the government to refuse to release death-scene photographs of a dead body, in the interest of protecting the sensibilities of the decedent's family members. The Court read "personal privacy" to embrace the interest, recognized in "the common law and our cultural traditions," of family members "to limit attempts to exploit pictures of the deceased family member's remains for public purposes." 541 U.S. at 167. This was no ordinary case. The decedent was Vincent Foster, Jr., deputy counsel to President Clinton and a long-time friend and confidant of the President and Mrs. Clinton. Foster was found dead in a federal park outside Washington, D.C. The U.S. Park Police investigation concluded that he had committed suicide by shooting himself with a revolver found in his hand. News of the death triggered sensationalistic speculation that he was murdered to cover up information adverse to the Clintons. The speculations persisted despite the findings of five subsequent federal investigations that Foster died by his own hand. Allan Favish, a citizen who believed that the government's investigations were "grossly incomplete and untrustworthy," sought disclosure of the death-scene photographs. The lower court had ordered disclosure of some of the photographs, finding that Favish's belief in government misfeasance was sufficient to outweigh the family's privacy interests. The Supreme Court reversed, concluding that, in order to overcome an established privacy interest, the requester must "produce evidence that would warrant a belief by a reasonable person that the alleged Government impropriety might have occurred." *Id.* at 174. Having produced no such evidence, there was nothing to "balance" against the privacy interest. Would the same reasoning apply to, say, a situation in which a defendant allegedly committed suicide in a federal prison and suspicions emerged about foul play? Could the Bureau of Prisons conduct an investigation and refuse to release death-scene photographs or other material from the investigation on the theory that it protects the family's privacy, even if the family had made no such claim or disputed that characterization?

4. *"Similar files."* Exemption 6 protects not only "personnel and medical files," but also "similar files." The Supreme Court gave an expansive reading to the latter phrase in the *Washington Post* case cited in the Court's footnote 21. In that case the Court upheld the State Department's refusal to disclose records of the Passport Office showing the citizenship of two named individuals. The

Court defined "similar files" to include any "'detailed Government records on an individual which can be identified as applying to that individual.'" 456 U.S. at 602, *quoting* H.R. Rep. No. 1497, 89th Cong., 2d Sess. 11 (1966).

5. *The Privacy Act.* Congressional concern to protect personal privacy did not cease with the enactment of FOIA Exemptions 2, 6, and 7. In the Privacy Act of 1974, *codified at* 5 U.S.C. §552a, Congress took steps to provide more affirmative protection to individuals against the unauthorized disclosure of personal information and the compilation and use of incorrect information. The heart of the Act is subsection (b) (§552a(b)), which provides:

> No agency shall disclose any record which is contained in a system of records by any means of communication to any person, or to another agency, except pursuant to a written request by, or with the prior consent of, the individual to whom the record pertains. . . .

There follow 11 instances in which disclosure is authorized, without the subject's consent, including disclosure to employees of the agency who use the record "in the performance of their duties," disclosure required by FOIA, "routine" agency use, and disclosure to various other branches or agencies of the government. Agencies are required to keep strict account of each disclosure made. The Act also sets out certain requirements that agencies must follow in collecting and maintaining systems of records on individuals, and requires that agencies must, upon request, grant individuals access to their records and to any information pertaining to them.

To avoid conflict between FOIA and the Privacy Act, §(b)(2) of the Privacy Act provides that the Act's disclosure restrictions do not apply when disclosure is required by the FOIA. Thus, when individual privacy concerns arise in a case where disclosure is arguably required by the FOIA, the individual is left to the balancing test performed pursuant to FOIA Exemption 6.

6. *Commercial "privacy."* Three of the FOIA exemptions—numbers 4, 8, and 9—reflect a congressional desire to protect the "privacy" of certain business information. The most important of these three is Exemption 4, which applies to "trade secrets and commercial or financial information obtained from a person and privileged or confidential." As this language has been uniformly interpreted by the courts, "trade secrets" are fully protected, whereas "commercial or financial information" is protected only if "obtained from a person and privileged or confidential." *See, e.g.,* Public Citizen Health Research Group v. FDA, 704 F.2d 1280 (D.C. Cir. 1983). In Food Marketing Inst. v. Argus Leader Media, 139 S. Ct. 2356 (2019), the Supreme Court had occasion to interpret the term "confidential" in Exemption 4. Echoing the *Milner* case, the Court applied the "ordinary, contemporary common meaning" test to reject an interpretive gloss that lower courts had grafted onto Exemption 4: namely, that commercial or financial information should be protected only if its disclosure would cause "substantial competitive harm" to the entity whose information was at issue. Rather, said the Court, "confidential" merely means "private" and "secret." The former condition was satisfied because petitioners did not publicly reveal the information; the latter was satisfied because the government agency provided assurances to petitioners that the information would not be disclosed.

There are many other federal statutes, such as the Trade Secrets Act, 18 U.S.C. §1905, that restrict the disclosure of specified kinds of commercial or financial information. Some of these statutes have been held to be qualifying statutes under FOIA Exemption 3 (discussed in the *Common Cause* case, *infra*), which exempts matters "specifically exempted from disclosure" by another federal statute that meets certain criteria. In Consumer Products Safety Commn. v. GTE Sylvania, Inc., 447 U.S. 102, 121-123 (1980), the Supreme Court found that Exemption 3 applied to §6(b)(1) of the Consumer Product Safety Act, 15 U.S.C. §2055(b)(1), which prohibits disclosure of certain product-related information until the manufacturer has an opportunity to comment on its accuracy. The Trade Secrets Act, on the other hand, has been held to be insufficiently "specific" to qualify as an Exemption 3 statute. *See, e.g.,* National Parks & Conserv. Assn. v. Kleppe, 547 F.2d 673 (D.C. Cir. 1976).

For an interesting decision concerning corporate privacy under FOIA, *see* FCC v. AT&T Inc., 562 U.S. 397 (2011). In this case, a trade association representing AT&T's competitors sought records related to an investigation of overcharging by AT&T in a program providing telecommunications to schools and libraries. The FCC denied access to some records under Exemption 4, relating to "trade secrets and commercial or financial information" but rejected AT&T's argument that additional records were shielded under Exemption 7(C) as records "compiled for law enforcement purposes" that "could reasonably be expected to constitute an unwarranted invasion of personal privacy." The FCC reasoned that corporations do not have personal privacy interests protected under the exemption. The Supreme Court, in an opinion by Chief Justice Roberts, agreed, concluding that while corporations may be "persons," the statutory context indicates that they do not have "personal privacy" interests under FOIA.

B. PUBLIC ACCESS TO ADMINISTRATIVE DELIBERATIONS

As mechanisms for opening up the administrative process to greater public scrutiny, FOIA and its state law counterparts are inherently limited in their reach. Focusing, as they do, on the disclosure of *written* information, they leave untouched that vast hidden province of governmental deliberations conducted solely by the spoken word. In an effort to remedy that shortcoming, many states enacted "open meeting" laws requiring public boards and commissions, elected and appointed, to conduct their business meetings in public. The federal government was slow to follow suit. It was not until the 1970s that Congress took significant steps to require that the meetings of federal instrumentalities be conducted in the open. The Federal Advisory Committee Act of 1972, Pub. L. No. 92-463, 86 Stat. 770, *codified at* 5 U.S.C. App. I, first applied that principle to the meetings of committees established to advise federal agencies. In 1973, the House of Representatives adopted House Resolution 259 to strengthen the presumption that all House committee sessions be open to public observation. 119 Cong. Rec. H6706-6720 (1973). The Senate followed suit two years later with

Senate Resolution 9. 121 Cong. Rec. S35,181-35,219 (1975). Finally, on September 13, 1976, after four years of hearings, debates, and amendments, Congress enacted a general open-meeting law, the Government in the Sunshine Act. Pub. L. No. 94-409, *codified at* 5 U.S.C. §552b.

The Sunshine Act requires the meetings of all federal agencies headed by "collegial bodies" to be open to public observation unless they fit into one of the ten exemptions in subsection (c). To close a meeting, an agency must publicly vote to do so, follow specific procedures, and keep a verbatim transcript of the proceedings. §552b(d), (f). The statute provides broad enforcement jurisdiction to the federal courts and authorizes the award of attorney's fees to successful litigants. §552b(h). The Act also (by inserting 5 U.S.C. §557(d)), specifically requires that an ex parte communication in a formal adjudicatory proceeding be made a part of the record of that proceeding.

Critics of the Act had expressed fears that open meetings would end candid discussions, induce grandstanding, and undermine efficiency and order in the conduct of business. While Congress was aware that the Sunshine Act would involve some costs, it was even more profoundly disturbed by the public's low opinion of government in the wake of the Watergate scandal. The Act's sponsors hoped that the public's faith in government would be restored by having better access to agency decisionmaking processes. As one supporter put it rather bluntly: "Most of those meetings are so boring that nobody would attend them anyway, so why not open them up and make the transcripts available and remove the cloud?" Government in the Sunshine Act: Hearings on H.R. 10315 and H.R. 9868, Before the Government Information and Individual Rights Subcomm. of the House Comm. on Government Operations, 94th Cong., 1st Sess. 41 (1974) (remarks of Representative Dante Fascell). Other proponents maintained, however, that the Act would achieve far more tangible improvements in the operation of government by encouraging better attendance, a higher level of preparation, and more succinct and articulate debate at administrative meetings.

1. "Meetings of an Agency"

Whether the Act has fulfilled the expectations of its more cynical or more optimistic supporters remains debatable. The answer depends in part on how the courts have interpreted its various limitations and exceptions. We focus on two important interpretive issues under the Act: what is a "meeting of an agency" and what meetings may be closed under the Act's ten exemptions. The first of these issues is taken up here; the other, in the subsection that follows.

FEDERAL COMMUNICATIONS COMMISSION
v. ITT WORLD COMMUNICATIONS, INC.
466 U.S. 463 (1984)

JUSTICE POWELL delivered the opinion of the Court.

The Government in the Sunshine Act, 5 U.S.C. §552b, mandates that federal agencies hold their meetings in public. This case requires us to consider whether the Act applies to informal international conferences attended by members of the Federal Communications Commission. . . .

I

Members of petitioner, the Federal Communications Commission (FCC), participate with their European and Canadian counterparts in what is referred to as the Consultative Process. This is a series of conferences intended to facilitate joint planning of telecommunications facilities through an exchange of information on regulatory policies. At the time of the conferences at issue in the present case, only three American corporations—respondents ITT World Communications, Inc. (ITT), and RCA Global Communications, Inc., and Western Union International—provided overseas record telecommunications services. Although the FCC had approved entry into the market by other competitors, European regulators had been reluctant to do so. The FCC therefore added the topic of new carriers and services to the agenda of the Consultative Process, in the hope that exchange of information might persuade the European nations to cooperate with the FCC's policy of encouraging competition in the provision of telecommunications services.

Respondents, opposing the entry of new competitors, . . . filed a rule-making petition with the FCC concerning the Consultative Process meetings. The petition . . . contended that the Sunshine Act required the Consultative Process sessions as "meetings" of the FCC, to be held in public. *See* 5 U.S.C. §552b(b). The FCC denied the rulemaking petition, and respondents filed an appeal in the Court of Appeals for the District of Columbia Circuit.

The Court of Appeals . . . held that the FCC had erred in concluding that the Sunshine Act did not apply to the Consultative Process sessions. . . .

We reverse. . . .

III

Section 552b(b) of the Sunshine Act requires that "meetings of an agency" be open to the public. Section 552b(a)(2) defines "meetings" as "the deliberations of at least the number of individual agency members required to take action on behalf of the agency where such deliberations determine or result in the joint conduct or disposition of official agency business." Under these provisions, the Sunshine Act does not require that Consultative Process sessions be held in public, as the participation by FCC members in these sessions constitutes neither a "meeting" as defined by §552b(a)(2) nor a meeting "of the agency" as provided by §552b(b).

A

Congress in drafting the Act's definition of "meetings" recognized that the administrative process cannot be conducted entirely in the public eye. "[I]nformal background discussions [that] clarify issues and expose varying views" are a necessary part of an agency's work. *See* S. Rep. No. 94-354, at 19 (1975). The

Act's procedural requirements[6] effectively would prevent such discussions and thereby impair normal agency operations without achieving significant public benefit.[7] Section 552b(a)(2) therefore limits the Act's application to meetings "where at least a quorum of the agency's members . . . conduct or dispose of official agency business." S. Rep. No. 94-354, at 2.

Three Commissioners, the number who attended the Consultative Process sessions, did not constitute a quorum of the seven-member Commission.[8] The three members were, however, a quorum of the Telecommunications Committee. That Committee is a "subdivision . . . authorized to act on behalf [of] the agency." The Commission had delegated to the Committee, pursuant to §155(d)(1) of the Communications Act, 47 U.S.C. §155(d), the power to approve applications for common carrier certification.[9] See 47 C.F.R. §0.215 (1983). The Sunshine Act applies to such a subdivision as well as to an entire agency. §552b(a)(1).

It does not appear, however, that the Telecommunications Committee engaged at these sessions in "deliberations [that] determine or result in the joint conduct or disposition of official agency business." This statutory language contemplates discussions that "effectively predetermine official actions." See S. Rep. No. 95-354, at 19; accord, id., at 18. Such discussions must be "sufficiently focused on discrete proposals or issues as to cause or be likely to cause the individual participating members to form reasonably firm positions regarding matters pending or likely to arise before the agency." R. Berg and S. Klitzman, An Interpretive Guide to the Government in the Sunshine Act 9 (1978) (hereinafter Interpretive Guide). On the cross motions for summary judgment, however, respondents alleged neither that the Committee formally acted upon applications for certification at the Consultative Process sessions nor that those sessions resulted in firm positions on particular matters pending or likely to arise before the Committee. Rather, the sessions provided general background information to the Commissioners and permitted them to engage with their foreign counterparts in an exchange of views by which decisions already reached by the

---

6. Meetings within the scope of the Act must be held in public unless one of the Act's exemptions is applicable. §552b(b). The agency must announce, at least a week before the meeting, its time, place and subject matter and whether it will be open or closed. §552b(e)(1). For closed meetings, the agency's counsel must publicly certify that one of the Act's exemptions permits closure. §552b(f)(1). Most closed meetings must be transcribed or recorded. *Ibid.*

7. The evolution of the statutory language reflects the congressional intent precisely to define the limited scope of the statute's requirements. *See generally* H.R. Rep. No. 94-880, Part 2, at 14 (1976). For example, the Senate substituted the term "deliberations" for the previously proposed terms—"assembly or simultaneous communication," H.R. 11656, 94th Cong, 2d Sess. §552b(a)(2) or "gathering," S. 5, 94th Cong, 1st Sess. §201(a) (1976)—in order to "exclude many discussions which are informal in nature." S. Rep. 94-354, at 10; *see id.*, at 18. Similarly, earlier versions of the Act had applied to any agency discussions that "concern[] the joint conduct or disposition of agency business," H.R. 11656, *supra*, §552b(a)(2). The Act now applies only to deliberations that *"determine or result in"* the conduct of *"official* agency business." The intent of the revision clearly was to permit preliminary discussion among agency members. *See* 122 Cong. Rec. 28474 (1976) (remarks of Rep. Fascell).

8. Since the Consultative Process sessions at issue here, held in October 1979, the Commission's membership has been reduced to five. Pub. L. No. 97-253, tit. V, §501(b), 96 Stat. 805 (effective July 1, 1983).

9. Common carriers "in interstate or foreign communication by wire or radio" or "radio transmission of energy," 47 U.S.C. §153(h), must obtain from the Commission a certificate of public convenience or necessity before undertaking construction or operation of additional communications lines. 47 U.S.C. §214. Permits must be obtained also for construction of radio broadcasting stations. 47 U.S.C. §319.

Commission could be implemented. As we have noted, Congress did not intend the Sunshine Act to encompass such discussions. . . .

B

The Consultative Process was not convened by the FCC and its procedures were not subject to the FCC's unilateral control. The sessions of the Consultative Process therefore are not meetings "of an agency" within the meaning of §552b(b) of the Sunshine Act. The Act prescribes procedures for the agency to follow when it holds meetings and particularly when it chooses to close a meeting. *See supra,* note 6. These provisions presuppose that the Act applies only to meetings that the agency has the power to conduct according to these procedures. And application of the Act to meetings not under agency control would restrict the types of meetings that agency members could attend. It is apparent that Congress, in enacting requirements for the agency's conduct of its own meetings, did not contemplate as well such a broad substantive restraint upon agency processes. *See* S. Rep. No. 95-354, at 1.

IV

For these reasons, we reverse the judgment of the Court of Appeals and remand the case for further proceedings consistent with this opinion.

It is so ordered.

NOTES AND QUESTIONS

1. *Deliberation, discussion, decision.* What precisely is the basis for the court's ruling? Must a meeting involve the making of a formal decision in order to be covered by the Sunshine Act? In Pacific Legal Found. v. CEQ, 636 F.2d 1259 (D.C. Cir. 1980), the D.C. Circuit struck down CEQ regulations that limited the open meeting requirement to matters requiring a formal vote. What counts, said the court, is the *effect,* not the *form,* of the deliberations. Is *Pacific Legal Foundation* still good law after *ITT World Communications?*

2. *Paper meetings?* Another case interpreting the Sunshine Act's "meeting" language was Communications Sys., Inc. v. FCC, 595 F.2d 797 (D.C. Cir. 1978). Plaintiff in that case attacked the FCC's practice of making many decisions by circulating written communications among its members ("notation voting") rather than by conducting open meetings. The court of appeals upheld the agency, agreeing that Congress could not have intended to deprive agencies of this common and expeditious device for handling routine business.

After *ITT World Communications* and *Communications Systems,* how difficult would it be for a determined collegial body to circumvent the Act?

2. *Exemptions*

The Sunshine Act permits collegial bodies to go into executive (private) session to discuss any of ten enumerated subjects. §552b(c). Seven of the ten exemptions track almost verbatim their counterparts in the FOIA (§§552(b)(1)-(4), (6)-(8)). The fifth exemption deals with discussions in which a person is accused of a crime or formally censured, and the tenth deals with discussions of litigation strategy. The exemption with the greatest potential for expansion into a gaping loophole is 9(B). §552b(c)(9)(B). That provision permits an agency to exclude the public from a discussion of any "information the premature disclosure of which would . . . be likely to significantly frustrate implementation of a proposed agency action. . . ." The following case illustrates the judicial response to this language.

COMMON CAUSE v. NUCLEAR REGULATORY COMMISSION
674 F.2d 921 (D.C. Cir. 1982)

Before WRIGHT, WILKEY and GINSBURG, Circuit Judges.
J. SKELLY WRIGHT, Circuit Judge: . . .

In these cases we must decide an important unresolved issue: whether any of the statutory exemptions from the Sunshine Act apply to agency budget deliberations. Interpreting the statutory language in light of the legislative history and underlying policies of the Act, we conclude that there is no blanket exemption for agency meetings at any stage of the budget preparation process. The availability of exemptions for specific portions of budgetary discussions must be determined upon the facts of each case. . . .

I. STATEMENT OF THE CASE

Three interrelated cases have been consolidated in this appeal. Each case turns on the lawfulness of a decision by the Nuclear Regulatory Commission to close a meeting to discuss the agency's budget proposals. In each case the District Court ruled against the Commission. In No. 81-1975 the District Court held that the agency had acted unlawfully in closing a meeting on July 18, 1980, and ordered the Commission to refrain in the future from closing all meetings "similar in nature." Subsequently, in No. 81-2002, the court ruled that the Commission had violated the injunction by closing a meeting on July 25, 1981, and adjudged the Commission in civil contempt, which it could purge by releasing the transcript of the meeting. Finally, in No. 81-2147 the court held that the Commission had acted without statutory authorization when it closed a meeting on October 15, 1981, and ordered release of the transcript. The orders in Nos. 81-2002 and 81-2147 have been stayed pending the determination of this appeal.

A. NO. 81-1975: COMMISSION MEETING ON JULY 18, 1980

In July 1980 the Commission scheduled a series of meetings to discuss preparation of the agency's annual budget request for fiscal year 1982, and announced that the sessions would be open to the public. Before the first of the meetings of July 18, 1980, however, the three Commissioners who were present voted unanimously to close all of the budget meetings scheduled to be held within the next 30 days. . . .

The Commission relied solely on Exemption 9(B) of the Sunshine Act, which permits closing of meetings if premature disclosure of the discussion would be "likely to significantly frustrate implementation of a proposed agency action." 5 U.S.C. §552b(c)(9)(B) (1976). A representative of appellee Common Cause, who wished to attend the July 18, 1980 meeting, was excluded. At that meeting the Commissioners received a preliminary briefing from the staff concerning the Commission's budgetary needs and the relationship of each office's budget requests to agency and Office of Management and Budget (OMB) guidelines and previous appropriation levels. . . .

B. NO. 81-2002: COMMISSION MEETING ON JULY 27, 1981

In July 1981 the Commission scheduled a series of meetings to discuss its budget request for fiscal year 1983. On the advice of its General Counsel it divided these meetings into two categories: preliminary staff briefings, designed to provide Commission members with background information and staff advice; and meetings in which the Commissioners would decide on specific funding levels for the agency's budget proposals to OMB (markup), and would also consider intra-agency appeals from initial markup decisions (reclama). It voted to hold the preliminary staff briefings, which it believed to be "similar in nature" to the July 18, 1980 meeting, in public. However, it decided to close the markup/reclama meeting, originally scheduled for July 23, which eventually took place on July 27. It relied on Exemptions 2 and 6 as well as Exemption 9(B). Common Cause was notified of this decision on July 17, 1981. . . .

On July 21, 1981 Common Cause sought an order from the District Court enforcing the July 2, 1981 injunction by requiring the scheduled markup/reclama meeting to be held in open session. . . . The court did not act immediately on the Common Cause motion. On July 27, 1981 the Commission held its markup/reclama meeting in closed session. The meeting discussed the Commission's final budget figures for submission to OMB, evaluated a number of regulatory programs, determined budgetary priorities, and selected strategies to maximize the budgetary resources that OMB might approve. . . .

C. NO. 81-2147: COMMISSION MEETING ON OCTOBER 15, 1981

The Commission submitted its budget request to OMB in September 1981. OMB proposed substantial reductions in the Commission's budget, but gave the agency an opportunity to appeal (reclama) the cutbacks on or before October 19, 1981. The Commission sought the District Court's permission to hold a closed session to discuss the reclama to OMB. It argued that unless the discussion of its priorities, negotiation strategy, and fallback positions could be closed the agency's goal of minimizing OMB's reductions would be "significantly frustrated" within the meaning of Exemption 9(B). It also invoked Exemptions 2, 6, and 10 of the Sunshine Act.[10]

---

10. Exemption 2 applies to information that "relate[s] solely to the internal personnel rules and practices of an agency[.]" 5 U.S.C. §552b(c)(2) (1976). Exemption 6 protects "information of a personal nature where disclosure would constitute a clearly unwarranted invasion of personal privacy[.]"

The District Court refused permission and ordered the meeting to be held in open session. . . . On an emergency motion for stay pending appeal this court granted a partial stay of the District Court's order. . . . The stay permitted the Commission to close those specific portions of the meeting during which it discussed material exempt under Exemptions 2, 6, 9(B), and 10. This court also ordered the Commission to submit a verbatim record of both open and closed portions of the meeting to the District Court within four days of the meeting, and instructed the District Court to rule on the Commission's action but to stay its orders pending review on appeal.

On October 15, 1981 the Commission held a two-part budget meeting to prepare its reclama to OMB. The first part, which dealt generally with the status of the Commission's budget request, was open to the public. The second part, which considered the specific budget items involved in the reclama, was held in closed session. . . .

III.   THE SUNSHINE ACT AND THE BUDGET PROCESS

. . . The Government in the Sunshine Act establishes the policy that "the public is entitled to the fullest practicable information regarding the decisionmaking processes of the Federal Government." Every meeting of a multimember agency must be open to the public, except that specific portions of a meeting may be closed if the discussion is reasonably likely to fall within one or more of ten narrowly defined exemptions. 5 U.S.C. §552b(c)(1)-(10) (1976). The Commission contends that these exemptions authorize closing of agency budget discussions. It places primary reliance on Exemption 9(B), which allows an agency to close a meeting or portion of a meeting which is likely to discuss matters whose "premature disclosure" would "be likely to significantly frustrate implementation of a proposed agency action." *Id.* §552b(c)(9)(B). The agency also contends that budget meetings may be closed because they encompass information protected under Exemption 2, matters related "solely to the internal personnel rules and practices of an agency," and Exemption 6, material of a personal nature whose disclosure would "constitute a clearly unwarranted invasion of personal privacy." *Id.* §§552b(c)(2), 552b(c)(6). In light of the language, legislative history, and underlying purposes of the Sunshine Act, we reject the Commission's proposed interpretations of the Sunshine Act exemptions.

A.   THE PURPOSES OF THE SUNSHINE ACT

Congress enacted the Sunshine Act to open the deliberations of multimember federal agencies to public view. It believed that increased openness would enhance citizen confidence in government, encourage higher quality work by government officials, stimulate well-informed public debate about government programs and policies, and promote cooperation between citizens and government. In short, it sought to make government more fully accountable

---

Id. §552b(c)(6). Exemption 10 shields discussions that "specifically concern an agency's issuance of a subpoena," or its participation in a civil proceeding or arbitration, or its conduct of formal agency proceedings. *Id.* §552b(c)(10).

to the people. In keeping with the premise that "government should conduct the public's business in public," the Act established a general presumption that agency meetings should be held in the open. Once a person has challenged an agency's decision to close a meeting, the agency bears the burden of proof. Even if exempt subjects are discussed in one portion of a meeting, the remainder of the meeting must be held in open session.

The Act went farther than any previous federal legislation in requiring openness in government. In general the Sunshine Act's exemptions parallel those in the Freedom of Information Act (FOIA), but there is an important difference. Unlike FOIA, which specifically exempts "predecisional" memoranda and other documents on the premise that government cannot "operate in a fishbowl," the Sunshine Act was designed to open the predecisional process in multi-member agencies to the public. During the legislative process a number of federal agencies specifically objected to the Sunshine Act's omission of an exemption for predecisional deliberations. Congress deliberately chose to forego the claimed advantages of confidential discussions among agency heads at agency meetings. . . .

Notwithstanding the omission of a deliberative process privilege from the Sunshine Act, the Commission asks us to hold that the deliberative process leading to formulation of an agency's budget request is exempt from the Sunshine Act. To resolve this question, we must examine the statutory underpinnings of the budget process and the specific exemptions from the Sunshine Act which the Commission invokes.

B.   THE BUDGET AND ACCOUNTING ACT OF 1921

The Budget and Accounting Act, 42 Stat. 21 (1921), was designed to centralize formulation of the Executive Branch budget. Previously Congress had received "uncompared, unrelated, and unrevised" estimates from individual departments and agencies, "representing the personal views and aspirations of bureau chiefs[.]" S. Rep. No. 524, 66th Cong., 2d Sess. 6 (1920). The disadvantages of this uncoordinated system led Congress to delegate to the President exclusive authority to submit budgetary requests on behalf of the Executive Branch. 31 U.S.C. §15 (1976). Congress thereby sought to enhance the government's ability to control the overall level of expenditures and to choose among conflicting priorities.[27]

The Commission contends that the . . . congressional goal of centralized budget formulation cannot be achieved without secrecy. If the proposals of individual agencies must be adopted in public, it suggests, development of the presidential budget would be "fragmented" and the President's discretion to choose

---

27. In the words of the Senate report, the budget "will be laid before Congress in the form of a proposed business program of government, already revised and coordinated in the interest of economy and efficiency and the reduction of taxation." S. Rep. No. 524, 66th Cong., 2d Sess. 6 (1920).

Typically each agency receives guidelines from the Director of OMB in the spring, setting out tentative overall budget ceilings. The agency allocates the tentative amount among its subdivisions and submits a budget request to OMB in September. OMB analyzes the agencies' requests, proposes changes, considers appeals from the agencies, and transmits a package to the President. After further analysis and discussion, which may include meetings between the President and agency heads, the President transmits his budget recommendations to the Congress in January for the following fiscal year. . . .

among alternatives would be impaired. Brief for appellants at 19-21. This contention reads too much into the 1921 Act, which simply requires that the President submit a single, unified Executive Branch budget proposal to Congress for consideration. It does not prescribe any method by which he must develop the consolidated budget figures which he submits. Nor does it require that the President's proposals be the only budgetary information available to the public. Even if agencies discuss their budget proposals at public sessions, the President remains capable of revising agency requests and combining them into a unified budget.

Indeed, the Sunshine Act itself affords persuasive evidence that Congress did not intend to allow presidential claims of confidentiality under the Budget and Accounting Act to override the Sunshine Act's specific provisions regarding openness and secrecy. Exemption 3, a provision which received extensive consideration in both houses, allows closing of a meeting or portion of a meeting which would "disclose matters specifically exempted from disclosure by statute," provided that such statute

> (A) requires that the matters be withheld from the public in such a manner as to leave no discretion on the issue, or (B) establishes particular criteria for withholding or refers to particular types of matters to be withheld[.]

5 U.S.C. §552b(e)(3) (1976). The Budget and Accounting Act of 1921, which contains no explicit references to confidentiality, does not qualify under the strict requirements of Exemption 3.

Therefore, the budget process is exempt from the open meeting requirement, in whole or in part, only if it fits within the terms of other specific Sunshine Act exemptions.

C.   NO BLANKET EXEMPTION FOR BUDGET MEETINGS

[T]he Commission claims that Exemption 9(B) permits closing of agency budget meetings in their entirety.

Exemption 9(B) permits closing of meetings to prevent "premature disclosure" of information whose disclosure would be likely to "significantly frustrate implementation of a proposed agency action." For two reasons, the precept of narrow construction applies with particular force to this exemption, upon which the Commission principally relies. First, as we have seen, Congress decided not to provide any exemption for predecisional deliberations because it wished the process of decision as well as the results to be open to public view. *See* Part III-A *supra*. Yet the agencies may attempt to seize upon the language of Exemption 9(B) to avoid the perceived discomfort and inconvenience that are, in the words of one commentary, "inherent in the open meeting principle. . . ." R. Berg & S. Klitzman, An Interpretive Guide to the Government in the Sunshine Act 24 (1978). Second, an overly broad construction of Exemption 9(B), which applies to all agencies subject to the Act, would allow agencies to "circumvent the spirit of openness which underlies this legislation." S. Rep. No. 94-354, *supra,* at 20.

The language of the exemption is not self-explanatory; we therefore turn to the legislative history for guidance. The House and Senate committee reports give four concrete examples of Exemption 9(B) situations. First, an agency might consider imposing an embargo on foreign shipment of certain goods; if this were publicly known, all of the goods might be exported before the agency had time to act, and the effectiveness of the proposed action would be destroyed. *Id.* at 24. Second, an agency might discuss whether to approve a proposed merger; premature public disclosure of the proposal might make it impossible for the two sides to reach agreement. *Id.* at 24-25. Third, disclosure of an agency's proposed strategy in collective bargaining with its employees might make it impossible to reach an agreement. *Id.* at 24. Fourth, disclosure of an agency's terms and conditions for purchase of real property might make the proposed purchase impossible or drive up the price. *Id.*

We construe Exemption 9(B) to cover those situations delineated by the narrow general principles which encompass all four legislative examples. In each of these cases, disclosure of the agency's proposals or negotiating position could affect private decisions by parties other than those who manage the federal government — exporters, potential corporate merger partners, government employees, or owners of real property. The private responses of such persons might damage the regulatory or financial interests of the government as a whole, because in each case the agency's proposed action is one for which the agency takes final responsibility as a governmental entity.

The budget process differs substantially from the examples given by the House and Senate reports. Disclosure of the agency's discussions would not affect private parties' decisions concerning regulated activity or dealings with the government. Rather, the Commission contends that opening budget discussions to the public might affect political decisions by the President and OMB. In addition, disclosure would not directly affect "agency action" for which the Commission has the ultimate responsibility. Instead, the Commission fears that disclosure of its time-honored strategies of item-shifting, exaggeration, and fall-back positions would give it less leverage in its "arm's-length" dealings with OMB and the President, who make the final budget decisions within the Executive Branch. The Commission argues that it would thereby be impaired in its competition with other government agencies — which also serve the public and implement federal legislation — for its desired share of budgetary resources. It is not clear, however, whether the interests of the government as a whole, or the public interest, would be adversely affected.

Moreover, in the budget context the public interest in disclosure differs markedly from its interest in the four situations described in the committee reports. In those cases disclosure would permit either financial gain at government expense or circumvention of agency regulation. In contrast, disclosure of budget deliberations would serve the affirmative purposes of the Sunshine Act: to open government deliberations to public scrutiny, to inform the public "what facts and policy considerations the agency found important in reaching its decision, and what alternatives it considered and rejected," and thereby to permit "wider and more informed public debate of the agency's policies. . . ." S. Rep. No. 94-354, *supra*, at 5-6.

The budget deliberation process is of exceptional importance in agency policymaking. The agency heads must review the entire range of agency programs and responsibilities in order to establish priorities. According to the Commission, a budget meeting "candidly consider[s] the merits and efficiencies of on-going or expected regulatory programs or projects" and then "decides upon the level of regulatory activities it proposes to pursue. . . ." Brief for appellants at 30-31. These decisions, the government contends, have a significant impact on "the Commission's ability to marshal regulatory powers in a manner which insures the greatest protection of the public health and safety with the most economical use of its limited resources." *Id.* at 31. . . .

D. PARTICULARIZED EXEMPTIONS

The Sunshine Act contains no express exemption for budget deliberations as a whole, and we do not read such an exemption into Exemption 9(B). We recognize, nevertheless, that specific items discussed at Commission budget meetings might be exempt from the open meetings requirement of the Act, and might justify closing portions of Commission meetings on an individual and particularized basis. After examining the transcripts of the Commission's closed meetings of July 27, 1981 and October 15, 1981, however, we conclude that none of the subject matter discussed at either meeting comes within any of the exemptions cited by the Commission. The Commission must therefore release the full transcripts of these meetings to the public. . . .

IV. CONCLUSION

For the reasons stated in this opinion the District Court's injunction issued July 2, 1981 and its contempt finding made on September 9, 1981 are vacated. Because the Commission has not carried its burden of proving that the July 27, 1981 and October 15, 1981 meetings were lawfully closed, the Commission shall release the transcripts of those meetings to the public forthwith.

So ordered. . . .

NOTES AND QUESTIONS

1. *"Significantly frustrate."* Suppose you were General Counsel of the Nuclear Regulatory Commission. The commission has asked you whether it may close a forthcoming meeting to discuss the agency's budget requests for the upcoming fiscal year. The subjects to be discussed include the following:

a. A staff proposal to eliminate NRC funding for outside research on the feasibility of safely disposing of nuclear waste in the ocean. The research is conducted exclusively by a private research firm that derives over half of its total revenues from the project. Premature disclosure of the project's elimination, it is thought, might make it difficult for the contractor to attract and retain key personnel.

b. A staff proposal to eliminate an internal research program as an economy move. Discussion of the proposal will involve identification of the staff positions to be eliminated and the salaries associated with those positions.

c. A discussion by the commission of the merit bonuses to be awarded to the agency's middle and senior managers under the agency's performance appraisal system.

d. A proposal to reduce the funding allocated to a research program on nuclear power plant cooling-system reliability jointly sponsored by the United States and Germany. The NRC's staff fears that premature revelation of the idea could cause embarrassment to the United States and could impair NRC's ability to renegotiate the cost allocation with its German counterpart.

How would you advise the commission? If these matters are scheduled to come up in the course of a meeting on NRC's entire budget proposal, can NRC close the entire meeting? How should it proceed?

2. *The Federal Advisory Committee Act.* A related "open government" statute is the Federal Advisory Committee Act (FACA), *codified at* 5 U.S.C. app. 2. Enacted in 1972 and amended in 1976 to conform to the Sunshine Act, FACA regulates the structure and operation of committees "established or utilized" by the President or a federal agency to give advice to the Executive Branch. Among other things, FACA requires advisory committees to publish advance notice of their meetings and open their meetings to the public, unless the President or relevant agency head determines that the meeting may be closed to the public in accordance with the Sunshine Act. Advisory Committees must also make their minutes, records, and reports available to the public to the same extent that they would be subject to mandatory disclosure under FOIA. In Public Citizen v. Department of Justice, 491 U.S. 440 (1989), the issue presented was whether FACA applies not only to committees specially constituted by an agency for the purpose of rendering advice to the agency, but also to independent private organizations to which agencies might turn from time to time for advice. For many years the Justice Department has requested the American Bar Association's Standing Committee on the Judiciary to review the qualifications of persons being considered for nomination to the federal judiciary by the President, and to provide a confidential evaluation of each candidate to the Justice Department. Two public interest organizations requested from the Department the names of persons being considered for appointment and the reports and minutes of meetings of the ABA Standing Committee. The Justice Department refused to release the information, arguing that FACA was not intended to apply to such organizations as the ABA. The Supreme Court agreed. While recognizing that the Justice Department "utilized" the advice of the ABA, the majority engaged in a rather tortured reading of the Act and its legislative history to conclude that Congress really didn't mean the Act to extend to such consultations. The majority also noted that its interpretation avoided the "difficult" constitutional issue of whether Congress could so deeply intrude into the President's constitutional appointment power. Justice Kennedy, joined by two colleagues, concurred. He rejected the Court's reading of the statute, finding it plainly applicable to the ABA Standing Committee, but argued that the statute, so construed, violated the Appointments Clause of the Constitution.

Section 3(2)(iii) exempts from FACA's provisions "any committee which is composed wholly of full-time officers or employees of the Federal Government." The meaning of that language has been featured in two cases involving high-profile presidential commissions. Both of these cases also presented the issue of whether the application of FACA to presidential advisory committees intrudes too deeply into the President's constitutional prerogatives. The first case, Association of American Physicians & Surgeons, Inc. v. Clinton, 997 F.2d 989 (D.C. Cir. 1993), involved the President's Task Force on National Health Care Reform, convened by President Clinton early in his first term to develop legislative proposals to address the growing problems of high costs and inadequate coverage in America's health care system. The case involved two FACA-exemption issues. The first arose because the President had appointed his wife, Hillary Rodham

Clinton, as chair of the task force. All other members were government officials. At issue was whether Mrs. Clinton, as First Lady, could be considered a "full-time officer or employee" for this purpose. Noting that applying FACA to the task force would present difficult constitutional questions, the court stretched to interpret the exemption language to apply to the First Lady (even though she was not a salaried employee of the government). The second exemption issue concerned a "working group" of the task force, which included not only government officials but also a group of private sector "consultants" who attended meetings intermittently. As to these participants, the court ruled that, regardless of their title, they should be considered "members" of the advisory committee (and thereby trigger the requirements of FACA) if their "involvement and role are functionally indistinguishable from those of the other members." 997 F.2d at 915. The court remanded to the district court to make that factual determination. This gave rise to the so-called "de facto membership" doctrine.

The second exemption case involved the National Energy Policy Development Group convened by President George W. Bush to prepare an energy policy for his administration. Although all of the named members (including its chair, Vice President Richard Cheney) were government officials, critics of the administration claimed that private energy-industry officials were participating in the group's deliberations to such an extent as to be de facto members. Judicial Watch and the Sierra Club brought actions against the Vice President to require compliance with FACA's public-disclosure requirements. The early stages of this saga, leading up to Justice Scalia's refusal to recuse himself, are described in Chapter VI, *supra*. On the merits, the Supreme Court ruled that the court of appeals did have authority to issue a writ of mandamus, but it should do so only if it were satisfied that such an action was necessary to protect the President's constitutional privilege to obtain candid advice from his closest advisors. On remand, the D.C. Circuit issued the writ, ordering the district court to dismiss the complaint. In re Cheney, 406 F.3d 723 (D.C. Cir. 2005) (en banc). Interpreting FACA "strictly" so as to avoid a constitutional issue, the court ruled that an advisory committee within the Executive Office of the President "is composed wholly of federal officials if the President has given no one other than a federal official a vote in or, if the committee acts by consensus, a veto over the committee's decisions." 406 F.3d at 728. Finding no allegation that any of the nonfederal participants had a "vote or veto," the court ordered the complaints dismissed.

Should the "vote or veto" test apply to committees convened to advise federal agencies other than the President? Does the new test gut the "de facto membership" test announced in *American Physicians*? Does it effectively gut FACA?

Consider how easy or difficult it might be to circumvent FACA (just like FOIA, and the Sunshine Act). Could the White House seek advice on a more ad hoc basis and come to a consensus more indirectly by consulting one party or person at a time? Might agencies sometimes decline to seek outside input precisely because of the burdens that would come with forming an advisory committee under FACA? Are there benefits to FACA even if sometimes the White House or the agencies avoid using it when they arguably ought to?

APPENDIX

THE CONSTITUTION OF THE UNITED STATES OF AMERICA (SELECTED PROVISIONS)

We the People of the United States, in Order to form a more perfect Union, establish Justice, insure domestic Tranquility, provide for the common defence, promote the general Welfare, and secure the Blessings of Liberty to ourselves and our Posterity, do ordain and establish this Constitution for the United States of America.

ARTICLE I

Section 1. All legislative Powers herein granted shall be vested in a Congress of the United States, which shall consist of a Senate and House of Representatives.

Section 2. [1] The House of Representatives shall be composed of Members chosen every second Year by the People of the several States, and the Electors in each State shall have the Qualifications requisite for Electors of the most numerous Branch of the State Legislature.

[2] No Person shall be a Representative who shall not have attained to the Age of twenty five Years, and been seven Years a Citizen of the United States, and who shall not, when elected, be an Inhabitant of that State in which he shall be chosen.

[3] Representatives and direct Taxes shall be apportioned among the several States which may be included within this Union, according to their respective Numbers, which shall be determined by adding to the whole Number of free Persons, including those bound to Service for a Term of Years, and excluding Indians not taxed, three fifths of all other Persons. The actual Enumeration shall be made within three Years after the first Meeting of the Congress of the United States, and within every subsequent Term of ten Years, in such Manner as they shall by Law direct. The Number of Representatives shall not exceed one

for every thirty Thousand, but each State shall have at Least one Representative; and until such enumeration shall be made, the State of New Hampshire shall be entitled to chuse three, Massachusetts eight, Rhode-Island and Providence Plantations one, Connecticut five, New-York six, New Jersey four, Pennsylvania eight, Delaware one, Maryland six, Virginia ten, North Carolina five, South Carolina five, and Georgia three.

[4] When vacancies happen in the Representation from any State, the Executive Authority thereof shall issue Writs of Election to fill such Vacancies.

[5] The House of Representatives shall chuse their Speaker and other Officers; and shall have the sole Power of Impeachment.

Section 3. [1] The Senate of the United States shall be composed of two Senators from each State, chosen by the Legislature thereof, for six Years; and each Senator shall have one Vote.

[2] Immediately after they shall be assembled in Consequence of the first Election, they shall be divided as equally as may be into three Classes. The Seats of the Senators of the first Class shall be vacated at the Expiration of the second Year, of the second Class at the Expiration of the fourth Year, and of the third Class at the Expiration of the sixth Year, so that one third may be chosen every second Year; and if Vacancies happen by Resignation, or otherwise, during the Recess of the Legislature of any State, the Executive thereof may make temporary Appointments until the next Meeting of the Legislature, which shall then fill such Vacancies.

[3] No Person shall be a Senator who shall not have attained to the Age of thirty Years, and been nine Years a Citizen of the United States, and who shall not, when elected, be an Inhabitant of that State for which he shall be chosen.

[4] The Vice President of the United States shall be President of the Senate, but shall have no Vote, unless they be equally divided.

[5] The Senate shall chuse their other Officers, and also a President pro tempore, in the Absence of the Vice President, or when he shall exercise the Office of President of the United States.

[6] The Senate shall have the sole Power to try all Impeachments. When sitting for that Purpose, they shall be on Oath or Affirmation. When the President of the United States is tried, the Chief Justice shall preside: And no Person shall be convicted without the Concurrence of two thirds of the Members present.

[7] Judgment in Cases of Impeachment shall not extend further than to removal from Office, and disqualification to hold and enjoy any Office of honor, Trust or Profit under the United States: but the Party convicted shall nevertheless be liable and subject to Indictment, Trial, Judgment and Punishment, according to Law.

Section 4. [1] The Times, Places and Manner of holding Elections for Senators and Representatives, shall be prescribed in each State by the Legislature thereof; but the Congress may at any time by Law make or alter such Regulations, except as to the Places of chusing Senators.

[2] The Congress shall assemble at least once in every Year, and such Meeting shall be on the first Monday in December, unless they shall by Law appoint a different Day.

Section 5. [1] Each House shall be the Judge of the Elections, Returns and Qualifications of its own Members, and a Majority of each shall constitute a Quorum to do Business; but a smaller Number may adjourn from day to day, and may be authorized to compel the Attendance of absent Members, in such Manner, and under such Penalties as each House may provide.

[2] Each House may determine the Rules of its Proceedings, punish its Members for disorderly Behaviour, and, with the Concurrence of two thirds, expel a Member.

[3] Each House shall keep a Journal of its Proceedings, and from time to time publish the same, excepting such Parts as may in their Judgment require Secrecy; and the Yeas and Nays of the Members of either House on any question shall, at the Desire of one fifth of those Present, be entered on the Journal.

[4] Neither House, during the Session of Congress, shall, without the Consent of the other, adjourn for more than three days, nor to any other Place than that in which the two Houses shall be sitting.

Section 6. [1] The Senators and Representatives shall receive a Compensation for their Services, to be ascertained by Law, and paid out of the Treasury of the United States. They shall in all Cases, except Treason, Felony and Breach of the Peace, be privileged from Arrest during their Attendance at the Session of their respective Houses, and in going to and returning from the same; and for any Speech or Debate in either House, they shall not be questioned in any other Place.

[2] No Senator or Representative shall, during the Time for which he was elected, be appointed to any civil Office under the Authority of the United States, which shall have been created, or the Emoluments whereof shall have been encreased during such time; and no Person holding any Office under the United States, shall be a Member of either House during his Continuance in Office.

Section 7. [1] All Bills for raising Revenue shall originate in the House of Representatives; but the Senate may propose or concur with Amendments as on other Bills.

[2] Every Bill which shall have passed the House of Representatives and the Senate, shall, before it become a Law, be presented to the President of the United States; If he approve he shall sign it, but if not he shall return it, with his Objections to that House in which it shall have originated, who shall enter the Objections at large on their Journal, and proceed to reconsider it. If after such Reconsideration two thirds of that House shall agree to pass the Bill, it shall be sent, together with the Objections, to the other House, by which it shall likewise be reconsidered, and if approved by two thirds of that House, it shall become a Law. But in all such Cases the Votes of both Houses shall be determined by yeas and Nays, and the Names of the Persons voting for and against the Bill shall be entered on the Journal of each House respectively. If any Bill shall not be returned by the President within ten Days (Sundays excepted) after it shall have been presented to him, the Same shall be a Law, in like Manner as if he had signed it, unless the Congress by their Adjournment prevent its Return, in which Case it shall not be a Law.

[3] Every Order, Resolution, or Vote to which the Concurrence of the Senate and House of Representatives may be necessary (except on a question of Adjournment) shall be presented to the President of the United States; and before the Same shall take Effect, shall be approved by him, or being disapproved by him, shall be repassed by two thirds of the Senate and House of Representatives, according to the Rules and Limitations prescribed in the Case of a Bill.

Section 8. [1] The Congress shall have Power To lay and collect Taxes, Duties, Imposts and Excises, to pay the Debts and provide for the common Defence and general Welfare of the United States; but all Duties, Imposts and Excises shall be uniform throughout the United States;

[2] To borrow Money on the credit of the United States;

[3] To regulate Commerce with foreign Nations, and among the several States, and with the Indian Tribes;

[4] To establish an uniform Rule of Naturalization, and uniform Laws on the subject of Bankruptcies throughout the United States;

[5] To coin Money, regulate the Value thereof, and of foreign Coin, and fix the Standard of Weights and Measures;

[6] To provide for the Punishment of counterfeiting the Securities and current Coin of the United States;

[7] To establish Post Offices and post Roads;

[8] To promote the Progress of Science and useful Arts, by securing for limited Times to Authors and Inventors the exclusive Right to their respective Writings and Discoveries;

[9] To constitute Tribunals inferior to the supreme Court;

[10] To define and punish Piracies and Felonies committed on the high Seas, and Offences against the Law of Nations;

[11] To declare War, grant Letters of Marque and Reprisal, and make Rules concerning Captures on Land and Water;

[12] To raise and support Armies, but no Appropriation of Money to that Use shall be for a longer Term than two Years;

[13] To provide and maintain a Navy;

[14] To make Rules for the Government and Regulation of the land and naval Forces;

[15] To provide for calling forth the Militia to execute the Laws of the Union, suppress Insurrections and repel Invasions;

[16] To provide for organizing, arming, and disciplining, the Militia, and for governing such Part of them as may be employed in the Service of the United States, reserving to the States respectively, the Appointment of the Officers, and the Authority of training the Militia according to the discipline prescribed by Congress;

[17] To exercise exclusive Legislation in all Cases whatsoever, over such District (not exceeding ten Miles square) as may, by Cession of particular States, and the Acceptance of Congress, become the Seat of the Government of the United States, and to exercise like Authority over all Places purchased by the Consent of the Legislature of the State in which the Same shall be, for the Erection of Forts, Magazines, Arsenals, dock-Yards, and other needful Buildings,—And

[18] To make all Laws which shall be necessary and proper for carrying into Execution the foregoing Powers, and all other Powers vested by this Constitution in the Government of the United States, or in any Department or Officer thereof.

Section 9. [1] The Migration or Importation of such Persons as any of the States now existing shall think proper to admit, shall not be prohibited by the Congress prior to the Year one thousand eight hundred and eight, but a Tax or duty may be imposed on such Importation, not exceeding ten dollars for each Person.

[2] The Privilege of the Writ of Habeas Corpus shall not be suspended, unless when in Cases of Rebellion or Invasion the public Safety may require it.

[3] No Bill of Attainder or ex post facto Law shall be passed.

[4] No Capitation, or other direct, Tax shall be laid, unless in Proportion to the Census or Enumeration herein before directed to be taken.

[5] No Tax or Duty shall be laid on Articles exported from any State.

[6] No Preference shall be given by any Regulation of Commerce or Revenue to the Ports of one State over those of another: nor shall Vessels bound to, or from, one State, be obliged to enter, clear, or pay Duties in another.

[7] No Money shall be drawn from the Treasury, but in Consequence of Appropriations made by Law; and a regular Statement and Account of the Receipts and Expenditures of all public Money shall be published from time to time.

[8] No Title of Nobility shall be granted by the United States: And no Person holding any Office of Profit or Trust under them, shall, without the Consent of the Congress, accept of any present, Emolument, Office, or Title, of any kind whatever, from any King, Prince, or foreign State.

Section 10. [1] No State shall enter into any Treaty, Alliance, or Confederation; grant Letters of Marque and Reprisal; coin Money; emit Bills of Credit; make any Thing but gold and silver Coin a Tender in Payment of Debts; pass any Bill of Attainder, ex post facto Law, or Law impairing the Obligation of Contracts, or grant any Title of Nobility.

[2] No State shall, without the Consent of the Congress, lay any Imposts or Duties on Imports or Exports, except what may be absolutely necessary for executing its inspection Laws: and the net Produce of all Duties and Imposts, laid by any State on Imports or Exports, shall be for the Use of the Treasury of the United States; and all such Laws shall be subject to the Revision and Controul of the Congress.

[3] No State shall, without the Consent of Congress, lay any Duty of Tonnage, keep Troops, or Ships of War in time of Peace, enter into any Agreement or Compact with another State, or with a foreign Power, or engage in War, unless actually invaded, or in such imminent Danger as will not admit of delay.

ARTICLE II

Section 1. [1] The executive Power shall be vested in a President of the United States of America. He shall hold his Office during the Term of four Years, and, together with the Vice President, chosen for the same Term, be elected, as follows

[2] Each State shall appoint, in such Manner as the Legislature thereof may direct, a Number of Electors, equal to the whole Number of Senators and Representatives to which the State may be entitled in the Congress: but no Senator or Representative, or Person holding an Office of Trust or Profit under the United States, shall be appointed an Elector.

[3] The Electors shall meet in their respective States, and vote by Ballot for two Persons, of whom one at least shall not be an Inhabitant of the same State with themselves. And they shall make a List of all the Persons voted for, and of the Number of Votes for each; which List they shall sign and certify, and

transmit sealed to the Seat of the Government of the United States, directed to the President of the Senate. The President of the Senate shall, in the Presence of the Senate and House of Representatives, open all the Certificates, and the Votes shall then be counted. The Person having the greatest Number of Votes shall be the President, if such Number be a Majority of the whole Number of Electors appointed; and if there be more than one who have such Majority, and have an equal Number of Votes, then the House of Representatives shall immediately chuse by Ballot one of them for President; and if no Person have a Majority, then from the five highest on the List the said House shall in like Manner chuse the President. But in chusing the President, the Votes shall be taken by States, the Representation from each State having one Vote; A quorum for this Purpose shall consist of a Member or Members from two thirds of the States, and a Majority of all the States shall be necessary to a Choice. In every Case, after the Choice of the President, the Person having the greatest Number of Votes of the Electors shall be the Vice President. But if there should remain two or more who have equal Votes, the Senate shall chuse from them by Ballot the Vice President.

[4] The Congress may determine the Time of chusing the Electors, and the Day on which they shall give their Votes; which Day shall be the same throughout the United States.

[5] No Person except a natural born Citizen, or a Citizen of the United States, at the time of the Adoption of this Constitution, shall be eligible to the Office of President; neither shall any Person be eligible to that Office who shall not have attained to the Age of thirty five Years, and been fourteen Years a Resident within the United States.

[6] In Case of the Removal of the President from Office, or of his Death, Resignation, or Inability to discharge the Powers and Duties of the said Office, the Same shall devolve on the Vice President, and the Congress may by Law provide for the Case of Removal, Death, Resignation or Inability, both of the President and Vice President, declaring what Officer shall then act as President, and such Officer shall act accordingly, until the Disability be removed, or a President shall be elected.

[7] The President shall, at stated Times, receive for his Services, a Compensation, which shall neither be increased nor diminished during the Period for which he shall have been elected, and he shall not receive within that Period any other Emolument from the United States, or any of them.

[8] Before he enter on the Execution of his Office, he shall take the following Oath or Affirmation: — "I do solemnly swear (or affirm) that I will faithfully execute the Office of President of the United States, and will to the best of my Ability, preserve, protect and defend the Constitution of the United States."

Section 2. [1] The President shall be Commander in Chief of the Army and Navy of the United States, and of the Militia of the several States, when called into the actual Service of the United States; he may require the Opinion, in writing, of the principal Officer in each of the executive Departments, upon any Subject relating to the Duties of their respective Offices, and he shall have Power to grant Reprieves and Pardons for Offences against the United States, except in Cases of Impeachment.

[2] He shall have Power, by and with the Advice and Consent of the Senate, to make Treaties, provided two thirds of the Senators present concur; and

he shall nominate, and by and with the Advice and Consent of the Senate, shall appoint Ambassadors, other public Ministers and Consuls, Judges of the Supreme Court, and all other Officers of the United States, whose Appointments are not herein otherwise provided for, and which shall be established by Law; but the Congress may by Law vest the Appointment of such inferior Officers, as they think proper, in the President alone, in the Courts of Law, or in the Heads of Departments.

[3] The President shall have Power to fill up all Vacancies that may happen during the Recess of the Senate, by granting Commissions which shall expire at the End of their next Session.

Section 3. He shall from time to time give to the Congress Information of the State of the Union, and recommend to their Consideration such Measures as he shall judge necessary and expedient; he may, on extraordinary Occasions, convene both Houses, or either of them, and in Case of Disagreement between them, with Respect to the Time of Adjournment, he may adjourn them to such Time as he shall think proper; he shall receive Ambassadors and other public Ministers; he shall take Care that the Laws be faithfully executed, and shall Commission all the Officers of the United States.

Section 4. The President, Vice President and all civil Officers of the United States, shall be removed from Office on Impeachment for, and Conviction of, Treason, Bribery, or other high Crimes and Misdemeanors.

ARTICLE III

Section 1. The judicial Power of the United States, shall be vested in one supreme Court, and in such inferior Courts as the Congress may from time to time ordain and establish. The Judges, both of the supreme and inferior Courts, shall hold their Offices during good Behaviour, and shall, at stated Times, receive for their Services, a Compensation, which shall not be diminished during their Continuance in Office.

Section 2. [1] The judicial Power shall extend to all Cases, in Law and Equity, arising under this Constitution, the Laws of the United States, and Treaties made, or which shall be made, under their Authority;—to all Cases affecting Ambassadors, other public Ministers and Consuls;—to all Cases of admiralty and maritime Jurisdiction;—to Controversies to which the United States shall be a Party;—to Controversies between two or more States;—between a State and Citizens of another State; between Citizens of different States,—between Citizens of the same State claiming Lands under Grants of different States, and between a State, or the Citizens thereof, and foreign States, Citizens or Subjects.

[2] In all Cases affecting Ambassadors, other public Ministers and Consuls, and those in which a State shall be Party, the supreme Court shall have original Jurisdiction. In all the other Cases before mentioned, the supreme Court shall have appellate Jurisdiction, both as to Law and Fact, with such Exceptions, and under such Regulations as the Congress shall make.

[3] The Trial of all Crimes, except in Cases of Impeachment, shall be by Jury; and such Trial shall be held in the State where the said Crimes shall have been committed; but when not committed within any State, the Trial shall be at such Place or Places as the Congress may by Law have directed.

Section 3. [1] Treason against the United States, shall consist only in levying War against them, or in adhering to their Enemies, giving them Aid and Comfort. No Person shall be convicted of Treason unless on the Testimony of two Witnesses to the same overt Act, or on Confession in open Court.

[2] The Congress shall have Power to declare the Punishment of Treason, but no Attainder of Treason shall work Corruption of Blood, or Forfeiture except during the Life of the Person attainted.

ARTICLE IV

Section 1. Full Faith and Credit shall be given in each State to the public Acts, Records, and judicial Proceedings of every other State. And the Congress may by general Laws prescribe the Manner in which such Acts, Records and Proceedings shall be proved, and the Effect thereof.

Section 2. [1] The Citizens of each State shall be entitled to all Privileges and Immunities of Citizens in the several States.

[2] A Person charged in any State with Treason, Felony, or other Crime, who shall flee from Justice, and be found in another State, shall on Demand of the executive Authority of the State from which he fled, be delivered up, to be removed to the State having Jurisdiction of the Crime.

[3] No Person held to Service or Labour in one State, under the Laws thereof, escaping into another, shall, in Consequence of any Law or Regulation therein, be discharged from such Service or Labour, but shall be delivered up on Claim of the Party to whom such Service or Labour may be due.

Section 3. [1] New States may be admitted by the Congress into this Union; but no new State shall be formed or erected within the Jurisdiction of any other State; nor any State be formed by the Junction of two or more States, or Parts of States, without the Consent of the Legislatures of the States concerned as well as of the Congress.

[2] The Congress shall have Power to dispose of and make all needful Rules and Regulations respecting the Territory or other Property belonging to the United States; and nothing in this Constitution shall be so construed as to Prejudice any Claims of the United States, or of any particular State.

Section 4. The United States shall guarantee to every State in this Union a Republican Form of Government, and shall protect each of them against Invasion; and on Application of the Legislature, or of the Executive (when the Legislature cannot be convened) against domestic Violence.

ARTICLE V

The Congress, whenever two thirds of both Houses shall deem it necessary, shall propose Amendments to this Constitution, or, on the Application of the Legislatures of two thirds of the several States, shall call a Convention for proposing Amendments, which, in either Case, shall be valid to all Intents and Purposes, as Part of this Constitution, when ratified by the Legislatures of three fourths of the several States, or by Conventions in three fourths thereof, as the one or the other Mode of Ratification may be proposed by the Congress;

Provided that no Amendment which may be made prior to the Year One thousand eight hundred and eight shall in any Manner affect the first and fourth Clauses in the Ninth Section of the first Article; and that no State, without its Consent, shall be deprived of its equal Suffrage in the Senate.

ARTICLE VI

[1] All debts contracted and engagements entered into, before the adoption of this Constitution, shall be as valid against the United States under this Constitution, as under the Confederation.

[2] This Constitution, and the laws of the United States which shall be made in pursuance thereof; and all treaties made, or which shall be made, under the authority of the United States, shall be the supreme law of the land; and the judges in every state shall be bound thereby, anything in the Constitution or laws of any State to the contrary notwithstanding.

[3] The Senators and Representatives before mentioned, and the members of the several state legislatures, and all executive and judicial officers, both of the United States and of the several states, shall be bound by oath or affirmation, to support this Constitution; but no religious test shall ever be required as a qualification to any office or public trust under the United States.

AMENDMENT I [1791]

Congress shall make no law respecting an establishment of religion, or prohibiting the free exercise thereof; or abridging the freedom of speech, or of the press; or the right of the people peaceably to assemble, and to petition the Government for a redress of grievances.

AMENDMENT IV [1791]

The right of the people to be secure in their persons, houses, papers, and effects, against unreasonable searches and seizures, shall not be violated, and no Warrants shall issue, but upon probable cause, supported by Oath or affirmation, and particularly describing the place to be searched, and the persons or things to be seized.

AMENDMENT V [1791]

No person shall be held to answer for a capital, or otherwise infamous crime, unless on a presentment or indictment of a Grand Jury, except in cases arising in the land or naval forces, or in the Militia, when in actual service in time of War or public danger; nor shall any person be subject for the same offence to be twice put in jeopardy of life or limb; nor shall be compelled in any criminal case to be a witness against himself, nor be deprived of life, liberty, or property, without due process of law; nor shall private property be taken for public use, without just compensation. . . .

AMENDMENT XIV [1868]

Section 1. All persons born or naturalized in the United States, and subject to the jurisdiction thereof, are citizens of the United States and of the State wherein they reside. No State shall make or enforce any law which shall abridge the privileges or immunities of citizens of the United States; nor shall any State deprive any person of life, liberty, or property, without due process of law; nor deny to any person within its jurisdiction the equal protection of the laws.

THE ADMINISTRATIVE PROCEDURE
ACT AND RELATED PROVISIONS
5 U.S.C. §§551-559, 701-706

CHAPTER 5—ADMINISTRATIVE PROCEDURE

§551. DEFINITIONS

For the purpose of this subchapter—

(1) "agency" means each authority of the Government of the United States, whether or not it is within or subject to review by another agency, but does not include—

(A) the Congress;

(B) the courts of the United States;

(C) the governments of the territories or possessions of the United States;

(D) the government of the District of Columbia;

or except as to the requirements of section 552 of this title—

(E) agencies composed of representatives of the parties or of representatives of organizations of the parties to the disputes determined by them;

(F) courts martial and military commissions;

(G) military authority exercised in the field in time of war or in occupied territory; or

(H) functions [relating to mortgage insurance, the termination of wartime contracts, and war and other national emergencies].

(2) "person" includes an individual, partnership, corporation, association, or public or private organization other than an agency;

(3) "party" includes a person or agency named or admitted as a party, or properly seeking and entitled as of right to be admitted as a party, in an agency proceeding, and a person or agency admitted by an agency as a party for limited purposes;

(4) "rule" means the whole or a part of an agency statement of general or particular applicability and future effect designed to implement, interpret, or prescribe law or policy or describing the organization, procedure, or practice requirements of an agency and includes the approval or prescription for the future of rates, wages, corporate or financial structures or reorganization thereof, prices, facilities, appliances, services or allowances therefor or of valuations, costs, or accounting, or practices bearing on any of the foregoing;

(5) "rule making" means agency process for formulating, amending, or repealing a rule;

(6) "order" means the whole or a part of a final disposition, whether affirmative, negative, injunctive, or declaratory in form, of an agency in a matter other than rule making but including licensing;

(7) "adjudication" means agency process for the formulation of an order;

(8) "license" includes the whole or a part of an agency permit, certificate, approval, registration, charter, membership, statutory exemption or other form of permission;

(9) "licensing" includes agency process respecting the grant, renewal, denial, revocation, suspension, annulment, withdrawal, limitation, amendment, modification, or conditioning of a license;

(10) "sanction" includes the whole or a part of an agency—

(A) prohibition, requirement, limitation, or other condition affecting the freedom of a person;

(B) withholding of relief;

(C) imposition of penalty or fine;

(D) destruction, taking, seizure, or withholding of property;

(E) assessment of damages, reimbursement, restitution, compensation, costs, charges, or fees;

(F) requirement, revocation, or suspension of a license; or

(G) taking other compulsory or restrictive action;

(11) "relief" includes the whole or a part of an agency—

(A) grant of money, assistance, license, authority, exemption, exception, privilege, or remedy;

(B) recognition of a claim, right, immunity, privilege, exemption, or exception; or

(C) taking of other action on the application or petition of, and beneficial to, a person;

(12) "agency proceeding" means an agency process as defined by paragraphs (5), (7), and (9) of this section;

(13) "agency action" includes the whole or a part of an agency rule, order, license, sanction, relief, or the equivalent or denial thereof, or failure to act; and

(14) "ex parte communication" means an oral or written communication not on the public record with respect to which reasonable prior notice to all parties is not given, but it shall not include requests for status reports on any matter or proceeding covered by this subchapter.

§552. PUBLIC INFORMATION; AGENCY RULES, OPINIONS, ORDERS, RECORDS, AND PROCEEDINGS

(a) Each agency shall make available to the public information as follows:

(1) Each agency shall separately state and currently publish in the Federal Register for the guidance of the public—

(A) descriptions of its central and field organization and the established places at which, the employees (and in the case of a uniformed service, the members) from whom, and the methods whereby, the public may obtain information, make submittals or requests, or obtain decisions;

(B) statements of the general course and method by which its functions are channeled and determined, including the nature and requirements of all formal and informal procedures available;

(C) rules of procedure, descriptions of forms available or the places at which forms may be obtained, and instructions as to the scope and contents of all papers, reports, or examinations;

(D) substantive rules of general applicability adopted as authorized by law, and statements of general policy or interpretations of general applicability formulated and adopted by the agency; and

(E) each amendment, revision, or repeal of the foregoing.

Except to the extent that a person has actual and timely notice of the terms thereof, a person may not in any manner be required to resort to, or be adversely affected by, a matter required to be published in the Federal Register and not so published. For the purpose of this paragraph, matter reasonably available to the class of persons affected thereby is deemed published in the Federal Register when incorporated by reference therein with the approval of the Director of the Federal Register.

(2) Each agency, in accordance with published rules, shall make available for public inspection and copying—

(A) final opinions, including concurring and dissenting opinions, as well as orders, made in the adjudication of cases;

(B) those statements of policy and interpretations which have been adopted by the agency and are not published in the Federal Register;

(C) administrative staff manuals and instructions to staff that affect a member of the public;

(D) copies of all records, regardless of form or format—(i) that have been released to any person under paragraph (3); and (ii) (I) that because of the nature of their subject matter, the agency determines have become or are likely to become the subject of subsequent requests for substantially the same records; or (II) that have been requested 3 or more times; and

(E) a general index of the records referred to under subparagraph (D); unless the materials are promptly published and copies offered for sale. [Agencies must make records created after November 1, 1996, available by "electronic means." Agencies may delete identifying details "to the extent required to prevent a clearly unwarranted invasion of personal privacy." Agencies must make indexes created pursuant to subparagraph (E) available to the public (by "computer telecommunications" after December 31, 1999).] A final order, opinion, statement of policy, interpretation, or staff manual or instruction that affects a member of the public may be relied on, used, or cited as precedent by an agency against a party other than an agency only if (i) it has been indexed and either made available or published as provided by this paragraph; or (ii) the party has actual and timely notice of the terms thereof.

(3) (A) Except with respect to the records made available under paragraphs (1) and (2) of this subsection, each agency, upon any request for records which (i) reasonably describes such records and (ii) is made in accordance with published rules stating the time, place, fees (if any), and procedures to be followed, shall make the records promptly available to any person.

(B) In making any record available to a person under this paragraph, an agency shall provide the record in any form or format requested by the person if the record is readily reproducible by the agency in that form or format. Each agency shall make reasonable efforts to maintain its records in forms or formats that are reproducible for purposes of this section.

(C) In responding under this paragraph to a request for records, an agency shall make reasonable efforts to search for the records in electronic form or format, except when such efforts would significantly interfere with the operation of the agency's automated information system.

(D) For purposes of this paragraph, the term "search" means to review, manually or by automated means, agency records for the purpose of locating those records which are responsive to a request.

(E) An agency, or part of an agency, that is an element of the intelligence community (as that term is defined in section 3(4) of the National Security Act of 1947 (50 U.S.C. 401a(4)) shall not make any record available under this paragraph to—

(i) any government entity, other than a State, territory, commonwealth, or district of the United States, or any subdivision thereof; or

(ii) a representative of a government entity described in clause (i).

(4) (A) [This subsection deals with the fees that agencies may charge for processing requests for records. The agency must use notice-and-comment rulemaking to establish a fee schedule. The agency may charge commercial requesters for "search" and "review," as well as "duplication," of records, whereas it may charge the media, academics, and scientists only for duplication. It must charge a reduced fee (or zero fee) if disclosure "is in the public interest because it is likely to contribute significantly to public understanding of the operations of activities of the government and is not primarily in the commercial interest of the requester."]

(B) On complaint, the district court of the United States in the district in which the complainant resides, or has his principal place of business, or in which the agency records are situated, or in the District of Columbia, has jurisdiction to enjoin the agency from withholding agency records and to order the production of any agency records improperly withheld from the complainant. In such a case the court shall determine the matter de novo, and may examine the contents of such agency records in camera to determine whether such records or any part thereof shall be withheld under any of the exemptions set forth in subsection (b) of this section, and the burden is on the agency to sustain its action. In addition to any other matters to which a court accords substantial weight, a court shall accord substantial weight to an affidavit of an agency concerning the agency's determination as to technical feasibility under paragraph (2)(C) and subsection (b) and reproducibility under paragraph (3)(B).

(C) Notwithstanding any other provision of law, the defendant shall serve an answer or otherwise plead to any complaint made under this subsection within thirty days after service upon the defendant of the pleading in which such complaint is made, unless the court otherwise directs for good cause shown.

(D) [Repealed.]

(E) (i) The court may assess against the United States reasonable attorney fees and other litigation costs reasonably incurred in any case under this section in which the complainant has substantially prevailed.

(ii) For purposes of this subparagraph, a complainant has substantially prevailed if the complainant has obtained relief through either— (I) a judicial order, or an enforceable written agreement or consent decree; or (II) a voluntary or unilateral change in position by the agency, if the complainant's claim is not insubstantial.

(F) [This section deals with institution of disciplinary action against any agency employee found by a court to have acted "arbitrarily or capriciously with respect to withholding" a disclosable record.]

(G) In the event of noncompliance with the order of the court, the district court may punish for contempt the responsible employee, and in the case of a uniformed service, the responsible member.

(5) Each agency having more than one member shall maintain and make available for public inspection a record of the final votes of each member in every agency proceeding.

(6) [This subsection deals with the timeliness of agency action in response to requests for records. Generally, the agency has 20 days to act on a request and, if a requester appeals a denial to the agency head, 20 days to act on the appeal. The agency may extend these limits in "unusual circumstances." If a requester petitions a court to enforce these time limits, the court may further extend the limits in "exceptional circumstances" if the agency exercises "due diligence" in attempting to comply. Agencies must also, by rulemaking, provide for "expedited processing" when a requester demonstrates a "compelling need."]

(7) Each agency shall —

(A) establish a system to assign an individualized tracking number for each request received that will take longer than ten days to process and provide to each person making a request the tracking number assigned to the request; and

(B) establish a telephone line or Internet service that provides information about the status of a request to the person making the request using the assigned tracking number, including— (i) the date on which the agency originally received the request; and (ii) an estimated date on which the agency will complete action on the request.

(8)(A) An agency shall— (i) withhold information under this section only if— (I) The agency reasonably foresees that disclosure would harm an interest protected by an exemption described in subsection (b); or (II) disclosure is prohibited by law; and (ii) (I) consider whether partial disclosure of information is possible whenever the agency determines that a full disclosure of a requested record is not possible; and (II) take reasonable steps necessary to segregate and release nonexempt information; and

(B) Nothing in this paragraph requires disclosure of information that is otherwise prohibited from disclosure by law, or otherwise exempted from disclosure under subsection (b)(3).

(b) This section does not apply to matters that are—

(1) (A) specifically authorized under criteria established by an Executive order to be kept secret in the interest of national defense or foreign policy and (B) are in fact properly classified pursuant to such Executive order;

(2) related solely to the internal personnel rules and practices of an agency;

(3) specifically exempted from disclosure by statute (other than section 552b of this title), provided that such statute (A) (i) requires that the matters be withheld from the public in such a manner as to leave no discretion on the issue; or (ii) establishes particular criteria for withholding or refers to particular types of matters to be withheld; and (B) if enacted after [2009], specifically cites to this paragraph.

(4) trade secrets and commercial or financial information obtained from a person and privileged or confidential;

(5) inter-agency or intra-agency memorandums or letters that would not be available by law to a party other than an agency in litigation with the agency, provided that the deliberative process privilege shall not apply to records created 25 years or more before the date on which the records were requested;

(6) personnel and medical files and similar files the disclosure of which would constitute a clearly unwarranted invasion of personal privacy;

(7) records or information compiled for law enforcement purposes, but only to the extent that the production of such law enforcement records or information

(A) could reasonably be expected to interfere with enforcement proceedings,

(B) would deprive a person of a right to a fair trial or an impartial adjudication,

(C) could reasonably be expected to constitute an unwarranted invasion of personal privacy,

(D) could reasonably be expected to disclose the identity of a confidential source, including a State, local, or foreign agency or authority or any private institution which furnished information on a confidential basis, and, in the case of a record or information compiled by criminal law enforcement authority in the course of a criminal investigation or by an agency conducting a lawful national security intelligence investigation, information furnished by a confidential source,

(E) would disclose techniques and procedures for law enforcement investigations or prosecutions, or would disclose guidelines for law enforcement investigations or prosecutions if such disclosure could reasonably be expected to risk circumvention of the law, or

(F) could reasonably be expected to endanger the life or physical safety of any individual;

(8) contained in or related to examination, operating, or condition reports prepared by, on behalf of, or for the use of an agency responsible for the regulation or supervision of financial institutions; or

(9) geological and geophysical information and data, including maps, concerning wells.

Any reasonably segregable portion of a record shall be provided to any person requesting such record after deletion of the portions which are exempt under this subsection. The amount of information deleted shall be indicated on the released portion of the record, unless including that indication would harm an interest protected by the exemption in this subsection under which the deletion is made. If technically feasible, the amount of the information deleted shall be indicated at the place in the record where such deletion is made.

(c)(1) Whenever a request is made which involves access to records described in subsection (b)(7)(A) and—

(A) the investigation or proceeding involves a possible violation of criminal law; and

(B) there is reason to believe that (i) the subject of the investigation or proceeding is not aware of its pendency, and (ii) disclosure of the existence of the records could reasonably be expected to interfere with enforcement proceedings, the agency may, during only such time as that circumstance continues, treat the records as not subject to the requirements of this section.

(2) Whenever informant records maintained by a criminal law enforcement agency under an informant's name or personal identifier are requested by a third party according to the informant's name or personal identifier, the agency may treat the records as not subject to the requirements of this section unless the informant's status as an informant has been officially confirmed.

(3) Whenever a request is made which involves access to records maintained by the Federal Bureau of Investigation pertaining to foreign intelligence or counterintelligence, or international terrorism, and the existence of the records is classified information as provided in subsection (b)(1), the Bureau may, as long as the existence of the records remains classified information, treat the records as not subject to the requirements of this section.

(d) This section does not authorize withholding of information or limit the availability of records to the public, except as specifically stated in this section. This section is not authority to withhold information from Congress.

(e) [This subsection requires agencies to submit annually to the Attorney General a detailed report on their activities under FOIA, and requires the Attorney General to prepare an annual report on cases arising under FOIA and actions undertaken by the Justice Department to improve compliance with FOIA.]

(f) For purposes of this section, the term—

(1) "agency" as defined in section 551(1) of this title includes any executive department, military department, Government corporation, Government controlled corporation, or other establishment in the executive branch of the Government (including the Executive Office of the President), or any independent regulatory agency; and

(2) "record" and any other term used in this section in reference to information includes—

(A) any information that would be an agency record subject to the requirements of this section when maintained by an agency in any format, including an electronic format; and

(B) any information described under subparagraph (A) that is maintained for an agency by an entity under Government contract, for the purposes of records management.

(g) The head of each agency shall prepare and make publicly available upon request, reference material or a guide for requesting records or information from the agency, subject to the exemptions in subsection (b), including—

(1) an index of all major information systems of the agency;

(2) a description of major information and record locator systems maintained by the agency; and

(3) a handbook for obtaining various types and categories of public information from the agency . . . under this section.

(h)-(m) [These sections establish and mandate the use of various administrative mechanisms to help enforce and implement the Act.]

§552A. RECORDS MAINTAINED ON INDIVIDUALS [OMITTED]

§552B. OPEN MEETINGS [OMITTED]

§553. RULE MAKING

(a) This section applies, according to the provisions thereof, except to the extent that there is involved—

(1) a military or foreign affairs function of the United States; or

(2) a matter relating to agency management or personnel or to public property, loans, grants, benefits, or contracts.

(b) General notice of proposed rule making shall be published in the Federal Register, unless persons subject thereto are named and either personally served or otherwise have actual notice thereof in accordance with law. The notice shall include—

(1) a statement of the time, place, and nature of public rule making proceedings;

(2) reference to the legal authority under which the rule is proposed; and

(3) either the terms or substance of the proposed rule or a description of the subjects and issues involved.

Except when notice or hearing is required by statute, this subsection does not apply—

(A) to interpretative rules, general statements of policy, or rules of agency organization, procedure, or practice; or

(B) when the agency for good cause finds (and incorporates the finding and a brief statement of reasons therefor in the rules issued) that notice and public procedure thereon are impracticable, unnecessary, or contrary to the public interest.

(c) After notice required by this section, the agency shall give interested persons an opportunity to participate in the rule making through submission of written data, views, or arguments with or without opportunity for oral presentation. After consideration of the relevant matter presented, the agency shall incorporate in the rules adopted a concise general statement of their basis and purpose. When rules are required by statute to be made on the record after opportunity for an agency hearing, sections 556 and 557 of this title apply instead of this subsection.

(d) The required publication or service of a substantive rule shall be made not less than 30 days before its effective date, except—

(1) a substantive rule which grants or recognizes an exemption or relieves a restriction;

(2) interpretative rules and statements of policy; or

(3) as otherwise provided by the agency for good cause found and published with the rule.

(e) Each agency shall give an interested person the right to petition for the issuance, amendment, or repeal of a rule.

§554. ADJUDICATIONS

(a) This section applies, according to the provisions thereof, in every case of adjudication required by statute to be determined on the record after opportunity for an agency hearing, except to the extent that there is involved—

(1) a matter subject to a subsequent trial of the law and the facts de novo in a court;

(2) the selection or tenure of an employee, except a[n] administrative law judge appointed under section 3105 of this title;

(3) proceedings in which decisions rest solely on inspections, tests, or elections;

(4) the conduct of military or foreign affairs functions;

(5) cases in which an agency is acting as an agent for a court; or

(6) the certification of worker representatives.

(b) Persons entitled to notice of an agency hearing shall be timely informed of—

(1) the time, place, and nature of the hearing;

(2) the legal authority and jurisdiction under which the hearing is to be held; and

(3) the matters of fact and law asserted.

When private persons are the moving parties, other parties to the proceeding shall give prompt notice of issues controverted in fact or law; and in other instances agencies may by rule require responsive pleading. In fixing the time and place for hearings, due regard shall be had for the convenience and necessity of the parties or their representatives.

(c) The agency shall give all interested parties opportunity for—

(1) the submission and consideration of facts, arguments, offers of settlement, or proposals of adjustment when time, the nature of the proceeding, and the public interest permit; and

(2) to the extent that the parties are unable so to determine a controversy by consent, hearing and decision on notice and in accordance with sections 556 and 557 of this title.

(d) The employee who presides at the reception of evidence pursuant to section 556 of this title shall make the recommended decision or initial decision required by section 557 of this title, unless he becomes unavailable to the agency. Except to the extent required for the disposition of ex parte matters as authorized by law, such an employee may not—

(1) consult a person or party on a fact in issue, unless on notice and opportunity for all parties to participate; or

(2) be responsible to or subject to the supervision or direction of an employee or agent engaged in the performance of investigative or prosecuting functions for an agency.

An employee or agent engaged in the performance of investigative or prosecuting functions for an agency in a case may not, in that or a factually related case, participate or advise in the decision, recommended decision, or agency review pursuant to section 557 of this title, except as witness or counsel in public proceedings. This subsection does not apply—

(A) in determining applications for initial licenses;

(B) to proceedings involving the validity or application of rates, facilities, or practices of public utilities or carriers; or

(C) to the agency or a member or members of the body comprising the agency.

(e) The agency, with like effect as in the case of other orders, and in its sound discretion, may issue a declaratory order to terminate a controversy or remove uncertainty.

§555. ANCILLARY MATTERS

(a) This section applies, according to the provisions thereof, except as otherwise provided by this subchapter.

(b) A person compelled to appear in person before an agency or representative thereof is entitled to be accompanied, represented, and advised by counsel or, if permitted by the agency, by other qualified representative. A party is entitled to appear in person or by or with counsel or other duly qualified representative in an agency proceeding. So far as the orderly conduct of public business permits, an interested person may appear before an agency or its responsible employees for the presentation, adjustment, or determination of an issue, request, or controversy in a proceeding, whether interlocutory, summary, or otherwise, or in connection with an agency function. With due regard for the convenience and necessity of the parties or their representatives and within a reasonable time, each agency shall proceed to conclude a matter presented to it. This subsection does not grant or deny a person who is not a lawyer the right to appear for or represent others before an agency or in an agency proceeding.

(c) Process, requirement of a report, inspection, or other investigative act or demand may not be issued, made, or enforced except as authorized by law. A person compelled to submit data or evidence is entitled to retain or, on payment of lawfully prescribed costs, procure a copy or transcript thereof, except that in a non-public investigatory proceeding the witness may for good cause be limited to inspection of the official transcript of his testimony.

(d) Agency subpoenas authorized by law shall be issued to a party on request and, when required by rules of procedure, on a statement or showing of general relevance and reasonable scope of the evidence sought. On contest, the court shall sustain the subpoena or similar process or demand to the extent that it is found to be in accordance with law. In a proceeding for enforcement, the court shall issue an order requiring the appearance of the witness or the production of the evidence or data within a reasonable time under penalty of punishment for contempt in cases of contumacious failure to comply.

(e) Prompt notice shall be given of the denial in whole or in part of a written application, petition, or other request of an interested person made in connection with any agency proceeding. Except in affirming a prior denial or when the denial is self-explanatory, the notice shall be accompanied by a brief statement of the grounds for denial.

§556. HEARINGS; PRESIDING EMPLOYEES; POWERS AND DUTIES; BURDEN OF PROOF; EVIDENCE; RECORD AS BASIS OF DECISION

(a) This section applies, according to the provisions thereof, to hearings required by section 553 or 554 of this title to be conducted in accordance with this section.

(b) There shall preside at the taking of evidence—

(1) the agency;

(2) one or more members of the body which comprises the agency; or

(3) one or more administrative law judges appointed under section 3105 of this title.

This subchapter does not supersede the conduct of specified classes of proceedings, in whole or in part, by or before boards or other employees specially provided for by or designated under statute. The functions of presiding employees and of employees participating in decisions in accordance with section 557 of this title shall be conducted in an impartial manner. A presiding or participating employee may at any time disqualify himself. On the filing in good faith of a timely and sufficient affidavit of personal bias or other disqualification of a presiding or participating employee, the agency shall determine the matters as a part of the record and decision in the case.

(c) Subject to published rules of the agency and within its powers, employees presiding at hearings may—

(1) administer oaths and affirmations;

(2) issue subpoenas authorized by law;

(3) rule on offers of proof and receive relevant evidence;

(4) take depositions or have depositions taken when the ends of justice would be served;

(5) regulate the course of the hearing;

(6) hold conferences for the settlement or simplification of the issues by consent of the parties;

(7) dispose of procedural requests or similar matters;

(8) make or recommend decisions in accordance with section 557 of this title; and

(9) take other action authorized by agency rule consistent with this subchapter.

(d) Except as otherwise provided by statute, the proponent of a rule or order has the burden of proof. Any oral or documentary evidence may be received, but the agency as a matter of policy shall provide for the exclusion of irrelevant, immaterial, or unduly repetitious evidence. A sanction may not be imposed or rule or order issued except on consideration of the whole record or those parts thereof cited by a party and supported by and in accordance with the reliable, probative, and substantial evidence. The agency may, to the extent consistent with the interests of justice and the policy of the underlying statutes administered by the agency, consider a violation of section 557(d) of this title sufficient grounds for a decision adverse to a party who has knowingly committed such violation or knowingly caused such violation to occur. A party is entitled to present his case or defense by oral or documentary evidence, to submit rebuttal evidence, and to conduct such cross-examination as may be required for a full and true disclosure of the facts. In rule making or determining claims for money or benefits or applications for initial licenses an agency may, when a party will not be prejudiced thereby, adopt procedures for the submission of all or part of the evidence in written form.

(e) The transcript of testimony and exhibits, together with all papers and requests filed in the proceeding, constitutes the exclusive record for decision in accordance with section 557 of this title and, on payment of lawfully prescribed costs, shall be made available to the parties. When an agency decision rests on official notice of a material fact not appearing in the evidence in the record, a party is entitled, on timely request, to an opportunity to show the contrary.

§557. INITIAL DECISIONS; CONCLUSIVENESS; REVIEW BY AGENCY; SUBMISSIONS BY PARTIES; CONTENTS OF DECISIONS; RECORD

(a) This section applies, according to the provisions thereof, when a hearing is required to be conducted in accordance with section 556 of this title.

(b) When the agency did not preside at the reception of the evidence, the presiding employee or, in cases not subject to section 554(d) of this title, an employee qualified to preside at hearings pursuant to section 556 of this title, shall initially decide the case unless the agency requires, either in specific cases or by general rule, the entire record to be certified to it for decision. When the presiding employee makes an initial decision, that decision then becomes the decision of the agency without further proceedings unless there is an appeal to, or review on motion of, the agency within time provided by rule. On appeal from or review of the initial decision, the agency has all the powers which it would have in making the initial decision except as it may limit the issues on notice or by rule. When the agency makes the decision without having presided at the reception of the evidence, the presiding employee or an employee qualified to preside at hearings pursuant to section 556 of this title shall first recommend a decision, except that in rule making or determining application for initial licenses—

(1) instead thereof the agency may issue a tentative decision or one of its responsible employees may recommend a decision; or

(2) this procedure may be omitted in a case in which the agency finds on the record that due and timely execution of its functions imperatively and unavoidably so requires.

(c) Before a recommended, initial, or tentative decision, or a decision on agency review of the decision of subordinate employees, the parties are entitled to a reasonable opportunity to submit for the consideration of the employees participating in the decisions—

(1) proposed findings and conclusions; or

(2) exceptions to the decisions or recommended decisions of subordinate employees or to tentative agency decisions; and

(3) supporting reasons for the exceptions or proposed findings or conclusions. The record shall show the ruling on each finding, conclusion, or exception presented. All decisions, including initial, recommended, and tentative decisions, are a part of the record and shall include a statement of—

(A) findings and conclusions, and the reasons or basis therefor, on all the material issues of fact, law, or discretion presented on the record; and

(B) the appropriate rule, order, sanction, relief, or denial thereof.

(d) (1) In any agency proceeding which is subject to subsection (a) of this section, except to the extent required for the disposition of ex parte matters as authorized by law—

(A) no interested person outside the agency shall make or knowingly cause to be made to any member of the body comprising the agency, administrative law judge, or other employee who is or may reasonably be expected to be involved in the decisional process of the proceeding, an ex parte communication relevant to the merits of the proceeding;

(B) no member of the body comprising the agency, administrative law judge, or other employee who is or may reasonably be expected to be involved in the decisional process of the proceeding, shall make or knowingly cause to be made to any interested person outside the agency an ex parte communication relevant to the merits of the proceeding;

(C) a member of the body comprising the agency, administrative law judge, or other employee who is or may reasonably be expected to be involved in the decisional process of such proceeding who receives, or who makes or knowingly causes to be made, a communication prohibited by this subsection shall place on the public record of the proceeding:

(i) all such written communications;

(ii) memoranda stating the substance of all such oral communications; and

(iii) all written responses, and memoranda stating the substance of all oral responses, to the materials described in clauses (i) and (ii) of this subparagraph;

(D) upon receipt of a communication knowingly made or caused to be made by a party in violation of this subsection, the agency, administrative law judge, or other employee presiding at the hearing may, to the extent consistent with the interests of justice and the policy of the underlying statutes, require the party to show cause why his claim or interest in the proceeding should not be dismissed, denied, disregarded, or otherwise adversely affected on account of such violation; and

(E) the prohibitions of this subsection shall apply beginning at such time as the agency may designate, but in no case shall they begin to apply later than the time at which a proceeding is noticed for hearing unless the person responsible for the communication has knowledge that it will be noticed, in which case the prohibitions shall apply beginning at the time of his acquisition of such knowledge.

(2) This subsection does not constitute authority to withhold information from Congress.

§558. IMPOSITION OF SANCTIONS; DETERMINATION OF APPLICATIONS FOR LICENSES; SUSPENSION, REVOCATION, AND EXPIRATION OF LICENSES

(a) This section applies, according to the provisions thereof, to the exercise of a power or authority.

(b) A sanction may not be imposed or a substantive rule or order issued except within jurisdiction delegated to the agency and as authorized by law.

(c) When application is made for a license required by law, the agency, with due regard for the rights and privileges of all the interested parties or adversely affected persons and within a reasonable time, shall set and complete proceedings required to be conducted in accordance with sections 556 and 557 of this title or other proceedings required by law and shall make its decision. Except in cases of willfulness or those in which public health, interest, or safety requires otherwise, the withdrawal, suspension, revocation, or annulment of a license is lawful only if, before the institution of agency proceedings therefor, the licensee has been given—

(1) notice by the agency in writing of the facts or conduct which may warrant the action; and

(2) opportunity to demonstrate or achieve compliance with all lawful requirements.

When the licensee has made timely and sufficient application for a renewal or a new license in accordance with agency rules, a license with reference to an activity of a continuing nature does not expire until the application has been finally determined by the agency.

§559. EFFECT ON OTHER LAWS; EFFECT OF SUBSEQUENT STATUTE

This subchapter, chapter 7, and [enumerated] sections . . . of this title that relate to administrative law judges, do not limit or repeal additional requirements imposed by statute or otherwise recognized by law. Except as otherwise required by law, requirements or privileges relating to evidence or procedure apply equally to agencies and persons. Each agency is granted the authority necessary to comply with the requirements of this subchapter through the issuance of rules or otherwise. Subsequent statutes may not be held to supersede or modify this subchapter, chapter 7, [or enumerated sections] that relate to administrative law judges, except to the extent that it does so expressly.

SUBCHAPTER III — NEGOTIATED RULEMAKING PROCEDURE [OMITTED]

CHAPTER 7 — JUDICIAL REVIEW

§701. APPLICATION; DEFINITIONS

(a) This chapter applies, according to the provisions thereof, except to the extent that—

(1) statutes preclude judicial review; or

(2) agency action is committed to agency discretion by law.

(b) For the purpose of this chapter—

(1) "agency" means each authority of the Government of the United States, whether or not it is within or subject to review by another agency, but does not include—

(A) the Congress;

(B) the courts of the United States;

(C) the governments of the territories or possessions of the United States;

(D) the government of the District of Columbia;

(E) agencies composed of representatives of the parties or of representatives of organizations of the parties to the disputes determined by them;

(F) courts martial and military commissions;

(G) military authority exercised in the field in time of war or in occupied territory; or

(H) functions [relating to mortgage insurance, termination of war contracts, disposal of surplus war property, defense housing, and foreign scholarships]; and

(2) "person," "rule," "order," "license," "sanction," "relief," and "agency action" have the meanings given them by section 551 of this title.

§702. RIGHT OF REVIEW

A person suffering legal wrong because of agency action, or adversely affected or aggrieved by agency action within the meaning of a relevant statute, is entitled to judicial review thereof. An action in a court of the United States seeking relief other than money damages and stating a claim that an agency or an officer or employee thereof acted or failed to act in an official capacity or under color of legal authority shall not be dismissed nor relief therein be denied on the ground that it is against the United States or that the United States is an indispensable party. The United States may be named as a defendant in any such action, and a judgment or decree may be entered against the United States: *Provided,* That any mandatory or injunctive decree shall specify the Federal officer or officers (by name or by title), and their successors in office, personally responsible for compliance. Nothing herein (1) affects other limitations on judicial review or the power or duty of the court to dismiss any action or deny relief on any other appropriate legal or equitable ground; or (2) confers authority to grant relief if any other statute that grants consent to suit expressly or impliedly forbids the relief which is sought.

§703. FORM AND VENUE OF PROCEEDING

The form of proceeding for judicial review is the special statutory review proceeding relevant to the subject matter in a court specified by statute or, in the absence or inadequacy thereof, any applicable form of legal action, including actions for declaratory judgments or writs of prohibitory or mandatory injunction or habeas corpus, in a court of competent jurisdiction. If no special statutory review proceeding is applicable, the action for judicial review may be brought against the United States, the agency by its official title, or the appropriate officer. Except to the extent that prior, adequate, and exclusive opportunity for judicial review is provided by law, agency action is subject to judicial review in civil or criminal proceedings for judicial enforcement.

§704. ACTIONS REVIEWABLE

Agency action made reviewable by statute and final agency action for which there is no other adequate remedy in a court are subject to judicial review. A preliminary, procedural, or intermediate agency action or ruling not directly reviewable is subject to review on the review of the final agency action. Except as otherwise expressly required by statute, agency action otherwise final is final for the purposes of this section whether or not there has been presented or determined an application for a declaratory order, for any form of reconsideration, or, unless the agency otherwise requires by rule and provides that the action meanwhile is inoperative, for an appeal to superior agency authority.

§705. RELIEF PENDING REVIEW

When an agency finds that justice so requires, it may postpone the effective date of action taken by it, pending judicial review. On such conditions as may be required and to the extent necessary to prevent irreparable injury, the reviewing court, including the court to which a case may be taken on appeal from or on application for certiorari or other writ to a reviewing court, may issue all necessary and appropriate process to postpone the effective date of an agency action or to preserve status or rights pending conclusion of the review proceedings.

§706. SCOPE OF REVIEW

To the extent necessary to decision and when presented, the reviewing court shall decide all relevant questions of law, interpret constitutional and statutory provisions, and determine the meaning or applicability of the terms of an agency action. The reviewing court shall—

(1) compel agency action unlawfully withheld or unreasonably delayed; and

(2) hold unlawful and set aside agency action, findings, and conclusions found to be—

(A) arbitrary, capricious, an abuse of discretion, or otherwise not in accordance with law;

(B) contrary to constitutional right, power, privilege, or immunity;

(C) in excess of statutory jurisdiction, authority, or limitations, or short of statutory right;

(D) without observance of procedure required by law;

(E) unsupported by substantial evidence in a case subject to sections 556 and 557 of this title or otherwise reviewed on the record of an agency hearing provided by statute; or

(F) unwarranted by the facts to the extent that the facts are subject to trial de novo by the reviewing court.

In making the foregoing determinations, the court shall review the whole record or those parts of it cited by a party, and due account shall be taken of the rule of prejudicial error.

Chapter 8 — Congressional Review of Agency Rulemaking [Omitted]

TABLE OF CASES

TABLE OF SECONDARY AUTHORITIES

Berry, Melissa M., Beyond *Chevron*'s Domain: Agency Interpretations of Statutory Procedural Provisions, 30 Seattle U.L. Rev. 541 (2007), 696

Biden, Joseph, Who Needs the Legislative Veto?, 35 Syracuse L. Rev. 685 (1984), 49

Blackstone, W., Commentaries, V.2 at *405, 660, 762

Boger, Jack, et al., The Federal Tort Claims Act Intentional Torts Amendment: An Interpretive Analysis, 54 N.C. L. Rev. 497 (1976), 837

Bonfield, Arthur E., The Federal APA and State Administrative Law, 72 Va. L. Rev. 297 (1986), 5

Bradley, Curtis A. & Posner, Eric A., Presidential Signing Statements and Executive Power, 23 Const. Commentary 307 (2006), 50

Bressman, Lisa, Judicial Review of Agency Inaction: An Arbitrariness Approach, 79 NYU L. Rev. 1657 (2004), 174

Breyer, Stephen, Breaking the Vicious Circle (1992), 587

_____, Judicial Review of Questions of Law and Policy, 38 Ad. L. Rev. 353, 391-393 (1986), 147

Bruff, Harold H., Judicial Review and the President's Statutory Powers, 68 Va. L. Rev. 1, 36 (1982), 64

Bryce, James, The American Commonwealth (1888), 3

Calame, Byron E., Everybody Favors Job Safety, but . . . , Wall St. J., Nov. 17, 1970, at 22, 12-13

Campbell, Jack W., Note, Revoking the "Fishing License": Recent Decisions Place Unwarranted Restrictions on Administrative Agencies' Power to Subpoena Personal Financial Records, 49 Vand. L. Rev. 395 (1996), 756

Cannon, Jonathan, The Sounds of Silence: Cost Benefit Analysis in *Entergy Corp. v. Riverkeeper, Inc.*, 34 Harv. Envtl. L. Rev. 425, 428-429 (2010), 580-581

Cass, Ronald A., *Auer* Deference: Doubling Down on Delegation's Defects, 87 Fordham L. Rev. 531 (2018), 242

_____, Delegation Reconsidered: A Delegation Doctrine for the Modern Administrative State, 40 Harv. J.L. & Pub. Pol'y 147 (2016), 34

_____, Models of Administrative Action, 72 Va. L. Rev. 363 (1986), 417

_____, Vive la Deference? Rethinking the Balance Between Administrative and Judicial Expression, 83 Geo. Wash. L. Rev. 1294 (2015), 189, 243

Cass, Ronald A. & Diver, Colin S., Administrative Law: Cases and Materials 714 (2d ed. 1987), 713

Cass, Ronald A. & Strauss, Peter, The Presidential Signing Statements Controversy, 17 William & Mary Bill of Rights J. 11 (2007), 49

Clark, Bradford R., Separation of Powers as a Safeguard of Federalism, 79 Tex. L. Rev. 1321 (2001), 822

Coglianese, Gary, Assessing Consensus: The Promise and Performance of Negotiated Rule-making, 46 Duke L.J. 1255, 1268 (1997), 572

Cohen, Mark A. & Rubin, Paul H., Private Enforcement of Public Policy, 3 Yale J. on Reg. 167, 169 (1985), 795-796

Comptroller General of the U.S., How Effective Are OSHA's Complaint Procedures?, 9 (1979), 744-745

Congressional Quarterly, 1968 Cong. Q. Almanac 677, 11

Commager, Henry Steele, The New York Review of Books, Oct. 5, 1972, at 7, 924

Convisser, Israel, Primary Jurisdiction: The Rule and Its Rationalizations, 65 Yale L.J. 315 (1956), 810

Cooper, Philip J., George W. Bush, Edgar Allan Poe, and the Use and Abuse of Presidential Signing Statements, 35 Presidential Stud. Q. 515 (2005), 50

Cooter, Robert, Models of Morality in Law and Economics: Self-Control and Self-Improvement for the "Bad Man" of Holmes, 78 B.U. L. Rev. 903 (1998), 740

Copeland, Curtis W., Length of Rule Reviews by the Office of Information and Regulatory Affairs (2013), 605

Corbin, A., on Contracts §§561-572A (1960), 653

Corwin, Edward S., The President: Office and Powers 102-114, 428 (3d ed. 1948), 85-86

Cox, Archibald, et al., Labor Law: Cases and Materials 112-151 (14th ed. 2006), 452

Cox, Edward R., et al., "The Nader Report" on the Federal Trade Commission (1969), 770, 853

Cross, Frank B. & Tiller, Emerson H., Judicial Partisanship and Obedience to Legal Doctrine: Whistleblowing on the Federal Courts of Appeals, 107 Yale L.J. 2155 (1998), 118

Currie, David P. & Goodman, Frank I., Judicial Review of Federal Administrative Action: Quest for the Optimum Forum, 75 Colum. L. Rev. 1 (1975), 281

Cushman, Robert E., The Independent Regulatory Commissions 101-114 (1941), 61

Davis, Kenneth C., A New Approach to Delegation, 36 U. Chi. L. Rev. 715 (1969), 32

_____, Administrative Law of the Seventies §11.00 at 317 (1976), 499

_____, Administrative Law Text §12.04, p. 250 (1972), 680

_____, Administrative Law Treatise (1958), 420, 345, 370, 406, 431, 473, 619, 623, 640

_____, Constitutional Torts §§6, 7-8, 11-16 (1984), 835

_____, The Information Act: A Preliminary Analysis, 34 U. Chi. L. Rev. 761, 797, (1967), 908

_____, The Liberalized Law of Standing, 37 U. Chi. L. Rev. 450 (1970), 354

Gellhorn, Ernest L., Rules of Evidence and Official Notice in Formal Administrative Hearings, 1971
    Duke L.J. 1, 703
Gellhorn, Ernest L. & Robinson, Glen O., Rulemaking "Due Process": An Inconclusive Dialogue, 48 U.
    Chi. L. Rev. 201 (1981), 846
Gellhorn, Walter, The Abuse of Occupational Licensing, 44 U. Chi. L. Rev. 6 (1976), 843
_____, Federal Administrative Proceedings 9 (1941), 8
_____, Individual Freedom and Governmental Restraints 106 (1956), 844
Gelpe, Marcia R., Exhaustion of Administrative Remedies: Lessons from Environmental Cases, 53 Geo.
    Wash. L. Rev. 1, 3 (1985), 407
Gerson, Jacob C. & O'Connell, Anne Joseph, Deadlines in Administrative Law, 156 U. Pa. L. Rev. 923
    (2008), 566
Goodnow, Frank, Comparative Administrative Law (1893), 4
_____, Politics and Administration (1900), 4
_____, The Principles of the Administrative Law of the United States (1905), 4
Green, Mark & Nader, Ralph, Economic Regulation vs. Competition: Uncle Same the Monopoly Man,
    82 Yale L.J. 871 (1973), 135
Grimaldi, James V. & Overberg, Paul, Millions of People Post Comments on Federal Regulations. Many
    Are Fake. Wall Street Journal Online (Dec. 12, 2017), 493

Hahn, Robert W. & Stavins, Robert N., Incentive-Based Environmental Regulation: A New Era from an
    Old Idea? 18 Ecology L.Q. 1 (1991), 741
Hamilton, Alexander, The Federalist No. 67 at 455, 83
_____, The Federalist No. 70 at 476, 107
_____, The Federalist No. 72 at 487, 107
_____, The Federalist No. 73 at 442, 457, 40, 98
_____, Works of Alexander Hamilton, V.7 at 76, 80-81 (C. Hamilton ed. 1851), 61
Hamilton, Robert W., Procedures for the Adoption of Rules of General Applicability: The Need for
    Procedural Innovation in Administrative Rulemaking, 60 Cal. L. Rev. 1276, 1287-1288 (1972),
    479-480
Harter, Philip J., Assessing the Assessors: The Actual Performance of Negotiated Rulemaking, 9 NYU
    Envtl. L.J. 32, 41, 56 (2000), 573
_____, Collaboration: The Future of Governance, 2009 J. Dispute Res. 411, 437, 577
_____, Negotiating Regulations: A Cure for the Malaise, 71 Geo. L.J. 1 (1981), 572
Havender, William R., Assessing and Controlling Risks, in Social Regulation: Strategies for Reform 21,
    22-23 (Eugene Bardach & Robert A. Kagan, eds., 1982), 272
Henderson, Gerald, The Federal Trade Commission: A Study in Administrative Law and Procedure
    (1924), 770
Hetherington, John A. C., State Economic Regulation and Substantive Due Process of Law II, 53 Nw. U.L.
    Rev. 226, 249 (1958), 843

Jaffe, Louis L., Judicial Control of Administrative Action 375 (1965), 339, 810
John F. Kennedy School of Government, Mike Pertschuk and the Federal Trade Commission (1981),
    517-518
Jordan, Ellen R., The Administrative Procedure Act's "Good Cause" Exemption, 36 Admin. L. Rev. 113
    (1984), 566
Jordan III, William S., *Chevron* and Hearing Rights: An Unintended Combination, 61 Admin. L. Rev. 249,
    288 (2009), 696
_____, Ossification Revisited: Does Arbitrary and Capricious Review Significantly Interfere with
    Agency Ability To Achieve Regulatory Goals Through Informal Rulemaking?, 94 Nw. U. L. Rev. 393,
    395 (2000), 147

Kagan, Elena, Presidential Administration, 114 Harv. L. Rev. 2245 (2001), 67-68, 514
Kalven, Harry, Broadcasting, Public Policy, and the First Amendment, 10 J.L. & Econ. 15 (1967), 865
Kaplow, Louis, An Economic Analysis of Legal Transitions, 99 Harv. L. Rev. 509 (1986), 767
Kavanaugh, Brett M., Two Challenges for the Judge as Umpire: Statutory Ambiguity and Constitutional
    Exceptions, 97 Notre Dame L. Rev. 1907, 1912 (2017), 244
Kerwin, Cornelius M. & Langbein, Lauri L., An Evaluation of Negotiated Rulemaking at the
    Environmental Protection Agency: Phase I (1995); and Phase II: A Comparison of Conventional
    and Negotiated Rulemaking (1997), 572
Kessler, David A., A Question of Intent: A Great American Battle with a Deadly Industry (2001), 70
Kolko, Gabriel, Railroads and Regulation: 1877-1916 (1965), 7

_____, OMB Interference with Agency Rulemaking: The Wrong Way to Write a Regulation, 99 Harv. L. Rev. 1059 (1986), 600

Moss, John E., Public Information Policies, The APA, and Executive Privilege, 15 Admin. L. Rev. 111 (1963), 888

Nader, Ralph, Why They Should Tell You the Octane Rating of the Gasoline You Buy, Popular Science Mag. (April 1970), 433

Nathanson, Nathaniel L., Probing the Mind of the Administrator: Hearing Variations and Standards of Judicial Review under the Administrative Procedure Act and Other Federal Statutes, 75 Colum. L. Rev. 721, 754-755 (1975), 389

National Research Council, Climate Change Science: An Analysis of Some Key Questions (2001), 169, 173

Nielson, Aaron L., Beyond Seminole Rock, 105 Geo. L.J. 943 (2017), 242, 474

Noll, Roger, Reforming Regulation: An Evaluation of the Ash Council Proposals (1971), 731, 853

Obama, Barack, Statement by the President on Signing the Omnibus Appropriations Act, 2009, March 11, 2009, 50

O'Connell, Anne Joseph, Agency Rulemaking and Political Transitions, 105 Nw. U. L. Rev. 471, 471-442, 568

Peck, Cornelius J., The Atrophied Rule-Making Powers of the National Labor Relations Board, 70 Yale L.J. 729 (1961), 441, 457

Pedersen, Jr., William F., Formal Records and Informal Rulemaking, 85 Yale L.J. 38 (1975), 504-05

Pertschuk, Michael, Revolt against Regulation 44 (1982), 517

Pierce, Jr., Richard J., Administrative Law Treatise §7.3, at 435 (4th ed. 2002), 545

_____, Chevron and Its Aftermath: Judicial Review of Agency Interpretations of Statutory Provisions, 41 Vand. L. Rev. 301 (1988), 188

_____, Seven Ways to Deossify Agency Rulemaking, 47 Admin. L. Rev. 59, 85 (1995), 473

_____, Two Problems in Administrative Law: Political Polarity on the District of Columbia Circuit and Judicial Deterrence of Agency Rulemaking, 1988 Duke L.J. 309, 493

_____, Use of Federal Rules of Evidence in Federal Agency Adjudications, 39 Admin. L. Rev. (1987), 702

Posner, Richard A., The Behavior of Administrative Agencies, 1 J. Legal Stud. 305 (1972), 726

Posner, Eric A. & Vermeule, Adrian, Interring the Nondelegation Doctrine, 69 U. Chi. L. Rev. 1721 (2002), 34

_____, The Federal Trade Commission, 37 U. Chi. L. Rev. 47, 82-84 (1969), 853

_____, Theories of Economic Regulation, 5 Bell J. Econ. & Mgmt. Sci. 335 (1974), 9, 865

President's Advisory Council on Executive Organization ("Ash Council"), A New Regulatory Framework: Report on Selected Independent Agencies (1971), 731

President's Committee on Administrative Management, Report with Special Studies (1937), 4-5

Rabin, Robert L., Job Security and Due Process: Monitoring Administrative Discretion through a Reasons Requirement, 44 U. Chi. L. Rev. 60 (1976), 660

Rao, Neomi, Administrative Collusion: How Delegation Diminishes the Collective Congress, 90 N.Y.U. L. Rev. 1463 (2015), 34

Raven-Hansen, Peter, Regulatory Estoppel: When Agencies Break Their Own "Laws," 64 Tex. L. Rev. 1 (1985), 477

Reich, Charles, Individual Rights and Social Welfare: The Emerging Legal Issues, 74 Yale L.J. 1245 (1965), 639

_____, The New Property, 73 Yale L.J. 733 (1964), 639,

Restatement (Second) of Torts §§286, 757, 908(1) (1979), 761-62

Revesz, Richard L. & Livermore, Michael A., Retaking Rationality: How Cost-Benefit Analysis Can Better Protect the Environment and Our Health (2008), 582

Robinson, Glen O., Access to Government Information: The American Experience, 14 Federal L. Rev. 35 (1983), 889

_____, The Making of Administrative Policy: Another Look at Rulemaking and Adjudication and Administrative Procedure Reform, 118 U. Pa. L. Rev. 485 (1970), 420, 441

Rodgers, Jr., William H., A Hard Look at Vermont Yankee: Environmental Law under Close Scrutiny, 67 Geo. L.J. 699, 722 (1979), 612

Rodriguez, Daniel B., Official Notice and the Administrative Process, 10 J. Natl. Assn. Admin. L. Judges 47 (1990), 703

Rose, Jonathan, Occupational Licensing: A Framework for Analysis, 1979 Ariz. St. L.J. 189, 843

INDEX